B
Bob Geldof
who raised £35 million for famine relief within two weeks through the globally televised 'Live Aid' concert.

BOB·GELDOF

D
Dr Robert Jarvick
inventor of the artificial heart.

Dr ROBERT·JARVICK

E
Edwin Moses
who was unbeaten in the 400 metre hurdles for nearly ten years.

EDWIN·MOSES

M
Marilyn Vos Savant
whose I.Q. is higher than that of any other human being.

MARILYN·VOS·SAVANT

ROLL·OF·HONOUR

1986 Inaugural Members and those inducted in 1987

Nineteen Eighty-Six

•

Vernon Craig

Sir Ranulph Fiennes, Bt

Billie-Jean King

Joseph Kittinger

Paul McCartney

Vesna Vulovic

•

Nineteen Eighty-Seven

Sir Donald Bradman

Sergey Bubka

Katharine Hepburn

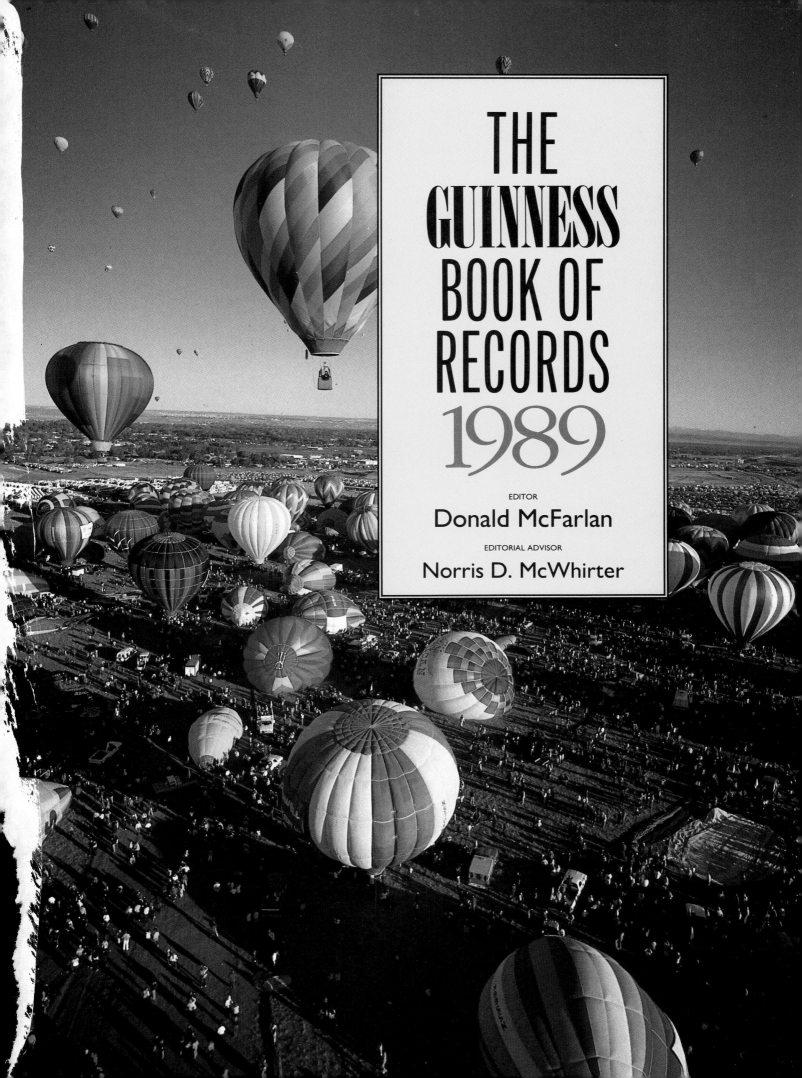

THE GUINNESS
BOOK OF RECORDS
1989

EDITOR

Donald McFarlan

EDITORIAL ADVISOR

Norris D. McWhirter

The Story Behind The Guinness Book

On Saturday 10 Nov 1951, Sir Hugh Beaver (1890–1967) was out shooting on The North Slob, by the river Slaney in County Wexford in the south–east of Ireland. Some golden plover were missed by the party. That evening at Castlebridge House it was realised that it was not possible to confirm in reference books whether or not the golden plover was Europe's fastest game bird.

In August 1954 argument arose as to whether grouse were even faster. Sir Hugh, managing director of Guinness thought that there must be numerous other questions debated nightly in the 81 400 pubs in Britain and in Ireland, but there was no book with which to settle arguments about records.

The Rt Hon. Earl of Iveagh

On 12 September 1954, Sir Hugh invited Norris and Ross McWhirter to see if their fact and figure agency in London could help. An office was set up at 107 Fleet Street and intense work began on the first slim 198 page edition. The printers bound the first copy on 27 August 1955. Well before Christmas the Guinness Book was No. 1 on the bestsellers list. It has occupied this position every year since except 1957 and 1959 when it was not republished.

The first US edition appeared in New York in 1956 followed by editions in French (1962) and German (1963).

In 1967 there were first editions in Japanese, Spanish, Danish and Norwegian, while the following year editions were published in Swedish, Finnish and Italian. In the 'seventies there followed Dutch (1971); Portuguese (1974); Czechoslovak (1976); Hebrew, Serbo-Croat and Icelandic (all in 1977) and Slovenian (1978).

In the 1980's translations into Greek, Indonesian, Chinese, Turkish, Hindi, Malay, Arabic, Thai, Tamil, Telugu, Malayalam, Kannada and Hungarian will bring the total to 262 editions in 35 languages.

In November 1974 the *Guinness Book* earned its own place in the *Guinness Book*. It had become the top selling copyright book in publishing history with sales of 23·9 million. In October 1988 the global sales surpassed 60 million which is equivalent to 168 stacks each as high as Mount Everest.

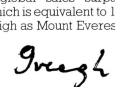

PRESIDENT
GUINNESS PLC
OCTOBER 1988

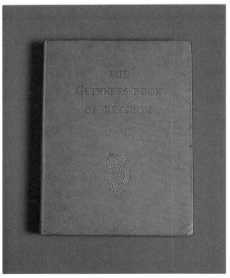

Above: The first edition of *The Guinness Book of Records* published in 1955. Below: Ross McWhirter (1925-75, left) and Norris McWhirter on BBC Television's *Record Breakers* in 1975.

British Library Cataloguing in Publication Data
Guinness book of records.-35th edition
1. Records of achievement-Collections-Serials
031'.02

ISBN 0-85112-878-5

Standard Book Number ISBN: 0-85112-878-5
Standard Book Number ISBN: 0-85112-883-1 (*Australian Edition*)

'Guinness' is a registered trade mark of Guinness Publishing Ltd.

Printed in England. Produced by Jarrold Printing, Norwich, Norfolk.

Is it a record ?

We are inclined to publish only those records which improve upon previous records or which are newly significant in having become the subject of widespread and preferably international competitiveness. However, in no circumstances will we *undertake* to publish any record and reserve the right to determine in our sole discretion the records to be published.

It should be stressed that unique occurrences, interesting peculiarites or 'firsts' are not in themselves necessarily records. Records in our sense essentially have to be both measurable and comparable. Records which are *qualified* in some way, for example, by age, day of the week, county etc, cannot be accommodated in a reference work so general as *The Guinness Book of Records.*

Claimants should send independent *written* corroboration in the form of local or national press coverage and signed authentication by independent adult witnesses or representatives of organisations of

Is it a record ?

This cake house consisted of 51 090 cake bricks, and measured 7·5 × 5·5 × 5·75 m *24 ft 7 in × 18 ft 1-in × 18 ft 10 in.*It was created by Nila Chandra. Next to it was a huge *garuda*—Indonesia's national symbol—created by Joyce Aswan. The *garuda*, made of icing sugar, was 12 m *39 ft 4 in* high. The cake and bird were displayed in Jakarta, Indonesia in Mar 1988 – one of the many new achievements recorded this year.

standing in their community. Signed log books should show there has been unremitting surveillance in the case of endurance events. Colour action photographs or transparencies should also be supplied and may be considered for publication. Five minute rest intervals (optional but aggregable) are *permitted* after each completed hour in marathon events except those very few 'non-stop' categories in which minimal intervals may be taken only for purposes other than for resting.

The publishers do not publish gratuitously dangerous categories such as the lowest height for a handcuffed free-fall parachutist or the thinnest burning rope suspending a man in a strait-jacket from a helicopter. If an activity is one controlled by a recognised world or national governing body, that body should be consulted and involved in ratifying it. Guidance and authentication notes are available from the publishers upon *postal* application and

Norris D. McWhirter

receipt of pre-paid postage and should be sought at *least* one month before completing plans for a record attempt. In addition, a last-minute check should also be made in case the published record has recently been broken.

Donald McFarlan

EDITOR

OCTOBER 1988

GUINNESS PUBLISHING LTD

33 LONDON ROAD
ENFIELD
MIDDLESEX EN2 6DJ
ENGLAND

Contents

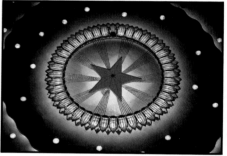

Stop Press

THE HUMAN BEING

CHAPTER·ONE

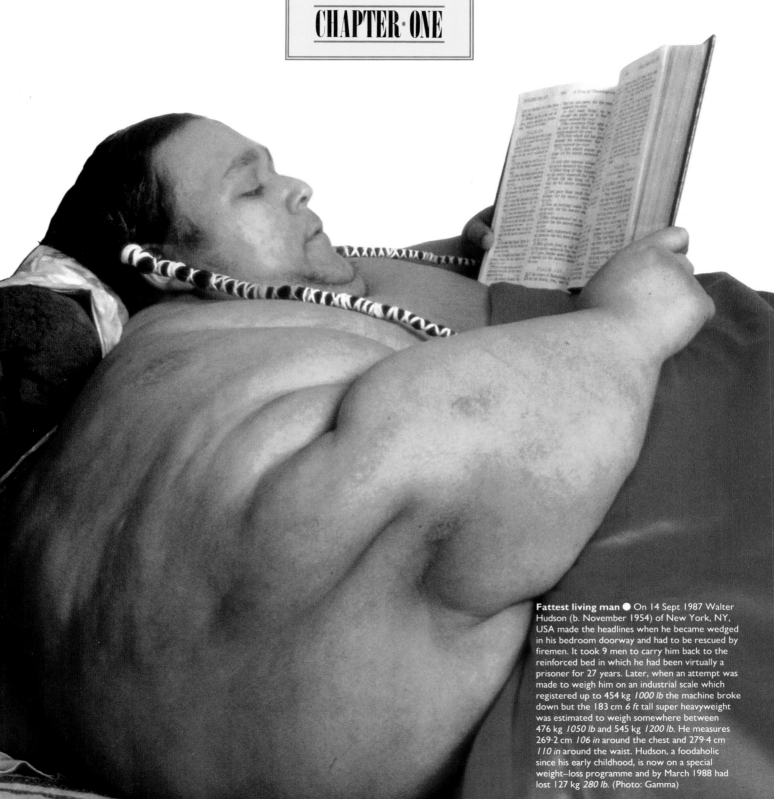

Fattest living man ● On 14 Sept 1987 Walter Hudson (b. November 1954) of New York, NY, USA made the headlines when he became wedged in his bedroom doorway and had to be rescued by firemen. It took 9 men to carry him back to the reinforced bed in which he had been virtually a prisoner for 27 years. Later, when an attempt was made to weigh him on an industrial scale which registered up to 454 kg *1000 lb* the machine broke down but the 183 cm *6 ft* tall super heavyweight was estimated to weigh somewhere between 476 kg *1050 lb* and 545 kg *1200 lb*. He measures 269·2 cm *106 in* around the chest and 279·4 cm *110 in* around the waist. Hudson, a foodaholic since his early childhood, is now on a special weight–loss programme and by March 1988 had lost 127 kg *280 lb*. (Photo: Gamma)

Dimensions

GIANTS

The true height of human giants is frequently obscured by exaggeration and commercial dishonesty. The only admissible evidence on the actual height of giants is that collected since 1870 under impartial medical supervision. Unfortunately medical authors are not blameless in including fanciful, as opposed to measured, heights.

The assertion that Goliath of Gath (c. 1060 BC) stood 6 cubits and a span (290 cm *9 ft 6½ in*) suggests a confusion of units or some over-zealous exaggeration by the Hebrew chroniclers. The Jewish historian Flavius Josephus (born AD 37/38, died c. AD 100) and some of the manuscripts of the Septuagint (the earliest Greek translation of the Old Testament) attribute to Goliath the wholly credible height of 4 Greek cubits and a span (208 cm *6 ft 10 in*).

Giants exhibited in circuses and exhibitions are routinely under contract not to be anthropometrically assessed and are, almost traditionally, billed by their promoters at heights up to 45 cm *18 in* in excess of their true heights.

TALLEST MEN

Modern opinion is that the tallest man in medical history of whom there is irrefutable evidence was the pre-acromegalic giant Robert Pershing Wadlow, born at 6.30 a.m. on 22 Feb 1918 in Alton, Illinois, USA. Weighing 3·85 kg, *8½ lb* at birth, his abnormal growth started at the age of two following a double hernia operation. On his 13th birthday he recorded a height of 218 cm *7 ft 1¾ in*, and at the age of 17 years he stood 245 cm *8 ft 0½ in*. On 27 June 1940 Dr C.M. Charles, Associate Professor of Anatomy at Washington University's School of Medicine in St. Louis, Missouri, and Dr Cyril MacBryde measured Robert Wadlow at 272 cm *8 ft 11·1 in* (arm-span 288 cm *9 ft 5¾ in*) in St Louis. Wadlow died 18 days later at 1.30 a.m. on 15 July 1940 weighing 199 kg *439 lb 31 st 5 lb* in an hotel in Manistee, Michigan, as a result of a septic blister on his right ankle, caused by a poorly-fitting brace. Because of his rapid growth he had limited feeling in his legs below the knees. Wadlow was still growing during his terminal illness and would probably have reached or just exceeded 274 cm *9 ft* in height if he had lived for another year. His greatest recorded weight was 222·7 kg *491 lb (35 st 1 lb)* on his 21st birthday, and scaled 199 kg *439 lb (31 st 5 lb)* at the time of his death. His shoes were size 37AA (47 cm *18½ in*) and his hands measured 32·4 cm *12¾ in* from the wrist to the tip of the middle finger (cf. the depth of this page at 29·7 cm *11 ¾ in*).

He was buried in Oakwood Cemetery, Alton, Illinois, in a coffin measuring 328 cm *10 ft 9 in* in length, 81 cm *32 in* wide and 76 cm *30 in* deep.

GIANTS

The only other men for whom heights of 244 cm *8 ft* or more have been reliably reported are the nine listed below. In seven cases, gigantism was followed by acromegaly, a disorder which causes an enlargement of the nose, lips, tongue, lower jaw, hands and feet, due to renewed activity by an already swollen pituitary gland, which is located at the base of the brain.

John William Rogan (1871–1905), of Gallatin, Tennessee, USA [1] 264 cm *8 ft 8 in*.

John F. Carroll (1932–69) of Buffalo, New York State, USA [2] 263·5 cm *8 ft 7¾ in*.

Väinö Myllyrinne (1909–63) of Helsinki, Finland [3] 251·4 cm *8 ft 3 in*.

Don Koehler (1925–81) of Denton, Montana, USA [4] 248·9 cm *8 ft 2 in*, latterly lived in Chicago.

Bernard Coyne (1897–1921) of Anthon, Iowa USA [5] 248·9 cm *8 ft 2 in*.

Patrick Cotter (O'Brien) (1760–1806) of Kinsale, County Cork, Ireland [6] 246 cm *8 ft 1 in*.

'Constantine' (1872–1902) of Reutlingen, West Germany [7] 245·8 cm *8 ft 0·8 in*.

Gabriel Estavao Monjane (b. 1944–fl. 1988) of Monjacaze, Mozambique [8] c. 245·7 cm *8 ft 0¾ in*.

Sulaimān 'Ali Nashnush (b. 1943–fl. 1968) of Tripoli, Libya [9] 245 cm *8 ft 0·4 in*.

[1] *Measured in a sitting position. Unable to stand owing to ankylosis (stiffening of the joints through the formation of adhesions) of the knees and hips. Weighed only 79 kg 175 lb.*

[2] *Severe kypho-scoliosis (two dimensional spinal curvature). The figure represents his height with assumed normal spinal curvature, calculated from a standing height of 244 cm 8 ft 0 in, measured on 14 Oct 1959. His standing height was 234 cm 7 ft 8¼ in shortly before his death.*

[3] *Stood 222 cm 7 ft 3½ in at the age of 21 years. Experienced a second phase of growth in his late thirties and measured 246·8 cm 8 ft 1·2 in at the time of his death. In 1931 he reportedly weighed 196·8 kg 31 st.*

[4] *Spinal curvature reduced his standing height to c. 238·4 cm 7 ft 10 in. Abnormal growth started at the age of 10. He had a twin sister who is 175 cm 5 ft 9 in tall. His father was 187 cm 6 ft 2 in and his mother 177 cm 5 ft 10 in.*

[5] *Eunuchoidal giant (Daddy long-legs syndrome). Rejected by Army in 1918 when 236 cm 7 ft 9 in. Still growing at time of death.*

[6] *Revised height based on skeletal remeasurement after bones exhumed on 19 Dec 1972.*

[7] *Eunuchoidal. Height estimated, as both legs were amputated after they turned gangrenous. He claimed a height of 259 cm 8 ft 6 in.*

[8] *Latest measurement taken in May 1987. Recently had a successful hip operation in South Africa.*

[9] *Operation to correct abnormal growth successfully carried out in Rome in 1960.*

EXAGGERATED HEIGHTS

The following lists a number of well-known giants whose heights have been exaggerated.

NAME	DATES	COUNTRY	CLAIMED cm	ft in	HEIGHT ACTUAL cm	ft in
Edouard Beaupre	1881–1904	Canada	251·4	8 3	236·2	7 9
Muhammad Aalam Channa[1]	1956–fl. 1987	Pakistan	250·8	8 2¾	233·6	7 8
Fernand (Atlas) Bacheland	1923–76	Belgium	279·4	9 2	234·3	7 8¼
Joachim Eleizegue	1822–fl. 1845	Spain	238·7	7 10	233·6	7 8
Chang Wu-Gow	1846–93	China	279·4	9 2	233·6	7 8
Johann Petrussen	1914–fl. 1986	Iceland	264·1	8 8	231·1	7 7
Max Palmer	1928–fl. 1986	USA	245·1	8 0½	231·1	7 7
Rigardus Riynhout	1922–fl. 1955	Netherlands	278·1	9 1½	229·8	7 6½
Baptiste Hugo	1879–1916	France	269·2	8 10	229·8	7 6½
Bernardo Gigli	1736–62	Italy	243·8	8 0	229·8	7 6½
James Toller	1795–1819	England	259·0	8 6	228·6	7 6
Eddie Carmel[2]	1938–72	Isreal	275·5	9 0½	228·6	7 6
Daniel Cajanus	1724–49	Finland	283·2	9 3½	222·2	7 3½
Patrick Murphy	1834–62	Ireland	269·2	8 10	222·2	7 3½
Jakop Loll (The Pomeranian Giant)	1783–1839	USSR	255·2	8 4½	220·9	7 3
Paul Henoch	1852–76	Germany	251·4	8 3	218·4	7 2

[1] *Channa was medically assessed in New York on 21 Aug 1987 and found to measure 233·6 cm 7 ft 8 in (238·7 cm 7 ft 10 in in his shoes)*
[2] *The height of Eddie Carmel was estimated from photographs and that of Cajanus from evidence by bones. Each of the other actual heights was obtained from independent medical authority. The embalmed body of Beaupre in the anatomical museum of the University of Montreal measures 217 cm 7 ft 1⅜ in in length.*

ROBERT WADLOW

Weighing 3·85 kg *8½ lb* at birth, the abnormal growth of Robert Wadlow started at the age of 2 following a double hernia operation. His height progressed as follows:

AGE	HEIGHT cm	ft in	WEIGHT kg	lb
5	163	5 4	48	105
8	183	6 0	77	169
9	189	6 2¼	82	180
10	196	6 5	95	210
11	200	6 7	–	–
12	210	6 10½	–	–
13	218	7 1¾	116	255
14	226	7 5	137	301
15	234	7 8	161	355
16	240	7 10¼	170	374
17	245	8 0½	143[1]	315
18	253	8 3½	–	–
19	258	8 5½	218	480
20	261	8 6¾	–	–
21	265	8 8¼	223	491
22·4[2]	272	8 11	199	439

[1] *Following severe influenza and infection of the foot.*

[2] *Still growing during his terminal illness.*

Living

The tallest living man is Gabriel Estavao Monjane (b. 1944) Monjacaze, Mozambique, East Africa. This acromegalic giant measured 226 cm *7 ft 5 in* at the age of 16 and was anthropometrically assessed by Dr Manuel Alberto in Lourenco Marques in December 1965, when his standing height was found to be 238·5 cm *7 ft 10 in*. Soon afterward he joined a Portuguese circus which billed him at 265 cm *8 ft 8 ⅓ in*, but his actual height today is 245·7 cm *8 ft ¾ in*, and he weighs 181 kg *400 lb*.

England

The tallest Englishman ever recorded was William Bradley (1787–1820), born in Market Weighton, now Humberside. He stood 236 cm *7 ft 9 in*. John Middleton (1578–1623), the famous Childe of Hale, from near Liverpool, was credited with a height of 282 cm *9 ft 3 in* but a life-size impression of his right hand (length 29·2 cm *11½ in*, cf. Wadlow's 32·4 cm *12¾ in*) painted on a panel in Brasenose College, Oxford indicates his true stature was nearer 236 cm *7 ft 9 in*. Albert Brough (1871–1919), a Nottingham publican, reached a height of 232 cm *7 ft 7½ in*. Frederick Kempster (1889–1918) of Avebury, Wiltshire, was reported to have measured 255 cm *8 ft 4½ in* at the time of his death, but photographic evidence suggests that his height was 235 cm *7 ft 8½ in.* He measured 234 cm *7 ft 8·1 in* in 1913. Henry Daglish, who stood 231 cm *7 ft 7 in* died in Upper Stratton, Wiltshire, on 15 Mar 1951, aged 25. The much-publicised Edward (Ted) Evans (1924–58) of Englefield Green, Surrey, was reputed to be 282 cm *9 ft 3 in* but actually stood 235 cm *7 ft 8½ in.*

The tallest man now living in Great Britain is Christopher Paul Greener (b. New Brighton, Merseyside, 21 Nov 1943) of Hayes, Kent, who measures 229 cm *7 ft 6¼ in* (weight 165 kg *364 lb*).

Scotland
The tallest Scotsman, and the tallest recorded 'true' (non-pathological) giant, was Angus Macaskill (1823–63), born on the island of Berneray, in the Sound of Harris, Western Isles. He stood 236 cm *7 ft 9 in* and died in St Ann's, on Cape Breton Island, Nova Scotia, Canada.

The tallest Scotsman now living is George Gracie (b. 1938) of Forth, Strathclyde. He stands 221 cm *7 ft 3 in* and weighs 203 kg *32 st.* His brother Hugh (b. 1941) is 215 cm *7 ft 0½ in.*

Wales
The tallest Welshman on record was William Evans (1599–1634) of Monmouthshire, now Gwent, who was porter to King James I. He stood 228·6 cm *7 ft 6 in.*

Ireland
The tallest Irishman was the 246 cm *8 ft 1 in* tall Patrick Cotter (O'Brien) (1760–1806), born in Kinsale, County Cork. He died at Hotwells, Bristol (See table opposite).

TALLEST WOMEN
Giantesses are rarer than giants but their heights are still spectacular. The tallest woman in history was the acromegalic giantess Zeng Jinlian (pronounced San Chunglin) (b. 26 June 1964) of Yujiang village in the Bright Moon Commune, Hunan Province, central China who was 247 cm *8 ft 1¾ in* when she died on 13 Feb 1982. This figure, however, represented her height with assumed normal spinal curvature because she suffered from severe scoliosis and could not stand up straight. She began to grow abnormally from the age of 4 months and stood 156 cm *5 ft 1½ in* before her 4th birthday (cf. 162·5 cm *5 ft 4 in* for Robert Wadlow at the age of 5) and 217 cm *7 ft 1½ in* when she was 13. Her hands measured 25·5 cm *10 in* and her feet 35·5 cm *14 in* in length. Both her parents and her brother are normal in size.

Living
The tallest living woman is a eunuchoidal giantess known only as Mulia (b. 1956) of Borneo, who stands 233 cm *7 ft 7¾ in* tall, (weight 77 kg *170 lb*) and is still growing. She measured 155 cm *5 ft 1 in* at the age of 13 years and began growing abnormally two years later. In April 1986 she was admitted to hospital in Surabaya, Jarva, for treatment to check her exceptional growth.

United Kingdom
The tallest British woman ever recorded in medical history was Jane ('Ginny') Bunford, born on 26 July 1895 at Bartley Green, Northfield, Birmingham. Her abnormal growth started at the age of 11 following a head injury, and on her 13th birthday she measured 198 cm *6 ft 6 in.* Shortly before her death on 1 Apr 1922 she stood 231 cm *7 ft 7 in* tall, but she had severe kyphoscoliosis and would have measured at least 241 cm *7 ft 11 in* if she had been able to stand fully erect. Her skeleton, now preserved in the Anatomical Museum in the Medical School at

Tallest woman in North America ● Sandy Allen (b. 18 June 1955, Chicago) of Niagara Falls, Ontario, Canada. On 14 July 1977 she underwent a pituitary gland operation, which inhibited further growth, at 231·7 cm *7 ft 7¼ in.* A 2·95 kg *6½ lb* baby, her acromegalic growth began soon after birth. She now weighs 209·5 kg *33 st* and takes a size 16EEE American shoe (= 14½ UK or 50PP Continental).

Birmingham University, has a mounted height of 223·5 cm *7 ft 4 in.*

Twins

The world's tallest identical twin are Michael and James Lanier (b. 27 Nov 1969) from Troy, Michigan, USA who stand 223·3 cm *7 ft 4 in.*

The tallest twins ever in Britain were the Knipe brothers (b. 1761) of Magherfelt, near Londonderry, Northern Ireland who both measured 218·4 cm *7 ft 2 in.* Britain's tallest living twins are Jonathan and Mark Carratt (b.11 June 1955) of Maltby, South Yorkshire, who are 203·3 cm *6 ft 8 in* and 205·7 cm *6 ft 9 in* respectively.

Married couple

Anna Hanen Swan (1846–88) of Nova Scotia, Canada, was billed at 246 cm *8 ft 1 in* but actually measured 227 cm *7 ft 5½ in.* At St Martin's-in-the-Fields, London on 17 June 1871 she married Martin van Buren Bates (1845–1919) of Whitesburg, Letcher County, Kentucky, USA, who stood 219 cm *7 ft 2½ in*, making them the tallest married couple on record.

DWARFS

The strictures which apply to giants apply equally to dwarfs, except that exaggeration gives way to understatement. In the same way as 274 cm *9 ft* may be regarded as the limit towards which the tallest giants

tend, so 58 cm *23 inches* must be regarded as the limit towards which the shortest mature dwarfs tend (cf. the average length of new-born babies is 46–50 cm *18–20 in*). In the case of child dwarfs their *ages* are often enhanced by their agents or managers.

Shortest

The shortest mature human of whom there is independent evidence was Pauline Musters ('Princess Pauline'), a Dutch midget. She was born at Ossendrecht, on 26 Feb 1876 and measured 30 cm *11·8 in* at birth. At the age of 9 she was 55 cm *21·65 in* tall and weighed only 1·5 kg *3 lb 5 oz.* She died on 1 Mar 1895 in New York City, at the age of 19, of pneumonia, with meningitis, her heart weakened from alcoholic excesses. Although she was billed at 48 cm *19 in*, she had earlier been medically assessed and found to be 59 cm *23.2 in* tall. A *post mortem* examination showed her to be exactly 61 cm *24 in* (there was some elongation after death). Her mature weight varied from 3·4–4 kg *7½–9 lb* and her 'vital statistics' were 47–48–43 cm *18½–19–17 in*, which suggests she was overweight.

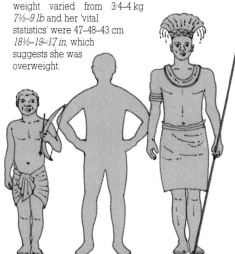

In 1938 a height of 48 cm *19 in* was attributed to Paul Del Rio (b. Madrid, 1920) by *Life Magazine* when he visited Hollywood, but the fact that his presence created no great impression among other dwarfs in the film capital and that he weighed as much as 5·4 kg *12 lb* suggests that he was closer to 66 cm *26 in* tall.

In 1979 a height of 50 cm *19·68 in* and a weight of 1·98 kg *4 lb 6 oz* were reported for a 9 year-old Greek girl named Stamatoula (b. Sept 1969 length 15 cm *5·9 in*). When she died on 22 Aug 1985 at the Lyrion Convent, Athens, she measured 67 cm *26·4 in* and weighed 5 kg *11 lb.* The child, believed to be the survivor of twins, suffered from Seckel's syndrome, also known as 'bird-headed dwarfism', because victims have prominent eyes and noses.

The shortest recorded adult male dwarf was Calvin Phillips, born on 14 Jan 1791 in Bridgewater, Massachusetts, USA. He weighed 907 g *2 lb* at birth and stopped growing at the age of 5. When he was 19 he measured 67 cm *26½ in* tall and weighed 5·4 kg *12 lb* with his clothes on. He died two years later, in April 1812, from progeria, a rare disorder characterised by dwarfism and premature senility.

William E. Jackson, *alias* 'Major Mite', born 2 Oct 1864 in Dunedin, New Zealand, measured 23 cm *9 in* long and weighed 340 g *12 oz* at birth. In November 1880 he stood 53 cm *21 in* and weighed 4 kg *9 lb.* He died in New York City on 9 Dec 1900, when he measured 69 cm *27 in.*

Smallest tribe ● The smallest pygmies are the Mbuti from Zaïre, with an average height of 137 cm *4 ft 6 in* for men and 135 cm *4 ft 5 in* for women, with some groups averaging only 132 cm *4 ft 4 in* for men and 124 cm *4 ft 1 in* for women. According to recent medical research pygmy children are not significantly shorter than the children of other tribes. But they do not grow in adolescence because they produce only a limited amount of the hormone called insulin–like growth factor (IGF). (Photo: Hutchinson Library)

Tallest tribe ● Some of the slender Tutsi (also known as the Watussi) of Rwanda and Burundi, Central Africa, one of the tallest major tribes in the world, below, dancing. As with the Dinka of the Sudan, the average adult male height just exceeds 183 cm *6 ft.* (Photo: Hutchinson Library)

In 1983 a height of 65 cm *25·6 in* was reported for Dimitris Morokos (b. 1963) of Poros, Greece, but this height has not yet been confirmed. He died two years later in 1985 aged 22 years.

The most famous midget in history was Charles Sherwood Stratton, *alias* 'General Tom Thumb', born on 4 Jan 1838. When he joined up with Phineas T. Barnum, the famous American showman, his birth date was changed to 4 Jan 1832 so that when billed at 77 cm *30½ in* at the age of 18 he was in fact 12. He died in his birthplace of Bridgeport, Connecticut, USA of apoplexy on 15 July 1883 aged 45 (not 51) and was 102 cm *3 ft 4 in* (31·7 kg *70 lb*).

Living

The world's shortest known mobile living adult human is believed to be Nelson de la Rosa (b. June 1968), of Santo Domingo, Dominican Republic, who suffers from Seckel's Syndrome. On 2 Apr 1987 he was examined by the Head of the Dominican Republic Medical Association who revealed that this tiny prodigy measured 72 cm *28·3 in* in height and weighed only 6·81 kg *15 lb*. (Compare 3·4 kg *7½ lb* for an average baby at birth.) Other statistics include a 44·4 cm *17½ in* chest and 40·6 cm *16 in* waist. The doctor also reported that Nelson had stopped growing. The rest of his family are all of normal size. In March 1988 an unconfirmed height of 64·7 cm *25·5 in* was reported for a woman named Mary Bester (b. 1965) living in South Africa.

United Kingdom

The shortest mature human ever recorded in Britain was Miss Joyce Carpenter (b. 21 Dec 1929), a rachitic dwarf of Charford, now Hereford & Worcester, who stood 74 cm *29 in* tall and weighed 13·60 kg *30 lb*. She died on 7 Aug 1973 aged 43. Hopkins Hopkins (1737–54) of Llantrisant, Mid-Glamorgan who suffered from progeria, was 79 cm *31 in* tall. He weighed 8·62 kg *19 lb* at the age of 7 and 6 kg *13 lb* at the time of his death. There are an estimated 3000 people of severely restricted growth (i.e. under 142 cm *4 ft 8 in*) living in Britain today.

The shortest adult living in Britain is Michael Henbury-Ballan (b. 26 Nov 1958) of Bassett, Southampton, who is 94 cm *37 in* tall and weighs 35 kg *5½ st*. A 2·66 kg *5 lb 14 oz* baby, he stopped growing at the age of 13 years. His fraternal twin brother Malcolm is 175 cm *5 ft 9 in* tall and weighs 73 kg *11 st 7 lb*. In 1981 a height of 96·5 cm *38 in* was reported for an unnamed woman (b. 1963) living in Brighton, Sussex.

Patrick Scanlan (b.1966) of Maida Vale, London stands 91·4 cm *36 in* tall and only weighs 19 kg *42 lb*, but he suffers from MPS (Mucopolysaccharide), an enzyme disease that causes severe bone abnormalities, including curvature of the spine and cannot stand erect. He stopped growing at the age of four years.

Twins

The shortest ever recorded were the primordial dwarfs Matjus and Bela Matina (b. 1903–*fl*. 1935) of Budapest, Hungary who later became naturalised Americans. They both measured 76 cm *30 in*.

The world's shortest living twins are John and Greg Rice (b. 3 Dec 1951) of West Palm Beach, Florida, who both measure 86·3 cm *34 in*. The shortest identical twin sisters are Dorene Williams of Oakdale and Darlene McGregor of Almeda, California, USA (b. 1948) who both stand 124·4 cm *4 ft 1 in* .

Oldest

There are only two centenarian dwarfs on record. The older was Hungarian-born Miss Susanna Bokoyni ('Princess Susanna') of Newton, New Jersey, who died aged 105 years on 24 Aug 1984. She was 101 cm *3 ft 4 in* tall and weighed 16·78 kg *37 lb*. The other was Miss Anne Clowes of Matlock, Derbyshire, who died on 5 Aug 1784 aged 103 years. She was 114 cm *3 ft 9 in* tall and weighed 21·7 kg *48 lb*.

Most variable stature

Adam Rainer, born in Graz, Austria, in 1899, measured 118 cm *3 ft 10·45 in* at the age of 21. He then suddenly started growing at a rapid rate, and by 1931 he had reached 218 cm *7 ft 1¾ in*. He became so weak as a result that he was bed-ridden for the rest of his life. At the time of his death on 4 Mar 1950 aged 51 he measured 234 cm *7 ft 8 in* and was the only person in medical history to have been both a dwarf and a giant.

Lord Adare (4th Earl of Dunraven and Mount-Earl, b. 12 Feb 1841, d. 14 June 1926) recorded that the Scots–born medium Daniel Home (b.1833) could elongate his body 28 cm *11 in*.

Most dissimilar couple

Nigel Wilks (200·6 cm *6 ft 7 in*) of Kingston upon Hull, Humberside married Beverly Russell (119·3 cm *3 ft 11 in*), both aged 21, on 30 June 1984. Their son Daniel, 4·22 kg *9 lb 5 oz*, was born on 22 Mar 1986.

SUPER HEAVYWEIGHTS

Jon Brower Minnoch (1941–83) USA 185 cm *(6 ft 1 in)*
635 kg *1400 lb 100 st*

Walter Hudson (b. 1944) USA 183 cm *(6 ft)*
545–476 kg *1200–1050 lb 85 st 7 lb–75 st†*

Michael Walker *né* Francis Lang (b. 1934) USA 188 cm *(6 ft 2 in)*[1]
538 kg *1187 lb 84 st 11 lb*

Robert Earl Hughes (1926–58) USA 184 cm *(6 ft 0½ in)*
485 kg *1069 lb 76 st 5 lb*

Mills Darden (1798–1857) USA 229 cm *(7 ft 6 in)*
462 kg *1020 lb 72 st 12 lb*

John Finnerty (b. 1952) USA
453 kg *1000 lb 71 st 6 lb†*

'Big Tex' (1902–*fl*1956) USA 186 cm *(6 ft 1½ in)*
419 kg *924 lb 66 st*

John Hanson Craig (1856–94) USA 195 cm *(6 ft 5 in)*[2]
411 kg *907 lb 64 st 11 lb*

Arthur Knorr (1914–60) USA 185 cm *(6 ft 1 in)*[3]
408 kg *900 lb 64 st 4 lb*

T. J. Albert Jackson (b. 1941) Canton, Mississippi, USA 193 cm *(6 ft 4 in)*
404 kg *891 lb 63 st 9 lb*

Albert Pernitsch (b. 1956) of Grafkorn, Austria 175 cm *(5 ft 9 in)*[4]
399 kg *880 lb 62 st 12 lb*

Ron High (b. 1953) of Chicago, USA
387 kg *853 lb 60 st 10 lb*[5]

T. A. Valenzuela (1895–1937) Mexico 180 cm *(5 ft 11 in)*
385 kg *850 lb 60 st 10 lb*

Joseph Shorr (1934–809) USA 193 cm *(6 ft 4 in)*
344 kg *60 st 6 lb*

[1] *Reduced to 167 kg 369 lb by Feb. 1980. Peak weight was only estimated in 1971.*

[2] *Won $1000 in a 'Bonny Baby' contest in New York City in 1858.*

[3] *Gained 136 kg 300 lb in the last 6 months of his life.*

[4] *His left arm tattoo proclaims 'Nobody is perfect'. In July 1984 his girth was 200 cm 78¾ in.*

[5] *Reduced by dieting to 154·2 kg 340 lb in 16 months to Jan 1987*

† *Weight estimated.*

WEIGHT

Heaviest men

The heaviest man in medical history was Jon Brower Minnoch (b. 29 Sept 1941) of Bainbridge Island, Washington, USA, who had suffered from obesity since childhood. The 185 cm *6 ft 1 in* tall former taxi-driver was 181 kg *400 lb* in 1963, 317 kg *700 lb* in 1966 and 442 kg *975 lb* in September 1976. Eighteen months later, in March 1978, Minnoch was rushed to University Hospital, Seattle, saturated with fluid and suffering from heart and respiratory failure. It took a dozen fire-fighters and an improvised stretcher to move him from his home to a ferry-boat. When he arrived at the hospital he was put in two beds lashed together. It took 13 people just to roll him over. By extrapolating his intake and elimination rates, consultant endocrinologist Dr Robert Schwartz calculated that Minnoch must have weighed more than 635 kg *1400 lb (100 st)* when he was admitted, a great deal of which was water accumulation due to his congestive heart failure. After nearly two years on a 1200-calories-a-day diet the choking fluid had gone, and he was discharged at 216 kg *476 lb (34 st)*. But the weight crept back again, and in October 1981 he had to be readmitted, after putting on 91 kg *200 lb (over 14 st)* in the previous 7 days. When he died on 10 Sept 1983 he weighed more than 363 kg *800 lb (just over 57 st)*.

Living

The heaviest living man is T. J. Albert Jackson (b. Kent Nicholson), also known as 'Fat Albert' of Canton, Mississippi, USA (*see table*). He recently tipped the scales at 402 kg *898 lb*. He has a 305 cm *120 in* chest, a 294 cm *116 in* waist, 178 cm *70 in* thighs and a 75 cm *29½ in* neck. Albert Pernitsch of Grafkorn, Austria also claims to be the world's heaviest man, but the greatest weight recorded for him so far is 399 kg *880 lb*.

The greatest weight attained by a living person is 538 kg *84 st 11 lb*. Michael Walker of Clinton, Iowa, USA, had reduced to 167 kg *369 lb* by February 1980.

Great Britain

The heaviest recorded man was Peter Yarnall of East Ham, London, who weighed 374 kg *59 st* and was 177·8 cm *5 ft 10 in* tall. The former docker began putting on weight at a very rapid rate in 1978 and for the last two years of his life he was completely bed-ridden. He died on 30 Mar 1984 aged 34 years. His coffin measured 233 cm *7 ft 4 in* in length, 122 cm *4 ft* across and had a depth of 83·8 cm *2 ft 9 in*.

Only two other British men had a recorded weight of more than 317·5 kg *50 st*. One of them was William Campbell (b. Glasgow 1856) who died on 16 June 1878 when a publican at High Bridge, Newcastle upon Tyne, Tyne and Wear. He was 190 cm *6 ft 3 in* tall and weighed 340 kg *53 st 8 lb* with an 216 cm *85 in* waist and a 244 cm *96 in* chest. The other was the celebrated Daniel Lambert (1770–1809) of Leicester, Leicestershire. He stood 180 cm *5 ft 11 in* tall and weighed 335 kg *52 st 11 lb* shortly before his death and had a girth of more than 233 cm *92 in*.

Britain's heaviest living man is the 210·8 cm *6 ft 11 in* professional wrestler Martin Ruane alias Luke McMasters ('Giant Haystacks') who was born in Camberwell, London in 1946. His weight now fluctuates between 286 kg *45 st* and 292 kg *46 st*, though he once claimed to have tipped the scales at 317 kg *50 st*. Arthur Armitage (b. 28 June 1929) of Knottingley, West Yorkshire, who weighed 305 kg *48 st* (height 175 cm *5 ft 9 in*) in October 1986. Since then, however, he has gone on another crash diet and by May 1988 he was down to 190 kg *30 st*. Norman Smith (b. 10 May 1957) of Slough, Berks reached a peak weight of 303 kg *47 st 11 lb* (height 184 cm *6 ft 0½ in*) on 10 March 1988, but since then he has also gone on a crash diet and was down to 265 kg *41 st 10 lb* nine weeks later.

Wales

The heaviest man ever recorded in Wales was Charles Dunbar of Aberdare, Glamorgan, who died on 22 Jan 1925 aged 24 years. He weighed 279 kg *44 st* and was 185·4 cm *6 ft 1 in* tall.

Ireland

The heaviest Irishman is reputed to have been Roger Byrne, who was buried in Rosenallis, County Laoighis

(Leix), on 14 Mar 1804. He died in his 54th year and his coffin and its contents weighed 330 kg *52 st.* Roly McIntyre (b. 1955) of Kesh, Fermanagh, Northern Ireland scaled a peak 262 kg *41 st 4 lb* in April 1983.

Heaviest women

The heaviest woman ever recorded was the late Mrs Percy Pearl Washington, 46 who died in hospital in Milwaukee, on 9 Oct 1972. The hospital scales registered only up to 362·8 kg *800 lb (57 st 2 lb)* but she was believed to weigh about 399·1 kg *880 lb (62 st 12 lb)*. She was 183 cm *6 ft* tall and wore a US size 62 dress. The previous feminine weight record had been set 84 years earlier at 385 kg *850 lb (60 st 10 lb)* although a wholly unsubstantiated report exists of a Mrs Ida Maitland (1898–1932) of Springfield, Mississippi, USA, who reputedly weighed 413·2 kg *65 st 1 lb (911 lb)*.

Mrs Flora Mae Jackson *(née King)* known in show business as 'Baby Flo' was born in 1930 at Shuqualak, Mississippi. She weighed 4·5 kg *10 lb* at birth and 381 kg *841 lb (60 st)* shortly before her death in Meridian, Mississippi, USA on 9 Dec 1965 when she stood 175 cm *5 ft 9 in* tall.

Great Britain and Ireland

The heaviest woman ever recorded in Britain was Mrs Muriel Hopkins (b. 1931) of Tipton, West Midlands, who weighed 278 kg *43 st 11 lb* (height 180 cm *5 ft 11 in*) in 1978. Shortly before her death on 22 Apr 1979 she reportedly scaled 330 kg *52 st*, but this was only an estimate, and her actual weight was found to be 301 kg *47 st 7 lb*. Her coffin measured 190 cm *6 ft 3 in* in length, 137 cm *4 ft 5 in* wide and was 114 cm *3 ft 9 in* deep.

Heaviest twins

The heaviest twins in the world were Billy Leon (1946–79) and Benny Loyd (b. 7 Dec 1946) McCrary *alias* McGuire of Hendersonville, North Carolina, who were normal in size until the age of 6 when they both contracted German measles. In November 1978 they were weighed at 337 kg *743 lb (53 st 1 lb)* (Billy) and 328 kg *723 lb (51 st 9 lb)* (Benny) and had 213 cm *84 in* waists. As professional tag wrestling performers they were *billed* at weights up to 349 kg *770 lb*. Billy died at Niagara Falls, Ontario, Canada on 13 July 1979 after a mini-motorcycle accident.

People suffering from the Prader–Willi syndrome, a rare brain disorder which makes them constantly crave for food, have been known to get so fat that they die from asphyxiation.

Lightest

The lightest adult human on record was Lucia Zarate (b. San Carlos, Mexico 2 Jan 1863, d. Oct 1889), an emaciated Mexican ateleiotic dwarf of 67 cm *26½ in*, who weighed 2125 kg *4·7 lb* at the age of 17. She 'fattened up' to 5·9 kg *13 lb* by her 20th birthday. At birth she weighed 1·1 kg *2½ lb*.

The thinnest recorded adults of normal height are those suffering from Simmonds' Disease (Hypophyseal cachexia). Losses up to 65 per cent of the original body-weight have been recorded in females, with a 'low' of 20 kg *3 st 3 lb* in the case of Emma Shaller (b. St Louis, Missouri 8 July 1868, d. 4 Oct 1890), who stood 157 cm *5 ft 2 in*. Edward C. Hagner (1892–1962), *alias* Eddie Masher (USA) is alleged to have weighed only 22 kg *3 st 6 lb* at a height of 170 cm *5 ft 7 in*. He was also known as ' Skeleton Dude'. In August 1825 the biceps measurement of Claude-Ambroise Seurat (b. 10 Apr 1797, d. 6 Apr 1826) of Troyes, France was 10 cm *4 in* and the distance between his back and his chest was less than 7·6 cm *3 in*. According to one report he stood 171 cm *5 ft 7½ in* and weighed 35 kg *5 st 8 lb*, but in another account he was described as 163 cm *5 ft 4 in* and only 16 kg *2 st 8 lb*. It was recorded that the American exhibitionist Rosa Lee Plemons (b. 1873) weighed 12 kg *27 lb* at the age of 18.

Great Britain

The lightest adult ever recorded in the United Kingdom was Hopkins Hopkins (Dwarfs, see p.9). Robert Thorn

(b. 1842) of March, Cambridgeshire weighed 22 kg *49 lb* at the age of 32. He was 137 cm *4 ft 6 in* tall and had a 68 cm *27 in* chest (expanded) 11·4 cm *4½ in* biceps, and a 7·6 cm *3 in* wrist. A doctor who examined him said he had practically no muscular development, 'although he could run along the road'.

In July 1977 the death was reported of an 83-year-old woman in Mexborough, South Yorkshire who scaled only 15 kg *2 st 5 lb* (height not recorded).

Slimming *Men*

The greatest slimming feat with published information was that of William J. Cobb (b. 1926), *alias* 'Happy Humphrey', a professional wrestler of Augusta, Georgia. It was reported in July 1965 that he had reduced from 364 kg *57 st 4 lb* to 105 kg *16 st 8 lb*, a loss of 259 kg *40 st 11 lb* in 32 months. His waist measurement declined from 256 to 112 cm *101 to 44 in*. In October 1973 it was reported that 'Happy' was back to his normal weight of 196 kg *31 st*. By July 1979 Jon Brower Minnoch (1941–83) (see p. 9) had reduced to 216 kg *34 st*, thus indicating a weight loss of at least 419 kg *66 st* in 2 years, or an average of 4 kg *8·8 lb* per week.

Paul M. Kimelman (b. 1943) of Pittsburgh, Pennsylvania, reduced from 216 kg *487 lb (34 st 11 lb)* to 59 kg *130 lb (9 st 4 lb)* between 1 Jan 1967 and 3 Aug 1967, a loss of 162 kg *357 lb* in 215 days. Roly McIntyre (b. 1952) of Kesh, Fermanagh, N. Ireland (see heaviest men) reduced from 262 kg *578 lb (41 st 4 lb)* to 84·8 kg *187 lb (13 st 5 lb)* during the 22-month period Apr 1983–Feb 1985.

On 14 March 1982 surgeons at a hospital in New York City, NY, USA removed 67 kg *147 lb* of tissue from a 362 kg *57 st* man. They had to use a hoist to lift the layers of fat as they were removed. Ron Allen (b. 1947) sweated off 9·7 kg *21½ lb* of his 113·4 kg *250 lb* in Nashville, Tennessee, in 24 hours in August 1984.

Women

The US circus fat lady Mrs Celesta Geyer (b. 1901), *alias* Dolly Dimples, reduced from 251 kg *553 lb* to 69 kg *152 lb* in 1950–51, a loss of 182 kg *401 lb* in 14 months. Her vital statistics diminished *pari passu* from 200–213–213 cm *79–84–84 in* to a svelte 86–71–91 cm *34–28–36 in*. Her book *'How I Lost 400 lbs'* was not a best-seller because of the difficulty of would-be readers identifying themselves with the dress-making and other problems of losing more than 178 kg *28 st* when 150 cm *4 ft 11 in* tall. In December 1967 she was reportedly down to 50 kg *7 st 12 lb*. In February 1951 Mrs Gertrude Levandowski (b. 1893) of Burnips, Michigan, successfully underwent a protracted operation for the removal of a ovarian cyst which subsequently reduced her weight from 280 kg *44 st* to 140 kg *22 st* (see also p. 20).

The feminine champion in Britain was Mrs Dolly Wager (b. 1933) of Charlton, London, who, between Sept 1971 and 22 May 1973 reduced from 200 kg *31 st 7 lb* to 69·8 kg *11 st* so losing 130 kg *20 st 7 lb* with Weight Watchers.

Weight gaining

The reported record for gaining weight was set by Jon Minnoch (see p. 9) in October 1981 when he was readmitted to University of Washington Hospital, Seattle, Washington State, having regained 91 kg *200 lb* in 7 days. Arthur Knorr (see table p.9) gained 136 kg *300 lb* in the last 6 months of his life. Miss Doris James of San Francisco, California, is alleged to have gained 147 kg *23 st 3 lb* in the 12 months before her death in August 1965, aged 38, at a weight of 306 kg *48 st 3 lb*. She was only 157 cm *5 ft 2 in* tall.

Greatest differential

The greatest weight differential recorded for a married couple is *c.* 589 kg *1300 lb (92 st 12 lb)* in the case of Jon Brower Minnoch (see p.9) and his 50 kg *110 lb (7 st 12 lb)* wife Jeannette in Mar 1978. The UK record is held by the wrestler Martin Ruane, 'Giant Haystacks', and his 47·6 kg *7½ st* wife Rita Their weight differential at one time may have been 270 kg *42½ st.*

Origins

EARLIEST MAN

SCALE OF TIME

If the age of the Earth-Moon system (latest estimate 4450 million years) is likened to a single year, Hominids appeared on the scene at about 4.15 p.m. on 31 December, Britain's earliest known inhabitants arrived at about 11.10 p.m., the Christian era began about 14 seconds before midnight and the life span of a 120-year-old person (pp 11 & 12) would be about three-quarters of a second. Present calculations indicate that the Sun's increased heat, as it becomes a 'red giant' will make life insupportable on Earth in about 5 500 million years. Meanwhile there may well be colder epicycles. The period of 1000 million years is often called an aeon.

Man (Homo sapiens) is a species in the sub-family Homininae of the family Hominidae of the super-family Hominoidea of the sub-order Simiae (or Anthropoidea) of the order Primates of the infra-class Eutheria of the sub-class Theria of the class Mammalia of the sub-phylum Vertebrata (Craniata) of the phylum Chordata of the sub-kingdom Metazoa of the animal kingdom.

Earliest *Primate*

The first primates appeared in the Palaeocene epoch about 69 million years ago. The earliest members of the sub-order Anthropoidea are known from both Africa and South America in the early Oligocene, 34–30 million years ago, when the two infra-orders, Platyrrhini and Catarrhini from the New and Old Worlds respectively were already distinct.

Earliest *Hominid*

Characteristics typical of the Hominidae such as the large brain and bipedal locomotion do not appear until much later. The earliest undoubted hominid relic found is an Australopithecine jaw bone with two molars 2 in *5 cm* in length found by Kiptalam Chepboi near Lake Baringo, Kenya in February 1984 and dated to 4 million years by associated fossils and to 5·6–5·4 million years through rock correlation by potassium-argón dating.

The most complete of the earliest hominid skeletons is that of 'Lucy' (40 per cent complete) found by Dr Donald C. Johanson and T. Gray at Locality 162 by the Awash river, Hadar, in the Afar region of Ethiopia on 30 Nov 1974. She was estimated to be *c.* 40 years old when she died 3 million years ago, and she was 106 cm *3½ ft* tall.

Parallel tracks of hominid footprints extending over 24 m *80 ft* were discovered at Laetoli, Tanzania in 1978, first by Paul Abell, in volcanic ash dating to 3·5 million years ago. The height of the smallest of the seemingly 3 individuals was estimated to be 120 cm *3 ft 11 in.*

Earliest genus *Homo*

The earliest species of the genus *Homo* is *Homo habilis* or 'Handy Man' so named by Professor Raymond Arthur Dart (b. Brisbane 4 Feb 1893) in 1964. The greatest age attributed to fossils of this genus is 1·9 million years for the skull KNM-ER (Kenya National Museum-East Rudolf) 1470 discovered in 1972 by Bernard Ngeneo at Koobi Fora by Lake Turkana, northern Kenya. It was reconstructed by Dr Meave Leakey *(née Epps).*

The earliest stone tools are abraded core-choppers dating from *c.* 2·5 million years. They were found at Hadar, Ethiopia in Nov-Dec 1976 by Hélène Roche (France). Finger-(as opposed to fist-) held quartz slicers found by Roche and Dr John Wall (NZ) close to the Hadar site by the Gona river are also put at the same date.

Earliest *Homo erectus*

The earliest *Homo erectus* (upright man), the species directly ancestral to *Homo sapiens*, was discovered by Kamoya Kimeu on the surface at the site of Nariokotome III to the west of Lake Turkana, Kenya in August 1985. The skeleton of this 1·64 m *5 ft 5 in* 12-year-old-boy is the most complete of this species ever found and only a very few of the small pieces have been found to be missing. It is dated to 1·6 million years.

Great Britain

A Lower Palaeolithic hand-axe factory and occupation site at Boxgrove, Sussex is thought to be possibly more than 450 000 years. This estimate is based on on an analysis of the remains of plants found on the site.

Evidence for the presence of hominids in Great Britain dates from *c.* 400 000 BC. Five worked flint artefacts showing features normally attributed to human workmanship were found in cave deposits near Westbury-sub-Mendip, Somerset, and described in 1975 by Michael J. Bishop.

The oldest actual human remains ever found in Britain are pieces of a brain case from a specimen of *Homo sapiens*, recovered in June 1935 and March 1936 by Dr Alvan T. Marston from the Boyn Hill terrace in the Barnfield Pit, near Swanscombe, Kent. The remains were associated with a middle Acheulian tool culture and probably date to the Holsteinian interglacial (*c.* 230 000 BC).
Three hominid teeth, mandible fragments and a vertebra were found in Pontnewydd Cave, Lower Elwy Valley, North Wales from October 1980. They were dated by the Thorium/Uranium disequilibrium method to a little over 200 000 years.

Europe

A *Homo erectus* skull from a site at Bilzingsleben, East Germany, has been dated by uranium dating techniques to more than 350 000 years and possibly more than 400 000 years.

Longevity

No single subject is more obscured by vanity, deceit, falsehood and deliberate fraud than the extremes of human longevity. Extreme claims are generally made on behalf of the very aged rather than *by* them.

Many hundreds of claims throughout history have been made for persons living well into their second century and some, insulting to the intelligence, for people living even into their third. Centenarians surviving beyond their 113th year are in fact of the extremest rarity and the present absolute proven limit of human longevity does not yet admit of anyone living to celebrate any birthday after their 120th.

The largest group of people in the world with reliable long pedigrees is the British peerage. After ten centuries this has produced only three centenarian peers, of whom only two reached their 101st birthdays. This poor record is possibly not unconnected with the extreme draughtiness of many of their residences and the amount of lead in their game.

Several celebrated super-centenarians (over 110 years) are believed to have been double lives (father and son, relations with the same names or successive bearers of a title). The most famous example was Christian Jakobsen Drackenberg allegedly born in Stavanger, Norway on 18 Nov 1626 and died in Aarhus, Denmark aged seemingly 145 years 326 days on 9 Oct 1772. A number of instances have been commercially sponsored, while a fourth category of recent claims are those made for political ends, such as the 100 citizens of the Russian Soviet–Federative Socialist Republic (population 117 494 000 at mid-1960) claimed in March 1960 to be between 120 and 156. From data on documented centenarians, actuaries have shown that only one 115-year life can be expected in 2100 million lives (cf. world population was estimated to be *c.* 5000 million by mid-1987).

The height of credulity was reached on 5 May 1933, when a news agency gullibly filed a story from China with a Peking date-line that Li Chung-yun, the 'oldest man on Earth', born in 1680, had just died aged 256 years (*sic*).

The most extreme case of longevity recently claimed in the USSR has been 168 years for Shirali 'Baba' Muslinov of Barzavu, Azerbaijan, who died on 2 Sept 1973 and was reputedly born on 26 Mar 1805. No interview of this man was ever permitted to any Western journalist or scientist. He was even said to have celebrated, in 1966, the 100th birthday of his third wife Hartun and that of one of his grandchildren in August 1973. It was reported in 1954 that in the Abkhasian Republic of Georgia, USSR, where aged citizens are invested with an almost saint-like status, 2.58 per cent of the population were aged over 90—24 times the proportion in the USA.

Dr Zhores Aleksandrovich Medvedev (b. Tbilisi, 14 Nov 1925), the Russian gerontologist who was refused a visa to return to the USSR in 1973, referring to USSR claims in Washington DC, on 30 Apr 1974 stated 'The whole phenomenon looks like a falsification' adding 'He [Stalin] liked the idea that [other] Georgians lived to be 100 or more. Local officials tried hard to find more and more cases for Stalin.' He points out (a) the *average* life-span in the regions claiming the highest incidence of centenarians is lower than the USSR average and (b) in contradistinction to the rest of the world, the incidence of centenarians claimed in the Caucasus had declined rapidly from 8000 in 1950 to 4500 in 1970.

It was announced in February 1984 that the 1982 census in China revealed only 2450 centenarians, of whom two-thirds were women. According to a 1985 census carried out in the Chinese Province of Xinjiang Urgur there were 850 centenarians in the area, four aged between 125 and 103 years. In the USA the mid-1983 figure was 32 000. Birth and death registration, however,

became complete only in 1933 and was only 30·9 per cent by 1915.

Oldest authentic centenarian
World

The greatest *authenticated* age to which any human has ever lived is a unique 120 years 237 days in the case of Shigechiyo Izumi of Asan on Tokunoshima, an island 1320 km *820 miles* South West of Tokyo, Japan. He was born at Asan on 29 June 1865 and recorded as a 6-year-old in Japan's first census of 1871. He died in his double-glazed bungalow at 12.15 GMT on 21 Feb 1986 after developing pneumonia.

Great Britain

The United Kingdom has an estimated population of some 4000 centenarians of whom only 22 per cent are male. While husbands have a better chance than bachelors, it appears that spinsters have a better chance than wives in reaching 100 years!

The only UK citizens with birth and death certificates more than 112 years apart have been Mrs Anna Williams (1873–1987) (114 years 208 days), Miss Alice Stevenson (1861–1973) (112 years 39 days) and Miss Janetta Jane Thomas (1869–1982) (112 years 35 days).

Britain's oldest proven man was John Mosley Turner (b. 15 June 1856), who died on 22 Mar 1968 aged 111 years 281 days. Thomas Abelson (allegedly born Britain 17 Oct 1844) died at Peoria, Illinois, USA on 23 Sept 1956 aged 112 years 350 days, but this claim has not yet been substantiated.

The oldest living person in the United Kingdom is Mrs Kate Begbie who was born on 9 Jan 1877 in Dundee, Tayside, Scotland where she now lives in a nursing home.

John Evans, of Llewitha, Swansea, West Glamorgan, is the oldest living man in Britain and was born on 19 Aug 1877. He was formerly a miner having first gone down the mines in 1889. He had a heart pacemaker fitted when he was 108 years old, on 19 Mar 1986, and celebrated his 110th birthday with his first ever visit to London.

The first recorded case in the UK of three siblings being centenarians occurred on 26 Nov 1982 when Miss Frances Adams MSc reached her 100th birthday. Her brother was Dr John Andrew Adams (1867–1967) and her sister Dr Elizabeth Hart (née Adams) (1876–1977). The family came from Omagh, Co. Tyrone, Northern Ireland.

Oldest quadruplets

The world's oldest quads are the Ottman quads of Munich, West Germany—Adolf, Anne-Marie, Emma and Elisabeth. They celebrated their 76th birthday on 5 May 1988.

Oldest triplets

The longest-lived triplets in the world on record were Faith, Hope and Charity Caughlin born at Marlboro, Massachusetts, on 27 Mar 1868. The first to die was Mrs (Ellen) Hope Daniels aged 93 on 2 Mar 1962.

The longest-lived triplets recorded in Great Britain were Faith Alice, Hope Fanny and Charity Sarah Stockdale of Cracoe, near Skipton, North Yorkshire, born on 28–9 Dec 1857. Charity was the first to die on 30 July 1944 aged 86 years 213 days.

Oldest twins

The oldest recorded twins were Eli Shadrack and John Meshak Phipps (b. 14 Feb 1803, Affington, Virginia). Eli died at Hennessey, Oklahoma on 23 Feb 1911 aged 108 years 9 days on which day John was still living in Shenandoah, Iowa. On 17 June 1984, identical twin sisters, Mildred Widman Philippi and Mary Widman Franzini of St Louis, Missouri, celebrated their 104th birthday. Mildred died on 4 May 1985, 44 days short of the twins' would-be 105th birthday. The chances of identical twins both reaching 100 are now probably about one in 50 million.

The oldest twins on record in Great Britain were the twins May and Marjorie Chavasse of Oxford, who were born on 29 Aug 1886. Their brother, Captain Noel Chavasse, was one of only three men ever to have been awarded a bar to the Victoria Cross. He won it posthumously in the First World War. Marjorie died on 27 July 1987 aged 100 years 332 days.

Most reigns

The greatest number of reigns during which any English subject could have lived is ten. A person born on the day (11 April) that Henry VI was deposed in 1471 had to live

AUTHENTIC NATIONAL LONGEVITY RECORDS

	Years	Days		Born		Died	
Japan	120	237	Shigechiyo Izumi	29 June 1865	21 Feb	1986
United Kingdom[1]	114	208	Anna Eliza Williams (Mrs) (née Davies)	2 June 1873	27 Dec	1987
United States[2]	114	93	Florence Knapp	10 Oct 1873	11 Jan	1988
Canada[3]	113	124	Pierre Joubert	15 July 1701	16 Nov	1814
Australia	112	330	Caroline Maud Mockridge	11 Dec 1874	6 Nov	1987
Spain[4]	112	228	Josefa Salas Mateo	14 July 1860	27 Feb	1973
France	112	66	Augustine Teissier (Sister Julia)	2 Jan 1869	9 Mar	1981
Morocco	>112		El Hadj Mohammed el Mokri (Grand Vizier)	1844	16 Sept	1957
Poland	112	+	Roswlia Mielczarak (Mrs)	1868	7 Jan	1981
Ireland	111	327	The Hon. Katherine Plunket	22 Nov 1820	14 Oct	1932
South Africa[5]	111	151	Johanna Booyson	17 Jan 1857	16 June	1968
Czechoslovakia	111	+	Marie Bernatkova	22 Oct 1857	fl. Oct	1968
Norway[6]	111	+	Maren Bolette Torp	21 Dec 1877	fl. Apr	1988
Channel Islands (Guernsey)	110	321	Margaret Ann Neve (née Harvey)	18 May 1792	4 Apr	1903
Northern Ireland	110	234	Elizabeth Watkins (Mrs)	10 Mar 1863	31 Oct	1973
Sweden[6]	110	200+	Wilhelmine Sande (Mrs)	24 Oct 1874	fl. 12 May	1985
Yugoslavia	110	150+	Demitrius Philipovitch	9 Mar 1818	fl. Aug	1928
Netherlands[7]	110	141	Gerada Hurenkamp-Bosgoed	5 Jan 1870	25 May	1980
Greece[8]	110	+	Lambrini Tsiatoura (Mrs)	1870	19 Feb	1981
USSR[9]	110	+	Khasako Dzugayev	7 Aug 1860	fl. Aug	1970
Italy	110	+	Dimiana Sette (Sig)	1884	25 Feb	1985
Tasmania (State of)	109	179	Mary Ann Crow (Mrs)	2 Feb 1836	31 July	1945
Scotland[10]	109	14	Rachel MacArthur (Mrs)	26 Nov 1827	10 Dec	1936
Belgium	108	327	Mathilda Vertommen-Hellemans	12 Aug 1868	4 July	1977
Germany[11]	108	128	Luise Schwarz	27 Sept 1849	2 Feb	1958
Iceland	108	45	Halldóra Bjarndóttir	14 Oct 1873	28 Nov	1981
Portugal[12]	108	+	Maria Luisa Jorge	7 June 1859	fl. July	1967
Finland	109	182	Andrei Akaki Kuznetsoff	17 Oct 1873	fl. 17 Apr	1983
Malaysia	106	+	Hassan Bin Yusoff	14 Aug 1865	fl. Jan	1972
Luxembourg	105	228	Nicolas Wiscourt	31 Dec 1872	17 Aug	1978

[1] London-born Miss Isabella Shepheard was allegedly 115 years old when she died at St Asaph, Clwyd, North Wales, on 20 Nov 1948, but her actual age was believed to have been 109 years 90 days. Charles Alfred Nunez Arnold died in Liverpool on 15 Nov 1941 reputedly aged 112 years 66 days based on a baptismal claim (London, 10 Sept 1829). Mrs Elizabeth Cornish (née Veale) who was buried at Stratton, Cornwall on 10 Mar 1691/2 was reputedly baptised on 16 Oct 1578, 113 years 4 months earlier.

[2] Ex-slave Mrs Martha Graham died at Fayetteville, North Carolina on 25 June 1959 reputedly aged 117 or 118. Census researches by Eckler show that she was seemingly born in Dec 1844 and hence aged 114 years 6 months. Mrs Rena Glover Brailsford died in Summerton, South Carolina, USA on 6 Dec 1977 reputedly aged 118 years. Mrs Rosario Reina Vasquez who died in California on 2 Sept 1980 was reputedly born in Sonora, Mexico on 3 June 1866, which would have made her 114 years 93 days. The 1900 US Federal Census for Crawfish Springs Militia District of Walker County, Georgia, records an age of 77 for a Mark Thrash. If the Mark Thrash (reputedly born in Georgia in December 1822) who died near Chattanooga, Tennessee on 17 Dec 1943 was he, and the age attributed was accurate, then he would have survived for 121 years.

[3] Mrs Ellen Carroll died in North River, Newfoundland, Canada on 8 Dec 1943, reputedly aged 115 years 49 days. Research is underway on the Ontario 1881 Census records on the claim of David Trumble to have been b. 15 Dec 1867.

[4] Snr Benita Medrana of Avila died on 28 Jan 1979 allegedly aged 114 years 335 days.

[5] Mrs Susan Johanna Deporter of Port Elizabeth, South Africa, was reputedly 114 years old when she died on 4 Aug 1954. Mrs Sarah Lawrence, Cape Town, South Africa was reputedly 112 on 3 June 1968.

[6] Mrs W. Sande was born in present-day Norway.

[7] Thomas Peters was recorded to have been born on 6 Apr 1745 in Leeuwarden and died aged 111 years 354 days on 26 Mar 1857 in Arnhem.

[8] The claim that Liakon Efdokia died 17 Jan 1982 aged 118 years 13 days is not substantiated by the censuses of 1971 or 1981. Birth registration before 1920 was fragmentary.

[9] There are allegedly 21 700 centenarians in the USSR (cf. 7000 in the USA). Of these 21 000 are ascribed to the Georgian SSR i.e. one in every 232. In July 1962 it was reported that 128, mostly male, were in the one village of Medini.

[10] Lachlen McDonald, who died 7 June 1858 in Harris, Outer Hebrides, was recorded as being '110 years' on his death certificate.

[11] West Germany: an unnamed female died in 1979 aged 112 years and an unnamed male died, aged also 112 years, in 1969. The Austrian record is 108 years (female d. 1975) and the Swiss record is also 108 years (female d. 1967).

[12] Senhora Jesuina da Conceicao of Lisbon was reputedly 113 years old when she died on 10 June 1965.

Note: fl is the abbreviation for floruit, Latin for he (or she) was living at the relevant date.

to only the comparatively modest age of 87 years 7 months and 6 days to see the accession of Elizabeth I on 17 Nov 1558. Such a person could have been Thomas Carn of London, reputedly born in 1471 and died 28 Jan 1578 in his 107th year.

Long spans

The last Briton with 18th-century paternity was Miss Alice J. Grigg of Belvedere, Kent (d. 28 Apr 1970) whose father William was born on 26 Oct 1799. The father of Baroness Elliot of Harwood (b. 15 Jan 1903), Sir Charles Tennant Bt, was born in Glasgow in the reign of George IV on 4 Nov 1823.

Oldest mummy

Mummification (from the Persian word múm, wax) dates from 2600 BC or the 4th dynasty of the Egyptian pharaohs. The oldest surviving mummy is of Wati, a court musician of c. 2400 BC from the tomb of Nefer in Saqqâra, Egypt found in 1944.

Reproductivity

MOTHERHOOD
Most children

The greatest officially recorded number of children produced by a mother is 69 by the first of the two wives of Feodor Vassilyev (b. 1707–*fl.* 1782), a peasant from Shuya, 241 km *150 miles* east of Moscow. In 27 confinements she gave birth to 16 pairs of twins, 7 sets of triplets and 4 sets of quadruplets. The case was reported by the Monastery of Nikolskiy on 27 Feb 1782 to Moscow. At least 67 survived infancy. Empress Ekaterina II (The Great) (1762–96) was said to have evinced interest. The children, of whom almost all survived to their majority, were born in the period *c.* 1725–65.

The world's most prolific mother is currently Leontina Albina (*née* Espinosa) (b. 1925) of San Antonio, Chile, who in 1981 produced her 55th and last child. Her husband Gerardo Secunda Albina (variously Alvina) (b. 1921) states that he was married in Argentina in 1943 and they had 5 sets of triplets (all boys) before coming to Chile. 'Only' 40 (24 boys and 16 girls) survive. Eleven were lost in an earthquake.

Great Britain
The British record is seemingly held by Elizabeth, wife of John Mott married in 1676 of Monks Kirby, Warwickshire, who produced 42 live-born children. She died in 1720, 44 years later. According to an inscription on a gravestone in Conway Church cemetery, Gwynedd, North Wales, Nicholas Hookes (d. 27 Mar 1637) was the 41st child of his mother Alice Hookes, but further details are lacking. It has not been possible to corroborate or refute this report. Mrs Elizabeth Greenhille (d. 1681) of Abbots Langley, Hertfordshire is alleged to have produced 39 children (32 daughters, 7 sons) in a record 38 confinements. Her son Thomas was author of *'Art of Embalming'* (1705). Mrs Rebecca Town (1805–51) of Keighley, Yorkshire, had 30 children, but only one survived to the age of 3. Mrs Ada Watson (b. 23 June 1886) of Cambridge gave birth to 25 children in 22 confinements, including 3 sets of twins, all of whom attained their majority, during the period 1904–31. She died in Roehampton, London, on 5 Feb 1974.

Great Britain's champion mothers of today are believed to be Mrs Margaret McNaught (b. 1923), of Balsall Heath, Birmingham (12 boys and 10 girls, all single births - 2 boys died in infancy) and Mrs Mabel Constable (b. 1920), of Long Itchington, Warwickshire who also has had 22 children including a set of triplets and two sets of twins. In December 1949 it was reported that Mrs Mabel Murphy (b. 1898) of Lisnaskea, Co. Fermanagh, N. Ireland had produced 28 children (12 still born) in 32 years of marriage, but this claim has not been fully substantiated.

Ireland's champion is Mrs. Kathleen Scott (b. 4 July 1914) of Dublin, who gave birth to her 24th child on the 9 Aug 1958. Twenty of her children are still alive.

Oldest mother
Medical literature contains extreme but unauthenticated cases of septuagenarian mothers, such as Mrs Ellen Ellis, aged 72, of Four Crosses, Clwyd, who allegedly produced a still-born 13th child on 15 May 1776 in her 46th year of marriage. Many very late maternities may be cover-ups for illegitimate grandchildren. The oldest recorded mother for whom the evidence satisfied medical verification was Mrs Ruth Alice Kistler (*née* Taylor), formerly Mrs Shepard (1899–1982), of Portland, Oregon, USA. A birth certificate indicates that she gave birth to a daughter, Suzan, at Glendale, near Los Angeles, California, on 18 Oct 1956, when her age was 57 years 129 days. In the *Gazette Médicale de Liège* (1 Oct 1891) Dr E. Derasse mentioned the case of one of his patients who gave birth to a healthy baby when aged 59 years 5 months. He had managed to obtain her birth certificate. The woman already had a married daughter aged 40 years.

Great Britain
The oldest British mother reliably recorded is Mrs Kathleen Campbell (b. 23 April 1932) of Ilkeston, Derbyshire, who gave birth to a 2·92 kg *6 lb 7 oz* baby boy at Nottingham City Hospital on 9 Sept 1987 aged 55 years 141 days. She already had six children aged 22 to 16 years. Mrs Elizabeth Pearce gave birth to a son when aged 54 years 40 days. According to a report in the *Lancet* (1867) a woman reputedly 62 gave birth to triplets. She had previously had 10 children.

According to figures published by the Office of Population Censuses and Surveys in 1986 a woman that year gave birth to a boy when aged 56 years, but at the moment further information is lacking.

Ireland
The oldest Irish mother recorded was Mrs Mary Higgins of Cork, County Cork (b. 7 Jan 1876) who gave birth to a daughter, Patricia, on 17 Mar 1931 when aged 55 years 69 days.

MULTIPLE BIRTHS

HIGHEST NUMBER REPORTED
AT SINGLE BIRTH *World*
10 (decaplets) (2 male, 8 female) Bacacay, Brazil, 22 Apr 1946 (also report from Spain, 1924 and China, 12 May 1936)

HIGHEST NUMBER MEDICALLY RECORDED[1]
World

9 (nonuplets) (5 male, 4 female) to Mrs Geraldine Brodrick at Royal Hospital, Sydney, Australia on 13 June 1971. 2 males stillborn. Richard (12 oz *340 g*) survived 6 days
9 (all died) to patient at University of Pennsylvania, Philadelphia 29 May 1972
9 (all died) reported from Bagerhat, Bangladesh, *c.* 11 May 1977 to 30-year-old mother

United Kingdom

7 (septuplets) (4 boys and 3 girls) to Mrs Susan Halton (b. 1960) at Liverpool Maternity Hospital on 15 Aug 1987. Last survivor Kane 680 g *1 lb 8 oz* died on 31 Aug 1987. 6 (sextuplets) (all female) to Mrs Janet Walton (b. 1952) at Liverpool Maternity Hospital on 18 Nov 1983. All survive. 6 (4 male, 2 female) to Mrs Jane Underhill (b. 1957) at Rosie Maternity Hospital, Cambridge, on 2 May 1985. After 9 months only 3 survived. 6 (3 male, 3 female) to Mrs Susan Coleman at Homerton, east London on 12 Nov 1986. All survive. 6 (2 male, 4 female) to Mrs Sheila Ann Thorns (*née* Manning) at New Birmingham Maternity Hospital on 2 Oct 1968. Three survive. 6 (1 male, 5 female) to Mrs Rosemary Letts (*née* Egerton) at University College Hospital, London, on 15 Dec 1969. One boy and 4 girls survive

HIGHEST NUMBER SURVIVING[2] *World*

6 out of 6 (3 males, 3 females) to Mrs Susan Jane Rosenkowitz (*née* Scoones) (b. Colombo, Sri Lanka, 28 Oct 1947) at Mowbray, Cape Town, South Africa on 11 Jan 1974. In order of birth they were: David, Nicolette, Jason, Emma, Grant and Elizabeth. They totalled 10·915 kg *24 lb 1 oz*
6 out of 6 (4 males, 2 females) to Mrs Rosanna Giannini (b. 1952) at Careggi Hospital, Florence, Italy on 11 Jan 1980. They are Francesco, Fabrizio, Giorgio Roberto, Letizia and Linda

United Kingdom
6 out of 6 (see above): Mrs Janet Walton and Mrs Susan Coleman

QUINTUPLETS *World Heaviest*

25 lb *11·35 kg* Mrs Lui Saulien, Chekiang, China, 7 June 1953
11·34kg *25 lb* Mrs Kamalammal, Pondicherry, India, 30 Dec 1956

Most premature ● Bouncing James Elgin was born to Brenda and James Gill on 20 May 1987 in Ottawa, Ontario, Canada 128 days premature and weighing 624 g *1 lb 6 oz.*

World Most Sets
No recorded case of more than a single set

QUADRUPLETS *World Heaviest*
10·35 kg *22 lb 13 oz* Mrs Ayako Takeda, Tsuchihashi Maternity Hospital, Kagoshima, Japan, 4 Oct 1978 (4 girls)
World Most Sets
4 Mde Feodor Vassilyev, Shuya, Russia (d. *ante* 1770)

TRIPLETS[3] *World Heaviest*
26 lb 6 oz *11,96 kg* (unconfirmed) Iranian case (2 male, 1 female) 18 Mar 1968
UK Heaviest
10·886 kg *24 lb* Mrs Mary McDermott, of Bearpark, Co Durham, 18 Nov 1914
World Most Sets
15 Maddalena Granata, Italy (1839–*fl.* 1886)

TWINS *World Heaviest*
12·590 kg *27 lb 12 oz* (surviving) Mrs J. P. Haskin, Fort Smith, Arkansas, USA, 20 Feb 1924
UK Heaviest
The 16·1 kg *35 lb 8 oz* reported in the *Lancet* from Derbyshire, on 6 Dec 1884 for the Warren Case (2 males liveborn) is believed to have been a misprint for 11·6 kg *25 lb 8 oz*
World Most Sets
16 Mde Vassilyev (see above). *Note also* Mrs Barbara Zulu of Barberton, South Africa bore 3 sets of girls and 3 mixed sets in 7 years (1967–73)
UK Most Sets
15 Mrs Mary Jonas of Chester (d. 4 Dec 1899)—all sets were boy and girl

[1] Mrs Edith Bonham (d. 1469) of Wishford Magna, Wiltshire reportedly had septuplets.
[2] The South African press were unable to verify the birth of 5 babies to Mrs Charmaine Craig (*née* Peterson) in Cape Town on 16 Oct 1980 and a sixth on 8 Nov. The reported names were Frank, Salome, John, Andrew, William and belatedly Deborah.
[3] Mrs Anna Steynvaait of Johannesburg produced 2 sets within 10 months in 1960.

Longest and shortest pregnancy

Claims up to 413 days have been widely reported but accurate data are bedevilled by the increasing use of oral contraceptive pills which is a cause of amenorrhoea. *The US Medical Investigator* of 27 Dec 1884 reported a case of 15 months 20 days and the *Histoire de l'Académie* of 1751 the most extreme case of 36 months. In the pre-pill era English law has accepted pregnancies with extremes of 174 days (*Clark* v. *Clark*, 1939) and 349 days (*Hadlum* v. *Hadlum*, 1949). In May 1961 a Burmese woman aged 54 had a 1·3 kg *3 lb* calcified foetus removed by caesarean section in Rangoon after 25 years' gestation. She had gone into labour in 1936, but no child was born.

MULTIPLE BIRTHS

Lightest twins

The lightest recorded birth weight for a pair of surviving twins has been 992 g *2 lb 3 oz* in the case of Mary 453 g *16 oz* and Margaret 538 g *19 oz* born on 16 Aug 1931 to Mrs Florence Stimson, Queens Road, Old Fletton, Peterborough, England.

'Siamese' twins

Conjoined twins derived the name 'Siamese' from the celebrated Chang and Eng Bunker (known in Thailand as Chan and In) born at Meklong on 11 May 1811 of Chinese parents. They were joined by a cartilaginous band at the chest and married in April 1843 the Misses Sarah and Adelaide Yates of Wilkes County, North Carolina, and fathered ten and twelve children respectively. They died within three hours of each other on 17 Jan 1874, aged 62. The only known British example to reach maturity were the pygopagus twins Daisy and Violet Hilton born in Brighton, now East Sussex, on 5 Feb 1908 (joined at the buttocks). They died in Charlotte, North Carolina, on 5 Jan 1969, aged 60, from Hong Kong flu. The earliest successful separation of Siamese twins was performed on xiphopagus (joined at the sternum) girls at Mt Sinai Hospital, Cleveland, Ohio by Dr Jac S. Geller on 14 Dec 1952.

The rarest form of conjoined twins is Dicephales tetrabrachius dipus (two heads, four arms and two legs). The only known examples are the pair Masha and Dasha born in the USSR on 4 Jan 1950, Nadir and Juraci Climerio de Oliverra of Santo Amaro de Purifcacao, Bahia, Brazil, born on 2 June 1957, an unnamed pair separated in a 10-hour operation in Washington DC, on 23 June 1977, Fonda Michelle and Shannon Elaine Beaver of Forest City, North Carolina, USA born on 9 Feb 1980 and successfully separated in February 1981. Hassan and Hussein (b. Sept 1986) of Sudan were successfully separated at Great Ormond Street Hospital, London on 29 Apr 1987. Britain's only known pair were the 'Scottish brothers', who were born near Glasgow in 1490. They were brought to the Court of King James IV of Scotland in 1491, and lived under the king's patronage for the rest of his reign. They died in 1518 aged 28 years, one 5 days before the other, who 'moaned piteously as he crept about the castle gardens, carrying with him the dead body of the brother from whom only death could separate him and to whom death would again join him'.

The oldest surviving unseparated twins are the craniopagus pair Yvonne and Yvette McCarther (b. 1949) of Los Angeles, California (heads are fused at the crown). They have rejected an operation to separate them.

Most twins *Geographically*

In Chungchon, South Korea it was reported in September 1981 that there were unaccountably 38 pairs in only 275 families—the highest ever recorded ratio. The highest ratio of twins in Britain is to be found on the island of North Uist in the Outer Hebrides, Scotland. In June 1985 there were 36 sets aged from 82 to 2 years, a ratio of 1 to 40. (Cf. the national average of 1 to 100.)

Longest separated twins

Twins Philip and Barbara McAuley of Preston, Lancashire (b. 27 May 1916) became separated when over a year old on 30 June 1917. Officers of the Salvation Army reunited them for the first time after almost exactly 70 years in London on 29 June 1987.

Fastest triplet birth

The fastest natural birth of triplets was 2 minutes for Mrs James E. Duck of Memphis, Tennessee (Bradley, Christopher and Carmon) on 21 Mar 1977.

Test-tube quintuplets

The world's first test-tube quintuplets, Alan, Brett, Connor, Douglas and Edward, were born to Linda and Bruce Jacobssen at University College Hospital, London on 26 Apr 1985.

Quindecaplets

It was announced by Dr Gennaro Montanino of Rome that he had removed by hysterotomy at 4 months of the pregnancy the foetuses of 10 girls and 5 boys from the womb of a 35-year-old housewife on 22 July 1971. A fertility drug was responsible for this unique and unsurpassed instance of quindecaplets.

Longest interval between twins

Mrs. Danny Berg (b. 1953) of Rome, Italy who had been on hormone treatment after suffering two miscarriages, gave birth normally to a baby girl, Diana, on 23 Dec 1987, but the other twin, Monica, was not delivered by Caesarian until 30 Jan 1988. Mrs Mary Wright, 38, gave birth to Amy and Elizabeth 18 months apart from eggs fertilised by her husband in March 1984. Elizabeth was born at Stoke-on-Trent, Staffordshire, on 22 April 1987 from an egg which had been in frozen storage for 29 months.

DESCENDANTS

In polygamous countries, the number of a person's descendants can become incalculable. The last Sharifian Emperor of Morocco, Moulay Ismail (1672–1727), known as 'The Bloodthirsty', was reputed to have fathered a total of 525 sons and 342 daughters by 1703 and a 700th son in 1721.

In April 1984 the death was reported of Adam Borntrager, aged 96, of Medford, Wisconsin, who had had 707 direct descendants of whom all but 32 were living. The total comprised 11 children, 115 grand, 529 great-grand and 20 great-great-grandchildren. The family is of the Amish Mennonite sect who eschew cars, telephones, electric light and higher education.

Mrs Sarah Crawshaw (d. 25· Dec 1844) left 397 descendants according to her gravestone in Stones Church, Ripponden, Halifax, West Yorkshire.

Multiple great-grandparents

The report in 1983 that Jane Kau Pung (1877–1982) had left 4 great-great-great-great-grandchildren has proved to be incorrect. She in fact proved to be one of many cases of great-great-great-grandparents. Of these cases the youngest person to learn that their great-granddaughter had become a grandmother was Mrs Ann V. Weirick (1888–1978) of Paxtonville, Pennsylvania, who received news of her great-great-great-grandson Matthew Stork (b. 9 Sept 1976) when aged only 88. She died on 6 Jan 1978. Britain's youngest 3 greats grandmother was Mrs Violet Lewis (1885–1982) of Southampton.

Most living ascendants

Megan Sue Austin (b. 16 May 1982) of Bar Harbor, Maine, had a full set of grandparents and great-grandparents and five great-great-grandparents, making 19 direct ascendants.

BABIES

Heaviest

The heaviest viable babies on record, of normal parentage, were boys 10·2 kg *22 lb 8 oz* born to Sig Carmelina Fedele of Aversa, Italy in September 1955 and by caesarian section to Mrs Christina Samane at Sipetu Hospital, Transkei, South Africa on 24 May 1982. The latter boy named Sithandive weighed 55·5 kg *8 st 10 lb* and stood 1·60 m *5 ft 3 in* on his 5th birthday.

Mrs Anna Bates *née* Swan (1846–88), the 227 cm *7 ft 5½ in* Canadian giantess (see also p. 8), gave birth to a boy weighing 10·77 kg *23 lb 12 oz* (length 76 cm *30 in*) at her home in Seville, Ohio, USA on 19 Jan 1879, but the baby died 11 hours later. Her first child, an 8·16 kg *18 lb* girl (length 61 cm *24 in*) was still-born when she was delivered in 1872.

On 9 Jan 1891 Mrs Florentin Ortega of Buenos Aires, Argentina produced a still-born boy weighing 11·3 kg *25 lb*. In May 1939 a deformed baby weighing 13·26 kg *29 lb 4 oz* was born in a hospital at Effingham, Illinois, USA, but died 2 hours later.

United Kingdom

The greatest recorded live birth weight in the United Kingdom is 9·53 kg *21 lb* for a child born on Christmas Day, 1852. It was reported in a letter to the *British Medical Journal* (1 Feb 1879) from a doctor in Torpoint, Cornwall. The only other reported birth weight in excess of 9·07 kg *20 lb* is 9·13 kg *20 lb 2 oz* for a boy with a 36·8 cm *14½ in* chest born to a 33-year-old schoolmistress in Crewe, Cheshire, on 12 Nov 1884. On 15 Oct 1785 the 'Irish Fairy', Mrs Catherine Kelly, who stood 86·3 cm *34 in* and weighed 9·97 kg *22 lb*, died in Norwich, Norfolk, after giving birth to a 3·17 kg *7 lb* baby which lived only 2 hours.

Most bouncing baby

Thomas Hills Everitt (b. 7 Feb 1779 – died ?) of Enfield, Middlesex weighed 57 kg *126 lb* at the age of 11 months. He stood 99 cm *3 ft 3 in* tall and had a girth of 94 cm *37 in*. T. J. Albert Jackson, the world's heaviest living man (see p. 9), weighed 47·6 kg *105 lb* and stood 124 cm *4 ft 1 in* tall at the age of 12 months. Therese Parentean, who died in Rouyn, Quebec, Canada on 11 May 1936 aged 9 years, weighed 154 kg *24 st 4 lb* (cf. 171 kg *27 st* for Robert Earl Hughes at the age of 10 [see table, and Chest measurements, p. 9).

Lightest

The lowest birth weight recorded for a surviving infant, of which there is definite evidence, is 283 g *10 oz* in the case of Mrs Marian Taggart *née* Chapman (b. 5 June 1938, d. 31 May 1983) who was born six weeks premature in South Shields, Tyne and Wear. She was born unattended (length 31 cm) and was nursed by Dr D. A. Shearer, who fed her hourly for the first 30 hours with brandy, glucose and water through a fountain-pen filler. At three weeks she weighed 821 g *1 lb 13 oz* and by her first birthday 6·29 kg *13 lb 14 oz*. Her weight on her 21st birthday was 48·08 kg *7 st 8 lb*.

A weight of 227 g *8 oz* was reported on 20 Mar 1938 for a baby born prematurely to Mrs John Womack, after she had been knocked down by a lorry in East St Louis, Illinois. The baby was taken alive to St Mary's Hospital, but died a few hours later. On 23 Feb 1952 it was reported that a 170 g *6 oz* baby only 17 cm *6½ in* long lived for 12 hours in a hospital in Indianapolis, Indiana. A twin was still-born.

Coincident birthdates

The only verified example of a family producing 5 single children with coincident birthdays is that of Catherine (1952), Carol (1953), Charles (1956), Claudia (1961) and Cecilia (1966), born to Ralph and Carolyn Cummins of Clintwood, Virginia, all on 20 February. The random odds against five single siblings sharing a birthdate would be one in 17 797 577 730—more than 3½ times the world's population.

The three children of the Henriksen family of Andenes, Norway, Heidi (b. 1960) Olav (b. 1964) and Lief-Martin (b. 1968) all celebrate their birthday infrequently, because these all fall on Leap Day – February 29. Ralph Bertram Williams was born on 4 July 1982 in Wilmington, North

Carolina. His father, grandfather and, in 1876, his great-grandfather were also born on 4 July.

Most southerly birth
Emilio Marcos Palma (Argentina), born 7 Jan 1978 at the Sargento Cabral Base, Antarctica, is the only person alive who can claim to be the first born on any continent. The mother was flown from Argentina at governmental expense.

Test-tube baby *Earliest*
Lesley Brown, 31, was delivered by caesarian section of Louise Brown (2·6 kg *5 lb 12 oz*) in Oldham General Hospital, Lancashire, at 11.47 p.m. on 25 July 1978. Louise was externally conceived on 10 Nov 1977.

Physiology and Anatomy

Hydrogen (63 per cent) and oxygen (25.5 per cent) constitute the commonest of the 24 elements in the human body. In 1972 four more trace elements were added—fluorine, silicon, tin and vanadium. The 'essentiality' of nickel has not yet been finally pronounced upon.

HANDS, FEET AND HAIR
Touch
The extreme sensitivity of the fingers is such that a vibration with a movement of 0·02 of a micron can be detected.

Longest finger nails
The longest finger nails ever reported are those of Shridhar Chillal (b. 1937) of Pune, India. The aggregate measurement, on 25 Mar 1988, was 413·5 cm *163 in* for the 5 nails on his left hand (thumb 96·5 cm *38 in*). He last cut his nails in 1952. Finger nails grow about 0·05 cm *0·02 in* a week—four times faster than toe nails.

Most fingers and toes (Polydactylism)
At an inquest held on a baby boy at Shoreditch, east London on 16 Sept 1921 it was reported that he had 14 fingers and 15 toes.

Least toes
The two-toed syndrome exhibited by some members of the Wadomo tribe of the Zambezi Valley, Zimbabwe, and the Kalanga tribe of the eastern Kalahari Desert, Botswana, is hereditary via a single mutated gene. These 'ostrich people', as they are known, are not handicapped by their deformity, and can walk great distances without discomfort.

Largest feet
John Thrupp (b.1964) of Stratford–upon–Avon, Warwickshire, wears a size 21 shoe. He is 2·11 m *6 ft 11 in* tall. Chris Greener, Britain's tallest man (see page 7) takes size 18.

Longest hair
Swami Pandarasannadhi, the head of the Tirudaduturai monastery, Tanjore district, Madras, India, was reported in 1949 to have hair 7·92 m *26 ft* in length but no photographic or scientific evidence has ever been supplied in order to support this extreme measurement. In 1780 a head of hair measuring 3·65 m *12 ft* in length and dressed in a style known as the Plica Polonica (hair closely matted together) was sent to Dresden after adorning the head of a Polish peasant woman for 52 years. The plait of hair was 12 in 30·4 cm in circumference. The length of hair of Miss Skuldfrid Sjorgren (b. Stockholm) was reported from Toronto in 1927 to have reached twice her height at 3·20 m *10 ft 6 in*. The hair of Diane Witt of Worcester, USA measured 312 cm *10 ft 3 in* in May 1988. She last cut her hair 16 years ago. Human hair grows at the rate of about 1·27 cm *0·5 in* a month. If left uncut it will usually grow to a maximum of 61–91 cm *2–3 ft*.

Strongest hair
In a test on BBC TV *Record Breakers* on 9 Sept 1984 a single hair from the head of Miss Pham Thy Lan broke at a strain of 178 g *6¼ oz*.

Most valuable hair
On 18 Feb 1988 a bookseller from Cirencester, Gloucestershire, paid £5575 for a lock of hair belonging to Lord Nelson (1758–1805) at an auction held at Crewkerne, Somerset.

Longest beard
The longest beard preserved was that of Hans N. Langseth (b. 1846 near Eidsroll, Norway) which measured 5·33 m *17½ ft* at the time of his burial at Kensett, Iowa in 1927 after 15 years' residence in the United States. The beard was presented to the Smithsonian Institution, Washington DC in 1967. Richard Latter (b. Pembury, Kent, 1831) of Tunbridge Wells, Kent, who died in 1914 aged 83, reputedly had a beard 4·87 m *16 ft* long but contemporary independent corroboration is lacking and photographic evidence indicates this figure was exaggerated. The beard of the bearded lady Janice Deveree (b. Bracken Co., Kentucky, 1842) was measured at 36 cm *14 in* in 1884. The beard of Mlle Hélène Antonia of Liège, Belgium, a 17th-century exhibitionist, was said to have reached to her hips.

Longest moustache
The longest moustache on record is that of Birger Pellas (b. 21 Sept 1934) of Malmö, Sweden, grown since 1973, which reached 281 cm *9 ft 2½ in* on 25 Jan 1988.

The longest moustache in Great Britain has been that of John Roy (b. 14 Jan 1910 d. 6 April 1988), of Weeley, near Clacton, Essex. It attained a peak span of 189 cm *74½ in* between 1939 and 2 Apr 1976. He accidentally sat on it in the bath in 1984 and chopped off 42 cm *16½ in*. He then took off the same amount from the other side to even the moustache. The current UK champion is Mike Solomons of Long Ditton, Surrey with 81·3 cm *32 in* as of March 88.

DENTITION
Earliest
The first deciduous or milk teeth normally appear in infants at 5–8 months, these being the mandibular and maxillary first incisors. There are many records of children born with teeth, the most distinguished example being Prince Louis Dieudonné, later Louis XIV of France, who was born with two teeth on 5 Sept 1638. Molars usually appear at 24 months, but in Pindborg's case published in Denmark in 1970, a 6-week premature baby was documented with 8 natal teeth of which 4 were in the molar region.

Most
Cases of the growth in late life of a third set of teeth have been recorded several times. A reference to a case in France of a fourth dentition, known as Lison's case, was published in 1896. A triple row of teeth was noted in 1680 by Albertus Hellwigius.

Most dedicated dentist
Brother Giovanni Battista Orsenigo of the Ospedale Fatebenefratelli, Rome, a religious dentist, conserved all the teeth he extracted in three enormous cases during the time he exercised his profession from 1868 to 1904. In 1903 the number was counted and found to be 2 000 744 teeth, indicating an average of 185 teeth or nearly 6 total extractions a day.

Strongest bite
In August 1986, Richard Hofmann (b. 1949) of Lake City, Florida, USA, achieved a bite strength of 442 kg *975 lb* for approx. 2 seconds in a research test using a gnathodynamometer at the College of Dentistry, University of Florida, USA. This figure is over 6 times normal biting strength.

Most valuable tooth
In 1816 a tooth belonging to Sir Isaac Newton (1643–1727) was sold in London for £730. It was purchased by a nobleman who had it set in a ring which he wore constantly.

Earliest false teeth
From discoveries made in Etruscan tombs, partial dentures of bridge-work type were being worn in what is now Tuscany, Italy, as early as 700 BC. Some were permanently attached to existing teeth and others were removable.

OPTICS
Smallest visible object
The resolving power of the human eye is 0·0003 of a radian or an arc of one minute (1/60th of a degree), which corresponds to 100 microns at 10 in. A micron is a thousandth of a millimetre, hence 100 microns is 0·003937, or less than four thousandths, of an inch. The

---

Longest moustache ● Karna Ram Bheel (1928–87) was granted permission by a New Delhi prison governor in February 1979 to keep his 238 cm *7 ft 10 in* moustache which he had grown since 1949 during his life sentence. He used mustard, oil, butter and cream to keep it in trim. (Photo: Gamma)

human eye can, however, detect a bright light source shining through an aperture only 3 to 4 microns across. Dentist Veronica Seider (b. 1951) of Ludwigsberg, West Germany, possesses a visual acuity of 20 times better than average. She can identify people at a distance of more than a mile *1·6 km*, and also specialises in micro-writing without the use of artificial aids. In one test she examined what seemed to be a thread of cotton and then announced that it was actually four threads twisted tightly together. Magnification proved her right.

Colour sensitivity

The unaided human eye, under the best possible viewing conditions, comparing large areas of colour, in good illumination, using both eyes, can distinguish 10 000 000 different colour surfaces. The most accurate photo-electric spectrophotometers possess a precision probably only 40 per cent as good as this. About 7·5 per cent of men and 0·1 per cent of women are colour blind. The most extreme form, monochromatic vision, is very rare. The highest rate of red-green colour blindness is in Czechoslovakia and the lowest rate among Fijians and Brazilian Indians.

BONES
Longest

Excluding a variable number of sesamoids (small rounded bones) there are 206 bones in the adult human body, compared with 300 for children (as they grow some bones fuse together to make one). The thigh bone or *femur* is the longest. It constitutes usually 27½ per cent of a person's stature, and may be expected to be 50 cm *19 ¾ in* long in a 183 cm *6 ft* tall man. The longest recorded bone was the femur of the German giant Constantine, who died in Mons, Belgium, on 30 Mar 1902, aged 30. It measured 76 cm *29·9 in.* The femur of Robert Wadlow, the tallest man ever recorded, measured an estimated 75 cm *29·5 in.*

Smallest

The *stapes* or stirrup bone, one of the three auditory ossicles in the middle ear, is the smallest human bone, measuring from 2·6 to 3·4 mm *0·10 to 0·17 in* in length and weighing from 2·0 to 4·3 mg *0.03 to 0·065 grains.*

MUSCLES
Largest

Muscles normally account for 40 per cent of the body weight and the bulkiest of the 639 named muscles in the human body is the *gluteus maximus* or buttock muscle, which extends the thigh.

Smallest

The smallest muscle is the *stapedius*, which controls the *stapes* (see above), an auditory ossicle in the middle ear, and which is less than 0·127 cm *1/20 th* of an inch long.

Largest chest measurements

The largest chest measurements are among endo-morphs (those with a tendency towards globularity). In the extreme case of Hughes (see table) this was 315 cm *124 in*, and William Campbell, Britain's second heaviest man, had a 244 cm *96 in* chest. George Macaree (formerly Britain's heaviest man) has a chest measurement of 190·5 cm *75 in* (waist 177·8 cm *70 in*), at a body weight of 196·8 kg *31 st* 177·8 cm *(height 5 ft 10 in)* and Martin Ruane has a chest measurement of 185·4 cm *73 in* (waist 172·7 cm *68 in*).

Among muscular subjects (mesomorphs) of normal height *expanded* chest measurements above 142 cm *56 in* are extremely rare. Arnold Schwarznegger (b.1948) of Graz, Austria, 185 cm *6 ft 11 in* former Mr Universe and 'the most perfectly developed man in the history of the world', had a chest measurement of 145 cm *57 in* (bicep 55·8 cm *22 in*) at his best bodyweight of 107 kg *235 lb.* This was exceeded by Vasiliy Alekseyev (b. 1942), the 186 cm *6 ft 1¼ in* Russian super-heavyweight weight-lifting champion, who had a 153·6 cm *60½ in* chest at his top weight of 158·7 kg *350 lb.*

Largest biceps

Isaac 'Dr Size' Nesser (b. 21 Apr 1962) has biceps of over 66·35 cm *26⅛ in* cold (not pumped). He has a chest measurement of 172·87 cm *68 1/16 in* and a waist of 110·06 cm *43 1/13 in.* He weighs 164·2 kg *362 lb.*

Smallest waists

Queen Catherine di Medici (1519–89) decreed a waist measurement of 33 cm *13 in* for ladies of the French Court, but this was at a time when females were more diminutive. The smallest recorded waist among women of normal stature in the 20th century is a reputed 33 cm *13 in* in the cases of the French actress Mlle Polaire (1881–1939) and Mrs Ethel Granger (1905–82) of Peter-borough, Cambridge, who reduced from a natural 56 cm *22 in* over the period 1929–39.

Longest necks

The maximum measured extension of the neck by the successive fitting of copper coils, as practised by the women of the Padaung or Kareni tribe of Burma, is 40 cm *15 ¾ in.* When the rings are removed the muscles developed to support the head and neck shrink to their normal length.

BRAINS
Heaviest

The brain of an average adult male (i.e. 20–55 years) weighs 1424 g *3 lb 2·2 oz*, decreasing gradually to 1395 g *3 lb 1·1 oz* with advancing age. The heaviest brain ever recorded was that of a 50-year-old male which weighed 2049 g *4 lb 8·29 oz* reported by Dr Thomas F. Hegert, chief medical examiner for District 9, State of Florida, USA, on 23 Oct 1975. The brain of Ivan Sergeyvich Turgenev (1818–83), the Russian author, weighed 2012 g *4 lb 6·9 oz.* In January 1891 the *Edinburgh Medical Journal* reported the case of a 75-year-old man in the Royal Edinburgh Asylum whose brain weighed 1829 g *4 lb 0·5 oz.* The largest female brain on record weighed 1565 g *3 lb 7·3 oz.* It belonged to a murderess.

Human brains are getting heavier. Examination of *post-mortem* records shows that the average male brain weight has increased from 1372 g *3 lb 0·4 oz* in 1860 to 1424 g *3 lb 2·2 oz* today. Women's brains have also put on weight, from 1242 g *2 lb 11·8 oz* to 1265 g *2 lb 12·6 oz* and in recent years have been growing almost as fast as men's.

Professor Marian Diamond of the University of California at Berkeley announced on 13 Feb 1985 that the neuron to glial cell ratio in Section 39 of the brain of Albert Einstein (1879–1955) was 1:12 as opposed to the standard 1:936—a difference of 72·8 per cent.

Lightest

The lightest 'normal' or non-atrophied brain on record was one weighing 1096 g *2 lb 6·7 oz* reported by Dr P. Davis and Professor E. Wright of King's College Hospital, London in 1977. It belonged to a 31-year-old woman.

Highest IQ

Intelligence quotients or IQs comprise the subject's mental age divided by his chronological or actual age multiplied by 100 such that an 8-year -old more gifted than an average 16-year-old would have an IQ of $^{16}/_8 \times 100 = 200$. The highest childhood score has been achieved by Marilyn vos Savant (b.1947) of St Louis, Missouri, who as a 10-year-old achieved a ceiling score for 23-year-olds thus giving her an IQ of 228. In December 1986 it was reported that 10–year old Andra-gone Eastwood Demello of Attos, California, USA had an estimated ceiling level of between 200 and 225. He spoke his first word 'hello' at the age of 7 weeks

The most exclusive ultra high IQ society is the Hoeflin Research Group, New York, USA, whose 17 members have an IQ which occurs at a 1 in 1 500 000 level in the population. The highest score in the admission test devised by Ronald K. Hoeflin, is 46 out of 48 by Marilyn vos Savant (see above), making her, with Eric Hart

(b.1956) and Keith Raniere (b.1960), both of New York, one of only three members who have scored higher than 45. This represents a performance at the level of 1 in 10 000 000.

The highest IQ published for a national population is 111 for the Japanese. For those born in 1960–61 a figure of 115 has been published. At least 10 per cent of their whole population has an IQ > 130.

Human computer

The fastest extraction of a 13th root from a 100– digit number is in 1 min 28·8 sec by the Dutchman Willem Klein (b. 1912, k. 1 Aug 1986) on 7 Apr 1981 at the National Laboratory for High Energy Physics (KEK), Tsukuba, Japan. Mrs Shakuntala Devi of India demonstrated the multiplication of two 13-digit numbers 7 686 369 774 870 × 2 465 099 745 779 picked at random by the Computer Department of Imperial College, London on 18 June 1980, in 28 seconds. Her correct answer was 18 947 668 177 995 426 462 773 730. Some experts on calculating prodigies refuse to give credence to Mrs Devi on the grounds that it is so vastly superior to the calculating feats of any other invigilated prodigy that the invigilation must have been defective.

Memory

Bhandanta Vicitsara recited 16 000 pages of Bhuddist canonical texts in Rangoon, Burma in May 1974. Gon Yang-ling, 26, has memorised more than 15 000 tele-phone numbers in Harbin, China according to the Xinhua News Agency. Rare instances of eidetic memory—the ability to re-project and hence 'visually' recall material—are known to science.

Creighton Herbert James Carvello (b. 19 Nov 1942, Middlesborough) memorised a random sequence of 6 separate packs (312) of cards on a single sighting with only 4 errors including an all correct straight run of 139 cards at the New Marske Institute Club, Cleveland, England on 21 Mar 1985. Jonathan Hancock (b. 12 Feb 1972) of Middlesbrough, Cleveland, memorised a random sequence of 6 packs shuffled together on 30 Apr 1988 with only 6 errors at the Dolphin Leisure Centre, Darlington, Durham.

The greater number of places of π

Hideaki Tomoyori (b. 30 Sept 1932), of Yokohama, Japan, recited 'pi' from memory to 40 000 places in 17 hr 21 min including 4 hr 15 min breaks on 9–10 Mar 1987 at the Tsukuba University Club House. On a Japanese TV programme, Mr Tomoyori also demonstrated his ability to recite correctly the 20 consecutive digits following a randomly selected series of numbers.

The British record is 20 013 by Creighton Carvello (see above) on 27 June 1980 in 9 hr 10 min at Saltscar Comprehensive School, Redcar, Cleveland. *Note:* It is only the *approximation* of π at $^{22}/_7$ which recurs after its sixth decimal place and can, of course, be recited *ad nauseam.* The true value is a string of random numbers fiendishly difficult to memorise. The average ability for memorising random numbers is barely more than 8, as proved by the common inability to memorise 9 or 10 digit telephone numbers.

VOICE
Highest and lowest

The highest and lowest recorded notes attained by the human voice before this century were a staccato E in *alt altissimo* (e[iv]) by Ellen Beach Yaw (US) (1869–1947) in Carnegie Hall, New York, on 19 Jan 1896, and an A₁ (55 Hz (cycles per sec)) by Kasper Foster (1617–73). Madeleine Marie Robin (1918–60) the French operatic coloratura could produce and sustain the B above high C in the Lucia mad scene in Donizetti's *Lucia di Lammer-moor.* Since 1950 singers have achieved high and low notes far beyond the hitherto accepted extremes. How-ever, notes at the bass and treble extremities of the register tend to lack harmonics and are of little musical value. Frl Marita Gunther, trained by Alfred Wolfsohn, has covered the range of the piano from the lowest note, A_{11} to c^v. Of this range of 7¼ octaves, 6 octaves were considered to be of musical value. Roy Hart, also trained by Wolfsohn, has reached notes below the range of the piano. Barry Girard of Canton, Ohio in May 1975 reached the E (4340 Hz) above the piano's top note. The highest note put into song is G^{iv} first occurring in Mozart's *Popoli di Tessaglia*. The lowest vocal note in the classical repertoire is in Mozart's *Il Seraglio* in Osmin's aria which calls for a low D (73.4 Hz). Dan Britton reached the 4th E below middle C at 20·6 Hz at Anoka County Fair, Minnesota, on 31 July 1984. Stefan Zucker sang A in *alt altissimo* for 3·8 sec in the tenor role of Salvini in the première of Bellini's *Adelson e Salvini* in New York on 12 Sept 1972.

Greatest range

The normal intelligible outdoor range of the male human voice in still air is 180 m *200 yd*. The *silbo*, the whistled language of the Spanish-speaking Canary Island of La Gomera, is intelligible across the valleys, under ideal conditions, at 8 km *5 miles*. There is a recorded case, under freak acoustic conditions, of the human voice being detectable at a distance of 17 km *10½ miles* across still water at night. It was said that Mills Darden (see table page 9) could be heard 9 km *6 miles* away when he bellowed at the top of his voice.

Because of their greater optimum frequency, female screams tend to record higher readings on decibel meters than male bellows. The annual World Shouting Championship record is 112·4 dBA by Anthony Fieldhouse on 9 Sept 1984 at Scarborough, North Yorkshire. The highest scientifically measured emission has been one of 123·2 dBA by the screaming of Neil Stephenson of Newcastle-upon-Tyne, Tyne and Wear on 18 May 1985.

Lowest detectable sound

The intensity of noise or sound is measured in terms of pressure. The pressure of the quietest sound that can be detected by a person of normal hearing at the most sensitive frequency of *c.* 2750 Hz is 2×10^{-5} pascal. One tenth of the logarithm to this standard provides a unit termed a decibel (dBA). A noise of 30 decibels is negligible.

Highest noise levels

Prolonged noise above 150 decibels will cause permanent deafness while above 192 dBA a lethal over-pressure shock wave can be formed. Equivalent continuous sound levels (LEQ) above 90 dBA are impermissible in factories, but this compares with 125 emitted by racing cars, 130 by amplified music and 170 by some toy guns.

Highest detectable pitch

The upper limit of hearing by the human ear is reckoned to be 20 000 Hz (cycles per sec), although it has been alleged that children with asthma can detect sounds of 30 000 Hz. Bats emit pulses at up to 90 000 Hz. It was announced in February 1964 that experiments in the USSR had conclusively proved that oscillations as high as 200 000 Hz can be detected if the oscillator is pressed against the skull.

Fastest talker

Few people are able to speak *articulately* at a sustained speed above 300 words per minute. The fastest broadcaster has been regarded as Gerry Wilmot (b. Victoria, BC, Canada, 6 Oct 1914), the ice hockey commentator in the late forties post-World War II period. Raymond Glendenning (1907–74), the BBC commentator, once spoke 176 words in 30 sec while commentating on a greyhound race. In public life the highest speed recorded is a 327 words per min burst in a speech made in December 1961 by John Fitzgerald Kennedy (1917–63), then President of the United States. Fran Capo, of New York, achieved a rate of 585 words per minute as a guest on the *Larry King Live* television programme of Cable News Network on 5 Mar 1986.

John Helm of Yorkshire TV can recite the 92 Football League clubs in 26 sec.

BLOOD
Groups

The preponderance of one blood group varies greatly from one locality to another. On a world basis Group O is the most common (46 per cent), but in some areas, for example Norway, Group A predominates.

The full description of the commonest sub-group in Britain is O MsNs, P+, Rr, Lu(a−), K−, Le(a−b+), Fy(a+b+), Jk(a+b+), which occurs in one in every 270 people.

Most expensive skull ● The skull of Emanuel Swedenborg (1688–1772), the Swedish philosopher and theologian, is kept in the Session Room of the Royal Swedish Academy of Sciences and was bought in London by the Academy for £5500 on 6 Mar 1978. (Photo: Ulf Blumenberg)

The rarest blood group on the ABO system, one of 14 systems, is AB, which occurs in less than 3 per cent of persons in the British Isles. The rarest type in the world is a type of Bombay blood (sub-type h-h) found so far only in a Czechoslovak nurse in 1961 and in a brother (Rh positive) and sister (Rh negative) named Jalbert in Massachusetts, reported in February 1968.

Richest natural resources

Joe Thomas of Detroit, Michigan, was reported in August 1970 to have the highest known count of Anti-Lewis B, the rare blood antibody. A US biological supply firm pays him $1500 per quart *1·13 l*. The Internal Revenue regard this income as a taxable liquid asset.

Donor and recipient

Since 1966, Allen Doster, a self-employed beautician, has, to March 1988, made a total of 984 platelet donations by both manual and machine plasmapheresis at Roswell Park Memorial Institute, New York. The current limit in the USA on machine platelet pheresis donations is 24 per year.

A 50-year-old haemophiliac Warren C. Jyrich required 2400 donor units *1080 l* of blood when undergoing open heart surgery at the Michael Reese Hospital, Chicago, in December 1970.

Largest vein

The largest vein in the human body is the *inferior vena cava*, which returns the blood from most of the body below the level of the heart.

Most alcoholic subject

California University Medical School, Los Angeles reported in December 1982 the case of a confused but conscious 24-year-old female, who was shown to have a blood alcohol level of 1510 mg per 100 ml— nearly 19 times the UK driving limit and triple the normally lethal limit. After two days she discharged herself.

The United Kingdom's legal limit for motorists is 80 mg of alcohol per 100 ml of blood (or 35 μg of alcohol per 100 ml of breath). The hitherto recorded highest figure in medical literature of 656 mg per 100 ml was submerged when the late Samuel Riley (b. 1922) of Sefton Park, Merseyside, was found by a disbelieving pathologist to have a level of 1220 mg on 28 Mar 1979.

William Pitt the younger (1759–1806) the British Prime Minister, once allegedly drank 574 bottles of claret, 854 bottles of Madeira and 2410 bottles of Port in one year!

BODY TEMPERATURE
Highest

Willie Jones, a 52– year-old blackman, was admitted to Grady Memorial Hospital, Atlanta, Georgia on 10 July 1980 with heat stroke on a day when the temperature reached 32·2° C *90° F* with 44 per cent humidity. His temperature was found to be 46·5° C *115·7° F*. After 24 days he was discharged 'at prior baseline status'.

Lowest

There are three recorded cases of patients surviving body temperatures as low as 16·0° C *60·8° F*. Dorothy Mae Stevens (1929–74) who was found in an alley in Chicago, Illinois on 1 Feb 1951 and whose pulse dropped to 12 beats per min; Vickie Mary Davis aged 2 years 1 month in an unheated house in Marshalltown, Iowa on 21 Jan 1956 and 2-year-old Michael Troke in the snow near his home in Milwaukee, Wisconsin, on 19 Jan 1985, all with this temperature. People may die of hypothermia with body temperatures of 35·0° C *95·0° F*.

ILLNESS AND DISEASE
Commonest

The commonest non-contagious disease in the world is periodontal disease, such as gingivitis (inflammation of the gums) which subclinically afflicts some 80 per cent of the US population. In Great Britain 13 per cent of people have lost all their teeth before they are 21 years old. During their lifetime few completely escape its effects. Infestation with pinworm (*Enterobius vermicularis*) approaches 100 per cent in some tropical areas of the world.

The commonest contagious disease in the world is coryza (acute nasopharyngitis) or the common cold. The greatest reported loss of working time in Britain is from neurotic disorders, which accounted for 28 101 200 or 8·56 per cent, of the total of 328 109 200 days lost from mid–1984 to mid–1985.

The most resistant recorded case to being infected at the Medical Research Council Common Cold Unit, Salisbury, Wiltshire is J. Brophy, who has had one mild reaction in 24 visits.

Rarest

Medical literature periodically records hitherto undescribed diseases. A disease as yet undiagnosed but predicted by a Norwegian doctor is podocytoma of the kidney—a tumour of the epithelial cells lining the glomerulus of the kidney.

The last case of endemic smallpox was recorded in Ali Maow Maalin in Merka, Somalia on 26 Oct 1977. Paul Braddon of Rusper, West Sussex was reported on 2 Aug 1983 to be the first person to contract malaria in Britain for more than 35 years.

Kuru, or laughing sickness, afflicts only the Fore tribe of

eastern New Guinea and is 100 per cent fatal. This was formally attributed to the cannibalistic practice of eating human brains.

The rarest fatal diseases in England and Wales have been those from which the last deaths (all males) were all recorded more than 40 years ago—yellow fever (1930), cholera nostras (1928) and bubonic plague (1926).

Most infectious

The most infectious of all diseases is the pneumonic form of plague, as evidenced by the Black Death of 1347–51. It had a mortality rate of about 99·99 per cent.

Highest mortality rate

The virus AIDS (acquired immune-deficiency syndrome), first recognised in 1978 was first identified in January 1983 at the Pasteur Institute, Paris by Luc Montagnier, Françoise Barré-Sinoussi and Jean-Claude Chermann as a Human T-lymphotrophic Type III (HTLV III) virus.

The US death toll from AIDS has been predicted to reach 179 000 by 1991, with care costs possibly reaching $16 000 million. Uncertainty on the percentage of seropositive HIV carriers and the duration of incubation only make it possible to assert that the toll will be of the order 100 000 to 300 000 by this date. The UK death roll figures reached 839 by 1 May 1988 with 1436 others with the virus.

Rabies in humans has been regarded as uniformly fatal when associated with the hydrophobia symptom. A 25-year-old woman, Candida de Sousa Barbosa of Rio de Janeiro, Brazil, after surgery by Dr Max Karpin, was believed to be the first ever survivor of the disease in November 1968. Some sources prefer the case of Matthew Winkler, 6, who, on 10 Oct 1970, survived a bite by a rabid bat.

Leading cause of death

The leading cause of death in industrialised countries is arteriosclerosis (thickening of the arterial wall) which underlies much coronary and cerebrovascular disease. Deaths from diseases of the circulatory system totalled 278 849 in England and Wales in 1984.

Most notorious carrier

The most publicised of all typhoid carriers has been Mary Mallon (real name Maria Anna Caduff), known as Typhoid Mary, who was born in Graubunden, Switzerland, in 1855 and arrived as an immigrant in New York City, NY, USA, on 11 Jan 1868. In her job as a cook she was the source of 53 outbreaks, including the 1903 epidemic of 1400 cases in Ithaca, and 3 deaths. She was placed under permanent detention at Riverside Hospital on North Brother Island, East River, from 1915 until her death from broncho-pneumonia on 11 Nov 1938.

Parkinson's disease

The most protracted case of Parkinson's disease (named after 'An Essay on the Shaking Palsy' of 1817 by Dr James Parkinson (1755–1824), for which the earliest treatments were not published until 1946, is 62 years in the case of Frederick G. Humphries (d. 23 Feb 1985) of Croydon, London. His symptoms were detected in 1923.

MEDICAL EXTREMES

Heart stoppage

The longest recorded heart stoppage is 4 hr in the case of a Norwegian fisherman, Jan Egil Refsdahl (b. 1936), who fell overboard in the icy waters off Bergen on 7 Dec 1987. He was rushed to nearby Haukeland Hospital after his body temperature fell to 24° C *77° F* and his heart stopped beating, but he made a full recovery after he was connected to a heart–lung machine normally used for heart surgery.

The longest gestation interval in a *post mortem* birth was one of 84 days in the case of a baby girl born on 5 July 1983 from a clinically dead woman in Roanoke, Virginia, who had been kept on life support since April.

Pulse rates

A normal adult pulse rate is 70–72 beats per min at rest for males and 78–82 for females. Rates increase to 200 or more during violent exercise. When Charles Thompson of Cwmbran, Gwent was admitted to hospital for a hip joint replacement operation on 16 Aug 1987 he was found to have a resting pulse rate of 28 beats per min.

Longest coma

The longest recorded coma was that undergone by Elaine Esposito (b. 3 Dec 1934) of Tarpon Springs, Florida. She never stirred after an appendicectomy on 6 Aug 1941, when she was 6, in Chicago, Illinois, and died on 25 Nov 1978 aged 43 years 357 days, having been in a coma for 37 years 111 days.

Longest dream

Dreaming sleep is characterised by rapid eye movements known as REM described in 1953 by William Dement of the University of Chicago. The longest recorded period of REM is one of 2 hr 23 min on 15 Feb 1967 at the Department of Psychology, University of Illinois, Chicago on Bill Carskadon, who had had his previous sleep interrupted. In July 1984 the Sleep Research Centre, Haifa, Israel recorded nil REM in a 33-year-old male who had a shrapnel brain injury.

Largest stone

The largest stone or vesical calculus reported in medical literature was one of 6·29 kg *13 lb 14 oz* removed from an 80-year-old woman by Dr Humphrey Arthure at Charing Cross Hospital, London, on 29 Dec 1952. In August 1987 it was reported that 23 530 gallstones has been removed from an 85–year old woman patient at St Thomas' Hospital, London, after she complained of severe abdominal pain.

Longest in iron lung

The longest recorded period in an 'iron lung' is 37 years 58 days by Mrs Laurel Nisbet (b. 17 Nov 1912) of La Crescenta, California, who died on 22 Aug 1985. She had been in an 'iron lung' continuously since 25 June 1948. The longest survival in an 'iron lung' in Britain was 30 years (1949–79) by Denis Atkin in Lodge Moor Hospital, Sheffield, South Yorkshire. John Prestwich (b. 24 Nov 1938) of Kings Langley, Hertfordshire has been dependent on a negative pressure respirator since 24 Nov 1955. Paul Bates of Horsham, West Sussex, was harnessed to a mechanical positive pressure respirator on 13 Aug 1954. From continuous respiration, he had received an estimated 252 141 743 respirations via his trachea up to 1 May 1988.

Longest on haemodialysis

Raymond Jones (b. 14 Apr 1929) of Slough, Berkshire, who has suffered from kidney failure from the age of 34, has received continuous haemodialysis since 13 Oct 1963 averaging three visits per week to the Royal Free Hospital, Hampstead, London. In this time he seen his children grow up, marry and themselves have children.

Fastest nerve impulses

The results of experiments published in 1966 have shown that the fastest messages transmitted by the human nervous system travel as fast as 288 km/h *180 mph*. With advancing age impulses are carried 15 per cent more slowly.

Fastest reactions

The fastest recorded apparent reaction times for sprinters at the 1980 Olympic Games were 0·120 sec for Romy Müller (GDR) in the women's 200 m semi-final and 0·124 sec for Wilbert Greaves (GB) in the 110 m hurdles heats. Both may have been anticipatory. These compare with 0·011 sec for the cockroach *Periplaneta americana*.

Hiccoughing

The longest recorded attack of hiccoughs or singultus is that afflicting Charles Osborne (b. 1894) of Anthon, Iowa, USA, for the past 66 years from 1922. He contracted it

when slaughtering a hog and has hiccoughed about 430 million times in the interim period. He has been unable to find a cure, but has led a reasonably normal life in which he has had two wives and fathered eight children. He has admitted, however, that he cannot keep in his false teeth. In July 1986 he was reported to be hiccoughing at 20–25 per minute from his earlier high of 40.

Sneezing

The most chronic sneezing fit ever recorded is that of Donna Griffiths (b. 1969) of Pershore, Hereford & Worcester. She started sneezing on 13 Jan 1981 and surpassed the previous duration record of 194 days on 27 July 1981. She sneezed an estimated million times in the first 365 days. She achieved her first sneeze-free day on 16 Sept 1983—the 978th day. The highest speed at which expelled particles have ever been measured to travel is 167 km/h *103·6 mph.*

Snoring

The highest measured sound level recorded by any chronic snorer is a peak of 87·5 decibels at Hever Castle, Kent in the early hours of 28 June 1984. Melvyn Switzer of Totton, Hants was 30 cm *1 ft* from the meter. His wife Julie is deaf in one ear. Research has shown that differences in lung capacity and pharynx shape account for snoring. In general the pharynx is smaller in snorers.

Yawning

In Lee's case, reported in 1888, a 15-year-old female patient yawned continuously for a period of 5 weeks.

Sleeplessness

Researches indicate that on the Circadian cycle (about every 24-hr) for the majority peak efficiency is attained between 8 and 9 p.m. and the low point comes at 4 a.m. The longest recorded period for which a person has voluntarily gone without sleep is 453 hr 40 min by Robert McDonald of California in a rocking chair on 14 Mar–2 Apr 1986 (see Chapter 10). Victims of the very rare condition chronic colestites (total insomnia) have been known to go without definable sleep for many years. Jesus de Frutos (b. 1925) of Segovia, Spain asserts that he has only dozed since 1954.

Sleepwalking

On 6 April 1987 Michael Dixon (b. 1976) was found wandering barefoot and in his pyjamas along a railway track in Peru, Indiana, USA. He had sleepwalked out of his home in Danville, Illinois, 160 km *100 miles* away after travelling on a freight train.

Motionlessness

Sunardi (b. 1960), an Indonesian teacher, continuously stood motionless for 15 hr 25 sec on 21 July 1986 at the Motionlessness Festival in Semarang, Indonesia. The longest recorded case of involuntarily being made to stand to attention was when Corporal Everett D. Reamer of the 60th Coast Artillery Regiment AA Battery F, USA FFE was so punished in Camp No 1, Osaka, Japan for 132 consecutive hours from 8.00 a.m. 15 Aug until 8.00 p.m. 20 Aug 1944.

Most voracious fire breathers and extinguishers

Reg Morris blew a flame from his mouth to a distance of 9·4 m *31 ft* at the Miner's Rest, Chasetown, Staffs on 29 Oct 1986. On 17 Mar 1987 Reg Morris also extinguished 20 035 torches of flame in his mouth in 1 hr 48 min 14 sec at Cinders Night Club, Willenhall, West Midlands. On 26 July 1986 at Port Lonsdale, Victoria, Australia, Sipra Ellen Lloyd set a female record of 8357.

Human salamanders

The highest dry-air temperature endured by naked men in the US Air Force experiments in 1960 was 204·4°C *400° F* and for heavily clothed men 260° C *500° F.* Steaks require only 162·8° C *325° F.* Temperatures of 140° C *284° F* have been found quite bearable in sauna baths.

A group of 11 people led by Steven Neil Bisyak of

Redmond, Washington, USA, participated in a firewalk with an average temperature of 841° C *1546° F* on 19 Dec 1987 at Redmond. There is an annual firewalk during the feast of St Constantine each May in Aghia Eleni, northern Greece.

Swallowing

The worst reported case of compulsive swallowing was an insane female Mrs H. aged 42, who complained of a 'slight abdominal pain'. She proved to have 2533 objects, including 947 bent pins, in her stomach. These were removed by Drs Chalk and Foucar in June 1927 at the Ontario Hospital, Canada. The heaviest object extracted from a human stomach has been a 2·53 kg *5 lb 3 oz* ball of hair in Swain's case from a 20-year-old female compulsive swallower in the South Devon and East Cornwall Hospital, England on 30 Mar 1895.

Sword

Edward Benjamin 'Count Desmond' (b. 1941 of Binghamton, NY, USA) swallowed thirteen 58·4 cm *23 in* long blades to below his xiphisternum and injured himself in the process.

No further claims will be published.

Heaviest smoker

In 1977 an English woman went to the Samaritans for help because she was afraid she was slowly committing suicide. She told astonished officials she was smoking 180 cigarettes a day, and said that during an 18-hour day she managed to light a fresh cigarette at least once every 6 minutes. It is not known whether she managed to 'kick the habit'.

Fasting

Most humans experience considerable discomfort after an abstinence from food for even 12 hr but this often passes off after 24–48 hr. The longest period for which anyone has gone without solid food is 382 days by Angus Barbieri (b.1940) of Tayport, Fife, who lived on tea, coffee, water, soda water and vitamins in Maryfield Hospital, Dundee, Angus, from June 1965 to July 1966. His weight declined from 214·1 kg *33 st 10 lb* to 80·74 kg *12 st 10 lb*.

Records claimed, unless there is unremitting medical surveillance, are inadmissible.

Hunger strike

The longest recorded hunger strike was 385 days from 28 June 1972 to 18 July 1973 by Denis Galer Goodwin in Wakefield Prison, West Yorkshire, protesting his innocence of a rape charge. He was fed by tube orally.

The longest recorded case of survival without food *and* water is 18 days by Andreas Mihavecz, then 18, of Bregenz, Austria who was put into a holding cell on 1 Apr 1979 in a local government building in Höchst, Austria but was totally forgotten by the police. On 18 Apr 1979 he was discovered close to death having had neither food nor water. He had been a passenger in a crashed car.

Underwater

The world record for voluntarily staying underwater is 13 min 42·5 sec by Robert Foster, then aged 32, an electronics technician of Richmond, California, who stayed under 3·05 m *10 ft* of water in the swimming pool of the Bermuda Palms Motel at San Rafael, California, on 15 Mar 1959. He hyperventilated with oxygen for 30 min before his descent. (See also Heart Stoppage, p 18).

g forces

The acceleration *g*, due to gravity, is 978·02 cm/sec^2 32 ft 1·05 in per sec^2 at sea level at the Equator. A *sustained* acceleration of 25 g was withstood in a dry capsule during astronautic research by Dr Carter Collins of California. The highest g value endured on a water-braked rocket sled is 82·6 g for 0·04 of a sec by Eli L. Beeding Jr at Holloman Air Force Base, New Mexico, on 16 May 1958. He was put in hospital for 3 days. A man who fell off a 56·39 m *5 ft* cliff survived a *momentary* g of 209 in

decelerating from 109 km/h *68 mph* to stationary in 0·015 of a sec.

Racing driver David Purley GM (1945–85) survived a deceleration from 173 km/h *108 mph* to zero in 66 cm *26 in* in a crash at Silverstone, Northamptonshire on 13 July 1977 which involved a force of 179·8 *g*. He suffered 29 fractures, 3 dislocations and 6 heart stoppages.

A land diver of Pentecost Island, New Hebrides dived from a platform 24·76 m *81 ft 3 in* high with liana vines attached to his ankles on 15 May 1982. The body speed was 15·24 m *50 ft* per sec 54 km/h *34 mph*. The jerk transmitted a momentary g force in excess of 110.

> **High *g* forces ●** One of the renowned land divers of Pentecost Island (see above) seen here making his death-defying leap. The terminal velocity which he reaches can be in excess of 50 km/h *30 mph* and is sufficient to cause the diver to experience a force of more than 110 times that of the Earth's gravitational pull.
> (Photo: Aspect)

Pill-taking

The highest recorded total of pills swallowed by a patient is 555 439 between 9 June 1967 and 31 Jan 1988 by C. H. A. Kilner (b. 1926) of Bindura, Zimbabwe, following a successful operation to remove a cancerous pancreas on 26 May 1966.

Most injections

A diabetic, Mrs Evelyn Ruth Winder (b. 1921) of Invercargill, New Zealand gave an estimated 60 028 insulin injections to herself over 58 years to May 1988.

Most tattoos

The seeming ultimate in being tattooed is represented by Wilfred Hardy of Huthwaite, Nottinghamshire, England. Not content with a perilous approach to within 96 per cent of totality, he has been tattooed on the inside of his cheek, his tongue, gums and eyebrows. Walter Stiglitz of North Plainfield, New Jersey, in March 1988 claimed 5473 separate tattoos by different artists. The world's most decorated woman is strip artiste Krystyne

Kolorful (b. 5 Dec 1952, Alberta, Canada). Her 95 per cent body suit took 10 years to complete and cost $15 000. Britain's most decorated woman is Rusty Field (b. 1944) of Norfolk, who after 12 years under the needle of Bill Skuse has come to 85 per cent of totality. Both the 1980 and 1981 World's Most Beautiful Tattooed Lady Contest in the USA were won by Britain's Susan James (b. 1959).

OPERATIONS

Longest

The most protracted reported operation, for surgical as opposed to medical control purposes, has been one of 96 hr performed on Mrs Gertrude Levandowski (see also p. 10) during the period 4–8 Feb 1951 in Chicago, Illinois, USA. The patient suffered from a weak heart and surgeons had to exercise the utmost caution during the operation. The 'most delayed' operation on record is one on the feet of Mrs Doreen Scott of Derby, England on 20 Nov 1981. She had been waiting since 10 March 1952—19 years 8 months.

Most

Padmabhushan Dr M. C. Modi, a pioneer of mass eye surgery in India since 1943, has performed as many as 833 cataract operations in one day and a total of 564 834 to January 1987.

Dr Robert B. McClure (b. 1901) of Toronto performed a career total of 20 423 major operations in 1924–78.

Joseph Ascough (b. 1935 d. 26 Sept 1987) of Nottingham, underwent his 341st operation (for the removal of papillomas from his wind pipe) in September 1987. These wart-like growths which impede breathing first formed when he was 18 months old. On 2 Mar 1977 Mr Jens Kjaer Jension (b. 1914) of Hoven, Denmark, was discharged from a local hospital after having had 32 131 thorns removed from his body over a period of six years and 248 visits. In 1967 he had tripped and fallen into a pile of spiky berberry cuttings in his garden and was rushed unconscious to hospital. Even today he is still troubled by thorns working their way out through the skin of his legs.

Oldest subject

The greatest recorded age at which anyone has undergone an operation is 111 years 105 days in the case of James Henry Brett, Jr (b. 25 July 1849, d. 10 Feb 1961) of Houston, Texas, USA. He underwent a hip operation on 7 Nov 1960. The oldest age established in Britain was the case of Miss Mary Wright (b. 28 Feb 1862) who died during a thigh operation at Boston, Lincolnshire on 22 Apr 1971 aged 109 years 53 days.

Transplant *Heart*

The first human heart transplant operation was performed on Louis Washkansky, aged 55, at the Groote Schuur Hospital, Cape Town, South Africa, between 1.00 a.m. and 6 a.m., on 3 Dec 1967, by a team of 30 headed by Professor Christiaan Neethling Barnard (b. Beaufort West, 8 Oct 1922). The donor was Miss Denise Ann Darvall, aged 25. Washkansky lived for 18 days. The longest surviving heart transplantee has been Emmanuel Vitria, of Marseilles, France (b. 24 Jan 1920) who received the heart of Pierre Ponson, 20, on 27 Nov 1968, and died on 9 May 1987. The surgeon, Edmon Herrig, died of a heart attack in 1972 aged 61.

Britain's longest-surviving heart transplant patient is Nigel Olney (b. 1944) who underwent surgery at Papworth Hospital, Cambridge on 29 Jan 1980.

The first transplantee to give birth was Betsy Sneith, 23, with a baby girl Sierra (3·45 kg *7 lb 10 oz*) at Stanford University, California on 17 Sept 1984. She had received a donor heart in February 1980.

Paul Holt of Vancouver, British Columbia, Canada underwent a heart transplant at Loma Linda Hospital, in California, USA on 16 Oct 1987 aged 2 hrs 34 min. He was born 6 weeks premature at 2·9 kg *6 lb 6 oz.*

The youngest transplant patient in the UK was Hollie Roffey who received a new heart when aged only 10

days at the National Heart Hospital in London in July 1984, but she survived only 18 days.

Heart—lung—liver

The first triple transplant took place on 17 Dec 1986 at Papworth Hospital, Cambridge, when Mrs Davina Thompson (b. 28 Feb 1951) of Rawmarsh, South Yorkshire, underwent surgery for 7 hours by a team of 15 headed by chest surgeon Mr John Wallwork and Professor Sir Roy Calne.

Kidney

R. H. Lawler (b. 1895) (USA) performed the first transplant of the kidney in the human in 1950. The longest survival, being between identical twins, has been 20 years.

Artificial heart

On 1–2 Dec 1982 at the Utah Medical Center, Salt Lake City, Dr Barney B. Clark, 61, of Des Moines, Iowa, USA, was the first recipient of an artificial heart. The surgeon responbsible was Dr William C. DeVries. The heart was a Jarvik 7 designed by Dr Robert K. Jarvik (b Midland, Michigan, USA, 11 May 1946). Dr Clark died on 23 Mar 1983, 112 days later. William J. Schroeder survived 620 days in Louisville, Kentucky, USA from 25 Nov 1984 to 7 Aug 1986.

Britain's first artificial heart patient was Raymond Cook of Hucknall, Notts who temporarily received a Jarvik 7 on 2 Nov 1986 at Papworth Hospital, Cambridge.

Earliest appendicectomy

The earliest recorded successful appendix operation was performed in 1736 by Claudius Amyand (1680–1740). He was Serjeant Surgeon to King George II (reigned 1727–60).

Earliest anaesthesia

The earliest recorded operation under general anaesthesia was for the removal of a cyst from the neck of James Venable by Dr Crawford Williamson Long (1815–78), using diethyl ether ($(C_2H_5)_2O$), in Jefferson, Georgia, on 30 Mar 1842.

The earliest amputation under an anaesthetic in Great Britain was by Dr William Scott and Dr James McLauchlan at the Dumfries and Galloway Infirmary, Scotland on 19 Dec 1846.

Most haunted village? ● Pluckley in Kent is generally thought to be the most haunted village in England boasting at least twelve spiritous inhabitants. These include both a White and a Red Lady at St Nicholas Church, a Highwayman at Fright Corner, a Screaming Man at the brickworks and a spectral Coach and Horses at various locations. Both pubs cater for more than one kind of spirit. Dancing round the Devil's Bush three times is supposed to guarantee the personal appearance of its namesake–provided the dancer is naked of course. (Photo: D L Roberts)

Most durable cancer patient

The most extreme recorded case of survival from diagnosed cancer is that of Mrs Winona Mildred Melick (*née* Douglass) (b. 22 Oct 1876) of Long Beach, California. She had four cancer operations in 1918, 1933, 1966 and 1968 but died from pneumonia on 28 Dec 1981, 67 days after her 105th birthday.

Laryngectomy

On 24 July 1924 John I. Poole of Plymouth, Devon after diagnosis of carcinoma, then aged 33, underwent total laryngectomy in Edinburgh. He died on 19 June 1979 after surviving nearly 55 years as a 'neck-breather'. Mr F. B. Harvey also of Plymouth has been a neck-breather since 1929.

Munchausen's syndrome

The most extreme recorded case of the rare and incurable condition known as 'Munchausen's syndrome' (a continual desire to have medical treatment) was William McIlroy (b. 1906), who cost the National Health Service an estimated £2·5 million during his 50-year career as a hospital patient. During that time he had 400 major and minor operations, and stayed at 100 different hospitals using 22 seperate alliases. The longest unbroken period for which he was ever out of hospital was only six months. In 1979 the Irishman hung up his bedpan for the last time, saying he was sick of hospitals, and retired to an old people's home in Birmingham, where he died in 1983.

Fastest amputation

The shortest time recorded for a leg amputation in the pre-anaesthetic era was 13–15 sec by Napoleon's chief surgeon Dominique Larrey. There could have been no ligation.

Largest tumour

The largest tumour ever recorded was Spohn's case of an ovarian cyst weighing 148·7 kg *328 lb (23 st 6 lb)* taken from a woman in Texas, in 1905. She made a full recovery.

The most extreme case reported in Britain was of a cyst weighing 135 kg *298 lb (21 st 4 lb)* removed from a woman in England in 1846. This time the patient did not survive.

Surgical instruments

The largest surgical instruments are robot retractors used in abdominal surgery, introduced by Abbey Surgical Instruments of Chingford, Essex in 1968 and weighing 5 kg *11 lb.* Some bronchoscopic forceps measure 60 cm *23½ in* in length. The smallest are Elliot's eye trephine, which has a blade 0·20 cm *0·078 in* in diameter and 'straight' stapes picks with a needle-type tip or blade of 0·3 mm *0·013 in* long.

PSYCHIC FORCES

Extra-sensory perception

The two most extreme published examples of ESP in scientific literature have been those of the Reiss case of a 26-year-old female at Hunter College, New York State, in 1936 and of Pavel Stepánek (Czechoslovakia) in 1967–68. Any importance which might be attached to their cases was diminished by subsequent developments. The Reiss subject refused to undergo any further tests under stricter conditions. When Stepánek was retested at Edinburgh University with plastic cards he 'failed to display any clairvoyant ability'. Much smaller departures from the laws of probability have however been displayed in less extreme cases carried out under strict conditions.

Most durable ghosts

Ghosts are not immortal and seem to deteriorate after 400 years. The most outstanding exception to their normal 'half-life' would be the ghosts of Roman soldiers thrice reported still marching through the cellars of the Treasurer's House, York Minster, after nearly 19 centuries.

THE LIVING WORLD

CHAPTER·TWO

Largest toad ● The largest known toad is the Marine toad (*Bufo marinus*) of tropical South America and Queensland, Australia (introduced). An average adult specimen weighs about 453 g *1 lb*. The largest toad ever recorded can be found on page 35. (Photo: Bruce Coleman)

Animal Kingdom General Records

Fastest and slowest growth

The fastest growth in the animal kingdom is that of the Blue whale calf. A barely visible ovum weighing a fraction of a milligramme grows to a weight of *c.* 26 tonnes in 22¾ months, made up of 10¾ months gestation and the first 12 months of life. This is equivalent to an increase of 30 000 million-fold. The slowest growth is that of the Deep-sea clam *Tindaria callistiformis* of the North Atlantic, which takes *c.* 100 years to reach a length of 8 mm *0·31 in.*

Fastest moving

The fastest living creature is the Peregrine falcon (*Falco peregrinus*) when stooping from great heights during territorial displays. In one series of experiments carried out in Germany the highest speed recorded for peregrines at a 30-degree angle of stoop was 270 km/h *168 mph*, and at 45 degrees the maximum velocity was 350 km/h *217 mph*.

Strongest

The strongest animals in the world in proportion to their size are the larger beetles of the Scarabaeidae, which are found mainly in the tropics. In tests carried out on one unnamed species it was found that it could support 850 times its own weight on its back (cf. compare 25 per cent of its bodyweight for an adult elephant).

Smelliest

The world's smelliest animal is the skunk-like Zorilla (*Ictonyx striatus*) of Africa. It can discharge a nauseous fluid from its anal glands which can be smelt over a radius of half a mile *1·6 km*, and there is one record of a zorilla taking possession of a zebra carcass and keeping nine fully-grown lions at bay for several hours.

Toughest

According to experiments carried out by Professor H. E. Hinton at Bristol University the larva of the Chironomid fly (*Polypedilum vanderplanki*) can tolerate temperatures ranging from −270°C to 102°C *−454°F to −215·6°F*, and is the most advanced organism so far known that can be totally dehydrated.

Largest colonies

The Black-tailed prairie dog (*Cynomys ludovicianus*) of the western USA and northern Mexico builds the largest colonies of any known animal. One single 'town' discovered in 1901 was estimated to cover an area measuring 384 × 160 km *240 × 100 miles*. It contained about 400 000 000 individuals.

Largest egg

The largest eggs laid by any known animal were those of the now extinct Elephant bird (*Aepyornis maximus*) of southern Madagascar. One huge example collected in 1841 and now in the Académie des Sciences, Paris, France measures 326 × 390 mm *12·8 × 15·4 in* and probably weighed about 12·24 kg *27 lb* with its contents.

Highest g force

The highest force encountered in nature is the 400 g *averaged* by the Click beetle *Athous haemorrhoidalis* (a common British species) when 'jack-knifing' into the air to escape predators. One example measuring 12 mm *0·47 in* in length and weighing 40 mg *0·00014 oz* which jumped to a height of 30 cm *11¾ in* was calculated to have 'endured' a peak brain deceleration of 2300 g by the end of the movement.

Most bizarre

The most bizarre animal in the mammalian world is the egg-laying Platypus (*Ornithorhynchus anatinus*) which is found in streams and lakes throughout eastern Australia and Tasmania. Apart from having the head and feet of a duck, the body of an otter and venomous spurs on its rear ankles (males), this freak of nature also has another claim to fame. It has a sensory system located in its broad flat bill that can pick up electrical charges as small as those caused by the flick of a shrimp's tail in muddy water.

Most prodigious eater

The most phenomenal eating machine in nature is the larva of the Polyphemus moth (*Antheraea polyphemus*) of North America which, in the first 48 hours of its life, consumes an amount equal to 86 000 times its own birth weight. In human terms, this would be equivalent to a 3·17 kg *7 lb* baby taking in 273 tonnes *269 tons* of nourishment!

Largest concentration

The largest single concentration of animals ever recorded was an enormous swarm of krill (*Euphausia superba*) estimated to weigh 10 million tonnes tracked by US scientists off Antarctica in March 1981. The swarm was so dense it equalled about one-seventh of the world's yearly catch of fish and shellfish.

Greatest size difference between sexes

The largest female marine worms of the species *Bonellia viridis* are at least 100 million times heavier than the smallest males. The female is up to 100 cm *39·3 in* long against the miserable 1·0 mm *0·04 in* of the male.

Thickest nerves

Fast-swimming squids (*Cephalopoda*) have the thickest nerve fibres (axons) of any living animal. In the case of the Humboldt squid (*Ommastrephes gigas*) they have been measured up to 18 mm *0·7 in* in diameter, about 100 times thicker than human nerves.

Most valuable

The most valuable animals in cash terms are thoroughbred racehorses. The most paid for a yearling is $13·1 m on 23 July 1985 at Keeneland, Kentucky, by Robert Sangster and Partners for *Seattle Dancer*. The most valuable zoo exhibit is the endangered Giant panda (*Ailuropoda melanoleuca*), and 'Chi-Lin' (b. Sept 1982) of Madrid Zoo has been valued at more than £1 000 000. There are only 14 Giant pandas living in captivity outside China, and the wild population may now be as low as 600–700 despite full protection.

The most valuable marine exhibits are 'Orky' and 'Corky', the world's only captive breeding pair of killer whales (*Orcinus orca*) at Marineland, Palos Verdes, Los Angeles. In 1985 they were valued at $2 000 000.

Mammals *Mammalia*

Largest and heaviest

The longest and heaviest mammal in the world, and the largest animal ever recorded, is the Blue or Sulphur-bottom whale (*Balaenoptera musculus*), also called Sibbald's rorqual. The longest specimen ever recorded was a female landed at the Compania Argentina de Pesca, Grytviken, South Georgia, in 1909 which measured 33·58 m *110 ft 2½ in* in length. Another female measuring 27·6 m *90 ft 6 in* caught in the Southern Ocean by the Soviet Slava whaling fleet on 20 Mar 1947 weighed 190 tonnes *187 tons*. Its tongue and heart weighed 4·29 tonnes *4·22 tons* and 698·5 kg *1540 lb* respectively.

The largest Blue whale ever recorded in the waters of Great Britain was probably a 26·8 m *88 ft* specimen killed near the Bunaveneader station in Harris in the Western Isles, Scotland in 1904. In December 1851 the carcase of a Blue whale measuring 28·87 m *94 ft 9 in* in length (girth 13·7 m *42 ft*) was brought into Bantry harbour, Co. Cork, after it had been found floating dead in the sea. A specimen stranded on the west coast of Lewis, Western Isles, *c.* 1870 was credited with a length of 32 m *105 ft* but the carcase was cut up by the local people before the length could be verified. The length was probably

exaggerated or taken along the curve of the body instead of in a straight line from the tip of the snout to the notch in the flukes.

Blue whales inhabit the colder seas and migrate to warmer waters in the winter for breeding. Observations made in the Antarctic in 1947–8 showed that a Blue whale can maintain a speed of 20 knots (37 km/h) for 10 min when frightened. It has been calculated that a 27 m *90 ft* Blue whale travelling at 20 knots *37 km/h* would develop 527 cv *520 hp*. Newborn calves measure 6·5–8·6 m *21 ft 3½ in–28 ft 6 in* in length and weigh up to 3000 kg *2·95 tons.*

It has been estimated that there are only about 12 000 blue whales roaming the world's oceans today as a result of over-hunting. This compares with a peak estimate of *c.* 220 000 at the turn of the century. The species has been protected *de jure* since 1967, although non-member countries of the International Whaling Commission, e.g. Panama and Taiwan, are not bound by this agreement. A world-wide ban on commercial whaling came into force at the start of the 1985/86 season, but Japan, Norway, Iceland and South Korea are still slaughtering Minke and Bryde's whales (*Balaenoptera acutorostrata* and *B. edeni*). The ban on commercial whaling will be re-assessed in 1990.

Deepest dive

The greatest *recorded* depth to which a whale has dived is 620 fathoms (1134 m) by a 14·32 m *47 ft* bull Sperm whale (*Physeter macrocephalus*) found with its jaw entangled with a submarine cable running between Santa Elena, Ecuador and Chorillos, Peru, on 14 Oct 1955. At this depth the whale withstood a pressure of 11 583 kPa *1680 lb/in²* of body surface. On 25 Aug 1969 another bull Sperm whale was killed 160 km *100 miles* south of Durban after it had surfaced from a dive lasting 1 hr 52 min, and inside its stomach were found two small sharks which had been swallowed about an hour earlier. These were later identified as *Scymnodon* sp., a species found only on the sea floor. At this point from land the depth of water is in excess of 1646 fathoms (3193 m) for a radius of 48–64 km *30–40 miles*, which suggests that the Sperm whale sometimes descends to a depth of over 3000 m *10 000 ft* when seeking food and is limited by pressure of time rather than by pressure of pressure.

Largest *Land*

The largest living land animal is the African bush elephant (*Loxodonta africana*). The average adult bull stands 3·2 m *10 ft 6 in* at the shoulder and weighs 5·7 tonnes *5·6 tons*. The largest specimen ever recorded was a bull shot by J. Oosterveen (Holland) south of Sesfontein in Damaraland, Namibia, south-west Africa on 4 April 1978. Lying on its side this mountain of flesh measured 4·42 m *14 ft 6 in* in a projected line from the shoulder to the base of the forefoot, indicating that its standing height must have been about 4·21 m *13 ft 10 in*. Other measurements included an overall length of 10·38 m *34 ft 1 in*, and a forefoot circumference of 1·57 m *5 ft 2 in*. The freakishly tall desert elephants of Damaraland (down to 84 in August 1981) have proportionally longer legs than other elephants, and this particular animal probably weighed less than 10·16 tonnes. Another enormous bull shot 40 km *25 miles* northnortheast of Mucusso, southern Angola, on 7 Nov 1974 had a pegged height of 4·16 m *13 ft 8 in* (standing height *c.* 3·96 m *13 ft*. It measured 10·67 m *35 ft* overall, had a forefoot circumference of 1·80 m *5 ft 11 in*, and its weight was computed to be 12 246 kg *26 998 lb* (12·24 tonnes *12·05 tons*).

The largest wild mammal in the British Isles is the Red deer (*Cervus elaphus*). A full-grown stag stands 1·11 m *3 ft 8 in* at the shoulder and weighs 104–113 kg *230–250 lb*. The heaviest ever recorded was a stag killed at Glenfiddich, Banff, Scotland in 1831, which weighed 238 kg *525 lb*. The heaviest park Red deer on record was a stag weighing 215 kg *476 lb* (height at shoulder 1·37 m *4 ft 6 in*) killed at Woburn, Bedfordshire in 1836. The so-called Wild pony (*Equus caballus*) may weigh up to 320 kg *700 lb* but there are no truly feral populations living today.

Marine

The largest toothed mammal ever recorded is the Sperm whale, also called the Cachalot. The largest accurately measured specimen on record was a 20·7 m *67 ft 11 in* bull captured off the Kurile Islands, north-west Pacific, by a USSR whaling fleet in the summer of 1950 but bulls of much larger size were reported in the early days of whaling. The 5 m *16 ft 4¾ in* long lower jaw of a Sperm whale exhibited in the British Museum (Nat. History) belonged to a bull measuring nearly 25·6 m *84 ft*, and similar lengths have been reported for other outsized individuals killed.

Thirteen Cachalots have been stranded on British coasts since 1913. The largest, a bull measuring 19 m *61 ft 5 in*, was washed ashore at Birchington, Kent on 18 Oct 1914. Another bull estimated at 19·8 m *65 ft* but badly decomposed was stranded at Derryloughan, Co. Galway, Ireland on 2 Jan 1952.

Tallest

The tallest living animal is the Giraffe (*Giraffa camelopardalis*), which is now found only in the dry savannah and semi-desert areas of Africa south of the Sahara. The tallest ever recorded was a Masai bull (*G. camelopardalis tippelskirchi*) named 'George', received at Chester Zoo, on 8 Jan 1959 from Kenya. His 'horns' *almost* grazed the roof of the 6·09 m *20 ft* high Giraffe House when he was 9 years old. George died on 22 July 1969. Less credible heights of up to 7 m *23 ft* (between pegs) have been claimed for bulls shot in the field.

Smallest

The smallest recorded mammal is the endangered Kitti's hog-nosed bat (*Craseonycteristhonglongyai*), also called the Bumblebee bat, which is confined to about 20 limestone caves on the Kwae Noi River, Kanchanaburi, Thailand. Mature specimens (both sexes) have a wing span of *c.* 160 mm *6·29 in* and weigh 1·75–2 g *0·062–0·071 oz*. The smallest insectivore is Savi's white-toothed pygmy shrew (*Suncus etruscus*), also called the Etruscan shrew, which is found along the coast of the Mediterranean and southwards to Cape Province, South Africa. Mature specimens have a head and body length of 36–52 mm *1·32–2·04 in*, a tail length of 24–29 mm *0·94–1·14 in* and weigh between 1·5 and 2·5 g *0·052–0·09 oz*.

The smallest mammal found in Britain is the European pygmy shrew (*Sorex minutus*). Mature specimens have a head and body length of 43–64 mm *1·69–2·5 in*, a tail length of 31–46 mm *1·22–1·81 in* and weigh between 2·4 and 6·1 g *0·084–0·213 oz*.

Marine

The smallest totally marine mammal in terms of weight is probably Commerson's dolphin (*Cephalorhynchus commersoni*), also known as Le Jacobite, which is found in the waters off the southern tip of South America. In one series of six adult specimens the weights ranged from 23 kg *50·7 lb* to 35 kg *77·1 lb*. The Sea otter (*Enhydra lutris*) of the north Pacific is of comparable size (25–38·5 kg *55–81·4 lb*), but this species sometimes comes ashore during storms.

Rarest *Land*

A number of mammals are known only from a single or type specimen. One of these is Garrido's hutia (*Capromys garridoi*), recognised from a single individual collected on the islet of Cayo Maja off southern Cuba in April 1967. The Thylacine or Tasmanian tiger (*Thylacinus cynocephalus*), feared extinct since the last captive specimen died in Beaumaris Zoo, Hobart, on 7 Sept 1936, was reportedly rediscovered in July 1982 when a wildlife ranger saw one of these predatory marsupials in the spotlight of his parked car. Since then, however, there have been no more positive sightings. The Red wolf (*Canis rufus*) of south-east USA became extinct in the

Most valuable mammal ● 'Du Du', the 6th cub of Giant panda 'Mei Mei' was born on Sept 20 1987 at Chengdu Zoo, Sichuan Province, China. This record-breaking birth has earned 'Mei Mei' a medal as 'Hero Mother of China'. (Photo: Gamma)

wild in the early 1970s, but there are now over 50 individuals (not all of them genetically pure) held by the US Fish and Wildlife Service. The Black-footed ferret (*Mustela nigripes*) of the northern USA is also extinct in the wild, but 25 are housed in a special centre in Cheyenne, Wyoming. By January 1988, seven offspring had been produced in captivity.

Marine

The rarest marine mammal is Longman's beaked whale (*Indopacetus pacificus*), which is known only from two skulls. The type specimen was discovered on a beach near MacKay, Queensland, Australia, in 1922, and the second near Muqdisho, Somalia, east Africa, in 1955. The Cochito or Gulf of California porpoise (*Phocoena sinus*)

has not been sighted since 1980, and may now be extinct. Many have been accidentally killed by gillnet fishing in the last 45 years.

Fastest *Land*

The fastest of all land animals over a short distance (i.e. up to 549 m *600 yd*) is the Cheetah or Hunting leopard (*Acinonyx jubatus*) of the open plains of east Africa, Iran, Turkmenia and Afghanistan, with a probable maximum speed of 96–101 km/h *60–63 mph* over suitably level ground. Speeds of 114, 135 and even 145 km/h *71, 84 and 90 mph* have been claimed for this animal, but these figures must be considered exaggerated. Tests in London in 1937 showed that on an oval greyhound track over 316 m *345 yd* a female Cheetah's average speed over three runs was 69·8 km/h *43·4 mph* (cf. 69·6 km/h *43·26 mph* for the fastest racehorse), but this specimen was not running flat out and had great difficulty negotiating the bends. The fastest land animal over a sustained distance (i.e. 914 m *1000 yd* or more) is the Pronghorn antelope (*Antilocapra americana*) of the western United States. Specimens have been observed to travel at 56 km/h for 6 km *35 mph for 4 miles*, at 67 km/h for 1·6 km *42 mph for 1 mile* and 88·5 km/h for 0·8 km *55 mph for half a mile*.

The fastest British land mammal over a sustained distance is the Roe deer (*Capreolus capreolus*), which can cruise at 40–48 km/h *25–30 mph* for more than 32 km *20 miles*, with occasional bursts of up to 64 km/h *40 mph*. On 19 Oct 1970 a frightened runaway Red deer registered a speed of 67·5 km/h *42 mph* on a police radar trap as it charged through a street in Stalybridge, Manchester.

Marine
The fastest marine mammal is the Killer whale (*Orcinus orca*). On 12 Oct 1958 a bull measuring an estimated 6·10–7·62 m *20–25 ft* in length was timed at 30 knots (*55·5 km/h*) in the east Pacific. Speeds of up to 30 knots in short bursts have also been reported for Dall's porpoise (*Phocoenoides dalli*).

Slowest

The slowest moving land mammal is the Ai or Three-toed sloth (*Bradypus tridactylus*) of tropical America. The average ground speed is 1·83–2·44 m *6–8 ft* a minute (0·109–0·158 km/h *0·068–0·098 mph*), but in the trees it can 'accelerate' to 4·57 m *15 ft* a minute (0·272 km/h *0·17 mph*) (cf. these figures with the 0·05 km/h *0·03 mph* of the common garden snail and the 0·27 km/h *0·17 mph* of the giant tortoise).

Sleepiest

Some armadillos (*Dasypodidae*), opossums (*Didelphidae*) and sloths (*Bradypodidae*) spend up to 80 per cent of their lives sleeping or dozing, and it is claimed that Dall's porpoise (*Phocoenoides dalli*) never sleeps at all.

Longest hibernation

The Barrow ground squirrel (*Spermophilus parryi barrowensis*) of Point Barrow, Alaska, USA, hibernates for nine months of the year. During the remaining three months it feeds, breeds and collects food for storage in its burrow.

Oldest

No other mammal can match the extreme proven 120 years attained by Man (*Homo sapiens*) (see pp 11 and 12). It is probable that the closest approach is made by the Asiatic elephant (*Elephas maximus*).

The greatest age that has been verified with absolute certainty is 78 years in the case of a cow named 'Modoc', who died at Santa Clara, California, USA, on 17 July 1975. She was imported into the USA from Germany in 1898 at the age of 2 years. Nepal's royal elephant 'Prem Prasad' was reportedly 81 when he died at Kasra, Chitwan, on 27 Feb 1985, but his actual age was believed to have been 65–70 years. Similarly, Sri Lanka's famous bull elephant 'Rajah', who had led the annual Perahera procession through Kandi carrying the Sacred Tooth of the Buddha since 1931, was reported to be dying in March 1988 aged 82 years, but another source the previous year gave his age as 75 years.

Highest living

The highest living wild mammal in the world is probably the Yak (*Bos grunniens*), of Tibet and the Szechwanese Alps, China, which occasionally climbs to an altitude of 6100 m *20 000 ft* when foraging.

Largest herds

The largest herds on record were those of the Springbok (*Antidorcas marsupialis*) during migration across the plains of the western parts of southern Africa in the 19th century. In 1849 John (later Sir John) Fraser observed a *trekbokken* that took three days to pass through the settlement of Beaufort West, Cape Province. Another herd seen moving near Nels Poortje, Cape Province in 1888 was estimated to contain 100 million head, although 10 million is probably a more realistic figure. A herd estimated to be 24 km *15 miles* wide and more than 160 km *100 miles* long was reported from Karree Kloof, Orange River, South Africa in July 1896.

The largest concentration of wild mammals found living anywhere in the world today is that of the Mexican free-tailed bat (*Tadarida brasiliensis*) in Bracken Cave,

San Antonio, Texas, where up to 20 million animals assemble after migration.

Britain's largest bat colony is in Greywell Canal Tunnel, Hampshire. It contains about 2000 individuals made up of six different species.

Longest and shortest gestation periods

The longest of all mammalian gestation periods is that of the Asiatic elephant (*Elephas maximus*), with an average of 609 days or just over 20 months and a maximum of 760 days—more than two and a half times that of a human. By 1981 only *c.* 35 000 survived. The gestation periods of the American opossum (*Didelphis marsupialis*), also called the Virginian opossum, the rare Water opossum or Yapok (*Chironectes minimus*) of central and northern South America, and the Eastern native cat (*Dasyurus viverrinus*) of Australia are all normally 12–13 days but they can be as short as 8 days.

Largest litter

The greatest number of young born to a *wild* mammal at a single birth is 31 (30 of which survived) in the case of the Tailless tenrec (*Tenrec ecaudatus*) found in Madagascar and the Comoro Islands. The normal litter size is 12–15, although females can suckle up to 24.

Youngest breeder

The Streaked tenrec (*Hemicentetes semispinosus*) of Madagascar is weaned after only 5 days, and females can breed 3–4 weeks after birth.

CARNIVORES

Largest

The largest living terrestrial carnivore is the Kodiak bear (*Ursus arctos middendorffi*), which is found on Kodiak Island and the adjacent Afognak and Shuyak islands in the Gulf of Alaska, USA. The average adult male has a nose-to-tail length of 2·4 m *8 ft* (tail about 10 cm *4 in*), stands 1·32 m *52 in* at the shoulder and weighs between 476 kg and 533 kg *1050 lb–1175 lb*. In 1894 a weight of 751 kg *1656 lb* was recorded for a male shot at English Bay, Kodiak Island, whose *stretched* skin measured 4·11 m *13 ft 6 in* from the tip of the nose to the root of the tail. This weight was exceeded by a 'cage-fat male' in the Cheyenne Mountain Zoological Park, Colorado Springs, Colorado, USA which scaled 757 kg *1670 lb* at the time of its death on 22 Sept 1955. In 1981 an unconfirmed weight of over 907 kg *2000 lb* was reported for a Peninsula giant bear (*Ursus a. gyas*) from Alaska on exhibition at the Space Farms Zoological Park at Beemerville, New Jersey, USA.

Weights in excess of 907 kg *2000 lb* have been reported for the Polar bear (*Ursus maritimus*), but the average adult male weighs 386–408 kg *850–900 lb* and measures 2·4 m *7¾ ft* nose-to-tail. In 1960 a Polar bear allegedly weighing 1002 kg *2210 lb* before skinning was shot at the polar entrance to Kotzebue Sound, north-west Alaska, by Arthur Dubs of Medford, Oregon, USA. In April 1962 the 3·38 m *11 ft 1¼ in* tall mounted specimen was put on display at the Seattle World Fair, but further details are lacking.

The largest land carnivore found in Britain is the Badger (*Meles meles*). The average adult boar (sows are slightly smaller) measures 90 cm *3 ft* in length and this includes a 10 cm *4 in* tail. It weighs some 12·3 kg *27 lb* in the early spring and 14·5 kg *32 lb* at the end of the summer when it is in 'grease'. In December 1952 a boar was reported weighing 27·2 kg *60 lb* which was killed near Rotherham, South Yorkshire.

Smallest

The smallest living member of the order Carnivora is the Least weasel (*Mustela rixosa*), also called the Dwarf weasel, which is circumpolar in distribution. Four races are recognised, the smallest of which is *M. r. pygmaea* of Siberia. Mature specimens have an overall length of 177–207 mm *6·96–8·14 in* and weigh between 35 and 70 g *1¼–2½ oz.*

Largest feline

The largest member of the cat family (Felidae) is the protected long-furred Siberian tiger (*Panthera tigris altaica*), also called the Amur or Manchurian tiger. Adult males average 3·15 m *10 ft 4 in* in length (nose to tip of extended tail), stand 99–107 cm *39–42 in* at the shoulder and weigh about 265 kg *585 lb*. In 1950 a male weighing 384 kg *846·5 lb* was shot in the Sikhote Alin Mts, Maritime Territory, USSR. In November 1967 David Hasinger of Philadelphia, Pennsylvania, USA shot an outsized Indian tiger (*Panthera tigris tigris*) in northern Uttar Pradesh which measured 3·22 m *10 ft 7 in* between pegs (3·37 m *11 ft 1 in* over the curves) and weighed 389 kg *857 lb* (cf. 2·82 m *9 ft 3 in* and 190 kg *420 lb* for an average adult male). This considerable specimen can now be seen on display in the US Museum of Natural History, Smithsonian Institution, Washington DC, USA.

The largest tiger ever held in captivity, and the heaviest 'big cat' on record, is an 8-year-old Siberian male named 'Jaipur', owned by animal trainer Joan Byron-Marasek of Clarksburg, New Jersey, USA. This specimen measures 3·32 m *10 ft 11 in* in total length and tipped the scales at 423 kg *932 lb* in October 1986.

The average adult African lion (*Panthera leo*) measures 2·7 m *9 ft* overall, stands 91–97 cm *36–38 in* at the shoulder and weighs 181–185 kg *400–410 lb*. The heaviest wild specimen on record was one weighing 313 kg *690 lb* shot by Lennox Anderson just outside Hectorspruit in the eastern Transvaal in 1936. In July 1970 a weight of 375 kg *826 lb* was reported for a black-maned lion named 'Simba' (b. Dublin Zoo, 1959) at Colchester Zoo, Essex. He died on 16 Jan 1973 at the now defunct Knaresborough Zoo, North Yorkshire, where his stuffed body had been on display. An adult male Litigon (an Indian lion/Tigon cross) named 'Cubanacan' at Alipore Zoological Gardens, Calcutta, India, is also believed to weigh at least 363 kg *800 lb*. This animal stands 1·32 m *52 in* at the shoulder (cf. 1·11 m *44 in* for the lion 'Simba') and measures a record 3·5 m *11 ft 6 in* in total length.

Smallest feline

The smallest member of the cat family is the Rusty-spotted cat (*Felis rubiginosa*) of southern India and Sri Lanka. The average adult male has an overall length of 64–71 cm *25–28 in* (tail 23–25 cm *9–10 in*) and weighs about 1·35 kg *3 lb.*

PINNIPEDS Seals, Sea-lions, Walruses

Largest

The largest of the 34 known species of pinniped is the Southern elephant seal (*Mirounga leonina*), which inhabits the sub-Antarctic islands. Adult bulls average 5 m *16½ ft* in length (tip of inflated snout to the extremities of the outstretched tail flippers), 3·7 m *12 ft* in maximum bodily girth and weigh about 2268 kg (*5000 lb*). The largest accurately measured specimen on record was a bull killed in Possession Bay, South Georgia on 28 Feb 1913 which measured 6·5 m *21 ft 4 in* after flensing (original length about 6·85 m *22½ ft*) and probably weighed at least 4 tonnes. There are old records of bulls measuring 7·62–9·14 m *25–30 ft* and even 10·66 m *35 ft* but these figures must be considered exaggerated. Adult cows are much smaller, averaging 3 m *10 ft* in length and weighing about 680 kg *1500 lb*.

The largest pinniped among British fauna is the Grey seal (*Halichoerus grypus*), also called the Atlantic seal. In one sample taken during the breeding season at the Farne Islands, Northumberland the heaviest (a male) weighed 310 kg *683½ lb* (length from nose to tip of flippers 2·45 m *8 ft 0½ in*).

Smallest

The smallest pinnipeds are the Ringed seal (*Phoca hispida*) of the Arctic and the closely-related Baikal seal (*P. sibirica*) of Lake Baikal and the Caspian seal (*P. caspica*) of the Caspian Sea, USSR. Adult specimens (males) measure up to 1·67 m *5 ft 6 in* in length and reach a maximum weight of 127 kg *280 lb*. Females are about two-thirds this size.

Britain's smallest pinniped is the Common seal (*Phoca vitulina*). Adult males measure 1·5–1·85 m *4 ft 11 in–6 ft 0¼ in* in length and weigh up to 105 kg *231 lb*. Females are four-fifths this size.

Most abundant

The most abundant species of pinniped is the Crabeater seal (*Lobodon carcinophagus*) of Antarctica. In 1978 the total population was believed to be nearly 15 000 000.

Rarest

The last reliable sighting of the Caribbean or West Indian monk seal (*Monachus tropicalis*) was on Serranilla Bank off the coast of Mexico's Yucatan peninsula in 1952. In 1974 two seals were seen near Cay Verde and Cay Burro, south-east Bahamas, but a search in 1979 found nothing. It has been suggested that these sightings (and others) may have been Californian sea-lions (*Zalophus californianus*) which had escaped from captivity and have been recorded in the Gulf of Mexico on several occasions.

Fastest

The highest swimming speed recorded for a pinniped is a 40 km/h *25 mph* short spurt by a Californian sea-lion. The fastest-moving pinniped on land is the Crabeater seal which has been timed at speeds up to 19 km/h *11·8 mph*.

Deepest

The deepest dive recorded for a pinniped is 630 m *2067 ft* by a female Northern elephant seal (*Mirounga anguistirostris*) off Ano Nuevo Point, California, USA on 1 Mar 1983. At this depth the seal withstood a pressure of 6335 kPa *919 lb/in²* of body area. The much larger bulls of this species can probably dive even deeper.

Oldest

A female Grey seal shot at Shunni Wick in the Shetland Islands on 23 Apr 1969 was believed to be 'at least 46 years old' based on a count of dentine rings. The captive record is an estimated 41 years for a bull Grey seal 'Jacob' held in Skansen Zoo (1901–42).

BATS

Largest

The only flying mammals are bats (order Chiroptera), of which there are about 950 living species. That with the greatest wing span is the Bismarck flying fox (*Pteropus neohibernicus*) of the Bismarck Archipelago and New Guinea. One specimen preserved in the American Museum of Natural History has a wing spread of 165 cm *5 ft 5 in*, but some unmeasured bats probably reach 183 cm *6 ft*.

The largest bat found in Britain is the very rare large Mouse-eared bat (*Myotis myotis*). Mature specimens have a wing span of 355–450 mm *13·97–17·71 in* and weigh up to 45 g *1·58 oz* in the case of females.

Smallest

The smallest bat in the world is Kitti's hog-nosed bat. See page 23.

The smallest native British bat is the Pipistrelle (*Pipistrellus pipistrellus*). Mature specimens have a wing span of 190–250 mm *7·48–9·84 in* and weigh between 3 and 8 g *0·1–0·28 oz*.

Rarest

At least three species of bat are known only from the type specimen. They are: the Small-toothed fruit bat (*Neopteryx frosti*) from Tamalanti, West Celebes (1938/39); *Paracoelops megalotis* from Vinh, Vietnam (1945); and *Latidens salimalii* from the High Wavy Mountains, southern India (1948).

The rarest bat on the British list (15 species) is now the large Mouse-eared bat of southern England, the population of which is down to a single male which has lived in Sussex for 14 years forlornly waiting for a mate. (The last known surviving female was killed by the felling of a tree in Sussex in 1977).

In 1987 a vagrant Northern bat (*Eptesicus nilssoni*) was found hibernating in Surrey by two journalists. A native of Europe and Russia, it was the first recorded example of this species in Britain.

Fastest

Because of the great practical difficulties few data on bat speeds have been published. The greatest velocity attributed to a bat is 51 km/h *32 mph* in the case of a Mexican free-tailed bat, but this may have been wind-assisted. In one American experiment using an artificial mine tunnel and 17 different kinds of bat, only four of them managed to exceed 20·8 km/h *13 mph* in level flight.

Oldest

The greatest age reliably reported for a bat is 31 years 5 months for an Indian flying fox (*Pteropus giganteus*) which died at London Zoo on 11 Jan 1979.

The greatest reliable age reported for a banded bat is at least 24 years for a female Little brown bat (*Myotis lucifugus*) found on 30 Apr 1960 in a cave on Mt Aeolus, Vermont, USA. It had been banded at a summer colony in Mashpee, Massachusetts, on 22 June 1937, at which time it was already fully grown.

Albino gorilla ● 'Snowflake' (born 1964), the world's first recorded albino gorilla, was captured in Equatorial Guinea in 1966 and later transferred to Barcelona, Spain. This blue-eyed prodigy shares his enclosure with 3 female gorillas, and has fathered a number of offspring with similar colouring. (Photo: Jaume Xampeng)

Highest detectable pitch

Because of their ultrasonic echolocation bats have the most acute hearing of any terrestrial animal. Vampire bats (*Desmodontidae*) and fruit bats (*Pteropodidae*) can hear frequencies as high as 120–210 kHz (cf. 20 kHz for the adult human limit but 280 kHz for the Common dolphin (*Delphinus delphis*)).

Deepest roost

A Little brown bat has been recorded at a depth of 1160 m *3805 ft* in a zinc mine in New York State, USA. The mine serves as winter quarters for 1000 members of this species, which normally roost at a depth of 200 m *656 ft.*

PRIMATES
Largest

The largest living primate is the Eastern lowland gorilla (*Gorilla g. graueri*) of the lowland forests of eastern Zaïre and south-western Uganda. The average adult male stands 175 cm *5 ft 9 in* tall and weighs 165 kg *360 lb*. The Mountain gorilla (*Gorilla g. beringei*) of the volcanic mountain ranges of western Rwanda, south-western Uganda and eastern Zaïre is also of comparable size i.e. 172·5 cm *5 ft 8 in* and 155 kg *343 lb*, and most of the exceptionally large gorillas taken in the field have been of this race. The greatest height (top of crest to heel) recorded for a gorilla in the wild is 1·88 m *6 ft 2 in* for a bull of the mountain race shot by T. Alexander Barns in the Eastern Congo (Zaïre) *c.* 1920. Another mountain gorilla called 'Baltimore Jack', who was received at Baltimore Zoo, Maryland, USA in 1956 and was sold to Phoenix Zoo, Arizona, USA in 1970 for breeding purposes, measured 1·91 m *6 ft 3 in* in the standing position. He had exceptionally long legs for a gorilla, and weighed only 126 kg *300 lb*. He died 2 years later and his body is now preserved in formaldehyde at Arizona State University. The heaviest gorilla ever kept in captivity was a male of the mountain race named 'N'gagi', who died in San Diego Zoo, California, on 12 Jan 1944 aged 18 years. He scaled 310 kg *683 lb* at his heaviest in 1943, and weighed 288 kg *636 lb* at the time of his death. He was 1·72 m *5 ft 7¾ in* tall and boasted a record chest measurement of 198 cm *78 in.*

Britain's largest captive gorilla is probably 'Djoum' (b. 1969) of Howletts Zoo, Kent, who scaled 213 kg *470 lb* in 1986. Another male example of the Western lowland gorilla (*Gorilla g. gorilla*) named 'Bukhama' (b. 1960) at Dudley Zoo, West Midlands, was reportedly 227 kg *500 lb* in 1969, but this animal has not been weighed since.

Smallest

The smallest known primate is the rare Pen-tailed shrew (*Ptilocercus lowii*) of Malaysia, Sumatra and Borneo. Adult specimens have a total length of 230–330 mm *9–13 in* (head and body 100–140 mm *3·93–5·51 in*, tail 130–190 mm *5·1–7·5 in*) and weigh 35–50 g *1·23–1·76 oz.* The Pygmy marmoset (*Cebuella pygmaea*) of the Upper Amazon Basin and the Lesser mouse-lemur (*Microcebus murinus*) of Madagascar are also of comparable length but heavier, adults weighing 50–75 g *1·76–2·64 oz* and 45–80 g *1·58–2·82 oz* respectively.

Rarest

The rarest living primate is the Greater bamboo Broadnosed gentle lemur (*Hapalemur simus*) of Madagascar, which reportedly became extinct in the early 1970s. In 1986 a group consisting of 60–80 individuals were discovered living in a remote rain forest near Ranomafana in the south-eastern part of the island by an expedition from Duke University, Durham, North Carolina, USA. The Golden-rumped tamarin (*Leontopithecus chrysopygus*), which is now restricted to two areas of forest in the state of Sao Paulo, south-east Brazil, is also on the verge of extinction, with only 75–100 surviving in 1986.

Oldest

The greatest irrefutable age reported for a non-human primate is *c.* 59 years in the case of a male Orang-utan (*Pongo pygmaeus*) named 'Guas', who died in Philadelphia Zoological Garden, Pennsylvania, USA on 9 Feb 1977. When he was received on 1 May 1931 he was at least 13 years of age. The oldest Chimpanzee (*Pan troglodytes*) on record was a male named 'Jimmy' at Seneca Zoo, Rochester, NY, who died on 17 Sept 1985 aged 55 years 6 months. The famous Western lowland Gorilla 'Massa' (b. July 1931) died on 30 Dec 1984 aged 53 years 5 months.

The oldest female gorilla on record was 'Carolyn' (b. 1939) of New York Zoological Park (Bronx Zoo), who died on 27 Sept 1986 aged 47 years.

Strongest

In 1924 'Boma', a 74·80 kg *165 lb* male Chimpanzee at Bronx Zoo, New York, USA recorded a right-handed pull (feet braced) of 384 kg *847 lb* on a dynamometer (cf. 95 kg *210 lb* for a man of the same weight). On another occasion an adult female Chimpanzee named 'Suzette' (estimated weight 61 kg *135 lb*) at the same zoo registered a right-handed pull of 572 kg *1260 lb* while in a rage. A record from the USA of a 45 kg *100 lb* Chimpanzee achieving a two-handed dead lift of 272 kg *600 lb* with ease suggests that a male gorilla could with training raise 907 kg *2000 lb*.

Oldest monkey ● The world's oldest monkey is a male White-throated capuchin (*Cebus capucinus*) called 'Bobo', owned by Dr Raymond T. Bartus of the American Cyanamid Company in Pearl River, NY, USA, who celebrated his 53rd birthday on 30 Oct 1987.

MONKEYS
Largest

The only species of monkey reliably credited with weights of more than 45 kg *100 lb* is the Mandrill (*Mandrillus sphinx*) of equatorial west Africa. The greatest reliable weight recorded is 54 kg *119 lb* for a captive male but an unconfirmed weight of 59 kg *130 lb* has been reported. (Adult females are about half the size of males.)

Smallest

The smallest known monkey is the Pygmy marmoset (*Cebuella pygmaea*) of the Upper Amazon Basin. (See Primate Smallest.)

Rarest

(see Primates, Rarest)

RODENTS
Largest

The world's largest rodent is the Capybara (*Hydrochoerus hydrochaeris*), also called the Carpincho or Water hog, which is found in tropical South America. Mature specimens have a head and body length of 0·99–1·4 m *3¼–4½ ft* and weigh up to 113 kg *250 lb* (cage-fat specimen). Britain's largest rodent until recently was the Coypu (*Myocastor coypus*), also known as the Nutria, which was introduced from Argentina by East Anglian fur-breeders in 1929. Three years later, the first escapes were recorded and by 1960 at least 200 000 Coypus were living in East Anglia. About 80 per cent were killed by the severe winter of 1963/4, and since then the Ministry of Agriculture has carried out a campaign of extermination against this species. In April 1988 the Government announced that the coypu had finally been eradicated, in Britain, but said the trapping campaign would continue until the end of 1989. Adult males measure 76–91 cm *30–36 in* in length (including short tail) and weigh up to 13 kg *28 lb* in the wild state (18 kg *40 lb* in captivity).

Smallest

The smallest known rodent is the Northern pygmy mouse (*Baiomys taylori*) of central Mexico and southern Arizona and Texas, which measures up to 109 mm *4·3 in* in total length and weighs 7–8 g *0·24–0·28 oz.*

Britain's smallest rodent is the Old World harvest mouse (*Micromys minutus*), which measures up to 135 mm *5·3 in* in total length and weighs 7–10 g *0·24–0·35 oz.*

Rarest

The rarest rodents in the world are Garrido's hutia (*Capromys garridoi*) of the Canarreos Archipelago, Cuba and the Little earth hutia (*C. sanfelipensis*) of Juan Garcia Cay, an islet off southern Cuba. The latter species has not been recorded since its discovery in 1970.

Oldest

The greatest reliable age reported for a rodent is 27 years 3 months for a Sumatran crested porcupine (*Hystrix brachyura*) which died in National Zoological Park, Washington DC, USA on 12 Jan 1965.

Fastest breeder

The female Meadow vole (*Microtus agrestis*), found in Britain, can reproduce from the age of 25 days and have up to 17 litters of 6–8 young in a year.

INSECTIVORES
Largest

The largest insectivore is the Moon rat (*Echinosorex gymnurus*), also known as Raffles' gymnure, which is found in Burma, Thailand, Malaysia, Sumatra and Borneo. Mature specimens have a head and body length of 265–445 mm *10·43–17·52 in*, a tail measuring 200–210 mm *7·87–8·26 in* and weigh up to 1400 g *3·08 lb*. The European hedgehog (*Erinaceus europaeus*) is much shorter in overall length (196–298 mm *7·71–11·73 in*), but well-fed examples have been known to scale as much as 1900 g *4·19 lb*. Although the much larger anteaters (families Tachyglossidae and Myrmecophagidae) feed on termites and other soft-bodied insects, they are not insectivores but belong to the orders Monotremata and Edentata ('without teeth').

Smallest

The smallest insectivore is Savi's white-toothed pygmy shrew (*Suncus etruscus*). (See Mammals, Smallest.)

Oldest

The greatest reliable age recorded for an insectivore is 16+ years for a Lesser hedgehog-tenrec (*Echinops telfairi*), which was born in Amsterdam Zoo, Netherlands in 1966 and was later sent to Jersey Zoo. It died on 27 Nov 1982.

ANTELOPES
Largest
The largest of all antelopes is the rare Giant eland (*Tragelaphus derbianus*), of western and central Africa, which may surpass 907 kg *2000 lb*. The Common eland (*T. oryx*) of eastern and southern Africa has the same shoulder height of up to 1·78 m *5 ft 10 in* but is not quite so massive, although there is one record of a 1·65 m *5 ft 5 in* bull shot in Malawi *c.* 1937 which weighed 943 kg *2078 lb*.

Smallest
The smallest known antelope is the Royal antelope (*Neotragus pygmaeus*) of western Africa. Mature specimens measure 25–31 cm *10–12 in* at the shoulder and weigh only 3–3·6 kg *7–8 lb* which is the size of a large Brown hare (*Lepus europaeus*). Salt's dik-dik (*Madoqua saltina*) of north-eastern Ethiopia and Somalia weighs only 2·2–2·7 kg *5–6 lb* when adult, but this species stands about 35·5 cm *14 in* at the withers.

Rarest
The world's rarest antelope is the Arabian oryx (*Oryx leucoryx*) which, until very recently, had not been reported in the wild since 1972 when three were killed and four others captured on the Jiddat-al-Harasis plateau, South Oman. Between March 1980 and August 1983 a total of 17 antelopes from the World Herd at San Diego Zoo, California, USA were released into the open desert in South Oman under the protection of a nomadic tribe. Since then there have been at least 15 live births, and two antelopes born in Oman have bred. Another release has also been carried out in Jordan. In January 1985 the first Arabian oryx was born at London Zoo.

Oldest
The greatest reliable age recorded for an antelope is 25 years 4 months for an Addax (*Addax nasomaculatus*) which died in Brookfield Zoo, Chicago, Illinois, USA on 15 Oct 1960.

DEER
Largest
The largest deer is the Alaskan moose (*Alces alces gigas*). Adult bulls average 1·83 m *6 ft* at the shoulder and weigh *c.* 500 kg *1100 lb*. A bull standing 2·34 m *7 ft 8 in* between pegs and weighing an estimated 816 kg *1800 lb* was shot on the Yukon River in the Yukon Territory, Canada in September 1897. Unconfirmed measurements up to 2·59 m *8 ft 6 in* at the shoulder and estimated weights up to 1180 kg *2600 lb* have been claimed. The record antler spread or 'rack' is 199 cm *78½ in* (skull and antlers 41 kg *91 lb*). They were taken from a moose killed near the headwaters of the Stewart River in the Yukon, Canada in October 1897 and are now on display in the Field Museum, Chicago, Illinois, USA.

Smallest
The smallest true deer (family Cervidae) is the Northern pudu (*Pudu mephistopheles*) of Ecuador and Colombia. Mature specimens measure 33–35 cm *13–14 in* at the shoulder and weigh 7·2–8·1 kg *16–18 lb*. The smallest ruminant is the Lesser Malay chevrotain (*Tragulus javanicus*) of south-east Asia, Sumatra and Borneo. Adult specimens measure 20–25 cm *8–10 in* at the shoulder and weigh 2·7–3·2 kg, *6–7 lb*.

Rarest
The rarest deer in the world is Fea's muntjac (*Muntiacus feae*) which, until recently, was known only from two specimens collected on the borders of southern Burma and western Thailand. In December 1977 a female was received at Dusit Zoo, Bangkok, followed by 2 females in 1981 and 3 males and 3 females from Xizang, Tibet, south-west China from February 1982–April 1983.

Oldest
The greatest reliable age recorded for a deer is 26 years

8 months for a Red deer (*Cervus elaphus scoticus*) which died in Milwaukee Zoo, Wisconsin, USA on 28 June 1954.

MARSUPIALS
Largest
The largest living marsupial is the Red kangaroo (*Macropus rufus*) of central, southern and eastern Australia. Adult males stand up to 213 cm *7 ft* tall, measure up to 245 cm *8 ft 0½ in* in total length and weigh up to 85 kg *187 lb*.

Smallest
The smallest known marsupial is the rare Long-tailed planigale (*Planigale ingrami*), a flat-skulled mouse, of north-eastern and north-western Australia. Adult males have a head and body length of 55–63 mm *2·16–2·48 in*, a tail length of 57–60 mm *2·24–2·36 in* and weigh 3·9–4·5 g *0·13–0·19 oz*.

Oldest
The greatest reliable age recorded for a marsupial is 26 years 22 days for a Common wombat (*Vombatus ursinus*) which died in London Zoo on 20 Apr 1906.

Fastest speed, highest and longest jumps
The highest speed recorded for a marsupial is 54 km/h *33·75 mph* for a Red kangaroo (*Macropus giganteus*). The greatest height cleared by a hunted kangaroo is 3·20 m *10 ft 6 in* over a pile of timber and during the course of a chase in January 1951 a female Red kangaroo made a series of bounds which included one of 12·80 m *42 ft*. There is also an unconfirmed report of an Eastern grey kangaroo jumping nearly 13·5 m *44 ft 8½ in* on the flat.

TUSKS
Longest
The longest recorded elephant tusks (excluding prehistoric examples) are a pair from Zaïre preserved in the National Collection of Heads and Horns kept by the New York Zoological Society in Bronx Park, New York City, USA. The right tusk measures 3·49 m *11 ft 5½ in* along the outside curve and the left 3·35 m *11 ft*. Their combined weight is 133 kg *293 lb*. A single tusk of 3·5 m *11 ft 6 in* has been reported. Ivory rose from $2·30 to $34/lb in the period 1970–80.

Heaviest
The heaviest recorded tusks are a pair in the British Museum (Natural History) which were collected from an aged bull shot by an Arab with a muzzle-loading gun at the foot of Mt Kilimanjaro, Kenya in 1897. They originally weighed 109 kg *240 lb* (length 3·11 m *10 ft 2½ in*) and

102 kg *225 lb* (length 3·18 m *10 ft 5½ in*) respectively, giving a total weight of 211 kg *465 lb*, but their combined weight today is 200 kg *440½ lb*.

The greatest weight ever recorded for a single elephant tusk is 117 kg *258 lb* for a specimen collected in Benin, west Africa and exhibited at the Paris Exposition in 1900.

HORNS
Longest
The longest horns grown by any living animal are those of the Water buffalo (*Bubalus arnee = B. bubalis*) of India. One huge bull shot in 1955 had horns measuring 4·24 m *13 ft 11 in* from tip to tip along the outside curve across the forehead. The longest single horn on record was one measuring 206 cm *81¼ in* on the outside curve found on a specimen of domestic Ankole cattle (*Bos taurus*) near Lake Ngami, Botswana.
The largest spread recorded for a Texas longhorn steer is 3·2 m *10 ft 6 in*. They are currently on exhibition at the Hermitage Museum, Big Springs, Texas, USA.

HORSES AND PONIES
The world's equine population is estimated to be 75 000 000.

Largest
The largest horse ever recorded was a 19.2-hand (*1·98 m*) pure-bred red roan Belgian (Brabant) stallion named 'Brooklyn Supreme' (1928–48) owned by C.G. Good of Ogden, Iowa, which weighed 1·44 tonnes *1·42 tons* at its heaviest in 1938 and had a chest girth of 259 cm *102 in*. Each of his 3·4 kg *7½ lb* shoes measured 35·5 cm *14 in* across and required 76·2 cm *30 in* of iron (cf. 55·8 cm *22 in* for 'Wandle Goliath' – see below).

In April 1973 a weight of 1459 kg *3218 lb* was reported for an 18.2-hand (*1·88 m*) Belgian (Brabant) mare named 'Wilma du Bos' (foaled 15 July 1966) shortly before she was shipped from Antwerp to her new owner, Mrs Virgie Arden of Reno, Nevada, USA, but at the time she

---

Largest mules ● The largest mules on record are 'Apollo' (born Tennessee 1977) and 'Anak' (born Kentucky 1976), both shown here with their 183 cm *6 ft* tall owner Herbert L. Mueller of Columbia, Illinois, USA. 'Apollo' (left) is 19.1 hands (*199·5 cm*) and weighs 998 kg *2200 lb* and 'Anak' is 18.3 hands (*190·5 cm*) and weighs 952·2 kg *2100 lb*, giving a combined weight of 1960·5 kg *4300 lb*. Both are the hybrid offspring of Belgian mares and Mammoth jacks. (Photo: Herbert L. Mueller)

was heavily in foal (maximum girth 3·65 m *12 ft*). When the horse arrived in New York she scaled 1399 kg *3086 lb*, but after foaling her weight returned to her normal 1088–1134 kg *2400–2500 lb*.

The British weight record is held by the 17.2-hand (*1·78 m*) Shire stallion 'Honest Tom 5123' (foaled in 1884), owned by James Forshaw of Littleport, Cambridgeshire, which scaled 1325 kg *2912 lb* in 1891. The heaviest horse living in Britain today is the 17.2-hand (*1·78 m*) champion Percheron stallion 'Pinchbeck Union Crest' (foaled 27 Jan 1964), whose peak weight fluctuated between 1143 kg *2520 lb* and 1194 kg *2632 lb*. His famous father 'Saltmarsh Silver Crest' (1955–78) scaled 1257 kg *2772 lb* at his heaviest.

Tallest

The tallest documented horse on record was the Shire gelding 'Sampson' (later renamed 'Mammoth') bred by Thomas Cleaver of Toddington Mills, Bedfordshire. This horse (foaled in 1846) measured 21.2½ hands (*2·19 m*) in 1850 and was later said to have weighed 1524 kg *30 cwt*.

Britain's tallest living horses are the Shires 'Wandle Goliath' (foaled 1977) owned by Young & Company's Brewery, Wandsworth, London, and 'Extra Stout' (foaled 1980) owned by Samuel Smith's Brewery, Tadcaster, Yorkshire, both of which measure 19.1½ hand (*1·97 m*).

Smallest

The smallest breed of horse is the Falabella of Argentina which was developed over a period of 70 years by inbreeding and crossing a small group of undersized horses originally discovered in the southern part of the country. Most adult specimens stand less than 76 cm *30 in* and average 36–45 kg *80–100 lb*. The smallest mature horse bred by Julio Falabella of Recco de Roca before he died in 1981 was a mare which stood 38 cm *15 in* and weighed 11·9 kg *26¼ lb*. On 30 Nov 1975 Dr T. H. Hamison of the Circle Veterinary Center, Spartenburg, South Carolina, USA certified that the stallion 'Little Pumpkin' (foaled 15 Apr 1973) owned by J. C. Williams Jr of Della Terra Mini Horse Farm, Inman, South Carolina, USA, stood 35·5 cm *14 in* and weighed 9·07 kg *20 lb*.

Fastest

A Lipizzaner stallion 'Siglavy Slava I' (foaled 17 June 1977) owned by Erich Dybal of Speicher, Switzerland, ran over a half-mile (*804·6 m*) course from a standing start and running free without a rider in 41·8 sec, so averaging 69·3 km/h *43·06 mph*.

Oldest

The greatest reliable age recorded for a horse is 62 years in the case of 'Old Billy' (foaled 1760), believed to be a cross between a Cleveland and Eastern blood, who was bred by Mr Edward Robinson of Wild Grave Farm in Woolston, Lancashire. In 1762 or 1763 he was sold to the Mersey and Irwell Navigation Company and remained with them in a working capacity (i.e. marshalling and towing barges) until 1819 when he was retired to a farm at Latchford, near Warrington, where he died on 27 Nov 1822. The skull of this horse is preserved in the Manchester Museum, and his stuffed head (fitted with false teeth) is now on display in Bedford Museum.

The greatest reliable age recorded for a pony is 54 years for a stallion owned by a farmer in central France (*fl.* 1919). A roan pony named 'Bonnie Lass' owned by twin sisters Sylvia Moore and Mrs Marion Atkinson of Old Harlow, Essex died on 2nd May 1987 aged 42 years.

Exactly a year to the day a moorland pony called 'Joey' belonging to June and Rosie Osborne of the Glebe Equestrian Centre, Wickham Bishop, Essex died aged 44 years.

The greatest age recorded for a thoroughbred racehorse is 42 years in the case of the chestnut gelding 'Tango Duke' (foaled 1935), owned by Mrs Carmen J. Koper of Barongarook, Victoria, Australia. The horse died on 25 Jan 1978.

Strongest

The greatest load ever hauled by a pair of draught–horses was allegedly one weighing 130·9 tonnes (*144 short tons*) which two Shires with a combined weight of 1587 kg *3500 lb* pulled on a sledge litter for a distance of 402 m *440 yd* along a frozen road at the Nester Estate near Ewen, Michigan, USA on 26 Feb 1893, but this tonnage was exaggerated. The load, which comprised 50 logs of white pine scaling 36 055 board feet, actually weighed in the region of 42·3 tonnes *53 short tons*.

On 23 Apr 1924 a shire gelding named 'Vulcan', owned by Liverpool Corporation, registered a pull equal to a starting load of 29·47 tonnes *29 tons* on a dynamometer at the British Empire Exhibition at Wembley, and a pair of

Shires *easily* pulled a starting load of 51 tonnes *50 tons*, the maximum registered on the dynamometer.

DOGS

UK canine population 6 500 000 (1988 estimate), compared with 55 000 000 for the USA and 400 000 000 for the world.

Heaviest

The heaviest breed of domestic dog (*Canis familiaris*) are the St Bernard and the Old English mastiff, both of which (males) regularly weigh 77–91 kg *170–200 lb* at maturity. The heaviest St. Bernard on record is 'Benedictine Jr. Schwarzwald Hof' (whelped 1982) owned by breeders Thomas and Anne Irwin of Grand Rapids, Michigan, USA. His last recorded weight was 140·6 kg *22 st 2 lb* (height at shoulder 99 cm *39 in*).

Tallest

The tallest breeds of dog are the Great Dane and the Irish wolfhound, both of which can exceed 99 cm *39 in* at the shoulder. In the case of the Great Dane the extreme recorded example was 'Shamgret Danzas' (whelped in 1975), owned by Mr and Mrs Peter Comley of Milton Keynes, Bucks. He stood 105·4 cm *41½ in* or 106·6 cm *42 in* when his hackles went up and weighed up to 108 kg *17 st*. He died on 16 Oct 1984. The Irish wolfhound 'Broadbridge Michael' (1920–29), owned by Mrs Mary Beynon of Sutton-at-Hone, Kent, stood 100·3 cm *39½ in* at the age of 2 years.

Smallest

The world's smallest breeds of dog are the Yorkshire terrier, the Chihuahua and the Toy poodle, *miniature* versions of which have been known to weigh less than 453 g *16 oz* when adult.

The smallest mature dog on record was a matchbox-sized Yorkshire terrier owned by Mr Arthur F. Marples of Blackburn, Lancs, a former editor of *Our Dogs*. This tiny atom, which died in 1945 aged nearly 2 years, stood 6·3 cm *2½ in* at the shoulder and measured 9·5 cm *3¾ in* from the tip of its nose to the root of its tail. Its weight was an incredible 113 g *4 oz*.

Oldest

Most dogs live between 8 and 15 years, and authentic records of dogs living over 20 years are rare. The greatest reliable age recorded for a dog is 29 years 5 months for an Australian cattle-dog named 'Bluey', owned by Mr Les Hall of Rochester, Victoria, Australia. The dog was obtained as a puppy in 1910 and worked among cattle and sheep for nearly 20 years. He was put to sleep on 14 Nov 1939.

The British record is 27 years 313 days for a Welsh collie named 'Taffy' owned by Mrs Evelyn Brown of Forge Farm, West Bromwich, West Midlands. He was whelped on 2 Apr 1952 and died on 9 Feb 1980.

Strength and endurance

The greatest load ever shifted by a dog was 2905 kg *6400½ lb* of railroad steel pulled by a 80 kg *176 lb* St Bernard named 'Ryettes Brandy Bear' at Bothell, Washington, USA on 21 July 1978. The 4-year-old dog, owned by Douglas Alexander of Monroe, Washington, pulled the weight on a four-wheeled carrier across a concrete surface for a distance of 4·57 m *15 ft* in less than 90 sec. Ten days earlier the same dog had moved 2993 kg *6600 lb*, but was 12·7 cm *5 in* short of the 4·5 m *15 ft* minimum distance when the 90 seconds were up.

At the American Dog Breeders' Association 'Weight-Pull' held at Conroe, Texas, USA on 7 Dec 1985 a 19·5 kg *43 lb* American Pit bull terrier bitch named 'Crazy II', owned by Bill Grimsley of Choctaw, Oklahoma, pulled 1383 kg *3050 lb* (32·19 kg per kg *70·98 lb per lb* of body weight).

The record time for the annual 1688 km *1049 mile* Iditarod Trail sled dog race from Anchorage to Nome, Alaska, USA (inaugurated 1973) is 11 days 2 hours 5 mins

13 sec by Susan Butcher's team of dogs in the 1987 race. It was her second consecutive win.

Guide dog

The longest period of *active service* reported for a guide dog is 14 years 8 months (August 1972 – March 1987) in the case of a Labrador-Retriever bitch named 'Cindy–Cleo' (whelped 20 Jan 1971), owned by Mr Aron Barr of Tel Aviv, Israel. The dog died on Apr 10 1987.

Largest litter

The largest recorded litter of puppies is one of 23 thrown on 19 June 1944 by 'Lena', an American foxhound bitch owned by Commander W. N. Ely of Ambler, Pennsylvania. All the puppies survived. On 6–7 Feb 1975 'Careless Ann', a St Bernard owned by Robert and Alice Rodden of Lebanon, Missouri, USA, also produced a litter of 23, 14 of which survived, and the same number (16 survived) was thrown by 'Shalimar Bootsie', a Great Dane owned by Mrs Marjorie Harris of Little Hall, nr. Colchester, Essex in June 1987.

Most prolific

The greatest sire of all time was the champion greyhound 'Low Pressure', nicknamed 'Timmy', whelped in September 1957 and owned by Mrs Bruna Amhurst of Regent's Park, London. From December 1961 until his death on 27 Nov 1969 he fathered 2414 registered puppies, with at least 600 others unregistered.

Most valuable

In 1907 Mrs Clarice Ashton Cross of Ascot, Berkshire turned down an offer of £32 000 (equivalent to £865 000 today!) from the American financier and industrialist J. Pierpont Morgan for her famous Pekingese 'Ch. Ch'êrh of Alderbourne' (1904–*fl.* 1914). Mr Morgan then came back with an 'open' cheque, but again she turned him down. The largest legacy devoted to a dog was by Miss Ella Wendel of New York who 'left' her standard poodle 'Toby' £15 million in 1931.

> **Heaviest dog** ● The heaviest (and longest) dog ever recorded is 'Alcama Zorba of La-Susa' (whelped Sept 26 1981), an Old English mastiff owned by Chris Eraclides of London. In September 1987 this canine super-heavyweight weighed 144·66 kg *22 st 6½ lb* (shoulder height 88·7 cm *35 in*) but, despite his enormous size, he does not carry any surplus fat. If his diet was not strictly controlled his owner believes he would reach 152·4 kg *24 st* without any trouble. Other statistics include a chest girth of 132 cm *52 in*, a 87·7 cm *36½ in* neck, and a nose to tail length of 254·4 cm *8 ft 3 in*. One of his sons 'Chandor' (whelped Aug 6 1987) weighed 85·9 kg *13½ st* (shoulder height 78·7 cm *31 in*) at the age of 8 months. (Photo: Gerald L. Wood)

> **Rarest dog** ● The rarest breed of dog in the world is currently the American hairless terrier. At the last count (18 March 1988) there were only 70 living examples, 68 owned by Willie and Edwin Scott of Trout, Louisiana, USA.

Highest and longest jump

The canine 'high jump' record for a leap and a scramble over a smooth wooden wall (without any ribs or other aids) is held by a German shepherd dog named 'Max of Pangoula', who scaled an 3·48 m *11 ft 5⅛ in* wall, at Chikurubi prison's dog training school near Harare, Zimbabwe on 18 Mar 1980. His trainer was Chief Prison Officer Alec Mann. 'Duke', a 3 year-old German shepherd dog, handled by Cpl Graham Urry of RAF Newton, Nottinghamshire, scaled a ribbed wall with regulation shallow slats to a height of 3·58 m *11 ft 9 in* on the BBC *Record Breakers* TV programme on 11 Nov 1986. The longest recorded canine long jump was one of 9·14 m *30 ft* by a greyhound named 'Bang' whilst coursing a hare at Brecon Lodge, Gloucestershire in 1849. He cleared a 1·4 m *4 ft 6 in* gate and landed on a hard road, but despite a damaged pastern bone he still managed to kill the hare.

Ratting

The greatest ratter of all time was a 11·8 kg *26 lb* 'bull and terrier' dog named 'Billy'. During the five-year period 1820–24 he despatched 4000 rats in 17 hr in matches, a remarkable feat considering that he was blind in one eye. His most notable feat was the killing of 100 rats in 5 min 30 sec at the cockpit in Tufton Street, Westminster, London on 23 Apr 1825. He died on 23 Feb 1829 aged 13

yrs. James Searle's famous 'bull and terrier' bitch 'Jenny Lind' was another outstanding ratter. On 12 July 1853 she was backed to kill 500 rats in under 3 hr at The Beehive in Old Crosshall Street, Liverpool, and completed the job in 1 hr 36 min.

Tracking

The greatest tracking feat on record was performed by a Dobermann pinscher named 'Sauer', trained by Detective-Sergeant Herbert Kruger. In 1925 he tracked a stock-thief 160 km *100 miles* across the Great Karroo, South Africa by scent alone. In 1923 a collie dog named 'Bobbie', lost by his owners while they were on holiday in Wolcott, Indiana, USA, turned up at the family home in Silverton, Oregon, USA 6 months later, after covering a distance of some 3200 km *2000 miles*. The dog, later identified by householders who had looked after him along the route, had apparently travelled back through the states of Illinois, Iowa, Nebraska and Colorado, before crossing the Rocky Mountains in the depths of winter.

Top show dogs

The greatest number of Challenge Certificates won by a dog is the 78 compiled by the famous chow chow 'Ch. U'Kwong King Solomon' (whelped 21 June 1968). Owned and bred by Mrs Joan Egerton of Bramhall, Cheshire, 'Solly' won his first CC at the Cheshire Agricultural Society Championship Show on 4 June 1969, and his 78th CC was awarded at the City of Birmingham Championship Show on 4 Sept 1976. He died on 3 April 1978. The greatest number of 'Best-in-Show' awards won by any dog in all-breed shows is the career total of 203 compiled by the Scottish terrier bitch 'Ch. Braeburn's Close Encounter' (whelped 22 Oct 1978) up to 10 Mar 1985. She is owned by Sonnie Novick of Plantation Acres,

Florida, USA. 'Ch. Clayfield's Mon Ami', a German Shepherd bitch whelped in 1973, won a unique 10 Dog Show championships on 4 continents from 1975 to 1987. She is owned by Neal, Sharon, Buffy and Holly Leas of West Des Moines, Iowa, USA.

Largest show

At the Ladies' Kennel Association Show (LKA) held at the Birmingham National Exhibition Centre on 14–15 Dec 1984 there were 21 212 entries and a total of 14 611 dogs exhibited.

Top trainer

The most successful dog trainer in the world is Mrs Barbara Woodhouse of Rickmansworth, Hertfordshire, who trained 19 000 dogs to obey the basic commands during the period 1951 to her retirement in 1985 following a stroke. The fastest trainer is Mr Armand Rabuttinio of Aston, Pennsylvania, USA. His highest total for a single day (9 a.m.–6 p.m.) is 132 dogs at a training marathon held at Upland, Pennsylvania on 12 June 1982.

Drug sniffing

The greatest drug-sniffing dog on record was a Golden retriever named 'Trep' (whelped 1969), owned by former policeman Tom Kazo of Dade County, Miami, Florida, USA. During the 5-year period 1973–77 'Agent K9-3', as he was also known, sniffed out $63 million worth of narcotics. His owner said he would retire his pet, who could detect 16 different drugs, when he reached the magic $100 million mark, but it is not known whether 'Trep' achieved this target. The only drug-sniffing dog with a 100 per cent arrest record was a German shepherd of the US Army called 'General'. During the period April 1974 to March 1976 this canine detective and his handler, SP4 Michael R. Harris of the 591st Military Police Company in Fort Bliss, Texas, USA, carried out 220 searches for narcotics, arrested 220 people for possession and uncovered 330 caches of drugs. The German shepherd 'Blue' of the Los Angeles Police Department was reported in January 1986 to have assisted in apprehending 253 suspected felons.

CATS

UK feline population 6 300 000 (1988 estimate), compared with 49 800 000 for the USA.

Largest

The largest of the 330 breeds of cat is the Ragdoll with males weighing 6·8–9·07 kg *15–20 lb*. In the majority of domestic cats (*Felis catus*), the average weight of the male (tom) at maturity is 2·81 kg *6·2 lb*, compared with 2·45 kg *5·4 lb* for the adult female or queen. Neuters and spays average out somewhat heavier. The heaviest domestic cat on record was a neutered male tabby named 'Himmy', owned by Thomas Vyse of Redlynch, Cairns, Queensland, Australia. At the time of his death on 12 Mar 1986 aged 10 years 4 months he weighed 21·3 kg *46 lb 15¼ oz* (neck 38·1 cm *15 in*, waist 83·8 cm *33 in*, length 96·5 cm *38 in*). In Feb 1988 an unconfirmed weight of 21·7 kg *48 lb* was reported for a cat named 'Edward Bear', owned by Miss Jackie Fleming of Sydney, NSW, Australia.

The heaviest cat ever recorded in Britain was an 11-year-old male tabby called 'Poppa' owned by Miss Gwladys Cooper of Newport, Gwent, South Wales. He scaled 20·19 kg *44½ lb* in November 1984 and died on 25 June 1985.

Smallest

The smallest breed of domestic cat is the Singapura or 'Drain Cat' of Singapore. Adult males average 2·72 kg *6 lb* in weight and adult females 1·81 kg *4 lb*. A male Siamese cross named 'Ebony-Eb-Honey Cat' owned by Miss Angelina Johnston of Boise, Idaho, USA tipped the scales at only 0·79 kg *1 lb 12 oz* in February 1984 when aged 23 months.

Oldest

Cats are generally longer-lived than dogs. The average

LARGEST PET LITTERS

Animal/Breed	No.	Owner	Date
CAT *Burmese/Siamese*	15[1]	Mrs Valerie Gane, Church Westcote, Kingham, Oxfordshire	7 Aug 1970
DOG *American foxhound*	23[2]	Cdr W. N. Ely, Ambler, Pennsylvania, USA	19 June 1944
DOG *St Bernard*	23[3]	R. and A. Rodden, Lebanon, Missouri, USA	6/7 Feb 1975
DOG *Great Dane*	23[4]	Mrs Marjorie Harris, Little Hall, Essex	June 1987
RABBIT *New Zealand white*	24	Joseph Filek, Sydney, Cape Breton, Nova Scotia, Canada	1978
GUINEA PIG (CAVY)	12	Laboratory specimen	1972
HAMSTER *Golden*	26[5]	L. and S. Miller, Baton Rouge, Louisiana, USA	28 Feb 1974
MOUSE *House*	34[6]	Marion Ogilvie, Blackpool, Lancs, England	12 Feb 1982
GERBIL *Mongolian*	14	Sharon Kirkman, Bulwell, Nottingham, England	May 1983
GERBIL *Mongolian*	15[7]	George Meares, geneticist-owner gerbil breeding farm, St Petersburg, Florida, USA	1960s

[1] 4 still born [2] all survived [3] 14 survived [4] 16 survived [5] 18 killed by mother [6] 33 survived [7] Used special food formula

---

CAGED PET LONGEVITY

Animal/Species	Name, Owner etc.	Years	Months
HAMSTER *Golden*	Reported 1984 Cambridge, England	19	—
RABBIT	*Flopsy* caught 6 Aug 1964 d.29 June 1983 (owner Mrs L.B. Walker) Longford, Tasmania	18	10¾
GUINEA PIG	*Snowball* d. 14 Feb 1979 (owner, M. A. Wall) Bingham, Notts.	14	10½
GERBIL *Mongolian*	*Sahara* May 1973–4 Oct 1981 (owner Aaron Milstone) Lathrup Village, Michigan, USA	8	4½
MOUSE *House*	*Fritzy* 11 Sept 1977–24 April 1985 (owner Mrs Bridget Beard) West House School, Edgbaston, Birmingham, England	7	7
RAT *Common*	Died: c. 1924 Philadelphia, Pennsylvania, USA.	5	8

---

life expectancy of entire well-fed males raised under household conditions, and receiving good medical attention, is 13–15 years (15–17 years for intact females), but neutered males and females live on the average one to two years longer.

The oldest cat ever recorded was probably the tabby 'Puss', owned by Mrs T. Holway of Clayhidon, Devon, who celebrated his 36th birthday on 28 Nov 1939 and died the next day. A more recent and better-documented case was that of the female tabby 'Ma', owned by Mrs Alice St George Moore of Drewsteignton, Devon. This cat was put to sleep on 5 Nov 1957 aged 34. The oldest cat living in Britain today is believed to be a female black moggy named 'Kitty' owned by Mr George Johnston of Croxton, Staffordshire. She was discovered as a stray (with four kittens) in November 1951, and celebrated her 31st birthday in 1988.

Largest kindle

The largest litter ever recorded was one of 19 kittens (4 stillborn) delivered by caesarean section to 'Tarawood Antigone', a 4-year-old brown Burmese, on 7 Aug 1970. Her owner, Mrs Valerie Gane of Church Westcote, Kingham, Oxfordshire, said the result was a mis-mating with a half-Siamese. Of the 15 survivors, 14 were males and one female.

The largest live litter (all of which survived) was one of 14 kittens born in December 1974 to a Persian cat named 'Bluebell', owned by Mrs Elenore Dawson of Wellington, Cape Province, South Africa.

Most prolific

The greatest number of kittens produced by a cat during her breeding life was 420 in the case of a tabby named 'Dusty' (b. 1935) living in Bonham, Texas, USA. She gave birth to her last kindle (a single kitten) on 12 June 1952. In May 1987 'Kitty' (see above) produced 2 kittens at the age of 30 years (breeding total to date 212 kittens), making her the oldest feline mother on record.

Most valuable

In 1988 Mr Carl Mayes, a breeder in Atlanta, Georgia,

USA turned down an offer of $10 000 for his male Singapura 'Bull', the best known example of its breed in the USA.

Best climber

On 6 Sept 1950 a four-month-old kitten belonging to Josephine Aufdenblatten of Geneva, Switzerland followed a group of climbers up to the top of the 4 478 m *14 691 ft* Matterhorn in the Alps.

Mousing champion

The greatest mouser on record was a female tortoise-shell cat named 'Towser' (b. 21 Apr 1963) owned by Glenturret Distillery Ltd near Crieff, Tayside, Scotland who notched up an estimated lifetime score of 28 899. She averaged a grand total of 3 mice per day until her death on 20 Mar 1987 at the ripe old feline age of 25.

RABBITS AND HARES

Largest

The largest breed of domestic rabbit (*Oryctolagus cuniculus*) is the Flemish giant. Adults weigh 7–8·5 kg *15·4–18·7 lb* (average toe-to-toe length when fully stretched 91 cm *36 in*), but weights up to 11·3 kg *25 lb* have been reliably reported for this breed. In April 1980 a 5 month-old French Lop doe weighing 12 kg *26·45 lb* was exhibited at the Reus Fair, north-east Spain. The heaviest recorded wild rabbit (av. weight 1·58 kg *3½ lb*) was one of 3·74 kg *8 lb 4 oz*, killed by Norman Wilkie of Markinch, Fife, Scotland while ferreting on 20 Nov 1982.

Smallest

The smallest breeds of domestic rabbit are the Nether-land dwarf and the Polish, both of which have a weight range of 0·9–1·13 kg *2–2½ lb* when fully grown. In 1975 Jacques Bouloc of Coulommière, France announced a new cross of the above breeds which weighed 396 g *14 oz*.

Most prolific

The most prolific domestic breeds are the New Zealand white and the Californian. Does produce 5–6 litters a year, each containing 8–12 kittens during their breeding life (cf. five litters and three to seven young for the wild rabbit).

Longest ears

The longest ears are found in the Lop family (four strains), and in particular the English Lop. The ears of a typical example measure about 61 cm *24 in* from tip to tip (taken across the skull), and 14 cm *5·51 in* in width. In 1901 Captain Youden exhibited a specimen in England which had 77·4 cm *30·5 in* ears; it is not known, however, if this was a natural attainment or weights had been used to stretch the ears and left the veins inside badly varicosed.

Largest hare

In November 1956 a Brown hare weighing 6·83 kg *15 lb 1 oz* was shot near Welford, Northamptonshire. The average adult weight is 3·62 kg *8 lb*.

Birds *Aves*

Largest *Ratite*

The largest living bird is the North African ostrich (*Struthio c. camelus*), which is found in reduced numbers south of the Atlas Mountains from Upper Senegal and Niger across to the Sudan and central Ethiopia. Male examples (adult hens are smaller) of this flightless or ratite sub-species have been recorded up to 2·74 m *9 ft* in height and 156·5 kg *345 lb* in weight.

Largest *Carinate*

The world's heaviest flying birds are the Kori bustard or Paauw (*Ardeotis kori*) of eastern South Africa and the Great bustard (*Otis tarda*) of Europe and Asia. Weights up to 18·14 kg *40 lb* have been reported for cock birds shot in South Africa, and there is an isolated record of 21 kg *46·2 lb* for a cock bird shot in Manchuria which was too heavy to fly. The Mute swan (*Cygnus olor*), which is resident in Britain, can also reach 18·14 kg *40 lb* on very rare occasions, and there is a record from Poland of a cob weighing 22·5 kg *49·6 lb* which had temporarily lost the power of flight. The heaviest bird of prey is the Andean condor (*Vultur gryphus*), adult males averaging 9·09–11·3 kg *20–25 lb*. A weight of 14·1 kg *31 lb* has been claimed for an outsized male Californian condor (*Gymnogyps californianus*) now preserved in the California Academy of Sciences, Los Angeles, USA. This species is appreciably smaller than the Andean condor and rarely exceeds 10·4 kg *23 lb*.

Largest wingspan

The Wandering albatross (*Diomedea exulans*) of the southern oceans has the largest wingspan of any living bird, adult males averaging 3·15 m *10 ft 4 in* with wings tightly stretched. The largest recorded specimen was a very old male 3·63 m *11 ft 11 in* caught by members of the Antarctic research ship USNS *Eltanin* in the Tasman Sea on 18 Sept 1965. Unconfirmed measurements up to 4·22 m *13 ft 10 in* have been claimed for this species. The only other bird reliably credited with a wingspan in excess of 3·35 m *11 ft* is the vulture-like Marabou stork (*Leptoptilus crumeniferus*) of tropical Africa. In 1934 an extreme measurement of 4·06 m *13 ft 4 in* was reported for a male shot in central Africa by the well-known naturalist Richard Meinertzhagen, but this species rarely exceeds 2·74 m *9 ft*.

Smallest

The smallest bird in the world is the Bee hummingbird (*Mellisuga helenae*) of Cuba and the Isle of Pines. Adult males (females are slightly larger) measure 57 mm *2·24 in* in total length, half of which is taken up by the bill and tail. It weighs 1·6 g *0·056 oz*, which means it is lighter than a Privet hawk-moth (2·4 g *0·084 oz*). The smallest bird of prey is the 35 g *1·23 oz* White-fronted falconet (*Microhierax latifrons*) of north-western Borneo, which is sparrow-sized. The smallest seabird is the Least storm petrel (*Halocyptena microsoma*), which breeds on many of the small islands in the Gulf of California, north-

Longest lived ● In 1987 an unconfirmed age of *c.* 82 years was reported for a male Siberian white crane (*Crus leucogeranus*) named 'Wolfe' at the International Crane Foundation, Baraboo, Wisconsin, USA. The bird was said to have hatched out in a zoo in Switzerland *c.* 1905.

western Mexico. Adult specimens average 140 mm *5½ in* in total length and weigh *c.* 28 g *1 oz*.

Most abundant

The most abundant species of wild bird is the Red-billed quelea (*Quelea quelea*), a seed-eating weaver of the drier parts of Africa south of the Sahara with an estimated adult breeding population of 1 500 000 000. One huge roost in the Sudan contained 32 000 000 birds. The most abundant sea bird is probably Wilson's storm petrel (*Oceanites oceanicus*) of the Antarctic. No population estimates have been published, but the numbers run into hundreds of millions.

The most abundant species of domesticated bird is the Chicken, the tame version of the wild Red jungle fowl (*Gallus gallus*) of south-east Asia. According to the FAO (Food and Agriculture Organisation of the United Nations), the world's chicken population stood at 8 295 760 000 in 1985, which means there are nearly two chickens for every member of the human race.

The most common nesting bird found in Britain is now the Blackbird (*Turdus merula*), with a peak breeding population of 15 million. It is followed by the Chaffinch (*Fringilla coelebs*), the Starling (*Sturnus vulgaris*), the House sparrow (*Passer domesticus*), the Robin (*Erithacus rubecula*) and the Blue tit (*Parus caeruleus*), all of which have a peak population of *c.* 10 million. Between 1964–74 the population of the Wren (*Troglodytes troglodytes*) increased tenfold, after a series of mild winters, and at the end of this period there were an estimated 20 million birds. This species, however, is severely affected by cold weather, and the harsh winter of 1978/9 alone reduced the Wren population by 40 per cent.

Rarest

Because of the practical difficulties in assessing bird populations in the wild, it is virtually impossible to establish the identity of the world's rarest living bird. The strongest contender, up until very recently, was the Dusky seaside sparrow (*Ammospiza nigrescens*), formerly of Titusville Marshes, Florida, USA, but the last living example (a male) died at Discovery Island, Disney World, Orlando on 16 May 1987. Some of its tissues has been frozen in the hope that future technology might allow a pure strain of Dusky seaside sparrow to be resurrected through genetic cloning. The Guam flycatcher (*Myiagra freycineti*) and the Rufous fantail (*Rhipidura rufifrons*), also of Guam, were last seen in 1984 and may now also be extinct, and the Guam rail (*Rallus owstoni*) has only been sighted 3 times since 1985. The Chatham Island black robin (*Petroica traversi*) is also on the verge of extinction with only 4 surviving in 1985. The

Smallest British bird ● The smallest regularly breeding bird is the Goldcrest (*Regulus regulus*) also known as the Golden crested wren. Adult specimens measure 90 mm *3·5 in* in total length and weigh between 3·8 and 4·5 g *0·108 and 0·127 oz*, which means it is half the weight of the Common wren (*Troglodytes troglodytes*). (Photo: Bruce Coleman)

last wild California condor (*Gymnogyps californianus*) was captured on 19 April 1987 in Kern County, California, USA to join 26 others held for captive breeding in San Diego Wildlife Park and Los Angeles Zoo. On 29 April 1988 the first California condor ever born in captivity was successfully hatched out at San Diego Wildlife Park.

The world's rarest, most restricted and most highly threatened bird is now probably the Aldabra brush warbler (*Nesillas aldabrabus*). Not discovered until 1967, 5 individuals (3 males and 2 females) were ringed between July 1974 and February 1977. One of the males was re-sighted in 1978 and again in September 1983, but that was the last confirmed record. This species is restricted to a coastal strip 2 km *1·24 miles* long and 50 m *54 yds* wide on the northern tip of Aldabra Atoll in the Indian Ocean.

According to the British Ornithologists' Union there are more than 40 species of birds which have been recorded only once in the British Isles – most of them since the end of the Second World War in 1945. That which has not recurred for the longest period is the Black-capped petrel (*Pterodroma hasitata*), of the West Indies. A specimen was caught alive on a heath at Southacre, near Swaffham, Norfolk in March or April 1850. On 28–29 May 1979 an Aleutian tern (*Sterna aleutica*) was sighted on the Farne Islands, Northumberland. This bird breeds on the coasts of Alaska and eastern Siberia, and until then had never been recorded outside the N. Pacific.

In August 1986 thousands of bird-watchers descended on Blackcroft Sands Nature Reserve on Humberside for a sighting of a Red-necked stint (*Calidris ruficollis*) from Siberia, the first ever recorded in Britain.

The most tenuously established British bird is the Snowy owl (*Nyctea scandiaca*). During the period 1967–75 one pair bred regularly on Fetlar, Shetland Isles and reared a total of 21 young, but soon afterwards the old male took off for an unknown destination, having driven off all the young males, and left the females without a mate. From 19–22 April 1979 an adult male was seen on Fair Isle some 129 km *80 miles* further south, but it did not find its way to Fetlar. In 1984 four females were seen on Fetlar, but once again no males were in evidence.

In 1916 an English vicar stole the eggs of the last White-tailed sea eagle (*Haliaeetus albicilla*) on Skye in the Inner Hebrides, Scotland. During the period 1975–7 an attempt to reintroduce this magnificent bird on the island of Rhum was made, and 13 eaglets from Norway were released. In the summer of 1985 the first specimen raised in the wild in Britain for more than 70 years took to the air, and it bred again successfully the following year.

Britain's rarest bird of prey is Montagu's harrier (*Circus pygargus*), which is confined to heathland and moorland areas of southern and eastern England. In 1974 there were no confirmed breeding pairs, but now they have re-established themselves, and in 1986 there were 7 pairs, 6 of which raised 13 chicks.

Fastest and slowest flying

The fastest fliers are found among the ducks and geese (*Anatidae*), and some powerful species such as the Red-breasted merganser (*Mergus serrator*), the Eider (*Somateria mollissima*), the Canvasback (*Aythya valisineria*) and the Spur-winged goose (*Plectropterus gambiensis*) can probably exceed an air speed of 104 km/h *65 mph* in level flight.

The White-throated spinetail swift (*Hirundapus caudacutus*) of Asia and the Alpine swift (*Apus melba*) are also extremely fast during courtship display flights, and the former has been timed at speeds up to 170 km/h *105·6 mph* in tests carried out in the USSR.

A record for sustained speed was set by a semi-palmated sandpiper (*Calidris pusilla*) tagged in Massachusetts, USA in August 1985 and shot by a hunter in Guyana 4425·5 km *2750 miles* distant within 4 days, thus averaging some 48km/h *30 mph* above 1524 m *5000 ft*.

Probably at least 50 per cent of the world's flying birds cannot exceed an air speed of 64 km/h *40 mph* in level flight.

The slowest flying bird is the American woodcock (*Scolopax minor*), which has been timed at 8 km/h *5 mph* without sinking during courtship flights.

Fastest and slowest wing beat

The fastest recorded wing beat of any bird is that of the Horned sungem (*Heliactin cornuta*) of tropical South America with a rate of 90 beats per sec. Large vultures (*Vulturidae*) sometimes exhibit a flapping rate as low as one beat per sec, and condors can cruise on air currents for up to 96 km *60 miles* without beating their wings once.

Longest lived

The greatest irrefutable age reported for any bird is 80+ years for a male Sulphur-crested cockatoo (*Cacatua galerita*) named 'Cocky', who died at London Zoo in 1982. He was presented to the Zoo in 1925, and had been with his previous owner since 1902 when he was already fully mature.

In 1987 an unconfirmed age of c. 82 years was reported for a male Siberian white crane (*Crus leucogeranus*) named 'Wolfe' at the International Crane Foundation, Baraboo, Wisconsin, USA. The bird was said to have hatched out in a zoo in Switzerland c. 1905.

In 1964 the death was reported of a male Andean condor called 'Kuzya' at Moscow Zoo, USSR, aged 72+ years. As this bird was already fully grown when it was received in 1892, it must have been at least 77. The oldest ringed bird on record is 'Blue White', a 59-year-old female Royal albatross (*Diomedea epomophora*), which nests at Taiaroa Head, Otago, New Zealand. She was banded as a breeding adult in the 1937/8 season when she was at least 9-years-old. Her mate 'Green White Green' is 46.

Longest flights

The greatest distance covered by a ringed bird is 22 530 km *14 000 miles* by an Arctic tern (*Sterna paradisea*), which was banded as a nestling on 5 July 1955 in the Kandalaksha Sanctuary on the White Sea coast and was captured alive by a fisherman 13 km *8 miles* south of Fremantle, Western Australia on 16 May 1956. The bird had flown south via the Atlantic Ocean and then circled Africa before crossing the Indian Ocean. It did not survive to make the return journey. There is also another report of an Arctic tern flying from Greenland to Australasia, but further details are lacking.

Highest flying

The highest acceptable altitude recorded for a bird is 11 277 m *37 000 ft* for a Ruppell's vulture (*Gyps rueppellii*) which collided with a commercial aircraft over Abidjan, Ivory Coast, western Africa, on 29 Nov 1973. The impact damaged one of the aircraft's engines, causing it to shut down, but the plane landed safely without further incident. Sufficient feather remains of the bird were recovered to allow the US Museum of Natural History to make a positive identification, but this was a freakish altitude even for this high-level soarer, which is rarely seen above 6096 m *20 000 ft*. Britain's highest flying bird is the Whooper swan (*Cygnus cygnus*). On 9 Dec 1967 about 30 of these birds were recorded at an altitude of just over 8230 m *27 000 ft* flying in from Iceland to winter at Loch Foyle, Northern Ireland. They were spotted by an airline pilot over the Outer Hebrides, and the height was also confirmed on radar by air traffic control.

Most airborne

The most aerial of all birds is the Sooty tern (*Sterna fuscata*) which, after leaving the nesting grounds, remains continuously aloft from 3 to 10 years as a sub-adult, before returning to land to breed. The most aerial land bird is the Common swift (*Apus apus*) which remains airborne for 2–3 years, during which time it sleeps, drinks, eats and even mates on the wing.

Fastest swimmer

The fastest swimming bird is the Gentoo penguin (*Pygoscelis papua*) which has a maximum burst speed of c. 27·4 km/h *17 mph*. The deepest diving bird is the Emperor penguin (*Aptenodytes forsteri*) of the Antarctic which can reach a depth of 265 m *870 ft* and remain submerged for up to 18 minutes.

Vision

Birds of prey (Falconiformes) have the keenest eyesight in the avian world, and their visual acuity is at least 3–5 times stronger than that of human vision. The Golden eagle (*Aquila chrysaetos*) can detect a 46 cm *18 in* long hare at a range of 3·2 km *2 miles* in good light and against a contrasting background, and a Peregrine falcon can spot a pigeon at a range of over 8 km *5 miles*.

g force

American scientific experiments have revealed that the beak of the Red-headed woodpecker (*Melanerpes erythrocephalus*) hits the bark of a tree with an impact velocity of 20·9 km/h *13 mph*. This means that when the head snaps back the brain is subject to a deceleration of about 10 g.

Longest feathers

The longest feathers grown by any bird are those of the Phoenix fowl or Onagadori (a strain of Red junglefowl *Gallus gallus*) which has been bred in south-western Japan since the mid-17th century. In 1972 a tail covert measuring 10·6 m *34 ft 9½ in* was reported for a rooster owned by Masasha Kubota of Kochi, Shikoku. Among flying birds the tail feathers of the male Crested pheasant (*Rheinhartia ocellata*) of south-east Asia regularly reach 173 cm *5 ft 8 in* in length and 13 cm *5 in* wide, and the central tail feathers of the Reeves' pheasant (*Syrmaticus reevesi*) of central and northern China have exceptionally reached 2·43 m *8 ft.*

Most feathers

In a series of 'feather counts' on various species of bird a Whistling swan (*Cygnus columbianus*) was found to have 25 216 feathers, 20 177 of which were on the head and neck. The Ruby-throated hummingbird (*Archilochus colubris*) has only 940.

Largest egg

The largest egg produced by any living bird is that of the Ostrich (*Struthio camelus*). The average example measures 15–20 cm *6–8 in* in length, 10–15 cm *4–6 in* in diameter and weighs 1·65–1·78 kg *3·63–3·88 lb* (around 2 dozen hens' eggs in volume). It requires about 40 min for boiling. The shell, though 1·5 mm *¹/₁₆ in* thick, can support the weight of a 127 kg *20 st* man.

The largest egg laid by any bird on the British list is that of the Mute swan (*Cygnus olor*), which measures 109–124 mm *4·3–4·9 in* in length, 71–78·5 mm *2·8–3·1 in* in diameter. The weight 340–368 g *12–13 oz.*

Smallest egg

The smallest egg laid by any bird is that of the Vervain hummingbird (*Mellisuga minima*) of Jamaica. Two specimens measuring less than 10 mm *0·39 in* in length weighed 0·365 g *0·0128 oz* and 0·375 g *0·0132 oz* respectively (cf. 0·5 g *0·017 oz* for the Bee hummingbird). The smallest egg laid by a bird on the British list is that of the Goldcrest, which measures 12·2–14·5 mm *0·48–0·57 in* in length and between 9·4 and 9·9 mm *0·37–0·39 in* in diameter with a weight of 0·6 g *0·021 oz.* Eggs emitted from the oviduct before maturity, known as 'sports', are not reckoned to be of significance.

Incubation

The longest normal incubation period is that of the Wandering albatross, with a normal range of 75–82 days. There is an isolated case of an egg of the Mallee fowl (*Leipoa ocellata*) of Australia taking 90 days to hatch against its normal incubation of 62 days.

The shortest incubation period is the 10 days of the Great spotted woodpecker (*Dendrocopus major*) and the Blackbilled cuckoo (*Coccyzus erythropthalmus*). The idlest of cock birds include hummingbirds (family Trochilidae), Eider duck (*Somateria mollissima*) and Golden pheasant (*Chrysolophus pictus*) among whom the hen bird does 100 per cent of the incubation, whereas the female Common kiwi (*Apteryx australis*) leaves this to the male for 75–80 days.

Bills

The largest bill or beak grown by any bird is that of the Australian pelican (*Pelicanus conspicillatus*), which measures 34–47 cm *13·3–18·5 in* long. The longest bill in relation to overall body length is that of the Sword-billed hummingbird (*Ensifera ensifera*) of the Andes from Venezuela to Bolivia. It measures 10·2 cm *4 in* in length and is longer than the bird's actual body if the tail is excluded.

Cuckoos

It is unlikely that the Cuckoo (*Culculus canorus*) has ever been *heard and seen* in Britain earlier than 2 March, on which date one was observed under acceptable conditions by Mr William A. Haynes of Trinder Road, Wantage, Oxfordshire in 1972. The two latest dates are

16 Dec 1912 at Anstey's Cove, Torquay, Devon and 26 Dec 1897 or 1898 in Cheshire.

Bird-spotter

The world's leading bird-spotter or 'twitcher' is Norman Chesterfield (b. 8 March 1913) of Wheatley, Ontario, Canada, who did not buy his first pair of binoculars until 1955. By March 1988 he had logged exactly 6260 of the 9016 known species.

The British life list record is 462 by Ron Johns (b. 1941) of Slough, Bucks who started spotting in 1952. The British year list record is 340 by Lee Evans (b. 1960) of Luton, Beds established in 1985. In an average year he travels 96 000 km *60 000 miles.*

The greatest number of species spotted in a 24-hour period is 342 by Kenyans Terry Stevenson, John Fanshawe and Andy Roberts on day two of the Birdwatch Kenya '86 event held on 29–30 November. The 48-hour record is held by Don Turner and David Pearson of Kenya who spotted 494 species at the same event.

Largest nest

The largest bird's nest on record is one 2·9 m *9½ ft* wide, 6 m *20 ft* deep built by a pair of Bald eagles (*Haliaeetus leucocephalus*) and possible their successors near St Petersburg, Florida, USA examined in 1963 and estimated to weigh more than 2 tonnes.

The Golden eagle (*Aquila chrysaetos*) also constructs huge nests, and one 4·57 m *15 ft* deep was reported from Scotland in 1954. It had been used for 45 years.

The incubation mounds built by the Mallee fowl (*Leipoa ocellata*) of Australia are much larger, having been measured up to 4·57 m *15 ft* in height and 10·6 m *35 ft* across, and it has been calculated that the nest site may involve the mounding of 289 m³ *300 yd³* of matter weighing 300 tonnes *295 tons.*

Smallest nest

The smallest nests are built by hummingbirds (Trochilidae). That of the Vervain hummingbird (*Mellisuga minima*) is about half the size of a walnut, while the deeper one of the Bee hummingbird is thimble–sized. The smallest British nest is that of the Goldcrest, which measures about 8–9 cm *3·14–3·54 in* in diameter.

DOMESTICATED BIRDS
Heaviest chicken

The heaviest breed of chicken is the White sully, which Mr Grant Sullens of West Point, California, USA developed over a period of 7 years by crossing and recrossing large Rhode Island Reds with other varieties. One monstrous rooster named 'Weirdo' reportedly weighed 10 kg *22 lb* in January 1973, and was so aggressive that he had already killed two cats and crippled a dog which came too close.

The heaviest chicken reported in Britain was a 5-month-old 7·78 kg *17 lb 3 oz* Cobb capon bred by Mr Henry Ransom of Brancaster Staithe, King's Lynn, Norfolk and weighed in December 1975 before ending up on the Christmas table.

Chicken flying

'Sheena', a barnyard bantam owned by Bill and Bob Knox, flew 192·07 m *630 ft 2 in* at Parkesburg, Pennsylvania, USA on 31 May 1985.

Oldest

The longest-lived domesticated bird (excluding the Ostrich which has lived up to 68 years) is the Domestic Goose (*Anser anser domesticus*) which normally lives about 25 years. On 16 Dec 1976 a gander named 'George' owned by Mrs Florence Hull of Thornton, Lancashire died aged 49 years 8 months. He was hatched out in April 1927.

The longest-lived small cagebird is the Canary (*Serinus canaria*). The oldest example on record was a 34-year-old cock bird named 'Joey' owned by Mrs K. Ross of Hull.

The bird was purchased in Calabar, Nigeria in 1941 and died on 8 Apr 1975. The oldest budgerigar (*Melopsittacus undulatus*) was a hen bird named 'Charlie' owned by Miss J. Dinsey of Stonebridge, London which died on 20 June 1977 aged 29 years 2 months.

Most talkative

The world's most talkative bird is a female African grey parrot (*Psittacus erythacus*) named 'Prudle', owned by Mrs Lyn Logue of Seaford, East Sussex, which won the 'Best talking parrot-like bird' title at the National Cage and Aviary Bird Show in London each December for 12 consecutive years (1965–76). Prudle, who has a vocabulary of nearly 800 words, was taken from a nest at Jinja, Uganda in 1958. She retired undefeated.

Reptiles *Reptilia*
(Crocodiles, snakes, turtles, tortoises, lizards.)

CROCODILIANS
Largest

The largest reptile in the world is the Estuarine or Saltwater crocodile (*Crocodylus porosus*) of south-east Asia, the Malay Archipelago, Indonesia, northern Australia, Papua New Guinea, Vietnam and the Philippines. Adult males average 4·2–4·8 m *14–16 ft* in length and scale about 408–520 kg *900–1150 lb.*

In July 1957 an unconfirmed – but probably reliable – length of 8·63 m *28 ft 4 in* was reported for an Estuarine crocodile shot by Mrs Kris Pawlowski on MacArthur Bank in the Norman River, Queensland, Australia.

At the present time there are 4 protected Estuarine crocodiles at the Bhitarkanika Wildlife Sanctuary, Orissa State, eastern India which measure more than 6 m *19 ft 8 in* in length. The largest individual has been measured at over 7 m *23 ft* long.

Smallest

The smallest living crocodilian is Osborn's dwarf crocodile (*Osteolaemus osborni*), found in the upper region of the Congo River, west Africa. It rarely exceeds 1·2 m *3 ft 11 in* in length.

Oldest

The greatest age authenticated for a crocodilian is 66 years for a female American alligator (*Alligator mississipiensis*) which arrived at Adelaide Zoo, South Australia, on 5 June 1914 as a 2-year-old, and died there on 26 Sept 1978 aged 66 years. Another female of this species at the Maritime Museum Aquarium, Gothenburg, Sweden, died on 10 Feb 1987 aged 65 years after the electricity heating its pool was accidentally cut off.

Rarest

The world's rarest crocodilian is the protected Chinese alligator (*Alligator sinensis*) of the lower Chang Jiang (Yangtse Kiang) River of Anhui, Zhejiang and Jiangsu Provinces. The total population is currently estimated at 700–1000 individuals.

LIZARDS
Largest

The largest of all lizards is the Komodo monitor or Ora (*Varanus komodoensis*), a dragonlike reptile found on the Indonesian islands of Komodo, Rintja, Padar and Flores. Adult males average 225 cm *7 ft 5 in* in length and weigh about 59 kg *130 lb.* Lengths up to 9·14 m *30 ft* (*sic*) have been claimed for this species, but the largest specimen to be accurately measured was a male presented to an American zoologist in 1928 by the Sultan of Bima which taped 3·05 m *10 ft 0·8 in.* In 1937 this animal was put on display in St Louis Zoological Gardens, Missouri, USA for a short period. It then measured 3·10 m *10 ft 2 in* in length and weighed 166 kg *365 lb.*

The longest lizard in the world is the slender Salvadori monitor (*Varanus salvadori*) of New Guinea which has been reliably measured up to 4·75 m *15 ft 7 in.*

Reptiles

Smallest

The smallest lizard in the world is believed to be *Sphaerodactylus parthenopion*, a tiny gecko indigenous to the island of Virgin Gorda, one of the British Virgin Islands. It is known only from 15 specimens, including some gravid females found between 10 and 16 Aug 1964. The three largest females measured 18 mm *0·67 in* from snout to vent, with a tail of approximately the same length. It is possible that another gecko, *S. elasmorhynchus*, may be even smaller. The only known specimen was an apparently mature female with a snout-vent length of 17 mm *0·67 in* and a tail of the same measurement. It was found on 15 Mar 1966 among

the roots of a tree in the western part of the Massif de la Hotte in Haiti.

Oldest

The greatest age recorded for a lizard is more than 54 years for a male Slow worm (*Anguis fragilis*) kept in the Zoological Museum in Copenhagen, Denmark from 1892 until 1946.

Fastest

The highest speed measured for any reptile on land is 29 km/h *18 mph* for a Six-lined race runner (*Cnemidophorus sexlineatus*) near McCormick, South Carolina, USA, in 1941.

CHELONIANS
Largest

The largest living chelonian is the Leatherback turtle (*Dermochelys coriacea*), which is circum-global in distribution. The average adult measures 1·83–2·13 m *6–7 ft* from the tip of the beak to the end of the tail (carapace 1·52–1·67 m *5–5½ ft*), about 2·13 m *7 ft* across the front flippers and weighs anything up to 453 kg *1000 lb*. The greatest weight reliably recorded is 865 kg *1908 lb* for a male captured off Monterey, California, USA on 29 Aug 1961 which measured 2·54 m *8 ft 4 in* overall.
The largest Leatherback turtle ever recorded in British waters was a male washed ashore dead near Lydd, Kent on 5 Oct 1987 which measured 2·51 m *8 ft 3 in* overall (over the curve) and 2·54 m *8 ft 4 in* across the front flippers. It weighed an estimated 580 kg *1280 lb*.

The largest living tortoise is Marion's tortoise *Geochelone gigantea* of the Indian Ocean islands of Aldabra, Mauritius, and the Seychelles (introduced 1874). A male named 'Marmaduke' received at London Zoo in 1951 recorded a peak weight of 279 kg *616 lb* before his death on 27 Jan 1963.

Smallest

The smallest marine turtle in the world is the Atlantic ridley (*Lepidochelys kempii*), which has a shell length of 50–70 cm *19·7–27·6 in* and does not exceed 36 kg *80 lb*.

Longest lived

The greatest authentic age recorded for a tortoise is over 152 years for a male Marion's tortoise (*Testudo*

sumeirii) brought from the Seychelles to Mauritius in 1766 by the Chevalier de Fresne, who presented it to the Port Louis army garrison. This specimen (it went blind in 1908) was accidentally killed in 1918. The greatest proven age of a continuously observed tortoise is more than 116 years for a Mediterranean spur-thighed tortoise (*Testudo graeca*). The oldest turtle on record was an Alligator snapping turtle (*Macrochelys temminckii*) at Philadelphia Zoo, Pennsylvania, USA. When it was accidentally killed on 7 Feb 1949 it was 58 years 9 months 1 day.

Fastest and slowest

The highest speed claimed for any reptile in water is 35 km/h *22 mph* by a frightened Pacific leatherback turtle. In a recent 'speed' test carried out in the Seychelles a male giant tortoise (*Geochelone gigantea*) could cover only 4·57 m *5 yd* in 43·5 sec (0·37 km/h *0·23 mph*) despite the enticement of a female. The National Tortoise Championship record is 5·48 m *18 ft* up a 1:12 gradient in 43·7 sec (0·45 km/h *0·28 mph*) by 'Charlie' at Tickhill, South Yorkshire on 2 July 1977.

Diving

In May 1987 it was reported by Dr Scott Eckert that a Leatherback turtle (*Dermochelys coriacea*) fitted with a pressure-sensitive recording device had dived to a depth of 1200 m *3973 ft* off the Virgin Islands in the West Indies.

Rarest

The world's rarest chelonian is the protected Short-necked swamp tortoise (*Pseudemydura umbrina*), which is confined to Ellen Brook and Twin reserves near Perth, Western Australia. The total wild population is now only 20–25, with another 22 held at Perth Zoo.

SNAKES
Longest

The longest of all snakes (average adult length) is the Reticulated python (*Python reticulatus*) of south-east Asia, Indonesia and the Philippines, which regularly exceeds 6·24 m *20 ft 6 in*. In 1912 a specimen measuring 10 m *32 ft 9½ in* was shot near a mining camp on the north coast of Celebes in the Malay Archipelago.

The longest snake found in Britian is the Grass snake (*Natrix natrix*), which is found throughout southern England, parts of Wales and in Dumfries and Galloway, Scotland. The longest accurately measured specimen was probably a female killed in South Wales in 1887

which measured 1·775 m *5 ft 10 in*. In September 1816 a 2·13 m *7 ft* female with a maximum girth of 55·8 cm *22 in* (sic) was allegedly killed by a labourer at Trebun, Anglesey, North Wales and 'left for public curiosity at Llangefni', but further details are lacking.

In captivity

The longest (and heaviest) snake ever held in captivity was a female Reticulated python named 'Colossus' who died in Highland Park Zoo, Pennsylvania, USA on 15 Apr 1963. She measured 8·68 m *28 ft 6 in* in length, and scaled 145 kg *320 lb* at her heaviest.

Shortest

The shortest snake in the world is the very rare thread snake *Leptotyphlops bilineata* which is known only from the islands of Martinique, Barbados and St Lucia in the West Indies. In one series of eight specimens the two longest both measured 108 mm *4·25 in*.

Heaviest

The heaviest snake is the Anaconda (*Eunectes murinus*), which is nearly twice as heavy as a Reticulated python (*Python reticulatus*) of the same length. A female shot in

> **Largest captive crocodile** ● The largest crocodile ever held in captivity is an Estuarine/Siamese hybrid named 'Yai' (b. 10 June 1972) at the famous Samutprakarn Crocodile Farm and Zoo, Thailand. He measures 6 m *19 ft 8 in* in length and weighs 1114·27 kg *2465 lb*.

Brazil *c.* 1960 was not weighed, but it measured 8·45 m *27 ft 9 in* in length with a girth of 111 cm *44 in* which implies it must have scaled nearly 227 kg *500 lb*.

The heaviest venomous snake is the Eastern diamond-back rattlesnake (*Crotalus adamanteus*) of the south-eastern United States. One specimen measuring 2·36 m *7 ft 9 in* in length weighed 15 kg *34 lb*. In February 1973 a posthumous weight of 12·75 kg *28 lb* was reported for a 4·39 m *14 ft 5 in* long King cobra (*Ophiophagus hannah*) at New York Zoological Park (Bronx Zoo). It had been ill for some time.

Oldest

The greatest irrefutable age recorded for a snake is 40 years 3 months and 14 days for a male Common boa (*Boa constrictor constrictor*) named 'Popeye' who died at Philadelphia Zoo, Pennsylvania, USA on 15 April 1977.

Fastest

The fastest-moving land snake is probably the slender Black mamba (*Dendroaspis polylepis*). A speed of 16–19 km/h *10–12 mph* may be possible for short bursts over level ground. The British grass snake has a maximum speed of 6·8 km/h *4·2 mph*.

Most venomous

The world's most venomous snake is the Sea snake (*Hydrophis belcheri*) which has a myotoxic venom a hundred times as toxic as that of the Australian taipan (*Oxyuranus scutellatus*). The snake abounds round Ashmore Reef in the Timor Sea, off the coast of north-west Australia. The most venomous land snake is the 2 m

6 ft 6 in long Inland taipan (*Oxyuranus microlepidotus*) of the Diamantina River and Cooper's Creek drainage basins in Channel County, Queensland, which has a venom nine times as toxic as that of the Tiger snake (*Notechis scutatus*) of South Australia and Tasmania. One specimen yielded 110 mg *0·00385 oz* of venom after milking, a quantity sufficient to kill 218 000 mice. More people die of snakebite in Sri Lanka than any comparable area in the world. An average of 800 people are killed annually on the island by snakes, and 97 per cent of the fatalities are caused by the Common krait (*Bungarus ceylonicus*), the Saw-scaled viper (*Echis carinatus*), the world's most dangerous snake, and the Asiatic cobra (*Naja naja*).

The only venomous snake in Britain is the adder (*Vipera berus*). Since 1890 ten people have died after being bitten by this snake, including six children. The most recent recorded death was on 1 July 1975 when a 5-year-old was bitten at Callander, Perthshire and died 44 hours later. The longest recorded specimen was a female measuring 110·5 cm *43½ in* which was killed by Graham Perkins of Paradise Farm, Pontrilas, Hereford & Worcester in August 1977.

Longest and shortest venomous

The longest venomous snake in the world is the King cobra (*Ophiophagus hannah*), also called the Hamadryad, of south-east Asia and the Philippines. An 5·54 m *18 ft 2 in* specimen, captured alive near Fort Dickson in the state of Negri Sembilan, Malaya in April 1937, later grew to 5·71 m *18 ft 9 in* in London Zoo. It was destroyed at the outbreak of war in 1939.

The shortest venomous snake is the Namaqua dwarf adder (*Bitis schneider*) of Namibia, south-west Africa, which has an average adult length of 200 mm *7·87 in.*

Longest fangs

The longest fangs of any snake are those of the highly venomous Gaboon viper (*Bitis gabonica*) of tropical Africa. In a 1·83 m *6 ft* long specimen they measured 50 mm *1·96 in.* On 12 Feb 1963 a Gaboon viper under severe stress sank its fangs into its own back at Philadelphia Zoo, Pennsylvania, USA and died as a result from traumatic injury to a vital organ. It did not, as has been widely reported, succumb to its own venom.

Rarest

The rarest snake in the world is probably the Keel-scaled boa (*Casarea dussumieri*) of Round Island, western Indian Ocean. In 1983 only 58 specimens were collected, marked and released and another 9 specimens are held at Jersey Zoo, Channel Islands. The other boa from Round Island *Bolyeria multicarinata*, is known from only 2 specimens collected in the past 40 years and probably became extinct in 1980. The rarest snake of Britain's three indigenous species is the Smooth snake (*Coronella austriaca*) of southern England with a total wild population of *c.* 2000.

Amphibians *Amphibia*

Largest

The largest species of amphibian is the Chinese giant salamander (*Andrias davidianus*), which lives in north-eastern, central and southern China. The average adult measures 114 cm *3 ft 9 in* in length and weighs 25–30 kg *55–66 lb.* One specimen collected in Hunan Province measured 1·8 m *5 ft 11 in* in length and scaled 65 kg *143 lb.*

The largest British amphibian is the Common toad (*Bufo bufo*) which is found throughout England, Scotland and Wales. A huge female collected from Marlpit Pond, Boxley, Kent, measured 99 mm *3·89 in* in snout to vent and weighed 118 g *4·16 oz.*

Smallest

The smallest known amphibian is the Short-headed toad

Psyllophryne didactyla (family *Brachycephalidae*) of south-eastern Brazil, adult specimens having an average snout-vent length of 9·8 mm *0·38 in.* The smallest found in Britain is the Palmate newt (*Triturus helveticus*). Adult specimens measure 7·5–9·2 cm *2·95–3·62 in* in length and weigh up to 2·39 g *0·083 oz.* The Natterjack or Running toad (*Bufo calamita*) has a maximum snout-vent length of only 80 mm *3·14 in* (female) but it is a bulkier animal.

Oldest

The greatest authentic age recorded for an amphibian is 55 years for a Japanese giant salamander which died in Amsterdam Zoo, Netherlands in 1881.

Rarest

The rarest amphibian in the world is the Israel painted frog (*Discoglossus nigriventer*) of Lake Huleh. Only 5 have been reported since 1940.

Britain's rarest amphibian is the *introduced* Green tree frog (*Hyla arborea*), which is now confined to a single site on the outskirts of London.

Highest and lowest

The greatest altitude at which an amphibian has been found is 8000 m *26 246 ft* for a Common toad collected in the Himalayas. This species has also been found at a depth of 340 m *1115 ft* in a coal mine.

Most poisonous

The most active known poison is the batrachotoxin derived from the skin secretions of the Golden poison-dart frog (*Phyllobates terribilis*) of western Colombia, South America which was not discovered until 1973. Its skin secretions are at least 20 times more toxic than those of any other known dart-poison frog, and an average adult specimen contains enough poison (1900 micrograms) to kill nearly 1500 people. Rather surprisingly, this species is preyed upon by the frog-eating snake *Leimadophis epinephelus*, which is thought to be immune to its poison.

Largest frog

The largest known frog is the rare Goliath frog (*Conraua goliath*) of Cameroun and Equatorial Guinea. A female weighing 3306 g *7 lb 4·5 oz* was caught in the River Mbia, Equatorial Guinea on 23 Aug 1960. It had a snout-vent length of 34 cm *13·38 in* and measured 81·5 cm *32·08 in* overall with legs extended. A slightly longer female (35·6 cm *14 in*) collected in the same river in December 1966 weighed 3100 g *6 lb 13¼ oz.*

The largest frog found in Britain is the *introduced* Marsh frog (*Rana r. ridibunda*). Adult males have been measured up to 96 mm *3·77 in* snout-vent, and adult females up to 133 mm *5·25 in*, the weight ranging from 60 to 95 g *1·7–3 oz.*

The largest captive frog living in Britain today is a male African bull frog (*Pyxicephalus adspersus*) named 'Colossus' (b. 1978) owned by Mr Steve Crabtree of Southsea, Hants. It has a snout-vent length of 22·2 cm *8¾ in*, a girth of 45·7 cm *18 in* and weighs 1·89 kg *4 lb 3 oz.*

Smallest frog

The smallest frog in the world, and the second smallest anuran, is *Sminthillus limbatus*, of Cuba. Adult specimens have a snout-vent length of 8·5–12·4 mm *0·44–0·48 in.*

Longest jump

(*Competition frog jumps are invariably the aggregate of three consecutive leaps.*)

The greatest distance covered by a frog in a triple jump is 10·3 m *33 ft 5½ in* by a South African sharp-nosed frog (*Ptychadena oxyrhynchus*) named 'Santjie' at a frog Derby held at Lurula Natal Spa, Paulpietersburg, Natal on 21 May 1977. At the famous annual Calaveras Jumping Jubilee held at Angels Camp, California, USA on 18 May 1986 an American bull frog (*Rana catesbeiana*) called 'Rosie the Ribeter', owned and trained by Lee Giudicci

of Santa Clara, California, USA leapt 6·55 m *21 ft 5¾ in.* 'Santjie' would have been ineligible for this contest because entrants must measure at least 10·16 cm *4 in* 'stem to stern'.

Largest toad

The largest toad ever recorded was a female Marine toad (*Bufo marinus*) nick-named 'Totally Awesome' (Toad A) owned by Blank Park Zoo, Des Moines, Iowa, USA. She was purchased from a Miami, Florida animal dealer on 11 May 1983, when she weighed about 0·9 kg *2 lb*, and attained a peak 2·31 kg *5 lb 1½ oz* (snout–vent length 24·13 cm *9½ in*) on Nov 19 1987. She died on 8 Apr 1988, most probably from old age.

Smallest toad

The smallest toad in the world is the Short-headed toad *Bufo beiranus*, first discovered *c.* 1906 near Beira, Mozambique, East Africa. Adult specimens have a maximum recorded snout-vent length of 24 mm *0·94 in.*

Fishes

Agnatha, Gnathostomata

World and British all-tackle records ratified by both the International Game Fish Association and Britain's National Association of Specialist Anglers, can be found in Sports Games and Pastimes (Chapter 12).

Largest marine

The largest fish in the world is the rare plankton-feeding Whale shark (*Rhincodon typus*), which is found in the warmer areas of the Atlantic, Pacific and Indian Oceans. This species was first discovered inApril 1828 when a small specimen was harpooned in Table Bay, South Africa after a fisherman had noticed its unusual coloration of greenish grey with white spots.More tha 40 years elapsed before this remarkable type of creature was heard of again.

The longest scientifically-measured Whale shark on record was a 12·65 m *41½ ft* specimen captured off Baba Island near Karachi, Pakistan on 11 Nov 1949. It measured 7 m *23 ft* round the thickest part of the body and weighed an estimated 15 tonnes.

The largest carnivorous fish (excluding plankton-eaters) is the comparatively rare Great white shark (*Carcharodon carcharias*), also called the 'Man-eater'. Adult speci-

Most ferocious fish● The razor-toothed piranhas of the genera *Serrasalmus*, *Pygocentrus* and *Pygopristis* are the most ferocious freshwater fish in the world. They live in the sluggish waters of the large rivers of South America, and will attack any creature, regardless of size, if it is injured or making a commotion in the water.

mens (females are larger than males) average 4·3–4·6 m *14–15 ft* in length and generally scale between 522–771 kg *1150–1700 lb*, but larger individuals have been recorded. The length record is 6·4 m *21 ft* for a female caught off Castillo de Cojimar, Cuba, in May 1945. It weighed 3312 kg *7302 lb*.

The longest of the bony or 'true' fishes (Pisces) is the Oarfish (*Regalecus glesne*), also called the 'King of the Herrings', which has a worldwide distribution. In *c.* 1885 a 7·6 m *25 ft* long example weighing 272 kg *600 lb* was caught by fishermen off Pemaquid Point, Maine, USA. Another Oarfish, seen swimming off Asbury Park, New Jersey, USA by a team of scientists from the Sandy Hook Marine Laboratory on 18 July 1963, was estimated to measure 15·2 m *50 ft* in length. The heaviest bony fish in the world is the Ocean sunfish (*Mola mola*), which is found in all tropical, sub-tropical and temperate waters. On 18 Sept 1908 a specimen was accidentally struck by the SS *Fiona* off Bird Island about 65 km *40 miles* from Sydney, New South Wales, Australia and towed to Port Jackson. It measured 4·26 m *14 ft* between the anal and dorsal fins and weighed 2235 kg *4927 lb*.

The largest fish ever recorded in the waters of the British Isles was a 11·12 m *36 ft 6 in* Basking shark (*Cetorhinus maximus*) washed ashore at Brighton, East Sussex in 1806. It weighed an estimated 8 tonnes. The largest bony fish found in British waters is the Ocean sunfish. A specimen weighing 363 kg *800 lb* stranded near Montrose, Angus on 14 Dec 1960 was sent to the Marine Research Institute in Aberdeen.

Largest freshwater

The largest fish which spends its whole life in fresh or brackish water is the rare Pa beuk or Pla buk (*Pangasianodon gigas*). This *was* exceeded by the European catfish or Wels (*Silurus glanis*) in earlier times (in the 19th century lengths up to 4·57 m *15 ft* and weights up to 336·3 kg *720 lb* were reported for Russian specimens), but today anything over 1·83 m *6 ft* and 91 kg *200 lb* is considered large. The Arapaima (*Arapaima glanis*), also called the Pirarucu, found in the Amazon and other South American rivers and often claimed to be the largest freshwater fish, averages 2 m *6½ ft* and 68 kg *150 lb*. The largest 'authentically recorded' measured 2·48 m *8 ft 1½ in* in length and weighed 147 kg *325 lb*. It was caught in the Rio Negro, Brazil in 1836. In September 1978, a Nile perch (*Lates niloticus*) weighing 188·6 kg *416 lb* was netted in the eastern part of Lake Victoria, Kenya.

The largest fish ever caught in a British river was a Common sturgeon (*Acipenser sturio*) weighing 230 kg *507½ lb* and measuring 2·74 m *9 ft*, which was accidentally netted in the Severn at Lydney, Gloucestershire on 1 June 1937. Larger specimens have been taken at sea—notably one weighing 317 kg *700 lb* and 3·18 m *10 ft 5 in* long netted by the trawler *Ben Urie* off Orkney and landed on 18 Oct 1956.

Smallest marine

The shortest recorded marine fish – and the shortest known vertebrate – is the dwarf goby *Trimmatom nanus* of the Chagos Archipelago, central Indian Ocean. In one series of 92 specimens collected by the 1978–9 Joint Services Chagos Research Expedition of the British Armed Forces the adult males averaged 8·6 mm *0·338 in* in length and the adult females 8·9 mm *0·35 in*. The lightest of all vertebrates and the smallest catch possible for any fisherman is the dwarf goby *Schindleria praematurus* from Samoa which measures 12–19 mm *0·47–0·74 in*. Mature specimens have been known to weigh only 2 mg, which is equivalent to *17·750 to the oz.*

The smallest British marine fish is Guillet's goby (*Lebutus guilleti*) which does not exceed 24 mm *0·94 in*. It has been recorded from the English Channel, the west coast of Ireland and the Irish sea.

The smallest known shark is the Long-faced dwarf shark (*Squaliolus laticaudus*) of the western Pacific which does not exceed 150 mm *5·9 in*.

Smallest freshwater

The shortest and lightest freshwater fish is the Dwarf pygmy goby (*Pandaka pygmaea*), a colourless and nearly transparent species found in the streams and lakes of Luzon in the Philippines. Adult males measure only 7·5–9·9 mm *0·28–0·38 in* in length and weigh 4–5 mg.

The world's smallest commercial fish is the now endangered Sinarapan (*Mistichthys luzonensis*), a goby found only in Lake Buhi, Luzon, Philippines. Adult males measure 10–13 mm *0·39–0·51 in* in length, and a dried 454 g *1 lb* fish cake contains about 70 000 of them!

Fastest

Some American fishermen believe that the Bluefin tuna (*Thunnus thynnus*) is the fastest fish in the sea, and burst speeds up to 56 knots *104km/h* have been claimed for this species, but the highest speed recorded so far is 70 km/h *43·4 mph* in a 20-second dash. The Yellowfin tuna (*Thunnus albacares*) and the Wahoo (*Acanthocy-* *bium solandri*) are also extremely fast, having been timed at 74·59 km/h *46·35 mph* and 77·05 km/h *47·88 mph* resepectively.

Oldest

Aquaria are of too recent origin to be able to establish with certainty which species of fish can be regarded as being the longest lived. Early indications are, however, that it may be the Lake sturgeon (*Acipenser fulvescens*) of North America. In one study of the growth rings (annuli) of 966 specimens caught in the Lake Winnebago region, Wisconsin, USA between 1951 and 1954 the oldest sturgeon was found to be a male (length 2·01 m *6 ft 7 in*), which gave a reading of 82 years and was still growing. The marine fish *Notothenia neglecta* of the Antarctic, whose blood

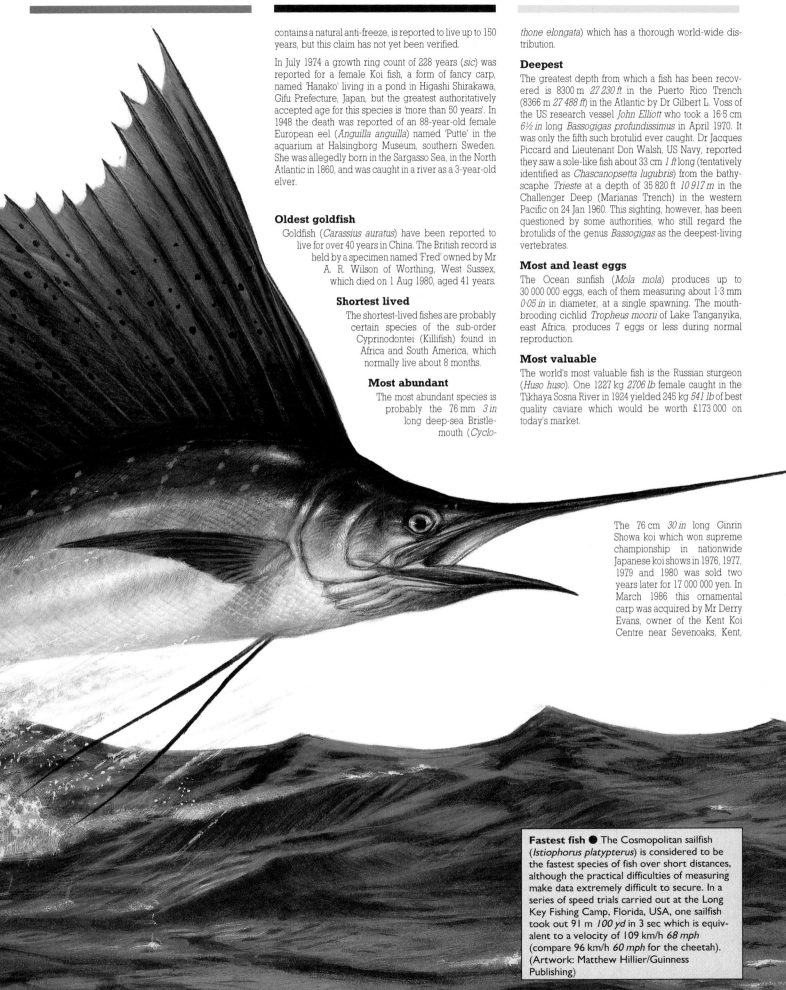

contains a natural anti-freeze, is reported to live up to 150 years, but this claim has not yet been verified.

In July 1974 a growth ring count of 228 years (*sic*) was reported for a female Koi fish, a form of fancy carp, named 'Hanako' living in a pond in Higashi Shirakawa, Gifu Prefecture, Japan, but the greatest authoritatively accepted age for this species is 'more than 50 years'. In 1948 the death was reported of an 88-year-old female European eel (*Anguilla anguilla*) named 'Putte' in the aquarium at Halsingborg Museum, southern Sweden. She was allegedly born in the Sargasso Sea, in the North Atlantic in 1860, and was caught in a river as a 3-year-old elver.

Oldest goldfish

Goldfish (*Carassius auratus*) have been reported to live for over 40 years in China. The British record is held by a specimen named 'Fred' owned by Mr A. R. Wilson of Worthing, West Sussex, which died on 1 Aug 1980, aged 41 years.

Shortest lived

The shortest-lived fishes are probably certain species of the sub-order Cyprinodontei (Killifish) found in Africa and South America, which normally live about 8 months.

Most abundant

The most abundant species is probably the 76 mm *3 in* long deep-sea Bristle-mouth (*Cyclo-*

thone elongata) which has a thorough world-wide distribution.

Deepest

The greatest depth from which a fish has been recovered is 8300 m *27 230 ft* in the Puerto Rico Trench (8366 m *27 488 ft*) in the Atlantic by Dr Gilbert L. Voss of the US research vessel *John Elliott* who took a 16·5 cm *6½ in* long *Bassogigas profundissimus* in April 1970. It was only the fifth such brotulid ever caught. Dr Jacques Piccard and Lieutenant Don Walsh, US Navy, reported they saw a sole-like fish about 33 cm *1 ft* long (tentatively identified as *Chascanopsetta lugubris*) from the bathyscaphe *Trieste* at a depth of 35 820 ft *10 917 m* in the Challenger Deep (Marianas Trench) in the western Pacific on 24 Jan 1960. This sighting, however, has been questioned by some authorities, who still regard the brotulids of the genus *Bassogigas* as the deepest-living vertebrates.

Most and least eggs

The Ocean sunfish (*Mola mola*) produces up to 30 000 000 eggs, each of them measuring about 1·3 mm *0·05 in* in diameter, at a single spawning. The mouth-brooding cichlid *Tropheus moorii* of Lake Tanganyika, east Africa, produces 7 eggs or less during normal reproduction.

Most valuable

The world's most valuable fish is the Russian sturgeon (*Huso huso*). One 1227 kg *2706 lb* female caught in the Tikhaya Sosna River in 1924 yielded 245 kg *541 lb* of best quality caviare which would be worth £173 000 on today's market.

The 76 cm *30 in* long Ginrin Showa koi which won supreme championship in nationwide Japanese koi shows in 1976, 1977, 1979 and 1980 was sold two years later for 17 000 000 yen. In March 1986 this ornamental carp was acquired by Mr Derry Evans, owner of the Kent Koi Centre near Sevenoaks, Kent,

Fastest fish ● The Cosmopolitan sailfish (*Istiophorus platypterus*) is considered to be the fastest species of fish over short distances, although the practical difficulties of measuring make data extremely difficult to secure. In a series of speed trials carried out at the Long Key Fishing Camp, Florida, USA, one sailfish took out 91 m *100 yd* in 3 sec which is equivalent to a velocity of 109 km/h *68 mph* (compare 96 km/h *60 mph* for the cheetah). (Artwork: Matthew Hillier/Guinness Publishing)

Fishes

England, for an undisclosed sum, but the 15-year-old fish died 5 months later. It has since been stuffed and mounted to preserve its beauty.

Most venomous

The most venomous fish in the world are the Stonefish (Synanceidae) of the tropical waters of the Indo-Pacific, and in particular *Synanceja horrida* which has the largest venom glands of any known fish. Direct contact with the spines of its fins, which contain a strong neurotoxic poison, often proves fatal.

Most electric

The most powerful electric fish is the Electric eel (*Electrophorus electricus*), which is found in the rivers of Brazil, Colombia, Venezuela and Peru. An average-sized specimen can discharge 400 volts at 1 ampere, but measurements up to 650 volts have been recorded.

Starfishes *Asteroidea*

Largest

The largest of the 1600 known species of starfish in terms of total arm span is the very fragile brisingid *Midgardia xandaros*. A specimen collected by the Texas A & M University research vessel *Alaminos* in the southern part of the Gulf of Mexico in the late summer of 1968 measured 1380 mm *54.33 in* tip to tip, but the diameter of its disc was only 26 mm *1.02 in*. Its dry weight was 70 g *2.46 oz*.

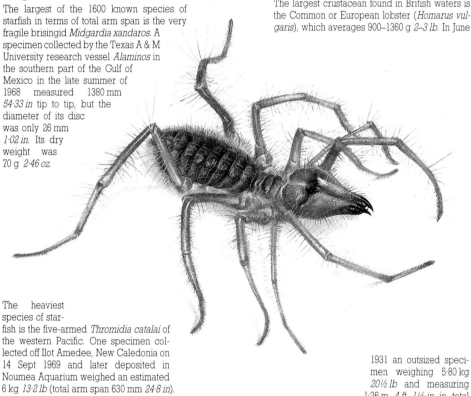

The heaviest species of starfish is the five-armed *Thromidia catalai* of the western Pacific. One specimen collected off Ilot Amedee, New Caledonia on 14 Sept 1969 and later deposited in Noumea Aquarium weighed an estimated 6 kg *13.2 lb* (total arm span 630 mm *24.8 in*).

The largest starfish found in British waters is the Spiny starfish (*Marthasterias glacialis*). In January 1979 Jonathon MacNeil from Isle of Barra, Western Isles, found a specimen which originally spanned 76.2 cm *30 in*.

Smallest

The smallest known starfish is the asterinid sea star *Patiriella parvivipara* discovered by Wolfgang Zeidler on the west coast of the Eyre peninsula, South Australia in 1975. It has a maximum radius of only 4.7 mm *0.18 in* and a diameter of less than 9 mm *0.35 in*.

Most destructive

The most destructive starfish in the world is the Crown of Thorns (*Acanthaster planci*) of the Indo-Pacific region and the Red Sea. It can destroy 300–400 cm² *46.5–62 in²* of coral a day.

Deepest

The greatest depth from which a starfish has been recovered is 7584 m *24 881 ft* for a specimen of *Porcellanaster ivanovi* collected by the USSR research ship *Vityaz* in the Marianas Trench, in the west Pacific *c*. 1962.

Crustaceans *Crustacea*

(Crabs, lobsters, shrimps, prawns, crayfish, barnacles, water fleas, fish lice, woodlice, sandhoppers, krill, etc.)

Largest

The largest of all crustaceans (although not the heaviest) is the Taka-ashi-gani or Giant spider crab (*Macrocheira kaempferi*), also called the Stilt crab, which is found in deep waters off the south-eastern coast of Japan. Mature specimens usually have a body measuring 254 × 305 mm *10 × 12 in* and a claw span of 2.43–2.74 m *8–9 ft*, but unconfirmed measurements up to 5.79 m *19 ft* have been reported. A specimen with a claw span of 3.69 m *12 ft 1½ in* weighed 18.6 kg *41 lb*.

The largest species of lobster, and the heaviest of all crustaceans, is the American or North Atlantic lobster (*Homarus americanus*). On 11 Feb 1977 a specimen weighing 20.14 kg *44 lb 6 oz* and measuring 1.06 m *3 ft 6 in* from the end of the tail-fan to the tip of the largest claw was caught off Nova Scotia, Canada, and later sold to a New York restaurant owner.

The largest crustacean found in British waters is the Common or European lobster (*Homarus vulgaris*), which averages 900–1360 g *2–3 lb*. In June 1931 an outsized specimen weighing 5.80 kg *20½ lb* and measuring 1.26 m *4 ft 1½ in* in total length was caught in a caisson during the construction of No 3 jetty at Fowey, Cornwall. Its crushing claw weighed 1188 g *2 lb 10 oz* after the meat had been removed. The largest crab found in British waters is the Edible or Great crab (*Cancer pagurus*). In 1895 a crab measuring 279 mm *11 in* across the shell and weighing 6.35 kg *14 lb* was caught off the coast of Cornwall.

Smallest

The smallest known crustaceans are water fleas of the genus *Alonella*, which may measure less than 0.25 mm *0.0098 in* in length. They are found in British waters. The smallest known lobster is the Cape lobster (*Homarus capensis*) of South Africa, which measures 10–12 cm *3.9–4.7 in* in total length. The smallest crabs in the world are Pea crabs (family Pinnotheridae). Some species have a shell diameter of only 6.3 mm *0.25 in*, including *Pinnotheres pisum* which is found in British waters.

Oldest

The longest lived of all crustaceans is the American lobster (*Homarus americanus*). Very large specimens may be as much as 50 years old.

Deepest

The greatest depth from which a crustacean has been recovered is 10 500 m *34 450 ft* for *live* amphipods from the Challenger Deep, Marianas Trench, west Pacific by the US research vessel *Thomas Washington* in November 1980. Amphipods and isopods have also been collected in the Ecuadorean Andes at a height of 4053 m *13 300 ft*.

Arachnids *Arachnida*

SPIDERS (order Araneae)

Largest

The world's largest known spider is the Goliath bird-eating spider (*Theraphosa leblondi*) of the coastal rainforests of Surinam, Guyana (formerly British Guyana) and French Guiana, north-eastern South America; isolated specimens have also been reported from Venezuela and Brazil. In February 1985 Charles J Seiderman of New York City, NY, USA, captured a huge female just north of Paramarido, Surinam. This spider had a maximum leg span of 266.7 mm *10½ in* (total body length 102 mm *4 in*), 25 mm *1 in* long fangs and weighed a peak 122.2 g *4.3 oz* before its death from moulting problems in Jan 1986. An outsized male example collected by members of the Pablo San Martin Expedition at Rio Cavro, Venezuela in April 1965 had a leg span of 280 mm *11.02 in*, but the female is built on much heavier lines.

> **The world's fastest spider** ● This long-legged Sun-spider of the genus *Solpuga* (left) from Africa and the Middle East can easily outstrip a sand lizard (right). It feeds on geckos and other lizards and can reach speeds of over 16 km/h *10 mph*. (Artwork: Matthew Hillier/Guinness Publishing)

Of the 617 known species of British spider covering an estimated population of over 500 000 000 000 the Cardinal spider (*Tegenaria gigantea*) of southern England has the greatest leg span. In October 1985 Mrs Lyndsay Jarrett of Marston Meysey, Wiltshire collected an outsized female in her home with a span of 139 mm *5.5 in*.

The well-known 'Daddy Longlegs' spider (*Pholcus phalangioides*) rarely exceeds 114 mm *4½ in* in leg span, but one outsized specimen collected in England measured 15.2 cm *6 in* across. The heaviest spider found in Britain is the orb weaver *Araneus quadratus*. On 10 Sept 1979 a female weighing 2.25 g *0.079 oz* was collected at Lavington, West Sussex by J. R. Parker.

Smallest

The smallest known spider is *Patu marplesi* (family Symphytognathidae) of Western Samoa in the Pacific. The type specimen (male) found in moss at *c*. 600 m *2000 ft* in Madolelei, Upolu, Western Samoa in Jan 1965 measured 0.43 mm *0.017 in* overall, which means that it was about the size of a full-stop on this page.

Britain's smallest spider is the extremely rare Money spider (*Glyphesis cottonae*) found only in a swamp near Beaulieu Road Station, Hampshire and on Thursley Common, Surrey. Adult specimens of both sexes have a body length of 1 mm *0.039 in*.

Most common

The most common spiders are the Crab spiders (family Thomisidae), which have a world-wide distribution. The commonest spider in Britain is the orb weaver *Araneus diadematus*, which has been recorded from all but four counties in Great Britain and Ireland.

Rarest

The most elusive of all spiders are the rare Trapdoor

spiders of the genus *Liphistius*, which are found in south-east Asia.

The most elusive spiders in Britain are the four species which are known only from the type specimen. These are the jumping spiders *Salticus mutabilis* (1 male Bloxworth, Dorset, 1860) and *Heliophanus melinus* (1 female Bloxworth, 1870); the Crab spider *Philodromus buxi* (1 female Bloxworth, pre-1879); and the Cobweb spider *Robertus insignis* (1 male Norwich, 1906).

Oldest

The longest lived of all spiders are the primitive *Mygalomorphae* (tarantulas and allied species). One female therasophid collected in Mexico in 1935 lived for an estimated 26–28 years. The longest-lived British spider is probably the Purse web spider (*Atypus affinis*). One specimen was kept in a greenhouse for 9 years.

Webs

The largest webs are aerial ones spun by the tropical orb weavers of the genus *Nephila*, which have been measured up to 573 cm *18 ft 9¾ in* in circumference. The smallest webs are spun by spiders such as *Glyphesis cottonae* (see above) which cover about 480 mm *0·75 in²*.

Most venomous

The most venomous spiders in the world are the Brazilian wandering spiders of the genus *Phoneutria*, and particularly *P. fera*, which has the most active neurotoxic venom of any living spider. These large and highly aggressive creatures frequently enter human

dwellings and hide in clothing or shoes. When disturbed they bite furiously several times, and hundreds of accidents involving these species are reported annually. Fortunately an effective antivenin is available, and when deaths do occur they are usually under the age of 7.

Insects *Insecta*

Heaviest

The heaviest living insects are the Goliath beetles (family Scarabaeidae) of Equatorial Africa. The largest members of the group are *Goliathus regius* and *G. goliathus* (=*G. giganteus*), and in one series of fully-grown males (females are smaller) the weight ranged from 70 to 100 g *2·5–3·5 oz.*

The heaviest insect found in Britain is the Stag beetle (*Lucanus cervus*) which is widely distributed over southern England. The largest specimen on record was a male collected at Sheerness, Kent in 1871 and now preserved in the British Museum (Natural History), which measures 87·4 mm *3·04 in* in length (body plus mandibles) and probably weighed over 6 g *0·21 oz* when alive.

Longest

The longest insect in the world is the Giant stick-insect (*Pharnacia serratipes*) of Indonesia, females of which have been measured up to 330 mm *13 in*. The longest known beetle (excluding antennae) is the Hercules beetle (*Dynastes hercules*) of Central and South America, which has been measured up to 190 mm *7·48 in*. Over half the length is prothoracic horn.

Smallest

The smallest insects recorded so far are the 'Hairy-

winged' beetles of the family Ptiliidae (=Trichopterygidae) and the 'Battledore-wing fairy flies' (parasitic wasps) of the family Myrmaridae. They are smaller than some of the protozoa (single-celled animals). The male Bloodsucking banded louse *Enderleinellus zonatus*, ungorged, and the parasitic wasp *Caraphractus cinctus* may each weigh as little as 0·005 mg, or *5 670 000 to an oz.* Eggs of the latter each weigh 0·0002 mg, *or 141 750 000 to an oz.*

Rarest

It has recently been estimated that there may be as many as 30 million species of insect – more than all other phylums and classes put together – but thousands are known only from a single or type specimen.

Fastest flying

Experiments have proved that the widely publicised claim by an American scientist in 1926 that the Deer bot-fly (*Cephenemyia pratti*) could attain a speed of 1316 km/h *818 mph* (sic) at an altitude of 3657 m *12 000 ft* was wildly exaggerated. If true the fly would have had to develop the equivalent of 1·1 kW *1·5 hp* and consume 1½ times its own weight in food per second to acquire the energy that would be needed, and even if this were possible it would still be crushed by the air pressure and incinerated by the friction. Acceptable modern experiments have now established that the highest maintainable air speed of any insect including the Deer bot-fly, hawk moths (*Sphingidae*), horse flies (*Tabanus bovinus*) and some tropical butterflies (*Hesperiidae*) is 39 km/h *24 mph*, rising to a maximum of 58 km/h *36 mph* for the Australian dragon fly *Austrophlebia costalis*, for short bursts.

Fastest moving

The fastest moving insects are large tropical cockroaches (*Dictyoptera*) and specimens measuring about 30 mm *1·18 in* in length have been timed at 120–130 cm/sec 4·28–4·64km/h *2·68–2·90 mph* or 40–43 body lengths per second.

Oldest

The longest-lived insects are the Splendour beetles (Buprestidae). On 27 May 1983 a *Buprestis aurulenta* appeared from the staircase timber in the home of Mr W. Euston of Prittlewell, Southend-on-Sea, Essex after 47 years as a larva.

Loudest

The loudest of all insects is the male cicada (family Cicadidae). At 7400 pulses/min its tymbal organs produce a noise (officially described by the US Department of Agriculture as 'Tsh-ee-EEEE-e-ou') detectable more than a quarter of a mile *400 m* distant.

The only British species is the very rare Mountain cicada (*Cicadetta montana*), which is confined to the New Forest area in Hampshire.

Largest cockroach

The largest cockroach in the world is the Giant burrowing cockroach (*Macropanesthia rhinoceros*) of the Atherton plateau, tropical northern Queensland, Australia. A female measuring 79 mm *3·11 in* in length, 35 mm

1·49 in across and weighing 21·9 g *0·77 oz* was collected at Agnes Water in December 1986.

Largest locust swarm

The greatest swarm of Desert locusts (*Schistocera gregaria*) ever recorded was one covering an estimated 5180 km² *2000 miles²* observed crossing the Red Sea in 1889. Such a swarm must have contained about 250 000 000 000 insects weighing about 508 000 tonnes *500 000 tons*. In 1958 in Somalia a swarm of *c.* 60 000 million covering a measured 1000 km² *400 miles²* was estimated to be devouring *c.* 120 000 tons of biomass daily.

Fastest wing beat

The fastest wing beat of any insect under natural conditions is 62 760 per min by a tiny midge of the genus *Forcipomyia*. In experiments with truncated wings at a temperature of 37° C *98·6° F* the rate increased to 133 080 beats/min. The muscular contraction–expansion cycle in 0·00045 or 1/2218th of a sec further represents the fastest muscle movement ever measured.

Slowest wing beat

The slowest wing beat of any insect is 300 per min by the Swallowtail butterfly (*Popilio machaon*). The average is 460–636 per min.

Dragonflies
Largest

The largest dragonfly in the world is *Megaloprepus caeruleata* of Central and South America, which has been measured up to 191 mm *7·52 in* across the wings and 120 mm *4·72 in* in body length.

The largest dragonfly found in Britain is *Anax imperator*, which has a wing span measurement of up to 106 mm *4·17 in*. The smallest is *Lestes dryas*, which has a wing span of 20–25 mm *0·78–0·98 in*.

Smallest

The smallest dragonfly in the world is *Agriocnemis naia* of Burma. A specimen in the British Museum (Natural History) had a wing expanse of 17·6 mm *0·69 in* and a body length of 18 mm *0·71 in*.

Largest flea

Siphonapterologists recognise 1830 varieties, of which the largest known is *Hystrichopsylla schefferi*, which was described from a single specimen taken from the nest of a Mountain beaver (*Aplodontia rufa*) at Puyallup, Washington, USA in 1913. Females measure up to 8 mm *0·31 in* in length, which is the diameter of a pencil.

The largest flea (61 species) found in Britain is the Mole and vole flea (*H. talpae*)—females have been measured up to 6 mm *0·23 in.*

The champion jumper among fleas is the Common flea (*Pulex irritans*). In one American experiment carried out in 1910 a specimen allowed to leap at will performed a long jump of 330 mm *13 in* and a high jump of 197 mm *7¾ in*. In jumping 130 times its own height a flea subjects itself to a force of 200 g.

BUTTERFLIES AND MOTHS
(order Lepidoptera)
Largest

The largest known butterfly is the protected Queen Alexandra's birdwing (*Ornithoptera alexandrae*) which is restricted to the Popondetta Plain in Papua New Guinea. Females may have a wing span exceeding 280 mm *11·02 in* and weigh over 25 g *0·88 oz*. The largest moth in the world (although not the heaviest) is the Hercules moth (*Cosdinoscera hercules*) of tropical Australia and New Guinea. A wing area of up to 263·2 cm² *40·8 in²* and a wing span of 280 mm *11 in* have been recorded. In 1948 an unconfirmed measurement of 360 mm *14·17 in* was reported for a female captured near the post office at the coastal town of Innisfail, Queensland, Australia, now in the Oberthur collection. The rare Owlet moth (*Thysania agrippina*) of Brazil has been measured up to 308 mm *12·16 in* wing span in the case of a female taken in 1934 and now in the collection of John G. Powers in Ontario, Canada.

The largest butterfly found in Britain is the Monarch butterfly (*Danaus plexippus*), also called the Milkweed or Black-veined brown butterfly, a rare vagrant which breeds in the southern United States and Central America. It has a wing span of up to 127 mm *5 in* and weighs about 1 g *0·04 oz.*

The largest *native* butterfly is the Swallowtail (*Papilio machaon britannicus*), females of which have a wing span up to 100 mm *3·93 in.* This species is now confined to fens in Suffolk, Cambridgeshire and the Norfolk Broads.

The largest (but not the heaviest) of the 21 000 species of insect found in Britain is the very rare Death's head hawkmoth (*Acherontia atropos*). One female found dead in a garden at Tiverton, Devon in 1931 had a wing span of 145 mm *5·75 in* and weighed nearly 3 g *0·10 oz.*

Smallest

The world's smallest known butterfly is the recently discovered *Micropsyche ariana*, which has a wing span of 7 mm *0·275 in.* The type specimen was collected on Mt Khwajaghar in the Koh-i-Baba range, Afghanistan.

The smallest of the 140 000 known species of Lepidoptera are the moths *Johanssonia acetosea* found in Britain, and *Stigmella ridiculosa* from the Canary Islands, which have a wing span of *c.* 2 mm *0·08 in* with a similar body length.

The smallest butterfly found in Britain is the Small blue (*Cupido minimus*), which has a wing span of 19–25 mm *0·75–1·0 in.*

Rarest

The birdwing butterfly *Ornithopteria* (= *Troides*) *allottei* of Bougainville, Solomon Islands is known from less than a dozen specimens. A male from the collection of C. Rousseau Decelle was auctioned for £750 in Paris on 24 Oct 1966.

Britain's rarest butterfly (59 species) is the Large tortoiseshell (*Nymphalis polychloros*) of southern England, which is now down to a dangerously low level.

The bog moth (*Choristoneura lafauryana*) breeds only on the proposed route of the Dersingham by-pass, Norfolk. The Chequered skipper (*Carterocephalus palaemon*), which is confined to a number of sites in Inverness-shire, Scotland, is now out of danger and making a comeback. The Large blue (*Maculinea arion*) was officially declared extinct in 1979, but eggs were brought over from the island of Oland, Sweden in 1984 and hatched successfully on a site in the West Country. In 1986 another 220 eggs were obtained from Sweden, and the caterpillars distributed. At least 75 butterflies emerged and flew the following summer, and it is estimated that at least 2000 eggs were laid by the butterflies in 1987. It is now planned to introduce them to other suitable sites.

Most acute sense of smell

The most acute sense of smell exhibited in nature is that of the male Emperor moth (*Eudia pavonia*) which, according to German experiments in 1961, can detect the sex attractant of the virgin female at the almost unbelievable range of 11 km *6·8 miles* upwind. This scent has been identified as one of the higher alcohols ($C_{16}H_{29}OH$), of which the female carries less than 0·0001 mg.

Largest butterfly farm

The Australian Butterfly Sanctuary at Kurunda, Queensland, Australia has an enclosed flight space of 3660 m³ *129 250 ft³.* The largest in Britain is Stratford-upon-Avon Butterfly Farm, which has a flight area of 582 m² *6264 ft²,* and can accommodate 2000 exotic butterflies in authentic rain forest conditions. The total of all flight areas at the farm, which opened on 15 June 1985, is 807 m² *8686 ft².*

Largest flea ● The largest known flea is the *Hystrichopsylla schefferi*. Females measure up to 8 mm *0·31 in* in length which is the diameter of a pencil.

Centipedes *Chilopoda*

Longest

The longest known species of centipede is a large variant of the widely distributed *Scolopendra morsitans,* found on the Andaman Islands in the Bay of Bengal. Specimens have been measured up to 330 mm *13 in* in length and 38 mm *1½ in* in breadth.

The longest centipede found in Britain is *Haplophilus subterraneus,* which has been measured up to 70 mm *2·75 in* in length and 1·4 mm *0·05 in* across the body.

Shortest

The shortest recorded centipede is an unidentified species which measures only 5 mm *0·19 in.*

The shortest centipede found in Britain is *Lithobius dubosequi,* which measures up to 9·5 mm *0·374 in* in length.

Most legs

The centipede with the greatest number of legs is *Himantarum gabrielis* found in southern Europe which has 171–177 pairs when adult.

Fastest

The fastest centipede is probably *Scrutigera coleoptrata* of southern Europe which can travel at 1·8 km/h *1·1 mph.*

Millipedes *Diplopoda*

Longest

The longest known species of millipede are *Graphidostreptus gigas* of Africa and *Scaphistostreptus seychellarum* of the Seychelles in the Indian Ocean, both of which have been measured up to 280 mm *11·02 in* in length and 20 mm *0·78 in* in diameter.

The longest millipede found in Britain is *Cylindroiulus londinensis* which measures up to 50 mm *1·96 in.*

Shortest

The shortest millipede in the world is the British species

Polyxenus lagurus, which measures 2·1–4·0 mm *0·082–0·15 in.*

Most legs

The greatest number of legs reported for a millipede is 375 pairs (750 legs) for *Illacme plenipes* of California, USA.

Segmented Worms

Annelida

Longest

The longest known species of earthworm is *Microchaetus rappi* (= *M. microchaetus*) of South Africa. In *c.* 1937 a giant measuring 6·70 m *22 ft* in length when naturally extended and 20 mm *0·78 in* in diameter was collected in the Transvaal.

The longest segmented worm found in Britain is the King rag worm (*Nereis virens*). On 19 Oct 1975 a specimen measuring 111·7 cm *44 in* when fully extended was collected by Mr James Sawyer in Hauxley Bay, Northumberland.

The longest earthworm found in Britain is *Lumbricus terrestris.* The normal range is 90–300 mm *3·54–11·81 in* but this species has been reliably measured up to 350 mm *13·78 in* when naturally extended. Measurements up to 508 mm *20 in* have been claimed, but in each case the body was probably macerated first.

On 2 Feb 1988 an 'earthworm' reported to measure 1·83 m *6 ft* in length was found on an allotment in Stratton St Margaret, Wiltshire. The specimen was later sent to the British Museum (Natural History) for identification, where it was found to be the intestine of a Hedgehog (*Erinaceus europaeus*).

Shortest

The shortest known segmented worm is *Chaetogaster annandalei,* which measures less than 0·5 mm *0·019 in* in length.

Worm charming

At the first World Worm Charming Championship held at Willaston near Nantwich, Cheshire, on 5 July 1980 a local farmer's son Tom Shufflebotham (b. 1960) charmed a record 511 worms out of the ground (a 3 × 3 m *3·28 × 3·28 yd* plot) in the alloted time of 30 minutes. Garden forks or other implements are vibrated in the soil by competitors to coax up the worms, but the use of water is banned.

Molluscs *Mollusca*

(Squids, octopuses, shellfish, snails, etc.)

Largest invertebrate

The Atlantic giant squid *Architeuthis dux* is the world's largest known invertebrate. The heaviest ever recorded was a 2 tonne monster which ran aground in Thimble Tickle Bay, Newfoundland, Canada on 2 Nov 1878.

There are numerous types of 10-armed cephalopods ranging in size from 1·5 cm *0·75 in* to the longest ever recorded – a 17·37 m *57 ft* giant *Architeuthis longimanus* which was washed up on Lyall Bay, Cook Strait, New Zealand in October 1887. Its long slender tentacles each possessed four rows of suckers which measured 15·01 m *49 ft 3 in.*

The largest squid ever recorded in British waters was an *Architeuthis monachus* found at the head of Whalefirth Voe, Shetland on 2 Oct 1959 which measured 7·31 m *24 ft* in total length.

Largest eye

The Atlantic giant squid has the largest eye of any animal – living or extinct. It has been estimated that the one recorded at Thimble Tickle Bay had eyes 400 mm *15·75 in* in diameter – almost the width of this open book !

Largest octopus

The largest octopus known to science is *Octopus apollyon* of the coastal waters of the North Pacific. One huge individual caught single-handed by skin-diver Donald E. Hagen in Lower Hoods Canal, Puget Sound, Washington, USA on 18 Feb 1973 had a relaxed radial spread of 7·01 m *23 ft* and weighed 53·8 kg *118 lb 10 oz.*

The largest octopus found in British waters is the Common octopus (*Octopus vulgaris*). It may span 2·13 m *7 ft* and weigh more than 4·5 kg *10 lb.*

Oldest mollusc

The longest-lived mollusc is the Ocean quahog (*Arctica islandica*), a thick-shelled clam found in mid-Atlantic. A specimen with 220 annual growth rings was collected in 1982.

SHELLS
Largest

The largest of all existing bivalve shells is the Marine giant clam *Tridacna gigas*, found on the Indo-Pacific coral reefs. A specimen measuring 110 cm *43·3 in* in length and weighing 333 kg *734 lb* collected off Ishigaki Island, Okinawa, Japan was found in 1956 but not formally measured until August 1984 by Dr Shohei Shirai.

The largest bivalve shell found in British waters is the Fan mussel (*Pinna fragilis*). One specimen found at Tor Bay, Devon measured 37 cm *14·56 in* in length and 20 cm *7·87 in* in breadth at the hind end.

Smallest

The smallest known shell-bearing species is the gastropod *Ammonicera rota*, which is found in British waters. It measures 0·5 mm *0·02 in* in diameter. The smallest bivalve shell is the Coinshell *Neolepton sykesi*, which is known only from a few examples collected off Guernsey, Channel Islands and western Ireland. It has an average diameter of 1·2 mm *0·047 in.*

Most expensive

The value of a sea-shell does not necessarily depend on its rarity or its prevalence. Some rare shells are inexpensive because there is no demand for them, while certain common shells fetch high prices because they are not readily accessible. In theory the most valuable shells in the world should be some of the unique examples collected in deep-sea trawls, but these shells are always dull and unattractive and hold very little interest for the collector. The most sought-after shell at present is probably *Cypraea fultoni.* In 1987 two live specimens were taken by a Russian trawler off Mozambique in the Indian Ocean. The larger of the two was later reportedly sold for a record $24 000 to a collector in Italy.

GASTROPODS
Largest

The largest known gastropod is the Trumpet or Baler conch (*Syrinx aruanus*) of Australia. One outsized specimen collected off Western Australia in 1979 and now owned by Don Pisor (who bought it from a fisherman in Kaoh-siung, Taiwan in November 1979) of San Diego, California measures 77·2 cm *30·39 in* in length and has a maximum girth of 101 cm *39·76 in.* It weighed nearly 18·14 kg *40 lb* when alive.

The largest known land gastropod is the African giant snail (*Achatina* sp.). A specimen named 'Gee Geronimo' owned by Christopher Hudson (1955–79) of Hove, East Sussex, measured 39·3 cm *15½ in* from snout to tail when fully extended (shell length 27·3 cm *10¾ in*) in December 1978 and weighed exactly 900 g *2 lb.* The snail was collected in Sierra Leone in June 1976.

The largest land snail found in Britain is the Roman or Edible snail (*Helix pomatia*), which measures up to 10 cm *4 in* in overall length and weighs up to 85 g *3 oz.*

Fastest

The fastest-moving species of land snail is probably the Common garden snail (*Helix aspersa*). According to

tests carried out in the United States the absolute top speed for this species is 0·05 km/h *0·0313 mph* (or 50·3 m *55 yd* per hr).

Ribbon Worms

Nemertina

Longest

The longest of the 550 recorded species of ribbon worms, also called nemertines (or nemerteans), is the 'Boot-lace' worm (*Lineus longissimus*), which is found in the shallow waters of the North Sea. A specimen washed ashore at St Andrews, Fife, Scotland, in 1864 after a severe storm measured more than 55 m *180 ft* in length.

Immolation

Some ribbon worms absorb themselves when food is scarce. One specimen under observation digested 95 per cent of its own body in a few months without apparently suffering any ill-effects. As soon as food became available the lost tissue was restored.

Jellyfishes and Corals *Cnidaria*

Largest jellyfish

The largest jellyfish is the Arctic giant jellyfish (*Cyanea capillata arctica*) of the north-western Atlantic. One washed up in Massachusetts Bay had a bell diameter of 2·28 m *7 ft 6 in* and tentacles stretching 36·5 m *120 ft.*

The largest cnidarian found in British waters is the rare 'Lion's mane' jellyfish (*Cyanea capillata*), also known as the Common sea blubber. One specimen measured at St Andrew's Marine Laboratory, Fife, had a bell diameter of 91 cm *35·8 in* and tentacles stretching over 13·7 m *45 ft.*

Most venomous cnidarian

The beautiful but deadly Australian sea wasp (*Chironex fleckeri*) is the most venomous jellyfish in the world. Its cardio-toxic venom has caused the deaths of 66 people off the coast of Queensland since 1880, with victims dying within 1–3 minutes if medical aid is not available. One effective defence is women's panty hose, outsize versions of which are now worn by Queensland lifesavers at surf carnivals.

Coral

The world's greatest stony coral structure is the Great Barrier Reef off Queensland, north-east Australia. It stretches 2028 km *1260 miles* and covers 207 000 km² *80 000 miles².*

The world's largest reported discrete coral is a stony colony of *Galaxea fascicularis* found in Sakiyama Bay off Irimote Island, Okinawa on 7 Aug 1982 by Dr Shohei Shirai. It measured more than 16 m *52½ ft* overall.

Sponges *Porifera*

Largest

The largest known sponge is the barrel-shaped Loggerhead sponge (*Spheciospongia vesparium*) of the West Indies and the waters off Florida, USA. Individuals measure up to 105 cm *3 ft 6 in* in height and 91 cm *3 ft* in diameter.

Neptune's cup or goblet (*Poterion patera*) of Indonesia grows to 120 cm *4 ft* in height, but this is a measurably less bulky animal.

In 1909 a Wool sponge (*Hippospongia canaliculata*) measuring 183 cm *6 ft* in circumference was collected off the Bahamas. When first taken from the water it weighed between 36 and 41 kg *80–90 lb* but after it had been dried and relieved of all excrescences it scaled 5·44 kg

12 lb (this sponge is now preserved in the US National Museum, Washington DC, USA).

Smallest

The smallest known sponge is the widely distributed *Leucosolenia blanca*, which measures 3 mm *0·11 in* in height when fully grown.

Deepest

Sponges have been recovered from depths of up to 5637 m *18 500 ft.*

Extinct Animals

The first dinosaur to be scientifically described was *Megalosaurus bucklandi* ('great fossil lizard') in 1824. The remains of this bipedal flesh-eater had been found by workmen before 1818 in a slate quarry near Woodstock, Oxfordshire and were later placed in the University Museum, Oxford. It was not until 1841, however, that the name Dinosauria ('terrible lizards') was given to these newly-discovered giants.

Largest

The largest terrestrial vertebrates of all time were the brachiosaurs ('arm lizards') of the Tendaguru and Morrison Formations of Africa and North America, which lumbered across the landscape 160 million years ago. Estimated weights up to 190 tonnes have been published for the biggest members of this family (*Brachiosauridae*), but analyses of limb bone mid-circumferences by palaeophysiologists (people who study the physical make-up of extinct animals) have revealed that these huge giraffe-like sauropods were nowhere near as heavy as previously claimed. Most of the brachiosaurs discovered so far weighed a more acceptable 35–40 tonnes, but they could have been up to 33 per cent heavier in prime fat-bearing condition. The largest (and tallest) species for which the whole skeleton is known was the gracile *Brachiosaurus (Giraffatitan) brancai* from the famous Tendaguru site in Tanzania, which was excavated by a German expedition during the period 1909–11. The bones were later shipped back to the Humboldt Museum for Naturkunde in East Berlin, Germany for preparation and assembly and the specimen was finally put on display in 1937. As it stands today the world's largest mounted dinosaur measures 22·2 m *72 ft 9½ in* overall length (height at shoulder 6 m *19 ft 8 in*) and has a raised head height of 14 m *46 ft.* It weighed an estimated 31·5 tonnes. Another skeleton (incomplete) in the same museum measures 25 m *82 ft* in total length (shoulder height 6·79 m *22 ft 3½ in*) and has an estimated height of 16 m *52½ ft.* It weighed 45 tonnes. *Brachiosaurus (B) altithorax* and its junior synonym *Ultrasaurus macintoshi* from the Uncompahgre plateau, western Colorado, USA was also in the same class but heavierbodied, and probably weighed about 50 tonnes in lean condition.

Trackways are also a good indication of size, and the print of the *Breviparopus* found at Taghbalout, Morocco together with those of the brachiosaur *Pleurocoelus* from the Paluxy River, Texas, USA, suggest that they were also in the very large size class i.e. 50 tonnes. Some of the diplodocids ('double beams') of the Morrison Formation were also massively heavy, including the long-necked barosaurus *Supersaurus viviane* ('super lizard') from Uncompahgre (discovered 1972), which weighed *c.* 50 tonnes. A small number of titanosaurs ('giant lizards') have also been described as super-sized, and *Antarctosaurus giganteus* ('Atlas lizard') of South America, India and Kazakhstan probably rivalled the largest brachiosaurs in terms of weight. There is also an enormous incomplete femur (original length at least 244 cm *8 ft*) in the Museum of La Plata, Argentina that must have come from a titanosaurus (*A. giganteus*) massing about 55 tonnes.

In 1985 the remains of a huge diplodocid said to be 'the

largest dinosaur ever known' (sic) were excavated from a site near Albuquerque, New Mexico, USA. According to a palaeontologist at the New Mexico Museum of Natural History this giant sauropod measured an estimated 30–36 m *100–120 ft* in total length and weighed at least 80 tonnes, but it is extremely doubtful whether this new species was as heavy as *Supersaurus viviane*. (It has been suggested that these two dinosaurs may represent one giant species.)

The largest known sauropods appear to weigh around the 50 tonne mark, but this doesn't necessarily represent the ultimate weight limit for a land vertebrate. New species yet to be discovered may well have weighed anything up to 100 tonnes, especially if they were carrying large amounts of seasonal fat.

Britain's largest known dinosaur was the diplodocid *Cetiosaurus oxoniensis* ('whale lizard'), from the upper beds of the Great Oolite at Enslow Bridge, near Oxford. This sauropod, which roamed across southern England about 150 million years BP, measured up to 21 m *69 ft* overall and weighed an estimated 27 tonnes.

This mass may have been matched or even exceeded by the brachiosaurus *Pelorosaurus* ('monstrous lizard') of the late Jurassic which, on the evidence of a haemal arch (the bone running beneath the vertebrae of the tail) found on the Isle of Wight may have reached 24 m *80 ft*.

Longest

Up until very recently the longest dinosaurs on record were believed to be certain attenuated diplodocids. A complete reconstruction of a *Diplodocus carnegii* in the Carnegie Museum of Natural History in Pittsburgh, Pennsylvania, USA measures 26·6 m *87 ft 6 in* in total length – head and body 6·7 m *22 ft*, body 4·5 m *15 ft*, tail 15·4 m *50 ft 6 in* – and has a mounted height of 3·58 m *11 ft 9 in* at the pelvis, the highest point on the body. But this giant was a lightweight relatively speaking and only weighed an estimated 10·7 tonnes. By comparison, *Supersaurus viviane* (see page 41) measured an estimated 42 m *138 ft* in total length, while *Breviparopus* (see page 41) attained the astonishing length of 48 m *157 ft* – making it the longest vertebrate on record!

Britain's longest known dinosaurs were *Cetiosaurus oxoniensis* and *Pelorosaurus* (see above).

Largest land predator

The largest flesh-eating dinosaur recorded so far is *Tyrannosaurus rex* ('king tyrant lizard'), which stalked across what are now the states of Montana, Wyoming and Texas in the USA, Alberta and Saskatchewan in Canada 135 million years ago. A composite skeleton of this nightmarish beast in the American Museum of Natural History, New York, USA has a bipedal height of 5·6 m *18 ft 6 in* (total length 10·6 m *34 ft 9 in*), and weighed an estimated 5·7 tonnes (close to 7 tonnes with large fat reserves).

This individual, however, may have been a sub-adult, because the upper jaw-bone (maxilla) of another tyrannosaurus in the Museum of Comparative Zoology at the University of California, Berkeley, is 29 per cent longer (90 cm *35·4 in*) than the one in the American Museum of Natural History. This indicated a 14 m *44 ft* carnosaur weighing anything up to 12 tonnes! Its counterparts which are found in Mongolia *Tarbosaurus bataar* ('alarming lizard') and *Dyna-*

Smallest dinosaurs ● The smallest dinosaurs so far recorded are the chicken–sized *Compsognathus* ('pretty jaw') of southern West Germany and south–east France, and an undescribed plant–eating fabrosaurid from Colorado, USA. Both measured 75 cm *29·5 in* from the snout to the tip of the tail and weighed about 6·8 kg *15 lb*. The illustration shows 'pretty jaw' and a typical 26–inch wheel bicycle for size comparison. (Artwork: Matthew Hillier FSCD/Peter Harper)

mosaurus imperiosus of Shandung Province, China, were also in the same size league, the former measuring up to 14 m *46 ft* overall (bipedal length 6·1 m *20 ft*), but these tyrannosaurids were not so heavily built as their North American relative.

Some of the allosaurs ('other lizards') of North America, Africa, Australia and China also reached exceptional sizes, and one individual excavated near Kenton, Oklahoma, USA in 1934 measured 12·8 m *42 ft* in total length and had a bipedal height of 4·9 m *16 ft*. It was built on even more massive lines than the tyrannosaurids and had arms more than twice as long.

Another allosaur from China, *Yanchuanosaurus magnus*, has been described as the largest non-tyrannosaurid carnosaur so far recorded, with a skull even more massive than that of *T. rex*. It measured over 10·36 m *34 ft* in length overall. *Spinosaurus aegyptiacus* ('thorn lizard') of Niger and Egypt was even longer than the largest-known tyrannosaurid, with a total length of *c.* 15 m *49 ft*, and combined its tremendous length with 1·6 m *5 ft 3 in* long blade-like spines running down its back, but it was a much more lightly-built theropod than the tyrannosaurids and probably did not exceed 4 tonnes.

The megalosaurids ('great lizards') also produced some enormities, including *Megalosaurus ingens* from the Tendaguru site in Tanzania, and *Bahariasaurus* from Egypt and Algeria, both of which were nearly as large as *T. rex*, while the extremely bulky *Torvosaurus* ('savage lizard') from the Uncompahgre, western Colorado, USA may have weighed as much as 5·5 tonnes, even though it was only 10 m *33 ft* long.

Longest trackway

In 1983 a series of four *Apatosaurus* (= *Brontosaurus*) trackways which ran parallel for a distance of over 215 m *705 ft* were recorded from 145-million-year-old Morrison strata in south-east Colorado, USA.

Fastest

Trackways can be used to estimate dinosaur speeds, and one from the Late Morrison of Texas discovered in 1981 indicated that a carnivorous dinosaur had been moving at 40 km/h *25 mph*. Some of the ornithomimids (ostrich dinosaurs) were even faster, and the large-brained 100 kg *220 lb Dromiceiomimus* ('emu mimic') of the late Cretaceous of southern Alberta, Canada could probably outsprint an ostrich, which has a top speed of 72 km/h *45 mph*.

Largest footprints

In 1932 the gigantic footprints of a large bipedal hadrosaurid (duckbill) measuring 1·36 m *53·5 in* in length and 81 cm *31·8 in* wide were discovered at Salt Lake City, Utah, USA, and other reports from Colorado and Utah refer to footprints 95–100 cm *37·4–39·4 in* wide. Footprints attributed to the largest brachiosaurids also range up to 100 cm *39·3 in* wide for the hind feet.

Earliest

The earliest known dinosaur is a yet unnamed plant-eating prosauropod which lived 230 million years ago. In 1984 a partial skeleton of this animal, which measured 2·4 m *8 ft* in length and weighed 67 kg *147 lb* when alive, was discovered in the Petrified Forest National Park, eastern Arizona, USA by a team from the University of California.

Most brainless

Stegosaurus ('plated lizard'), which roamed across the states of Colorado, Oklahoma, Utah and Wyoming, USA about 150 million years ago, measured up to 9 m *30 ft* in total length but had a walnut-sized brain weighing only 70 g *2½ oz*. This represents only 0·004 of 1 per cent of its computed body weight of 1¾ tonnes (cf. 0·074 of 1 per cent for an elephant and 1·88 per cent for a human).

Largest eggs

The largest known dinosaur eggs are those of *Hypselo-*

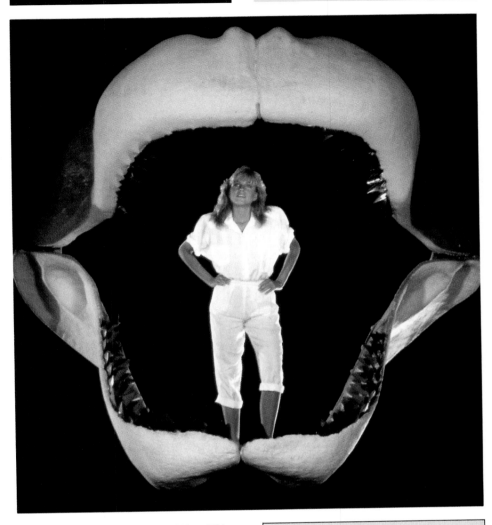

saurus priscus ('high ridge lizard'), a 12·19 m *40 ft* long titanosaurid which lived about 80 000 000 years ago. Some examples found in the valley of the Durance near Aix-en-Provence, southern France in October 1961 would have had, uncrushed, a length of 300 mm *12 in* and a diameter of 255 mm *10 in* (capacity 3·3 litre *5·8 pints*).

Largest claws

The therizinosaurids ('scythe lizards') from the Late Cretaceous of the Nemegt Basin, southern Mongolia, had the largest claws of any known animal, and in the case of *Therizinosaurus cheloniformis* measured up to 91·4 cm *36 in* round the outer curve (cf. 20·3 cm *8 in* for *T. rex*). It has been suggested that these sickle claws were designed for grasping and tearing apart large victims, but this creature had a feeble skull partially or entirely lacking teeth and probably lived on termites.

In January 1982, amateur fossil collector William Walker found a 30 cm *11·8 in* long claw-bone in a clay pit near Dorking, Surrey. Further excavations by a team from the British Museum (Natural History) revealed that the owner of this claw (believed to be a spinosaur) measured more than 6 m *19 ft 8 in* overall (estimated weight 2 tonnes) and had a bipedal height of 3–4 m *9 ft–13 ft*. It was also distinguished from other carnosaurs by having 128 teeth instead of the usual 64. This enigma, said to be the most important dinosaur fossil found in Europe this century, was subsequently named *Baryonyx walkeri* ('heavy claw').

Largest skull

The skulls of the long-frilled ceratopsids were the largest of all known land animals and culminated in the long-frilled *Torosaurus sp.*, ('bull lizard'). This herbivore, which measured *c.* 7·6 m *25 ft* in total length and weighed up to 8 tonnes, had a skull measuring up to 3 m *9 ft 10 in* in

Largest prehistoric fish ● An over-sized reconstruction of the jaws of the extinct giant shark *Carchardon megalodon* in the American Museum of Natural History. This giant marine predator, which abounded in the Miocene seas some 15 million years ago, reportedly measured 24·38 m *80 ft* in length based on ratios from fossil teeth, but the modern estimate is that this shark did not exceed 13·1 m *43 ft*. (Photo: Seaphot)

length (including fringe) and weighing up to 2 tonnes. It ranged from Montana to Texas, USA.

Largest flying creature

The largest flying creature was the pterosaur *Quetzalcoatlus northropi* ('feathered serpent') which glided over what is now Texas, USA and Alberta, Canada about 65 million years ago. Partial remains discovered in Big Bend National Park, western Texas in 1971 indicate that this reptile must have had a wing span of 11–12 m *36–39 ft* and weighed about 86 kg 190 lb.

Britain's largest known flying reptile was *Ornithodesmus latidens*, which soared over what is now Hampshire and the Isle of Wight about 90 million years ago. It had a wing expanse of *c.* 5 m *16 ft 4¼ in* allowing for the natural curve.

Largest marine reptile

The largest marine reptile ever recorded was *Kronosaurus queenslandicus*, a short-necked pliosaur from the Early Cretaceous (135 million years BP) of Australia. It had a 3·04 m *10 ft* long skull containing 80 massive teeth and measured up to 15·2 m *50 ft* in length.

Britain's largest marine reptile was *Stretosaurus macromerus*, a short-necked pliosaur from the Kim-

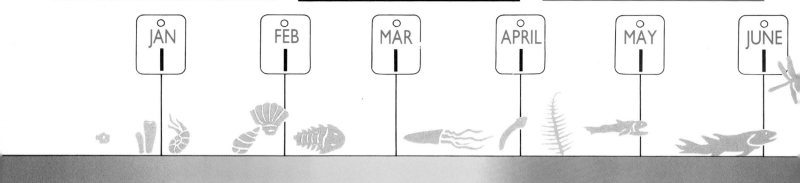

JAN	FEB	MAR	APRIL	MAY	JUNE

millions of years ago   570   500   435   395   345

The Age of the Dinosaurs ● Recognisable animal life began 570 million years ago.

Imagine that this were the beginning of a calendar year – January 1st. One year later – December 31st – a remarkable comparison can be made between the dinosaur domination of time and man's insignificant period of existence.

In terms of a year, the dinosaurs arrived in August and became extinct towards the end of November. Homo Sapien man, however, did not arrive until half an hour before the end of December. Some sources quote 11·24 pm on 31 December, and others 11·50 pm on 31 December.

If this chart were to continue back through the book, you would need to turn to page 32, i.e. for a further 11½ pages (*2·59 m*) to arrive at the formation of planet Earth. (Artwork: Rhoda and Robert Burns)

meridge Clay of Stretham, Cambridgeshire and Oxfordshire. A mandible found at Cumnor, Oxfordshire and now in the University Museum, Oxford has a restored length of over 3 m *9 ft 10 in* and must have belonged to a reptile measuring at least 14 m *46 ft* in total length.

Largest crocodile

The largest known crocodile was the euschian *Deinosuchus riograndensis*, which lived in the lakes and swamps of what is now the state of Texas, USA about 75 million years ago. Fragmentary remains discovered in Big Bend National Park, western Texas, indicate a hypothetical length of 16 m *52 ft 6 in*, compared with the 15·2 m *50 ft* of the huge gharial *Rhamphosuchus* of northern India (2 million years ago) and the 14 m *46 ft* of *Sarcosuchus imperator* of Niger.

Largest chelonians

The largest prehistoric chelonian was *Stupendemys geographicus*, a pelomedusid turtle which lived about 5 million years ago. Fossil remains discovered by Harvard University palaeontologists in northern Venezuela in 1972 indicate that this turtle had a carapace (shell) measuring 218–230 cm *7 ft 2 in–7 ft 6½ in* in mid-line length and measured 3 m *9 ft 10 in* in overall length. It had a computed weight of 2041 kg *4500 lb* in life.

Largest tortoise

The largest prehistoric tortoise was probably *Geochelone* (= *Colossochelys*) *atlas*, which lived in what is now northern India, Burma, Java, the Celebes and Timor, about 2 million years ago. In 1923 the fossil remains of a specimen with a carapace 180 cm *5 ft 11 in* long (223 cm *7 ft 4 in* over the curve) and 89 cm *2 ft 11 in* high were discovered near Chandigarh in the Siwalik Hills, India. This animal had a total length of 2·44 m *8 ft* and is computed to have weighed 852 kg *2100 lb* when it was alive.

Longest snake

The longest prehistoric snake was the python-like *Gigantophis garstini*, which inhabited what is now Egypt about 55 million years ago. Parts of a spinal column and a small piece of jaw discovered at Fayum in the Western Desert indicate a length of *c*. 11 m *37 ft*.

Largest amphibian

The largest amphibian ever recorded was the gharial-like *Prionosuchus plummeri* which lived 230 million years ago. In 1972 the fragmented remains of a specimen measuring an estimated 9 m *30 ft* in life were discovered in northern Brazil.

Largest insect

The largest prehistoric insect was the dragonfly *Meganeura monyi*, which lived about 280 million years ago. Fossil remains (i.e. impressions of wings) discovered at Commentry, central France, indicate a wing extending up to 70 cm *27·5 in*.

Britain's largest dragonfly was *Pupus diluculum* (family Meganeuridae), which is known only from a wing impression found on a lump of coal in Bolsover colliery, Derbyshire in July 1978. It had an estimated wing span of 50–60 cm *19·68–23·62 in* and lived about 300 million years ago, making it the oldest flying creature so far recorded.

Largest bird

The largest prehistoric true bird was the flightless *Dromornis stirtoni*, a huge emu-like creature which lived in central Australia 11 million years ago. Fossil leg bones found near Alice Springs in 1974 indicate that the bird must have stood *c*. 3 m *10 ft* in height and weighed *c*. 500 kg *1100 lb*. The giant moa *Dinornis maximus* of New Zealand was even taller, attaining a maximum height of 3·6 m *12 ft*, but it weighed only about 227 kg *500 lb*.

The largest known flying bird was the Giant teratorn (*Argentavis magnificens*) which lived in Argentina about 6 million years ago. Fossil remains discovered at a site 160 km *100 miles* west of Buenos Aires, Argentina in 1979 indicate that this gigantic vulture had a wing span of 7·0–7·6 m *23–25 ft* and weighed about 120 kg *265 lb*.

In 1987 an expedition from the Charleston Museum of South Carolina, USA discovered the fossil remains of a 30 million-year-old giant sea-bird (*Pseudodontorns sp.*), which was related to the pelicans and cormorants. It had a wingspan of *c*. 5·8 m *19 ft* and weighed about 41 kg *90 lb*.

● For purposes of comparison here is a scale drawing of a mammoth, African elephant and Indian elephant. (Artwork: Suzanne Alexander)

Largest mammal

The largest land mammal ever recorded was *Paraceratherium* (= *Baluchitherium*), a long-necked hornless rhinocerotid which roamed across western Asia and Europe (Yugoslavia) about 35 million years ago. A restoration in the American Museum of Natural History, New York, USA measures 5·41 m *17 ft 9 in* to the top of the shoulder hump and 11·27 m *37 ft* in total length, and this particular specimen must have weighed about 20 tonnes. The bones of this gigantic browser were first discovered in the Bugti Hills in east Baluchistan, Pakistan in 1907–8.

The largest marine mammal was the serpentine *Basilosaurus* (*Zeuglodon*) *cetoides*, which swam in the seas over modern-day Arkansas and Alabama 50 million years ago. It measured up to 21·3 m *70 ft* in length.

Largest mammoth

The largest prehistoric elephant was the Steppe mammoth *Mammuthus* (*Parelephas*) *trogontherii*, which roamed over what is now central Europe a million years ago. A fragmentary skeleton found in Mosbach, West Germany indicates a shoulder height of 4·5 m *14 ft 9 in*.

Largest primate

The largest known primate was *Gigantopithecus*, which lived in Asia about 7 million years ago. The only remains that have been discovered so far are partial lower jaws and single teeth, but if this giant ape's body was in proportion to its massive jaw then it would have stood about 2·74 m *9 ft* tall when erect and weighed at least 272 kg *600 lb*.

Antlers

The prehistoric Giant deer (*Megaceros giganteus*), which lived in northern Europe and northern Asia as recently as 8000 BC, had the longest horns of any known animal. One specimen recovered from an Irish bog had greatly palmated antlers measuring 4·3 m *14 ft* across.

Tusks

The longest tusks of any prehistoric animal were those of the Straight-tusked elephant *Palaeoloxodom antiquus germanicus*, which lived in northern Germany about 300 000 years ago. The average length in adult bulls was 5 m *16 ft 5 in*. A single tusk of a Woolly mammoth (*Mammuthus primigenius*) preserved in the Franzens Museum at Brno, Czechoslovakia measures 5·02 m *16 ft 5½ in* along the outside curve. In *c*. August 1933, a single tusk of an Imperial mammoth (*Mammuthus imperator*) measuring 4·87+ m *16+ ft* (anterior end missing) was unearthed near Post, Gorza County, in Texas, USA. In 1934 this tusk was presented to the American Museum of Natural History in New York City.

The heaviest single fossil tusk on record is one weighing 150 kg *330 lb* with a maximum circumference of 89 cm *35 in* now preserved in the Museo Civico di Storia Naturale in Milan, Italy. The specimen (in two pieces) measures 3·58 m *11 ft 9 in* in length.

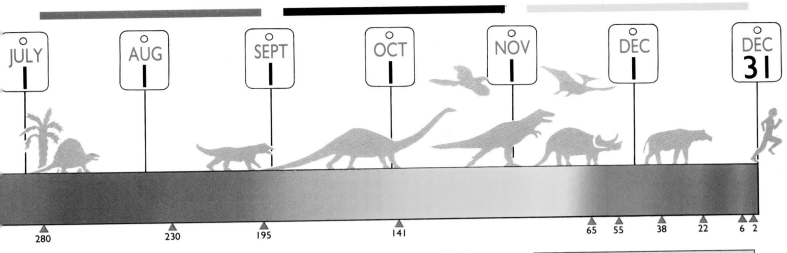

JULY | AUG | SEPT | OCT | NOV | DEC | DEC 31

280 | 230 | 195 | 141 | 65 | 55 | 38 | 22 | 6 | 2

The heaviest recorded fossil tusks are a pair belonging to a 4·06 m *13 ft 4 in* tall Columbian mammoth (*Mammuthus columbi*) in the State Museum, Lincoln, Nebraska, USA, which have a combined weight of 226 kg *498 lb* and measure 4·21 m *13 ft 9 in* and 4·14 m *13 ft 7 in* respectively. They were found near Campbell, Nebraska, USA in April 1915.

Plant Kingdom *Plantea*

PLANTS

The medicinal value of plants was known to Neanderthal man in Iraq *c.* 60 000 BC. The earliest evidence for a garden is a relief of proto-dynastic age *c.* 3000 BC in Egypt depicting a specimen palm in a protective enclosure amid irrigation or decorative waterways. Though the Romans had gardens in England from AD 43 the earliest surviving garden is at Romsey Abbey, Hampshire laid out *c.* 1092.

Oldest

'King Clone', the oldest known clone of the Creosote plant (*Larrea tridentata*), found in south-west California, USA, was estimated in February 1980 by Professor Frank C. Vasek to be 11 700 years old. It is possible that crustose lichens in excess of 500 mm *19·6 in* in diameter may be as old. In 1981 it was estimated that Antarctic lichens of more than 100 mm *3·9 in* in diameter are at least 10 000 years old.

Rarest

Plants thought to be extinct are rediscovered each year and there are thus many plants of which specimens are known in but a single locality. Cuttings from a Cafe marron tree (*Ramosmania heterophylla*), a single specimen growing on Rodriguez Island, Indian Ocean, reported in April 1986 were flown to the Royal Botanical Gardens, Kew, west London in an attempt to propagate it and preserve the species. *Pennantia baylisiana*, a tree found in 1945 on Three Kings Island, off New Zealand, only exists as a female and cannot fruit.

Northernmost

The Yellow poppy (*Papaver radicatum*) and the Arctic willow (*Salix arctica*) survive, the latter in an extremely stunted form, on the northernmost land (83° N).

Southernmost

Lichens resembling *Rhinodina frigida* have been found in Moraine Canyon in 86°09′S 157°30′W in 1971 and in the Horlick Mountain area, Antarctica in 86°09′S 131°14′W in 1965. The southernmost recorded flowering plant is the Antarctic hair grass (*Deschampsia antarctica*) which was found in latitude 68°21′S on Refuge Island, Antarctica on 11 Mar 1981.

Highest

The greatest certain altitude at which any flowering plants have been found is 6400 m *21 000 ft* on Kamet (7756 m *25 447 ft*) by N. D. Jayal in 1955. They were *Ermania himalayensis* and *Ranunculus lobatus.*

Roots

The greatest reported depth to which roots have penetrated is a calculated 120 m *400 ft* in the case of a wild fig tree at Echo Caves, near Ohrigstad, eastern Transvaal, South Africa. An elm tree root of at least 110 m *360 ft* was reported from Auchencraig, Largs, Ayrshire *c.* 1950. A single Winter rye plant (*Secale cereale*) has been shown

Largest cactus ● The largest of all cacti is the Saguaro (*Cereus giganteus* or *Carnegiea gigantea*), found in Arizona, south-eastern California and Sonora, Mexico. The green fluted column is surmounted by candelabra-like branches rising to a height of 16 m *52 ft 6 in* in the case of a specimen measured on the boundary of the Saguaro National Monument, Arizona. Waxy white blooms are followed by edible crimson fruit. (Photo: Bruce Coleman Limited)

to produce 622·8 km *387 miles* of roots in 0·051 m³ *1·83 ft³* of earth.

Worst weeds

The most intransigent weed is the mat-forming Water weed *Salvinia auriculata*, found in Africa. It was detected on the filling of Kariba Lake in May 1959 and within 11 months had choked an area of 199 km² *77 miles²* rising by 1963 to 1002 km² *387 miles²*. The world's worst land weeds are regarded as Purple nut sedge, Bermuda grass, Barnyard grass, Jungle-rice, Goose grass, Johnson grass, Guinea grass, Cogon grass and lantana.

The most damaging and widespread cereal weeds in Britain are the wild oats *Avena fatua* and *A. ludoviciana*. Their seeds can withstand temperatures of 115·6° C *240° F* for 15 min and remain viable. The largest weed in Britain is the Giant hogweed (*Heracleum manteggazzianum*) which established itself from seeds brought from the Caucasus before 1862. It reaches 3·65 m *12 ft*.

Most spreading

The greatest area covered by a single clonal growth is that of the wild Box huckleberry (*Gaylussacia brachyera*), a mat-forming evergreen shrub first reported in 1796. A colony covering about 40 ha *100 acres* was found on 18 July 1920 near the Juniata River,

Heaviest onion ● This 4·01 kg *8 lb 13½ oz* onion was grown by Ivor Mace of Treorci, Rhondda, Mid Glamorgan, Wales in 1987 !

UNITED KINGDOM FRUIT, VEGETABLES, FLOWERS

Many data subsequent to 1958 come from the annual *Garden News* and Phostrogen Ltd Giant Vegetable and Fruit Contest and the Super Sunflower Contest.

TYPE	SIZE (Weight/Dimensions)		GROWER	LOCATION	YEAR
APPLE	1·357 kg	*3 lb 1 oz*	V. Loveridge	Ross-on-Wye, H & W	1965
ARTICHOKE	3·625 kg	*8 lb*	A. R. Lawson	Tollerton, North Yorkshire	1964
BEETROOT	13·154 kg	*29 lb*	F. A. Pulley	Maidstone, Kent	1964
BROAD BEAN	59·3 cm	*23⅜ in*	T. Currie	Jedburgh, Borders	1963
	59·3 cm	*23⅜ in*	Mrs M. Adrian	Irvine, Strathclyde	1982
BROCCOLI	13·100 kg	*28 lb 14¾ oz*	J. T. Cooke	Funtington, W. Sussex	1964
BRUSSELS SPROUT[1]	7·285 kg	*16 lb 1 oz*	E. E. Jenkins	Shipston-on-Stour, Warwickshire	1974
CABBAGE	53·52 kg	*118 lb 0 oz*	E. Stone	East Woodyates, Wiltshire	1987
CABBAGE, RED [2]	19·05 kg	*42 lb*	R. Straw	Staveley, Derbyshire	1925
CARROT[3]	4·649 kg	*10 lb 4 oz*	E. Stone	East Woodyates, Wiltshire	1984
CAULIFLOWER	23·900 kg	*52 lb 11½ oz*	J. T. Cooke	Funtington, W. Sussex	1966
CELERY	16·1 kg	*35 lb 8 oz*	E. Stone	East Woodyates, Wiltshire	1986
CUCUMBER[4]	6·201 kg (indoor)	*13 lb 10¾ oz*	A. Emery	Rochester, Kent	1984
	3·740 kg (outdoor)	*8 lb 4 oz*	C. Bowcock	Willaston, Merseyside	1973
	110 cm	*43½ in*	A. C. Rayment	Chelmsford, Essex	1984-6
DAHLIA[5]	3·17 m	*10 ft 5 in*	R. Lond	Diss, Norfolk	1985
DWARF BEAN	43·4 cm	*17½ in*	C. Bowcock	Willaston, Merseyside	1973
GLADIOLUS	2·55 m	*8 ft 4½ in*	A. Breed	Melrose, Roxburgh	1981
GOOSEBERRY	58·5 g	*2.06 oz*	A. Dingle	Macclesfield, Cheshire	1978
GOURD	88·900 kg	*196 lb*	J. Leathes	Herringfleet Hall, Suffolk	1846
GRAPEFRUIT*[6]	1·673 kg	*3 lb 11 oz*	Willington G.C.	Willington, Bedfordshire	1986
HOLLYHOCK	7·39 m	*24 ft 3 in*	W. P. Walshe	Eastbourne, E. Sussex	1961
KALE[7]	3·65 m tall	*12 ft*	B. T. Newton	Mullion, Cornwall	1950
LEEK, BLANCH	4·235 kg	*9 lb 5½ oz*	C. Bowcock	Willaston, Merseyside	1973
LEEK, POT	5·5 kg	*12 lb 2 oz*	P. Harrigan	Linton, Northumberland	1987
LEMON[8]	2·13 kg	*4 lb 11 oz*	Pershore College	Pershore, H & W	1986
LETTUCE	11·335 kg	*25 lb*	C. Bowcock	Willaston, Merseyside	1974
LUPIN*	1·84 m	*6 ft 0½ in*	J. Lawlor	New Malden, Surrey	1971
MANGOLD	24·720 kg	*54½ lb*	P. F. Scott	Sutton, Humberside	1971
MARROW	47·85 kg	*105 lb 8 oz*	D. C. Payne	Tewkesbury, Glos.	1982
MELON[9]	6·42 kg	*14 lb 2¾ oz*	R. D. Sainsbury	Paull, Hull, Humberside	1985
MUSHROOM[10]	1·72 m diam.	*68 in*	G. Long	Listowel, Co. Kerry	1987
ONION	4·01 kg	*8 lb 13½ oz*	I. Mace	Treorci, Rhondda	1987
PARSNIP[11]	3·62 m	*142¾ in*	K. Lloyd	Cydweli, Dyfed	1984
PEAPOD[12]	25·7 cm	*10⅛ in*	T. Currie	Jedburgh, Borders	1964
PEAR[13]	1·200 kg	*2 lb 10½ oz*	Mrs K. Loines	Hythe, Hampshire	1973
PETUNIA*[14]	2·53 m	*8 ft 4 in*	G. A. Warner	Dunfermline, Fife	1978
POTATO[15]	3·200 kg	*7 lb 1 oz*	J. H. East	Spalding, Lincolnshire	1963
	3·200 kg	*7 lb 1 oz*	J.P. Busby	Atherstone, Warwickshire	1982
PUMPKIN[16]	201·4 kg	*444 lb*	R. A. Butcher	Stockbridge, Hampshire	1984
RADISH[17]	7·711 kg	*17 lb*	K. Ayliffe	Brecon, Powys	1976
RHUBARB	2·665 kg	*5 lb 14 oz*	E. Stone	East Woodyates, Wiltshire	1985
RUNNER BEAN	100·3 cm	*39½ in*	J. Taylor	Shifnal, Salop	1986
SAVOY CABBAGE	17·450 kg	*38 lb 8 oz*	W. H. Neil	Retford, Nottinghamshire	1966
SHALLOT*	2·636 kg (4 bulbs)	*5 lb 13 oz*	R. Miller	Exeter, Devon	1987
STRAWBERRY	231 g	*8.17 oz*	G. Anderson	Folkestone, Kent	1983
SUGAR BEET[18]	13·9 kg	*30 lb 10 oz*	K. McLean	Meldreth, Hertfordshire	1984
SUNFLOWER[19]	7·17 m tall	*23 ft 6½ in*	F. Kelland	Exeter, Devon	1976
SWEDE	22·11 kg	*48 lb 12 oz*	A. Foster	Alnwick, Northumberland	1980
TOMATO[20]	2·537 kg	*5 lb 9½ oz*	R. G. Burrows	Huddersfield, West Yorkshire	1985
TOMATO PLANT[21]	13·96 m (length)	*45 ft 9½ in*	Chosen Hill School	Gloucester, Glos.	1981
TOMATO TRUSS	9·175 kg	*20 lb 4 oz*	C. Bowcock	Willaston, Merseyside	1973
TURNIP[22]	15·975 kg	*35 lb 4 oz*	C. W. Butler	Nafferton, Humberside	1972

[1] A Brussels sprout plant measuring 3·55 m *11 ft 8 in* was grown by Ralph G. Sadler of Watchbury Farm, Barford, Warwickshire on 6 July 1978.

[2] The Swalwell, County Durham red cabbage of 1865 grown by William Collingwood (d. 8 Oct 1867) reputedly weighed 55·7 kg *123 lb* and was 6·57 m *259 in* in circumference.

[3] A specimen of 7 kg *15 lb 7 oz* was grown by Miss I. G. Scott of Nelson, New Zealand in October 1978. A 2·99 m *118 in* specimen grown by Ken Ayliffe of Brecon, Powys was recorded in September 1986.

[4] A Vietnamese variety 1·83 m *6 ft* long was reported by L. Szabo of Debrecen, Hungary in September 1976.

[5] A 5·0 m *16 ft 5 in* dahlia was grown by Sam and Pat Barnes of Chattahoochee, Florida, USA in 1982.

[6] A 2·966 kg *6 lb 8½ oz* specimen was weighed for Joshua and Allison Sosnow in Tucson, Arizona, USA on 21 Dec 1984.

[7] Gosse Haisma grew a stalk to 4·77 m *15 ft 7¾ in*.

[8] An 3·88 kg *8 lb 8 oz* lemon with a 74·9 cm *29½ in* in girth was grown by Charlotte and Donald Knutzen of Whittier, California, USA in August 1983.

[9] Jason Bright, 10, of Hope, Arkansas, USA, grew a watermelon reported by Grace's Gardens in September 1985 to weigh 118 kg *260 lb* and overtaking the joint record set by his father and grandfather.

[10] This mushroom weighed 10·8 kg *24 lb*. A specimen of the edible Termitomyces titanicus found near Kitwe, Zambia on 18 Dec 1978 measured 63 cm *26 in* in diameter and weighed 2·5 kg *5·5 lb*. A mushroom of 'nearly 100 lb' and 51 cm *20 in* thick was reported from Potenza, Italy on 30 Oct 1985.

[11] One 152 cm *60 in* long was reported by M. Zaninovich of Waneroo W. Australia.

[12] A 63·5 cm *25 in* peapod was grown by Chad McInville in July 1986.

[13] A specimen weighing 1·405 kg *3.09 lb* was harvested on 10 May 1979 at Messrs K. & R. Yeomans, Arding, Armidale, NSW, Australia.

[14] Bert Lawrence of Windham, New York, USA grew a petunia plant measured on 19 Sept 1985 at 4·16 m *13 ft 8 in*.

[15] One weighing 8·275 kg *18 lb 4 oz* reported dug up by Thomas Siddal in his garden in Chester on 17 Feb 1795. A yield of 233·5 kg *515 lb* was achieved from a 1·1 kg *2½ lb* parent seed by Bowcock planted in April 1977. Six tubers weighing 24·72 kg *54 lb 8 oz* by Alan Nunn of Rhodes, Middleton, Lancs were reported on 18 Sept 1949.

[16] A pumpkin (C. maxima) of 304·3 kg *671 lb* (3·63 m *143¼ in* girth) grown by Robert Gancarz of Jacobstown, New Jersey, USA won the World Pumpkin Federation contest at Collins, New York, on 13 Oct 1986.

[17] A radish of 12·25 kg *27 lb* and 69·8 cm *27½ in* long was grown by Ron Whitford in Wollongong, Australia in November 1985.

[18] One weighing 20·63 kg *45½ lb* was grown by R. Meyer of Brawley, California, USA in 1974.

[19] A sunflower of 7·76 m was grown by Martien Heijms of Oirschot, Netherlands in 1986. A sunflower with a head measuring 82 cm *32¼ in* in diameter was grown by Mrs Emily Martin of Maple Ridge, British Columbia, Canada in Sept 1983.

[20] Gordon Graham of Edmond, Oklahoma, grew a tomato of 3·51 kg *7 lb 12 oz* in 1986.

[21] Gordon Graham of Edmond, Oklahoma, grew a tomato plant of 16·3 m *53 ft 6 in* in 1985. Charles H. Wilber grew a cherry tomato plant with a height of 8·71 m *28 ft 7 in* recorded in November 1985. It was reported at the Tsukuba Science Expo Centre, Japan on 28 Feb 1988 that a single plant produced 16 897 tomatoes.

[22] A 33·1 kg *73 lb* turnip was reported in December 1768 and one of 23·1 kg *51 lb* from Alaska in 1981.

* Not in official contest.

The heaviest orange ever reported is one weighing 2·50 kg *5 lb 8 oz* exhibited in Nelspruit, South Africa on 19 June 1981. It was the size of a human head, but was stolen.

Pennsylvania, USA. It has been estimated that this colony began 13 000 years ago.

Smallest flowering and fruiting

The floating flowering Aquatic duckweed (*Wolffia angusta*) of Australia, described in 1980, is only 0·6 mm $\frac{1}{42}$ *of an inch* in length and 0·33 mm $\frac{1}{85}$ *of an inch* in width. It weighs about 0·00015 g *1/190 000 of an oz*, its fruit resembling a minuscule fig weighing 0·00007 g or *400 000 to the oz.*

The smallest land plant regularly flowering in Britain is the Chaffweed (*Cetunculus minimus*), a single seed of which weighs 0·00003 of a gramme.

Fastest growing

The case of a *Hesperogucca whipplei* of the family Liliaceae growing 3·65 m *12 ft* in 14 days was reported from Tresco Abbey, Isles of Scilly in July 1978.

Slowest flowering

The slowest flowering of all plants is the rare *Puya raimondii*, the largest of all herbs, discovered at 3960 m *13 000 ft* in Bolivia in 1870. The panicle emerges after about 80–150 years of the plant's life. One planted near sea level at the University of California's Botanical Garden, Berkeley, USA in 1958 grew to 7·6 m *25 ft* and bloomed as early as August 1986 after only 28 years. It then dies. (See also below under Largest blooms.)

Oldest pot plant

The oldest known pot plant is the succulent *Fockea crispa* potted by Baron Jacquin (1728–1817) at the Schönbrunn gardens, Vienna *c.* 1801.

Biggest collection

Dr Julian A. Steyermark of the Herbario Nacional, Caracas, Venezuela had by April 1988 made a total of 138 000 collections of which 132 500 were solo.

Largest aspidistra

The aspidistra (*Aspidistra elatior*) was introduced to Britain as a parlour palm from Japan and China in 1822.

The biggest aspidistra in the world measures 142 cm *56 in* and belongs to Cliff Evans of Kiora, Moruya, New South Wales, Australia.

The biggest aspidistra known in Britain is one 127 cm *50 in* tall with more than 500 leaves spanning 1·52 m *5 ft* grown by Gertie James in Staveley, Chesterfield.

Earliest flower

The oldest fossil of a flowering plant with palm-like imprints was found in Colorado, USA in 1953 and dated about 65 million years old.

Largest cactus

An armless cactus 24 m *78 ft* in height was measured in April 1978 by Hube Yates in Cave Creek, Arizona. It was toppled in a windstorm in July 1986 at an estimated age of 150 years.

Mosses

The smallest of mosses is the microscopic Pygmy moss (*Ephemerum*) and the longest is the Brook moss (*Fontinalis*), which forms streamers up to 91 cm *3 ft* long in flowing water.

SEAWEED
Longest

The longest species is the Pacific giant kelp (*Macrocystis pyrifera*), which, although it does not exceed 60 m *196 ft* in length, can grow 45 cm *18 in* in a day.

The longest of the 700 species of British seaweed is the Brown seaweed *Chorda filum* which grows up to a length of 6·10 m *20 ft*. The Japanese *Sargassum muticum* introduced *c.* 1970 can grow to 9·0 m *30 ft*.

Deepest

The greatest depth at which plant life has been found is 269 m *884 ft* by Mark and Diane Littler (USA) off San

Salvadore Island, Bahamas in October 1984. These maroon-coloured algae survived though 99·9995 per cent of sunlight was filtered out.

VINES AND VINEYARDS
Largest

This was planted in 1842 at Carpinteria, California, USA. By 1900 it was yielding more than 9 tonnes of grapes in some years, and averaging 7 tonnes per year. It died in 1920. A single bunch of grapes (Red Thomson seedless) weighing 9400 grammes *20 lb 11½ oz* was weighed in Santiago, Chile in May 1984.

Britain's largest vine (1898–1964) was at Kippen, Stirling with a girth, measured in 1956, of 1·52 m *5 ft*. England's largest vine is the Great Vine, planted in 1768 at Hampton Court, London. Its girth is 215·9 cm *85 in* with branches up to 34·7 m *114 ft* long and an average yield of 318·8 kg *703 lb*. In 1986 Leslie Stringer of Dartford, Kent obtained a yield of 1016·5 kg *2241 lb* from a vine in Banstead, Surrey planted in 1962.

Most northerly and southerly

A vineyard at Sabile, Latvia, USSR is just north of Lat. 57° N. The most southerly commercial vineyards are to be found in central Otago, South Island, New Zealand south of Lat. 45° S.

Renton Burgess Vineyard, south of Alexandra, South Island, New Zealand, is in Lat. 44°36′S.

The most northerly commercial vineyard in Britain is that at Renishaw Hall, Nr Chesterfield, Derbyshire with 2600 vines, at Lat. 53° 18′N.

BLOOMS AND FLOWERS
Largest

The largest of all blooms are the parasitic Stinking corpse lily (*Rafflesia arnoldii*). They attach themselves to the cissus vines of the jungle in south-east Africa and measure up to 91 cm *3 ft* across and 1·9 cm *¾ in* thick, and attain a weight of 7 kg *15 lb*. True to name, the plant is extremely offensive in scent.

The largest known inflorescence as distinct from the largest of all blooms is that of *Puya raimondii*, a rare Bolivian monocarpic member of the Bromeliaceae family with an erect panicle (diameter 2·4 m *8 ft*) which emerges to a height of 10·7 m *35 ft*. Each of these bears up to 8000 white blooms (see also Slowest flowering plant above).

The flower-spike of an agave was in 1974 measured to be 15·8 m *52 ft* long in Berkeley, California, USA.

The world's largest blossoming plant is the giant Chinese wisteria (*Wisteria sinensis*) at Sierra Madre, California, USA. It was planted in 1892 and now has branches 152 m *500 ft* long. It covers nearly an acre, weighs 228 tonnes *225 tons* and has an estimated 1 500 000 blossoms during its blossoming period of 5 weeks, when up to 30 000 people pay admission to visit it.

The largest bloom of any indigenous British flowering plant is that of the Wild white water lily (*Nymphaea alba*), which measures 15 cm *6 in* across.

Most valuable

The Burpee Co $10 000 prize offered in 1954 for the first all-white marigold was won on 12 Aug 1975 by Alice Vonk of Sully, Iowa, USA.

Largest arrangement

The largest arrangement of a single variety of flower was made by Johan Weisz, floral designer of Amsterdam, and 15 assistants at the City Hall, Aalsmeer, Netherlands from 23–25 Sept 1986. It consisted of 35 000 'Zurella' roses and measured 21·8 m *71 ft 6 in* in length, 7·68 m *25 ft 2 in* in width and 7·59 m *24 ft 11 in* high.

Largest bouquet

Thirty-six people took 335 hr to make an 11·23 m *36 ft 10 in* high bouquet of 9299 flowers at Annecy, France on 19 Sept 1986.

Largest wreath

The largest wreath constructed was the wreath built by The Farm Stand, wholesale nurserymen of Walworth, New York, USA in November 1985 measuring 30·68 m *100 ft 8 in* in diameter and weighing 4463 kg *9840 lb*.

Longest daisy chain

The longest daisy chain, made in 7 hr, was one of 2·12 km *6980 ft 7 in* by villagers of Good Easter, Chelmsford, Essex on 27 May 1985. The team is limited to 16.

Largest rhododendron

The largest species of rhododendron is the scarlet *Rhododendron arboreum*, examples of which reach a height of 19·8 m *65 ft* on Mt Japfu, Nagaland, India. The cross-section of the trunk of a *Rhododendron giganteum*, reputedly 27·43 m *90 ft* high from Yunnan, China is preserved at Inverewe Gardens, Highland, Scotland.

The largest in the United Kingdom is one 7·60 m *25 ft* tall and 82·90 m *272 ft* in circumference at Government House, Hillsborough, Co. Down, Northern Ireland. A specimen 10·65 m *35 ft* high and 99 cm *3 ft 3 in* in circumference has been measured at Tregothan, Truro.

Longest philodendron

A philodendron 224·0 m *735 ft* in length grows in the home of Mr M J Linhart in Thornton, Leicestershire.

Largest rose tree

A 'Lady Banks' rose tree at Tombstone, Arizona, USA has a trunk 101 cm *40 in* thick, stands 2·74 m *9 ft* high and covers an area of 499 m² *5380 ft²* supported by 68 posts and several thousand feet of piping. This enables 150 people to be seated under the arbour. The cutting came from Scotland in 1884.

Smallest sunflower

A fully-mature sunflower measuring a mere 5·6 cm *2·2 in* tall was grown by Michael Lenke in Lake Oswego, Oregon, USA in 1985 using a patented 'Bonsai' technique.

ORCHIDS
Tallest

The largest of all orchids is *Grammatophyllum speciosum*, native to Malaysia. Specimens have been recorded up to 7·62 m *25 ft* in height.

Largest flower

The largest orchid flower is that of *Phragmipedium caudatum*, found in tropical areas of America. Its petals grow up to 46 cm *18 in* long, giving it a maximum outstretched diameter of 91 cm *3 ft*. The flower is, however, much less bulky than that of the Stinking corpse lily (see above). *Galeola foliata*, a saprophyte of the Vanilla family, has been recorded at a height of 15 m *49 ft*. It grows in the decaying rain forests of Queensland, Australia but is not free standing.

The first flowering in Britain of *Grammatophyllum wallisii* from Mindanao, Philippines at Burnham Nurseries, Kingsteignton, Devon in 1982 produced 557 flowers.

Smallest

The smallest orchid is *Platystele jungermannoides*, found in Central America. Its flowers are 1 mm *0·04 in* across.

Most expensive

The highest price ever paid for an orchid is 1150 guineas (£1207·50), paid by Baron Schröder to Sanders of St Albans for an *Odontoglossum crispum* (variety *pittianum*) at an auction by Protheroe & Morris of Bow Lane, London on 22 Mar 1906. A Cymbidium orchid called 'Rosanna Pinkie' was sold in the United States for $4500 in 1952.

FRUITS AND VEGETABLES
Most and least nutritive

An analysis of the 38 commonly eaten raw (as opposed to dried) fruits shows that the one with the highest calorific value is avocado (*Persea americana*), with 741 calories per edible pound or *163 cals per 100 g*. That with the lowest value is cucumber with 73 calories per pound *16 cals per 100 g*. Avocados probably originated in Central and South America and also contain vitamins A, C and E and 2·2 per cent protein.

Chilli

The tallest chilli plant was one of 6·6 m *21 ft 7 in* grown by Shri Kishan Joshi of Almora, India in 1985–6.

Cucumber

Mrs Eileen Chappel of Bowen Hills, Queensland, Australia grew a cucumber weighing 26·8 kg *59 lb* in March 1988.

Rarest plant ● In May 1983 it was reported that there was a sole surviving specimen of the Lady's slipper orchid (*Cypripedium calceolus*) in Britain. (Photo: Bruce Coleman)

Peach

The largest peach reported in Britain is one of 411 g *14½ oz*, 30·4 cm *12 in* in August 1984 from a 26-year-old Italian tree grown by Mrs Jean Bird of London SW6.

Pineapple

A pineapple weighing 7·96 kg *17 lb 8 oz* was harvested by Dole Philippines Inc. at South Cotabato, Philippines in November 1984. Pineapples up to 13 kg *28·6 lb* were reported in 1978 from Tarauaca, Brazil.

Potato

A record display of 369 varieties of potato (*Solanum tuberosum*) was mounted on BBC *Record Breakers* by Donald MacLean on 16 Sept 1984.

HERBS

Herbs are not botanically defined but consist of plants whose leaves or roots are of culinary or medicinal value. The most heavily consumed is coriander (*Coriandrum sativum*). It is used in curry powder, confectionery, in bread and in gin.

FERNS
Largest

The largest of all the more than 6000 species of fern is the Tree fern (*Alsophila excelsa*) of Norfolk Island, in the South Pacific, which attains a height of up to 18·28 m *60 ft*.

The highest in Britain is a bracken *Pteridium aquilinum* measuring over 4·8 m *16 ft* in Ruislip, Middlesex in 1970.

Smallest

The world's smallest ferns are *Hecistopteris pumila*, found in Central America, and *Azolla caroliniana*, which is native to the United States and has fronds down to 12 mm *½ in*.

GRASSES
Commonest

The world's commonest grass is *Cynodon dactylon* or Bermuda grass. The 'Callie' hybrid, selected in 1966, grows as much as 15·2 cm *6 in* a day and stolons reach 5·5 m *18 ft* in length.

Fastest growing

Some species of the 45 genera of bamboo have been measured to grow at up to 91 cm *36 in* per day (0·00003 km/h *0·00002 mph*).

Tallest

A Thorney bamboo culm (*Bambusa arundinacea*) felled at Pattazhi, Travancore, India in November 1904 measured 37·0 m *121½ ft*. The tallest of the 160 grasses found in Great Britain is the Common reed (*Phragmites communis*), which reaches a height of 2·97 m *9 ft 9 in*.

Shortest

The shortest grass native to Great Britain is the very rare sand bent (*Mibora minima*) from Anglesey, which has a maximum growing height of under 15 cm *6 in*.

LEAVES
Largest

The largest leaves of any plant belong to the Raffia palm (*Raphia raffia*) of the Mascarene Islands in the Indian Ocean, and the Amazonian bamboo palm (*R. toedigera*) of South America, whose leaf blades may measure up to 19·81 m *65 ft* in length with petioles up to 3·96 m *13 ft*.

The largest undivided leaf is that of *Alocasia macrorrhiza*, found in Sabah, East Malaysia. One found in 1966 was 3·02 m *9 ft 11 in* long and 1·92 m *6 ft 3½ in* wide, with a unilateral area of 3·17 m² *34·2 ft²*.

The largest leaves to be found in outdoor plants in Great Britain are those of *Gunnera manicata* from Brazil with leaves 1·82–3·04 m *6–10 ft* across on prickly stems 1·52–2·43 m *5–8 ft* long.

Fourteen-leafed clover

A fourteen-leafed white clover (*Trifolium repens*) was found by Randy Farland near Sioux Falls, South Dakota, USA on 16 June 1975. A fourteen-leafed red clover (*Trifolium pratense*) was also reported by Paul Haizlip, 12 at Bellevue, Washington, USA on 22 June 1987.

SEEDS
Largest

The largest seed in the world is that of the Double coconut or Coco de mer (*Lodoicea seychellarum*), the single-seeded fruit of which may weigh 18 kg *40 lb*. This grows only in the Seychelles, in the Indian Ocean.

Smallest

The smallest seeds are those of epiphytic orchids, at 35 000 000 to the oz (cf. grass pollens at up to 6 000 000 000 grains/oz). A single plant of the American ragweed can generate 8 000 000 000 pollen grains in 5 hours.

Most viable

The most protracted claim for the viability of seeds is that made for the Arctic lupin (*Lupinus arcticus*) found in frozen silt at Miller Creek in the Yukon, Canada in July 1954 by Harold Schmidt. The seeds were germinated in 1966 and were dated by the radiocarbon method of associated material to at least 8000 BC and more probably to 13 000 BC.

Most conquering conker

The highest recorded battle honours for an untreated conker (fruit of the Common horse-chestnut or *Aesculus hippocastanum*) is a 'five thousander plus', which won the BBC Conker Conquest in 1954. A professor of botany has however opined that this heroic specimen might well have been a 'ringer', probably an ivory or tagua nut (*Phytelephas macrocarpa*). The Guinness Book of Records *will not publish any category for the largest collection of conkers for fear that trees might suffer wholesale damage.*

HEDGES

Tallest

The world's tallest hedge is the Meikleour beech hedge in Perthshire. It was planted in 1746 and has now attained a trimmed height of 26 m *85 ft.* It is 550 m *600 yd* long. Some of its trees now exceed 32 m *105 ft.*

Tallest yew

The tallest yew hedge in the world is in Earl Bathurst's Park, Cirencester, Gloucestershire, England. It was planted in 1720, runs for 155 m *170 yd*, reaches 11 m *36 ft*, is 4·5 m *15 ft* thick at its base and takes 20 man-days to trim.

Tallest box

The tallest box hedge is 10·7 m *35 ft* in height at Birr Castle, Offaly, Ireland dating from the 18th century.

TREES AND WOOD

Tallest

According to the researches of Dr A. C. Carder, the tallest tree ever measured was an Australian Eucalyptus (*Eucalyptus regnans*) at Watts River, Victoria, Australia, reported in 1872 by trained forester William Ferguson. It measured 132·58 m *435 ft* and almost certainly measured over 152·4 m *500 ft* originally. A *Eucalyptus regnans* at Mt Baw Baw, Victoria, Australia is believed to have measured 143 m *470 ft* in 1885. The closest measured rivals to these champions have been:

m	ft	
126·5	415	Douglas-Fir *Pseudotsuga menziesii*, Lynn Valley, British Columbia, 1902
119·7	393	The Mineral Douglas-fir *Pseudotsuga menziesii*, Washington State, USA, 1905
115·8	380	Nisqually fir *Pseudotsuga menziesii*, Nisqually River, Washington State, USA, 1899
114·3	375	Cornthwaite Mountain ash *Eucalyptus regnans*, Thorpdale, Victoria, Australia, 1880
*112	367·6	Coast redwood *Sequoia sempervirens*, Guerneville, California, USA, 1873

* Tallest standing tree in the world. It is possible that the 'Harry Cole' tree, Humboldt County, California, is at least 112·77 m *370 ft* tall since it still has a growing top; it measured 111·98 m *367·4 ft* in 1964.

Currently the tallest standing broadleaf tree is a Mountain ash in the Styx Valley, Tasmania at 99 m *325 ft.*

The tallest trees in Great Britain are a Grand fir (*Abies grandis*) at Strone, Cairndow, Argyllshire and Douglas-firs at The Hermitage, Perth, and in Moniac Glen, Inverness. In June 1985 all were 61–62 m *200–203 ft*. Only the Strone Grand fir can be measured from both sides. At 62 m *203 ft* and still making visible annual increase, this is the best claimant. The tallest in England is a Douglas-fir (*Pseudotsuga menziesii*) measured at 53·0 m *174 ft* at Broadwood, Dunster, Somerset. The tallest measured in Northern Ireland is a Giant Sequoia (*Sequoiadendron giganteum*), measured in 1983 to be 50 m *164 ft* tall at Caledon Castle, County Tyrone. The tallest in Wales is a grand fir at Leighton Park, Powys (pl. 1886) measured in 1982 to be 58 m *190 ft.*

The tallest tree in Ireland is a Sitka spruce (*Picea sitchensis*) 50·59 m *166 ft* tall at Curraghmore, Waterford, measured in March 1974.

TALLEST TREES IN THE BRITISH ISLES
(By species)

		m	ft
ALDER (Italian)	Westonbirt, Gloucester	30	98
ALDER (Common)	Ashburnham Park, East Sussex	32	105
ASH	Old Roar Ghyll, St. Leonards, East Sussex	41	135
BEECH	Beaufront Castle, Hexham, Northumberland	44	144
BEECH (Copper)[1]	Chart Park Golf Course, Dorking, Surrey	38	124
BIRCH (Swedish)	Taymouth Castle, Perthshire	29	110
CEDAR (Blue Atlas)	Brockhampton Pk, Hereford & Worcs	38	125
CEDAR (of Lebanon)	Leaton Knolls, Shropshire	42	140
CHESTNUT (Horse)	Ashford Chase, Petersfield, Hampshire	39	130
CHESTNUT (Sweet)	Godinton Park, Ashford, Kent	37	122
CYPRESS (Lawson)	Endsleigh, Tavistock, Devon	40	133
CYPRESS (Leyland)	Bicton, Sidmouth, Devon	36	118
CYPRESS (Monterey)	Bicton, Sidmouth, Devon	38	124
DOUGLAS FIR	The Hermitage, Perth, Tayside	61+	200+
ELM[2] (Huntingdon)	Howlett's Park Zoo, Canterbury, Kent	40	132
ELM[2] (Smooth Leaf)	North Inch, Perth, Tayside	40	132
ELM (Wych)[2]	Rossie Priory, Tayside	42	138
EUCALYPTUS (Blue Gum)	Glencormack, Co. Wicklow	44	144
GRAND FIR	Strone, Cairndow, Strathclyde	62	203
GINK-GO	Linton Park, Maidstone, Kent	30	98
HEMLOCK (Western)	Murthly Castle, Dunkeld, Tayside	52	170
HOLLY	Ashburnham Park, Battle, East Sussex	24	80
HORNBEAM	Wrest Park, Shefford, Bedfordshire	32	105
LARCH (European)	Glenlee, Dumfries & Galloway	46	150
LARCH (Japanese)	Blair Castle, Tayside	37	123
LIME	Duncombe Park, Helmsley, North Yorkshire	45	150
METASEQUOIA	Leonardslee, West Sussex	29	95
MONKEY PUZZLE	Lochnaw, Dumfries & Galloway	29	95
OAK (Common)	Leeds Castle, Maidstone, Kent	41	135
OAK (Sessile)	Whitfield Ho., Hereford & Worcs	42	140
OAK (Red)	Cowdray Park, Midhurst, West Sussex	35	115
OAK (Turkey)	Knightshayes, Tiverton, Devon	42	138
PEAR	Borde Hill, Cuckfield, West Sussex	19	64
PINE (Corsican)	Adhurst, St. Mary, Petersfield, Hampshire	46	150
PLANE	Bryanston School, Blandford, Dorset	48	156
POPLAR (Black Italian)	Fairlawne, Kent	46	150
POPLAR (Black, native)	Longner Hall, Shrewsbury, Shropshire	37	124
POPLAR (Lombardy)	Marble Hill, Twickenham, G. London	39	130
REDWOOD (Coast)	Bodnant, Conway, Gwynedd	45	148
SILVER FIR	Arninglas Ho, Strathclyde	54	176
SPRUCE (Sitka)	River Findhorn, Nairn	59	195
SYCAMORE	Lennoxlove, Haddington, Lothian	40	132
TULIP-TREE	Taplow House, Buckinghamshire	36	120
WALNUT	Gayhurst, Newport Pagnell, Buckinghamshire	24	80
WALNUT (Black)	Bisham Abbey, Buckinghamshire	36	118
WELLINGTONIA	Castle Leod, Strathpeffer, Easter Ross	51	167
WILD SERVICE	Gatton Manor, Surrey	26	87
WILLOW (Weeping)	Ashford Chase, Petersfield, Hampshire	24	79
WINGNUT (Caucasian)	Abbotsbury, Weymouth, Dorset	35	115
YEW	Close Walks, Midhurst, West Sussex	29	95

[1] It was toppled by severe winds on 16th Oct 1987. On the night of 16–17 Oct 1987 an estimated 15 million trees were destroyed by high winds at an estimated cost of £15 million.

[2] It was estimated in 1980 that more than 17 million of the 23 million elms in southern England had since 1968 been killed by the fungus that causes Dutch elm disease Ceratocystis ulmi.

Christmas

The world's tallest cut Christmas tree was a 67·36 m *221 ft* tall Douglas-fir (*Pseudotsuga menziesii*) erected at Northgate Shopping Center, Seattle, Washington, USA in December 1950.

The tallest Christmas tree erected in Britain was an 25·98 m *85 ft 3¼ in* long spruce from Norway erected for the Canterbury Cathedral appeal on the South Bank, London on 20 Nov 1975.

Most massive

The most massive living thing on Earth is the biggest known Giant Sequoia (*Sequoiadendron giganteum*) named the 'General Sherman', standing 83·8 m *274·9 ft* tall, in the Sequoia National Park, California, USA. It has a true girth of 34·9 m *114·6 ft* (1980) (at 1·52 m *5 ft* above the ground). The 'General Sherman' has been estimated to contain the equivalent of 600 120 board feet of timber, sufficient to make 5 000 000 000 matches. The foliage is blue-green, and the red-brown tan bark may be up to 61 cm *24 in* thick in parts. Estimates place its weight, including its root system, at 2500 tonnes but the timber is light (288·3 kg/m³ *18 lb/ft³*). This 2500-year-old monster has an annual growth rate of almost a millimetre (¹/₂₅ *in*)–the volume contained in a tree 15 m *49·2 ft* tall and 30 cm *1 ft* in diameter. The largest known petrified tree is one of this species with a 89·9 m *295 ft* trunk near Coaldale, Nevada, USA.

The seed of a 'big tree' weighs only 4·7 mg *1/6000th of an oz*. Its growth at maturity may therefore represent an increase in weight of 1 300 000 million-fold.

The tree canopy covering the greatest area is the great Banyan *Ficus benghalensis* in the Indian Botanical Garden, Calcutta with 1775 prop or supporting roots and a circumference of 412 m *1350 ft*. It covers overall some 1·2 ha *3 acres* and dates from *ante* 1787. However, it is reported that a 550-year-old Banyan tree (known as 'Thimmamma Marrimanu') in Gutibayalu village near Kadiri Taluk, Andhra Pradesh, India spreads over 2·1 ha *5·2 acres.*

Greatest girth

'El Arbol del Tule', in the state of Oaxaca, in Mexico is a 41 m *135 ft* tall Montezuma cypress (*Taxodium mucronatum*) with a girth of 35·8 m *117·6 ft* at a height of 1·52 m *5 ft* above the ground in 1982. A figure of 51 m *167 ft* in circumference was reported for the pollarded European chestnut (*Castanea sativa*) – the 'Tree of the 100 Horses' (Castagno di Cento Cavalli) on Mount Etna, Sicily, Italy in 1972. Measurements to 54·5 m *180 ft* have been attributed to Baobab trees (*Adansonia digitata*).

The tree of greatest girth in Britain is a sweet ('Spanish') chestnut (*Castanea sativa*) in the grounds of Canford School, near Poole, Dorset, with a bole 13·33 m *43 ft 9 in* in circumference. The largest-girthed living British oak is one at Bowthorpe Farm near Bourne, south Lincolnshire, measured in September 1973 to be 11·91 m *39 ft 1 in*. The largest 'maiden' (i.e. not pollarded) oak is the Majesty Oak at Fredville Park, near Nonington, Kent, with girth 11·60 m *38 ft 1 in* (1973). The largest yew with a clear bole at 1·52 m *5 ft* is 10·79 m *35 ft 5 in* at Ulcombe Church, Kent.

Fastest growing

Discounting bamboo, which is not botanically classified as a tree but as a woody grass, the fastest rate of growth recorded is 10·74 m *35 ft 3 in* in 13 months by an *Albizzia falcata* planted on 17 June 1974 in Sabah, Malaysia. The youngest recorded for a tree to reach 30·48 m *100 ft* is 64 months for one of the species planted on 24 Feb 1975, also in Sabah.

Slowest growing

The speed of growth of trees depends largely upon conditions, although some species, such as box and yew, are always slow-growing. The extreme is represented by the *Dioon edule* (Cycadaceae) measured in Mexico in 1981–86 by Dr Charles M. Peters. He found the average annual growth rate to be 0·76 mm *0.03 in* and a 120-year old specimen of 9·9 cm *3·9 in* tall. The growing of miniature trees or *bonsai* is an oriental cult mentioned as early as *c.* 1320.

Greatest storm damage *UK*

An estimated 15 million trees, many of which will not be replaced for at least a century, were destroyed by the high winds which swept across southern and eastern England on the night of 16–17 October 1987. The severity of the of the storm had not been predicted.

The worst affected area was Kent; at Manston, a mean wind speed of 111 km/h *69 mph* (Beaufort Scale Hurricane Force: 117 km/h *73 mph* and over) was recorded although gusts of 177 km/h *110 mph* were experienced elsewhere. The town of Sevenoaks, Kent was reduced to 'Oneoak' when it lost 6 of its famous trees. At the Royal Botanical Gardens, Kew, west London a third of the trees were uprooted, and an estimated 1000 trees fell in London's Hyde Park, St James's Park and Green Park.

The devastation is certainly the worst that has occurred since the outbreak of Dutch elm disease *Ceratocystis ulmi* in the late 1960s which destroyed over 17 million elms in southern England.

Oldest

The oldest recorded tree was a Bristlecone pine (*Pinus longaeva*) designated WPN-114, which grew at 3275 m *10 750 ft* above sea level on the north-east face of Mt Wheeler, eastern Nevada, USA. It was found to be 5100 years old. The oldest known *living* tree is the Bristlecone pine named 'Methuselah' at 3050 m *10 000 ft* in the California side of the White Mountains, confirmed as 4600 years old. In March 1974 it was reported that this tree had produced 48 live seedlings. Dendrochronologists estimate the *potential* life-span of a Bristlecone pine at nearly 5500 years, but that of a California big tree (*Sequoia giganteum*) at perhaps 6000 years. No single cell lives more than 30 years.

Of all British trees that with the longest life is the Yew (*Taxus baccata*), for which a maximum age well in excess of 1000 years is usually conceded. The oldest known is the Fortingall Yew near Aberfeldy, Perthshire, part of which still grows. In 1777 this tree was over

15·24 m *50 ft* in girth and it cannot be much less than 3500 years old today.

Earliest species

The earliest species of tree still surviving is the Maidenhair tree (*Ginkgo biloba*), of Zhexiang, China, which first appeared about 160 000 000 years ago, during the Jurassic era. It was 'rediscovered' by Kaempfer (Netherlands) in 1690 and reached England *c.* 1754. It has been grown in Japan since *c.* 1100 where it was known as *ginkyō* ('silver apricot') and is now known as *icho*.

Most leaves

Little work has been done on the laborious task of establishing which species has most leaves. A large oak has perhaps 250 000 but a cypress may have some 45–50 million leaf scales.

Remotest

The tree believed to be the remotest from any other is a Norwegian spruce, the only one on Campbell Island, Antarctica. Its nearest companion would be over 145 km *120 miles* away on the Auckland Islands.

Rarest

A single specimen of the cafe marron bush *Romosmania heterophylla* survives at the Royal Botanical Gardens, Kew, west London. It is 12·7 cm *5 in* tall and was last seen in Mauritius in 1940.

Most expensive

The highest price ever paid for a tree is $51 000 for a single Starkspur Golden Delicious apple tree from near Yakima, Washington, USA, bought by a nursery in Missouri in 1959.

Largest forest

The largest afforested areas in the world are the vast coniferous forests of the northern USSR, lying between latitude 55° N and the Arctic Circle. The total wooded area amounts to 1100 million ha *2 700 000 000 acres* (25 per cent of the world's forests), of which 38 per cent is Siberian larch. The USSR is 34 per cent afforested.

The largest forest in England is Kielder Forest (29 273 ha *72 336 acres*), in Northumberland. The largest in Wales is the Coed Morgannwg (Forest of Glamorgan) (17 221 ha *42 555 acres*). Scotland's most extensive forest is the Glen Trool Forest (20 791 ha *51 376 acres*) in Kirkcudbright, Dumfries & Galloway. The United Kingdom is 7 per cent afforested.

Longest avenue

The longest avenue of trees has been the now partly felled private avenue of 1750 beeches in Savernake Forest near Marlborough, Wiltshire. It measures 5·79 km *3·6 miles*.

Heaviest wood

The heaviest of all woods is Black ironwood (*Olea laurifolia*), also called South African ironwood, with a specific gravity of up to 1·49, and weighing up to 1490 kg/m³ *93 lb/ft³*.

The heaviest British wood is boxwood (*Buxus sempervirens*) with an extreme of 1025 kg/m³ *64 lb/ft³*.

Lightest wood

The lightest wood is *Aeschynomene hispida*, found in Cuba, which has a specific gravity of 0·044 and a weight of only 44 kg/m³ *2¾ lb/ft³*.

Largest private park ● The largest private park in the United Kingdom is Woburn Park (1200 ha *3000 acres*), near Woburn Abbey, the seat of the Dukes of Bedford. The world famous herd of rare Père David's deer can be seen to the left of the picture. (Photo: Woburn Abbey)

The wood of the Balsa tree (*Ochroma pyramidale*) is of very variable density—between 40 and 384 kg/m³ *2½ and 24 lb/ft³*. The density of cork is 240 kg/m³ *15 lb/ft³*.

Kingdom Protista

Largest

The largest protozoans in terms of volume which are known to have existed were calcareous foraminifera (Foraminiferida) belonging to the genus *Nummulites*, a species of which, in the Middle Eocene rocks of Turkey, attained 22 cm *8·6 in* in diameter. The largest existing protozoan, a species of the fan-shaped *Stannophyllum* (Xenophyophorida), can exceed this in length (25 cm *9·8 in* has been recorded) but not in volume.

Smallest Protophytes

The smallest is the marine microflagellate alga *Micromonas pusilla*, with a diameter of less than 2 microns or micrometres (2×10^{-6} m) or *0·00008 in*.

Fastest

The protozoan *Monas stigmatica* has been measured to move a distance equivalent to 40 times its own length in a second. No human can cover even 7 times his own length in a second.

Fastest reproduction

The protozoan *Glaucoma*, which reproduces by binary fission, divides as frequently as every three hours. Thus in the course of a day it could become a '6 greats grandparent' and the progenitor of 510 descendants.

Kingdom Fungi

Largest

Martin Mortenson, a science teacher at Dodgeland Junior High, Reeseville, Wisconsin, USA, found a Puff ball (*Calvatia gigantea*) 194·3 cm *76½ in* in circumference in 1985. A 32·6 kg *72 lb* example of the edible mushroom (*Polyporus frondosus*) was reported by Joseph Opple near Solon, Ohio, USA in September 1976. The largest officially recorded tree fungus was a specimen of *Oxyporus* (*Fomes*) *nobilissimus*, measuring 142 cm *56 in* by 94 cm *37 in* and weighing at least 136 kg *300 lb* found by J. Hisey in Washington State, USA in 1946.

The largest recorded in the United Kingdom is an Ash fungus (*Fomes fraxineus*) measuring 127 cm by 38 cm *50 in* by *15 in* wide, found by the forester A. D. C. LeSueur on a tree at Waddesdon, Buckinghamshire in 1954.

Most poisonous toadstool

The yellowish-olive Death cap (*Amanita phalloides*) is regarded as the world's most poisonous fungus. It is found in England. From 6 to 15 hours after tasting, the effects are vomiting, delirium, collapse and death. Among its victims was Cardinal Giulio di' Medici, Pope Clement VII (b. 1478) on 25 Sept 1534.

In the United Kingdom there were 39 fatalities from fungus poisoning between 1920 and 1950. As the poisonous types are mostly *Amanita* varieties, it is reasonable to assume that the deaths were predominantly due to *Amanita phalloides*. The most recent fatality was probably in 1960.

Aeroflora

Fungi were once classified in the subkingdom Protophyta of the kingdom Protista. The highest total fungal spore count was 161 037 per m³ near Cardiff on 21 July 1971. A plant tree pollen count of 2160 per m³ was recorded near London on 9 May 1971. The lowest counts of airborne allergens are nil.

The highest recorded grass pollen count in Britain was one of 2824 per m³ recorded at Aberystwyth on 29 June 1961.

Kingdom Procaryota

Earliest

The earliest life form reported from Britain is *Kakabekia barghoorniana*, a micro-organism similar in form to an orange slice, found near Harlech, Gwynedd, Wales in 1964 and this has been dated to 4000 million years ago in July 1986.

BACTERIA

Antonie van Leeuwenhoek (1632–1723) was the first to observe bacteria, in 1675. The largest of the bacteria is the sulphur bacterium *Beggiatoa mirabilis*, which is from 16 to 45 microns in width and which may form filaments several millimetres long.

The bacteria *Thermoactinomyces vulgaris* have been found alive in cores of mud taken from the bottom of Windermere, Cumbria, England and have been dated to 1500 years before the present.

Smallest free-living entity

The smallest of all free-living organisms are pleuropneumonia-like organisms (PPLO) of the *Mycoplasma*. One of these, *Mycoplasma laidlawii*, first discovered in sewage in 1936, has a diameter during its early existence of only 100 millimicrons, or *0·000004 in*. Examples of the strain known as H.39 have a maximum diameter of 300 millimicrons and the weight is estimated at $1·0 \times 10^{-16}$ gramme. Thus a 190-tonne Blue whale would weigh $1·9 \times 10^{24}$ or 1·9 quadrillion times as much.

Highest

In April 1967 the US National Aeronautics and Space Administration (NASA) reported that bacteria had been discovered at an altitude of 41 100 m (41·13 km) *135 000 ft (25·56 miles)*.

Oldest

The oldest deposits from which living bacteria are claimed to have been extracted are salt layers near Irkutsk, USSR, dating from about 600 000 000 years ago, but the discovery was not accepted internationally. The US Dry Valley Drilling Project in Antarctica claimed resuscitated rod-shaped bacteria from caves up to a million years old.

Fastest

The rod-shaped bacillus *Bdellovibrio bacteriovorus*, by means of a polar flagellum rotating 100 times/sec, can move 50 times its own length of 2 μm per sec. This would be the equivalent of a human sprinter reaching 320 km/h *200 mph* or a swimmer crossing the English Channel in 6 min.

Toughest

The bacterium *Micrococcus radiodurans* can withstand atomic radiation of 6·5 million röntgens or 10 000 times that fatal to the average man. In March 1983 John Barras (University of Oregon, USA) reported bacteria from sulphurous sea bed vents thriving at 306°C *583°F* in the East Pacific Rise at Lat. 21°N.

VIRUSES

Largest

Dmitriy Ivanovsky (1864–1920) first reported filterable objects in 1892 but Martinus Willem Beijerink (1851–1931) first confirmed the nature of viruses in 1898. These are now defined as aggregates of two or more types of chemical (including either dna or rna) which are infectious and potentially pathogenic. The longest known is the rod-shaped *Citrus tristeza* virus with particles measuring 200×10 nm (1 nanometre $= 1 \times 10^{-9}$ m).

Smallest

The smallest known viruses are the nucleoprotein plant viruses such as the satellite of tobacco *Necrosis virus*

with spherical particles 17 nm in diameter. A putative new infectious submicroscopic organism but without nucleic acid, named a 'prion', was announced from the University of California in February 1982. Viroids (rna cores without protein coating) are much smaller than viruses. They were discovered by Theodor O. Diener (USA) in February 1972. Dr Rohwer of Bethesda, Maryland, USA stated in September 1984 that scrapie-specific protein was smaller than the concept of a 'yet to be identified prion'.

Parks, Zoos, Oceanaria, Aquaria

PARKS

Largest

The world's largest park is the Wood Buffalo National Park in Alberta, Canada (established 1922), which has an area of 45 211 197 ha *11 172 000 acres* (45 480 km² *17 560 miles²*).

The largest national park in Great Britain is the Lake District National Park which has an area of 2240 km² *866 miles²*.

ZOOS

It has been estimated that throughout the world there are some 500 zoos with an estimated annual attendance of 330 000 000.

Largest game reserve

The world's largest zoological reserve is the Etosha National Park, Namibia. Established in 1907 its area has grown to 99 525 km² *38 427 miles²*.

Oldest

The earliest known collection of animals was that set up by Shulgi, a 3rd-dynasty ruler of Ur from 2097–2094 BC at Puzurish in south-east Iraq. The oldest known zoo is that at Schönbrunn, Vienna, Austria, built in 1752 by the Holy Roman Emperor Franz I for his wife Maria Theresa. The oldest existing privately-owned zoo in the world is that of the Zoological Society of London, founded in 1826. Its collection, housed partly in Regent's Park, London (14·5 ha *36 acres*) and partly at Whipsnade Park, Bedfordshire (219 ha *541 acres*) (opened 23 May 1931), is the most comprehensive in the United Kingdom. The stocktaking on 1 Jan 1988 accounted for a total of 11 243 specimens. These comprised 2715 mammals, 1812 birds, 526 reptiles, 155 amphibians, an estimated total of 2380 fish and an estimated total of 3655 invertebrates excluding some common species. The record annual attendances are 3 031 571 in 1950 for the zoo at Regent's Park and 756 758 in 1961 in the case of that at Whipsnade.

OCEANARIA

Earliest

The world's first oceanarium is Marineland of Florida, opened in 1938 at a site 29 km *18 miles* south of St Augustine, Florida, USA. Up to 26·3 million litres *5 800 000 gal* of sea-water are pumped daily through two major tanks, one rectangular (30·48 m *100 ft* long by 12·19 m *40 ft* wide by 5·48 m *18 ft* deep) containing 1·7 million litres *375 000 gal*, and one circular (71 m *233 ft* in circumference and 3·65 m *12 ft* deep) containing 1·5 million litres *330 000 gal*. The tanks are seascaped, and thewy include coral reefs and there is even a shipwreck to be seen.

AQUARIA

Largest aquarium

The world's largest aquarium, is the Sydney Aquarium, Australia holding a total of 3 315 398 litres *875 838 gal* of water. It contains over 5000 fish displayed in a variety of habitats including 2 massive floating oceanariums, 21 major aquarium tanks and 29 smaller aquarium tanks.

THE NATURAL WORLD

CHAPTER·THREE

Longest stalactite ● The longest known stalactite in the world is this wall-supported column, which extends 59 m *195 ft* from roof to floor in the Cueva de Nerja, near Málaga, in Spain. (Photo: Juan A. Fernandez)

THE EARTH

The Earth is not a true sphere, but flattened at the poles and hence an oblate spheroid. The polar diameter of the Earth, which is 12 713·505 km *7899·806 miles*, is 42·769 km *26·575 miles* less than the equatorial diameter (12 756·274 km *7926·381 miles*). The Earth has a pear-shaped asymmetry with the north polar radius being 45 m *148 ft* longer than the south polar radius. There is also a slight ellipticity of the equator since its long axis (about longitude 37° W) is 159 m *522 ft* greater than the short axis. The greatest departures from the reference ellipsoid are a protuberance of 73 m *240 ft* in the area of Papua New Guinea and a depression of 105 m *344 ft* south of Sri Lanka, in the Indian Ocean. The greatest circumference of the Earth, àt the equator, is 40 075·02 km *24 901·46 miles*, compared with 40 007·86 km *24 859·73 miles* at the meridian. The area of the surface is estimated to be 510 065 600 km² *196 937 400 miles²*. The period of axial rotation, sidereal day, is 23 hr 56 min 4·0996 sec, mean time.

The first person to assess the mass of the Earth was Dr Nevil Maskelyne (1732–1811), who did so in Perthshire, Scotland in 1774. The modern value is $5·937 \times 10^{21}$ tonnes *5 879 000 000 000 000 000 000 tons* and its density is 5·515 times that of water. The volume is an estimated 1 083 207 000 000 km³ *259 875 300 000 miles³*. The Earth picks up cosmic dust but estimates vary widely with 30 000 tonnes/*tons* a year being the upper limit. Modern theory is that the Earth has an outer shell or lithosphere 80 km *50 miles* thick, then an outer and inner rock layer or mantle extending 2809 km *1745 miles* deep, beneath which there is an iron-rich core of radius 3482 km *2164 miles*. If the iron-rich core theory is correct, iron would be the most abundant element in the Earth. At the centre of the core the estimated density is 13·09 g/cm³, the temperature 4500°C and the pressure 364 GPa or 23 600 tons f/in².

Highest rock pinnacle ● The world's highest rock pinnacle is Ball's Pyramid near Lord Howe Island in the Pacific, which is 561 m *1843 ft* high, but has a base axis of only 200 m *220 yd*. It was first scaled in 1965. (Photo: Fotostock)

Structure and Dimensions

OCEANS

The area of the Earth covered by sea is estimated to be 361 740 000 km² *139 670 000 miles²* or 70·92 per cent of the total surface. The mean depth of the hydrosphere was once estimated to be 3795 m *12 450 ft*, but recent surveys suggest a lower estimate, of 3554 m *11 660 ft*. The total weight of the water is estimated to be $1·3 \times 10^{18}$ tons, or 0·022 per cent of the Earth's total weight. The volume of the oceans is estimated to be 1 285 600 000 km³ *308 400 000 miles³* compared to 35 000 000 km³ *8 400 000 miles³* of fresh water.

Largest

The largest ocean in the world is the Pacific. Excluding adjacent seas, it represents 45·8 per cent of the world's oceans and covers 166 240 000 km² *64 186 300 miles²* in area. The average depth is 3939 m *12 925 ft*. The shortest navigable trans-Pacific distance from Guayaquil, Ecuador to Bangkok, Thailand is 17 550 km *10 905 miles*.

Deepest

The deepest part of the ocean was first pinpointed in 1951 by HM Survey Ship *Challenger* in the Marianas Trench in the Pacific Ocean. The depth was measured by wide-band sounding at 5940 fathoms *(10 863 m)*. Subsequent visits have resulted in slightly deeper measurements by multi-beam sonar now refined to 6034 fathoms *(11 034 m)* or 6·85 miles made by the Soviet research ship *Vityaz* in 1959. On 23 Jan 1960 the US Navy bathyscaphe *Trieste* descended to the bottom at 5970 fathoms *(10 917 m)*.

A metal object, say a pound ball of steel, dropped into water above this trench would take nearly 64 min to fall to the sea bed, where hydrostatic pressure is over 1250 bars *18 000 lb/in²*.

The deepest point in the territorial waters of the United Kingdom is an area 6 cables *(1100 m)* off the island of Raasay, off Skye, in the Inner Sound at Lat. 57° 30′ 33″ N, Long. 5° 57′ 27″ W.

Largest sea

The largest of the world's seas is the South China Sea, with an area of 2 974 600 km² *1 148 500 miles²*.

Largest gulf

The largest gulf in the world is the Gulf of Mexico, with an area of 1 500 000 km² *580 000 miles²* and a shoreline of 4990 km *3100 miles* from Cabo Sable, Florida, USA, to Cabo Catoche, Mexico.

Largest bay

The largest bay in the world measured by shoreline length is Hudson Bay, northern Canada, with a shoreline of 12 268 km *7623 miles* and with an area of 822 300 km² *317 500 miles²*. The area of the Bay of Bengal is however 2 172 000 km² *839 000 miles²*.

Great Britain's largest bay is Cardigan Bay which has a 225 km *140 mile* long shoreline and measures 116 km *72 miles* across from the Lleyn Peninsula, Gwynedd to St David's Head, Dyfed in Wales.

Longest fjord

The world's longest fjord is the Nordvest Fjord arm of the Scoresby Sund in eastern Greenland, which extends inland 313 km *195 miles* from the sea. The longest Norwegian fjord is the Sogne Fjord, which extends 183 km *113·7 miles* inland from Sygnefest to the head of the Lusterfjord arm at Skjolden. It averages barely 4·75 km *3 miles* in width and has a deepest point of 1245 m *4085 ft*. If measured from Huglo along the Bømlafjord to the head of the Sørfjord arm at Odda, Hardangerfjorden can also be said to extend 183 km *113·7 miles*. The longest Danish fjord is Limfjorden (160 km *100 miles*).

Longest sea loch

Loch Fyne, Scotland, extends 67·5 km *42 miles* inland into Strathclyde.

Highest seamount

The highest known submarine mountain, or seamount, is one discovered in 1953 near the Tonga Trench, between Samoa and New Zealand. It rises 8690 m *28 500 ft* from the sea bed, with its summit 365 m *1200 ft* below the surface.

Remotest spot from land

The world's most distant point from land is a spot in the South Pacific, approximately 48° 30′ S, 125° 30′ W, which is about 2670 km *1660 miles* from the nearest points of land, namely Pitcairn Island, Ducie Island and Cape Dart, Antarctica. Centred on this spot, therefore, is a circle of water with an area of about 22 421 500 km² *8 657 000 miles²*—about 18 000 km² *7000 miles²* larger than the USSR, the world's largest country.

Most southerly

The most southerly part of the oceans is 85° 34′ S, 154° W, at the snout of the Robert Scott Glacier, 490 km *305 miles* from the South Pole.

Temperature

The temperature of the water at the surface of the sea varies from −2° C *28·5° F* in the White Sea to 35·6° C *96° F* in the shallow areas of the Persian Gulf in summer. Ice-focused solar rays have been known to heat lake water to nearly 26·8° C *80° F*. The normal Red Sea temperature is 22° C *71·6° F*. The highest temperature recorded in the ocean is 404° C *759° F*, for a spring measured by an American research submarine some 480 km *300 miles* off the American west coast, in an expedition under the direction of Professor Jack Diamond of Oregon State University, USA. Remote probes measured the temperature of the spring which was kept from vaporising by the weight of water above it.

STRAITS

Longest

The longest straits in the world are the Tatarskiy Proliv or Tartar Straits between Sakhalin Island and the USSR mainland running from the Sea of Japan to Sakhalinsky

Zaliv: 800 km *497 miles*, thus marginally longer than the Malacca Straits.

Broadest

The broadest named straits in the world are the Davis Straits between Greenland and Baffin Island with a minimum width of 338 km *210 miles*. The Drake Passage between the Diego Ramirez Islands, Chile and the South Shetland Islands is 1140 km *710 miles* across.

Narrowest

The narrowest navigable straits are those between the Aegean island of Euboea and the mainland of Greece. The gap is only 40 m *45 yd* wide at Khalkis. The Seil Sound, Inner Hebrides, Scotland narrows to a point only 6 m *20 ft* wide where the Clachan bridge joins the island of Seil to the mainland and so in consequence is said to span the Atlantic.

WAVES
Highest

The highest officially-recorded sea wave was calculated at 34 m *112 ft* from trough to crest; it was measured by Lt Frederic Margraff USN from the USS *Ramapo* proceeding from Manila, Philippines, to San Diego, California, USA, on the night of 6–7 Feb 1933, during a 68-knot (*126 km/h*) hurricane.

The highest instrumentally measured wave was one 26·2 m *86 ft* high, recorded by the British ship *Weather Reporter*, in the North Atlantic on 30 Dec 1972 in Lat. 59° N, Long. 19° W. It has been calculated on the statistics of the Stationary Random Theory that one wave in more than 300 000 may exceed the average by a factor of 4.

On 9 July 1958 a landslip caused a 160 km/h *100 mph* wave to wash 524 m *1720 ft* high along the fjord-like Lituya Bay in Alaska, USA.

Highest seismic

The highest estimated height of a *tsunami* (often wrongly called a tidal wave) was one of 85 m *278 ft*, which appeared off Ishigaki Island, Ryukyu Chain on 24 Apr 1771. It tossed a 750-ton block of coral more than 2·5 km *1·3 miles*. Tsunami (a Japanese word meaning *nami*, a wave; *tsu*, overflowing) have been observed to travel at 790 km/h *490 mph*.

Evidence for a 300 m *1000 ft* ocean wave breaking on the southern shore of Lanai, Hawaiian Islands was reported on 4 Dec 1984. This occurred about 100 000 years ago due to a meteorite, a volcanic eruption or a submarine landslide.

CURRENTS
Greatest

The greatest current in the oceans is the Antarctic Circumpolar Current or West Wind Drift Current which was measured in 1969 in the Drake Passage between South America and Antarctica to be flowing at a rate of 270 000 000 m^3 *9500 million ft^3* per sec—nearly treble that of the Gulf Stream. Its width ranges from 300–2000 km *185–1240 miles* and has a proven surface flow rate of $^4/_{10}$ of a knot *0·75 km/h*.

Strongest

The world's strongest currents are the Nakwakto Rapids, Slingsby Channel, British Columbia, Canada (Lat. 51° 05′ N, Long. 127° 30′ W) where the flow rate may reach 16 knots *29·6 km/h*.

The fastest current in British territorial waters is 10·7 knots *19·8 km/h* in the Pentland Firth between the Orkney Islands and Caithness.

TIDES

Extreme tides are due to lunar and solar gravitational forces affected by their perigee, perihelion and syzygies. Barometric and wind effects can superimpose an added 'surge' element. Coastal and sea-floor configurations can accentuate these forces. The normal interval between tides is 12 hr 25 min.

Greatest

The greatest tides occur in the Bay of Fundy, which divides the peninsula of Nova Scotia, Canada, from the United States' north-easternmost state of Maine and the Canadian province of New Brunswick. Burncoat Head in the Minas Basin, Nova Scotia, has the greatest mean spring range with 14·50 m *47·5 ft*. A range of 16·6 m *54½ ft* was recorded at springs in Leaf Basin in 1953. Tahiti experiences virtually no tide.

The place with the greatest mean spring range in Great Britain is Beachley, on the Severn, with a range of 12·40 m *40·7 ft*, compared with the British Isles' average of 4·57 m *15 ft*. Prior to 1933, tides as high as 8·80 m *28·9 ft* above and 6·80 m *22·3 ft* below datum (total range 15·60 m *51·2 ft*) were recorded at Avonmouth though an extreme range of 15·90 m *52·2 ft* for Beachley was officially accepted. In 1883 a freak tide of greater range was reported from Chepstow, Gwent.

ICEBERGS
Largest and tallest

The largest iceberg on record was an antarctic tabular 'berg of over 31 000 km^2 *12 000 miles^2* (*335 km 208 miles* long and 97 km *60 miles* wide and thus larger than Belgium) sighted 240 km *150 miles* west of Scott Island, in the South Pacific Ocean, by the USS *Glacier* on 12 Nov 1956. The 61 m *200 ft* thick arctic ice island T.1 (360 km^2 *140 miles^2*), discovered in 1946, was tracked for 17 years. The tallest iceberg measured was one of 167 m *550 ft* reported off western Greenland by the US icebreaker *East Wind* in 1958.

Most southerly arctic

The most southerly arctic iceberg was sighted in the Atlantic by a USN weather patrol in Lat. 28° 44′ N, Long. 48° 42′ W in April 1935. The southernmost iceberg reported in British home waters was sighted 96 km *60 miles* from Smith's Knoll, on the Dogger Bank, in the North Sea.

Most northerly antarctic

The most northerly antarctic iceberg was a remnant sighted in the Atlantic by the ship *Dochra* in Lat. 26° 30′ S, Long. 25° 40′ W, on 30 Apr 1894.

LAND

There is satisfactory evidence that at one time the Earth's land surface comprised a single primeval continent of 2×10^8 km^2 *80 million miles^2*, now termed Pangaea, and that this split about 190 million years ago, during the Jurassic period, into two super-continents, which are termed Laurasia (Eurasia, Greenland and Northern America) and Gondwanaland (Africa, Arabia, India, South America, Oceania and Antarctica) and named after Gondwana, India, which itself split 120 million years ago. The South Pole was apparently in the area of the Sahara as recently as the Ordovician period of *c.* 450 million years ago.

ROCKS

The age of the Earth is generally considered to be within the range of 4430 ± 20 million years, by analogy with directly measured ages of meteorites and of the Moon. However, no rocks of this great age have yet been found on the Earth since geological processes have presumably destroyed them.

Oldest

The greatest reported age for any scientifically dated rock is 4300 million years in the case of zircon crystals found by Bob Pidgeon and Simon Wilde 700 km *935 miles* in the Jack Hills, north-east of Perth, Western Australia. The find was reported in July 1986.

On 6 Apr 1988 Japanese scientists claimed that 10 small diamonds found in Zaire were 6000 million years old.

The oldest rocks in Great Britain are the original volcanic products from which were formed the gneiss and granulite rocks of the Scourian complex in the north-west Highlands and the Western Isles which were crystallised 2800 million years ago.

Largest

The largest isolated monolith in the world is the 377 m *1237 ft* high Mount Augustus (1105 m *3627 ft* above sea level), discovered on 3 June 1858, 320 km *200 miles* east of Carnarvon, Western Australia. It is an upfaulted monoclinal gritty conglomerate 8 km *5 miles* long and 3 km *2 miles* across and thus twice the size of the celebrated monolithic arkose Ayer's Rock (335 m *1100 ft*), 400 km *250 miles* south-west of Alice Springs, in Northern Territory, Australia. It was estimated in 1940 that La Gran Piedra, a volcanic plug located in the Sierra Maestra, Cuba weighs 61 355 tonnes.

CONTINENTS
Largest

Of the Earth's surface 41·25 per cent, or 210 400 000 km^2 *81 200 000 miles^2* is covered by continental masses of which only about two-thirds or 29·08 per cent of the Earth's surface (148 328 000 km^2 *57 270 000 miles^2*) is land above water, with a mean height of 756 m *2480 ft* above sea level. The Eurasian land mass is the largest, with an area (including islands) of 53 698 000 km^2 *20 733 000 miles^2*. The Afro-Eurasian land mass, separated artificially only by the Suez Canal, covers an area of 84 702 000 km^2 *32 704 000 miles^2* or 57·1 per cent of the Earth's land mass.

Smallest

The smallest is the Australian mainland, with an area of 7 618 493 km^2 *2 941 526 miles^2*, which, together with Tasmania, New Zealand, New Guinea and the Pacific Islands, is described sometimes as Oceania.

Land remotest from the sea

The point of land remotest from the sea is at Lat. 46° 16·8′ N Long. 86° 40·2′ E in the Dzoosotoyn Elisen (desert), northern Xinjiang Uygur Zizhiqu (Sin Kiang), China's most north-westerly province. It was visited by Nicholas Crane and Dr Richard Crane (GB) on 27 June 1986 and is at a straight-line distance of 2648 km *1645 miles* from the nearest open sea.

The point furthest from the sea in Great Britain is a point near Meriden, West Midlands, England, which is 117 km *72 ½ miles* equidistant from the Severn Bridge, the Dee and Mersey estuaries and the Welland estuary in the Wash. The equivalent point in Scotland is in the Forest of Atholl, north-west Tayside, 65 km *40 ½ miles* equidistant from the head of Loch Leven, Inverness Firth and the Firth of Tay.

Peninsula

The world's largest peninsula is Arabia, with an area of about 3 250 000 km^2 *1 250 000 miles^2*.

ISLANDS
Largest

Discounting Australia, which is usually regarded as a continental land mass, the largest island in the world is Greenland (renamed Kalaatdlit Nunaat on 1 May 1979), with an area of about 2 175 000 km^2 *840 000 miles^2*. There is evidence that Greenland is in fact several islands overlaid by an ice cap without which it would have an area of 1 680 000 km^2 *650 000 miles^2*. The largest sand island in the world is Fraser Island, Queensland, Australia with a 120 km *75 mile* long sand dune.

The mainland of Great Britain is the eighth largest island in the world, with an area of 218 024 km^2 *84 186 miles^2*. It stretches 971 km *603½ miles* from Dunnet Head in the north to Lizard Point in the south and 463 km *287½ miles* across from Porthaflod, Dyfed to Lowestoft, Suffolk. The island of Ireland (84 418 km^2 *32 594 miles^2*) is the 20th largest in the world.

Freshwater

The largest island surrounded by fresh water is

Structure

the Ilha de Marajó (48 000 km² *18 500 miles²*), in the mouth of the Amazon, Brazil. The world's largest inland island (i.e. land surrounded by rivers) is Ilha do Bananal, Brazil (18 130 km² *7000 miles²*). The largest island in a lake is Manitoulin Island (2766 km² *1068 miles²*) in the Canadian (Ontario) section of Lake Huron.

The largest lake island in Great Britain is Inchmurrin in Loch Lomond, Dunbarton/Stirling, Scotland with an area of 115 ha *284 acres*.

Remotest

The remotest island in the world is Bouvet Øya (formerly Liverpool Island), discovered in the South Atlantic by J. B. C. Bouvet de Lozier on 1 Jan 1739, and first landed on by Capt George Norris on 16 Dec 1825. Its position is 54° 26′ S, 3° 24′ E. This *uninhabited* Norwegian dependency is about 1700 km *1050 miles* from the nearest land—the uninhabited Queen Maud Land coast of eastern Antarctica.

The remotest *inhabited* island in the world is Tristan da Cunha, discovered in the South Atlantic by Tristão da Cunha, a Portuguese admiral, in March 1506. It has an area of 98 km² *38 miles²* (habitable area 31 km² *12 miles²*). The first permanent inhabitant was Thomas Currie, who landed in 1810. The island was annexed by the United Kingdom on 14 Aug 1816. After evacuation in 1961 (due to volcanic activity), 198 islanders returned in November 1963. The nearest *inhabited* land to the group is the island of St Helena, 2120 km *1320 miles* to the north-east. The nearest continent, Africa, is 2735 km *1700 miles* away.

The remotest of the British islets is Rockall. It is officially given as being 307 km *191 miles* west of St Kilda, Western Isles, although in June 1986 it was found by an RAF *Nimrod* to be 1509 m *4950 ft* to the south-east of its official location. This 21 m *70 ft* high rock measuring 25 m *83 ft* across was not formally annexed until 18 Sept 1955. It was 'occupied' by Tom McClean for 38 days 22 hr 52 min from 25 May to 4 July 1985. The remotest British island which has ever been inhabited is North Rona which is 70·8 km *44 miles* from the next nearest land at Cape Wrath and the Butt of Lewis. It was evacuated *c.* 1844. Muckle Flugga, off Unst, in the Shetlands, is the northernmost inhabited with a population of 3 (1971) and is in a latitude north of southern Greenland. Just to the north of it is the rock of Out Stack in Lat. 60° 51′ 35.7″ N.

Depressions ● The deepest exposed depression on land is the shore surrounding the Dead Sea, shown here, which is now 400 m *1312 ft* below sea level. The deepest point on the bed of this saltiest of all lakes is 728 m *2388 ft* below sea level. The rate of fall in the lake surface since 1948 has been 350 mm *13·78 in* per annum. The deepest part of the bed of Lake Baykal in Siberia, USSR is 1485 m *4872 ft* below sea level.

Greatest archipelago

The world's greatest archipelago is the 5600 km *3500 mile* long crescent of more than 13 000 islands which forms Indonesia.

Northernmost land

On 26 July 1978 Uffe Petersen of the Danish Geodetic Institute observed the islet of Oodaq Ø 30 m *100 ft* across, 1·36 km *1478 yd* north of Kaffeklubben Ø off Pearyland, Greenland in Lat. 83° 40′ 32.5″ N. Long. 30° 40′ 10.1″ W. It is 706·4 km *438·9 miles* from the North Pole.

Southernmost land

The South Pole, unlike the North Pole, is on land. The Amundsen–Scott South Polar station was built there at an altitude of 2855 m *9370 ft* in 1957. It is drifting bodily with the ice cap 8–9 m *27–30 ft* per annum in the direction 43° W and was replaced by a new structure in 1975.

Newest

The world's newest island is the lava islet of Fukuto Kuokanoba near Iwo Jima in the Pacific reported in January 1986. It measures 650 × 450 m *2132 × 1476 ft* and is 12 m *40 ft* above sea level.

Largest atoll

The largest atoll in the world is Kwajalein in the Marshall Islands, in the central Pacific Ocean. Its slender 283 km *176 mile* long coral reef encloses a lagoon of 2850 km² *1100 miles²*. The atoll with the largest land area is Christmas Atoll, in the Line Islands, in the central Pacific Ocean. It has an area of 642 km² *248 miles²* of which 323 km² *125 miles²* is land. Its principal settlement, London, is only 4·0 km *2½ miles* distant from another settlement, Paris.

Longest reef

The Great Barrier Reef off Queensland, north-eastern

Australia, is 2027 km *1260 statute miles* in length. Between 1959 and 1971 a large section between Cooktown and Townsville was destroyed by the Crown of Thorns starfish (*Acanthaster planci*).

DEPRESSIONS
Deepest

The deepest depression so far discovered is the bed rock in the Bentley sub-glacial trench, Antarctica at 2538 m *8326 ft* below sea level. The greatest submarine depression is an area of the north-west Pacific floor which has an average depth of 4570 m *15 000 ft*.

The lowest-lying area in Great Britain is in the Holme Fen area of the Great Ouse, in Cambridgeshire, at 2·75 m *9 ft* below sea level. The deepest depression in England is the bed of part of Lake Windermere, 28·65 m *94 ft* below sea level, and in Scotland the bed of Loch Morar, Inverness, 300·8 m *987 ft* below sea level.

Largest

The largest exposed depression in the world is the Caspian Sea basin in the Azerbaydzhani, Russian, Kazakh and Turkmen Republics of the USSR and northern Iran (Persia). It is more than 518 000 km² *200 000 miles²*, of which 371 800 km² *143 550 miles²* is lake area. The preponderant land area of the depression is the Prikaspiyskaya Nizmennost, lying around the northern third of the lake and stretching inland for a distance of up to 450 km *280 miles*.

RIVERS
Longest

The two longest rivers in the world are the Nile (*Bahr-el-Nil*) flowing into the Mediterranean, and the Amazon (*Amazonas*), flowing into the South Atlantic. Which is the longer is more a matter of definition than simple measurement. (See map)

The longest river in Great Britain is the Severn, which empties into the Bristol Channel and is 354 km *220 miles* long. (See map)

The longest river wholly in England is the Thames, which is 346 km *215 miles* long to the Nore. Its remotest source is at Seven Springs, Gloucestershire, whence the River Churn joins the other head waters. The source of the Thames proper is Trewsbury Mead, Coates,

Cirencester, Gloucestershire. The basin measures 9948 km² *3841 miles²*. The 11 tributaries of the Yorkshire Ouse aggregate 1012 km *629 miles*.

The longest river wholly in Wales is the Usk, with a length of 104·5 km *65 miles*. It rises on the border of Dyfed and Powys and flows out via Gwent into the Severn Estuary. The longest river in Scotland is the Tay, with Dundee, Tayside, on the shore of the estuary. It is 188 km *117 miles* long from the source of its remotest head-stream, the River Tummel, Tayside and has the greatest volume of any river in Great Britain, with a flow of up to 1387 m³/sec *49 000 cusec*. Of Scottish rivers the Tweed and the Clyde have most tributaries with 11 each.

The longest river in Ireland is the Shannon, which is longer than any river in Great Britain. It rises 78·6 m *258 ft* above sea level, in County Cavan, and flows through a series of loughs to Limerick. It is 386 km *240 miles* long, including the 90 km *56 mile* long estuary to Loop Head. The basin area is 15 695 km² *6060 miles²*.

Shortest

The world's shortest river with a name is the D River, Lincoln City, Oregon, USA which connects Devil's Lake to the Pacific Ocean and is 134 m *440 ft* long at low tide. It also has the shortest name of any river.

Largest basin

The largest river basin in the world is that drained by the Amazon (6448 km *4007 miles*). It covers about 7 045 000 km² *2 720 000 miles²*. It has about 15 000 tributaries and subtributaries, of which four are more than 1609 km *1000 miles* long. These include the Madeira, the longest of all tributaries, with a length of 3380 km *2100 miles*, which is surpassed by only 14 rivers in the whole world.

Longest sub-tributary

The longest sub-tributary is the Pilcomayo (1609 km *1000 miles*) in South America. It is a tributary of the Paraguay (2415 km *1500 miles* long), which is itself a tributary of the Paraná (4025 km *2500 miles*).

Longest estuary

The world's longest estuary is that of the often frozen Ob', in the northern USSR, at 885 km *550 miles*. It is up to 80 km *50 miles* wide.

AMAZON V. NILE

Longest river ● Amazonian boats at Vero-Peso market, Belem, Para State, Brazil. The picture shows the River Amazon–not the sea! Is the Amazon longer, or is the Nile? (Photo: L.C. Marigo)

Longest river ● A felucca at sunset on the River Nile, near Aswan, Egypt. Is the Nile longer, or is the Amazon? (Photo: Spectrum Colour Library)

The longest rivers
● This map shows Britain, Africa and South America in their appropriate geographical positions on the world map. The two longest rivers in the world are the Nile (*Bahr-el-Nil*) which flows into the Mediterranean, and the Amazon (*Amazonas*), flowing into the South Atlantic. With differing definitions, some people would claim that the Nile is longer, others the Amazon. The longest in Great Britain is the Severn.

The length of the Nile watercourse, as surveyed by M. Devroey (Belgium) before the loss of a few miles of meanders due to the formation of Lake Nasser, behind the Aswan High Dam, was 6670 km *4145 miles*.
This course is unitary from a hydrological standpoint and runs from the source in Burundi of the Luvironza branch of the Kagera feeder of the Victoria Nyanza via the White Nile (*Bahrel-Jebel*) to the delta in the Mediterranean.

The true source of the Amazon was discovered in 1953 to be a stream named Huarco, deriving from the Misuie Glacier (5400 m *17 715 ft*) in the Arequipa Andes of Peru. This stream progressively becomes the Toro then the Santiago then the Apurimac, which in turn is known as the Ene and then the Tambo before its confluence with the Amazon prime tributary the Ucayali. The length of the Amazon from this source to the South Atlantic via the Canal do Norte was measured in 1969 and found to be 6448 km *4007 miles* (usually quoted to the rounded-off figure of 6437 km *4000 miles*).

If a vessel navigating down the river follows the 'arm' (carrying 10 per cent of the river's water) to the south of Ilha de Marajó through the Furo Tajapuru and Furo dos Macacos into the Pará, the total length of the water-course becomes 6750 km *4195 miles*. The Rio Pará is not however a tributary of the Amazon, being hydrologically part of the basin of the Tocantins which itself flows into the Bahía de Marajó and out into the South Atlantic.

The longest river in Great Britain is the Severn, which empties into the Bristol Channel and is 354 km *220 miles* long. Its basin extends over 11 419 km² *4409 miles²*. It rises in north-western Powys, Wales, and flows through Shropshire, Hereford & Worcester, Gloucestershire and Avon and has a record 17 tributaries.

Map by Eddie Botchway.

Largest delta

The world's largest delta is that created by the Ganges (Ganga) and Brahmaputra in Bangladesh and West Bengal, India. It covers an area of 75 000 km^2 *30 000 miles^2*.

Greatest flow

The greatest flow of any river in the world is that of the Amazon, which discharges an average of 120 000 m^3/sec *4 200 000 cusec* into the Atlantic Ocean, increasing to more than 200 000 m^3/sec *7 000 000 cusec* in full flood. The lowest 1450 km *900 miles* of the Amazon average 90 m *300 ft* in depth.

Submarine

In 1952 a submarine river 400 km *250 miles* wide, known as the Cromwell current, was discovered flowing eastward 90 m *300 ft* below the surface of the Pacific for 5625 km *3500 miles* along the equator. Its volume is 1000 times that of the Mississippi.

Subterranean

In August 1958 a crypto-river was tracked by radio isotopes flowing under the Nile with 6 times its mean annual flow or 500 000 million m^3 *20 million million ft^3*.

Largest swamp

The world's largest tract of swamp is in the basin of the Pripet or Pripyat River—a tributary of the Dnieper in the USSR. These swamps cover an estimated area of 46 950 km^2 *18 125 miles^2*.

RIVER BORES

The bore on the Ch'ient'ang'kian (Hang-chou-fe) in eastern China is the most remarkable of the 60 in the world. At spring tides the wave attains a height of up to 7·5 m *25 ft* and a speed of 13–15 knots *24–27 km/h*. It is heard advancing at a range of 22 km *14 miles*. The annual downstream flood wave on the Mekong sometimes reaches a height of 14 m *46 ft*. The greatest volume of any tidal bore is that of the Canal do Norte (16 km *10 miles* wide) in the mouth of the Amazon.

The most notable of the 8 river bores in the United Kingdom is that on the Severn, which attained a measured height of 2·8 m *9¼ ft* on 15 Oct 1966 downstream of Stonebench, and a speed of 20 km/h *13 mph*. It travels from Framilode towards Gloucester.

CAVES

Longest

The most extensive cave system in the world is that under the Mammoth Cave National Park, Kentucky, USA, first discovered in 1799. On 9 Sept 1972 an exploration group led by Dr John P. Wilcox completed a connection, pioneered by Mrs Patricia Crowther on 30 Aug, between the Flint Ridge Cave system and the Mammoth Cave system, so making a combined system with a total mapped passageway length which is now over 530 km *330 miles*.

The longest cave system in Great Britain is the Ease Gill system, West Yorkshire which now has 52·4 km *32·5 miles* of explored passage.

Largest

The world's largest cave chamber is the Sarawak Chamber, Lubang Nasib Bagus, in the Gunung Mulu National Park, Sarawak, discovered and surveyed by the 1980 British–Malaysian Mulu Expedition. Its length is 700 m *2300 ft*, and its average width is 300 m *980 ft*, and it is nowhere less than 70 m *230 ft* high. It would be large enough to garage 7500 buses.

Longest stalactite

Probably the longest free-hanging stalactite in the world is one of 7 m *23 ft* in the Poll, an Ionian cave in County Clare, Ireland.

Tallest stalagmite

The tallest known stalagmite in the world is La Grande Stalagmite in the Aven Armand cave, Lozère, France, which has attained a height of 29 m *98 ft* from the cave floor. It was found in September 1897.

The tallest cave column is considered to be the 39 m *128 ft* high Flying Dragon Pillar in Nine Dragons Cave (Daji Dong), Guizhou, China.

DEEPEST CAVES

WORLD

m	ft		
1535	5036	Réseau Jean Bernard	France
1408	4619	Puerta de Illamina	Spain
1370	4495	Snieznaja Piezcziera	USSR
1353	4439	Sistema Huautla	Mexico
1219	3999	Schwersystem	Austria
1215	3986	Complesso Fighiera Corchia	Italy
1159	3802	Anou Ifflis	Algeria
1020	3346	Siebenhengste System	Switzerland
897	2943	Jama u Vjetrena brda	Yugoslavia
889	2917	Nettlebed System	New Zealand
783	2569	Jaskinia Sniezna	Poland
751	2464	Ghar Parau, Zagros	Iran

BRITISH ISLES

m	ft		
308	1010	Ogof Ffynnon Ddu	Wales
214	702	Giant's Hole System	England
179	587	Reyfad Pot	N. Ireland
140	459	Carrowmore Cavern	Rep. of Ireland
76	249	Cnoc nan Uamh	Scotland

MOUNTAINS

Highest

An eastern Himalayan peak of 8848 m *29 028 ft* above sea level on the Tibet–Nepal border (in an area first designated Chu-mu-lang-ma on a map of 1717) was discovered to be the world's highest mountain in 1852 by the Survey Department of the Government of India, from theodolite readings taken in 1849 and 1850. In 1860 its height was computed to be 8840 m *29 002 ft*. On 25 July 1973 the Chinese announced a height of 8848·2 m *29 029 ft 3 in*. It was named Mount Everest after Col. Sir George Everest, CB. (1790–1866), formerly Surveyor-General of India.

Everest's status as the world's highest mountain, maintained for 135 years (1852–1987), was challenged by K2 (formerly Godwin Austen), also known as Chogori, in the disputed Kashmiri Northern Areas of Pakistan, on 6 Mar 1987 by the US K2 Expedition. Their satellite transit surveyor yielded altitudes of between 8858 and 8908 m *29 064–29 228 ft* as against the hitherto official 19th-century figure of 8611 m *28 250 ft*, and the 20th-century proposed height of 8760 m *28 740 ft*. However, on 13 Aug 1987 the Chinese reaffirmed their heights of 8848·2 m *29 029 ft 3 in* for Everest and 8611 m *28 250 ft* for K2. The research Council in Rome announced on 23 Oct 1987 that new satellite measurements restored Everest to primacy, at 8863 m *29 078 ft*, and put K2 down to 8607 m *28 238 ft*. It was on 31 July 1954 that K2 was first climbed, by A. Campagnoni and L. Lacedelli of Italy, 14 months after the summit of Everest had been reached. (For details of Everest ascents, see under Mountaineering in Chapter 12.)

The mountain whose summit is farthest from the Earth's centre is the Andean peak of Chimborazo (6267 m *20 561 ft*), 158 km *98 miles* south of the equator in Ecuador, South America. Its summit is 2150 m *7057 ft* further from the Earth's centre than the summit of Mt Everest. The highest mountain on the equator is Volcán Cayambe (5878 m *19 285 ft*), Ecuador, in Long. 77° 58' W. A mountaineer atop the summit would be moving at 1671 km/h *1038 mph* relative to the Earth's centre due to the Earth's rotation.

The highest insular mountain in the world is Puncak Jayak (formerly Puncak Sukarno, formerly Carstensz Pyramide) in Irian Jaya, Indonesia. A survey by the Australian Universities' Expedition in 1973 yielded a height of 4884 m *16 023 ft*. Ngga Pula, now 4861 m *15 950 ft*, was in 1936 possibly c. 4910 m c. *16 110 ft* before the melting of its snow cap.

The highest mountain in the United Kingdom is Ben Nevis (1343 m *4406 ft* excluding the 3·65 m *12 ft* cairn), 6·85 km *4¼ miles* south-east of Fort William, Argyll, Scotland. It was climbed before 1720 but though acclaimed the highest in 1790 was not confirmed to be higher than Ben Macdhui (1310 m *4300 ft*) until 1847. In 1834 Ben Macdhui and Ben Nevis (Gaelic, *Beinn Nibheis*) (first reference, 1778) were respectively quoted as 1393 m *4570 ft* and 1332 m *4370 ft*. The highest mountain in England is Scafell Pike (978 m *3210 ft*) in Cumbria; in Wales the highest is Snowdon (*Yr Wyddfa*) (1085 m *3560 ft*) in Gwynedd; and the highest peak in the island of Ireland is Carrauntual (1041 m *3414 ft*) in County Kerry.

There is some evidence that, before being ground down by the ice cap, mountains in the Loch Bà area of the Isle of Mull, Strathclyde were 4575 m *15 000 ft* above sea level.

There are 577 peaks and tops over 915 m *3000 ft* in the whole British Isles and 165 peaks and 136 tops in Scotland higher than England's highest point, Scafell Pike. The highest mountain off the mainland is Sgùrr Alasdair (1008 m *3309 ft*) on Skye, named after Alexander (Gaelic, *Alasdair*) Nicolson, who made the first ascent in 1873. Mountains over 914 m *3000 ft* are called Munros and named after Mounro's Tables which were first published in 1891 by one Hugh Munro.

Unclimbed

The highest unclimbed mountain is now only the 31st highest—Zemu Gap Peak (7780 m *25 526 ft*) in the Sikkim Himalaya.

Tallest

The world's tallest mountain measured from its submarine base (3280 fathoms *6000 m*) in the Hawaiian Trough to its peak is Mauna Kea (Mountain White) on the island of Hawaii, with a combined height of 10 203 m *33 476 ft* of which 4205 m *13 796 ft* are above sea level. Another mountain whose dimensions, but not height, exceed those of Mount Everest is the volcanic Hawaiian peak of Mauna Loa (Mountain Long) at 4170 m *13 680 ft*. The axes of its elliptical base, 4975 m *16 322 ft* below sea level, have been estimated at 119 m *74 miles* and 85 km *53 miles*. It should be noted that Cerro Aconcagua (6960 m *22 834 ft*) is more than 11 826 m *38 800 ft* above the 4875 m *16 000 ft* deep Pacific abyssal plain or 13 055 m *42 834 ft* above the Peru-Chile Trench which is 290 km *180 miles* distant in the South Pacific.

Greatest ranges

The world's greatest land mountain range is the Himalaya-Karakoram, which contains 96 of the world's 109 peaks of over 7315 m *24 000 ft*. Himalaya derives from the sanskrit *him*, snow; *alaya*, home. The greatest of all mountain ranges is, however, the submarine Indian/East Pacific Oceans Cordillera extending 30 900 km *19 200 miles* from the Gulf of Aden to the Gulf of California by way of the seabed between Australia and Antarctica with an average height of 2430 km *8000 ft* above the base ocean depth.

Longest lines of sight

Vatnajökull (2118 m *6952 ft*), Iceland has been seen by refracted light from the Faeroe Islands 550 km *340 miles* distant. In Alaska Mt McKinley (6193 m *20 320 ft*) has been sighted from Mt Sanford (4949 m *16 237 ft*) from a distance of 370 km *230 miles*. McKinley, so named in 1896, was called Denali (Great One) in the Athabascan language of North American Indians and is the highest mountain in the United States.

Greatest plateau

The most extensive high plateau in the world is the Tibetan Plateau in Central Asia. The average altitude is 4875 m *16 000 ft* and the area is 200 000 km^2 *77 000 miles^2*.

Sheerest wall

Mount Rakaposhi (7772 m *25 498 ft*) rises 5·99 vertical kilometres *3·72 miles* from the Hunza Valley, Pakistan in 10 horizontal kilometres *6·21 miles* with an overall gradient of 31°.

The 975 m *3200 ft* wide north-west face of Half Dome, Yosemite, California, USA is 670 m *2200 ft* high but nowhere departs more than 7 degrees from the vertical. It was first climbed (Class VI) in 5 days in July 1957 by Royal Robbins, Jerry Gallwas and Mike Sherrick.

Highest halites

Along the northern shores of the Gulf of Mexico for 1160 km *1725 miles* there exist 330 subterranean 'mountains' of salt, some of which rise more than 18 300 m *60 000 ft* from bed rock and appear as the low salt domes first discovered in 1862.

Lowest hill

Official maps of Seria, Brunei show an artificial hillock named Bukit Thompson by the 13th hole on the Panaga Golf Course at 4·5 m *15 ft*.

WATERFALLS
Highest

The highest waterfall (as opposed to vaporised 'Bridal Veil') in the world is the Salto Angel in Venezuela, on a branch of the River Carrao, an upper tributary of the Caroni, with a total drop of 979 m *3212 ft*—the longest single drop is 807 m *2648 ft*. The 'Angel Falls' were named after the United States pilot Jimmy Angel (d. 8 Dec 1956), who recorded them in his log book on 14 Nov 1933. The falls, known by the Indians as Cherun-Meru, were first reported by Ernesto Sanchez La Cruz in 1910.

The tallest waterfall in the United Kingdom is Eas a'Chùal Aluinn, from Glas Bheinn (774 m *2541 ft*), Sutherland, Scotland, with a drop of 200 m *658 ft*. England's highest fall above ground is Caldron (or Cauldron) Snout, on the Tees, with a fall of 60 m *200 ft* in 135 m *450 ft* of cataracts, but no sheer leap. It is on the border of Durham and Cumbria. The cascade in the Gaping Gill Cave descends 111 m *365 ft*. The highest Welsh waterfall is the Pistyll-y-Llyn on the Powys-Dyfed border which exceeds 90 m *300 ft* in descent. The highest falls in Ireland are the Powerscourt Falls (106 m *350 ft*), on the River Dargle, County Wicklow.

Highest lake ● The highest steam-navigated lake in the world is Lake Titicaca, partly in Peru, and partly in Bolivia, in South America. Its maximum depth is 370 m *1214 ft* and its area about 8285 km² *3200 miles²*. (Photo: Spectrum Colour Library)

Greatest

On the basis of the average annual flow, the greatest waterfalls in the world are the Boyoma (formerly Stanley) Falls in Zaïre with 17 000 m³/sec *600 000 cusec*. The peak flow of the Guaíra (Salto das Sete Quedas) on the Alto Paraná river between Brazil and Paraguay at times attained a peak flow rate of 50 000 m³/sec *1 750 000 cusec*.

It has been calculated that, when some 5 500 000 years ago the Mediterranean basins began to be filled from the Atlantic through the Straits of Gibraltar, a waterfall 26 times greater than the Guaíra and perhaps 800 m *2625 ft* high was formed.

Widest

The widest waterfalls in the world are the Khône Falls (15–21 m *50–70 ft* high) in Laos, with a width of 10·8 km *6·7 miles* and a flood flow of 42 500 m³/sec *1 500 000 cuséc*.

LAKES AND INLAND SEAS
Largest

The largest inland sea or lake in the world is the Kaspiskoye More (Caspian Sea) in the southern USSR and Iran. It is 1225 km *760 miles* long and its total area is 360 700 km² *139 000 miles²*. Of the total area some 143 200 km² *55 280 miles²* (38·6 per cent) are in Iran, where it is named the Darya-ye-Khazar. Its maximum depth is 1025 m *3360 ft* and its surface is 28·5 m *93 ft* below sea level. Its estimated volume is 89 600 km³ *21 500 miles³* of saline water. Its surface has varied between 32 m *105 ft* (11th century) and 22 m *72 ft* (early 19th century) below sea level.

Deepest

The deepest lake in the world is Ozero (Lake) Baykal in central Siberia, USSR. It is 620 km *385 miles* long and between 32–74 km *20–46 miles* wide. In 1957 the lake's Olkhon Crevice was measured to be 1940 m *6365 ft* deep and hence 1485 m *4872 ft* below sea level.

The deepest lake in Great Britain is the 16·57 km *10·30 mile* long Loch Morar, in Inverness. Its surface is 9 m *30 ft* above sea level and its extreme depth 310 m *1017 ft*. England's deepest lake is Wast Water (78 m *258 ft*), in Cumbria. The lake with the greatest mean depth is Loch Ness with 130 m *427 ft*.

Highest

There is an unnamed glacial lake near Mount Everest at 5880 m *19 300 ft*. Tibet's largest lake, Nam Tso, with an area of 1956 km² *722 miles²*, is at 4578 m *15 060 ft*.

The highest lake in the United Kingdom is the 0·76 ha *1·9 acre* Lochan Buidhe at 1097 m *3600 ft* above sea level in the Cairngorm Mountains, Scotland. England's highest is Broad Crag Tarn (837 m *2746 ft* above sea level) on Scafell Pike, Cumbria and the highest named freshwater lake in Wales is The Frogs Pool, a tarn near the summit of Carnedd Llywelyn, Gwynedd at 830 m *2723 ft*.

Freshwater

The freshwater lake with the greatest surface area is Lake Superior, one of the Great Lakes of North America. The total area is 82 350 km² *31 800 miles²*, of which 53 600 km² *20 700 miles²* are in Minnesota, Wisconsin and Michigan, USA and 27 750 km² *11 100 miles²* in Ontario, Canada. It is 182 m *1600 ft* above sea level. The freshwater lake with the greatest volume is Lake Baykal in Siberia, USSR with an estimated volume of 23 000 km³ *5520 miles³*.

The largest lake in the United Kingdom is Lough Neagh (14·60 m *48 ft* above sea level) in Northern Ireland. It is 28·9 km *18 miles* long and 17·7 km *11 miles* wide and has an area of 381·73 km² *147·39 miles²*. Its extreme depth is 31 m *102 ft*.

Freshwater loch

The largest lake in Great Britain, and the largest inland loch in Scotland is Loch Lomond (7·0 m *23 ft* above sea level), which is 36·44 km *22·64 miles* long and has a surface area of 70·04 km² *27·45 miles²*. It is situated in the Strathclyde and Central regions and its greatest depth is 190 m *623 ft*. The lake or loch with the greatest volume is Loch Ness with 7 443 000 000 m³ *262 845 000 000 ft³*. The longest lake or loch is Loch Ness which measures 38·99 km *24·23 miles*, although the three arms of the Y-shaped Loch Awe, Argyll aggregate 40·99 km *25·47 miles*. The largest lake in England is Windermere,

Natural arches

The largest natural arch in the world is the Rainbow Bridge, Utah, USA discovered on 14 Aug 1909 with a span of 84·7 m *278 ft* and a width of more than 6·7 m *22 ft*. The highest natural arch is the sandstone arch 40 km *25 miles* west-north-west of K'ashih, Sinkiang, China, estimated in 1947 to be nearly 312 m *1000 ft* tall with a span of about 45 m *150 ft*.

Longest glaciers

It is estimated that 15 600 000 km² *6 020 000 miles²*, or 10½ per cent of the Earth's land surface, is permanently glaciated. The world's longest known glacier is the Lambert Glacier, discovered by an Australian aircraft crew in Australian Antarctic Territory in 1956–7. It is up to 64 km *40 miles* wide and, with its upper section, known as the Mellor Glacier, it measures at least 402 km *250 miles* in length. With the Fisher Glacier limb, the Lambert forms a continuous ice passage about 514 km *320 miles* long. The longest Himalayan glacier is the Siachen (75·6 km *47 miles*) in the Karakoram range, though the Hispar and Biafo combine to form an ice passage 122 km *76 miles* long. The fastest-moving major glacier is the Quarayaq in Greenland flowing 20–24 m *65–80 ft* per day.

Greatest avalanches

The greatest natural avalanches, though rarely observed, occur in the Himalayas but no estimates of their volume have been published. It was estimated that 3 500 000 m³ *120 000 000 ft³* of snow fell in an avalanche in the Italian Alps in 1885. The 400 km/h *250 mph* avalanche triggered by the Mount St. Helens eruption in Washington, USA on 18 May 1980 was estimated to measure 2800 million m³ *96 000 million ft³* (see Disasters, Chapter 11).

Natural Phenomena

EARTHQUAKES

(Seismologists record all dates with the year *first*, based not on local time but on Greenwich Mean Time).

Greatest

It is estimated that each year there are some 500 000 detectable seismic or micro-seismic disturbances of which 100 000 can be felt and 1000 cause damage. The deepest recorded hypocentres are of 720 km *447 miles* in Indonesia in 1933, 1934 and 1943.

An inherent limitation in the widely used Gutenberg–Richter scale (published in 1954) precludes its usefulness when extended to the relative strengths of the strongest earthquakes ever recorded.

The scale was named after Dr Beno Gutenberg (1889–1960) and Dr Charles Robert Richter (1900–1985). Its use of surface-wave Magnitudes, based on amplitudes of waves of a period of 20 sec, results in the 'damping' of any increase in amplitude where fault ruptures break over a length much above 60 km *37 miles*. These, however, provenly may reach a length of 800 to 1000 km *500 to 620 miles*.

This 'overload' or 'saturation effect' has resulted in the adoption since 1977 of the Kanamori scale for comparing the most massive earthquakes. Magnitudes are there defined in terms of energy release using the concept of the seismic moment, devised by K-Aki in 1966. The most massive instrumentally recorded earthquake was the cataclysmic Lebu shock south of Concepción, Chile on 1960 May 22 estimated at 10^{26} ergs. While this uniquely rates a Magnitude of 9·5 on the Kanamori scale, it ranks in only equal 4th place (with the 1922 Chilean earthquake) at Magnitude 8·3 on the Gutenberg–Richter scale.

Worst death toll

The greatest chronicled loss of life occurred in the earthquake which rocked every city of the Near East and eastern Mediterranean *c.* July 1201. Contemporary accounts estimate the loss of life at 1 100 000. Less

---

in Cumbria. It is 17 km *10½ miles* long and has a surface area of 14·74 km² *5·69 miles²*. Its greatest depth is 66·75 m *219 ft* in the northern half. The largest *natural* lake in Wales is Llyn Tegid, with an area of 4·38 km² *1·69 miles²*, although the largest lake in Wales is that formed by the reservoir at Lake Vyrnwy, where the total surface area is 453·25 ha *1120 acres*.

Freshwater loughs

The largest lough in the Republic of Ireland is Lough Corrib in Mayo and Galway. It measures 43·5 km *27 miles* in length and is 11·25 km *7 miles* across at its widest point with a total surface area of 168 km² *(65·0 miles²)*.

Lake in a lake

The largest lake in a lake is Manitou Lake (106·42 km² *41·09 miles²*) on the world's largest lake island Manitoulin Island (2766 km² *1068 miles²*) in the Canadian part of Lake Huron. The lake itself contains a number of islands.

Underground

Reputedly the world's largest underground lake is the Lost Sea, 91 m *300 ft* subterranean in the Craighead Caverns, Sweetwater, Tennessee, USA measuring 1·8 ha *4½ acres* and discovered in 1905.

Largest lagoon

Lagoa dos Patos in southernmost Brazil is 254 km *158 miles* long and extends over 10 645 km² *4110 miles²*.

OTHER FEATURES
Desert

Nearly an eighth of the world's land surface is arid with a rainfall of less than 25 cm *9·8 in* per annum. The Sahara in North Africa is the largest in the world. At its greatest length it is 5150 km *3200 miles* from east to west. From north to south it is between 1275 and 2250 km *800 and 1400 miles*. The area covered by the desert is about 8 400 000 km² *3 250 000 miles²*. The land level varies from 132 m *436 ft* below sea level in the Qattâra Depression, Egypt to the mountain Emi Koussi (3415 m *11 204 ft*) in Chad. The diurnal temperature range in the western Sahara may be more than 45° C or *80° F.*

Sand dunes

The world's highest measured sand dunes are those in the Saharan sand sea of Isaouane-n-Tifernine of east central Algeria in Lat. 26° 42′ N, Long. 6° 43′ E. They have a wave-length of 5 km *c. 3 miles* and attain a height of 430 m *1410 ft*.

Longest natural arch ● The longest natural arch in the world is the Landscape Arch in the Arches National Park, 40 km *25 miles* north of Moab in Utah, USA. This natural sandstone arch spans 88 m *291 ft* and is set about 30 m *100 ft* above the canyon floor. In one place erosion has narrowed its section to 1·82 m *6 ft*. (Photo: Spectrum Colour Library)

Largest gorge

The largest land gorge in the world is the Grand Canyon on the Colorado River in north-central Arizona, USA. It extends from Marble Gorge to the Grand Wash Cliffs, over a distance of 349 km *217 miles*. It varies in width from 6–20 km *4–13 miles* and is some 1615 m *5300 ft* deep. The submarine Labrador Basin canyon is 3440 km *c. 2150 miles* long.

Deepest canyon

The deepest canyon is El Cañón de Colca, Peru, reported in 1929 which is 3223 m *10 574 ft* deep. It was first traversed by the Polish Expedition CANOANDES' 79-kayak team from 12 May–14 June 1981. A stretch of the Kali River in central Nepal flows 5485 m *18 000 ft* below its flanking summits of the Dhaulagiri and Annapurna groups.

The deepest submarine canyon yet discovered is one 40 km *25 miles* south of Esperance, Western Australia, which is 1800 m *6000 ft* deep and 32 km *20 miles* wide.

Cliffs

The highest sea cliffs yet pinpointed anywhere in the world are those on the north coast of east Moloka'i, Hawaii near Umilehi Point, which descend 1005 m *3300 ft* to the sea at an average gradient of >55°.

The highest cliffs in north-west Europe are those on the north coast of Achill Island, in County Mayo, Ireland, which are 668 m *2192 ft* sheer above the sea at Croaghan. The highest cliffs in the United Kingdom are the 396 m *1300 ft* Conachair cliffs on St Kilda, Western Isles (425 m *1397 ft*).

The highest sheer sea cliffs on the mainland of Great Britain are at Clo Mor, 4·8 km *3 miles* south-east of Cape Wrath, Sutherland, Scotland which drop 280·7 m *921 ft*.

England's highest cliff (gradient >45°) is Great Hangman Hill, near Combe Martin, in north Devon, which descends from 318 m *1043 ft* to the sea in 300 m *984 ft*, the last 213 m *700 ft* of which is sheer.

WORLD'S STRONGEST EARTHQUAKES

Progressive list of instrumentally recorded earthquakes

Kanamori Scale Magnitudes M_s*	Gutenberg–Richter Scale Magnitude M_w*	Location	Date	
8·8	8·6	Colombia coast	1906	31 Jan
(8·6)	8·6	Assam, India	1950	15 Aug
9·0	(8¼)	Kamchatka, USSR	1952	4 Nov
9·1	(8·3)	Andreanol, Aleutian Is., USA	1957	9 Mar
9·5	(8·3)	Lebu, Chile	1960	22 May

Where $M_s = \frac{2}{3}(\log_{10}E - 11\cdot8)$ and $M_w = \frac{2}{3}[\log_{10}(2E \times 10^4) - 10\cdot7]$. Where E = energy released in dyne/cm

uncertain is the figure of 830 000 fatalities in a prolonged 'quake (ti chen) in the Shensi, Shansi and Honan provinces of China, of 1556 Feb 2 (new style) (Jan 23 os). The highest death toll in modern times has been in the Tangshan 'quake (Mag. 8·2) in eastern China on 1976 July 27 (local time was 3 a.m. July 28). A first figure published on 4 Jan 1977 revealed 655 237 killed, later adjusted to 750 000. On 22 Nov 1979 the New China News Agency unaccountably reduced the death toll to 242 000. As late as January 1982 the site of the city was still a prohibited area.

Material damage

The greatest physical devastation was in the 'quake on the Kwanto plain, Japan, of 1923 Sept 1 (Mag. 8.2, epicentre in Lat. 35° 15′ N, Long. 139° 30′ E) in Sagami Bay the sea bottom in one area sank 400 m *1310 ft*. The official total of persons killed and missing in this *Shinsai* or great 'quake and the resultant fires was 142 807. In Tōkyō and Yokohama 575 000 dwellings were destroyed. The cost of the damage was estimated at £1000 million (now £17 000 million).

Great Britain and Ireland

The total of the undisputed death toll for Great Britain is two—an apprentice, Thomas Grey, struck by falling masonry from Christ's Hospital Church, near Newgate, London at 6 p.m. on 6 Apr 1580, and another youth, Mabel Everet, who died of injuries 4 days later.

The East Anglian or Colchester earthquake of 1884 Apr 22 (9.18 a.m.) (epicentres Lat. 51° 48′ N, Long. 0° 53′ E, and Lat. 51° 51′ N, Long. 0° 55′ E) caused damage estimated at more than £12 000 to 1250 buildings. Langenhoe Church was wrecked. Windows and doors were rattled over an area of 137 250 km² *53 000 miles²* and the shock was felt in Exeter and Ostend, Belgium. It has been estimated to have been of Magnitude 5·2 on the Richter scale.

The highest instrumentally measured Magnitude is 6·0 for the Dogger Bank event of 1931 June 7. The strongest Scottish tremor occurred at Inverness at 10.45 p.m. on 1816 Aug 13, and was felt over an area of 130 000 km² *50 000 miles²*. The strongest Welsh tremor occurred in Swansea at 9.45 a.m. on 1906 June 27 (epicentre Lat. 51° 38′ N, Long. 4° W). It was felt over an area of 97 900 km² *37 800 miles²*.

No earthquake with its epicentre in Ireland has ever been instrumentally measured, though the effects of the North Wales shock of 1984 July 19 (Mag. 5 to 5·5) dislocated traffic lights in Dublin. However, there was a shock in August 1734 which damaged 100 dwellings and 5 churches.

VOLCANOES

The total number of known active volcanoes in the world is 850 of which many are submarine. The greatest active concentration is in Indonesia, where 77 of its 167 volcanoes have erupted within historic times. The name volcano derives from the now dormant Vulcano Island (from the god of fire Vulcanus) in the Mediterranean.

Greatest explosion

The greatest explosion (possibly since Santorini in the Aegean Sea, 96 km *60 miles* north of Crete, in 1628 BC) occurred at c. 10 a.m. (local time), or 3.00 a.m. GMT, on 27 Aug 1883, with an eruption of Krakatoa, an island (then 47 km² *18 miles²*) in the Sunda Strait, between Sumatra and Java, in Indonesia. 163 villages were wiped out, and 36 380 people killed by the wave it caused. Rocks were thrown 55 km *34 miles* high and dust fell 5330 km *3313 miles* away 10 days later. The explosion was recorded 4 hours later on the island of Rodrigues, 4776 km *2968 miles* away, as 'the roar of heavy guns', and was heard over 1/13th part of the surface of the globe. This explosion, estimated to have had about 26 times the power of the greatest H-bomb test (conducted by the USSR), was still only a fifth part of the intensity of the Santoríni cataclysm.

Greatest eruption

The total volume of matter discharged in the eruption of Tambora, a volcano on the island of Sumbawa, in Indonesia, 5–7 Apr 1815, was 150–180 km³. The energy of this 2245 km/h *1395 mph* eruption, which lowered the height of the island by 1250 m *4100 ft* from 4100 m *13 450 ft* to 2850 m *9350 ft*, was 8·4×10¹⁹ joules. A crater 11 km *7 miles* in diameter was formed. Some 90 000 were killed or died of famine. This compares with a probable 60–65 km³ ejected by Santorini (see above) and 20 km³ ejected by Krakatoa (see above). The internal pressure at Tambora has been estimated at 3270 kg/cm² or *20·76 tons/in²*.

The ejecta in the Taupo eruption in New Zealand c. AD 130 has been estimated at 30 000 million tonnes of pumice moving at one time at 700 km/h *400 mph*. It flattened 16 000 km² *6180 miles²* (over 26 times the devastated area of Mount St Helens which erupted in Washington State on 18 May 1980). Less than 20 per cent of the 14×10⁹ tonnes of pumice ejected in this most violent of all documented volcanic events fell within 200 km *125 miles* of the vent.

Longest lava flow

The longest lava flow in historic times is a mixture of pahoehoe ropey lava (twisted cord-like solidifications) and aa blocky lava, resulting from the eruption of Laki in 1783 in south-east Iceland which flowed 65–70 km *40·5–43·5 miles*. The largest known prehistoric flow is the Roza basalt flow in North America c. 15 million years ago, which had an unsurpassed length (480 km *300 miles*), area (40 000 km² *15 400 miles²*) and volume (1250 km³ *300 miles³*).

Largest active

Mauna Loa (meaning 'long mountain') in Hawaii has a dome 120 km *75 miles* long and 103 km *64 miles* wide with a lava flow that occupies more than 5180 km² *2000 miles²* of the island. Its pit crater, Mokuaweoweo, measures 10·4 km² *4 miles²* and is 150–180 m *500–600 ft* deep. It rises 4168 m *13 677 ft* and has averaged one eruption every 3½ years since 1832, most recently in April 1984.

Highest active

The highest volcano regarded as active is Ojos del Salado (which has fumaroles), at a height of 6885 m *22 588 ft*, on the frontier between Chile and Argentina.

Highest dormant

The highest dormant volcano is Volcán Llullaillaco (6739 m *22 109 ft*), on the frontier between Chile and Argentina.

Highest extinct

The highest extinct volcano in the world is Cerro Aconcagua ('stone sentinel') (6960 m *22 834 ft*) on the Argentinian side of the Andes. It was first climbed on 14 Jan 1897 by Mathias Zurbriggen—the highest summit climbed until 12 June 1907.

Northernmost and southernmost

The northernmost volcano is Beeren Berg (2276 m *7470 ft*) on the island of Jan Mayen (71° 05′ N) in the Greenland Sea. It erupted on 20 Sept 1970 and the island's 39 inhabitants (all male) had to be evacuated. It was possibly discovered by Henry Hudson the English navigator and explorer (d. 1611) in 1607 or 1608, but was definitely visited by Jan Jacobsz Mayen (Netherlands) in 1614. It was annexed by Norway on 8 May 1929. The Ostenso seamount (1775 m *5825 ft*) 556 km *346 miles* from the North Pole in Lat. 85° 10′ N, Long. 133° W was volcanic.

The most southerly known active volcano is Mount Erebus (3795 m *12 450 ft*) on Ross Island (77° 35′ S), in Antarctica. It was discovered on 28 Jan 1841 by the expedition of Captain (later Rear-Admiral Sir) James Clark Ross, RN (1800–62), and first climbed at 10 a.m. on 10 Mar 1908 by a British party of five, led by Professor (later Lieut-Col Sir) Tannatt William Edgeworth David (1858–1934).

Largest crater

The world's largest *caldera* or volcano crater is that of Toba, north-central Sumatra, Indonesia covering 1775 km² *685 miles²*.

GEYSERS
Tallest

The Waimangu (Maori, *'black water'*) geyser, in New Zealand, erupted to a height in excess of 457 m *1500 ft* in 1904, but has not been active since it erupted violently at 6.20 a.m. on 1 Apr 1917 and killed 4 people. Currently the world's tallest active geyser is the US National Parks' Service Steamboat Geyser, in Yellowstone National Park, Wyoming, which from 1962 to 1969 erupted with intervals ranging from 5 days to 10 months to a height of 76–115 m *250–380 ft*.

The greatest measured water discharge has been 37 850 hl *825 000 gal* by the Giant Geyser, also in Yellowstone National Park, which has been dormant since 1955. The *Geysir* ('gusher') near Mount Hekla in south-central Iceland, from which all others have been named, spurts, on occasions, to 55 m *180 ft*, while the adjacent Strokkur, reactivated by drilling in 1963, spurts at 10–15 min intervals.

Weather

The meteorological records given below necessarily relate largely to the last 140–160 years, since data before that time are both sparse and often unreliable.

Reliable registering thermometers were introduced as recently as c. 1820. The longest continuous observations have been maintained at the Radcliffe Observatory, Oxford since 1815 though discontinuous records have enabled the Chinese to assert that 903 BC was a very bad winter.

Palaeo-entomological evidence is that there was a southern European climate in England c. 90 000 BC, while in c. 6000 BC the mean summer temperature reached 19·4° C *67° F*, or 3·3° C *6° F* higher than the present. It is believed that 1·2 million years ago the world's air temperature averaged 35° C *95° F*. The earliest authentic recording of British weather which is

Hottest place ● The worst place in the world to run out of petrol or have a breakdown? In Death Valley, California, USA maximum temperatures of over 48·9° C *120° F* were recorded on 43 consecutive days, between 6 July and 17 Aug 1917. (Photo: Art Directors Photo Library)

available relates to the period 26 Aug–17 Sept 55 BC. The earliest reliably known hot summer was in AD 664 during our driest-ever century and the earliest known severe winter was that of AD 763–4. In 1683–4 there was frost in London from November to April. Frosts were recorded during August in the period 1668–89.

Most equable temperature

The location with the most equable recorded temperature over a short period is Garapan, on Saipan, in the Mariana Islands, Pacific Ocean. During the 9 years from 1927 to 1935, inclusive, the lowest temperature recorded was 19·6° C *67·3° F* on 30 Jan 1934 and the highest was 31·4° C *88·5° F* on 9 Sept 1931, giving an extreme range of 11·8° C *21·2° F*.

Between 1911 and 1966 the Brazilian off-shore island of Fernando de Noronha had a minimum temperature of 18·6° C *65·5° F* on 17 Nov 1913 and a maximum of 32·0° C *89·6° F* on 2 Mar 1965, an extreme range of 13·4° C *24·1° F*.

Greatest temperature ranges

The greatest recorded temperature ranges in the world are around the Siberian 'cold pole' in the eastern

USSR. Temperatures in Verkhoyansk (67° 33′ N, 133° 23′ E) have ranged 106·7° C *192° F* from −70°C–*94° F* (unofficial) to 36·7° C *98° F*. The greatest temperature variation recorded in a day is 55·5° C *100° F* (a fall from 6·7° C *44° F* to −48·8° C *−56° F*) at Browning, Montana, USA on 23–24 Jan 1916. The most freakish rise was 27·2° C *49° F* in 2 min at Spearfish, South Dakota, USA from −20° C *−4° F* at 7.30 a.m. to 7·2° C *45° F* at 7.32 a.m. on 22 Jan 1943. The British record is 29° C *52·2° F* (−7° C *19·4° F* to 22° C *71·6° F*) at Tummel Bridge, Tayside on 9 May 1978.

Longest freeze

The longest recorded unremitting freeze in the British Isles was one of 40 days at the Great Dun Fell radio station, Appleby, Cumbria, from 23 Jan to 3 Mar 1986. Less rigorous early data include a frost from 5 Dec 1607 to 14 Feb 1608 and a 91-day frost on Dartmoor, Devon in 1854–5. No temperature lower than 1° C *34° F* has ever been recorded on Bishop Rock, Isles of Scilly.

Upper atmosphere

The lowest temperature ever recorded in the atmosphere is −143° C *−225·4° F* at an altitude of about

80·5–96·5 km *50–60 miles*, during noctilucent cloud research above Kronogård, Sweden from 27 July to 7 Aug 1963. A jet stream moving at 656 km/h *408 mph* at 47 000 m *154 200 ft* (46 km *29·2 miles*) was recorded by Skua rocket above South Uist, Outer Hebrides, Scotland on 13 Dec 1967.

Thickest ice

The greatest recorded thickness of ice is 4776 m *2·97 miles (15 670 ft)* measured by radio echo soundings from a US Antarctic research aircraft at 69° 9′ 38″ S 135° 20′ 25″ E 400 km *250 miles* from the coast in Wilkes Land on 4 Jan 1975.

Deepest permafrost

The deepest recorded permafrost is more than 1370 m *4500 ft* reported from the upper reaches of the Viluy River, Siberia, USSR in February 1982.

Most recent white Christmas and Frost Fair

London has experienced 8 'white' or snowing Christmas Days since 1900. These have been 1906, 1917 (slight), 1923 (slight), 1927, 1938, 1956 (slight), 1970 and 1981.

These were more frequent in the 19th century and even more so before the change of the calendar which by removing 3–13 Sept brought forward all dates subsequent to 2 Sept 1752 by 11 days. The last of the 9 recorded Frost Fairs held on the Thames since 1564/5 was from December 1813 to 26 Jan 1814.

Most intense rainfall

Difficulties attend rainfall readings for very short periods but the figure of 38·1 mm *1·50 in* in 1 min at Barst, Guadeloupe on 26 Nov 1970, is regarded as the most intense recorded in modern times. The cloudburst of 'near 609 mm *2 ft* in less than a quarter of half an hour' at Oxford on the afternoon of 31 May (old style) 1682 is regarded as unacademically recorded.

The most intense rainfall in Britain recorded to modern standards has been 51 mm *2·0 in* in 12 min at Wisbech, Cambridgeshire on 27 June 1970.

Falsest St. Swithin's Days

The legend that the weather on St. Swithin's Day, celebrated on 15 July (old and new style) since AD 912, determines the rainfall for the next 40 days is one which has long persisted. There was a brilliant 13½ hr sunshine in London on 15 July 1924, but 30 of the next 40 days were wet. On 15 July 1913 there was a 15-hr downpour, yet it rained on only 9 of the subsequent 40 days in London.

Best and worst British summers

According to Professor Gordon Manley's survey over the period 1728–1978 the best (*i.e.* driest and hottest) British summer was that of 1976 and the worst (*i.e.* wettest and coldest) that of 1879. Temperatures of >32° C *89·8° F* were recorded on 13 consecutive days (25 June–7 July 1976) within Great Britain including 35·9° C *96·6° F* at Cheltenham on 3 July. In 1983 there were 40 days >26·6° C *80°F* in Britain between 3 July–31 Aug including 17 consecutively (3–19 July). London experienced its hottest month (July) since records began in 1840.

Humidity and discomfort

Human comfort or discomfort depends not· merely on temperature but on the combination of temperature, humidity, radiation and wind-speed. The United States Weather Bureau uses a Temperature-Humidity Index, which equals two-fifths of the sum of the dry and wet bulb thermometer readings plus 15. A THI of 98·2 has been twice recorded in Death Valley, California—on 27 July 1966 (119° F and 31 per cent) and on 12 Aug 1970 (117° F and 37 per cent). A person driving at 72 km/h *45 mph* in a car without a windscreen in a temperature of −42·7° C *−45°F* would, by the chill factor, experience the equivalent of −87· 2° C *−125° F*, i.e. within 2·0° C *3·5° F* of the world record.

Largest mirage

The largest mirage on record was that sighted in the Arctic at 83° N 103° W by Donald B. MacMillan in 1913. This type of mirage, known as the Fata Morgana, appeared as the same 'hills, valleys, snow-capped peaks extending through at least 120 degrees of the horizon' that Peary had misidentified as Crocker Land 6 years earlier. On 17 July 1939 a mirage of Snaefells Jokull (1437 m *4715 ft*) on Iceland was seen from the sea at a distance of 539–563 km *335–350 miles.*

Longest-lasting rainbow

A rainbow lasting over 3 hours was reported from the coastal border of Gwynedd and Clwyd, North Wales on 14 Aug 1979.

Lightning

The visible length of lightning strokes varies greatly. In mountainous regions, when clouds are very low, the flash may be less than 91 m *300 ft* long. In flat country with very high clouds, a cloud-to-earth flash may measure 6 km *4 miles* though in the most extreme cases such flashes have been measured at 32 km *20 miles*. The intensely bright central core of the lightning channel is extremely narrow. Some authorities suggest that its diameter is as little as 1·27 cm *half an inch*. This core is surrounded by a 'corona envelope' (glow discharge) which may measure 3–6 m *10–20 ft* in diameter.

The speed of a discharge varies from 160 to 1600 km/sec *100 to 1000 miles/sec* for the downward leader track, and reaches up to 140 000 km/sec *87 000 miles/sec* (nearly half the speed of light) for the powerful return stroke. In Britain there is an average of 3·7 strikes per km² per annum (6 strikes per mile²), and an average of 4200 per annum over London alone. Every few million strokes there is a giant discharge, in which the cloud-to-earth and return strokes flash from and to the top of the thunder clouds. In these 'positive giants' energy of up to 3000 million joules (3×10^{16} ergs) has been recorded. The temperature reaches about 30 000° C, which is more than 5 times greater than that of the surface of the Sun.

Highest waterspout

The highest waterspout of which there is a reliable record was one observed on 16 May 1898 off Eden, New South Wales, Australia. A theodolite reading from the shore gave its height as 1528 m *5014 ft*. It was about 3 m *10 ft* in diameter. The Spithead waterspout off Ryde, Isle of Wight on 21 Aug 1878 was measured by sextant to be 1600 m *or 'about a mile'* in height. A waterspout moved around Tor Bay, Devon on 17 Sept 1969 which, according to press estimates, was 300 m *1000 ft* in height.

Cloud extremes

The highest standard cloud form is cirrus, averaging 8250 m *27 000 ft* and above, but the rare nacreous or mother-of-pearl formation sometimes reaches nearly 24 000 m *80 000 ft* (see also Noctilucent clouds, Chapter 4). Cirrus cloud at 8075 m *26 500 ft* contains unfrozen but super-cooled water at −35° C *−31° F*. The lowest is stratus, below 1066 m *3500 ft*. The cloud form with the greatest vertical range is cumulo-nimbus, which has been observed to reach a height of nearly 20 000 m *68 000 ft* in the tropics.

Tornadoes (see also Accidents and Disasters, Chapter 11)

Britain's strongest tornado was at Southsea, Portsmouth on 14 Dec 1810 (Force 8 on the Meaden-TORRO scale). The Newmarket tornado (Force 6) of 3 Jan 1978 caused property damage estimated at up to £1 000 000. On 23 Nov 1981, 58 tornadoes were reported in one day from Anglesey to eastern England.

Highest shade temperature

The highest ever recorded shade temperature is 58° C *136·4° F* at al'Azīzīyah, Libya (alt. 111 m *367 ft*) on 13 Sept 1922. The highest in Britain is 36·8° C *98·2° F* at Raunds (Northants), Epsom (Surrey), and Canterbury (Kent) on 9 Aug 1911. The 38·6° C *100·5° F* which was once reported from Tonbridge (Kent) was a non-standard exposure and is estimated to be equivalent to 36–36·7° C *97–98° F*.

Lowest screen temperature

A record low of −89·2° C *−128·6° F* was registered at Vostok, Antarctica (alt. 3419 m *11 220 ft*) on 21 July 1983. The coldest permanently inhabited place is the Siberian village of Oymyakon (pop. 4000) (63° 16′ N., 143° 15′ E.), (700 m *2300 ft*) in the USSR where the temperature reached −71·1° C *−96° F* in 1964. Britain's lowest was −27·2° C *−17° F* on 11 Feb 1895 and again on 10 Jan 1982, both times at Braemar, Grampian, Scotland. The −30·5° C *−23° F* at Blackadder, Borders, on 4 Dec 1879, and the −28·9° C *−20° F* at Grantown-on-Spey on 24 Feb 1955, were not standard exposures. The lowest official temperature in England is −26·1° C *−15° F* at Newport, Shropshire on 10 Jan 1982. The lowest maximum temperature for a day ·was −19·1° C *−2·3° F* at Braemar, again on 10 Jan 1982.

Greatest rainfall

A record 1870 mm *73·62 in* of rain fell in 24 hours in Cilaos (alt. 1200 m *3937 ft*), La Réunion, Indian Ocean on 15 and 16 Mar 1952. This is equal to 7554 tonnes *7435 tons* of rain per acre. For a calendar month, the record is 9300 mm *366·14 in* at Cherrapunji, Meghalaya, India in July 1861, and the 12 month record was also at Cherrapunji with 26 461 mm *1041·78 in* between 1 Aug 1860 and 31 July 1861.

In Great Britain, the 24 hour record is 279 mm *11·00 in* at Martinstown, Dorset, on 18 and 19 July 1955. 1436 mm *56·54 in* fell in October 1909 at Llyn Llydau, Snowdon, Gwynedd, and over a 12 month period 6527 mm *257·0 in* fell at Sprinkling Tarn, Cumbria, in 1954.

Wettest place

By average annual rainfall, the wettest place in the world is Tutunendo, in Colombia, with 11 770 mm *463·4 in* per annum. Styhead Tarn (487 m *1600 ft*), in Cumbria, with 4391 mm *172·9 in*, is Britain's wettest place.

Greatest snowfall

31 102 mm *1224·5 in* of snow fell over a 12 month period from 19 Feb 1971 to 18 Feb 1972 at Paradise, Mt Rainier, in Washington, USA. The record for a single snowstorm is 4800 mm *189 in* at Mt. Shasta, Ski Bowl, in California, USA and for 24 hr, 1930 mm *76 in* at Silver Lake, Colorado, USA on 14 and 15 April 1921. The greatest depth of snow on the ground was 8407 mm *27 ft 7 in* at Helen Lake, Mount Lassen, USA in April 1983. Britain's 12 month record is the 1524 mm *60 in* which fell both in Upper Teesdale and also in the Denbighshire Hills, Clwyd, in 1947. London's earliest recorded snow was on 25 Sept 1885, and the latest on 27 May 1821. Less reliable reports suggest snow on 12 Sept 1658 (old style) and on 12 June 1791.

Maximum sunshine

The annual average in the eastern Sahara is more than 97 per cent (over 4300 hours). St Petersburg, Florida, USA, recorded 768 consecutive sunny days from 9 Feb 1967 to 17 Mar 1969. The best in Britain was 78·3 per cent of the maximum possible in one month (382 hours out of 488) at Pendennis Castle, Falmouth, Cornwall in June 1925.

Minimum sunshine

At the North Pole the figure is nil, for winter stretches of 186 days. In December 1890, a figure of nil was registered at Westminster, London, whilst from 18 Nov to 8 Feb each winter the south-eastern end of the village of Lochranza, Isle of Arran, Strathclyde is in shadow of mountains.

Barometric pressure

The highest barometric pressure ever recorded was 1083·8 mb *(32·00 in)*, at Agata, Siberia, USSR (alt. 262 m *862 ft*) on 31 Dec 1968. The highest in Britain was 1054·7 mb *(31·15 in)*, in Aberdeen on 31 Jan 1902.

The lowest was 870 mb *(25·69 in)*, 482 km *300 miles* west of Guam, Pacific Ocean, in Lat. 16°44′ N, Long. 137°46′ E on 12 Oct 1979. The USS Repose, a hospital ship, recorded 856 mb *25·55 in* in the eye of a typhoon, in 25°35′ N 128°20′ E, off Okinawa on 16 Sept 1945. Britain's lowest is 925·5 mb *(27·33 in)*, at Ochtertyre, near Crieff, Tayside on 26 Jan 1884.

Highest surface wind-speed

A surface wind-speed of 371 km/h *231 mph* was recorded at Mt. Washington (1916 m *6288 ft*), New Hampshire, USA on 12 Apr 1934. The highest speed measured to date in a tornado is 450 km/h *280 mph* at Wichita Falls, Texas, USA on 2 Apr 1958. The record high surface wind-speed for Britain is 278 km/h *172 mph* (150 knots), on Cairn Gorm Summit (1245 m *4084 ft*), on 20 Mar 1986. A figure of 285·2 km/h *177·2 mph* at RAF Saxa Vord, Unst, in the Shetlands, Scotland on 16 Feb 1962, was not recorded with standard equipment. British tornadoes may reach 290 km/h *180 mph*. There were gales of great severity on 15 Jan 1362, 26 Nov 1703 and 16 Oct 1987.

Thunder-days

In the period from 1916 to 1919 there were on average 322·4 days of thunder each year at Bogor (formerly

Britain's mildest climate ● An aerial shot of Penzance, in Cornwall, where annual mean temperatures of 11·5°C *52·7°F* were recorded in the period 1931 to 1960. Both ferry and helicopter services provide a link with the equally mild Isles of Scilly (see right).

Buitenzorg), Java, Indonesia. Between Lat. 35° N and 35° S there are some 3200 thunderstorms each 12 night-time hours, some of which can be heard at a range of 29 km *18 miles*. The record number of thunder-days recorded in a specific place in a calendar year in Britain is 38, twice. The first time was in 1912, at Stonyhurst, in Lancashire, and the second was in 1967, at Huddersfield, in West Yorkshire.

Hottest place

On an annual mean basis, with readings taken over a six year period from 1960 to 1966, the temperature at Dallol, in Ethiopia, was 34·4° C *94° F*. At Marble Bar, Western Australia (maximum 49·4° C *121° F*), 160 consecutive days with maximum temperatures of over 37·8° C *100° F* were recorded between 31 Oct 1923 and 7 Apr 1924. At Wyndham, also in Western Australia, the temperature reached 32·2° C *90° F* or more on 333 days in 1946. In Britain, annual mean temperatures of 11·5° C *52·7° F* were recorded both at Penzance, in Cornwall, and the Isles of Scilly in the period 1931 to 1960.

Coldest place

Polus Nedostupnosti, Pole of Cold (78° S, 96° E), Antarctica is the coldest place in the world, with an extrapolated annual mean of −57·8° C *−72° F*. The coldest measured mean is −56·6° C *−70° F*, at Plateau Station, Antarctica. For Britain it is 6·34° C *43·41° F*, at Braemar, Grampian, Scotland based on readings taken between 1952 and 1981.

Most rainy days

Mt. Wai-'ale-'ale (1569 m *5148 ft*), Kauai, Hawaii, has up to 350 rainy days per annum. The place in the British Isles which has had the most rainy days in a calendar year is Ballynahinch, in Galway, Ireland with 309 in 1923.

Driest place

The annual mean rainfall in the Desierto de Atacama, near Calama, Chile is nil. In Britain, the lowest annual mean rainfall on record is at St Osyth, Lee Wick Farm, Essex, with 513 mm *20·2 in*, based on the period 1964 to 1982. The lowest rainfall recorded in a single year was 236 mm *9·29 in* at one station in Margate, Kent in 1921.

Longest drought

Desierto de Atacama, in Chile experienced a drought for some 400 years up to 1971. Britain's longest drought lasted 73 days, from 4 Mar to 15 May 1893, at Mile End, Greater London.

Heaviest hailstones

The heaviest hailstones on record, weighing 1·02 kg *2·25 lb*, are reported to have killed 92 people in the Gopalganj district of Bangladesh on 14 Apr 1986. The *Canton Evening News* reported 5 killed and 225 injured by a hailstorm on 14 Apr 1981, with stones weighing up to 13·6 kg *30 lb* (sic). The heaviest hailstones in Britain fell on 5 Sept 1958, at Horsham, West Sussex, and weighed 141 g *5 oz*. Much heavier ones are sometimes reported, but usually these are coalesced rather than single stones. An ice block of 1–2 kg *35–70 oz* was reputed at Withington, Manchester on 2 Apr 1973.

Longest sea level fogs

Sea level fogs–with visibility less than 914·4 m *1000 yd*–persist for weeks on the Grand Banks, Newfoundland, Canada, with the average being more than 120 days per year. The duration record for Britain is 4 days 18 hours, twice, in both cases in London. The first time was from 26 Nov to 1 Dec 1948 and the second from 5 to 9 Dec 1952. Lower visibilities occur at higher altitudes. Ben Nevis is reputedly in cloud 300 days per year.

Windiest place

The Commonwealth Bay, George V Coast, Antarctica, where gales reach 320 km/h *200 mph* is the world's windiest place. In Britain, an average reading of 33·1 km/h *20·6 mph* was registered at Fair Isle in the period 1974 to 1978.

EXTREME TEMPERATURES
(Progressive recordings)
HIGH

53·0° C	127·4°F	Ouargla, Algeria	27 Aug	1884
54·4° C	130°F	Amos, California, USA	17 Aug	1885
54·4° C	130°F	Mammoth Tank, California, USA	17 Aug	1885
56·7° C	134°F	Death Valley, California, USA	10 July	1913
58·0° C	136·4°F	Al'Aziziyah (el-Azizia), Libya*	13 Sept	1922

* Obtained by the US National Geographical Society but not officially recognised by the Libyan Ministry of Communications.

A reading of 60°C 140°F at Delta, Mexico, in August 1953 is not now accepted because of over-exposure to roof radiation. The official Mexican record of 58·0°C 136·4°F at San Luis, Sonora on 11 Aug 1933 is not internationally accepted.

A freak heat flash reported from Coimbra, Portugal, in September 1933 said to have caused the temperature to rise to 70°C 158°F for 120 sec is apocryphal.

LOW

−58·3° C	−73°F	Floeberg Bay, Ellesmere I., Canada		[1]1852
−68° C	−90·4°F.	Verkhoyansk, Siberia, USSR	3 Jan	1885
−68° C	−90·4°F.	Verkhoyansk, Siberia, USSR	5 & 7 Feb	1892
−68° C	−90·4°F.	Oymyakon, Siberia, USSR[2]	6 Feb	1933
−73·5° C	−100·4°F.	South Pole, Antarctica	11 May	1957
−74·5° C	−102·1°F.	South Pole, Antarctica	17 Sept	1957
−78·3° C	−109·1°F.	Sovietskaya, Antarctica	2 May	1958
−80·7° C	−113·3°F.	Vostok, Antarctica	15 June	1958
−81·2° C	−114·1°F.	Sovietskaya, Antarctica	19 June	1958
−83·0° C	−117·4°F.	Sovietskaya, Antarctica	25 June	1958
−85·7° C	−122·4°F.	Vostok, Antarctica	7–8 Aug	1958
−86·7° C	−124·1°F.	Sovietskaya, Antarctica	9 Aug	1958
−87·4° C	−125·3°F.	Vostok, Antarctica	25 Aug	1958
−88·3° C	−126·9°F.	Vostok, Antarctica	24 Aug	1960
−89·2° C	−128·6°F.	Vostok, Antactica	21 July	1983

[1] The earliest recorded occasion that mercury froze (at −40°C or −40°F) was by M. V. Lomonosov, near Moscow c. 1750.

[2] Population in 1986 reported to be 4000—the world's coldest inhabited place.

THE UNIVERSE AND SPACE

CHAPTER·FOUR

Sunspots ● An ultraviolet image of the largest observed solar prominence which protruded 588 000 km *365 000 miles*, photographed on 19 Dec 1973 during the 3rd and final manned Skylab mission. The distribution of helium gas just above the Sun's visible surface can be clearly seen. The 'ghost' images to left and right of the full disc were recorded at nearby ultraviolet wavelengths and show radiation from atoms in the solar atmosphere. (Photo: NASA/Science Photo Library)

LIGHT-YEAR—defined as the distance travelled by light (speed 299 792·458 km/s *186 282·397 miles/sec* or 1 079 252 848·8 km/h *670 616 629·2 mph in vacuo*) in one tropical year (365·24219878 mean solar days at January 0·12 hours Ephemeris time in AD 1900) and is equivalent to 9 460 528 405 000 km *5 878 499 814 000 miles*. The unit was first used in March 1888 and fixed at this constant in October 1983.

MAGNITUDE—a measure of stellar brightness such that the light of a star of any magnitude bears a ratio of 2·511 886 to that of a star of the next magnitude. Thus a fifth magnitude star is 2·511 886 times as bright, while one of the first magnitude is exactly 100 (or 2·511 886⁵) times as bright, as a sixth magnitude star. In the case of such exceptionally bright bodies as Sirius, Venus, the Moon (magnitude −12·71) or the Sun (magnitude −26·78), the magnitude is expressed as a minus quantity.

PROPER MOTION—that component of a star's motion in space which, at right angles to the line of sight, constitutes an apparent change of position of the star in the celestial sphere.

The universe is the entirety of space, matter and anti-matter. An appreciation of its magnitude is best grasped by working outward from the Earth, through the Solar System which is revolving around the centre of the Milky Way once in every 225 000 000 years, at a speed of 792 000 km/h 492 000 mph and has a velocity of 72 000 km/h 44 700 mph relative to stars in our immediate region and then on to the remotest extra-galactic nebulae and quasars.

METEOROIDS

Meteoroids are of cometary or asteroidal origin. A meteor is the light phenomenon caused by the entry of a meteoroid into the Earth's atmosphere.

Meteor shower

The greatest meteor 'shower' on record occurred on the night of 16–17 Nov 1966, when the Leonid meteors (which recur every 33¼ years) were visible between western North America and eastern USSR. It was calculated that meteors passed over Arizona, USA, at a rate of 2300 per min for a period of 20 min from 5 a.m. on 17 Nov 1966.

METEORITES

Oldest

The oldest dated meteorites are from the fall in Allende, Coahuila, Mexico on 8 Feb 1969 dating back 4610 million years.

It was reported in August 1978 that dust grains in the Murchison meteorite which fell in Australia in September 1969 also pre-date the formation of the Solar System 4600 million years ago.

Largest

There was a mysterious explosion of 12½ megatons in Lat. 60° 55′ N, Long. 101° 57′ E, in the basin of the Podkamennaya Tunguska river, 40 miles north of Vanavar, in Siberia, USSR, at 00 hrs 17 min 11 sec UT on 30 June 1908. The cause was variously attributed to a meteorite (1927), a comet (1930), a nuclear explosion (1961) and to anti-matter (1965). This devastated an area of about 3885 km² *1500 miles²* and the shock was felt as far as 1000 km (more than *600 miles*) away. The theory is now favoured that this was the terminal flare of stony debris from a comet, possibly Encke's comet, at an altitude of only 6 km or less than *20 000 ft*. A similar event may have occurred over the Isle of Axholm, Humberside, England a few thousand years before. A stony meteorite with a diameter of 10 km *6·2 miles* striking the Earth at 55 925 mph *25 km/sec* would generate an explosive energy equivalent to 100 million megatons. Such events should not be expected to recur more than once in 75 million years.

The largest meteorite exhibited by any museum is the

> **Largest known meteorite ●** This was found in 1920 at Hoba West, near Grootfontein in south-west Africa and is a block 2·75 m *9 ft* long by 2·43 m *8 ft* broad, estimated to be 59 tonnes *132 000 lb*.
> (Photo: Patrick Moore)

'Tent' meteorite, which weighed 30 883 kg *68 085 lb (30·39 tons)* found in 1897 near Cape York, on the west coast of Greenland, by the expedition of Commander (later Rear-Admiral) Robert Edwin Peary (1856–1920). It was known to the Eskimos as the Abnighito and is now exhibited in the Hayden Planetarium in New York City, NY, USA. The largest piece of stony meteorite recovered is a piece of 1770 kg *3902 lb*, part of a 4 tonne shower which struck Jilin (formerly Kirin), China on 8 Mar 1976.

The heaviest of the 22 meteorites known to have fallen on the British Isles since 1623 was one weighing at least 46·25 kg *102 lb* (largest piece 7·88 kg *17 lb 6 oz*), which fell at 4.12 p.m. on 24 Dec 1965 at Barwell, Leicestershire. Scotland's largest recorded meteorite fell in Strathmore, Tayside on 3 Dec 1917. It weighed 10·09 kg *22¼ lb* and was the largest of four stones totalling 13·324 kg *29 lb 6 oz*. The largest recorded meteorite to fall in Ireland was the Limerick Stone of 29·5 kg *65 lb*, part of a shower weighing more than 48 kg *106 lb* which fell near Adare, County Limerick, on 10 Sept 1813. The larger of the two recorded meteorites to land in Wales was one weighing 794 g *28 oz* of which a piece weighing 723 g *25½ oz* went through the roof of the Prince Llewellyn Hotel in Beddgelert, Gwynedd, shortly before 3.15 a.m. on 21 Sept 1949. Debris from the Bovedy Fall in Northern Ireland in 1969 spread over 80 km *50 miles*.

Craters

Largest

It has been estimated that some 2000 asteroid-Earth collisions have occurred in the last 600 million years. 102 collision sites or astroblemes have been recognised. A crater 241 km *150 miles* in diameter and 805 m *½ mile* deep was postulated in 1962 in Wilkes Land, Antarctica. It would be caused by a 13 000 million ton meteorite striking at 70 811 km/h *44 000 mph*. Soviet scientists reported in December 1970 an astrobleme with a 95 km

60 mile diameter and a maximum depth of 400 m *1300 ft* in the basin of the River Popigai. There is a crater-like formation or astrobleme 442·5 km *275 miles* in diameter on the eastern shore of the Hudson Bay, Canada, where the Nastapoka Islands are just off the coast.

Evidence was published in 1963 discounting a meteoric origin for the crypto-volcanic Vredefort Ring (diameter 41·8 km *26 miles*), to the south-west of Johannesburg, South Africa, but this has now been re-asserted. The New Quebec (formerly the Chubb) 'Crater', first sighted on 20 June 1943 in northern Ungava, Canada, is 404 m *1325 ft* deep and measures 10·9 km *6·8 miles* round its rim.

Tektites

The largest tektite of which details have been published has been of 3·2 kg *7·04 lb* found in 1932 at Muong Nong, Saravane Province, Laos and now in the Paris Museum. Eight SNC meteorites named after their find sites at Shergotty, India; Nakla, Egypt and Chassigny, France, are believed to have emanated from Mars.

Fireball
Brightest

The brightest fireball ever photographically recorded was by Dr Zdenek Ceplecha over Sumava, Czechoslovakia on 4 Dec 1974 with a momentary magnitude of −22 or 10 000 times brighter than a full Moon.

AURORAE
Most frequent

Polar lights, known since 1560 as Aurora Borealis or Northern Lights in the northern hemisphere and since 1773 as Aurora Australis in the southern hemisphere, are caused by electrical solar discharges in the upper atmosphere and occur most frequently in high latitudes. Aurorae are visible at some time on *every* clear dark night in the polar areas within 20 degrees of the magnetic poles. The extreme height of aurorae has been measured at 1000 km *620 miles,* while the lowest may descend to 72·5 km *45 miles.* Reliable figures exist only from 1952, since when the record high and low number of nights of auroral displays in Shetland (geomagnetic Lat. 63°) has been 203 (1957) and 58 (1965). The most

recent great display in north-west Europe was that of 4–5 Sept 1958.

Lowest latitudes

Extreme cases of displays in very low latitudes are Cuzco, Peru (2 Aug 1744); Honolulu, Hawaii (1 Sept 1859) and, questionably, Singapore (25 Sept 1909).

Noctilucent clouds

These clouds remain sunlit long after sunset owing to their great altitude and are thought to consist of ice crystals or meteoric dust .

Regular observations (at heights of *c.* 85 km *52 miles*) in Western Europe date only from 1964, since when the record high and low number of nights on which these phenomena have been observed have been 43 (1979) and 15 (1970).

THE MOON

The Earth's closest neighbour in space and its only natural satellite is the Moon: this is at a mean distance of 384 399·1 km *238 854·5 miles* from centre to centre or 376 283 km *233 811 miles* from surface to surface. The average orbital speed is of the Moon is 3680 km/h *2287 mph.* In the present century the closest approach (smallest perigee) was 348 259 km *216 398 miles* surface-to-surface or 356 375 km *221 441 miles* centre-to-centre on 4 January 1912, and the farthest distance (largest apogee) was 398 598 km *247 675 miles* surface-to-surface or 406 711 km *252 718 miles* centre-to-centre on 2 Mar 1984. The Moon was only a few Earth radii distant during the 'Gerstenkorn period' 3900 million years ago. It has a diameter of 3475·1 km *2159·3 miles* and has a mass of $7·348 \times 10^{19}$ tonnes *$7·232 \times 10^{19}$ tons* with a mean density of 3·344. The first direct hit on the Moon was achieved at 2 min 24 sec after midnight (Moscow time) on 14 Sept 1959, by the Soviet space probe *Luna II* near the *Mare Serenitatis.* The first photographic images of the hidden side were collected by the USSR's *Luna III* from 6.30 a.m. on 7 Oct 1959, from a range of up to 70 400 km *43 750 miles* and transmitted to the Earth from a distance of 470 000 km *292 000 miles.* The oldest of the Moon material brought back to Earth by the *Apollo* programme crews has been soil dated to 4720 million years.

Crater
Largest and deepest

Only 59 per cent of the Moon's surface is directly visible from the Earth because it is in 'captured rotation', i.e. the period of rotation is equal to the period of orbit. The largest wholly visible crater is the walled plain Bailly, towards the Moon's South Pole, which is 295 km *183 miles* across, with walls rising to 4250 m *14 000 ft.* The Orientale Basin, partly on the averted side, measures more than 965 km *600 miles* in diameter. The deepest crater is the Newton crater, with a floor estimated to be between 7000 and 8850 m *23 000–29 000 ft* below its rim and 2250 m *14 000 ft* below the level of the plain outside. The brightest directly visible spot on the Moon is *Aristarchus.*

Highest mountains

In the absence of a sea level, lunar altitudes are measured relative to an adopted reference sphere of radius 1 738·000 km *1079·943 miles.* Thus the greatest elevation attained on this basis by any of the 12 US astronauts has been 7830 m *25 688 ft* on the Descartes Highlands by Capt John Watts Young USN and Major Charles M. Duke Jr on 27 Apr 1972.

Temperature extremes

When the Sun is overhead the temperature on the lunar equator reaches 117·2°C *243°F* (17·2 deg C *31 deg F* above the boiling point of water). By sunset the temperature is 14·4°C *58°F* but after nightfall it sinks to −162·7°C *−261°F.*

THE SUN
Distance extremes

The Earth's 107 210 km/h *66 620 mph* orbit of 939 885 500 km *584 017 800 miles* around the Sun is elliptical, hence our distance from the Sun varies. The orbital speed varies between 105 450 km/h *65 520 mph* (minimum) and 109 030 km/h *67 750 mph.* The average distance of the Sun is 1·000 000 230 astronomical units or 149 597 906 km *92 955 829 miles.*

Our closest approach (perihelion) is 147 097 000 km *91 402 000 miles* and our farthest departure (aphelion) is 152 099 000 km *94 510 000 miles.*

IF THE CENTRE OF THE SUN IS CHARING CROSS LONDON . . .

The diagram shows, as the crow flies, the relative distances of all the planets in our Solar System from the sun which is imagined to be centred at Charing Cross, London. The size of each planet has been drawn to scale.

JUPITER
Sun: 483,634,000 miles
778 833 000 km
BLENHEIM PALACE
Charing Cross, London:
60.14 miles
96.78 km

PLUTO
Sun: 3,674,490,000 miles
5 913 510 000 km
INVERNESS
Charing Cross, London:
456.6 miles
737.83 km

NEPTUNE
Sun: 2,794,350,000 miles
4 497 070 000 km
FORTH ROAD BRIDGE
Charing Cross, London:
347.23 miles
558.82 km

URANUS
Sun: 1,783,951,000 miles
2 870 991 000 km
MIDDLESBROUGH
Charing Cross, London:
221.68 miles
356.75 km

MARS
Sun: 141,635,700 miles
227 940 500 km
HATFIELD HOUSE
Charing Cross, Lon
17.60 miles
28.32 km

MERCURY
Sun: 35,983,100 mile
57 909 100 km
FINSBURY PARK
Charing Cross, London:
4.47 miles
7.19 km

SYON HOUSE BRENTFORD
Charing Cross, London:
8.35 miles
13.45 km

VENUS
108 208 900 km

SATURN
Sun: 886,683,000 miles
1 426 978 000 km
BRISTOL
Charing Cross, London:
110.18 miles
177.32 km

EARTH
Sun: 92,955,800 miles
149 597 900 km

HAMPTON COURT PALACE
Charing Cross, London:
11.55 miles
18.59 km

THE SUN

Artwork: Rhoda and Robert Burns

Temperature and dimensions

The Sun has a central temperature of about 15 400 000 K, a core pressure of some 25·4 PPa *1 650 000 000 tons/in²* and uses up 4 000 000 tonnes/*tons* of hydrogen per sec, thus providing a luminosity of 3×10^{27} candlepower, with an intensity of 1 530 000 candelas *1 500 000 candles/in².* The Sun has the stellar classification of a 'yellow dwarf' and, although its density is only 1·407 times that of water, its mass is 332 946 times as much as that of the Earth. It has a mean diameter of 1 392 520 km *865 270 miles.* The Sun with a mass of $1·9889 \times 10^{27}$ tonnes *$1·9575 \times 10^{27}$ tons* represents more than 99 per cent of the total mass of the Solar System but will exhaust its energy in 10 000 million years.

Sunspots

To be visible to the *protected* naked eye, a sunspot must cover about one two-thousandth part of the Sun's disc and thus have an area of about 1300 million km² *500 000 000 miles².* The largest sunspot ever noted was in the Sun's southern hemisphere on 8 Apr 1947. Its area was about 18 000 million km² *7000 million miles²* with an extreme longitude of 300 000 km *187 000 miles* and an extreme latitude of 145 000 km *90 000 miles.* Sunspots appear darker because they are more than 1500 deg C cooler than the rest of the Sun's surface temperature of 5525° C. In October 1957 a smoothed sunspot count showed 263, the highest recorded index since records started in 1755 (cf. previous record of 239 in May 1778). In 1943 one sunspot lasted for 200 days from June to December.

ECLIPSES
Earliest recorded

For the Middle East, lunar eclipses have been extrapolated to 3450 BC and solar ones to 4200 BC. No centre of the path of totality for a solar eclipse crossed London for the 575 years from 20 Mar 1140 to 3 May 1715. On 14 June 2151 at 18.25 GMT the eclipse will be 99 per cent total in central London but total in Sheffield and Norfolk. The most recent occasion when a line of totality of a solar eclipse crossed Great Britain was on 29 June 1927 for 24·5 sec at 6.23 a.m. at West Hartlepool, Cleveland and the next instance will clip the coast at St Just, Cornwall at 10.10 a.m. on Wednesday 11 Aug 1999. On 30 June 1954 a total eclipse was witnessed from Unst, Shetland Islands but the centre of the path of totality was to its north.

Longest duration

The maximum *possible* duration of an eclipse of the Sun is 7 min 31 sec. The longest actually *measured* was on 20 June 1955 (7 min 8 sec), seen from the Philippines. One of 7 min 29 sec should occur in mid-Atlantic on 16 July 2186, which will then be the longest for 1469 years. The longest possible in the British Isles is 5 min 30 sec. That of 15 June 885 lasted nearly 5 min, as will that of 20 July 2381 in the Borders area. Durations can be extended by observers being airborne as on 30 June 1973 when an eclipse was 'extended' to 72 min aboard Concorde. An annular eclipse may last for 12 min 24 sec. The longest totality of any lunar eclipse is 104 minutes and has occurred many times.

Most and least frequent

The highest number of eclipses possible in a year is seven, as in 1935, when there were five solar and two lunar eclipses; or four solar and three lunar eclipses, as occurred in 1982. The lowest possible number in a year is two, both of which must be solar, as in 1944 and 1969.

COMETS
Earliest recorded

The earliest records of comets date from the 7th century BC. The speeds of the estimated 2 000 000 comets vary from 1125 km/h *700 mph* in outer space to 2 000 000 km/h *1 250 000 mph* when near the Sun. The successive appearances of Halley's Comet have been traced back to 467 BC. It was first depicted in the Nuremberg Chronicle of AD 684. The first prediction of its return by Edmund Halley (1656–1742) proved true on Christmas Day 1758, 16 years after his death. On 13–14 Mar 1986, the European satellite *Giotto* (launched 2 July 1985) penetrated to within 540 km *335 miles* of the nucleus of Halley's Comet. It was established that this was 15 km *9·3 miles* in length and velvet black in colour.

Closest approach

On 1 July 1770, Lexell's Comet, travelling at a speed of 38·5 km/sec *23·9 miles/sec* (relative to the Sun), came to within 1 200 000 km *745 000 miles* of the Earth. However, the Earth is believed to have passed through the tail of Halley's Comet, most recently on 19 May 1910.

Largest

The tail of the brightest of all comets, the Great Comet of 1843, trailed for 330 000 000 km *205 000 000 miles.* The bow shock of Holmes Comet of 1892 once measured 2 400 000 km *1 500 000 miles* in diameter.

Shortest period

Of all the recorded periodic comets (these are members of the Solar System), the one which most frequently returns is Encke's Comet, first identified in 1786. Its period of 1206 days (3.3 years) is the shortest established. Not one of its 53 returns (including that of 1983) has been missed by astronomers. Now increasingly faint, it is expected to 'die' by February 1994. The most frequently observed comets are Schwassmann-Wachmann I, Kopff and Oterma which can be observed every year between Mars and Jupiter.

Longest period

At the other extreme is Delavan's Comet of 1914, whose path was not accurately determined. It is not expected to return for perhaps 24 million years.

PLANETS
Largest

The nine major planets (including the Earth) are bodies within the Solar System and which revolve round the Sun in definite orbits. The search for Planet X continues. Jupiter, with an equatorial diameter of 142 984 km *88 846 miles* and a polar diameter of 133 708 km *83 082 miles* is the largest of the nine major planets, with a mass 317·828 times, and a volume 1323·3 times that of the Earth. It also has the shortest period of rotation resulting in a Jovian day of only 9 hr 50 min 30·003 sec in the equatorial zone.

Smallest, coldest and outermost

Pluto was first recorded by Clyde William Tombaugh (b. 4 Feb 1906) at Lowell Observatory, Flagstaff, Arizona, USA on 18 Feb 1930 from photographs he took on 23 and 29 Jan. His find was announced on 13 March. Pluto's companion Charon was announced on 22 June 1978 from the US Naval Observatory, Flagstaff, Arizona. Pluto, with a mass of about 1/500th of that of the Earth, has a diameter of 2245 km *1395 miles* and Charon 1199 km *745 miles.* Their surface temperature is an estimated −214°C *−353°F.* Their mean distance from the Sun is 5 913 514 000 km *3 674 488 000 miles* with a period of revolution of 248·54 years. Because of their orbital eccentricity they were temporarily closer to the Sun than Neptune in the period from 23 Jan 1979 to 15 Mar 1999.

Fastest

Mercury, which orbits the Sun at an average distance of 57 909 200 km *35 983 100 miles,* has a period of revolution of 87·9686 days, so giving the highest average speed in orbit of 172 248 km/h *107 030 mph.*

Hottest

For Venus a surface temperature of 462° C *864°F* has been estimated from measurements made from the USSR *Venera* and US Pioneer Cytherean surface probes.

Nearest

The fellow planet closest to the Earth is Venus, which is, at times, only 41 360 000 km *25 700 000 miles* inside the Earth's orbit, compared with Mars's closest approach of 55 680 000 km *34 600 000 miles* outside the Earth's orbit. Mars, known since 1965 to be cratered, has temperatures ranging from 29·4° C *85° F* to −123° C −*190° F.*

Surface features

By far the highest and most spectacular is Olympus Mons (formerly Nix Olympica) in the Tharsis region of Mars with a diameter of 500–600 km *310–370 miles* and a height of 26±3 km *75 450–95 150 ft* above the surrounding plain. Venus has a canyon some 1600 km *1000 miles* south of Venusian equator 6·4 km *21 000 ft* deep and 400 km *250 miles* long. The ice cliff on the Uranian moon Miranda is 5·20 km *65 000 ft* high.

Brightest and faintest

Viewed from the Earth, by far the brightest of the five planets visible to the naked eye is Venus, with a maximum magnitude of −4·4. Uranus, the first to be discovered by telescope when it was sighted by Sir William Herschel from his garden at 19, New King St., Bath on 13 Mar 1781, is marginally visible with a magnitude 5·5. Pluto is faintest, with a magnitude of 15·0.

Densest and least dense

Earth is the densest planet with an average figure of 5·515 times that of water, whilst Saturn has an average density only about one-eighth of this value or 0·685 times that of water.

Conjunctions

The most dramatic recorded conjunction (coming together) of the other seven principal members of the Solar System (Sun, Moon, Mercury, Venus, Mars, Jupiter and Saturn) occurred on 5 Feb 1962, when 16° covered all seven during an eclipse in the Pacific area. It is possible that the seven-fold conjunction of September 1186 spanned only 12°. The next notable conjunction will take place on 5 May 2000.

SATELLITES
Most

Of the nine major planets, all but Venus and Mercury have satellites. Saturn has most with at least 17 satellites. The Earth and Pluto are the only planets with a single satellite. The distance from their parent planets varies from the 9377 km *5827 miles* of *Phobos* from the centre of Mars to the 23 700 000 km *14 700 000 miles* of Jupiter's outer satellite *Sinope* (Jupiter IX). The Solar System has a total of 54 established satellites.

Largest and smallest

The largest and heaviest satellite is *Ganymede* (Jupiter III), which is 2·017 times heavier than our own Moon and has a diameter of 5262 km *3270 miles.* The smallest satellite is *Leda* (Jupiter XIII) with a diameter of less than 15 km *9·3 miles.*

Largest asteroids

In the belt which lies between Mars and Jupiter, there are some 45 000 (about 3900 numbered to October 1988) minor planets or asteroids which are, for the most part, too small to yield to diameter measurement. The largest and first discovered (by G. Piazzi at Palermo, Sicily on 1 Jan 1801) of these is *Ceres*, which has a diameter of 936 km *582 miles.* The only one visible to the naked eye is asteroid 4 *Vesta* (diameter 519 km *322 miles*) discovered on 29 Mar 1807 by Dr Heinrich Wilhelm Olbers (1758–1840), a German amateur astronomer. The closest measured approach to the Earth by an asteroid was 780 000 km *485 000 miles* in the case of *Hermes* on 30 Oct 1937 (asteroid now lost). The most distant detected is 2060 *Chiron*, found between Saturn and Uranus on 18–19 Oct 1977, by Charles T. Kowal from the Hale Observatory, California, USA.

STARS
Largest and most massive

The variable star *Eta Carinae*, which is 9100 light-years

THE MOST DISTANT MEASURED HEAVENLY BODIES

The possible existence of galaxies external to our own Milky Way system was mooted in 1789 by Sir William Herschel (1738–1822). These extra-galactic nebulae were first termed 'island universes'. Sir John Herschel (1792–1871) opined as early as 1835 that some might be more than 250 000 000 000 million miles distant. The first direct measurement of any body outside our Solar System was in 1838. Distances in the table below assume that the edge of the observable Universe is at a distance of 14 000 million light years.

Estimated Distance in Light-years[1]	Object	Method	Astronomers	Observatory	Date
about 6 (now 11·08)	61 Cygni	Parallax	F. Bessel	Königsberg, Germany	1838
>20 (now 26)	Vega	Parallax	F. G. W. Struve	Dorpat (now Tartu), Estonia	1840
c. 200	Limit	Parallax			by 1900
900 000 (now 2·15 million)[2]	Galaxy M31	Cepheid variable	E. P. Hubble (1889–1953)	Mt. Wilson, Cal., USA	

Millions of Light–Years	Recession Speed % of c	Object	Redshift[3]	Astronomers	Observatory	Date
c.200	1·4	NGC 7619		M. L. Humason	Mt. Wilson, Cal., USA	early 1928
>2100	>15·0	Ursa Major No. 2		Humason & E. P. Hubble	Mt. Wilson, Cal., USA	by 1936[4]
4600	32·6	Cluster 1448	0·403		Palomar, Cal., USA	1956
5100	36·2	3C 295 in Boötes	0·461	R. Minkowski	Palomar, Cal., USA	June 1960
5700	41·0	QSO 3C 147	0·545	M. Schmidt & T. A. Matthews	Palomar, Cal., USA	Feb 1964[5]
11 200	80·1	QSO 3C 9	2·01	M. Schmidt	Palomar, Cal., USA	Apr 1965
11 400	81·3	QSO 0106+01	2·11	E. M. Burbridge et al.	Palomar, Cal., USA	Dec 1965
11 400	81·4	QSO 1116+12	2·12	C. R. Lynds & A. N. Stockton	Steward, Ariz., USA	Mar 1966
				M. Schmidt	Palomar, Cal., USA	Mar 1966
11 500	82·4	QSO Pks 0237–23	2·22	H. C. Arp et al.	Palomar, Cal., USA	Dec 1966
11 700	83·7	QSO 4C 25.05	2·36	E. T. Olsen & M. Schmidt	Palomar, Cal., USA	Dec 1967[6]
12 300	87·5	QSO 4C 05.34	2·88	R. Lynds & D. Wills	Kitt Peak, Arizona, USA	Mar 1970
12 600	90·2	QSO OH 471	3·40	R. F. Carswell & P. A. Strittmatter	Steward, Ariz., USA	Mar 1973
12 700	90·7	QSO OQ 172	3·53	E. J. Wampler et al.	Lick, Cal., USA	May 1973
12 800	91·6	QSO Pks 2000–330	3·78	B. A. Peterson et al.	Siding Spring, NSW, Australia	Apr 1982[7]
12 800	91·7	QSO Pks 1208+1011	3·80	C. Hazard et al	Siding Spring, NSW, Australia	Feb 1986[8]
12 900	92·3	QSO 0046–293	4·01	S. J. Warren et al	Siding Spring, NSW, Australia	Sept 1986[8]
12 900	92·4	QSO PC0910+5625	4·04	M. Schmidt et al	Palomar, Cal., USA	June 1987
13 000	92·6	QSO 0000–2620	4·11	C. Hazard et al	Siding Spring, NSW, Australia	Aug 1987[8]
13 100	93·4	QSO 0051–279	4·43	S. J. Warren et al	Siding Spring, NSW, Australia	Nov 1987[8]

Note: c is the notation for the speed of light. (see p. 66). [1] Term first utilised in March 1888. [2] Re-estimate by G. de Vaucouleurs in Dec 1983. [3] Discovered by Vesto Slipher (1875–1969) from Flagstaff, Arizona, USA 1920. Redshift, denoted by z, is the measure of the speed of recession indicated by the ratio resulting from the subtraction of the rest wavelength of an emission line from the observed wavelength divided by the rest wavelength. [4] In 1934 Hubble opined that the observable horizon would be 3000 m light-years. [5] In Dec 1963 Dr I. S. Shklovsky's (USSR) suggestion that QSO 3C2 was more distant was subsequently confirmed with a value of 0·612 c. [6] In Oct 1968 Dr Margaret Burbidge (GB) published a tentative redshift of 2·38 for QSO 5C 2.56. [7] Anglo-Australian telescope. [8] UK Schmidt telescope.

distant in the Carina Nebula in our own galaxy, has a mass at least 200 times greater than our own Sun. Betelgeux (top left star of Orion) has a diameter of 700 million km 400 million miles or about 500 times greater than the Sun. In 1978 it was found to be surrounded not only by a dust 'shell' but also an outer tenuous gas halo up to 8·5 × 10^11 km 5·3 × 10^11 miles in diameter, that is over 1100 times the diameter of the star. The light from Betelgeux left in AD 1680.

Smallest and lightest

A mass of 0·014 that of the Sun is estimated for the very faint star RG 0058.8-2807 which was discovered by I. Neill Reid and Gerard Gilmore using the UK Schmidt telescope and was announced in April 1983. The white dwarf star L362-81 has an estimated diameter of 5600 km 3500 miles or only 0·0040 that of the Sun.

Brightest

Sirius A (Alpha Canis Majoris), also known as the Dog Star, is apparently the brightest star of the 5776 stars of naked eye visibility in the heavens, with an apparent magnitude of −1·46. It is in the constellation Canis Major and is visible in the winter months of the northern hemisphere, being due south at midnight on the last day of the year. The Sirius system is 8·64 light-years distant and has a luminosity 26 times as much as that of the Sun. It has a diameter of 2·33 million km 1 450 000 miles and a mass of 4·26 × 10^27 tonnes 4·20 × 10^27 tons. The faint white dwarf companion Sirius B has a diameter of only 10 000 km 6000 miles but is 350 000 times heavier than the Earth. The magnitude of Sirius should rise to a maximum of −1·67 by c. AD 61 000.

Farthest

The Solar System, with its Sun's nine principal planets, 54 satellites, asteroids and comets, was estimated in 1982 to be 28 000 light-years from the centre of the lens-shaped Milky Way galaxy (diameter 70 000 light-years) so that the most distant stars in our galaxy are estimated to be 63 000 light-years distant.

Nearest

Excepting the special case of our own Sun (q.v. above) the nearest star is the very faint Proxima Centauri, discovered in 1915, which is 4·22 light-years (4·00 × 10^13 km 24 800 000 000 000 miles) away. The nearest 'star' visible to the naked eye is the southern hemisphere binary Alpha Centauri, or Rigel Kentaurus (4·35 light-years distant), with an apparent magnitude of −0·29. It was discovered by Nicolas L. da Lacaille (1713–62) in c. 1752. In AD 29 700 this binary will reach a minimum distance of 2·84 light-years and should then be the second brightest 'star' with an apparent magnitude of −1·20.

Most and least luminous

If all the stars could be viewed at the same distance the most luminous would be the variable Eta Carinae (see Most Massive Star), which now has a total luminosity 6 500 000 times that of the Sun but at its peak brightness in 1843 was at least ten times more luminous than this. The visually brightest star is the hypergiant Cygnus OB2 No.12, 5900 light-years distant, which has an absolute visual magnitude of −9·9 and is therefore visually 810 000 times more luminous than the Sun. This brightness may be matched by the supergiant IV b 59 in the nearby galaxy Messier 101 but this would depend on the distance adopted for this galaxy (estimates varying between 15 600 000 and 19 700 000 light-years). The variable eta Carinae in 1843 had an absolute brightness 4 million times that of the Sun. The faintest star detected is the recently discovered RG 0058.8-2807 (see Lightest Star) which has a total luminosity only 0·000 21 that of the Sun and an absolute visual magnitude of 20·2 so that the visual brightness is less than one millionth of the Sun.

Brightest and latest supernova

The brightest supernova ever seen by historic man is believed to be SN 1006 in April 1006 near Beta Lupi, which flared for 2 years and attained a magnitude of −9 to −10. The remnant is believed to be the radio source G.327·6+14·5 nearly 3000 light-years distant. Others have occurred in 1054, 1604, 1885 and most recently on 23 Feb 1987 when Ian Shelton sighted that designated −69 202 in the Large Magellanic Cloud 170 000 light-years distant.

Constellations

The largest of the 89 constellations is Hydra (the Sea Serpent), which covers 1302·844 °² or 6·3 per cent of the hemisphere and contains at least 68 stars visible to the naked eye (to 5·5 mag.). The constellation Centaurus (Centaur), ranking ninth in area embraces however at least 94 such stars. The smallest constellation is Crux Australis (Southern Cross) with an area of only 0·16 per cent of the whole sky viz 68·477 deg² compared with the 41 252·96 deg² of the whole sky.

Stellar planets

The first direct evidence of a planet-like companion, announced in January 1985 by D. McCarthy Jr, F. J. Law and R. G. Probst (US), is now a subject of serious dispute. It concerned an object in orbit 1000 million km 600 million miles from the very faint red dwarf star Van Biesbroeck 8 (VB8), 21 light-years distant in Ophiuchus.

Three Canadian astronomers, Bruce Campbell of the Dominion Astrophysical Laboratory, Victoria, British Columbia, Gordon Walker and Stephenson Yang of the University of British Columbia in Vancouver reported in June 1987 the tentative detection of planet-like companions to two stars Epsilon Eridani and Gamma Cephei and they suspect the existence of companions to a further five stars. Their observations suggest that these bodies are between one and ten times the mass of Jupiter.

Longest name

The longest name for any star is *Shurnarkabtishashutu*, the Arabic for 'under the southern horn of the bull'.

Black Holes

The concept of superdense bodies was first adumbrated by the Marquis de LaPlace (1749–1827). This term for a star that has undergone complete gravitational collapse was first used by Prof John Archibald Wheeler at an Institute for Space Studies meeting in New York City on 29 Dec 1967.

The first tentative identification of a Black Hole was announced in December 1972 in the binary-star X-ray source Cygnus X-1. The best candidate is LMC X–3 of 10 solar masses and 180 000 light-years distant reported in Jan 1983. The critical size has been estimated to be as low as a diameter of 5·90 km *3·67 miles*. One at the centre of the Seyfert galaxy, NGC 4151 in *Canes Venatici*, was estimated by Michael Preston (GB) in Oct 1983 to be of between 50–100 million solar masses or up to 2×10^{35} tonnes.

THE UNIVERSE

Outside the Milky Way galaxy, which is part of the so-called Local Group of galaxies moving at a speed of 2 300 000 km/h *1 400 000 mph* relative to the microwave background radiation in a direction offset 44° from the centre of the Virgo cluster, there exist 10 000 million other galaxies. In March 1985 David J. Batuski and Jack O. Burns of the University of New Mexico, Albuquerque, announced the discovery of the largest discrete object in the Universe—a filamentary arrangement of Abell clusters stretching across the South Galactic Cap and measuring 1000 million light-years, $9·46 \times 10^{21}$ km *$5·88 \times 10^{21}$ miles* in length.

Farthest visible object

The remotest heavenly body visible with the *naked eye* is the Great Galaxy in *Andromeda* (mag. 3·47), known as Messier 31. It was first noted by the German Simon Marius (1570–1624). This is a rotating nebula in spiral form, and its distance from the Earth is about 2 150 000 light-years away or $20·3 \times 10^{18}$ km *c. 12 600 000 000 000 000 000 miles* and is moving towards us. It is just possible however that, under ideal seeing conditions, Messier 33, the Spiral in Triangulum (mag. 5·79), can be glimpsed by the naked eye of keen-sighted people at a distance of 2 360 000 light-years.

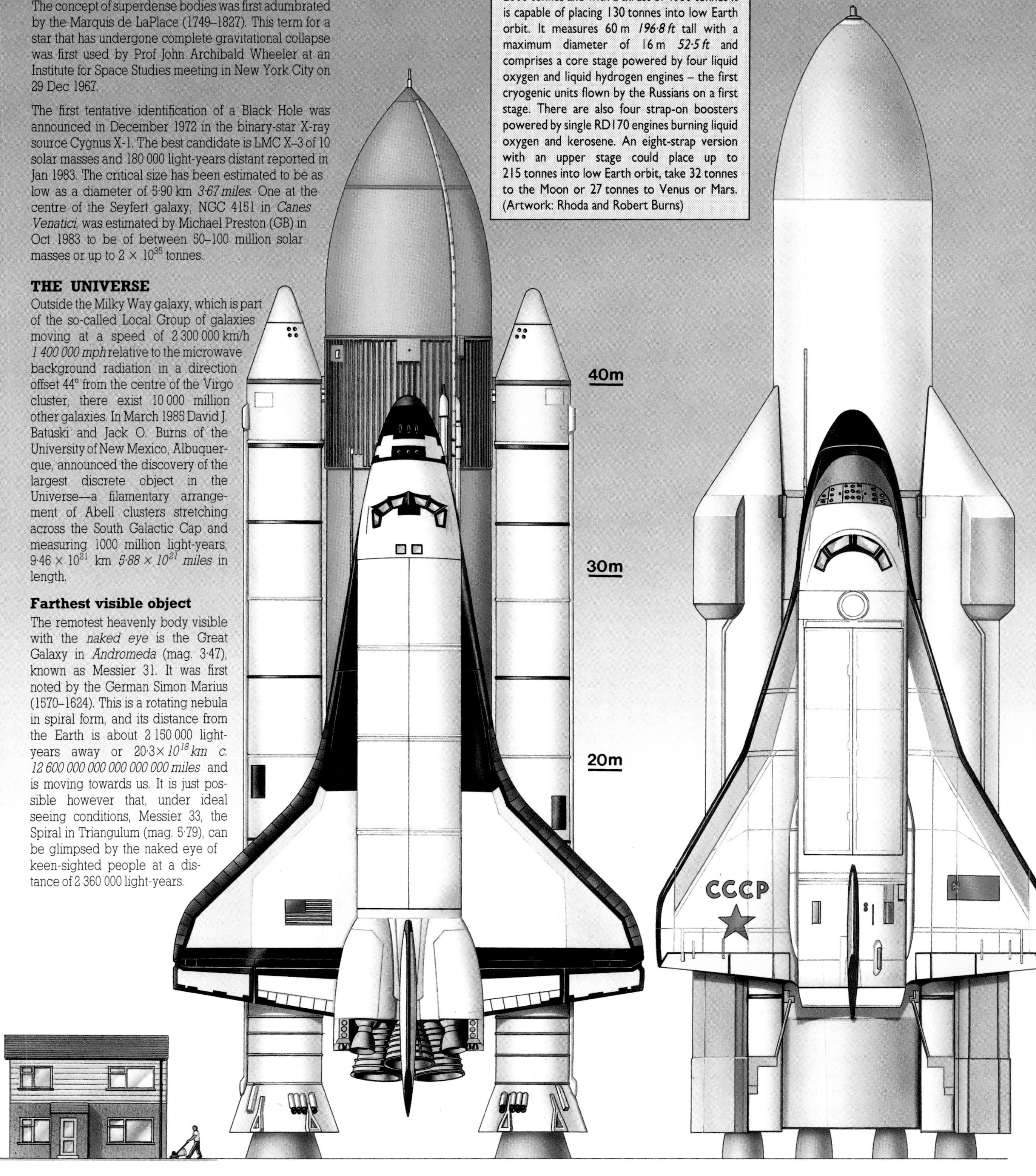

Most powerful rocket ● The USSR's *Energya*, first launched on 15 May 1987 from the Baikonur Cosmodrome, is seen here with the Space Shuttle due to be launched in 1988 and alongside the US Shuttle and an average domestic house for comparison. Weighing 2000 tonnes and with a thrust of 4000 tonnes it is capable of placing 130 tonnes into low Earth orbit. It measures 60 m *196·8 ft* tall with a maximum diameter of 16 m *52·5 ft* and comprises a core stage powered by four liquid oxygen and liquid hydrogen engines – the first cryogenic units flown by the Russians on a first stage. There are also four strap-on boosters powered by single RD170 engines burning liquid oxygen and kerosene. An eight-strap version with an upper stage could place up to 215 tonnes into low Earth orbit, take 32 tonnes to the Moon or 27 tonnes to Venus or Mars. (Artwork: Rhoda and Robert Burns)

40m

30m

20m

PROGRESSIVE ROCKET ALTITUDE RECORDS

HEIGHT		ROCKET	PLACE	LAUNCH DATE	
MILES	KM				
0·71	1·14	A 3 in 7·62 cm rocket	near London, England	Apr	1750
1·24	2	Reinhold Tiling[1] (Germany) solid fuel rocket	Osnabruck, Germany	Apr	1931
3·1	5	GIRD-X liquid fuel (USSR)	USSR	25 Nov	1933
8·1	13	USSR 'Stratosphere' rocket	USSR		1935
52·46	84·42	A.4 rocket (Germany)[2]	Peenemünde, Germany	3 Oct	1942
c. 85	c. 136	A.4 rocket (Germany)[2]	Heidelager, Poland	early	1944
118	190	A.4 rocket (Germany)[2]	Heidelager, Poland	mid	1944
244	392·6	V-2/W.A.C. Corporal (2-stage) Bumper No. 5 (USA)	White Sands, NM, USA	24 Feb	1949
318	512	Geophysical rocket V-5-V (USSR)	Tyuratam, USSR		1950–52
682	1097	Jupiter C (USA)	Cape Canaveral, Florida, USA	20 Sept	1956
>800	>1300	ICBM test flight R-7 (USSR)	Tyuratam, USSR	Aug	1957
>2700	>4345	Farside No. 5 (4-stage) (USA)	Eniwetok Atoll	20 Oct	1957
70 700	113 770	Pioneer 1-B Lunar Probe (USA)	Cape Canaveral, Florida, USA	11 Oct	1958
215 300 000*	346 480 000	Luna 1 or Mechta (USSR)	Tyuratam, USSR	2 Jan	1959
242 000 000*	389 450 000	Mars 1 (USSR)	USSR	1 Nov	1962
3 666 000 000[3]	5 900 000 000	Pioneer 10 (USA) (see also this page)	Kennedy Space Center, Cape Canaveral, Florida, USA	2 Mar	1972

* Apogee in solar orbit.
[1] There is some evidence that Tiling may shortly after have reached 9500 m (5·90 miles) with a solid fuel rocket at Wangerooge, East Friesian Islands, West Germany.
[2] The A4 was latterly referred to as the V2 rocket, a code for second revenge weapon (vergeltungswaffe) following upon the V1 'flying bomb'.
[3] Distance on crossing Pluto's orbit on 17 Oct 1986

Quasars

An occultation of 3C-273, observed from Australia on 5 Aug 1962, enabled the existence of quasi-stellar radio sources ('quasars' or QSOs) to be announced by Maarten Schmidt (b. Netherlands 1929). The red shift proved to be z = 0·158. Quasars have immensely high luminosity for bodies so distant and of such small diameter. It was announced in May 1983 that the quasar S5 0014+81 had a visual luminosity $1·1 \times 10^{15}$ times greater than that of the Sun. The first double quasar (0957+56) among 1500 known quasars, was announced in May 1980.

Pulsars

The earliest observation of a pulsating radio source or 'pulsar' CP 1919 (now PSR 1919+21) by Dr Jocelyn Burnell (née Bell, 1943) was announced from the Mullard Radio Astronomy Observatory, Cambridgeshire, England, on 24 Feb 1968. It had been detected on 28 Nov 1967. The fastest spinning is pulsar 1937+214 which is in the region of the minor constellation Vulpecula (The Fox) 16 000 light-years distant. It has a pulse period of 1·557806449 milli-sec and a spin-down rate of $1·0511 \times 10^{-19}$ sec/sec. However, the most accurate stellar clock is the pulsar PSR 1855+09 which has a spin-down rate of only $2·1 \times 10^{-20}$ sec/sec.

Remotest object

Both the interpretation of the very large redshifts exhibited by quasars and the estimation of equivalent distances remain controversial. The record red shift of z = 4·43 for quasar 0051-279 (see Table) was announced by Stephen Warren et al on November 1987 from analysis of plates from the UK Schmidt telescope, Siding Spring, NSW, Australia. Assuming an 'observable horizon', where the speed of recession very closely approaches the speed of light c, 14 000 million light years or $1·32 \times 10^{23}$ km 82 300 000 000 000 000 000 miles, this quasar would be more than 13 100 million light-years distant. The 3 K background radiation or primordial hiss discovered in 1965 by Arno Penzias and Robert Wilson of Bell Laboratories appears to be moving at a velocity of 99·9998 per cent of the speed of light.

Work in the near infra-red spectrum by Richard Elston and George H and Marcia J Rieke, from April 1987 at the University of Arizona's Steward Observatory, revealed two very dim, fuzzy proto-galaxies, seemingly lying beyond the most distant quasars. It was suggested in February 1988 that these might be 17 000 million light-years distant but the high red shift value of at least Z= 6 has not yet been confirmed.

Age of the Universe

For the age of the Universe a consensus value of 14±3 aeons or gigayears (an aeon or gigayear being 1000 million light years) is obtained from various cosmological techniques. The equivalent value of the Hubble constant based on a Friedman model of the Universe without cosmological constant is 70±15 km/s/Mpc. In 1973 an ex nihilo creation was postulated by Edward P. Tryon (US). Modified versions of the Inflationary Model, originally introduced by Alan Guth (US) in 1981, now rival the 'Big Bang' theory of creation.

ROCKETRY AND MISSILES

Earliest uses

War rockets, propelled by a charcoal-saltpetre-sulfur gun-powder, were described by Tseng Kung Liang of China in 1042. This early form of rocket became known in Europe by 1258.

The pioneer of military rocketry in Britain was Col Sir William Congreve, Bt, MP (1772–1828), Comptroller of the Royal Laboratory, Woolwich, London and Inspector of Military Machines. His '2·72 kg (6 lb) rocket' was developed to a range of 1825 m 2000 yd by 1805 and first used by the Royal Navy against Boulogne, France on 8 Oct 1806.

The first launching of a liquid-fuelled rocket (patented 14 July 1914) was by Dr Robert Hutchings Goddard (1882–1945) of the United States, at Auburn, Massachusetts, USA, on 16 Mar 1926, when his rocket reached an altitude of 12·5 m 41 ft and travelled a distance of 56 m 184 ft. The USSR's earliest rocket was the semi-liquid fuelled GIRD-IX (Gruppa Izucheniya Reaktivnogo Dvizheniya) begun in 1931 and tested on 17 Aug 1933.

Longest ranges

On 16 Mar 1962, Nikita Khrushchyov, then Prime Minister of the USSR, claimed in Moscow that the USSR possessed a 'global rocket' with a range of 30 000 km (about 19 000 miles) i.e. more than the Earth's semi-circumference and therefore capable of hitting any target from either direction.

Highest velocity

The first space vehicle to achieve the Third Cosmic velocity sufficient to break out of the Solar System was Pioneer 10 (see table above). The Atlas SLV-3C launcher with a modified Centaur D second stage and a Thiokol Te-364-4 third stage left the Earth at an unprecedented 51 682 km/h 32 114 mph on 2 Mar 1972.

The highest recorded velocity of any space vehicle has been 240 000 km/h 149 125 mph in the case of the US-German solar probe Helios B launched on 15 Jan 1976.

Remotest man-made object

Pioneer 10, launched from Kennedy Space Center, Cape Canaveral, Florida, crossed the mean orbit of Pluto on 17 Oct 1986 being then at a distance of 5900 million km 3670 million miles. It will be beyond the furthest extension of Pluto's orbit by April 1989 and will continue into space at 49 000 km/h 30 450 mph. In AD 34 593 it will make its nearest approach to the Star Ross 248, 10.3 light-years distant. Before 1991, Voyager 1, travelling faster, will surpass Pioneer 10 in remoteness from the Earth.

The spacecraft carries a plaque designed to communicate with any possible interstellar humanoids. This shows a man and a woman and, diagrammatically, where the spacecraft comes from in our Solar System and how our Sun relates to the pulsars.

SPACE FLIGHT

The physical laws controlling the flight of artificial satellites were first propounded by Sir Isaac Newton (1642–1727) in his Philosophiae Naturalis Principia Mathematica ('Mathematical Principles of Natural Philosophy'), begun in March 1686 and first published in the summer of 1687. The first artificial satellite was successfully put into orbit at an altitude of 228·5/946 km 142/588 miles and a velocity of more than 28 565 km/h 17 750 mph from Baikonur, north of Tyuratam, 275 km 170 miles east of the Aral Sea on the night of 4 Oct 1957. This spherical satellite Sputnik ('Fellow Traveller') 1, officially designated 'Satellite 1957 Alpha 2', weighed 83·6 kg 184·3 lb, with a diameter of 58 cm 22·8 in, and its lifetime is believed to have been 92 days, ending on 4 Jan 1958. The 29·5 m 96 ft 8 in SL-1 launcher was designed under the direction of former Gulag prisoner Dr Sergey Pavlovich Korolyov (1907–66).

Earliest manned satellite

The earliest manned space flight ratified by the world governing body, the Fédération Aéronautique Internationale (FAI founded 1905), was by Cosmonaut Flight Major (later Colonel) Yuriy Alekseyevich Gagarin (b. 9 Mar 1934) in Vostok 1 on 12 Apr 1961.

Details filed showed take-off to be from Baikonur at 6.07 a.m. GMT and the landing near Smelovka, near Engels, in the Saratov region, USSR, 108 minutes later. The maximum altitude reached during Vostok I's 40 868·6 km

25 394·5 miles flight was listed at 327 km *203·2 miles*, with a maximum speed of 28 260 km/h *17 560 mph*.

Colonel Gagarin, invested a Hero of the Soviet Union and awarded the Order of Lenin and the Gold Star Medal, was killed in a low level jet plane crash near Moscow on 27 Mar 1968.

First woman in space

The first woman to orbit the Earth was Junior Lieutenant (now Lt-Col Eng) Valentina Vladimirovna Tereshkova (b. 6 Mar 1937), who was launched in *Vostok 6* from Tyuratam, USSR, at 9.30 a.m. GMT on 16 June 1963, and landed at 8.16 a.m. on 19 June, after a flight of 2 days 22 hr 50 min, during which she completed over 48 orbits (1 971 000 km *1 225 000 miles*) and passed momentarily within 4·8 km *3 miles* of *Vostok 5*.

Space fatalities

The greatest published number to perish in any of the 117 attempted space flights to date is seven (five men and two women) aboard the ill-fated *Challenger* 51L on 28 Jan 1986 when an explosion occurred 73 sec after lift off, at a height of 14 326 m *47 000 ft*. There is no evidence to suggest that manned space flight explosions have occurred in the Soviet Union except for the *Soyuz T10* launch pad abort in September 1983 which did not result in fatalities.

First 'walk' in space

Lt-Col (now Maj-Gen) Aleksey A. Leonov (b. 20 May 1934) from *Voskhod 2* was the first person to engage in 'extra-vehicular activity' on 18 Mar 1965. Capt Bruce McCandless II (b. 8 Jun 1937) USN, from the space shuttle *Challenger*, was the first to engage in untethered EVA, at an altitude of 264 km *164 miles* above Hawaii, on 7 Feb 1984. His MMU (Manned Manoeuvering Unit) back-pack cost $15 million to develop.

Astronaut

Oldest and youngest

The oldest of the 204 people in space has been Karl G. Henize (US), aged 58 while on the 19th Space Shuttle mission aboard the *Challenger* on 29 Jul 1985. The youngest has been Major (later Lt-Gen) Gherman Stepanovich Titov (b. 11 Sept 1935), who was aged 25 years 329 days when launched in *Vostok 2* on 6 Aug 1961.

Most journeys

Capt John Watts Young (b. 24 Sept 1930) (USN ret) completed his sixth space flight on 8 Dec 1983 when he relinquished command of *Columbia* STS 9/Spacelab after a space career of 34 days 19 hr 42 min 13 sec.

Largest crew

The most crew on a single space mission is eight. This included one female and was launched on Space Shuttle STS 61A, *Challenger 9*, the 22nd shuttle mission, on 30 Oct 1985, carrying the West German Spacelab D1 laboratory. The mission, commanded by Hank Harts-field, lasted 7 days 44 min 51 sec.

Most in space

The greatest number of people in space at any one time is 11: five Americans aboard a Shuttle and five Russians and an Indian aboard *Salyut 7* in April 1984; and the eight STS 61A astronauts above and three Russians aboard *Salyut 7* in October 1985.

Lunar conquest

By FAI (Fédération Aéronautique Internationale) definition 'space' starts at an altitude of 100 km *62·137 miles* or *328 083 ft*. Neil Alden Armstrong (b. Wapakoneta, Ohio, of Scottish [via Ireland] and German ancestry, on 5 Aug 1930), command pilot of the *Apollo 11* mission, became the first man to set foot on the Moon, on the Sea of Tranquillity, at 02.56 and 15 sec GMT on 21 July 1969. He was followed out of the Lunar Module *Eagle* by Col Edwin Eugene Aldrin, Jr, USAF (b. Montclair, New Jersey, USA of Swedish, Dutch and British ancestry, on 20 Jan 1930), while the Command Module *Columbia* piloted

First men on the Moon ● Edwin Eugene Aldrin seen here beside the footpad of the lunar module when he and the command pilot of the *Apollo 11* mission, Neil Alden Armstrong, became the first to set foot on the lunar surface on 21 July 1969.

by Lt Col Michael Collins, USAF (b. Rome, Italy, of Irish and pre-Revolutionary American ancestry, on 31 Oct 1930) orbited above.

Eagle landed at 20.17 and 42 sec GMT on 20 July and lifted off at 17.54 GMT on 21 July, after a stay of 21 hr 36 min. *Apollo 11* had blasted off from Cape Canaveral, Florida at 13.32 GMT on 16 July and was a culmination of the US space programme which, at its peak, employed 376 600 people and attained in 1966–7 a peak budget of $5 900 000 000 .

There is evidence that Pavel Belyayev was the cosmonaut selected by the USSR for a manned circumlunar flight in *Zond 7* on 9 Dec 1968, 12 days before the *Apollo 8* flight, but no launch took place.

Longest manned space flight ● Col Yuri Romanenko (b. 1 Aug 1944) has made the longest manned space flight of 326 days on board the Russian *Soyuz TM2*, the Mir space station and *Soyuz TM3* between 5 Feb and 29 Dec 1987 landing in southern Kazakhstan. He also became the most experienced space traveller, his three spaceflights in 1977-8, 1980 and 1987 having amassed 430 days flight time. The medical research supporting these achievements was preparatory to the manned flight to Mars planned for 1991. Two of the three *Soyuz TM4* cosmonauts launched on 21 Dec 1987 to the Mir space station, Vladimir Titov and Musa Manarov, are expected to end an attempted 400 day flight in 1989.
(Photo: V. Shone)

THE SCIENTIFIC WORLD

CHAPTER FIVE

High speed photography ● A flash of less than 2 millionths of a second duration was used to stop this bullet in its tracks. But see also page **77**. (Photo: Robert Harding Picture Library)

Elements

All known matter in, on and beyond the Earth is made up of chemical elements. It is estimated that there are 10^{87} electrons in the known Universe. The total of naturally-occurring elements is 94, comprising, at ordinary temperatures, 2 liquids, 11 gases and 81 solids. The so-called 'fourth state' of matter is plasma, when negatively-charged electrons and positively-charged ions are in flux.

Lightest and heaviest sub-nuclear particles

By April 1986 the existence was accepted of 29 'stable' particles, 56 meson resonance multiplets, and 48 baryon resonance multiplets, representing the eventual discovery of 224 particles and an equal number of anti-particles. The heaviest stable particle fully accepted is the neutral weak gauge boson, the $Z°$, of mass 92·6 GeV which was first detected in May 1983 by the UA1 Collaboration, CERN, Geneva, Switzerland using the 540 GeV Super Proton Synchrotron proton-antiproton beam collider. The heaviest hadron accepted is the upsilon (6S) meson resonance of mass 11·02 GeV and lifetime $8·3 \times 10^{-24}$ sec., which consists of a bottom or beauty quark and its anti-quark, and which was first identified in October 1984 by two groups using the electron storage ring facilities at Cornell University, Ithaca, New York, USA. Sub-atomic concepts require that the masses of the graviton, photon and neutrino should all be zero. Based on the sensitivities of various cosmological theories, upper limits for the masses of these particles are $7·6 \times 10^{-67}$ g for the graviton, $3·0 \times 10^{-53}$ g for the photon, and $1·4 \times 10^{-32}$ g for the neutrino (cf. electron mass $9·10939 \times 10^{-28}$ g).

Most and least stable

Experiments from 1982 to 1985 have finally confirmed that the proton has a lifetime in excess of 1×10^{30} years compared to theoretical predictions based on the 'grand unified theory' which suggests that the lifetime may be less than 1×10^{34} years.

The half-life of Selenium 84 was estimated at the University of California at Irvine by Michael K Moes, Alan A Hahn and Steven R Elliott to be $1·1 \times 10^{20}$ year and announced in September 1987.

Least stable or shortest-lived particles are the two baryon resonances N(2220) and N(2600), both with $1·6 \times 10^{-24}$ sec although the *predicted* lifetimes of both the weak gauge bosons, the $W^{\pm}$ and $Z°$, are $2·4 \times 10^{-25}$ sec.

Smelliest substance

The most evil-smelling substance, of the 17 000 smells so far classified, must be a matter of opinion but ethyl mercaptan (C_2H_5SH) and butyl seleno-mercaptan (C_4H_9SeH) are powerful claimants, each with a smell reminiscent of a combination of rotting cabbage, garlic, onions and sewer gas.

Most expensive perfume

The retail prices of the most expensive perfumes tend to be fixed with an eye to public relations rather than levels solely dictated by the cost of ingredients and packaging.

The Chicago-based firm Jōvan marketed from March 1984 a cologne called Andron which contains a trace of the attractant pheromone androstenol which has a cost of $2750 per oz $97 per gramme.

Most potent poison

The rickettsial disease, Q-fever, can be instituted by a *single* organism though it is fatal in only 1 in 1000 cases.

About 10 organisms of *Francisella tularenesis* (formerly *Pasteurella tularenesis*) can institute tularaemia, variously called alkali disease, Francis disease or deerfly fever. This is fatal in upwards of 10 cases in 1000.

Most powerful nerve gas

VX, 300 times more toxic than phosgene ($COCl_2$) used in World War I, was developed at the Chemical Defence Experimental Establishment, Porton Down, Wiltshire in 1952. Patents were applied for in 1962 and published in February 1974 showing it to be Ethyl S-2-diisopropylam-inoethylmethylphosphonothiolate. The lethal dosage is 10 mg-minute/m^3 airborne or 0·3 mg orally.

Most absorbent substance

The US Department of Agriculture Research Service announced on 18 Aug 1974 that 'H-span' or Super Slurper composed of one half starch derivative and one fourth each of acrylamide and acrylic acid can, when treated with iron, retain water 1300 times its own weight.

Finest powder

The ultimate in fine powder is solid helium which was first postulated to be a monatomic powder as early as 1964.

THE 109 ELEMENTS

There are 94 naturally—occurring elements comprising, at ordinary temperatures, two liquids, 11 gases, 72 metals and 9 other solids. To date the discovery of a further 15 transuranic elements (Elements 95 to 109) has been claimed of which 10 are undisputed.

Category	Name	Symbol	Discovery of Element		Record
Commonest (lithosphere)	Oxygen	O	1771	Scheele (Germany-Sweden)	46·60% by weight
Commonest (atmosphere)	Nitrogen	N	1772	Rutherford (GB)	78·09% by volume
Commonest (extra-terrestrial)	Hydrogen	H	1776	Cavendish (GB)	90% of all matter
Rarest (of the 94)[1]	Astatine	At	1940	Corson (US) *et al.*	1/100th oz *0·35 g* in Earth's crust
Lightest	Hydrogen	H	1776	Cavendish (GB)	0·005 612 lb/ft^3 *0·000 089 89 g/cm^3*
Lightest (metal)	Lithium	Li	1817	Arfwedson (Sweden)	33·30 lb/ft^3 *0·5334 g/cm^3*
Densest	Osmium	Os	1804	Tennant (GB)	1410 lb/ft^3 *22·59 g/cm^3*
Heaviest (Gas)	Radon	Rn	1900	Dorn (Germany)	0·6274 lb/ft^3 *0·0100 5 g/cm^3* at 0°C
Newest[2]	Unniloctium	Uno	1984	G. Munzenberg *et al.* (W. Germany) and at Dubna Research Institute, Moscow, USSR	Element 108
Purest[3]	Helium	^{4}He	1868	Lockyer (GB) & Janssen (France)	2 parts in 10^{15} (1978)
Hardest	Carbon	C	prehistoric		Diamond allotrope, Knoop value 8400
Most Expensive	Californium	Cf	1950	Seaborg (US) *et al.*	Sold in 1970 for $10 per µg
Most Stable[4]	Tellurium	^{128}Te	1782	von Reichenstein (Austria)	Half-life of $1·5 \times 10^{24}$ years
Least Stable	Lithium (isotope 5)	Li 5	1817	Arfwedson (Sweden)	Lifetime of $4·4 \times 10^{-22}$ sec.
Most Isotopes	Xenon	Xe	1898	Ramsay & Travers (GB)	36
	Caesium	Cs	1860	Bunsen & Kirchoff (Germany)	36
Least Isotopes	Hydrogen	H	1776	Cavendish (GB)	3 (confirmed)
Most Ductile	Gold	Au	*ante* 3000 BC		1 oz drawn to 43 miles *1 g/2.4 km*
Highest Tensile Strength	Boron	B	1808	Gay-Lussac & Thenard (France) & H. Davy (GB)	$3·9 \times 10^6$ lb f/in^2 *26·8 GPa*
Lowest Melting/Boiling Point (non-metallic)[3,5]	Helium	^{4}He	1868	Lockyer (GB) & Janssen (France)	−272·375° C under pressure (*2532 kPa*) and −268·928° C
Lowest Melting/Boiling Point (metallic)	Mercury	Hg	protohistoric		−38·836° C/356·661° C
Highest Melting/Boiling Point (non-metallic)	Carbon (carbyne 6)	C	prehistoric[6]		3530° C/3870° C
Highest Melting/Boiling Point (metallic)[6]	Tungsten	W	1783	J. J. & F. d'Elhuyar (Spain)	3420° C and 5730° C
Largest Expansion (negative)	Plutonium	Pu	1940	Seaborg (US) *et al.*	−5·8 × 10^{-5} cm/cm/deg C between 450–480° C (Delta prime allotrope disc. 1953)
Lowest Expansion (positive)	Carbon (diamond)	C	prehistoric		1·0 × 10^{-6} cm/cm/deg C (at 20° C)
Highest Expansion (metal)	Caesium	Cs	1860	Bunsen & Kirchoff (Germany)	9·7 × 10^{-5} cm/cm/deg C (at 20° C)
Highest Expansion (solid)	Neon	Ne	1898	Ramsay & Travers (GB)	1·94 × 10^{-3} cm/cm/deg C at −248·59° C
Most Toxic	Radium	^{224}Ra	1898	The Curies & Bemont (France)	Naturally occurring isotope 17 000 × more toxic than plutonium 239

[1] *The naturally-occuring isotope astatine 215 occurs only to the extent of $1·6 \times 10^{-10}$ oz 4·5 nanograms.*

[2] *Provisional IUPAC name. A single atom of Unnilennium 109) was created by bombardment of bismuth by iron ions at the GSI laboratory, Dormstadt, West Germany on 29 Aug 1982. It had the highest atomic number (element 109) and also had the highest atomic mass (266).*

[3] *Identified on Earth by Ramsay (GB) in 1895. There is a very tentative Soviet claim to have observed the formation of an isotope of mass 276 of element 110 (provisional name 'Ununnilium' symbol Uun).*

[4] *Double beta decay estimate. Alpha particle record is Samarium 148 at 8×10^{15} years and beta particle record is Cadmium 113 at 9×10^{15} years.*

[5] *Monatomic hydrogen H is expected to be a non-liquefiable superfluid gas.*

[6] *The carbyne forms of carbon were discovered by A. E. Goresy and G. Donnay (USA) and A. M. Sladkov and Yu. P. Koudrayatsev (USSR) in 1968.*

Drink and Drugs

As from 1 Jan 1981 the strength of spirits has been expressed only in terms of percentae volume of alcohol at 20° C. Absolute or '100 per cent vol' alcohol was formerly expressed to be 75·5 ° over proof or 75·35°OP. In the USA proof is double the actual percentage of alcohol by volume at 15·6° C *60° F* such that absolute alcohol is 200 per cent proof spirit.

'Hangovers' are said to be aggravated by the presence of such toxic congenerics as amyl alcohol ($C_5H_{11}OH$).

Most alcoholic

During independence (1918–40) the Estonian Liquor Monopoly marketed 98 per cent potato alcohol (196 proof US). In 31 US states *Everclear,* 190 proof or 95 per cent vol alcohol, is marketed by the American Distilling Co 'primarily as a base for home-made cordials'. Royal Navy rum, introduced in 1655, was 40° OP (79 per cent vol) before 1948, but was reduced to 4·5° UP (under proof) or 46 per cent vol before its abolition on 31 July 1970. Full strength Pusser's naval rum was again sold by E. D. & F. Man from 1984.

Strongest beers

The strongest beer as measured by alcoholic content is Roger & Out brewed at the Frog & Parrot in Sheffield, South Yorkshire, from a recipe devised by W.R. Nowill and G.B. Spencer. It contains 16·9 per cent alcohol by volume with an original gravity of 1125°. It was first brewed in July 1985 and has been on sale ever since.

The strongest as measured by original gravity is Domesday Ale brewed by the Cornish Brewery Company Ltd, Redruth, Cornwall with an alcohol content of 15·86 per cent by volume. It has an original gravity of 1143·5 °.

The strongest lager is Samichlaus Dark 1987 brewed by Brauerei Hürlimann of Zürich, Switzerland. It has an original gravity of 1123 °and is 14·93 per cent alcohol by volume at 20° C.

Most ductile element ● Gold, which is the most ductile of the elements, can be worked into thin sheets of foil as can be seen here. Goldleaf with a thickness of only a few hundred atoms can be produced and this looks yellow in reflected light but appears green by transmitted light. (Photo: Bruce Coleman)

Weakest beer

The weakest liquid ever marketed as beer was a sweet ersatz beer which was brewed in Germany by Sunner, Colne-Kalk, in 1918. It had an original gravity of 1000·96° and a strength 1/30th that of the weakest beer now obtainable in the UK.

Oldest wine

The oldest datable wine ever found were two bottles from Xinyang, Hunan, China in 1980 from a tomb dated to 1300 BC. A wine jar recovered in Rome has been found to bear the label 'Q. Lutatio C. Mario Cos' meaning that it was produced in the consulship of Q. Lutatius and C. Marius i.e. in 102 BC. A bottle of .1748 Rudesheimer Rosewein was auctioned at Christie's, London for £260 on 6 Dec 1979.

Most expensive wine

The highest price paid for any bottle has been £105 000 for a 1787 Château Lafite claret sold to Christopher Forbes (USA) at Christie's, London on 5 Dec 1985. The price was affected insofar as the bottle was initialled by Thomas Jefferson (1743–1826), 3rd President of the United States. In Nov 1986 its cork, dried out by exhibition lights, slipped thus making the wine undrinkable.

A bottle of white wine – Château d'Yquem of 1784 and also initialled by Thomas Jefferson – was sold at auction by Christie's, London on 4 Dec 1986 for £36 900 to Iyad Shiblaq, Jordan, a teetotaller.

A half bottle of 1784 Château Margau bearing the initials

---

of Thomas Jefferson was sold by Christie's, at Vinexpo, on 26 June 1987 at Bordeaux, France for FF180 000 .

Wine auction

The largest single sale of wine was conducted by Christie's of King Street, St James's, London on 10–11 July 1974 at Quaglino's Ballroom, London when 2325 lots comprising 432 000 bottles realised £962 190.

Wine tasting

The largest ever reported wine tasting was that staged by the Wine Institute at St Francis Hotel, San Francisco, California on 17 July 1980 with 125 pourers, 90 openers and a consumption of 3000 bottles.

Most expensive spirits

A 60-year-old bottle of' The Macallan' was sold by the Rotary Club of Elgin, Grampian, for £6000 on 2 June 1988. The purchaser was Sheraton Caltrust of Glasgow.

In Britain *Hennessy Private Reserve Grande Champagne* retails for £120 (including VAT) for a standard bottle.

Largest bottles

The largest bottle ever made was unveiled at the *Guinness World of Records,* Piccadilly, London on 31 Mar 1987 measuring 1·83 m *6 ft* tall and 1·46 m *4 ft 9½ in* in circumference. The bottle, built by independent family whisky company William Grant & Sons as part of its centenary celebrations, contained 40·7 gal *185 litres* of William Grant's Family Reserve Finest Scotch Whisky.

The largest bottles normally used in the wine and spirit trade are the Jeroboam (equal to 4 bottles of champagne or, rarely, of brandy and from 5 to 6½ bottles of claret according to whether blown or moulded) and the double magnum (equal, since *c.* 1934 to 4 bottles of claret or, more rarely, red Burgundy). A complete set of champagne bottles would consist of a quarter bottle, through the half bottle, bottle, magnum, Jeroboam, Rehoboam, Methuselah, Salmanazer and Balthazar, to the Nebuchadnezzar, which has a capacity of 16 litres *28·14 pt,* and is equivalent to 20 bottles.

Martell Cognac is available in a range of 21 bottle sizes from 3 cl *0·05 pt* to 3·78 l *6·6 pt.*

THE BEAUJOLAIS RUN

Largest single shipment....In the early hours of 19 Nov 1987 the 'Pride of Dover' carried 1 646 340 bottles from Calais to Dover thus constituting the largest ever shipment of Beaujolais Nouveau. The bottles were packed in 91 trailers and 2 vans. This was part of a total shipment of 3 234 804 bottles carried on the same night by P&O European Ferries in five vessels.

Fastest run....Steve Morgan and Ron Porter of The Principality Wine Co with 15 cases of Beaujolais Nouveau achieved a time of 36 minutes and 21 seconds from Dinard to touch down at Cardiff airport, South Glamorgan by Lear jet. The wine was in British airspace 13 minutes after take-off.

Fastest by electric power....Ron Haggerty and a team from Unigate Dairies completed the 792 km *492 miles* from Beaune, France to Trafalgar Square, London in 30 hr 40 min (average speed- 25·82 km/h *16·04 mph*) in a Wales & Edwards milk float powered by lead-acid batteries.

Smallest bottle

The smallest bottles of liquor now sold are of Whyte and Mackay Scotch Whisky standing just over 5 cm *2 in* tall and containing 1·3 ml *22 minims*. A mini case of 12 bottles is also available and measuring 4·67 × 3·33 × 2·69 cm *1·84 × 1·31 × 1·06 in* and costs £5.50 including VAT, distributed by Cumbrae Supply Co. Paisley, Scotland.

Bottle collections

David L. Maund of Upham, Hampshire, has a collection of unduplicated miniature Scotch whisky bottles amounting to 7014. Over the past 30 years he has also collected 323 different miniature Guinness bottles.

George E. Terren of Southboro, Massachusetts, USA, has a collection of 29 508 miniature and distilled spirit and liquor bottles as at 1 Mar 1988

The collection of unduplicated labels by Ian Boasman of Bistro French, Preston, Lancashire had reached 2067 by April 1988.

The world's greatest collection of whisky bottles is one of 3100 unduplicated labels assembled by Sig Edward Giaccone at his whiskyteca, Salo, Lake Garda, Italy.

Champagne cork flight

The longest distance for a champagne cork to fly from an untreated and unheated bottle 1·22 m *4 ft* from level ground is 54·18 m *177 ft 9 in* by Professor Emeritus Heinrich Medicus, RPI, at the Woodbury Vineyards Winery, New York, USA on 5 June 1988 .

Most powerful drugs

The most powerful commonly available drug is d-Lysergic Acid Diethylamide tartrate (LSD-25, $C_{20}H_{25}N_3O$) first produced in 1938 for common cold research and as a hallucinogen by Dr Albert Hoffman (Swiss) on 16–19 Apr 1943.

The most potent analgesic drug is the morphine-like R33799 confirmed in 1978 to have almost 12 000 times the potency of morphine. Interferon was reported available for $10 per millionth of a microgramme.

Most prescribed drug

The top-selling prescription drug is the anti-ulcer drug Zantac, manufactured by Glaxo Holdings plc. London. Worldwide sales in 1987 were $1·59 billion. Zantac is also the top seller in the UK, with sales of £80 million in the prescribed drug market.

Most lethal man-made chemical

TCDD (2,3,7,8-tetrachlorodibenzo-p-dioxin), discovered in 1872, is admitted to be 150 000 times more deadly than cyanide at $3,1 \times 10^{-9}$ moles/kg.

Photography

CAMERAS

Earliest

The earliest veiled reference to a photograph on glass taken in a camera was in a letter dated 19 July 1822 from Joseph Nicéphore Niépce (1765–1833), a French scientist. It was of a copper engraving of Pope Pius VII taken at Gras, near Chalon-sur-Saône and it was rediscovered in London in February 1952 by the photohistorian Helmut Gernsheim after 6 years' research.

The earliest photograph taken in England was one of a diamond-paned window in Laycock (or Lacock) Abbey, Wiltshire, taken in August 1835 by William Henry Fox Talbot, MP (1800–77), the inventor of the negative-positive process. The negative of this was donated to the Science Museum, London in 1937 by his grand–daughter Matilda.

The world's earliest aerial photograph was taken in 1858 by Gaspard Félix Tournachon (1820–1910), *alias* Nadar, from a balloon near Villacoublay, on the outskirts of Paris.

Largest

The largest and most expensive industrial camera ever built is the 27 tonne Rolls Royce camera now owned by BPCC Graphics Ltd of Derby, England commissioned in 1956. It measures 2·69 m *8 ft 10 in* high, 2·51 m *8 ft 3 in* wide and 14·02 m *46 ft* in length. The lens is a 160 cm *63 in* f 16 Cooke Apochromatic. In 1988 it was still in full use.

Smallest

Apart from cameras built for intra-cardiac surgery and espionage, the smallest camera that has been marketed is the circular Japanese 'Petal' camera with a diameter of 2·9 cm *1·14 in* and a thickness of 1·65 cm *0·65 in*. It has a focal length of 12 mm *0·47 in*. The BBC TV programme *Record Breakers* showed prints from this camera on 3 Dec 1974.

Fastest

A camera built for research into high-power lazers by The Blackett Laboratory of Imperial College of Science and Technology, London, registers images at a rate of 33 000 million per sec.

Most expensive

The most expensive complete range of camera equipment in the world is that of Nikon of Tokyo, Japan, who marketed in April 1988 their complete range of 24 cameras with 72 lenses and 553 accessories. Fox Talbot

of London quoted £218 167·50 excluding VAT. The highest auction price for an antique camera is £21 000 for a J. B. Dancer stereo camera, patented in 1856 and sold at Christie's, South Kensington on 12 Oct 1977.

Longest negative

On 22 June 1985 Robert J. Paluzzi using a 40·6 cm *16 in* Century Cirkut camera captured a 200 degree view of Las Vegas in a single shot. The resulting negative measured 40·6 cm *16 in* by 274 cm *9 ft.*

Most expensive photograph

A photograph taken on 9 Feb 1864 of Abraham Lincoln and his son Tad was sold at Sotheby's New York, USA, in May 1985 to Malcolm Forbes Jr for $104 500 .

Telescopes

Earliest

Although there is evidence that early Arabian scientists understood something of the magnifying power of lenses, their first use to form a telescope has been attributed to Roger Bacon (*c.* 1214–92) in England. The prototype of modern refracting telescopes was completed by Johannes Lippershey for the Netherlands government on 2 Oct 1608.

Largest reflector

On 12 Sept 1985, work started on the W. M. Keck 10 m *393·7 in* reflector for Caltech and the University of California on Mauna Kea, Hawaii. It is due to be completed by 1989 and will comprise 36 independently-controlled fitting hexagonal mirrors.

Note: The attachment of an electronic charge-coupled device (CCD) increases the 'light-grasp' of a telescope

Largest wine bottle ● The French ambassador in Norway, M Phillipe Peltier, on the occasion of the launching of the passenger liner *Sovereign of the Seas* in January 1988, unveiling a bottle provided by the champagne producers, Taittinger, equal in volume to 35 whole wine bottles i.e. 26 litres. It was suggested that this be known as a 'Sovereign'.

by a factor up to 100 fold. Thus a 508 cm *200 in* telescope achieves the light-gathering capacity of a 25·4 m *1000 in* telescope.

Largest refractor

The largest refracting (i.e. magnification by lenses) telescope in the world is the 18·90 m *62 ft* long 101·6 cm *40 in* telescope completed in 1897 at the Yerkes Observatory, Williams Bay, Wisconsin, and belonging to the University of Chicago, Illinois, USA. In 1900 a 125 cm *49·2 in* refractor 54·85 m *180 ft* in length was built for the Paris Exposition but its optical performance was too poor to justify attempts to use it.

Britain's largest refractor is the 71·12 cm *28 in* Great Equatorial Telescope of 1893 installed in the Old Royal Observatory, Greenwich, South east London.

Largest radio dish

Radio waves of extra-terrestrial origin were first detected by Karl Jansky of Bell Telephone Laboratories, Holmdel, New Jersey, USA using a 30·48 m *100 ft* long shortwave rotatable antenna in 1932. The world's largest dish radio telescope is the partially-steerable ionospheric assembly built over a natural bowl at Arecibo, Puerto Rico, completed in November 1963 at a cost of about $9 000 000 . The dish has a diameter of 304·8 m *1000 ft* and covers 7·48 ha *18½ acres*. Its sensitivity was raised by a factor of 1000 and its range to the edge of the observable Universe at some 15 000 million light-years by the fitting of new aluminium plates at a cost of $8·8 million. Rededication was on 16 Nov 1974.

The world's largest trainable dish-type radio telescope is the 100 m *328 ft* diameter, 3048 tonnes *3000 ton* assembly at the Max Planck Institute for Radio Astronomy of Bonn in the Effelsberger Valley, West Germany; it became operative in May 1971. Begun in November 1967, the cost was 36 920,000 DM.

Largest radio installation

It was reported in October 1986 that radio astronomers first linked the NASA deep-space installation at Tidbinbilla, Australia with the tracking stations at Usuda and Kashima, Japan and with the TDRS (Tracking and Data Relay Satellite) which is in a geosynchronous orbit. This has now been developed to create a radio telescope with an effective diameter of 2·16 Earth diameters, 27 523 km *17 102 miles*.

The world's largest terrestrial radio-telescopic installation is the US National Science Foundation VLA (Very Large Array). It is Y-shaped with each arm 20·9 km *13 miles* long with 27 mobile antennae (each of 25 m *82 ft* diameter) on rails. It is 80 km *50 miles* west of Socorro in the Plains of San Augustin, New Mexico, USA and was dedicated on 10 Oct 1980 at a cost of $78 million .

Oldest observatory

The oldest astronomical observatory building extant in the world is 'Tower of the Winds' used by Andronichus of Cyrrhos in Athens, Greece *c.* 70 BC, and equipped with sundials and clepsydra.

Highest observatory

The highest observatory in the world is the University of Denver's High Altitude Observatory at 4297 m *14 100 ft*, opened in 1973. The principal instrument is a 60·48 cm *24 in* Ealing Beck reflecting telescope.

Planetaria

The ancestor of the planetarium is the rotatable Gottorp Globe, built by Andreas Busch in Denmark between 1654 and 1664 to the orders of Olearius, court mathematician to Duke Frederick III of Holstein. It is 10·54 m *34·6 ft* in circumference, weighs nearly 3½ tonnes and is now preserved in Leningrad, USSR. The stars were painted on the inside. The earliest optical installation was not until 1923 in the Deutsches Museum, Munich, by Zeiss of Jena, East Germany. The world's largest planetarium is in Miyazaki, Japan. Construction was completed on 30 June 1987 and the dome has a diameter of 27 m *88 ft 7 in.*

Space telescope

The first space observatory was the Orbiting Solar observatory 0504 launched on 18 Oct 1967. The largest will be the $1·2 billion NASA Edwin P Hubble Space Telescope of 11 tonnes *10·8 tons* and 13·1 m *43 ft* in overall length with a 240 cm *94·5 in* reflector eventually to be placed in orbit at *c.* 480 km *300 miles* altitude aboard a US Space Shuttle. The cost of maintaining it and its staff after the launch postponment of October 1986 has been $230 000.

Numbers

In dealing with large numbers, scientists use the notation of 10 raised to various powers to eliminate a profusion of noughts. For example, 19 160 000 000 000 miles would be written 1·916×10^{13} miles. Similarly, a very small number, for example 0·000 015 432 4 of a gram, would be written 1·543 24×10^{-5}. Of the prefixes used before numbers the smallest is 'tredo' from the Danish *tredyvo* for 30, indicating 10^{-30} of a unit, and the highest is 'dea' (*Greek*, deca, ten), symbol D, indicating ten groups of 3 zeros 10^{30} or a quintillion (*UK*) or a nonillion (*US*).

Highest numbers

The highest lexicographically accepted named number in the system of successive powers of ten is the centillion, first recorded in 1852. It is the hundredth power of a million, or one followed by 600 noughts. The highest named number outside the decimal notation is the Buddhist *asankhyeya*, which is equal to 10^{140} and mentioned in Jaina works of *c.* 100 BC.

The number 10^{100} is designated a Googol. The term was devised by Dr Edward Kasner (US) (d. 1955). Ten raised to the power of a Googol is described as a Googolplex. Some conception of the magnitude of such numbers can be gained when it is said that the number of electrons in some models of the observable Universe does not exceed 10^{87}.

The highest number ever used in a mathematical proof is a bounding value published in 1977 and known as Graham's number. It concerns bi-chromatic hypercubes and is inexpressible without the special 'arrow' notation, devised by Knuth in 1976, extended to 64 layers. Mr Candelaria ('the only man infinity fears') of Loma Linda, California, USA has devised a Large Number Denomination System concluding with a milli-decillifiveillion-illion.

Prime numbers

A prime number is any positive integer (excluding 1) having no integral factors other than itself and unity, e.g. 2, 3, 5, 7 or 11. The lowest prime number is thus 2. The highest known prime number is 2^{216,091}−1, discovered in September 1985 by analysts using a Cray X-MP/24 computer at Chevron Geosciences Co in Houston, Texas, USA. It is the 30th known Marsenne prime, and contains 65 050 digits. The lowest non-prime or composite number (excluding 1) is 4.

Perfect numbers

A number is said to be perfect if it is equal to the sum of its divisors other than itself, e.g. 1+2+4+7+14=28. The lowest perfect number is 6 (=1+2+3). The highest known and the 30th so far discovered, is (2^{216,091}−1)×2^{216,090}. It is a consequence of the highest known prime (see above).

Most-proved theorem

A book published in 1940 contained 370 different proofs of Pythagoras's Theorem including one by President Garfield of the United States of America.

Longest proof

The longest mathematical proof is the proof of the classification of all finite simple groups. It is spread over more than 14 000 pages in nearly 500 papers in mathematical journals contributed by more than 100 mathematicians over a period of more than 35 years.

Largest claimed accurate number in physics

Sir Arthur Eddington announced in 1938 that there are exactly 15 747 724 136 275 002 577 605 653 961 181 555 468 044 717 914 527 116 709 366 231 425 076 185 631 031 296 protons in the universe, and the same number of electrons. Unfortunately for Eddington, no one else believed his theory, which is now discredited.

Largest prize ever offered

Dr Paul Wolfskell left prize money in his will for the first person to solve Fermat's Last Theorem. This prize was worth 100 000 deutschmarks in 1908. As a result of inflation, the prize is now just over 10 000 deutschmarks.

Most innumerate

The most innumerate people are the Nambiquara of the north-west Matto Grosso of Brazil who lack any system of numbers. They do, however, have a verb which means 'they are alike'.

Most accurate and most inaccurate version of 'pi'

The greatest number of decimal places to which *pi* (π) has been calculated is 208 326 000 on 8 Mar 1988 by Yasumasa Kanada of Tokyo University, Japan using a Hitachi supercomputer Hitacs-802/80. The computation took 5 hr 57 min. In 1897 the General Assembly of Indiana enacted in House Bill No. 246 that *pi* was *de jure* 4. Places 762 – 767 are 6 consecutive '9's'.

Earliest measures

The earliest known measure of weight is the *beqa* of the Amratian period of Egyptian civilisation *c.* 3800 BC found at Naqada, Egypt. The weights are cylindrical with rounded ends from 188·7 to 211·2 g *6·65–7.45 oz.* The unit of length used by the megalithic tomb-builders in north western Europe *c.* 3500 BC appears to have been 82·90 cm ± 0·09 cm *2·72±0·003 ft*. This was deduced by Professor Alexander Thom (1894–1985) in 1966.

Time measure

Owing to variations in the length of a day, which is estimated to be increasing irregularly at the average rate of about a millisecond per century due to the Moon's tidal drag, the second has been redefined. Instead of being 1/86 400th part of a mean solar day, it has, since 1960, been reckoned as 1/31 556 925 9747th part of the solar (or tropical) year at AD 1900, January 0·12 hr, Ephemeris time. In 1958 the second of Ephemeris time was computed to be equivalent to 9 192 631 770 ± 20 cycles of the radiation corresponding to the transition of caesium 133 atoms when unperturbed by exterior fields. The greatest diurnal change recorded has been 10 milliseconds on 8 Aug 1972 and this was due to the most violent solar storm which had been recorded in 370 years of observations.

The accuracy of the caesium beam frequency standard approaches 8 parts in 10^{14} compared to 2 parts in 10^{13} for the methane-stabilised helium-neon laser and 6 parts in 10^{13} for the hydrogen maser.

The longest measure of time is the *kalpa* in Hindu chronology. It is equivalent to 4320 million years. In astronomy a cosmic year is the period of rotation of the Sun around the centre of the Milky Way galaxy i.e. 225 million years. In the Late Cretaceous Period of *c.* 85 million years ago the Earth rotated faster so resulting in 370·3 days per year while in Cambrian times some 600 million years ago there is evidence that the year extended over 425 days.

Gems, Jewels and Precious Stones

OPAL

Largest. 220 troy oz. The 17 700 carat *Olympic Australis* (SiO$_2$nH$_2$O) found in Coober Pedy, South Australia in August 1956, owned by Altmann and Cherny Pty Ltd, is on public display in Melbourne and valued at $1·8 million (US).

DIAMOND

Largest. 3106 carats. Found on 25 Jan 1905 in the Premier Mine, Pretoria, South Africa and named *The Cullinan* after the mine's discoverer Sir Thomas Cullinan. Presented to King Edward VII in 1907. Currently the largest uncut stone is of 599 carats, found near Pretoria, South Africa in July 1986 and was revealed by De Beers on 11 Mar 1988. It is expected to yield a 350 carat cut stone.

Rarest colour. Blood red. The largest is a 5·05 carat flawless stone found in Tichtenburg, South Africa in 1927 and now in a private collection in the United States.

Highest priced. $9 130 000. The flawless pear-shaped 85·91 carat, sold to Laurence Gaff of London at Sotheby's New York City on 19 Nov 1988. The record for carat is $192 000 for a 52·59 carat stone sold to a Saudi Arabian at Christies', New York on 20 Apr 1988 for $7 980 000

Largest cut. 530·2 carats. A 74 facets pear-shaped gem named *The Star of Africa*, cleaved from *The Cullinan* by Jak Asscher and polished by Henri Koe in Amsterdam in 1908. Now in the Royal Sceptre. The uncut 890 carat Zale Corporation stone may yield a larger cut stone.

JADE

Largest. 143 tons/*tonnes*. On 17 Sept 1978 a boulder of nephrite jade was reported Ca$_2$(Mg,Fe)$_5$(Sl$_4$O$_{11}$)$_2$(OH)$_2$ of 603 m^3 *21 300 ft^3* found in China.

TOPAZ

Largest. 21·327 carats. The light blue *Brazilian Princess* is cut from a 33·4 kg *75 lb* crystal and has resided in the American Museum of Natural History, New York, USA from 10 Dec 1985. Valued at $1 006 350 and with 221 facets, this is the world's largest faceted stone.

GOLD

Largest nugget. 214·32 kg *7560 oz* .The *Holtermann Nugget* found on 19 Oct 1872 in the Beyers & Holtermann Star of Hope mine, Hill End, New South Wales, Australia, contained some 99·8 kg *220 lb* of gold in a 285·7 kg *630 lb* slab of slate.

Largest pure nugget. The *Welcome Stranger* found at Moliagul, Victoria, Australia in 1869 yielded 69·92 kg *2248 troy oz* of pure gold from 70·92 kg *2280 ¼ oz*.

EMERALD

Largest cut. 86 136 carats. This natural beryl Gleim [Be$_3$Al$_2$(SiO$_3$)$_6$] was found in Carnaiba, Brazil in August 1974. It was carved by Richard Chan in Hong Kong and valued at £718 000 in 1982.

RUBY

Largest star. 2475 carats. *Rajarathna*, India, displays an animated star of 6 lines and is cut as a cabochon.

Largest double star. 1370 carats. A cabochon cut gem, *Neelanjahi* owned by G. Vidyaraj, Bangalore, India, displays 12 star lines and measures 7·62 cm *3 in* in height and 5·08 cm *2 in* in diameter.

Largest. 8500 carats. In July 1985 jeweller James Kazanjian of Beverly Hills, California, displayed a 14 cm *5½ in* tall red corundum (Al$_2$O$_3$) carved into the Liberty Bell.

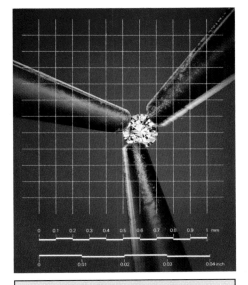

Smallest diamond ● D. Drukker & Zn NV of Amsterdam, Netherlands have produced a 57–facet brilliant with a diameter of 0·22 mm *0·009 in* and weight of 0·001 2 carat *0·000 24 g.*

PEARL

Largest. 14 lb 6·37 kg *I oz.* The *Pearl of Laotze* was found at Palawan, Philippines on 7 May 1934 in the shell of a giant clam. The property of Wilburn Dowell Cobb until his death, this 24 cm *9½ in* long by 14 cm *5½ in* diameter *molluscan concretion* was bought at auction on 15 May 1980 in San Francisco by Peter Hoffman and Victor Barbish for $200 000 . An appraisal by the San Francisco Gem Laboratory in May 1982 suggested a value of $32 640 000.

SAPPHIRE

Largest. 2302 carats. Found at Anakie, Queensland, Australia in *c.* 1935, this corundum (Al$_2$O$_3$) was carved into a 1318 carat head of Abraham Lincoln and is now in the custody of the Kazanjian Foundation of Los Angeles, California, USA. A sapphire crystal found by Steve Meyer and Craig Peden near Canton, North Carolina in December 1987 has been provisionally estimated at 3500 carats.

Largest cut. 1444 carats. A bust of General Dwight David Eisenhower that was carved in 1953–5 from a 2097-carat black star stone.

Largest Star. The 1154 carat pale lavender 'Star of America', appraised at $2 290 000 was unveiled by its owner Roy Whestone of Kilgore, Texas at Tucson, Arizona on 5 Feb 1987.

Highest priced. £579 300. A step-cut single stone of 66·03 carats from the Rockefeller Collection was sold by auction on 8 May 1980 at Sotheby's, Zurich.

AMBER

Largest. 15·25 kg 33 lb 10 oz. The 'Burma Amber' is located in the Natural History Museum, London. Amber is a fossil resin derived from extinct coniferous trees, and often contains trapped insects.

Physical Extremes

Highest temperature

The highest man-made temperatures yet attained are those produced in the centre of a thermonuclear fusion bomb, which are estimated to be in the order of 300 000 000 – 400 000 000° C. Of controllable temperatures the highest effective laboratory figure reported is 200 million degrees C achieved in the Tokamak Fusion Test Reactor at the Princeton Plasma Physics Laboratory, USA in June 1986. A figure of 3000 million degrees C was reportedly achieved in the USSR with Ogra injection-mirror equipment *c.* 1962.

Lowest temperature

The lowest temperature reached is 3×10^{-8} Kelvin above absolute zero attained in a two-stage nuclear demagnetisation cryostat at Espoo, Finland by the team led by Professor Olli V. Lounasmaa (b. 1930) and announced in June 1984. Absolute or thermodynamic temperatures are defined in terms of ratios rather than as differences reckoned from the unattainable absolute zero, which on the Kelvin scale is −273·15° C or −459·67° F. Thus the lowest temperature ever attained is 1 in 9·1×10^9 of the melting point of ice (0° C or 273·15 K or 32° F). Tokyo University's Institute of Solid State Physics announced on 15 Feb 1983 that a team led by Prof Kazuo Ono had attained a temperature within 0·000 03 of a degree of absolute zero at which molecular motion ceases.

Smallest thermometer

Dr Frederich Sachs, a biophysicist at the State University of New York at Buffalo, USA, has developed an ultra-microthermometer for measuring the temperature of single living cells. The tip is one micron in diameter, about one fiftieth the diameter of a human hair.

Largest barometer

A water barometer 12 m *39 ft* in height was constructed by Bert Bolle, Curator of the Barometer Museum, Maartensdijk, Netherlands where the instrument is situated.

Highest pressures

The highest sustained laboratory pressures yet reported are of 1·70 megabars (170 GPa *11 000 tons force/in^2*) achieved in the giant hydraulic diamond-faced press at the Carnegie Institution's Geophysical Laboratory, Washington DC reported in June 1978. This laboratory announced solid hydrogen achieved at 57 kilobars pressure on 2 Mar 1979. If created, metallic hydrogen is expected to be silvery white but soft with a density of 1·1 g/cm^3. The pressure required for the transition is estimated by H. K. Mao and P. M. Bell to be 1 megabar at 25° C. Using dynamic methods and impact speeds of up to 29000 km/h *18 000 mph,* momentary pressures of 75 000 000 atmospheres (7000 GPa *490 000 tons/in^2*) were reported from the United States in 1958.

Highest velocity

The highest velocity at which any solid visible object has been projected is 150 km/sec *335 000 mph* in the case of a plastic disc at the Naval Research Laboratory, Washington DC, reported in August 1980.

Finest balance

The most accurate balance in the world is the Sartorius Model 4108 manufactured in Göttingen, West Germany, which can weigh objects of up to 0·5 g to an accuracy of 0·01 μg or 0·000 000 01g, equivalent to little more than one sixtieth of the weight of the ink on this full stop .

Largest bubble chamber

The largest bubble chamber in the world is the $7 million installation completed in October 1973 at Weston, Illinois. It is 4·57 m *15 ft* in diameter and contains 33 000 litres *7259 gal* of liquid hydrogen at a temperature of −247° C with a super conducting magnet of 3 tesla.

Fastest centrifuge

Ultra-centrifuges were invented by Theodor Svedberg (b. 30 Aug 1884) (Sweden) in 1923. The highest man-made rotary speed ever achieved and the fastest speed of any earth-bound object is 7250 km/h *4500 mph* by a swirling tapered 15·2 cm *6 in* carbon fibre rod in a vacuum at Birmingham University on 24 Jan 1975.

Finest cut

The $13 million Large Optics Diamond Turning Machine

at the Lawrence Livermore National Laboratory, California, USA was reported in June 1983 to be able to sever a human hair 3000 times lengthwise.

Longest echo

The longest recorded echo in any building is one of 15 sec following the closing of the door of the Chapel of the Mausoleum, Hamilton, Lanarkshire built 1840–55.

Most powerful electric current

The most powerful electric current generated is that from the Zeus capacitor at the Los Alamos Scientific Laboratory, New Mexico, USA. If fired simultaneously the 4032 capacitors would produce, for a few microseconds, twice as much current as that generated elsewhere on Earth.

Hottest flame

The hottest flame that can be produced is from carbon subnitride (C_4N_2) which at one atmosphere pressure is calculated to reach 5261 K.

Highest measured frequency

The highest *directly* measured frequency is a visible yellow-green light at 520·2068085 terahertz (a terahertz being a million million hertz or cycles per second) for the o-component of the 17–1 P(62) transition line of iodine 127. The highest measured frequency determined by precision metrology is a green light at 582·491703 terahertz for the b_{21} component of the R(15) 43–0 transition line of iodine 127. However, with the decision on 20 Oct 1983 by the Conférence Générale des Poids et Mesures (CGPM) to define exactly the metre (m) in terms of the velocity of light (c) such that 'the metre is the length of the path travelled by light in vacuum during a time interval of 1/299 792 458 of a second' then frequency (f) and wavelength (ξ) are exactly interchangeable through the relationship $f\xi = c$.

Lowest friction

The lowest coefficient of static and dynamic friction of any solid is 0·02, in the case of polytetrafluoroethylene ($[C_2F_4]_n$), called PTFE — equivalent to wet ice on wet ice. It was first manufactured in quantity by E. I. du Pont de Nemours & Co Inc. in 1943, and is marketed from the USA as Teflon. In the United Kingdom it is marketed by ICI as Fluon. In the centrifuge at the University of Virginia a 13·60 kg *30 lb* rotor magnetically supported has been spun at 1000 rev/sec in a vacuum of 10^{-6} mm of mercury pressure. It loses only one revolution per second per day, thus spinning for years.

Smallest hole

A hole of 40 Å (4×10^{-6} mm) was shown visually using a JEM 100C electron microscope and Quantel Electronics devices at the Dept of Metallurgy, Oxford on 28 Oct 1979. To find such a hole is equivalent to finding a pinhead in a haystack with sides of 1·93 km *1·2 miles*. An electron microscope beam on a sample of sodium beta-alumina at the University of Illinois, USA, in May 1983 accidentally bored a hole 2×10^{-9} m in diameter.

Most powerful laser beams

The first illumination of another celestial body was achieved on 9 May 1962, when a beam of light was successfully reflected from the Moon by the use of a laser (light amplification by stimulated emission of radiation) attached to a· 121·9 cm *48 in* telescope at Massachusetts Institute of Technology, Cambridge, Massachusetts, USA. The spot was estimated to be 6·4 km *4 miles* in diameter on the Moon. The device was propounded in 1958 by the American Dr Charles Hard Townes (b. 1915). Such a flash for 1/5000th of a second can bore a hole through a diamond by vaporisation at 10 000° C, produced by 2×10^{23} photons. The 'Shiva' laser at the Lawrence Livermore Laboratory, California, USA concentrated $2·6 \times 10^{13}$ watts into a pinhead-sized target for $9·5 \times 10^{-11}$ sec in a test on 18 May 1978.

Brightest light

The brightest artificial light sources are 'laser' pulses

generated at the US Los Alamos National Laboratory, New Mexico announced in March 1987 by Dr Robert Graham. An ultra-violet flash lasting 1 picosecond (1×10^{-12} sec) is intensified to an energy of 5×10^{15} watts. Of continuously burning sources, the most powerful is a 313 kW high-pressure argon arc lamp of 1 200 000 candle-power, completed by Vortek Industries Ltd of Vancouver, BC, Canada in March 1984.

The most powerful searchlight ever developed was one produced during the 1939–45 war by the General Electric Company Ltd at the Hirst Research Centre in Wembley, London. It had a consumption of 600 kW and gave an arc luminance of 46 500 candelas/cm² *300 000 candles/in²* and a maximum beam intensity of 2 700 000 000 candles from its parabolic mirror (diameter 3·04 m *10 ft*).

Shortest light pulse

Charles Z. Shank and colleagues of the AT & T Laboratories in New Jersey, USA achieved a light pulse of 8 femtoseconds (8×10^{-15} sec) announced in April 1985. The pulse comprised only 4 or 5 wavelengths of visible light or 2·4 micrometres long.

Most durable light

The average bulb lasts for 750–1000 hr. There is some evidence that a 5 watt carbide filament bulb made by the Shelby Electric Co and presented by Mr Bernell in the Fire Department, Livermore, south Alameda County, California, USA was first shedding light in 1901.

Heaviest magnet

The heaviest magnet in the world is one measuring 60 m *196 ft* in diameter, with a weight of 36 000 tonnes for the 10 GeV synchrophasotron in the Joint Institute for Nuclear Research at Dubna, near Moscow, USSR.

Magnetic fields

The strongest continuous magnetic field strength achieved was a total of 35·3 ± 0·3 teslas at the Francis Bitter National Magnet Laboratory, Massachusetts Institute of Technology, on 26 May 1988 employing a hybrid magnet with holmium pole pieces. This had the effect of enhancing the central magnetic field which itself had reached 31·8 teslas.

The weakest magnetic field measured is one of 8×10^{-15} tesla in the heavily shielded room at the same laboratory. It is used by Dr David Cohen for research into the very weak magnetic field generated in the heart and brain.

Most powerful microscope

The world's most powerful microscope is the scanning tunnelling microscope invented at the IBM Zürich research laboratory in 1981. It has the magnifying ability of 100 million and is capable of resolving down to one hundredth the diameter of an atom (3×10^{-10} m). The fourth generation of the scanning tunnelling microscope now being developed is said to be 'about the size of a finger tip'.

By using field ion microscopy the tips of probes of scanning tunnelling microscopes have been shaped to end in a single atom—the last three layers constituting the world's smallest man-made pyramid consisting of 7, 3 and 1 atoms. It was announced in July 1986 from AT & T Bell Laboratories, Murray Hill, New Jersey, USA that they had successfully deposited a single atom (probably of germanium) from the tungsten tip of a scanning tunnelling microscope back on to a germanium surface.

Loudest noise

The loudest noise created in a laboratory has been 210 decibels or 400 000 acoustic watts reported by NASA from a 14·63 m *48 ft* steel and concrete test bed for the Saturn V rocket static with 18·3 m *60 ft* deep foundations at Marshall Space Flight Center, Huntsville, Alabama, USA in October 1965. Holes could be bored in solid material by this means. and the audible range was in excess of 161 km *100 miles*.

Smallest microphone

Professor Ibrahim Kavrak of Bogazici University, Istanbul, Turkey developed a microphone for a new technique of pressure measurement in fluid flow in 1967. It has a frequency response of 10 Hz to 10 KHz and measures 1·5 mm × 0·76 mm *0·06 in × 0·03 in*.

Highest note

The highest note yet attained is one of 60 gigahertz generated by a 'laser' beam striking a sapphire crystal at the Massachusetts Institute of Technology, USA in September 1964.

Most powerful particle accelerator

The 2 kilometre *6562 ft* diameter proton synchrotron at the Fermi National Accelerator Laboratory east of Batavia, Illinois, USA is the highest energy 'atom-smasher' in the world. On 14 May 1976 an energy of 500 giga electron volts (5×10^{11}) was achieved for the first time. On 13 Oct 1985 a centre of mass energy of 1.6 tera electron volts ($1·6 \times 10^{12}$ electron volts) was achieved by colliding beams of protons and anti-protons. This involves 1000 super-conducting magnets maintained at a temperature of $-268·8°C$ *$-452°F$* by means of the world's largest 4500 litre *990 gal* per hour helium liquefying plant which began operating on 18 Apr 1980.

The aim of CERN (*Conseil Européan pour la Recherche Nucléaire*) to collide beams of protons and anti-protons in their Super Proton Synchroton (SPS) near Geneva, Switzerland at 270 GeV × 2 = 540 GeV was achieved at 4.55 a.m. on 10 July 1981. This was the equivalent of striking a fixed target with protons at 150 TeV or 150 000 GeV. The US Department of Energy set up a study for a $6 billion Super Superconductivity Collider (SSC) 1995 with two 20 TeV proton and anti-proton colliding beams on 16 Aug 1983 with a diameter of 83·6 km *52 miles*. White House approval was announced on 30 Jan 1987.

Quietest place

The 'dead room', measuring 10·67 × 8·50 m *35 ft by 28 ft* in the Bell Telephone System laboratory at Murray Hill, New Jersey, USA, is the most anechoic room in the world, eliminating 99·98 per cent of reflected sound.

Sharpest objects and smallest tubes

The sharpest objects yet made are glass micropipette tubes used in intracellular work on living cells. Techniques developed and applied by Professor Kenneth T. Brown and Dale G. Flaming of the Department of Physiology, University of California, San Francisco, USA achieved by 1977 bevelled tips with an outer diameter of 0·02 κm and 0·01 κm inner diameter. The latter is smaller than the smallest known nickel tubing by a factor of 340 and is 6500 times thinner than human hair.

Smallest man-made object

It was announced by Texas Instruments, Dallas, Texas, USA on 8 Feb 1988 that they had succeeded in making 'quantam dots' indium and gallium arsenide only 100 millionths of a millemetre in diameter

Highest vacuum

The highest (or 'hardest') vacuums obtained in scientific research are of the order of 10^{-14} torr at the IBM Thomas J. Watson Research Center, Yorktown Heights, New York, USA in October 1976 in a cryogenic system with temperatures down to $-269 °C$ *$-452 °F$*. This is equivalent to depopulating (baseball-sized) molecules from 1 metre apart to 80 km apart or from 1 yard to 50 miles.

Lowest viscosity

The California Institute of Technology announced on 1 Dec 1957 that there was no measurable viscosity, i.e. perfect flow, in liquid helium II.

Highest voltage

The highest potential difference ever obtained in a laboratory has been 32 ± 1·5 million volts by the National Electrostatics Corporation at Oak Ridge, Tennessee, USA on 17 May 1979.

Janet Jackson

Whitesnake

Heart

THE ARTS AND ENTERTAINMENT

CHAPTER·SIX

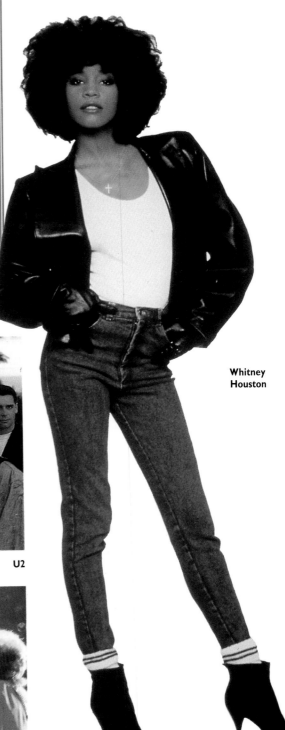

Whitney
Houston

U2

Fleetwood Mac

Painting

Oldest

Evidence of Palaeolithic art was first found in 1833 at Veyrier, 5 km *3 miles* south-west of Geneva, Switzerland, when François Mayor (1779–1854) found two harpoon-like objects decorated with geometric figures. Recently discovered pieces of bone with geometric engraved marks on them from an Old Stone Age site at Bilzingsleben, near Erfurt, East Germany, could possibly be the world's oldest examples of art. They are dated to *c.* 350 000 years ago. The oldest known dated examples of representational art come from La Ferrassie, near Les Eyzies in the Périgord, France in layers dated to *c.* 25 000 BC. Blocks of stone were found with engraved animals and female symbols; some of the blocks also had symbols painted in red ochre. Pieces of ochre with ground facets have been found at Lake Mungo, NSW, Australia in a context *ante* 30 000 BC but there is no evidence whether these were used for body-painting or pictorial art.

Largest

Panorama of the Mississippi, completed by John Banvard (1815–91) in 1846, showing the river for 1930 km *1200 miles* in a strip probably 1524 m *5000 ft* long and 3·66 m *12 ft* wide, was the largest painting in the world, with an area of more than 5575 m² *60 000 ft²*. The painting is believed to have been destroyed when the rolls of canvas, stored in a barn at Cold Spring Harbor, Long Island, New York State, USA, caught fire shortly before Banvard's death on 16 May 1891.

The Battle of Gettysburg, completed in 1883, after 2½ years of work, by Paul Philippoteaux (France) and 16 assistants, was 125 m *410 ft* long, 21·3 m *70 ft* high and weighed 5·45 tonnes *5·36 tons*. It depicts the climax of the battle, in southern Pennsylvania, USA, on 3 July 1863. In 1964 it was bought by Joe King of Winston-Salem, North Carolina, USA after being stored by E. W. McConnell in a Chicago warehouse since 1933 but, owing to deterioration, the sky was trimmed so decreasing the area.

Jackson Bailey's *Life of Christ* exhibited by Religious Art Institute of America Inc. of Atlanta, Georgia comprises 50 panels 3·35 × 6·09 m *11 × 20 ft* and was complete by 1971 with an area of 1022 m² *11 000 ft²*.

Kimiko Hibino (b. 1942) painted over 800 species of the animal kingdom on a canvas 3 km *1·86 miles* long and 2·2 m *7·2 ft* wide. On 27 Oct 1985, it was unveiled with the help of 3000 volunteers along the bank of the Tamagawa River in Tokyo, Japan.

The largest 'Old Master' is *Il Paradiso*, by Jacopo Robusti, *alias* Tintoretto (1518–94), and his son Domenico (1565–1637) on the east wall of the Sala del Maggior Consiglio in the Palazzo Ducale (Doge's Palace) in Venice, Italy between 1587 and 1590. The work is 22 m *72 ft 2 in* long and 7 m *22 ft 11½ in* high and contains some 350 human figures.

The largest painting in Great Britain is the oval *Triumph of Peace and Liberty* by Sir James Thornhill (1676–1734), on the ceiling of the Painted Hall in the Royal Naval College, Greenwich. It measures 32·3 m *106 ft* by 15·4 m *51 ft* and took 20 years (1707–1727) to complete.

The largest painting ever auctioned was Carl Larsson's *Midvinterblot* painted in Stockholm, Sweden in 1911–15 and sold at Sotheby's on 25 Mar 1988 for £880 000 to the Umeda Gallery of Japan.

Most valuable

The 'Mona Lisa' (*La Gioconda*) by Leonardo da Vinci (1452–1519) in the Louvre, Paris, was assessed for insurance purposes at $100 000 000 for its move to Washington DC, and New York City, NY, USA for exhibition from 14 Dec 1962 to 12 Mar 1963. However, insurance was not concluded because the cost of the closest security precautions was less than that of the premiums. It was painted *c.* 1503–7 and measures 77 × 53 cm *30·5 × 20·9 in.* It is believed to portray either Mona (short for Madonna) Lisa Gherardini, the wife of Francesco del Giocondo of Florence, or Constanza d'Avalos, coincidentally nicknamed La Gioconda, mistress of Giuliano de Medici. Francis I, King of France, bought the painting for his bathroom in 1517 for 4000 gold florins or 15·30 kg *92 oz* of gold.

Most repetitious painter

William Allen Bixler (1876–1961) of Andersen, Indiana, USA reproduced his painting *The Old Swimmin' Hole* over 5000 times between the years 1912–1918. The painting was inspired by James Whitcomb Riley's poem of the same name.

Oldest and youngest RA

The oldest ever Royal Academician has been (Thomas) Sidney Cooper CVO, who died on 8 Feb 1902 aged 98 yr 136 days, having exhibited 266 paintings over the record span of 69 consecutive years (1833–1902). The youngest ever RA has been Mary Moser (1744–1819) (later Mrs Hugh Lloyd), who was elected on the foundation of the Royal Academy in 1768 when aged 24.

Youngest exhibitor

The youngest ever exhibitor at the Royal Academy of Arts Annual Summer Exhibition was Lewis Melville 'Gino' Lyons (b. 30 Apr 1962). His *Trees and Monkeys* was painted on 4 June 1965, submitted on 17 Mar 1967 and exhibited to the public on 29 Apr 1967.

Most prolific art teacher

Constance G. Gordon (Mrs Robert Asch) (b. New Britain, Connecticut) first devised a 4-step system of teaching painting in 1944/45. On 16 Aug 1965 she conducted the longest ever art class (for Tupperware) in Orlando, Florida, USA taking the 'pain' out of painting for 2500 'first-time' artists. Through the medium of large movie screens, TV series and 17 art books she has subsequently taught uncountable millions.

Largest galleries

The world's largest art gallery is the Winter Palace and the neighbouring Hermitage in Leningrad, USSR. One has to walk 24 km *15 miles* to visit each of the 322 galleries, which house nearly 3 000 000 works of art and objects of archaeological interest. The world's largest modern art museum is the Georges Pompidou National Centre for Art and Culture, Beauborg, opened in Paris in 1977 with 17 700 m² *183 000 ft²* of floor space.

Finest brush

The finest standard brush sold is the 000 in Series 7 by Winsor and Newton known as a 'triple goose'. It is made of 150–200 Kolinsky sable hairs weighing 15 mg *0·000529 oz.*

MURALS
Earliest

The earliest known murals on man-made walls are the clay relief leopards at Catal Hüyük in southern Anatolia, Turkey, discovered by James Malaart at level VII in 1961 and dating from *c.* 6200 BC.

Largest

The longest recorded continuous mural is one stretching 497·7 m *1633 ft* on the walls of the Royal Liverpool Children's Hospital, Alder Hey, Liverpool, England. It covers an area of 1668·7 m² *17 963 ft². Future entries for this category will be assessed on overall area only.*

Largest mosaic

The world's largest mosaic is on the walls of the central library of the Universidad Nacional Autónoma de Mexico, Mexico City. There are four walls, the two largest measuring 1203 m² *12 949 ft²* each representing the pre-Hispanic past.

The largest Roman mosaic in Britain is the Woodchester Pavement, Gloucestershire of *c.* AD 325, excavated in 1793, now re-covered with protective earth. It measured

Most prolific painter ● Morris Katz (b. 1932) of Greenwich Village, New York City is the most prolific painter of saleable portraits in the world. His sales total as of 5 March 1986 was 153 629. Described as the 'King of Schlock Art', he sells his paintings 'cheap and often'. On the NBC 'Today' TV programme in Nov 1985 Katz demonstrated he could paint at a rate of 0·25 m² *2·64 ft²* per min.

HIGHEST PRICE PAINTINGS

Price	Painter, title, sold by and sold to	Date
£6500	Antonio Correggio's *The Magdalen Reading* (in fact spurious) to Elector Friedrich Augustus II of Saxony.	1746
£8500	Raphael's *The Sistine Madonna* (1513–14) from Piacenza to Elector Friedrich Augustus II of Saxony.	1759
£16 000	Van Eyck's *Adoration of the Lamb*, 6 outer panels of Ghent altarpiece by Edward Solby to the government of Prussia.	1821
£24 600*	Murillo's *The Immaculate Conception* by estate of Marshal Soult to the Louvre (against Czar Nicholas I) in Paris.	1852
£70 000	Raphael's *Ansidei Madonna* (1506) from Perugia by the 8th Duke of Marlborough to the National Gallery.	1885
£100 000	Raphael's *The Colonna Altarpiece* (1503–05) from Perugia by Seldemeyer to J. Pierpont Morgan.	1901
£102 880	Van Dyck's *Elena Grimaldi-Cattaneo* (portrait) by Knoedler to Peter Widener (1834–1915).	1906
£102 880	Rembrandt's *The Mill* by 6th Marquess of Lansdowne to Peter Widener.	1911
£116 500	Raphael's smaller *Panshanger Madonna* by Joseph (later Baron) Duveen (1869–1939) to Peter Widener.	1913
£310 400	Leonardo da Vinci's *Benois Madonna* (c. 1477) to Czar Nicholas II in Paris.	1914
£821 429	Rembrandt's *Aristotle Contemplating the Bust of Homer* by estate of Mr and Mrs Alfred W. Erickson to New York Metropolitan Museum of Art.	1961
£1 785 714	Leonardo da Vinci's *Ginevra de' Benci* (c. 1475) by Prince Franz Josef II of Liechtenstein to National Gallery of Art, Washington DC, USA.	1967
£2 310 000*	Velázquez's *Portrait of Juan de Pareja* by the Earl of Radnor to the Wildenstein Gallery, New York.	1970
£2 729 000*	Turner's *Juliet and her Nurse* by Trustees of Whitney Museum, New York to undisclosed bidder at Sotheby Parke Bernet, New York.	1980
£7 470 500*	Turner's *Seascape: Folkestone* from estate of Lord Clark (1903–83) to Leggatt's of London for an unknown buyer.	1984
£8 100 000*	Mantegna's *The Adoration of the Magi* by the Marquess of Northampton to the J. Paul Getty Museum, Malibu, California.	1985
£22 500 000	Van Gogh's *Sunflowers* from Lady Beatty to Yasuda Fire and Marine Insurance Co, Tokyo.	1987
£30 187 623*	Van Gogh's *Irises* from Mr John Whitney Payson to an undisclosed bidder at Sotheby's, New York.	1987

* Indicates price at auction, otherwise prices were by private treaty.

14·3 m² *47 ft²* comprising 1·6 million tesserae. A total reconstruction carried out by Robert and John Woodward of Stroud, Gloucestershire was completed in June 1987.

'WORK OF ART'

Largest

The largest work of art was the wrapping in 1983 of 11 islands in Biscayne Bay, Florida, USA in flamingo pink plastic tutus for Christo's work entitled *Surrounded Islands*. The amount of plastic sheeting used was 603 000 m² *6 500 000 ft²*.

HIGHEST PRICE

Abstract

The auction record is $5·06 million for *Composition in a Square with Red Corner* painted in 1938 by Piet Mondrian (1872–1944) at Sotheby's, New York on 18 Nov 1986. The purchaser was an anonymous Japanese businessman.

Miniature portrait

The highest price ever is the £75 000 paid by an anonymous buyer at Sotheby's, London on 24 Mar 1980 for a miniature of Jane Broughton, aged 21, painted on vellum by Nicholas Hilliard (1547–1619) in 1574. The painted surface measures 42 mm *1·65 in* in diameter.

20th century painting

The record bid at auction for a 20th century painting is £2 235 294 for Jackson Pollock's (1912–1956) *Search* spatter painted in 1955 and sold at Sotheby's, New York City on 4 May 1988. It was sold from the estate of Andy Warhol (1927–1987).

Living artist

The highest price at auction for a work by a living artist was $4 180 000 for *Diver* by Jasper Johns at Christie's, New York on 4 May 1988.

The highest price for any painting by a living United Kingdom-born artist has been £1 035 294 for *Study for Portrait II* by Francis Bacon (b. Dublin, Ireland, 1909, then part of the United Kingdom), sold on 6 May 1987 at Christie's, New York.

Print

The record price for a print at auction was £561 600 for a 1655 print of *Christ Presented to the People* by Rembrandt at Christie's, London on 5 Dec 1985, sold by Chatsworth Settlement Trustees.

Drawing

The highest price ever paid for any drawing is £3 546 000 for a study of an apostle's head and hand for the Transfiguration in the Vatican by Raphael (Raffaello Santi 1483–1520) and sold for the 11th Duke of Devonshire (b. 1920) at Christie's, London on 3 July 1984.

Poster

The record price for a poster is £62 000 for an adver-

Most expensive painting ● *Irises* by Vincent Van Gogh (b. 30 Mar 1853, Zundert, Netherlands–d. 29 July 1890, Auvers-sur-Oise, France) was sold for a record $53·9 million (including buyer's premium) at Sotheby's, New York on 11 Nov 1987. It took less than 4 minutes to sell the 71·1 cm × 92·7 cm *28 in × 36½ in* canvas which Van Gogh had painted in 1889 whilst a voluntary patient at the Saint Remy Mental Asylum in Provence, France. The successful bid was by telephone from Europe. (Photo: Sotheby's)

tisement for the 1902 Vienna Exhibition by Koloman Moser (b. Vienna 30 Mar 1868—d. 18 Oct 1918), sold at Christie's, South Kensington, London on 1 Apr 1985.

Sculpture

Earliest

A piece of ox rib found in 1973 at Pech de l'Aze, Dordogne, France in an early Middle Palaeolithic layer of the Riss glaciation *c.* 105 000 BC has several engraved lines on one side, thought to be possibly intentional. A churingo or curved ivory plaque rubbed with red ochre from the Middle Palaeolithic Mousterian site at Tata, Hungary has been dated to 100 000 BC by the thorium/uranium method. The earliest known examples of sculpture date from the Aurignacian culture *c.* 28 000–22 000 BC and include the so-called Venus figurines from Austria and the numerous figurines from northern Italy and central France. A carving in mammoth ivory from the Magdalenian culture of a horse 6·3 cm *2½ in* long was found in the Vogelherd cave in south-west Germany.

The earliest example of an engraving found in Britain is of a horse's head on a piece of rib-bone from Robin Hood Cave, Creswell Crag, Derbyshire. It dates from the Upper Palaeolithic period (*c.* 15 000 to 10 000 BC). The earliest Scottish rock carving from Lagalochan, Argyll dates from *c.* 3000 BC.

Most expensive

The record price paid for a sculpture at auction is $10·12 million for *Petite danseuse de quatorze ans* by Edgar Degas (1834–1917), by an anonymous European bidder at Sotheby's, New York on 10 May 1988. This ballerina is the most famous of the Degas bronzes and the only sculpture he exhibited in his lifetime.

The highest price paid for the work of a sculptor during his lifetime is the $1 265 000 given at Sotheby Parke Bernet, New York on 21 May 1982 for the 190·5 cm *75 in* long elmwood *Reclining Figure* by Henry Moore, OM, CH (b. 30 July 1898 d. 31 Aug 1986).

Largest

The world's largest sculptures are the mounted figures of Jefferson Davis (1808–89), Gen. Robert Edward Lee (1807–70) and Gen. Thomas Jonathan (Stonewall) Jackson (1824–63), covering 0·5 ha *1·33 acres* on the face of Stone Mountain, near Atlanta, Georgia, USA. They are 27·4 m *90 ft* high. Roy Faulkner was on the mountain face for 8 years 174 days with a thermo-jet torch working with the sculptor Walker Kirtland Hancock and other helpers from 12 Sept 1963 to 3 Mar 1972.

If completed, the world's largest sculpture will be that of the Indian chief Tashunca-Uitco (*c.* 1849–77), known as Crazy Horse, of the Oglala tribe of the Dakota or Nadowessioux (Sioux) group, on horseback. The sculpture was begun on 3 June 1948 near Mount Rushmore, South Dakota, USA. A projected 171·6 m *563 ft* high and 195 m *641 ft* long, it was the uncompleted life work of one man, Korczak Ziólkowski (1908–82). The horse's nostril is 15·2 m *50 ft* deep and 10·7 m *35 ft* in diameter. In 1985–86 another 400 000 tons of granite blasted off the mountain face brought the total to 8·2 million tons.

Ground figures

In the Nazca Desert, 300 km *185 miles* south of Lima, Peru there are straight lines (one more than 11·2 km *7 miles* long), geometric shapes and shapes of plants and animals drawn on the ground some time between 100 BC and AD 600 for an uncertain but probably religious, astronomical, or even economic purpose by a imprecisely identified civilisation. They were first detected from the air *c.* 1928 and have also been described as the world's longest works of art.

Hill figures

In August 1968, a 100 m *330 ft* tall figure was found on a hill above Tarapacá, Chile.

The largest human hill carving in Britain is the 'Long Man' of Wilmington, East Sussex, 68 m *226 ft* in length.

There are many giant horse carvings in Britain and the oldest of these is the Uffington White Horse in Oxfordshire, dating from the late Iron Age (*c.* 150 BC) and measuring 114 m *374 ft* from nose to tail and 36 m *120 ft* high.

Most massive mobile

The most massive mobile is *White Cascade* weighing 8 tonnes and measuring 30·48 m *100 ft* from top to bottom installed on 24–25 May 1976 at the Federal Reserve Bank of Philadelphia, Pennsylvania, USA. It was designed by Alexander Calder (1898–1976), whose first mobiles were exhibited in Paris in 1932 and whose *Big Crinkley* sold for a record £555 572 at Sotheby's, New York on 10 May 1984.

Language and Literature

Earliest

The ability to speak is believed to be dependent upon physiological changes in the height of the larynx between *Homo erectus* and *Homo sapiens sapiens* as developed *c.* 45 000 BC. The earliest written language discovered has been on Yangshao culture pottery from

Paa-t'o, near Xi'an (Sian) in the Shaanxi (Shensi) province of China found in 1962. This bears proto-characters for the numbers 5, 7 and 8 and has been dated to 5000–4000 BC. The earliest dated pictographs are on clay tablets from Nippur, southern Iraq from one of the lowest excavation levels equivalent to Uruk V/VI and dated in 1979 to *c.* 3400 BC. Tokens or tallies from Tepe Asiab and Ganji-I-Dareh Tepe in Iran have however been dated to 8500 BC. The earliest known piece of writing from the British Isles (*c.* AD 630) is a fragment of Irish uncial script in an ecclesiastical history sold for £75 000 by the Folger Shakespeare Library, Washington DC to the British Rail Pension Fund at Sotheby's, London on 25 June 1985.

Fragments of Roman wooden writing tablets found in the 1970s at Vindolandia near Newcastle-upon-Tyne have been shown to make up the earliest known substantial written records in British history. These contain letters and a quotation from the Roman poet Virgil and are dated to *c.* AD 100.

Oldest English words

It was first suggested in 1979 that languages ancestral to English and to Latvian (both Indo-European) split *c.* 3500 BC. About 40 words of a pre-Indo-European substrate survive in English e.g. apple (apal), bad (bad), gold (gol) and tin (tin) according to researches completed in 1988.

Commonest language

Today's world total of languages and dialects still spoken is about 5000 of which some 845 come from India. The language spoken by more people than any other is Mandarin, by an estimated 68 per cent of China's population, hence 715 million people in 1988. The so-called national language (*Guóyǔ*) is a standardised form of Northern Chinese (*Běifānghuà*) as spoken in the Peking area. This was alphabetised into *zhùyīn fúhào* of 37 letters in 1913 by Wa Chih-hui (1865–1953). On 11 Feb 1938 the *Hanyu-Pinyin-Fang'an* system, which is a phonetic pronunciation guide, was introduced. The next most commonly spoken language, and the most widespread, is English, with an estimated 330 000 000 as a mother tongue and nearly twice as many using it as a second or third language.

In Great Britain and Ireland there are 6 indigenous tongues: English, Cornish, Scots Gaelic, Welsh, Irish Gaelic and Romany (Gipsy). Mr Edward (Ned) Maddrell (1877–1974) of Glen Chass, Port St Mary, Isle of Man died as the last islander whose professed tongue was Manx. Cornish, of which there are now some 300 students, came within an ace of extinction. A dictionary was published in 1887, 4 years before the death of the then

last fluent speaker John Davey. A Cornish novel by Melville and Kitty Bennetto, *An Gurun Wosek a Geltya*, was published in November 1984. In the Channel Islands, apart from Jersey and Guernsey *normand*, there survive words of Sarkese or *Sèrtchais* in which the Parable of the Sower, as recited by some fishermen, was noted and published by Prince Louis Lucien Bonaparte (1813–91) in 1862.

Most complex

The following extremes of complexity have been noted: Chippewa, the North American Indian language of Minnesota, USA, has the most verb forms with up to 6000; Haida, the North American Indian language, has the most prefixes with 70; Tabassaran, a language in Daghestan, USSR, uses the most noun cases with 37, while Eskimos use 63 forms of the present tense and simple nouns have as many as 252 inflections. In Chinese the 40-volume *Chung-wén Tà Tz'u-tiên* dictionary lists 49 905 characters. *The Dictionary of Chinese Characters* (Sichuan and Huber) in 8 volumes will contain 20 million characters when completed in 1989. The fourth tone of 'i' has 84 meanings, varying as widely as 'dress', 'hiccough' and 'licentious'. The written language provides 92 different characters of 'i⁴'. The most complex written character in Chinese is that representing *xiè* consisting of 64 strokes, meaning 'talkative'. The most complex in current use is *nang* with 36 strokes, meaning a blocked-up nose.

Most and least irregular verbs

Esperanto was first published by its inventor Dr Ludwig Zamenhof (1859–1917) of Warsaw in 1887 without irregular verbs and is now estimated (by text book sales) to have a million speakers. The even earlier interlanguage Volapük, invented by Johann Martin Schleyer (1831–1912), also has absolutely regular configuration. The Turkish language has a single irregular verb—*olmak*, to be. According to *The Morphology and Syntax of Present-day English* by Professor Olu Tomori, English has 283 irregular verbs of which 30 are merely formed with prefixes.

Rarest and commonest sounds

The rarest speech sound is probably the sound written ř in Czech which occurs in very few languages and is the last sound mastered by Czech children. In the southern Bushman language !xo there is a click articulated with both lips, which is written ☉ The *l* sound in the Arabic word *Allah*, in some contexts, is pronounced uniquely in that language. The commonest sound is the vowel *a* (as in the English father); no language is known to be without it.

Vocabulary

The English language contains about 490 000 words plus another 300 000 technical terms, the most in any language, but it is doubtful if any individual uses more than 60 000. Those in Great Britain who have undergone a full 16 years of education use perhaps 5000 words in speech and up to 10 000 words in written communications. The membership of the International Society for Philosophical Enquiry (no admission for IQs below 148) have an average vocabulary of 36 250 words. Shakespeare employed a vocabulary of *c.* 33 000 words.

Greatest linguist

If the yardstick of ability to speak with fluency and reasonable accuracy is adhered to, it is doubtful whether any human could maintain fluency in more than 20–25 languages concurrently or achieve fluency in more than 40 in a lifetime.

Historically the greatest linguists have been proclaimed as Cardinal Mezzofanti (1774–1849) of Italy (fluent in 26 or 27); Professor Rask (1787–1832) of Denmark, Sir John Bowring (1792–1872) and Dr Harold Williams of New Zealand (1876–1928), who were all fluent in 28 languages.

The most multi-lingual living person is Georges Henri Schmidt (b. Strasbourg, France, 28 Dec 1914), the Chief of the UN Terminology Section in 1965–71. The 1975

edition of *Who's Who in the United Nations* listed 'only' 19 languages because he was then unable to find time to 'revive' his former fluency in 12 others. Powell Alexander Janulus (b. 1939) has worked with 41 languages in the Provincial Court of British Columbia, Vancouver, Canada.

Britain's greatest linguist is George Campbell (b. 9 Aug 1912), who is retired from the BBC Overseas Service where he *worked* with 54 languages.

ALPHABET
Earliest

The earliest example of alphabetic writing has been found at Ugarit (now Ras Sharma), Syria dated to *c.* 1450 BC. It comprised a tablet of 32 cuneiform letters.

The oldest letter is 'O', unchanged in shape since its adoption in the Phoenician alphabet *c.* 1300 BC. The newest letters added to the English alphabet are 'j' and 'v' which are of post-Shakespearean use *c.* 1630. Formerly they were used only as variants of 'i' and 'u'. There are 65 alphabets now in use.

Longest and shortest

The language with most letters is Cambodian with 72 (including useless ones) and Rotokas in central Bougainville Island has least with 11 (just a, b, e, g, i, k, o, p, ř, t and u).

Most and least consonants and vowels

The language with most distinct consonantal sounds is that of the Ubykhs in the Caucasus, with 80–85, and that with least is Rotokas, which has only 6 consonants. The language with the most vowels is Sedang, a central Vietnamese language with 55 distinguishable vowel sounds, and that with the least is the Caucasian language Abkhazian with 2. The record in written English for consecutive vowels is 6 in the musical term *euouae*. The Estonian word *jäääärre*, meaning the edge of the ice, has the same 4 consecutively. The name of a language in Pará State, Brazil consists solely of 7 vowels—*uoiauai*. The English word 'latchstring' has 6 consecutive letters which are consonants, but the Georgian word *gvprtskvnis* (he is feeling us) has 8 separately pronounced consonants.

Largest letters

The largest permanent letters in the world are giant 183 m *600 ft* letters spelling READYMIX on the ground in the Nullarbor Plain near East Balladonia, Western Australia. These were constructed in December 1971.

Smallest letters

The 16 letters MOLECULAR DEVICES have been etched into a salt crystal by an electron beam so that the strokes were only 2 to 3 nm (10^{-9}) wide—the width of 20 hydrogen atoms. This was done by Michael Isaacson at Cornell University, Ithaca, New York in February 1982.

WORDS
Longest

Lengthy concatenations and some compound or agglutinative words or nonce words are or have been written in the closed-up style of a single word e.g. the 182-letter fricassee of 17 sweet and sour ingredients in Aristophanes' comedy *The Ecclesiazusae* in the 4th century BC. A compound 'word' of 195 sanskrit characters (which transliterates into 428 letters in the Roman alphabet) describing the region near Kanci, Tamil Nadu, India appears in a 16th-century work by Tirumalâmbâ, Queen of Vijayanagara.

The longest real word in the Oxford English Dictionary is floccipaucinihilipilification (alternatively spelt in hyphenated form with 'n' in seventh place), with 29 letters, meaning 'the action of estimating as worthless', first used in 1741, and later by Sir Walter Scott (1771–1832). The longest factitious word in the Oxford English Dictionary is pneumonoultramicroscopicsilicovolcanoconiosis (–koniosis) with 45 letters -alleged to mean 'a lung

disease caused by the inhalation of very fine silica dust'. Webster's Third International Dictionary lists among its 450 000 entries: pneumonoultramicroscopicsilicovolcanoconiosises (47 letters), the plural of the above-mentioned disease.

The longest regularly formed English word is praetertranssubstantiationalistically (37 letters), used by Mark McShane in his 1963 novel *Untimely Ripped*. The medical term hepaticocholangiocholecystenterostomies (39 letters) refers to the surgical creations of new communications between gallbladders and hepatic ducts and between intestines and gallbladders. The longest words in common use are disproportionableness and incomprehensibilities (21 letters). Interdenominationalism (22 letters) is found in Webster's Dictionary and hence perhaps interdenominationalistically (28 letters) is permissible. Simon Proctor of Maidstone, Kent has compiled 15 592 lesser words (excluding plurals) from its 28 letters.

Longest palindromes

The longest known palindromic word is *saippuakivikauppias* (19 letters), Finnish for a dealer in lye (i.e. caustic soda). The longest in English is *redivider* (9 letters). The 9-letter word *Malayalam* is a proper noun given to the language of the Malayali people in Kerala, southern India, while *Kanakanak* near Dillingham, Alaska is a 9-lettered palindromic place-name. The contrived chemical term *detartrated* has 11 letters. Some baptismal fonts in Greece and Turkey bear the circular 25-letter inscription NIψON ANOMHMATA MH MONAN OψIN meaning 'wash (my) sins not only (my) face'. This appears at St Mary's Church, Nottingham, St Paul's, Woldingham, Surrey and other churches. The longest palindromic composition devised is one of 77 777 words completed by Edward Benbow of Bewdley, Hereford & Worcs in November 1987. It begins 'Al, sign it, "Lover"! . . .' and hence predictably ends '. . . . revolting, Isla'. The longest palindromic novel, *Dr Awkward and Olson in Oslo* contains 31 594 words and was written by Lawrence Levine, New York, New York, USA in 1986.

Longest scientific name

The systematic name for deoxyribonucleicacid of the human mitochondria contains 16 569 nucleotide residues and is thus *c.* 207 000 letters long. It was published in key form in *Nature* on 9 Apr 1981.

Longest anagrams

The longest non-scientific English words which can form anagrams are the 18-letter transpositions 'conservationalists' and 'conversationalists'.

The longest scientific transposals are 'hydroxydesoxycorticosterone' and also with 27 letters, 'hydroxydeoxycorticosterones'.

Longest abbreviation

The longest known abbreviation is S.K.O.M.K.H.P.K.J.C.D.P.W.B., the initials of the Syarikat Kerjasama Orang-orang Melayu Kerajaan Hilir Perak Kerana Jimat Cermat Dan Pinjam-meminjam Wang Berhad. This is the Malay name for The Cooperative Company of the Lower State of Perak Government's Malay People for Money Savings and Loans Ltd, in Teluk Anson, Perak, West Malaysia (formerly Malaya). The abbreviation for this abbreviation is Skomk. The 55-letter full name of Los Angeles (El Pueblo de Nuestra Señora la Reina de los Angeles de Porciuncula) is abbreviated to LA or 3·63 per cent of its length.

Longest acronym

The longest acronym is NIIOMTPLABOPARMBETZHELBETRABSBOMONIMONKONOTDTEKHSTROMONT with 56 letters (54 in Cyrillic) in the *Concise Dictionary of Soviet Terminology*, meaning: the laboratory for shuttering, reinforcement, concrete and ferroconcrete operations for composite-monolithic and monolithic constructions of the Department of the Technology of Building—assembly operations of the Scientific

Research Institute of the Organisation for building mechanisation and technical aid of the Academy of Building and Architecture of the USSR.

Commonest words and letters

In written English the most frequently used words are, in order: the, of, and, to, a, in, that, is, I, it, for and as. The most used in conversation is I. The commonest letter is 'e' and the commonest initial letter is 'T'.

Most meanings

The most over-worked word in English is the word *set* which has 58 noun uses, 126 verbal uses and 10 as a participial adjective.

Most succinct word

The most challenging word for any lexicographer to define briefly is the Fuegian (southernmost Argentina and Chile) word 'mamihlapinatapai' meaning 'looking at each other hoping that either will offer to do something which both parties desire but are unwilling to do'.

Most synonyms

The condition of being inebriated has more synonyms than any other condition or object. Delacourt Press of New York City, USA has published a selection of 1224 from 2241 compiled by Paul Dickson of Garrett Park, Maryland, USA.

Most homophones

The most homophonous sounds in English are *air* and *sol* which, according to the researches of Dora Newhouse of Los Angeles, USA, both have 38 homophones. The homonym with most variant spellings is *air* with Aire, are, Ayer, Ayr, Ayre, err, e'er, ere, eyre and heir.

Most accents

Accents were introduced in French in the reign of Louis XIII (1601–43). The word with most accents is *újjáépítésére*, the Hungarian word meaning 'for its reconstruction'. Two runners up each with 5 accents are the French *hétérogénéité*, meaning heterogeneity, and an atoll in the Pacific Ocean 516 km *320 miles* east-south-east of Tahiti which is named Héréhérétué.

Shortest pangram (holoalphabetic sentence)

Pangrammists who endeavour to produce meaningful sentences of minimal length utilising all the letters in the alphabet have now attained the ultimate of 26-letter brevity. Michael Jones of Chicago, Illinois, USA compiled in 1984 the sentence to describe the situation in which a wryneck woodpecker from the grasslands of Africa climbed up the side of an ox which is grazing on sacred Muslim-owned land, viz. 'Veldt jynx grimps waqf zho buck'. The number of ways 26 letters can be combined is 4.0329×10^{26}.

PERSONAL NAMES

Earliest

The earliest personal name which has survived is seemingly that of a predynastic king of Upper Egypt *ante* 3050 BC, who is indicated by the hieroglyphic sign for a scorpion. It has been suggested that the name should be read as Sekhen. The earliest known name of any resident of Britain is Divitiacus, King of the Suessiones, the Gaulish ruler of the Kent area *c.* 100 BC under the name Prydhain. Scotland, unlike England, was never fully conquered by the Roman occupiers (AD 43–410). Calgacus (b. *c.* AD 40), who led the final resistance in Scotland, was the earliest native whose name has been recorded.

Longest pedigree

The only non-royal English pedigree that can with certainty show a clear pre-Conquest descent is that of the Arden family. Shakespeare's mother was a Mary Arden. It is claimed on behalf of the Clan Mackay that their clan can be traced to Loarn, the Irish invader of south-west Pictland, now Argyll, *c.* AD 501.

LONGEST WORDS

JAPANESE[1]
Chi-n-chi-ku-ri-n (12 letters)
a very short person (slang)

SPANISH
Superextraordinarisimo (22 letters)
extraordinary

FRENCH
Anticonstitutionnellement (25 letters)
anticonstitutionally

CROATIAN
Prijestolonasljednikovica (25 letters)
wife of an heir apparent

ITALIAN
Precipitevolissimevolmente (26 letters)
as fast as possible

PORTUGUESE
Inconstitucionalissimamente (27 letters)
with the highest degree of unconstitutionality

ICELANDIC
Haecstaréttarmálaflutningsmaður (29 letters)
supreme court barrister

RUSSIAN
Ryentgyenoelyektrokardiografichyeskogo
(33 Cyrillic letters, transliterating as 38)
of the radioelectrocardiographic

HUNGARIAN
Megszentségtelenithetetlenségeskedéseitekért
(44 letters)
for your unprofanable actions

TURKISH[4]
Cekoslovakyalılastıramadıklarımızdanmıymıssınız (47 letters)
'are you not of that group of persons that we were said to be unable to Czechoslovakianise?'

DUTCH[4]
Kindercarnavalsoptochtvoorbereidingswerkzaamheden (49 letters)
preparation activities for a children's carnival procession

MOHAWK[2]
Tkanuhstasrihsranuhwe'tsraaksahsrakaratattsrayeri' (50 letters)
the praising of the evil of the liking of the finding of the house is right

GERMAN[3,4]
Donaudampfschiffahrtselectrizitaetenhauptbetriebswerkbauunterbeamtengesellschaft (80 letters)
The club for subordinate officials of the head office management of the Danube steamboat electrical services (name of a pre-war club in Vienna)

SWEDISH[4]
Nordöstersjökustartilleriflygspaningssimulatoranläggningsmaterielunderhållsuppföljningssystemdiskussionsinläggsförberedelsearbeten (130 letters)
Preparatory work on the contribution to the discussion on the maintaining system of support of the material of the aviation survey simulator device within the north-east part of the coast artillery of the Baltic

[1] Patent applications sometimes harbour long compound 'words'. An extreme example is one of 13 kana which transliterates to the 40-letter Kyūkitsürohekimenfuchakunenryōsekisanryō meaning 'the accumulated amount of fuel condensed on the wall face of the air intake passage'.

[2] Lengthy concatenations are a feature of Mohawk. Above is an example.

[3] The longest dictionary word in everyday usage is Rechtsschutzversicherungsgesellschaften (39 letters) meaning 'insurance companies which provide legal protection'.

[4] Agglutinative words are limited only by imagination and are not found in standard dictionaries. The first 100-letter such word was published in 1975 by the late Eric Rosenthal in Afrikaans.

Longest personal name

The longest name appearing on a birth certificate is that of Rhoshandiatellyneshiaunneveshenk Koyaanfsquatsiuty Williams born to Mr and Mrs James L. Williams in Beaumont, Texas, USA on 12 Sept 1984. On 5 Oct 1984 the father filed an amendment which expanded his daughter's first name to 1019 letters and the middle name to 36 letters.

The longest surname in the United Kingdom was the six-barrelled one borne by the late Major L.S.D.O.F. (Leone Sextus Denys Oswolf Fraudatifilius) Tollemache-Tollemache de Orellana-Plantagenet-Tollemache-Tollemache, who was born on 12 June 1884 and died of pneumonia in France on 20 Feb 1917. At school he was known as Tolly. The current record is for 4-barrelled names – examples include the family names of Lord Thurlow (Hovell-Thurlow-Cumming-Bruce) and the Earl of Wharncliffe (Montagu-Stuart-Wortley-Mackenzie). Of non-repetitious surnames, the last example of a 5-barrelled one was that of the Lady Caroline Jemima Temple-Nugent-Chandos-Brydges-Grenville (1858–1946). The longest single English surname is Featherstonehaugh (17 letters), variously pronounced Featherstonehaw or Festonhaw or Fessonhay or Freestonhugh or Feerstonhaw or Fanshaw. In Scotland the surname Nin (feminine of Mac) Achinmacdholicachinskerray (29 letters) was recorded in an 18th-century parish register.

Most Christian names

The great-great-grandson of Carlos III of Spain, Don Alfonso de Borbón y Borbón (1866–1934) had 94 Christian names of which several were lengthened by hyphenation.

John and Margaret Nelson of Chesterfield, Derbyshire gave their daughter Tracy Nelson (b. 31 Dec 1985) a total of 139 other Christian names. In Nov 1986 the Registrar agreed that the names would have to be accommodated on a document separate from the birth certificate.

Shortest

The commonest single-letter surname is O, prevalent in Korea but with 52 examples in US phone books (1973–81) and 12 in Belgium. This name causes most distress to those concerned with the prevention of cruelty to computers. Every other letter, except Q, has been traced in US phone books (used as a surname) by A. Ross Eckler. There are two one-lettered Burmese names: E (calm), pronounced aye, and U (egg), pronounced Oo. U *before* the name means 'uncle'.

There exist among the 47 000 000 names on the Dept of Health & Social Security index 6 examples of a one-lettered surname. Their identity has not been disclosed, but they are 'A', 'B', 'J', 'N', 'O' and 'X'. Two-letter British surnames include By and On and have recently been joined by Oy, Za and others. The Christian name 'A' has been used for 5 generations in the Lincoln Taber family of Fingringhoe, Essex.

Commonest family name

The commonest family name in the world is the Chinese name Chang which is borne, according to estimates, by between 9·7 and 12·1 per cent of the Chinese population, so indicating even on the lower estimate that there are at least some 104 million Changs—more than the entire population of all but 7 of the 170 other sovereign countries of the world.

The commonest surname in the English-speaking world is Smith. The most recent published count showed 659 050 nationally insured Smiths in Great Britain, of whom 10 102 were plain John Smith and another 19 502 were John (plus one or more given names) Smith. Including uninsured persons there were over 800 000 Smiths in England and Wales alone, of whom 81 493 were called A. Smith. There were an estimated 2 382 509 Smiths in the USA in 1973. It is no secret that by 1984 there were some 90 000 Singhs in Britain—the name means 'in secret'.

'Macs'

There are estimated to be 1 600 000 persons in Britain with M', Mc or Mac (Gaelic, 'son of') as part of their surnames. Macdonald is the commonest accounting for about 55 000 of the Scottish population.

Most versions

Mr Edward A. Nedelcov of Regina, Saskatchewan,

Canada has collected 1085 versions of the spelling of his family name since January 1960. Mzilikazi of Zululand (b. c. 1795) had his name chronicled in 325 spellings, according to researches by Dr R. Kent Rasmussen.

Most changed

Excluding members of the royal family the living monogamous woman who has most times changed her name is Lady Home of the Hirsel, formerly Lady Douglas-Home; Countess of Home; Lady Dunglass, and originally Miss Elizabeth Alington.

Most contrived

In the United States the determination to derive commercial or other benefit from being the last listing in the local telephone book has resulted in self-given names, starting with up to 9 Z's—an extreme example being Zachary Zzzzzzzzzzra in the San Francisco book. The alpha and omega of Britain's 82 directories are Mrs Maude E. Aab of Hull, Humberside and the Zzzzzz Coffee Shop in Gray's Inn Road, London WC1.

PLACE-NAMES

Earliest

The world's earliest known place-names are pre-Sumerian e.g. Kish, Ur and Attara and therefore earlier than c. 3500 BC. The earliest recorded British place-name is Belerion, the Penwith peninsula of Cornwall, referred to as such by Pytheas of Massilia c. 308 BC. The name Salakee on St Mary's, Isles of Scilly is however arguably of a pre-Indo-European substrate meaning *tin island*. There are reasons to contend that Leicester (Roman, Ligora Castrum) contains an element reflecting its founding by the western Mediterranean navigators, the Ligurians, as early as c. 1200 BC. The earliest distinctive name for what is now Great Britain was Albion by Himilco c. 500 BC. The oldest name among England's 46 counties is Kent, first mentioned in its Roman form of Cantium (from the Celtic *canto*, meaning a rim, i.e. a coastal district), from the same circumnavigation by Pytheas. The earliest mention of England is the form *Angelcymn*, which appeared in the Anglo-Saxon Chronicle in AD 880.

Longest

The official name for Bangkok, the capital city of Thailand, is Krungthep Mahanakhon. The full name is however: Krungthep Mahanakhon Bovorn Ratanakosin Mahintharayutthaya Mahadilokpop Noparatratchathani Burirom Udomratchanivetmahasathan Amornpiman Avatarnsathit Sakkathattiyavisnukarmprasit (167 letters), which in its most scholarly transliteration emerges with 175 letters. Cauaiauaia in Angola has 9 consecutive vowel letters.

The longest place-name now in use in the world is Taumatawhakatangihangakoauauotamateaturipukakapikimaungahoronukupokaiwhenuakitanatahu, the unofficial 85-letter version of the name of a hill (305 m *1002 ft* above sea level) in the Southern Hawke's Bay district of North Island, New Zealand. The Maori translation means 'The place where Tamatea, the man with the big knees, who slid, climbed and swallowed mountains, known as landeater, played his flute to his loved one.'

Great Britain

The longest place-name in the United Kingdom is the concocted 58-letter version of Llanfairpwllgwyngyllgogerychwyrndrobwllllantysiliogogogoch, which is translated: 'St Mary's Church by the pool of the white hazel trees, near the rapid whirlpool, by the red cave of the Church of St Tysilio'. This is the name used for the reopened (April 1973) village railway station in Anglesey, Gwynedd, Wales, and was coined by a local bard, Y Bardd Cocos–John Evans (1827–95) as a hoax. The *official* name consists of only the first 20 letters. The longest Welsh place-name listed in the Ordnance Survey Gazetteer is Lower Llanfihangel-y-Creuddyn (26 letters), a village near Aberystwyth, Dyfed. For commercial rather than toponymic reasons the proprietors of the Fairbourne Steam Railway, near Barmouth, North Wales

have posted a 67-letter-long name on a station board 19·5 m *64 ft* long. It reads Gorsafawddachaidraigddanheddogleddollonpenrhynarefrdraethceredigion though the 'll' should read 'l' making 66 letters or 65 if 'ch' is regarded as a single letter.

England

The longest single-word (unhyphenated) place-name in England is Blakehopeburnhaugh, a hamlet between Byrness and Rochester in Northumberland, of 18 letters. The nearby Cottonshopeburnfoot (19 letters) is locally rendered as one word though not by the Ordnance Survey. The hyphenated Sutton-under-Whitestonecliffe, North Yorkshire has 27 letters on the Ordnance Survey but with the insertion of 'the' and the dropping of the final 'e' it has 29 letters in the Post Office list. The longest parish name is Saint Mary le More and All Hallows with Saint Leonard and Saint Peter, Wallingford (68 letters) in Oxfordshire, formed on 5 Apr 1971.

Scotland

The longest single-word place-name in Scotland is Coignafeuinternich in Inverness-shire. Kirkcudbrightshire (also 18 letters) became merged into Dumfries and Galloway on 16 May 1975. A 5 ha *12 acre* loch 14 km *9 miles* west of Stornoway on Lewis, Western Isles is named Loch Airidh Mhic Fhionnlaidh Dhuibh (31 letters).

Ireland

The longest place-name in Ireland is Muckanaghederdauhaulia (22 letters), 6 km *4 miles* from Costello in Camus Bay, County Galway. The name means 'soft place between two seas'.

Shortest

The shortest place-names in the world are the French village of Y (population 143), so named since 1241, the Danish village Å on the island Fyn, the Norwegian village of Å (pronounced 'Aw'), the Swedish place Å in Vikholandet, U in the Caroline Islands, Pacific Ocean, and the Japanese town of Sosei which is alternatively called Aioi or O. There was once a '6' in West Virginia, USA. The shortest place-names in Great Britain are the two-lettered places of Ae (population 199 in 1961), Dumfries and Galloway; Oa on the island of Islay, Strathclyde, and Bu on Wyre, Orkney Islands. In the Shetland Islands there are skerries called Ve and two stacks called Aa. The island of Iona was originally I. The River E flows into the southern end of Loch Mhór, Inverness-shire, and O Brook flows on Dartmoor, Devon. The shortest place-name in Ireland is Ta (or Lady's Island) Lough, a sea inlet on the coast of County Wexford. Tievelough, in County Donegal, is also called Ea.

Most spellings

The spelling of the Dutch town of Leeuwarden has been recorded in 225 versions since AD 1046. Bromesberrow, Hereford and Worcester, is recorded in 161 spellings since the 10th century as reported by local historian Lester Steynor.

Literature

Oldest

The oldest surviving printed work is the Dharani scroll or *sutra* from wooden printing blocks found in the foundations of the Pulguk Sa pagoda, Kyŏngju, South Korea on 14 Oct 1966. It has been dated to no later than AD 704. It was claimed in November 1973 that a 28-page book of Tang dynasty poems at Yonsei University, Korea was printed from metal type c. 1160.

The oldest medical literature, a small clay tablet in the Sumerian script from Nippur (now in Iraq), is dated to c. 2100 BC. It is now in the University Museum of Philadelphia and gives details of various ointments and plasters made of crushed turtle shell, nagasi plant, salt and mustard. Beer formed an ingredient of some of the ointments.

Oldest mechanically printed

It is widely accepted that the earliest mechanically printed full-length book was the 42-line per page Gutenberg Bible, printed in Mainz, West Germany, c. 1454 by Johann Henne zum Gensfleisch zur Laden, called 'zu Gutenberg' (c. 1398– 1468). Work on water marks published in 1967 indicates a copy of a surviving printed 'Donatus' Latin grammar was made from paper of c. 1450. The earliest exactly dated printed work is the Psalter completed on 14 Aug 1457 by Johann Fust (c. 1400–66) and Peter Schöffer (1425–1502), who had been Gutenberg's chief assistant. The earliest printing by William Caxton (c. 1422–1491) though undated would appear to be *The Recuyel of the Historyes of Troye* in Cologne in late 1473 to spring 1474.

Largest book

The largest book in the world is the *Super Book* measuring 2·74 × 3·07 m *9 ft × 10 ft 2⅛ in* weighing 252·6 kg *557 lb* consisting of 300 pages, published in Denver, Colorado, USA in 1976.

Largest publication

The largest publication in the world is the 1112-volume set of *British Parliamentary Papers* published by the Irish University Press in 1968–72. A complete set weighs 3·3 tonnes *3¼ tons*, costs £50 000 and would take 6 years to read at 10 hours per day. The production involved the death of 34 000 Indian goats, and the use of £15 000 worth of gold ingots. The total print is 500 sets and the price per set in 1987 was £49 500.

Largest dictionary

Deutsches Wörterbuch started by Jacob and Wilhelm Grimm in 1854 was completed in 34 519 pages and 33 volumes in 1971. Today's price is DM5425. The largest English-language dictionary is the 12-volume Royal quarto *The Oxford English Dictionary* of 15 487 pages published between 1884 and 1928 and edited by Sir James Murray until his death in 1915. A first supplement of 963 pages was published in 1933. Of the 4-volume supplement, edited by R. W. Burchfield, the final (Se-Z) volume and the Bibliography were published in 1986. The work contains 414 825 words, 1 827 306 illustrative quotations and reputedly 227 779 589 letters and figures, 63·8 times more than the Bible. The greatest outside contributor has been Marghanita Laski (1915–1988) with 175 000 quotations from 1958 till her death.

The *New Grove Dictionary of Music and Musicians* edited by Stanley Sadie CBE (b. 30 Oct 1930), published in 20 volumes by Macmillan in February 1981, contains over 22 million words and 4500 illustrations and is the largest specialist dictionary priced in 1987 at £1100.

Smallest book

The smallest marketed bound printed book is one printed on 22 gsm paper which measures 1 mm × 1 mm $\frac{1}{25} \times \frac{1}{25}$ *in*, comprising the children's story *Old King Cole!* and published in 85 copies in March 1985 by The Gleniffer Press of Paisley, Renfrew, Scotland. The pages can be turned (with care) only by the use of a needle.

Longest novel

The longest important novel ever published is *Les hommes de bonne volonté* by Louis Henri Jean Farigoule (1885–1972), *alias* Jules Romains, of France, in 27 volumes in 1932–46. The English version *Men of Good Will* was published in 14 volumes in 1933–46 as a 'novel-cycle'. The 4959-page edition published by Peter Davies Ltd has an estimated 2 070 000 words excluding a 100-page index. The novel *Tokuga-Wa Ieyasu* by Sohachi Yamaoka has been serialised in Japanese daily newspapers since 1951. Now completed, it will require nearly 40 volumes.

Earliest encyclopaedias

The earliest known encyclopaedia was compiled by Speusippus (*post* 408–c. 338 BC), a nephew of Plato, in Athens c. 370 BC. The earliest encyclopaedia compiled by a Briton was *Liber exerptionum* by the Scottish monk Richard (d. 1173) at St Victor's Abbey, Paris *c.* 1140.

Largest encyclopaedia

The largest encyclopaedia is *La Enciclopedia Universal Ilustrada Europeo-Americana* (J. Espasa & Sons, Madrid and Barcelona) totalling 105 000 pages and an annual supplement since 1935 comprising 165 200 000 words. The number of volumes in the set in August 1983 was 104, and the price $2325.

Most comprehensive encyclopaedia

The most comprehensive English-language encyclopaedia is the *Encyclopaedia Britannica*, first published in Edinburgh in December 1768. A group of booksellers in the United States acquired reprint rights in 1898 and completed ownership in 1899. In 1943 the *Britannica* was given to the University of Chicago, Illinois, USA. The current 32-volume 15th edition contains 32 330 pages and 44 000 000 words from more than 4000 contributors. It is now edited in Chicago and London.

Longest index

The Tenth Collective Index of *Chemical Abstracts* completed in June 1983 contains 23 948 253 entries in 131 445 pages and 75 volumes, and weighs 172·3 kg *380 lb.*

MAPS

The oldest known map of any kind is a clay tablet depicting the river Euphrates flowing through northern Mesopotamia, Iraq, dated *c.* 3800 BC. The earliest surviving product of English map-making is the Anglo-Saxon *mappa mundi*, known as the Cottonian manuscript, from the late 10th century. The earliest printed map in the world is one of western China dated to 1115. The earliest printed map of Britain was Ptolemy's outline printed in Bologna, Italy in 1477.

A *Giant Relief Map of California*, by Reuben Hall, weighing 39 tonnes *38·4 tons*, was displayed in the Ferry Building, San Francisco, USA from 1924 until 1960. Now in storage in Hamilton Air Force Base, Novato, California, USA it measures 137·1 × 5·48 m *450 × 18 ft.* Known as *Paradise in Panorama* it required 29 man years and $147 000 to build.

HIGHEST PRICES
Most expensive book

The highest price paid for any book has been £8 140 000 for the 226-leaf manuscript *The Gospel Book of Henry the Lion, Duke of Saxony* at Sotheby's, London on 6 Dec, 1983. The book, 34·3 × 25·4 cm *13½ × 10 in*, was illuminated by the monk Herimann *c.* 1170 at Helmershansen Abbey with 41 full-page illustrations, and was bought by Hans Kraus for the Hermann Abs consortium.

Printed book

The highest price ever paid for a printed book has been $5 390 000 for an Old Testament (Genesis to the Psalms) of the Gutenberg Bible printed in 1455 in Mainz, Germany. It was bought by the Maruzen Co Ltd, Tokyo booksellers, at Christie's, New York on 22 Oct 1987. The most expensive new book is the reproduction of the full set of ornithological prints *The Birds of America* by John James Audubon (1785–1851) by Abbeville Press, at $15 000.

Broadsheet

The highest price ever paid for a broadsheet was $412 500 for one of the 22 known copies of *The Declaration of Independence*, printed in Philadelphia, Pennsylvania, USA in 1776 by Samuel T. Freeman & Co, and sold to the Chapin Library, Williams College, Williamstown, Massachusetts, USA at Christie's, New York City on 22 Apr 1983.

Manuscript

The highest price ever paid for a complete manuscript has been £2·2 million by Armand Hammer at Christie's, London on 12 Dec 1980 for Leonardo da Vinci's 36-page Codex Leicester illustrated manuscript on cosmology compiled *c.* 1507. It was sold by the trustees of the Holkham estate.

The highest price paid for a British manuscript has been £1 540 000 paid by London dealer Quarritch at Sotheby's, London on 21 June 1988 for a 14th-century elaborately illuminated Hours and Psalter of Elizabeth de Bohun, Countess of Northampton .

The auction record for a musical manuscript (including buyer's premium) was £2 585 000 for a 508-page 21·6 × 16·5 cm *8½ × 6½ in* bound volume of 9 complete symphonies in Mozart's hand by London dealer James Kirkman at Sotheby's, London on 22 May 1987. The seller was an anonymous European.

The earliest known manuscript written in Britain is a bifolium of Eusebius' *Historia Ecclesiastica* from *c.* AD 625, possibly from the Jarrow library.

> **Most letters** ● The Rev Canon Bill Cook and his fiancée/wife Helen of Diss, Norfolk, exchanged 6000 love letters during their 4½-year wartime separation from March 1942 – May 1946. (Photo: Leslie Ward)

Atlas

The highest price paid for an atlas has been £340 000 for a Gerardus Mercator atlas of *c.* 1571 of Europe, sold at Sotheby's, London on 13 Mar 1979.

BIBLE
Oldest

The earliest biblical texts are from two silver amulets found under the Scottish Church, Jerusalem in 1979 bearing Numbers Ch. 6 v. 22–27 dated to *c.* 587 BC. The oldest known bible is the *Codex Vaticanus* written in Greek *ante* AD 350 and preserved in the Vatican Museum, Rome. The earliest complete bible *printed* in English was one edited by Miles Coverdale, Bishop of Exeter (*c.* 1488–1569), while living in Antwerp, and printed in 1535. William Tyndale's New Testament in English had, however, been printed in Cologne and in Worms, Germany in 1525 while John Wycliffe's first manuscript translation dates from 1382.

Longest and shortest books

The longest book in the Authorised version of the Bible is the Book of Psalms, while the longest book including prose is the Book of the Prophet Isaiah, with 66 chapters. The shortest is the Third Epistle of John, with 294 words in 14 verses. The Second Epistle of John has only 13 verses but 298 words.

Longest and shortest psalm and verse

Of the 150 psalms, the longest is the 119th, with 176 verses, and the shortest is the 117th, with two verses. The shortest verse in the Authorised version (King James) of the Bible is verse 35 of Chapter XI of the Gospel according to St John, consisting of the two words 'Jesus wept'. The longest is verse 9 of Chapter VIII of the Book of Esther, which extends to a 90-word description of the Persian empire.

Total letters and words, longest name

The total number of letters in the Bible is 3 566 480. The total number of words depends on the method of counting hyphenated words, but is usually given as between 773 692 and 773 746. The word 'and' according to Colin McKay Wilson of the Salvation Army appears 46 227 times. The longest actual name in English language bibles is the 18-letter Maher-shalal-hash-baz, symbolic name of the second son of Isaiah (Isaiah, Chapter VIII, verses 1 and 3). The caption of Psalm 22, however, contains a Hebrew title sometimes rendered Al-Ayyeleth Hash-Shahar (20 letters).

DIARIES AND LETTERS
Longest kept diary

Col. Ernest Loftus CBE of Harare, Zimbabwe began his daily diary on 4 May 1896 at the age of 12 and continued it until his death on 7 July 1987 aged 103 years 178 days.

George C. Edler (b. 13 Dec 1889) of Bethesda, Maryland, USA, has kept a diary with no breaks since 1 Jan 1912.

The diary of T. C. Baskerville of Chorlton-cum-Hardy, Manchester, maintained since 1939, comprises an estimated 5 500 000 words in 157 volumes occupying 35 000 pages.

Longest and most letters

The longest personal letter based on a word count is one of 1 402 344 words started on 3 Jan 1982 by Alan Foreman of New Barn, Dartford, Kent, England and posted to his wife Janet on 25 Jan 1984.

Vichi Noda, former Vice Minister of Treasury and Minister of Construction in Japan, from July 1961 until his bedridden wife Mitsu's death in March 1985, wrote her 1307 letters amounting to 50 000 characters during his overseas trips. These letters have been published in 25 volumes totalling 12 404 pages.

Longest letter to an editor

The *Upper Dauphin Sentinel* of Pennsylvania, USA published a letter of 25 513 words over 8 issues from

August to November 1979, written by John Sultzbaugh of Lykens, Pennsylvania.

Most letters to an editor
David Green, a solicitor, of Castle Morris, Dyfed had 118 letters published in the main correspondence columns of *The Times* by 15 June 1988. His record year was 1972 with 12.

Shortest correspondence
The shortest correspondence on record was that between Victor Marie Hugo (1802–85) and his publisher Hurst and Blackett in 1862. The author was on holiday and anxious to know how his new novel *Les Misérables* was selling. He wrote '?'. The reply was '!'.

The shortest letter to *The Times* comprised the single abbreviated symbol 'Dr^2?' in the interrogative from R. S. Cookson of London NW11, on 30 July 1984, in a correspondence on the correct form of recording a plurality of academic doctorates. On 8 Jan 1986 a letter was sent to *The Times* by a 7-year-old girl from the Isle of Man. It read 'Sir, Yours faithfully Caroline Sophia Kerenhappuch Parkes'. The brief epistle was intended to inform readers of her unusual name, Kerenhappuch, mentioned in a letter the previous week from the Rev. John Ticehurst on the subject of common 19th century names.

Most personal mail
The highest confirmed mail received by any private citizen in a year is 900 000 letters by the baseball star Hank Aaron (b. 1934) reported by the US Postal Department in June 1974. About a third were letters of hate engendered by his bettering of 'Babe' Ruth's career record for 'home runs' set in 1927. (See Chapter 12.)

Pen pals
The longest sustained correspondence on record is one of 75 years from 11 Nov 1904 between Mrs Ida McDougall of Tasmania, Australia and Miss R. Norton of Sevenoaks, Kent until Mrs McDougall's death on 24 Dec 1979.

Birthday card
Mrs Amelia Finch (b. 18 Apr 1912) of Lakehurst, New Jersey, USA and Mr Paul E. Warburgh (1902–80) of Huntington, New York exchanged the same card from 1 Feb 1927 to 18 Apr 1980.

Christmas cards
The greatest number of personal Christmas cards sent out is believed to be 62 824 by Mrs Werner Erhard of San Francisco, California, USA in December 1975. Many must have been to unilateral acquaintances. The earliest known Christmas card was sent out by Sir Henry Cole (1808–82) in 1843 but did not become an annual ritual until 1862.

AUTOGRAPHS AND SIGNATURES
Earliest
The earliest surviving examples of an autograph are those made by scribes on cuneiform clay tablets from Tell Abu Salābikh, Iraq dated to the early Dynastic III A *c.* 2600 BC. A scribe named 'a-du' has added 'dub-sar' after his name thus translating to 'Adu, scribe'. The earliest surviving signature on a papyrus is that of the scribe Amen-'aa dated to the Egyptian middle kingdom which began *c.* 2130 BC and which is in the Leningrad Museum, USSR. A signum exists for William I (the Conqueror) *c.* 1070. The earliest English sovereign whose handwriting is known to have survived is Edward III (1327–77). The earliest full signature extant is that of Richard II (dated 26 July 1386). The Magna Carta does not bear even the mark of King John (reigned 1199–1216), but carries only his seal affixed on 19 June 1215.

Most expensive
The highest price ever paid on the open market for a single autograph letter signed has been $360 000 paid on 29 Oct 1986 at Sotheby's, New York for a letter by Thomas Jefferson condemning prejudice against Jews in 1818. It was sold by Charles Rosenbloom of Pittsburgh, Pennsylvania, USA.

The highest price paid for an autograph letter signed by a living person is $12 500 at the Hamilton Galleries on 22 Jan 1981 for a letter from President Ronald Reagan praising Frank Sinatra.

A record $4250 was paid at a Hamilton sale on 12 Aug 1982 by Barry D. Hoffman for the signed portrait of Al Capone (1899–1947).

Rarest and most valuable
Only one example of the signature of Christopher Marlowe (1564–93) is known. It is in the Kent County Archives on a will of 1583. It is estimated that a seventh Shakespearean signature, should it ever come to light, might realise at least £1 million at auction.

The only known document which bears 9 US presidential signatures is a letter sent by President F. D. Roosevelt to Mr Richard C. Corbyn, then of Dallas (now of Amarillo), Texas, USA dated 26 Oct 1932. It was subsequently signed by Herbert Hoover, Harry Truman, General Eisenhower, Gerald Ford, Lyndon Johnson, Jimmy Carter and Ronald Reagan. Nixon's first signature was signed with an auto-pen but was later re-signed.

AUTHORS
Most prolific
The champion of the goose quill era was Józef Ignacy Kraszewski (1812–87) of Poland who produced more than 600 volumes of novels and historical works. Until recently very high productivity had been attributed to Charles Hamilton, *alias* Frank Richards (1876–1961), the

> **Top-selling** ● Barbara Cartland, currently the top-selling authoress with global sales of over 500 000 000 for 470 titles in 24 languages. She has averaged 23 titles per year for the last 12 years.

creator of Billy Bunter with up to 80 000 words a week in 1913 including the whole of the periodicals *Gem* (founded 1907) and *Magnet* (1908–40). In 1984 George Samways (b. 1894) asserted that Hamilton used him and others as 'ghost-writers'.

Soho Tokutomi (1863–1957) wrote the history *Kinsei Nippon Kokuminshi* in 100 volumes of 42 468 pages and 19 452 952 letters in 35 years.

Most novels
The greatest number of novels published by an authoress is 904 by Kathleen Lindsay (Mrs Mary Faulkner) (1903–73) of Somerset West, Cape Province, South Africa. She wrote under 2 other married names and 8 pen names. Baboorao Arnalkar (b. 9 June 1907) of Maharashtra State, India between 1936 and 1984 has published 1092 short mystery stories in book form and several non-fiction books.

After receiving a probable record 743 rejection slips the British novelist John Creasey MBE (1908–73), under his own name and 25 *noms de plume* had 564 books totalling more than 40 000 000 words published from 1932 to his death. The British authoress with the greatest total of full-length titles was Ursula Harvey Bloom (Mrs A. C. G. Robinson, formerly Mrs Denham-Cookes, 1892–1984), who reached 560 in 1976, starting in 1924 with *The Great Beginning* and including the best sellers *The Ring Tree* (novel) and *The Rose of Norfolk* (non-fiction).

Enid Mary Blyton (1898–1968) (Mrs Darrell Waters) completed 600 titles of children's stories, many of them brief, with 59 in 1955. She was translated into a record 128 languages.

Most text books
Britain's most successful writer of text books is ex-schoolmaster Ronald Ridout (b. 23 July 1916) who between 1948 and April 1988 had 515 titles published with sales of 88 070 000. His *The First English Workbook* has sold 5 238 000 copies.

Literature

Highest paid

In 1958 Mrs Deborah Schneider of Minneapolis, Minnesota, USA wrote 25 words to complete a sentence in a competition for the best blurb for Plymouth cars. She won from about 1 400 000 entrants the prize of $500 every month for life. On normal life expectations she should collect $12 000 per word. No known anthology includes Mrs Schneider's deathless prose but it is in her deed box at her bank 'Only to be opened after death'. She passed $6000 a word by 1983.

Greatest advance

The greatest advance paid for any book is $5 000 000 for *Whirlwind* to James Clavell at auction in New York City on 11 Jan 1986 by William Morrow & Co and Avon Books.

On 5 May 1988 Mary Higgins Clark (USA) signed a contract for $10 100 000 for 4 novels and a book of short stories.

Top selling

It was announced on 13 Mar 1953 that 672 058 000 copies of the works of Generalissimo Stalin (born Yózef Vissarionovich Dzhugashvili) (1879–1953), had been sold or distributed in 101 languages.

Currently the top-selling authoress is Barbara Cartland with global sales of over 500 000 000 for 470 titles in 24 languages. She has averaged 23 titles per year for the last 12 years.

The all-time estimate of book sales by Erle Stanley Gardner (1889–1970) (US) to 1 Jan 1987 is 319 884 707 copies in 37 languages. The top-selling lady crime writer has been Dame Agatha Christie (*née* Miller) (later Lady Mallowan) (1890–1976) whose 87 crime novels sold an estimated 300 000 000 in 103 languages. *Sleeping Murder* was published posthumously in 1977. An estimated 500 000 000 copies of Georges Simenon's works had been printed by 1973.

Longest biography

The longest biography in publishing history is that of Sir Winston Churchill by his son Randolph (4832 pages) and Martin Gilbert (16 745 pages) to date comprising some 9 244 000 words. George Simenon (b. 1903) wrote 22 autobiographical books from 1972.

Most rejections

The greatest recorded number of publishers' rejections for a manuscript is 242 (by December 1987) for the 150 000-word manuscript *World Government Crusade* written in 1966 by Gilbert Young (b. 1906) of Bath, England. The record for rejections before publication is from 176 publishers (and non-acknowledgement from many others) in the case of Bill Gordon's *How Many Books Do You Sell in Ohio?* from 19 Oct 1983 to 20 Nov 1985. Mr Gordon then spoiled his record by himself rejecting a publishers written offer from Aames-Allen.

Oldest authoress

The oldest authoress in the world was Mrs Alice Pollock (*née* Wykeham-Martin) (1868–1971), of Haslemere, Surrey, whose book *Portrait of My Victorian Youth* (Johnson Publications) was published in March 1971 when she was aged 102 years 8 months.

Literary luncheons

Literary luncheons were inaugurated by Christina Foyle (Mrs Ronald Batty) in October 1930 at the Old Holborn Restaurant, London. Attendances were over 1500 at the Grosvenor House, Park Lane, London at lunches for Mistinguett (1873–1956) and Dr Edvard Benes (1884–1948) both in 1938.

Longest literary gestation

The standard German dictionary *Deutsches Wörterbuch*, begun by the brothers Grimm in 1854, was finished in 1971. *Acta Sanctorum* begun by Jean Bolland in 1643, arranged according to saints' days, reached the month of November in 1925 and an introduction for December was published in 1940. Oxford University Press received

back their proofs of *Constable's Presentments* from the Dugdale Society in December 1984. They had been sent out for correction 35 years earlier in December 1949.

Youngest and oldest Poet Laureate

The youngest Poet Laureate was Laurence Eusden (1688–1730), who 'received the bays' on 24 Dec 1718 at the age of 30 years and 3 months. The greatest age at which a poet has succeeded is 73 in the case of William Wordsworth (1770–1850) on 6 Apr 1843. The longest-lived Laureate was John Masefield, OM, who died on 12 May 1967, aged 88 years 345 days. The longest any poet has worn the laurel is 41 years 322 days, in the case of Alfred (later the 1st Lord) Tennyson (1809–92), who was appointed on 19 Nov 1850 and died in office on 6 Oct 1892.

Longest Poem

The lengthiest poem ever published has been the Kirghiz folk epic *Manas*, which appeared in printed form in 1958 but which has never been translated into English. It runs to 'more than 500 000 lines'. Short translated passages appear in *The Elek Book of Oriental Verse*.

The longest poem ever written in the English language is one on the life of King Alfred by John Fitchett (1766–1838) of Liverpool which ran to 129 807 lines and took 40 years to write. His editor Robert Riscoe added the concluding 2585 lines.

Roger Brien's (b. Montreal, 1910) *Prométhée—dialogue des vivants et des morts* runs to 456 047 lines written from 1964–81. Brien has written another 497 000 lines of French poetry in over 90 published works.

Most successful poem

If by Joseph Rudyard Kipling (1865–1936), first published in 1910, has been translated into 27 languages and, according to Kipling, 'anthologised to weariness'.

HIGHEST PRINTINGS

The world's most widely distributed book is the Bible, which has been translated into 303 languages and portions of it into a further 1581 languages. This compares with 222 languages for Lenin. It has been estimated that between 1815 and 1975 some 2 500 000 000 copies were printed of which 1 500 000 000 were handled by Bible societies. In the period 1976–1987 combined world-wide sales of Today's English Version (*Good News*) New Testament and Bible (which is copyright of the Bible societies) exceeded 100 000 000 copies.

Apart from the King James version (averaging some 13 million copies printed annually) there are at least 14 other copyrights on other versions of the Bible. The oldest publisher of bibles is the Cambridge University Press which began with the Geneva version in 1591.

It has been reported that 800 000 000 copies of the red-covered booklet *Quotations from the Works of Mao Tse-tung* were sold or distributed between June 1966, when possession became virtually mandatory in China, and September 1971 when its promoter Marshal Lin Piao died in an air crash.

It is believed that in the USA Van Antwerp Bragg and Co printed some 60 million copies of the 1879 edition of *The McGuffey Reader*, compiled by Henry Vail in the pre-copyright era for distribution to public schools.

The total disposal through non-commercial channels by Jehovah's Witnesses of *The Truth that Leads to Eternal Life* published by the Watchtower Bible and Tract Society of Brooklyn, New York on 8 May 1968, reached 106 669 155 in 116 languages by April 1988.

BEST-SELLING BOOKS

Excluding versions of the Bible, the world's all-time best-selling book is *The Guinness Book of Records* first published in September 1955 by the Guinness Brewery and edited by Norris Dewar McWhirter (b. 12 Aug 1925) and his twin brother Alan Ross McWhirter (k. 27 Nov

1975). Global sales in 31 languages will surpass 60 million in late 1988.

Best-seller lists

The longest duration on the *New York Times* best-seller list (founded 1935) has been for *A Light in the Attic* by Shelby Silverstein (b. 1932) which on 10 Jan 1985 had its 112th week on the lists.

The Country Diary of an Edwardian Lady (Michael Joseph, Webb & Bower) by Edith Holden (1871–1920) held the No. 1 position in the *Sunday Times* best-seller list (which excludes books published annually) for 64 weeks. Its global sales in 13 languages reached 2 820 231 copies by January 1988.

Fiction

The novel with the highest sales has been *Valley of the Dolls* (first published Mar 1966) by Jacqueline Susann (Mrs Irving Mansfield) (1921–74) with a world-wide total of 28 712 000 to 30 March 1987. In the first 6 months Bantam sold 6·8 million. In the United Kingdom the highest print order has been 3 000 000 by Penguin Books Ltd for their paperback edition of *Lady Chatterley's Lover*, by D. H. (David Herbert) Lawrence (1885–1930). The total sales to May 1988 were 4 760 000. Alistair Stuart MacLean (1922–87) wrote 30 books of which 28 each sold over a million in the United Kingdom alone. His books have been translated into 28 languages and 13 have been filmed. It has been estimated that a 'MacLean' novel is purchased every 18 seconds. *The Cruel Sea* by Nicholas Monsarrat (1910–79), published in 1951 by Cassell, reached sales of 1 200 000 in its *original* edition.

Fastest publisher

The ITN Election Factbook published by Michael O'Mara was printed by Hazell, Watson & Viney in less than 24 hours of the general election date of 11 June 1987 being announced.

Slowest seller

The accolade for the world's slowest-selling book (known in US publishing as slooow sellers) probably belongs to David Wilkins's translation of the New Testament from Coptic into Latin published by Oxford University Press in 1716 in 500 copies. Selling an average of one each 139 days, it remained in print for 191 years.

PUBLISHERS AND PRINTERS

Oldest publisher

Cambridge University Press has a continuous history of printing and publishing since 1584. The University received Royal Letters Patent to print and sell all manner of books on 20 July 1534.

In 1978 the Oxford University Press celebrated the 500th anniversary of the printing of the first book in the City of Oxford in 1478. This was before OUP was itself in existence.

Most prolific publisher

In terms of new titles per annum Britain's most prolific publisher in 1987 was Oxford University Press with 1012. The UK published a record 59 837 book titles in 1987 of which a record 14 185 were reprints.

Largest printer

The largest printers in the world are R. R. Donnelley & Sons Co of Chicago, Illinois, USA. The company, founded in 1864, has plants in 24 main centres, turning out $2 482 000 000 worth of work per year. More than 1 927 000 short tons of paper are consumed every year. The largest printer under one roof is the United States Government Printing Office (founded 1861) in Washington DC. Encompassing 13·35 ha *33 acres* of floor space the central office processes an average of 2000 print orders daily, and consumes 45 360 tonnes *100 million lb* of paper annually. The Superintendent of Documents sells almost $73 million worth of US government publications every year and maintains an inventory of over 20 000 titles in print, receiving 5800 mail orders each day.

Largest print order

The initial print order for the 55th Automobile Association *Members' Handbook* (1987–8) was 4 820 000 copies stacked one on top of another, 35 times the height of Ben Nevis. The total print since 1908 has been 91 520 000. It is currently printed by web offset by Petty & Sons of Leeds. The aggregate print of *The Highway Code* (instituted 1931) reached 106 350 000 in April 1988.

LIBRARIES

Earliest

One of the earliest known collections of archival material was that of King Ashurbanipal at Nineveh, (668–627 BC). He had day tablets referring to events and personages as far back as the Dynasty of Agode *c.* 23rd century BC.

Largest

The largest non-statutory library in the world is the New York Public Library (founded 1895) on Fifth Avenue with a floor space of 48 800 m² *525 276 ft²* and 141·6 km *88 miles* of shelving. Its collection including 82 branch libraries embraces 11 952 450 volumes, 14 466 478 manuscripts and 363 679 maps.

The greatest personal library ever amassed was that of Sir Thomas Phillipps. Dispersal began in 1886. The residue was bought largely unseen by the brothers Lionel Robinson CBE, MC and Philip Robinson for £100 000. Sales began on 1 July 1946.

The largest library in the United Kingdom is the British Library, dispersed among more than 20 buildings in London and a 24·3 ha *60 acre* site at Boston Spa, West Yorkshire, with a total staff of some 2500. The Library contains over 16 million volumes. Stock increases involve over 12·8 km *8 miles* of new shelving annually. The Newspaper Library at Colindale, north London, opened in 1932, has 562 300 volumes and parcels comprising 70 000 different titles on 35·4 km *22 miles* of shelving. The Document Supply Centre in West Yorkshire (shelf capacity 157·7 km *98 miles*) runs the largest library inter-lending operation in the world; it handles annually nearly 3 million requests from other libraries (UK and overseas) for items they do not hold in stock. The National Sound Archive holds 1 000 000 discs and 50 000 hours of recorded tape. The largest public reference library in Europe is the extended Mitchell Library, North Street, Glasgow with a floor area of 50 00 m² *538 200 ft²* or 4·9 ha *12·3 acres* and an ultimate capacity for 4 000 000 volumes.

Overdue books

The record for an unreturned and overdue library book was set when a book in German on the Archbishop of Bremen, published in 1609, was borrowed from Sidney Sussex College, Cambridge by Colonel Robert Walpole in 1667–68. It was found by Professor Sir John Plumb in the library of the then Marquess of Cholmondeley at Houghton Hall, Norfolk and returned 288 years later. No fine was exacted.

Oldest museum

The oldest museum still extant in the world is the Ashmolean Museum in Oxford built from 1679–83 and named after the collector Elias Ashmole (1617–1692). Since 1924 it has housed an exhibition of historic scientific instruments.

Largest museum

The world's largest complex of museums is the Smithsonian Institution comprising 15 museums with 6000 employees. It contains over 134 million objects and specimens. The largest and most visited museum in the United Kingdom is the British Museum (founded in 1753), which was opened to the public in 1759. The main building in Bloomsbury, London was begun in 1823 and has a total floor area of 8·7 ha *21·5 acres*. In 1987, 3 725 073 people passed through its doors.

The American Museum of Natural History is situated between 77th and 81st Streets and Central Park West and Columbus Avenue in New York. It was founded in 1869 and comprises 22 interconnected buildings. The buildings of the Museum and the Planetarium contain an area of 139 350 m² *1·5 million ft²* of floor space accommodating more than 36 million artifacts and specimens. Its exhibits are viewed by more than 2·6 million visitors each year.

Most popular

The highest attendance for any museum is that at the Smithsonian Air and Space Museum, Washington DC opened in July 1976. The record-setting day in 1984 required the doors to be temporarily closed with an attendance of 118 437.

NEWSPAPERS

Oldest

A copy has survived of a news pamphlet published in Cologne, West Germany in 1470. The oldest existing newspaper in the world is the Swedish official journal *Post och Inrikes Tidningar*, founded in 1645. It is published by the Royal Swedish Academy of Letters. The oldest existing commercial newspaper is the *Haarlems Dagblad/Oprechte Haarlemsche Courant*,

Largest library ● The largest library in the world is the United States Library of Congress (founded on 24 Apr 1800), on Capitol Hill, Washington DC, USA. By 1988 it contained 86 million items, including 22 million volumes and pamphlets. The buildings contain 26·14 ha *64·6 acres* of floor space and 856 km *532 miles* of shelving. (Photo: Spectrum)

published in Haarlem in the Netherlands. First issued as the *Weeckelycke Courante van Europa* on 8 Jan 1656, a copy of issue No. 1 survives.

The newspaper with the earliest origins in the United Kingdom is *Berrow's Worcester Journal* (originally the *Worcester Post Man*), published in Worcester. It was traditionally founded in 1690 and has appeared weekly since June 1709. No complete file exists. The earliest date of foundation for any British newspaper published under the same title is the *Stamford Mercury*, printed since 1712 and traditionally even 1695. The *London Gazette* (originally the *Oxford Gazette*) was first published on 16 Nov 1665. The oldest Sunday newspaper is *The Observer*, first issued on 4 Dec 1791. The earliest known edition of the Belfast-based *News Letter* was dated 6 Mar 1738 and has been a daily since 1855. *The Daily Universal Register* was founded in 1785 and changed its name to *The Times* in 1788.

Largest newspapers

The most massive single issues of a newspaper have been of the *Sunday New York Times* which by August 1987 had reached 6·35 kg *14 lb* with a prediction that 7·7 kg *17 lb* was a probability. The largest page size ever used has been 130 cm × 89 cm *51 in × 35 in* for The *Constellation*, printed in 1859 by George Roberts as part of the 4 July celebrations in New York City, NY, USA. The *Worcestershire Chronicle* was the largest British newspaper. A surviving issue of 16 Feb 1859 measures 82 cm × 57 cm *32¼ in × 22½ in.*

Smallest newspapers

The smallest original page size has been the 7·6 × 9·5 cm *3 × 3¾ in* of the *Daily Banner* (25 cents per month) of Roseberg, Oregon, USA, issues of which, dated 1 and 2 Feb 1876, survive. The *Answers to Correspondents* published by Messrs Carr & Co, Paternoster Square, London in 1888 was 9 × 11 cm *3½ × 4½ in.* The British Library Newspaper Library has the *Watford News and Advertiser* of 1 Apr 1899 measuring 7·5 × 10 cm *2·9 × 3·9 in.*

Most expensive

Britain's most expensive papers are *The Observer* and *The Sunday Times* at 50p or double the price of the original 1955 fully bound edition of *The Guinness Book of Records.*

The United States had 1657 English-language daily newspapers at 30 Sept 1986 with a combined net paid circulation of 62 766 232 copies per day. The peak year for US newspapers was 1910, when there were 2202.

The leading newspaper readers in the world are the people of Sweden, where 580 newspapers are sold for each 1000 compared with the UK figure of 410.

Longest editorship

Sir Etienne Dupuch OBE (b. 16 Feb 1899) of Nassau, Bahamas, Editor-in-Chief of *The Tribune* since 1 Apr 1919 to 1972, and Contributing Editor to the present time, entered his 70th year as an editor on 1 Apr 1988.

The longest editorship of any United Kingdom national newspaper was more than 59 years by C. P. Scott (1846–1932) of the *Manchester Guardian*, who was appointed, aged 26, in 1872 and who died on 1 Jan 1932.

Most durable feature

Eric Hardy of Liverpool is now in his 61st year as a regular natural history contributor to the *Daily Post* of Liverpool with a weekly 'Countryside' feature. Albert E. Pool (b. 1909) was a part-time journalist for the *Lincolnshire and South Humberside* (formerly *Hull*) *Times* from March 1923 until the paper closed on 26 July 1985.

Longest-lived strip

The most durable newspaper comic strip has been the 'Katzenjammer Kids' (Hans and Fritz) created by Rudolph Dirks and first published in the *New York Journal* on 12 Dec 1897.

The earliest strip cartoon was 'The Yellow Kid', which first appeared in the *New York Journal* on 18 Oct 1896. The most widely syndicated is 'Peanuts' by Charlie Schulz of Santa Rosa, California, USA appearing in more than 2000 newspapers in 68 countries in 26 languages starting in October 1950. In 1986 his income was estimated at $1 million per month.

Most misprints

The record for misprints in *The Times* was set on 22 Aug 1978 when on page 19 there were 97 in 5½ single column inches. The passage concerned 'Pop' (Pope) Paul VI.

Most durable advertiser

The Jos Neel Co, a clothing store in Macon, Georgia, USA (founded 1880) has run an 'ad' in the *Macon Telegraph* every day in the upper left corner of page 2 since 22 Feb 1889 or 35 760 times to March 1987.

CIRCULATION

Earliest 1 000 000

The first newspaper to achieve a circulation of 1 000 000 was *Le Petit Journal*, published in Paris, France, which reached this figure in 1886, when selling at 5 centimes. The *Daily Mail* first reached a million on 2 Mar 1900.

Highest

The highest circulation for any newspaper in the world is that for the *Yomiuri Shimbun* (founded 1874) of Japan which attained a figure of 14 474 573 copies on 1 April 1988. This is achieved by totalling the figures for editions published in various centres with a morning figure of 9 456 625 and an evening figure of 5 017 948. It reaches 38 per cent of Japan's 34 million households. It has a staff of 10 205 and 121 bureaux. In Japan 569 newspapers are printed for each 1000 people. *Trud*, the Soviet trade union daily, is printed in 53 cities in 18 million copies of which only 70 000 are bought at news-stands.

The highest circulation of any single newspaper in Britain is that of *The News of the World*. Single issues have attained a sale of 9 000 000 copies with an estimated readership of more than 19 000 000. The paper first appeared on 1 Oct 1843, and surpassed the million mark in 1905. The latest sales figure is 5 290 000 copies per issue (mid-May 1988), with an estimated readership of 13 099 000.

The highest net sale of any daily newspaper in the United Kingdom is that of *The Sun*, founded in London in 1964. The latest sales figure is 4 134 454 (mid-May 1988), with an estimated readership of 11 517 000. It is not surprising therefore that the record number of entrants received for a newspaper competition was by *The Sun* for its game entitled 'Lotto'. In the 3-week period 18 Jan–8 Feb 1988, a total of 4 305 162 entries were registered — equivalent to to 3000 full-to-the-brim standard pillar boxes.

Most read

The national newspaper which achieves the closest to a saturation circulation is the *Sunday Post*, established in Glasgow in 1914. In 1987 its estimated readership in Scotland of 2 505 000 represented 61 per cent of the entire population aged 15 and over. The *Arran Banner* (founded March 1974) has a readership of 97+ per cent on Britain's 7th largest offshore island.

PERIODICALS

Oldest

The oldest continuing periodical in the world is *Philosophical Transactions of the Royal Society*, published in London, which first appeared on 6 Mar 1665.

The bi-monthly *Gospel Magazine* has been published since 1766. Curtis's *Botanical Magazine* has been in continuous publication since 1 Feb 1787, as several 'parts' a year forming a series of continuously numbered volumes. Britain's oldest weekly periodical is *The Lancet*, first published in 1823. The *Scots Magazine* began in 1739 and ran until 1826, and with only three breaks has been produced since 1924.

Largest circulations

The largest circulation of any weekly periodical is that of *TV Guide* (USA) which in 1974 became the first magazine in history to sell a billion (1000 million) copies in a year. The weekly average for July–Dec 1987 was 16 969 260. In its 39 basic international editions *Reader's Digest* (established February 1922) circulates 28 000 000 copies monthly in 15 languages, including a United States edition of more than 16 250 000 copies and a United Kingdom edition (established 1939) of 1 555 791 copies (ABC July–Dec 1987).

Parade, the American syndicated Sunday newspaper colour magazine, is distributed with 135 newspapers every Sunday. The current circulation is 32·5 million (May 1988).

The highest circulation of any periodical in Great Britain is that of the *Radio Times* (instituted on 28 Sept 1923). The average weekly sale for July–Dec 1987 was 3 209 697 copies with a readership of 9 009 000. The highest sale of any issue was 11 057 818 copies for the Christmas issue of 1987. *TV Times* averaged sales of 3 156 011 in the period July–Dec 1987 with an estimated readership of 9 177 000 (Jan–Dec 1987).

Weightiest

The heaviest magazine ever published was the September 1987 USA issue of the women's fashion journal *Vogue* which ran to 828 hernia-inducing pages.

Annual

Old Moore's Almanack has been published annually since 1697, when it first appeared as a broadsheet by Dr Francis Moore (1657–1715) of Southwark, London to advertise his 'physiks'. The annual sale certified by its publishers W. Foulsham & Co Ltd of Slough, England is one million copies and its aggregate sale is estimated to be in excess of 108 million.

CROSSWORDS

First

The earliest known crossword was a 9 by 9 Double Diamond published in *St Nicholas* for September 1875 in New York City. This was discovered by Dr Kenneth Miller of Newcastle-upon-Tyne, England, inventor of the colour crossword in 1983.

The first crossword published in a British newspaper was one furnished by C. W. Shepherd in the *Sunday Express* of 2 Nov 1924. However, a 25-letter acrostic of Roman provenance was discovered on a wall in Cirencester, Gloucestershire in 1868.

Largest crossword

The world's largest published was one compiled in July 1982 by Robert Turcot of Québec, Canada. It comprised 82 951 squares, contained 12 489 clues across and 13 125 down and covered 3·55 m² *38·28 ft²*.

Fastest and slowest solution

Dr John Sykes won *The Times* championship 8 times between 1972 and 1985. In May 1966 *The Times* of London received an announcement from a Fijian woman that she had just succeeded in completing their crossword No. 673 in the issue of 4 Apr 1932.

Most durable compilers

Adrian Bell (1901–1980) of Barsham, Suffolk contributed a record 4520 crosswords to *The Times* from 2 Jan 1930 until his death.

The most prolific crossword compiler is Roger F. Squires of Ironbridge, Shropshire, who compiles 37 published puzzles single-handedly each week. His total output to August 1988 was over 31 000.

ADVERTISING RATES

The highest ever price for a single page was $408 900 for a four-colour back cover in *Parade* (circulation 32·5 million per week) in May 1988 (see above). The record for a four-colour inside page is $355 600 in *Parade* (summer 1988). The advertising revenue from the November 1982 US edition of *Reader's Digest* was a peak $14 716 551.

The highest expenditure ever incurred on a single advertisement in a periodical has been $3 200 000 by Gulf and Western Industries on 5 Feb 1979 for insertions in *Time* magazine (US and selected overseas editions).

The British record is some £100 000 for a 20-page colour supplement by Woolworths in the *Radio Times* of 16 Nov 1972 (approximately £470 000 at today's prices). The rate for a single page in the *News of the World SunDay* magazine is £28 500, and £57 000 for a centre spread

(April 1987). The world's highest newspaper advertising rate is 39 210 000 yen for a full page in the morning edition and 32 205 000 yen for the evening edition of the *Yomiuri Shimbun* of Tokyo (April 1988).

The highest rate in Britain is a full page in colour in the *Sunday Times* at £60 000 (March 1988).

Music

Whistles and flutes made from perforated phalange bones have been found at Upper Palaeolithic sites of the Aurignacian period (*c.* 25 000–22 000 BC) e.g. at Istalló-óskö, Hungary and in Molodova, USSR. The world's earliest surviving musical notation dates from *c.* 1800 BC. A heptatonic scale deciphered from a clay tablet by Dr Duchesne-Guillemin in 1966–7 was found at a site in Nippur, Sumer, now Iraq. An Assyrian love song also *c.* 1800 BC to an Ugaritic god from a tablet of notation and lyric was reconstructed for an 11-string lyre at the University of California, Berkeley, USA on 6 Mar 1974. Musical history can be traced back to the 3rd millennium BC, when the yellow bell (*huang chung*) had a recognised standard musical tone in Chinese temple music.

INSTRUMENTS
Earliest piano
The earliest pianoforte in existence is one built in Florence, Italy in 1720 by Bartolommeo Cristofori (1655–1731) of Padua, and now preserved in the Metropolitan Museum of Art, New York City.

Grandest piano
The grandest grand piano was one of 1¼ tonnes 3·55 m *11 ft 8 in* in length made by Chas H. Challen & Son Ltd of London in 1935. The longest bass string measured 3·02 m *9 ft 11 in* with a tensile strength of 30 tonnes.

Most expensive piano
The highest price ever paid for a piano has been $390 000 at Sotheby Parke Bernet, New York on 26 Mar 1980 for a Steinway grand of *c.* 1888 sold by the Martin Beck Theater. It was bought by a non-pianist.

Smallest piano
The smallest playable piano is a ⅛ th scale model of a 1910 Knabe. It measures 19·05 × 8·57 × 16·5 cm *7½ × 3⅜ × 6½ in* and was built by Emil J. Cost.

Largest organ
The largest and loudest musical instrument ever constructed is the now only partially functional Auditorium Organ in Atlantic City, New Jersey, USA. Completed in 1930, this heroic instrument had 2 consoles (one with 7 manuals and another movable one with 5), 1477 stop controls and 33 112 pipes ranging in tone from 4·7 mm *³⁄₁₆ of an inch* to the 19·5 m *64 ft* tone. It had the volume of 25 brass bands, with a range of 7 octaves. The world's largest fully functional organ is the 6 manual 30 067 pipe Grand Court Organ installed in the Wanamaker Store, Philadelphia, Pennsylvania, USA in 1911 and enlarged between then and 1930. It has a 19·5 m *64 ft* tone gravissima pipe.

The world's largest church organ is that in Passau Cathedral, West Germany. It was completed in 1928 by D. F. Steinmeyer & Co and has 16 000 pipes and 5 manuals. The world's most powerful electronic organ is the 5000-watt Royal V. Rodgers organ, designed by Virgil Fox and with 465 speakers, installed by Orient Shoji Co in the Founders Hall of the Shingi Shumai Kai, near Kyoto, Japan in June 1983. The chapel organ at West Point US Military Academy, NY has, since 1911, been expanded from 2406 to 18 200 pipes.

The largest organ in Great Britain is that completed in Liverpool Anglican Cathedral on 18 Oct 1926, with two 5-manual consoles of which only one is now in use, and 9704 speaking pipes (originally 10 936) ranging from tones 1·9 cm to 9·75 m *¾ in to 32 ft.*

Largest guitar ● The largest and presumably also the loudest playable guitar in the world is one 4·35 m *14 ft 3¼ in* tall, and 140 kg *309 lb* in weight, built by Joe Kovacic of Lado Musical Inc., Scarborough, Ontario, Canada.

Loudest organ stop
The loudest organ stop in the world is the Ophicleide stop of the Grand Great in the Solo Organ in the Atlantic City Auditorium (see above). It is operated by a pressure of water 24 kPa (3½ lb/in²) and has a pure trumpet note of ear-splitting volume, more than 6 times the volume of the loudest locomotive whistles.

Most durable musicians
Elsie Maude Stanley Hall (1877–1976) gave piano recitals for 90 years, giving her final concert in Rustenburg, Transvaal, South Africa aged 97. Charles Bridgeman (1779–1873) of All Saints Parish Church, Hertford, England, was appointed organist in 1792, was still playing 81 years later in 1873. Norwegian pianist Reidar Thommesen (1889–1986) played over 30 hours a week in theatre cafés when a nonagenarian.

Largest brass instrument
The largest recorded brass instrument is a tuba standing 2·28 m *7½ ft* tall, with 11·8 m *39 ft* of tubing and a bell 1 m *3 ft 4 in* across. This contrabass tuba was constructed for a world tour by the band of American composer John Philip Sousa (1854–1932), *c.* 1896–8. It is now owned by a circus promoter in South Africa.

Largest stringed instrument
The largest movable stringed instrument ever constructed was a pantaleon with 270 strings stretched over 4·6 m² *50 ft²* used by George Noel in 1767. The greatest number of musicians to operate an instrument was the 6 required to play the gigantic orchestrion, known as the Apollonican, built in 1816 and played until 1840.

Most expensive guitar
The most expensive standard sized guitar is the German chittara battente by Jacob Stadler, dated 1624, which was sold for £10 500 at Christie's, London on 12 June 1974.

Largest double bass
The largest double bass ever constructed was one 4·26 m *14 ft* tall, built in 1924 in Ironia, New Jersey, USA by Arthur K. Ferris, allegedly on orders from the Archangel Gabriel. It weighed 590 kg *11·6 cwt* with a sound box 2·43 m *8 ft* across, and had leathern strings totalling 31·7 m *104 ft*. Its low notes could be felt rather than heard. On 27 June 1984 5 members of 'Bass Ten' from Bournemouth, Dorset bowed and six-fingered a double bass simultaneously in a rendition of Monti's *Czardas* at Hever Castle, Kent.

Most valuable 'cello
The highest auction price for a violoncello or any musical instrument is £682 000 at Sotheby's, London on 22 June 1988 for a Stradivarius known as 'The Cholmondely made in Cremona, Italy *c.* 1698.

Most valuable violin
The Lady Blunt Stradivarius violin of 1721 failed at £820 000 to reach its undisclosed 'reserve' at Sotheby's, London on 14 Nov 1985. The highest price ever *paid* at auction for a violin is £473 000 for Marie Hall Stradivarius dated 1709 at Sotheby's, London on 31 March 1988. Some 700 of the 1116 violins by Stradivarius (1644–1737) have survived. His Alard violin was confirmed by Jacques Français to have been sold by private treaty by W. E. Hill for $1·2 million to a Singaporean.

Most durable fiddlers
Rolland S. Tapley retired as a violinist from the Boston Symphony Orchestra after reputedly playing for an unrivalled 58 years from February 1920 to 27 August 1978. Otto E. Funk, 62, walked 6702 km *4165 miles* from New York City to San Francisco, California, USA playing

his Hopf violin every step of the way westward. He arrived on 16 June 1929 after 183 days on the road.

Largest drum

The largest drum ever constructed was one 3·96 m *13 ft* in diameter, built by the Supreme Drum Co, London, and played at the Royal Festival Hall, London on 31 May 1987.

The largest drum kit is professional rock star Luis Cardenas' 'Status Cymbal' – a 75-piece (excluding the stool) custom-made kit. Drummer with the Los Angeles-based group 'Renegade' as well as a solo artiste, Luis' kit includes 2 suspended overhead toms, 2 Agogo percussion bells, 15 finger cymbals and a 1948 Black Beauty snare drum.

Longest alphorn

The longest alphorn is one of 35·96 m *118 ft* (excluding mouthpiece) weighing 83 kg *183 lb* built by Swiss-born Peter Wutherich, of Boise, Idaho, USA. The sound takes 105·7 milliseconds to emerge from the bowl after entry into the mouthpiece.

Highest and lowest notes

The extremes of orchestral instruments (excluding the organ) range between a handbell tuned to g^v (6272 cycles/sec) and the sub-contrabass clarinet, which can reach C_{11} or 16·4 cycles/sec. The highest note on a standard pianoforte is c^v (4186 cycles/sec), which is also the violinist's limit. In 1873 a sub double bassoon able to reach $B_{111}\pm$ or 14·6 cycles/sec was constructed but no surviving specimen is known. The extremes for the organ are g^{vi} (the sixth G above middle C) (12·544 cycles/sec) and C_{111} (8·12 cycles/sec) obtainable from 1·9 cm ¾ *in* and 19·5 m *64 ft* pipes respectively.

Easiest and most difficult instruments

The American Music Conference announced in September 1977 that the easiest instrument is the ukulele, and the most difficult are the French horn and the oboe, which latter has been described as 'the ill woodwind that no one blows good'.

Fastest bagpipe playing

Sgt Mick Maitland, Pipe Major of No. 111 RAF Fighter Squadron played 'Scotland the Brave' on his pipes at a speed of Mach 2·0 and a height of 12 190 m *40 000 ft.* He was flown in a Phantom XV 574 by Wing Commander Phil W. Roser, the Squadron Commander. This supersonic performance was given 64·3 km *40 miles* south of RAF Akrotiri, Cyprus on 3 June 1986.

ORCHESTRAS
Largest orchestra

On 17 June 1872, Johann Strauss the younger (1825–99) conducted an orchestra of 987 pieces (including 400 first violinists) supported by a choir of 20 000, at the World Peace Jubilee in Boston, Massachusetts, USA.

Largest band

The most massive band ever assembled was one of 20 100 bandsmen at the Ullevaal Stadium, Oslo from Norges Musikkorps Forbund bands from all Norway on 28 June 1964. On 17 Apr 1982, 6179 'musicians' congregated at Bay Shore Mall, Milwaukee, Wisconsin, USA for a rendering of Sousa's 'Stars and Stripes Forever'. According to one music critic, the 'instruments' included 'kazoos, 7-Up bottles, one-man-band contraptions, coffee cans, bongo drums and anything-you-can-thump-on'. 'At times' the report concludes, 'you could almost tell what they were playing.'

Largest marching band

The largest marching band was one of 4524 including 1342 majorettes under the direction of Danny Kaye (1913–87) at Dodger Stadium, Los Angeles on 15 Apr 1985. The longest recorded musical march is one of 61 km *37·9 miles* from Lillehammer to Hamar, Norway in 15 hours when, on 10 May 1980, 26 of 35 members of the Trondheim Brass Band survived the playing of 135 marches.

Most durable conductor

The Cork Symphony Orchestra performed under the baton of Dr Aloys Fleischmann for 52 seasons (1935–86).

Most successful bands

Most British Open Brass Band Championship titles (inst. 1853) have been won by the Black Dyke Mills Band which has won 22 times from 1862 to 1974 including 3 consecutive wins in 1972–4. The most successful pipe band is the Shotts & Dykehead Caledonian Pipe Band with their 10th world title in August 1980.

ATTENDANCES
Classical
Pop festival

The greatest attendance has been 725 000 for Steve Wozniak's 1983 US Festival. The attendance at the 3rd Pop Festival at East Afton Farm, Freshwater, Isle of Wight, England on 30 Aug 1970 was claimed by its promoters, Fiery Creations, to be 400 000.

Solo performer

The largest paying audience ever attracted by a solo performer was an estimated 175 000 in the Maracaña Stadium, Rio de Janeiro, Brazil to hear Frank Sinatra (b. 1915) on 26 Jan 1980. Jean-Michel Jarre entertained an estimated 1·3 million at downtown Houston, Texas, USA at a free concert on 5 Apr 1986.

Greatest choir

Excluding 'sing alongs' by stadium crowds, the greatest choir is one of 60 000 which sang in unison as a finale of a choral contest among 160 000 participants in Breslau, Germany on 2 Aug 1937.

Most successful concert tour

Bruce Springsteen's tour which began in April 1984 grossed an estimated $117 million. He played 158 dates in 61 cities spread over 11 countries and was seen by 4 767 854 people.

COMPOSERS
Most prolific

The most prolific composer of all time was probably Georg Philipp Telemann (1681–1767) of Germany. He composed 12 complete sets of services (one cantata every Sunday) for a year, 78 services for special occasions, 40 operas, 600 to 700 orchestral suites, 44 Passions, plus concertos and chamber music. The most prolific symphonist was Johann Melchior Molter (*c.* 1695–1765) of Germany who wrote 169. Joseph Haydn (1732–1809) of Austria wrote 108 numbered symphonies, many of which are regularly played today.

Most rapid

Among composers of the classical period the most prolific was Wolfgang Amadeus Mozart (1756–91) of Austria, who wrote *c.* 1000 operas, operettas, symphonies, violin sonatas, divertimenti, serenades, motets, concertos for piano and many other instruments, string quartets, other chamber music, masses and litanies, of which only 70 were published before he died aged 35. His opera *La Clemenza di Tito* (1791) was written in 18 days, and three symphonic masterpieces, *Symphony No. 39 in E flat major, Symphony No. 40 in G minor* and the *Jupiter Symphony No. 41 in C major,* were reputedly written in the space of 42 days in 1788. His overture *Don Giovanni* was written in full score at one sitting in Prague in 1787 and finished on the day of its opening performance.

Longest symphony

The longest of all single classical symphonies is the orchestral symphony No. 3 in D minor by Gustav Mahler (1860–1911) of Austria. This work, composed in 1896, requires a contralto, a women's and a boys' choir in addition to a full orchestra. A full performance requires 1 hr 40 min, of which the first movement alone takes between 30 and 36 min. The Symphony No. 2 (the

Gothic), composed from 1919–22 by William Havergal Brian (1876–1972), was played by over 800 performers (4 brass bands) in the Victoria Hall, Hanley, Staffordshire on 21 May 1978 (conductor Trevor Stokes). A recent broadcast required 1 hr 45½ min. Brian wrote an even vaster work based on Shelley's 'Prometheus Unbound' lasting 4 hr 11 min but the full score has been missing since 1961. The symphony *Victory at Sea* written by Richard Rodgers and ' arranged by Robert Russell Bennett for NBC TV in 1952 lasted for 13 hours.

Longest piano composition

The longest continuous non-repetitious piano piece ever published has been *The Well-Tuned Piano* by La Monte Young, first presented by the Dia Art Foundation at the Concert Hall, Harrison St, New York on 28 Feb 1980. The piece lasted 4 hr 12 min 10 sec. *Symphonic Variations,* composed in the 1930s by Kaikhosru Shapurji Sorabji (b. 1892) on 500 pages of close manuscript in 3 volumes, would last for 6 hours at the prescribed tempo.

Longest silence

The longest interval between the known composition of a major composer and its performance in the manner intended is from 3 Mar 1791 until 9 Oct 1982 (over 191 years), in the case of Mozart's *Organ Piece for a Clock,* a fugue fantasy in F minor (K 608), arranged by the organ builders Wm Hill & Son and Norman & Beard Ltd at Glyndebourne, East Sussex, England.

PERFORMERS
Highest-paid pianist

Wladziu Valentino Liberace (1917–87) earned more than $2 million each 26-week season with a peak of $138 000 for a single night's performance at Madison Square Garden, New York in 1954. The highest-paid classical concert pianist was Ignace Jan Paderewski (1860–1941), Prime Minister of Poland (1919–20), who accumulated a fortune estimated at $5 000 000, of which $500 000 was earned in a single season in 1922–23. The *nouveau riche* wife of a US industrialist once required him to play in her house behind a curtain. For concerts Artur Rubinstein (1887–1982), between 1937 and 1976, commanded 70 per cent of the gross.

Greatest span

Sergei Vassilievitch Rachmaninov (1873–1943) had a span of 12 white notes and could play a left-hand chord of C, E♭, G, C, G.

Most successful singer

Of great fortunes earned by singers, the highest on record are those of Enrico Caruso (1873–1921), the Italian tenor, whose estate was about $9 000 000 and the Italian-Spanish coloratura soprano Amelita Galli-Curci (1889–1963), who received about $3 000 000. The Irish tenor Count John Francis McCormack (1884–1945) gave up to 10 concerts to capacity audiences in a single season in New York.

David Bowie drew a fee of $1·5 million for a single show at the US Festival in Glen Helen Regional Park, San Bernardino County, California, USA on 26 May 1983. The 4-man Van Halen rock band attracted a matching fee. The total attendance at Michael Jackson's 'Victory Tour' in the United States, July–Dec 1984, brought in a tour gross revenue of $81 million.

Singer's pulling power

In 1850, up to $653 was paid for a single seat at the US concerts of Johanna ('Jenny') Maria Lind (1820–87), the 'Swedish nightingale'. She had a range from g to e^{111} of which the middle register is still regarded as unrivalled.

Worst singer

While no agreement exists as to the identity of history's greatest singer, there is unanimity on the worst. The excursions of the soprano Florence Foster Jenkins (1868–1944) into lieder and even high coloratura culminated on 25 Oct 1944 in her sell-out concert at the

Carnegie Hall, New York. The diva's (already high) high F was said to have been made higher in 1943 by a crash in a taxi. It is one of the tragedies of musicology that Madame Jenkins' *Clavelitos*, accompanied by Cosme McMoon, was never recorded for posterity.

OPERA

Longest

The longest of commonly performed operas is *Die Meistersinger von Nürnberg* by Wilhelm Richard Wagner (1813–83) of Germany. A normal uncut performance of this opera as performed by the Sadler's Wells company between 24 Aug and 19 Sept 1968 entailed 5 hr 15 min of music. *The Heretics* by Gabriel von Wayditch (1888–1969), a Hungarian-American, is orchestrated for 110 pieces and lasts 8½ hr.

Shortest

The shortest opera published was *The Deliverance of Theseus* by Darius Milhaud (1892–1972), first performed in 1928, which lasted for 7 min 27 sec.

Longest aria

The longest single aria, in the sense of an operatic solo, is Brünnhilde's immolation scene in Wagner's *Gotterdam-merung*. A well-known recording of this has been precisely timed at 14 min 46 sec.

Largest opera houses

The largest opera house in the world is the Metropolitan Opera House, Lincoln Center, New York, completed in September 1966 at a cost of $45 700 000. It has a capacity of 3800 seats in an auditorium 137 m *451 ft* deep. The stage is 71 m *234 ft* wide and 44·5 m *146 ft* deep. The tallest opera house is one housed in a 42-storey building on Wacker Drive in Chicago, Illinois, USA. The Teatro della Scala (La Scala) in Milan, Italy shares with the Bolshoi Theatre in Moscow the distinction of having the greatest number of tiers. Each has 6, with the topmost being nicknamed the *Galiorka* by Russians.

Youngest and oldest opera singers

The youngest opera singer in the world has been Ginetta Gloria La Bianca, born in Buffalo, New York on 12 May 1934, who sang Rosina in *The Barber of Seville* at the Teatro dell'Opera, Rome on 8 May 1950 aged 15 years 361 days, having appeared as Gilda in *Rigoletto* at Velletri 45 days earlier. Ginetta La Bianca was taught by Lucia Carlino and managed by Angelo Carlino. The tenor Giovanni Martinelli sang Emperor Altoum in *Turandot* in Seattle, Washington State, USA on 4 Feb 1967 when aged 81.

Danshi Toyotake (b. 1 Aug 1891) has been singing *Musume Gidayu* for 91 years.

Longest encore

The longest operatic encore, listed in the *Concise Oxford Dictionary of Opera*, was of the entire opera Cimarosa's *Il Matrimonio Segreto* at its première in 1792. This was at the command of the Austro-Hungarian Emperor Leopold II (reigned 1790–2).

Most curtain calls

On 24 February 1988 Luciano Pavarotti received 115 curtain calls and was applauded for 1 hr 2 min after singing the part of Nemorino in Gaetano Donizetti's *L'elisir d'amore* at the Deutsche Oper in West Berlin, Germany.

SONG

Oldest

The oldest known song is the *shaduf* chant, which has been sung since time immemorial by irrigation workers on the man-powered pivoted-rod bucket raisers of the Nile water mills (or *saqiyas*) in Egypt. The oldest known harmonised music performed today is the English song *Sumer is icumen in* which dates from *c.* 1240.

National anthems

The oldest national anthem is the *Kimigayo* of Japan, in which the words date from the 9th century, whilst the oldest music belongs to the Netherlands.

The anthem of Greece constitutes the first two verses of the Solomos poem, which has 158 stanzas. The shortest anthems are those of Japan, Jordan and San Marino, each with only 4 lines. Of the 11 wordless national anthems the oldest is that of Spain dating from 1770.

Longest rendering

'God Save the King' was played non-stop 16 or 17 times by a German military band on the platform of Rathenau railway station, Brandenburg, Germany on the morning of 9 Feb 1909. The reason was that King Edward VII was struggling inside the train with the uniform of a German field-marshal before he could emerge.

Top songs

The most frequently sung songs in English are *Happy Birthday to You* (based on the original *Good Morning to All*), by Mildred and Patty S. Hill of New York (published in 1935 and in copyright until 2010); *For He's a Jolly Good Fellow* (originally the French *Malbrouk*), known at least as early as 1781, and *Auld Lang Syne* (originally the Strathspey *I Fee'd a Lad at Michaelmass*), some words of which were written by Robert Burns (1759–96). *Happy Birthday* was sung in space by the Apollo IX astronauts on 8 Mar 1969.

Top-selling sheet music

Sales of three non-copyright pieces are known to have exceeded 20 000 000, namely *The Old Folks at Home* by Stephen Foster (1855), *Listen to the Mocking Bird* (1855) and *The Blue Danube* (1867). Of copyright material the two top sellers are *Let Me Call You Sweetheart* (1910, by Whitson and Friedman) and *Till We Meet Again* (1918, by Egan and Whiting) each with some 6 000 000 by 1967. Other huge sellers have been *St Louis Blues*, *Stardust* and *Tea for Two*.

Most successful songwriters

The songwriters responsible for the most number one singles are John Lennon and Paul McCartney. In America McCartney is credited as writer on 32 number one hits, 6 more than Lennon. In Britain Lennon authored 28 number ones, McCartney 27. In America 23 of their number ones were jointly written, in Britain, 24. After Lennon/McCartney the most successful songwriters in terms of number one hits in Britain are Benny Andersson and Bjorn Ulvaeus of the group ABBA, who have written 10. In America Barry Gibb of the Bee Gees has written or co-written 16 number ones. The most successful female songwriter in America is Carole King with 8 number ones – in Britain it is Madonna with 4.

HYMNS

Earliest

There are more than 950 000 Christian hymns in existence. The music and parts of the text of a hymn in the *Oxyrhynchus Papyri* from the 2nd century are the earliest known hymnody. The earliest exactly datable hymn is the *Heyr Himna Smióur* (*Hear, the maker of heaven*) from 1208 by the Icelandic bard and chieftain Kolbeinn Tumason (1173–1208).

Longest and shortest

The longest hymn is *Hora novissima tempora pessima sunt; vigilemus* by Bernard of Cluny (12th century),

Theatre

which runs to 2966 lines. In English the longest is *The Sands of Time are Sinking* by Mrs Anne Ross Cousin, *née* Cundell (1824–1906), which is in full 152 lines, though only 32 lines in the Methodist Hymn Book. The shortest hymn is the single verse in long metre *Be Present at our Table Lord*, anon., but attributed to 'J. Leland'.

Most prolific hymnists

Mrs Frances (Fanny) Jane van Alstyne, *née* Crosby (1820–1915) (USA) wrote 8500 hymns although she had been blinded at the age of 6 weeks. She is reputed to have knocked off one hymn in 15 minutes. Charles Wesley (1707–88) wrote about 6000 hymns. In the 7th (1950) edition of *Hymns Ancient and Modern* the works of John Mason Neale (1818–66) appear 56 times.

BELLS
Oldest

The oldest bell in the world is the tintinnabulum found in the Babylonian Palace of Nimrod in 1849 by Mr (later Sir) Austen Henry Layard (1817–94) dating from *c.* 1100 BC. The oldest known tower bell is one in Pisa, Italy dated MCVI (1106).

The fragile hand bell known as the Black or Iron Bell of St Patrick is dated *c.* AD 450. The oldest tower bell in Great Britain is one of 50 kg *1 cwt* at St Botolph, Hardham, Sussex, still in use but dated *ante* 1100. The oldest inscribed bell is the Gargate bell at Caversfield church, Oxfordshire and is dated *c.* 1200–1210. The oldest *dated* bell in England is one hanging in Lissett church, near Bridlington, Humberside discovered in October 1972 to bear the date MCCLIIII (1254).

Heaviest

The heaviest bell in the world is the Tsar Kolokol, cast on 25 Nov 1735 in Moscow. It weighs 196 tonnes *193 tons*, measures 5·9 m *19 ft 4½ in* in diameter and 5·87 m *19 ft 3 in* high, and its greatest thickness is 60 cm *24 in*. The bell is cracked, and a fragment, weighing about 11 tonnes was broken from it. The bell has stood, unrung, on a platform in the Kremlin in Moscow since 1836.

The heaviest bell in use is the Mingun bell, weighing 55 555 viss or *90·52 tons* with a diameter of 5·09 m *16 ft 8½ in* at the lip, in Mandalay, Burma, which is struck by a teak boom from the outside. It was cast at Mingun late in

the reign of King Bodawpaya (1782–1819). The heaviest swinging bell in the world is the Petersglocke in the south-west tower of Cologne Cathedral, West Germany, cast in 1923 with a diameter of 3·40 m *11 ft 1¾ in* weighing 25·4 tonnes *25·0 tons*.

The heaviest bell hung in Great Britain is 'Great Paul' in the south-west tower of St Paul's Cathedral, London, cast in 1881. It weighs 17 002 kg *16 tons 14 cwt 2 qrs 19 lb*, has a diameter of 2·90 m *9 ft 6½ in* and sounds note E-flat. 'Big Ben', the hour bell in the clock tower of the House of Commons, was cast in 1858 and weighs 13 761 kg *13 tons 10 cwt 3 qrs 15 lb*. It is the most broadcast bell in the world and is note E.

Peals

A ringing peal is defined as a diatonic 'ring' of 5 or more bells hung for full-circle change ringing. Of 5500 rings so hung only 70 are outside the United Kingdom and Ireland.

The heaviest ring in the world is that of 13 bells cast in 1938–39 for the Anglican Cathedral, Liverpool. The total bell weight is 16·76 tonnes *16½ tons* of which Emmanuel, the tenor bell note A, weighs 4170·8 kg *82 cwt 11 lb*.

Largest carillon

The largest carillon (minimum of 23 bells) in the world is the Laura Spelman Rockefeller Memorial Carillon in Riverside Church, New York with 74 bells weighing 102 tons. The bourdon, giving the note lower C, weighs 18 563 kg *40 926 lb*. This 18·27 ton bell, cast in England, with a diameter of 3·09 cm *10 ft 2 in* is the largest *tuned* bell in the world.

The heaviest carillon in Great Britain is in St Nicholas Church, Aberdeen. It consists of 48 bells, the total weight of which is 25 838 kg *25 tons 8 cwt 2 qrs 13 lb*. The bourdon bell weighs 4571 kg *4 tons 9 cwt 3 qrs 26 lb* and is the note G-sharp.

Oldest theatre ● The theatre of Epidauros, Greece, built by Polycleitos in the 4th century BC, is an extremely well-preserved example of the earliest amphitheatres which date from the 5th century BC. (Photo: Ronald Sheridan/ AA & A)

Bell ringing

Eight bells have been rung to their full 'extent' (40 320 unrepeated changes of Plain Bob Major) only once without relays. This took place in a bell foundry at Loughborough, Leicestershire, beginning at 6.52 a.m. on 27 July 1963 and ending at 12.50 a.m. on 28 July, after 17 hr 58 min. The peal was composed by Kenneth Lewis of Altrincham, Manchester, and the 8 ringers were conducted by Robert B. Smith, aged 25, of Marple, Manchester. Theoretically it would take 37 years 355 days to ring 12 bells (maximus) to their full extent of 479 001 600 changes. The greatest number of peals (minimum of 5040 changes, all in tower bells) rung in a year is 209 by Mark William Marshall of Ashford, Kent in 1973. The late George E. Fearn rang 2666 peals from 1928 to May 1974. Matthew Lakin (1801–1899) was a regular bell-ringer at Tetney Church near Grimsby for 84 years.

Theatre

Oldest

Theatre in Europe has its origins in Greek drama performed in honour of a god, usually Dionysus. The earliest amphitheatres date from the 5th century BC. The first stone-built theatre in Rome erected in 55 BC could accommodate 40 000 spectators.

Oldest indoor theatre

The oldest indoor theatre in the world is the Teatro Olimpico in Vicenza, Italy. Designed in the Roman style by Andrea di Pietro, *alias* Palladio (1508–80), it was begun 3 months before his death and finished by his pupil Vicenzo Scamozzi (1552–1616) in 1583. It is preserved today in its original form.

The earliest London theatre was James Burbage's 'The Theatre', built in 1576 near Finsbury Fields, London. The oldest theatre still in use in Great Britain is The Royal, Bristol. The foundation stone was laid on 30 Nov 1764, and the theatre was opened on 30 May 1766 with a 'Concert of Musick and a Specimen of Rhetorick'. The City Varieties Music Hall, Leeds was a singing room in 1762 and so claims to outdate the Theatre Royal. Actors had the legal status of rogues and vagabonds until the passing of the Vagrancy Act in 1824. The oldest amateur dramatic

society is the Old Stagers inaugurated in Canterbury, Kent in 1841. They have performed in every year except the years of World Wars I and II.

Largest

The world's largest building used for theatre is the National People's Congress Building (*Ren min da hui tang*) on the west side of Tian an men Square, Peking, China. It was completed in 1959 and covers an area of 5·2 ha *12·9 acres*. The theatre seats 10 000 and is occasionally used as such, as in 1964 for the play *The East is Red*. The highest capacity purpose-built theatre is the Perth Entertainment Centre, Western Australia completed at a cost of $A8·3 million in November 1976 with 8003 seats. The stage area is 1148 m² *12 000 ft²*.

The highest capacity theatre is the Odeon, Hammersmith, London, with 3483 seats. The largest theatre stage in Great Britain is the Opera House in Blackpool, Lancashire. It was rebuilt in July 1939 and has seats for 2975 people. Behind the 14 m *45 ft* wide proscenium arch, the stage is 33 m *110 ft* high, 18 m *60 ft* deep and 30 m *100 ft* wide, and there is dressing-room accommodation for 200 artistes.

Smallest

The smallest regularly operated professional theatre in the world is the Piccolo in Juliusstrasse, Hamburg, West Germany. It was founded in 1970 and has a maximum capacity of 30 seats.

Largest amphitheatre

The largest amphitheatre ever built is the Flavian amphitheatre or Colosseum of Rome, Italy, completed in AD 80. Covering 2 ha *5 acres* and with a capacity of 87 000, it has a maximum length of 187 m *612 ft* and a maximum width of 175 m *515 ft*.

Largest stage

The largest stage in the world is in the Ziegfeld Room, Reno, Nevada, USA with 53·6 m *176 ft* passerelle, 3 main lifts each capable of raising 1200 show girls (65·3 tonnes *64¼ tons*), two 19·1 m *62½ ft* circumference turntables and 800 spotlights.

Longest runs

Plays

The Vicksburg Theater Guild, Mississippi, USA has been playing the melodrama *Gold in the Hills* by J. Frank Davis discontinuously but every season since 1936.

Revue

The greatest number of performances of any theatrical presentation is 47 250 (to April 1986) in the case of *The Golden Horseshoe Revue*—a show staged at Disneyland Park, Anaheim, California, USA. It started on 16 July 1955, closed on 12 Oct 1986 and has been seen by 16 million people. The three main performers were Fulton Burley, Dick Hardwick and Betty Taylor who played as many as 5 houses a day in a routine that lasted 45 minutes.

Broadway

A Chorus Line which opened on 25 July 1975 entered its 13th year in August 1987. It was created by Michael Bennet (b.1943) who died of AIDS, aged 44, in Arizona, USA on 2 July 1987.

The off-Broadway musical show *The Fantasticks* by Tom Jones and Harvey Schmidt opened on 3 May 1960 and the total number of performances to 3 May 1987 is 11 240 at the Sullivan Street Playhouse, Greenwich Village, New York.

Musical shows

The longest-running musical show ever performed in Britain was *The Black and White Minstrel Show* later *Magic of the Minstrels*. The aggregate but discontinuous number of performances was 6464 with a total attendance of 7 794 552. The show opened at the Victoria Palace, London on 25 May 1962 and closed on 4 Nov 1972. It reopened for a season in June 1973 at the New Victoria and finally closed on 8 Dec 1973.

Longest run ● The longest continuous run of any show in the world is *The Mousetrap* by Dame Agatha Mary Clarissa Christie DBE (*née* Miller, later Lady Mallowan) (1890–1976). This thriller opened on 25 Nov 1952, at the Ambassadors Theatre (capacity 453) and moved after 8862 performances 'down the road' to St Martin's Theatre on 25 Mar 1974. The 35th anniversary performance on 25 Nov 1987 was the 14 566th. The Box Office reached £13 million from more than 7 million attenders.
The above photograph shows a scene from the 1987/88 production with (from left to right) Hazel McBride, Paul Bacon, Helen Christie, Rupert Bates and David Beale.

Jesus Christ Superstar, which opened at the Palace Theatre, London on 8 Aug 1972, closed on 23 Aug 1980 after 3357 performances having played to 2 million people with box office receipts of £7 million. By 1984 it had been produced in 37 other countries.

Comedy

The British record for long-running comedy is held by *No Sex Please We're British* by Anthony Marriott and Alistair Foot and presented by John Gale, which opened at the Strand Theatre on 3 June 1971, transferred to the Duchess Theatre on 2 Aug 1986, and finally ended its run on 5 Sept 1987 after 17 years and 6761 performances. Its director Allan Davis had his name in lights from the start.

Shortest runs

The shortest run on record was that of *The Intimate Revue* at the Duchess Theatre, London, on 11 Mar 1930. Anything which could go wrong did. With scene changes taking up to 20 min apiece, the management scrapped 7 scenes to get the finale on before midnight. The run was described as 'half a performance'.

The opening and closing nights of many Broadway shows have coincided. Spectacular failures are known as 'turkeys'. The most spectacular was the Royal Shakespeare Company's musical *Carrie* which closed after 5 performances at the Virginia Theatre, Broadway on 17 May 1988 with a loss of £4 250 000.

Lowest attendance

The ultimate in low attendances was in December 1983 when the comedy *Bag* in Grantham, Lincolnshire opened to a nil attendance.

Youngest Broadway producer

Margo Feiden (Margo Eden) (b. New York, 2 Dec 1944) produced the musical *Peter Pan*, which opened on 3 Apr 1961, when she was 16 years 5 months old. She wrote *Out Brief Candle*, which opened on 18 Aug 1962. She is now a leading art dealer.

One-man shows

The longest run of one-man shows is 849 by Victor Borge (b. Copenhagen, 3 Jan 1909) in his *Comedy in Music* from 2 Oct 1953 to 21 Jan 1956 at the Golden Theater, Broadway, New York City. The world aggregate record for one-man shows is 1700 performances of *Brief Lives* by Roy Dotrice (b. Guernsey, 26 May 1923) including 400 straight at the Mayfair Theatre, London ending on 20 July 1974. He was on stage for more than 2½ hr per performance of this 17th-century monologue and required 3 hr for make-up and 1 hr for removal of make-up so aggregating 40 weeks in the chair.

Most durable actors and actresses

Kanmi Fujiyama (b. 1929) played the lead role in 10 288 performances by the comedy company Sochiku Shikigeki from November 1966 to June 1983. Dame Anna Neagle DBE (1904–86) played the lead role in *Charlie Girl* at the Adelphi Theatre, London for 2062 of 2202 performances between 15 Dec 1965 and 27 Mar 1971. She played the role a further 327 times in 327 performances in Australasia. Frances Etheridge has played Lizzie, the housekeeper, in *Gold in the Hills* (see Longest runs) more than 660 times over a span of 47 years since 1936. David Raven played Major Metcalfe in *The Mousetrap* on 4575 occasions between 22 July 1957 and 23 Nov 1968. Jack Howarth MBE (1896–1984) was an actor on the stage and in television for 76 years from 1907 until his last appearance after 23 years as Albert Tatlock in *Coronation Street* on 25 Jan 1984.

Least insecure

Ben Vereen was given a 20-week guarantee of $52 500 per week plus a cut of the 'box office' in the Broadway production *Pippin* in 1986.

Most roles

The greatest recorded number of theatrical, film and television roles is 3382 from 1951 to March 1988 by Jan Leighton (US).

Most theatrical roles

Kanzaburo Nakamura (b. July 1909) has performed in 806 Kabuki titles from November 1926 to January 1987. As each title in this classical Japanese theatrical form lasts 25 days, he has therefore played 20 150 performances.

Longest play

The longest recorded theatrical production has been *The Acting Life* staged in the Tom Mann Theatre, Sydney, Australia on 17–18 Mar 1984 with a cast of 10. The production required 19½ hours or 21 hours with intervals.

Shakespeare

The first all-amateur company to have staged all 37 plays was The Southsea Shakespeare Actors, Hampshire (founded 1947) in October 1966 when, under K. Edmonds Gateley MBE, they presented *Cymbeline*. The longest is *Hamlet* with 4042 lines and 29 551 words. Of Shakespeare's 1277 speaking parts the longest is Hamlet with 11 610 words.

Longest chorus line

The longest chorus line in performing history numbered up to 120 in some of the early Ziegfeld's Follies. In the finale of *A Chorus Line* on the night of 29 Sept 1983 when it broke the record as the longest-running Broadway show ever, 332 top-hatted 'strutters' performed on stage.

Highest cabaret fee

Dolly Parton received up to $400 000 per live concert. Johnny Carson's fee for the non-televised Sears Roebuck Centenary Gala in October 1984 was set at $1 million.

Ice shows

Holiday on Ice Production Inc., founded by Morris Chalfen in 1945, stages the world's most costly live entertainment with up to 7 productions playing simultaneously in several of 75 countries. By 8 March 1988 the show had been seen by 250 000 000 spectators. The total skating and other staff exceeds 900. The most prolific producer of ice shows was Gerald Palmer (1908–83) with 137 since 1945 including 34 consecutive shows at the Empire Pool, Wembley, London with attendances up to 850 000. Hazel Wendy Jolly (b. 1933) has appeared in the Wembley Winter Pantomime for 27 years.

Most ardent theatre-goers

Dr H. Howard Hughes (b. 1902), Professor Emeritus of Texas Wesleyan College, Fort Worth, Texas, USA has attended 5720 shows in the period 1956–86. Britain's leading 'first nighter' Edward Sutro MC (1900–78) saw 3000 first-night productions from 1916–56 and possibly more than 5000 in his 60 years of theatre-going. The highest precisely recorded number of theatre attendances in Britain is 3687 shows in 33 years from 28 Mar

1953 to his death on 10 Sept 1986 by John Iles of Salisbury, Wiltshire.

Arts festival

The world's largest arts festival is the annual Edinburgh Festival Fringe (instituted in 1947). In 1985, 510 groups gave 9424 performances of 1091 shows between 9 and 31 Aug. Professor Gerald Berkowitz of Northern Illinois University attended a record 145 separate performances at the 1979 Festival from 15 Aug–8 Sept.

Fashion shows

The most prolific producer of fashion shows is Adalene Ross of San Francisco, California, USA with totals over 4711 to mid-1988.

Professional wrestling

The professional wrestler who has received most for a single bout has been Kanii Antonio Inoki of Japan on 26 June 1976. He received $2 million for the drawn wrestler v boxer bout against Muhammad Ali in the Budokan Arena, Tokyo. Lou Thesz has won 7 of wrestling's many 'world' titles. 'Fabulous' Moolah won major US women's alliance titles over the longest span starting in 1956. The heaviest ever wrestler has been William J. Cobb of Macon, Georgia, USA (b. 1926), who was billed in 1962 as the 363 kg *57 st 4 lb* 'Happy' Humphrey. Ed 'Strangler' Lewis (1890–1966) né Robert H. Friedrich fought 6200 bouts in 44 years losing only 33 matches. He won world titles in 1921, 1922, 1928 and 1931–32. (See also Chapter 12 Heaviest sportsmen).

Recorded Sound

The gramophone (phonograph) was first *conceived* by Charles Cros (1842–88), a French poet and scientist, who described his idea in sealed papers deposited in the French Academy of Sciences on 30 Apr 1877. However, the realisation of a practical device was first *achieved* by Thomas Alva Edison (1847–1931) of the USA.

The first successful wax cylinder machine was constructed by his mechanic, John Kruesi on 4–6 Dec 1877, demonstrated on 7 Dec and patented on 19 Feb 1878. The horizontal disc was introduced by Emile Berliner (1851–1929) and first demonstrated in Philadelphia on 18 May 1888.

Earliest recordings

The earliest birthdate of anyone whose voice is recorded is that of Lajos Kossuth (b. 9 Sept 1802 d. 24 Mar 1894), former Governor of Hungary whose speech in Torino, Italy on 20 Sept 1890 is still preserved on a wax cylinder in the National Széchényi Library in Budapest. The earliest-born recorded singer was Peter Schram, the Danish baritone of whom a cylinder was made in the role of Don Giovanni on his 70th birthday on 5 Sept 1889.

Tape recording

Magnetic recording was invented by Valdemar Poulsen (1869–1942) of Denmark with his steel wire Telegraphone in 1898 (US Pat. No. 661619). Fritz Pfleumer (German Patent 500900) introduced tape in 1928. Tapes were first used at the Blattner Studios, Elstree, Hertfordshire in 1929. Plastic tapes were devised by BASF of Germany in 1932–35, but were not marketed until 1950 by Recording Associates of New York. In April 1983 Olympic Optical Industry Co of Japan marketed a micro-cassette recorder measuring $10·7 \times 5·1 \times 1·4$ cm $4·2 \times 2 \times 0·55$ in weighing 125 g *4·4 oz*.

Oldest records

The BBC record library contains over 1 000 000 records, including 5250 with no known matrix. The oldest records in the library are white wax cylinders dating from 1888. The earliest commercial disc recording was manufactured in 1895. The world's largest private collection is believed to be that of Stan Kilarr (b. 1915) of Klamath Falls, Oregon, USA with some 500 000.

Smallest record

The smallest functional gramophone record are 6 titles of 33·3 mm *1 5/16 in* diameter recorded by HMV's studio at Hayes, Middlesex on 26 Jan 1923 for Queen Mary's Dolls' House. Some 92 000 of these miniature records were pressed including 35 000 of 'God Save The King' (Bb 2439).

Phonographic identification

Dr Arthur B. Lintgen (b. 1932) of Rydal, Pennsylvania has an as yet unique and proven ability to identify the music on phonograph records purely by visual inspection without hearing a note.

Earliest jazz records

The earliest jazz record made was *Indiana* and *The Dark Town Strutters Ball*, recorded for the Columbia label in New York on or about 30 Jan 1917, by the Original Dixieland Jazz Band, led by Dominick (Nick) James La Rocca (1889–1961). This was released on 31 May 1917. The first jazz record to be released was the ODJB's *Livery Stable Blues* (recorded 24 Feb), backed by *The Dixie Jass Band One-Step* (recorded 26 Feb), released by Victor on 7 Mar 1917.

Most successful singer

The most successful singer is Madonna (Madonna Louise Veronica Ciccone, Mrs Sean Penn, b. 16 Aug 1959). Her album *True Blue*, with sales of over 11 million, was a number one LP in 28 countries – a totally unprecedented achievement. Up to August 1987 she had a total of 15 British Top Ten hits. *Who's That Girl?* gave her her 5th No. 1 single, increasing her lead over her nearest female rival, Sandie Shaw, who has 3. Her first three albums together sold 3 million copies in Britain. In 1986 she became the first woman ever to top the annual sales tabulations for both singles and albums, massively outselling all other recording artists. Each of her last two albums *Like a Virgin* (1985), and *True Blue* (1986) have contained 5 Top Five singles.

Most successful solo recording artist

No independently audited figures have ever been published for Elvis Aron Presley (1935–77). In view of Presley's world-wide tally of over 170 major hits on singles and over 80 top-selling albums from 1956 continuing after his death, it may be assumed that it was he who must have succeeded Bing Crosby as the top-selling solo artist of all time.

On 9 June 1960 the Hollywood Chamber of Commerce presented Harry Lillis (*alias* Bing) Crosby Jr (1904–77) with a platinum disc to commemorate the alleged sale of 200 000 000 records from the 2600 singles and 125 albums he had recorded. On 15 Sept 1970 he received a second platinum disc when Decca claimed a sale of 300 650 000 discs. No independently audited figures of his global lifetime sales have ever been published and figures are considered exaggerated.

Most successful group

The singers with the greatest sales of any group have been The Beatles. This group from Liverpool, Merseyside, England comprised George Harrison MBE (b. 25 Feb 1943), John Ono (formerly John Winston) Lennon MBE (b. 9 Oct 1940–k. 8 Dec 1980), James Paul McCartney MBE (b. 18 June 1942) and Richard Starkey MBE *alias* Ringo Starr (b. 7 July 1940). The all-time Beatles sales by May 1985 have been estimated by EMI at over 1000 million discs and tapes.

All 4 ex-Beatles sold many million further records as solo artists. Since their break-up in 1970, it is estimated that the most successful group in the world in terms of record sales is the Swedish foursome ABBA (Agnetha Faltskog, Anni-Frid Lyngstad, Bjorn Ulvaeus and Benny Andersson) with total sales of 215 million discs and tapes by May 1985.

Earliest golden discs

The earliest recorded piece eventually to aggregate a

total sale of a million copies was performances by Enrico Caruso (b. Naples, Italy, 1873, d. 2 Aug 1921) of the aria 'Vesti la giubba' ('On with the Motley') from the opera *I Pagliacci* by Ruggiero Leoncavallo (1858–1919), the earliest version of which was recorded with piano on 12 Nov 1902.

The first single recording to surpass the million mark was Alma Gluck's *Carry Me Back to Old Virginny* on the Red Seal Victor label on the 12-inch *30·48 cm* single faced (later backed) record 74420.

The first actual golden disc was one sprayed by RCA Victor for the US trombonist and band-leader Alton 'Glenn' Miller (1904–44) for his *Chattanooga Choo Choo* on 10 Feb 1942.

Most golden discs

The only *audited* measure of gold, platinum and multi-platinum singles and albums within the United States is certification by the Recording Industry Association of America introduced 14 Mar 1958. Out of the 2582 RIAA awards made to 1 Jan 1985, The Beatles with 47 (plus one with Billy Preston) have most for a group. Paul McCartney has 27 more awards outside the group and with Wings (including one with Stevie Wonder and one with Michael Jackson).

The most awards to an individual is 51 to Elvis Presley (1935–77) spanning the period 1958 to 1 Jan 1986. Globally, however, Presley's total of million-selling singles has been authoritatively placed at 'approaching 80'.

Most recordings

Miss Lata Mangeshker (b. 1928) between 1948 and 1987 has reportedly recorded not less than 30 000 solo, duet and chorus-backed songs in 20 Indian languages. She frequently had 5 sessions in a day and has 'backed' in excess of 2000 films.

Biggest sellers *Singles*

The greatest seller of any gramophone record to date is *White Christmas* by Irving Berlin (b. Israel Bailin, at Tyumen, Russia, 11 May 1888) and recorded by Bing Crosby on 29 May 1942. It was announced on Christmas eve 1987 that North American sales alone reached 170 884 207 copies by 30 June 1987.

The highest claim for any 'pop' record is an unaudited 25 000 000 for *Rock Around the Clock*, copyrighted in 1953 by James E. Myers under the name Jimmy DeKnight and the late Max C. Freedmann and recorded on 12 Apr 1954 by Bill Haley (1927–1981) and the Comets.

The top-selling British record of all time is *I Want to Hold Your Hand* by The Beatles, released in 1963, with world sales of over 13 000 000.

The top selling single of all time in the United Kingdom is *Do They Know It's Christmas* written and produced by Bob Geldof and Midge Ure with 3·6 million by May 1987 with a further 8·1 million world-wide. The profits were in aid of the Ethiopian Famine Relief Fund and are now estimated to be over £90 million.

The only female solo artist to have a million-selling single in the UK is Jennifer Rush, whose single *The Power of Love* was certified in 1985. Forty-five other singles by groups, duos or male soloists have sold a million copies in the UK. The best-selling female duet in the UK is *I Know Him So Well* by Elaine Page and Barbara Dickson with sales of over 820 000 to May 1987.

Biggest sellers *Albums*

The best selling album of all time is *Thriller* by Michael Jackson (b. Gary, Indiana, 29 Aug 1958) with global sales of 40 million copies by May 1988. His earnings for the first week of Sept 1987 from his album *Bad* (CBS-Epic) which sold 6 million were about £12 million.

The best selling album by a group is Fleetwood Mac's *Rumours* with over 20 million sales to May 1987.

The best selling album by a British group is *Dark Side of*

the Moon by Pink Floyd with sales audited at 19·5 million to December 1986.

The best selling album by a woman is *Whitney Houston* by Whitney Houston released in 1985. It had sold over 14 million copies by May 1987, including over 9 million in America, one million in the UK, and a further million in Canada. This is also the best selling debut album of all time.

The best-selling album in Britain is Dire Straits' *Brothers in Arms*, with over 3 million sold by May 1988.

The best-selling movie soundtrack is *Saturday Night Fever* with sales of over 26·5 million to May 1987.

The charts—*US Singles*

Singles record charts were first published by *Billboard* on 20 July 1940 when the No. 1 was *I'll Never Smile Again* by Tommy Dorsey (b. 19 Nov 1905, d. 26 Nov 1956). *Near You* by Francis Craig stayed at the No. 1 spot for 17 weeks in 1947. *Tainted Love* by Soft Cell stayed on the chart for 43 consecutive weeks from January 1982.

The Beatles have had the most No. 1s (20), Conway Twitty the most Country No. 1s (35) and Aretha Franklin the most Black No. 1s (20). Aretha Franklin is also the female solo artist with the most million-selling singles with 14 between 1967 and 1973. Elvis Presley has had the most hit singles on *Billboard*'s Hot 100–149 from 1956 to May 1988.

US Albums

Billboard first published an album chart on 15 Mar 1945 when the No. 1 was *King Cole Trio* featuring Nat 'King' Cole (b. 17 Mar 1919, d. 15 Feb 1965). *South Pacific* was No. 1 for 69 weeks (non-consecutive) from May 1949. *Dark Side of the Moon* by Pink Floyd (see above) enjoyed its 730th week on the *Billboard* charts in May 1988.

The Beatles had the most No. 1s (15), Elvis Presley was the most successful male soloist (9), and Simon and Garfunkel the top duo with 3. Elvis Presley has had the most hit albums (94 from 1956 – May 1988).

The woman with the most No. 1 albums (6), and most hit albums in total (39 between 1963 and May 1988), is Barbra Streisand, 29 of which have been certified gold (500 000 sales) or platinum (1 million sales) by the RIAA,

making Streisand the best-selling female singer of all time.

UK Singles

Singles record charts were first published in Britain on 14 Nov 1952 by *New Musical Express*. *I Believe* by Frankie Laine (b. 30 Mar 1913) held No. 1 position for 18 weeks (non-consecutive) from April 1953, with *Rose Marie* by Slim Whitman (b. 20 Jan 1924) the consecutive record holder with 11 weeks from July 1955.

The longest stay has been the 122 weeks of *My Way* by Francis Albert Sinatra (b. 12 Dec 1915) in 10 separate runs from 2 Apr 1969 to 1972.

The record for most consecutive weeks on the chart is 56 weeks for Engelbert Humperdinck's *Release Me* from 26 Jan 1967. The Beatles and Presley hold the record for most No. 1 hits with 17 each, with Presley having an overall record of 106 hits in the UK singles chart from 1956 to May 1987.

UK Albums

The first British album chart was published on 8 Nov 1958 by *Melody Maker*. The first No. 1 LP was the film soundtrack *South Pacific* which held the position for a record 70 consecutive weeks and eventually achieved a record 115 weeks at No. 1.

The album with the most total weeks on chart is *Rumours* by Fleetwood Mac with 420 weeks by May 1988. The Beatles have had most No 1 albums—12; and Elvis Presley the most hit albums—91.

Fastest-selling albums

The fastest-selling record of all time is *John Fitzgerald Kennedy—A Memorial Album* (Premium Albums), recorded on 22 Nov 1963, the day of Mr Kennedy's assassination, which sold 4 000 000 copies at 99 cents in 6 days (7–12 Dec 1963), thus ironically beating the previous speed record set by the satirical LP *The First Family* in 1962–3.

The fastest-selling British record is the Beatles' double album *The Beatles* (Apple) with 'nearly 2 million' in its first week in November 1968.

Advance sales

The greatest advance sale for a single world-wide is 2 100 000 for *Can't Buy Me Love* by the Beatles. Released 21 March 1964, it also holds the British record of 1 million jointly with another Beatles single, *I Want to Hold Your Hand*, released 29 Nov 1963. The UK record for advance sales of an album is 1 100 000 for *Welcome to the Pleasure Dome*, the debut album by Frankie Goes To Hollywood from 1984.

The fastest live performance to cut disc played on radio

On 10 Mar 1988, a live performance of 'Make my Heart

Most successful all-girl group *UK* ● The most successful all-girl group in the history of the UK singles chart is Bananarama. Between 1982 and 1988 the group, comprising Keren Woodward, Sarah Dallin and Siobhan Fahey, scored 14 consecutive chart hits on their own, and a further 2 in partnership with the Funboy Three. Fahey left the group to pursue a solo career after marrying Eurythmics' Dave Stewart in 1988, and was replaced by Jacqui O'Sullivan.

Fly' by The Proclaimers was recorded on to master tape at The Trocadero, Piccadilly, London and then put to disc by EMI M & D Services, Hayes, Middlesex. The completed disc was ferried back to the Trocadero where it was played on the BBC Radio 1 'Steve Wright Show'. The total time taken from the final chord of the live performance to the first note of the disc being played live on air was 2 hr 19 min 31 sec.

Compact discs

Announced by Philips in 1978, and introduced by the same company in 1982, the compact disc (CD) increasingly challenges the LP and cassette as a recording medium. After sales of 20·7 million units (£127 million) in 1987 CD's are expected to surpass LP's in the British market in 1988.

The first CD to sell a million copies world-wide was Dire Straits' *Brothers in Arms* in 1986. It subsequently topped a million sales in Europe alone including over 250 000 in Britain–both records.

Most Grammy awards

The all time record of 26 awards is held by Sir Georg Solti KBE the British conductor born in Budapest 22 Oct 1912 which he has won since 1958.

The greatest number won in a year is 8 by Michael Jackson in 1984.

Cinema

FILMS

The earliest motion pictures ever taken were by Louis Aimé Augustin Le Prince (1842–1890). He was attested to have achieved dim moving outlines on a whitewashed wall at the Institute for the Deaf, Washington Heights, New York, USA as early as 1885–87. The earliest surviving film (sensitised 53·9 mm *2⅛ in* wide paper roll) is from his camera, patented in Britain on 16 Nov 1888, taken in early October 1888 of the garden of his father-in-law, Joseph Whitley, in Roundhay, Leeds, West Yorkshire at 10 to 12 frames per second. The first commercial presentation of *motion pictures* was at Holland Bros' Kinetoscope Parlor at 1155 Broadway, New York City on 14 April 1894. Viewers could see 5 films for

25 cents or 10 for 50 cents from a double row of Kinetoscopes developed by William Kennedy Laurie Dickson (1860–1935), assistant to Thomas Alva Edison (1847–1931) in 1889–91.

The earliest publicly presented film on a *screen* was *La Sortie des Ouvriers de l'Usine Lumière* probably shot in August or September 1894 in Lyon, France. It was exhibited at 44 rue de Rennes, Paris on 22 Mar 1895 by the Lumière brothers, Auguste Marie Louis Nicholas (1862–1954) and Louis Jean (1864–1948).

Earliest 'talkie'

The earliest sound-on-film motion picture was achieved by Eugene Augustin Lauste (1857–1935) who patented his process on 11 Aug 1906 and produced a workable system using a string galvanometer in 1910 at Benedict Road, Stockwell, London. The earliest public presentation of sound on film was by the Tri-ergon process at the Alhambra cinema, Berlin, Germany on 17 Sept 1922.

Most expensive film

The highest ever budgeted film has been $69 million for *Rambo III* released in May 1988 starring Sylvester Stallone. He thereby became history's highest paid actor with receipts of £10 500 000 (see below).

Least expensive full–length feature film

The total cost of production for the 1927 film *The Shattered Illusion*, by Victorian Film Productions, was £300. It took twelve months to complete and included spectacular scenes of a ship overwhelmed in a storm.

Most expensive film rights

The highest price ever paid for film rights was $9 500 000 announced on 20 Jan 1978 by Columbia for *Annie*, the Broadway musical by Charles Strouse starring Andrea McCardle, Dorothy Loudon and Reid Shelton.

Longest film

The longest film ever premièred was the 48-hr-long *The Longest Most Meaningless Movie in the World* in 1970. It was British made and later compassionately cut to 90 minutes.

Longest-running film

Emmanuelle opened on 26 June 1974 at the Paramount City, Paris and closed on 26 Feb 1985 – the longest continuous run of any one film at one cinema.

Highest box office gross

The box office gross championship for films is susceptible to inflated ticket prices. Calculations based on the 1983 value of the dollar show that *Gone with the Wind* with Clark Gable (1901–1960) and Vivien Leigh (1913–1967) released in 1939 is unsurpassed at $312 million. The highest numerical (as opposed to value) dollar champion is Steven Spielberg's *ET: The Extra-Terrestrial*, released on 11 June 1982, which has earned a gross $700 million. On 27 May 1984 *Indiana Jones and the Temple of Doom* (Paramount) grossed $9 324 760 for a single day record. The highest opening day gross was scored by *Return of the Jedi* on 25 May 1983 with a take of $6 219 629 at 1002 sites.

Largest loss

Michael Cimino's 1980 production *Heaven's Gate* absorbed $35 190 718 causing United Artists to write the film off at final cost of $44 000 000.

Most violent

A study on the portrayal of violence showed the worst film on record was *Red Dawn*, released in the USA in 1984, with acts of violence occurring at the rate of 134 per hour (2·23 per min).

Most destructive chase sequence

Over 150 vehicles including 2 Cadillac Eldorados, 2 Chrysler Magnums, numerous boats, trucks and motorcycles and 2 Pitts high-performance aeroplanes were wrecked in H. B. Halicki's 1982 film *The Junkman*.

UK FILM TOP 20

TITLE	WEEKS ON CHART
1. CROCODILE DUNDEE	47
2. THE LIVING DAYLIGHTS	14
3. BEVERLY HILLS COP II	7
4. PLATOON	20
5. POLICE ACADEMY IV	10
6. THE GOLDEN CHILD	6
7. LABYRINTH	11
8. SUPERMAN IV	7
9. FULL METAL JACKET	11
10. BLIND DATE	14
11. THE UNTOUCHABLES	9
12. STAR TREK IV	8
13. THE MISSION	23
14. THE FLY	9
15. LETHAL WEAPON	6
16. THE COLOR OF MONEY	10
17. MANNEQUIN	10
18. NIGHTMARE ON ELM STREET III	4
19. PERSONAL SERVICES	12
20. THE WITCHES OF EASTWICK	5

This list was compiled and provided by Screen International

The 1987 Screen International *Top 20 chart covers the 12 months from Dec 1, 1986, to Nov 30, 1987. Chart positions are based on the gross box office revenues for the period – as indicated in the chart – for which each film was tracked by its distributors.*

Highest earnings

The highest rate of pay in cinema history is that paid to Sylvester Stallone (b. New York, 6 July 1946). Having received $12 million each for *Cobra* and *Over the Top* plus, shares of box office, Stallone received $19 500 000 for *Rambo III* (see above) which surpassed the $18·5 million received by Marlon Brando for his nine minutes of screen time in *Superman*. The highest-paid actresses are Meryl Streep (b. Summit, NJ, USA 1949) with $4 million for *Out of Africa* and the same for *Heartburn*, and Barbra Streisand with $5 million for *Nuts*.

Stuntman Dar Robinson was paid $100 000 for the 335 m *1100 ft* leap from the CN Tower, Toronto in November 1979 for *High Point*. His parachute opened just 91 m *300 ft* above ground. He died 21 Nov 1986 (aged 39).

Longest series still continuing

Japan's *Tora-San* films have now stretched from *Tora-San I* in August 1969 to *Tora-San XL* in 1988 with Kiyoshi Atsumi (b. 1929) starring in each for Shochiku Co.

Most portrayed character

In horror films the character most often portrayed is Count Dracula created by the Irish writer Bram Stoker (1847–1912). Representations of the Count or his immediate descendants outnumber those of his closest rival, Frankenstein's monster, by 155 to 109.

THE·MANY·FACES·OF
Sherlock Holmes

Robert
Stephens

Raymond
Massey

Peter
Cook

Christopher
Plummer

H.A.
Saintsbury

Most portrayed character on screen ● Sherlock Holmes, created by Sir Arthur Conan Doyle 1859-1930) has been portrayed by 69 actors in 194 films produced between 1900 and 1988. Illustrated here are just 19 of the 69 actors

Eille
Norwood

James
Barrington

Nicholas
Rowe

Viggo
Larsen

Clive
Brook

William
Gillette

John
Neville

Nicol
Williamson

Douglas
Wilmer

Jeremy
Brett

John
Barrymore

Basil
Rathbone

Peter
Cushing

Arthur
Wontner

All-Time Film Rental Champs
(Of US-Canada Market)
Compiled and researched by Variety -to 31 Dec 1987.

TITLE	DIRECTOR	TOTAL RENTALS ($)
1. E.T. THE EXTRA-TERRESTRIAL	S. SPIELBERG	228 379 346
2. STAR WARS	G. LUCAS	193 500 000
3. RETURN OF THE JEDI	R. MARQUAND	168 002 414
4. THE EMPIRE STRIKES BACK	I. KERSHNER	141 600 000
5. JAWS	S. SPIELBERG	129 549 242
6. GHOSTBUSTERS	I. REITMAN	128 264 005
7. RAIDERS OF THE LOST ARK	S. SPIELBERG	115 598 000
8. INDIANA JONES AND THE TEMPLE OF DOOM	S. SPIELBERG	109 000 000
9. BEVERLY HILLS COP	M. BREST	108 000 000
10. BACK TO THE FUTURE	R. ZEMECKIS	104 237 346
11. GREASE	R. KLEISER	96 300 000
12. TOOTSIE	S. POLLACK	95 268 806
13. THE EXORCIST	W. FRIEDKIN	89 000 000
14. THE GODFATHER	F.F. COPPOLA	86 275 000
15. SUPERMAN	R. DONNER	82 800 000
16. CLOSE ENCOUNTERS OF THE THIRD KIND	S. SPIELBERG	82 750 000
17. BEVERLY HILLS COP II	T. SCOTT	80 857 776
18. THE SOUND OF MUSIC	R. WISE	79 748 000
19. GREMLINS	J. DANTE	79 500 000
20. TOP GUN	T. SCOTT	79 400 000
21. RAMBO: FIRST BLOOD PART II	G.P. COSMATOS	78 919 250
22. GONE WITH THE WIND	V. FLEMING	77 612 077
23. ROCKY IV	S. STALLONE	75 974 593
24. SATURDAY NIGHT FEVER	J. BADHAM	74 100 000
25. THE STING	G.R. HILL	71 366 309
26. CROCODILE DUNDEE	P. FAIMAN	70 227 000
27. PLATOON	O. STONE	69 742 143
28. ROCKY III	S. STALLONE	66 235 909
29. SUPERMAN II	R. LESTER	65 100 000
30. SNOW WHITE AND THE SEVEN DWARFS	ANIM	62 750 000
31. NATIONAL LAMPOON'S ANIMAL HOUSE	J. LANDIS	62 400 928
32. ON GOLDEN POND	M. RYDELL	61 174 744
33. FATAL ATTRACTION	A. LYNE	60 000 000
34. KRAMER VS KRAMER	R. BENTON	59 986 335
35. ONE FLEW OVER THE CUCKOO'S NEST	M. FORMAN	59 930 732
36. NINE TO FIVE	C. HIGGINS	59 100 000
37. SMOKEY AND THE BANDIT	H. NEEDHAM	58 949 900
38. STIR CRAZY	S. POITIER	58 364 420
39. THE KARATE KID PART II	J. AVILDSEN	57 700 000
40. STAR TREK IV: THE VOYAGE HOME	L. NIMOY	56 820 071

Oscar speech ● In 1942 Greer Garson (b. County Down, N. Ireland 29 Sept 1908) took over 1½ hours to say 'Thank you' for *Mrs Miniver.* Acceptance speeches are now limited to 45 sec. (Photo: Ronald Sheridan)

Largest number of extras
It is believed that over 300 000 extras appeared in the funeral scene of Sir Richard Attenborough's *Gandhi* (1982).

Largest studios
The largest complex of film studios in the world is that at Universal City, Los Angeles, California, USA. The Back Lot contains 561 buildings and there are 34 sound stages on the 170 ha *420 acre* site.

Largest studio stage
The world's largest studio stage is the 007 stage at Pinewood Studios, Buckinghamshire. It was designed by Ken Adam and Michael Brown and built in 1976 for the James Bond film *The Spy Who Loved Me.*. It measures 102 m × 42 m × 12 m (*336 ft × 139 ft × 41 ft*) and accommodated 4·54 million litres *1·2 million gallons* of water, a full-scale 600 000-ton oil tanker and 3 nuclear submarines.

Largest film set
The largest film set ever built was the 400 m × 230 m (*1312 ft × 754 ft*) Roman Forum designed by Veniero Colosanti and John Moore for Samuel Bronston's production of *The Fall of the Roman Empire* (1964). It was built on a 22·25 ha *55 acre* site outside Madrid, Spain. 1100 workmen spent 7 months laying the surface of the Forum with 170 000 cement blocks, erecting 6705 m *22 000 ft* of concrete stairways, 601 colums and 350 statues, and constructing 27 full-size buildings.

The largest indoor set was the UFO landing site built for the climax of Steven Spielberg's *Close Encounters of the Third Kind.* The 137 m × 786 m × 27 m (*450 ft × 250 ft × 90 ft*) set was constructed inside a 3·53 million m³ *10 million ft³* dirigible hangar at Mobile, Alabama, USA. The structure included 6·4 km (*4 miles*) of scaffolding, 1570 m² (*16 900 ft²*) of fibreglass, 2740 m² (*29 500 ft²*) of nylon canopy and 'enough concrete to make a full-scale replica of the Washington monument'.

Longest directorial career
The directorial career of King Vidor (1894–1982) lasted for 66 years, beginning with the two-reel comedy *The Tow* and culminating in another short, a documentary called *The Metaphor.*

Oldest director
Joris Ivens (b. Netherlands 1898) directed the Franco-Italian co-production *Le Vent* in 1988 at the age of 89. He made his directorial debut with the Dutch film *De Brug* in 1928.

George Cukor (1899–1983) was Hollywood's oldest director. In October 1980, at 81 years old, he was signed by MGM to direct the film *Rich and Famous* starring Jacqueline Bisset and Candice Bergen.

Most generations of screen actors in a family
There are 4 generations of screen actors in the Redgrave family.

Roy Redgrave (1872–1922) made his screen debut in 1911 and continued to appear in Australian films until 1920. Sir Michael Redgrave married actress Rachel Kempson and their two daughters Vanessa and Lynn and son Corin all went into films. Vanessa's two daughters Joely and Natasha and Corin's daughter Jemma are already successful actresses with films such as *Wetherby*, *A Month in the Country* and *The Dream Demon* to their respective credit.

Largest number of costumes
The largest number of costumes for any one film was 32 000 for the 1951 film *Quo Vadis.*

Longest Make-up Jobs

Name of Film	Actor	Time (hours)
THE ILLUSTRATED MAN (USA, 1969)	Rod Steiger	20
AN AMERICAN WEREWOLF IN LONDON (GB, 1981)	David Naughton	10
THE BRIDE OF FRANKENSTEIN (USA, 1935)	Boris Karloff	7
THE ELEPHANT MAN (GB, 1980)	John Hurt	7
THE HUNCHBACK OF NOTRE DAME (USA, 1939)	Charles Laughton	5½
THE PLANET OF THE APES (USA, 1968)	Roddy McDowall*	5
LITTLE BIG MAN (USA, 1970)	Dustin Hoffman	5
NOSFERATU (WEST GERMANY, 1979)	Klaus Kinski	5
THE HUNCHBACK OF NOTRE DAME (USA, 1923)	Lon Chaney	4½
THE LOST WORLD (USA, 1925)	Bull Montana	4½

and other principal apes.

Most expensive costume

The most expensive costume worn in a film was Constance Bennett's sable coat in *Madam X* valued at $50 000. The most expensive costume designed and made specially for a film was Edith Head's mink and sequins dance costume worn by Ginger Rogers in *Lady in the Dark*. It cost Paramount $35 000.

Most Oscars

Walter (Walt) Elias Disney (1901–66) won more 'Oscars', the awards of the United States Academy of Motion Picture Arts and Sciences, instituted on 16 May 1929 and named after Mr Oscar Pierce of Texas, USA—than any other person. The physical count comprises 20 statuettes and 12 other plaques and certificates including posthumous awards. The only person to win 4 Oscars in a starring role has been Miss Katharine Hepburn, formerly Mrs Ludlow Ogden Smith (b. Hartford, Conn., USA, 9 Nov 1909) in *Morning Glory* (1932–3), *Guess Who's Coming to Dinner* (1967), *The Lion in Winter* (1968) and *On Golden Pond* (1981). She has been nominated 12 times. Only 4 actors have won 2 Oscars in starring roles—Frederic March in 1931/32 and 1946, Spencer Tracy in 1937 and 1938, Gary Cooper in 1941 and 1952, and Marlon Brando in 1954 and 1972. Edith Head (Mrs Wiard B. Ihnen) (1907–1981) won 8 individual awards for costume design. The film with most awards has been *Ben Hur* (1959) with 11. That with the highest number of nominations was *All About Eve* (1950) with 14. It won 6. The youngest ever winner was Shirley Temple (b. 24 Apr 1928) aged 5 with her honorary Oscar, and the oldest George Burns (b. 20 Jan 1896) aged 80 for *The Sunshine Boys* in 1976.

Versatility show-business awards

The only 3 performers to have won Oscar, Emmy, Tony and Grammy awards have been Helen Hayes (b. 1900) in 1932–1976; Richard Rodgers (1902–1979), composer of musicals, and Rita Moreno (b. 1931) in 1961–1977. Barbra Streisand (b. 24 Apr 1942 in Brooklyn, NY, USA) received Oscar, Grammy and Emmy awards in addition to a special 'Star of the Decade' Tony award.

Most honoured entertainer

The most honoured entertainer in history is Bob Hope (né Leslie Townes Hope, Eltham, London; 29 May 1903). He has been uniquely awarded the USA's highest civilian honours – the Medal of Freedom (1969); Congressional Gold Medal (1963); Medal of Merit (1966); Distinguished Public Service Medal (1973); Distinguished Service Gold Medal (1971) and is also an Hon. CBE (1976) and was appointed Hon. Brigadier of the US Marine Corps. He also has 44 honorary degrees.

CINEMAS
Earliest

The earliest structure designed and exclusively used for exhibiting projected films is believed to be one erected at the Atlanta Show, Georgia, USA in October 1895 to exhibit C. F. Jenkins' phantoscope. The earliest attempt at establishing a cinema in Britain was made by Birt Acres, whose Kineopticon opened at 2 Piccadilly Mansions at the junction of Piccadilly Circus and Shaftesbury Avenue on 21 Mar 1896. After only a few weeks, the cinema was gutted by fire.

Largest

The largest cinema in the world is the 5041-seat Fox Theater in Detroit, Michigan, USA. Originally opened in 1928, the Fox is now principally a live entertainment theatre but still shows films on an occasional basis. Cineplex, opened at the Toronto Eaton Centre, Canada on 19 Apr 1979, has 18 separate theatres with an aggregate capacity of 1700.

Great Britain's largest cinema is the Odeon, Leicester Square, London, with 1983 seats.

Most and least cinemas

Saudi Arabia (population 8·4 million) has no cinemas. San Marino has a total of 7 cinemas, one for every 3190 inhabitants. The USA has most cinemas with one for every 11 000 inhabitants. The UK had 1250 screens in 1987. Admissions in 1987 reached 75 000 000 compared with the 1946 peak of 1640 million.

Highest cinema-going

The Chinese Ministry of Culture reported in September 1987 that there were 21 000 million cinema attendances in 1986—or nearly 21 per person per annum.

Biggest screen

The permanently installed cinema screen with the largest area is one of 28·28 × 21·48 m *92 ft 9 in × 70 ft 6 in* installed in the Keong Emas Imax Theatre, Taman Mini Park, Jakarta, Indonesia opened on 20 Apr 1984. It was made by Harkness Screens Ltd at Borehamwood, Herts, England. A temporary screen 90·5 × 10 m *297 ft × 33 ft* was used at the 1937 Paris Exposition.

Most films seen

Albert E. van Schmus (b. 1921) saw 16 945 films in 32 years (1949–1982) as a rater for Motion Picture Association of America Inc.

Radio

The earliest patent for telegraphy without wires (wireless) was received by Dr Mahlon Loomis (USA) (1826–86). It was entitled 'Improvement in Telegraphy' and was dated 20 July 1872 (US Pat. No. 129 971). He in fact demonstrated only potential differences on a galvanometer between two kites 22 km *14 miles* apart in Loudoun County, Virginia, USA in October 1866.

Earliest patent

The first patent for a system of communication by means of electro-magnetic waves, numbered No. 12039, was granted on 2 June 1896 to the Italian-Irish Marchese Guglielmo Marconi (1874–1937). A public demonstration of wireless transmission of speech was, however, given in the town square of Murray, Kentucky, USA in 1892 by Nathan B. Stubblefield. He died destitute on 28 March 1928. The first permanent wireless installation was at The Needles on the Isle of Wight, by Marconi's Wireless Telegraph Co Ltd, in November 1897.

Earliest broadcast

The world's first advertised broadcast was made on 24 Dec 1906 by the Canadian-born Professor Reginald Aubrey Fessenden (1868–1932) from the 128 m *420 ft* mast of the National Electric Signalling Company at Brant Rock, Massachusetts, USA. The transmission included Handel's *Largo*. Fessenden had achieved distorted broadcast speech by November 1900 .

Transatlantic transmissions

The earliest claim to have received wireless signals (the letter S in Morse Code) across the Atlantic was made by Marconi, George Stephen Kemp and Percy Paget from a 10 kW station at Poldhu, Cornwall, to Signal Hill, St John's, Newfoundland, Canada, at 12.30 p.m. on 12 Dec 1901. Human speech was first heard across the Atlantic in November 1915 when a transmission from the US Navy station at Arlington, Virginia was received by US radio-telephone engineers on the Eiffel Tower.

Earliest radio-microphones

The radio-microphone, which was in essence also the first 'bug', was devised by Reg Moores (GB) in 1947 and first used on 76 MHz in the ice show *Aladdin* at Brighton Sports Stadium, East Sussex, England in September 1949.

Longest BBC national broadcast

The longest BBC national broadcast was the Coronation of Queen Elizabeth II on 2 June 1953. It began at 10.15 a.m. and finished at 5.30 p.m., after 7 hr 15 min.

Longest continuous broadcast

The longest continuous broadcast (excluding disc-jockeying) has been one of 484 hr (20 days 4 hr) by Larry Norton of WGRQ FM Buffalo, New York, USA from 19 Mar–8 Apr 1981. *No further claims for the above category will be entertained.* Radio Telefís Éireann transmitted an unedited reading of *Ulysses* by James Joyce (1882–1941) for 29 hr 38 min 47 sec on 16–17 July 1982.

Topmost prize

Mary Buchanan, 15, on WKRQ, Cincinnati, USA won a prize of $25 000 for 40 years (*viz* $1 million) on 21 Nov 1980.

Brain of Britain quiz

The youngest person to become 'Brain of Britain' on BBC radio was Anthony Carr, 16, of Anglesey in 1956. The oldest contestant has been the author and translator Hugh Merrick (1898–1980) in his 80th year in August 1977. The record score is 35 by the 1981 winner Peter Barlow of Richmond, Surrey and Peter Bates of Taunton who won the title in 1984.

Most durable programmes

CKNW's 'Roving Mike' programme with Bill Hughes has been broadcast 6 days a week in New Westminster, British Columbia, Canada since 1944. On Oct 8 1987, the programme celebrated its 13 000th consecutive broadcast. The weekly sports report 'The Tenpin Tattler' was first broadcast on WCFL, Chicago, USA on Aug 24, 1935. Fifty three-years and 2756 broadcasts later, it still continues on WGN, Chicago, USA.

BBC
The longest-running BBC radio series is *The Week's Good Cause* which began on 24 Jan 1926. The St Martin-in-the-Fields Christmas appeal by Canon Geoffrey Brown on 14 Dec 1986 raised a record £138 039. The longest running record programme is *Desert Island Discs* which began on 29 Jan 1942 and on which programme only one guest, Arthur Askey CBE (1900–82), has been stranded a fourth time (on the 1572nd show on 20 Dec 1980). The programme was originally presented by its creator, Roy Plomley OBE, who died on 28 May 1985 having presented 1791 editions. The longest-running solo radio feature is *Letter from America* by (Alfred) Alistair Cooke, Hon. KBE, (b. Salford 20 Nov 1908), first broadcast on 24 Mar 1946. In June 1987 he filed his 2000th edition.

The longest-running radio serial is *The Archers* which was created by Godfrey Baseley and was first broadcast on 29 May 1950. Up to May 1987 the signature tune *Barwick Green* had been played over 38 680 times. The only role which has been played without interruption from the start has been that of Philip Archer by Norman Painting OBE (b. Leamington Spa, 23 Apr 1924).

Most heard broadcaster

Larry King has broadcast on network for 27½ hours a week since 30 Jan 1978 from Washington DC on Mutual Broadcasting Systems to all 50 US States (now on 272 stations).

Earliest antipodal reception

Frank Henry Alfred Walker (b. 11 Nov 1904), on the night of 12 Nov 1924 at Crown Farm, Cuttimore Lane, Walton-on-Thames, Surrey, received on his home-made 2-valve receiver on 75 metres, signals from Marconi's yacht *Electra* (call sign ICCM) in Australian waters.

Most assiduous radio ham

The late Richard C. Spenceley of KV4AA at St Thomas, Virgin Islands built his contacts (QSOs) to a record level of 48 100 in 365 days in 1978.

Most stations

The country with the greatest number of radio broadcasting stations is the United States, where there were 9512 authorised broadcast stations as at April 1985 made up of both AM (amplitude modulation) and FM (frequency modulation).

Highest listening

The peak recorded listenership on BBC Radio was 30 000 000 adults on 6 June 1950 for the boxing match between Lee Savold (US) and Bruce Woodcock (GB) (b. Doncaster, S. Yorks, 1921).

Highest response

The highest recorded response from a radio show occurred on 27 Nov 1974 when, on a 5-hr talk show on WCAU, Philadelphia, USA, astrologer Howard Sheldon registered a call count of 388 299 on the *Bill Corsair Show*.

Smallest set

The Toshiba AM-FM RP-1070 with inbuilt loudspeaker measures 9·0×5·4×1·3 cm *3·5×2·1×0·5 in* and with battery weighs 70 g *2·5 oz*.

Television

Invention

The invention of television, the instantaneous viewing of distant objects by electrical transmissions, was not an act but a process of successive and interdependent discoveries. The first commercial cathode ray tube was introduced in 1897 by Karl Ferdinand Braun (1850–1918), but was not linked to 'electric vision' until 1907 by Professor Boris Rosing (disappeared 1918) of Russia in St Petersburg (Leningrad). A. A. Campbell Swinton FRS (1863–1930) published the fundamentals of television transmission on 18 June 1908 in a brief letter to *Nature* entitled 'Distant Electric Vision'. The earliest public demonstration of television was given on 27 Jan 1926 by John Logie Baird (1888–1946) of Scotland, using a development of the mechanical scanning system patented by Paul Gottlieb Nipkow (1860–1940) on 6 Jan 1884. He had achieved the transmission of a Maltese Cross over 3·05 m *10 ft* at 8 Queen's Arcade, Hastings, East Sussex, England by February 1924 and the first facial image (of William Taynton, 15) at 22, Frith Street, London on 30 Oct 1925. Taynton had to be bribed with 2s6d. A patent application for the Iconoscope had been filed on 29 Dec 1923 by Dr Vladimir Kosma Zworykin (1889–1982) but was not issued until 20 Dec 1938. Kenjiro Takayanagi (b. 20 Jan 1899) succeeded in transmitting a 40-line electronic picture on 25 Dec 1926 with a Braun cathode ray tube and a Nipkow disc at Hamamatsu Technical College, Japan. Baird launched his first television 'service' via a BBC transmitter on 30 Sept 1929 and marketed the first sets, Baird Televisors, at 26 guineas in May 1930. Public transmissions on 30 lines were made from 22 Aug 1932 until 11 Sept 1935. It has been estimated that 6 million billion (6 × 10^{15}) electrons traverse a television tube each second.

Earliest service

The world's first high-definition (i.e. 405 lines) television broadcasting service was opened from Alexandra Palace, north London, on 2 Nov 1936, when there were about 100 sets in the United Kingdom. The chief engineer was Mr Douglas Birkinshaw. A television station in Berlin, Germany made a low-definition (180-line) transmission from 22 Mar 1935 but the transmitter burnt out in August that year.

Transatlantic transmission

On 9 Feb 1928 the image of J. L. Baird and of a Mrs Howe was transmitted from Station 2 KZ at Coulsdon, Surrey, England to Station 2 CVJ, Hartsdale, NY, USA. The earliest transatlantic transmission by satellite was achieved at 1 a.m. on 11 July 1962, via the active satellite *Telstar 1* from Andover, Maine, USA to Pleumeur Bodou, France. The picture was of Frederick R. Kappell, chairman of the American Telephone and Telegraph Company, which owned the satellite. The first 'live' broadcast was made on 23 July 1962 and the first woman to appear was the *haute couturière* Ginette Spanier, directrice of Balmain, the next day.

Longest telecast

The longest pre-scheduled telecast on record was a continuous transmission for 163 hr 18 min by GTV 9 of Melbourne, Australia covering the Apollo XI moon mission from 19–26 July 1969. The longest continuous TV transmission under a single director was the York student television production 'Breaker 88' transmitted from 29–30 Jan 1988 for 28 hr 2 min under the direction of Keith Hide-Smith. The programme's producer was Lawrence De'Ath and the technical co-ordinator John Mills.

Earliest video-tape recording

Alexander M. Poniatoff first demonstrated video-tape recording known as Ampex (his initials plus 'ex' for excellence) in 1956. The earliest demonstration of a home video recorder was on 24 June 1963 at the BBC News Studio at Alexandra Palace, London of the Telcan developed by Norman Rutherford and Michael Turner of the Nottingham Electronic Valve Co.

Fastest video production

Tapes of the Royal Wedding of HRH Prince Andrew and Miss Sarah Ferguson on 23 July 1986 were produced by Thames Video Collection. Live filming ended with the departure of the honeymoon couple from Chelsea Hospital by helicopter at 4.42 p.m. The first fully edited and packaged VHS tapes were purchased 5 hr 41 min later by Fenella Lee and Lucinda Burland of West Kensington at the Virgin Megastore in Oxford Street, London at 10.23 p.m.

Most durable shows

The world's most durable TV show is NBC's *Meet the Press*, first transmitted on 6 Nov 1947 and weekly since 12 Sept 1948, originated by Lawrence E. Spivak, who appeared weekly as either moderator or panel member until 1975. On 1 June 1986 Joe Franklin presented the 21 700th version of his show started in 1951. Since 1949 over 150 000 individual episodes of the TV show 'Bozo the Clown', by Larry Harmon Pictures, have been aired daily on 150 stations in the US and abroad. The greatest number of hours on camera on US national commercial television is 10 000 by the TV personality Hugh Downs in over 42 years to 1 Jan 1987.

Great Britain

Andy Pandy was first transmitted on 11 July 1950 but consisted of repeats of a cycle of 26 shows until 1970. *Come Dancing* was first transmitted on 29 Sept 1950 but is seasonal. *The Good Old Days* ran from 20 July 1953 to 31 Dec 1983. Barney Colehan MBE produced all 244 programmes. The *BBC News* was inaugurated in vision on 5 July 1954. Richard Baker OBE read the news from 1954 to Christmas 1982. Of current affairs programmes BBC's weekly *Panorama* was first transmitted on 11 Nov 1953 but has summer breaks, whereas Granada's *What the Papers Say* was transmitted weekly from 5 Nov 1956 until Sept 1988. The monthly *Sky at Night* has been presented by Patrick Moore OBE without a break or a miss since 24 Apr 1957. The BBC's *Farming* programme was transmitted weekly from 3 Oct 1957 until its end in late spring 1988. The longest-serving TV quizmaster is Bamber Gascoigne of Granada's *University Challenge* which ran from 21 Sept 1962 until 31 Dec 1987. The longest-running domestic drama serial is Granada's *Coronation Street* which has run twice weekly since 9 Dec 1960. William Roache had played Ken Barlow without a break since the outset for 27 years by 9 Dec 1987.

Most sets

The USA had, by January 1987, 89·13 million TV households, with 42·82 million on cable TV. The number of homes with colour sets was 82 680 000 (91 per cent) by January 1987. More than 57 per cent of the total homes own 2 or more TV sets. The number of licences current in the United Kingdom was 19 332 342 on 29 Feb 1988 of which 17 093 576 were for colour sets. Black and white licences became less commonplace than colour in 1976. On 15 Feb 1988 the new China News Agency announced

that China's number of TV viewers had risen to 600 million from 100 million sets.

TV watching

The National Coalition on TV Violence published an estimate in June 1985 that, by its 16th birthday, the *average* American child will have seen 50 000 TV murders or attempted murders and 200 000 acts of violence. Between the ages of 2 and 11 the average viewing time is 25¾ hours per week. The global total of homes with television surpassed 500 million in 1987 led by the USA with 89·13 million. There are 8250 TV transmitting stations world-wide of which 1241 are in the USA. There are 364 TV sets per 1000 people in the USA compared with 348 in Sweden and 330 in Britain. In Britain in winter the average male views 26 hr 4 min and the average female 30 hr 38 min per week.

Greatest audience

The greatest estimated number of viewers worldwide for a televised event is 2500 million for the live and recorded transmissions of the XXIIIrd Olympic Games in Los Angeles, California from 27 July to 13 Aug 1984. The American Broadcasting Co airing schedule comprised 187½ hours of coverage on 56 cameras. The estimated viewership for the 'Live Aid' concerts organised by Bob Geldof and Bill Graham, via a record 12 satellites, was 1·6 billion or nearly one third of the world's population.

The programme which attracted the highest ever viewership was the *Goodbye, Farewell and Amen* final episode of M*A*S*H (the acronym for Mobile Army Surgical Hospital 4077) transmitted by CBS on 28 Feb 1983 to 60·3 per cent of all households in the United States. It was estimated that some 125 million people tuned in, taking a 77 per cent share of all viewing. The UK record is 39 million for the wedding of TRH the Prince and Princess of Wales in London on 29 July 1981.

Most expensive production

The Winds of War, a 7-part Paramount World War II saga aired by ABC, was the most expensive ever TV production costing $42 million over 14 months' shooting. The final episode on 13 Feb 1983 attracted a rating of 41·0 per cent (percentage of total number of viewers), and a share of 56 per cent (percentage of total sets turned on that were tuned in).

Largest contracts

Currently television's highest-paid performer is John William Carson (b. 23 Oct 1925), the host of *The Tonight Show*. His current NBC contract reportedly calls for annual payment of $5 000 000 for his one-hour evening show aired 4 times weekly. The highest-paid current affairs or news performer is Dan Rather of CBS who reportedly signed an $8 million contract for 5 years from 1982.

Marie Osmond signed a contract worth $7 million for 7 hours of transmission, paid by NBC on 9 Mar 1981. The figure includes talent and production costs.

Great Britain

The largest contract in British television was one of a reported £9 000 000, inclusive of production expenses, signed by Tom Jones (b. Thomas Jones Woodward, 7 June 1940) of Treforest, Mid Glamorgan, Wales in June 1968 with ABC-TV of the United States and ATV in London for 17 one-hour shows per annum from January 1969 to January 1974.

Highest-paid TV performer

The highest paid newscaster and journalist is Dan Rather of the CBS' *Nightly News* reported in February 1986 to be paid $2 500 000 per annum.

It was reported in September 1987 that Bill Cosby earned $57 million in 1987 on US TV shows and concerts and from advertisements, albums and endorsements.

Largest TV prizes

On 24 July 1975 WABC-TV, New York City transmitted

the first televised Grand Tier draw of the State Lottery in which the winner took the grand prize of $1 000 000. This was, however, taxable.

Most successful telethon

The Jerry Lewis Labor Day Telethon on 2 Sept 1984 raised $32 074 566 in pledges for the Muscular Dystrophy Association. The Victims of Famine in East Africa and the Sahel appeal raised a record £9 518 736 from 17 July 1984 to 6 Feb 1985.

Biggest sale

The greatest number of episodes of any TV programme ever sold has been 1144 episodes of *Coronation Street* by Granada Television to CBKST Saskatoon, Saskatchewan, Canada, on 31 May 1971. This constituted 20 days 15 hr 44 min continuous viewing. A further 728 episodes (Jan 1974–Jan 1981) were sold to CBC in August 1982.

Most rented video *UK*

The video which in 1987 attracted most home viewers was *Ghostbusters* with an audience of 13 100 000. The percentage of families hiring videos rose to 46 per cent.

Most prolific scriptwriter

The most prolific television writer in the world is the Rt Hon. Lord Willis (b. 13 Jan 1918), who from 1949–87 has created 35 series, including the first 7 years and 2 250 000 words of *Dixon of Dock Green* which ran on BBC television from 1955 to 1976, 30 stage plays and 38 feature films. He has had 24 plays produced. His total output since 1942 is estimated at 19 000 000 words.

'Mastermind' records

Mrs Jennifer Keaveney (on 'The life and work of E. Nesbit') scored a record 40 points in a 1986 semi-final

Most durable show ● *Sooty* was first presented on BBC by its deviser Harry Corbett (b. 1918) in 1952. In 1968, *Sooty* moved to Thames Television and when Harry retired in 1975, the show was, and is continued to this very day by his son Matthew. Over the years Sooty acquired some very popular new friends - Sweep, who first appeared in 1957, and Soo, in 1962. *The Sooty Show* also holds the record for the longest run of consecutive Christmas seasons at the same theatre. It has been running annually at The Mayfair Theatre, London since 1966. (Photo: Dori Horlock for Guinness Publishing)

and equalled her semi-final score of 40 points when she won the 1986 final with 'The life and works of Elizabeth Gaskell' of this BBC TV series which began on 11 Sept 1972. Sir David Hunt KCMG, OBE won the 'Mastermind Champions' contest on 3 May 1982.

TV producer

Aaron Spelling (b. 1928) has produced more than 1770 TV episodes totalling 2250 hours of air time, as well as 207½ hours of TV movies and 8 feature films. The total 2467 broadcast hours is equal to 3688 km *13·7 million ft* of film and, projected 24 hours a day, it would take 103·9 days – just 3½ months – to screen it all. The average American TV is turned on 6 hours per day. At that rate, Spelling has produced enough film to last 374 days.

Highest TV advertising rates

The highest TV advertising rate has been $600 000 per ½ min for NBC network prime time during the transmission of Super Bowl XXI on 25 Jan 1987, watched by a record 127 million viewers. In Great Britain the peak time weekday 60-sec spot rate (8.00–11.20 p.m.) for

Thames Television is £74 113 + VAT (January 1988). The longest run was 7 min 10 sec by Great Universal Stores on TV-am's *Good Morning Britain* for £100 000 on 20 Jan 1985.

Most takes

The highest number of 'takes' for a TV commercial is 28 in 1973 by Pat Coombs, the comedienne. Her explanation was 'Every time we came to the punch line I just could not remember the name of the product'.

Commercial records

It was reported in March 1988 that Pepsi Cola had paid Michael Jackson £7 million to do 4 TV commercials for them.

Largest and smallest sets

The Sony Jumbo Tron colour TV screen at the Tsukuba International Exposition '85 near Tokyo in March 1985 measured 24·3 m × 45·7 m *80 ft × 150 ft*.

The largest cathode ray tubes for colour sets are 94 cm *37 in* models made by Mitsubishi Electric of Japan.

The Seiko TV-Wrist Watch launched on 23 Dec 1982 in Japan has a 30·5 mm *1·2 in* screen and weighs only 80 g *2·8 oz*. Together with the receiver unit and the headphone set the entire black and white system, costing 108 000 yen, weighs only 320 g *11·3 oz*. The smallest single-piece set is the Casio-Keisanki TV-10 weighing 338 g *11·9 oz* with a 6·85 cm *2·7 in* screen, launched in Tokyo in July 1983.

The smallest colour set is the liquid crystal display (LCD) Japanese Epson launched in 1985 with dimensions of 7·6 × 17·1 × 2·8 cm *3 × 6¾ × 1⅛ in* weighing, with batteries and its 52 800 crystals, only 453 g *16 oz*.

Largest mound ● Statues on the eastern terrace of the gravel mound built as a memorial to the Seleucid King Antiochus I (reigned 69–34 BC). On the summit of Nemrud Dagi (8205 ft *2494 m*) in south-east of Malatya, eastern Turkey this measures 197 ft *59.8 m* tall and covers 7.5 acres *3 ha*. (Photo: Tim Butcher)

THE WORLD'S STRUCTURES

CHAPTER·SEVEN

EARLIEST STRUCTURES

World

The earliest known human structure is a rough circle of loosely piled lava blocks found on the lowest cultural level at the Lower Palaeolithic site at Olduvai Gorge in Tanzania revealed by Dr Mary Leakey in January 1960. The structure was associated with artifacts and bones on a work-floor, dating from c. 1 750 000 BC. The earliest evidence of *buildings* yet discovered is that of 21 huts with hearths or pebble-lined pits and delimited by stake-holes found in October 1965 at the Terra Amata site in Nice, France, thought to belong to the Acheulian culture of c. 400 000 years ago. Excavation carried out between 28 June and 5 July 1966 revealed one hut with palisaded walls with axes of 15 m *49 ft* and 6 m *20 ft.* The remains of a stone tower 6·1 m *20 ft* high originally built into the walls of Jericho have been excavated and are dated to 5000 BC. The foundations of the walls themselves have been dated to as early as 8350 BC.

Earliest structures ● The oldest free-standing structures in the world are now believed to be these megalithic temples at Mgarr and Skorba in Malta. With those at Ggantija in Gozo they date from c. 3250 BC.

Cape Canaveral, Florida. Construction began in April 1963 by the Ursum Consortium. It is a steel-framed building measuring 218 m *716 ft* in length, 158 m *518 ft* in width and 160 m *525 ft* high. The building contains four bays, each with its own door 140 m *460 ft* high. Its floor area is 31 911 m² *343 500 ft²* and its capacity is 3 666 500 m³ *129 482 000 ft³.* The building was 'topped out' on 14 Apr 1965 at a cost of $108 700 000.

Administrative

The largest ground area covered by any office building is that of the Pentagon, in Arlington, Virginia, USA. Built to house the US Defense Department's offices it was completed on 15 Jan 1943 and cost an estimated $83 000 000. Each of the outermost sides is 281 m *921 ft* long and the perimeter of the building is about 1370 m *1500 yd.* Its five storeys enclose a floor area of 604 000 m² *6 500 000 ft².* The corridors measure 27 km *17 miles* in length and there are 7748 windows to be cleaned. Twenty-nine thousand people work in the building which has over 44 000 telephones connected by 257 500 km *160 000 miles* of cable.

Two hundred and twenty staff handle 280 000 calls a day. Two restaurants, six cafeterias and ten snack bars and a staff of 675 form the catering department.

Great Britain

Twelve small stone clusters, associated with broken bones and charcoal in stratum C of the early Palaeolithic site at Hoxne, near Eye, Suffolk may be regarded as Britain's earliest structural remains, dated c. 250 000 BC. Remains of the earliest dated stone shelter and cooking pit were discovered in 1967 at Culver Well, Isle of Portland, Dorset (mesolithic, 5200 BC±135). On the Isle of Jura, Argyll, a hearth consisting of three linked stone circles has been dated to the Mesolithic period 6013±200 BC. The earliest surviving piece of Roman building is the bottom 4·25 m *14 ft* of their beacon at Dover, Kent dating from the 1st century AD.

Ireland

The earliest known evidence of human occupation in Ireland dates from the Mesolithic period c. 7500 at the Carrowmore site in County Sligo. Ireland became enisled or separated from Great Britain c. 9050 BC. Nearby there are megalithic burials dated to 3800±80 BC.

Buildings for Working

LARGEST

Construction project

The Madinat Al-Jubail Al-Sinaiyah project in Saudi Arabia (1976–1996) covering 932 45·7 ha *230 412·8 acres* is the largest in history. The work force on the city and industrial port complex is increasing to a peak of 33 187 from the mid-1982 figure of 17 200. The total earth moving and dredging volume will reach 345 million m³ or *0·82 of a cubic mile.*

The London docklands development has been described as 'the world's largest commercial development'. The first phase will cost about £3500 million.

Industrial

The largest industrial plant in the world is the Nizhniy Tagil Railroad Car and Tank Plant, 136 km *85 miles* north-west of Sverdlovsk, USSR which has 827 000 m² or *204·3 acres* of floor space. It has an annual capacity to produce 2500 T-72 tanks.

Commercial

The greatest ground area covered by any commercial building in the world under one roof is the flower auction building of the Co-operative VBA (Verenigde Bloemenveilingen Aalsmeer, Aalsmeer, Netherlands, which was built with dimensions of 776 × 547 m *2546 × 1794 ft.* The floor surface of 343 277 m² *84·82 acres* was extended in 1986 to 368 477 m² *91·05 acres.* The building with the largest cubic capacity in the world is the Boeing Company's main assembly plant at Everett, Washington State, USA completed in 1968 with a capacity of 5·6 million m³ *200 million ft³.*

The largest building in Britain is the Ford Parts Centre at Daventry, Northamptonshire, which measures 602 × 7 m *1978 × 780 ft* or 14·86 ha *36·7 acres.* It was opened on 6 Sept 1972 and cost nearly £8 million. It employs 1600 people and is fitted with 14 000 fluorescent lights.

Scientific

The most capacious scientific building in the world is the Vehicle Assembly Building (VAB) at Complex 39, the selected site for the final assembly and launching of the Apollo moon spacecraft on the Saturn V rocket, at the John F. Kennedy Space Center (KSC) on Merritt Island,

Office

The office buildings with the largest rentable space in the world are The World Trade Center in New York, with a total of 406 000 m² *4 370 000 ft²* in each of the twin towers of which the taller Tower Two (formerly B) is 415·22 m *1362 ft 3¼ in.* The tip of the TV antenna on Tower One is 521·2 m *1710 ft* above street level and is thus 46 m *151 ft* taller than the antennae atop the Sears Tower (see below).

The largest single open plan office in the United Kingdom is that of British Gas West Midlands at Solihull, built by Spooners (Hull) Ltd in 1962. It now measures 230 by 49 m *753 ft by 160 ft,* accommodating 2125 clerical and managerial staff.

TALLEST

The tallest office building in the world is the Sears Tower, national headquarters of Sears, Roebuck & Co in Wacker Drive, Chicago, Illinois with 110 storeys rising to 443 m *1454 ft* and begun in August 1970. Its gross area is 408 760 m² *4 400 000 ft².* It was 'topped out' on 4 May 1973, having surpassed the World Trade Center in New York in height at 2.35 p.m. on 6 Mar 1973 with the first steel column reaching to the 104th storey. The addition of two TV antennae brought the total height to 475·18 m *1559 ft.* The building's population is 16 700 served by 103 elevators and 18 escalators. It has 16 000 windows. Tentative plans for a 169-storey 701 m *2300 ft* tall building, projected to cost $1250 million, for the Chicago Loop, Illinois, USA were drawn up and published on 27 Oct 1981.

Demolition on the Central Place site in Brisbane, Queen-

Buildings for Working

sland, began on 9 Aug 1987 for the erection of the 120 storey world's tallest building 445 m *1460 ft* in height for completion at a cost of $A800 million by late 1990.

The tallest office block in Britain and the tallest cantilevered building in the world is the £72 million National Westminster tower block in Bishopsgate, City of London completed in 1979. It has 49 storeys and 3 basement levels, serviced by 21 lifts, and is 183 m *600 ft 4 in* tall. The gross floor area is 59 121 m² *636 373 ft²*.

The Canary Wharf development plans in London Docklands included three 50-storey office towers of up to 259 m *850 ft*. The tallest will probably be finally built to 243.8 m *800 ft* because of air safety.

SHALLOWEST

The shallowest commercial building is the 1.8 m *6 ft* wide, 30 m *100 ft* long Sam Kee Building at 8 West Pender, Vancouver, Canada. It was erected in 1912.

HABITATIONS
Greatest altitude

The highest inhabited buildings in the world are those in the Indo–Tibetan border fort of Bāsisi by the Māna Pass (Lat. 31° 4'N; Long. 79° 24' E) at *c.* 5988 m *19 700 ft*. In April 1961, however, a 3-room dwelling was discovered at 6600 m *21 650 ft* on Cerro Llullaillaco (6723 m *22 058 ft*), on the Argentine–Chilean border, believed to date from the late pre-Columbian period *c.* 1480. A settlement on the T'e-li-mo trail in southern Tibet is sited at an apparent altitude of 6019 m *19 800 ft*.

Northernmost

The most northerly habitation in the world is the Danish Scientific station set up in 1952 in Pearyland, northern Greenland (Kalaalit Nunaat), over 1450 km *900 miles* north of the Arctic Circle. Eskimo hearths dated to before 1000 BC were discovered in Pearyland in 1969. Polar Eskimos were discovered in Inglefield Land, NW Greenland in 1818. The USSR's drifting research station 'North Pole 15' passed within 2.8 km *1¼ miles* of the North Pole in December 1967. The most northerly continuously inhabited place is the Canadian Department of National Defense outpost at Alert on Ellesmere Island, Northwest Territories in Lat. 82° 30' N, Long. 62° W, set up in 1950.

Southernmost

The most southerly permanent human habitation is the United States' Amundsen–Scott South Polar Station (see Chapter 10) completed in 1957 and replaced in 1975.

EMBASSIES AND CIVIC BUILDINGS
Largest

The largest embassy in the world is the USSR embassy on Bei Xiao Jie, Beijing, China, in the north-eastern corner of the northern walled city. The whole 18.2 ha *45 acre* area of the old Orthodox Church Mission (established 1728), now known as the *Bei guan*, was handed over to the USSR in 1949.

The largest in Great Britain is the United States of America embassy in Grosvenor Square, London. The Chancery Building alone, completed in 1960, has 600 rooms for a staff of 700 on seven floors with a usable floor area of 236 895 m² *255 000 ft²*.

EXHIBITION CENTRES
Largest *World*

The International Exposition Center in Cleveland, Ohio, USA, the world's largest, is situated on a 70.8 ha *175 acre* site adjacent to Cleveland Hopkins International Airport in a building which measures 232 250 m² *2.5 million ft²*. An indoor terminal provides direct rail access and parking for 10 000 cars.

Great Britain

Britain's largest exhibition centre is the National Exhibition Centre, Birmingham opened in February 1976. Five halls which inter-connect cover 87 180 m²

938.397 ft² with a combined volume of 1 168 466 m³ or 41.26 million ft³.

INDUSTRIAL STRUCTURES
Tallest chimneys

The world's tallest chimney is the $5.5 million International Nickel Company's stack 379.6 m *1245 ft 8 in* tall at Copper Cliff, Sudbury, Ontario, Canada, completed in 1970. It was built by Canadian Kellogg Ltd in 60 days and the diameter tapers from 35.4 m *116.4 ft* at the base to 15.8 m *51.8 ft* at the top. It weighs 39 006 tonnes *38 390 tons* and became operational in 1971.

The world's most massive chimney is one of 350 m *1148 ft* at Puentes de Garcia Rodriguez, north-west Spain, built by M. W. Kellogg Co. It contains 15 750 m³ *20 600 yd³* of concrete and 1315 tonnes *2.9 million lb* of steel and has an internal volume of 189 720 m³ *6.7 million ft³*. Europe's tallest chimney serves the Zasavje thermo-power plant in Trboulje, Yugoslavia and was completed to 350 m *1181 ft* on 1 June 1976.

The tallest chimney in Great Britain is one of 259 m *850 ft* at Drax Power Station, North Yorkshire, begun in 1966 and topped out on 16 May 1969. It has an untapered diameter of 26 m *87 ft 9 in* and has the greatest capacity of any chimney. The architects were Clifford Tee & Gale of London. The oldest known industrial chimney in Britain is the Stone Edge Chimney, near Chesterfield, Derbyshire built to a height of 16.76 m *55 ft ante* 1771.

Cooling towers

The largest cooling tower in the world is that adjacent to the nuclear power plant at Uentrop, West Germany which is 179.8 m *590 ft* tall, completed in 1976. The largest in the United Kingdom are of the Ferrybridge and Didcot type and measure 114 m *375 ft* tall and 91 m *300 ft* across the base.

HANGARS
Largest

The world's largest hangar is Hangar 375 ('Big Texas') at Kelly Air Force Base, San Antonio, Texas, USA completed on 15 Feb 1956. It has 4 doors each 76.2 m *250 ft* in width and 18.28 m *60 ft* high with a weight of 608 tonnes *598 tons*. The high bay area measures 609.6 × 91.4 × 27.4 m *2000 × 300 × 90 ft* and is surrounded by a 17.8 ha *44 acre* concrete apron. Delta Airlines' jet base on a 56.6 ha *140 acre* site at Hartsfield International Airport, Atlanta, Georgia, has 14.5 ha *36 acres* under roof.

The largest hangar building in the United Kingdom is the Britannia assembly hall at the former Bristol Aeroplane Company's works at Filton, Avon, now part of British Aerospace. The overall width of the hall is 321 m *1054 ft* and the overall depth of the centre bay is 128 m *420 ft*. It encloses a floor area of 3.0 ha *7½ acres*. The cubic capacity of the hall is 934 000 m³ *33 000 000 ft³*. The building was begun in April 1946 and completed by September 1949. (See also Largest Doors.)

GLASSHOUSE
Largest *Great Britain*

The largest glasshouse in the United Kingdom is one covering 9.10 ha *22.5 acres* owned by van Heyningen Bros at Waterham, Herne Bay, Kent completed in October 1982. A crop of 160 000 tomato plants is grown under 1155 tons of glass.

GRAIN ELEVATOR
Largest

The world's largest single-unit grain elevator is operated by the C-G-F Grain Company at Wichita, Kansas. Consisting of a triple row of storage tanks, 123 on each side of the central loading tower or 'head house', the unit is 828 m *2 717 ft* long and 30 m *100 ft* wide. Each tank is 37 m *120 ft* high, with an inside diameter of 9 m *30 ft* giving a total storage capacity of 7.3 million hl *20 000 000 bushels* of wheat. The largest collection of elevators in the world are the 23 at City of Thunder Bay, Ontario,

Canada, on Lake Superior with a total capacity of 37.4 million hl *103.9 million bushels*.

SEWAGE WORKS
Largest

The largest single full treatment sewage works in the world is the West-Southwest Treatment Plant, opened in 1940 on a site of 203 ha *501 acres* in Chicago, Illinois. It serves an area containing 2 940 000 people and it treated an average of 3160 million litres *835 000 000 US gal* of wastes per day in 1973. The capacity of its sedimentation and aeration tanks is 1 280 000 m³ *1.6 million yd³*.

The largest full treatment works in Britain and probably in Europe is the Beckton Works, East London which serves a 2 966 000 population and handles a daily flow of 941 million litres *207 million gal* in a tank capacity of 21 400 m³ *757 000 ft³*.

WOODEN BUILDING
Largest

The world's largest buildings in timber are the two US Navy airship hangars built in 1942–3 at Tillamook, Oregon. Now used by the Louisiana-Pacific Corporation as a sawmill the measurements are 304.8 m *1000 ft* in length, 51.8 m *170 ft* in height at the crown and 90.22 m *296 ft* wide at the base.

What is believed to be the oldest complete wooden building in England was discovered in December 1986 in the Fenlands, Cambridgeshire. It measures 8 m *26.2 ft* × 2 m *6.65 ft* and was a burial chamber of the Neolithic period *c.* 5000 years ago.

AIR-SUPPORTED BUILDING
Largest

The world's largest air-supported roof has been that of the 80 600 capacity octagonal Pontiac Silverdome Stadium, Michigan, 159 m *522 ft* wide and 220 m *722 ft* long. The air pressure was 34.4 kPa *5 lb/in²* supporting the 4 ha *10 acre* translucent 'Fiberglas' roofing. The structural engineers were Geiger-Berger Associates of New York City.

The largest standard size air hall was one 262 m *860 ft* long, 42.6 m *140 ft* wide and 19.8 m *65 ft* high. One was first sited at Lima, Ohio, USA, made by Irvin Industries of Stamford, Connecticut.

Buildings for Living

WOODEN BUILDINGS
Oldest

The oldest extant wooden buildings in the world are those comprising the Pagoda, Chumanar gate and the Temple of Horyu (Horyu-ji), at Nara, Japan, dating from *c.* AD 670 and completed in 715. The wood used were beams from 1000 year old Hinoki trees. The nearby Daibutsuden, built in 1704–11, measured 87 m long, 51 m wide and 46.75 m tall *285.4 ft × 167.3 ft × 153.3 ft*. The present dimensions measure some 57.3 × 50.4 × 48.6 m *188 × 165.3 × 159.4 ft*.

CASTLES
Earliest

The oldest castle in the world is at Gomdan, in the Yemen, which originally had 20 storeys and dates from before AD 100.

The oldest stone castle extant in Great Britain is Richmond Castle, Yorkshire, built *c.* 1075.

The oldest Irish castle is Ferrycarrig near Wexford dating from *c.* 1180. The oldest castle in Northern Ireland is Carrickfergus Castle, County Antrim, Northern Ireland, which dates from before 1210.

Largest

The largest inhabited castle in the world is the royal residence of Windsor Castle at New Windsor, Berkshire. It is primarily of 12th century construction and is in the form of a waisted parallelogram 576 by 164 m *1890 by 540 ft*.

The total area of Dover Castle, however, covers 13·75 ha *34 acres* with a width of 335·2 m *1100 ft* and a curtain wall of 550 m *1800 ft* or if underground works are taken in, 700 m *2300 ft*. The overall dimensions of Carisbrooke Castle (110 by 137 m *450 ft by 360 ft*), Isle of Wight, if its earthworks are included, are 411 m by 251 m *1350 ft by 825 ft*. The largest castle in Scotland is Edinburgh Castle with a major axis of 402 m *1320 ft* and measuring 1025 m *3360 ft* along its perimeter wall including the Esplanade. The most capacious of all Irish castles is Carrickfergus (see above) but that with the most extensive fortifications is Trim Castle, County Meath, built *c.* 1205 with a curtain wall 443 m *1455 ft* long.

Forts

The largest ancient castle in the world is Hradčany Castle, Prague, Czechoslovakia, originating in the 9th century. It is an oblong irregular polygon with an axis of 570 m *1870 ft* and an average traverse diameter of 128 m *420 ft* with a surface area of 7·28 ha *18 acres*. Fort George, Ardersier, Inverness-shire built in 1748–69 measures 640 m *2100 ft* in length and has an average width of 189 m *620 ft*. The total site covers 17·2 ha *42½ acres*.

Thickest walls

Urnammu's city walls at Ur (now Muqayyar, Iraq), destroyed by the Elamites in 2006 BC, were 27 m *88½ ft* thick in mud brick. The walls of the Great Tower or Donjon of Flint Castle, built 1277–80 are 7·0 m *23 ft* thick.

PALACES
Largest

The largest palace in the world is the Imperial Palace (Gu gong) in the centre of Peking (*Beijing*, the northern

---

---

capital), China, which covers a rectangle 960 by 750 m *1050 yd by 820 yd*, an area of 72 ha *177·9 acres*. The outline survives from the construction of the third Ming Emperor, Yung Lo of 1402–24, but due to constant rearrangements most of the intra-mural buildings are 18th-century. These consist of 5 halls and 17 palaces of which the last occupied by the last Empress until 1924 was the Palace of Accumulated Elegance (*Chu xia gong*).

The Palace of Versailles, 23 km *14 miles* south-west of Paris has a façade with 375 windows, 580 m *634 yards* in length. The building, completed in 1682 for Louis XIV occupied over 30 000 workmen under Jules Hardouin-Mansert (1646–1708).

Residential

The largest palace in the United Kingdom in royal use is Buckingham Palace, London, so named after its site, bought in 1703 by John Sheffield, the 1st Duke of Buckingham and Normanby (1648–1721). Buckingham House was reconstructed in the Palladian style between 1835 and 1836, following the design of John Nash (1752–1835). The 186 m *610 ft* long East Front was built in 1846 and refaced in 1912. The Palace, which stands in 15·8 ha *39 acres* of garden, has 600 rooms including a ballroom 34 m *111 ft* long. The largest ever royal palace has been Hampton Court, Middlesex, acquired by Henry VIII from Cardinal Wolsey in 1525 and greatly enlarged by him and later by William III, Anne and George I, whose son George II was its last resident monarch. It covers 1·6 ha *4 acres* of a 270·7 ha *669 acre* site.

Largest moat

The world's largest moats are those which surround the Imperial Palace in Beijing (see above). From plans drawn by French sources it appears to measure 49 m *54 yd* wide and have a total length of 3290 m *3600 yd*. The city's moats total in all 38 km *23½ miles*.

HOTELS
Largest

The world's largest hotel is The Las Vegas Hilton, Nevada, USA built on a 25·5 ha *63 acre* site in 1974–81 with 3174 rooms, 13 international restaurants and a staff of 3600. It has a 2·47 ha *10 acre* rooftop recreation deck, a 4460 m^2 *48 000 ft^2* pillar-free ballroom and 11600 m^2 *125 000 ft^2* of convention space.

The Hotel Rossiya in Moscow opened in 1967 with 3200 rooms but owing to its proportion of dormitory accommodation, is not now internationally listed among the largest hotels. The Izmailovo Hotel complex opened in July 1980 for the XXIInd Olympic Games in Moscow, was designed to accommodate 9500 people.

The lobby at the Hyatt Regency, San Francisco, USA, is 106·6 m *350 ft* long, 48·7 m *160 ft* wide and at 51·8 m *170 ft* is the height of a 17 storey building.

The greatest sleeping capacity of any hotel in Great Britain is 1859 in the London Forum Hotel, Cromwell Road, London which has a staff of 419 and was opened in 1973. The Regent Palace Hotel, Piccadilly Circus, London, opened 20 May 1915, has, however, 225 more rooms totalling 1140. The largest hotel is the Grosvenor House Hotel, Park Lane, London, which was opened in 1929. It is 8 storeys high covering 1 ha *2½ acres* and caters for more than 100 000 visitors per year in 470 rooms. The Great Room is the largest single hotel room measuring 55 by 40 m *181 ft by 131 ft* with a height of 7 m *23 ft*. Banquets for 1500 are frequently handled.

The Regent Hotel, Royal Leamington Spa, Warwickshire when first opened in 1819 with 100 bedrooms and only one bathroom, was acclaimed to be the largest in the world.

Tallest

The tallest hotel in the world, measured from the street level of its main entrance to the top, is the 226·1 m *741·9 ft* tall 73-storey Westin Stamford in Raffles City, Singapore topped out in March 1985. The $235 million hotel is operated by Westin Hotel Company and owned by Raffles City Pte Ltd. Their Detroit Plaza measuring from the rear entrance level is however 227·9 m *748 ft* tall.

Britain's tallest hotel is the 27-storey 132·24 m *380 ft* tall 914-bedroom London Forum Hotel (see above).

Narrowest

The Star Hotel in Moffat, Dumfries & Galloway, Scotland, the narrowest detached hotel is only 6·1 m *20 ft* wide. The 8-bedroom hotel, which has two bars, is owned by Douglas and Monica House and by Tim and Allison Leighfield.

Most remote

Garvault Hotel, by Kinbrace, Sutherland, is claimed to be the most isolated in mainland Britain being some 25·7 km *16 miles* from its nearest competitor at Forsinard, also in Sutherland.

Most expensive

The world's costliest hotel accommodation is the roof-top Royal Suite at 500 000 Pesetas per day excluding VAT in the Marbella–Dinamar, Spain. It has 2 halls, 2 dining rooms, 5 double bedrooms, 7 bathrooms, a kitchen, a service area, a study/library/office, a lounge, an 8 metre heated swimming pool with a massage system, 2 solariums, a sauna and an 18-hole putting green. The most expensive hotel suite in Britain is the Royal Suite of the Hotel Inter-Continental, London, at £1235 per day (incl. VAT)

Mobile

The 3-storey brick Hotel Fairmount (built 1906) in San Antonio, Texas which weighed 3 200 000 lb, was moved on 36 dollies with pneumatic tyres over city streets approximately 5 blocks and over a bridge, which had to be reinforced. The move by Emmert International of Portland, Oregon, took 4 days, 30 Mar–2 Apr, 1985, and cost $650 000.

Spas

The largest spa in the world measured by number of available hotel rooms is Vichy, Allier, France, with 14 000 rooms. Spas are named after the watering place in the Liège province of Belgium where hydropathy was developed from 1626. The highest French spa is Bareges, Hautes-Pyrénées, at 1240 m *4068 ft* above sea level.

HOUSING
Largest estate

The largest housing estate in the United Kingdom is the 675 ha *1670 acre* Becontree Estate, on a site of 1214 ha *3000 acres* in Barking and Redbridge, London, built between 1921 and 1929. The total number of homes is 26 822, with an estimated population of nearly 90 000.

New towns

Of the 32 new towns set up in Great Britain, that with the largest eventual planned population is Milton Keynes, Buckinghamshire, with a projected 210 000 for 1992.

Largest house *World*

The largest private house in the world is the 250-room Biltmore House in Asheville, North Carolina, USA. It is owned by George and William Cecil, grandsons of George Washington Vanderbilt II (1862–1914). The house was built between 1890 and 1895 in an estate of 48 160 ha *119 000 acres*, at a cost of $4 100 000. The property is currently valued at $55 000 000 with 4856 ha *12 000 acres*.

The most expensive private house ever built is the Hearst Ranch at San Simeon, California. It was built from 1922–39 for William Randolph Hearst (1863–1951), at a total cost of more than $30 000 000. It has more than 100 rooms, a 32 m *104 ft* long heated swimming pool, an 25 m

> **Most rooms ●** Knole, near Sevenoaks, Kent, believed to have had 365 rooms, one for each day of the year, is in the care of the National Trust. Built round seven courtyards, the total depth from front to back is about 120 m *400 ft* . Thomas Bourchier, Archbishop of Canterbury (1454–86), bought the estate in 1456 and commenced building. Sir Thomas Sackville who leased it in 1566 put the finishing touches between 1603 – 1608 being then Earl of Dorset. (Photo: NT/National Trust/Rob Matheson)

83 ft long assembly hall and a garage for 25 limousines. The house required 60 servants to maintain it.

Great Britain

The largest house in Great Britain is Wentworth Woodhouse, near Rotherham, South Yorkshire, formerly the seat of the Earls Fitzwilliam and now a teachers' training college. The main part of the house, built over 300 years ago, has more than 240 rooms with over 1000 windows, and its principal façade is 183 m *600 ft* long. The royal residence Sandringham House, Norfolk, has been reported to have had 365 rooms before the demolition of 73 surplus rooms in 1975. The largest house in Ireland is Castletown in County Kildare, owned by the Hon. Desmond Guinness and is the headquarters of the Irish Georgian Society. Scotland's largest house is Hopetoun House, West Lothian, built between 1696 and 1756 with a west façade 206 m *675 ft* long.

Most expensive

The most expensive private house is The Kenstead Hall with the adjoining Beechwood property in The Bishop's Avenue, Hampstead, London, residence of the late King of Saudi Arabia. It was put on the market for £16 million in August 1982.

Oldest

The oldest house in Britain is Eastry Court near Sandwich, Kent dating from AD 603. Some of the original timbers and stone infill still survive behind its present Georgian façade.

Most visited stately home

The most visited stately home in the United Kingdom in 1987 was Warwick Castle, near Stratford-on-Avon, Warwickshire, with 642 549 visitors. Built by the Beauchamp family it dates from the 14th century.

Barracks

The oldest purpose-built barracks are believed to be Collins Barracks, formerly the Royal Barracks, Dublin, Ireland, completed in 1704 and still in use.

FLATS
Tallest

The tallest block of flats in the world is the 218 m *716 ft* Metropolitan Tower on West 57 Street, New York, USA. It consists of a towering 78 storeys, of which the upper 48 are residential.

Largest

The largest blocks of private flats in Britain form the Barbican Estate, in the City of London with 2011 flats on a 16 ha *40 acre* site with covered parking space for 2000 cars. The architects were Chamberlain, Powell and Bon.

The tallest residential block in Great Britain is Shakespeare Tower in the Barbican in the City of London, which has 116 flats on 44 storeys and rises to a height of 127·77 m *419 ft 2½ in* above the street. The first of the three Barbican towers was 'topped out' in May 1971.

Most expensive

The largest of the four flats at Rutland Gate, Kensington, London designed by YRM Architects for occupation in 1988 is reputed to be worth around £6 million. The flat has a private swimming pool, seven bedrooms, and overlooks Hyde Park.

Mobile

The Cudecom Building, an eight storey apartment block in Bogota, Colombia, South America weighing 7700 tonnes was moved intact 28·95 m *95 ft* on 6 Oct 1974 to make way for a road.

Buildings for Entertainment

STADIUM
Largest

The world's largest stadium is the open Strahov Stadium in Prague (Praha), Czechoslovakia. It was completed in 1934 and can accommodate 240 000 spectators for mass displays of up to 40 000 Sokol gymnasts.

Football

The largest football stadium in the world is the Maracaña Municipal Stadium in Rio de Janeiro, Brazil, where the football ground has a normal capacity of 205 000, of whom 155 000 was accommodated for the World Cup final between Brazil and Uruguay on 16 July 1950. A crowd of 199 854 was accommodated for the World Cup final between Brazil and Uruguay on 16 July 1950. A dry moat, 2·13 m *7 ft* wide and more than 1·5 m *5 ft* deep, protects players from spectators and *vice versa*. Britain's most capacious football stadium is Hampden Park, Glasgow, opened on 31 Oct 1903 and once surveyed to accommodate 184 000 compared with a record attendance of 149 547 on 17 Apr 1937 and the present licensed limit of 74 400.

Covered

The Azteca Stadium, Mexico City, Mexico, opened in 1968, has a capacity of 107 000 of whom nearly all are under cover. The world's largest retractable roof is being constructed to cover the 60 000-capacity Toronto Blue Jays new stadium near the CN Tower for completion by August 1988. The diameter will be 207 m *679 ft*.

The largest covered stadium in Britain is the Empire Stadium, Wembley, Middlesex, opened in April 1923. It was the scene of the 1948 Olympic Games and the final of the 1966 World Cup. In 1962–3 the capacity under cover was increased to 100 000 of whom 45 000 may be seated. The original cost was £1 250 000.

Largest roof

The transparent acryl glass 'tent' roof over the Munich Olympic Stadium, West Germany measures 84 997·9 m^2 *914 940 ft^2* in area resting on a steel net supported by masts. The roof of longest span in the world is the 207·2 m *680 ft* diameter of the Louisiana Superdome (see below). The major axis of the elliptical Texas Stadium completed in 1971 at Irving, Texas is, however, 240 m *787 ft 4 in*.

Indoor

The world's largest indoor stadium is the 5·26 ha *13 acre* $173 million 83·2 m *273 ft* tall Superdome in New Orleans,

The smallest house in Britain ● This 19th-century fisherman's cottage at The Quay, Conwy, Gwynedd seen here has a 72 in *182 cm* frontage, is 122 in *309 cm* high, 100 in *254 cm* front to back and has two tiny rooms and a staircase. The narrowest known house frontage is of 47 inches *1·19 m* at 50 Stuart Street, Millport, Great Cumbrae, Bute. (Photo: D. Redfearn)

Louisiana, completed in May 1975. Its maximum seating capacity for conventions is 97 365 or 76 791 for football. Box suites rent for $35 000 excluding the price of admission. A gondola with six 7·92 m *312 in* TV screens produces instant replay.

Amusement resort

The world's largest amusement resort is Disney World in 11 332 ha *28 000 acres* of Orange and Osceola counties, 32 km *20 miles* south west of Orlando in central Florida, USA. It was opened on 1 Oct 1971 with a $400 million investment. The attendance in 1987 was 22 500 000.

The most attended resort is Disneyland, Anaheim, California (opened 1955) which received its 250 millionth visitor on 24 Aug 1985 at 9.52 a.m. The attendance is expected to be increased from 12 620 million with the completion of the 80–acre Magic Kingdom announced in July 1987.

Largest pleasure beach

The largest pleasure beach in the world is Virginia Beach, Virginia, USA. It has 45 km *28 miles* of beach front on the Atlantic and 16 km *10 miles* of estuary frontage. The area embraces 600 km^2 *255 miles^2* and 134 hotels and motels.

The most visited pleasure beach in Britain is at Blackpool, Lancashire which attracts 6½ million visitors annually.

Piers

A pleasure pier was completed at Great Yarmouth, Norfolk in 1808 but was washed away in 1953. The Old Pier, Weymouth, Dorset dates back to 1812.

The longest pleasure pier in the world is Southend Pier at Southend-on-Sea in Essex. It is 2·15 km *1·34 miles* in length and it was first opened in August 1889 with final extensions made in 1929. In 1949–50 the pier had a peak 5 750 000 visitors. The pier railway closed in October 1978, and reopened on 2 May 1986.

The resort with most piers is Atlantic City, New Jersey

with 6 pre-war and 5 currently. In Britain only Blackpool has as many as three—North, Central and South.

Earliest fair

The earliest major international fair was the Great Exhibition of 1851 in the Crystal Palace, Hyde Park, London which in 141 days attracted 6 039 195.

Largest fair

The largest ever International Fair site was that for the St Louis, Missouri, Louisiana Purchase Exposition which covered 514·66 ha *1271·76 acres*. It also staged the 1904 Olympic Games and drew an attendance of 19 694 855.

Record fair attendance

The record attendance for any fair was 64 218 770 for Expo 70 held on an 330 ha *815 acre* site at Osaka, Japan from March to 13 Sept 1970. It made a profit of 19 439 402 017 yen.

Big wheel

The original Ferris Wheel, named after its constructor, George W. Ferris (1859–96), was erected in 1893 at the Midway, Chicago, Illinois, at a cost of $385 000. It was 76 m *250 ft* in diameter, 240 m *790 ft* in circumference, weighed 1087 tonnes *1070 tons* and carried 36 cars each seating 60 people, making a total of 2160 passengers. The structure was removed in 1904 to St Louis, Missouri, and was eventually sold as scrap for $1800. In 1897 a Ferris Wheel with a diameter of 86·5 m *284 ft* was erected for the Earl's Court Exhibition, London. It had ten 1st-class and 30 2nd-class cars. The largest diameter wheels now operating are 'The Giant Peter' at Himeji Central Park, Himeji City, Hyogo, and that at the city of Tsukuba, both in Japan and with a height of 85 m *278 ft 10 in*. The latter has a capacity for 384 riders.

Fastest switchbacks

The maximum speeds claimed for switchbacks, scenic railways or roller coasters have in the past been exaggerated for commercial reasons. The twin-track triple-helix American Eagle at Six Flags Great America, Gurnee, Illinois, opened on 23 May 1981, has a vertical drop of 44·92 m *147·4 ft* on which a speed of 106·73 km/h *66·31 mph* is reached. The longest roller coaster in the world is *The Beast* at Kings Island near Cincinnati, Ohio. Measurements at the bottom of its 42·98 m *141 ft* high drop returned a speed of 104·23 km/h *64·77 mph* on 5 Apr 1980. The run of 2·25 km *1·40 miles* incorporates 243·8 m *800 ft* of tunnels and a 540-degree banked helix. The tallest is the *Moonsault Scramble* at the Fujikyu Highland Park, near Kawaguchi Lake, Japan opened on 24 June 1983. It is 75 m *246 ft* tall (with a speed of 105 km/h *65·2 mph*).

Longest slide

The longest dry slide in the world is the Bromley Alpine Slide on Route 11 in Peru, Vermont. This has a length of 1402 m *4600 ft* and a vertical drop of 250 m *820 ft*.

Largest harem

The world's most capacious harem is the Winter Harem of the Grand Seraglio at Topaki, Istanbul, Turkey completed in 1589 with 400 rooms. By the time of the deposing of Abdul Hamid II in 1909 the number of *carge* (those who serve) had dwindled from 1200 to 370 odalisques with 127 eunuchs.

Night club *Oldest*

The earliest night club (*boîte de nuit*) was 'Le Bal des Anglais' at 6 rue des Anglais, Paris, 5^e, France. Founded in 1843, it closed *c.* 1960.

Largest

The largest night club in the world is 'Gilley's Club', (formerly 'Shelly's') built in 1955 and extended in 1971 on Spencer Highway, Houston, Texas, with a seating capacity of 6000 under one roof covering 1·6 ha *4 acres*. In the more classical sense the largest night club in the world is 'The Mikado' in the Akasaka district of Tokyo, with a seating capacity of 2000. It is 'manned' by 1250

THE OLD THIRTEENTH CHESHIRE AS

Longest pub name ● This pub in Astley Street, Stalybridge, Manchester, has the longest name with 55 letters – 'The Old Thirteenth Cheshire Astley Volunteer Rifleman Corps Inn'. (Photo: Simon Kench)

---

hostesses. Binoculars are essential to an appreciation of the floor show.

Lowest

The lowest night club is the 'Minus 206' in Tiberias, Israel on the shores of the Sea of Galilee. It is 206 m *676 ft* below sea level. An alternative candidate is the oft-raided 'Outer Limits', opposite the Cow Palace, San Francisco, California. It has been called 'The Most Busted Joint' and 'The Slowest to Get the Message'.

Restaurants

The earliest restaurant, named 'Casa Botin', was opened in 1725 in Calle de Cuchilleros 17, Madrid. The 'Tump Nak' Thai restaurant in Bangkok consists of 65 adjoining houses built on 4 ha *10 acres*. A thousand waiters are available to serve the 3000 potential customers. The highest restaurant in the world is at the Chacaltaya ski resort, Bolivia at 5340 m *17 519 ft*. The highest in Great Britain is the 'Ptarmigan Observation Restaurant' at 1112 m *3650 ft* above sea level on Cairngorm (1244 m *4084 ft*) near Aviemore, Inverness-shire.

PUBLIC HOUSES
Oldest

There are various claimants to the title of the United Kingdom's oldest inn. A foremost claimant is 'The Fighting Cocks', St Albans, Hertfordshire (an 11th-century structure on an 8th-century site). The timber frame of The Royalist Hotel, Digbeth Street, Stow-on-the-Wold, Gloucestershire has been dated to even earlier. It

was the inn 'The Eagle and the Child' in the 13th century and known to exist in AD 947. An origin as early as AD 560 has been claimed for 'Ye Olde Ferry Boat Inn' at Holywell, Cambridgeshire. There is some evidence that it antedates the local church, built in 980, but the earliest documents are not dated earlier than 1100. There is evidence that the 'Bingley Arms', Bardsey, near Leeds, West Yorkshire, restored and extended in 1738, existed as the 'Priest's Inn', according to Bardsey Church records, dated 905.

The oldest pub in Northern Ireland is 'Grace Neill's Bar', Donaghadee, County Down built in 1611. An inn has stood on the site of the 'Brazen Head Inn', Lower Bridge Street, Dublin since the late 12th century. The present structure dates from 1668.

Largest *World*

The largest beer-selling establishment in the world is the 'Mathäser', Bayerstrasse 5, Munich, West Germany, where the daily sale reaches 48 000 litres *84 470 pts*. It was established in 1829, was demolished in World War II and rebuilt by 1955, and now seats 5500 people. The through-put at the Dube beer halls in the Bantu township of Soweto, Johannesburg, South Africa may, however, be higher on some Saturdays when the average daily consumption of 27 280 litres *48 000 pts* of beer is far exceeded.

Great Britain

The largest public house in Great Britain is the 'Courage' house, Downham Tavern, Downham Way, Bromley, Kent built in 1930. Two large bars (counter length 13·7 m *45 ft*) accommodate 1000 customers with 18–20 staff.

Smallest

The Smith's Arms, Godmanstone, Dorset has external

dimensions of 12·04 m *39 ft 6 in* in length 3·5 m *11 ft 6 in* in width and 3·65 m *12 ft* in height.

The pub with the smallest bar room is the 'Earl Grey', Quenington, Gloucestershire, measuring 3·73 m × 2·89 m *12 ft 3 in × 9 ft 6 in*.

Longest bars

The world's longest permanent bar is the 103·6 m *340 ft* long bar in 'Lulu's Roadhouse', Kitchener, Ontario, Canada opened on 3 Apr 1984. The 'Bar at Erickson's', on Burnside Street, Portland, Oregon, in its heyday (1883–1920) possessed a bar which ran continuously around and across the main saloon measuring 208·48 m *684 ft*. The chief bouncer Edward 'Spider' Johnson had an assistant named 'Jumbo' Reilly who weighed 23 stone and was said to resemble 'an ill-natured orang-utan'. Beer was 5 cents for 16 fluid ounces. Temporary bars have been erected of greater length.

The longest bar in the United Kingdom with beer pumps is the Long Bar at The Cornwall Coliseum Auditorium at Carlyon Bay, St Austell, Cornwall measuring 31·8 m *104 ft 4 in* and having 34 dispensers (beer and lager). The longest bar in a pub is of 31·77 m *104 ft 3 in* in 'The Horse Shoe', Drury Street, Glasgow. The Grand Stand Bar at Galway Racecourse, Ireland, completed in 1955, measures 64 m *210 ft*.

Shortest name

The public house in the United Kingdom with the shortest name was the 'X' at Westcott, Cullompton, Devon but in October 1983 the name was changed to the 'Merry Harriers'.

Commonest name

The commonest pub name in Britain is 'Red Lion' of

THE WORLD'S TALLEST STRUCTURES

HEIGHT m	ft	STRUCTURE	LOCATION	MATERIAL	BUILDING OR COMPLETION DATES
62	204	Djoser step pyramid (earliest Pyramid)	Saqqâra, Egypt	Tura limestone casing	c. 2650 BC
91·7	300·8	Pyramid of Meidum	Meidum, Egypt	Tura limestone casing	c. 2600 BC
101·1	331·6	Snefru Bent pyramid	Dahshûr, Egypt	Tura limestone casing	c. 2600 BC
104	342	Snefru North Stone pyramid	Dahshûr, Egypt	Tura limestone casing	c. 2600 BC
146·5	480·9[1]	Great Pyramid of Cheops (Khufu)	El Gizeh, Egypt	Tura limestone casing	c. 2580 BC
160	525[2]	Lincoln Cathedral, Central Tower	Lincoln, England	lead sheathed wood	c. 1307–1548
149	489[3]	St Paul's Cathedral spire	City of London, England	lead sheathed wood	1315–1561
141	465	Minster of Notre Dame	Strasbourg, France	Vosges sandstone	1420–1439
153	502[4]	St Pierre de Beauvais spire	Beauvais, France	lead sheathed wood	–1568
144	475	St Nicholas Church	Hamburg, Germany	stone and iron	1846–1847
147	485	Rouen Cathedral spire	Rouen, France	cast iron	1823–1876
156	513	Köln Cathedral spires	Cologne, W. Germany	stone	–1880
169	555[5]	Washington Monument	Washington, DC, USA	stone	1848–1884
300·5	985·9[6]	Eiffel Tower	Paris, France	iron	1887–1889
318	1046	Chrysler Building	New York City, USA	steel and concrete	1929–1930
381	1250[7]	Empire State Building	New York City, USA	steel and concrete	1929–1930
479	1572	KWTV Television Mast	Oklahoma City, USA	steel	Nov 1954
490	1610[8]	KSWS Television Mast	Roswell, New Mexico, USA	steel	Dec 1956
493	1619	WGAN Television Mast	Portland, Maine, USA	steel	Sept 1959
510	1676	KFVS Television Mast	Cape Girardeau, Missouri, USA	steel	June 1960
533	1749	WTVM & WRBL Television Mast	Columbus, Georgia, USA	steel	May 1962
533	1749	WBIR-TV Mast	Knoxville, Tennessee, USA	steel	Sept 1963
628	2063	KTHI-TV Mast	Fargo, North Dakota, USA	steel	Nov 1963
646·38	2120·6	Warszawa Radio Mast	Plock, Poland	galvanised steel	22 July 1974

[1] Original height. With loss of pyramidion (topmost stone) height now 137 m 449 ft 6 in.
[2] Fell in a storm.
[3] Struck by lightning and destroyed 4 June 1561.
[4] Fell April 1573, shortly after completion.
[5] Sinking at a rate of 0·0047 ft per annum or 5 in 12·7 cm since 1884.
[6] Original height. With addition of TV antenna in 1957, now 320·75 m 1052 ft.
[7] Original height. With addition of TV tower on 1 May 1951, now 449 m 1472 ft. Exterior is clad in limestone from the Empire Quarry, Indiana.
[8] Fell in gale in 1960.

Y VOLUNTEER RIFLEMAN CORPS INN

which there are probably about 630. Arthur Amos of Bury St Edmunds, Suffolk, has recorded 21 516 differently-named pubs continuously since 1938. On his death in June 1986, his son John took over the collection which now numbers 23 563.

Highest

The highest public house in the United Kingdom is the 'Tan Hill Inn'. It is 528 m *1732 ft* above sea level, just in Co. Durham on the moorland road between Reeth, North Yorkshire and Brough, Cumbria. The 'Snowdon Summit' licensed bar and cafeteria is when open the highest at 1085 m *3560 ft.*

Most visits

Stanley House of Totterdown, Bristol has visited 3309 differently named pubs in Britain by way of public transport only, from 1969 to 1988. Jimmy Young GM, BEM, of Better Pubs Ltd, claims to have visited 23 741 different pubs by 15 May 1988.

HIGHEST STRUCTURES IN GREAT BRITAIN

Metres	Feet		
123	*404*	Salisbury Cathedral Spire	*c.* 1305–
160	*525*	Lincoln Cathedral	1307–1548
149	*489*	St Paul's Cathedral, London	1315–1561
158·1	*518·7*	Blackpool Tower, Lancashire	1894–
171·29	*562*	New Brighton Tower, Merseyside	1898–1919
250	*820*	GPO Radio Masts, Rugby	1925–
304·8	*1000**	ITA Mast, Mendlesham, Suffolk	July 1959
385	*1265*	IBA Mast, Emley Moor, West Yorkshire	1965–1969†
385	*1265*	IBA Mast, Belmont, Lincolnshire	1965–
387·1	*1272*	IBA Mast, Belmont, Lincolnshire	Sept 1967

* ITA masts of the same height followed at Lichfield, Staffordshire; Black Hill, Strathclyde; Caldbeck, Cumbria; and Durris, Grampian.
† Severely damaged by icing and replaced.

Towers and Masts

TALLEST STRUCTURES
World

The tallest structure in the world is the guyed Warszawa Radio mast at Konstantynow near Gabin and Plock 96 km *60 miles* north-west of the capital of Poland. It is 646·38 m *2120 ft 8 in* tall or more than four-tenths of a mile. It was completed on 18 July 1974 and put into operation on 22 July 1974. It was designed by Jan Polak and weighs 550 tonnes. The mast is so high that anyone falling off the top would reach their terminal velocity and hence cease to be accelerating before hitting the ground. Work was begun in July 1970 on this tubular steel construction, with its 15 steel guy ropes. It recaptured for Europe, after 45 years, a record held in the USA since the Chrysler Building surpassed the Eiffel Tower in 1929.

The tallest structure in the United Kingdom is the Independent Broadcasting Authority's mast north of Horncastle, Lincolnshire completed in 1965 to a height of 385 m *1265 ft* with 2·13 m *7 ft* added by meteorological equipment installed in September 1967. It serves Yorkshire TV and weighs 210 tonnes.

TALLEST TOWERS

The tallest self-supporting tower (as opposed to a guyed mast) in the world is the $44 million CN Tower in Metro Center, Toronto, Canada, which rises to 555·33 m *1822 ft 1 in.* Excavation began on 12 Feb 1973 for the 130 000 tonne structure of reinforced, post-tensioned concrete topped out on 2 Apr 1975. The 416-seat restaurant revolves in the Sky Pod at 347·5 m *1140 ft* from which the visibility extends to hills 120 km *74½ miles* distant. Lightning strikes the top about 200 times (30 storms) per annum.

The tallest tower built before the era of television masts is the Eiffel Tower in Paris, France, designed by Alexandre Gustav Eiffel (1832–1923) for the Paris Exhibition and completed on 31 Mar 1889. It was 300·51 m *985 ft 11 in* tall, now extended by a TV antenna, to 320·75 m *1052 ft 4 in* and weighs 7340 tonnes *7224 tons.* The maximum sway in high winds is 12·7 cm *5 in.* The whole iron edifice, which has 1792 steps, took 2 years, 2 months and 2 days to build and cost 7 799 401 francs 31 centimes.

The tallest self-supported tower in Great Britain is the 329·18 m *1080 ft* tall Independent Broadcasting Authority transmitter at Emley Moor, West Yorkshire, completed in September 1971. The structure, which cost £900 000, has an enclosed room at the 263·65 m *865 ft* level and weighs with its foundations more than 15 000 tonnes. The tallest tower of the pre-television era was the New Brighton Tower of 171·29 m *562 ft* built on Merseyside in 1897–1900 and dismantled in 1919–21.

Bridges

Oldest

Arch construction was understood by the Sumerians as early as 3200 BC and a reference exists to a Nile bridge in 2650 BC. The oldest surviving datable bridge in the world is the slab stone single arch bridge over the River Meles in Smyrna (now Izmir), Turkey, which dates from *c.* 850 BC.

The clapper bridges of Dartmoor and Exmoor (e.g. the Tarr Steps over the River Barle, Exmoor, Somerset) are thought to be of prehistoric types although none of the existing examples can be certainly dated. They are made of large slabs of stone placed over boulders. The Romans built stone bridges in England and remains of these have been found at Corbridge (Roman, Corstopitum), Northumberland dating to the 2nd century AD; Chesters, Northumberland; and Willowford, Cumbria. Remains of a very early wooden bridge have been found at Aldwinkle, Northamptonshire.

LONGEST
Cable suspension

The world's longest bridge span is the main span of the Humber Estuary Bridge, England at 1410 m *4626 ft.* Work began on 27 July 1972, after a decision announced on 22 Jan 1966. The towers are 162·5 m *533 ft 1⅝ in* tall from datum and are 36 mm *1⅜ in* out of parallel, to allow for the curvature of the Earth. Including the Hessle and the Barton side spans, the bridge stretches 2220 m or *1·37 miles.* It was structurally completed on 18 July 1980 at a cost of £96 million and was opened by H M the Queen on 17 July 1981. Tolls, ranging between 70 pence for motorcycles and £8 for heavy vehicles, as at January 1988, are the highest in Britain. By 1995 the debt is expected to grow to £500 million.

The double-deck road Akashi-Kaikyo bridge linking Honshū and Shikoku, Japan is planned to be completed in 1998. The main span will be 1980 m *6496 ft* in length with an overall suspended length with side spans totalling 3560 m *11 680 ft.* The Seto-Ohashi double-deck road and rail bridge linking Kojima, Honshu with Sakaide, Shikoku, Japan opened on 10 Apr 1988 at a cost of £4900 million and 17 lives. The tolls for cars are £24 each way for the 12·7 km *7·9 miles* on spans and viaducts.

Work on the Messina Bridge linking Sicily with Calabria on the Italian mainland is due to start in 1989. The single span will be the world's largest by far at 3 320 m *10 892 ft.* The escalating cost of such a project was estimated by 1982 already to have passed the £10 250 million mark. Plans for a £183 million second Severn Bridge were published in July 1986 from Sudbrook, Gwent to Redwick in Avon. Completion is scheduled for *c.* 1995.

Cantilever

The Quebec Bridge (Pont de Québec) over the St Lawrence River in Canada has the longest cantilever truss span of any in the world—549 m *1800 ft* between the piers and 987 m *3239 ft* overall. It carries a railway track and 2 carriageways. Begun in 1899, it was finally opened to traffic on 3 Dec 1917 at a cost of 87 lives, and $Can. 22 500 000.

The longest cantilever bridge in Great Britain is the Forth Bridge. Its two main spans are 521 m *1710 ft* long. It carries a double railway track over the Firth of Forth 47·5 m *156 ft* above the water level. Work commenced in November 1882 and the first test trains crossed on 22 Jan 1890 after an expenditure of £3 million. It was officially opened on 4 Mar 1890. Of the 4500 workers who built it, 57 were killed in various accidents.

Steel arch

The longest steel arch bridge in the world is the New River Gorge Bridge, near Fayetteville, West Virginia, completed in 1977 with a span of 518·2 m *1700 ft.*

The longest steel arch bridge in Great Britain is the Runcorn–Widnes bridge, Cheshire opened on 21 July 1961. It has a span of 329·8 m *1082 ft.*

Floating bridge

The longest floating bridge in the world is the Second Lake Washington Bridge, Evergreen, Seattle, Washington State. Its total length is 3839 m *12 596 ft* and its floating section measures 2291 m *7518 ft.* It was built at a total cost of $15 000 000 and completed in August 1963.

Covered bridge

The longest covered bridge in the world is that at

Hartland, New Brunswick, Canada measuring 390·8 m *1282 ft* overall, completed in 1899.

Railway bridge

The longest railway bridge in the world is the Huey P. Long Bridge, Metairie, Louisiana, with a railway section 7009 m *22 996 ft (7 km 4·35 miles)* long It was completed on 16 Dec 1935 with a longest span of 241 m *790 ft.*

The longest railway bridge in Britain is the second Tay Bridge (3552 m *11 653 ft*), across the Firth of Tay at Dundee opened on 20 June 1887. Of the 85 spans, 74 (length 3136 m *10 289 ft*) are over the waterway. The 878 brick arches of the London Bridge to Deptford Creek viaduct built in 1836 extend for 6·0 km *3¾ miles.*

Longest bridging

The world's longest bridging is the Second Lake Pontchartrain Causeway, completed on 23 Mar 1969, joining Lewisburg and Metairie, Louisiana. It has a length of 38 422 m *126 055 ft.* It cost $29 900 000 and is 69 m *228 ft* longer than the adjoining First Causeway completed in 1956.

The longest railway viaduct in the world is the rock-filled Great Salt Lake Railroad Trestle, carrying the Southern Pacific Railroad 19 km *11·85 miles* across the Great Salt Lake, Utah. It was opened as a pile and trestle bridge on 8 Mar 1904, but converted to rock fill in 1955–60.

The longest stone arch bridging is the 1161 m *3810 ft* long Rockville Bridge north of Harrisburg, Pennsylvania,

---

Widest bridge ▲ An aerial view of the traffic-laden Sydney Harbour Bridge – helping to keep the beer moving! (Photo: Aspect)

Aqueduct ▼ The triple-tiered aqueduct Pont du Gard, built in AD 19 near Nîmes, France, is 160 ft *48 m* high. (Photo: Ancient Art and Architecture Collection)

---

with 48 spans containing 196 000 tonnes of stone and completed in 1901.

Widest bridge

The world's widest long-span bridge is the 502·9 m *1650 ft* span Sydney Harbour Bridge, Australia (48·8 m *160 ft* wide). It carries two electric overhead railway tracks, 8 lanes of roadway and a cycle and footway. It was officially opened on 19 Mar 1932. The Crawford Street Bridge in Providence, Rhode Island, has a width of 350 m *1147 ft.* The River Roch is bridged for a distance of 445 m *1460 ft* where the culvert passes through the centre of Rochdale, Manchester and this is sometimes claimed to be a breadth.

Bridge Building

A 10-man team of the 2nd Field Support Squadron, 26th Regiment of Royal Engineers constructed a bridge across a 9-metre gap using a 5-bay MGB in 9 min 41 sec at their training area at Iserlohn, West Germany on 10 Mar 1988. A 546·13 m *1792 ft* long rope suspension bridge was erected at Spaarnwoude, Holland by 1500 boy scouts and girl guides from 28 Jul–6 Aug 1987.

HIGHEST

The highest bridge in the world is the bridge over the Royal Gorge of the Arkansas River in Colorado which is 321 m *1053 ft* above the water level. It is a suspension bridge with a main span of 268 m *880 ft* and was constructed in 6 months, ending on 6 Dec 1929. The highest railway bridge in the world is the single-track span at Fades, outside Clermont-Ferrand, France. It was built in 1901–9 with a span of 144 m *472 ft* and is 132·5 m *435 ft* above the River Sioule. The road bridge at the highest altitude in the world, 5602 m *18 380 ft,* is the 30 m *98·4 ft* long Bailey Bridge built by the Indian Army in Aug 1982 near Khardung La, in Ladakh, India.

The highest railway bridge in Great Britain is the Ballochmyle viaduct over the River Ayr, Ayrshire built 51·5 m *169 ft* over the river bed in 1846–8 with the then world's longest masonry arch span of 55·16 m *181 ft.*

AQUEDUCTS
Longest ancient

The greatest of ancient aqueducts was the Aqueduct of Carthage in Tunisia, which ran 141 km *87·6 miles* from the springs of Zaghouan to Djebel Djougar. It was built by the Romans during the reign of Publius Aelius Hadrianus (AD 117–138). By 1895, 344 arches still survived. Its original capacity has been calculated at 31·8 million litres *7 000 000 gal* per day. The tallest of the 14 arches of Aguas Livres Aqueduct, built in Lisbon, Portugal, in 1784 is 65 m *213 ft 3 in.*

Longest modern

The world's longest aqueduct, in the non-classical sense of water conduit, excluding irrigation canals, is the

California State Water Project aqueduct, completed in 1974, to a length of 1329 km *826 miles* of which 619 km *385 miles* is canalised.

The longest bridged aqueduct in Britain is the Pont Cysylltau in Clwyd on the Frankton to Llantisilio branch of the Shropshire Union Canal. It is 307 m *1007 ft* long, has 19 arches up to 36 m *121 ft* high above low water on the Dee. Designed by Thomas Telford (1757–1834) it was opened in 1805. The oldest is the Dundas aqueduct on the Kennet and Avon canal near Bath. It was built in 1810 and restored in 1984.

Canals

Earliest

Relics of the oldest canals in the world, dated by archaeologists c. 4000 BC, were discovered near Mandali, Iraq early in 1968.

The earliest canals in Britain were first cut by the Romans. In the Midlands the 17 km *11 mile* long Fossdyke Canal between Lincoln and the River Trent at Torksey was built in about AD 65 and was scoured in 1122. It is still in use today.

Though the Exeter Canal was cut as early as 1564–6, the first wholly artificial major navigation canal in the United Kingdom was the 29·7 km *18½ mile* long canal with 14 locks from Whitecoat Point to Newry, Northern Ireland opened on 28 Mar 1742. The Sankey Navigation Canal in Lancashire, 12·8 km *8 miles* in length, with 10 locks, was opened in November 1757.

Longest

The longest canalised system in the world is the Volga–Baltic Canal opened in April 1965. It runs 2300 km *1850 miles* from Astrakhan up the Volga, via Kuybyshev, Gor'kiy and Lake Ladoga, to Leningrad.

The longest canal of the ancient world has been the Grand Canal of China from Peking (Beijing) to Hangchou. It was begun in 540 BC and not completed until 1327 by which time it extended (including canalised river sections) for 1781 km *1107 miles*. The estimated work force c. AD 600 reached 5 000 000 on the Pien section. Having been allowed by 1950 to silt up to the point that it was nowhere more than 1·8 m *6 ft* deep, it is now, however, plied by vessels of up to 2000 tonnes.

The Beloye More (White Sea) Baltic Canal from Belomorsk to Povenets, in the USSR, is 227 km *141 miles* long with 19 locks. It was completed with the use of forced labour in 1933. It cannot accommodate ships of more than 5 m *16 ft* in draught.

The world's longest big ship canal is the Suez Canal linking the Red and Mediterranean Seas, opened on 16 Nov 1869 but inoperative from June 1967 to June 1975. The canal was planned by the French diplomatist Comte Ferdinand de Lesseps (1805–94) and work began on 25 Apr 1859. It is 161·9 km *100·6 miles* in length from Port Said lighthouse to Suez Roads and 60 m *197 ft* wide. The work force consisted of 8213 men and 368 camels. The largest vessel to transit has been SS *Settebello* of 322 446 tonnes dwt (length 338·43 m *1110·3 ft*, beam 57·35 m *188·1 ft* at a maximum draft of 22·35 m *73·3 ft*). This was southbound in ballast on 6 Aug 1986. USS *Shreveport* transited southbound on 15–16 Aug 1984 in a record 7 hr 45 min.

Canals and river navigations in Great Britain amount to approximately 5630 km *3 500 miles* with 290 km *150 miles* being restored. Of this total 4000 km *2500 miles* are inter-linked.

The geographical north-south extreme is Ripon, North Yorks, to Goldalming, Surrey at 670 km *415 miles*.

Busiest

The busiest big ship canal is the Kiel Canal linking the North Sea with the Baltic Sea in West Germany with over 45 000 transits recorded in 1987. Next comes the Suez Canal with over 20 000 transits and third the Panama Canal with over 10 000 transits. Busiest in terms of tonnage of shipping using it is the Suez Canal with nearly 440 000 000 grt.

Longest seaway

The world's longest artificial seaway is the St Lawrence Seaway (304 km *189 miles* long) along the New York State–Ontario border from Montreal to Lake Ontario, which enables ships up to 222 m *728 ft* long and 8 m *26·2 ft* draught, some of which are of 26 400 tonnes *26 000 tons*, to sail 3769 km *2342 miles* from the North Atlantic up the St Lawrence estuary and across the Great Lakes to Duluth, Minnesota, on Lake Superior (183 m *602 ft* above sea level). The project, begun in 1954, cost $470 000 000 and was opened on 25 Apr 1959.

Irrigation canal

The longest irrigation canal in the world is the Karakumskiy Kanal, stretching 850 km *528 miles* from Haun-Khan to Ashkhabad, Turkmenistan, USSR. In September 1971 the 'navigable' length reached 450 km *280 miles*. The length of the £370 million project will reach 1300 km *930 miles*.

LOCKS
Largest

The world's largest single lock is the sea lock at Zeebrugge, Belgium which measures 500 × 57 × 23 m *1640 × 187 × 75·4 ft* giving a volume of 655 300 m³ *857 066 yd³*. The Berendrecht Lock, Antwerp will have the same length but a width of 68 m *223 ft* at a depth of 21·5 m *70·5 ft* giving a volume of 731 000 m³ *956 000 yd³*.

The largest and deepest lock in the United Kingdom is the Royal Portbury Entrance Lock, Bristol which measures 366 × 42·7 m *1200 × 140 ft* and has a depth of 20·2 m *66 ft*. It was opened in August 1977.

Deepest

The world's deepest lock is the John Day dam lock on the Columbia river, Oregon and Washington, USA completed in 1963. It can raise or lower barges 34·4 m *113 ft* and is served by a 998 tonne *982 ton* gate.

Highest rise and longest flight

The world's highest lock elevator overcomes a head of 68·58 m *225 ft* at Ronquières on the Charleroi–Brussels Canal, Belgium. The two 236-wheeled caissons, each able to carry 1350 tons, take 22 min to cover the 1432 m *4698 ft* long ramp. The highest rise of any boat-carrying plane in Britain was the 68·6 m *225 ft* of the 285 m *935 ft* long Hobbacott Down plane on the Bude Canal, Cornwall.

The longest flight of locks in the United Kingdom is on the Worcester and Birmingham Canal at Tardebigge, Hereford and Worcester, where in a 4 km *2½ mile* stretch there are the Tardebigge (30 locks) and Stoke (6 locks) flights which together drop 78·9 m *259 ft*. The flight of locks on the Huddersfield Canal, closed in 1944, on the 11·6 km *7¼ mile* stretch to Marsden numbered 42.

Largest cut

The Gaillard Cut (known as 'the Ditch') on the Panama Canal is 82 m *270 ft* deep between Gold Hill and Contractor's Hill with a bottom width of 152 m *500 ft*. In one day in 1911 as many as 333 dirt trains each carrying 363 tonnes *357 tons* left this site. The total amount of earth excavated for the whole Panama Canal as of 1 Oct 1979 was 509 338 960 m³ *666 194 450 yd³* which total will be raised by the further widening of the Gaillard Cut.

Dams

Earliest

The earliest known dams were those uncovered by the British School of Archaeology in Jerusalem in 1974 at Jawa in Jordan. These stone-faced earth dams are dated to c. 3200 BC.

Most massive

Measured by volume, the largest dam in the world is the earth and rock fill Pati dam on the Pavanã river, Argentina which has a volume of 238 180 000 m³ *311 527 000 yd³*. It is 174·9 km *108·6 miles* in length and 36 m *118 ft* high. The Chapetón dam also on the Pavanã is planned to have a volume of 296 200 000 m³ *387 400 000 yd³* and a crest length of 224 km *139 miles*. Both will be surpassed in volume by the Syncrude Tailings Dam in Canada with 540 000 000 m³ *706 000 000 yd³*.

Largest concrete

The world's largest concrete dam, and the largest concrete structure in the world, is the Grand Coulee Dam on the Columbia River, Washington State, USA. Work on the dam was begun in 1933, it began working on 22 Mar 1941, and was completed in 1942 at a cost of $56 million. It has a crest length of 1272 m *4173 ft* and is 167 m *550 ft* high. It contains 8 092 000 m³ *10 585 000 yd³* of concrete and weighs approximately 19 595 000 tonnes *19 285 000 tons*.

Highest

The highest dam in the world will be the 335 m *1098 ft* high Rogunsky earth-fill dam across the Vakhsh river, Tadzhikistan, USSR with a crest length of only 602 m *1975 ft* and a volume of 85 million m³. Building since 1973, the completion date is still unconfirmed. Meanwhile the tallest completed is the 300 m *984 ft* high Nurek dam, USSR of 58 million m³ volume.

Longest

The 41 m *134·5 ft* high Yacyreta–Apipe dam across the Paraná on the Paraguay–Argentina borders extends for 72 km *44·7 miles*. In the early 17th century an impounding dam of moderate height was built in Lake Hungtze, Kiangsu, China, to a reputed length of 100 km *62 miles*.

The longest sea dam is the Afsluitdijk stretching 32·5 km *20·195 miles* across the mouth of the Zuider Zee in two sections of 2·499 km *1·553 miles* (mainland of North Holland to the Isle of Wieringen) and 30 km *18·641 miles* from Wieringen to Friesland. It has a sea-level width of 89 m *293 ft* and a height of 7·5 m *24 ft 7 in*.

Strongest

The world's strongest structure will be the 242 m *793 ft* high Sayano-Shusenskaya dam on the River Yenisey, USSR which is designed to bear a load of 18 000 000 tonnes from a fully-filled reservoir of 31 300 million m³ *41 000 million yd³* capacity.

The most massive dam in Britain is the Northumbrian Water Authority's Kielder Dam, a 52 m *170 ft* high earth embankment measuring 1140 m *3740 ft* in length and 5 300 000 m³ *6 932 000 yd³*. There are longer low dams or barrages of the valley cut-off type, notably the Hanningfield Dam, Essex, built from July 1952 to August 1956 to a length of 2088 m *6850 ft* and a height of 19·7 m *64·5 ft*. The rock-fill Llyn Brianne Dam, Dyfed is Britain's highest dam reaching 91 m *298½ ft* in Nov 1971. It became operational on 20 July 1972.

Largest reservoir

The most voluminous man-made reservoir is the Kakhovskaya Reservoir, USSR, with a volume of 182 km³ *147 550 000 acre-feet*. The world's largest artificial lake measured by surface area is Lake Volta, Ghana, formed by the Akosombo Dam completed in 1965. By 1969 the lake had filled to an area of 8482 km² *3275 miles²* with a shoreline 7250 km *4500 miles* in length.

The completion in 1954 of the Owen Falls Dam near Jinja, Uganda, across the northern exit of the White Nile from the Victoria Nyanza marginally raised the level of that *natural* lake by adding 270 km³ *218 900 000 acre-feet*, and technically turned it into a reservoir with a surface area of 6·9 million ha *17 169 920 acres*.

Tunnels

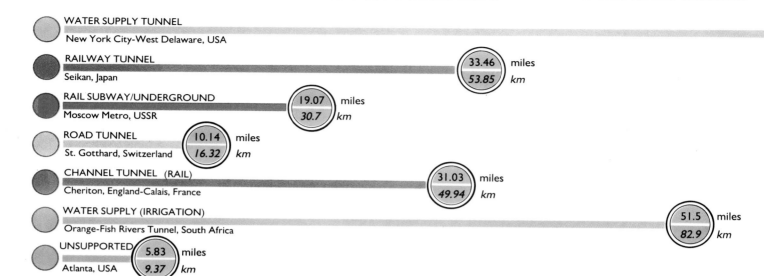

WATER SUPPLY TUNNEL
New York City-West Delaware, USA

RAILWAY TUNNEL
Seikan, Japan — **33.46** miles / **53.85** km

RAIL SUBWAY/UNDERGROUND
Moscow Metro, USSR — **19.07** miles / **30.7** km

ROAD TUNNEL
St. Gotthard, Switzerland — **10.14** miles / **16.32** km

CHANNEL TUNNEL (RAIL)
Cheriton, England-Calais, France — **31.03** miles / **49.94** km

WATER SUPPLY (IRRIGATION)
Orange-Fish Rivers Tunnel, South Africa — **51.5** miles / **82.9** km

UNSUPPORTED
Atlanta, USA — **5.83** miles / **9.37** km

The $4-billion Tucurui Dam in Brazil of 64·3 million m³, had, by 1984, converted the Tocantins River into a 1900 km *1180 mile* long chain of lakes.

The most capacious reservoir in Britain is Kielder Water in the North Tyne Valley, Northumberland, which filled to 2000 million hl *44 000 million gallons* from 15 Dec 1980 to mid-1982, and which acquired a surface area of 1086 ha *2684 acres* and a perimeter of 43·4 km *27 miles* to become England's second largest lake. Rutland Water has a lesser capacity (124 106 million l *27 300 million gallons*) and a lesser perimeter (38·6 km *24 miles*) but a greater surface area of 1254 ha *3100 acres*. The deepest reservoir in Europe is Loch Morar, Inverness-shire, Scotland, with a maximum depth of 310 m *1017 ft* (see also page 59).

The largest wholly artificial reservoir in Great Britain is the Queen Mary Reservoir, built from August 1914 to June 1925, at Littleton, near Staines, Surrey, with an available storage capacity of 369·6 million hl *8130 million gal* and a water area of 286 ha *707 acres*. The length of the perimeter embankment is 6329 m *20 766 ft* (6·32 km *3·93 miles*).

Largest polder (*Reclaimed land*)
The largest of the five great polders in the old Zuider Zee, Netherlands, will be the 60 300 ha *149 000 acre* (603 km² *232·8 miles²*) Markerwaard. Work on the 106 km *66 mile* long surrounding dyke was begun in 1957. The water area remaining after the erection of the 1927–32 dam (32 km *20 miles* in length) is called IJssel meer, which will have a final area of 1262·6 km² *487·5 miles²*.

Largest levees
The most massive levees ever built are the Mississippi levees begun in 1717 but vastly augmented by the US Federal Government after the disastrous floods of 1927. These extend for 2787 km *1732 miles* along the main river from Cape Girardeau, Missouri, to the Gulf of Mexico and comprise more than 765 million m³ *1000 million yd³* of earthworks. Levees on the tributaries comprise an additional 3200 km *2000 miles*. The Pine Bluff, Arkansas to Venice, Louisiana segment of 1046 km *650 miles* is continuous.

Tunnels

LONGEST

Vehicular (*Rail*)
The 53·85 km *33·46 mile* long Seikan Rail Tunnel has been bored 240 m *787 ft* beneath sea level and 100 m *328 ft* below the sea bed of the Tsugaru Strait between Tappi Saki, Honshū, and Fukushima, Hokkaidō, Japan. Tests started on the sub-aqueous section (23·3 km

14·5 miles) in 1964 and construction in June 1972. It was holed through on 27 Jan 1983 after a loss of 34 lives. The cost by the finish of tunnelling after 20 years 10 months in March 1985 and subsequent maintenance to Feb 1987 was 800 000 million yen. The fast test run took place on 13 Mar 1988.

Great Britain's longest main-line railway tunnel is the Severn Tunnel (6 km *4 miles 628 yd*), linking Avon and Gwent completed with 76 400 000 bricks between 1873 and 1886.

Subway
The world's longest continuous subway tunnel is the Moscow Metro underground railway line from Belyaevo to Medvedkovo. It is *c.* 30·7 km *19·07 miles* long and was completed in 1978/9.

Road
The longest road tunnel is the 16·32 km *10·14 mile* long two-lane St Gotthard Road Tunnel from Göschenen to Airolo, Switzerland, opened to traffic on 5 Sept 1980. Nineteen lives were lost during the construction, begun in autumn 1969, at a cost of SF 686 million.

The longest road tunnel in the United Kingdom is the Mersey Tunnel, joining Liverpool and Birkenhead, Merseyside. It is 3·43 km *2·13 miles* long, or 4·62 km *2·87 miles* including branch tunnels. Work was begun in December 1925 and it was opened by HM King George V on 18 July 1934. The total cost was £7¾ million. The 11 m *36 ft* wide 4-lane roadway carries nearly 7½ million vehicles a year. The first tube of the second Mersey Tunnel was opened on 24 June 1971.

Excavation of the projected £6000 million Eurotunnel under the English Channel between Cheriton near Folkestone, Kent and Sargatte by Calais, France began on 1 July 1987 and should be completed by 1993. The length of the twin rail tunnels of 7·6 m *24 ft 11 in* diameter will be 49·94 km *31·03 miles*.

Largest
The largest diameter road tunnel in the world is that blasted through Yerba Buena Island, San Francisco, California. It is 23 m *76 ft* wide, 17 m *58 ft* high and 165 m *540 ft* long. More than 80 000 000 vehicles pass through on its two decks every year.

Water supply
The world's longest tunnel of any kind is the New York City West Delaware water-supply tunnel, begun in 1937 and completed in 1944. It has a diameter of 4·1 m *13 ft 6 in* and runs for 168·9 km *105 miles* from the Rondout Reservoir into the Hillview Reservoir, on the border of Yonkers and New York City.

The longest water-supply tunnel in the United Kingdom is the Kielder Water tunnel system. These tunnels have

been driven through the rock to link the Tyne Valley with the Wear Valley. A pipe passes under the River Wear and the tunnel then proceeds to link up with the Tees Valley for 32·18 km *20·2 miles*.

Hydro-electric, irrigation or sewerage
The longest irrigation tunnel in the world is the 82·9 km *51·5 mile* long Orange-Fish Rivers Tunnel, South Africa, begun in 1967 at an estimated cost of £60 million. The boring was completed in April 1973. The lining to a minimum thickness of 23 cm *9 in* will give a completed diameter of 5·33 m *17 ft 6 in*.

The Majes project in Peru involves 98 km *60·9 miles* of tunnels for hydro-electric and water-supply purposes. The dam is at 4200 m *13 780 ft* altitude. The Chicago TARP (Tunnels and Reservoir Plan) in Illinois, involves 193 km *120 miles* of sewerage tunnelling.

Bridge-tunnel
The world's longest bridge-tunnel system is the Chesapeake Bay Bridge-Tunnel, extending 28·40 km *17·65 miles* from Eastern Shore, Virginia Peninsula to Virginia Beach, Virginia, USA. It cost $200 000 000 and was completed after 42 months and opened to traffic on 15 Apr 1964.

The longest bridged section is Trestle C (7·34 km *4·56 miles* long) and the longest tunnel is the Thimble Shoal Channel Tunnel (1·75 km *1·09 miles*).

Canal-tunnel
The world's longest and largest canal tunnel is the Rove Tunnel on the Canal de Marseille au Rhône in the South of France. Completed in 1927 it is 7120 m *23 359 ft* long, 22 m *72 ft* wide and 11·4 m *37 ft* high. Built to be navigated by sea-going ships, it was closed in 1963 following a collapse of the structure and has not been re-opened.

The world's oldest navigable canal tunnel is the Malpas Tunnel on the Canal du Midi in south-west France. Completed in 1681, it is 161 m *528 ft* long. Its completion enabled vessels to navigate from the Atlantic Ocean to the Mediterranean Sea via the river Garonne to Toulouse and the Canal du Midi to Sete.

The longest canal tunnel in Great Britain is the Standedge (more properly Stanedge) Tunnel in West Yorkshire on the Huddersfield Narrow Canal built from 1794 to 4 Apr 1811. It measures 5·21 km *3 miles 418 yd* in length and was closed on 21 Dec 1944. However it is currently undergoing restoration.

The British canal system has contained 84 tunnels exceeding 27·4 m *30 yd* of which 48 are still open. The longest of these is the 2·79 km *3056 yd* long Blisworth Tunnel on the Grand Union in Northamptonshire.

The now closed Huddersfield Narrow Canal is the

highest in the United Kingdom, at 194 m *638 ft* above sea level.

Tunnelling

The longest unsupported example of a machine-bored tunnel is the Three Rivers Water Tunnel driven 9·37 km *30 769 linear feet* with a 3·2 m *10·5 ft* diameter for the city of Atlanta, Georgia, from April 1980 to February 1982.

S & M Constructors Inc of Cleveland, Ohio achieved 54·5 m *179 ft* in a day through the granite, schist and gneiss.

The NCB record of 251·4 m *824·8 ft* for a 3·80 m *12½ ft* wide, 2 m *6½ ft* high roadway by a team of 35 pitmen in 5 days was set at West Cannock, Staffordshire No 5 Colliery from 30 Mar–3 Apr 1981.

Specialised Structures

Advertising signs

Highest

The highest advertising signs in the world are the four Bank of Montreal logos atop the 72-storey 285 m *935 ft* tall First Canadian Place, Toronto. Each sign, built by Claude Neon Industries Ltd, measures 6·09×6·70 m *20×22 ft* and was lifted by helicopter.

Largest

The most conspicuous sign ever erected was the electric Citroën sign on the Eiffel Tower, Paris. It was switched on on 4 July 1925, and could be seen 38 km *24 miles* away. It was in six colours with 250 000 lamps and 90 km *56 miles* of electric cables. The letter 'N' which terminated the name 'Citroën' between the second and third levels measured 20·8 m *68 ft 5 in* in height. The whole apparatus was taken down after 11 years in 1936. For the largest ground sign see Chapter 6, page 85, 'Largest letter'.

The letter 'M' installed on the Great Mississippi River Bridge is 548·6 m *1800 ft* long and comprises 200 high intensity lamps. The world's largest neon sign measures 64 × 16·7 m *210 × 55 ft* built for Marlboro cigarettes at Hung Hom, Kowloon, Hong Kong in May 1986. It contains 10 668 m *35 000 ft* of neon tubing and weighs approximately 113 tons *114·7 tonnes*. The world's largest reported hoarding is one 44·5 m *146 ft* long and 17·5 m *57 ft 5 in* tall erected by Propaganda Campanella on Route N9, Buenos Aires, Argentina. The largest 'hoarding' in Britain measures 68·9 m *226 ft* by 16·5 m *54 ft* and was produced by Forwardair Ltd. The site is the roof of the Brentford Football Club stand, at its Griffin Park, Middlesex ground which is on the flight path of London, Heathrow airport. Britain's largest illuminated sign is the name NEI NUCLEAR SYSTEMS LTD extending 52 m *170 ft 6 in* installed at their factory in Gateshead, Tyne and Wear, in June 1983. It can be seen from the air at a distance of 32 km *20 miles*.

An interior lit fascia advertising sign in Clearwater, Florida, completed by Adco Sign Corp in April 1983 measures 356·17 m *1168 ft 6½ in* in length.

The world's most massive animated sign is reputed to be that outside the Circus Circus Hotel, Reno, Nevada named Topsy, the Clown. It is 38·7 m *127 ft* tall and weighs over 40 tons *40·8 tonnes* with 2·25 km *1·4 miles* of neon tubing. His smile measures 4·26 m *14 ft* across.

Barn

The largest barn in Britain is one at Frindsbury, Kent. Its length is 66·7 m *219 ft* and it is still wholly roofed. The Ipsden Barn, Oxfordshire, is 117 m *385½ ft* long but 9 m *30 ft* wide 1074 m² (*11 565 ft²*). The longest tithe barn in Britain is one measuring 81 m *268 ft* long at Wyke Farm, near Sherborne, Dorset.

Bonfire

The largest recorded bonfire constructed was in Espel, in the Noordoost Polder, Netherlands. It stood 27·87 m 91 ft 5 in high with a base circumference of 84·40 m *276 ft 11 in* and was lit on 19 Apr 1987.

The largest in Britain was the Coronation bonfire atop Arrowthwaite Brows, Whitehaven, Cumbria lit in 1902 with 800 tons *812 tonnes* of timber, 4546 litres *1000 gal* each of petroleum and tar. It was octagonal in shape and built to a height of 36·67 m *120 ft* with a base circumference of 47·2 m *155 ft* tapering to 6·1 m *20 ft*.

Longest breakwater

The world's longest breakwater is that which protects the Port of Galveston, Texas, USA. The granite South Breakwater is 10·85 km *6·74 miles* in length.

The longest breakwater in Great Britain is the North Breakwater at Holyhead, Anglesey, which is 2395 m (*1·48 miles 7860 ft*) in length and was completed in 1873.

Buildings demolished by explosives

The largest building demolished by explosives has been the 21-storey Traymore Hotel, Atlantic City, New Jersey, on 26 May 1972 by Controlled Demolition Inc of Towson, Maryland. This 600-room hotel had a cubic capacity of 181 340 m³ *6 495 500 ft³*. The tallest chimney ever demolished by explosives was the Matla Power Station chimney, Kriel, South Africa on 19 July 1981. It stood 275 m *902 ft* and was brought down by The Santon (Steeplejack) Co Ltd of Manchester, England.

Cemetery

The world's largest cemetery is that in Leningrad, which contains over 500 000 of the 1 300 000 victims of the German army's siege of 1941–3. The largest cemetery in the United Kingdom is Brookwood Cemetery, Brookwood, Surrey. It is owned by the London Necropolis Co and is 200 ha *500 acres* in extent with more than 225 000 interments.

Column

The tallest columns (as opposed to obelisks) in the world are the 36 fluted pillars 27·43 m *90 ft* tall, of Vermont marble in the colonnade of the Education Building, Albany, New York. Their base diameter is 1·98 m *6½ ft*. The tallest load-bearing stone columns in the world are those measuring 21 m *69 ft* in the Hall of Columns of the Temple of Amun at Karnak, opposite Thebes on the Nile, the ancient capital of Upper Egypt. They were built in the 19th dynasty in the reign of Rameses II *c.* 1270 BC.

Crematorium

The oldest crematorium in Britain was built in 1879 at Woking, Surrey. The first cremation took place there on 26 Mar 1885, the practice having been found legal after the cremation of Iesu Grist Price on Caerlan Fields, Llantrisant, Mid Glamorgan on 13 Jan 1884. The total number of people cremated in Britain since has been 11 172 452 (to 31 Dec 1985), and the percentage is now 68%. The percentage in Japan is 93·4%.

The largest crematorium in the world is at the Nikolo-Arkhangelskoye Cemetery, East Moscow, with 7 twin cremators of British design, completed in March 1972. It has several Halls of Farewell for atheists. Currently, Britain's largest is the City of London Crematorium, E.12.

The all-time total of 264 312 cremations at Golders Green Crematorium, London, since 1902, remains unsurpassed as does its record 7509 in 1957.

Dome

The world's largest dome is the Louisiana Superdome, New Orleans. It has a diameter of 207·26 m *680 ft*. (See pages 111 for further details.) The largest dome of ancient architecture is that of the Pantheon, built in Rome in AD 112, with a diameter of 43 m *142½ ft*.

The largest dome in Britain is that of the Bell Sports Centre, Perth, Scotland, with a diameter of 67 m *222 ft* designed by D. B. Cockburn and constructed in Baltic whitewood by Muirhead & Sons Ltd of Grangemouth, Central, Scotland.

Door

The largest doors in the world are the four in the Vehicle Assembly Building near Cape Canaveral, Florida, with a height of 140 m *460 ft* (see page 107). The world's heaviest door is that leading to the laser target room at Lawrence Livermore National Laboratory, California. It weighs 321·4 tons *326·5 tonnes*, is up to 2·43 m *8 ft* thick and was installed by Overly.

The largest doors in Great Britain are those to the Britannia Assembly Hall, at Filton airfield, Avon. The doors are 315 m *1035 ft* in length and 20 m *67 ft* high, divided into three bays each 105 m *345 ft* across. The largest simple hinged door in Britain is that of Ye Old Bull's Head, Beaumaris, Anglesey, which is 3·35 m *11 ft* wide and 3·96 m *13 ft* high.

The oldest doors in Britain are those of Hadstock Church, near Saffron Walden, Essex, which date from *c.* 1040 AD and exhibit evidence of Danish workmanship.

Dry dock

The largest dry dock in the world with a maximum shipbuilding capacity of 1 200 000 tons deadweight is the Okpo No 1 Dry Dock, Chojé Island in South Korea. It measures 525 m *1722·4 ft* long by 131 m *430 ft* wide and was completed in 1979. The dock gates 14 m *46 ft* high and 10 m *32·8 ft* thick at the base are the world's largest.

The largest shipbuilding dry dock in the UK is the Belfast Harbour Commission and Harland and Wolff building dock in Belfast, Northern Ireland. It was excavated by Wimpey to a length of 556 m *1825 ft* and a width of 93 m *305 ft* and can accommodate tankers of 1 000 000 tons deadweight. Work was begun on 26 Jan 1968 and completed on 30 Nov 1969 and involved the excavation of 306 000 m³ *400 000 yd³*.

Earthworks

The largest earthworks in the world carried out prior to the mechanical era were the Linear Earth Boundaries of the Benin Empire in the Bendel state of Nigeria. These were first reported in 1900 and partially surveyed in 1967. In April 1973 it was estimated by Patrick Darling that the total length of the earthworks was probably between 6400–12 800 km *4000 and 8000 miles* with the amount of earth moved estimated at from 380–460 million m³ *500 to 600 million yd³*.

The greatest prehistoric earthwork in Britain is Wansdyke, originally Wodensdic, which ran 138 km *86 miles* from Portishead, Avon to Inkpen Beacon and Ludgershall, south of Hungerford, Berkshire. It was built by the Belgae as their north boundary. The most extensive single site earthwork is the Dorset Cursus near Gussage St Michael 8 km *5 miles* SW of Cranborne, dating from *c.* 1900 BC. The workings are 9·7 km *6 miles* long, involving an estimated 191 000 m³ *250 000 yd³* of excavations. The largest of the Celtic hill-forts is that known as Mew Dun, or Maiden Castle, 3 km *2 miles* SW of Dorchester, Dorset. It covers 46·5 ha *115 acres* and was abandoned shortly after AD 43.

Fence

The longest fence in the world is the dingo-proof fence enclosing the main sheep areas of Australia. The wire fence is 1·8 m *6 ft* high, 30 cm *1 ft* underground and

stretches for 5531 km *3437 miles*. The Queensland State Government discontinued full maintenance in 1982 but 500 km *310 miles* is now being repaired.

The world's tallest fences are security screens 20 m *65·6 ft* high erected by Harrop-Allin of Pretoria in November 1981 to protect fuel depots and refineries at Sasolburg, South Africa.

Flagstaff

The tallest flagstaff ever erected was that outside the Oregon Building at the 1915 Panama-Pacific International Exposition in San Francisco, California. Trimmed from a Douglas fir, it stood 91 m *299 ft 7 in* in height and weighed 47 tonnes *45 tons*. The tallest unsupported flag pole in the world is the 85·95 m *282 ft* tall steel pole weighing 54 430 kg *120 000 lb* which was erected on 22 Aug 1985 at the Canadian Expo 86 exhibition in Vancouver, British Columbia and supporting a gigantic ice hockey stick 62·5 m *205 ft* in length. Mr Sherrold Haddad of Flag Chevrolet Oldsmobile Ltd was instrumental in moving and reconstructing the flagstaff where it has been relocated at the company's premises in 104th Avenue, Surrey, British Columbia, Canada.

The tallest flagstaff in Great Britain is a 68 m *225 ft* tall Douglas fir staff at Kew, Richmond upon Thames. Cut in

> **Longest 'fire dragon'** ● This dragon structure is suspended over the Metroplex Mall, the shopping complex in Kuala Lumpur, Malaysia to celebrate the year of the dragon. It measures 118·54 m *388 ft 11 in* in length and is 91·4 cm *3 ft* in diameter. Its length, when 'translated' into the Cantonese dialect, means 'wishes that you will be prosperous day after day'.

Canada, it was shipped across the Atlantic and towed up the River Thames on 7 May 1958, to replace the old 65 m *214 ft* tall staff of 1919.

Fountain

The world's tallest fountain is the Fountain at Fountain Hills, Arizona built at a cost of $1 500 000 for McCulloch Properties Inc. At full pressure of 26·3 kg/cm² *375 lb/in²* and at a rate of 26 500 litres/min *5828 imp. gal/min* the 170 m *560 ft* tall column of water weighs more than 8 tonnes. The nozzle speed achieved by the three 600 hp pumps is 236 km/h *146·7 mph*.

Britain's tallest fountain is the Emperor Fountain at Chatsworth, Bakewell, Derbyshire. When first tested on 1 June 1844, it attained the then unprecedented height of

79 m *260 ft*. Since the war it has not been played to more than 76 m *250 ft* and rarely beyond 55 m *180 ft*.

Garbage dump

Reclamation Plant No 1, Fresh Kills, Staten Island, New York opened in March 1974, is the world's largest sanitary landfill. In its first 4 months 457 000 tonnes *450 000 tons* of refuse from New York City was dumped on the site by 700 barges.

Gasholder

The world's largest gasholder is that at Fontaine l'Eveque, Belgium, where disused mines have been adapted to store up to 500 million m³ *17 650 million ft³* of gas at ordinary pressure. Probably the largest conventional gasholder is that at Wien-Simmering, Vienna, completed in 1968, with a height of 84 m *274 ft 8 in* and a capacity of 300 000 m³ *10·59 million ft³*.

The largest gasholder ever constructed in Great Britain is the East Greenwich Gas Works No 2 Holder built in 1891 with an original capacity for 346 000 m³ *12 200 000 ft³*. As constructed its capacity is 252 000 m³ *8·9 million ft³* with a water tank 92 m *303 ft* in diameter and a full inflated height of 45 m *148 ft*. The No 1 holder (capacity 243 500 m³ *8·6 million ft³*) has a height of 61 m

200 ft. The River Tees Northern Gas Board's 361 m *1186 ft* deep underground storage in use since January 1959 has a capacity of 9300 m³ *330 000 ft³.*

Globe

The world's largest revolving globe is the 21½ tonne 8·50 m *27 ft 11 in* diameter sphere in Babson College Wellesley, Massachusetts, completed at a cost of $200 000 in 1956.

Jetty

The longest deep-water jetty in the world is the Quai Hermann du Pasquier at Le Havre, France, with a length of 1524 m *5000 ft.* Part of an enclosed basin, it has a constant depth of water of 9·8 m *32 ft* on both sides.

Kitchen

The largest kitchen ever set up has been an Indian government field kitchen set up in April 1973 at Ahmadnagar, Maharashtra a famine area, which daily provided 1·2 million subsistence meals.

Lamppost

The tallest lighting columns ever erected are four of 63·5 m *208 ft 4 in* made by Petitjean & Cie of Troyes, France and installed by Taylor Woodrow at Sultan Qaboos Sports Complex, Muscat, Oman.

Lighthouse

The word's tallest lighthouse is the 106 m 348 ft steel tower near Yamashita Park in Yokohama, Japan. It has a power of 600 000 candles and a visibility range of 32 km *20 miles.* The lights with the greatest range are those 332 m *1092 ft* above the ground on the Empire State Building, New York City. Each of the four-arc mercury bulbs has a rated candlepower of 450 000 000, visible 130 km *80 miles* away on the ground and 490 km *300 miles* away from aircraft. They were switched on on 31 Mar 1956.

Fumigation ▼ The largest fumigation in the world was carried out during the restoration of the Mission Inn complex in Riverside, California, USA on 28 June–1 July to rid the buildings of termites. It was performed by Fume Masters Inc of Riverside with over 350 tarpaulins weighing up to 160 kg *350 lb* and involved completely covering the 6500 m² *70 000 ft²* site and buildings – domes, minarets, chimneys and balconies – some of which exceeded 30 m *100 ft* in height.

Largest Lego statue ▲ This sculpture of the Indian chief Sitting Bull at the Legoland Park, Billund, Denmark, measures 7·6 m *25 ft* to the top of the feather. Requiring 1 500 000 bricks each individually glued to withstand the weather, it is the largest Lego statue ever constructed and the only one of the chief.

The most remote Trinity House lighthouse is The Smalls, about 16 sea miles (29·6 km *18·4 statute miles*) off the Dyfed coast.

The most remote Scottish lighthouse is Sule Skerry, 56 km *35 miles* off shore and 72 km *45 miles* north-west of Dunnet Head, Caithness. The most remote Irish light is Blackrock, 14 km *9 miles* off the Mayo coast.

The world's tallest lighthouse is the steel tower 106 m *348 ft* tall near Yamashita Park in Yokohama, Japan. It has a power of 600 000 candles and a visibility range of 32 km *20 miles.*

Bishop Rock, Isles of Scilly measures 47·8 m *156·8 ft* high to its helipad. The tallest Scottish lighthouse is the 42·3 m *139 ft* tall North Ronaldsay lighthouse, Orkney Islands.

The lighthouse in Great Britain with the most powerful light is the shorelight at Strumble Head, near Fishguard, Dyfed. It has an intensity of 6 000 000 candelas. The Irish light with the greatest intensity is Aranmore on Rinrawros Point, County Donegal.

Largest marquee

The largest tent ever erected was one covering an area of 17 500 m² *188 368 ft²* (1·7 ha *4·32 acres*) put up by the firm of Deuter from Augsburg, West Germany, for the 1958 'Welcome Expo' in Brussels, West Belgium.

The largest single-unit tent in Britain covers a ground area of more than 12 000 m² *129 170 ft²* and was manufactured by Clyde Canvas Ltd of Edinburgh, Scotland.

The largest marquee in Britain was one made by Piggot Brothers in 1951 and used by the Royal Horticultural Society at their annual show (first held in 1913) in the grounds of the Royal Hospital in Chelsea, London. The marquee is 94 m *310 ft* long by 146 m *480 ft* wide and consists of 30 km *18¾ miles* of 91 cm *36 in* wide canvas covering a ground area of 13 820 m² *148 800 ft².*

Manor Marquees Ltd, of Maidstone, Kent, erected a 143 m *470 ft* long marquee in one lift on 16 May 1987.

The Offshore Europe 1983 exhibition at Bridge of Don, Aberdeenshire, was housed in 15 contiguous air tents covering 6·91 acres *28 400 m².*

Maypole

The tallest reported Maypole erected in England was one of Sitka spruce 32·12 m *105 ft 7 in* tall put up in Pelynt, Cornwall on 1 May 1974. The permanent pole at Paganhill, near Stroud, Gloucestershire is 27·43 m *90 ft* tall.

Maze

The oldest datable representation of a labyrinth is that on a clay tablet from Pylos, Greece from *c.* 1200 BC.

The world's largest hedge maze is that at Longleat, near Warminster, Wilts, which has 2·72 km *1·69 miles* of paths flanked by 16 180 yew trees. It was opened on 6 June 1978 and measures 116 × 57 m *381 × 187 ft.* 'Il Labirinto' at Villa Pisani, Stra, Italy, in which Napoleon was 'lost' in 1807, had 6·4 km *4 miles* of pathways.

Menhir

The tallest menhir found is the 380 tonnes Grand Menhir Brisé, now in 4 pieces, which originally stood 22 m *69 ft* high at Locmariaquer, Brittany, France. Recent research suggests a possible 22·8 m *75 ft* high menhir, in 3 pieces, also at Locmariaquer. Britain's tallest is one of 7·6 m *25 ft* at Rudston, Humberside.

Monument

Britain's largest megalithic prehistoric monument and largest existing henge are the 11·5 ha *28½ acre* earthworks and stone circles of Avebury, Wiltshire, 'rediscovered' in 1646. The earliest calibrated date in the area of this Neolithic site is *c.* 4200 BC. The work is 365 m *1200 ft* in diameter with a 12 m *40 ft* ditch around the perimeter and required an estimated 15 million manhours of work. The henge of Durrington Walls, Wiltshire, obliterated by road building, had a diameter of 472 m

1550 ft. It was built from *c.* 2500 BC and required some 900 000 man-hours.

The largest trilithons exist at Stonehenge, to the south of Salisbury Plain, Wiltshire, with single sarsen blocks weighing over 45 tonnes and requiring over 550 men to drag them up a 9° gradient. The earliest stage of the construction of the ditch has been dated to 2800 BC. Whether Stonehenge, which required some 30 million man-years for its construction was a lunar calendar, a temple, an eclipse-predictor or a navigation school is still debated.

The world's tallest monument is the stainless steel Gateway to the West Arch in St Louis, Missouri, USA, completed on 28 Oct 1965 to commemorate the westward expansion after the Lousiana Purchase of 1803. It is a sweeping arch spanning 192 m *630 ft* and rising to the same height of 192 m *630 ft* and costing $29 000 000 . It was designed in 1947 by the American architect Eero Saarinen (d.1961).

The tallest monumental column commemorates the battle of San Jacinto (21 Apr 1836), on the bank of the San Jacinto River near Houston, Texas. General Sam Houston (1793–1863) and his force of 743 Texan troops killed 630 Mexicans (out of a total force of 1600) and captured 700 others, for the loss of nine men killed and 30 wounded. Constructed from 1936–9, at a cost of $1 500 000, the tapering column is 173 m *570 ft* tall, 14 m *47 ft* square at the base, and 9 m *30 ft* square at the observation tower, which is surmounted by a star weighing 196·4 tons *199·6 tonnes.* It is built of concrete and is faced with buff limestone having a weight of 31 384 tons *31 888 tonnes.*

The newest scheduled ancient monuments are a hexagonal pill box and 48 concrete tank traps south of Christchurch, Dorset built in World War II and protected since 1973.

Mound

The largest artificial mound in Europe is Silbury Hill, 9·7 km *6 miles* west of Marlborough, Wiltshire, which involved the moving of an estimated 670 000 tons *681 000 tonnes* of chalk, at a cost of 18 million man-hours to make a cone 39 m *130 ft* high with a base of 2 ha *5½ acres.* Professor Richard Atkinson in charge of the 1968 excavations showed that it is based on an innermost central mound, similar to contemporary round barrows, and is now dated to 2745±185 BC. The largest long barrow in England is that inside the hill-fort at Maiden Castle near Dorchester (see Earthworks). It originally had a length of 548 m *1800 ft* and had several enigmatic features such as a ritual pit with pottery, limpet shells and animal bones, but the date of these is not certain. The longest long barrow containing a megalithic chamber is that at West Kennet (*c.* 2200 BC), near Silbury, measuring 117 m *385 ft* in length.

Naturist resorts

The oldest resort is Der Freilichtpark, Klingberg, West Germany established in 1903. The largest in area in the world is the Beau Valley Country Club, Warmbaths, South Africa extending over 4 million m² *988 acres* with up to 20 000 visitors a year. However, 100 000 people visit the smaller centre Helio-Marin at Cap d'Agde, southern France, which covers 90 ha *222 acres.* The appellation 'nudist camp' is deplored by naturists.

Obelisk (monolithic)

The largest standing obelisk (from the Gk *obeliskos,* skewer or spit) in the world is the obelisk of Tuthmosis III brought from Aswan, Egypt by Emperor Constantius in the spring of AD 357. It was repositioned in the Piazza San Giovanni in Laterane, Rome on 3 Aug 1588. Once 36 m *118·1 ft* tall, it now stands 32·81 m *107·6 ft* and weighs 455 tonnes. The unfinished obelisk, probably commissioned by Queen Hatshepsut *c.* 1490 BC, at Aswan, is 41·75 m *136·8 ft* in length and weighs 1168 tonnes. The largest obelisk in the United Kingdom is Cleopatra's Needle on the Embankment, London, which at 20·88 m *68 ft 5 in* is the world's 11th tallest. It weighs 186·3 tons

189·35 tonnes and was towed up the Thames from Egypt on 21 Jan 1878 and positioned on 13 Sept. The longest an obelisk has remained *in situ* is that still at Heliopolis, near Cairo, erected by Senusret I *c.* 1750 BC.

Pier

The world's longest pier was the Dammam Pier, Saudi Arabia, on the Persian Gulf with an overall length of 10·93 km *6·79 miles*. The work was begun in July 1948 and completed on 15 Mar 1950. The area was subsequently developed by 1980 into the King Abdul Aziz Port with 39 deep-water berths. The original causeway, much widened, and the port extend for 12·8 km *7·95 miles*.

Longest Roman wall in Britain ▲ Hadrian's Wall, built AD 122–6 and 4·5 to 6 m *15 to 20 ft* tall crossed the Tyne-Solway isthmus for 118 km *73½ miles* from Bowness-on-Solway, Cumbria, to Wallsend-on-Tyne, Tyne and Wear. It was abandoned in AD 383. (Photo: Images Colour Library)

Largest surviving ziggurat ▼ The Ziggurat of Ur (now Muquyyar, Iraq) built *c.* 2113–2096 BC, with a base of 61×45·7 m *200×150 ft* built to three storeys surmounted by a summit temple. The first and part of the second storeys now survive to a height of 18 m *60 ft*. (Photo: Ancient Art & Architecture Collection)

The longest pier in Great Britain is the Bee Ness Jetty, completed in 1930, which stretches 2500 m *8200 ft* along the west bank of the River Medway, 5 to 8 to 9·6 km *6 miles* below Rochester, at Kingsnorth, Kent.

Largest pyramid

The largest pyramid, and the largest monument ever constructed, is the Quetzacóatl at Cholula de Rivadabia, 101 km *63 miles* south-east of Mexico City. It is 54 m *177 ft* tall and its base covers an area of nearly 18·2 ha *45 acres*. Its total volume has been estimated at 3 300 000 m³ *4 300 000 yd³* compared with 2·5 million m³ *3 360 000 yd³*

for the Pyramid of Cheops (see Seven Wonders of the World). The pyramid-building era here was between the 2nd and 6th centuries AD.

Oldest pyramid

The oldest known pyramid is the Djoser step pyramid at Saqqâra, Egypt constructed by Imhotep to a height of 62 m *204 ft* originally with a Tura limestone casing *c.* 2650 BC. The largest known single block comes from the Third Pyramid (the pyramid of Mycerinus) and weighs 290 tonnes *285 tons*.

The oldest New World pyramid is that on the island of La Venta in south-eastern Mexico built by the Olmec people *c.* 800 BC. It stands 30 m *100 ft* tall with a base dimension of 128 m *420 ft*.

Scarecrow

The largest scarecrow in the world was built by Stephen Speers and family of Paris, Ontario, Canada on 5 Sept 1987. 'Stretch' measured 22·39 m *73 ft 5¾ in* in height and 11·88 m *39 ft* in width.

Snow and ice constructions

A snow palace 26·5 m *87 ft* high and one of four structures which spanned 214·2 m *702·7 ft* wide was unveiled on 7 Feb 1987 Asahikawa City, Hokkaido, Japan.

The world's largest ice construction is the Ice Palace built in January 1986 using 9 000 blocks of ice at St Paul, Minnesota, during the Winter Carnival. Designed by Ellerbe Associates Inc, it stood 39·24 m *128 ft 9 in* high— the equivalent of a 13-storey building.

A snow palace, Galliber's Dream Castle, was unveiled on 7 Feb 1987 at the Asahikawa Winter Festival at Asahikawa City, Hokkaido, Japan. It measured 95·4 m *312·9 ft* wide, 26·5 m *86·9 ft* high and 30 m *98·4 ft* deep and was one of four such structures which altogether spanned a width of 214·2 m *702·7 ft* and which took 6500 people to construct.

The biggest snowman, 'Super Frosty', was one built by a team in Anchorage, Alaska, USA led by Myron L. Ace between 20 Feb and 5 Mar 1988 and stood 19·37 m *63·56 ft*.

Stairs

The world's longest stairway is the service staircase for the Niesenbahn funicular which rises to 2365 m *7759 ft* near Spiez, Switzerland. It has 11 674 steps and a bannister. The stone-cut T'ai Chan temple stairs of 6600 steps in the Shantung Mountains, China ascend 1428 m in 8 km *4700 ft in 5 miles*. The longest spiral staircase is one 336·2 m *1103 ft* deep with 1520 steps installed in the Mapco–White County Coal Mine, Carmi, Illinois, by Systems Control Inc in May 1981.

The longest stairs in Britain are those from the transformer gallery to the surface 324 m *1065 ft* in the Cruachan Power Station, Argyll. They have 1420 steps and the plant's work study unit allows 27 min 41·4 sec for the ascent.

Longest statue

Near Bamiyan, Afghanistan there are the remains of the recumbent Sakya Buddha, built of plastered rubble, which was 'about 305 m' *1000 ft* long and is believed to date from the 3rd or 4th century AD.

Tallest statue

The tallest full-figure statue in the world is that of 'Motherland', an enormous pre-stressed concrete female figure on Mamayev Hill, outside Volgograd, USSR, designed in 1967 by Yevgeniy Vuchetich, to commemorate victory in the Battle of Stalingrad (1942–3). The statue from its base to the tip of the sword clenched in her right hand measures 82·30 m *270 ft*.

Swing

The tallest is a glider swing 9 14 m *30 ft* high, constructed by Kenneth R. Mack, Langenburg, Saskatchewan, Canada for Uncle Herb's Amusements. The swing is capable of taking its 4 sides 7·62 m *25 ft* off the ground.

Tidal river barrier

The largest tidal river barrier in the world is the Thames Barrier at Woolwich, London. It has 9 piers and 10 gates. There are 6 rising sector gates 61 m *200 ft 1½ in* wide and 4 falling radial gates 31·5 m *103 ft 4 in* wide. It was opened by HM Queen on 8 May 1984.

Tomb

The largest tomb yet discovered is the Mount Li tomb, belonging to Zheng, the first Emperor of China. It dates to 221 BC and is situated 40 km *25 miles* east of Xianyang. The two walls surrounding the grave measure 2173 × 974 m *7129 × 3195 ft* and 685 × 578 m *2247 × 1896 ft*. Several pits in the tomb contained a vast army of an estimated 8000 life-size terracotta soldiers.

Totem pole

A totem pole 52·73 m *173 ft* tall was raised on 6 June 1973 at Alert Bay, British Columbia, Canada. It tells the story of the Kwakiutl and took 36 man-weeks to carve.

Vats

The largest vat in the world is named 'Strongbow', and used by H.P. Bulmer Ltd, the English cider makers of Hereford. It measures 19·65 m *64½ ft* in height and 23·0 m *75½ ft* in diameter with a capacity of 74 099 hl *1 630 000 gallons*.

The largest wooden wine cask in the world is the Heidelberg Tun completed in 1751 in the cellar of the Friedrichsbau Heidelberg, West Germany. Its capacity is 1855 hl *40 790 gal*. The world's oldest is that in use since 1715 at Hugelet Fils (founded 1639) Riquewihr, Haut-Rhin by the most recent of the 12 generations of the family.

Wall

The Great Wall of China has a main-line length of 3460 km *2150 miles* – nearly three times the length of Britain. Completed during the reign of Ch'in Shih Huang-ti (221–210 BC), it has a further 2860 km *1780 miles* of branches and spurs. Its height varies from 4·5 m–12 m *15–39 ft* and it is up to 9·8 m *32 ft* thick. It runs from Shanhaikuan, on, the Gulf of Pohai, to Yumenkuan and Yang-kuan and was kept in repair up to the 16th century. Some 51·5 km *32 miles* of the wall have been destroyed since 1966 and part of the wall was blown up to make way for a dam in July 1979. On 6 Mar 1985 a report from China stated that a five-year-long survey proved that the total length had been 9980 km *6200 miles*.

The longest of the Roman walls in Britain was the 4 5–6 m *15–20 ft* tall Hadrian's Wall, built AD 122–126. It crossed the Tyne-Solway isthmus for 118 km *73½ miles* from Bowness-on-Solway, Cumbria, to Wallsend-on-Tyne, Tyne and Wear, being abandoned in AD 383.

Water tower

The world's tallest water tower is that at Union, New Jersey, built in 1965 to a height of 64 m *210 ft* with a capacity of 9462 hl *250 000 gal*. The tower is owned and operated by the Elizabethtown Water Company.

Waterwheel

The largest waterwheel in the world is the Mohamma-dieh Noria wheel at Hamah, Syria with a diameter of 40 m *131 ft* dating from Roman times.

The Lady Isabella wheel at Laxey, Isle of Man is the largest in the British Isles and was built for draining a lead mine. It was completed on 27 Sept 1854, and has been disused since 1929. It has a circumference of 69 m *228 ft*, a diameter of 22 m *72½ ft* and an axle weighing 9 tonnes. The largest waterwheel in Britain is the 15·36 m *50 ft 5 in* diameter wheel built in 1870 at Caernarfon, Gwynedd. It worked until 1925 and is 1·52 m *5 ft* in width. It is exhibited and can be seen working at the Welsh Slate Museum, Dinorwic, Llanberis, Gwynedd.

Window

The largest sheet of glass ever manufactured was one of 50 m² *538·2 ft²*, or 20 m *65 ft 7 in* by 2·5 m *8 ft 2¼ in*, exhibited by the Saint Gobin Company in France at the *Journées Internationales de Miroiterie* in March 1958. The largest single windows in the world are those in the Palace of Industry and Technology at Rondpoint de la Défense, Paris, with an extreme width of 218 m *715·2 ft* and a maximum height of 50 m *164 ft*.

The record for Pilkington of St Helens, Merseyside is a sheet of 2·5 × 15·2 m *8 ft 2¼ × 49 ft 10½ in* made for the Festival of Britain in 1951.

Wine cellar

The largest wine cellars in the world are at Paarl, those of the Ko-operative Wijnbouwers Vereeniging, known as KWV, near Cape Town, in the centre of the wine-growing district of South Africa. They cover an area of 10 ha *25 acres* and have a capacity of 136 million litres *30 million gal*.

The Cienega Winery of the Almaden Vineyards in Hollister, California, covers 1·6 ha *4 acres* and can house 37 300 oak barrels containing 1·83 million gallons of wine.

Ziggurat

The largest ziggurat ever built was by the Elamite King Untash *c.* 1250 BC known as the Ziggurat of Choga Zanbil, 30 km *18·6 miles* from Haft Tepe, Iran. The outer base was 105 × 105 m *344 ft* and the fifth 'box' 28 × 28 m *91·8 ft* nearly 50 m *164 ft* above.

Borings and Mines

Deepest

Man's deepest penetration into the Earth's crust is a geological exploratory drilling near Zapolarny, Kola peninsula, USSR begun in 1970. By 1987 a depth of 13 km *8·07 miles or 42 650 ft* was surpassed. Progress has understandably greatly slowed to 500 m *1640 ft* per annum as the eventual target of 15 000 m *49 212 ft* in 1989–90 is neared. The drill bit is mounted on a turbine driven by a mud pump. The temperature at 11 km *6·83 miles* was already 200°C *392° F*.

The West Germans announced the test drilling of the Erbendorf hole, Upper Bavaria on 9 Oct 1986. The planned depth of the £150 million project is 14 km *45 900 ft 8·69 miles*.

Ocean drilling

The deepest recorded drilling into the sea bed by the *Glomar Challenger* of the US Deep Sea Drilling Project is one of 1740 m *5709 ft* off north-west Spain in 1976. The deepest site is now 7034 m *23 077 ft* below the surface on the western wall of the Marianas Trench (see page 54) in May 1978.

Oil fields

The world's largest oil field is the Ghawar field, Saudi Arabia developed by ARAMCO which measures 240 km by 35 km *150 miles by 22 miles*.

The area of the designated parts of the UK Continental shelf as at mid-1987 was 651 650 km² *252 000 miles²* with proven and probable reserves of 1330 million tonnes of oil and 634 000 million m³ *22 400 000 million ft³* of gas. Gas was first discovered in the West Sole Field in October 1965 and oil in commercial quantities in the Forties Field (Block 22/17) at 3352 m *11 000 ft* from the drilling barge *Sea Quest* on 18 Sept 1970, though a small gas field was detected near Whitby, North Yorkshire in 1937. The most productive field is BP's Forties Field with 224·7 million tonnes. Production peaked for the U.K.'s 32 oil fields at 127·5 million tonnes.

The deepest drilling in the North Sea is in 795·8 m *2611 ft* of water on 11-12 June 1986 by the British-built *Sovereign Explorer*, a propulsion-assisted semisubmersible drilling unit operated by Scotdrill Offshore Company, Aberdeen, and contracted to Chevron Petroleum.

Gas deposits

The largest gas deposit in the world is at Urengoi, USSR with an eventual production of 261 600 million yd³ *200 000 million m³* per year through 6 pipelines from proved reserves of 9 155 600 million yd³ *7 000 000 million m³*. The trillionth (10¹²) cubic metre was produced on 23 Apr 1986.

Oil platforms

The world's most massive oil platform is the *Statfjord B* concrete gravity-base platform built at Stavanger, Norway owned by the Statfjord Group and operated by Mobil Exploration Norway Inc until 31 Dec 1986. Tow-out to its permanent field took place between 1 and 5 Aug 1981 and it was the heaviest object ever moved—816 000 tonnes or 803 000 long tons ballasted weight. The £1·1 billion structure was towed by 8 tugs with a combined power of 115 000 hp. The height of the concrete structure is 204 m *670 ft* and the overall height 271 m *890 ft*. It thus weighs almost three times the weight of each of the towers of the World Trade Center, New York City (290 000 long tons). The world's tallest production platform is the 345 m *1132 ft* Shell Cognac platform built in 1976 and placed outside the Mississippi delta in Louisiana.

Gusher

The greatest wildcat ever recorded blew at Alborz No 5 well, near Qum, Iran on 26 Aug 1956. The uncontrolled oil gushed to a height of 52 m *170 ft* at 120 000 barrels per day at a pressure of 62 055 kPa *9000 lb/in²*. It was closed after 90 days work by B. Mostofi and Myron Kinley of Texas. The Lake View No 1 gusher in California on 15 Mar 1910 may have yielded 125 000 barrels in its first 24 hours.

Oil spills

The slick from the Mexican marine blow-out beneath the drilling rig *Ixtoc I* in the Gulf of Campeche, Gulf of Mexico, on 3 June 1979 reached 640 km *400 miles* by 5 Aug 1979. It eventually was capped on 24 Mar 1980 after a loss of 3 000 000 barrels (535 000 tons).

The worst oil spill in history was of 236 000 tonnes of oil from two super-tankers *Atlantic Empress* and *Aegean Captain* when they collided off Tobago on 19 July 1979. The worst oil spill in British waters was from the 118 285-dwt *Torrey Canyon* which struck the Pollard Rock off Land's End on 18 Mar 1967 resulting in a loss of 106 000 tons of oil.

Flare

The greatest gas fire was that which burnt at Gassi Touil in the Algerian Sahara from noon on 13 Nov 1961 to 9.30 a.m. on 28 Apr 1962. The pillar of flame rose 137 m *450 ft* and the smoke 182 m *600 ft*. It was eventually extinguished by Paul Neal ('Red') Adair (b. 1932), of Houston, Texas, using 245 kg *550 lb* of dynamite. His fee was understood to be about $1 000 000 .

Water well

The world's deepest water bore is the Stensvad Water Well 11-W1 of 2231 m *7320 ft* drilled by the Great Northern Drilling Co Inc in Rosebud County, Montana, in October–November 1961. The Thermal Power Co geothermal steam well begun in Sonoma County, California in 1955 is now down to 2752 m *9029 ft*.

The deepest well in Great Britain is a water table well 866 m *2842 ft* deep in the Staffordshire coal measures at Smestow 8 km *5 miles* south-west of Wolverhampton. The deepest artesian well in Britain is that at the White Heather Laundry, Stonebridge Park, Brent, London, bored in 1911 to a depth of 678 m *2225 ft*. The deepest known hand-dug well is one dug to a depth of 391 6 m *1285 ft* in 1858 to March 1862 on the site of Fitzherbert School, Woodingdean, Brighton, East Sussex.

Largest uranium mine ● A satellite photograph of the coast line of Namibia, including the uranium mine at Rossing (see Table right). A large part of the Namib desert can be seen in the lower part of the picture. (Photo: Science Photo Library)

MINE RECORDS

EARLIEST *World* ● 41 250 BC ± 1600 Lion Cavern, Haematite (red iron ore) at Ngwenya, Hhohho, Swaziland.
GB ● 3390 BC ± 150 Flint at Church Hill, Findon, W. Sussex.

DEEPEST *World* [1] ● 3777 m *12 391 ft (2·34 miles)* Gold, Western Deep Levels (temp 55°C *131°F*) at Carletonville, South Africa.
GB ● 1315 m *4314 ft* Coal, Plodder Seam, Bickershaw Colliery at Leigh, Lancashire.
Cornwall ● 1097 m *3600 ft* Tin, Williams Shaft at Dolcoath (1910) near Camborne, Cornwall.

COPPER *Deepest, open pit* ● 800 m *2625 ft* Bingham Canyon (begun 1906), *Location* near Salt Lake City, Utah, USA.
Largest underground ● 573 km *356 miles* tunnels, San Manuel Mine, Magma Copper Co in Arizona, USA.

LEAD *Largest* ● > 10 per cent of world output Viburnum Trend in south-east Missouri, USA.

GOLDMINING *Area* ● >51 per cent of world output, 38 mines of the Witwatersrand Discovery, South Africa in 1886.

GOLD *Largest World* [2] ● 4900 ha *12 100 acres* East Rand Proprietary Mines Ltd at Boksburg, Transvaal, South Africa.
Largest, GB ● 120 000 fine oz (1854–1914), Clogau, St David's (discovered 1836) at Gwynedd, Wales.
Richest ● 49·4 million fine oz, Crown Mines (all-time yield) in Transvaal, South Africa.

IRON *Largest* ● 20 300 million tonnes rich ore Lebedinsky (45–65% ore), Kursk region, USSR.

PLATINUM *Largest* ● 28 tonnes *1 000 000 oz* per annum, Rustenburg Platinum Mines Group, Rustenburg Platinum Mine *Location* Western Transvaal, South Africa.

TUNGSTEN *Largest* ● 2000 tonnes per day, Union Carbide Mount Morgan mine, near Bishop, California, USA.

URANIUM *Largest* ● 5000 tons of uranium oxide, Rio Tinto Zinc open cast pit at Rössing, Namibia, SW Africa.

SPOIL DUMP *Largest, World* ● 275 million yd³ *210 million m³* New Cornelia Tailings at Ten Mile Wash, Arizona, USA.
Largest, GB [3] ● 46 ha *114 acre* 40 m *130 ft* high, Cutacre Clough Colliery tip (18 million tonnes), Lancashire.

QUARRY *Largest, World* ● 7·21 km² *2·81 miles²*. *3700 million short tons 3355 million tonnes* extracted. Bingham Canyon, Utah, USA.
Largest, GB ● 150 m *500 ft* deep, 2·6 km *1·6 mile* circumference, Old Delabole Slate Quarry (since *c.* 1570), Cornwall.

COAL, OPEN CAST MINE ● 325 m deep *1130 ft* 21 km² *8 mile²* area Fortuna-Garsdorf (lignite) (begun 1955), near Bergheim, West Germany.

COAL MINE *Oldest, UK* ● *c.* 1822 founded by William Stobart at Wearmouth, near Sunderland.

OCEAN DRILLING ● 5709 ft *1740 m* by *Glomar Challenger*, off north-west Spain, 1976.

[1] *Sinking began in June 1957. Scheduled to reach 3880 m 12 730 ft by 1992 with 14 000 ft or 2·65 miles regarded as the limit. No 3 vertical ventilation shaft is the world's deepest shaft at 2948·9 m 9675 ft. This mine requires 130 000 tons of air per day and refrigeration which uses the energy it would take to make 37 000 short tons of ice. An underground shift comprises 11 150 men. The deepest exploratory coal mining shaft is one reaching 6700 ft 2042 m near Thorez in the Ukrainian Donbas field, USSR in Aug 1983.*

[2] *The world's most productive gold mine may be Muruntau, Kyzyl Kum, Uzbekistan, USSR. According to one Western estimate it produces 80 tonnes of gold in a year. It has been estimated that South Africa has produced in 96 years (1886–1982) 36 400 tons or more than 31 per cent of all gold mined since 3900 BC.*

[3] *Reclamation plan announced 13 Sept 1982 for 1983–1996.*

THE MECHANICAL WORLD

CHAPTER·EIGHT

Longest railway straight ● An impressive single-track straight in Australia. The longest in the world is on the Commonwealth Railways Trans-Australian line over the Nullarbor Plain from Mile 496 between Nurina and Loongana, Western Australia, to Mile 793 between Ooldea and Watson, South Australia, 478 km *297 miles* dead straight although not level. The longest straight on British Rail is the 29 km *18 miles* between Barlby Junction and Brough on the 'down' line on the Selby, North Yorkshire, to Kingston-upon-Hull, Humberside, line. (Photo: Ace Photo Agency)

Ships

EARLIEST SEA-GOING BOATS

Aborigines are thought to have been able to cross the Torres Strait from New Guinea to Australia, then at least 70 km *43½ miles* across, at least as early as 40 000 BC. They are believed to have used double canoes. The earliest *surviving* 'vessel' is a pinewood dug-out found in Pesse, Netherlands and dated to *c.* 6315±275 BC and now in the Provincial Museum, Assen. The earliest representation of a boat is disputed between possible rock art outlines of Mesolithic skin-boats in Høgnipen, Norway (*c.* 8000–7000 BC); Minateda, Spain (7000–3000 BC) and Kobystan, USSR (8000–6000 BC). An 45 cm *18 in* long paddle was found at the Star Carr, North Yorkshire site, described in 1948. It has been dated to *c.* 7600 BC and is now in the Cambridge Museum of Archaeology.

The oldest surviving boat is a 8·2 m *27 ft* long 0·76 m *2·5 ft* wide wooden eel-catching canoe discovered at Tybrind Vig on the Baltic Island of Fünen which is dated to *c.* 4490 BC.

The oldest shipwreck ever found is one of a Cycladic trading vessel located off the islet of Dhókós, near the Greek island of Hydra, reported in May 1975 and dated to 2450 BC±250.

Earliest power

Propulsion by steam engine was first achieved when in 1783 the Marquis Jouffroy d'Abbans (1751–1832) ascended a reach of the river Saône near Lyon, France, in the 180-tonne paddle steamer *Pyroscaphe*.

The tug *Charlotte Dundas* was the first successful power-driven vessel. She was a stern paddle-wheel steamer built for the Forth and Clyde Canal, Scotland in 1801–2 by William Symington (1763–1831), using a double-acting condensing engine constructed by James Watt (1736–1819). The screw propeller was invented and patented by a Kent farmer, Sir Francis Pettit Smith (1808–71) on 31 May 1836 (Brit. Pat. No 7104).

The world's oldest active steam ship is the paddle steamer *Skibladner*, which has plied Lake Mjøsa, Norway since 1856. She was built in Motala, Sweden and has two major refits.

Oldest vessel

The sail training ship HMS *Foudroyant*, built in Bombay in 1857, was taken from Portsmouth Harbour to West Hartlepool in 1987 to undergo repairs and restoration.

Earliest turbine

The first turbine ship was the *Turbinia*, built in 1894 at Wallsend-on-Tyne, Tyne and Wear, to the design of the Hon. Sir Charles Parsons OM, KCB (1854–1931). The *Turbinia* was 30·48 m *100 ft* long and of 45·2 tonnes *44½ tons* displacement with machinery consisting of

three steam turbines totalling about 2000 shaft horsepower. At her first public demonstration in 1897 she reached 34·5 knots (*63·9 km/h*) and is now preserved at Newcastle-upon-Tyne.

WARSHIPS
Largest battleships

The largest battleship in service in the world is the 270·6 m *887 ft 9 in* long USS *New Jersey* with a full load displacement of 58 000 tonnes. She was the last fire support ship on active service off the Lebanon coast with her nine 16-in guns from 14 Dec 1983 to 26 Feb 1984. The $405-million refit of USS *Iowa* was completed in May 1984. USS *Missouri* and USS *Wisconsin* have also been re-activated. The 16-inch projectiles of 1225 kg *2700 lb* can be fired 39 km *23 miles*.

The Japanese battleships *Yamato* (completed on 16 Dec 1941 and sunk south-west of Kyūshū, Japan, by US planes on 7 Apr 1945) and *Musashi* (sunk in the Philippine Sea by 11 bombs and 16 torpedoes on 24 Oct 1944) were the largest battleships ever commissioned, each with a full load displacement of 72 809 tons *73 977 tonnes*. With an overall length of 263 m *863 ft*, a beam of 38·7 m *127 ft* and a full load draught of 10·8 m *35½ ft* they mounted nine 460 mm *18·1 in* guns in three triple turrets. Each gun weighed 164·6 tonnes *162 tons* and was 22·8 m *75 ft* in length firing a 1451 kg *3200 lb* projectile.

Britain's largest ever and last battleship was HMS *Vanguard* (1944–1960) with a full load displacement of 52 245 tonnes *51 420 tons* and an overall length of 248·1 m *814 ft*. She mounted eight 38 cm *15 in* guns.

Earliest 'Ironclad'

H.M.S. *Warrior*, put on show in Portsmouth on 16 June 1987 was launched in 1860.

Guns and armour

The largest guns ever mounted in any of HM ships were the 45 cm *18 in* pieces in the light battle cruiser (later aircraft carrier) HMS *Furious* in 1917. In 1918 they were transferred to the monitors HMS *Lord Clive* and *General Wolfe*. The thickest armour ever carried was in HMS *Inflexible* (completed 1881), measuring 60 cm *24 in* backed by teak up to a maximum thickness of 106·6 cm *42 in*.

Fastest destroyer

The highest speed attained by a destroyer was 45·25 knots (*83·42 km/h*) by the 2830 tonne French destroyer *Le Terrible* in 1935. She was built in Blainville and powered by four Yarrow small tube boilers and two Rateau geared turbines giving 100 000 shaft horsepower. She was removed from the active list at the end of 1957.

AIRCRAFT CARRIERS
Largest

The warships with the largest full load displacement in the world are the Nimitz class US Navy aircraft carriers USS *Nimitz, Dwight D. Eisenhower, Carl Vinson, Theodore Roosevelt* and *Abraham Lincoln* at 91 487 tons. They are 322·9 m *1092 ft* in length overall with 1·82 ha *4½ acres* of flight deck and have a speed well in excess of 30 knots *56 km/h* from their 4 nuclear-powered 260 000 shp geared steam turbines. They have to be refuelled

after about 1 450 000 km *900 000 miles* steaming. Their complement is 5684.

The total cost of the *Abraham Lincoln*, laid down at Newport News on 3 Nov 1984, will exceed, together with the *George Washington*, $3¼ billion, excluding the 90-plus aircraft carried. USS *Enterprise* is, however, 335·8 m *1102 ft* long and thus still the longest warship ever built.

The Royal Navy's largest fighting ship is HMS aircraft carrier HMS *Ark Royal*, commissioned 1 Nov 1983. She has a 167·6 m *550 ft* long flight deck and is 209·3 m *685·8 ft* long overall, and has a top speed of 28 knots being powered by 4 Rolls Royce Olympus TM3B gas turbines delivering 94 000 shp.

Most landings

The greatest number of landings on an aircraft carrier in one day was 602 achieved by Marine Air Group 6 of the United States Pacific Fleet Air Force aboard the USS *Matanikau* on 25 May 1945 between 8 a.m. and 5 p.m.

SUBMARINES
Largest

The world's largest submarines are of the USSR Typhoon class. The launch of the first at the secret covered shipyard at Severodvinsk in the White Sea was announced by NATO on 23 Sept 1980. They are believed to have a dived displacement of 25 000 tonnes, measure 170 m *557·6 ft* overall and be armed with twenty SS NX 20 missiles with a 4800 nautical mile *8895 km* range, each with 7 warheads. By late 1987 two others built in Leningrad are expected to be operational, each deploying 140 warheads.

The largest submarines ever built for the Royal Navy are the four atomic-powered nuclear missile R class boats with a surface displacement of 7620 tonnes *7500 tons* and 8534 tonnes *8400 tons* submerged, a length of 129·5 m *425 ft*, a beam of 10 m *33 ft* and a draught of 9·1 m *30 ft*. The longest submarine patrol ever spent dived and unsupported is 111 days by H M Submarine *Warspite* (Cdr J. G. F. Cooke RN) in the South Atlantic from 25 Nov 1982 to 15 Mar 1983. She sailed 30 804 nautical miles *57 085 km*.

Fastest

The Russian Alfa-class nuclear-powered submarines have a reported maximum speed of 42 knots *77·8 km/h* plus. With use of titanium alloy they are believed to be able to dive to 762 m *2500 ft*. A US spy satellite over Leningrad's naval yard on 8 June 1983 showed they were being lengthened and are now 79·3 m *260·1 ft* long.

Deepest

The two USN vessels able to descend 3650 m *12 000 ft* are the 3-man *Trieste II* (DSV I) of 303 tons (recommissioned in November 1973) and the DSV 2 (deep submergence vessel) USS *Alvin*. The *Trieste II* was reconstructed from the record-breaking bathyscaphe *Trieste* but without the Krupp-built sphere, which enabled it to descend to 10 917 m *35 820 ft*. (See Chapter 10, Greatest ocean descent).

PASSENGER LINERS
Largest

The world's largest passenger ship (by tonnage) is the 73 219 grt Norwegian cruise ship *Sovereign of the Seas*. Built at the French shipyard Chantiers de l'Atlantique at St Nazaire, she entered service from Miami in January 1988.

The world's longest ever liner is the *Norway* of 70 202 19 grt and 315 66 m *1035 ft 7½ in* in overall length with a capacity of 2400 passengers. She was built as the *France* in 1961 and renamed after purchase in June 1979 by Knut Kloster of Norway. Her second maiden voyage was from Southampton on 7 May 1980. Britain's largest liner is RMS *Queen Elizabeth 2* at 67 140 gross tons and with an overall length of 293 m *963 ft*, completed for

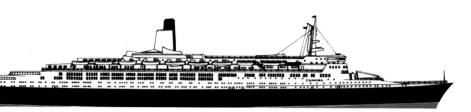

● Britain's largest passenger liner – RMS *Queen Elizabeth 2*.

Cunard Line in 1969. She set a 'turn round' record of 5 hr 47 min at New York on 21 Nov 1983. Her original steam turbine machinery was replaced with diesel electric units in April 1987.

The RMS *Queen Elizabeth* (finally 82 998 but formerly 83 673 gross tons), of the Cunard fleet, was the largest passenger vessel ever built and had the largest displacement of any liner in the world. She had an overall length of 314 m *1031 ft*, was 36 m *118 ft 7 in* in breadth and was powered by steam turbines which developed 168 000 hp. Her last passenger voyage ended on 15 Nov 1968. In 1970 she was removed to Hong Kong to serve as a floating marine university and renamed *Seawise University*. She was burnt out on 9 Jan 1972 when 3 *simultaneous* outbreaks of fire strongly pointed to arson. The gutted hull had been cut up and removed by 1978. *Seawise* was a pun on the owner's initials—C. Y. Tung (1911–1982).

TANKERS
Largest
The world's largest tanker and ship of any kind was the 564 739 tonne deadweight *Seawise Giant* completed for C. Y. Tung in 1976. She was 458 45 m *1504 ft* long overall with a beam of 68 86 m *225 ft 11 in* and a draught of 24·61 m *80 ft 9 in*. She had been lengthened by Nippon Kokan in 1980 by adding an 81 m *265 ft 8 in* midship section. She was attacked by Iraqi Mirage jets off Larak Island in the Gulf on 5 Oct 1987 and was destroyed in another attack on 14 May 1988.

CARGO VESSELS
Largest
The largest vessel in the world capable of carrying dry cargo is the Norwegian ore carrier *Berge Stahl* of 364·767 dwt built in South Korea for the Norwegian owner Sig Bergesen. It has a length of 343 m *1125 ft*, a beam measuring 63·5 m *208 ft* and was launched on 5

Tallest mast ● The *Astra*, a Class J sailing vessel built about 50 years ago, has been refitted with the tallest mast in the world. At 50 m *164 ft* in length and constructed of extruded aluminium this weighs 2·5 tons and can support a sail area of 1500 m² *16 140 ft²*. (Photo: Rex Features)

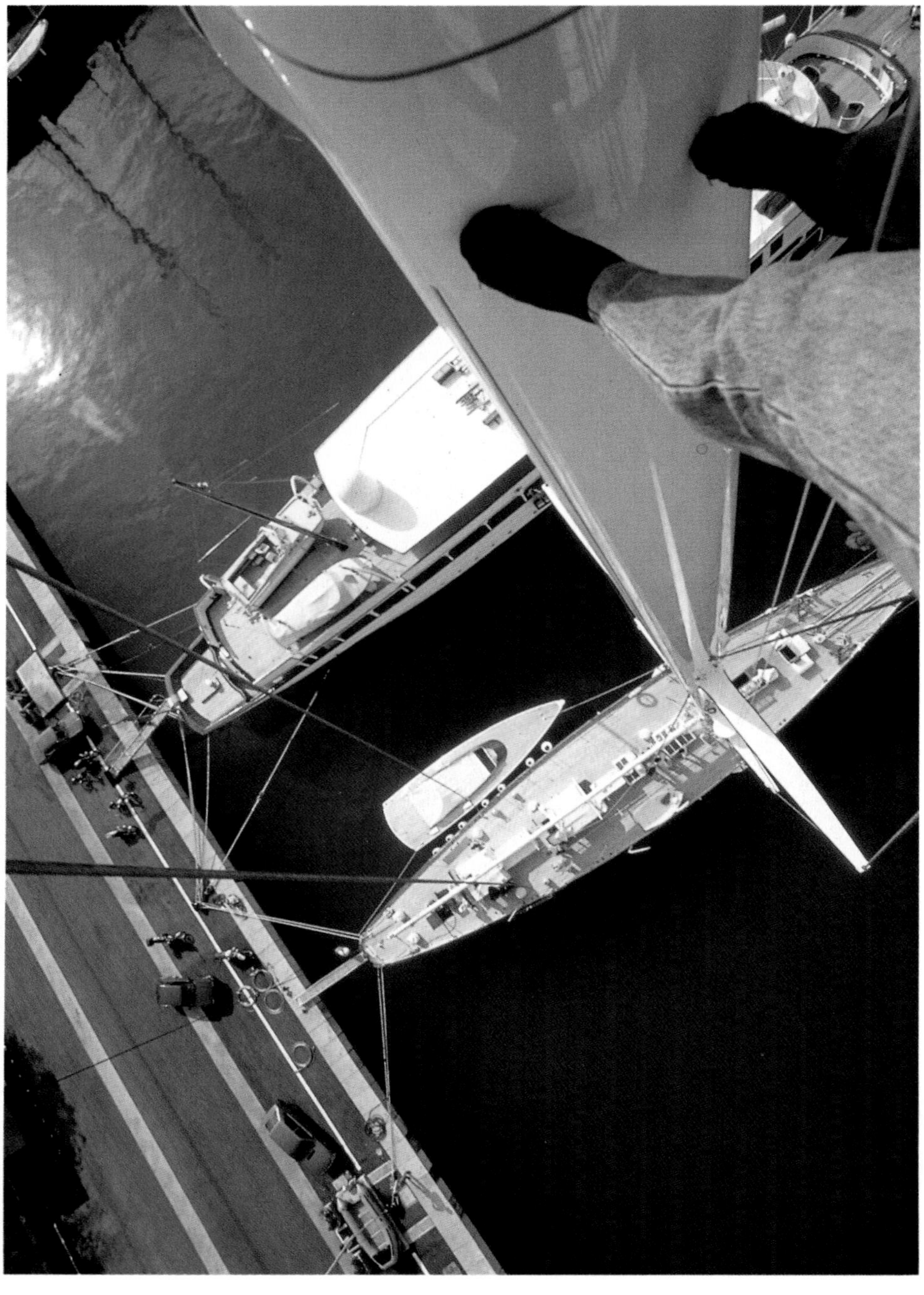

Nov 1986. The largest British ore/oil carriers (registered in the Isle of Man) are Lombard North Central Leasing's *Rapana* and *Rimula* built in Sweden in 1973 and 1974 of 227 412 dwt, *121 166 grt* with lengths of 332 77 m *1091 ft 9 in*.

Whale factory
The largest whale factory ship is the USSR's *Sovietskaya Ukraina* (32 034 gross tons) with a summer deadweight of 46 738 tonnes *46 000 tons* completed in October 1959. She is 217·8 m *714 ft 6 in* in length and 25·8 m *84 ft 7 in* in the beam.

Barges
The world's largest RoRo (roll-on, roll-off) ships are four *El Rey* class barges of 16 700 tons and 176·78 m *580 ft* in length. They were built by the FMC Corp of Portland, Oregon, and are operated by Crowley Maritime Corp of San Francisco between Florida and Puerto Rico with tri-level lodging of up to 376 truck-trailers.

Container ship
Shipborne containerisation began in 1955 when the tanker *Ideal X* was converted by Malcom McLean (US). She carried containers only on deck.

The world's largest container ships are the twelve built for United States Lines in Korea in 1984–5. They are capable of carrying 4482 TEU (6·1 m *20ft equivalent units—20 ft* containers) and have a gross tonnage of 57 075. They were named *American Alabama, American California, Illinois, Kentucky*, etc. Following the financial collapse of United States Lines, the fleet was sold and the twelve ships now have names such as *Sea-Land Atlantic, Sea-Land Achiever, Commitment, Integrity* etc, while others carry names either with the prefix 'Nedlloyd' (*Nedlloyd Holland*) or the suffix 'Bay' (*Galveston Bay*).

Tugs
The world's most powerful tug is the *Smit Singapore* commissioned in April 1984 by Smit Tak International, of 22 000 horsepower and 189 tons bollard pull at full power. It is 75·2 m *246·72 ft* long and 15·68 m *51·44 ft* wide.

Ferries
The world's largest car and passenger ferry is the 37 800 grt M/S *Mariella* which entered service across the Baltic between Helsinki and Stockholm, Sweden in May, 1985. Built in Turku, Finland for the Viking Line, she is 177·10 m *581 ft* long, 29 m *95 ft* in the beam and can carry 2500 passengers and 580 cars.

The world's fastest car and passenger ferry is the 24 065 grt gas turbine-powered *Finnjet*. Built in 1977, she operates in the Baltic between Helsinki and Trave-munde, W. Germany and is capable of exceeding 30 knots.

The 9700-dwt 21-knot *Railship II* went into service on the Baltic run in November 1984. She can carry 8820 m *65 ft 7 in* long rail cars, is 186·5 m *611 ft 10 in* overall and was built for HM Gehrckens of Hamburg.

Propeller
The world's largest ship propeller is the triple- bladed screw of 11·0 m *36 ft 1 in* diameter made by Kawasaki Heavy Industries on 17 Mar 1982 for the 208 739 ton bulk carrier *Hoei Maru*.

Hydrofoil
The world's largest naval hydrofoil is the 64·6 m *212 ft* long *Plainview* (310 tonnes *314 tons* full load), launched by the Lockheed Shipbuilding and Construction Co at Seattle, Washington, USA on 28 June 1965. She has a service speed of 50 knots (*92 km/h*).

Three 165-ton Supramar PTS 150 Mk III hydrofoils carry 250 passengers at 40 knots *74 km/h* across the Öre Sound between Malmö and Copenhagen. They were built by Westermoen Hydrofoil Ltd of Mandal, Norway. A 500-ton wing ground effect vehicle capable of carrying 900 tons has been reported in the USSR.

River boat

The world's largest inland river boat is the 116 m *382 ft Mississippi Queen* designed by James Gardner of London. The vessel was commissioned on 25 July 1976 in Cincinatti, Ohio, USA and is now in service on the Mississippi River.

Fastest building

The fastest times in which complete ships of more than 10 000 tons were ever built were achieved at Kaiser's Yard, Portland during the war-time programme for building 2 742 Liberty ships in 18 yards from 27 Sept 1941. In 1942 No 440, named *Robert E. Peary*, had her keel laid on 8 Nov, was launched on 12 Nov and was operational after 4 days 15 hrs on 15 November. She was broken up in 1963.

Largest and most powerful icebreakers

A 61 000 tonne nuclear-powered barge-carrying merchantman designed for work along the USSR's arctic coast was completed in early 1982 and is known to be designed to break ice. The longest purpose-built icebreaker is the 25 000 ton 140 m *460 ft* long *Rossiya*, powered by 75 000 hp nuclear engines built in Leningrad and completed in 1985. A $(Can)500 million, 100 000 hp, 194 m *636 ft* long Polar class 8 icebreaker was ordered by Canada in October 1985.

The largest *converted* icebreaker has been the 306·9 m *1007 ft* long SS *Manhattan* (43 000 shp), which was converted by the Humble Oil Co into a 152 407 tonne *150 000 ton* icebreaker with an armoured prow 69 ft 2 in long. She made a double voyage through the Passage in arctic Canada from 24 Aug to 12 Nov 1969. The North-West Passage was first navigated by Roald Engebereth Gravning Amundsen (Norway) (1872–1928) in the sealing sloop *Gjöa* on 11 July 1906.

Yacht

The fitting out of the 143·2 m *470 ft* Saudi Arabian royal yacht *Abdul Aziz*, built in Denmark, was completed on 22 June 1984 at Vospers Yard, Southampton. It was estimated in September 1987 to be worth more than $100 million. The longest private (non-Royal) yacht is the 85·9 m *282 ft Nabila* originally costing some $29 million. She was sold in September 1987 by the Sultan of Brunei to New York property dealer Donald Trump (b. 1946) for close to this price and renamed *Trump Princess*. Her original owner was Adnan Kashoggi who installed a helicopter pad and an operating theatre.

Dredger

The world's most powerful dredger is the 142·7 m *468·4 ft* long *Prins der Nederlanden* of 10 586 grt. She can dredge 20 000 tonnes of sand from a depth of 35 m *115 ft* via two suction tubes in less than an hour.

Wooden ship

The heaviest wooden ship ever built was the *Richelieu*, 101·70 m *333 ft 8 in* long and of 8534 tons launched in Toulon, France on 3 Dec 1873. HM battleship *Lord Warden*, completed in 1869, displaced 7940 tonnes *8060 tons*. The longest modern wooden ship ever built was the New York-built *Rochambeau* (1867–72) formerly *Dunderberg*. She measured 115 m *377 ft 4 in* overall. *It should be noted that the biblical length of Noah's Ark was 300 cubits or, at 45·7 cm 18 in to a cubit, 137 m 450 ft.*

Human powered

The largest human-powered ship was the giant *Tessarakonteres* 3-banked catamaran galley with 4000 rowers built for Ptolemy IV *c.* 210 BC in Alexandria, Egypt. It measured 128 m *420 ft* with up to 8 men to an oar of 38 cubits (17·5 m *57 ft*) in length.

The world's longest canoe is the 35·7 m *117 ft* long 20 ton Kauri wood Maori war canoe *Nga Toki Matawhaorua* built by adzes at Kerikeri Inlet, New Zealand in 1940 for a crew of 70 or more. The 'Snake Boat' *Nadubhagóm* 41·1 m *135 ft* long from Kerala, southern India has a crew of 109 rowers and 9 'encouragers'.

Light Vessels

The earliest station still marked by a light vessel is the Newarp in the North Sea, off Great Yarmouth in 1791. A Nore light vessel was first placed in the Thames estuary in 1732.

SAILING SHIPS

Largest

The largest vessel ever built in the era of sail was the *France II* (5806 gross tons), launched at Bordeaux in 1911. The *France II* was a steel-hulled, five-masted barque (square-rigged on four masts and fore and aft rigged on the aftermost mast). Her hull measured 127·4 m *418 ft* overall. Although principally designed as a sailing vessel with a stump topgallant rig, she was also fitted with two steam engines. She was wrecked off New Caledonia on 13 July 1922.

The only seven-masted sailing schooner ever built was the 114·4 m *375·6 ft* long *Thomas W. Lawson* (5218 gross tons) built at Quincy, Massachusetts, in 1902 and lost off the Isles of Scilly on 15 Dec 1907.

The largest sailing ship in service is the 104 m *342 ft Krusenstern*. She was launched in 1926 as the *Padua* and is used by the USSR marine schools of Kaliningrad and Murmansk.

The world's only surviving First Rate Ship-of-the-Line is the Royal Navy's 104-gun battleship HMS *Victory* laid down at Chatham, Kent on 23 July 1759 and constructed from the wood of some 2200 oak trees. She bore the body of Admiral Nelson from Gibraltar to Portsmouth arriving 44 days after serving as his victorious flagship at the Battle of Trafalgar of 21 Oct 1805. In 1922 she was moved to No 2 dock, Portsmouth—site of the world's oldest graving dock. The length of her cordage (both standing and running rigging) is 30·77 km *19·12 miles*).

The longest is the 134 m *440 ft* long French built *Wind Song* with 4 aluminium masts each 62·17 m *204 ft* high. The polyester sails are computer-controlled. It is operated as a Pacific cruise vessel for 150 passengers by Windstar Sail Cruises Ltd.

Largest junks

The largest junk on record was the sea-going *Cheng Ho*, flagship of Admiral Cheng Ho's 62 treasure ships, of *c.* 1420, with a displacement of 3150 tonnes *3100 tons* and a length variously estimated up to 164 m *538 ft* and believed to have had 9 masts.

A river junk 110 m *361 ft* long, with treadmill-operated paddle-wheels, was recorded in AD 1161. In *c.* AD 280 a floating fortress 182·8 m *600 ft* square, built by Wang Chün on the Yangtze, took part in the Chin-Wu river war. Present-day junks do not, even in the case of the Chiangsu traders, exceed 51·8 m *170 ft* in length.

Longest day's run under sail

The longest day's run calculated for any commercial vessel under sail was one of 462 nautical miles (856·16 km) by the clipper *Champion of the Seas* (2722 registered tons) of the Liverpool Black Ball Line running before a north-westerly gale in the south Indian Ocean

under the command of Capt Alex Newlands in 1854. The elapsed time between the fixes was 23 hr 17 min giving an average of 19·97 knots *37·00 km/h* (see Chapter 12 Yachting for sporting record).

Largest sails

Sails are known to have been used for marine propulsion since 3500 BC. The largest spars ever carried were those in HM Battleship *Temeraire*, completed at Chatham, Kent, on 31 Aug 1877. She was broken up in 1921. The fore and main yards measured 35 m *115 ft* in length. The foresail contained 1555 m *5100 ft* of canvas, weighing 2·03 tonnes *2 tons* and the total sail area was 2322 m² *25 000 ft²*. HM Battleship *Sultan* was ship-rigged when completed at Chatham, Kent on 10 Oct 1871 and carried 3168 m² *34 100 ft²* of sails plus 1421 m² *15 300 ft²* of stunsails. She was broken up in 1946.

Largest wreck

The largest ship ever wrecked has been the 312 186 dwt VLCC (Very Large Crude Carrier) *Energy Determination* which blew up and broke in two in the Straits of Hormuz on 12 Dec 1979. Her full value was $58 million. The largest wreck removal was carried out in 1979 by Smit Tak International who removed the remains of the French tanker *Betelgeuse*, 120 000 tons, from Bantry Bay, Ireland, within 20 months.

Most massive collision

The closest approach to an irresistible force striking an immovable object occurred on 16 Dec 1977, 35 km *22 miles* off the coast of southern Africa when the tanker *Venoil* (330 954 dwt) struck her sister ship *Venpet* (330 869 dwt).

OCEAN CROSSINGS

Atlantic *Earliest*

The earliest crossing of the Atlantic by a power vessel, as opposed to an auxiliary-engined sailing ship, was a 22-day voyage begun in April 1827, from Rotterdam, Netherlands, to the West Indies by the *Curaçao*. She was a 38·7 m *127 ft* wooden paddle boat of 438 ton, built as the *Calpe* in Dover in 1826 and purchased by the Dutch Government for the West Indian mail service.

The earliest Atlantic crossing completed entirely under steam power (with essential intervals for desalting the boilers) was by HMS *Rhadamanthus* from Plymouth to Barbados in 1832. The earliest crossing under continuous steam power was by the condenser-fitted packet ship *Sirius* (714 tonnes *703 tons*) from Queenstown (now Cóbh), Ireland, to Sandy Hook, New Jersey, USA, in 18 days 10 hr from 4–22 Apr 1838.

Atlantic *Fastest*

The fastest Atlantic crossing was made by the *United States* (then 51 988, now 38 216 gross tons), former flagship of the United States Lines. On her maiden voyage between 3 and 7 July 1952 from New York, to Le Havre and Southampton, England, she averaged 35·39 knots, or 65·95 km/h for 3 days 10 hr 40 min (6.36 p.m. GMT, 3 July to 5.16 a.m., 7 July) on a route of 2949 nautical miles *5465 km* from the Ambrose Light Vessel to the Bishop Rock Light, Isles of Scilly, Cornwall. During this run, on 6–7 July 1952, she steamed the greatest distance ever covered by any ship in a day's run (24 hr)—868 nautical miles *1609 km*, hence averaging 36·17 knots *67·02 km/h*. The maximum speed attained from her 240 000 shp engines was 38·32 knots (*71·01 km/h*) in trials on 9–10 June 1952.

Pacific *Fastest*

The fastest crossing of the Pacific Ocean from Yokohama to Long Beach, California (4840 nautical miles *8960 km*) was 6 days 1 hr 27 min (30 June–6 July 1973) by the container ship *Sea-Land Commerce* (50 315 tons) at an average of 33·27 knots (*61·65 km/h*).

Channel crossing *Fastest*

The fastest crossing of the English Channel by a commercial ferry is 52 min 49 sec from Dover to Calais by Townsend Thoresen's *Pride of Free Enterprise* in a near gale of Force 7 on 9 Feb 1982.

HOVERCRAFT (skirted air-cushion vehicles)

Earliest

The ACV (air-cushion vehicle) was first made a practical proposition by Sir Christopher Sydney Cockerell CBE, FRS (b. 4 June 1910), a British engineer who had the idea in 1954, published his Ripplecraft report 1/55 on 25 Oct 1955 and patented it on 12 Dec 1955. The earliest patent relating to air-cushion craft was applied for in 1877 by John I. Thornycroft (1843–1928) of Chiswick, London and the Finn Toivo Kaario developed the idea in 1935. The first flight by a hovercraft was made by the 4 tonne Saunders-Roe SR-N1 at Cowes on 30 May 1959. With a 680 kg *1500 lb* thrust Viper turbojet engine, this craft reached 68 knots *126 km/h* in June 1961. The first hovercraft public service was run across the Dee estuary by the 60 knot *111 km/h* 24-passenger Vickers-Armstrong VA-3 between July and September 1962.

Largest

The world's largest civil hovercraft is the 305 ton British-built SRN4 Mk III. It has a capacity of 418 passengers and 60 cars. It is 56·38 m *185 ft* in length, is powered by 4 Bristol Siddeley Marine Proteus engines giving a maximum speed in excess of the permitted cross-Channel operating speed of 65 knots.

Fastest warship

The world's fastest warship is the 23·7 m *78 ft* long 100 tonne US Navy test vehicle SES-100B. She attained a world record 91·9 knots *105·8 mph* on 25 Jan 1980 on the Chesapeake Bay Test Range, Maryland, USA. The 3000 ton US Navy Large Surface Effect Ship (LSES) was built by Bell Aerospace under contract from the Department of Defense in 1977–81.

Longest flight

The longest hovercraft journey was one of 8047 km *5000 miles* through eight West African countries between 15 Oct 1969 and 3 Jan 1970 by the British Trans-African Hovercraft Expedition.

Cross-Channel

The fastest crossing of the Channel was achieved by an SRN 4 Mark II Mountbatten Class Hovercraft operated by Hoverspeed on 1 Sept 1984 when *The Swift* completed the Dover–Calais run in 24 min 8·4 sec.

Highest

The greatest altitude at which a hovercraft (HM2 Hoverferry) is operating is on Lake Titicaca, Peru, at 3811 m *12 506 ft* above sea level.

Road Vehicles

COACHING

Before the widespread use of tarred road surfaces from 1845 coaching was slow and hazardous. The zenith was reached on 13 July 1888 when J. Selby Esq. drove the *Old Times* coach 173 km *108 miles* from London to Brighton and back with 8 teams and 14 changes in 7 hr 50 min to average 22·19 km/h *13·79 mph*. Four-horse carriages could maintain a speed of 34 km/h *21 ⅓ mph* for nearly an hour. The *Border Union* stage coach, built c. 1825, ran 4 in hand from Edinburgh to London (632 km *393 miles*). When it ceased in 1842, due to competition from railways, the allowed schedule was 42 hr 23 min to average better than 14·9 km/h *9¼ mph*.

John Parker (b. July 1939) drove a mail coach and horses 218·8 km *136 miles* from Bristol to London in 17 hr 30 mins on 1–2 Aug 1984. Norwich Union's six teams of greys were changed 11 times while an estimated 1 million people lined the route.

The record for changing a team of four horses by a team of 12 ostlers is 24·53 sec set at Olympia, London, on 18 Dec 1987, for the Norwich Union Charity Mail Coach team led by driver John Parker.

The longest horse drawn procession was a cavalcade of 68 carriages which measured 'nose to tail' 920 m *3018 ft* organised by the Spies Travelling Company of Denmark on 7 May 1986. It carried 810 people through the woods around Copenhagen to celebrate the coming of Spring.

MOTOR CARS

Most cars

For 1987 it was estimated that the United States, with 176 532 000 vehicles, passed 37·9 per cent of the total world stock of 411 113 000. In 1986 the American automobile industry sold an all-time record 16·3 million vehicles including 8 214 671 domestically-built cars retail. Of the latter General Motors sold 4 532 798.

Earliest automobiles *Model*

The earliest automobile of which there is record is a two-foot-long steam-powered model constructed by Ferdinand Verbiest (d. 1687), a Belgian Jesuit priest, and described in his *Astronomia Europaea*. His model of 1668 was possibly inspired either by Giovanni Branca's description of a steam turbine, published in his *La Macchina* in 1629, or by writings on 'fire carts' or *Nan Huai-Jen* in the Chu dynasty (c. 800 BC).

Passenger-carrying

The earliest full-scale automobile was the first of two military steam tractors, completed at the Paris Arsenal in 1769 by Nicolas-Joseph Cugnot (1725–1804). This reached 3·6 km/h *2 ¼ mph*. Cugnot's second, larger tractor, completed in May 1771, today survives in the *Conservatoire nationale des arts et métiers* in Paris. The world's first passenger-carrying automobile was a steam-powered road vehicle carrying eight passengers and built by Richard Trevithick (1771–1833). It first ran on 24 Dec 1801 in Camborne, Cornwall.

Internal combustion

The Swiss Isaac de Rivaz (d. 1828) built a carriage powered by his 'explosion engine' in 1805. The first practical internal-combustion-engined vehicle was that built by the Londoner Samuel Brown (Patent 5350, 25 Apr 1826) whose 4·05 cv *4 hp* two-cylinder atmospheric gas 88 litre engined carriage climbed Shooters Hill, Blackheath, Kent in May 1826.

Britain's continuous motoring history started in November 1894 when Henry Hewetson drove his imported Benz Velo in the south-eastern suburbs of London. The first successful petrol-driven car, the Motorwagen, built by Karl-Friedrich Benz (1844–1929) of Karlsruhe, ran at Mannheim, Germany, in late 1885. It was a 250 kg *5 cwt* 3-wheeler reaching 13–16 km/h *8–10 mph*. Its single-cylinder 4-stroke chain-drive engine (bore 91·4 mm, stroke 160 mm) delivered 0·86 cv *0·85 hp* at 200 rpm. It was patented on 29 Jan 1886. Its first 1 km road test was reported in the local newspaper, the *Neue Badische Landeszeitung*, of 4 June 1886, under the heading 'Miscellaneous'. Two were built in 1885 of which one has been preserved in 'running order' at the Deutsches Museum, Munich.

Registrations *Earliest and most expensive*

The world's first plates were probably introduced by the Parisian police in 1893. Registration plates were introduced in Britain in 1903. The original A1 plate was secured by the 2nd Earl Russell (1865–1931) for his 12·1 cv *12 hp* Napier. This plate, willed in September 1950 to Trevor T. Laker of Leicester, was sold in August 1959 for £2500 in aid of charity. By April 1986, prices for plates reached £25 000. Licence plate No 8 was sold at a Hong Kong government auction for HK$5 million on 13 Feb 1988 to Law Ting-pong, a textile manufacturer. The number 8 is considered a lucky number.

FASTEST CARS

Diesel engined

The prototype 230 hp 3 litre Mercedes C 111/3 attained 327·3 km/h *203·3 mph* in tests on the Nardo Circuit, southern Italy on 5–15 Oct 1978, and in April 1978 averaged 314·462 km/h *195·398 mph* for 12 hours, so covering a world record 3773·55 km *2399·76 miles*.

Rocket-powered sleds

The highest speed recorded on ice is 399·00 km/h *247·93 mph* by *Oxygen* driven by Sammy Miller (b. 15 Apr 1945) on Lake George, NY, USA on 15 Feb 1981.

Steam car

On 19 Aug 1985 Robert E. Barber broke the 79-year old record for a steam car driving No 744 *Steamin' Demon*, built by the Barber-Nichols Engineering Co, 234·33 km/h *145·607 mph* at Bonneville Salt Flats, Utah, USA.

Road cars

Various detuned track cars have been licensed for road use but are not for-sale production models. Manufacturers of very fast and very expensive models understandably limit speed tests to stipulated engine revs. Jaguar cars announced a £100 000 330 km/h *205 mph* two-door coupe being developed at their Engineering Design Centre, Coventry on 25 May 1988. Ferrari asserted a speed of 323·5 km/h *201 mph* for their £140 000 F40 in July 1987. The highest road-tested acceleration

FASTEST CARS

CATEGORY	KM/H	MPH	CAR	DRIVER	PLACE	DATE
JET ENGINED *official*	1019·4	633·468	Thrust 2	Richard Noble (GB)	Black Rock Desert Nevada, USA	4 Oct 1983
ROCKET ENGINED *official*	1001·473	622·287	Blue Flame	Gary Gabelich (USA)	Bonneville, Utah, USA	23 Oct 1970
*unofficial**	1190·377	739·666	Budweiser Rocket	Stan Barrett (USA)	Edwards Air Force Base, California, USA	17 Dec 1979
WHEEL DRIVEN *turbine*	690·909	429·311	Bluebird	Donald Campbell (UK)	Lake Eyre, Australia	17 July 1964
multi piston engine	673·516	418·504	Goldenrod	Robert Summers (USA)	Bonneville, Utah, USA	12 Nov 1965
single piston engine	575·149	357·391	Herda-Knapp-Milodon	Bob Herda (USA)	Bonneville, Utah, USA	2 Nov 1967

* This published speed of Mach 1·0106 is *not* officially sanctioned by the USAF whose Digital Instrumented Radar was not calibrated or certified. The radar information was *not* generated by the vehicle directly but by an operator aiming the dish by means of a TV screen. To claim a speed to 6 significant figures appears quite unsustainable.

reported is 0–96·5 km/h *0–60 mph* in 4·1 sec for an MG Metro 6R4 International Rally Car in 1986.

LARGEST CARS

Of cars produced for private road use, the largest has been the Bugatti 'Royale' type 41, known in Britain as the 'Golden Bugatti', of which only six (not seven) were made at Molsheim, France by the Italian Ettore Bugatti, and all survive. First built in 1927, this machine has an 8-cylinder engine of 12·7 litres capacity, and measures over 6·7 m *22 ft* in length. The bonnet is over 2 m *7 ft* long.

Of custom-built cars the longest is the 16-wheeled 18·3 m *60 ft* long Cadillac limousine 'American Dream' created by Jay Ohrberg Show Cars of Newport Beach, California. It features a swimming pool, hot tub, helipad, satellite dish, crystal chandelier and has 'ample luggage space'.

Largest engines

The world's most powerful piston engine car is 'Quad Al'. It was designed and built in 1964 by Jim Lytle and was first shown in May 1965 at the Los Angeles Sports Arena. The car featured four Allison V12 aircraft engines with a total of 112 087 cc *6840 in³* displacement and 12 000 hp. It

> **Fastest car** ● The highest road tested speed for any road car is for the Porsche 959, a limited edition road car announced in April 1986 with a top road-tested speed of 317 km/h *197 mph.* (Photo: Porsche)

has 4-wheel drive, 8 wheels and tyres, and dual 6-disc clutch assemblies. The wheelbase is 406·4 cm *160 in,* and weighs 2658 kg *5860 lb.* It also has 96 spark plugs and 96 exhaust pipes.

The largest car ever used was the 'White Triplex', sponsored by J. H. White of Philadelphia, Pennsylvania, USA. Completed early in 1928, after two years' work, the car weighed about 4·06 tonnes *4 tons* and was powered by three Liberty V12 aircraft engines with a total capacity of 81188 cc, developing 1500 bhp at 2000 rpm. It

> **Most expensive** *GB* ● In Great Britain £5·5 million was paid at auction by Christie's at the Royal Albert Hall, London for a 1931 Bugatti Type 41 Royale Sports Coupé on 19 Nov 1987 by Nicholas Harley, a London dealer. (Photo: Bob Masters for Christie's)

was used to break the world speed record but crashed at Daytona, Florida, on 13 Mar 1929.

Currently the most powerful car on the road is the 6-wheeled Jameson-Merlin, powered by a 27000 cc 1760 hp Rolls Royce V12 Merlin aero-engine, governed down to a maximum speed of 298 km/h *185 mph.* It has a range of 480 km *300 miles* with tanks of 272 litres *60 gal* capacity. The vehicle weighs 2·69 tonnes *2·65 tons* overall.

Production car

The highest engine capacity of a production car was 13½ litres *824 in³,* for the US Pierce-Arrow 6–66 Racea-bout of 1912–18, the US Peerless 6–60 of 1912–14 and the Fageol of 1918. The most powerful current production car is the Lamborghini Countach 50005 quattro-valvole with a 5167 cc V12 engine developing 455 bhp.

Engine change

The fastest time recorded for removing a car engine and replacing it is 42 sec for a Ford Escort by a Royal Marine team of five from Portsmouth, on 21 Nov 1985 on the BBC *Record Breakers* programme.

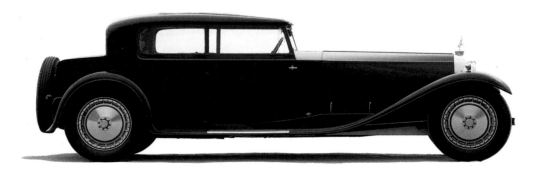

Petrol consumption

On 29 May 1986 at the Shell Oakville Research Center test track at Ontario, Canada, Tim Leier of the University of Saskatchewan, Saskatoon covered a distance of 9158 km *5691 miles* on 4·54 litre *1 gallon* although subsequently figures of 5107 mpg and 5691 mpg have been reported from Australia and Canada respectively.

Longest fuel range

The greatest distance driven without refuelling on a tankful of fuel (88·12 l *19·41 gal*) is 1851·2 km *1150·3 miles* by an Audi 100 turbo diesel driven by Stuart

Bladon with his son Bruce (navigator) and Bob Proctor (RAC observer) from Land's End to John O'Groats and back to West Falkirk in 22 hrs 28 min in July 1984. The average speed was 82·33 km/h *51·17 mph* giving 4·77 l/100 km *59·27 mpg*.

Most durable car

The highest recorded mileage for a car was 1 906 879 km *1 184 880 authenticated miles* by August 1978 for a 1957 Mercedes 180 D owned by Robert O'Reilly of Olympia, Washington State. Its subsequent fate is unknown. R. L. Bender of Madison, Wisconsin, U.S.A., who had been driving since

Crawler ● The most massive vehicle ever constructed is the Marion eight-caterpillar crawler used for conveying *Saturn V* rockets to their launching pads at Cape Canaveral, Florida (see Chapter 4, Most powerful rocket). It measures 40 m *131 ft 4 in* by 34·7 m *114 ft* and the two built cost $12 300 000). The loaded train weight is 8036 tons *8165 tonnes*. The windscreen wipers were 106 cm *42 in* blades and were the world's largest. (Photo: Ken Brookes)

1958, has claimed 1 643 206 km *1 021 041 miles* by 9 June 1984 for his car.

Taxis

The largest taxi fleet is that in Mexico City, Mexico with 60 000 'normal' taxis, pesaros (communal fixed route taxis) and settas (airport taxis) in mid-1984. On 31 Dec 1987 there were 14 792 taxis and 19 685 drivers in London. The longest fare on record is one of 12 133 km *7533 miles* through 10 countries from Marble Arch, London from 19 Sept–18 Oct 1981. The trip was sponsored for charity and the driver was Stephen Tillyer. Francis Edward

Kenyon (b. 1904) was continuously licensed as a taxi driver in Manchester for 57 years 36 days from 1924–81.

MOST EXPENSIVE CARS
Special
The most expensive car to build has been the US Presidential 1969 Lincoln Continental Executive delivered to the US Secret Service on 14 Oct 1968. It has an overall length of 6·56 m *21 ft 6·3 in* with a 4·06 m *13 ft 4 in* wheel-base and with the addition of 2·03 tonnes *2 tons* of armour plate, weighs 5·43 tonnes *5·35 tons* (5443 kg *12 000 lb*). The estimated cost of research, development and manufacture was $500 000 but it is rented at $5000 per annum. Even if all four tyres were shot out it can travel at 80 km/h *50 mph* on inner rubber-edged steel discs. Carriage House Motor Cars of New York in March 1978 completed 4 years' work on converting a 1973 Rolls Royce including lengthening it by 76·2 cm *30 in*. The price tag was $500 000.

Standard
The most expensive British standard car is the Rolls-Royce 8-cylinder 6750 cc Phantom VI quoted in 1987 at £207 133 (including tax). More expensive are custom-built models. Jack Barclay Ltd of Berkeley Square, London quote £350 000 for an armour-plated Rolls-Royce Phantom VI.

The unrivalled collector of Rolls-Royces was Bhagwan Shri Rajneesh (b. 1931), the Indian mystic lately of Rajneeshpuram, Oregon. His disciples bestowed 93 of these upon him before his deportation in November 1985.

Used
The greatest price paid for any used car is $8·1 million for the 1931 Berline de Voyage Royale, one of six Bugatti Royales, by Thomas Monaghan of Ann Arbor, Michigan, USA. The car, formerly part of the William F. Harrah collection, was first sold to property developer Jerry Moore for $6·5 million when the collection was cut down from 1700 to 1300 cars in June 1986, then on to Mr Monaghan some months later.

> **Largest Ambulance** ● The world's largest ambulances are the 18 m *59 ft 0½ in* long articulated Alligator Jumbulances Mark VI, VII and VIII and IX, operated by The ACROSS Trust to convey the sick and handicapped on holidays and pilgrimages across Europe. Built by Van Hool of Belgium with Fiat engines, they cost £200 000 for 44 patients and staff.

Most inexpensive
The cheapest car of all time was the 1922 Red Bug Buckboard, built by Briggs and Stratton Co of Milwaukee, Wisconsin, USA listed at $150–$125. It had a 1·57 m *62 in* wheel base and weighed 111 kg *245 lb*. Early models of the King Midget cars were sold in kit form for self-assembly for as little as $100 as late as 1948. By May 1987 the cheapest quoted new car price in Britain was £2431 for a Fiat 126, 652-cc 2-door car.

Longest in production
The longest any car has been in mass production is 50 years (1938 to date), including wartime interruptions, for the Volkswagen 'Beetle' series, originally designed by Ferdinand Porsche. The 20-millionth car came off the final production line in Mexico on 15 May 1981, and more than 21 million had been built by January 1987. Residual production continues in South America. Britain's all-time champion is the Morgan series 4/4 from 27 Dec 1935 from the Morgan Motor Car of Malvern (founded 1910). Britain's champion seller has been the Mini, designed by Sir Alec Issigonis (b. 1906) which originally sold for £496 19s 2d in August 1959. Sales reached 5 000 000 on 19 Feb 1986.

DRIVING
Round the world
The fastest circumnavigation embracing more than an equator's length of driving (40 075·0 km *24 901·47 road miles*) is one of 74 days 1 hr 11 min by Garry Sowerby (driver) and Ken Langley (navigator) of Canada from 6 Sept to 19 Nov 1980 in a Volvo 245 DL westwards from Toronto, Canada through 4 continents and 23 countries. The distance covered was 43 030 km *26 738 miles* (see below for their Cape to Cape record). Between 30 Mar 1964 and 23 Apr 1984 entertainers Manfred Müller and Paul-Ernst Luhrs drove round the world in their 1963 Citroen 2CV covering 83 countries and 350 000 km *217 490 miles*. They started and finished in Bremerhaven, West Germany.

Cape to Cape
The first traverse of the world's greatest land mass (Afro-Eurasia) was achieved by Richard Pape, who left the North Cape in an Austin A90 on 28 July and arrived in Cape Town on 22 Oct 1955 with the milometer recording 28 160 km *17 500 miles* after 86 days. The speed record was set by Ken Langley and Garry Sowerby of Canada driving north in 28 days 13 hr 10 min for 20 166 km *12 531 miles* from 4 Apr—2 May 1984.

Cape to London
The record for the 18 787 km *11 674 mile* road route from Cape Town, South Africa, to London is 14 days 19 hr 26 min set by husband and wife team Brig John and Dr Lucy Hemsley from 8 to 22 Jan 1983 in a Range Rover. Apart from the Channel crossing they were the first to drive entirely overland from Capetown, South Africa, to London.

Cape to Cairo
Brig Hemsley and his wife, in the course of establishing the above Cape to London record drove from Capetown to Cairo, Egypt in 10 days 12 hr 16 min from 8 to 18 Jan 1983, a distance of 11 159 km *6934 miles*. During the course of the drive, their's was the first car to cross the Allenby Bridge between Israel and Jordan for 7 years This bridge has not been traversed by car subsequently.

British counties
Richard and Rachel Parkhouse of Gwynedd covered all 62 mainland counties of Great Britain by car (BMW 325i Touring) on a 2423 km *1506 mile* route on 11–12 June 1988 in 25 hr 6 min, averaging exactly 96·5 km/h *60 mph*. This broke his 1984 record of 28 hr 52 min by motorcycle.

Round Britain economy
A diesel-powered Ford Fiesta 1600 was driven by Rod Lambert and Ray Hancox with navigator John Taylor around the 5808 km *3609 mile* course from 14–21 June 1987 returning a fuel consumption of 30·16 km/litre *85·2 mpg*.

Mountain driving
Vehicles have been driven up Ben Nevis, Invernessshire, Scotland (1343 m *4406 ft*) on six occasions. The record times are 7 hr 23 min (ascent) and 1 hr 55 min (descent) by George F. Simpson in an Austin 7 on 6 Oct 1928. Henry Alexander accomplished the feat twice in May 1911 (Model T Ford) and on 13 Sept 1928 (Model A Ford). The most recent ascent was on 11 Sept 1987 when two Suzuki 4-wheel ATV Quad Runner vehicles drove from Old Inverlochy Castle to the summit in 2 hr 21 min. They were driven by Jerome Fack of Wadebridge, Cornwall, Paul Hunt of Egham, Surrey David Kirke of London and Rod Shand of Fort William.

Driving in reverse
Charles Creighton (1908–70) and James Hargis of Maplewood, Missouri, USA· drove their Ford Model A 1929 roadster in reverse from New York 5375 km *3340 miles* to Los Angeles, California, USA from 26 July–13 Aug 1930 without once stopping the engine. They arrived back in New York in reverse on 5 Sept so completing 11 555 km *7180 miles* in 42 days. The highest average speed attained in any non-stop reverse drive exceeding 800 km *500 miles* was achieved by Gerald Hoagland who drove a 1969 Chevrolet Impala 806·2 km *501 miles* in 17 hr 38 min at Chemung Speed Drome, New York, USA on 9–10 July 1976 to average 45·72 km/h *28·41 mph*.

Brian 'Cub' Keene and James 'Wilbur' Wright drove their Chevrolet Blazer 14 533 km *9031 miles* in 37 days (1 Aug–6 Sept 1984) through 15 US states and Canada. Though it was prominently named 'Stuck in Reverse' law enforcement officers in Oklahoma refused to believe it and insisted they drove in reverse reverse, i.e. forwards, out of the state.

Battery-powered vehicle
Robert Dodds and Ian Pridding with the support of the Pontllanfraith Rotary Club travelled 1479 km *919 miles* from John O'Groats to Land's End in a Sinclair C5 in 80 hr 47 min from 18–21 May 1987. David Turner and Tim Pickhard of Turners of Boscastle Ltd, Cornwall, travelled 1408 km *875 miles* from Land's End to John O'Groats in 63 hours in a Freight Rover Leyland Sherpa powered by a Lucas electric motor from 21–23 Dec 1985.

Joe Schwarzkopf-Bowers, 37, of Watford, Herts drove his modified battery-powered Bond Equipe from Heathrow Airport, London to Crewkerne, Somerset on 16 May 1986, a distance of 212·4 km *132 miles* on a single charge costing an estimated 60p.

Two-side-wheel driving
Gilbert Bataille of Paris drove a Leyland T45 Road Runner Truck on two wheels for 4·60 km *2·864 miles* at the British Truck Grand Prix, Silverstone, Northants on 17 Aug 1986.

Kenneth Eriksson (b. 13 May 1956) of Äppelbo, Sweden, drove a standard production 1986 Opel Kadett GSI 1·8 litre on two wheels for a distance of 24·299 km *15·1 miles* on 28 Sept 1985 at the Anderstorp Motor Circuit, Sweden. Göran Eliason (b. 7 Dec 1946) of Boras, Sweden achieved 143·027 km/h *88·87 mph* on the two wheels of a standard Volvo 760 at Anderstorp on 24 May 1987.

Wheelie
Steve Murty drove a Multi-Part Skytrain truck on its rear wheels for 412·5 m *1353 ft 4 in* at Mondello Park, Co Kildare, Ireland on 23 Aug 1987. The 60 tonne truck was powered by a 500 bhp Cummins turbo-charged 14-litre engine and had a ZF-Ecomat hp 600 5-speed automatic gearbox.

Oldest driver
Roy M. Rawlins (b. 10 July 1870) of Stockton, California, was warned for driving at 152 km/h *95 mph* in a 88·5 km/h *55 mph* zone in June 1974. On 25 Aug 1974 he was

C. Kocich drove 5 056 470 km *3 141 946 miles* from 5 Feb 1953 to 28 Feb 1986 so averaging 153 226 km *95 210 miles* per year.

Driving tests

The record for persistence in taking the Ministry of Transport's Learner's Test is held by Mrs Miriam Hargrave (b. 3 Apr 1908) of Wakefield, West Yorkshire, who failed her 39th driving test in eight years on 29 Apr 1970 after 'crashing' a set of red lights. She triumphed at her 40th attempt after 212 lessons on 3 Aug 1970. The examiner was alleged not to have known about her previous 39 tests. In 1978 she was reported still to disdain right-hand turns. The world's easiest tests have been those in Egypt in which the ability to drive 6 m *19·64 ft* forward and the same in reverse has been deemed sufficient. In 1979 it was reported that accurate reversing had been added between two rubber traffic cones. 'High cone attrition' soon led to the substitution of white lines. Mrs Fannie Turner (b. 1903) of Little Rock, Arkansas, passed the *written* test for drivers on her 104th attempt in October 1978.

SERVICES

Car parks

The world's largest car park is the West Edmonton Mall, Edmonton, Alberta, Canada, which can hold 20 000 vehicles. There are overflow facilities on an adjoining lot for 10 000 more cars.

The largest parking area in Great Britain is that for 15 000 cars and 200 coaches at the National Exhibition Centre, Birmingham (see p.108).

Britain's highest capacity underground car park is under the Victoria Centre, Nottingham with a capacity of 1650 cars, opened in June 1972.

The largest private garage is one of two storeys built outside Bombay for the private collection of 176 cars owned by Pranlal Bhogilal (b. 1939).

Filling stations

Little America, west of Cheyenne, Wyoming, at the junction of Interstate Routes 80 and 25 claims to be the world's biggest gas station with 52 diesel and gas pumps—none self-service. The largest filling station of the 36 000 in the United Kingdom is the Esso service area on the M4 at Leigh Delamere, Wiltshire, opened on 3 Jan 1972. It has 48 petrol and diesel pumps and extends over 17·4 ha *43 acres*. The highest in the world is at Leh, Ladakh, India at 3658 m *12 001 ft* operated by the Indian Oil Corporation.

Unleaded petrol

The first unleaded petrol to be available in the United

---

awarded a California State licence valid till 1978, but Mr Rawlins died on 9 July 1975, one day short of his 105th birthday. Mrs Maude Tull of Inglewood, California, who took to driving aged 91 after her husband died, was issued a renewal on 5 Feb 1976 when aged 104. Britain's oldest known driver have been Benjamin Kagan (1878–1988) of Leeds who was still driving at the age of 102 in 1983. Currently the record is held by the Reverend Albert Thomas Humphrey (b. 18 May 1886) from Bridgwater, Somerset in a white Mini. The oldest age at which a man has passed the Department of Transport driving test has been 89 years 2 months by David Coupar (b. 9 Feb 1898) on 4 Mar 1987 in Perth, Perthshire. The oldest woman to pass was Mrs Gerty Edwards Land (b. 9 Sept 1897) on 27 Apr 1988 in Colne, Lancs. She was aged 90 years 229 days.

The holder of the earliest driving licence to be issued in Britain is Mr Reginald 'Gerry' Bond (b. 16 July 1889) of Bournemouth, Dorset whose first licence is dated Oct 1907.

Youngest driver

Instances of drivers have been recorded in HM Armed Forces much under 17 years. Mrs P. L. M. Williams (b. 3 Feb 1926), now of Risca, Gwent, as Private Patterson in the ATS, drove a 5-ton truck in 1941 aged 15. Mark Blackbourn of Lincoln, having passed his driving test the

> **Snowmobiles ●** Tony Lenzini of Duluth, Minnesota, USA, seen here with his 1986 Arctic Cat Cougar snowmobile drove a total of 11 604·6 km *7211 miles* in 60 riding days between 28 Dec 1985 and 20 Mar 1986.
> Richard and Raymond Moore and Loren Matthews drove their snowmobile 9456 km *5876 miles* from Fairbanks, Alaska to Fenton, Michigan, USA, in 39 days from 3 Feb–13 Mar 1980.

day after his 17th birthday, went on to pass the advanced test less than 48 hours later on 7 Aug 1985.

Clare Howard of Rainham, Essex, passed her test on 2 Sept 1987 aged 16 years 102 days. Mark Collins Hall of Otley, West Yorkshire passed his test on 24 July 1985 aged 16 years 103 days.

Most durable

The Goodyear Tire and Rubber Co test driver Weldon

> **Most powerful truck ●** This 1987 Ford L + L 9000 truck, owned and driven by Ken Warby of Cincinnati, Ohio, USA, is equipped with a General Electric J 79 tuned to produce 88 950 N *20 000 lbf* of thrust. Weighing 4 tonnes it has achieved 338·27 km/h *210·2 mph* in 7·7 sec over a quarter mile standing start.

Solar-powered car ● The highest speed attained by a solely solar-powered land vehicle is 78·37 km/h *48·71 mph* by Molly Brennan driving the General Motors *Sunraycer* at Mesa, Arizona, USA on 24 June 1988. On the same day *Sunraycer* also attained a top speed of 129·04 km/h *80·2 mph* using both solar ands battery power.

In November 1987 *Sunraycer* won the 3138 km *1950 mile* solar challenge race in Australia, finishing two and a half days ahead of its nearest competitor. (Photo: All-Sport)

Kingdom went on sale on 24 June 1986. Minister of State for the Environment, William Waldegrave, made the first fill at Stamford Bridge Service Station, London.

Largest garage
The KMB Overhaul Centre operated by the Kowloon Motor Bus Co (1933) Ltd, Hong Kong, is the world's largest multi-storeyed service centre. Purpose built for double deck buses, its 4 floors occupy in excess of 47·00 m² *11·6 acres*.

Tow
The longest tow on record was one of 7658 km *4759 miles* from Halifax, Nova Scotia to Canada's Pacific coast, when Frank J. Elliott and George A. Scott of Amherst, Nova Scotia, Canada, persuaded 168 passing motorists in 89 days to tow their Model T Ford (in fact engineless) to win a $1000 bet on 15 Oct 1927.

After his 1969 MGB, TJN 405H, broke down in the vicinity of Moscow, Eddie McGowan of Chipping Warden, Oxfordshire, was towed a distance of 2343 km *1456 miles* from Moscow to West Berlin on a 2 m *7 ft* single nylon tow rope on 12–17 July 1987

Tyres
The world's largest tyres ever manufactured were by the Goodyear Tire & Rubber Co for giant dumper trucks. They measure 3·65 m *12 ft* in diameter, weigh 5670 kg *12 500 lb* and cost $74 000. A tyre 5·18 m *17 ft* in diameter is believed to be the limitation of what is practical.

Skid marks
The longest recorded skid marks on a public road have been those 290 m *950 ft* long left by a Jaguar car involved in an accident on the M1 near Luton, Bedfordshire, on 30 June 1960. Evidence given in the High Court case *Hurlock* v. *Inglis* et al. indicated a speed 'in excess of 160 km/h *100 mph* before the application of the brakes'.

The skid marks made by the jet-powered *Spirit of America*, driven by Norman Craig Breedlove, after the car went out of control at Bonneville Salt Flats, Utah, USA, on 15 Oct 1964, were nearly 9·6 km *6 miles* long.

VEHICLES
Land
The most massive automotive land vehicle is 'Big Muskie' the 10 890 tonne *10 700 ton* mechanical shovel built by Bucyrus Erie for the Musk mine. It is 148·43 m *487 ft* long, 46·02 m *151 ft* wide and 67·66 m *222 ft* high with a grab capacity of 325 tons.

Longest
The longest vehicle ever built is the Arctic Snow Train owned by the world-famous wire-walker Steve McPeak (US). This 54-wheeled 174·3 m *572 ft* long vehicle was built by R.G. Le Tourneau Inc of Longview, Texas for the US Army. Its gross train weight is 400 tons with a top speed of 32 km/h *20 mph* and it was driven by a crew of 6 when used as an 'overland train' for the military. McPeak repaired it and every punctured wheel single-handed in often sub-zero temperatures in Alaska.

It generates 4680 shp and has a capacity of 29 648 litres *6522 imperial gallons*.

Amphibious circumnavigation
The only circumnavigation by an amphibious vehicle was achieved by Ben Carlin (Australia) (d. 7 Mar 1981) in an amphibious jeep *Half-Safe*. He completed the last leg of the Atlantic crossing (the English Channel) on 24 Aug 1951. He arrived back in Montreal, Canada on 8 May 1958 having completed a circumnavigation of 62 765 km *39 000 miles* over land and 15 450 km *9600 miles* by sea and river. He was accompanied on the trans-Atlantic stage by his ex-wife Elinore (US) and on the long trans-Pacific stage (Tokyo to Anchorage) by Broye Lafayette De-Mente (b. Missouri, 1928).

Buses *Earliest*
The first municipal motor omnibus service in the world was inaugurated on 12 Apr 1903 between Eastbourne railway station and Meads, East Sussex, England. A steam-powered bus named *Royal Patent* ran between Gloucester and Cheltenham for 4 months in 1831.

Longest
The longest buses in the world are the 10 870 kg *10·72 ton*, 23·16 m *76 ft* articulated buses, with 121 passenger seats and room also for 66 'strap-hangers', built by the Wayne Corporation of Richmond, Indiana for use in the Middle East.

Longest route
The longest regularly scheduled bus route is by 'Across Australia Coach Lines', who inaugurated a regular scheduled service between Perth and Brisbane on 9 Apr 1980. The route is 5455 km *3389 miles* taking 75 hr 55 min. The longest route in Great Britain is 1089 km *677 miles* between Plymouth and Aberdeen.

The 806 service is operated jointly by Western National Ltd and Northern Scottish Omnibuses Ltd, each company allocating coaches on alternate days.

Trolleybuses
The last trolleybus in Britain, owned by Bradford Corporation, ran in 1972. Plans have been made to reintroduce trolleybuses by both West Yorkshire and South Yorkshire Passenger transport Executives.

Caravans *Longest journey*
The longest continuous motor caravan journey is one of 231 288 km *143 716 miles* by Harry B. Coleman and Peggy Larson in a Volkswagen Camper from 20 Aug 1976 to 20 Apr 1978 through 113 countries. Saburo Ouchi (b. 7 Feb 1942) of Tokyo, Japan drove 270 000 km *167 770 miles* in 91 countries from 2 Dec 1969 to 10 Feb 1978.

Largest
The largest caravans built in Britain for exhibition purposes are the £300 000 'State Super Caravans', 18 m *59 ft 0½ in* in length and 3·5 m *11 ft 5¾ in* wide built since 1977 by Coventry Steel Caravans of Newport Pagnell, Buckinghamshire. Firm in liquidation now.

Fastest
The world speed record for a caravan is 201·02 km/h *124·91 mph* by an Alpha 14 towed by a Le Mans Aston Martin V8 saloon driven by Robin Hamilton at RAF Elvington, North Yorkshire on 14 Oct 1980.

Dumper truck
The world's largest dump-truck is the Terex Titan 33–19 manufactured by the Terex Division of General Motors Corporation. It has a loaded weight of 548·6 tonnes *539·9 tons* and a capacity of 317·5 tonnes *312½ tons.* When tipping its height is 17·06 m *56 ft.* The 16-cylinder engine delivers 3300 hp. The fuel tank holds 5904·6 litres *1300 imperial gallons.* It went into service in November 1974.

Earth mover
The world's largest earth mover is the 100-tonne T-800 built at the Lenin Tractor Works in Chelyabinsk, USSR, announced in September 1984.

Fire engine
The world's most powerful fire appliance is the 860 hp 8-wheel Oshkosh firetruck used for aircraft fires. It can discharge 190 000 l *41 600 gal* of foam through two turrets in just 150 sec. It weighs 60 tonnes *59 tons.* The fastest on record is the Jaguar XJ12 – 'Chubb Firefighter', which, in Nov 1982, attained a speed of 210·13 km/h *130·57 mph* in tests when servicing the *Thrust 2* land speed record trials (see pp. 128)

Go-karting
The highest mileage recorded in 24 hours on a closed twisting circuit for go-karts driven by a 4-man team is 1638·3 km *1018 laps of a mile* at Erbsville Kartway, Waterloo, Ontario, Canada. The 5-hp 140-cc Honda engined kart was driven by Owen Nimmo, Gary Ruddock, Jim Timmins and Danny Upshaw on 4–5 Sept 1983.

The highest distance recorded in a 48 hour marathon is 2730 km *1696·3 miles* by Denis Wedes, Stephen Mantle, Len Nicholson and Janice Bennett driving a Yamaha RC100SE kart powered by a KT100J 100 cc engine at Mount Sugarloaf Circuit, Newcastle, NSW, Australia on 25–7 Mar 1983.

The highest mileage of the 100-cc non-gearbox solo six-hour record is 313·51 km *194·81 miles* by Emily Newman at Rye House Raceway, Hoddesdon, Hertfordshire on 25 July 1986.

Lawn mowers
The widest gang mower in the world is the 5-ton 18·28 m *60 ft* wide 27-unit 'Big Green Machine' used by the sod farmer Jay Edgar Frick of Monroe, Ohio. It mows an acre in 60 sec. The longest drive on a lawn mower was 4877 km *3031 miles* when Steve Perritt of Standlake,

Oxfordshire drove a Kubota G3HST from Windsor, Berkshire to Great Dunmow, Essex via Inverness, Highland, in 30 driving days from 14 Feb to 18 Mar 1988. The greatest distance covered in the annual 12-hour Lawn Mower Race (under the rules of the BLMRA, the British Lawn Mower Racing Association) is 444·1 km *276 miles* by Tony Hazelwood, Derek Bell, Tony Smith and Ray Kilminster at Wisborough Green, W. Sussex on 21–22 June 1980. A 12-hour run-behind record of 162·7 km *101·15 miles* was set at Wisborough Green on 8–9 July 1984 by the 'Super Gnome' team.

Tractor
The world's largest tractor is the $459 000 US Department of Agriculture Wide Tractive Frame Vehicle completed by Ag West of Sacramento, California in June 1982. It measures 10·05 m *33 ft* between its wheels which are designed to run on permanent paths and weighs 22·22 tonnes *21·87 tons.*

The sport of tractor-pulling was put on a national US championship basis in 1967 at Bowling Green, Ohio where the winner was 'The Purple Monster' built and driven by Roger E. Varns. Today there are 12 classes ranging up to '12 200 lb unlimited'.

Wrecker
The world's most powerful wrecker is the Twin City Garage and Body Shop's 20·6 tonne *21 ton* 10·9 m *36 ft* long 1969 International M6-23 'Hulk' stationed at Scott City, Missouri. It can lift in excess of 295 tonnes *300 tons* on its short boom.

Fastest road machine ●The 115–bhp Japanese Honda V65 Magna with a liquid –cooled, in–line V–4, 16–valve DoHC engine of 1098–cc capacity has a design speed of 283·2 km/h *176 mph.* (Photo: Honda)

ROAD LOADS
Heaviest load
On 14–15 July 1984 John Brown Engineers & Contractors BV moved the Conoco Kotter Field production deck with a roll-out weight of 3805 tonnes for the Continental Netherlands Oil Company of Leidsenhage, Netherlands.

The heaviest road load moved in the United Kingdom has been a 1305 tonne *1284 ton* module for the semi-submersible drilling rig *Ocean Alliance 2002.* It measured 21 m *70 ft* high by 30·5 m *100 ft* long by 27·4 m *90 ft* wide and was drawn by four tractor units developing a total of 0·8 km *0·49 mile* of public road on its journey from the River Tees to the River Clyde on 5 Nov 1985. The longest item moved has been a 83·8 m *275 ft* long high-pressure steel gas storage vessel weighing 233 tonnes *229 tons* transported to a new site at Beckton gasworks in east London on 10 July 1985. The overall train length was 99 m *325 ft.*

MOTORCYCLES
(see also Chapter 12)
Earliest
The earliest internal combustion-engined motorised bicycle was a wooden-framed machine built at Bad Cannstatt in Oct–Nov 1885 by Gottlieb Daimler (1834–1900) of Germany and first ridden by Wilhelm Maybach

(1846–1929). It had a top speed of 19 km/h *12 mph* and developed one-half of one horsepower from its single-cylinder 264-cc four-stroke engine at 700 rpm. Known as the 'Einspur', it was lost in a fire in 1903. The first motorcycles of entirely British production were the 1046-cc Holden flat-four and the 2¾-hp Clyde single both produced in 1898. The earliest factory which made motorcycles in quantity was opened in 1894 by Heinrich and Wilhelm Hildebrand and Alois Wolfmüller at Munich, West Germany. In its first two years this factory produced over 1000 machines, each having a water-cooled 1488-cc twin-cylinder four-stroke engine developing about 2·5-bhp at 600 rpm—the highest capacity motor cycle engine ever put into production.

Fastest racing machine
There is no satisfactory answer to the identity of the fastest track machine other than to say that the current Kawasaki, Suzuki and Yamaha machines have all been geared to attain speeds marginally in excess of 300 km/h *186·4 mph* under race conditions.

Most expensive motorcycle
The Harley Davidson FLHTC Electra Glide Classic, with a four-stroke 45-degree V-Twin engine of 1340 cubic capcity, a sound system with handlebar controls, adjustable three-position rider floorboards, a seat with a 'floating' rubber-mounted backrest and a choice of five two-tone colours, costs £8930 including tax and VAT.

Duration
The longest time a solo motorcycle has been kept in non-stop motion is 560 hr by Norberto Naummi, Foppiani Maurizio and Roberto Ghillani who covered 30 370 km *18 000 miles* at an average speed of 54·23 km/h *33·69 mph* in Varano do Melegari, Italy from 16 Aug–8 Sept 1986.

Biggest fan
The White Helmets, the Royal Signals Motorcycle Display Team, successfully achieved an 8-bike, 36-man pyramid for 300 m *328 yds* on 2 Sept 1986 at Catterick, North Yorkshire.

Wheelie
Doug Domokos on the Alabama International Speedway, Talladega, USA on 27 June 1984 covered 233·34 km *145 miles* non-stop on the rear wheel of his Honda XR 500. He stopped only when the gas ran out. The highest speed attained on a back wheel is 221·43 km/h *137·6 mph* by Richard Almot (France) on 15 Aug 1986 at the Multi-Part British Truck Grand Prix, Silverstone, Northants.

Most on one machine
The record for the most people on a single machine is for 46 members of the Illawarra Mini Bike Training Club, New South Wales, Australia. They rode on a 1000 cc motorcycle and travelled a distance of 1·7 km *1 mile* on 11 Oct 1987.

Oldest motorcyclist
Arthur Merrick Cook (b. 13.6.1895) still regularly rides his Suzuki 125 GS Special motorcycle every day.

BICYCLES
Earliest
The first design for a machine propelled by cranks and pedals with connecting rods has been attributed to Leonardo da Vinci (1452–1519), or one of his pupils, dated *c.* 1493. The earliest such design actually built was in 1839–40 by Kirkpatrick Macmillan (1810–78) of Dumfries, Scotland. It is now in the Science Museum, Kensington and Chelsea, London. The first practical bicycle was the *vélocipède* built in March 1861 by Pierre and his son Ernest Michaux of rue de Verneuil, Paris. In 1870, James Starley, in Coventry, constructed the first 'penny-farthing' or Ordinary bicycle. It had wire-spoked wheels for lightness and was available with an optional speed gear.

Trishaw

The longest trishaw parade on record was when 177 trishaw pedlars rode in single convoy in Penang, Malaysia on 23 Nov 1986.

Longest

The longest true tandem bicycle ever built (i.e. without a third stabilising wheel) is one of 20·4 m *66 ft 11 in* for 35 riders built by the Pedaalstompers Westmalle of Belgium. They rode *c.* 60 m *195 ft* in practice on 20 Apr 1979. The machine weighs 1100 kg *2425 lb.*

Smallest

The world's smallest wheeled ridable bicycle is one with wheels of 1·95 cm *0·76 in* diameter which was ridden by its constructor Neville Patten of Gladstone, Queensland, Australia for a distance of 4·1 m *13 ft 5½ in* on 25 Mar 1988. Jacques Puyoou of Pau, Pyrénées-Atlantiques, France has built a tandem 36 cm *14·1 in* ridden by him and Madame Puyoou.

Largest

A classic Ordinary bicycle with wheels of 165·7 cm *65¼ in* diameter front and 45·7 cm *18 in* back was constructed by the Coventry Machinists Co in 1881. It is now owned by Paul Foulkes-Halbard of Crowborough, Sussex.

A bicycle with an 2·50 m *8 ft 2½ in* front wheel with pedal extenders was built in 1878 for circus demonstrations.

Fastest *HPV's*

The world speed records for human-powered vehicles (HPVs) are 99·68 km/h *61·94 mph* (single rider) by John Seibert at La Garita, Colorado on 27 Oct 1980; and 101·25 km/h *62·92 mph* (multiple riders) by Dave Grylls and Leigh Barczewski at the Ontario Speedway, California on 4 May 1980.

A British 200 m record was set by S. Poulter in *Poppy Flyer*, in 9·10 sec at Greenham Common, Berkshire on 2 Aug 1981.

Endurance

From 10–21 July 1983, 24 City and Guilds College, London, students drove an HPV round Great Britain on a 5914 km *3675 mile* route to average 23·19 km/h *14·41 mph.*

Unicycles

The tallest unicycle ever mastered is one 31·01 m *101 ft 9 in* tall ridden by Steve McPeak (with a safety wire or mechanic suspended to an overhead crane) for a distance of 114·6 m *376 ft* in Las Vegas in October 1980. The freestyle riding of ever taller unicycles (i.e. without any safety harness) must inevitably lead to serious injury or fatality. Deepak Lele of Maharashtra, India unicycled 6378 km *3963 miles* from New York to Los Angeles from 6 June–25 Sept 1984.

Brian Davis, 33 of Tillicoultry, Clackmannan, Scotland rode 1450 km *901 miles* from Land's End to John O'Groats from 16 May to 4 June 1980 in 19 days 1 hr 45 min. Takayuki Koike of Kanagawa, Japan set a record for 160·9 km *100 miles* in 6 hr 44 min 21·84 sec on 9 Aug 1987. The sprint record from a standing start over 100 metres is 13·71 sec by John Foss of Westbury, New York, USA, in Tokyo, Japan on 1 Aug 1987.

Wheelie

A world duration record of 4 hr 21 min 1 sec was set by Robert Hurd at the Recreation Centre, Winchester, Hants on 18 Nov 1986.

Penny-farthing

The record for riding from Land's End to John O'Groats on Ordinary bicycles, more commonly known in the 1870s as Penny-farthings, is 9 days 6 hr 52 min by police officer Clive Flint, 31 of Manchester from 1–10 June 1984. G. P. Mills (Anfield BC) rode this course in 5 days 1 hr 45 min on a 53-inch Humber from 4–10 July 1886.

Smallest motorcycle ● Paul Ashley of Basildon, Essex, with the motorcycle he has constructed. It has a wheelbase of 175 mm *6·88 in*, a seat height of 175 mm *6·88 in* and with wheels 50 mm *1·96 in* in diameter. Powered by a 3·5 cc engine he has ridden it over 120 m *400 ft* reaching 8 km/h *5 mph.*

Underwater cycling

Thirty-two certified Scuba divers in 60 hours from 27–29 Nov 1981 rode a submarine tricycle 104·54 km *64·96 miles* on the bottom of Amphi High School pool, Tucson, Arizona, USA, in a scheme devised by Lucian Spataro to raise money for the Casa De Los Niños Nursery. A team of 32 in 72 underwater hours achieved 141·322 km *87·81 miles* in Navik, Norway from 28–31 Mar 1984.

Railways

TRAINS
Earliest

Wagons running on wooden rails were used for mining as early as 1550 at Leberthal, Alsace, and in Britain for conveying coal at Wollaton near Nottingham from 1603–15 and at Broseley Colliery, Shropshire, in October 1605. The earliest commercially successful steam locomotives worked on the Middleton Colliery Railway to Leeds, Yorkshire, authorised by Britain's first Railway Act on 9 June 1758. Richard Trevithick (1771–1833) built his first steam locomotive for the 914 mm *3 ft* gauge iron plateway at Coalbrookdale, Shropshire, in 1803, but there is no evidence that it ran. His second locomotive drew wagons in which men rode on a demonstration run at Penydarren, Mid-Glamorgan, Wales, on 22 Feb 1804, but it broke the plate rails. The first permanent public railway to use steam traction was the Stockton & Darlington, from its opening on 27 Sept 1825 from Shildon to Stockton via Darlington, in Cleveland. The 7 tonne *Locomotion* could pull 48 tonnes at a speed of 24 km/h *15 mph.* It was designed and driven by George Stephenson (1781–1848). The first regular steam passenger service was inaugurated over a one-mile section (between Bogshole Farm and South Street in Whitstable) on the 10·05 km *6¼ mile* Canterbury & Whitstable Railway in Kent on 3 May 1830, hauled by the engine *Invicta.* The first practical electric railway was Werner von Siemens' oval metre-gauge demonstration track about 300 m *328 yd* long at the Berlin Trades Exhibition on 31 May 1879.

Fastest

The highest speed attained by a railed vehicle is 9851 km/h *6121 mph* or Mach 8 by an unmanned rocket sled over the 15·2 km *9½ mile* long rail track at White Sands Missile Range, New Mexico, USA on 5 Oct 1982. The world's fastest speed with passengers in a non-railed vehicle is 400·7 km/h *249 mph* by the Maglev (magnetic levitation) MLU-001 test train over the 7 km *4·3 mile* long JNR experimental track at Miyazaki, Japan on 4 Feb.1987. On 1 May 1988 West Germany's Intercity Experimental train attained 405 km/h *252 mph* on a test run between Würzburg and Fulda. The highest speed recorded on any national rail system is 380 km/h *236 mph* by the French SNCF high-speed train TGV-PSE on trial near Tonnerre on 26 Feb 1981. The TGV (Train à Grande Vitesse) inaugurated on 27 Sept 1981 by Sept 1983 had reduced its scheduled time for the Paris–Lyon run of 425 km *264 miles* to 2 hr exactly, so averaging 212·5 km/h *132 mph.* The peak speed attained is 270 km/h *168 mph.*

The highest speed ever ratified for a steam locomotive was 202·8 km/h *126 mph* over 402 m *440 yd* by the LNER 4-6-2 No 4468 *Mallard* (later numbered 60022) which hauled seven coaches weighing 243 tonnes *240 tons* gross down Stoke Bank, near Essendine, between Grantham, Lincolnshire, and Peterborough, Cambridgeshire, on 3 July 1938. Driver Joseph Duddington was at the controls with Fireman Thomas Bray. The engine suffered some damage.

British Rail inaugurated their HST (High Speed Train) daily services between London–Bristol and South Wales on 4 Oct 1976. The electric British Rail APT-P (Advanced Passenger Train-Prototype) attained 261 km/h *162 mph* between Glasgow and Carlisle on its first revenue-earning run on 7 Dec 1981. It covered the 644 km *400 miles* from Glasgow to London in 4¼ hr.

British Rail set a new world speed record for diesel traction on 1 Nov 1987 when a special train testing the prototype SIG bogies for the Mk IV Inter City coaches reached 283·9 km/h *176·4 mph* between Darlington and York, with two Inter City 125 power cars.

Longest non-stop

The longest run on British Rail without any advertised stop is the Night Motorail Service from Inverness to Euston. The distance is 913·7 km *567·75 miles* and the time taken is 11 hr 4 min. The longest passenger journey without a stop is the re-inaugurated Flying Scotsman's 432·1 km *268·5 miles* run from King's Cross to Newcastle en route to Edinburgh.

Most powerful

The world's most powerful steam locomotive, measured by tractive effort, was No 700, a triple-articulated or triplex 2–8–8–8–4, 6-cylinder engine built by the Baldwin Locomotive Works in 1916 for the Virginian Railroad. It had a tractive force of 75 434 kg *166 300 lb* working compound and 90 520 kg *199 560 lb* working simple.

Probably the heaviest train ever hauled by a single engine was one of 15 545 tonnes *15 300 tons* made up of 250 freight cars stretching 2·5 km *1·6 miles* by the *Matt H. Shay* (No 5014), a 2–8–8–8–2 engine which ran on the Erie Railroad from May 1914 until 1929. On 16 Feb 1986, a single locomotive, No 59001, one of four diesels built by General Motors and privately owned by quarry company Foster Yeoman of Minehead, Somerset, hauled a 4639 tonne *4565 ton* train, the heaviest on record, during trials on Savernake Bank, Wiltshire.

Greatest load

The heaviest single pieces of freight ever conveyed by rail are limited by the capacity of the rolling stock. The world's strongest rail carrier with a capacity of 807 tonnes is the 336 tonne 36 axle 92 m *301 ft 10 in* long 'Schnabel' built for a US railway by Krupp, West Germany, in March 1981.

The heaviest load carried by British Rail was a 37·1 m *122 ft* long boiler drum, weighing 279 tonnes *275 tons* which was carried from Immingham Dock to Killingholme, Humberside, in September 1968.

The heaviest load ever moved on rails is the 10 700-ton Church of the Virgin Mary built in 1548 in the village of Most, Czechoslovakia, in October–November 1975 because it was in the way of coal workings. It was moved 730 m *800 yd* at 0·002 km/h *0·0013 mph* over 4 weeks at a cost of £9 million.

Freight trains

The longest and heaviest freight train on record was about 6 km *4 miles* in length. It comprised 500 coal cars with three 3600-hp diesels pulling and three more in the middle, on the Iaeger, West Virginia, to Portsmouth, Ohio, stretch of 252 km *157 miles* on the Norfolk and Western Railway on 15 Nov 1967. The total weight was nearly 42 674 tonnes *42 000 tons*. British Rail's heaviest freight train began its regular run on 16 Sept 1983 from Merehead Quarry, Somerset, to Acton, west London, with 3300 tonnes of limestone in 43 wagons and 2 engines stretching nearly 800 m *½ mile*. Since Feb 1986 this has been hauled by a single '59' class diesel.

TRACKS

Longest

The world's longest run is one of 9438 km *5864½ miles* on the Trans-Siberian line from Moscow to Nakhodka, USSR, in the Soviet Far East. There are 97 stops on the journey which takes 8 days 4 hr 25 min. The 3145 km *1954 mile* Baykal-Amur northern main line (BAM), begun with forced labour in 1938, was restarted in 1974 and put into service on 27 Oct 1984. A total of 382 million m³ *13 500 million ft³* of earth had to be moved and 3901 bridges built in this £8000 million project.

Longest straight

The longest straight in the world is on the Common-

Gauges ● A local train at Atocha Station, Madrid operating on a 1·676 m *5 ft 6 in* track. This is the widest gauge in the world and is used throughout Spain and also in Portugal, India, Pakistan, Bangladesh, Sri Lanka, Argentina and Chile. The narrowest gauge on which public services are operated is 260 mm *10¼ in* on the Wells Harbour (1·12 km *0·7 mile*) and the Wells–Walsingham Railways (6·5 km *4 miles*) in Norfolk, England. (Photo: Colour Library International)

wealth Railways Trans-Australian line over the Nullarbor Plain from Mile 496 between Nurina and Loongana, Western Australia, to Mile 793 between Ooldea and Watson, South Australia, 478 km *297 miles* dead straight although not level. The longest straight on British Rail is the 29 km *18 miles* between Barlby Junction and Brough on the 'down' line on the Selby, North Yorkshire, to Kingston-upon-Hull, Humberside, line.

Widest and narrowest gauge

The widest gauge in standard use is 1·676 m *5 ft 6 in*. This width is used in Spain, Portugal, India, Pakistan, Bangladesh, Sri Lanka, Argentina and Chile. The narrowest gauge on which public services are operated is 260 mm *10¼ in* on the Wells Harbour (1·12 km *0·7 mile*) and the Wells–Walsingham Railways (6·5 km *4 miles*) in Norfolk, England.

Highest line

At 4817 m *15 806 ft* above sea level the standard gauge (1435 mm *4 ft 8½ in*) track on the Morococha branch of the Peruvian State Railways at La Cima is the highest in the world

The highest point on the British Rail system is at the pass of Drumochter on the Perthshire–Inverness border, where the track reaches an altitude of 452 m *1484 ft* above sea-level. The highest railway in Britain is the Snowdon Mountain Railway, which rises from Llanberis, Gwynedd to 1064 m *3493 ft* above sea-level, just below the summit of Snowdon (*Yr Wyddfa*). It has a gauge of 800 mm *2 ft 7½ in*.

Lowest

The lowest point on British Rail is in the Severn Tunnel—43·8 m *144 ft* below sea level.

Steepest gradient

The steepest standard-gauge gradient by adhesion is 1:11 between Chedde and Servoz on the metre gauge SNCF Chamonix line, France.

The steepest sustained adhesion-worked gradient on main line in the United Kingdom is the 3·2 km *2 mile* Lickey incline of 1:37·7 just south-west of Birmingham.

From the tunnel bottom to James Street, Liverpool, on the former Mersey Railway, there is a stretch of 1:27; 1:30 between Folkestone Junction and Harbour 1·6 km *1 mile*.

Slightest gradient

The slightest gradient posted on the British Rail system is one indicated as 1 in 14 400 between Pirbright Junction and Farnborough, Hampshire. This could be described alternatively as England's most obtuse summit.

Busiest system

The world's most crowded rail system is Japanese National Railways, which in 1987 carried 13 848 000 passengers daily. Among articles lost in 1987 were 1 296 840 umbrellas, 146 191 clothing items, 134 372 books and stationery items, 4233 accessories and 89 555 purses.

RAIL TRAVEL

Calling All Stations

Alan M. Witton (b. 1943) of Chorlton, Manchester visited every open British Rail station (2362) in a continuous tour for charity of 26 703 km *16 592¾ miles* in 27 136 minutes from 13 July–28 Aug 1980. Colin M. Mulvany and Seth N. Vafiadis of west London, visited every British Rail station (2 378) embracing also the Tyne and Wear, Glasgow and London underground systems (333 stations) for charity in 31 days 5 hr 8 min 58 sec over 24 989 km *15 527·6 miles* to average 61·2 km/h *38·05 mph* from 4 June–5 July 1984. Carl Lombardelli of Romford, Essex traversed the extreme points of the compass for stations in Great Britain—Thurso (north), Lowestoft (east), Penzance (south) and Arisaig (west) in 48 hrs 15 mins from 8–10 Sept 1985.

Most countries in 24 hours

The record number of countries travelled through entirely by train in 24 hours is 10 by Aaron Kitchen on 16–17 Feb 1987. His route started in Yugoslavia and continued through Austria, Italy, Liechtenstein, Switzerland, France, Luxembourg, Belgium, Netherlands arriving in West Germany 22 hr 42 min later.

Super Traveller

Andrew Kendall of Moreton, Wirral, Lancs, has clocked up an amazing 109 884·75 miles by train in 1987 to become British Rail's Super Traveller of the year.

Handpumped railcars

A speed of 20 mph for a 300 m *984 ft* course was first surpassed at Port Moody, British Columbia, Canada by the 5-man team (1 pusher, 4 pumpers) from Port Moody Motors with 33·54 sec on 27 June 1982. They averaged 32·20 km/h *20·008 mph*.

Longest journey

The greatest distance travelled on British Rail within 24 hours is 2782·5 km *1729 miles* on 16–17 June 1987 by Martyn Tebbutt and Ian Buttery of Leeds.

Charles Starling of Gorton, Manchester, travelled a total distance of 10 124·5 km *6291¼ mile* on British Rail in a 7-day period leaving Manchester, Piccadilly on 27 Oct 1986 at 12.30 a.m. and arriving at London, Euston on 2 Nov at 11.30 p.m. John Byrne of Dublin, Ireland, travelled the length of the entire Irish rail system – Iarnród Éireann in connection with the Cheeverstown Rail Marathon from Dublin to Dublin in 3 days 14 hr 50 min on 21–4 Sept 1987. In the course of some 73 years commuting on British Rail from Kent to London, Ralph Ransome of Birchington travelled an equivalent of an estimated 39 times round the world. He retired early, aged 93, on 5 Feb 1986.

STATIONS
Largest

The world's largest railway station is Grand Central Terminal, Park Avenue and 43rd Street, New York City, built 1903–13. It covers 19 ha *48 acres* on two levels with 41 tracks on the upper level and 26 on the lower. On average more than 550 trains and 180 000 people per day use it, with a peak of 252 288 on 3 July 1947. The largest railway station in extent on the British Rail system is the 17-platform Clapham Junction, London, extending over 11·22 ha *27¾ acres* with a total face of 3409 m *11 185 ft*. The station with the largest number of platforms is London Waterloo (9·9 ha *24½ acres*), with 21 main and two Waterloo and City Line platforms, with a total face of 4679 m *15 352 ft*. Victoria Station (8·80 ha *21¾ acres*) has, however, a total face length of 5611 m *18 412 ft* for its 17 platforms.

Oldest

The oldest station in the world is Liverpool Road Station, Manchester, England first used on 15 Sept 1830 and now partly turned into a museum.

Busiest

The busiest railway junction in Great Britain is Clapham Junction, London, on the Southern Region of British Rail, with an average of 2200 trains passing through each 24 hr.

Highest

The highest station in the world is Condor, Bolivia at 4786 m *15 705 ft* on the metre-gauge Rio Mulato to Potosi line. The highest passenger station on British Rail is Corrour, Inverness-shire, at an altitude of 410·5 m *1347 ft* above sea level.

Waiting rooms

The world's largest waiting rooms are the four in Peking Station, Chang'an Boulevard, Peking, China, opened in September 1959, with a total standing capacity of 14 000.

Platform

The longest railway platform in the world is the Khargpur platform, West Bengal, India, which measures 833 m *2733 ft* in length. The State Street Center subway platform staging on 'The Loop' in Chicago, Illinois measures 1066 m *3500 ft* in length. The longest in the British Rail system is the 602·69 m *1977 ft 4 in* long platform at Gloucester. The two platforms comprising the New Nisato railway station on the Musashino line, Saitama, Japan are 300 m *984 ft 3 in* apart and are connected by a bridge.

UNDERGROUND RAILWAYS
Most extensive

The earliest (first section between Farringdon St and Edgware Road, opened 10 Jan 1863) and one of the most extensive underground or rapid transit railway systems of the 67 in the world is the London Underground with 408 km *254 miles* of route, of which 135 km *85 miles* is bored tunnel and 32 km *20 miles* is 'cut and cover'. The whole system is operated by a staff of 20 600 serving 273

stations. The 457 trains comprising 3875 cars carried 769 000 000 passengers in 1986/7. The greatest depth is 67·4 m *221 ft* near Hampstead on the Northern Line. The longest journey without a change is Epping to West Ruislip—54·8 km *34·1 miles*. The record for touring the 272 stations including Heathrow Terminal 4 station opened 12 Apr 1986 is 18 hr 41 min 41 sec set by a team of five: Robert A. Robinson, Peter D. Robinson, Timothy J. Robinson, Timothy J. Clark and Richard J. Harris on 30 July 1986. Peter Robinson (b. 19 July 1974) was the youngest to tour all stations on 22 July 1982 aged 8.

The subway with most stations in the world is the New York City Transport Authority subway (first section opened on 27 Oct 1904) with a total of 372·93 km *231·73 route miles* and 1 096 006 529 passengers in 1979. The 458 stations are closer set than London's. The record for travelling the whole system is 21 hr 8½ min set by Mayer Wiesen and Charles Emerson on 8 Oct 1973.

Busiest

The world's busiest metro system is that in Greater Moscow with as many as 6½ million passengers per day. To mid-1985 it had 123 stations and 198 km *123 miles* of track. The record transit (with 18 changes) in 1982 (115 stations) was 8 hr 10 min 22 sec by Eric Rudkin of Chaddesden, Derbyshire.

MODEL RAILWAYS

The non-stop duration record for a model train (loco plus 6 coaches) is 864 hr 30 min from 1 June–7 July 1978, covering 1091 km *678 miles*, organised by Roy Catton at 'Pastimes' Toy Store, Mexborough, S. Yorkshire.

The longest recorded run by a model *steam* locomotive is 231·7 km *144 miles* in 27 hr 18 min by the 18·4 cm *7¼ in* gauge 'Winifred', built in 1974 by Wilf Grove at Thames Ditton, Surrey, on 8–9 Sept 1979. 'Winifred' works on 5·6 kg/cm² *80 lb/in²* pressure and is coal fired with cylinders 54 mm *2⅛ in* in diameter and 79 mm *3⅛ in* stroke.

The most miniature model railway ever built is one of 1:1000 scale by Jean Damery (b. 1923) of Paris. The engine ran on a 4½-volt battery and measures 7·9 mm *⁵⁄₁₆ in* overall.

TRAMS
Longest journey

The longest tramway journey now possible is from Krefeld St Tönis to Witten Annen Nord, West Germany. With luck at the 8 inter-connections the 105·5 km *65·5 mile* trip can be achieved in 5½ hr. By late 1987 there were more than 320 tramway systems surviving of which the most extensive is that of Leningrad, USSR with 2500 cars on 53 routes. The only system in Great Britain until the £43 million Greater Manchester Rapid Transit System opens. The Glasgow system was scrapped in 1962 and that in London in 1952.

Oldest

The oldest trams in revenue service in the world are motor cars 1 and 2 of the Manx Electric Railway dating from 1893.

Aircraft

Note—The use of the Mach scale for aircraft speeds was introduced by Prof Ackeret of Zürich, Switzerland. The Mach number is the ratio of the velocity of a moving body to the local velocity of sound. This ratio was first employed by Dr Ernst Mach (1838–1916) of Vienna, Austria in 1887. Thus Mach 1·0 equals 1224·67 km/h *760·98 mph* at sea level at 15°C, and is assumed, for convenience, to fall to a constant 1061·81 km/h *659·78 mph* in the stratosphere, i.e. above 11 000 m *36 089 ft*. In 1986 the speed of sound was revised to 1192·64 km/h *741·07 mph*.

EARLIEST FLIGHTS

The first controlled and sustained power-driven flight occurred near the Kill Devil Hill, Kitty Hawk, North Carolina, USA, at 10.35 a.m. on 17 Dec 1903, when Orville

Wright (1871–1948) flew the 12-hp chain-driven *Flyer I* for a distance of 36·5 m *120 ft* at an air speed of 48 km/h *30 mph*, a ground speed of 10·9 km/h *6·8 mph* and an altitude of 2·5–3·5 m *8–12 ft* for about 12 sec watched by his brother Wilbur (1867–1912), 4 men and a boy. Both brothers, from Dayton, Ohio, were bachelors because, as Orville put it, they had not the means to 'support a wife as well as an aeroplane'. The *Flyer* is now in the National Air and Space Museum at the Smithsonian Institution, Washington DC.

The first hop by a man-carrying aeroplane entirely under its own power was made when Clément Ader (1841–1925) of France flew in his *Eole* for about 50 m *164 ft* at Armainvilliers, France, on 9 Oct 1890. It was powered by a lightweight steam engine of his own design which developed about 20 hp (15 kW). The earliest 'rational design' for a flying machine, according to the Royal Aeronautical Society, was that published by Emanuel Swedenborg (1688–1772) in Sweden in 1717.

The first officially recognised flight in the British Isles was made by the US citizen Samuel Franklin Cody (1861–1913) who flew 423 m *1390 ft* in his own biplane at Farnborough, Hampshire, on 16 Oct 1908. Horatio Frederick Phillips (1845–1924) almost certainly covered 152 m *500 ft* in his Phillips II '*Venetian blind*' aeroplane at Streatham, in 1907.

The first Briton to fly was George Pearson Dickin (1881–1909), a journalist from Southport, Lancashire as a passenger to Wilbur Wright at Auvóur, France on 3 Oct 1908. The first resident British citizen to fly in Britain was J. T. C. Moore-Brabazon (later Lord Brabazon of Tara PC, GBE, MC) (1884–1964) with 3 short but sustained flights from 30 Apr–2 May 1909.

Cross-Channel

The earliest cross-Channel flight by an aeroplane was made on Sunday, 25 July 1909 when Louis Blériot (1872–1936) of France flew his *Blériot XI* 23-hp monoplane 41·8 km *26 miles* from Les Baraques, near Northfall Meadow near Dover Castle, England, in 36½ min, after taking off at 4.41 a.m.

Jet-engined

Proposals for jet propulsion date back to Captain Marconnet (1909) of France, and Henri Coanda (1886–1972) of Romania, and to the turbojet proposals of Maxime Guillaume in 1921. The earliest tested run was that of the British Power Jets Ltd's experimental WU1 (Whittle Unit) on 12 Apr 1937, invented by Flying Officer (later Air Commodore Sir) Frank Whittle OM, KBE (b. Coventry, 1 June 1907), who had applied for a patent on jet propulsion in 1930. The first flight by an aeroplane powered by a turbojet engine was made by the Heinkel He 178, piloted by Flug Kapitan Erich Warsitz, at Marienehe, Germany, on 27 Aug 1939. It was powered by a Heinkel He S3b engine (378 kg *834 lb* as installed with long tailpipe) designed by Dr Hans 'Pabst' von Ohain and first tested in August 1937.

The first British jet flight occurred when Fl-Lt P. E. G. 'Jerry' Sayer OBE (k. 1942) flew the Gloster-Whittle E.28/39 (wing span 8·84 m *29 ft*, length 7·70 m *25 ft 3 in*) fitted with an 390 kg *860 lbs*. t. Whittle W-1 engine for 17 min at Cranwell, Lincolnshire, on 15 May 1941. The maximum speed was *c*. 560 km/h *350 mph*. This aircraft (W404i/G) is now in the Science Museum, London.

Supersonic flight

The first supersonic flight was achieved on 14 Oct 1947 by Capt (later Brig Gen) Charles ('Chuck') Elwood Yeager, (b. 13 Feb 1923), over Edwards Air Force Base, Muroc, California, in a Bell XS-1 rocket plane ('Glamorous Glennis') with Mach 1·015 (1078 km/h *670 mph*) at an altitude of 2 800 m *142 000 ft*. The first British aircraft to attain Mach 1 in a dive was the de Havilland D. H. 108 tail-less research aircraft on 6 Sept 1948, piloted by John Derry. The XS-1 is now in the National Air and Space Museum at the Smithsonian Institution, Washington DC, USA.

Trans-Atlantic

The first crossing of the North Atlantic by air was made by Lt-Cdr (later Rear Admiral) Albert Cushion Read (1887–1967) and his crew (Stone, Hinton, Rodd, Rhoads and Breese) in the 84 knot *155 km/h* US Navy/Curtiss flying boat NC-4 from Trepassey Harbor, Newfoundland, via the Azores, to Lisbon, Portugal, from 16–27 May 1919. The whole flight of 7591 km *4717 miles*, originating from Rockaway Air Station, Long Island, NY on 8 May, required 53 hr 58 min, terminating at Plymouth, England, on 31 May. The Newfoundland–Azores flight of 1930 km *1200 miles* took 15 hr 18 min at 81·7 knots *151·4 km/h*.

Non-stop

The first non-stop trans-Atlantic flight was achieved 18 days later from 4.13 p.m. GMT on 14 June 1919, from Lester's Field, St John's, Newfoundland, 3154 km *1960 miles* to Derrygimla bog near Clifden, County Galway, Ireland, at 8.40 a.m. GMT, 15 June, when the pilot, Capt John William Alcock DSC (1892–1919), and the navigator Lt Arthur Whitten Brown (1886–1948) flew across in a Vickers *Vimy*, powered by two 360-hp Rolls-Royce *Eagle VIII* engines. Both men were created civil KBE's on 21 June 1919 when Alcock was aged 26 years 227 days, and they shared a *Daily Mail* prize of £10 000.

Solo

The 79th man to achieve a trans-Atlantic flight but the first to do so solo was Capt (later Brig) Charles Augustus Lindbergh (Hon AFC) (1902–74) who took off in his 220 hp Ryan monoplane *Spirit of St Louis* at 12.52 p.m. GMT on 20 May 1927 from Roosevelt Field, Long Island, NY, USA. He landed at 10.21 p.m. GMT on 21 May 1927 at Le Bourget Airfield, Paris, France. His flight of 5810 km *3610 miles* lasted 33 hr 29½ min and he won a prize of $25 000 . The *Spirit of St Louis* is now in the National Air and Space Museum at the Smithsonian Institution, Washington DC, USA.

Most flights

Between March 1948 and his retirement on 1 Sept 1984 Flight Service Manager Charles M. Schimpf logged a total of 2 880 Atlantic crossings—a rate of 6·4 per month.

Trans-Pacific

The first non-stop trans-Pacific flight was by Major Clyde Pangborn and Hugh Herndon in the Bellanca cabin plane *Miss Veedol* from Sabishiro Beach, Japan 7335 km *4558 miles* to Wenatchee, Washington in 41 hr 13 min from 3–5 Oct 1931. (For earliest crossing see Circumnavigational flights below.)

Circumnavigational flights

Strict circumnavigation requires passing through two antipodal points thus with a minimum distance of 40 007·89 km *24 859·75 miles*.

The earliest such flight of 26 345 miles *42 398 km* was by two US Army Douglas DWC amphibians in 57 'hops'. The *Chicago* was piloted by Lt Lowell H. Smith and Lt Leslie P. Arnold and the *New Orleans* by Lt Erik H. Nelson and Lt John Harding between 6 Apr and 28 Sept 1924 beginning and ending at Seattle, Washington.

The fastest flight was the 37 216 km *23 125 mile* eastabout flight of 36 hr 54 min 15 sec by the Boeing 747 SP 'Friendship One' (Capt. Clay Lacy) from Seattle, Washington with 141 passengers on 28–30 Jan 1988. The plane reached 1292 km/h *803 mph* over the Atlantic and refuelled only in Athens and Taipei.

The first circumnavigation without refuelling was achieved by Dick Rutan and Jeana Yeager in their specially constructed aircraft *Voyager*, designed by Dick's brother Burt Rutan. They flew from Edwards Air Force Base, California, USA from 14–23 Dec 1986. Their flight took 9 days 3 min 44 sec and they covered a distance of 40 212·139 km *24 986·665 miles* averaging 186·1 km/h *115·64 mph*. The plane, with a wing span of 33·77 m *110·8 ft*, was capable of carrying 5636 litres *1240 gal* of fuel weighing 4052 kg *8934 lb*. It took over 2 years and 22 000 man-hours to construct. The pilot flew from a cockpit measuring 1·7 × 0·54 m *5·6 × 1·8 ft* and the off-duty crew member occupied a cabin 2·3 × 0·6 m *7·5 × 2·0 ft*. *Voyager* is now in the National Air and Space Museum at the Smithsonian Institution, Washington DC, USA.

The first circum-polar flight was solo by Capt Elgen M. Long, 44, in a Piper Navajo from 5 Nov–3 Dec 1971. He covered 62 597 km *38 896 miles* in 215 flying hours. The cabin temperature sank to −40° C −40° F over Antarctica.

Largest wing span

The aircraft with the largest ever wing span is the $40-million Hughes H.4 Hercules flying boat ('Spruce Goose'), which was raised 21·3 m *70 ft* into the air in a test run of 914 m *1000 yd*, piloted by Howard Hughes (1905–76) off Long Beach Harbor, California, on 2 Nov 1947. The eight-engined 193 tonne *190 ton* aircraft had a wing span of 97·51 m *319 ft 11 in* and a length of 66·64 m *218 ft 8 in*, and never flew again. In a brilliant engi-

---

Circum-polar flight ● Richard Norton, an American airline captain, and Calin Rosetti, head of satellite navigation systems at the European Space Agency, are seen here with their Piper PA-46-310P Malibu in which they made the first single-engined circum-polar flight. This began and finished at Le Bourget Airport, Paris from 21 Jan to 15 Jun 1987. They travelled 55 266 km *34 342 miles* in a flying time of 185 hr 41 min. The so-called 'Flight of the Arctic Tern' also set 16 other point-to-point records.

---

neering feat she was moved bodily by Goldcoast Corp aided by the US Navy barge crane YD-171 on 22 Feb 1982 to her final resting place 9·6 km *6 miles* across the harbour under a 213·4 m *700 ft* diameter dome. Among current aircraft, the Soviet Antonov An-124 has a span of 73·3 m *240 ft 5¾ in* and the Boeing 747-400 one of 64·92 m *213 ft*.

The $34-million Piasecki Heli-Stat, comprising a framework of light-alloy and composite materials to mount four Sikorsky SH-34J helicopters and the envelope of a Goodyear ZPG-2 patrol airship, was exhibited on 26 Jan 1984 at Lakehurst, New Jersey. Designed for use by the US Forest Service and designated Model 94-37J Logger, it has an overall length of 104·55 m *343 ft* and was intended to carry a payload of 21·4 tons. It crashed on 1 July 1986.

Heaviest

The aircraft with the highest standard maximum take-off weight is the Antonov An-124 (NATO code name: Condor) at 405 000 kg *892 872 lb* or 405 tonne *398·6 tons*. This aircraft lifted a payload of 171 219 kg *377 473 lb* to a height of 10 750 m *35 269 ft* on 26 July 1985. A Boeing 747-300 operated by the manufacturer took off at a weight of 395 086 kg *871 000 lb* during noise-level certification flights from Glasgow, Montana, USA on 19 July 1987.

Solar powered

The solar-powered *Solar Challenger*, designed by a team led by Dr Paul MacCready, was flown for the first time entirely under solar power on 20 Nov 1980. On 7 July 1981, piloted by Steve Ptacek (USA), the *Solar Challenger* became the first aircraft of this category to achieve a crossing of the English Channel. Taking off from Pontois-Cormeilles, Paris, the 262·3 km *163 mile* journey to Manston, Kent was completed in 5 hr 23 min at a maximum altitude of 3353 m *11 000 ft*. The aircraft has a wing span of 14·3 m *47 ft*.

Ultralight

On 3 Aug 1985 Anthony A. Cafaro (b. 30 Nov 1951) flew a ULA (max weight 111 kg *245 lb*, max speed 104·6 km/h *65 mph*, capacity 18·93 l *5 US gal*) single-seater Gypsey Skycycle for 7 hr 31 min at Dart Field, Mayville, NY. Nine fuel 'pick-ups' were completed during the flight.

Smallest

The smallest aeroplane ever flown is the *Baby Bird*, designed and built by Donald R. Stits. It is 3·35 m *11 ft* long, with a wing span of 1·91 m *6 ft 3 in*, and weighs 114·3 kg *252 lb* empty. It is powered by a 55-hp 2-cylinder Hirth engine, giving a top speed of 177 km/h *110 mph*. It was first flown by Harold Nemer on 4 Aug 1984 at Camarillo, California. The smallest jet is the 450 km/h *280 mph Silver Bullet* weighing 196 kg *432 lb* with a 5·18 m *17 ft* wing span built by Bob Bishop (USA).

Bombers *Heaviest*

The world's heaviest bomber is the eight-jet swept-wing Boeing B-52H Stratofortress, which has a maximum take-off weight of 221·35 tonnes *217·86 tons*). It has a wing span of 56·38 m *185 ft* and is 48·02 m *157 ft 6¾ in* in length, with a speed of over 1046 km/h *650 mph*. The B-52 can carry twelve SRAM thermonuclear short-range attack missiles or twenty-four 340 kg *750 lb* bombs under its wings and eight more SRAMs or eighty-four 226 kg *500 lb* bombs in the fuselage.

The ten-engined Convair B-36J, weighing 185 tonnes *183 tons*, had a greater wing span, at 70·10 m *230 ft* but is no longer in service. Its top speed was 700 km/h *435 mph*.

Fastest

The world's fastest operational bombers are the French Dassault Mirage IV, which can fly at Mach 2·2 (2333 km/h *1450 mph*) at altitude 11 000 m *36 000 ft*. The American General Dynamics FB-111A has a maximum speed of Mach 2·5; and the Soviet swing-wing Tupolev Tu-22M known to NATO as 'Backfire' has an estimated over-

target speed of Mach 2·0 but which may reach Mach 2·5.

Largest airliner

The highest capacity jet airliner is the Boeing 747 'Jumbo Jet', first flown on 9 Feb 1969 (see Heaviest aircraft) and has a capacity of from 385 to more than 500 passengers with a maximum speed of 969 km/h *602 mph.* Its wing span is 59·64 m *231·8 ft* and its length 70·7 m *195·7 ft.* It entered service on 22 Jan 1970. The first 747-400 was rolled out on 26 Jan 1988 for service with Northwest Airlines with a wing span of 64·92 m *213 ft* and a range exceeding 12 875 km *8000 miles* and a capacity for 422 passengers.

The greatest passenger load recorded was one of 306 adults, 328 children and 40 babies (total 674) from the cyclone-devastated Darwin to Sydney, New South Wales, Australia on 29 Dec 1974.

The largest ever British aircraft was the experimental Bristol Type 167 Brabazon, which had a maximum take-off weight of 131·4 tonnes *129·4 tons,* a wing span of 70·10 m *230 ft* and a length of 53·94 m *177 ft.* This eight-engined aircraft first flew on 4 Sept 1949. Concorde has a maximum take-off weight of 185 065 kg *408 000 lb.*

Fastest airliner

The supersonic BAC/Aérospatiale Concorde, first flown on 2 Mar 1969, with a capacity of 100 passengers, cruises at up to Mach 2·2 (2333 km/h *1450 mph*). It flew at Mach 1·05 on 10 Oct 1969, exceeded Mach 2 for the first time on 4 Nov 1970 and became the first supersonic airliner used on passenger services on 21 Jan 1976. A New York–London record of 2 hr 55 min 15 sec was set on 6 Feb 1988 to average 1955 km/h *1215 mph.*

Most capacious

The Aero Spacelines Super Guppy has a cargo hold with a usable volume of 1410 m³ *49 790ft³* and a maximum take-off weight of some 79·38 tonnes *78·12 tons.* Wing span is 47·62 m *156 ft 3 in,* length 43·05 m *141 ft 3 in.* Its cargo compartment area measures 33·17 m *108 ft 10 in* in length with a cylindrical section of 7·62 m *25 ft* in diameter.

The Soviet Antonov An-124 Ruslan has a cargo hold with a usable volume of 1014 m³ *35 800 ft³* and a maximum take-off weight of 405 tonnes *398·6 tons.* It is powered by four Lotarev D-18T turbofans giving a cruising speed of up to 850 km/h *528 mph* at 12 000 m *39 370 ft* and a range of 4500 km *2796 miles.*

Largest propeller

The largest aircraft propeller ever used was the 6·9 m *22 ft 7½ in* diameter Garuda propeller, fitted to the Linke-Hofmann R II built in Breslau, Germany (now Wroclaw, Poland), which flew in 1919. It was driven by four 260-hp Mercedes engines and turned at only 545 rpm.

Scheduled flights *Longest*

The longest scheduled non-stop flight is the United Airlines and Qantas Los Angeles–Sydney non-stop 14 hr 50 min flight in a Boeing 747 SP (Special Performance), over 12 050 km *7487 statute miles.*

The longest delivery flight by a commercial jet is 8936 nautical miles or 16 560 km *10 290 statute miles* from Seattle, Washington, USA to Cape Town, South Africa by the South African Airways' Boeing 747 SP (Special Performance) 'Matroosberg' using 178 400 kg *175·5 tons* of pre-cooled fuel in 17 hr 22½ min on 23–24 Mar 1976.

Shortest

The shortest scheduled flight in the world is that by

Electric plane ● The MB-E1 is the first electrically propelled aircraft. A Bosch 8-kW motor *10·7 hp* is powered by Varta FP25 nickel-cadmium 25 Ah batteries. The plane, with a wingspan of 12 m *39·4 ft* is 7 m *23 ft* long and weighs 400 kg *882 lb.* It was designed by the model aircraft constructor American Fred Militky and made its maiden flight on 21 Oct 1973. (Photo: K.J.A.Brookes)

Loganair between the Orkney Islands of Westray and Papa Westray which has been flown with Britten-Norman Islander twin-engined 10-seat transports since September 1967. Though scheduled for 2 min, in favourable wind conditions it has been accomplished in 58 sec by Capt Andrew D. Alsop.

United Airlines provide the shortest scheduled flight by jet, a Boeing 727 between San Francisco and Oakland, California. There are three flights daily and return, the flight time averaging 5 minutes for the 19·3 km *12 mile* journey.

Gary W. Rovetto of Island Air on 21 Mar 1980 flew on the scheduled flight from Center Island to Decatur Island, Washington, USA in 41 sec.

Fastest intercontinental scheduled airline

GB Airways have, since 1931, been operating a scheduled service from Gibraltar in Europe to Tangier in Africa on an almost daily basis. The flight by Vickers Viscount averages 15 minutes and covers a distance of 60 km *37 miles.*

Paris–London

The fastest time to travel the 344 km *214 miles* from central Paris to central London (BBC TV centre) is 38 min 58 sec by David Boyce of Stewart Wrightson (Aviation) Ltd on 24 Sept 1983 by motorcycle–helicopter to Le Bourget; Hawker Hunter jet (piloted by the late Michael Carlton) to Biggin Hill, Kent; helicopter to the TV centre car park.

London–New York

The record for central London to downtown New York City by helicopter and Concorde is 3 hr 59 min 44 sec and the return in 3 hr 40 min 40 sec both by David J. Springbett, 1981 Salesman of the Year, and David Boyce (see above) on 8 and 9 Feb 1982.

John O'Groats–Land's End

The record time for an End to End over Great Britain where supersonic overflying is banned is 46 min 44 sec by a Phantom Jet (Wing-Cdr John Brady and Flt Lt Mike Pugh) on 24 Feb 1988.

HIGHEST SPEED
Official record

The official air speed record is 3529·56 km/h *2193·167 mph* by Capt Eldon W. Joersz and Maj George T. Morgan, Jr, in a Lockheed SR-71A near Beale Air

Force Base, California over a 15 to 25 km *9·3 to 15·5 mile* course on 28 July 1976.

Air-launched record

The fastest fixed-wing aircraft in the world was the US North American Aviation X-15A-2, which flew for the first time (after modification from X-15A) on 25 June 1964 powered by a liquid oxygen and ammonia rocket propulsion system. Ablative materials on the airframe once enabled a temperature of 3000°F to be withstood. The landing speed was momentarily 210 knots (389·1 km/h *242 mph*).

The highest speed attained was 7274 km/h *4520 mph* (Mach 6·7) when piloted by Maj William J. Knight, USAF (b. 1930), on 3 Oct 1967. An earlier version which was piloted by Joseph A. Walker (1920–66) reached 107 960 m *354 200 ft* (67·08 miles) also over Edwards Air Force Base, California, on 22 Aug 1963. The programme was suspended after the final flight of 24 Oct 1968.

Following a production programme stretching back to the early 1970's the US NASA Rockwell International Space Shuttle Orbiter *Columbia* was launched from the Kennedy Space Center, Cape Canaveral, Florida commanded by Cdr John W. Young USN and piloted by Robert L. Crippen on 12 Apr 1981 after expenditure of $9900 million since 1972. *Columbia* broke all records for space by a fixed-wing craft with 26 715 km/h *16 600 mph* at main engine cut-off. After re-entry from 122 km *400 000 ft,* experiencing temperatures of 2160° C *3920° F,* she glided home weighing 97 tonnes with the highest ever landing speed of 347 km/h *216 mph* on Rogers Dry Lake, California on 14 Apr 1981.

Under a new FAI (Fédération Aéronautique Internationale) Category P for Aerospacecraft, the *Columbia* is holder of the current absolute world record for duration of 10 days 7 hr 47 min 23 sec to main touchdown when launched on its sixth mission, STS 9 Spacelab 1, with six crewmen on 28 Nov 1983. *Challenger* was destroyed soon after launch from Cape Canaveral on 28 Jan 1986 (see Chapter 4). *Atlantis* holds the Shuttle altitude record of 515 km *320 miles* achieved on 3 Oct 1985 on its maiden flight STS 51J.

The greatest mass lifted by Shuttle and placed in orbit was 118 697 kg *261 679 lb* by *Discovery* on STS 51A, launched on 8 Nov 1984.

Fastest jet

The USAF Lockheed SR-71, a reconnaissance aircraft, is the world's fastest jet (See Official Record above and diagram on p.140). First flown on 22 Dec 1964, it is reportedly capable of attaining an altitude ceiling of close to 30 480 m *100 000 ft.* It has a wing span of 16·94 m *55·6 ft* and a length of 32·73 m *107·4 ft* and weighs 75·9 tons *170 0000 lb* at take-off. Its reported range ·is 4800 km *2982 miles* at Mach 3 at 24 000 m *78 750 ft.* At least 30 jets are believed to have been built. It was reported on 15 Jan 1988 that the US Air Force was developing secretly a Mach 5 6115 km/h *3800 mph* high altitude (above 30 480 m *100 000 ft*) stealth aircraft.

Fastest combat jet

The fastest combat aircraft in the world is the USSR Mikoyan MiG-25 fighter (NATO code name 'Foxbat'). The reconnaissance 'Foxbat-B' has been tracked by radar at about Mach 3·2 (3395 km/h *2110 mph*). When armed with four large underwing air-to-air missiles known to NATO as 'Acrid', the fighter 'Foxbat-A' is limited to Mach 2·8 (2969 km/h *1845 mph*). The single-seat 'Foxbat-A' spans 13·95 m *45 ft 9 in,* is 3·82 m *278 ft 2 in* long and has an estimated maximum take-off weight of 37 421 kg *82 500 lb.*

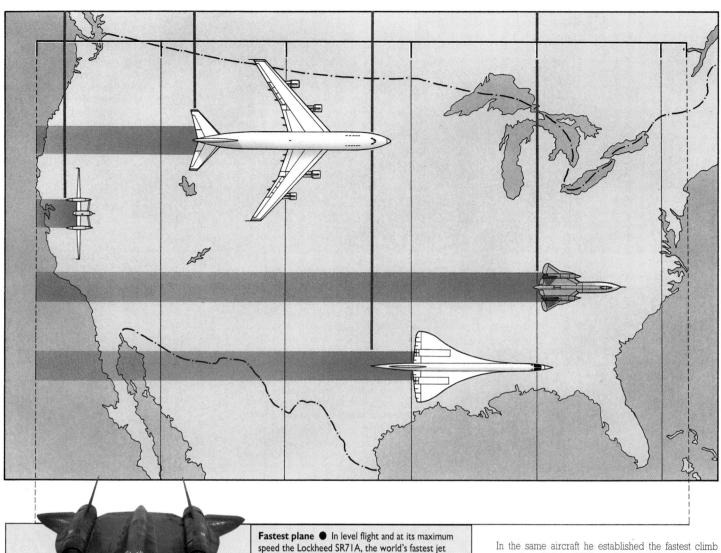

Fastest plane ● In level flight and at its maximum speed the Lockheed SR71A, the world's fastest jet aircraft, would have flown in excess of 3220 km *2000 miles* in 1 hour; almost equivalent to the crossing of the United States. In the same time, an Aérospatiale/BAe Concorde would have travelled 2180 km *1335 miles*, a Boeing 747 'Jumbo' 997 km *620 miles*. At its average world circumnavigation speed, *Voyager*, with the greatest fuel range of them all, would have covered 196 km *122 miles*. (Artwork: Peter Harper)

Fastest biplane
The fastest recorded biplane was the Italian Fiat C.R.42B, with a 1010-hp Daimler-Benz DB601A engine, which attained 520 km/h *323 mph* in 1941. Only one was built.

Fastest piston-engined aircraft
The fastest speed for a piston-engined aeroplane is for a cut-down privately-owned Hawker Sea Fury which attained 836 km/h *520 mph* in level flight over Texas, USA, in August 1966. It was piloted by Mike Carroll (k. 1969) of Los Angeles. The FAI accredited record for a piston-engined aircraft is 832·12 km/h *517·055 mph* over Mojave, California by Frank Taylor (US) in a modified North American P-51D Mustang powered by a 3000-hp Packard Merlin, over a 15 to 25 km *9·3 to 15·5 mile* course, on 30 July 1983.

Fastest propeller-driven aircraft
The Soviet Tu-114 turboprop transport achieved a recorded speed of 877·212 km/h *545·076 mph* carrying heavy payloads over measured circuits. It is developed from the Tupolev Tu-95 bomber, known in NATO as the

'Bear', and has four 14,795-hp engines. The turboprop-powered Republic XF-84H prototype US Navy fighter which flew on 22 July 1955 had a top *design* speed of 1078 km/h *670 mph* but was abandoned. McDonnell Douglas expects its projected MD-91X, powered by counter-rotating multi-bladed fans, to cruise at about Mach 0·78 814 km/h *514 mph.*

Fastest trans-Atlantic flight
The trans-Atlantic flight record is 1 hr 54 min 56.4 sec by Maj James V. Sullivan, 37, and Maj Noel F. Widdifield, 33, flying a Lockheed SR-71A eastwards on 1 Sept 1974. The average speed, slowed by refuelling by a KC-135 tanker aircraft, for the New York–London stage of 5570·80 km *3461·53 miles* was 2908·026 km/h *1806·963 mph.* The solo record (Gander to Gatwick) is 8 hr 47 min 32 sec by Capt John J. A. Smith in a Rockwell 685 on 12 Mar 1978.

Altitude
The official world altitude record by an aircraft taking off from the ground under its own power is 37 650 m (*123 524 ft*) by Aleksandr Fedotov (USSR) in a Mikoyan E.266M (MiG-25) aircraft, powered by two 14 000 kg *30 865 lb* thrust turbojet engines, on 31 Aug 1977.

In the same aircraft he established the fastest climb record on 17 May 1975 reaching 30 000 m *98 425 ft* in 4 min 11·7 sec after take off.

Duration
The flight duration record is 64 days 22 hr 19 min and 5 sec, set up by Robert Timm and John Cook in a Cessna 172 'Hacienda'. They took off from McCarran Airfield, Las Vegas, Nevada, just before 3.53 p.m. local time on 4 Dec 1958, and landed at the same airfield just before 2.12 p.m. on 7 Feb 1959. They covered a distance equivalent to six times round the world with continued refuellings, without landing.

AIRPORTS
Largest
The world's largest airport is the £2100-million King Khalid International Airport outside Riyadh, Saudi Arabia covering an area of 221 km² *86 miles²,* opened on 14 Nov 1983. It also has the world's largest control tower, 74 m *243 ft* in height. The Hajj Terminal at the £2800-million King Abdul-Aziz airport near Jeddah is the world's largest roofed structure covering 1·5 km² *370 acres.* The present 6 runways and 5 terminal buildings of Dallas/Fort Worth Airport, Texas are planned to be extended to 9 runways and 13 terminals with 260 gates with an ultimate capacity for 150 million passengers. The world's largest airport terminal is Hartsfield Atlanta International Airport, Georgia, USA, opened on 21 Sept 1980 with floor space covering 20·43 ha *50·50 acres.* It has 138 gates handling nearly 50 million passengers a year but has a capacity for 75 million. The new airport planned for Denver, Colorado was expected to occupy an area of 116·5 km² *45 miles²* and in early 1988 was the only new major airport being

planned. It was to have 12 runways. Construction of new homes within the expected 60 dB noise 'contour' was banned.

Sixty-eight airline companies from 61 countries operate scheduled services into Heathrow Airport, London (1197 ha *2958 acres*), and during 1987 there was a total of 330 098 air transport movements, including 303 591 passenger flights, handled by a staff of 53 241 employed by the various companies, government departments and Heathrow Airport Ltd, a subsidiary of the British Airports Authority plc. The total number of passengers, both incoming and outgoing, was 34 742 051 (35 080 417 including transit passengers). The most flights yet handled by Heathrow in a day was 1 080 on 25 Sept 1987 and the largest number of passengers yet handled in a day was 129 368 on 31 July 1987. A record 11 787 passengers were handled in one hour (1200–1300 hrs GMT) on 30 August 1987. The Airport's busiest single hour for aircraft movements was 1000–1100 hours GMT on 5 July 1984 when 81 flights were handled using two active runways. Aircraft fly to 213 destinations direct in 84 countries. Heathrow Airport is the UK's number 2 port – behind Dover – in terms of visible trade, handling £21 805·5 million worth of imports and exports. This represents some 13·7 per cent of visible trade through all UK ports and 72·8 per cent through all airports.

Busiest

The world's busiest airport is Chicago International Airport, O'Hare Field, Illinois, with a total of 795 026 movements and 54 770 673 passengers in the year 1986. This represents a take-off or landing every 39·66 sec round the clock. Heathrow Airport, London handles more *international* traffic than any other.

The busiest landing area ever has been Bien Hoa Air Base, South Vietnam, which handled more than 1 000 000 take-offs and landings in 1970. The world's largest 'helipad' was An Khe, South Vietnam.

The heliport at Morgan City, Louisiana, USA, one of a string used by helicopters flying energy-related offshore operations into the Gulf of Mexico, has pads for 46 helicopters.

Highest and lowest

The highest airport in the world is La Sa (Lhasa) Airport, Tibet at 4363 m *14 315 ft*.

The highest landing ever made by a fixed-wing plane is 6080 m *19 947 ft* on Dhaulagiri, Himalaya by a Pilatus Porter named 'Yeti', supplying the 1960 Swiss expedition. The lowest landing field is El Lisan on the east shore of the Dead Sea, 360 m *1180 ft* below sea level, but during World War II BOAC Short C-class flying boats operated from the surface of the Dead Sea 394 m *1292 ft* below sea level. The lowest international airport is Schiphol, Amsterdam, at 3·9 m *13 ft* below sea level. Rotterdam's airport is fractionally lower at 4·5 m *15 ft*.

Farthest and nearest to city or capital centres

The airport farthest from the city centre it allegedly serves is Viracopos, Brazil, which is 96 km *60 miles* from São Paulo. Gibraltar Airport is 800 m *880 yd* from the centre.

Longest runway

The longest runway in the world is one of 11 km *7 miles* in length (of which 4572 m *15 000 ft* is concreted) at Edwards Air Force Base on the bed of Rogers Dry Lake at Muroc, California, USA. The whole test centre airfield extends over 168km^2 *65 miles^2*. In an emergency an auxiliary 19 km *12 mile* strip is available along the bed of the Dry Lake. The *Voyager* aircraft, taking off on its round-the-world unrefuelled flight (see Circumnavigational flights) used 4328 m *14 200 ft* of concrete runway

---

Nearest and farthest airports ● Gibraltar Airport is a mere 800 m *880 yd* from the city centre. The runway is seen here with Spain in the background. The airport farthest from the city centre it allegedly serves is Viracopos, Brazil, which is 96 km *60 miles* from São Paulo. (Photo: Ace Photo Agency)

---

at Edwards AFB. The world's longest civil airport runway is one of 4·89 km *3·04 miles* at Pierre van Ryneveld Airport, Upington, South Africa constructed in five months from August 1975 to January 1976. A paved runway 6·24 km *3·88 miles* long appears on maps of Jordan at Abu Husayn. The longest runway normally available to civil aircraft in the United Kingdom is No 1 at Heathrow Airport, London, measuring 3·90 km *2·42 miles*. The most southerly major runway (2·57 km *1·6 miles*) in the world is at Mount Pleasant, East Falkland (Lat 51° 50′S) built in 16 months to May 1985.

HELICOPTERS
Fastest

Trevor Eggington, 53, averaged 400·87 km/h *249·10 mph* over Somerset on 11 Aug 1986 in a Westland Lynx company demonstrator helicopter.

Largest

The world's largest helicopter is the Soviet Mil Mi-12 (NATO code-name 'Homer'), also known as the V-12. It is powered by four 6500-hp turboshaft engines and has a span of 67 m *219 ft 10 in* over its rotor tips with a length of 37·00 m *121 ft 4½ in* and it weighs 103·3 tonnes.

Greatest load

On 3 Feb 1982 at Podmoscovnoé in the Soviet Union, a Mil Mi-26 heavy-lift helicopter, crewed by G. V. Alfeurov and L. A. Indeyev (co-pilot), lifted a total mass of 56·77 tonnes *55·87 tons* to 2000 m *6560 ft*.

Smallest

The Aerospace General Co one-man rocket-assisted minicopter weighs about 72·5 kg *160 lb* cruising 400 km *250 miles* at 37 km/h *185 mph*.

Highest

The altitude record for helicopters is 12 442 m *40 820 ft* by an Aérospatiale SA315B *Lama*, over France on 21 June 1972. The highest recorded landing has been at 7000 m *23 000 ft* below the south-east face of Everest in a rescue sortie in May 1971. The South Tower of the World

Trade Center helipad is 422 m *1385 ft* above street level in New York City, USA.

Circumnavigation

H. Ross Perot and Jay Coburn, both of Dallas, Texas made the first helicopter circumnavigation in 'Spirit of Texas' on 1–30 Sept 1982. The first solo round-the-world flight in a helicopter was completed by Dick Smith (Australia) on 22 July 1983. Flown from and to the Bell Helicopter facility at Fort Worth, Texas, USA in a Bell Model 206L *Long Ranger III*, his unhurried flight began on 5 Aug 1982 and covered a distance of 56 742 km *35 258 miles.*

AUTOGYROS
Earliest

The autogyro or gyroplane, a rotorcraft with an unpowered rotor turned by the airflow in flight, preceded the practical helicopter with engine-driven rotor. Juan de la Cierva (Spain) made the first successful autogyro flight with his model C.4 (commercially named an *Autogiro*) at Getafe, Spain, on 9 Jan 1923.

Speed, altitude and distance records

Wing-Cdr Kenneth H. Wallis (GB) holds the straight-line distance record of 874·32 km *543·27 miles* set in his WA-116F autogyro on 28 Sept 1975 non-stop from Lydd, Kent to Wick, Caithness. Wing-Cdr Wallis flew his WA-116, with a 72-hp McCulloch engine, to a record speed of 193·9 km/h *120·5 mph* over a 3 km *1·86 mile* straight course on 18 Sept 1986. On 20 July 1982, flying from Boscombe Down, Wiltshire, he established a new autogyro altitude record of 5643·7 m *18 516 ft* in his WA-121/Mc. It was reported that on 8 Apr 1931 Amelia Earhart (US) reached a height in excess of 5791 m *19 000 ft* at Pitcairn Aviation Field, Pennsylvania, USA.

FLYING-BOAT
Fastest

The fastest flying-boat ever built has been the Martin XP6M-1 Seamaster, the US Navy 4-jet-engined minelayer flown in 1955–59 with a top speed of 1040 km/h *646 mph.* In September 1946 the Martin JRM-2 Mars flying-boat set a payload record of 30 992 kg *68 327 lb.* The official flying-boat speed record is 912 km/h *566·69 mph,* set up by Nikolay Andreyevskiy and crew of two in a Soviet Beriev M-10, powered by two AL-7 turbojets, over a 15 to 25 km *9·3 to 15·5 mile* course on 7 Aug 1961. The M-10 holds all 12 records listed for jet-powered flying-boats, including an altitude of 14 962 m *49 088 ft* set by Georgiy Buryanov and crew over the Sea of Azov on 9 Sept 1961.

AIRSHIPS
Earliest

The earliest flight in an airship was by Henri Giffard from Paris in his steam-powered coal-gas 2500 m³ *88 300 ft³* 43·8 m *144 ft* long airship on 24 Sept 1852. The earliest British airship was a 566 m³ *20 000 ft³* 22·8 m *75 ft* long craft built by Stanley Spencer whose maiden flight was from Crystal Palace, London on 22 Sept 1902. The latest airship to be built in Britain is the 6666 m³ *235 400 ft³* 59 m *193·6 ft* long Skyship 600 designed and built by Airship Industries. This 20-passenger dirigible (G-SKSC) was flown for the first time at RAE Cardington, Bedfordshire on 6 Mar 1984.

Largest *Rigid*

The largest rigid airship ever built was the 213·9 tonne *210·5 ton* German *Graf Zeppelin II* (LZ 130), with a length of 245 m *803·8 ft* and a capacity of 199 981 m³ *7 062 100 ft³.* She made her maiden flight on 14 Sept 1938 and in May and August 1939 made radar spying missions in British air space. She was dismantled in April 1940. Her sister ship *Hindenburg* was 1·70 m *5·6 ft* longer.

The largest British airship was the R101 built by the Royal Airship Works, Cardington, Bedfordshire, which first flew on 14 Oct 1929. She was 236·8 m *777 ft* in length and had a capacity of 155 995 m³ *5 508 800 ft³.* She

crashed near Beauvais, France, killing 48 aboard on 5 Oct 1930.

Non-rigid

The largest non-rigid airship ever constructed was the US Navy ZPG 3-W which had a capacity of 42 937 m³ *1 516 300 ft³,* was 122·9 m *403· ft* long and 25·93 m *85·1 ft* in diameter, with a crew of 21. She first flew on 21 July 1958, but crashed into the sea in June 1960.

Hot-air

The world altitude, duration and distance records, of 3159 m *10 365 ft,* 1 hr 26 min 52 sec, and 37·07 km *23·03 miles* respectively, are held by the Cameron D-38 hot-air airship flown at Cunderdin, Western Australia on 27 Aug 1982 by R. W. Taaffe (Australia).

Greatest passenger load

The most people ever carried in an airship was 207 in the US Navy *Akron* in 1931. The trans-Atlantic record is 117 by the German *Hindenburg* in 1937.

Distance records

The FAI (Fédération Aéronautique Internationale) accredited straight-line distance record for airships is 6384·5 km *3967·1 miles,* set up by the German *Graf Zeppelin,* captained by Dr Hugo Eckener, between 29 Oct and 1 Nov 1928. The German Zeppelin L59 flew from Yambol, Bulgaria to south of Khartoum, Sudan and returned from 21–25 Nov 1917 to cover a minimum of 7250 km *4500 miles.*

Duration record

The longest recorded flight by a non-rigid airship (without refuelling) is 264 hr 12 min by a US Navy Goodyear-built ZPG-2 class ship (Cdr J. R. Hunt USN) from South Weymouth NAS, Massachusetts, USA from 4–15 Mar 1957 landing back at Key West, Florida having flown 15 205 km *9448 miles.*

BALLOONING
Earliest

I. William Deiches (b. 1934) of Brentwood, Essex, has adduced that the 'mace-head' of the Scorpion King *c.* 3100 BC found at Hierakonpolis, Egypt is in reality a depiction of a panelled hot-air balloon of papyrus construction. The earliest recorded ascent was by a model hot-air balloon invented by Father Bartolomeu de Gusmão (né Lourenço) (1685–1724), which was flown indoors at the Casa da India, Terreiro do Paço, Portugal on 8 Aug 1709.

Distance record *(Great-circle distance between take-off and first landing point)*

The record distance travelled by a balloon is 8382·54 km *5208·68 miles* by the Raven experimental helium-filled balloon *Double Eagle V* (capacity 11 300 m³ *399·053 ft³*) from 9–12 Nov 1981, from Nagashima, Japan to Covello, California, USA.

The crew for this the first manned balloon crossing of the Pacific Ocean were Ben L. Abruzzo, 51, Rocky Aoki, 43 (Japan), Ron Clark, 41 and Larry M. Newman, 34.

Ex-USAF Colonel Joe Kittinger (see Parachuting, Chapter 10) became the first man to complete a solo trans-Atlantic crossing by balloon. Accomplished in the 3000 m³ helium-filled balloon *Rosie O'Grady* between 14–18 Sept 1984, Kittinger lifted off from Caribou, Maine and completed a distance of approximately 5701 km *3543 miles* before landing at Montenotte, Italy in 86 hr.

The first balloon crossing of the North Atlantic had been made during 12–17 Aug 1978 (137 hr 6 min) in the gas balloon *Double Eagle II* crewed by Ben L. Abruzzo, Maxie L. Anderson and Larry M. Newman.

The first balloon crossing of the United States was by the helium-filled *Super Chicken III* (pilots Fred Gorell and John Shoecraft) from Costa Mesa, California, 4047 km *2515 miles* to Blackbeard's Island, Georgia from 9–12 Oct 1981.

Highest
Unmanned

The highest altitude attained by an unmanned balloon was 51 815 m *170 000 ft* by a Winzen balloon of 1·35 million m³ *47·8 million ft³* launched at Chico, California in October 1972.

Manned

The greatest altitude reached in a manned balloon is an unofficial 37 735 m *(123 800 ft)* by Nicholas Piantanida (1933–66) of Bricktown, New Jersey, from Sioux Falls, South Dakota on 1 Feb 1966. He landed in a cornfield in Iowa but did not survive.

The official record is 34 668 m *113 740 ft* by Cdr Malcolm D. Ross, USNR and the late Lt-Cdr Victor A. Prother, USN in an ascent from the deck of USS *Antietam* on 4 May 1961, over the Gulf of Mexico in a balloon of 339 804 m³ *12 million ft³.*

Owing to an oversight, Harold Froelich and Keith Lang, scientists from Minneapolis, ascended in an open gondola and without the protection of pressure suits to a height of 12·84 km *42 150 ft,* just under 8 miles, on 26 Sept 1956. During their 6½-hour flight, the temperature at maxiuum altitude (measured with a laboratory thermometer) was −57·7°C *−72°F.*

Largest

The largest balloons built have an inflatable volume of 2 million m³ *70 million ft³* by Winzen Research Inc, Minnesota. These stand 300 m *1000 ft* tall and are unmanned.

Hot-air

Richard Branson (GB) with his pilot Per Lindstrand (Sweden), the first to cross the Atlantic in a hot-air balloon, flew on 2–3 July 1987 from Sugarloaf, Maine, USA to Limavady, Co Londonderry, N Ireland, a distance of 4947 km *3075 miles.* Their balloon, *Virgin Atlantic Challenger,* of 65 000 m³ *2·3 million ft³* capacity was the largest ever flown and reached speeds in excess of 209 km/h *130 mph.*

The duration record of 40 hr 12 min 5 sec was established by the French pair Hélène Dorigny and her co-pilot Michel Arnould on 6–7 July 1984 in the balloon *Le Primagaz* flying from Germaine to Le Mele-sur-Sarthe, France.

On 31 Oct 1980 Julian Nott (GB) attained an altitude, which has been ratified by the FAI, of 16 805 m *55 137 ft,* taking off from Longmont, near Denver, Colorado in the Cameron-built ICI balloon *Innovation.*

The FAI endurance and distance record for a gas and hot-air balloon is 96 hr 24 min and 3339·086 km *2074·817 miles* by *Zanussi* crewed by Donald Allan Cameron (GB) and Major Christopher Davey which failed by only 166 km *103 miles* to achieve the first balloon crossing of the Atlantic on 30 July 1978.

The record altitude in an open basket and with the use of a pressure suit is 16 154·4 m *53 000 ft* by Chauncey M. Dunn (US) on 1 Aug 1979.

Miss Champagne a balloon of 73 625 m³ *2·6 million ft²* capacity was built by Tom Handcock of Portland, Maine, USA. Tethered, it rose to a height of 12 ·25 m *50 ft* with 61 passengers on board on 19 Feb 1988.

The greatest mass ascent of hot-air balloons from a single site took place when 128 participants at the 9th Bristol International Balloon Festival at Ashton Court, Bristol, Avon on 15 Aug 1987 took off all within a period of 1 hour.

PERSONAL AVIATION RECORDS
Oldest and youngest passengers

Airborne births are reported every year. The oldest person to fly has been Mrs Jessica S. Swift (b. Anna Stewart 17 Sept 1871) aged 110 yrs 3 months, from Vermont to Florida in Dec 1981. The oldest Briton to fly was Charlotte Hughes (b. 1 Aug 1877) on a Concorde flight to New York on 4 Aug 1987 as a 110th birthday present. She returned 4 days later.

Youngest and oldest pilots

The youngest age at which anyone has ever qualified as a military pilot is 15 years 5 months in the case of Sgt Thomas Dobney (b. 6 May 1926) of the RAF. He had overstated his age (14 years) on entry. A wholly untutored James A. Stoodley aged 14 years 5 months took his 13-year-old brother John on a 29-minute joy ride in an unattended US Piper Cub trainer aircraft near Ludgershall, Wiltshire in December 1942.

The world's oldest pilot is Ed McCarty (b. 18 Sept 1885) of Kimberly, Idaho who in 1979 was flying his rebuilt 30-year-old Ercoupe, aged 94. The oldest British pilot is Air Commodore Harold 'Daddy' Probyn (b. 8 Dec 1891), who first flew with the RFC in 1916 and was flying in Kenya on his 92nd birthday 67 years later in 1983.

Longest interval between trans-Atlantic flights

Wing-Cdr A. G. Evenden first flew the Atlantic as a crew member on the British airship R-34 on the first airship crossing between 2–6 July 1919. Sixty years later he made the crossing on 2 July 1979 by Concorde.

Most flying hours

Max Conrad (1903–79) (USA) between 1928 and mid-1974 totalled 52 929 hr 40 min logged flight more than 6 years airborne. He completed 150 trans-Atlantic crossings in light aircraft. The record as a supersonic passenger is held by Fred Finn who made his 604 th Concorde crossing in June 1986.

Since Sept 1970 Maisie Muir of Orkney, Scotland has flown over 8000 times with Loganair.

Most airport take-offs and landings

Al Yates and Bob Phoenix of Texas made 193 take-offs and daylight landings at unduplicated airfields in 14 hr 57 min in a Piper Seminole, on 15 June 1979.

E. K. Coventry (pilot) and D. Bullen (navigator) made full-stop landings in a Piper Arrow in all of England's 45 counties between dawn and dusk on 24 July 1984.

Human-powered flight

The first man-powered Channel crossing was achieved on 12 June 1979 by Bryan Allen (US) in the *Gossamer Albatross*, designed by Dr Paul MacCready. The 35·82 km *22·26 mile* flight from Folkestone to Cape Gris Nez set the duration record of 2 hr 49 mins. The Daedalus Project, centred on the Massachusetts Institute of Technology, achieved its goal of human-powered flight from Crete to the island of Santorini 119 km *74 miles* distant on 23 Apr 1988 when Kanellos Kanellopoulos (b. 25 Apr 1957) averaged 29·7 km/h *18·5 mph* in his 34·1 m *112 ft* wingspan machine.

MODEL AIRCRAFT

Altitude, speed and duration

Maynard L. Hill (US) flying radio-controlled models established the world record for altitude of 8208 m *26 929 ft* on 6 Sept 1970 and on 4 July 1983 set a closed-circuit distance record of 765 km *1231 miles*. The free-flight speed record is 343·92 km/h *213·70 mph* by V. Goukoune and V. Myakinin (both USSR) with a radio-controlled model at Klementyeva, USSR, on 21 Sept 1971. The record duration flight is one of 32 hr 7 min 40 sec by Eduard Svoboda (Czechoslovakia), flying a radio-controlled glider on 23–24 Aug 1980. An indoor model with a rubber motor designed by J. Richmond (USA) set a duration record of 52 min 14 sec on 31 Aug 1979.

The first cross-Channel model helicopter flight was achieved by an 5 kg *11 lb* model Bell 212 radio controlled by Dieter Zeigler for 52 km *32 miles* between Ashford, Kent and Ambleteuse, France on 17 July 1974.

Smallest

The smallest model aircraft to fly is one weighing 0·1 g

0·004 oz powered by attaching a horsefly and designed by insectonaut Don Emmick of Seattle, Washington on 24 July 1979. One flew for 5 minutes at Kirkland, Washington.

Paper aircraft

The flight duration record for a paper aircraft is 16·89 sec by Ken Blackburn in the Reynolds Coliseum, North Carolina State University on 29 Nov 1983. The indoor record with a 3·65 m *12 ft* ceiling is 1 min 33 sec set in the Fuji TV studios, Tōkyō, Japan on 21 Sept 1980. A paper plane was reported and witnessed to have flown 2·0 km *1¼ miles* by 'Chick' C. O. Reinhart from a 10th-storey office window at 60 Beaver Street, New York across the East River to Brooklyn in August 1933, helped by a thermal from a coffee-roasting plant. An indoor distance of 58·82 m *193 ft* was recorded by Tony Felch at the La Crosse Center, Wisconsin on 21 May 1985.

The largest flying paper aeroplane was constructed on 26 Apr 1986 by Grahame Foster, David Broom and Andrew Barkas at the Old Warden Aerodrome, Biggleswade, Bedfordshire. With a wing span of 1·8 m *6 ft* it was launched from a platform of height 3·04 m *10 ft* and flew for 16·4 m *54 ft* during the course of the BBC television programme *The Great Egg Race*.

Power

Steam engines

The oldest steam engine in working order is the 1812 Boulton & Watt 26-hp 1066 mm *42 in* bore beam engine on the Kennet & Avon Canal at Great Bedwyn, Wiltshire. It was restored by the Crofton Society in 1971 and still runs periodically.

The largest single-cylinder steam engine ever built was that designed by Matthew Loam of Cornwall and made by the Hayle Foundry Co in 1849 for installation for land draining at Haarlem, Netherlands. The cylinder was 3·65 m *12 ft* in diameter such that each stroke, also of 3·65 m *12 ft*, lifted 61 096 l *13 440 gallons* or .60 tons of water.

The most efficient steam engine recorded was Taylor's engine built by Michael Loam for United Mines, Gwennap, Cornwall in 1840. It registered only 1·7 lb of coal per horsepower per hour.

Earliest atomic pile

The world's first atomic pile was built in a disused doubles squash court at Stagg Field, University of Chicago, Illinois. It went 'critical' at 3.25 p.m. on 2 Dec 1942.

Largest power plant

Currently, the world's most powerful installed power station is the Grand Coulee, Washington State, USA with 9·7 million kilowatt hours (ultimately 10 080 MW) which began operating in 1942.

The $11-billion Itaipu power station on the Paraná river by the Brazil-Paraguay border began generating power formally on 25 Oct 1984 and will by 1988/89 attain 12 600 000 kW from 18 turbines. Construction began in 1975 with a workforce reaching 28 000. A 20 000-MW power station project on the Tunguska River, USSR was announced in February 1982.

The world's largest coal-fired power complex at Ekibastuz, Kazakhstan, USSR began generating in May 1982.

The power station with the greatest installed capacity in Great Britain is Drax, North Yorkshire, with 5 of its 6660-MW sets yielding 3300-MW in mid-1986. The sixth set will be operational in early 1987. A 3300-MW oil-fired installation is under construction on the Isle of Grain, Kent.

The largest hydroelectric plant in the UK is the North of Scotland Hydroelectricity Board's Power Station at Loch Sloy, Dumbartonshire. The installed capacity of this

station is 130 MW. The Ben Cruachan pumped storage scheme was opened on 15 Oct 1965 at Loch Awe, Argyllshire, Scotland. It has a capacity of 400 MW and cost £24 000 000.

The 1880-MW underground pumped storage scheme at Dinorwig, Gwynedd is the largest in Europe with a head of 530 m *1739 ft* and a capacity of 390 m³/sec *13 770 ft³/sec*. The £425-million plant was completed in 1984 with a capacity of 1681 MW.

Nuclear power station

The first nuclear power station producing electricity was the ERR-1 in the USA on 20 Dec 1951. Britain's earliest was Calder Hall (Unit 1), Cumbria on 27 Aug 1956.

The world's largest nuclear power station with 10 reactors and an output of 9096 MW is the station in Fukushima, Japan.

Nuclear reactor

The largest single nuclear reactor in the world is the 1450-MW (net) reactor at the Ignalina station, Lithuania, USSR, put on full power in January 1984. The largest under construction is the CHOOZ-B1 reactor in France which is scheduled for operation in 1991 and will have a net capacity of 1457 MW.

Fusion power

Tokamak-7, the experimental thermonuclear apparatus, was declared in January 1982 by USSR academician Velikhov to be operating 'reliably for months on end'. An economically featured thermonuclear reactor is not anticipated in the near future.

Solar power plant

The largest solar furnace in the world is the $141-million 10 megawatt 'Solar I', 19·3 km *12 miles* south-east of Barstow, California, first tested in April 1982. It comprises 1818 mirrors in concentric circles focused on a boiler atop a 77·7 m *255 ft* high tower. Sunlight from 222 heliostats is concentrated on a target 34·7 m *114 ft* up in the power tower. The $30-million thermal solar energy system at Pakerland Packing Co, Bellevue Plant, Green Bay, Wisconsin completed in January 1984 comprises 9750 1·21 x 2· 43 m *4 x 8 ft* collectors covering 28 985 m² *7·16 acres*. It will yield up to 8000 million BTUs a month.

Tidal power station

The world's first major tidal power station is the *Usine marémotrice de la Rance*, officially opened on 26 Nov 1966 at the Rance estuary in the Golfe de St Malo, Brittany, France. It was built in five years at a cost of 420 000 000 francs , and has a net annual output of 544 000 000 kWh. The 804 m *880 yd* barrage contains 24 turbo alternators. The $1000-million Passamaquoddy project for the Bay of Fundy in Maine, USA, and New Brunswick, Canada, remains a project. A $46-million pilot Annapolis River project for the Bay of Fundy was begun in 1981.

Largest boiler

The largest boilers ever designed are those ordered in the United States from Babcock & Wilcox (USA) with a capacity of 1330 MW so involving the evaporation of 4 232 000 kg *9 330 000 lb* of steam per hour. The largest boilers now being installed in the United Kingdom are five 660-MW units for the Drax Power Station, designed and constructed by Babcock & Wilcox.

Largest generator

Generators in the 2 000 000-kW (or 2000-MW) range are now in the planning stages both in the UK and the USA. The largest operational is a turbo-generator of 1450 MW (net) being installed at the Ignalina Atomic Power Station in Lithuania .

Largest turbines

The largest hydraulic turbines are those rated at 815 000 kW (equivalent to 1·1 million hp), 9·7 m *32 ft* in diameter with a 407 tonne *401 ton* runner and a 317·5 tonne *312½ ton* shaft installed by Allis-Chalmers at the Grand Coulee 'Third Powerplant', Washington, USA.

Pump
The world's largest reversible pump-turbine is that made by Allis-Chalmers for the Bath County project, Virginia, USA. It has a maximum rating of 457 MW as a turbine and maximum operating head of 393 m *1289 ft*. The impeller/runner diameter is 6349 mm *20 ft 9 in* with a synchronous speed of 257·1 rpm.

Gas
The largest gas turbine is type GT 13 E from BBC Brown Boveri AG with a maximum output of 140MW. The first machine is being installed in Holland in order to increase the general output of a 500MW steam-powered plant (Hemweg 7) by more than 46 per cent.

Largest battery
The world's largest battery is a 10 MW lead-acid battery at Chino, California, USA. With design capacity of 40 MWh, it will be used at an electrical sub-station for levelling peak demand loads. This $13 million project is a co-operative effort by Southern California Edison Company, Electric Power Research Institute, and International Lead Zinc Research Organization Inc.

Longest-lasting battery
The zinc foil and sulfur dry-pile batteries made by Watlin and Hill of London in 1840 have powered ceaseless tintinnabulation inside a bell jar at the Clarendon Laboratory, Oxford since that year.

Largest gasworks
The flow of natural gas from the North Sea is diminishing the manufacture of gas by the carbonisation of coal and the reforming process using petroleum derivatives. Britain's largest ever gasworks, 120 ha *300 acres*, were at Beckton, Newham, east London. Currently, the largest gasworks in the UK are the Breakwater Works at Oreston, Plymouth, Devon which opened in 1966–7 and cover an area of 7·6 ha *19 acres*. They convert complex hydrocarbons into methane and produce 1 415 850 m³ *50 million ft³* per day.

Biggest black-out
The greatest power failure in history struck seven north-eastern US states and Ontario, Canada, on 9–10 Nov 1965. About 30 000 000 people in 207 200 km² *80 000 miles²* were plunged into darkness. Only two were killed. In New York the power failed at 5.27 p.m. and was not fully restored for 13½ hr.

The total consequential losses in the 52-min New York City power failure of 13 July 1977 including looting was put at $1 billion .

Windmill
Earliest
The earliest recorded windmills are those used for grinding corn in Iran in the 7th century AD.

The earliest date attributed to a windmill in England is 1185 for one at Weedley, near Hull, Humberside. The oldest Dutch mill is the towermill at Zeddam, Gelderland built in *c.* 1450. The oldest working mill in England is the post-mill at Outwood, near Redhill, Surrey, built in 1665, though the Ivinghoe Mill in Pitstone Green Farm, Buckinghamshire, dating from 1627, has been restored. The post-mill in North Ronaldsay, Orkney Islands operated until 1905.

Largest
The world's first 3000-kW wind generator was the 150 m *492 ft* tall turbine, built by Grosse Windenergie–Anlage which was set up in 1982 on the Friesian coast of West Germany. The £12 million 3000-kW aerogenerator LS1 with 60 m *196 ft 10 in* blades on a 37 m *121 ft* tall tower on Burgar Hill, Evie, Orkney built by Taylor Woodrow was switched on in a gale on 10 Nov 1987. It should yield 9 million kW/h per annum. The $14·2-million GEC MOD-5A installation on the north shore of Oahu, Hawaii will produce 7300 kW when the wind reaches 51·5 km/h

32 mph with 122 m *400 ft* rotors. Installation started in March 1984.

The largest Dutch windmill is the Dijkpolder in Maasland built in 1718. The sails measure 29 m *95¾ ft* from tip to tip. De Noord windmill in Schiedam, Netherlands at 33·33 m *109 ft 4 in*, is the tallest in Europe. The tallest windmill still standing in Britain is the 9-storey Sutton mill, Norfolk built in 1853 which (before being struck by lightning in 1941) had sails 22·2 m *73 ft* in diameter with 216 shutters.

Water mill
There has been a water-powered corn-mill at Priston Mill near Bath, Avon since pre-Norman times. The earliest recorded is dated AD 931.

Tidal Mill
On 1 May 1988 the Eling Tide Mill, Hampshire attained 15 hr 26 min rotation of the waterwheel in one day. It is the only surviving mill in the world harnessing the power of the tide for regular production of wholemeal flour.

Engineering

Oldest machinery
The earliest mechanisms still in use are the *dâlu*—a water-raising instrument known to have been in use in the Sumerian civilisation which originated *c.* 3500 BC in lower Iraq thus even earlier than the *Saqiyas* on the Nile.

The oldest piece of machinery (excluding clocks) operating in the United Kingdom is the snuff mill driven by a water wheel at Messrs Wilson & Co's Sharrow Mill in Sheffield, South Yorkshire. It is known to have been operating in 1797 and more probably since 1730.

Blast furnace
The largest blast furnace has an inner volume of 5070 m³ *179 040 ft³* and 14·8 m *48 ft 6½ in* diameter hearth at the Oita Works, Kyūshū, Japan completed in October 1976 with 4 380 000 tonnes annual capacity.

Cat cracker
The world's largest catalyst cracker is Exxon's Bayway Refinery plant at Linden, New Jersey, USA with a fresh feed rate of 19 077 000 litres *5 040 000 US gal* per day.

Conveyor belt
The world's longest single-flight conveyor belt is one of 29 km *18 miles* in Western Australia installed by Cable Belt Ltd of Camberley, Surrey. The longest in Great Britain is also by Cable Belt and of 8·9 km *5½ miles* underground at Longannet Power Station, Fife, Scotland. The world's longest multi-flight conveyor is one of 100 km *62 miles* between the phosphate mine near Bucraa and the port of El Aaiun, Morocco, built by Krupps and completed in 1972. It has 11 flights of between 9 and 11 km *5·6–6·8 miles* and was driven at 4·5 m/sec *10·06 mph* but has since been closed down.

Most powerful crane
The world's most powerful cranes are the two aboard the semi-submersible vessel *Micoperi 7000* (190 m *623·35 ft* in length and 89 m *292 ft* in breadth) operated by Officine Meccaniche Reggiane, built by Monfalcone, Gorizia, Italy and launched 15 Dec 1986. Each has a capacity of 7000 tonne.

Gantry crane
The 28·14 m *92·3 ft* wide Rahco (R. A. Hanson Disc. Ltd) gantry crane at the Grand Coulee Dam Third Powerplant was tested to lift a load of 2232 long tonnes in 1975. It lowered a 1789 tonne *3 944 000 lb* generator rotor with an accuracy of 0·8 mm *1/32 in*.

Tallest mobile crane
The tallest mobile crane in the world is the 810-tonne Rosenkranz K10001 with a lifting capacity of 1000 tonnes, and a combined boom and jib height of 202 m *663 ft*. It is

carried on 10 trucks each limited to 23·06 m *75 ft 8 in* and an axle weight of 118 tonnes . It can lift 30 tonnes to a height of 160 m *525 ft*.

The Taklift 4 craneship of the Smit International fleet based in Rotterdam, Netherlands has boom jib reaching a height of 95 m *312 ft*.

Dragline
The Ural Engineering Works at Ordzhonikdze, USSR, completed in March 1962, has a dragline known as the ES-25(100) with a boom of 100 m *328 ft* and a bucket with a capacity of 24 m³ *31·5 yd³*. The world's largest walking dragline is 'Big Muskie', the Bucyrus-Erie 4250W with an all-up weight of 12 000 tonnes and a bucket capacity of 168 m³ *220 yd³* on a 94·4 m *310 ft* boom. This, the largest mobile land machine, is now operating on the Central Ohio Coal Company's Muskingum site in Ohio, USA.

The largest dragline excavator in Britain is 'Big Geordie', the Bucyrus-Erie 1550W 6250 gross hp, weighing 3000 tonnes with a forward mast 48·7 m *160 ft* high. On open-cast coal workings at Butterwell, Northumberland in September 1975 it proved able to strip 100 tonnes of overburden in 65 sec with its 49·7 m³ *65 yd³* bucket on a 80·7 m *265 ft* boom. This excavator is owned by Derek Crouch (Contractors) Ltd of Peterborough, Cambridgeshire.

Escalator
The term was registered in the US on 28 May 1900 but the earliest 'Inclined Escalator' was installed by Jesse W. Reno on the pier at Coney Island, New York in 1896. The first installation in Britain was at Harrods department store, London in November 1898. The escalators on the Leningrad underground, USSR at Lenin Square have 729 steps and a vertical rise of 59·68 m *195 ft 9½ in*.

The longest escalators in operation in Britain are the four in the Tyne Tunnel, Tyne and Wear which were installed in 1951. They measure 58·7 m *192 ft 8 in* between combs with a vertical lift of 25·9 m *85 ft* and a step speed of up to 2·7 km/h *1·7 mph*.

The world's longest 'moving sidewalks' are those installed in 1970 in the Neue Messe Centre, Dusseldorf, West Germany which measure 225 m *738 ft* between comb plates. The longest in Great Britain is the 114·3 m *375 ft* long Dunlop Starglide at London's Heathrow Airport Terminal 3 installed in March – May 1970.

The world's longest *ride* is on the 4-section outdoor escalator at Ocean Park, Hong Kong which has an overall length of 227 m *745 ft* and a total vertical rise of 115 m *377 ft*.

Excavator
The world's largest excavator is the 13 000-tonne bucket wheel excavator being assembled at the open-cast lignite mine of Hambach, West Germany with a rating of 200 000 m³ *260 000 yd³* per 20-hr working day. It is 210 m *690 ft* in length and 82 m *269 ft* tall. The wheel is 67·88 m *222 ft* in circumference with 5 m³ *6·5 yd³* buckets.

Forging
The largest forging on record is one of a 204·4 tonne *450 600 lb* 16·76 m *55 ft* long generator shaft for Japan, forged by the Bethlehem Steel Corp of Pennsylvania, USA in October 1973.

Fork lift truck
Kalmar LMV of Sweden manufactured in 1985 ten counterbalanced fork lift trucks capable of lifting loads up to 80 tonnes at a load centre of 2300 mm *90·5 in*. They were built to handle the large-diameter pipeline in the Libyan Great Man-made River Project.

Lathe
The largest is the 38·4 m *126 ft* long 416·2 tonne giant lathe built by Waldrich Siegen of West Germany in 1973 for the South African Electricity Supply Commission at Rosherville with a capacity for 300 tonne work pieces and a swing-over bed of diameter 5 m *16 ft 5 in*.

Largest wheeled loader ● This giant earthmover is 16·8 m *55·1 ft* in length, weighs 180 tonnes and its rubber tyres are 3·5 m *11·5 ft* in diameter. The bucket has a capacity of 19 m³ *671 ft³* and it was developed for open-air coal mining in Australia by SMEC, a consortium of eleven manufacturers in Tōkyō, Japan.

Greatest lift

The heaviest lifting operation in engineering history was the raising of the entire 1·6 km *0·745 mile* long offshore Ekofisk complex in the North Sea owing to subsidence of the sea bed. The complex consists of eight platforms weighing some 40 000 tonne and was raised 6·5 m *21 ft 4 in* by 122 hydraulic jacks during 17–18 Aug 1987. Hydraudyne Systems & Engineering bv of Boxtel, Netherlands developed and supplied the computer-controlled hydraulic system.

Slowest machine

A nuclear environmental machine for testing stress corrosion has been developed by Nene Instruments of Wellingborough, Northants that can be controlled at a speed as slow as one million millionth of a millimetre per minute, or one metre *3·28 ft* in about 2000 million years.

Nut

The largest nuts ever made weigh 4·74 tonnes *93·4 cwt* each with an outside diameter of 132 cm *52 in* and a 63·5 cm *25 in* thread. Known as 'Pilgrim Nuts', they are manufactured by Pilgrim Moorside Ltd of Oldham, Lancashire for use on the columns of a large forging press.

Oil tank

The largest oil tanks ever constructed are the five Aramco 1½-million-barrel storage tanks at Ju'aymah, Saudi Arabia. They are 21·94 m *72 ft* tall with a diameter of 117·6 m *386 ft* and were completed in March 1980.

Passenger lift

The fastest domestic passenger lifts in the world are the express lifts to the 60th floor of the 240 m *787·4 ft* tall 'Sunshine 60' building, Ikebukuro in Tōkyō, Japan completed 5 Apr 1978. They were built by Mitsubishi Corp and operate at a speed of 609·6 m/min *2000 ft/min* or 36·56 km/h *22·72 mph*. Much higher speeds are achieved in the winding cages of mine shafts. A hoisting shaft 2072 m *6800 ft* deep, owned by Western Deep Levels Ltd in South Africa, winds at speeds of up to 65·2 km/h *40·9 mph* (1095 m *3595 ft* per min). Otitis-media (popping of the ears) presents problems much above even 16 km/h *10 mph*.

The longest lift in the United Kingdom is one 930 ft long inside the BBC Television Tower at Bilsdale, West Moor, North Yorkshire, built by J. L. Eve Construction. It runs at 39·6 m/min *130 ft/min*. The longest fast lifts are the two 15-passenger cars in the British Telecom Tower, London which travel 164 m *540 ft* at up to 304 m/min *1000 ft/min*.

Graham Coates established an involuntary duration record when trapped in a lift for 62 hr in Brighton, East Sussex on 24–26 May 1986.

Pipelines *Oil*

The world's earliest pipeline of 5 cm *2 in* cast iron, laid at Oil Creek, Pennsylvania in 1863 was torn up by Luddites.

The longest crude oil pipeline in the world is the Interprovincial Pipe Line Company's installation from Edmonton, Alberta, Canada to Buffalo, New York State, USA, a distance of 2856 km *1775 miles*. Along the length of the pipe 13 pumping stations maintain a flow of 31 367 145 litres *6 900 000 gal* of oil per day. The eventual length of the Trans-Siberian Pipeline will be 3732 km *2319 miles*, running from Tuimazy through Omsk and Novosibirsk to Irkutsk. The first 48 km *30 mile* section was opened in July 1957.

Submarine

The world's longest submarine pipeline is that of 425 km *264 miles* for natural gas from the Union Oil Platform to Rayong, Thailand opened on 12 Sept 1981. The longest North Sea pipeline is the Ekofisk–Emden line stretching 418 km *260 miles* and completed in July 1975. The deepest North Sea pipeline is that from the Cormorant Field to Firths Voe, Shetland at 162 m *530 ft.*

Natural gas

The longest natural gas pipeline in the world is the Trans-Canada Pipeline which by 1974 had 9099 km *5654 miles* of pipe up to 106·6 cm *42 in* in diameter. The Tyumen–Chelyabinsk–Moscow–Brandenburg gasline stretches 4330 km *2690 miles.*

The large-calibre Urengoi-Uzhgorod line to Western Europe, begun in November 1982, stretches 4451 km *2765 miles* and was completed on 25 July 1983. It has a capacity of 32 000 million m³ *42 000 million yd³* per annum.

Water

The world's longest water pipeline runs a distance of 563 km *350 miles* to the Kalgoorlie gold fields from near Perth in Western Australia. Engineered in 1903, the system has since been extended five-fold by branches.

Most expensive

The world's most expensive pipeline is the Alaska Pipeline running 1284 km *798 miles* from Prudhoe Bay to Valdez. By completion of the first phase in 1977 it had cost at least $6000 million . The pipe is 1·21 m *48 in* in diameter and will eventually carry up to 2 million barrels of crude oil per day.

Press

The world's two most powerful production machines are forging presses in the USA. The Loewy closed-die forging press, in a plant leased from the US Air Force by the Wyman-Gordon Company at North Grafton, Massachusetts weighs 9469 tonnes and stands 34·79 m *114 ft 2 in* high, of which 20·1 m *66 ft* is sunk below the operating floor. It has a rated capacity of 44 600 tonnes, and became operational in October 1955. The other similar press is at the plant of the Aluminum Company of America in Cleveland, Ohio. In Jan 1986 ASEA's QUINTUS Dept delivered a sheet metal forming press to BMW AG, Munich, West Germany. This press, which is the largest in the world in terms of forming pressure and press force is a QUINTUS Fluid Cell Press with a press force of 106 000 tonnes. The Bêché and Grohs counter-blow forging hammer, manufactured in West Germany is rated at 60 000 tonnes.

The most powerful press in Great Britain is the closed-die forging and extruding press installed in 1967 at the Cameron Iron Works, Livingston, West Lothian. The press is 28 m *92 ft* tall (8·2 m *27 ft* below ground) and exerts a force of 30 000 tonnes.

Printer

The world's fastest printer is the Radiation Inc electro-sensitive system at the Lawrence Radiation Laboratory, Livermore, California, USA. High-speed recording of up to 30 000 lines, each containing 120 alphanumeric characters, per minute is attained by controlling electronic pulses through chemically-impregnated recording paper which is rapidly moving under closely-spaced fixed styli. It can thus print the wordage of the whole Bible (773 692 words) in 65 seconds—3306 times as fast as the world's fastest typist.

Radar installation

The largest scientific radar installation is the 84 000 m² *21 acre* ground array at Jicamarca, Peru.

Ropeway or téléphérique

The longest ropeway in the world is the Compagnie Minière de l'Ogooué or COMILOG installation built in 1959–62 for the Moanda manganese mine in Gabon which extends 76 km *47·2 miles.* It has 858 towers and 2800 buckets with 155 km *96·3 miles* of wire rope running over 6000 idler pulleys.

The highest and longest passenger-carrying aerial ropeway in the world is the Teleférico Mérida (Mérida téléphérique) in Venezuela, from Mérida City (1639·5 m *5379 ft*) to the summit of Pico Espejo (4763·7 m *15 629 ft*),

a rise of 3124 m *10 250 ft.* The ropeway is in four sections, involving 3 car changes in the 12·8 km *8 mile* ascent in 1 hr. The fourth span is 3069 m *10 070 ft* in length. The two cars work on the pendulum system—the carrier rope is locked and the cars are hauled by means of three pull ropes powered by a 230 hp *233 cv* motor. They have a maximum capacity of 45 persons and travel at 9·7 m *32 ft* per sec (35·08 km/h *21·8 mph*). The longest-single span ropeway is the 4114 m *13 500 ft* span from the Coachella Valley to Mt San Jacinto (3298 m *310 821 ft*), California, USA, inaugurated on 12 Sept 1963.

Britain's longest cabin lift is that at Llandudno, Gwynedd, opened in June 1969. It has 42 cabins with a capacity of 1000 people per hour and is 1621 m *5320 ft* in length.

Shovel

The Marion 6360 has a reach of 72·16 m *236·75 ft,* a dumping height of 46·63 m *153 ft* and a scooping capacity of 45·87 m³ *1620 ft³.* Manufactured in 1963 by the Marion Power Shovel Company, Ohio, USA, it weighs 11 million kg *24 250 000 lb* and uses 20 electric motors that generate 45 000 horse power to operate its 67·2 m *220·5 ft* long boom arm.

Transformer

The world's largest single-phase transformers are rated at 1 500 000 kVA of which eight are in service with the American Electric Power Service Corporation. Of these, five stepdown from 765 to 345 kV. Britain's largest transformers are those rated at 1 000 000 kVA 400/275 kV built by Hackbridge & Hewittic, Walton-on-Thames, Surrey first commissioned for the CEGB in October 1968.

Transmission lines *Longest*

The longest span between pylons of any power line in the world is that across the Sogne Fjord, Norway, between Rabnaberg and Fatlaberg. Supplied in 1955 by Whitecross of Warrington, Cheshire, and projected and erected by A. S. Betonmast of Oslo as part of the high-tension power cable from Refsdal power station at Vik, it has a span of 4888 m *16 040 ft* and a weight of 12 tonnes. In 1967 two further high-tensile steel/aluminium lines 4878 m *16 006 ft* long, and weighing 33 tonnes, manufactured by Whitecross and BICC were erected here. The longest in Britain are the 1618 m *5310 ft* lines built by J. L. Eve across the Severn with main towers each 148 m *488 ft* high.

Highest

The world's highest are those across the Straits of Messina, with towers of 205 m *675 ft* (Sicily side) and 224 m *735 ft* (Calabria) and 3627 m *11 900 ft* apart. The highest lines in Britain are those made by BICC at West Thurrock, Essex, which cross the Thames estuary suspended from 192 m *630 ft* tall towers at a minimum height of 76 m *250 ft,* with a 130 tonne breaking load. They are 1371 m *4500 ft* in length.

Highest voltages

The highest voltages now carried are 1 330 000 volts 1970 km *1224 miles* on the DC Pacific Inter-tie in the United States. The Ekibastuz DC transmission lines in Kazakhstan, USSR are planned to be 2400 km *1490 miles* long with 1 500 000 volt capacity.

Valve

The world's largest valve is the 9·75 m *32 ft* diameter, 170 tonne butterfly valve designed by Boving & Co Ltd of London for use at the Arnold Airforce Base engine test facility in Tennessee .

Wire ropes

The longest wire ropes in the world are the 4 made at British Ropes Ltd, Wallsend, Tyne and Wear each measuring 24 000 m *14·9 miles.* The ropes are 35 mm *1·3 in* in diameter, weigh 108·5 tonnes *106·8 tons* each and were ordered by the CEGB for use in the construction of the 2000-MW cross-Channel power cable. The thickest ever made are spliced crane strops from wire ropes 28·2 cm *11¼ in* thick made of 2392 individual wires in March 1979 by British Ropes Ltd of Doncaster at

Willington Quay, also Tyne and Wear, designed to lift loads of up to 3000 tonnes. The heaviest ever wire ropes (4 in number) are each of 130 tonnes, made for the twin shaft system of Western Deep Levels Gold Mine, South Africa, by Haggie Rand Ltd of Johannesburg.

The suspension cables on the Seto Grand Bridge, completed in 1988, Japan are 104 cm *41 in* thick.

Wind tunnels

The world's largest wind tunnel is that on the NASA-Ames Research Centre in Mountain View, Palo Alto, California, USA reopened on 11 Dec 1987 with a 12 × 24 m *40 × 80 ft* tunnel powered by six 22 500 hp motors enabling a best speed of 555 km/h *345 mph.*

COMPUTERS

A geared calculator dated *c.* 80 BC was found in the sea by Antikythera Island off north-west Crete in April 1900.

The earliest programmable electronic computer was the 1500-valve Colossus formulated by Prof Max H. A. Newman FRS (1897–1985) and built by T. H. Flowers MBE. It was run in December 1943 at Bletchley Park, Buckinghamshire to break the German coding machine Enigma. It arose from a concept published in 1936 by Dr Alan Mathison Turing OBE, FRS (1912–54) in his paper *On Computable Numbers with an Application to the Entscheidungsproblem.* Colossus was declassified on 25 Oct 1975. The world's first stored-program computer was the Manchester University Mark I which incorporated the Williams storage cathode ray tube (pat. 11 Dec 1946). It ran its first program, by Prof Tom Kilburn CBE FRS (b. 1921) for 52 min on 21 June 1948. Computers were greatly advanced by the invention of the point-contact transistor by John Bardeen and Walter Brattain announced in July 1948, and the junction transistor by R. L. Wallace, Morgan Sparks and Dr William Bradford Shockley (b. 1910) in early 1951. The concept of the integrated circuit, which has enabled micro-miniaturisation, was first published on 7 May 1952 by Geoffrey W. A. Dummer MBE (b. 1909) in Washington, DC. The microcomputer was achieved in 1969–73 by M. E. Hoff Jr of Intel Corporation with the production of the microprocessor chip '4004'.

Most powerful and fastest

The world's most powerful and fastest computer is the liquid-cooled CRAY-2, named after Seymour R. Cray of Cray Research, Inc, Minneapolis, Minnesota, USA. Its memory has a capacity of 256 million 64-bit words, resulting in a capacity of 32 million bytes of main memory. (NB a 'byte' is a unit of storage comprising 8 'bits' which are collectively equivalent to one alphabetic symbol or two numericals.) It attains speeds of 250 million floating point operations per second. The cost of a mid-range system was quoted in October 1985 at $17 million. The most powerful British computer is the International Computer's Distribution Array Processor—the ICL DAP. Sondia Laboratory, New Mexico on 18 Mar 1988 announced a 'massively parallel' .hypercube computer with 1024 parallel processors which, by breaking down problems into parts for simultaneous solution, proved 1019 times faster than a conventional mainframe computer. In May 1988 NEC (Nippon Electric Co.) announced a £1600 million research programme for a fifth generation computer able to read handwriting and understand speech in many languages and incorporating super conduction and Josephson functions.

Megabits

The megabit barrier was broken in February 1984, with the manufacture of a 1024K-bit integrated circuit the size of a drawing pin head and as thin as a human hair, by 4 Japanese companies, Hitachi, NEC, NTT Atsugi Electrical Communications and Toshiba.

Fastest Transistor

A transistor capable of switching 230 000 million times per second was announced by Illinois State University, USA on 5 Oct 1986.

Largest vineyard ● The world's largest vineyard
extends over the Mediterranean façade between the
Rhône and the Pyrenees in the *départements* Hérault,
Gard, Aude, and Pyrénées-Orientaies in an area of
840 000 ha *2 075 685 acres* of which 52·3 per cent is
monoculture viticole. (Photo: Food & Wine from
France Ltd)

THE
BUSINESS
WORLD
CHAPTER · NINE

Commerce

Oldest industry

The oldest known industry is flint knapping, involving the production of chopping tools and hand axes, dating from 2·5 million years ago in Ethiopia. The earliest evidence of trading in exotic stone and amber dates from *c.* 28 000 BC in Europe.

Agriculture is often described as 'the oldest industry in the world', whereas in fact there is no firm evidence yet that it was practised before *c.* 11 000 BC.

Oldest company

The oldest company in the world is the Faversham Oyster Fishery Co, referred to in the Faversham Oyster Fishing Act 1930 as existing 'from time immemorial', i.e. in English law, from before 1189.

The Royal Mint has origins going back to AD 287. The Oxford University Press celebrated a 500th anniversary in 1978 not of itself but of the earliest origin of printing in Oxford in 1478. The Shore Porters' Society of Aberdeen, a haulier, shipping and warehouse partnership, is known to have been established before 4 June 1498. The Whitechapel Bell Foundry of Whitechapel Road, east London, has been in business since *c.* 1570. It has, through Master Founder Thomas Mears II, indirect successions, since 1810, via Rudhalls of Gloucester back to 1270.

The retail business in Britain with the oldest history is the Oxford ironmonger Gill & Co of 127–8, High Street founded by Abel Smythe *c.* 1530. R. Durtnell & Sons, builders, of Brasted, Kent, has been run by the same family since 1591. Mr Richard Durtnell is of the 12th generation. The first bill of adventure, signed by the English East India Co was dated 21 Mar 1601.

Greatest assets

The business with the greatest amount in physical assets has been the Bell System, which comprised the American Telephone and Telegraph Company and its subsidiaries. The Bell System's total assets on the consolidated balance sheet at the time of its divestiture and break-up into 8 companies on 31 Dec 1983 reached $149 529 million. The plant involved included more than 142 million telephones. The number of employees was 1 036 000. The company's market value of $47 989 million was held among 3 055 000 share-holders. A total of 20 109 shareholders had attended the Annual Meeting in April 1961, thereby setting a world record.

Currently the largest assets of any manufacturing corporation are the $74 042 000 000 of Exxon Corporation, the world's largest oil company, on 1 Jan 1988. They have 100 000 employees. The first company to have assets in excess of $1 billion was the United States Steel Corporation with $1400 million at the time of its creation by merger in 1917.

The net assets of Shell Transport and Trading Company PLC at 31 Dec 1987 were £9207 million comprising mainly its 40 per cent share in the net assets of the Royal Dutch Shell Group of Companies which stood at £22 975 million. Group companies employ some 136 000. Shell Transport was formed in 1897 by Marcus Samuel (1853–1927), later the 1st Viscount Bearsted.

The largest rights issue on record was one amounting to £921 million by Barclays Bank. It was announced on 7 April 1988.

The biggest British manufacturing company is Imperial Chemical Industries PLC with assets employed of £8787 million as at 1 Jan 1988. Its staff and payroll averaged 127 800 during the year. The company, which has more than 400 UK and overseas subsidiaries, was formed on 7 Dec 1926 by the merger of 4 concerns—British Dyestuffs Corporation Ltd; Brunner, Mond & Co Ltd; Nobel Industries Ltd and United Alkali Co Ltd. The first chairman was Sir Alfred Moritz Mond (1868–1930), later the 1st Lord Melchett.

Greatest profit and loss

The greatest net profit ever made by any corporation in 12 months is $7647 million by American Telephone and Telegraph Co from 1 Oct 1981 to 30 Sept 1982.

The Argentine petroleum company YPF (Yacimientos Petrolíferos) (government owned) made a trading record loss of US $4 643 995 000 in 1983. The loss for the National Coal Board (now British Coal) in the tax year ending on 31 Mar 1985 was £2225 million.

Largest employer

The world's largest employer is Indian Railways with 1 613 280 staff in 1985/6. Europe's largest employer is the UK's National Health Service with 1 237 383 staff as at 30 Sep 1986.

Greatest sales

The first company to surpass the $1 billion (US) mark in annual sales was the United States Steel Corporation in 1917. Now there are 570 corporations with sales exceeding £1000 million including 272 from the United States. The *Fortune 500 List* of April 1988 is headed by the General Motor Corporation of Detroit with $101 781 900 000 for 1987.

The world's largest private company is Cargill Inc, the Minneapolis, Minnesota grain-trading company, with sales of $32 000 million in 1985/86.

The top gross profits in the United Kingdom in *The Times 1000 1986–87* were those of British Petroleum with £7053 million.

Largest take-over

The largest corporate take-over agreement in commercial history is by Chevron (formerly Standard Oil Co of California) which on 15 June 1984 bought Gulf Oil Corporation for $13 231 253 000. The fees of the financial intermediaries were estimated by *Fortune* to be $63·9 million.

The greatest acquisition by a British company was that achieved in stages by British Petroleum of American Standard Oil (formerly Sohio). BP offered $7·7 billion for the unacquired 45 per cent of shares by 13 May 1987. The Guinness PLC takeover of the Distillers Company PLC on 18 Apr 1986 was £2·695 billion.

Greatest bankruptcy

Rajendra Sethia (b. 1950) was arrested in New Delhi on 2 Mar 1985 on charges including criminal conspiracy and forgery. He had been declared bankrupt by the High Court in London on 18 Jan 1985 when Esal Commodities was stated to be in debt for a record £170 million. His personal debts were estimated at £140 million. William G. Stern (b. Hungary, 1936) of Golders Green, north London, a US citizen since 1957, who set up Wilstar Group Holding Co in the London property market in 1971, was declared bankrupt for £104 390 248 in February 1979. This figure rose to £142 978 413 by February 1983. He was discharged for £500 000 suspended for 2½ years on 28 Mar 1983.

Companies

The number of companies on the register in Great Britain at 31 Mar 1988 was 1 117 517 of which 6721 were public and the balance private.

Most directorships

The record for directorships was set in 1961 by Hugh T. Nicholson (1914–85), formerly senior partner of Harmood Banner & Sons, London who, as a liquidating chartered accountant, became director of all 451 companies of the Jasper group in 1961 and had 7 other directorships.

Accountancy firms

The largest firm of accountants world-wide is that resulting from the merger of Peat Marwick International and Klynveld Main Goerdeler of the Netherlands announced on 3 Sept 1986 with a combined annual revenue of £1·8 billion and a total of 58 000 employees.

Advertising agency

The largest advertising agency group in the world is Saatchi & Saatchi PLC of London. *Advertising Age* lists the group's billings for 1987 at about $11 360 million.

Biggest advertiser

The world's biggest advertiser is Sears, Roebuck and Co, spending $1 165 100 000 in 1987 excluding its catalogue.

Aerospace company

The world's largest aerospace company is Boeing with 1987 sales of $15 355 000 000 and a workforce of 118 500. Cessna Aircraft Company of Wichita, Kansas, USA, in 1987, had total sales of $469 000 000. The company has produced more than 177 000 aircraft since Clyde Cessna's first was built in 1911.

Airline

The largest airline in the world is the USSR state airline 'Aeroflot', so named since 1932. This was instituted on 9 Feb 1923, with the title of Civil Air Fleet of the Council of Ministers of the USSR, abbreviated to 'Dobrolet'. It operates 1650 aircraft over 1 000 000 km *620 000 miles* of routes, employs 500 000 people and carried 119 million passengers and 3 million tonnes of freight in 1987. Seventy per cent of its routes are international and it serves 122 towns or cities in 97 countries. Its domestic network covers 3600 towns. The commercial airline carrying the greatest number of passengers (Dec 1984) was United Airlines Inc. of Illinois with 41 273 000 passengers. The company had 47 900 employees and a fleet of 319 jet planes. On 1 Apr 1987 British Airways operated a fleet of 165 aircraft. Airline staff employed totalled 39 000 and 19 681 000 passengers were carried in 1986–7 on 550 000 km *341 754 miles* of unduplicated routes.

The oldest existing national airline is Koninklijke-Luchtvaart-Maatschappij NV (KLM) of the Netherlands, which opened its first scheduled service (Amsterdam–London) on 17 May 1920, having been established on 7 Oct 1919. One of the original constituents of BOAC, Handley-Page Transport Ltd, was founded in May 1919 and merged into Imperial Airways in 1924. Delag (Deutsche Luftschiffahrt AG) was founded at Frankfurt am Main on 16 Nov 1909 and started a scheduled airship service in June 1910. Chalk's International Airline has been flying amphibians from Miami, Florida to the Bahamas since July 1919. Albert 'Pappy' Chalk flew from 1911 to 1975.

Aluminium producer

The world's largest producer of primary aluminium is Alcan Aluminum Ltd of Montreal, Canada with its affiliated companies. The company shipped 2 197 000 tonnes *2 162 000 tons* in 1987.

Art auctioneering

The largest and oldest firm of art auctioneers in the world is the Sotheby Group of London and New York, founded in 1744 although their trading until 1778 was primarily in books. Christie's held their first art auction in 1766. Sotheby's turnover in 1986–87 was a record £853 000 000. A single session record of £40 100 000 million was set at Sotheby's, London in November 1986.

Bank

The International Bank for Reconstruction and Development (founded 27 Dec 1945), the 'World Bank', the world's largest multilateral development bank, at 1818 H Street NW, Washington DC, had an authorised share capital of $169·7 billion at 27 April 1988. There were 151 members with a subscribed capital of $87·4 billion at 31 Dec 1986. The International Monetary Fund also in Washington DC, USA had 151 members with total quotas of SDR 89 987·6 million (*£51 233·77 million* or *$122 277·60 million*) as at Feb 1988.

The world's biggest commercial bank is Dai-Ichi Kongyo Bank Ltd of Japan with assets on 1 Jan 1987 of

$236 600 million. The world's oldest bank is C. Hoare & Co started in 1633 by Lawrence Hoare, a goldsmith, in London. The bank with most branches is the State Bank of India with 11 171 on 1 Jan 1987 with assets of £17 800 million.

The bank with the largest network in the United Kingdom is the National Westminster with consolidated total assets of £87 027 000 000 and 3167 branches as at 31 Dec 1987.

Banquet

It was estimated that some 30 000 attended a military feast at Radewitz, Poland on 25 June 1730 thrown by King August II (1709–33).

The greatest number of people served indoors at a single sitting was 18 000 municipal leaders at the Palais de l'Industrie, Paris on 18 Aug 1889. At the wedding of cousins Menachem Teitelbaum, and Brucha Sima Melsels, both 18, conducted by their grandfather Grand Rabbi Moses at Uniondale, Long Island, New York on 5 Dec 1984, the attendance of the Satmar sect of Hasidic Jews was estimated at between 17 000 and 20 000. Meal Mart of Brooklyn, a kosher caterer, provided the food including 2 tons of gefilte fish.

The most expensive menu ever served was for the main 5½-hr banquet at the Imperial Iranian 2500th Anniversary gathering at Persepolis in October 1971. It comprised quail eggs stuffed with Iranian caviar, a mousse of crayfish tails in Nantua sauce, stuffed rack of roast lamb, with a main course of roast peacock stuffed with *foie gras,* fig rings and raspberry sweet champagne sherbet, with wines including *Château Lafite-Rothschild* 1945 at £40 (now £235) per bottle from Maxime's, Paris.

Bicycle manufacturers

The world's biggest manufacturer of bicycles is Hero Cycles of Ludhiana, Punjab, India founded in 1956 by the Munjal brothers. In 1986 they turned out 2 220 000 units. China is estimated to have 210 million bicycles.

Book shop

The book shop with most titles and the longest shelving (48 km *30 miles*) in the world is W. & G. Foyle Ltd, London. First established in 1904 in a small shop in Islington, the company is now at 113–119 Charing Cross Road. The area on one site is 7044 m^2 *75 825 ft^2*. The most capacious individual bookstore in the world measured by square footage is Barnes & Noble Bookstore of Fifth Ave at 18th Street, New York City, USA with 14 330 m^2 *154 250 ft^2* and with 20·71 km *12·87 miles* of shelving.

Brewer

The oldest brewery in the world is the Weihenstephan Brewery, Freising, near Munich, West Germany, founded in AD 1040.

The largest single brewing organisation in the world is Anheuser-Busch Inc. of St Louis, Missouri, USA, with 12 breweries in the USA. In 1987 the company sold 76 100 000 US barrels, equivalent to *8931 million litres,* the greatest annual volume ever produced by a brewing company. The company's St Louis plant covers 40·5 ha *100 acres* and after completion of current modernisation projects will have an annual capacity in excess of 13 000 000 US barrels *1525·183 million litres.*

The largest brewery on a single site is Adolph Coors Co of Golden, Colorado, USA where 15 658 000 barrels *1837·1 million litres* were sold in 1987.

The largest brewing company in the United Kingdom, based on its 7300 public houses, 646 off-licences and over 100 hotels, is Bass PLC. The company has net assets of £2 433 600 000, it controls 13 breweries and has 76 348 employees. Its sales figure for the year ending 30 Sept 1986 was £3 214 400 000.

Brickworks

The largest brickworks in the world is the London Brick Company Limited plant at Stewartby, Bedfordshire. The

works, established in 1898, now cover 90 ha *221 acres* and have a production capacity of 10·5 million bricks and brick equivalent each week.

Building societies

The world's biggest lender is the Japanese government-controlled House Loan Corporation. The biggest building society in the world is the Halifax Building Society of Halifax, West Yorkshire. Established in 1853 it has total assets exceeding £33 000 000 000. Lending during 1987 was £7 310 000 000. It has 14 816 employees and over 2981 offices.

Building contractors ● The largest construction company in the United Kingdom is George Wimpey PLC (founded 1880) with a turnover of work was £1482 million in 1987 and 17 000 staff in 20 countries. The above photograph shows a view of the shopping complex at The Market Place, Bolton recently completed by Wimpey Construction Management. (Photo: Len Dance Associates Limited)

Chemist shop chain

The largest chain of chemist shops in the world is Boots The Chemists, which has 1026 retail branches. The firm was founded by Jesse Boot (b. Nottingham, 1850), later the 1st Baron Trent, who died in 1931.

Chocolate factory

The largest chocolate and confectionery factory is that built by Hershey Chocolate Company in Hershey, Pennsylvania, USA in 1903–5. It has 185 800 m^2 *2 000 000 ft^2* of floor space.

Computer company

The world's largest computer firm is International Business Machines (IBM) Corporation of New York. In December 1987 assets were $63 688 000 and gross income was $54 217 000. In October 1979 it made the largest borrowing in corporate history with $1 billion. Its world-wide employees number 389 348 and there are 787 988 stockholders.

Department stores

F. W. Woolworth, which celebrated its centenary year in 1979, now operates a total of 6799 stores world-wide. Frank Winfield Woolworth opened his first store 'The Great Five Cent Store' in Utica, New York State on 22 Feb 1879. The 1987 income was $251 million.

The world's largest department store is R.H. Macy & Co Inc. at Broadway and 34th Street, New York. It covers 20·3 ha *50·5 acres* and employs 14 000 who handle 400 000 items. The sales of the company and its subsidiaries in 1986–1987 were $5 210 416 000. Mr Rowland

Hussey Macy's sales on his first day at his fancy goods store on 6th Avenue, on 27 Oct 1858, were recorded as $11·06.

The largest department store in the United Kingdom is Harrods Ltd of Knightsbridge, London named after Henry Charles Harrod (1800–85), who opened a grocery in Knightsbridge Village in 1849. It has a total selling floor space of 8·09 ha *20 acres,* (50 lifts and 36 escalators) employs between 4000 and 6000 people depending on the time of year, and achieved record sales of over £312 million for the year ending 1 Feb 1987. The record for a day is £6·7 million. The record time from the opening of the doors to the crockery department, on the first day of the sale, is 11 sec by Mr Ian Bach on 6 Jan 1988.

Highest sales per unit area
The department store with the fastest-moving stock in the world is the Marks & Spencer premier branch, at Marble Arch, London. The figure of £1600-worth of goods per square foot of selling space per year is believed to be an understatement. The selling area is 12 025 m^2 *129 300 ft^2.* The company has 274 branches in the UK and operates on over 660 300 m^2 *7·1 million ft^2* of selling space and has stores on the Continent and in Canada and the United States.

Longest wait for a sale

Kevin Mellish (b. 2 Aug 1948) queued for a carpet reduced in price by more than 86 per cent for 20 days outside Arding and Hobbs, Clapham, London, from 7 to 27 Dec 1986.

Distillery

The world's largest distilling company is the Seagram Company Ltd, of Canada. Its sales in the year ending 31 Jan 1988 totalled US $3 815 480 000. The group employs about 13 400 people.

The largest blender and bottler of Scotch whisky is United Distillers' Shieldhall plant in Glasgow, with a capacity to fill 234 million bottles of Scotch a year, equivalent to 40 million gallons most of which is exported. The world's largest-selling brand of gin is Gordon's. Old Bushmills Distillery, County Antrim, Northern Ireland, licensed in 1608, claims to have been in production in 1276.

Employment agency

The world's largest employment group became Blue Arrow when on 5 Sept 1987 it bid successfully for the US company Manpower at £825 million.

Fisheries

The greatest catch ever recorded with a single throw is 2471 tonnes by the purse seine-net boat M/S *Flømann* from Hareide, Norway in the Barents Sea on 28 Aug 1986. It was estimated that more than 120 million fish were caught in this shoal.

The catch record of a single trawler is £278 798 from a 37 300 ton catch by the Icelandic *Videy* at Hull, England on 11 Aug 1987.

Grocery stores

The largest grocery chain in the world is the Kroger Co of the United States with 1987 sales of $17·7 billion, and total current assets valued at $4·46 billion. Kroger operates 1320 supermarkets and 890 convenience stores, and employs 170 000 people.

Hotelier

The top revenue-earning hotel business is Holiday Inns with a total revenue of $5 billion, from 1600 hotels (320 000 rooms), at 1 Jan 1988, in 53 countries. The business was founded by Charles Kemmons Wilson with his first Holiday Inn hotel on Summer Avenue, Memphis, Tennessee, USA in 1952.

Insurance

The company with the highest volume of insurance in force in the world is the Prudential Insurance Company of America of Newark, New Jersey with $702·8 billion at 31 Dec 1987. The total consolidated assets are $140·9 billion.

The largest single association in the world is the Blue Cross and Blue Shield Association, the US-based hospital insurance organisation, with a membership of 76·8 million on 31 Dec 1987. Benefits paid out in 1987 totalled $44 500 billion.

The largest life assurance group in the United Kingdom is the Prudential Corporation PLC. At 1 Jan 1988 the tangible assets were £26 475 100 000.

The largest life-assurance policy ever written was one for $44 million for a Calgary land developer Victor T. Uy in February 1982 by Transamerica Occidental Life Assurance Co. The salesman was local manager Lorenzo F. Reyes. The highest payout on a single life has been some $18 million to Mrs Linda Mullendore, wife of an Oklahoma rancher, reported on 14 Nov 1970. Her murdered husband had paid $300 000 in premiums in 1969.

The largest ever marine insurance loss was £46 million for the self-propelled semi-submersible drilling platform *Ocean Ranger* (14 914 gross tons) built for Ocean Drilling & Exploration Co of New Orleans in 1976. On 15 Feb 1982 she was lost with 84 lives in the Hibernia Field, off Newfoundland. Underwriters face a claim that may reach $330 million as a result of the effective total loss in April 1988 of the Enchova platform in the Campos Basin 290 km *180 miles* east of Rio de Janeiro, Brazil.

The largest sum claimed for consequential losses is £890 million (*$1700 million*) against owning, operating and building corporations and Claude Phillips resulting from the 66-million-gallon oil spill from M. T. *Amoco Cadiz* on the Brittany coast on 16 Mar 1978.

Jewellery auction

The world's largest jewellery auction, which included the Van Cleef and Arpels 1939 ruby and diamond necklace, brought £31 380 197 on 3 Apr 1987 when the Duchess of Windsor's (1896–1986) collection was auctioned at Sotheby's, Geneva, Switzerland.

Landowner

The world's largest landowner is the United States Government, with a holding of 294 209 630 ha *727 000 000 acres* (2 942 076 km² *1 135 937 miles²*) which is bigger

than the world's 8th largest country, Argentina, and 12 times larger than the United Kingdom. It has been suggested that the USSR Government constitutionally owned all the land in the entire country excepted perhaps that on which foreign embassies stand. The world's largest *private* landowner is reputed to be International Paper Co with 3·64 million ha *9 million acres.*

The United Kingdom's greatest ever private landowner was the 3rd Duke of Sutherland, George Granville Sutherland-Leveson-Gower KG(1828–92), who owned 549 560 ha *1 358 000 acres* in 1883. Currently the largest landholder in Great Britain is the Forestry Commission (instituted 1919) with 1 156 554 ha *2 857 844 acres.* The landowner with the largest known acreage is the 9th Duke of Buccleuch (b. 1923) with 136 035 ha *336 000 acres.* The longest tenure is that by St Paul's Cathedral of land at Tillingham, Essex, given by King Ethelbert before AD 616.

The world's most expensive land is in the central Giza district of Tokyo, Japan, where the capital cost had risen to £175 000 per m² by August 1987.

The record price per acre for agricultural land in Great Britain is £12 000 at Elm Road, March, Cambridgeshire. It was sold by J. Collingwood & Son of March on 31 Dec 1973. In Jersey a record of £10 454 per acre (where 2¼ vergées equal 1 acre) was paid at Les Landes, St Martin on 5 July 1984.

The highest rentals in the world for prime offices, according to *World Rental Levels* by Richard Ellis of London, are in Tokyo, Japan at £92·31 and in the City of London at £60·00 per ft² p.a. (May 1988). With added service charges and rates Tokyo is top at £102·25.

Greatest auction

The greatest auction was of the Hughes Aircraft Co for $5000 million by General Motors of Detroit, Michigan, USA on 5 June 1985.

Greatest barter deal

The biggest barter in trading history was 36 million barrels of oil valued at £900 million exchanged for 10 Boeing 747s for the Royal Saudi Airline in July 1984.

Motor car manufacturer

The largest manufacturing company in the world is General Motors Corporation of Detroit, Michigan, USA, which operates manufacturing and assembly plants throughout the world. Apart from motor cars, it produces defence and aerospace materials, mining and heavy engineering machinery and household appliances. During 1987 world wide sales totalled $101 781 900 000. Its assets at 31 Dec 1987 were valued at $87 421 900 000. Its total 1987 payroll was $27 146 000 000 to an average

813 000 employees. Dividends paid in 1987 were $1 667 900 000.

Britain

The largest British manufacturer was the Rover Group PLC with 471 504 vehicles produced in 1987 and a sales turnover of £3096 million of which £1269 million were overseas sales. Direct exports were £1043 million. The company produced 4 out of every 10 cars built in Britain and accounted for 7 out of 10 cars exported from the UK.

Largest plant

The largest single automobile plant in the world is the Volkswagenwerk, Wolfsburg, West Germany, with 60 000 employees and a capacity for 4000 vehicles daily. The surface area of the factory buildings is 150 ha *371 acres* and that of the whole plant 1980 ha *4892 acres* with 70 km *43·5 miles* of rail sidings.

Salesmanship

The all-time record for automobile salesmanship in units sold individually is 1425 in 1973 by Joe Girard of Michigan. His lifetime total of one-at-a-time 'belly to belly' selling was 13 001 sales, all retail with a record 174 in a month. His *How To Close Any Sale* was published in 1988.

Oil refineries *Largest*

The world's largest refinery has been the Amerada Hess refinery in St Croix, Virgin Islands producing 345 000 barrels per day in 1987.

The largest oil refinery in the United Kingdom is the Esso Refinery at Fawley, near Southampton. Opened in 1921 and much expanded in 1951, it has a capacity of 15·6 million tonnes per year. The total investment, together with the associated chemical plant, on the 1295 ha *3200 acre* site is in excess of £1·7 billion on a replacement cost basis. The area occupied by the Shell Stanlow Refinery at Ellesmere Port, Cheshire, founded in 1922 and now with a capacity of 18 million tonnes per year, is 810 ha *2000 acres.*

Paper company

The world's largest company in paper, fibre and wood products is Georgia-Pacific of Atlanta, Georgia, USA with sales in 1987 of $8603 million employing 42 000 workers.

The largest uncoated woodfree paper machine in the United Kingdom is PM6 at New Thames Paper Company, located at Kemsley near Sittingbourne, Kent with a capacity in excess of 125 000 tonnes a year. The paper manufacturing and converting complex covers an area of 60·7 ha *150 acres.*

Pharmaceuticals

The world's largest pharmaceutical company is Johnson & Johnson of New Brunswick, New Jersey, USA with sales of $8 012 000 000 in 1987.

Britain's largest pharmaceutical turnover in 1986–87 was by Glaxo with £1730 million.

Photographic store

The photographic store with the largest selling area is Jessop of Leicester Ltd's Photo Centre, Hinckley Road, Leicester opened in June 1979 with an area now of 2508 m² *27 000 ft².*

Public relations

The world's largest public relations firm is Burson Marsteller with headquarters in New York and a 1987 net fee income of $137 214 000. Hill and Knowlton Inc. have most offices world wide with 56 including one in Beijing, China.

The world's pioneer public relations publication is *Public Relations News,* founded by Mrs Denny Griswold in 1944 and which now circulates in 91 countries.

Publishing

The publishing company generating most net revenue is Time Inc. of New York with $4193 million in 1987. The largest educational book publishing concern in the

world is the Book Division of McGraw-Hill Inc. of New York with sales of $1 751 230 000 in 1988 with 1685 new books and educational products.

Restaurateurs

The largest restaurant chain in the world is that operated by McDonald's Corporation of Oak Brook, Illinois, USA founded on 15 April 1955 in Des Plaines, Chicago by Ray A. Kroc BH (Bachelor of Hamburgerology) (1902–84), after buying out the McDonald brothers' restaurants. 'Mac' McDonald, who with his brother Dick opened his first fast food drive-in outlet in Pasadena, California in 1937, died in 1971. By 3 Apr 1988 the number of McDonald's restaurants licensed and owned in 47 countries and territories around the world reached 10 000, serving 22 million customers per day, with an aggregate throughput of 65 billion 100 per cent pure beef hamburgers. Sales system-wide in 1987 surpassed $14·3 billion.

Britain's largest hotel and catering group is Trusthouse Forte with 800 hotels worldwide. It employs 57 300 full and part-time staff in the UK, 13 700 overseas, and which had a turnover of £1 778 000 000 in 1986–87.

Fish and chip restaurant

The world's largest fish and chip shop is Harry Ramsden's, White Cross, Guiseley, West Yorkshire, England with 140 staff serving 1 000 000 customers per annum, who consumed 210 tons of fish and 350 tons of potatoes.

Record store

HMV opened the world's largest record store at 150 Oxford Street, London on 24 Oct 1986. Its trading area measures 3407·9 m² *36 684 ft²*.

Retailer

The largest retailing firm in the world is Sears, Roebuck and Co (founded by Richard Warren Sears in North Redwood railway station, Minnesota, USA in 1886) of Chicago, Illinois, USA. World-wide revenues were $28·09 billion in the year ending 31 Dec 1987 when Sears Merchandise Group had 813 retail stores, 1100 sales offices and 1701 independent catalogue merchants in the USA. Total assets stood at $23·82 billion.

Shipbuilding

In 1987 there was 12 259 419 gross tonnage of ships, excluding sailing ships, non-propelled vessels and vessels of less than 100 gross tonnage, completed throughout the world. The figures for the USSR, Romania and the People's Republic of China are incomplete. Japan completed 5 707 898 gross tonnage (46·56 per cent of the world total).

The world's leading shipbuilder in 1987 was Hyundai of South Korea, which completed 34 vessels of 1 261 079 gross tonnage.

Physically the largest shipyard in the United Kingdom is Harland and Wolff of Queen's Island, Belfast, which covers some 120 ha *300 acres*. The United Kingdom completions totalled 98 895 gross tonnage.

Shipping line

The largest shipping owners and operators are Exxon Corporation (see p. 148) whose fleets of owned/managed and chartered tankers in 1987 totalled a daily average of 9 200 000 deadweight tons.

Shopping centre

The world's largest shopping centre is the $1·2 billion West Edmonton Mall, Alberta, Canada first opened on 15 Sept 1981 and completed 4 years later which covers 483 080 m² *5·2 million ft²* on a 44·5 ha *110 acre* site. It encompasses 828 stores and services as well as 6 major department stores. Parking is provided for 20 000 vehicles for more than 500 000 shoppers per week.

The world's first shopping centre was Roland Park Shopping Center, Baltimore, Maryland, USA built in 1896. The world's largest wholesale merchandise mart is the Dallas Market Center, located on Stemmons Free-

Longest mall ● The longest mall in the world can be found at the £40-million shopping centre at Milton Keynes, Buckinghamshire. It measures 650 m *710 yds 2 ft.* (Photo: Stewart Newport)

way, Dallas, Texas, USA with nearly 864 000 m² *9·3 million ft²* in 8 buildings. The complex covers 60 ha *150 acres* with some 3400 permanent showrooms displaying merchandise of more than 26 000 manufacturers. The Center attracts 600 000 buyers each year to its 38 annual markets and trade shows.

The largest covered city centre shopping complex in Britain is Manchester's Arndale Centre which has a floor area of 208 672 m² *2 246 200 ft²* including a 44 713 m² *481 300 ft²* car park for 1800 cars. It was built from 1976–79, has a gross shopping area of 110 270 m² *1 187 000 ft²* and is the first such centre in Europe with its own radio station.

Soft drinks

The world's most popular soft drink is Coca-Cola with over 301 000 000 drinks sold per day by early 1985 in more than 155 countries. Coke was launched as a tonic by Dr John S. Pemberton of Atlanta, Georgia, USA in 1886. The Coca-Cola Company was formed in 1892. The secret '7X' formula was unchanged until 1985 when Coca-Cola had 21·7 per cent of the $28 billion market to Pepsi's 18·8 per cent.

Steel company

The non-communist world's largest producer of steel has been Nippon Steel Corporation of Japan, which produced 26·03 million tons of crude steel in 1987. Its workforce is 64 000. The Mizushima works of Kawasaki Steel produced 6 418 000 tons of crude steel during 1987, the highest amount produced in a single integrated steel works in Japan.

Sugar mill

The highest recorded output for any sugar mill was set in 1966–67 by Ingenio de San Cristobal y Anexas, S.A., Veracruz, Mexico with 247 900 tonnes refined from 2 886 074 tonnes of cane ground. The world's largest cane sugar plant is that of the California & Hawaii Sugar

Co founded in 1906 at Crockett, California, USA with an output of 8 million lb per day.

Largest supermarket

The world's largest supermarkets (self-service with check-outs) were the Piggly Wiggly chain started in 1916 by Clarence Saunders (1881–1953) in Memphis, Tennessee, USA. Above 2500 m² *25 000 ft²* net shopping area, stores are usually termed superstores, and above 5000 m² *50 000 ft²*—hypermarkets.

The largest such in Britain is the 8396 m² *90 377 ft²* Tesco hypermarket at Weston Favell, Northants opened in October 1974 with parking for 1300 cars.

Tobacco plant

The world's largest and most automated cigarette plant is that of the $1-billion Reynolds Tobacco Co at Tobaccoville, North Carolina, USA opened in September 1986 which produces more than 110 billion cigarettes p.a..

Toy shop

The world's biggest toy shop is Hamleys, founded in 1760 in Holborn, London and removed to Regent Street, London W1 in 1901. It has selling space of 4180 m² *45 000 ft²* on 6 floors with over 300 employees during the Christmas season.

Undertaker (or Mortician)

The world's largest undertaking business is the SCI (Service Corporation International), Houston, Texas, USA with 454 funeral homes and 73 flower shops with associated limousine fleets and cemeteries. Its annual revenue in this most recession-proof of industries in the year ending 30 Apr 1987 was $386 632 000.

Vintners

The oldest champagne firm is Ruinart Père et Fils founded in 1729. The oldest cognac firm is Augier Frères & Cie, established in 1643.

STOCK EXCHANGES

The oldest Stock Exchange of the 138 listed throughout the world is that of Amsterdam, in the Netherlands, founded in 1602 with dealings with printed shares of the United East India Company of the Netherlands in the Oude Zijds Kapel. The largest in trading volume in 1987 was Tokyo with $1750 billion moving ahead of New York City with $1590 billion.

Most bargains

The highest number of equity bargains in one day on the London Stock Exchange was 114 973 on 22 Oct 1987. The record for a year is 13 021 337 bargains in the year ending 31 Dec 1987. There were 6756 securities (cf. 9749 peak in June 1973) listed at 31 Dec 1987. Their total nominal value was £350 826 million (gilt-edged £142 857 million) with a market value of £1 427 397 million (gilt-edged £151 207 million).

The highest closing figure for the FT–SE Share Index was 2443·4 on 16 July 1987. The greatest rise in a day has been 142·2 points to 1943·8 on 21 Oct 1987 and the greatest fall in a day was 250·7 to 1801·6 on 20 Oct 1987.

Most highly valued UK company

The market capitalisation of British Petroleum as at 31 Mar 1987 was £16 749·4 million.

Highest par value

The highest denomination of any share quoted in the world is a single share in Moeara Enim Petroleum worth £42 846 (*Dfl 143 000*) on 8 April 1987.

US records

The highest index figure on the Dow Jones average (instituted 8 Oct 1896) of selected industrial stocks at the close of a day's trading was 2722·42 on 25 Aug 1987. The record day's trading was 608 148 710 shares on 20 Oct 1987. The old record trading volume in a day on the New York Stock Exchange of 16 410 030 shares on 29 Oct 1929,

the 'Black Tuesday' of the famous 'crash', was unsurpassed until April 1968. The Dow Jones industrial average, which reached 381·71 on 3 Sept 1929, plunged 30·57 points on 29 Oct 1929, on its way to the Depression's lowest point of 41·22 on 8 July 1932.

The largest decline in a day, 508·00 points (22·6 per cent), occurred on 19 Oct 1987. The total lost in security values from 1 Sept 1929 to 30 June 1932 was $74 000 million. The greatest paper loss in a year was $209 957 million in 1974. The record daily increase of 69·89 on 3 Apr 1986 was most recently bettered on 21 Oct 1987 with 186·84 points to 2027·85. The percentage record was 15·34 per cent between 3 Mar (53·84) and the next opening on 15 Mar 1933 (62·10).

The largest stock trade in the history of the New York Exchange was a 48 788 800-share block of Navistar International Corporation stock at $10 in a $487 888 000 transaction on 10 Apr 1986. The highest price paid for a seat on the NY Stock Exchange was $1 150 000 in 1987. The lowest 20th-century price was $17 000 in 1942. The market value of stocks listed on the New York Stock Exchange reached an all-time high at the end of Aug 1986—$2 945 883 381 839.

Largest and smallest equity

The greatest aggregate market value of any corporation at year end was £26 million for IBM on 31 Dec 1985.

Britain's smallest company ever was Frank Davies Ltd, incorporated on 22 Aug 1924 with ½ d share capital divided into 2 ¼ d shares. Converting to decimal coinage (£0·002 divided into 2 shares of £0·001), it was finally dissolved in 1978 without ever having increased its share capital.

Greatest personal loss

The highest recorded personal paper losses on stock values have been those of the late Ray A. Kroc, chairman of McDonald's Corporation, with $64 901 718 on 8 July 1974 (see page 151).

Largest flotation

The largest ever flotation in stock-market history has been that of British Gas PLC with an equity offering producing proceeds of £7750 million to 4½ million

shareholders. Allotment letters were dispatched on 15 Dec 1986.

Largest investment house

The largest securities company in the USA, and once the world's largest partnership with 124 partners, before becoming a corporation in 1959, is Merrill, Lynch, Pierce, Fenner & Smith Inc. (founded 6 Jan 1914) of New York. Its parent, Merrill, Lynch and Co., Inc., has assets of over $55 billion, approximately 44 000 employees, more than 1000 offices and 5 million customer accounts.

Names

The longest name on the British Index of Company Names is The Australian Academy of the Humanities for the Advancement of Scholarship in Language, Literature, History, Philosophy and the Fine Arts, a company incorporated by Royal Charter.

The longest name on the Index registered under the Companies Acts is The Liverpool and Glasgow Association for the Protection of Commercial Interest as Respects Wrecked and Damaged Property Ltd, company number 15147. The shortest names on the Index are G Ltd, company number 1656906, and U Ltd, company number 1910886.

ANTIQUE PRICE RECORDS

ANCIENT SCULPTURE

An eight-inch 6000-year-old neolithic sculpture of a seated goddess from the estate of James Johnson Sweeney was sold for $1·32 million, at auction by Sotheby's, New York on 24 Nov 1986. The purchaser was Mrs Shelby White Levy, a New York financial writer.

ART NOUVEAU

The highest auction price for any piece of art nouveau is $360 000 for a spider-web leaded glass mosaic and bronze table lamp by L. C. Tiffany at Christie's, New York on 8 Apr 1980.

BED

A 1930 black lacquer kingsize bed made by Jean Durand was auctioned at Christie's, New York on 2 Oct 1983 for £49 668.

BLANKET

The most expensive blanket was a Navajo Churro hand-spun serape of c. 1852 sold for $115 500 with premium at Sotheby's, New York on 22 Oct 1983.

CARPET

In 1946 the Metropolitan Museum, New York, privately paid $1 million for the 807×414 cm 26·5 × 13·6 ft Anhalt Medallion carpet made in Tabriz or Kashan, Persia c. 1590. The highest price ever paid at auction for a carpet is £231 000 for a 17th-century 'Polonaise' silk and metal thread carpet at Sotheby's, London on 13 Oct 1982.

CERAMICS

The Greek urn painted by Euphronios and thrown by Euxitheos c. 530 was bought by private treaty by the Metropolitan Museum of Art, New York, for $1·3 million in August 1972.

CHAMBER POT

A 935 g 33 oz silver pot, made by David Willaume and engraved for the 2nd Earl of Warrington, made £9500 at Sotheby's, London on 14 June 1984.

CIGARETTE CARD

The most valuable card is one of the 6 known baseball series cards of Honus Wagner, who was a non-smoker, which was sold in New York in December 1981 for $25 000.

DOLLS

The highest price at auction for a doll is £67 100 for a 14-in wooden 17th-century doll of c. 1690 at Sotheby's, London on 24 Mar 1987. It was purchased by Mme Didi Vierny for a planned doll museum in Paris, France.

FURNITURE

The highest price ever paid for a single piece of furniture is $2·75 million at Sotheby's, New York on 31 Jan 1987 for a Chippendale carved mahogany, wing armchair, made by Philadelphia cabinetmaker Thomas Affleck for General John Cadwalader by New York dealer Leigh Keno.

The English furniture record was set by a black-japanned bureau-bookcase of c. 1705. Formerly owned by Queen Mary, it made $860 000 at Christie's, New York on 18 Oct 1981. The record in the UK was set on 10 Apr 1986 when twin silver Chippendale mirrors were sold at Christie's, London for £280 000 to Roy Miles, the London dealer.

GLASS

The auction record is £520 000 for a Roman glass cage-cup of c. AD 300 measuring 17·78 cm 7 in in diameter and 10·16 cm 4 in in height, sold at Sotheby's, London, on 4 June 1979 to Robin Symes.

GOLD PLATE

The highest price for any gold artefact is £950 400 for the 22-carat font made by Paul Storr to the design of Humphrey Repton in 1797. It was sold at Christie's by Lady Anne Cavendish-Bentinck and bought by Armitage of London on 11 July 1985.

GUNS

See 'Pistol' below.

HAT

The highest price ever paid for a hat is $66 000 by the Alaska State Museum at a New York City auction in November 1981 for a Tlingit Kiksadi ceremonial frog helmet from c. 1600.

ICON

The record auction price for an icon is $150 000 paid at Christie's, New York on 17 Apr 1980 for the Last Judgement (from the George R. Hann collection, Pittsburgh, USA) made in Novgorod in the 16th century.

JADE

The highest price ever paid for an item in jade is $396 000 (with premium) at Sotheby's, New York on 6 Dec 1983 for a mottled brownish-yellow belt-hook and pendant mask of the Warring States Period of Chinese history.

JEWELS

The highest auction price for any jewels is £2 825 000 (or £3·1 million with the buyer's premium) for two pear-shaped diamond drop earrings of 58·6 and 61 carats at Sotheby's, Geneva on 14 Nov 1980. Neither the buyer nor seller was disclosed.

MECHANICAL TOY

The auction record for a toy is £25 500 for a model train set of Stephenson's Rocket made by Marklin of Germany in tin plate in 1909 sold at Sotheby's, London on 29 May 1984.

MUSICAL BOX

The highest price paid for a musical box is £20 900 (with premium) for a Swiss-made example made for a Persian prince in 1901, sold at Sotheby's, London on 23 Jan 1985.

PAPERWEIGHT

The highest price for a glass paperweight is $143 000 (with premium) at Sotheby's, New York, USA on 2 Dec 1983 for a blue glass weight made at Pantin, Paris post 1850.

PISTOL

The highest price paid at auction for a pistol is $242 000 at Christie's, New York on 14 May 1987 for a .45 calibre Colt single-action army revolver, Serial No. 1 for 1873.

PLAYING CARDS

The highest price paid for a deck of playing cards is $143 352 (with premium) by the New York Metropolitan Museum of Art at Sotheby's, London on 6 Dec 1983.

POT LID

The highest price paid for a pot lid is £3960 for one depicting 'Eastern Lady with Black Attendant', sold at Phillips, London on 7 Jan 1987.

ENGLISH SILVER

The record for a single piece of English silver is £770 000 for an epergne by de Lamerie sold at Christie's, London by the Earl of Portarlington and bought by Jacques Koopman on 17 Dec 1986. The 100-piece Paul de Lamerie service made for the 7th Earl of Thanet *c.* 1745 was sold by Lord Hothfield at Sotheby's, London on 22 Nov 1984 for £825 000 (with premium).

SCIENTIFIC INSTRUMENT

The highest auction price for a scientific instrument is £181 500 for a gilt, brass and silver astronomical compendium by Erasmus Habermal made in Prague in 1597 at Sotheby's, London on 16 Nov 1987

SNUFF BOX

The highest price ever paid for a snuff box is £764 826 in a sale at Christie's, Geneva on 11 Nov 1986 for a pale-green chrysoprase and diamond gold box once owned by Frederick the Great of Prussia. It was purchased by a London dealer.

SPOONS

A Wiener werkstaffe spoon by Josef Hoffmann, Austria *c.* 1905 was sold at Sotheby's, London for £17 600 (with premium) on 28 Apr 1983. A set of 13 Henry VIII Apostle spoons owned by Lord Astor of Hever was sold for £120 000 on 24 June 1981 at Christie's, London.

STUFFED BIRD

The highest price ever paid for a stuffed bird is £9000. This was given on 4 Mar 1971 at Sotheby's, London by the Iceland Natural History Museum for a specimen of the Great Auk (*Alca impennis*) in summer plumage, which was taken in Iceland *c.* 1821; it stood 57 cm *22½ in* high. The Great Auk was a flightless North Atlantic seabird which was finally exterminated on Eldey, Iceland in 1844, becoming extinct through hunting. The last British sightings were at Co. Waterford in 1834 and St Kilda, Western Isles *c.* 1840.

SWORD

The highest price paid for a sword is £823 045 for the Duke of Windsor's Royal Navy officer's sword (presented to him by King George V in 1913) at Sotheby's in Geneva on 3 Apr 1987.

TAPESTRY

The highest price paid for a tapestry is £550 000 for a Swiss Medieval tapestry frieze in two parts dated 1468–1476 at Sotheby's, Geneva, on 10 Apr 1981 by the Basle Historische Museum.

THIMBLE

The record auction price for a thimble is £8000 paid by London dealer Winifred Williams at Christie's, London on 3 Dec 1979 for a Meissen dentil-shaped porcelain piece of *c.* 1740.

TOY SOLDIER

The highest price paid for a single toy soldier is £1 200 for an extremely rare 70 mm scale figure of the Colonel–in–Chief, the Welsh Guards at Phillips, London on 9 Sept 1987.

TYPEWRITER

The highest price paid for an antique machine is £3000 for an 1886 Daw and Tait machine auctioned at Sotheby's, London on 12 Dec 1980.

WALKING STICK

The highest auction price for a walking stick has been $24 200 at Sotheby Parke Bernet, New York in 1983 for an octagonal whale ivory nobbed stick decorated by Scrimshanders in 1845.

Manufactured Articles

Amplifier

The largest working guitar amplifier is 2·75 m *9·04 ft* high, weighs 325·68 kg *718 lb*, houses 32 25·4 cm *10 in* speakers driven by 600 watts of all tube power. However, it can handle 1400 watts output. This Ampeg Mega SVT Bass Amp System was unveiled at the NAMM EXPO in Chicago, Illinois by St Louis Music of St Louis, Misssouri, USA.

Armour

The highest auction price paid for a suit of armour was £1 925 000 by B. H. Trupin (US) on 5 May 1983 at Sotheby's, London for a suit made in Milan by Giovanni Negroli in 1545 for Henri II of France. It came from the Hever Castle Collection in Kent.

Astrolabe

The Astrolabium Galileo Galilei wristwatch, made by Ulysse Nardin, is the only wristwatch that indicates the time of the day, local time, month, zodiac, length of the day and night, Moon phases and Sun and Moon eclipses. The mechanism for indicating the tropical year is accurate to one day in 144 000 years. The retail price is £17 850.

Basket

The biggest basket ever made was 4·57 m *15 ft* tall, woven by Nineteenth Century Basket Company, Warren, Ohio, USA in 1986.

Beds

In Bruges, Belgium, Philip, Duke of Burgundy had a bed 3·81 m wide and 5·79 m long *12½ ft × 19 ft* erected for the perfunctory *coucher officiel* ceremony with Princess Isabella of Portugal in 1430.

The largest bed in Great Britain is the Great Bed of Ware, dating from *c.* 1580, from the Crown Inn, Ware, Hertfordshire, now preserved in the Victoria and Albert Museum, London. It is 3·26 wide, 3·37 long and 2·66 m tall *10 ft 8½ in × 11 ft 1 in × 8 ft 9 in.*

The largest bed currently marketed in the United Kingdom is a Super Size Diplomat bed, 2·74 m wide by 2·74 m long, *9 ft × 9 ft* from The London Bedding Centre, Sloane Street. It costs more than £4000. A promotional 1500 kg *1½ ton* bed 6 m × 4·40 m *19 ft 8 in × 14 ft 5 in* pinewood bed accommodating 39 people was exhibited by a French company in August 1986.

Beer cans

Beer cans date from a test marketing by Krueger Beer of Newark, New Jersey at Richmond, Virginia, USA in 1935. The largest collection has been made by John F. Ahrens of Mount Laurel, New Jersey, USA with nearly 15 000 different cans. A Rosalie Pilsner can sold for $6000 in the USA in April 1981.

Beer labels (*Labology*)

Jan Solberg of Oslo, Norway has amassed 218 600 different labels from around the world.

The greatest collection of different British beer labels is 30 722 (to April 1987) by Keith Osborne, Hon. Sec. of The Labologists' Society (founded by Guinness Exports Ltd in 1958). His oldest is one from A. B. Walker & Co, Warrington of *c.* 1846.

Beer mats (*Tegestology*)

The world's largest collection of beer mats is owned by Leo Pisker of Vienna, who had collected over 123 200 different mats from 151 countries by April 1988. The largest collection of British mats is 38 875 formed by Timothy J. Stannard of Birmingham.

Beer tankard

The largest tankard was made by the Selangor Pewter Co, Kuala Lumpur, Malaysia and unveiled on 30 Nov 1985. It measures 198·7 cm *6 ft 6 in* in height and has a capacity of 2796 litres *615 gal.*

Blanket

The largest blanket measured 21·3 × 46·3 m *70 × 152 ft* (988·45 m² *10 640 ft²*) and consisted of 1100 squares. It was made by Adolph Coors Company Volunteers, Denver, Colorado, USA and took 13 000 hours to complete. It was displayed at the Denver Broncos practice stadium on 12 Dec 1987.

Bottle caps

Since 1950 Helge Friholm (b. 1910) of Soborg, Denmark has amassed 38 570 different bottle caps (to April 1986) from 145 countries.

Pyramid

A pyramid consisting of 223 300 bottle caps was constructed by 16 students of the Economische Hogeschool Saint-Aloysius, Brussels, Belgium from 22 Feb–3 Mar 1988.

Cans

A Colosseum-shaped structure consisting of 1 250 000 empty beverage cans was built in Coccaglio, Brescia, Italy by members of AVIS–AIDO with the co–operation of Rail (producers of aluminium cans). It was completed on 18 Oct 1987 after 1500 hours of man-hours.

Candle

A candle 24·38 m *80 ft* high and 2·59 m *8½ ft* in diameter was exhibited at the 1897 Stockholm Exhibition by the firm of Lindahls. The overall height was 38·70 m *127 ft.* Currently the largest is that made by the Atletiek-en Trimvereniging Tegelen Sportsclub of Tegelen, Netherlands on 1 June 1986. This Dutch giant stands 27·15 m *89 ft 1 in* high.

Card

The world's largest greeting card was produced by Valentine Sands Greetings and students of the Melbourne College of Decoration. It measured 5·2 m × 3·4 m *17 ft × 11 ft* and weighed 136·63 kg *301 lb.* It was delivered by Australia Post to the Eastland Shopping Centre, Victoria. The largest greeting card delivered by the Royal Mail in the UK measured 3·05 m × 1·8 m *10 ft × 6 ft.* It was painted by Rolf Harris for Heartbeat '86 at the NEC, Birmingham, West Midlands and sent to Birmingham Children's Hospital.

Carpets and rugs

The earliest carpet known is a Seythian woollen pile-knotted carpet measuring 1·8 m by 1·8 m (*6 ft × 6 ft*) and dating from the 4th-3rd centuries BC. It was discovered by the Russian archaeologist Sergey Ivanovich Rudenko in 1947 in the Pazyryk Valley in southern Siberia and is now preserved in the Hermitage, Leningrad.

Of ancient carpets the largest was a gold-enriched silk carpet of Hashim (dated AD 743) of the Abbasid caliphate in Baghdad, Iraq. It is reputed to have measured 54·86 by 91·44 m *180 × 300 ft.* A 4851 m² *52 225 ft²* or 1·23 acre 28 ton red carpet was laid on 13 Feb 1982, by the Allied Corporation, from Radio City Music Hall to the New York Hilton along the Avenue of the Americas.

The most finely woven old carpet known is one having more than 403 knots per cm² *2600 per in²* produced in March 1985 by the Bikaner Woollen Mills of Bhadohi, Varanasi, Uttar Pradesh, India. It was displayed at the 1986 *Heimtextil* International Trade Fair in Frankfurt, West Germany, where a consensus of expert opinion declared the 'knottage' to be close to 465 per cm² *3000 per in².* The most magnificent carpet ever made was the Spring carpet of Khusraw made for the audience hall of the Sassanian palace at Ctesiphon, Iraq. It was about 650 m² *7000 ft²* of silk and gold thread, and encrusted with emeralds. It was cut up as booty by looters in AD 635 and from the known realisation value of the pieces must have had an original value of some £100 000 000.

Chair

The largest chair is a 12·71 m *41 ft 8½ in* tall, 7·26 m *23 ft 9½ in* wide deck-chair constructed by Luigi Bernasconi & Co, Mendrisio, Switzerland. It was exhibited from 11–13 Apr 1987.

Chandelier

The largest set of chandeliers was built for the palace of HM Sir Muda Hassanal Bolkiah of Brunei in 1983. His palace or Istana Nurul Iman is in the capital Bandar Seri Begawan. Britain's largest chandelier measures 9·1 m *30 ft* and is in the Chinese Room at the Royal Pavilion, Brighton. It was made in 1818 and weighs 1 tonne.

Largest clock ● 'Timepiece', which measures 15·54 m × 15·54 m × 15·54 m *51 ft × 51 ft × 51 ft*, is suspended over five storeys in the atrium of the International Square building in Washington, DC, USA. Computer driven and accurate to within 1/100th of a second, it weighs 2 tonnes.It is lit by 122 m *400 ft* of neon tube lighting and requires 460 m *1500 ft* of cable and wiring. Twelve tubes at its base light to tell the hour and the minute. The clock, designed by the sculptor John Safer, also indicates when the sun is directly overhead in twelve international cities.

Christmas cracker

The largest functional cracker ever constructed was one measuring 24·384 m *80 ft* long by 3 m *9 ft 10 in* diameter built by Markson Sparks, Sydney for Christmas 1986.

Cigars

The largest cigar ever made measures 5·095 m *16 ft 8½ in* in length and weighs 262 kg *577 lb 9 oz* (over ¼ ton) taking 243 hours and using 3330 full tobacco leaves. It was made by Tinus Vinke and Jan Weijmer in February 1983 and is in the Tobacco Museum in Kampen, Netherlands. The largest marketed cigar in the world is the 35·5 cm *14 in* Valdez Emperado by San Andres Cigars.

The most expensive standard cigar in the world is the 23·5 cm *9¼ in* long Montecristo 'A' which retails in Britain at £13·50.

Joseph Hruby of Lyndhurst, Ohio, USA has the largest known collection of cigar bands with 175 391 different examples dating from *c.* 1895.

Cigarettes

World production in 1985 was 9873 billion cigarettes. The people of China were estimated to consume 1180 million in 1985. In Senegal 80 per cent of urban males smoke. The peak consumption in the United Kingdom was 3230 cigarettes per adult in 1973. The peak volume was 110·2 million kg *243 100 000 lb* in 1961, compared with 79·4 million kg *175 million lb* in 1987 when 95 000 million cigarettes were sold. In the United Kingdom in 1987 44 per cent of adult males were smokers, averaging 136 cigarettes per week each. Of women 34 per cent smoked.

Of the 147 brands most recently analysed for the Dept of Health and Social Security, the one with highest tar/nicotine content is *Capstan Full Strength* with 23/2·5 mg per cigarette. *Silk Cut Ultra Low King Size, Embassy Ultra Mild King Size* and *John Player King Size Ultra Mild* with < 4/0·3 are at the lower risk end of the league table. In the Philippines there is a brand with 71 mg nicotine per cigarette.

The world's most popular cigarette is *Marlboro*, a filter cigarette made by Philip Morris, which sold 237 000 million units in 1982. The largest-selling British cigarette in 1987 *Benson and Hedges Special Filter*. The oldest brand still available on the British market is Wills Woodbine, introduced in 1888.

The longest cigarettes ever marketed were *Head Plays*, each 27·9 cm *11 in* long and sold in packets of 5 in the United States in about 1930, to save tax. The shortest were *Lilliput* cigarettes, each of which was 31·7 mm *1¼ in* in length and 3 mm *⅛ in* in diameter. They were manufactured in Great Britain in 1956.

The world's largest collection of cigarettes is that of Robert E. Kaufman MD, of 950 Park Avenue, New York City, USA. In April 1988 he had 8200 different cigarettes made in 172 countries. The oldest brand represented is *Lone Jack*, made in the USA *c.* 1885. Both the longest and shortest (see above) are represented.

Cigarette cards

The earliest known tobacco card is 'Vanity Fair' dated 1876, issued by Wm S. Kimball & Co, Rochester, New York. The earliest British example appeared *c.* 1883 in the form of a calendar issued by Allen & Ginter, of Richmond, Virginia, trading from Holborn Viaduct, City of London. The largest known collection is that of Mr Edward Wharton-Tigar MBE (b. 1913) of London with a collection of more than 1 000 000 cigarette and trade cards in about 45 000 sets. For most valuable (see page 156)

Cigarette lighter

The Leader Lighthouse Table Lighter is made in 18-ct gold—designed in the shape of a lighthouse set on an island base of amethyst which alone weighs 50 kg *1 cwt.* It weighs 1600 g *51·4 oz troy* and the windows on the

lighthouse stem are amethyst. Priced at £37 500, it was sold by Alfred Dunhill, St James's, London in 1986.

Since 1970 Bent Hansen of Præsto, Denmark has collected 7060 cigarette lighters from all over the world.

Cigarette packets

The earliest surviving cigarette packet is a Finnish *Petit Canon* packet for 25, made by Tollander & Klärich in 1860, from the Ventegodt Collection. The rarest is the Latvian 700-year anniversary (1201–1901) *Riga* packet, believed to be unique, from the same collection. The largest verified private collection is one of 60 955 from over 150 countries owned by Vernon Young of Farnham, England.

Clocks

Oldest

The earliest mechanical clock, that is, one with an escapement, was completed in China in AD 725 by I Hsing and Liang Lingtsan. The oldest surviving working clock in the world is the faceless clock dating from 1386, or possibly earlier, at Salisbury Cathedral, Wiltshire, which was restored in 1956 having struck the hours for 498 years and ticked more than 500 million times. Earlier dates, ranging back to *c.* 1335, have been attributed to the weight-driven clock in Wells Cathedral, Somerset, but only the iron frame is original. A model of Giovanni de Dondi's heptagonal astronomical clock of 1348–64 was completed in 1962.

Largest

The world's most massive clock is the Astronomical Clock in the Cathedral of St Pierre, Beauvais, France, constructed between 1865 and 1868. It contains 90 000 parts and measures 12·1 m *40 ft* high, 6·09 m *20 ft* wide and 2·7 m *9 ft* deep. The Su Sung Clock, built in China at K'aifeng in 1088–92, had a 20·3 tonne *20 ton* bronze armillary sphere for 1· 52 tonnes *1½ tons* of water. It was removed to Beijing in 1126 and was last known to be working in its 12·1 m *40 ft* high tower in 1136.

The world's largest clock face is that of the floral clock at Tokachigaoka Park, Otofuke, Hokkaido, Japan, completed on 1 Aug 1982 with a diameter of 18 m *59 ft 0⅝ in.* The largest four-faced clock in the world is that on the building of the Allen-Bradley Company of Milwaukee, Wisconsin. Each face has a diameter of 12·28 m *40 ft 3½ in* with a minute hand 6·09 m *20 ft* in overall length. The largest single-faced clock is the octagonal Colgate Clock in Jersey, New Jersey with a diameter of 15·24 m *50 ft* and a minute hand 8·31 m *27 ft 3 in* in length. The tallest four-faced clock in the world is that of the Williamsburgh Savings Bank in Brooklyn, New York City. It is 131 m *430 ft* above street level. The digital, electronic, two-sided clock which revolves on top of the Texas Building in Fort Worth, Texas, USA, has dimensions of 13·4 × 13·4 × 8·5 m *44 × 44 × 28 ft*

The largest clock in the United Kingdom is that on the Royal Liver Building, Liverpool (built 1908–11) with dials 7·62 m *25 ft* in diameter and the 4 minute hands each 4·26 m *14 ft* long. The mechanism and dials weigh 22 tons and are 67 m *220 ft* above street level.

Most accurate

The most accurate and complicated clockwork in the world is the Olsen Clock, completed for Copenhagen Town Hall, Denmark in December 1955. The clock, which has more than 14 000 units, took 10 years to make and the mechanism functions in 570 000 different ways. The celestial pole motion will take 25 753 years to complete a full circle and is the slowest-moving designed mechanism in the world. The clock is accurate to 0·5 sec in 300 years—50 times more accurate than the previous record.

Most expensive

The highest price paid for any clock is the sum of £500 000 for a Thomas Tompion (1639–1713) bracket clock bought by the British Museum by private treaty on 15 July 1982.

Longest stoppage 'Big Ben'

The longest stoppage of the clock in the House of Commons clock tower, London since the first tick on 31 May 1859 has been 13 days from noon on 4 Apr to noon on 17 Apr 1977. In 1945 a host of starlings slowed the minute hand by 5 minutes.

Pendulum

Longest

The longest pendulum in the world is 22·5 m *73 ft 9¾ in* on the water-mill clock installed by Hattori Tokeiten Co in the Shinjuku NS building in Tokyo in 1983.

Most accurate time measurer

The most accurate time-keeping devices are the twin atomic hydrogen masers installed in 1964 in the US Naval Research Laboratory, Washington, DC. They are based on the frequency of the hydrogen atom's transition

period of 1 420 450 751 694 cycles/sec. This enables an accuracy to within 1 sec in 1 700 000 years.

Coathanger

The world's largest coathanger measures 4·6 m × 2·06 m × 0·5 m *15 ft × 6·75 ft × 1·6 ft* and weighs 200 kg *440 lb*. It was made of Oregon pine and plywood by Stefan Geir Karlsson of Reykjavik, Iceland.

Credit card collection

The largest is one of 1199 (all different) by Walter Cavanagh (b. 1943) of Santa Clara, California. The cost to him was nil, and he keeps them in the longest wallet— 76·2 m *250 ft* long weighing 15·87 kg *35 lb* and worth more than $1·40 million in credit.

Curtain

The largest curtain ever built was a bright orange-red

Most expensive cigarette cards ● On July 30 1987, a complete set of Taddy's Clowns and Circus Artistes was sold at Phillips, London for £15 500 (£17 050 including buyer's premium of £1550), a record price for cigarette cards at auction. Only a handful of complete sets of 20 are known. James Taddy & Co, a small London tobacco firm founded *c.* 1740, was renowned for its beautifully produced cards. (Photo: Phillips)

4064 kg *4 ton* 56 m *185 ft* high curtain suspended 411 m *1350 ft* across the Rifle Gap, Grand Hogback, Colorado, USA by Bulgarian-born sculptor Christo (*né* Javacheff) on 10 Aug 1971. It blew apart in a 80 km/h *50 mph* gust 27 hr later. The total cost involved in displaying this work of art was $750 000.

The world's largest functional curtain is one 167·6 long ×

19·8 m high *550 ft × 65 ft* in the Brabazon hangar at British Aerospace, Filton, Bristol, used to enclose aircraft in the paint-spraying bay. It is electrically drawn.

Dress

The dress with the highest price tag ever exhibited by a Paris fashion house was one in the Schiaparelli spring/summer collection on 23 Jan 1977. 'The Birth of Venus' designed by Serge Lepage with 512 diamonds was priced at FFr. 7 500 000. The world's longest wedding dress train measured 22·86 m *75 ft*. The dress was created by seamstress Mona Dunn of Belles Bridal, Lynwood, Lancashire and was made of taffeta, lace, beads and sequins. It took 34½ hours to complete.

Fabrics

The oldest surviving fabric discovered from Level VI A at Çatal Hüyük, Turkey has been radio-carbon dated to

5900 BC. The most expensive fabric is Vicuña cloth manufactured by Fuji Keori Ltd of Osaka, Japan at £2087 per metre in July 1983. The most expensive evening wear fabric was that designed by Alan Hershman of Duke Street, London at £775 per metre. Each square metre, despite 155 000 hand-sewn sequins, weighs less than 198 g *7 oz*.

The most expensive cloth, the brown-grey throat hair of Indian goats, is Shatoosh (or Shatusa), finer and more expensive than Vicuña. It was sold by Neiman-Marcus of Dallas, Texas, USA at $1000 per yard but supplies have now dried up.

Firework

The largest firework ever produced has been *Universe I* exploded for the Lake Toya Festival, Hokkaido, Japan on 28 Aug 1983. The 421 kg *928 lb* shell was 108 cm *42·5 in* in diameter and burst to a diameter of 860 m *2830 ft*, with a 5-colour display.

The longest firecracker display was produced by the Hyatt Regency Hotel, the President Hotel and the Department of Tourism, Macau on June 27 1987. The total length of the

display was 3988 m (*13 083 ft*) and consisted of 2 788 000 firecrackers and 600 kg (*1322 lb*) of gunpowder. It burned for 6 hr 45 min.

Flags

The oldest known flag is one dated to *c.* 3000 BC found in 1972 at Khabis, Iran. It is of metal and measures 23×23 cm *9×9 in* and depicts an eagle, 2 lions and a goddess, 3 women and a bull. The oldest national flags are claimed by Austria, Denmark, Malta, Japan, Sri Lanka and Mali. The largest flag in the world, the 'Great American Flag', was displayed at Evansville, Indiana, USA on 22 Mar 1980 measuring 125 m *411 ft* by 64 m *210 ft* with a weight of 7 tonnes/*tons*. It was donated to the White House and was the brainchild of Len Silverfine. The largest Union Flag (or Union Jack) was

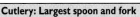

> **Cutlery: Largest spoon and fork**
> ● A giant spoon measuring 2·04 m *6 ft 8 in* and a giant fork measuring 2·15 m *7 ft ¾ in* were unveiled at the Taubame-Koike Industrial Park Co-op, Tsubame, Niigata, Japan on 30 August 1986. They were made of stainless steel and weighed 20 kg *44 lb* and 16 kg *35 lb 4½ oz* respectively.

one 73·15×32·91 m *240×108 ft* displayed at the Royal Tournament, Earl's Court, London in July 1976. It weighed more than a ton and was made by Form 4Y at Bradley Rowe School, Exeter, Devon.

The largest flag *flown* from a flagstaff is a Brazilian national flag measuring 70×100 m *229 ft 8 in×328 ft 1 in* in Brasilia. The study of flags is known as vexillology from Latin *vexillum*, a flag, and was coined by Dr Whitney Smith of Winchester, Massachusetts, USA.

Float

The largest float was the 47·24 m *155 ft* long, 7·32 m *24 ft* wide 'Merry Christmas America' float bearing 3 double arches, a 5·18 m *17 ft* Christmas tree, two 4·57 m *15 ft* peppermint candy sticks and 500 m² *5380 ft²* of wrapping paper, used at the 40th Annual Christmas Parade, Baton Rouge, Louisiana, USA on 5 Dec 1986.

Furniture

The largest item of furniture in the world is a wooden bench along the Masuhoura Beach, Ishikawa, Japan which can seat over 1400 people and measures 460·9 m *1512 ft* long. It was

completed by a team of 800 on 9 Mar 1987 as an additional tourist attraction for this area.

Garden gnome

The earliest recorded garden gnome was one placed in the rockery at Lamport Hall, Northamptonshire, England in 1847 by Sir Charles Isham Bt (1819–1903) who believed they were real people.

Glass

The most priceless example of the art of glass-making is usually regarded as the glass Portland Vase which dates from late in the 1st century BC or 1st century AD. It was made in Italy, and was in the possession of the Barberini family in Rome from at least 1642. It was eventually bought by the Duchess of Portland in 1792 but smashed while in the British Museum by William Lloyd on 7 Feb 1845. The thinnest glass, type D263, has a minimum thickness of 0·035 mm *0·00137 in* and a maximum thickness of 0·055 mm *0·0021 in.* It is made by Deutsche Spezialglas AG, Grünenplan, West Germany for use in electronic and medical equipment.

Gold

The gold coffin of the 14th-century BC Pharaoh Tutankhamun discovered by Howard Carter on 16 Feb 1923 in the Valley of the Kings, western Thebes, Egypt weighed 110·4 kg *243 lb.* The exhibition at the British Museum from 30 Mar to 30 Dec 1972 attracted 1 656 151 people (of whom 45·7 per cent bought catalogues), resulting in a profit of £657 731·22.

Grill

A 100·2 m *328·7 ft* long grill was made for a barbecue at Esplugnes de Llobregat, Barcelona, Spain on 22 Sept 1986. A single *butifarra* (sausage) 1803·6 m *5 917 ft* in length was cooked on it.

Jigsaw

The earliest jigsaws were made as 'dissected maps' by John Spilsbury (1739–69) in Russell Court off Drury Lane, London *c.* 1762.

The largest jigsaw ever made is one measuring 25·87 × 16·83 m *84 ft 10½ in × 55 ft 2½ in* with 15 520 pieces constructed by the Monadnock United Way of Keene, New Hampshire, USA from 21–23 Sept 1985.

In July 1986 'L'Association l'Arbre aux Mille Sources' constructed a jigsaw consisting of 150 000 pieces and measuring 25 × 14·64 m *82 × 48 ft.* Fujisankei Communications Group of Japan commissioned Yanoman Co to produce a puzzle 3·24 × 5·88 m *10·63 × 19·29 ft* with 61 752 pieces. Each piece was sold for charity. Custom-made Stave puzzles made by Steve Richardson of Norwich, Vermont, USA of 2640 pieces cost $5620 in March 1988.

Kettle

The largest antique copper kettle was one standing 0·9 m *3 ft* high with a 1·8 m *6 ft* girth and a 90 l *20 gal* capacity, built in Taunton, Somerset, England for the hardware merchants Fisher and Son *c.* 1800.

Lamp

The smallest electric bulb is one 3 mm *0·12 in* long by 0·5 mm *0·02 in* in diameter made by the Hamai Electric Lamp Co, Tokyo, Japan.

Matchbox labels

The oldest match label of accepted provenance is that of Samuel Jones *c.* 1830. The finest collection of trade mark labels (excluding any bar or other advertising labels) is some 280 000 pieces collected by the phillumenist Robert Jones of Indianapolis, USA. The greatest British prize is a Lucifer & Congreve label of *c.* 1835.

Photographs with stars ● During the past 4 years, Barbara Ann Thomas of Fredericksburg, Virginia, USA has had her photograph taken with 160 Hollywood stars. Husband John acts as photographer whilst they holiday at film locations in Hollywood, Los Angeles, California, USA. In this selection of 6 photographs Barbara can be seen with (from top to bottom) Larry Hagman, Pierce Brosnan, Joan Collins, Clint Eastwood, Linda Evans and James Stewart. (Photos: J W Thomas)

Most expensive fountain pen ● A Japanese collector paid 1·3 million FF in Feb 1988 for the 'Anémone' fountain pen made by Réden, France. It was encrusted with 600 precious stones including emeralds, amethysts, rubies, sapphires and onyx and took skilled craftsmen over a year to complete. (Photo: Gamma)

Needles

Needles made of bone have been found in sites of the Upper Palaeolithic Aurignacian period in France dated *c.* 28 000–24 000 BC. The longest is one 185·5 cm *6 ft 1 in* long made by George Davies of Thomas Somerfield, Bloxwich, England for stitching on mattress buttons lengthways. One is preserved in the National Needle Museum at Forge Mill, Redditch, Worcestershire.

Nylon

The lowest denier nylon yarn ever produced is the 6 denier used for stockings exhibited at the Nylon Fair in London in February 1956. The sheerest stockings normally available are 9 denier. A hair from the average human head is about 50 denier.

Penknife

The penknife with the greatest number of blades is the Year Knife made by cutlers Joseph Rodgers & Sons, of Sheffield, England, whose trade mark was granted in 1682. The knife was made in 1822 with 1822 blades and a blade was added every year until 1973 when there was no further space. It was acquired by Britain's largest hand tool manufacturers, Stanley Works (Great Britain) Ltd of Sheffield, South Yorkshire, in 1970.

Pens

The most expensive writing pen is the 5003.002 Caran d'Ache 18-carat solid gold Madison slimline ballpoint pen incorporating white diamonds of 6.35 carats made by Jakar International Ltd, London. Its recommended retail price is £19 950 (incl. VAT).

The world's leading pen is the BiC Crystal with 14 000 000 being manufactured daily by the BiC organisation world-wide. 500 000 are sold daily in the UK, which, if used, would offer a write-out length of at least 1 250 000 km *776 735·2 miles* – the equivalent of drawing a line around the world 31 times or alternatively to the Moon and back and back to the Moon again.

Pistol

In Dec 1983 it was reported that Ray Bily (US) owned an initialled gold pistol made for Hitler which was valued for insurance at $375 000. The pistol with the largest magazine capacity is the .22LR M.100P with 103 rounds of continuous firepower, manufactured by Calico, Bakersfield, California, USA.

Postcards

Deltiology is claimed to be the third largest collecting hobby next only to stamps and coins. Austria issued the first cards in 1869 followed by Britain in 1872. The highest price paid for a postcard was $4400 for one of the 5 known Mucha Waverly Cycle postcards. It was sold by Susan Brown Nicholson of Lisle, Illinois, USA in September 1984.

Most words on the back of a postcard

Jon Mears of Worle, Weston super Mare, England managed to squeeze 5998 words on to the back of a 15·24 cm × 10·16 cm *6 in × 4 in* postcard in March 1988.

Quilting

The world's largest quilt was made by 10 000 people in memory of those who died of AIDS-related illnesses exhibited at Pauley Pavilion, Los Angeles on 7 April 1988. It had by this time reached 4200 panels covering 0·67 ha *1·73 acres.*

Robe

A robe for Emperor Field-Marshal Jean-Bédel Bokassa with a 11·8 m *39 ft* long train was encrusted with 785 000

pearls and 1 220 000 crystal beads by Guiselin of Paris for £77 125. It was for his coronation at Bangui, Central African Empire (now Republic) on 4 Dec 1977. He also wore pearl-studded shoes commissioned from the House of Berluti, Paris at a cost of £38 800.

Ropes

The largest rope ever made was a coir fibre launching rope with a circumference of 119 cm *47 in* made in 1858 for the British liner *Great Eastern* by John and Edwin Wright of Birmingham. It consisted of 4 strands, each of 3780 yarns. The longest fibre rope ever made without a splice was one of 10 000 fathoms or 18 288 m *11·36 miles* of 16·5 cm *6½ in* circumference manila by Frost Brothers (now British Ropes Ltd) in London in 1874. (See also Wire ropes, Chapter 8.) The strongest cable-laid wire rope strop made is one 282 mm *11·1 in* in diameter with a breaking strain of 3250 tonnes.

Longest scarf

The longest scarf ever knitted measured an amazing 32 km *3·9 m* *20 miles 13 ft* long. It was knitted by residents of Abbeyfield Houses for the Abbeyfield Society and was completed on 29 May 1988.

Shoes

James Smith, founder of James Southall & Co of Norwich, introduced sized shoes in 1792. The firm began making 'Start-rite' children's shoes in 1923.

The most expensive shoes are mink-lined golf shoes with 18-carat gold embellishments and ruby-tipped spikes made by Stylo Matchmakers International, of Northampton, England, which retail for £9250 (*$17 000*) per pair in the USA. A pair of women's cream kid and braid high-heeled shoes *c.* 1660 sold by Lord Hereford at Sotheby's in September 1987 to Mrs Sonia Bata fetched £21 000. (See also 'Robe', above.)

Excluding cases of elephantiasis, the largest shoes ever sold are a pair size 42 built for the giant Harley Davidson of Avon Park, Florida. The normal limit is size 14. For advertising and display purposes facsimiles of shoes weighing up to 1·5 tonnes have been constructed.

Silver

The largest single pieces of silver are a pair of water jugs of 242·7 kg *10 408 troy oz 4·77 cwt* made in 1902 for the Maharaja of Jaipur (1861–1922). They are 160 cm *5 ft 3 in* tall, with a circumference of 2·48 m *8 ft 1½ in*, and have a capacity of 8182 litres *1800 gallons*. Now in the City Palace, Jaipur, India, the silversmith was Gorind Narain.

Snuff

The most expensive snuff obtainable in Britain is 'Café Royale' sold by G. Smith and Sons (est. 1869) of 74, Charing Cross Road, London. The price was £2·18 per oz in April 1987.

Sofa

The longest standard sofa manufactured for market is the Augustus Rex Sofa, 3·74 m *12 ft 3 in* in length made by Dodge & Son of Sherborne, Dorset. Barton Grange Hotel, near Preston, Lancashire, bought a 4·26 m *14 ft* long pink leather settee for £3250 on 4 Oct 1984.

Suit

EVA suits for extra-vehicular activity worn by Space Shuttle crews from 1982 had a unit cost of $2·3 million.

Sundial

The world's largest sundial is the Samrat Yantra with gnomon height of 27 m *88·5 ft* and a vertical height of 36 m *118 ft* built in 1724 at Jaipur, India.

Table and table cloth

The longest table was set up from La Punta to The Terramar, Sitges, Spain on 4 Oct 1986. It was 2410·6 m *2636·2 yd* in length and was used to seat 6400 people. The world's largest table cloth is one 300·5 m *328·6 yd*

Largest postcard collection ● The world's largest collection is owned by Mario Morby, 12, of Streetly, West Midlands, consisting of 1 000 265 postcards.

long by 184 cm *72 in* wide made of damask by Tonrose Limited of Manchester in June 1988.

Tapestry

The earliest known examples of tapestry woven linen are 3 pieces from the tomb of the Egyptian pharaoh Thutmose IV and dated to 1483–1411 BC.

The largest tapestry ever woven is the 'History of Irak', with an area of 1242·1 m² *13 370·7 ft²*. It was designed by the Yugoslavian artist Frane Delale and produced by the Zivtex Regeneracija Workshop in Zabok, Yugoslavia.

Longest Soft toy ● 'Lots-a-Lots-a-Legggggggs', the 1000-legged pink caterpillar, measures 76·2 m *250 ft* and weighs 136·08 kg *300 lb*. It was created by Commonwealth Toy & Novelty Co, Inc, New York, .

The tapestry was completed in 1986 and it now adorns the wall of an amphitheatre in Baghdad.

Britain's largest single piece of tapestry is 'Christ in His Majesty', measuring 21·94 by 11·88 m *72 ft × 39 ft* designed by Graham Vivian Sutherland OM (1903–80) for an altar hanging in Coventry Cathedral. It cost £10 500, weighs 760 kg *¾ ton* and was delivered from Pinton Frères of Felletin, France on 1 Mar 1962. The famous Bayeux *Telle du Conquest, dite tapisserie de la reine Mathilde*, a hanging 49·5 cm *19½ in* wide by 70·40 m *231 ft* in length depicts events of 1064–6 in 72 scenes and was probably worked in Canterbury, Kent, *c.* 1086. It was 'lost' for 2½ centuries from 1476 until 1724. The Overlord Embroidery of 34 panels each 2·43×0·91 m *8×3 ft*, commissioned by Lord Dulverton CBE, TD (b. 1915) from the Royal School of Needlework in London, was completed in 1979 after 100 man-years of work and is 12·49 m *41 ft* longer than the Bayeux. It has the largest area of any embroidery with 75·8 m² *816 ft²*. An uncompleted 20·3 cm *8 in* deep 407·82 m *1338 ft* long embroidery of scenes from C. S. Lewis's 'Narnia' children's stories has been worked by Mrs Margaret S. Pollard of Truro, Cornwall, England to the order of Michael Maine.

Tartan

The earliest evidence of tartan is the so-called Falkirk tartan, found stuffed in a jar of coins in Bells Meadow, Falkirk, Stirlingshire, Scotland. It is of a dark and light brown pattern and dates from *c.* AD 245. The earliest reference to a specific named tartan is to a Murray tartan in 1618 although Mackay tartan was probably worn earlier. There are 1300 tartans known to the Museum of Scottish Tartans at Comrie, Perthshire. HRH Prince of Wales is eligible to wear 11 including the Balmoral which has been exclusive to the royal family since 1852.

Tea towels

The largest reported collection of unduplicated tea towels was 5967 formed by Tony Judkin of Luton,

Bedfordshire, England. In April 1986 a fire destroyed 'over a thousand' of them.

Ticket

The smallest ticket was one measuring 3 mm × 7 mm × 1 mm for admission to the Asian-Pacific Exposition Fukuoka '89, Fukuoka, Japan. It was made of ceramic on which letters of 85–280 microns were printed.

Time capsule

The world's largest time capsule is the Tropico Time Tunnel of 283 m³ *10 000 ft³* in a cave in Rosamond, California, USA sealed by the Kern Antelope Historical Society on 20 Nov 1966 and intended for opening in AD 2866.

Toy construction

The tallest Lego tower, 15·01 m *49 ft 2⅜ in*, was built in the forecourt of Waterloo Station, London on 29–30 Oct 1985.

Typewriters

The first patent for a typewriter was by Henry Mill in 1714 but the earliest known working machine was made by Pellegrine Turri (Italy) in 1808.

Vase

The largest vase on record is one 2·78 m *8 ft* in height, weighing 294·8 kg *650 lb*, thrown by Sebastiano Maglio at Haeger Potteries of Dundee, Illinois, USA (founded 1872) during August 1976. The Chinese ceramic authority Chingwah Lee of San Francisco was reported in August 1978 to have appraised a unique 99 cm *39 in* Kang Hsi 4-sided vase then in a bank vault in Phoenix, Arizona, USA at '$60 million'.

Wallet

The most expensive wallet ever made is a platinum-cornered, diamond-studded crocodile creation made by Louis Quatorze of Paris and Mikimoto of Tokyo selling in September 1984 at £56 000.

Watches

Oldest

The oldest watch (portable clockwork time-keeper) is one made of iron by Peter Henlein in Nürnberg (Nüremberg), Bavaria, Germany, *c.* 1504. The earliest wrist watches were those of Jacquet-Droz and Leschot of Geneva, Switzerland, dating from 1790.

Largest

A facsimile 'Swatch' watch was draped from the roof of the Comme Bank building, Frankfurt, West Germany in December 1985. It was 143 m *469 ft* in length, had a weight of 13 tonnes and its face had a diameter of some 16·45 m *54 ft*.

A 'Swatch' 162 m *531 ft 6 in* long and 20 m *65 ft 7½ in* in diameter, made by D. Tomas Feliu, was set up on the Bank of Bilbao building, Madrid, Spain from 7–12 Dec 1985.

The Eta 'watch' which could be seen on the Swiss pavilion at Expo 86 in Vancouver, British Columbia from May–Oct weighed 35 tonnes *34·4 tons* and stood 24·3 m *80 ft* high.

Smallest

The smallest watches in the world are produced by Jaeger le Coultre of Switzerland. Equipped with a 15-jewelled movement they measure just over 1·2 cm *½ in* long and 0·476 cm *³/₁₆ in* in width. Movement and case weigh under 7 g *0·25 oz*.

Thinnest

The world's thinnest wrist watch is the Swiss Concord Delirium IV. It measures 0·98 mm *0·0385 in* thick and retailed for $16 000 (including 18-carat gold strap) in June 1980.

Most expensive

Excluding watches with jewelled cases, the most expensive standard man's pocket watch is the Swiss *Grande*

Complication by Audemars-Piguet which retailed for £210 000 in March 1988. Its movement is made up of 416 tiny parts and production time is 8–12 months per piece. It is also a perpetual calendar, it chimes the hours, quarters and minutes, and indicates the phases of the moon. Despite the price, there is currently a year's waiting list. The record price for an antique watch is SwFr1 870 000 paid at Christie's, Geneva on 13 May 1986 by a European collector for a gold-enamelled and diamond-set pocket watch with a movement *c.*1650 by the Parisian maker Jehan Cremfdorff.

Wreath

The most expensive wreath on record was that presented to Sri Chinmoy in New York on 11 July 1983 by Ashrita Furman and Pahar Meltzer. It was handled by the Garland of Divinity's Love Florist, contained 10 000 flowers, and cost $3500.

Zip-fastener

The world's longest zip-fastener is 632·45 m *2074 ft* long made for covers of aquatic cables by RIRI of Mendrisio, Italy in January 1985. It has 119 007 nylon teeth.

Agriculture

Origins

It has been estimated that only 21 per cent of the world's land surface is cultivable and that only 7·6 per cent is actually under cultivation. Evidence adduced in 1971 from Nok Nok Tha and Spirit Cave, Thailand tends to confirm that plant cultivation and animal domestication were part of the Hoabinhian culture *c.* 11 000 BC. Goats were herded on Mount Carmel, Palestine as early as 16 000 BC.

Goat was domesticated at Asiab, Iran by *c.* 8050 BC and dog at Star Carr, North Yorkshire by *c.* 7700 BC; the earliest definite date for sheep *c.* 7200 BC at Argissa-Magula, Thessaly, Greece and for pig and cattle *c.* 7000 BC at the same site. The earliest date for horse is *c.* 4350 BC from Dereivka, Ukraine, USSR.

FARMS

Earliest

The earliest dated British farming site is Neolithic and is enclosed within the Iron-Age hill fort at Hembury, Devon, excavated during 1934–5 and now dated to 4210–3990 BC. Pollen analysis from 2 sites, Oakhanger, Hampshire and Winfrith Heath, Dorset (Mesolithic *c.* 5000 BC), indicates that Mesolithic man may have had deer herds which were fed on ivy during the winter months.

Largest

The largest farms in the world are collective farms (*sovkhozes*) in the USSR. These have been reduced in number from 235 500 in 1940 to only 18 000 in 1980 and have been increased in size so that units of over 25 000 ha *60 000 acres* are not uncommon. The pioneer farm owned by Laucidio Coelho near Campo Grande, Mato Grosso, Brazil *c.* 1901 was 8700 km² *3358 miles²* or 2·15 million acres with 250 000 head of cattle at the time of his death in 1975.

The largest farms in the British Isles are Scottish hill farms in the Grampians. The largest arable farm is that at Elveden, Suffolk, farmed by the Earl of Iveagh. Here 4513·1 ha *11 151·9 acres* are farmed on an estate of 9112·45 ha *22 517 acres*, the greater part of which was formerly derelict land. The 1987 production included 9514 tonnes *9344 tons* of grain and 56 246 tonnes *55 234 tons* of sugar beet. The livestock includes 1030 ewes and 6322 pigs.

Cattle station

The world's largest cattle station is the Anna Creek station of 30 113·5 km² *11 626·8 miles²*, South Australia owned by the Kidman family. It is thus 23 per cent of the

size of England. The biggest component is Strangway at 14 114 km² *5449 miles²*. Until 1915 the Victoria River Downs Station, Northern Territory had an area of 22 400 000 acres (90 650 km² *35 000 miles²*), the same as England's 20 largest counties put together.

Sheep station

The largest sheep station in the world is Commonwealth Hill, in the north-west of South Australia. It grazes between 60 000 and 70 000 sheep, *c.* 700 cattle and 54 000 uninvited kangaroos in an area of 10 567 km² *4080 miles²*, i.e. larger than the combined area of Norfolk and Suffolk. The head count on Sir William Stevenson's 12 140 ha *30 000 acre* Lochinver Station in New Zealand was 117 500 on 1 Jan 1983 on 8500 ha *21 000 acres*. The largest sheep move on record occurred when 27 horsemen moved a mob of 43 000 sheep 64 km *40 miles* from Barcaldine to Beaconsfield Station, Queensland, Australia in 1886.

Rice farming

The largest contiguous wild rice (*Zizania aquatica*) farm in the world is Clearwater Rice Inc. at Clearbrook, Minnesota, USA with 809 ha *2000 acres*. In 1986 it yielded 261 727 kg *577 000 lb*, the largest to date.

Turkey farm

The world's largest turkey farm is that of Bernard Matthews PLC, at Great Witchingham, Norfolk, England with 2500 staff tending 8 000 000 turkeys.

Chicken ranch

The world's largest chicken ranch is the Croton Egg Farm in Ohio, USA, which has 4·8 million hens laying some 3·7 million eggs daily.

Piggery

The world's largest piggery is the Sljeme pig unit in Yugoslavia which is able to process 300 000 pigs in a year.

Cow shed

The longest cow shed in Britain is that of the Yorkshire Agricultural Society at Harrogate, North Yorkshire. It is 139 m *456 ft* in length with a capacity of 686 cows. The National Agricultural Centre, Kenilworth, Warwickshire, completed in 1967, has, however, capacity for 782 animals.

Foot-and-mouth disease

The worst outbreak of foot-and-mouth disease in Great Britain was that from Shropshire on 25 Oct 1967 to 25 June 1968 in which there were 2364 outbreaks and 429 632 animals slaughtered at a direct and consequential loss of £150 000 000. The outbreak of 1871, when farms were much smaller, affected 42 531 farms. The disease first appeared in Britain at Stratford, east London in August 1839.

Sheep shearing

The highest speed for sheep shearing in a working day was that recorded for John Fagan who machine-sheared 804 lambs (average 89·3 per hour) in 9 hr at Hautora Rd, Pio Pio, New Zealand on 8 Dec 1980. Peter Casserly of Christchurch, New Zealand achieved a solo blade (i.e. hand-shearing) record of 353 lambs in 9 hours on 13 Feb 1976. In a shearing marathon, 4 men machine-shore 2519 sheep in 29 hr at Stewarts Trust, Waikia, Southland, New Zealand on 11 Feb 1982.

Mr Lavor Taylor (b. 27 Feb 1896) of Ephraim, Utah claims to have sheared 515 000 sheep to May 1984.

British records for 9 hr have been set at 555 by Roger Poyntz-Roberts (300) and John Savery (255) on 9 June 1971 (sheep caught *by* shearers), and 610 by the same pair (sheep caught *for* shearers) in July 1970.

Sheep survival

The longest recorded survival by a sheep buried in snow is 50 days when Alex Maclennan uncovered 15 dead and 1 live sheep near the River Skinsdale on Mrs

Agriculture

Tyser's Gordonbush Estate, Sutherland, Scotland on 24 Mar 1978 during the great January blizzard.

Mushroom farm

The largest single mushroom farm in the world is that of Moonlight Mushroom Inc., founded in 1937 in a disused limestone mine near Worthington, Pennsylvania, USA. It employs over 900 in a maze of underground galleries 177 km *110 miles* long, producing over 20 412 000 kg *20 090 tons* of mushrooms per year. The French annual consumption is unrivalled at 3·17 kg *7 lb* per caput.

Wheat field

The largest single fenced field sown with wheat was one of 14 160 ha *35 000 acres* sown in 1951 south-west of Lethbridge, Alberta, Canada.

Vineyard

The world's largest vineyard extends over the Mediterranean façade between the Rhône and the Pyrenees in the *départements* Hérault, Gard, Aude, and Pyrénées-Orientales in an area of 840 000 ha *2 075 685 acres* of which 52·3 per cent is *monoculture viticole.*

Hop field

The largest is one of 773·8 ha *1912 acres* near Toppenish, Washington State, USA. It is owned by John I. Haas Inc., the world's largest hop growers, with hop farms in Idaho, Oregon, Washington State and Tasmania, with a total net area of 1699·3 ha *4199 acres.*

Community garden

The largest such project is that operated by the City Beautiful Council, and the Benjamin Wegerzyn Garden Center at Dayton, Ohio, USA. It comprises 1173 allotments each of 74·45 m² *812¼ ft².*

CROP YIELDS
Wheat

Crop yields for highly tended small areas are of little significance. The British record is 13·99 tonnes/ha *111·4 cwt/acre* at 15·5 per cent moisture on a field of 17·49 ha *43·24 acres* by Gordon Rennie of Clifton Mains, Newbridge, Midlothian.

Barley

A yield of 11 762 kg/ha *93·7 cwt/acre* of Gerbel Winter Barley was achieved in August 1984 by the Brewster family farm at Kirknewton, Midlothian from a 8·29 ha *20·48 acre* field.

Potato

The greatest number of US barrels picked in a 9½ hr day is 235 by Walter Sirois (b. 1917) of Caribou, Maine on 30 Sept 1950.

Corn

A yield of 352·64 US bushels (15½ per cent moisture) from an acre, using De Kalb XL-54, was achieved by Roy Lynn Jr near Kalamazoo, Michigan, USA on 30 Sept 1977.

Sugar beet

The highest recorded yield for sugar beet is 139·9 tonnes/ha *62·4 short tons (55·71 long tons) per acre* by Andy Christensen and Jon Giannini in the Salinas Valley, California, USA.

Field-to-loaf

The fastest time for producing loaves from growing wheat is 40 min 44 sec at O. S. North's Bakery at Heydon, near Royston, Hertfordshire, England on 10 Sept 1983. Two one-pound loaves (1 white, 1 wholemeal) and 115 gm *4·05 oz* of butter (from 9 litres *15·8 pints* of milk produced by 'Daffodil') were produced in 29 min 37 sec at Thriplow Farm, Cambridgeshire, England on 18 April 1986.

Ploughing

The world championship (instituted 1953) has been staged in 18 countries and won by ploughmen of 11 nationalities of which the United Kingdom has been most successful with 8 championships. The only man to take the title 3 times has been Hugh B. Barr of Northern Ireland in 1954–5–6. The 1984 champion was Desmond Wright, 48 (Northern Ireland). The fastest recorded time for ploughing an acre *0·404 ha* (minimum 32 right-hand turns and depth 22 cm *9 in*) is 11 min 21·8 sec by Robert Dee using a Fiat 180-90 DT tractor at Hodstock Priory Farm, Blythe, Nottinghamshire, England on 1 Nov 1984. Frank Allinson of Leyburn, North Yorkshire, ploughed for 250 hr 9 min 50 sec from 14–24 Nov 1981. DMI Inc of Goodfield, Illinois, USA marketed a 'Hydrawide' plough with 21 furrows in 1978.

24-hour ploughing

The greatest recorded acreage ploughed with a 6-furrow plough to a depth of 22·86 cm *9 in* in 24 hr is 63·43 ha *156·74 acres* by Christiaan Mauritius Van Den Heever using a 158-hp Fiat 160/90DT tractor at Swerwerskraal No. 733 farm, Potgietersrus, South Africa on 8–9 Jan 1988.

Rick

A rick of 40 400 bales of straw was completed from 22 July to 3 Sept 1982 by Nick and Tom Parsons with a gang of 8 at Cuckoo-pen Barn Farm, Birdlip, Gloucestershire. It measured 45·7 × 9·1 × 18·2 m *150 × 30 × 60 ft* high and weighed 711 tonnes *700 tons.* They baled, hauled and ricked 24 200 bales in 7 days from 22–29 July.

LIVESTOCK

Note: Some exceptionally high livestock auction prices are believed to result from collusion between buyer and seller to raise the ostensible price levels of the breed concerned. Others are marketing and publicity exercises with little relation to true market prices.

Highest priced *Bull*

The highest price has been $2 500 000 for the beefalo (a ⅜ bison, ⅜ charolais, ¼ Hereford) 'Joe's Pride' sold by D. C. Basalo of Burlingame, California to the Beefalo Cattle Co of Canada, of Calgary on 9 Sept 1974. A young 14-month-old Canadian Holstein bull 'Pickland Elevation B. ET' was bought by Premier Breeders of Stamfordham, Northumberland, England for £233 000. The highest price in Britain has been 60 000 guineas (£63 000), paid on 5 Feb 1963 at Perth, Scotland by James R. Dick (1928–74), co-manager of Black Watch Farms, for 'Lindertis Evulse', an Aberdeen-Angus owned by Sir Torquil and Lady Munro of Lindertis, Kirriemuir, Angus. This bull failed a fertility test in August 1963, thus becoming the world's most expensive piece of beef.

Cow

The highest price for a cow has been $1 300 000 for a Holstein at auction in East Monpelier, Vermont, USA in 1985. The British record is £33 600 for 'Ullswater Beatexus 8th', a British Friesian sold to the British Livestock Embryo Syndicate of Royston, Hertfordshire by Sir Keith and Lady Showering of West Horrington, Wells, Somerset on 9 May 1981 (auctioneers: Hobsons).

Goat

An angora goat was sold for £14 700 at a sale at Longhope, Gloucestershire, England on 23 May 1987.

Sheep

The highest price ever paid for a ram was $A79 000 by the Gnowangerup Animal Breeding Centre, Western Australia for a Merino ram from the Collinsville Stud, South Australia at the Royal Adelaide Show on 10 Sept 1981. The British auction record is £21 000 paid by Mr W. Sheddon of Brighouse, Kirkcudbrightshire, Scotland for A. W. Carswell & Son's Blackface ram on 4 Oct 1978. The highest price ever paid for wool was $A320 per kg greasy for a bale of Tasmania superfine at the wool auction in Tasmania, Australia on 25 Feb 1988 by Fujii Keori Ltd of Osaka, Japan — top bidders since 1973.

Pig

The highest price ever paid for a pig is $56 000 for a cross-bred barrow named 'Bud' owned by Jeffrey Roemisch of Hermleigh, Texas, USA and bought by E. A.

'Bud' Olson and Phil Bonzio on 5 Mar 1983. The UK record is 3300 guineas (£3465), paid by Malvern Farms for a Swedish Landrace gilt 'Bluegate Ally 33rd' owned by Davidson Trust in a draft sale at Reading, Berkshire on 2 Mar 1955.

Horse

The highest price for a draught horse was $47 500 paid for the 7-year-old Belgian stallion 'Farceur' by E. G. Good at Cedar Falls, Iowa, USA on 16 Oct 1917. A Welsh mountain pony stallion 'Coed Cock Bari' was sold to an Australian builder in Wales in September 1978 for 21 000 guineas (then £22 050).

Turkey

The highest price recorded at auction for a turkey was the £4200 paid by Dewhurst the butchers, for a 37·59 kg *82 lb 14⅜ oz* stag at Smithfield, London, on 8 Dec 1987.

Donkey

The lowest ever price for livestock was at a sale at Kuruman, Cape Province, South Africa in 1934 where donkeys were sold for less than 2p each.

Heaviest *Cattle*

The heaviest on record was a Holstein-Durham cross named 'Mount Katahdin' exhibited by A. S. Rand of Maine, USA from 1906–10 and frequently weighed at an even 2267 kg *5000 lb.* He was 1·88 m *6 ft 2 in* at the shoulder with a 3·96 m *13 ft* girth and died in a barn fire c. 1923. The British record is the 2032 kg *4480 lb* of 'The Bradwell Ox' owned by William Spurgin of Bradwell, Essex. He was 4·57 m *15 ft* from nose to tail and had a girth of 3·35 m *11 ft* when 6 years old in 1830. The largest breed of heavyweight cattle is the Chianini, brought to the Chiana Valley, central-west Italy, from the Middle East in pre-Roman times. Four types of the breed exist, of which the largest is the Val di Chianini, found on the plains and low hills of Arezzo and Sienna. Mature bulls average 1·73 m *5 ft 8 in* at the forequarters and weigh 1300 kg *2865 lb.* In 1965 a prize bull named 'Donetto' recorded a weight of 1739 kg *3834 lb* at the Arezzo Show – a world record for any bull of any breed. The Airedale Heifer of East Riddlesdon, near Keighley, South Yorkshire c. 1820 was 3·62 m *11 ft 10·6 in* long and weighed 1197·5 kg *2640 lb.*

The heaviest recorded live birthweight for a calf is

102 kg *225 lb* from a British Friesian cow at Rockhouse Farm, Bishopston, Swansea, West Glamorgan, in 1961. On 29 May 1986 a Holstein cow owned by Sherlene O'Brien of Henryetta, Oklahoma, USA gave birth to a perfectly formed still-born calf weighing 122·4 kg *270 lb*. The lowest live birthweight recorded for a calf is 8 kg *17 lb 10 oz* for a bull (breed not identified) born on Jan van Rensberg's farm at Kankus, Orange Free State, South Africa, in August 1972. It stood 40 cm *15·74 in* at the hindquarters and measured 55 cm *21·6 in* overall.

Pigs

The heaviest hog recorded was a Poland-China hog 'Big Bill' of 1157·5 kg *2552 lb* or *22¾ cwt* measuring 2·75 m *9 ft* long with a belly on the ground, owned by Burford Butler of Jackson, Tennessee, USA and chloroformed in 1933. Raised by W. J. Chappall he was mounted and displayed in Weekly County, Tennessee until 1946. The heaviest pig ever bred in Britain was the Rudgewick, which scaled about 453 kg *1000 lb* at the age of two years. In 1805 a weight of 660·4 kg *1456 lb* was recorded for a boar bred at Godstone, Surrey. The highest recorded weight for a piglet at weaning (8 weeks) is 36·7 kg *81 lb* for a boar, one of 9 piglets farrowed on 6 July 1962 by the Landrace gilt 'Manorport Ballerina 53rd', *alias* 'Mary', and sired by a Large White named 'Johnny' at Kettle Lane Farm, West Ashton, Trowbridge, Wiltshire.

The smallest breed of pig is the 'Mini Maialino' developed by Stefano Morini of St Golo d'Enza, northern Italy, after ten years of experimentation with Vietnam pot-bellied pigs. The piglets weigh 400 g *14 oz* at birth and 9 kg *20 lb* at maturity.

Sheep

The heaviest sheep ever recorded was an old Leicester Longwool ram which scaled 214 kg *472 lb*.

The highest recorded birthweight for a lamb is 17·2 kg *38 lb* at Clearwater, Sedgwick County, Kansas, USA in 1975, but neither lamb nor ewe survived. Another lamb of the same weight was born on 7 Apr 1975 in Howard, South Dakota, USA but died soon afterwards. The British record is 11·79 kg *26 lb* for a lamb delivered on 9 Feb 1967 by Alan F. Baldry from an ewe belonging to J. L. Arkwright of Winkleigh, Devon.

The lowest live birthweight recorded for a lamb is 1·02 kg *2 lb 4 oz* for a ram named 'Tiny' owned by Jeanette Fox of Daisy Bank Farm, Barthomley, Cheshire, in April 1980. It was nursed to full health.

Goats

The largest goat ever recorded was a British Saanen named 'Mostyn Moorcock' owned by Pat Robinson of Ewyas Harold, Herefordshire, which reached a weight of 181·4 kg *400 lb* (shoulder height 111·7 cm *44 in* and overall length of 167·6 cm *66 in*). He died in 1977 aged 4 years. Some Pygmy goats only weigh 15–20 kg *33–44 lb*.

Turkey

The greatest dressed weight recorded for a turkey (*Meleagris gallapavo*) is 37·59 kg *82 lb 14⅜ oz* for a stag reared by British United Turkeys of Chester, Cheshire. It won the annual 'heaviest turkey' competition held in London on 8 Dec 1987. Turkeys were introduced into Britain via Spain from Mexico in 1549.

Broiler growth

The record for growth for flocks of at least 2400 at 56 days is 2·901 kg *6·396 lb* with a conversion rate of 2·17 by D. B. Marshall (Newbridge) Ltd of Newbridge, Midlothian, Scotland reported in October 1981.

Prolificacy *Cattle*

On 25 Apr 1964 it was reported that a cow named 'Lyubik' had given birth to 7 calves at Mogilev, USSR. Five live and one dead calf were recorded from a Friesian at Te Puke, North Island, New Zealand on 27 July 1980, but none survived. A case of 5 live calves at one birth was reported in 1928 by T. G. Yarwood of Manchester. The life time prolificacy record is 39 in the case of 'Big Bertha' (b. 17 March 1944), a Dremon owned by Jerome O'Leary of Blackwatersbridge, Co. Kerry, Ire-

land. 'Soender Jylland's Jens', a Danish black and white bull, left 220 000 surviving progeny by artificial insemination when he was put down aged 11 in Copenhagen in September 1978. 'Bendalls Adema', a Friesian bull, died aged 14 at Clondalkin, County Dublin, Ireland on 8 Nov 1978 having sired an estimated 212 000 progeny by artificial insemination.

Pigs

The highest recorded number of piglets in one litter is 34, thrown on 25–26 June 1961 by a sow owned by Aksel Egedee of Denmark. In February 1955 a Wessex sow owned by Mrs E. C. Goodwin of Paul's Farm, Leigh, near Tonbridge, Kent, England had a litter of 34, of which 30 were born dead. The highest number of live births in Britain is 30 reported by W. Ives of Dane End Fruit Farm, near Ware, Hertfordshire from a white Welsh sow in September 1979. A Large White owned by H. S. Pedlingham farrowed 385 pigs in 22 litters (Dec 1923–Sept 1934). In 1930 this sow farrowed 65 piglets in 3 litters within the space of 12 months. During the period 1940–1952 a Large Black sow belonging to A. M. Harris of Lapworth, Birmingham, farrowed 26 litters.

Sheep

A case of 8 lambs at a birth was reported by D. T. Jones of Priory Farm, Gwent, in June 1956 and by Ken Towse of Buckton near Bridlington in March 1981 but none lived. A Border Leicester-Merino cross-bred sheep owned by Roger Saunders gave birth to 4 ram and 3 ewe live lambs at Strathdownie, Victoria, Australia on 19 June 1984. Seven live lambs (4 rams and 3 ewes) were also reported for a Finn ewe owned by Elsward Meine of Crookston, Minnesota, USA on 24 March 1980. A case of a sheep living to 26 years was recorded in flock book records by H. Poole, Wexford, Ireland.

Egg-laying

The highest authenticated rate of egg-laying is by a White Leghorn chicken hen, No. 2988 at the College of Agriculture, University of Missouri, USA, with 371 eggs in 364 days in an official test conducted by Professor Harold V. Biellier ending on 29 Aug 1979. The UK record is 353 eggs in 365 days in a National Laying Test at Milford, Surrey in 1957 by a Rhode Island Red 'Wonderful Lady' owned by W. Lawson of Welham Grange, Retford, Nottinghamshire.

The heaviest egg reported is one of 454 g *16 oz*, with double yolk and double shell, laid by a White Leghorn at Vineland, New Jersey, USA on 25 Feb 1956. The largest recorded was one of 'nearly 12 oz' for a 5-yolked egg 31 cm *12¼ in* around the long axis and 22·8 cm *9 in* around the short, laid by a Black Minorca at Mr Stafford's Damsteads Farm, Mellor, Lancs, England in 1896. An egg of 1·47 g *0·05 oz* (27 × 22 mm *1·06 × 0·86 in*) was laid by a Leghorn/Ranger cross named 'Obedience' owned by Miss Verity Nicholson of Adstock Fields Farm House, Buckingham, Bucks, England on 12 Mar 1986.

The highest recorded annual average for a flock is 313 eggs in 52 weeks from a flock of 1000 Warren-Stadler SSL layers (from 21 weeks of age) by Eric Savage, White Lane Farm, Albury, Surrey, England in 1974–5.

Most yolks

The highest claim for the number of yolks in a chicken's egg is 9 reported by Mrs Diane Hainsworth of Hainsworth Poultry Farms, Mount Morris, New York in July 1971 and also from a hen in Kirgizya, USSR in August 1977.

Goose egg

The white goose 'Speckle' owned by Donny Brandenberg, of Goshen, Ohio, USA on 3 May 1977 laid a 680 g *24 oz* egg measuring 34 × 24 cm *13½ × 9½ in* in circumferences.

Duck

An Aylesbury duck belonging to Annette and Angela Butler of Princes Risborough, Bucks, England laid 457 eggs in 463 days including an unbroken run of 375 in as many days. The duck died on 7 Feb 1986. Another duck

of the same breed owned by Edmond Walsh of Gormanstown, Co Kildare, Ireland laid eggs every year right up to her 25th birthday. She died on 3 Dec 1978 aged 28 years 6 months.

Milk yields *Cows*

The highest recorded world lifetime yield of milk is 211 025 kg (207·68 tons *465 224 lb*) by the unglamorously named cow No. 289 owned by M. G. Maciel & Son of Hanford, California to 1 May 1984. The greatest yield of any British cow was that given by 'Winton Pel Eva 2' owned by John Waring of Glebe House, Kilnwick near Pocklington, Humberside, with 165 tonnes. The greatest recorded yield for one lactation (maximum 365 days) is 25 247 kg *55 661 lb* by the Holstein 'Beecher Arlinda Ellen' owned by Mr and Mrs Harold L. Beecher of Rochester, Indiana in 1975. The British lactation record (305 days) was set by 'Michaelwood Holm Emoselle 25' (b. 1 Aug 1973), a Friesian, owned by Mr and Mrs M. T. Holder of Aylesmore Farm, Newent, Gloucestershire with 19 400 kg *42 769 lb* in 1984–5.

The Irish lactation record (305 days) is held by 'Oriel Freda 10'(b.21 Feb 1978), a Friesian owned by Mellifont Abbey Trust, Collon, Co. Louth, Ireland with 21 513 kg in 1986. The highest reported milk yield in a day is 109·3 kg *241 lb* by 'Urbe Blanca' in Cuba on or about 23 June 1982.

Hand milking

Andy Faust at Collinsville, Oklahoma, USA in 1937 achieved 99·92 UK gal *120 US gal* in 12 hr.

Goats

The highest recorded milk yield for any goat is 3499 kg *7714 lb* in 365 days by 'Osory Snow-Goose' owned by Mr and Mrs G. Jameson of Leppington, NSW, Australia in 1977. A 15-year-old goat owned by Mrs Nanbui Meghani of Bhuj, Gujarat, India was reported in November 1984 to have lactated continuously for 12 years.

Butter fat yield

The world record lifetime yield is 7425 kg *16 370 lb* by the US Holstein 'Breezewood Patsy Bar Pontiac' in 3979 days. Her lactation record for 365 days of 1011 kg *2230 lb* was reported on 8 Oct 1976.

The British record butter fat yield in a lifetime is 5518 kg *12 166 lb* by the Ayrshire cow 'Craighead Welma' owned by W. Watson Steele from 273 072 lb at 4·45 per cent.

The British record for 365 days is 852 kg *1878 lb* by 'Michaelwood Holm Emoselle 25', a Friesian owned by Mick and Linda Holder of Aylesmore Farm, Newent, Gloucestershire. 'Michaelwood Holm Emoselle 25' went on to milk for a total of 295 days in her 8th lactation, producing an incredible 1 012 kg *2231 lb* of butterfat. The United Kingdom record for butter fat in one day is 4·53 kg *10 lb* by British Friesian 'Michaelwood Holm Emoselle 25'.

Cheese

The most active cheese-eaters are the people of France, with an annual average in 1983 of 19·8 kg *43·6 lb* per person. The world's biggest producer is the United States with a factory production of 4 773 500 000 lbs (2 200 000 tonnes *2 165 000 tons*) in 1980. The UK cheese consumption where 67 per cent is Cheddar in 1987 was 7·2 kg *15·87 lb* per head.

The oldest and most primitive cheeses are the Arabian *kishk*, made of dried curd of goats' milk. There are today 450 named cheeses in 18 major varieties, but many are merely named after different towns and differ only in shape or the method of packing. France has 240 varieties.

The world's most expensive cheese in its home market is Le Leruns made from ewes' milk at 90FF per kilo. Cheese made to the Liederkranz formula in Van Wert, USA retails for $2·25 per 4 oz; equivalent to $9·00 per lb. Britain's most costly cheese is Lanark Blue which is obtainable from some shops for £7·50 per lb.

HUMAN ACHIEVEMENTS

CHAPTER·TEN

555.3 m

Human fly ● Daniel Goodwin, 30, of California, USA climbed a record 342·9 m *1125 ft* up the outside of the 555·33 m *1822 ft* CN Tower in Toronto, Canada—the tallest self-supporting tower in the world—using neither climbing aids nor safety equipment. (Photo: Anne Marie Weber/ T.K.O. IMAGES)

Endurance and Endeavour

For the fastest speed at which humans have travelled, see Chapter 4.

Land speed

The highest reputed land speed is 1190·377 km/h *739·666 mph* or Mach 1·0106 by Stan Barrett (US) in *The Budweiser Rocket*, a rocket-engined 3-wheeled car at Edwards Air Force Base, California, USA on 17 Dec 1979 (see also p. 128).

The *official* one-mile land-speed record is 1019·467 km/h *633·468 mph* set by Richard Noble OBE (b. 1946) on 4 Oct 1983 over the Black Rock Desert, Nevada, USA, in his 17 000 lb thrust Rolls Royce Avon 302 jet-powered *Thrust 2*, designed by John Ackroyd.

The highest land speed attained in Britain is 424·74 km/h *263·92 mph* by Richard Noble in *Thrust 2* at Greenham Common, Berkshire on 25 Sept 1980.

The highest land speed recorded by a woman is 843·323 km/h *524·016 mph* by Mrs Kitty Hambleton *née* O'Neil (US) in the 48 000-hp rocket-powered 3-wheeled S.M.1 *Motivator* over the Alvard Desert, Oregon, USA on 6 Dec 1976. Her official two-way record was 825·126 km/h *512·710 mph* and she probably touched 965 km/h *600 mph* momentarily.

Water speed

The highest speed ever achieved on water is an estimated 300 knots (556 km/h *345 mph*) by Kenneth Peter Warby MBE (b. 9 May 1939) on the Blowering Dam Lake, NSW, Australia on 20 Nov 1977 in his unlimited hydroplane *Spirit of Australia*. The official world water speed record is 275·80 knots (511·11 km/h *317·60 mph*) set on 8 Oct 1978 by Warby on Blowering Dam Lake.

The fastest woman is Mary Rife (US), who has driven her drag boat *Proud Mary* at more than 305 km/h *190 mph*.

The highest speed recorded by a propeller-driven boat is 368·54 km/h *229·00 mph* by *The Texan*, a Kurtis top fuel hydro drag boat, driven by Eddie Hill on 5 Sept 1982 at Chowchilla, California, USA.

Most travelled

The world's most travelled man is Parke G. Thompson, a lawyer from Akron, Ohio, USA, who has visited all of the 170 sovereign countries and the 63 non-sovereign or other territories (see heading COUNTRIES, in Chapter Eleven, page 188). He is a member of the Travelers Century Club of Los Angeles, and his choice for the '7 wonders of the modern world' are Tahiti, Antarctica, the Himalaya mountain region, Hong Kong, the south island of New Zealand, Rio de Janeiro and the Alps.

The most travelled man in the horseback era was probably the Methodist preacher Francis Asbury (b. Birmingham, England), who travelled 424 850 km *264 000 miles* in North America from 1771 to 1815 preaching 16 000 sermons.

Most isolated

The farthest any human has been removed from his nearest living fellow man is 3596·4 km *2233·2 miles* in the case of the Command Service Module pilot Alfred M. Worden on the US *Apollo 15* lunar mission of 30 July–1 Aug 1971.

Round the world

The fastest time for a round-the-world trip on scheduled flights for a circumnavigation is 44 hr 6 min by David J. Springbett (b. 2 May 1938) of Taplow, Buckinghamshire. His route took him from Los Angeles eastabout via London, Bahrain, Singapore, Bangkok, Manila, Tokyo and Honolulu from 8–10 Jan 1980 over a 37 124 km *23 068 mile* course.

LONGEST WALKS

The first person reported to have 'walked round the world' is George Matthew Schilling (US) from 3 Aug 1897 to 1904, but the first verified achievement was by David Kunst (b. 1939, USA) from 10 June 1970 to 5 Oct 1974.

Tomas Carlos Pereira (b. Argentine, 16 Nov 1942) spent 10 years, 6 Apr 1968 to 8 Apr 1978, walking 48 000 km *29 825 miles* around all 5 continents.

Steven Newman of Bethal, Ohio, USA spent 4 years walking 36 200 km *22 500 miles* around the world, 1 Apr 1983 to 1 Apr 1987, covering 20 countries and all 5 continents.

Rick Hansen (b. Canada, 1957), who was paralysed from the waist down in 1973 as a result of a motor accident, wheeled his wheelchair over 40 074·06 km *24 901·55 miles*, through 4 continents and 34 countries. He started his journey from Vancouver on 21 Mar 1985 and arrived back on 22 May 1987.

George Meegan (b. 2 Oct 1952) from Rainham, Kent walked 30 431 km *19 019 miles* from Usuaia, the southern tip of South America, to Prudhoe Bay in northern Alaska, taking 2426 days from 26 Jan 1977 to 18 Sept 1983, and thus completed the first traverse of the western hemisphere.

Sean Eugene Maguire (b. USA, 15 Sept 1956) walked 11 791 km *7327 miles* from the Yukon River, north of Livengood, Alaska, to Key West, Florida, in 307 days, 6 June 1978 to 9 Apr 1979.

The trans-Canada (Halifax to Vancouver) record walk of 6057 km *3764 miles* is 96 days by Clyde McRae, 23, from 1 May to 4 Aug 1973.

John Lees (b. 23 Feb 1945) of Brighton, East Sussex between 11 Apr and 3 June 1972 walked 4628 km *2876 miles* across the USA from City Hall, Los Angeles to City Hall, New York in 53 days 12 hr 15 min (average 86·49 km *53·75 miles* a day).

Britain

The longest continuous walk in Britain is one of 10 982 km *6824 miles*, around the British coast by John N. Merrill (b. 19 Aug 1943), from 3 Jan to 8 Nov 1978.

Cathryn Townsend set a record for the longest continuous female walk in Britain by walking for a total distance of 8714 km *5416 miles* around the British coast, between 26 Oct 1986 and 2 Aug 1987, starting and finishing at the Palace Pier, Brighton.

North Pole conquest

The claim of neither of the 2 US Arctic explorers, Dr Frederick Albert Cook (1865–1940) and Cdr (later Rear-Ad.) Robert Edwin Peary (1856–1920), of the US Naval Civil Engineering branch, in reaching the North Pole is subject to positive proof. Cook, accompanied by the Eskimos Ah-pellah and Etukishook, 2 sledges and 26 dogs, struck north from a point 96·5 km *60 miles* north of Svartevoeg, on Axel Heiberg I., Canada, 740 km *460 miles* from the Pole on 21 Mar 1908, allegedly reaching Lat. 89° 31′ N on 19 Apr and the Pole on 21 Apr. Peary, accompanied by his assistant, Matthew Alexander Henson (1866–1955, USA) and the 4 Eskimos Ooqueah, Eginwah, Seegloo and Ootah (1875–1955), struck north from his Camp Bartlett (Lat. 87° 44′ N) at 5

MILESTONES IN ABSOLUTE HUMAN ALTITUDE RECORDS

Altitude m	ft	Pilot	Vehicle	Place		Date
24*	80	Jean François Pilâtre de Rozier (1757–85) (France)	Hot Air Balloon (tethered)	Fauxbourg, Paris	15 & 17	Oct 1783
c.100	c.330	de Rozier and the Marquis d'Arlandes (1742–1809) (France)	Hot Air Balloon (free flight)	LaMuette, Paris[1]	21	Nov 1783
c.900	c.3000	Dr Jacques-Alexandre-César Charles (1746–1823) and Ainé Robert (France)	Charlière Hydrogen Balloon	Tuileries, Paris	1	Dec 1783
c.2750	c.9000	Dr J.-A.-C. Charles (France)	Hydrogen Balloon	Nesles, France	1	Dec 1783
c.4000	c.13 000	James Sadler (GB)	Hydrogen Balloon	Manchester		May 1785
7740[2]	*25 400*	James Glaisher (1809–1903) (GB)	Hydrogen Balloon	Wolverhampton	17	July 1862
9615	31 500	Prof A. Berson (Germany)	Hydrogen Balloon Phoenix	Strasbourg, France	4	Dec 1894
11 145	36 565	Sadi Lecointe (France)	Nieuport Aircraft	Issy-les-Moulineaux, France	30	Oct 1923
15 837	51 961	Prof Auguste Piccard and Paul Kipfer (Switzerland)	FNRS I Balloon	Augsburg, Germany	27	May 1931
22 066	72 395	Capts Orvill A. Anderson and Albert W. Stevens (US Army Air Corps)	US Explorer II Helium Balloon	Rapid City, South Dakota, USA	11	Nov 1935
24 262	79 600	William Barton Bridgeman (USA)	US Douglas D558—11 *Skyrocket*	California, USA	15	Aug 1951
38 465	126 200	Capt Iven C. Kincheloe, Jr (USAF)	US Bell X-2 Rocket plane	California, USA	7	Sept 1956
51 694	169 600	Joseph A. Walker (USA)	US X-15 Rocket plane	California, USA	30	Mar 1961

km	Statute miles					
327	203·2	Flt-Major Yuriy A. Gagarin (USSR) (1934–68)	USSR *Vostok I Capsule*	Orbital flight	12	Apr 1961
377 657	234 672	Col Frank Borman, USAF, Capt James Arthur Lovell, Jr, USN and Major William A. Anders, USAF	US *Apollo VIII* Command Module	Circum-lunar flight	25	Dec 1968
400 171	248 655	Capt James Arthur Lovell Jr, USN, Frederick Wallace Haise Jr and John L. Swigert Jr (1931–82)	US *Apollo XIII*	Abortive lunar landing mission	15	Apr 1970

* There is some evidence that Father Bartolomeu de Gusmo flew in his hot-air balloon in his 4th experiment post August 1709 in Portugal.

[1] Duration c.1.54 to 2.16 pm from Château de LaMuette to Butte aux Cailles, Paris 13e. Volume of the 21·3 m 70 ft high balloon was 60 000 'piedcubes' c.1700 m³.

[2] Glaisher, with Henry Tracey Coxwell (1819–1900) claimed 11 275 m 37 000 ft from Wolverhampton on 5 Sept 1862. Some writers accept 9145 m 30 000 ft.

A complete progressive table comprising entries from 1783 to date was published in the 1977 edition.

PROGRESSIVE SPEED RECORDS

km/h	Speed mph	Person and Vehicle	Place	Date
40	25	Sledging	Heinola, Finland	c.6500 BC
55	35	Horse-riding	Anatolia, Turkey	c.1400 BC
70	45	Mountain Sledging	Island of Hawaii (now USA)	ante AD 1500
80	50	Ice Yachts (earliest patent)	Netherlands	AD 1600
95	56·75	Grand Junction Railway 2–2–2: *Lucifer*	Madeley Banks, Staffs, England	13 Nov 1830
141·3	87·8	Tommy Todd, downhill skier	La Porte, California, USA	Mar 1873
144·8	90·0	Midland Railway 4–2–2 2·36 m *7 ft 9 in* single	Ampthill, Bedford, England	Mar 1897
210·2	130·61	Siemens and Halske electric engine	Marienfeld-Zossen, near Berlin	27 Oct 1903
c.257·5	c.150	Frederick H. Marriott (fl. 1957) Stanley Steamer *Wogglebug*	Ormond Beach, Florida, USA	26 Jan 1907
339	210·64	Sadi Lecointe (France) Nieuport-Delage 29	Villesauvage, France	25 Sept 1921
668·2	415·2	Flt Lt (Later Wing Cdr) George Hedley Stainforth AFC *Supermarine S.6B*	Lee-on-Solent, England	29 Sept 1931
1004	623·85	Flugkapitan Heinz Dittmar *Me. 163V–1*	Peenemunde, Germany	2 Oct 1941
1078	670	Capt Charles Elwood Yeager, USAF *Bell XS–1*	Muroc Dry Lake, California, USA	14 Oct 1947
1556	967	Capt Charles Elwood Yeager, USAF *Bell XS–1*	Muroc Dry Lake, California, USA	26 Mar 1948
4675·1	2905	Major Robert M. White, North American *X–15*	Muroc Dry Lake, California, USA	7 Mar 1961
c.28 260	c.17 560	Flt Maj Yuriy Alekseyevich Gagarin, *Vostok 1*	Earth orbit	12 Apr 1961
38 988	24 226	Col Frank Borman, USAF, Capt James Arthur Lovell, Jr, USN, Major William A. Anders, USAF *Apollo VIII*	Trans-lunar injection	21 Dec 1968
39 897	24 790·8	Cdrs Eugene Andrew Cernan and John Watts Young, USN and Col Thomas P. Stafford, USAF *Apollo X*	Re-entry after lunar orbit	26 May 1969

A complete progressive table comprising entries from prehistoric times to date was published in the 1977 edition.

a.m. on 2 Apr 1909. After travelling another 215 km *134 miles*, he allegedly established his final camp, Camp Jessup, in the proximity of the Pole at 10 a.m. on 6 Apr and marched a further 67·5 km *42 miles* quartering the sea-ice before turning south at 4 p.m. on 7 Apr. On excellent pack ice and modern sledges Wally Herbert's 1968–9 expedition (see heading 'Arctic crossing') attained a best day's route mileage of 37 km *23 miles* in 15 hr. Cook claimed 41·8 km *26 miles* twice while Peary claimed a surely unsustainable average of 61 km *38 miles* over 8 consecutive days.

The earliest indisputable attainment of the North Pole over the sea-ice was at 3 p.m. (Central Standard Time) on 19 Apr 1968 by Ralph Plaisted (US) and 3 companions after a 42-day trek in 4 Skidoos (snow-mobiles). Their arrival was independently verified 18 hr later by a US Air Force weather aircraft. The sea bed is 4087 m *13 410 ft* below the North Pole.

Naomi Uemura (1941–84), the Japanese explorer and mountaineer, became the first person to reach the North Pole in a solo trek across the Arctic ice cap at 4.45 a.m. GMT on 1 May 1978. He had travelled 725 km *450 miles* setting out on 7 Mar from Cape Edward, Ellesmere Island in northern Canada. He averaged nearly 13 km *8 miles* per day with his sled 'Aurora' drawn by 17 huskies.

Dr Jean-Louis Etienne, 39, was the first to reach the Pole solo and without dogs, on 11 May 1986 after 63 days. On 20 Apr 1987 Fukashi Kazami, 36, of Tokyo reached the North Pole from Ward Hunt Island, northern Canada in 44 days having started on his 250-cc motorcycle on 8 March.

The first woman to set foot on the North Pole was Mrs Fran Phipps on 5 Apr 1971. Galina Aleksandrovna Lastovskaya (b. 1941) and Lilia Vladislavovna Minina (b. 1959) were crew members of the USSR atomic ice-breaker *Arktika* which reached the Pole on 17 Aug 1977.

The Soviet scientist Dr Pavel A. Gordienko and 3 companions were arguably the first ever to stand on the exact point Lat. 90° 00′ 00″ N (±300 metres) on 23 Apr 1948.

South Pole conquest

The first men to cross the Antarctic circle (Lat. 66° 33′S) were the 193 crew of the *Resolution* (462 tonnes/*tons*) (Capt James Cook, RN (1728–79)) and *Adventure* (336 tonnes/*tons*) (Lt T. Furneaux) on 17 Jan 1773 in 39° E. The first person known to have sighted the Antarctic ice shelf was Capt. F. F. Bellinghausen (USSR) (1778–1852) on 27 Jan 1820 from the vessels *Vostock* and *Mirnyi*. The first known to have sighted the mainland of the continent was Capt. William Smith (1790–1847) and Master Edward Bransfield, RN, in the brig *Williams*. They saw the peaks of Trinity Land 3 days later on 30 Jan 1820.

The South Pole (alt. 2779 m *9186 ft* on ice and 102 m *336 ft* bed rock) was first reached at 11 a.m. on 16 Dec 1911 by a Norwegian party led by Capt. Roald Engebereth Gravning Amundsen (1872–1928), after a 53-day march with dog sledges from the Bay of Whales, to which he had penetrated in the *Fram*. Subsequent calculations showed that Olav Olavson Bjaaland (the last survivor, dying in June 1961, aged 88) and Helmer Hanssen probably passed within 400–600 m *1310–1970 ft* of the exact pole. The other 2 members were Sverre H. Hassell (d. 1928) and Oskar Wisting (d. 1936).

The first woman to set foot on Antarctica was Mrs Karoline Mikkelsen on 20 Feb 1935. No woman stood on the South Pole until 11 Nov 1969. On that day Lois Jones, Eileen McSaveney, Jean Pearson, Terry Lee Tickhill (all US), Kay Lindsay (Australia) and Pam Young (NZ) arrived by air.

First on both Poles

Dr Albert P. Crary (US) (1911-87) reached the North Pole in a Dakota aircraft on 3 May 1952. On 12 Feb 1961 he arrived at the South Pole by Sno Cat on a scientific traverse party from the McMurdo Station.

Arctic crossing

The first crossing of the Arctic sea-ice was achieved by the British Trans-Arctic Expedition which left Point Barrow, Alaska on 21 Feb 1968 and arrived at the Seven Island archipelago north-east of Spitzbergen 464 days later on 29 May 1969 after a haul of 4699 km *2920 statute miles* and a drift of 1126 km *700 miles* compared with the straight-line distance of 2674 km *1662 miles*. The team comprised Wally Herbert (leader), 34, Major Ken Hedges, 34, RAMC, Allan Gill, 38, and Dr Roy Koerner, 36 (glaciologist), and 40 huskies. The only crossing achieved in a single season was that by Fiennes and Burton (see heading 'Polar circumnavigation') from Alert via the North Pole to the Greenland Sea in open snowmobiles.

Antarctic crossing

The first surface crossing of the Antarctic continent was completed at 1.47 p.m. on 2 Mar 1958, after a trek of 3473 km *2158 miles* lasting 99 days from 24 Nov 1957, from Shackleton Base to Scott Base via the Pole. The crossing party of 12 was led by Dr (now Sir) Vivian Ernest Fuchs (b. 11 Feb 1908). The 4185 km *2600 mile* trans-Antarctic leg from Sanae to Scott Base of the 1980–82 Trans-Globe Expedition was achieved in 66 days from 26 Oct 1980 to 11 Jan 1981 having passed through the South Pole on 23 Dec 1980. The 3-man party on snowmobiles comprised Sir Ranulph Fiennes (b. 1944), Oliver Shepard and Charles Burton.

Polar circumnavigation

The first polar circumnavigation was achieved by Sir Ranulph Fiennes, Bt and Charles Burton of the British Trans-Globe Expedition who travelled south from Greenwich (2 Sept 1979), via the South Pole (17 Dec 1980) and the North Pole (11 Apr 1982), and back to Greenwich arriving after a 56 325 km *35 000 mile* trek on 29 Aug 1982.

Longest sledge journeys

The longest totally self-supporting Polar sledge journey ever made was one of 1738 km *1080 miles* from west to east across Greenland (now Kalaallit Nunaat) from 18 June to 5 Sept 1934 by Capt. M. Lindsay (1905–1981) (later Sir Martin Lindsay of Dowhill, Bt, CBE, DSO), Lt Arthur S. T. Godfrey, RE (later Lt. Col., k. 1942), Andrew N. C. Croft (later Col., DSO) and 49 dogs. The Ross Sea Party of 10 (3 died) sledged over 3220 km *2000 miles* in 300 days from 6 May 1975.

Greatest ocean descent

The record ocean descent was achieved in the Challenger Deep of the Marianas Trench, 400 km *250 miles* south-west of Guam, in the Pacific Ocean, when the Swiss-built US Navy bathyscaphe *Trieste*, manned by Dr Jacques Piccard (b. 1914) (Switzerland) and Lt Donald Walsh, USN reached 10 917 m (*35 820 ft 6·78 miles*) down, at 1.10 p.m. on 23 Jan 1960 (see page 54). The pressure of the water was 1183 kgf/cm^2 *16 883 lbf/in^2* and the temperature 3° C *37·4° F*. The descent took 4 hr 48 min and the ascent 3 hr 17 min.

Deep diving records

The record depth for the extremely dangerous activity of breath-held diving is 105 m *344 ft* by Jacques Mayol (France) off Elba, Italy, in December 1983. He descended on a sled in 104 seconds and ascended in 90 seconds. The record for women is 75 m *246 ft ¾ in* by Rossana Majorca off Syracuse, Sicily on 31 July 1987.

The record dive with scuba (self-contained under-water breathing apparatus) is 133 m *437 ft* by John J. Gruener and R. Neal Watson (US) off Freeport, Grand Bahama on 14 Oct 1968. For women it is 105·16 m *345 ft* by Marty Dunwoody (US) off Bimini, Bahama Islands.

The record dive utilising gas mixtures (nitrogen, oxygen and helium) is a simulated dive of 685·8 m *2250 ft* in a dry chamber by Stephen Porter, Len Whitlock and Erik Kramer at Duke University Medical Center in Durham, North Carolina, USA on 3 Feb 1981 in a 43-day trial in a sphere of 2·43 m *8 ft*. Patrick Raude and 5 Comex divers left and returned to the bell 'Petrel' at 501 m *1643 ft*, off Cavalaire, France, in 1982.

Deepest underwater escapes

The deepest underwater rescue achieved was of the *Pisces III* in which Roger R. Chapman, 28, and Roger Mallinson, 35, were trapped for 76 hr when it sank to 480 m *1575 ft*, 240 km *150 miles* south-east of Cork, Ireland on 29 Aug 1973. She was hauled to the surface by the cable ship *John Cabot* after work by *Pisces V*, *Pisces II* and the remote control recovery vessel US CURV on 1 Sept. The greatest depth of an actual escape without any equipment has been from 68·58 m *225 ft* by Richard A. Slater from the rammed submersible *Nekton Beta* off Catalina Island, California, USA on 28 Sept 1970. The record for an escape with equipment was by Norman Cooke and Hamish Jones on 22 July 1987. During a naval exercise they escaped from a depth of 183 m *601 ft* from the submarine HMS *Otus* in Bjornefjorden, off Bergen, Norway, wearing standard suits with a built-in lifejacket, from which air expanding during the ascent passes into a hood over the escaper's head.

MARINE CIRCUMNAVIGATION RECORDS

(Compiled by Sq Ldr D. H. Clarke DFC, AFC)

A true circumnavigation entails passing through two antipodal points which are at least 20 000 km *12 429 statute miles* apart. A non-stop circumnavigation is entirely self-maintained; no water supplies, provisions, equipment or replacements of any sort may be taken aboard en route. Vessel may anchor, but no physical help may be accepted apart from passing mail or messages.

CATEGORY	VESSEL	NAME	START	FINISH
EARLIEST	*Vittoria* Expedition of Fernão de Magalhães, *c.* 1480–k. 1521	Juan Sebastián de Elcano or del Cano (d. 1526) and 17 crew	Seville, Spain 20 Sept 1519	San Lucar, 6 Sept 1522, 49 400 km *30 700 miles*
EARLIEST BRITISH	*Golden Hind* (ex *Pelican*) 100 tonnes	Francis Drake (*c.* 1540–96) (Knighted 4 April 1581)	Plymouth, 13 Dec 1577	26 Sept 1580
EARLIEST WOMAN	*Etoile* (Storeship for Bougainville's La Boudeuse)	Crypto-female valet of M. de Commerson, named Baré	St Malo, 1766	1769
EARLIEST FORE-AND-AFT RIGGED VESSEL	*Union* 98 tons (Sloop)	John Boit Junior, 19–21, (US) and 22 crew	Newport, RI 1794 (via Cape Horn westabout)	Newport, RI 1796
EARLIEST YACHT	*Nancy Dawson* Schooner	Robert Shedden (GB) and crew	Thames, 1847	Thames, 1850 (owner died in Mexico, 1849)
EARLIEST YACHT OWNERS	*Sunbeam* 51·8 m *170 ft* 3 Mast Topsail schooner	Lord and Lady Brassey (GB) passengers and crew	Cowes, Isle of Wight 1876	Cowes, Isle of Wight 1877
EARLIEST SOLO	*Spray* 11·20 m *36¾ ft* Gaff yawl	Capt Joshua Slocum, 51, (US) (a non-swimmer) (No 1 solo circum)	Newport, RI, via Magellan Straits, 24 Apr 1895	3 July 1898 74 000 km *46 000 miles* (100 mpd)
EARLIEST TRIMARAN	*Victress* 12·19 m *40 ft* Bermudan ketch	Nigel Tetley (GB) (b. S. Africa)	Plymouth 1968 (W–E via Horn)	1969 (trimaran sank after circumnavigation was completed)
EARLIEST SOLO CATAMARAN	*Amon-Re* 7·97 m *26 ft 2 in* Bermudan sloop	Alan Butler (Canada)	Barbados 1980 (E–W via Panama)	Barbados 1986 (also smallest catamaran to circumnavigate)
EARLIEST MOTOR BOAT	*Speejacks* 29·87 m *98 ft*	Albert Y. Gowen (US) wife and crew	New York City 1921	New York City 1922
EARLIEST SOLO MOTOR BOAT	*Mabel E. Holland* 12·8 m *42 ft* (no sails)	David Scott Cowper (GB)	Plymouth 1984 (via Panama Canal)	Plymouth 170 days 2 hr 15 min (165·7 mpd)
EARLIEST WOMAN SOLO	*Mazurek* 9·5 m *31 ft 2 in* Bermudan sloop	Krystyna Chojnowska-Liskiewicz (Poland) (No 58 solo circum)	Las Palmas 28 Mar 1976 (westabout via Panama)	Tied knot 21 Mar 1978
EARLIEST WOMAN NON-STOP SOLO	*First Lady* 11·24 m *37 ft* Bermudan sloop	Kay Cottee (Australia)	Sydney 1987 (W–E via Horn)	Sydney 1988
SMALLEST BOAT	*Acrohc Australis* 3·6 m *11 ft 10 in* Bermudan sloop	Sergio Testa (Australia)	Brisbane, 1984	Brisbane, 1987 (500 sailing days)
EARLIEST KNIGHT	*Glory* 6 m *19 ft 8 in* Junk sloop	Sir Henry Pigott Bt	Poole June 1983	Poole Feb 1986
EARLIEST SUBMERGED	US Submarine *Triton*	Capt Edward L. Beach USN plus 182 crew	New London, Connecticut 16 Feb 1960	10 May 1960 49 422 km *39 708 miles*
EARLIEST NON-STOP SOLO (Port to Port)	*Suhaili* 9·87 m *32·4 ft* Bermudan ketch	Robin Knox Johnston CBE (b. 1939) (No 25 solo circum)	Falmouth, 14 June 1968	22 Apr 1969 (312 days)
MOST NON-STOP SOLO CIRCUMNAVIGATIONS	*Parry Endeavour* 13·92 m *44 ft* Bermudan sloop	Jon Sanders (Australia)	Fremantle, 25 May 1986	Fremantle, 13 Mar 1988 (3 circumnavigations in 657 days)
FASTEST SOLO (speed) (multihull)	*Kriter Brut de Brut* 23·5 m *75 ft* Trimaran	Philippe Monnet (France) (No 120 solo circum)	Brest 1986 (via Cape Town)	Brest 1987 127 days 12 hr 11 min (210·4 mpd)
EARLIEST SOLO IN BOTH DIRECTIONS	*Solitaire* 10·36 m *34 ft* Bermudan sloop	Leslie Thomas Powles (GB) (Nos 62 & 71 solo circum)	Falmouth 1975 (E–W) Lymington 1980 (W–E)	(via Panama) Lymington 1978 (via Horn) Lymington 1981
EARLIEST SOLO IN BOTH DIRECTIONS (via Horn)	*Ocean Bound* 12·52 m *41 ft 1 in* Bermudan sloop	David Scott Cowper (GB) (Nos 66 & 78 solo circum)	Plymouth 1979 (W–E) Plymouth 1981 (E–W)	Plymouth 1980 Plymouth 1982 (see below)
FASTEST SOLO NON-STOP (time and speed)	*American Promise* 18·3 m *60 ft* Bermudan sloop	Dodge Morgan (US)	Bermuda 12 Nov 1985 (W–E via Horn)	Bermuda 11 Apr 1986 150 days 1 hr 6 min (171·1 mpd)
FASTEST TIME AND FASTEST SPEED (yacht)	UBS *Switzerland* 24·38 m *80 ft* Bermudan sloop	Pierre Fehlmann (Swiss) and crew	Portsmouth 1985	Portsmouth 1986 117 days 14 hr 31 min (238 mpd)
FASTEST (clipper)	*James Baines* 81·07 m *266 ft*	Capt C. McDonald (GB) and crew	Liverpool to Melbourne (58 days) 1854	Melbourne to Liverpool (69 days) 1855
FASTEST SOLO WESTABOUT (via Cape Horn)	*Ocean Bound* 12·52 m *41 ft 1 in* Bermudan sloop	David Scott Cowper (GB) (No 78 solo circum)	Plymouth 22 Sept 1981 (south of 5 capes)	Plymouth 17 May 1982 221 days (141·85 mpd)
FASTEST-EVER TIME (yacht) (short circumnavigation)	*Awahnee II* 16·15 m *53 ft* Bermudan cutter	Bob Griffith (US) (5 crew)	Bluff, NZ 1970 (W–E via Horn)	Bluff, NZ, 1971 (88 sailing days plus 23 days stopovers)
FASTEST-EVER TIME (clipper)	*Red Jacket* 79·24 m *260 ft*	Capt S. Reid (GB) and crew	From/to Lat 26° 25' W (via Horn)	62 days 22 hr 1854
MOST SOLO CIRCUMNAVIGATIONS	*Perie Banou* and *Parry Endeavour*	Jon Sanders (Australia)	Fremantle 1981 Fremantle 1986	Fremantle 1982 (twice) Fremantle 1988 (thrice)
MOST CIRCUMNAVIGATIONS ALONE BY HUSBAND/WIFE	*Myomie* 11 m *36 ft* Gaff ketch	Al Gehrman (US) Helen (wife)	Florida 1961, 1966, 1972, 1979	Florida 1964, 1970, 1976, 1983

* Eduard Roditi, author of *Magellan of the Pacific*, advances the view that Magellan's slave, Enrique, was the first circumnavigator. He had been purchased in Malacca and it was shown that he already understood the Filipino dialect Vizayan, when he reached the Philippines from the east. He 'tied the knot' off Limasawa on 28 Mar 1521. The first to circumnavigate in both directions was Capt Tobias Furneaux, RN (1735–81) as second lieutenant aboard the *Dolphin* from/to Plymouth east to west via the Magellan Straits from 1766–68 and as captain of the *Adventure* from/to Plymouth west to east via Cape Horn in 1772–4.

Deepest salvage

The greatest depth at which salvage has been achieved is 5029 m *16 500 ft* by the bathyscaphe *Trieste II* (Lt Cdr Mel Bartels, USN), to attach cables to an 'electronic package' on the sea bed 645 km *400 miles* north of Hawaii on 20 May 1972.

Flexible dress divers

The deepest salvage operation ·ever achieved with divers was on the wreck of HM cruiser *Edinburgh* sunk on 2 May 1942 in the Barents Sea off northern Norway inside the Arctic Circle in 244·7 m *803 ft* of water. Twelve divers dived on the wreck in pairs using a bell from the *Stephaniturm* (1423 tons) over 32 days under the direction of former RN officer Michael Stewart from 17 Sept to 7 Oct 1981.

A total of 460 gold ingots was recovered and was divided thus: £14·6 million to the USSR, £7·3 million to HM Government and some £22 million to the salvage contractors, Jessop Marine Recoveries Ltd (10 per cent) and Wharton Williams Ltd (90 per cent). John Rossier, 28, was the first to touch the gold. The longest decompression time was 7 days 10 hr 27 min. The £43·4 million is an all-time 100 per cent record.

Greatest penetration into the earth

The deepest penetration made into the ground by man is in the Western Deep Levels Mine at Carletonville, Transvaal, South Africa where a record depth of 3777 m (*12 391 ft 2·34 miles*) was attained, temperature 55° C *131° F.*

Longest on a raft

The longest recorded survival alone on a raft is 133 days (4½ months) by Second Steward Poon Lim (b. Hong Kong) of the UK Merchant Navy, whose ship, the SS *Ben Lomond*, was torpedoed in the Atlantic 910 km *565 miles* west of St Paul's Rocks in Lat. 00° 30′ N Long. 38° 45′ W at 11.45 a.m. on 23 Nov 1942. He was picked up by a Brazilian fishing boat off Salinópolis, Brazil on 5 Apr 1943 and could walk ashore. In July 1943 he was awarded the BEM and now lives in New York City.

Maurice and Maralyn Bailey of Derby survived 118⅓ days in an inflatable dinghy 1·37 m *4½ ft* in diameter in the Pacific from 4 Mar to 30 June 1973.

Shaft-sinking record

The one-month (31 days) world record is 381·3 m *1251 ft* for a standard shaft 7·92 m *26 ft* in diameter at Buffelsfontein Mine, Transvaal, South Africa, in March 1962. The British record of 131·2 m *430 ft* of 7·92 m *26 ft* diameter

shaft was set in No. 2 Shaft of the NCB's Whitemoor Mine Selby, North Yorkshire in 31 days (15 Nov–16 Dec 1982).

Most marriages

The greatest number of marriages accumulated in the monogamous world is 27 by former Baptist minister Glynn 'Scotty' Wolfe (b. 25 July 1908) of Blythe, California, USA, who first married in 1927. His latest wife is Daisy Delgado (b. 29 Dec 1970), a Filipino from Liloan, Cebu. His previous oldest wife was 38. His total number of children is, he says, 41. Mrs Beverly Nina Avery, then aged 48, a barmaid from Los Angeles, California, USA, set a monogamous world record in October 1957 by obtaining her 16th divorce from her 14th husband, Gabriel Avery. She alleged outside the court that five of the 14 had broken her nose.

The record for bigamous marriages is 104 by Giovanni Vigliotto, one of some 50 aliases used by either Fred Jipp (b. New York City, 3 Apr 1936) or Nikolai Peruskov (b. Siracusa, Sicily, 3 Apr 1929) during 1949–81 in 27 US states and 14 other countries. Four victims were aboard one ship in 1968 and two in London. On 28 Mar 1983 in Phoenix, Arizona, USA he received 28 years for fraud, 6 for bigamy and was fined $336 000.

> **Atlantic crossing ●** The fastest east to west sailing of the Atlantic was achieved by Philippe Poupon (France) in the 1988 single-handed transatlantic race. He left Plymouth on 7 June in his 18·29 m *60 ft* trimaran *Fleury Michon (IX)* and reached Newport, Rhode Island on 16 June, in a record time of 10 days 9 hrs 15 mins. (Photo: Gamma)

In Britain, the only monogamous citizen who married eight men is Olive Joyce Wilson of Marston Green, Birmingham. She has consecutively been Mrs John Bickley; Mrs Don Trethowan; Mrs George Hundley; Mrs Raymond Ward; Mrs Harry Latrobe; Mrs Leslie Harris; Mrs Ray Richards, and now Mrs John Grassick. All were divorced except Mr Hundley, who died.

Oldest bride and bridegroom

The oldest bridegroom has been Harry Stevens, 103, who married Thelma Lucas, 84, at the Caravilla Retirement Home, Wisconsin on 3 Dec 1984.

The British record was set by Sir Robert Mayer CH, KCVO (1879–1985) who married Jacqueline Noble, 51, in London on 10 Nov 1980 when aged 101 years. Mrs Winifred Clark (b. 13 Nov 1871) became Britain's oldest recorded bride when she married Albert Smith, 80, at St

CATEGORY	NAME	VESSEL	START	FINISH	DURATION	DATE
FASTEST (Trans-Pac)	Bob Hanel (US) & 6 crew	*Double Bullet* (BM Sloop—Cat)	Los Angeles	Hawaii	7 days 7 hr 31 min 325·5 mpd	1983
FASTEST YACHT (Australia–Horn)	O. K. Pennendreft (Fr) & 13 crew	*Kriter II* 24·38 m *80 ft*	Sydney	Cape Horn	21 days (275 mpd)	1975–6
FASTEST CLIPPER (Australia–Horn)	Capt J. N. Forbes (GB) & crew	*Lightning* 74·36 m *244 ft*	Melbourne	Cape Horn	19 days 1 hr (315 mpd)	1854
FASTEST SOLO MONOHULL (Australia–Horn)	Philippe Jeantot (Fr)	*Crédit Agricole* 17·07 m *56 ft*	Sydney	Cape Horn	29 days 23 hr (5709 miles=190·6 mpd)	1982–3
EARLIEST SOLO (Woman)	Sharon Sites Adams (US)	*Sea Sharp II* 9·45 m *31 ft*	Yokohama, Japan	San Diego, Cal.	75 days (5911 miles)	1969
EARLIEST ROWING	John Fairfax (GB) Sylvia Cook (GB)	*Britannia II* 10·66 m *35 ft*	San Francisco 26 Apr 1971	Hayman I., Australia 22 Apr 1972	362 days	1971–2
EARLIEST ROWING SOLO	Peter Bird (GB)	*Hele-on-Britannia* 9·75 m *32 ft*	San Francisco 23 Aug 1982	Gt Barrier Reef, Australia 14 June 1983	294 days 14 480 km 9000 miles	1982–3
FASTEST 2-CREW ROW	Curtis Saville (US) Kathleen (wife)	*Excalibur Pacific* 7·75 m *25 ft 5 in*	Callao, Peru	Australia	193 days rowing (approx 43 mpd)	1984–6
EARLIEST SOLO (Totally Blind)	Hank Dekker (US)	*Dark Star* 7·79 m *25 ft 7 in* (BM Sloop)	San Francisco	Honolulu	23 days (Braille charts, compass and loran)	1983
EARLIEST RAFT (Shore to shore)	Vital Alsar (Sp) & 3 crew	*La Balsa* (Balsa logs) 12·8 m *42 ft*	Guayaquil Ecuador	Mooloolaba Australia	160 days	1970

TRANS–PACIFIC MARINE RECORDS
(Compiled by Sq Ldr D. H. Clarke DFC, AFC)

N.B.——The earliest single-handed Pacific crossings were achieved East–West by Bernard Gilboy (US) in 1882 in the 5·48 m *18 ft* double-ender *Pacific* to Australia and West–East by Fred Rebel (Latvia) in the 5·48 m *18 ft Elaine*, (from Australia) and Edward Miles (US) in the 11·2 m *36¾ ft Sturdy II* (from Japan) both in 1932, the latter via Hawaii.

Endurance and Endeavour

TRANS–ATLANTIC MARINE RECORDS

(Compiled by Sq Ldr D. H. Clarke DFC, AFC)

CATEGORY	NAME	VESSEL	START	FINISH	DURATION	DATE
EARLIEST SOLO SAILING (E–W)	Josiah Shackford (US)	15-ton Gaff sloop	Bordeaux, France	Surinam (Guiana)	35 days	1786
EARLIEST ROWING (fastest crew row)	John Brown & 5 British deserters from garrison	Ship's boat c. 6·1 m 20 ft	St Helena (10 June)	Belmonte, Brazil (fastest ever row)	28 days (83 mpd) (see 2-crew row)	1799
EARLIEST CROSSING (2 men)	C. R. Webb & 1 crew (US)	Charter Oak 13·1 m 43 ft	New York	Liverpool	35 days 15 hr	1857
EARLIEST TRIMARAN (Raft)	John Mikes & 2 crew (US)	Non Pareil, 7·62 m 25 ft	New York	Southampton	51 days	1868
EARLIEST SOLO SAILING (W–E)	Alfred Johnson (US)	Centennial 6·09 m 20 ft	Glos., Mass	Wales	46 days	1876
EARLIEST WOMAN (with US husband)	Mrs Joanna Crapo (b. Scotland) (Thomas Crapo)	New Bedford 6·09 m 20 ft (Bermudan ketch)	Chatham, Mass.	Newlyn, Cornwall	51 days (Earliest with Bermudan rig)	1877
EARLIEST SINGLE-HANDED RACE	J. W. Lawlor (US) (winner)	Sea Serpent 4·57 m 15 ft	Boston (21 June)	Coverack, Cornwall	45 days	1891
EARLIEST ROWING BY 2 MEN (fastest 2-crew)	Georg Harboe & Frank Samuelsen (Nor)	Fox 5·58 m 18⅓ ft	New York City (6 June)	Isles of Scilly (1 Aug)	55 days (56 mpd) (see solo rows)	1897
EARLIEST MOTOR-BOAT	William C. Newman (US) Edward (son)	Abiel Abbott Low 11·58 m 38 ft (Engine: 10hp kerosene)	New York	Falmouth	36 days (83·3 mpd)	1902
EARLIEST OUTBOARD	Al Grover (US) Dante (son)	Trans-Atlantic 7·92 m 26 ft (2·65 hp Evinrudes)	St Pierre NF	Lisbon	34 days (88 mpd approx)	1985
EARLIEST CANOE (with sail)	Franz Romer (Germany)	Deutscher Sport 6·55 m 21½ ft	Las Palmas	St Thomas	58 days (47 mpd)	1928
EARLIEST WOMAN SOLO (East–West)	Ann Davison (GB)	Felicity Ann 7·01 m 23 ft	Portsmouth Las Palmas	Dominica (20 Nov 1952)	65 days	1952–3
EARLIEST WOMAN SOLO (W–E)	Gladys Gradeley (US)	Lugger 5·5 m 18 ft	Nova Scotia	Hope Cove, Devon	60 days	1903
EARLIEST WOMAN SOLO (both directions)	Ingeborg von Heister (Ger)	Ultima Ratio 10·67 m 35 ft (Tri)	Las Palmas Bermuda	Barbados Gibraltar	33 days 46 days	1969 1970
EARLIEST WOMAN SOLO (across 2 oceans)	Anna Woolf (SA)	Zama Zulu 13·1 m 43 ft (Ferroconcrete)	Cape Town	Bowling, Scotland	8920 miles in 109 days	1976
FASTEST 2-WOMAN CREW	Annick Martin (Fr) Annie Cordelle (Fr)	Super Marches Bravo 13·7 m 45 ft	Plymouth	Newport, R.I.	21 days 4 hr 28 min	1981
SMALLEST WEST–EAST	Wayne Dickinson (US)	God's Tear 2·71 m 8 ft 11 in	Allerton, Mass. (30 Oct)	Aranmore Is. NW Eire (20 Mar)	142 days	1982–3
SMALLEST EAST–WEST (Southern)	Eric Peters (GB)	Toniky-Nou 1·79 m 5 ft 10½ in (barrel)	Las Palmas (25 Dec)	St Françoise, Guadeloupe (8 Feb)	46 days	1982–3
FASTEST CROSSING SAILING (East–West)	Philippe Poupon (France)	Fleury Michon (IX) Trimaran 18·29 m 60 ft	Plymouth	Newport, R.I.	10 days 9 hr 15 min	1988
FASTEST CROSSING UNDER SAIL (West–East)	Serge Madec (France) & crew	Jet Services 5 Catamaran 22·86 m 75 ft	Ambrose	Lizard	7 days 6 hr 30 min	1988
FASTEST CROSSING (power) (West–East)	Richard Branson and crew (GB)	Virgin Atlantic Challenger II	Ambrose	Bishops Rock	3 days 8 hr 31 min	1986
FASTEST CROSSING SAILING SHIP (West–East)	A. Eldridge (US) & crew	Red Jacket (Clipper) 79·24 m 260 ft	Sandy Hook, NJ	Liverpool Bar	12 days 277·7 mpd	1854
FASTEST SOLO EAST–WEST (Northern) (monohull)	Kazimierz Jaworski (Poland)	Spaniel II 17·06 m 56 ft	Plymouth	Newport, R.I.	19 days 13 hr 25 min	1980
FASTEST EAST–WEST (Northern) monohull	Bruno Bacilieri (It) Marc Vallin	Faram Serenissima 20·27 m 66½ ft	Plymouth	Newport, R.I.	16 days 1 hr 25 min	1981
FASTEST SOLO EAST–WEST (Northern) (multihull)	Philip Weld (US)	Moxie Trimaran 15·54 m 51 ft	Plymouth	Newport, R.I.	17 days 23 hr 12 min	1980
FASTEST EVER YACHT SAIL (N. route) (East–West)	Loic Caradec (Fr) Oliver Despaigne	Royale 25·9 m 85 ft (Sloop—catamaran)	Plymouth	Newport, R.I.	13 days 6 hr 12 min (approx 235 mpd)	1986
FASTEST 24-HOUR RUN	Michael Birch (Can) & 8 crew	Formula Tag (BM Sloop—Cat)	Quebec	St Malo	512·3 miles in 23 hr 42 min	1984
FASTEST SOLO ROWING EAST–WEST	Sidney Genders (51 years) (GB) (oldest rower)	Khaggavisana 6·02 m 19¾ ft	Penzance, Cornwall	Miami, Florida via Antigua	60·8 km 37·8 miles/day 160 days 8 hr	1970
YOUNGEST ROWERS	Mike Nestor (22 years 299 days) Sean Crowley (23 years 146 days)	In Finnegans Wake 6·7 m 22 ft (GB)	Canaries (Pasito Blanco)	Guyana (Hague)	74 days	1986
FASTEST SOLO ROWING WEST–EAST	Tom McClean (Ireland)	Skol 1080 6·1 m 20 ft	St John's Newfoundland	Bishop's Rock, Falmouth 10 Aug	54 days 18 hr 74 km 46 miles/day	1987
EARLIEST SOLO ROWING EAST–WEST	John Fairfax (GB)	Britannia 6·70 m 22 ft	Las Palmas (20 Jan)	Ft Lauderdale, Florida (19 July)	180 days	1969
EARLIEST SOLO ROWING WEST–EAST	Tom McClean (Ireland)	Super Silver 6·1 m 20 ft	St John's, Newfoundland	Black Sod Bay, Ireland (27 July)	70·7 days	1969
YOUNGEST SOLO SAILING	David Sandeman (17½ years) (GB)	Sea Raider 10·67 m 35 ft	Jersey, C.I.	Newport, R.I.	43 days	1976
OLDEST SOLO SAILING	Monk Farnham (74 years 276 days)	Seven Bells 8·53 m 28 ft	Shannon, Ireland	Rhode Is.	72 days (3 stops)	1983
EARLIEST BY SAILBOARD	Christian Marty (Fr) (Escorted by yacht Assiduous)	Sodim (type)	Dakar Senegal	Kourou Fr. Guiana	37 days 16 hr 4 min (slept on board)	1981–2
UNACCOMPANIED SOLO SAILBOARD	Stephane Peyron (Fr)	No name 7·62 m 25 ft	New York	Cap la Rochelle	46 days	1987
SMALLEST RAFT	Henri Beaudout (Fr) & 2 crew	L'Egaré 5·2 m 17 ft (Cedar logs)	Halifax N.S.	Falmouth	87 days	1956

Hugh's Church, Cantley, South Yorkshire the day before her 100th birthday.

Longest engagement

The longest engagement on record was between Octavio Guillen and Adriana Martinez. They finally took the plunge after 67 years in June 1969 in Mexico City, Mexico. Both were then aged 82.

Longest marriage

The longest recorded marriages are of 86 years, one between Sir Temulji Bhicaji Nariman and Lady Nariman from 1853 to 1940 resulting from a cousin marriage when both were 5. Sir Temulji (b. 3 Sept 1848) died, aged 91 years 11 months, in August 1940 at Bombay. Lazurus Rowe (b. Greenland, New Hampshire, USA, 1725) and Molly Webber were recorded as marrying in 1743. He died first in 1829 after 86 years of marriage. The British record is for a marriage of 82 years, between James Frederick Burgess (b. 3 Mar 1861, d. 27 Nov 1966) and his wife Sarah Ann, née Gregory (b. 11 July 1865, d. 22 June 1965) who were married on 21 June 1883 at St James's, Bermondsey, London.

Golden weddings

Despite the advent of the computer, records on golden (or 50-year-long) weddings remain largely uncollated. Unusual cases reported include that of Mrs Agnes Mary Amy Mynott (b. 25 May 1887) who attended the golden wedding of her daughter Mrs Violet Bangs of St Albans on 20 Dec 1980, 23 years after her own. The 3 sons and 4 daughters of Mr and Mrs J. Stredwick of East Sussex *all* celebrated golden weddings between May 1971 and April 1981. Triplets Lucille (Mrs Vogel), Marie (Mrs McNamara) and Alma (Mrs Prom) Pufpaff all celebrated their golden weddings on 12 Apr 1982 having all married in Cleveland, Minnesota, USA in 1932.

Most married

Jack V. and Edna Moran of Seattle, Washington, USA have married each other 40 times since the original and only really necessary occasion on 27 July 1937 in Seaside, Oregon, USA. Subsequent ceremonies have included those at Banff, Canada (1952), Cairo, Egypt (1966) and Westminster Abbey, London (1975).

Youngest married

It was reported in 1986 that an 11-month-old boy was married to a 3-month-old girl in Bangladesh to end a 20-year feud between two families over a disputed farm.

Mass ceremony

The largest mass wedding ceremony was one of 5837 couples from 83 countries officiated over by Sun Myung Moon (b. 1920) of the Holy Spirit Association for the Unification of World Christianity in the Chamsil Gymnasium, Seoul, South Korea on 14 Oct 1982. The response to the question 'Will you swear to love your spouse for ever?' is 'Ye'.

Most expensive wedding

The wedding of Mohammed, son of Shaik Rashid Bin Saeed Al Maktoum, to Princess Salama in Dubai in May 1981 lasted 7 days and cost an estimated £22 million in a purpose-built stadium for 20 000.

Oldest divorced

On 2 Feb 1984 a divorce was granted in Milwaukee, Wisconsin, USA between Ida Stern, aged 91, and her husband Simon, 97. The British record age is 101 years by Harry Bidwell at Brighton, East Sussex. He divorced on 21 Nov 1980 from a younger wife.

Dining out

The world champion for eating out has been Fred E. Magel of Chicago, Illinois, USA who since 1928 has dined out 46 000 times in 60 nations as a restaurant grader (to 21 June 1983). He asserts the one which served largest helpings was Zehnder's Hotel, Frankenmuth, Michigan, USA. Mr Magel's favourite dishes were South African rock lobster and mousse of fresh English strawberries.

Party giving

The 'International Year of the Child' children's party in Hyde Park, London was attended by the royal family and 160 000 children on 30–31 May 1979.

The world's largest birthday party was attended by 8534 people on 8 Dec 1987 in Indianapolis, Indiana, USA. The party was held to mark the 100th birthday of the United Way.

The largest Christmas Party ever staged was that thrown by the Boeing Company in the 65 000-seat Kingdome, Seattle, Washington, USA, in two shows totalling 103 152 people on 15 Dec 1979. During St Patrick's week of 11–17 Mar 1985, Houlihan's Old Place hosted St Pat's Parties at the 48 Kansas City, Missouri-based Gilbert/Robinson restaurants for a total of 206 854 documented guests.

Toastmasters

The Guild of Professional Toastmasters (founded 1962) has only 12 members. Its founder and president, Ivor Spencer, once had to listen to a speech in excess of 2 hr by the maudlin guest of honour of a retirement luncheon. The Guild also elects the most boring speaker of the year, but for professional reasons will not publicise the winners' names until a decent interval has elapsed. Red coats were introduced by the pioneer professional William Knight-Smith (d. 1932) c. 1900.

Lecture agency

In 1980 Bob Jones of Wellington, New Zealand addressed a seminar of 1048 people in Auckland, New Zealand on the subject of property. He received $NZ200 000 or $NZ16 666 per hour. In March 1981 it was reported that both Johnny Carson and Bob Hope commanded fees of $40 000. The author Tom Peters of

Beer keg lifting ● Denis McKeown raised a keg of beer weighing 62·5 kg *137·79 lb* above his head 292 times in 6 hr in Dundalk, Co. Louth, Ireland on 13 Dec 1987.

Palo Alto, California, USA made 275 speeches in 1986 generating $1·5 million in fees.

Working week

A case of a working week of 142 hours (with an average each day of 3 hr 42 min 51 sec for sleep) was recorded in June 1980 by Dr Paul Ashton, 32, the anaesthetics registrar at Birkenhead General Hospital, Merseyside. He described the week in question as 'particularly bad but not untypical'. Some non-consultant doctors are contracted to work 110 hours a week or be available for 148 hours. Some contracts for fully salaried university lecturers call for a 3-hr week or a 72-hr year spread over 24 weeks.

Working career

The longest working life has been that of 98 years by Mr Izumi (see p. 11) who began work goading draft animals at a sugar mill at Isen, Tokunoshima, Japan in 1872. He retired as a sugar cane farmer in 1970 aged 105.

The longest working life recorded in the UK was that of Susan O'Hagan (1802–1909) who was in domestic service with 3 generations of the Hall family of Lisburn, near Belfast, Northern Ireland for 97 years from the age of 10 to light duties at 107.

The writer who has interviewed most heads of state and heads of government in the world is Brian Rossiter Crozier (GB) (b. 4 Aug 1918) with 58 from 36 countries in the period 1948–85.

The longest recorded industrial career in one job in Britain was that of Miss Polly Gadsby who started work with Archibald Turner & Co of Leicester aged 9. In 1932, after 86 years' service, she was still at her bench wrapping elastic, at the age of 95. Theodore C. Taylor (1850–1952) served 86 years with J. T. & T. Taylor of Batley, West Yorkshire including 56 years as chairman.

The longest serving chairman (appointed July 1926) of any board of directors was Mrs Mary Henrietta Anne Moody (b. 7 Apr 1881) of Mark & Moody Ltd, printers and booksellers of Stourbridge, West Midlands having completed 59 years at her death on 5 Aug 1985.

Edward William Beard (1878–1982), a builder of Swindon, Wiltshire, retired in October 1981 from the firm he had founded in 1896 after 85 years.

Commissioner Catherine Bramwell-Booth (b. 20 July 1883, d. 4 Oct 1987) had been serving the Salvation Army since 1903.

Richard John Knight (b. 2 Apr 1881) was company secretary to 7 companies at the time of his death on 12 Nov 1984 aged 103 years.

Most durable coal miner

George Stephenson (b. 21 Apr 1833) worked at William Pit, a Whitehaven colliery, Cumbria from 1840 (aged 7) for 82 years until his retirement in 1922. He died on 18 Mar 1926 aged 92 years 10 months having received a testimonial of £54 12s.

Longest pension

Miss Millicent Barclay, daughter of Col. William Barclay was born posthumously on 10 July 1872 and became eligible for a Madras Military Fund pension to continue until her marriage. She died unmarried on 26 Oct 1969 having drawn the pension for every day of her life of 97 years 3 months.

Medical families

The 4 sons and 5 daughters of Dr Antonio B. Vicencio of Los Angeles, USA all qualified as doctors during 1964–82. Eight sons of John Robertson of Benview, Dumbarton, Scotland graduated as medical doctors between 1892 and 1914. Henry Lewis Lutterloh and Elizabeth Grantham of Chatham County, North Carolina, USA were the grandparents of 19 medical doctors. From 1850 to 1962 they practised a total of 704 man-years. The Maurice family of Marlborough, Wiltshire have had the same practice for 6 generations since 1792.

Miscellaneous Endeavours

Accordion Playing

Pieter van Loggerenberg of Hoedspruit, Transvaal, South Africa played an accordion for 85 hr from 7–10 July 1987 as part of the Wildlife Festival of Hoedspruit.

Apple Peeling

The longest single unbroken apple peel on record is one of 52·51 m *172 ft 4 in* peeled by Kathy Wafler of Wolcott, NY, USA in 11 hr 30 min at Long Ridge Mall, Rochester, NY, USA on 16 Oct 1976. The apple weighed 567 g *20 oz.*

Apple Picking

The greatest recorded performance is 128·80 hectolitres (*365½ US bushels 354·1 imperial bushels*) picked in 8 hr by George Adrian of Indianapolis, Indiana, USA on 23 Sept 1980.

Auctioneering

The longest one-man auction on record is one of 53½ hr by Reg Coates at the *Guinness World of Records* exhibition, Piccadilly, London from 3–5 July 1986.

Bag-Carrying

The greatest non-stop bag-carrying feat carrying 50·8 kg *1 cwt* of household coal in an open bag is 54·7 km *34 miles* by Neil Sullivan, 37, of Small Heath, Birmingham, in 12 hr 45 min on 24 May 1986.

The record for the 1012·5 m *1107·2 yd* course annual Gawthorpe, West Yorkshire race is 4 min 19 sec by Terry Lyons on 16 Apr 1979.

Bagpipes

The duration record pipe has been one of 100 hr by Neville Workman, Clive Higgins, Patrick Forth and Paul Harris of Churchill School Pipe Band, Harare, Zimbabwe, playing 2 at a time in shifts from 9–13 July 1976.

Balancing on One Foot

The longest recorded duration for balancing on one foot is 34 hr by Shri N. Ravi in Sathyamangalam City, Tamil Nadu, India on 17–18 Apr 1982. The disengaged foot may not be rested on the standing foot nor may any object be used for support or balance.

Balloon Release

The largest mass balloon release ever was one of 1 429 643 balloons at Public Square in Cleveland, Ohio, USA on 27 Sept 1986.

The British record was 68 000 helium balloons released simultaneously on 18 Sept 1987 from Battersea Park, south London.

Band Marathons

The longest recorded 'blow-in' is 102 hr 43 min 43 sec by the Band of the West Midlands Fire Service, at the National Exhibition Centre in Birmingham from 22–26 Oct 1986.

Band, One-Man

Rory Blackwell, aided by his left-footed perpendicular percussion-pounder and his right-footed horizontal 4 pronged differential beater, played 24 (4 melody, 20 percussion) instruments in Plymouth, Devon on 2 May 1985. He also played in a single rendition 314 instruments in 1 min 23·07 sec at Dawlish, Devon on 27 May 1985. Sadhak Hurst of Brisbane, Queensland, Australia played his one-man band (which must include at least 3 instruments played simultaneously) for 131 hr from 16–21 Nov 1987, in Melbourne, Australia. Nicki Clarke of Chester, Cheshire created the women's record of 100 hr 20 min from 24–28 Mar 1986 at the Hotel Leofric, Coventry, West Midlands.

Barrel Jumping *on Ice Skates*

The official distance record is 8·99 m *29 ft 5 in* over 18 barrels by Yvon Jolin at Terrebonne, Quebec, Canada on 25 Jan 1981. The feminine record is 6·21 m *20 ft 4½ in* over 11 barrels by Janet Hainstock in Michigan, USA on 15 Mar 1980.

Barrel Rolling

The record for rolling a full 36-gallon metal beer barrel over a measured mile is 8 min 7·2 sec by Phillip Randle, Steve Hewitt, John Round, Trevor Bradley, Colin Barnes and Ray Glover of Haunchwood Collieries Institute and Social Club, Nuneaton, Warwickshire on 15 Aug 1982. A team of 10 rolled a 63½ kg *140 lb* barrel 240·35 km *150 miles* in 30 hr 31 min in Chlumcany, Czechoslovakia on 27–28 Oct 1982.

Barrow Pushing

The heaviest loaded one-wheeled barrow pushed for a minimum 60·96 level metres *200 level feet* is one loaded with bricks weighing a gross 3·753 tonnes *8275 lb* through 74·06 m *243 ft* by John Sarich at London, Ontario, Canada on 19 Feb 1987.

Barrow Racing

The fastest time attained in a 1·609 km *1 mile* wheelbarrow race is 4 min 48·51 sec by Piet Pitzer and Jaco Erasmus at the Transvalia High School, Vanderbijlpark, South Africa on 3 Oct 1987. Brothers-in-law Malcolm Shipley and Adrian Freeburg pushed each other from John O'Groats to Land's End for charity in 30 days from 28 July to 26 Aug 1981.

Bath Tub Racing

The record for a 57·9 km *36 mile* bath tub race is 1 hr 22

Bricklifting ● Geoff Capes lifting 26 bricks at the Kendrick Hire Open Day in Brockley, south London on 16 June 1988. Before rules were standardised, Geoff had lifted 28 bricks on 18 Sept 1987.

---

min 27 sec by Greg Mutton at the Grafton Jacaranda Festival, New South Wales, Australia on 8 Nov 1987. Tubs are limited to 1·90 m *75 in* and 6-hp motors. The greatest distance for paddling a hand-propelled bath tub in 24 hr is 145·6 km *90·5 miles* by 13 members of Aldington Prison Officers Social Club, nr Ashford, Kent on 28–29 May 1983.

Baton Twirling

Victor Cerda, Sol Lozano, Harry Little III (leader) and Manuel Rodriguez twirled batons for 122½ hours from 24–29 June 1984 in El Seveno, California, USA.

The greatest number of complete spins done between tossing a baton into the air and catching it is 10, by Donald Garcia, on the BBC *Record Breakers* programme on 9 Dec 1986. The record for women is 7, by Lisa Fedick on the same programme, and also by Joanne Holloway, at the UK National Baton Twirling Association Championships in Paignton, Devon on 29 Oct 1987.

Bed Making

The record time set under the rigorous rules of the Australian Bedmaking Championships is 28·2 sec solo by Wendy Wall, 34, of Hebersham, Sydney, NSW on 30 Nov 1978. The British pair record with 1 blanket, 2 sheets, an undersheet, an uncased pillow, 1 counterpane and 'hospital' corners is 19·0 sec by Sisters Jill Bradbury and Chris Humpish of Hammersmith Hospital, London on 8 Oct 1985 on BBC TV's *Record Breakers* programme.

Bed of Nails

The Reverend Ken Owen, 48, of Pontypridd, Mid Glamorgan lay on a bed of nails for a total of 300 hr, including 132 hr 30 min without a break, from 3–14 May 1986 starting at Bridgend Hotel, Pontygwaith and concluding at the The Three Horse Shoes, Tonteg, Pontypridd. Much longer durations are claimed by uninvigilated *fakirs*—the most extreme case being *Silki* who claimed 111 days in São Paulo, Brazil ending on 24 Aug 1969.

Bed Pushing

The longest recorded push of a normally sessile object is of 5204 km *3233 miles 1150 yd* in the case of a wheeled hospital bed by a team of 9 employees of Bruntsfield Bedding Centre, Edinburgh from 21 June to 26 July 1979.

Bed Race

The record time for the annual Knaresborough Bed Race (established 1966) in North Yorkshire is 12 min 36 sec for the 3·27 km *2 mile 63 yd* course crossing the River Nidd by the Beavers' Team on 9 June 1984. The course record for the 16·09 km *10 mile* Chew Valley Lake race (established 1977) in Avon is 50 min by the Westbury Harriers' 3-man bed team.

Beer Mat Flipping

Dean Gould of Felixstowe, Suffolk flipped and caught a pile of 102 mats (1·2 mm-thick 490 gsm wood pulp board) through 180 degrees in Hamburg, West Germany on 18 Mar 1988.

Beer Stein Carrying

Barmaid Rosie Schedelbauer covered a distance of 15 m *49 ft 2½ in* in 4·0 sec with 5 full steins in each hand in a televised contest at Königssee, West Germany on 29 June 1981.

Best Man

The world champion is Wally Gant, a bachelor fishmonger from Wakefield, West Yorkshire, who officiated for the 50th time since 1931 in December 1964.

Bicycle *Most mounting simultaneously*

On 2 Apr 1984 at Mito, Ibaragi, Japan 16 members of the Mito-Itomi Unicycle Club mounted and rode a single bicycle a distance of 50 m *164 ft.*

Boat Trot

The 'City of Dublin' Appeal Committee of the Royal

National Lifeboat Institution organised 329 sailing boats belonging to members of Dublin sailing clubs to be moored into a double ring pattern in the shape of a sunflower in Dun Laoghaire Harbour, Dublin, Republic of Ireland on 14 June 1987.

BOOMERANG THROWING

World championships and codified rules were not established until 1970. The Boomerang Association of Australia's championship record for distance reached before return is 111 m *364.1 ft* diameter by Bob Burwell in November 1981 at Albury, NSW. The longest unofficial out and return distance on record is one of 114.3 m *375 ft* by Peter Ruhf (US) at Randwick, Sydney, NSW on 28 June 1982. The longest flight duration (with self-catch) is one of 28.19 sec by Bob Burwell at Albury, NSW on 7 Apr 1984. The greatest number of consecutive 2-handed catches is 653 by Bob Croll (Victoria) on the same occasion.

BRICK CARRYING

The greatest distance achieved for carrying a brick 4.08 kg *9 lb* in a nominated ungloved hand in an uncradled downward pincher grip is 99.37 km *61¾ miles* by Reg Morris of Walsall, West Midlands on 16 July 1985.

The feminine record for carrying a 4.422 kg *9 lb 12 oz* brick is 36.2 km *22½ miles* by Wendy Morris of Walsall, West Midlands on 28 Apr 1986. The British feminine record for a 2.97 kg *6 lb 9 oz* smooth-sided brick is 9.6 km *6 miles* by Karen Stevenson of Wallasey, Merseyside on 17 Aug 1984.

BRICKLAYING

Tony Gregory of Horndon on the Hill, Essex laid 747 bricks, each weighing 2.00 kg *4.41 lb*, in 60 min at Grays, Essex on 18 Apr 1987. This was achieved in accordance with the rules of the Brick Development Association and the Guild of Bricklayers.

BRICK THROWING

The greatest reported distance for throwing a standard 2.268 kg *5 lb* building brick is 44.54 m *146 ft 1 in* by Geoff Capes at Braybrook School, Orton Goldhay, Cambridgeshire on 19 July 1978.

BUBBLE

Garry Thomas of Gainesville, Florida, USA created a 10.67 m *35 ft* long bubble in San Antonio, Texas, USA on 31 July 1987. He made the bubble just using a simple bubble wand, washing-up liquid and water.

BUBBLE GUM BLOWING

The greatest reported diameter for a bubble gum bubble under the strict rules of this highly competitive activity is 55.8 cm *22 in* by Susan Montgomery Williams of Fresno, California, USA in June 1985. The British record is 42 cm *16½ in* by Nigel Fell, 13, from Derriaghy, Northern Ireland in November 1979. This was equalled by John Smith of Willingham, Cambridgeshire on 25 Sept 1983.

BURIAL ALIVE

Voluntary burial alive claims (of which claims up to 217 days have been published) are inadmissible unless the depth of the coffin is a minimum 2 m *6 ft 6¾ in* below ground; the coffin has a maximum cubic capacity of 1.5 million cc *54 ft³*, and the single aperture for communication and feeding has a maximum dimension of 10 cm *4 in*. 'Country' Bill White, 50, was so buried from 31 July to 19 Dec 1981 (141 days) in Killeen, Texas, USA.

CAMPING OUT

The silent Indian *fakir* Mastram Bapu ('contented father') remained on the same spot by the roadside in the village of Chitra for 22 years from 1960–82.

CANAL JUMPING (DYKE VAULTING)

In the sport of Fierljeppen at Winsam, Friesland, Netherlands, the record is 18.61 m *61 ft 0¾ in* across the water with a 12.2 m *40 ft* aluminium pole set by Aarth de Wit in August 1983.

Circus Records

The largest permanent circus is Circus Circus, Las Vegas, Nevada opened on 18 Oct 1968 at a cost of $15 000 000. It covers an area of 11984 m² *129 000 ft²* with a tent-shaped flexiglass roof 27.43 m *90 ft* high. The largest travelling circus is the Circus Vargas in the USA which can hold 5000 people under its Big Top.

Flying trapeze

Downward circles or 'muscle grinding'—1350 by Sarah Denu (aged 14) (US) Madison, Wisconsin, USA, 21 May 1983. Single-heel hang on swinging bar, Angela Revelle (Angelique), Australia, 1977.

Highest aerial act

Ian Ashpole (b. 15 Jan 1956) of Ross-on-Wye, Hereford and Worcester performed a trapeze act suspended from a hot-air balloon between St Neots, Cambridgeshire and Newmarket, Suffolk at 5004.8 m *16 420 ft* on 16 May 1986.

Triple twisting double somersault

Tom Robin Edelston to catcher John Zimmerman, Circus World, Florida, 20 Jan 1981.

Full twisting triple and the quadruple somersault

Vasquez Troupe. Miguel Vasquez to catcher Juan Vasquez at Ringling Bros, Amphitheater, Chicago, Illinois, USA in November 1981. On 20 Sept 1984 he performed a triple somersault in a layout position (no turn) to catcher Juan Vasquez at the Sports Arena, Los Angeles, USA.

Triple back somersault with 1½ twists

Terry Cavaretta Lemus (now Mrs St Jules). At Circus Circus, Las Vegas, Nevada, USA in 1969.

Trampoline

Septuple twisting back somersault to bed and quintuple twisting back somersault to shoulders by Marco Canestrelli to Belmonte Canestrelli at Madison Square Gardens, New York, USA on 5 Jan and 28 Mar 1979. Richard Tison (France) performed a triple twisting triple back somersault for television near Berchtesgaden, West Germany on 30 June 1981.

Flexible pole

Double full twisting somersault to a 5.08 cm *2 in* diameter pole by Roberto Tabak (aged 11) in Sarasota, Florida, USA in 1977. Triple full twisting somersault by Corina Colonelu Mosoianu (aged 13) at Madison Square Garden, New York, USA on 17 Apr 1984.

Human pyramid (or tuckle)

Twelve (3 high) supported by a single under-stander. Weight 771 kg *1700 lb* or *121.4 stone* by Tahar Douis of the Hassani Troupe at BBC TV Pebble Mill Studio, Birmingham on 17 Dec 1979. Nine high by top-mounter Josep-Joan Martínez Lozano, aged 10, of the Colla Vella dels Xiquets, 12 m *39 ft* tall on 25 Oct 1981 in Valls, Spain.

Oldest clown

Charlie Revel (b. Andrea Lassere, Spain, 24 Apr 1896) performed for 82 years (1899–1981).

JUGGLING RECORDS

7 clubs: Albert Petrovski (USSR), 1963; Sorin Munteanu (Romania), 1975; Jack Bremlov (Czechoslovakia), 1985; Albert Lucas (US), 1985. **8 plates**: Enrico Rastelli (Italy), 1896–1931; Albert Lucas (US), 1984. **10 balls**: Enrico Rastelli (Italy), 1896–1931; Albert Lucas (US), 1984. **12 rings**: Albert Lucas (US), 1985. **Pirouettes with 3 cigar boxes**: Kris Kremo (Switzerland) (quadruple turn with 3 boxes in mid-air), 1977. **Duration 5 clubs**: 37 min 10 sec, Albert Lucas (US), 1984. **3 objects while running—joggling**: Owen Morse (US), 100 m in 12.12 sec, 1987. Scott Damgaard (US), 1.6 km *1 mile* in 4 min 37 sec, 1981. Marty Gardella (US), 5 km *3.1 miles* in 18 min 47.95 sec, 1982. **5 objects while running—joggling**: Owen Morse (US), 100 m in 15.25 sec, 1987. **7 ping-pong balls with mouth**: Tony Ferko (Czechoslovakia), 1987. **5 balls inverted**: Bobby May (US), since 1953

CARD THROWING

Kevin St Onge threw a standard playing card 56.41 m *185 ft 1 in* at the Henry Ford Community College Campus, Dearborn, Michigan, USA on 12 June 1979.

CARRIAGE DRIVING

The only man to drive 48 horses in a single hitch is Dick Sparrow of Zearing, Iowa, USA from 1972–77. The lead horses were on reins 41 m *135 ft* long.

CAR WRECKING

The greatest number of cars wrecked in a stunting career is 1983 to 1 June 1988 by Dick Sheppard of Gloucester, England.

CATAPULTING

The greatest recorded distance for a catapult shot is 415 m *1362 ft* by James M. Pfotenhauer using a patented 5.22 m *.17 ft 1½ in* 'Monarch IV Supershot' and a 53-calibre lead musket ball on Ski Hill Road, Escanaba, Michigan, USA on 10 Sept 1977.

CHAMPAGNE FOUNTAIN

The greatest number of storeys achieved in a champagne fountain, successfully filled from the top and using 10 404 traditional long-stem glasses, is 44 (height 7.52 m *24.7 ft*), achieved by Pascal Leclerc at the Biltmore Hotel, Los Angeles, USA on 18 June 1984.

CHICKEN AND TURKEY PLUCKING

Ernest Hausen (1877-1955) of Fort Atkinson, Wisconsin, USA died undefeated after 33 years as champion. On 19 Jan 1939 he was timed at 4.4 sec and reputedly twice did 3.5 sec a few years later. The record time for plucking 12 chickens clean by a team of 4 women at the annual Chicken Plucking Championship at Masaryktown, Florida, USA is 32.9 sec set on 9 Oct 1976 by Doreena Cary, Diane Grieb, Kathy Roads and Dorothy McCarthy.

Vincent Pilkington of Cootehill, County Cavan, Ireland killed and plucked 100 turkeys in 7hr 32 min on 15 Dec 1978. His record for a single turkey is 1 min 30 sec on RTE television in Dublin on 17 Nov 1980.

On 23 May 1983 Joe Glaub (USA) killed 7300 turkeys in a 'working' day. Mrs Madge Colenso gutted 94 turkeys in 60 mins at Rivington Farm, Burstow, Horley, Surrey on 20 Dec 1984.

CIGAR BOX BALANCING

Bruce Block balanced 134 King Edward boxes on his chin for 15 sec in the Hilton Hotel, Akron, Ohio, USA on 15 July 1987.

CLAPPING

The duration record for continuous clapping (sustaining an average of 160 claps per min audible at 109.7 m *120 yd*) is 54 hr by V. Jeyaraman of Tamil Nadu, India from 13–15 Dec 1985.

CLUB SWINGING

Albert Rayner set a world record of 17 512 revolutions (4.9 per sec) in 60 min at Wakefield, West Yorkshire on 27 July 1981. M. Dobrilla swung continuously for 144 hr at Cobar, NSW, Australia finishing on 15 Sept 1913.

COAL CUTTING

The individual record is 218 tons in a week of 5 shifts by Jim Marley (b. 1914) at East Walbottle Colliery, Tyne and Wear, England in 1949. This included 47½ tons in 6 hr. The NCB record for a week's production by a 48-man team is 32 333 tonnes at the biggest pit at Kellingley Colliery, Knottingley, West Yorkshire in the pre-Christmas 'Bull Week' in December 1982.

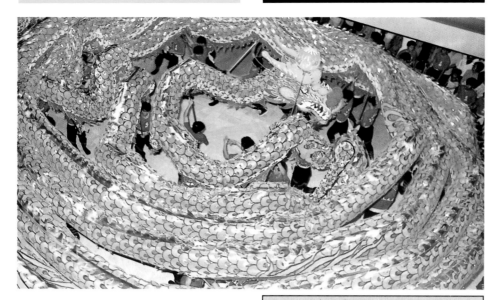

COAL SHOVELLING

The record for filling a 508 kg ½ *ton* hopper with coal is 29·4 sec by Piet Groot at the Inangahua A and P Show, New Zealand on 1 Jan 1985.

COIN BALANCING

The tallest column of coins ever stacked on the edge of a coin is 205 Canadian 25-cent pieces on top of a Canadian Olympic commemorative coin which was freestanding vertically on the base of a coin flat on the surface, by Bruce McConachy (b. 1963) of West Vancouver, BC, Canada for Fuji-TV in Tokyo, Japan on 24 Feb 1985. Alex Chervinsky (b. 22 Feb 1908) of Lock Haven, Pennsylvania, USA achieved a pyramid of 390 coins on his 75th birthday.

COIN SNATCHING

The greatest number of 10p pieces clean caught from being flipped from the back of a forearm into the same downward palm is 140 by Dean Gould in Hamburg, West Germany on 19 Mar 1988.

COMPETITION WINNINGS

The largest individual competition prize win on record is $307 500 by Herbert J. Idle, 55, of Chicago in an encyclopaedia contest run by Unicorn Press Inc., on 20 Aug 1953. The highest value first prize offered in Britain has been a £172 950 new house in a £491 000 competition run by the *London Evening Standard* in April and May 1987.

COW CHIP TOSSING

The record distances in the country sport of throwing dried cow chips depend on whether or not the projectile may be 'moulded into a spherical shape'. The greatest distance achieved under the 'non-sphericalisation and 100 per cent organic' rule (established in 1970) is 81·07 m *266 ft* by Steve Urner at the Mountain Festival, Tehachapi, California, USA on 14 Aug 1981.

CRAWLING

The longest continuous voluntary crawl (progression with one or other knee in unbroken contact with the ground) on record is 45·05 km *28 miles* by Bob DiSalle and Bobby Kunkle of Miami University from 4–6 Aug 1987. The crawl took place on a measured course 816·56 m *2679 ft* long. It took 32 hr 27 min and over 55 laps of the track to gain the record. Over a space of 15 months ending on 9 Mar 1985 Jagdish Chander, 32, crawled 1400 km *870 miles* from Aligarh to Jamma, India to propitiate his favourite Hindu goddess, Mata.

CROCHET

Mrs Barbara Jean Sonntag (b. 1938) of Craig, Colorado, USA crocheted 330 shells plus 5 stitches (equivalent to

> **Dancing dragon** ● The longest dancing dragon in the world was 136·84 m *448 ft 10 in* in length, commissioned by Raffles City Pte Ltd and made by 30 members of the Singapore Dragon and Lion Athletic Association in January 1988. The head was made from cloth, bamboo, cane, aluminium strips, papier mâché, gauze and paints, and the body from cloth. Some 3 000 tinkling bells were sewn on its body, as were over 20 000 pieces of scale-shaped silver sequins to give it a shimmering effect. 49 people then brought it to life in dance as part of the Lunar New Year celebrations.

4412 stitches) in 30 min at a rate of 147 stitches a minute on 13 Jan 1981. Miss Ria van der Honing of Wormerveer, Netherlands, completed a crochet chain 62·50 km *38·83 miles* in length on 14 July 1986. Mrs Sybille Anthony completed a 120-hr crochet marathon at Toombul Shopping-town, Queensland, Australia on 7 Oct 1977.

CUCUMBER SLICING

Norman Johnson of Blackpool College, Lancashire set a record of 13·4 sec for slicing a 30·48 cm *12 in* cucumber, 3·81 cm *1½ in* in diameter, at 22 slices to the inch (total 244 slices) at *West Deutscher Rundfunk* in Cologne on 3 Apr 1983.

CUSTARD PIE THROWING

The most times champion in the annual World Custard Pie Championships, now at Ditton, Maidstone, Kent (instituted 1968) have been 'The Birds' ('The Bashers') and the 'Coxheath Men' ('Custard Kings') each with 3 wins. The target (face) must be 2·53 m *8 ft 3⅜ in* from the thrower who must throw a pie no more than 26·03 cm *10¼ in* in diameter. Six points are scored for a square hit full in the face.

DEBATING

The Oxford Union Society, Oxford University debated the motion that ''This House Believes That Without Beck's Bier 1992 Will Be Just Another Year' for 315 hours 15 mins from 12–25 May 1988.

DEMOLITION WORK

Fifteen members of the Black Leopard Karate Club demolished a 7-room wooden farmhouse west of Elnora, Alberta, Canada in 3 hr 18 min by foot and empty hand on 13 June 1982.

DOMINO STACKING

Leard Wayne Woodruff, 76, of McFarland, California, USA successfully stacked 242 dominoes on a single supporting domino on 15 Sept 1986.

DOMINO TOPPLING

The greatest number set up single-handed and toppled

is 281 581 out of 320 236 by Klaus Friedrich, 22, in Bayern, West Germany on 27 Jan 1984. The dominoes fell within 12 min 57·3 sec having taken 31 days (10 hours daily) to set up.

Thirty students at Delft, Eindhoven and Twente Technical Universities in the Netherlands set up 1 500 000 dominoes depicting all of the EC member countries. Of these, 1 380 650 were toppled by one push on 2 Jan 1988.

DRINK ROUND

Liam Fallon treated 1613 people to a free drink at a charity fund-raising gathering on 4 July 1987 at Lord Byron's Wine Bar, Solihull, Warwickshire.

DRUMMING

The world duration drumming record is 44 days 1 hour by Trevor Mitchell at the Brown Cow Hotel, Scunthorpe, Humberside from 5 July to 18 Aug 1986.

Four hundred separate drums were played in 31·78 seconds by Rory Blackwell at Finlake Country Park, Chudleigh, Devon on 30 May 1988.

DUCKS AND DRAKES

The best is 29 skips (14 plinkers and 15 pitty-pats) by Arthur Ring, 69, at Midway Beach, California, USA on 4 Aug 1984 and Jerdone 'Jerry' McGhee, 42, at Wimberley, Texas, USA on 18 Nov 1986.

EGG AND SPOON RACING

Chris Riggio of San Francisco, California, USA completed a 45·86 km *28·5 mile* fresh egg and dessert spoon marathon in 4 hr 34 min on 7 Oct 1979.

EGG DROPPING

The greatest height from which fresh eggs have been dropped (to earth) and remained intact is 198 m *650 ft* by David S. Donoghue from a helicopter on 2 Oct 1979 on a Tokyo Golf Course, Japan.

EGG HUNT

The greatest egg hunt on record involved 72 000 hard-boiled eggs and 40 000 candy eggs at the 26th annual Garrison Egg Hunt at Homer, Georgia, USA on 7 Apr 1985.

EGG SHELLING

Two kitchen hands, Harold Witcomb and Gerald Harding, shelled 1050 dozen eggs in a 7¼ hr shift at Bowyers, Trowbridge, Wiltshire on 23 Apr 1971. Both were blind.

EGG THROWING

The longest authenticated distance for throwing a fresh hen's egg without breaking it is 96·90 m *317 ft 10 in* by Risto Antikainen to Jyrki Korhonen at Siilinjarvi, Finland on 6 Sept 1981.

ESCALATOR RIDING

The record for travelling a pair of 'up' and 'down' escalators is 84 hr, by a team of 9 from Metro Theatres Alberton, Johannesburg, South Africa, from 5–8 Dec 1987. The total distance travelled was 164·54 km *102·25 miles.*

ESCAPOLOGY

The most renowned of all escape artists has been Ehrich Weiss *alias* Harry Houdini (1874–1926), who pioneered underwater escapes from locked, roped and weighted containers while handcuffed and shackled with irons.

A manufacturer of strait-jackets acknowledges that an escapologist 'skilled in the art of bone and muscle manipulation' could escape from a standard jacket in seconds. There are, however, methods by which such circumvention can itself be circumvented. Nick Janson of Benfleet, Essex can escape from handcuffs locked on him by more than 1000 different police officers.

FAMILY TREE

The farthest back the lineage of any family has been traced is that of K'ung Ch'iu or Confucius (551–479 BC). His 4 greats grandfather K'ung Chia is known from the

8th century BC. This man's 85th lineal descendants Wei-yi (b. 1939) and Wei-ning (b. 1947) live today in Taiwan (Formosa).

FASHION SHOW

The longest distance covered by girl models is 114·4 km *71·1 miles* from 19–21 Sept 1983 by Roberta Brown and Lorraine McCourt at Parke's Hotel, Dublin, Ireland. Male model Eddie Warke covered a further 19·1 km *11·9 miles* on the catwalk. The compère was Marty Whelan of Radio 2.

FAUX PAS

If measured by financial consequence, the greatest *faux pas* on record was that of the young multi-millionaire James Gordon Bennett, committed on 1 Jan 1877 at the family mansion of his demure fiancée one Caroline May, in Fifth Avenue, New York, USA. Bennett arrived in a 2-horse cutter late and obviously in wine. By dint of intricate footwork, he gained the portals to enter the withdrawing room where he was the cynosure of all eyes. He mistook the fireplace for a plumbing fixture more usually reserved for another purpose. The May family broke the engagement and Bennett (1841–1918) was obliged to spend the rest of his foot-loose and fancy-free life based in Paris with the resultant non-collection of millions of tax dollars by the US Treasury.

FEMININE BEAUTY

Female pulchritude, being qualitative rather than quantitative, does not lend itself to records. It has been suggested that, if the face of Helen of Troy (c. 1200 BC) was capable of launching 1000 ships, a unit of beauty sufficient to launch one ship should be a millihelen. The earliest international beauty contest was staged by P. T. Barnum (with the public to be the judges) in the United States in June 1855. The Miss America contest was staged at Atlantic City, New Jersey, USA in 1921 and was won by a thin blue-eyed blonde with a 76·2 cm *30 in* chest, Margaret Gorman. The world's largest annual beauty pageants are the Miss World (inaugurated 1951) and Miss Universe (1952) contests. The most successful country in the latter contest has been the USA with winners in 1954–56–60–67–70–80. The number of countries represented has reached 80. The United Kingdom is the only country to have produced 5 winners in the Miss World contest. They were Rosemarie Frankland (1961); Ann Sidney (1964); Lesley Langley (1965); Helen Morgan (1974), who resigned, and Sarah-Jane Hutt (1983). The maximum number of contestants was 72 in November 1983. The shortest reign was 18 hours by Miss Germany (Gabriella Brum) in 1980.

FIELD GUN PULL

3 teams of 8 members from 55 Ordnance Company (Volunteers) Royal Army Ordnance Corps pulled a 25-pounder field gun over a distance of 137·92 km *85·7 miles* in 24 hours in Hounslow, Middlesex on 15–16 Apr 1988.

FIRE PUMPING

The greatest gallonage stirrup-pumped by a team of 8 in an 80-hr charity pump is 93 887 litres *20 863 gal* by firefighters representing Grampian Fire Brigade from 13–16 Aug 1987 at Langstane Kirk, Aberdeen, Grampian.

FIRE PUMP MANHANDLING

The longest unaided tow of a fire appliance in excess of 508 kg *10 cwt* in 24 hr on a closed circuit is 358·8 km *223 miles* by a 32-man team of the Dublin Fire Brigade with an 520 kg *1144 lb* fire pump on 20–21 June 1987.

FLUTE MARATHON

The longest recorded marathon by a flautist is 61 hr by Joseph Shury of the Sri Chinmoy Marathon Team, Toronto, Ontario, Canada from 21–23 Mar 1986.

FLYING DISC THROWING (FORMERLY FRISBEE)

The World Flying Disc Federation indoor records are, men: 121·6 m *399 ft* by Van Miller (US) at Flagstaff, Arizona, USA on 18 Sept 1982; and women: 69·8 m *229·0 ft*

by Suzanne Fields (US) at Cedar Falls, Iowa, USA on 26 Apr 1981. The outdoor records are, men: 186·83 m *612·8 ft* by Michael Canci (Australia), 11 Apr 1987 at Bunbury, Australia; and women: 124·73 m *409 ft* by Bethany Porter (US), 21 Aug 1987 at Fort Collins, Colorado, USA. The throw, run and catch records are, men: 88·70 m *290·9 ft* by Pekka Ranta (Finland), 7 June 1986 at Tali, Finland; and women: 60·02 m *196·91 ft* by Judy Horowitz (US), 29 June 1985 at La Mirada, California, USA. The group marathon record is 1198 hr by Prince George's Community College Club from 1 June–21 July 1981 at Largo, Maryland, USA (see Throwing p.183).

Belly dancing ● Eileen Foucher, dancing her way to the belly dancing marathon record of 106 hr, at Rush Green Hospital, Romford, Essex from 30 July–3 Aug 1984.

Dancing

Marathon dancing must be distinguished from dancing mania, or tarantism, which is a pathological condition. The worst outbreak of this was at Aachen, Germany in July 1374, when hordes of men and women broke into a frenzied and compulsive choreomania in the streets. It lasted for many hours until injury or complete exhaustion ensued.

Largest and longest dances

An estimated 25 000 attended a 'Moonlight Serenade' outdoor evening of dancing to the music of the Glenn Miller Orchestra in Buffalo, New York, USA on 20 July 1984. An estimated total of 20 000 dancers took part in the National Square Dance Convention at Louisville, Kentucky, USA on 26 June 1983.

The most severe marathon dance staged as a public spectacle was one by Mike Ritof and Edith Boudreaux who logged 5148 hr 28½ min to win $2000 at Chicago's Merry Garden Ballroom, Belmont and Sheffield, Illinois, USA from 29 Aug 1930 to 1 Apr 1931. Rest periods were progressively cut from 20 to 10 to 5 to nil minutes per hour with 10-inch steps and a maximum of 15 seconds for closure of eyes.

Will Kemp in 1599 Morris-danced his way from London to Norwich in 9 days.

'Rosie Radiator' (Rose Marie Ostler) on 16 Aug 1986 claimed a mileage of 9·6 km *6 miles* in leading a column of 17 tap dancers across San Francisco.

Ballet

In the *entrechat* (a vertical spring from the fifth position with the legs extended criss-crossing at the lower calf), the starting and finishing position each count as one such that in an *entrechat douze* there are *five* crossings and uncrossings. This was performed by Wayne Sleep for the BBC *Record Breakers* programme on 7 Jan 1973. He was in the air for 0·71 of a second.

Most turns

The greatest number of spins called for in classical ballet choreography is 32 *fouettés rond de jambe en tournant* in 'Swan Lake' by Pyotr Ilyich Chaykovskiy (Tschaikovsky) (1840–93). Miss Rowena Jackson MBE (b. Invercargill, NZ, 1925) achieved 121 such turns at her class in Melbourne, Victoria, Australia in 1940.

Most curtain calls

The greatest recorded number of curtain calls ever received is 89 by Dame Margaret Evelyn Arias DBE, *née* Hookham (born Reigate, Surrey, 18 May 1919) *alias* Margot Fonteyn, and Rudolf Hametovich Nureyev (born on a train near Irkutsk, USSR, 17 Mar 1938) after a performance of 'Swan Lake' at the Vienna Staatsoper, Austria in October 1964.

Largest cast

The largest number of ballet dancers used in a production in Britain has been 2000 in the London Coster Ballet of 1962, directed by Lillian Rowley, at the Royal Albert Hall, London.

Ballroom *Marathon*

The individual continuous world record for ballroom dancing is 126 hr by Scott Michael, 31, a dancing instructor of Huntington Beach, California, USA, on 20–25 June 1986 at the Dance Masters Ballroom Studio, Stanton, California, USA. 27 girls worked shifts as his partner.

Champions

The world's most successful professional ballroom dancing champions have been Bill Irvine MBE and Bobbie Irvine MBE, who won 13 world titles between 1960 and 1972. The oldest competitive ballroom dancer is Albert J. Sylvester CBE, JP (b. 24 Nov 1889) of Corsham, Wiltshire, who retired aged 94. In 1977 he won the topmost amateur Alex Moore award for a 10-dance test with his partner Paula Smith in Bath on 26 Apr 1977. By 1981 he had won nearly 50 medals and trophies since he began dancing in 1964.

Charleston

The charleston duration record is 110 hr 58 min by Sabra Starr of Lansdowne, Pennsylvania, USA from 15–20 Jan 1979.

Conga

The longest recorded conga was the Miami Super Conga, held in conjunction with Calle Ocho—a party to which Cuban-Americans invite the rest of Miami for a celebration of life together. Held on 13 Mar 1988, the conga consisted of 119 986 people.

The longest one in Britain comprised a 'snake' of 8659 people from the South Eastern Region of the Camping and Caravanning Club of Great Britain and Ireland on 4 Sept 1982 at Brands Hatch, Kent.

Country dancing

The most complex Scottish country dance ever held was a 256-some reel, choreographed by Ian Price, which took place on 24 Apr 1988 in Vancouver, Canada.

Disco

The longest recorded disco dancing marathon is one of 462 hr 30 min by Alfie Turner of Romford, Essex from 28 Apr–17 May 1985.

Flamenco

The fastest flamenco dancer ever measured is Solero de Jerez, aged 17, who in Brisbane, Australia in September 1967 in an electrifying routine attained 16 heel taps per second.

High kicking

The world record for high kicks (heel to ear level) is 10 502 in 5 hr 30 min by Shawn Kovacich at Butte, Montana, USA on 27 Sept 1986. Tony Higo set heel to ear level high kick records of 90 in 25 sec and 51 in 10 sec on Yorkshire TV's *Calendar Lunchtime Live* on 17 Dec 1987, and 147 in 1 min on the same programme on 23 Dec 1987.

Jiving

The duration record for non-stop jiving is 97 hr 42 min by Richard Rimmer (with a relay of partners) of Caterham, Surrey from 11–16 Nov 1979. Under the strict rules of the

Limbo on roller skates ● Kelly Foley, one of the joint holders of the record for limbo on roller skates (see heading 'limbo' below).

European Rock 'n' Roll Association the duration pair record is 24 hr 5 min by 5 couples at the Clayton Community Festival, Victoria, Australia from 11–12 October 1986.

Limbo

The lowest height for a bar (flaming) under which a limbo dancer has passed is 15·5 cm *6⅛ in* off the floor by Marlene Raymond, 15, at the Port of Spain Pavilion, Toronto, Canada on 24 June 1973. Junior J. Renaud (b. 7 June 1954), Australia became the first Official World Limbo Champion at the inaugural International Limbo Competition on 19 Feb 1974 at Port of Spain, Trinidad.

The record on roller skates is 13·33 cm *5¼ in*, first achieved by Denise Culp of Rock Hill, South Carolina, USA on 22 Jan 1984. This has since been equalled by Tracey O'Callaghan on 2 June 1984 and Sandra Siviour on 30 Mar 1985, both at Bexley North, NSW, Australia, Jessie Ball on 27 June 1985 at Beverley Hills, NSW, Australia, and Kelly Foley on 22 May 1987, Magdalena Petrik and Meegan Anderson, both on 13 Apr 1988, and Michelle Boyle, Donna Bray and Jessica McLeish, on 21 May 1988, all at Parramatta, NSW, Australia.

Tap

The fastest *rate* ever measured for tap dancing is 1440 taps per min (24 per sec) by Roy Castle on BBC TV *Record Breakers* programme on 14 Jan 1973. On 31 Oct–1 Nov 1985 he achieved one million taps in 23 hr 44 min at the *Guinness World of Records* exhibition, London, an average of 11·7 per second. The greatest ever assemblage of tap dancers in a single routine is 4000 at Glasgow Airport, Stratchclyde, on 29 May 1988.

The world record for keeping a footbag airborne is 36 230 consecutive kicks or hacks by Andy Linder (US) in Palatine, Illinois, USA on 24 Aug 1986. The feminine record is held by Tricia Sullivan with 12 838 on 31 July 1985 at Golden, Colorado, USA. The sport originated in Oregon, USA in 1972 and was invented by John Stalberger (US).

GIRNING

The only girner to have won 6 national titles is Ron Looney of Egremont, Cumbria from 1979–84.

GLADIATORIAL COMBAT

Emperor Trajan of Rome (AD 98–117) staged a display involving 4941 pairs of gladiators over 117 days. Publius Ostorius, a freed-man, survived 51 combats in Pompeii.

GOLD PANNING

The fastest time for 'panning' 8 planted gold nuggets in a 25·4 cm *10 in* diameter pan is 9·23 sec by Bob Box of Ahwahnee, California, USA, and the female record is 10·03 sec by Susan Bryeans of Fullerton, California, both in the 23rd World Gold Panning Championship on 6 Mar 1983 at Knotts Berry Farm, Buena Park, California, USA.

GOLF BALL BALANCING

Lang Martin balanced 7 golf balls vertically without

adhesive at Charlotte, North Carolina, USA on 9 Feb 1980.

GRAPE CATCHING

The greatest distance at which a grape thrown from level ground has been caught in the mouth is 97·43 m *319 ft 8 in* by Arden Chapman at Northeast Louisiana University, Monroe, USA on 18 July 1980.

GRAVE DIGGING

It is recorded that Johann Heinrich Karl Thieme, sexton of Aldenburg, Germany, dug 23 311 graves during a 50-year career. In 1826 his understudy dug *his* grave.

GUITAR PLAYING

The longest recorded solo guitar-playing marathon is one of 300 hr by Vincent Paxton at the Lord Nelson public house, Winterslow, Wiltshire from 23 Nov–6 Dec 1986.

GUM BOOT THROWING

The longest recorded distance for 'Wellie wanging' (size 8 Challenger Dunlop Boot) is 52·73 m *173 ft* by Tony Rodgers of Warminster, Wilts on 9 Sept 1978. Rosemary Payne established the feminine record at Cannon Hill Park, Birmingham on 21 June 1975 with 39·60 m *129 ft 11 in.*

GUM WRAPPER CHAIN

Cathy Ushler of Redmond, Washington, USA has made the longest gum wrapper chain, which measured 1819·9 m *5967 ft* as of October 1987.

GUN RUNNING

The record for the Royal Tournament Naval Field Gun Competition (instituted 1907, with present rules since 1913) is 2 min 40·6 sec by the Portsmouth Command Field Gun crew at Earl's Court, London on 19 July 1984. The barrel alone weighs 406 kg *8 cwt*. The wall is 1·52 m *5 ft* high and the chasm 8·53 m *28 ft* across.

HAGGIS HURLING

The longest recorded distance for throwing a haggis (min. weight 680 g *1 lb 8 oz*) is 55·11 m *180 ft 10 in* by Alan Pettigrew on Inchmurrin, Loch Lomond, Strathclyde on 24 May 1984.

HAIRDRESSING

Colin Watson and André Douglas each cut, set and styled hair continuously for 408 hr from 4–21 Aug 1986 in Northcliff, Transvaal, South Africa.

HAIR SPLITTING

The greatest reported achievement in hair splitting has been that of the former champion cyclist and craftsman Alfred West (1901–85) who succeeded in splitting a human hair 17 times into 18 parts on 8 occasions.

HANDBELL RINGING

The longest recorded handbell-ringing recital has been one of 56 hr 3 min by 12 handbell ringers of Ecclesfield School, Sheffield from 21–23 July 1985.

HANDSHAKING

Rainer Vikström of Turku, Finland shook 19 592 different hands in 8 hours on 15 May 1988 during Turku's Fourth Annual Spring Market 'Manun Markkinat'. The record number of hands shaken by a public figure at an official function was 8513 by President Theodore Roosevelt (1858–1919) at a New Year's Day White House presentation in Washington DC, USA on 1 Jan 1907.

HEDGE LAYING

John Williams of Sennybridge and David James of Llanwern, both in Brecon, hedged by the 'stake and pleach' method a total of 241·4 m *264 yd* in 11 hr 24 min on 28 April 1986.

Food

APPLE PIE
The largest apple pie ever baked was that by ITV chef Glynn Christian in a 12 m × 7 m *40 ft × 23 ft* dish at Hewitts Farm, Chelsfield, Kent from 25–27 Aug 1982. Over 600 bushels of apples were included in the pie which weighed 13·66 tonnes *30 115 lb*. It was cut by Rear Admiral Sir John Woodward.

BANANA SPLIT
The longest banana split ever made was one of 7·32 km *4·55 miles* in length made by residents of Selinsgrove, Pennsylvania, USA on 30 Apr 1988.

BARBECUE
On 31 Jan 1981, 46 386 chicken halves supplied by Ernie Morgado were barbecued for 15 000 people at Iolani School, Honolulu, Hawaii, USA.

At the Sertoma Club Barbecue, New Port Richey, Florida, USA 9576 kg *21 112 lb* of beef was sold from 7–9 Mar 1986.

At the St Patrick's Irish Picnic, McEwen, Tennessee, USA, 7171 kg *15 810 lb* of pork was sold on 25 July 1986.

CAKES
The largest cake ever created weighed 40·82 tonnes *90 000 lb*, included 13·61 tonnes *30 000 lb* of vanilla icing, was 33·5 × 24·3 m *110 × 80 ft* in size and was baked in 32 hours by Chef Franz Eichenauer at the City Coliseum, Austin, Texas, USA on 20 Feb 1986. It was cut by HRH the Prince of Wales and the Governor of Texas, Mark White Jr. The tallest recorded free-standing cake is one of 83 tiers, 21·43 m *70 ft 4½ in* completed by a team of 20 chefs at the Collins Hotel, Melbourne, Australia on 18 June 1987.

A cake house consisting of 51 090 cake bricks and measuring 7·5 × 5·5 × 5·75 m *24 ft 7 in × 18 ft 1 in × 18 ft 10 in* was created by Nila Chandra. Next to it was a huge *garuda*—Indonesia's national symbol—created by Joyce Aswan. The *garuda*, made of icing sugar, was 12 m *39 ft 4 in* high. The cake and bird were displayed in Jakarta, Indonesia in March 1988. (See p. 3 for illustration).

CHEESE
The largest cheese ever made was a cheddar of 15 190 kg *34 591 lb* made in 43 hr from 20–22 Jan 1964 by the Wisconsin Cheese Foundation for exhibition at the New York World's Fair, USA. It was transported in a specially designed tractor trailer, 'Cheese Mobile', 13·71 m *45 ft* long.

CHERRY PIE
The largest cherry pie ever made was one weighing a total of 12 861·82 kg *12·64 tons* and containing 11 754·06 kg *25 890 lb* of cherry filling. It measured 5·33 m *17 ft 6 in* in diameter, 66·04 cm *26 in* in depth, and was baked by Chef Pierre Bakeries in conjunction with the Michigan Cherry Committee in Traverse City, Michigan, USA on 25 July 1987.

CHOCOLATE MODEL
The largest chocolate model was one measuring 10 × 5 m *32 ft 9½ in × 16 ft 4 ³⁄₅ in* and 73 cm *28·7 in* high of the 1992 Olympic Centre, Barcelona, Spain by Gremi Provincial de Pastigeria i Confiteria School in November 1985.

CHRISTMAS PUDDING
The largest was one of 1390 kg *3064·37 lb*, made by employees of Herbert Adams in Kensington, Victoria, Australia. They started preparing it on 16 Nov 1987 and finished the decorating on 9 Dec 1987.

COCKTAIL
The largest cocktail on record was one of 1 300 litre *285·96 gal* created by Ernst Lechthaler at the Hilton International Hotel, Munich, West Germany on 29 Jan 1988, and named 'Benetton Formula Uno'.

CONDIMENT RAREST
The world's most prized condiment is Cà Cuong, a secretion recovered in minute amounts from beetles in North Vietnam. Owing to war conditions, the price had risen to $100 per 28 g *1 oz* before supplies virtually ceased in 1975.

CUSTARD PIE
The largest custard pie made was one of 203·2 kg *448 lb* made in the kitchen of Jury's Hotel, Dublin under the supervision of Derek McLoughlin and John Clancy on 6 Feb 1987.

DISH
The largest menu item in the world is roasted camel, prepared occasionally for Bedouin wedding feasts. Cooked eggs are stuffed into fish, the fish stuffed into cooked chickens, the chickens stuffed into a roasted sheep's carcass and the sheep stuffed into a whole camel.

EASTER EGGS
The heaviest Easter egg ever made was one weighing 3430 kg *7561 lb 13½ oz*, measuring 3·04 m *10 ft* high, by Siegfried Berndt at 'Macopa' Patisserie, Leicester, and completed on 7 Apr 1982. An egg 5·78 m *18 ft 11½ in* tall was constructed by Tobler Suchard of Bedford, on 10 April 1987.

FOOD MOST EXPENSIVE
The most expensively priced food (as opposed to spice) is First Choice Black Périgord truffle (*Tuber melanosporum*), retailed at £8·50 per 12·5 g *0·44 oz* tin.

> **Strawberry bowl ●** Children from Hazelrigg School picked a record 569·72 kg *1256 lb* of strawberries at Hewitts Farm, Chelsfield, Kent, England on 2 July 1987.

However, in January 1985 in the Hafr El-Baten market, Riyadh, Saudi Arabia local truffles sold for SR 5000 for 3 kg, equivalent to £50·16 for 12·5 g.

FRUIT MOST EXPENSIVE
On 5 Apr 1977 John Synnott of Ashford, County Wicklow, Ireland sold 453 g *1 lb* of strawberries (a punnet of 30 berries) to the restaurateur Leslie Cooke, at auction by Walter L. Cole Ltd in the Dublin Fruit Market for £530 or £17·70 a berry.

HAGGIS
The largest haggis (encased in 8 ox stomach linings) on record was one weighing 273·5 kg *603 lb* made for the ASDA Superstore, Corby, Northants by David A. Hall Ltd of Broxburn, Lothian on 6 Nov 1986.

HAMBURGER
The largest hamburger on record was one of 2270·66 kg *5005 lb 13·8 oz* made on 13 Oct 1985 by Spur Steak Ranches (Pty) Ltd at Three Anchor Bay, Cape Town, South Africa. The burger had a diameter of 7·10 m *23 ft 3½ in* and was cut into over 15 750 portions after grilling.

ICE CREAM SUNDAE
The largest ice cream sundae was one weighing 15 248·32 kg *33 616·75 lb* made by the Knudsen Corp. of Los Angeles and Smucker's at Ohio at Disneyland Hotel in Anaheim, California, USA on 28 July 1985. It consisted of 11 802·4 kg *26 020 lb* of ice-cream, 3414·12 kg *7 521·75 lb* of topping and 34·02 kg *75 lb* of whipped cream.

JELLY
The world's largest jelly, a 35 000 litre *7700 gal* water-melon flavoured pink jelly made by Paul Squires and Geoff Ross worth $14 000, was set at Roma Street Forum, Brisbane, Queensland, Australia on 5 Feb 1981 in a tank by Pool Fab.

KEBAB
The longest kebab ever made was one 19·2 m *63 ft* long, at Leeudoringstad Primary School in Leeudoringstad, South Africa on 26 Sept 1987.

LOAF
The longest loaf ever baked was a rosca de Reyes 649·90 m *2132 ft 2½ in* in length and 1173 kg *1·15 tons* in weight at the Exelaris Hyatt Regency Hotel, Acapulco, Mexico on 6 Jan 1985. If a consumer of the rosca (twisted loaf) finds the embedded bread doll he has to throw the next rosca party. The longest pan loaf baked was one of 138·46 kg *3051 lb 4 oz* measuring 2·7 × 1·5 m *9 ft × 5 ft* by the Calgary Italian Bakery and Southern Alberta Bakers' Association on 7 July 1986 at Calgary, Alberta, Canada.

LOLLIPOP
The world's largest iced lollipop was one of 2608 kg *5750 lb* constructed for the Westside Assembly of God Church, Davenport, Iowa, USA on 7 Sept 1975.

The largest 'regular' lollipop was one of 931 kg *2052·5 lb* made by the Hyatt Regency Memphis Hotel, Tennessee, USA on 20 Feb 1986.

MEAT PIE
The largest ever made was 'The Chuck Wagon Gang's Chili Meat Pie', which weighed 6061 kg *13 362·9 lb*, on 17 Oct 1986 at Odessa, Texas, USA. It was baked in a half cylinder 6 m *20 ft* long and 1·2 m *4 ft* in diameter, and had a 907 kg *2000 lb* crust. Britain's largest weighed 5¾ tonnes/*tons* and measured 5·48 × 1·83 × 0·45 m *18 ft × 6 ft × 18 in*. Baked on 5 Sept 1964 to mark 4 royal births, it was the 8th in the series of Denby Dale, West Yorkshire pies. The first was in 1788 to celebrate King George III's return to sanity, but the 4th (Queen Victoria's Jubilee, 1887) went a bit 'off' and had to be buried in quick-lime.

MILK SHAKE
The largest milk shake was one of 340·96 litre *75 gal* containing 136·08 kg *300 lb* of vanilla ice cream, 136·38 litre *30 gal* of milk and 3·63 kg *8 lb* of vanilla syrup, made by airmen and base officials at Sheppard Air Force Base, Texas, USA on 16 Apr 1988.

MINCE PIE
The largest mince pie recorded was one of 1025 kg *2260 lb* 6·09 × 1·52 m *20 × 5 ft*, baked at Ashby-de-la-Zouch, Leicestershire on 15 Oct 1932.

OMELETTE
The largest omelette in the world was one made of 54 763 eggs with 240 kg *531 lb* cheese in a skillet 9·1 m *30 ft* in diameter cooked by Michael McGowan assisted by his staff and the Sunrise Jaycees of Las Vegas, Nevada, USA on 25 Oct 1986.

A Spanish omelette weighing 300 kg *660 lb* was made by Jose Antonio Rivera Casal at Caracacia, Padron, Spain on 17 May 1987 and consisted of 5000 eggs, 500 kg *1102 lb* of potatoes, 80 kg *176 lb* of red peppers, 10 kg *22 lb* of salt and 150 litre *33 gal* of oil.

PANCAKE
A crew representing Birkett Mills baked and flipped a buckwheat pancake 8·56 m *28 ft 1 in* in diameter and 5·08 cm *2 in* deep at Penn Yan, New York, USA on 27 Sept 1987. The pancake weighed 1924 kg *4238 lb*.

PASTRY
The longest pastry in the world was the 'record' pastry 513·04 m *1683 ft 2½ in* in length made by chefs at the Hyatt Regency Ravinia, Atlanta, Georgia, USA on 26 July 1986.

PIZZA PIE
The largest pizza ever baked was one measuring 30·51 m *100 ft 1 in* in diameter, organised by Lorenzo Amato and Louis Piancone and completed at Highway 27, Havana, Florida, USA on 11 Oct 1987.

POTATO CRISPS
Charles Chip Inc. of Mountville, Pennsylvania, USA, produced

crisps 10 × 17·5 cm *4 × 7 in* from outsize potatoes in February 1977.

POTATO MASH

A single serving of 8·26 tonnes *18 260 lb* of potato mash was prepared in a concrete mixer for the 17th Annual Potato Bowl at Grand Forks, North Dakota, USA on 4 Sept 1982.

SALAMI

The longest salami on record was one 17·9 m *58 ft 9 in* long with a circumference of 52·7 cm *20¾ in*, weighing 391·6 kg *863·5 lb*, made by Kutztown Bologna Company, Pennsylvania, USA on 21 Aug 1986.

SAUSAGE (SEE ALSO GRILL P.158)

The longest continuous sausage ever made was one of 15·91 km *9·89 miles* prepared by Messrs Dewhurst in 21 hr 17 min on 17–18 June 1987, and transported to Hyde Park, London and cooked by scouts on 20 June 1987. Nearly 100 000 portions weighing 4½ tonnes/*tons* were served as part of the St John Ambulance Brigade centenary.

SMÖRGÅSTÅRTA

A *smör*-(butter)*gås*-(goose)*tårta*(cake) 510·69 m *1675 ft 6 in* long was set up by Hans Pettersson and a team on 9 Mar 1985 in Köping, Sweden. It was demolished in short order.

SPICE MOST EXPENSIVE

Prices for wild ginseng (root of *Panax quinquefolius*), from the Chan Pak Mountain area of China, thought to have aphrodisiac qualities, were reported in November 1977 to be as high as $23 000 per ounce in Hong Kong. Total annual shipments from Jilin Province do not exceed 4 kg *140 oz* a year. A leading medical journal in the USA has likened its effects to 'corticosteroid poisoning'.

SPICE 'HOTTEST'

The hottest of all spices is claimed to be Siling labuyo from the Philippines.

The chili pepper or capsicum known as Tepin, of south-west USA, comes in pods 7 mm *⅜ in* in diameter. A single dried gram will produce detectable 'heat' in 31 kg *68·3 lb* of bland sauce.

STICK OF ROCK

The mightiest piece was a stick weighing more than 305 kg *673·5 lb*, 3·6 m *12 ft* long and 40·6 cm *16 in* thick made by Carshalton Confectionery Company of St. Annes-on-Sea, Lancashire on 21 May 1987.

SWEET TOP-SELLING

The world's top-selling sweets (candies) are Life Savers with 33 431 236 300 rolls between 1913 and May 1987. A tunnel formed by the holes in the middle placed end to end would stretch to the Moon and back more than 3 times.

Thomas Syta of Van Nuys, California, USA made one last 7 hr 10 min (with hole intact) on 15 Jan 1983.

TRIFLE

The largest sherry trifle on record was one weighing 886·31 kg *1954 lb* including 81·83 litre *18 gal* of sherry made on 30 May 1988 by staff and students of Weymouth College,

> **Largest paella ●** This monster measured 16 m *52·48 ft* in diameter and was made by Josep Gruges 'Pepitu' on 25 Aug 1987 in the Playa de Aro, Gerona, Spain. The ingredients included 3700 kg *8140 lb* of rice, 3000 kg *6600 lb* of meat, 1500 kg *3300 lb* of mussels, 700 kg *1540 lb* each of beans and peppers, 200 kg *440 lb* of garlic and 400 litres *88 gal* of oil. The paella was eaten by 40 000 people who washed it all down with 8000 bottles of Catalan champagne.

Dorset under the leadership of Roland Foote and Graham Chesher.

YORKSHIRE PUDDING

The largest was one measuring 15·42 m² *166 ft²* made by staff of the Guide Post Hotel, Bradford, West Yorkshire with 50 dozen eggs 63·50 kg *140 lb* of flour and 105·7 litre *186 pints* of milk on 17 Aug 1986.

Gluttony Records

Records for eating and drinking by trenchermen do not match those suffering from the rare disease of bulimia (morbid desire to eat) and polydipsia (pathological thirst). Some bulimics exceed 20 000 calories a day and others eat all their waking hours. An extreme consumption of 174·236 kg *384 lb 2 oz* in 6 days by Matthew Daking, 12 (known as Mortimer's case), was reported in 1743. Fannie Meyer of Johannesburg, South Africa, after a skull fracture, was stated in 1974 to be unsatisfied by less than 160 pints of water a day. By October 1978 he was down to 52 pints. Miss Helge Andersson (b. 1908) of Lindesberg, Sweden was reported in January 1971 to have drunk 22·73 litres *40 pints* of water a day since 1922—a total of 3982 hectolitres *87 600 gal*.

The world's greatest trencherman has been Edward Abraham ('Bozo') Miller (b. 1909) of Oakland, California, USA. He consumes up to 25 000 calories per day or more than 11 times that recommended. He stands 1·71 m *5 ft 7½ in* tall but weighs from 127 to 139 kg *20 to 21½ st* with a 144 cm *57 in* waist. He had been undefeated in eating contests since 1931 (see below). He ate 27 (907 g *2 lb*) pullets at a sitting in Trader Vic's, San Francisco, USA in 1963. Phillip Yadzik (b. 1912) of Chicago, USA in 1955 ate 77 large hamburgers in 2 hours and in 1957 101 bananas in 15 min. The bargees on the Rhine are reputed to be the world's heaviest eaters with 5200 calories a day. However, the New Zealand Sports Federation of Medicine reported in December 1972 that a long-distance road runner consumed 14 321 calories in 24 hr.

While no healthy person has been reported to have succumbed in any contest for eating non-toxic food or

drinking non-alcoholic drinks, such attempts, from a medical point of view, must be regarded as *extremely* inadvisable, particularly among young people. Gluttony record attempts should aim at improving the *rate* of consumption rather than the volume. The *Guinness Book of Records* will not list any records involving the consumption of more than 2 litres *3·52 imperial pints* of beer nor any at all involving spirits. Nor will records for such potentially dangerous categories as live ants, chewing gum, marshmallow or raw eggs with shells be published. The ultimate in stupidity—the eating of a bicycle—has however been included in the book since it is unlikely to attract competition (see **GREATEST OMNIVORE p.177**).

Liquidising, processing or puréeing foodstuffs is not permitted. However, drinking during attempts is permissible.

Records have been claimed as follows:

BAKED BEANS

2780 cold baked beans one by one with a cocktail stick in 30 min by Karen Stevenson, of Wallasey, Merseyside on 4 Apr 1981.

BANANAS

17 (edible weight minimum 128 g *4½ oz* each) in 2 min by Dr Ronald L. Alkana at the University of California, Irvine, USA on 7 Dec 1973.

BEER

Steven Petrosino drank one litre of beer in 1·3 sec on 22 June 1977 at The Gingerbreadman, Carlisle, Pennsylvania, USA.

Peter G. Dowdeswell (b. London, 29 July 1940) of Earls Barton, Northants holds the following records:
2 pints—2·3 sec Zetters Social Club, Wolverton, Bucks, 11 June 1975. *2 litres*—6·0 sec Carriage Horse Hotel, Higham Ferrers, Northants, 7 Feb 1975.

Yards of Ale

2½ pints—5·0 sec RAF Upper Heyford, Oxfordshire, 4 May 1975.

3 pints—5·0 sec Royal Oak, Bishops Cleeve, Gloucestershire, 6 July 1985.

3½ pints—4·49 sec Silver Stadium, Rochester, New York, USA, 19 June 1986.

Upside-down

1 pint—3 sec BBC Radio Leicester studios, 16 Feb 1988.

CHAMPAGNE

1000 bottles per annum by Bobby Acland of the Black Raven, Bishopsgate, London.

CHEESE

453 g *16 oz* of Cheddar in 1 min 13 sec by Peter Dowdeswell in Earls Barton, Northants on 14 July 1978.

CHICKEN

2·1 kg *4 lb 10 oz* in 10 min 37 sec by Valentin Florentino

Muñoz Muñoz at Kortezubi, Vizcaya, Spain on 27 Apr 1986. Sean Barry ate 1·7 kg *3 lb 12 oz* of chicken in 8 min 5 sec at the Royal Oak, Bishops Cleeve, Cheltenham, Gloucestershire on 5 July 1986.

CLAMS
397 (Littlenecks) in 8 min by Dave Barnes at Seattle, Washington, USA on 24 May 1988.

COCKLES
113·5 centilitres *2 pints* in 60·8 sec by Tony Dowdeswell at Kilmarnock, Ayrshire on 1 June 1984.

DOUGHNUTS
12¾ (1·445 kg *51 oz*) in 5 min 46 sec by James Wirth, and 13 (1·474 kg *52 oz*) in 6 min 1·5 sec by John Haight, both at the Sheraton Inn, Canandaigua, New York, USA on 3 Mar 1981.

EELS
453 g *1 lb* of elvers in 13·7 sec by Peter Dowdeswell at Reeves Club, Bristol on 20 Oct 1978.

EGGS
(Hard Boiled) 14 in 14·42 sec by John Kenmuir on Scottish Television's *Live at 1.30* programme on 17 Apr 1987.
(Soft Boiled) 38 in 75 sec by Peter Dowdeswell in Kilmarnock, Ayrshire on 28 May 1984.
(Raw) 13 in 1·0 sec by Peter Dowdeswell at Kilmarnock, Ayrshire on 16 May 1984.

FRANKFURTERS
30 (56·6 g *2 oz*) in 64 sec by Reg Morris at the Miners Rest, Burntwood, Staffordshire on 10 Dec 1986.

GHERKINS
453 g *1 lb* in 41·60 sec by Peter Dowdeswell at Ronelles Discotheque, Cambridge on 8 Feb 1986.

GRAPES
1·39 kg *3 lb 1 oz* of grapes in 34·6 sec by Jim Ellis of Montrose, Michigan, USA on 30 May 1976.

HAGGIS
680 g *24 oz* in 31·94 sec by John Kenmuir at the Bully Inn, near Hamilton, Lanarkshire on 30 Nov 1986.

HAMBURGERS
21 hamburgers (each weighing 100 g *3½ oz*) and buns in 9 min 42 sec by Peter Dowdeswell at Cockshut Hill School, Yardley, Birmingham on 30 June 1984.

ICE CREAM
1·53 kg *3 lb 6 oz* in 31·67 sec by Tony Dowdeswell at the Guinness Museum of World Records, New York on 16 July 1986. The ice cream must be unmelted.

JELLY
56·8 centilitres *20 fl oz* in 8·25 sec by Peter Dowdeswell at the Royal Oak, Bishops Cleeve, Gloucestershire on 5 July 1986. The jelly must be gelatinous.

KIPPERS
27 (self-filleted) in 16 min 52·66 sec by Reg Morris at Walsall, West Midlands on 30 May 1988.

LEMONS
12 quarters (3 lemons) whole (including skin and pips) in 15·3 sec by Bobby Kempf of Roanoke, Virginia, USA on 2 May 1979.

MEAT
One whole roast ox in 42 days by Johann Ketzler of Munich, Germany in 1880.

MEAT PIES
22 (each weighing 156 g *5½ oz*) in 18 min 13 sec by Peter Dowdeswell of Earls Barton, Northants on 5 Oct 1978.

MILK
113·5 centilitres (*2 pt* or *1 imperial quart*) in 3·2 sec by Peter Dowdeswell at Dudley Top Rank Club, West Midlands on 31 May 1975.

OYSTERS (*Eating, Opening*)
2·72 kg *6 lb* (edible mass of 288) in 1 min 33 sec by Tommy Greene in Annapolis, Maryland, USA on 6 July 1985. The record for opening oysters is 100 in 2 min 22·17 sec by Mike Racz in Invercargill, New Zealand on 25 Aug 1987.

PANCAKES
(15·2 cm *6 in* diameter buttered and with syrup) 62 in 6 min

58·5 sec by Peter Dowdeswell at The Drapery, Northampton on 9 Feb 1977.

PEANUTS
100 (whole unshelled) singly in 46 sec by Jim Kornitzer, 21, at Brighton, East Sussex on 1 Aug 1979.

PEAS
7175 petit pois one by one in 60 min using chopsticks by Mrs Janet Harris, Seal Hotel, Selsey, West Sussex on 16 Aug 1984.

PICKLED ONIONS
91 pickled onions (total weight 850 g *30 oz*) in 1 min 8 sec by Pat Donahue in Victoria, British Columbia, Canada on 9 Mar 1978.

PIZZA
907 g *2 lb* in 32 sec by John Kenmuir at Confettis Nightclub, Derby on 18 Mar 1988.

POTATOES
1·36 kg *3 lb* in 1 min 22 sec by Peter Dowdeswell in Earls Barton, Northants on 25 Aug 1978.

POTATO CRISPS
30 bags, at 56·6 g *2 oz* per bag, in 24 min 33·6 sec, without a drink, by Paul G. Tully of Brisbane University, Australia in May 1969.

PRUNES
144 in 31·27 sec by Peter Dowdeswell at Silver Stadium, Rochester, New York, USA on 20 June 1986.

RAVIOLI
2·25 kg *5 lb* (170 squares) in 5 min 34 sec by Peter Dowdeswell at Pleasurewood Hills American Theme Park, Lowestoft, Suffolk on 25 Sept 1983.

SANDWICHES
40 in 17 min 20 sec (jam 'butties' 15·2 × 10·16 × 1·27 cm *6 × 4 × ½ in*) by Reg Morris at the Miners Rest, Burntwood, Staffordshire on 25 Nov 1986.

SAUSAGE MEAT
2·72 kg *6 lb* (96 28·3 g *1 oz* pieces) in 3 min 10 sec by Reg Morris at Spring Cottage, Shelfield, Walsall, West Midlands on 28 Dec 1986. No 'Hot Dog' contest results have been remotely comparable.

SHEEP'S BRAINS
1·16 kg *2·55 lb* in 3 min by William Michael Burke at Balmain, NSW, Australia on 10 Nov 1986.

SHRIMPS
1·36 kg *3 lb* in 3 min 10 sec by Peter Dowdeswell at Weymouth, Dorset on 7 Aug 1985.

SNAILS
1·1 kg *38·8 oz* in 1 min 5.6 sec by Andoni Basterrechea Dominguez at Kortezubi, Vizcaya, Spain on 27 Apr 1986.

SPAGHETTI
91·44 m *100 yd* in 12·02 sec by Peter Dowdeswell at 42nd St Disco, Halesowen, West Midlands on 3 July 1986.

STRAWBERRIES
907 g *2 lb* in 12·95 sec by Peter Dowdeswell at Easby Street, Nottingham on 5 July 1985.

SUSHI
680 g *1½ lb* of nigiri-sushi in 1 min 13·5 sec in Tokyo, Japan by Peter Dowdeswell on 22 February 1985.

TORTILLA
74 (total weight 1·85 kg *4 lb 1½ oz*) in 30 min by Tom Nall in the 2nd World Championship at Mariano's Mexican Restaurant, Dallas, Texas, USA on 16 Oct 1973.

WHELKS
100 (unshelled) in 5 min 17 sec by John Fletcher at The Apples and Pears public house, Liverpool Street Station, London on 18 Aug 1983.

WINKLING
50 shells picked (with a straight pin) in 3 min 15 sec by Mrs B. Charles at Eastbourne, East Sussex on 4 Aug 1982.

GREATEST OMNIVORE
Michel Lotito (b. 15 June 1950) of Grenoble, France, known as Monsieur Mangetout, has been eating metal and glass since 1959. Gastroenterologists have X-rayed his stomach and have described his ability to consume 900 g *2 lb* of metal per

day as unique. His diet since 1966 has included 10 bicycles, a supermarket trolley in 4½ days, 7 TV sets, 6 chandeliers and a low-calorie Cessna light aircraft which he ate in Caracas, Venezuela. He is said to have provided the only example in history of a coffin (handles and all) ending up inside a man.

The highest regularly performed head-first dives are those of professional divers from La Quebrada ('the break in the rocks') at Acapulco, Mexico, a height of 26·7 m *87½ ft*. The leader of the 27 divers in the Club de Clavadistas is Raul Garcia (b. 1928) with more than 35 000 dives. The first feminine accomplishment was by Mrs Barbara Winters (b. 12 Nov 1953), *née* Mayer, on 7 Dec 1976. The base rocks, 6·40 m *21 ft* out from the take-off, necessitate a leap of 8·22 m *27 ft* out. The water is 3·65 m *12 ft* deep.

The world record high dive is 53·23 m *174 ft 8 in* by Randal Dickison (US) at Ocean Park, Hong Kong on 6 Apr 1985. The feminine record is 36·57 m *120 ft* by Lucy Wardle (US) at the same exhibition. The highest witnessed in Britain is one of 32·9 m *108 ft* into 2·43 m *8 ft* of water at the Aqua Show at Earl's Court, London on 22 Feb 1946 by Roy Fransen (1915–85).

On 8 May 1885, Sarah Ann Henley, 24, jumped from the Clifton Suspension Bridge, which crosses the Avon. Her 76 m *250 ft* fall was slightly cushioned by her voluminous dress and petticoat acting as a parachute. She landed, bruised and bedraggled, in the mud on the north bank and was carried to hospital by 4 policemen. On 11 Feb 1968 Jeffrey Kramer, 24, leapt off the George Washington Bridge 76 m *250 ft* above the Hudson River, New York City, USA, and survived. Of the 696 identified people who have made 73 m *240 ft* suicide dives from the Golden Gate Bridge, San Francisco, California, USA since 1937, 12 survived of whom Todd Sharratt was the only one who managed to swim ashore unaided.

Col. Harry A. Froboess (Switzerland) jumped 110 m *360 ft* into the Bodensee from the airship *Graf Hindenburg* on 22 June 1936.

The greatest height reported for a dive into an air bag is 99·36 m *326 ft* by stuntman Dan Koko from the top of Vegas World Hotel and Casino into a 6·1 × 12·2 × 4·2 m *20 × 40 × 14 ft* target on 13 Aug 1984. His impact speed was 141 km/h *88 mph*. Kitty O'Neill dived 54·8 m *180 ft* from a helicopter over Northridge, California, USA on 9 Sept 1979 on to an air cushion measuring 9·14 × 18·28 m *30 × 60 ft* for a TV film stunt.

Henri La Mothe (b. 1904) set a record diving 8·53 m *28 ft* into 31·43 cm *12⅜ in* of water in a child's paddling pool in

Hay bale rolling ● 'Cressy Rangers' Mark Eastoe and Paul Bowles—winners of the Hay Bale Rolling Championship held at Cressy, Tasmania, Australia on 12 March 1988. They rolled a 400 kg *882 lb* round bale over a 50 m *164 ft* course in 20·53 sec. The event was organised by the Parish Council of Cressy as part of their Bicentennial celebrations.

Northridge, California, USA on 7 Apr 1979. He struck the water chest first at a speed of 45·7 km/h *28·4 mph.*

High-Wire Act

The greatest height above street level of any high-wire performance has been a 42·6 m *140 ft* long wire between the 411 m *1350 ft* tall twin towers of the World Trade Center, New York, USA, by Philippe Petit, 24, of Nemours, France on 7 Aug 1974. He was charged with criminal trespass after a 75 min display of at least 7 crossings. The police psychiatrist opined 'Anyone who does this 110 storeys up can't be entirely right.'

Hitch-Hiking

The title of world champion hitch-hiker is claimed by Bill Heid of Allen Park, Michigan, USA who from 1964 to 1985 obtained free rides of 492 248 km *305 870 miles.* Stephen Burns of Melbourne, Australia hitched round all 48 co-terminous states of the USA in 26 days 6 hr in an 18 407 km *11 438 mile* trip in 56 vehicles from 8 Sept to 4 Oct 1984.

The hitch-hiking record for the 1406 km *874 miles* from Land's End, Cornwall to John O'Groats, Caithness is 17 hr 8 min by Martin Clark and Graham Beynon of Guildford, Surrey on 14–15 September 1987. The time before the first 'hitch' on the first day is excluded. The fastest time recorded for the round trip is 41 hr 42 min by Anthony D. Sproson of Wolverhampton from 17–19 Sept 1984.

Hod Carrying

Jim Ford of Bury, Lancs carried bricks totalling 161 kg *355 lb* up the minimum 3·65 m *12 ft* ladder (17 rungs) on 28 June 1984 at Hever Castle, Kent on the *International Guinness TV Show* presented by David Frost. Eric Stenman of Jakobstad, Finland carried 74 bricks of 4 kg *8·8 lb* each, so totalling 296 kg *651 lb,* in a 4 kg *8·8 lb* hod 5 metres *16·4 ft* on the flat before ascending a runged ramp to a height of 2·13 m *7 ft* on 25 July 1939.

Homework—Longest on Ice

In 1967, Thomas Litz, a teacher in Switzerland, set some homework which he marked but forgot to return. It was only in 1988, while sorting through old papers, that he came across the exercises. One of the pupils, Mark Johnson, had by this time himself become a teacher at the school, and on 1 Feb 1988 was given his homework back, 21 years late.

Hoop Rolling

In 1968 it was reported that Zolilio Diaz (Spain) had rolled a hoop 965 km *600 miles* from Mieres to Madrid, Spain and back in 18 days.

Hop-Scotch

The longest recorded hop-scotch marathon is one of 101 hr 15 min by Mark Harrison and Tony Lunn at the Studio Night Club, Leicester from 30 Sept to 4 Oct 1985.

House of Cards

The greatest number of storeys achieved in building freestanding houses of standard playing cards is 68 to a height of 3·9 m *12 ft 10 in* built by John Sain, 15, of South Bend, Indiana, USA in May 1984.

Hula Hooping

The highest claim for sustaining gyrating hoops between shoulders and hips is 81 by William Kleeman 'Chico' Johnson (b. 8 July 1939) on BBC TV's *Record Breakers* on 18 Sept 1983. Three complete gyrations are mandatory. The women's record is 75 by Desai Kehaiovi of the Kehaiovi Troupe of Bulgaria on Wellington Pier, Great Yarmouth on 12 July 1987.

The longest marathon for a single hoop is 90 hr by Roxann Rose of Pullman, Washington, USA from 2–6 Apr 1987.

Human Cannonball

The first human cannonball was Emilio Onra *né* Mai-trejean at Cirque d'Hiver, Paris, France on 21 Nov 1875. The record distance for firing a human from a cannon is

53·3 m *175 ft* in the case of Emanuel Zacchini, son of the pioneer Hugo Zacchini in the Ringling Bros and Barnum & Bailey Circus, Madison Square Gardens, New York City, USA in 1940. His muzzle velocity has been estimated at 86·9 km/h *54 mph.* On his retirement the management were fortunate in finding that his daughter Florinda was of the same calibre. An experiment on Yorkshire TV on 17 Aug 1978 showed that when Miss Sue Evans, 17, was fired she was 9·5 mm *⅜ in* shorter on landing.

Human Centipede

The largest 'human centipede' to move 30 m *98 ft 5 in* (with ankles firmly tied together) consisted of 475 people. Not one single person fell over in the course of the walk, which took place on 5 Feb 1988 in Southampton, Hampshire.

Human Fly

Lead climber Jean-Claude Droyer (b. 8 May 1946) of Paris, France, and Pierre Puiseux (b. 2 Dec 1953) of Pau, France climbed up the outside of the Eiffel Tower to a height of 300 m *984 ft* with no dynamic mechanical assistance on 21 July 1980. Jean-Claude took 2 hr 18 min 15 sec to complete the climb.

Jaromir Wagner (b. Czechoslovakia 1941) became the first man to fly the Atlantic standing on the wing of an aircraft. He took off from Aberdeen, Grampian on 28 Sept 1980.

Joke Cracking

T. R. (Tim) Benker of Chicago told jokes unremittingly for 48 hr 30 min in the window of the Marshall Field store, Chicago, Illinois, USA from 17–19 Nov 1985. The duo record is 52 hr by Wayne Malton and Mike Hamilton at the Howard Johnson Motor Hotel, Toronto airport, Ontario, Canada from 13–16 Nov 1975.

Jumble Sale

Britain's largest jumble sale was 'Jumbly '79' sponsored by *Woman's Own* at Alexandra Palace, London from 5–7 May 1979 in aid of the Save The Children Fund. The attendance was 60 000 and the gross takings in excess of £60 000. The Winnetka Congregational Church, Illinois, USA raised $147 378·74 in their 54th one-day rummage sale on 8 May 1986.

The Cleveland Convention Center, Ohio, USA White Elephant Sale (instituted 1933) on 18–19 Oct 1983 raised $427 935·21.

Kiss of Life

Two teams, one consisting of Frank Blake and Kevin McKeown, and the other of Les Williams and David Bailey, each completed a 77 hr CPR (cardiopulmonary resuscitation—15 compressions alternating with 2 breaths) marathon between 31 Dec 1987 and 3 Jan 1988 in Melbourne, Florida, USA.

Kissing

The most prolonged osculatory marathon in cinematic history is one of 185 sec by Regis Toomey and Jane Wyman (b. Sarah Jane Faulks 4 Jan 1914, later Mrs Ronald Reagan) in *You're in the Army Now* released in 1940. Eddie Levin and Delphine Crha celebrated the breaking of the record for the longest ever kiss of 17 days 10½ hr in Chicago, USA on 24 Sept 1984 with a kiss. John McPherson kissed 4444 women in 8 hr in Eldon Square, Newcastle-upon-Tyne on 8 Mar 1985, a rate of 1 each 6·48 sec. The most protracted kiss underwater was one of 2 min 18 sec by Toshiaki Shirai and Yukiko Nagata on Channel 8, Fuji TV in Tokyo, Japan on 2 Apr 1980.

Kite Flying

The largest kite flown was the Thai Snake flown by Herman van den Broek and Jan Pieter Kuil for 22 min 50 sec at Uithuizen, Netherlands on 11 Aug, 1984. It was 650 m *2133 ft* long, with an area of 770 m² *8288 ft².*

The most kites flown on a single line is 7150 by Sadao Harada, 69, at Kagoshima, Japan on 27 Apr 1987.

The classic record height is 9740 m *31 955 ft* by a chain of 8 kites over Lindenberg, Germany on 1 Aug 1919. The record for a single kite is 6860 m (min.)–8530 m (max.) *22 500 ft (min.)–28 000 ft (max.)* by Professor Philip R. and Jay P. Kunz of Laramie, Wyoming, USA on 21 Nov 1967. *Kite Lines* magazine of Baltimore, Maryland, USA does not accept triangulation by line angle and length but only range-finder sightings or radar.

The longest recorded flight is one of 180 hr 17 min by the Edmonds Community College team at Long Beach, Washington, USA from 21–29 Aug 1982. Managing the flight of the J-25 parafoil was Harry N. Osborne.

Knitting

The world's most prolific hand-knitter of all time has been Mrs Gwen Matthewman of Featherstone, West Yorkshire. She attained a speed of 111 stitches per min in a test at Phildar's Wool Shop, Central Street, Leeds on 29 Sept 1980. Her technique has been filmed by the world's only Professor of Knitting—a Japanese.

The Exeter Spinners—Audrey Felton, Christine Heap, Eileen Lancaster, Majorie Mellis, Ann Sandercock and Maria Scott—produced a jumper by hand from raw fleece in 1 hr 55 min 50·2 sec on 25 Sept 1983 at BBC Television Centre, London.

Knot-Tying

The fastest recorded time for tying the 6 Boy Scout Handbook Knots (square knot, sheet bend, sheep shank, clove hitch, round turn and 2 half hitches and bowline) on individual ropes is 8·1 sec by Clinton R. Bailey Sr, 52, of Pacific City, Oregon, USA on 13 Apr 1977.

Leap Frogging

Fourteen students at the University of Szczecin, Poland covered 1068·93 km *663·8 miles* in 132 hr 38 min from 23–28 May 1987.

Life Saving

In November 1974 the city of Galveston, Texas, USA and the Noon Optimist Club unveiled a plaque to the deaf-mute lifeguard Leroy Colombo (1905–74) who saved 907 people from drowning in the waters around Galveston Island from 1917 to his death. The greatest single rescue in Britain was on 17 Mar 1907 when 4 lifeboats lifted 456 shipwreck survivors to safety off The Lizard, Cornwall.

Lightning—Most Times Struck

The only man in the world to be struck by lightning 7 times is ex-park ranger Roy C. Sullivan (US), the human lightning conductor of Virginia, USA. His attraction for lightning began in 1942 (lost big toe nail), and was resumed in July 1969 (lost eyebrows), in July 1970 (left shoulder seared), on 16 Apr 1972 (hair set on fire), on 7 Aug 1973 (new hair refired and legs seared), on 5 June 1976 (ankle injured), and he was sent to Waynesboro Hospital with chest and stomach burns on 25 June 1977 after being struck while fishing. In September 1983 he died by his own hand, reportedly rejected in love.

Lion-Taming

The greatest number of lions mastered and fed in a cage by an unaided lion-tamer was 40, by 'Captain' Alfred Schneider in 1925. Clyde Raymond Beatty handled more than 40 'cats' (mixed lions and tigers) simultaneously. Beatty (b. Bainbridge, Ohio, USA, 10 June 1903, d. Ventura, California, USA, 19 July 1965) was the featured attraction at every show he appeared with for more than 40 years. He insisted upon being called a lion-trainer. More than 20 lion-tamers have died of injuries since 1900.

Log Rolling

The record number of International Championships is 10 by Jubiel Wickheim (of Shawnigan Lake, British Columbia, Canada) between 1956 and 1969. At Albany, Oregon, USA on 4 July 1956 Wickheim rolled on a 35·5 cm *14 in* log against Chuck Harris of Kelso, Washington, USA for 2 hr 40 min before losing. The youngest international log-rolling champion is Cari Ann Hayer (b. 23 June 1977), who won her first championship on 15 July 1984 at Hayward, Wisconsin, USA.

MAGICIAN—FASTEST

Paul Ricksecker performed 91 different tricks in 2 min 12·5 sec at the 57th Annual Magi-Fest, Columbus, Ohio, USA on 6 Feb 1988.

MERRY-GO-ROUND

The longest merry-go-round marathon on record is one of 312 hr 43 min by Gary Mandau, Chris Lyons and Dana Dover in Portland, Oregon, USA from 20 Aug-2 Sept 1976.

MESSAGE IN A BOTTLE

The longest recorded interval between drop and pick-up is 73 years in the case of a message thrown from the SS *Arawatta* out of Cairns, Queensland, Australia on 9 June 1910 in a lotion bottle and reported to be found on Moreton Island on 6 June 1983.

METEOROLOGICAL BALLOON INFLATION

The inflation of a standardised 1000-gramme meteorological balloon to a diameter of 2·43 m *8 ft* against time was achieved by Nicholas Berkeley Mason in 57 min 7 sec for a Fuji TV programme in Tokyo, Japan on 9 Mar 1986.

MILK BOTTLE BALANCING

The greatest distance walked by a person continuously balancing a full pint milk bottle on the head is 38·6 km *24 miles* by Ashrita Furman of Jamaica, NY, USA on 10 July 1983.

MORSE

The highest recorded speed at which anyone has received Morse code is 75·2 words per minute—over 17 symbols per second. This was achieved by Ted R. McElroy of the United States in a tournament at Asheville, North Carolina, USA on 2 July 1939.

The highest speed recorded for hand key transmitting is 175 symbols a minute by Harry A. Turner of the US Army Signal Corps at Camp Crowder, Missouri, USA on 9 Nov 1942. Thomas Morris, a GPO operator, is reputed to have been able to send at 39–40 wpm *c.* 1919 but this is not verifiable.

MUSICAL CHAIRS

The largest game on record was one starting with 6003 participants, ending with Tamara van der Schans on the last chair, which was held in the market place at Etten-Leur, Netherlands on 15 Feb 1988.

NOODLE MAKING

Mark Pi of the China Gate Restaurant, Columbus, Ohio, USA made 2048 noodle strings (over 1·52 m *5 ft*) in 34·5 sec on 12 Feb 1983.

OMELETTE MAKING

The greatest number of 2-egg omelettes made in 30 min is 315 by John Elkhay at the City Lights Restaurant in Providence, Rhode Island, USA on 29 June 1985.

ONION PEELING

The record for peeling 22·67 kg *50 lb* of onions is 3 min 18 sec by Alain St. John in Plainfield, Connecticut, USA on 6 July 1980. Under revised rules stipulating a minimum of 50 onions, Alfonso Salvo of York, Pennsylvania, USA peeled 22·67 kg *50 lb* of onions (52 onions) in 5 min 23 sec on 28 Oct 1980.

ORGAN

The longest recorded electric organ marathon is one of 440 hr by Tony Peters at Sheppey Beach Social Club, Isle of Sheppey, Kent from 20 Apr–8 May 1987.

The longest church organ recital ever sustained has been 119 hr by Martin Stanley at St. Mary the Virgin, Brixham, Devon from 25–30 Aug 1986.

PADDLE BOATING

The longest recorded voyage is 3582 km *2226 miles* in

103 days by the foot power of Mick Sigrist and Brad Rud down the the Mississippi River from the headwaters in Minnesota to the Gulf of Mexico from 4 Aug to 11 Nov 1979.

PANCAKE TOSSING

The greatest number of times a pancake has been tossed in 2 minutes is 232 by Philip Artingstall on 16 Feb 1988 at the Hawthorne Restaurant, Fordyce, Grampian.

PIANO PLAYING

The record for piano playing is 1218 hr (50 days 18 hr) playing 22 hr every day (with 5 min intervals each playing hour) from 7 May to 27 June 1982 by David Scott at Wagga Wagga League Football Club, NSW, Australia. *The non-stop category is now discontinued.*

PIANO SMASHING

The record time for demolishing an upright piano and passing the entire wreckage through a circle 22·8 cm *9 in* in diameter is 1 min 37 sec by 6 members of the Tinwald Rugby Football Club, Ashburton, New Zealand led by David Young on 6 Nov 1977. Messrs Anthony

> **Mantle of bees** ● Max Beck was covered all over by a mantle of an estimated 100 000 swarming bees weighing 12·48 kg *27½ lb* at Bob Harvey's Bee Farm, New Jersey, USA on 19 Aug 1987.

> **Needle threading** ● The record number of times that a strand of cotton has been threaded through a number 13 needle (eye 12·7 mm × 1·6 mm, *½ in × ¹⁄₁₆ in*) in 2 hr is 5370, set by Diane Sharp (right) on 1 Aug 1987 at the Charitable Union's centenary event, Battle Creek, Michigan, USA.

Fukes, Mike Newman and Terry Cullington smashed a piano with bare hands and feet in 2 min 53 sec in Nottingham on 25 Aug 1979. All wreckage was passed through the circle.

PIANO TUNING

The record time for pitch raising (one semi-tone or 100 cents) and then returning a piano to a musically acceptable quality is 4 min 20 sec by Steve Fairchild at the Piano Technicians Guild contest at the Dante Piano Co factory, NY, USA on 5 Feb 1980.

PILLAR BOX MOUNTING

The record number to pile on top of or hang from a standard double pillar box (oval top of 0·55 m² *6 ft²*) is 32, all students of Wentworth College, York University in Parliament St, York on 27 Feb 1985.

PIPE SMOKING

The duration record for keeping a pipe (3·3 g *0·1 oz* of tobacco) continuously alight with only an initial match under IAPSC (International Association of Pipe Smokers Clubs) rules is 126 min 39 sec by 5-time champion William Vargo of Swartz Creek, Michigan, USA at the 27th World Championships in 1975. The only other 5-time champion is Paul T. Spaniola (US) (1951–66–70–73–77). On 18 Aug 1984 Joe Oetli achieved 130 min 11 sec at the 15th Iowa State Fair contest using *two* matches. Longer durations have been recorded in less rigorously invigilated contests in which the foul practices of 'tamping' and 'gardening' are not unknown.

PLANE PULLING

Dave Gauder, 30, frustrated the take-off of 2 Piper Cherokees by holding 2 tow ropes despite a pull of 612 kg *1349 lb* at Bobbington, Staffs on 16 July 1985.

Dave Wilkins of Burntwood, Staffs single-handedly pulled a BAC 1-11 over 22·86 m *75 ft* at Birmingham Airport on 25 May 1986.

PLATE SPINNING

The greatest number of plates spun simultaneously is 84 by Dave Spathaky on BBC TV's *Record Breakers* on 21 Oct 1986.

POGO STICK JUMPING

The greatest number of jumps achieved is 130 077 by Gary Stewart in Reading, Ohio, USA on 8–9 Mar 1985.

Ashrita Furman of New York, USA set a distance record of 18·68 km *11·53 miles* in 8 hr 21 min on 8 Jan 1986. His 'route' up and down the foothills of Mt Fuji, Japan was from the Gotemba railroad station, west along the Gotembaguchi Tozando Road, to an elevation of 90 m *295·28 ft*, and return.

POLE-SQUATTING

Modern records do not, in fact, compare with that of St

Simeon the Elder (c. AD 390–459), called 'Stylites', a monk who spent his last 39 years up a stone pillar on The Hill of Wonders, near Antioch, Syria. This is probably the longest-lasting example of record setting.

There being no international rules, the 'standards of living' atop poles vary widely. Mark Sutton finally descended from his pole on 1 July 1985 in Victoria, BC, Canada after 488 days.

Pat Bowen stayed in a barrel (max. capacity 150 gallons) atop a pole (5·48 m *18 ft*) outside the Bull Hotel, Ludlow, Shropshire for 40 days 1 hr from 28 May to 7 July 1986.

POP GROUP

The duration record for a 4-man group is 147 hr by the 'Dekorators' at Becketts Bar, Bexhill-on-Sea, East Sussex from 8–14 Jan 1984. *From next year this category is being combined with the 'Rock Band' entry, and only one marathon will be listed.*

POTATO PEELING

The greatest amount of potatoes peeled by 5 people to an institutional cookery standard with standard kitchen knives in 45 min is 310·84 kg *685 lb 4 oz* (net) by Lia Sombroek, Marlene Guiamo, Walijem Kertoidjojo, Judith van Druenen and Wijna Scheringa at Emmeloord, Netherlands on 17 Sept 1987.

PRAM PUSHING

The greatest distance covered in pushing a pram in 24 hr is 555·62 km *345·25 miles* by Runner's Factory of Los Gatos, California, USA with an all-star team of 57 Californian runners on 23–24 June 1979. A 10-man Royal Marine team from the Commando Training Centre, Lympstone, Devon, with an adult 'baby', covered 406·60 km *252·65 miles* in 24 hr from 31 Mar to 18 Apr 1984.

'PSYCHIATRIST' FASTEST

The world's fastest 'psychiatrist' was Dr Albert L. Weiner of Erlton, New Jersey, USA, trained solely in osteopathy but who dealt with up to 50 psychiatric patients a day in 4 treatment rooms. He relied heavily on narco-analysis, muscle relaxants and electro-shock treatments. In December 1961 he was found guilty on 12 counts of manslaughter from using unsterilised needles.

QUIZZES

The highest number of participants was 80 977 in the All-Japan High School Quiz Championship televised by NTV on 31 Dec 1983. The most protracted contest was that lasting 110 hr in Long Hanborough, Oxfordshire from 27 Mar to 1 Apr 1986. The 2 teams answered correctly 22 483 of the 37 310 questions.

QUOIT THROWING

The world record for rope quoit throwing is an unbroken sequence of 4002 pegs by Bill Irby Sr of Australia in 1968.

RAMP JUMPING

The longest distance ever achieved for motorcycle long jumping is 74·98 m *246 ft* by Todd Seeley at a World of Wheels show in Tampa, Florida, USA on 28 Feb 1988.

The pioneer of this form of exhibition—Evel Knievel (b. Robert Craig Knievel, 17 Oct 1938 at Butte, Montana, USA)—had suffered 433 bone fractures by his 1975 season. His abortive attempt to cross the 485 m *1600 ft* wide and 180 m *600 ft* deep Snake River Canyon, Idaho, USA on 8 Sept 1974 in a rocket reputedly increased his lifetime earnings by $6 million.

The longest ramp jump in a car by a professional stunt driver is 70·73 m *232 ft* by Jacqueline De Creed (née Creedy) in a 1967 Ford Mustang at Santa Pod Raceway, Bedfordshire on 3 Apr 1983.

> **Rock band** ● The duration record for a rock group is 107 hrs by 4-piece heavy metal band Vengence K.S.A. at Take Two, Sheffield, South Yorkshire from 7–11 Sept 1987.

RAPPELING (or ABSEILING)

The west face of Thor Peak, Baffin Island, northern Canada allowed an abseiling or rappeling record of 990 m *3250 ft* by Steve Holmes (US) in July 1982. The longest descent down the side of a skyscraper is one of 176·7 m *580 ft* (52 storeys) in Hong Kong by Capt. Martin Fuller (1st Bn Cheshire Regt) on 1 Sept 1984.

RIDING IN ARMOUR

The longest recorded ride in full armour (50·8 kg *8 stone*) is one of 268·7 km *167 miles* from Edinburgh to Dumfries in 3 days (riding time 28 hr 30 min) by Dick Brown, 48, from 13–15 June 1979.

RIVETING

The world's record for riveting is 11 209 in 9 hr by John Moir at the Workman Clark Ltd shipyard, Belfast, Northern Ireland, in June 1918. His peak hour was his 7th with 1409, an average of nearly 23½ per min.

ROCK BAND

See photograph. *From next year this category is being combined with the 'Pop Group' entry, and only one marathon will be listed.*

ROCKING CHAIR

The longest recorded 'Rockathon' is 453 hr 40 min by Robert McDonald at Mariposa, California, USA from 14 Mar–2 Apr 1986.

ROLLING PIN

The record distance for a woman to throw a 907 g *2 lb* rolling pin is 53·4 m *175 ft 5 in* by Lori La Deane Adams, 21, at Iowa State Fair, Iowa, USA on 21 Aug 1979.

SAND CASTLE

A sand castle 8·37 km *5·2 miles* long was made by staff and pupils of Ellon Academy, near Aberdeen, Grampian, on 24 March 1988.

SAND SCULPTURING

The longest sand sculpture ever made—with a water-saturated mound of sand mechanically piled up and the sculpture meticulously carved out—was a 3279 m *10 760 ft* long 'Millerpede' which meandered along South Padre Island, Texas, USA on 18 Mar 1987, organised by Walter McDonald and Lucinda Wierenga and built by college students and local members of the Sons of the Beach organisation. The tallest was the 'Lost City of Atlantis' which was 16·08 m *52 ft 9 in* tall and was built by Sand Sculptors International of California on Treasure Island, Florida, USA from 21–26 Apr 1986.

SCOOTER RIDING

The greatest distance covered by a team of 25 in 24 hr is 540·93 km *336·11 miles* by Wimmera Young Farmers, Victoria, Australia on 22–23 Mar 1980.

SEARCH LONGEST

Walter Edwin Percy Zillwood (b. Deptford, London, Dec 1900) traced his missing sister Lena (Mrs Elizabeth Eleanor Allen, b. Nov 1897, d. Jan 1982) after 79 years through the agency of the Salvation Army on 3 May 1980.

SEE-SAW

George Partridge and Tamara Marquez of Auburn High School, Washington, USA on a suspension see-saw completed 1101 hr 40 min (indoor) from 28 Mar to 13 May 1977. Georgia Chaffin and Tammy Adams of Goodhope Junior High School, Cullman, Alabama, USA completed 730 hr 30 min (outdoor) from 25 June to 25 July 1975.

SERMON

The longest sermon on record was delivered by the Reverend Ronald Gallagher at the Baptist Temple, Appomattox, Virginia, USA for 120 hr from 26 June–1 July 1983. From 31 May to 10 June 1969 the 14th Dalai Lama (b. 6 July 1934 as Tenzin Gyalto), exiled ruler of Tibet, completed a sermon on Tantric Buddhism for 5–7 hr per day to total 60 hr, in India.

SHAVING

The fastest demon barber on record is Gerry Harley, who shaved 987 men in 60 min with a safety razor in Gillingham, Kent on 28 Apr 1983 taking a perfunctory 3·64 sec per volunteer. On 13 Aug 1984 he shaved 235 even braver volunteers with a cut-throat razor in a less perfunctory 15·3 sec per face. He drew blood only once.

SHEAF TOSSING

The world's best performance for tossing a 3·63 kg *8 lb* sheaf for height is 19·77 m *64 ft 10¼ in* by Trond Ulleberg of Skolleborg, Norway on 11 Nov 1978. Such pitchfork contests date from 1914.

SHEEP TO SHOULDER

At the International Wool Secretariat Development Centre, Ilkley, West Yorkshire, a team of 8 using commercial machinery produced a jumper from shearing sheep to the finished article in 2 hr 28 min 32 sec on 3 Sept 1986.

SHOESHINE BOYS

In this category (limited to a team of 4 teenagers; duration of 8 hr; shoes 'on the hoof') the record is 6780 pairs by the Sheffield Citadel Band of the Salvation Army, South Yorkshire, on 27 Feb 1982.

SHORTHAND FASTEST

The highest recorded speeds ever attained under championship conditions are: 300 words per min (99·64 per cent accuracy) for 5 minutes and 350 wpm (99·72 per cent accuracy, that is, 2 insignificant errors) for 2 minutes by Nathan Behrin (US) in tests in New York in December 1922. Behrin (b. 1887) used the Pitman system invented in 1837. Morris I. Kligman, official court reporter of the US Court House, New York has taken 50 000 words in 5 hr (a sustained rate of 166·6 wpm). Rates are much dependent upon the nature, complexity and syllabic density of the material. Mr G. W. Bunbury of Dublin, Ireland held the unique distinction of writing at 250 wpm for 10 minutes on 23 Jan 1894.

Mr Arnold Bradley achieved a speed of 309 wpm without error using the Sloan-Duployan system with 1545 words in 5 minutes in a test in Walsall, West Midlands on 9 Nov 1920.

SHOUTING

Donald H. Burns of St George's, Bermuda, USA won the Loudest Cry trophy in the Seventh International Town Criers' Championship in Halifax, Nova Scotia, Canada on 15 Sept 1984 with a shout recorded at 113 decibels.

The greatest number of wins in the national Town Criers' Contest is 11 (between 1939–73) by Ben Johnson of Fowey, Cornwall. The first national feminine champion has been Mrs Henrietta Sargent, towncrier, of The Three Horse Shoes, Cricklade, Wiltshire in 1980. On being told she had beaten the other 31 contestants she said 'I'm speechless'. (See also page 17)

SHOWERING

The most prolonged continuous shower bath on record is one of 340 hr 40 min by Kevin McCartney of State University College at Buffalo, New York, USA, from 29 Mar to 12 Apr 1985. The feminine record is 121 hr 1 min by Lisa D'Amato from 5–10 Nov 1981 at Harpur College, Binghamton, also New York, USA. Desquamation can be a positive danger.

SINGING

The longest recorded solo-singing marathon is one of 200 hr 20 min by Jorge António Hidalgo Chamorro at the Piano Bar, Barcelona, Spain, from 7–15 Nov 1985. The marathon record for a choir has been 78 hr 28 min by the Barnsley Junior Operatic and Dramatic Society at the Globe Theatre, Barnsley, South Yorkshire from 29 Aug–1 Sept 1987. Acharya Prem Bhikuji (d.18 Apr 1970) started chanting the Akhand Rama-Dhoon at Jamnagar, Gujarat, India on 31 July 1964 and devotees were continuing in January 1988.

PARACHUTING RECORDS

It is estimated that the human body reaches 99 per cent of its low-level terminal velocity after falling 573 m *1880 ft*, which takes 13–14 sec. This is 188–201 km/h *117–125 mph* at normal atmospheric pressure in a random posture, but up to 298 km/h *185 mph* in a head-down position.

FIRST ● **Tower**[1] ● Louis-Sébastien Lenormand (1757–1839), quasi-parachute, Montpellier, France, 1783.
Balloon ● André-Jacques Garnerin (1769–1823), 680 m *2230 ft* Monceau Park, Paris, France, 22 Oct 1797.
Aircraft ● *Man*; 'Captain' Albert Berry, an aerial exhibitionist, St. Louis, Missouri, USA, 1 Mar 1912. *Woman*; Mrs Georgina 'Tiny' Broadwick (b. 1893), Griffith Park, Los Angeles, USA, 21 June 1913.

LONGEST DURATION FALL ● Lt Col Wm H. Rankin, USMC, 40 min due to thermals, North Carolina, USA, 26 July 1956.

LONGEST DELAYED DROP ● **World**
● *Man*; Capt Joseph W. Kittinger[2], 25 816 m *84 700 ft 16·04 miles*, from balloon at 31 333 m *102 800 ft*, Tularosa, New Mexico, USA, 16 Aug 1960. *Woman*; E. Fomitcheva (USSR) 14 800 m *48 556 ft* over Odessa, USSR, 26 Oct 1977.
Over UK ● *Man (Civilian)*; P. Halfacre, R. O'Brien, R. James, 8321 m *27 300 ft* from an aircraft at 9144 m *30 000 ft*, Sibson, Peterborough, Cambridgeshire, 27 Aug 1983. *Woman (Civilian)*; Francesca Gannon and Valerie Slattery, 6520 m *21 391 ft* from 7600 m *24 934 ft*, Netheravon, Wiltshire, 11 Mar 1987. *Group*; S/Ldr J. Thirtle AFC, Fl Sgt A. K. Kidd AFM, Sgts L. Hicks (d. 1971), P. P. Keane AFM BEM, K. J. Teesdale AFM, 11 943 m *39 183 ft* from 12 613 m *41 383 ft*, Boscombe Down, Wiltshire, 16 June 1967.

BASE JUMP[3] ● **Longest (Spire)** ● Carl Ronald Boenische and Jean K. Campbell Boenische, 1763 m *5784 ft*, Trollveggan Spire, Romsdal, Norway, 4 July 1984.
Bridge ● Donald R. Boyles, 320 m *1053 ft*, Royal Gorge, Colorado, USA, 7 Sept 1970.
Tower ● Herbert Leo Schmidtz (USA), KTUL-TV mast 604 m *1984 ft*, Tulsa, Oklahoma, USA, 4 Oct 1970.

MID-AIR RESCUE ● **Earliest** ● Miss Dolly Shepherd brought down Miss Louie May on her single 'chute from balloon at 3350 m *11 000 ft*, Longton, Staffordshire, 9 June 1908.
Lowest ● Gregory Robertson saved Debbie Williams (unconscious), collision at 2750 m *9000 ft*, pulled her ripcord at 1065 m *3500 ft*—10 secs from impact, Coolidge, Arizona, USA, 18 Apr 1987.

HIGHEST LANDING ● Ten USSR parachutists[4], 7133 m *23 405 ft*, Lenina Peak, May 1969.

[1] *The king of Ayutthaya, Siam in 1687 was reported to have been diverted by an ingenious athlete parachuting with two large umbrellas. Faustus Verancsis is reputed to have descended in Hungary with a framed canopy in 1617.*

[2] *Maximum speed in rarefied air was 1006 km/h*

LOWEST INDOOR JUMP ● Andy Smith and Phil Smith, 58·5 m *192 ft*, Houston Astrodome, Texas, USA, 16–17 Jan 1982.

MOST SOUTHERLY ● T/Sgt Richard J. Patton (d. 1973), Operation Deep Freeze, South Pole, 25 Nov 1956.

MOST NORTHERLY ● Dr Jack Wheeler (US); pilot Capt Rocky Parsons, −31·6° C (−25° F), in Lat. 90° 00' N, 15 Apr 1981.

CROSS-CHANNEL (LATERAL FALL) ● Sgt Bob Walters with 3 soldiers and 2 Royal Marines, 35·4 km *22 miles* from 7600 m *25 000 ft*, Dover, Kent to Sangatte, France, 31 Aug 1980.

TOTAL SPORT PARACHUTING DESCENTS ● *Man*; Roch Charmet (France), 14 000, various, to Feb 1988. *Woman*; Valentina Zakoretskaya (USSR), 8000, over USSR, 1964–Sept 1980.

24-HOUR TOTAL ● David Huber (USA), 250, Issaquah, Washington, USA, 3–4 July 1985.

MOST TRAVELLED ● Kevin Seaman from a Cessna Skylane (pilot Charles E. Merritt), 19 611 km *12 186 miles*, jumps in all 50 US States, 26 July–15 Oct 1972.

HEAVIEST LOAD ● US Space Shuttle *Columbia*, external rocket retrieval, 80 ton capacity, triple array, each 36·5 m *120 ft* diameter, Atlantic, off Cape Canaveral, Florida, USA, 12 April 1981.

HIGHEST COLUMN ● 24 Royal Marine Team, Dunkeswell, Devon, 20 Aug 1986.

LARGEST FREE FALL FORMATION ● 126, held for 4·68 sec, from 5800 m *19 029 ft*, Koksijde, Belgium, 11 July 1987.

OLDEST ● *Man*; Edwin C. Townsend (d. 7 Nov 1987), 89 years, Vermillion Bay, Louisiana, USA, 5 Feb 1986. *Woman*; Mrs Sylvia Brett (GB), 80 years 166 days, Cranfield, Bedfordshire, 23 Aug 1986.

LONGEST FALL WITHOUT PARACHUTE ● **World** ● Vesna Vulovic (Yugoslavia), air hostess in DC-9 which blew up at 10 160 m *33 330 ft* over Serbska Kamenice, Czechoslovakia, 26 Jan 1972.
UK ● Flt-Sgt Nicholas Stephen Alkemade (d. 22 June 1987), from blazing RAF *Lancaster* bomber, at 5485 m *18 000 ft* over Germany (near Oberkürchen), 23 Mar 1944.

625·2 mph *at 27 430 m 90 000 ft—marginally supersonic.*

[3] *'Base' is an acronym for jumping from fixed objects—Building, Antenna, Span and Earth. Carl Boenische was killed on 7 July 1984.*

[4] *Four were killed.*

SKATE BOARDING

'World' championships have been staged intermittently since 1966. David Frank, 25, covered 435·3 km *270·5 miles* in 36 hr 43 min 40 sec in Toronto, Canada on 11–12 Aug 1985.

The highest speed recorded on a skate board under USSA rules is 115·53 km/h *71·79 mph* on a course at Mt Baldy, California, USA in a prone position by Richard K. Brown, 33, on 17 June 1979. The stand-up record is 86·01 km/h *53·45 mph* by John Hutson, 23, at Signal Hill, Long Beach, California, USA on 11 June 1978. The high-jump record is 1·67 m *5 ft 5·7 in* by Trevor Baxter (b. 1 Oct 1962) of Burgess Hill, East Sussex at Grenoble, France on 14 Sept 1982. At the 4th US Skateboard Association Championship, at Signal Hill on 25 Sept 1977, Tony Alva, 19, jumped 17 barrels (5·18 m *17 ft*).

SLINGING

The greatest distance recorded for a sling-shot is 437·13 m *1434 ft 2 in* using a 129·5 cm *51 in* long sling and a 56·5 g *2 oz* stone by Lawrence L. Bray at Loa, Utah, USA on 21 Aug 1981.

SMOKE RING BLOWING

The highest recorded number of smoke rings formed from the lips from a single pull of a cigarette (cheek-tapping is disallowed) is 355 by Jan van Deurs Formann of Copenhagen, Denmark, achieved in Switzerland in August 1979.

SNOW SHOEING

The USSA record for covering 1609·34 m *1 mile* is 7 min 56 sec by Mark Lessard at Corinth, New York in 1979.

T-Bone dive ● Joe Delaney drove a Rover SDI for a record leap of 60·98 m *200 ft* at Long Marston Raceway, Warwickshire, England on 18 July 1987. (Photo: Avon studios)

The so-called T-bone dives or Dive Bomber crashes by cars off ramps over and on to parked cars are often measured by the number of cars, but owing to their variable size and that their purpose is purely to cushion the shock, distance is more significant.

Walking on water ● Wearing 3·36 m *11 ft* water ski shoes, called Skijaks, and using a twin-bladed paddle, David Kiner walked 249·44 km *155 miles* on the Hudson River from Albany to Battery Park, New York, USA. His walk took him 57 hr, between 22 and 27 June 1987. (Photo: Forbes Museum)

SPEAR THROWING

The greatest distance achieved throwing a spear with the aid of a woomera is 99·51 m *326 ft 6 in* by Bailey Bush on 27 June 1982 at Camden, NSW, Australia.

SPIKE DRIVING

In the World Championship Professional Spike Driving Competition held at the Golden Spike National Historic Site in Utah, USA, Dale C. Jones, 49, of Lehi, drove six 7-in railroad spikes in a time of 26·4 sec on 11 Aug 1984. He incurred no penalty points under the official rules.

SPINNING BY HAND

The duration record for spinning a clock-balance wheel by unaided hand is 5 min 26·8 sec by Philip Ashley, 16, of Leigh, Lancashire on 20 May 1968. The record using 91·4 cm *36 in* of string with a 205·5 g *7¼ oz* top is 58 min 20 sec by Peter Hodgson at Southend-on-Sea, Essex on 4 Feb 1985.

SPITTING

The greatest distance achieved at the Annual Tobacco Spitting Classic (instituted 1955) at Raleigh, Mississippi, USA is 10·24 m *33 ft 7½ in* by Jeff Barber on 25 July 1981. (In 1980 he reached 13·71 m *45 ft* at Fulton, Missouri, USA, and on 29 June 1985 he won a record 13th National Spitting title at Raleigh.) In the 3rd International Spittin', Belchin' and Cussin' Triathlon, Harold Fielden reached 10·36 m *34 ft 0¼ in* at Central City, Colorado, USA, on 13 July 1973. Distance is dependent on the quality of salivation, absence of cross wind, the two-finger pucker and coordination of the back arch and neck snap. Sprays or wads smaller than a dime are not measured. Randy Ober of Bentonville, Arkansas, USA spat a tobacco wad 14·50 m *47 ft 7 in* at the Calico 5th Annual Tobacco Chewing and Spitting Championships north of Barstow, California, USA on 4 Apr 1982. The record for projecting a melon seed under WCWSSCA rules is 19·91 m *65 ft 4 in* by John Wilkinson in Luling, Texas, USA, on 28 June 1980. The furthest recorded distance for a cherry stone is 20·26 m *66 ft 6 in* by Rick Krause, at Eau Claire, Michigan, USA on 4 July 1987.

SQUARE DANCE CALLING

Alan Covacic called continuously for 24 hr 2 min for the Wheelers and Dealers SDC at St John's Hospital, Stone, Bucks from 23–24 Nov 1984.

STAIR CLIMBING

The 100-storey record for stair climbing was set by Dennis W. Martz in the Detroit Plaza Hotel, Detroit, Michigan, USA on 26 June 1978 at 11 min 23·8 sec. Dale Neil, 22, ran a vertical mile on the stairs of the Peachtree Plaza Hotel, Atlanta, Georgia, USA in continuous action of 2 hr 1 min 24 sec on 9 Mar 1984. *These records can only be attempted in buildings with a minimum of 70 storeys.*

The record for the 1760 steps (vertical height 342 m *1122 ft*) in the world's tallest free-standing structure, Toronto's CN Tower, Canada, is 8 min 28 sec by George Kapenyes on 27 Oct 1985. Robert C. Jezequel ran 17 round trips in 11 hr 20 min on 18 Oct 1985 without use of the elevator for a vertical height of 4787 m *15 708 ft*.

Pete Squires raced up the 1575 steps of the Empire State Building, New York, USA on 12 Feb 1981 in 10 min 59 sec.

In the line of duty Bill Stevenson mounted 334 of the 364 steps of the tower in the Houses of Parliament 4000 times in the 15 years 1968–83—equivalent to 24·9 ascents of Everest.

A team of 200 ran up the 1336 stairs of the world's tallest hotel, the Westin Stamford, Singapore, on 3 May 1987. The fastest time was recorded by Kenneth Keng at 7 min 20 sec.

STAMP LICKING

Ian Thomas of Brisbane, Australia licked and affixed 204 stamps in 4 min at the Sunpex '85 Exhibition, Brisbane on 5 Oct 1985.

STANDING

The longest period on record that anyone has continuously stood is for more than 17 years in the case of Swami Maujgiri Maharij when performing the *Tapasya* or penance from 1955 to November 1973 in Shahjahanpur, Uttar Pradesh, India. When sleeping he would lean against a plank. He died aged 85 in September 1980.

STILT-WALKING

Hop stringers use stilts up to 4·57 m *15 ft*. In 1892 M. Garisoain of Bayonne stilt-walked 8 km *4·97 miles* into Biarritz in 42 min to average 11·42 km/h *7·10 mph*. In 1891 Sylvain Dornon stilt-walked from Paris, France to Moscow, USSR via Vilno in 50 stages for the 2945 km *1830 miles*. Another source gives his time as 58 days. Even with a safety or Kirby wire very high stilts are *extremely* dangerous—25 steps are deemed to constitute 'mastery'. Eddy Wolf ('Steady Eddy') of Loyal, Wisconsin, USA mastered stilts measuring 12·36 m *40 ft 6½ in* from ground to ankle over a distance of 27 steps without touching his safety handrail wires, at Yokohama Dreamland Park, Yokohama on 9 Mar 1986. His aluminium stilts weighed 25 kg *55 lb* each. Joe Long (b.

Kenneth Caesar), who has suffered 5 fractures, mastered 25·4 kg *56 lb* 7·31 m *24 ft* stilts at BBC Television Centre, London on 8 Dec 1978. The endurance record is 4804 km *3008 miles* from Los Angeles, California, USA to Bowen, Kentucky, USA, from 20 Feb to 26 July 1980 by Joe Bowen. Masaharu Tatsushiro, 28 (Japan), ran 100 m *328 ft* on 30·48 cm *1 ft* high stilts in 14·15 sec in Tokyo, Japan on 30 Mar 1980.

STOWAWAY

The most rugged stowaway was Socarras Ramirez who escaped from Cuba on 4 June 1969 by stowing away in an unpressurised wheel well in the starboard wing of a Douglas DC8 from Havana, Cuba to Madrid, Spain in a 9010 km *5600 mile* Iberian Airlines flight.

STRETCHER BEARING

The longest recorded carry of a stretcher case with a 63·5 kg *10 st* 'body' is 209·21 km *130 miles* in 45 hr 5 min by two four-man teams from the British Services 3 Squadron, 9th Signal Regiment (Radio), in Cyprus, from 6–8 Feb 1988.

The record limited to Youth Organisations (under 20 years of age) and 8-hr carrying is 67·62 km *42·02 miles* by 8 members of the Henry Meoles School, Moreton, Wirral, Cheshire on 13 July 1980.

STRING BALL LARGEST

The largest ball of string on record is one of 3·88 m *12 ft 9 in* in diameter, 12·19 m *40 ft* in circumference and weighing 10 tonnes/*tons*, amassed by Francis A. Johnson of Darwin, Minnesota, USA between 1950–78.

SUBMERGENCE

The *continuous* duration record (*i.e.* no rest breaks) for 'scuba' (*i.e.* self-contained and without surface air hoses) is 212 hr 30 min by Michael Stevens of Birmingham in a Royal Navy tank at the National Exhibition Centre, Birmingham from 14–23 Feb 1986. Measures have to be taken to reduce the risk of severe desquamation in such endurance trials.

SUGGESTION BOXES

The most prolific example on record of the use of any suggestion box scheme is that of John Drayton (1907–87) of Newport, Gwent who plied the British rail system with a total of 31 316 suggestions from 1924 to May 1987 of which over 100 were accepted by London Transport. In 1983 he was presented with a chiming clock by British Rail to mark almost 60 years of suggestions.

SWINGING

The record duration for continuous swinging in a hammock is 240 hr by John David Joyce of Bryan, Texas, USA from 29 July to 8 Aug 1986.

SWITCHBACK RIDING

The endurance record for rides on a roller coaster is 503 hr by M. M. Daniel Glada and Normand St-Pierre at Parc Belmont, Montreal, Canada from 18 July to 10 Aug 1983. The minimum qualifying average speed required is 40 km/h *25 mph.*

TAILORING

The highest speed in which the manufacture of a 3-piece suit has been executed from sheep to finished article is 1 hr 34 min 33·42 sec by 65 members of the Melbourne College of Textiles, Pascoe Vale, Victoria, Australia on 24 June 1982. Catching and fleecing took 2 min 21 sec, and carding, spinning, weaving and tailoring occupied the remaining time.

TALKING

The world record for non-stop talking has been 240 hours by N.S. Viswanathan at the Jalakandeswarar Temple, Tamil Nadu, India from 24 Dec 1987 to 3 Jan 1988. The subject of the talk was a discourse on Ramayanam, Mahabharatham and Kandapuranam. The women's non-stop talking record was set by Mrs Mary E. Davis, who on 2 Sept 1958 started at a radio station in

Buffalo, New York, USA and did not draw breath until 110 hr 30 min 5 sec later on 7 Sept in Tulsa, Oklahoma, USA. (See also Filibusters, Chapter 11.)

The longest recorded after-dinner speech was one of 32 hr 25 min by Dr Donald Thomas at City College, New York, USA from 1 to 3 April 1988. Historically the longest recorded after-dinner speech with *unsuspecting* victims was one of 3 hr by the Reverend Henry Whitehead (d. March 1896) at the Rainbow Tavern, Fleet Street, London on 16 Jan 1874.

TEETH-PULLING

'Hercules' Walter Arfeuille of Vlamertinge-Ieper, Belgium raised a weight of 247·5 kg *545·64 lb* 16 cm *6·3 in* from the ground with a tooth bit at Diksmuide, Belgium on 11 Sep 1983. 'Hercules' John Massis (b. Wilfried Oscar Morbée, 4 June 1940) of Oostakker, Belgium prevented a helicopter from taking off using only a tooth bit harness in Los Angeles, California, USA on 7 Apr 1979 for a *Guinness Spectacular* TV show.

THROWING

The longest independently authenticated throw of any inert object heavier than air is 383·13 m *1257 ft*, for an Aerobie flying ring, by Scott Zimmerman on 8 July 1986 at Fort Funston, California, USA.

TIGHTROPE WALKING

The greatest 19th-century tightrope walker was Jean François Gravelet, *alias* Charles Blondin (1824–97), of France, who made the earliest crossing of the Niagara Falls on a 76 mm *3 in* rope, 335 m *1100 ft* long, 48·75 m *160 ft* above the Falls on 30 June 1859. He also made a crossing with Harry Colcord pick-a-back on 15 Sept 1860. Though other artistes still find it difficult to believe, Colcord was his agent. The oldest wirewalker was 'Professor' William Ivy Baldwin (1866–1953), who crossed the South Boulder Canyon, Colorado, USA on a 97·5 m *320 ft* wire with a 38·1 m *125 ft* drop on his 82nd birthday on 31 July 1948.

The world tightrope endurance record is 185 days by Henri Rochetain (b. 1926) of France on a wire 120 m *394 ft* long, 25 m *82 ft* above a supermarket in Saint Etienne, France from 28 Mar–29 Sept 1973. His ability to sleep on the wire has left doctors puzzled. Ashley Brophy, of Neilborough, Victoria, Australia, walked 11·57 km *7·18 miles* on a wire 45 m *147·64 ft* long 10 m *32·81 ft* high at the Adelaide Grand Prix, Australia on 1 Nov 1985 in 3 hr 30 min.

Steve McPeak (b. 21 April 1945) of Las Vegas, Nevada, USA ascended the 46·6 mm *1·83 in* diameter Zugspitzbahn cable for a vertical height of 705 m *2313 ft* in 3 stints aggregating 5 hr 4 min on 24/25/28 June 1981. The maximum gradient over the stretch of 2282 m *7485 ft* was above 30 degrees. Earlier on 28 June 1981 he had walked on a thinner stayed cable 181 steps across a gorge at the top of the 2963 m *9721 ft* mountain with a sheer drop of 960 m *3150 ft* below him.

The first crossing of the River Thames was achieved by Charles Elleano (b. 1911) of Strasbourg, France on a 320 m *1050 ft* wire 18·2 m *60 ft* above the river in 25 min on 22 Sept 1951.

TOP SPINNING

A team of 25 from the Mizushima Plant of Kawasaki Steel Works in Okayama spun a giant top 2 m *6 ft 6¾ in* tall and 2·6 m *8 ft 6¼ in* in diameter weighing 360 kg *793·6 lb* for 1 hr 21 min 35 sec on 3 Nov 1986.

TRAIN SPOTTING

Bill Curtis of Clacton-on-Sea, Essex is acknowledged as the world champion train spotter—or 'gricer' (after Richard Grice, the first champion). His totals include some 60 000 locomotives, 11 200 electric units and 8 300 diesel units, clocked up over a period of 40 years in a number of different countries.

TREE CLIMBING

The fastest speed climb up a 30·4 m *100 ft* fir spar pole

and return to the ground is one of 27·16 sec by Ed Johnson of Victoria, BC, Canada in July 1982 at the Lumberjack World Championships in Hayward, Wisconsin, USA.

The fastest time up a 9 m *29·5 ft* coconut tree barefoot is 4·88 sec by Fuatai Solo, 17, in Sukuna Park, Fiji on 22 Aug 1980.

TREE EATING

In an 'Outrageous Contest' organised by WKQX Chicago from 11–15 Sept 1980, Jay Gwaltney, 19, ate a birch tree that was 3·35 m *11 ft* in length and had a 12 cm *4·7 in* diameter trunk. It took him 89 hr.

TREE SITTING

The duration record for sitting in a tree is 431 days by Timothy Roy at Golf N'Stuff Amusement Park, Norwalk, California, USA from 4 July 1982–8 Sept 1983.

TREE TOPPING

Guy German climbed a 30·5 m *100 ft* spar and sawed off the top in a record time of 70·87 sec at Albany, Oregon, USA on 5 July 1987.

TYPEWRITING

The world duration record for typewriting on an electric machine is 264 hr by Violet Gibson Burns at The Royal Easter Show, Sydney, Australia from 29 Mar–9 Apr 1985.

The longest duration in a typing marathon on a manual machine is 123 hr by Shambhoo Govind Anbhawane of Bombay, India from 18–23 Aug 1986 on a Godrej Prima manual machine, aggregating 806 000 strokes. Les Stewart of Mudjimba Beach, Queensland, Australia has typed the numbers 1 to 544 000 in *words* on 10 770 quarto sheets as of 23 May 1988. His target is to become a 'millionaire'.

The highest recorded speeds attained with a ten-word penalty per error on a manual machine are:

Five Min: 176 wpm net Mrs Carole Forristall Waldschlager Bechen at Dixon, Illinois, USA on 2 Apr 1959. **One Hour**: 147 wpm net Albert Tangora (US) (Underwood Standard), 22 Oct 1923.

The official hour record on an electric machine is 9316 words (40 errors) on an IBM machine, giving a net rate of 149 words per min, by Margaret Hamma, now Mrs Dilmore (US), in Brooklyn, New York, USA on 20 June 1941. Mary Ann Morel (South Africa) set a numerical record at the CABEX '85 Exhibition in Johannesburg, South Africa on 6 Feb 1985 by typing spaced numbers from 1 to 781 in 5 min. In an official test in 1946 Stella Pajunas, now Mrs Garnard, attained a rate of 216 words in a minute on an IBM machine.

TYRE SUPPORTING

The greatest number of motor tyres supported in a free-standing 'lift' is 96 by Gary Windebank of Romsey, Hants in February 1984. The total weight was 653 kg *1440 lb.* The tyres used were Michelin XZX 155 × 13.

UNSUPPORTED CIRCLE

The highest recorded number of people who have demonstrated the physical paradox of all being seated without a chair is an unsupported circle of 10 323 employees of the Nissan Motor Company at Komazawa Stadium, Tokyo, Japan on 23 Oct 1982.

The British record is 7402 participants at Goodwood Airfield, West Sussex on 25 May 1986, as part of a Sport Aid event.

VERSATILITY

Ashrita Furman (b. 1959) of Jamaica, NY, USA set 10 competitive stamina records in the period 1983–87, ranging from juggling, step running and somersaulting to pogo-stick jumping in water.

WALKING ON HANDS

The duration record for walking on hands is 1400 km *871 miles* by Johann Hurlinger, of Austria, who in 55 daily

10-hr stints, averaged 2·54 km/h *1·58 mph* from Vienna to Paris in 1900. Shin Don-mok of South Korea completed a 50 m *54·68 yd* inverted sprint in 17·44 sec at the Toda Sports Centre, Saitama, Japan on 14 Nov 1986.

A four-man team of David Lutterman, Brendan Price, Philip Savage and David Scannel covered 1·609 km *1 mile* in 24 min 48 sec on 15 March 1987 at Knoxville, Tennessee, USA. This compares with the record of 3 min 2 sec the right way up.

WALL OF DEATH

The greatest endurance feat on a wall of death was 6 hr 7 min 38 sec by Hugo Dabbert (b. Hildesheim, 24 Sept 1938) at Rüsselsheim, West Germany on 14 Aug 1980. He rode 6841 laps on the 10 m *32·8 ft* diameter wall on a Honda CM 400T averaging 35·2 km/h *21·8 mph* for the 214·8 km *133·4 miles.*

WHIP CRACKING

The longest stock whip ever 'cracked' (*i.e.* the end made to travel above the speed of sound—1223 km/h *760 mph*) is one of 42·67 m *140 ft* (excluding the handle) wielded by Garry Brophy at Adelaide, Australia on 31 Oct 1985.

WHISTLING *Loudest and longest*

Roy Lomas achieved 122·5 decibels at 2½ m *8·20 ft* in the Deadroom at the BBC studios in Manchester on 19 Dec 1983. The marathon record is held by David Frank of Toronto, Canada, who completed 35 hr non-stop at the Washington Monument, Washington DC, USA on 17–18 July 1987.

WINDOW CLEANING

On 19 Oct 1984 at the Clearview Challenge Cup contest, Sydney, Australia Roy Ridley achieved 18·92 sec without a smear for 3 standard 1040 × 1153 mm *40·94 × 45·39 in* office windows with a 300 mm *11·8 in* long squeegee and 9 litres *15·83 pts* of water.

WIRE SLIDE

The greatest distance recorded in a wire slide is from the London Weekend TV building to the barge 'Driftwood' 112·7 m *370 ft* below and 281·9 m *925 ft* distant on the Thames on 27 Oct 1986. This 'death slide' set up by the Royal Marines was traversed by Lady Nourse *née* Lavinia Malim for charity. The estimated run length was 305 m *1000 ft.*

WOOD CUTTING

The earliest competitions date from Tasmania in 1874. The records set at the Lumberjack World Championships at Hayward, Wisconsin, USA (founded 1960) are:

Power Saw	8·73 sec	
Sven Johnson (US)		1983
One-Man Bucking	21·70 sec	
Merv Jensen (NZ) (d. Apr 1983)		1982
Standing Block Chop	25·38 sec	
Mel Lentz (US)		1982
Underhand Block Chop	18·66 sec	
Mel Lentz (US)		1982
Two-Man Bucking	9·44 sec	
Merv Jensen (NZ), Cliff Hughes (NZ)		1982
Hand Splitting a Cord into Quarters	53 min 40 sec	
Richard Sawyer (US)		1982

WRITING MINUSCULE

In 1926 an account was published of Alfred McEwen's pantograph record in which the 56-word version of the Lord's Prayer was written by diamond point on glass in the space of 0·04 × 0·02 mm *0·0016 × 0·0008 in.*

Frank C. Watts of Felmingham, Norfolk demonstrated for photographers on 24 Jan 1968 his ability, without mechanical or optical aid, to write the Lord's Prayer 34 times (9452 letters) within the size of a definitive UK postage stamp *viz* 21·33 × 18·03 mm *0·84 × 0·71 in.* Tsutomu Ishii of Tokyo demonstrated the ability to write the names of 44 countries (184 letters) on a single grain of rice and TOKYO JAPAN in Japanese on a human hair in April 1983.

WRITING UNDER HANDICAP

The ultimate feat in 'funny writing' appears to be the ability to write extemporaneously and decipherably backwards, upside down, laterally inverted (mirror-style), while blindfolded, with both hands simultaneously. Three claims to this ability with both hands and feet simultaneously, by Mrs Carolyn Webb of Thirlmere, NSW, Australia, Mrs Judy Hall of Chesterfield, Virginia, USA, and Robert Gray of Toronto, Ontario, Canada, are outstanding.

YODELLING

The most protracted yodel on record was that of Errol Bird for 26 hr in Lisburn, Northern Ireland on 27–28 Sept 1984. Yodelling has been defined as 'repeated rapid changes from the chest-voice to falsetto and back again'. The most rapid recorded is 5 tones (3 falsetto) in 1·9 sec by Donn Reynolds of Canada on 25 July 1984.

Yo-Yo

A yo-yo was a toy in Grecian times and is depicted on a bowl dated 450 BC. It was also a Filipino jungle fighting weapon recorded in the 16th century weighing 1·81 kg *4 lb* with a 6 m *20 ft* thong. The word means 'come-come'. Though illustrated in a book in 1891 as a bandalore the craze did not begin until it was started by Donald F. Duncan of Chicago, Illinois, USA in 1926. The most difficult modern yo-yo trick is the 'whirlwind' incorporating both inside and outside horizontal loop-the-loops. The individual continuous endurance record is 121 hr 10 min by Bob Brown of Boston, Massachusetts, USA from 24–29 June 1985. Dr Allen Bussey in Waco, Texas, USA on 23 Apr 1977 completed 20 302 loops in 3 hr (including 6886 in a single 60-min period). He used a Duncan Imperial with a 87·6 cm *34½ in* nylon string. Spins of 8000 rpm have been recorded.

The largest yo-yo ever constructed was one by Dr Tom Kuhn weighing 116·11 kg *256 lb* test launched from a 52·2 m *150 ft* crane in San Francisco, California, USA on 13 Oct 1979.

Honours, Decorations and Awards

Oldest order

The earliest honour known was the 'Gold of Honour' for extraordinary valour awarded in the 18th dynasty *c.* 1440–1400 BC. A statuette was found at Qan-el-Kebri, Egypt. The order which can trace its origins furthest back is the Military Hospitaller Order of St Lazarus of Jerusalem founded by St Basil the Great in the 4th century AD. A date as early as AD 809 has been attributed to the Most Ancient Order of the Thistle, but is of doubtful provenance. The Order of St John in Scotland, founded in 1124, was suppressed in the 16th century but revived in 1947. The prototype of the princely Orders of Chivalry is the Most Noble Order of the Garter founded by King Edward III *c.* 1348.

Eponymous record

The largest object to which a human name is attached is the Universe itself—in the case of 3 different cosmological models, known as Friedmanian models, devised in 1922 by the Russian mathematician Aleksandr Aleksandrovitch Friedman (1888–1925).

Most titles

The most titled person in the world is the 18th Duchess of Alba (Alba de Tormes), Doña Maria del Rosario Cayetana Fitz-James Stuart y Silva. She is 8 times a duchess, 15 times a marchioness, 21 times a countess and is 19 times a Spanish grandee.

Versatility

The only person to win a Victoria Cross and an Olympic Gold Medal has been Lt Gen. Sir Philip Neame VC, KBE, CB, DSO (1888–1978). He won the VC in 1914 and was an Olympic gold medallist for Britain for rifle shooting in 1924 though under the illusion at the time that he was shooting for the British Empire. The only George Cross holder who was also a Fellow of the Royal Society was Professor Peter Victor Danckwerts GC, MBE, FRS F Eng (1916–85) who defused 16 parachute mines in under 48 hr in the London docks during the Battle of Britain as a Sub Lt RNVR in August 1940.

Victoria Cross *Double awards*

The only 3 men ever to have been awarded a bar to the Victoria Cross (instituted 29 Jan 1856) are:

Surg.-Capt. (later Lt-Col.) Arthur Martin-Leake VC*, VD, RAMC (1874–1953) (1902 and bar 1915).
Capt. Noel Godfrey Chavasse VC*, MC, RAMC (1884–1917) (1916 and bar posthumously 31 July–2 Aug 1917).
Second Lt (later Capt.) Charles Hazlitt Upham VC*, NZMF (b. 21 Sept 1908) (1941 and bar 1942).

The most VCs awarded in a war were the 634 in World War I (1914–18). The greatest number won in a single action was 11 at Rorke's Drift in the Zulu War on 22–23 Jan 1879. The school with most recipients is Eton College, Col. H. H. Jones being the 36th (posthumously in the Falklands campaign).

Youngest

The lowest established age for a VC is 15 years 100 days for hospital apprentice Andrew (wrongly gazetted as Arthur) Fitzgibbon (born at Peteragurh, northern India, 13 May 1845) of the Indian Medical Services for bravery at the Taku Forts in northern China on 21 Aug 1860. The youngest living VC is Capt. Rambahadur Limbu (b. 1 Nov 1939, Chyangthapu, Nepal) of the 10th Princess Mary's Own Gurkha Rifles. The award was for his courage as a L/Cpl while fighting in the Bau district of Sarawak, east Malaysia on 21 Nov 1965. He retired on 25 Mar 1985 as Lieutenant.

Oldest

Capt. William Raynor was the oldest person to be awarded the medal, given for gallantry when he was aged 69. The medal dates from the Indian Mutiny on 11 May 1857, when he risked life to blow up an arms store used by Indian insurgents. The medal was retrieved from an auction by his great-grandson Mr William Raynor in December 1987.

Longest lived

The longest lived of all the 1351 winners of the Victoria Cross has been Lt Col. Harcus Strachan VC. He was born in Bo'ness, West Lothian, Scotland on 7 Nov 1884 and died in Vancouver, British Columbia, Canada on 1 May 1982 aged 97 years 175 days.

Most highly decorated

The 6 living persons to have been twice decorated with any of the United Kingdom's topmost decorations are Capt. C. H. Upham VC and bar; the Viscount de l'Isle VC, KG; HM the Queen Mother CI, GCVO, GBE, who is a Lady of the Garter and a Lady of the Thistle; HRH the Duke of Edinburgh KG, KT, OM, GBE; HRH Prince Charles KG, KT, GCB and HM King Olaf V of Norway KG, KT, GCB, GCVO. Lord De L'Isle is the only person who has both the highest military and highest civil honour. Britain's most highly decorated woman is the World War II British agent Mrs Odette Hallowes GC, MBE, Légion d'Honneur, Ordre St George (Belge), who survived imprisonment and torture at the hands of the Gestapo from 1943–45. Violette Reine Elizabeth Szabo (*née* Bushnell) GC (1921–45) lost her husband in the French Legion at El Alamein in 1942. He was Etienne Szabo, Médaille Militaire, Légion d'Honneur and Croix de Guerre.

Top jet ace

The greatest number of kills in jet to jet battles is 16 by Capt. Joseph Christopher McConnell, Jr USAF (b. Dover, New Hampshire, USA, 30 Jan 1922) in the Korean war (1950–3). He was killed on 25 Aug 1954. It is possible that an Israeli ace may have surpassed this total in the period

1967–70 but the identity of pilots is subject to strict security.

Top woman ace

The record score for any woman fighter pilot is 12 by Jnr Lt Lydia Litvak (USSR) (b. 1921) on the Eastern Front between 1941 and 1943. She was killed in action on 1 Aug 1943.

Top-scoring air aces (World Wars I and II)

The 'scores' of air aces in both wars are *still* hotly disputed. The highest figures officially attributed have been:

World	United Kingdom
World War I	
75[1] Col. René Paul Fonck (France) Gr Cordon Ld'H, C de G (26 palms), Méd. Mil., MC*, C de G (Belge) (d. 1953)	73 Major Edward Mannock VC, DSO**, MC*
World War II	
352 Major Erich Hartmann (Germany)	38 Wg Cdr (now AVM) James Edgar Johnson CB, CBE, DSO**, DFC*[2]

[1] A total of 80 was attributed to Rittmeister Manfred Freiherr (Baron) von Richthofen (Germany) but more than 20 of these are not fully verifiable from German records, leaving Col.-Gen. Ernst Udet (d. 1941) Ordre pour le Mérite, Iron Cross with the highest number of unquestioned victories at 62.

[2] The greatest number of successes against flying bombs (V1s) was by Sqn Ldr Joseph Berry DFC** (b. Nottingham, 1920, k. 2 Oct 1944) who brought down 60 in 4 months. The most successful fighter pilot in the RAF was Sqn Ldr Marmaduke Thomas St John Pattle DFC*, of South Africa, with a known total of at least 40. In the Battle of Leyte Gulf, Cdr David McCampbell, USN shot down 9 aircraft in one mission on 24 Oct 1944.

Youngest award

The youngest age at which an official gallantry award has ever been won is 8 years in the case of Anthony Farrer who was given the Albert Medal on 23 Sept 1916 for fighting off a cougar at Cowichan Lake, Vancouver Island, Canada to save Doreen Ashburnham. She was also awarded the AM, which, in 1971, was exchanged for the George Cross.

Most lifeboat medals

Manxman Sir William Hilliary (1771–1847), founder of the Royal National Lifeboat Institution in 1824, was personally and uniquely awarded 4 RNLI Gold Medals, in 1825, 1828 and 1830 (twice). The only triple award this century has been to Coxwain Henry Blogg GC, BEM (1876–1954) of Cromer, Norfolk, who also had 4 Silver Medals. The record for Silver Medals is 5 by Sydney Harris of Great Yarmouth and Gorleston, both Norfolk (1905 (twice), 1909, 1912 and 1916).

Most mentions in despatches

The record number of 'mentions' is 24 by Field Marshal the Rt Hon. Sir Frederick Sleigh Roberts Bt, the Earl Roberts VC, KG, PC, KP, GCB, OM, GCSI, GCIE, VD (1832–1914).

Most post-nominal letters

Lord Roberts, who was also a privy counsellor, was the only non-royal holder of 8 sets of *official* post-nominal letters. Currently the record number is 7 by Marshal of the RAF the Rt Hon. Lord Elworthy KG, GCB, CBE, DSO, LVO, DFC, AFC (b. 23 Mar 1911) of New Zealand. HRH the Duke of Windsor (1894–1972) when Prince of Wales had 10 sets and was also a privy counsellor *viz* KG, PC, KT, KP, GCB, GCSI, GCMG, GCIE, GCVO, GBE, MC. He later appended the ISO but never did so in the cases of the OM, CH or DSO of which orders he had also been sovereign.

Civilian gallantry

Reginald H. Blanchford of Guernsey received the MBE

for gallantry in 1950; the Queen's Commendation in 1957; the George Medal in 1958; the OBE for gallantry in 1961 for saving life from cliff tops. He was also awarded the Life Saving Medal in Gold 1957 with golden bar 1963 and was made a Knight of Grace of the Order of St John in 1970.

USSR

The USSR's highest award for valour is the Gold Star of a Hero of the Soviet Union. Over 10 000 were awarded in World War II. Among the 109 awards of a second star were those to Marshal Iosif Vissarionovich Dzhugashvili, *alias* Stalin (1879–1953), and Lt-General Nikita Sergeyevich Khrushchyov (1894–1971). The only war-time triple awards were to Marshal Georgiy Konstantinovich Zhukov, Hon. GCB (1896–1972) (subsequently awarded a fourth Gold Star) and to the leading air aces Guards Colonel (later Marshal of Aviation) the late Aleksandr Ivanovich Pokryshkin and Aviation Maj. Gen. Ivan Nikitovich Kozhedub (b. 8 June 1920) (Order of the Red Banner, 7 times). Zhukov also uniquely had the Order of Victory (twice), the Order of Lenin (6 times) and the Order of the Red Banner (thrice). Leonid Ilich Brezhnev (1907–1982) was 4 times Hero of the Soviet Union and Hero of Socialist Labour, Order of Victory, Order of Lenin (8 times) and Order of the Red Banner (twice).

Germany

The Knight's Cross of the Iron Cross with swords, diamonds and golden oak-leaves was uniquely awarded to Col. Hans Ulrich Rudel (1916–82) for 2530 operational flying missions on the Eastern Front in the period 1941–5. He destroyed 519 Soviet armoured vehicles.

USA

The highest US military decoration is the Medal of Honor. Five marines received both the Army and Navy Medals of Honor for the same acts in 1918 and 13 officers and men from 1863 to 1915 have received the medal on 2 occasions. Maj. Audie Murphy (1929–1971) received in World War II the Medal of Honor, the Distinguished Service Cross, the Silver Star (thrice), the Legion of Merit, the Bronze Star Medal (twice) and the Purple Heart (thrice).

Record price

The highest price ever paid for a VC group has been £110 000 for the medals of the Battle of Britain fighter pilot Wing Cdr J. B. Nicholson VC, DFC (k. 1945), one of only 3 men ever to win the VC actually defending Britain. The auction was at Glendining & Co, London on 27 Apr 1983.

The record for a George Cross is £20 250 at Christie's on 14 Mar 1985, for that of Sgt Michael Willets (3rd Battalion

Parachute Regiment), killed by an IRA bomb in Ulster in 1971.

Order of Merit

The Order of Merit (instituted on 23 June 1902) is limited to 24 members. The longest lived of the 153 holders has been the Rt Hon. Bertrand Arthur William Russell, 3rd Earl Russell, who died on 2 Feb 1970 aged 97 years 260 days. The oldest recipient was Admiral of the Fleet the Hon. Sir Henry Keppel GCB, OM (1809–1904), who received the Order aged 93 years 56 days on 9 Aug 1902. The youngest recipient has been HRH the Duke of Edinburgh KG, PC, KT, OM, GBE, who was appointed on his 47th birthday on 10 June 1968.

Anti-submarine successes

The highest number of U-boat kills attributed to one ship in the 1939–45 War was 15 to HMS *Starling* (Capt. Frederic John Walker CB, DSO***, RN). Captain Walker was in command at the sinking of a total of 25 U-boats between 1941 and the time of his death on 9 July 1944. The US Destroyer Escort *England* sank 6 Japanese submarines in the Pacific between 18 and 30 May 1944.

Most successful submarine captains

The most successful of all World War II submarine commanders was Leutnant Otto Kretschmer, captain of the U.23 and U.99 who up to March 1940 sank one destroyer and 44 allied merchantmen totalling 266 629 gross registered tons. In World War I Kapitän-Leutnant (later Vize-admiral) Lothar von Arnauld de la Périère, in the U.35 and U.139, sank 195 allied ships totalling 458 856 gross tons. The most successful boats were U.35, which in World War I sank 54 ships of 90 350 grt in a single voyage and 224 ships of 539 711 grt all told, and U.48, which sank 51 ships of 310 007 grt in World War II. The largest target ever sunk by a submarine was the Japanese aircraft carrier *Shinano* (59 000 tons) by USS *Archerfish* (Cdr Joseph F. Enright, USN) on 29 Nov 1944.

AWARDS

Most valuable annual prize

The value of each of the 1988 Nobel Prizes (see p.186) was Sw Kr 2 500 000, which at the time of printing was equivalent to nearly £237 000. The ceremonial presentations for physics, chemistry, medicine and physiology, literature and economics take place in Stockholm, Sweden and that for peace in Oslo, Norway.

Most statues

The world record for raising statues to oneself was set by Generalissimo Dr Rafael Leónidas Trujillo y Molina (1891–1961), former President of the Dominican Republic. In March 1960 a count showed that there were 'over 2000'. The country's highest mountain was named Pico Trujillo (later Pico Duarte). One province was called Trujillo and another Trujillo Valdez. The capital was named Ciudad Trujillo (Trujillo City) in 1936, but

NOBEL PRIZES

Earliest 1901 for Physics, Chemistry, Medicine and Physiology, Literature and Peace

Most Prizes USA outright or shared 120 including most for Medicine–Physiology (34); Physics (31); Peace (13); Economics (14); Chemistry (22). France has most for Literature (11). The United Kingdom total is 75 (all classes) comprising Physics (18); Chemistry (20); Medicine (16); Peace (9); Literature (7); Economics (5)

Oldest Laureate Professor Francis Peyton Rous (US) (1879–1970) in 1966 shared in Medicine prize aged 87

Youngest Laureates *At time of award:* Professor Sir William Bragg CH, OBE, MC (1890–1971) 1915 Physics prize at 25 *At time of work:* Bragg, and Theodore W. Richards (US) (1868–1928) 1914 Chemistry prize at 23 *Literature:* Rudyard Kipling (UK) (1865–1936) 1907 prize at 41 *Peace:* Mrs Mairead Corrigan-Maguire (Northern Ireland) (b. 27 Jan 1944) 1976 prize (shared) at 32

Most 3 Awards: International Committee for Red Cross (founded 1863) Peace 1917, 1944 and 1963 (shared); 2 Awards: Dr Linus Carl Pauling (US) (b. 28 Feb 1901) Chemistry 1954 and Peace 1962; Mme Marja Sklodowska Curie (Polish-French) (1867–1934) Physics 1903 (shared) and Chemistry 1911; Professor John Bardeen (US) (b. 23 May 1908) Physics 1956 (shared) and 1972 (shared); Professor Frederick Sanger OM, CBE, FRS (b. 13 Aug 1918) Chemistry 1958 (shared) and 1980 (shared)

Highest Prize Sw Kr 2 500 000 (for 1988) equivalent to £237 000

Lowest Prize Sw Kr 115 000 (1923) equivalent to £6 620

reverted to its old name of Santo Domingo de Guzmán on 23 Nov 1961. Trujillo was assassinated in a car ambush on 30 May 1961, and 30 May is now celebrated as a public holiday. The man to whom most statues have been raised is Buddha. The 20th-century champion is Vladimir Ilyich Ulyanov, *alias* Lenin (1870–1924), busts of whom have been mass-produced, as also has been the case with Mao Tse-tung (1893–1976) and Ho Chi Minh (1890–1969).

PEERAGE
Most ancient
The oldest extant peerage is the premier Earldom of Scotland, held by the Rt Hon. Margaret of Mar, the Countess of Mar and 31st holder of this Earldom (b. 19 Sept 1940), who is the heir-at-law of Roderick or Rothri, 1st Earl (or Mormaer) of Mar, who witnessed a charter in 1114 or 1115 as 'Rothri *comes*'.

Oldest creation
The greatest age at which any person has been raised to the peerage is 93 years 337 days in the case of Sir William Francis Kyffin Taylor GBE, KC (b. 9 July 1854), created Baron Maenan of Ellesmere, County Shropshire, on 10 June 1948, and died, aged 97, on 22 Sept 1951. The oldest elevation to a life peerage has been that of Emanuel Shinwell PC, CH (b. 18 Oct 1884) on 2 June 1970 when aged 85 years 227 days. He died on 8 May 1986 aged 101.

Longest-lived peer
The longest-lived peer ever recorded was the Rt Hon. Emanuel Shinwell PC, CH (b. 18 Oct 1884), created a life

baron in 1970. He died in London aged 101 years 202 days on 8 May 1986. The oldest peeress recorded was the Countess Desmond, who was alleged to be 140 when she died in 1604. This claim is patently exaggerated but it is accepted that she may have been 104. Currently the oldest peer is the Rt Hon. Major the Earl of Southesk of Kinnaird Castle, Brechin, Angus (b. 23 Sept 1893).

Youngest peers
Twelve Dukes of Cornwall became (in accordance with the grant by the Crown in Parliament) peers at birth as the eldest sons of a sovereign; and the 9th Earl of Chichester inherited his earldom at his birth on 14 Apr 1944, 54 days after his father's death. The youngest age at which a person has had a peerage conferred on him is 7 days old in the case of the Earldom of Chester on HRH the Prince George (later George IV) on 19 Aug 1762. The youngest to be created a life peer or peeress is Baroness Masham of Ilton, Countess of Swinton (b. 19 Apr 1935) aged 34, in 1970.

Longest and shortest peerages
The longest tenure of a peerage has been 87 years 10 days in the case of Charles St Clair, Lord Sinclair, born 30 July 1768, succeeded 16 Dec 1775 and died aged 94 years 243 days on 30 Mar 1863.

The shortest enjoyment of a peerage was the 'split second' by which the law assumes that the Hon. Wilfrid Carlyl Stamp (b. 28 Oct 1904), the 2nd Baron Stamp, survived his father, Sir Josiah Charles Stamp GCB, GBE, the 1st Baron Stamp, when both were killed as a result of German bombing of London on 16 Apr 1941. Apart from this legal fiction, the shortest recorded peerage was one of 30 min in the case of Sir Charles Brandon KB, the 3rd Duke of Suffolk, who died, aged 13 or 14, just after succeeding his brother, Henry, both suffering a fatal illness, at Buckden, Cambridgeshire, on 14 July 1551.

Highest numbering
The highest succession number borne by any peer is that of the present 35th Baron Kingsale (John de Courcy, b. 27 Jan 1941), who succeeded to the then 746-year-old Barony on 7 Nov 1969. His occupations have included barman, bingo-caller and plumber.

Most creations
The largest number of new hereditary peerages created in any year was the 54 in 1296. The record for all peerages (including 40 life peerages) is 55 in 1964. The greatest number of extinctions in a year was 16 in 1923 and the greatest number of deaths was 44 in 1935.

Most prolific
The most prolific peers of all time are believed to be the 1st Earl Ferrers (1650–1717) and the 3rd Earl of Winchilsea (*c.* 1627–89), each with 27 legitimate children. In addition, the former reputedly fathered 30 illegitimate children. Currently the peer with the largest family is the Rt Hon. Bryan Walter Guinness, 2nd Baron Moyne (b. 27 Oct 1905) with 6 sons (1 now deceased) and 5 daughters. The most prolific peeress is believed to be Mary Fitzgerald, wife of Patrick, 19th Baron Kingsale, who bore 23 children (no twins) who survived to baptism. She died in 1663.

Baronets
The greatest age to which a baronet has lived is 101 years 188 days, in the case of Sir Fitzroy Donald Maclean, 10th Bt KCB (1835–1936). He was the last survivor of the Crimean campaign of 1853–56. Capt. Sir Trevor Wheler, 13th Baronet (b. 20 Sept 1889) entered his 83rd year as a baronet on 11 Aug 1984 but died aged 96 on 14 Jan 1986. The only baronetess is Dame Maureen Dunbar of Hempriggs, who succeeded in her own right as 8th in line of a 1706 baronetcy in 1965. There are some 1 350 baronets.

Knights *Youngest and oldest*
The youngest age for the conferment of a knighthood is

29 days for HRH the Prince George (b. 12 Aug 1762) (later George IV) by virtue of his *ex officio* membership of the Order of the Garter (KG) consequent upon his creation as Prince of Wales on 17 or 19 Aug 1762.

The greatest age for the conferment of a knighthood is on a 100th birthday, in the case of the Knight Bachelor Sir Robert Mayer CH (1879–1985), who was additionally made a KCVO by the Queen at the Royal Festival Hall, London on 5 June 1979.

Most brothers
George and Elizabeth Coles of Australia had 5 sons knighted—Sir George CBE (1885–1977); Sir Arthur (b. 1892); Sir Kenneth (b. 1896); Sir Edgar (b. 1899) and Sir Norman (b. 1907).

Most freedoms
Probably the greatest number of freedoms ever conferred on any man was 57 in the case of Andrew Carnegie (1835–1919), who was born in Dunfermline, Fife but emigrated to the United States in 1848. The most freedoms conferred upon any citizen of the United Kingdom is 42, for Sir Winston Churchill (1874–1965).

Most honorary degrees
The greatest number of honorary degrees awarded to any individual is 111, given to Reverend Father Theodore M. Hesburgh (b. 1918), president of the University of Notre Dame, Indiana, USA. These were accumulated from 1954 to June 1987.

Greatest vote
The largest monetary vote made by Parliament to a subject was the £400 000 given to the 1st Duke of Wellington (1769–1852) on 12 Apr 1814. He received in all £864 000. The total received by the 1st, 2nd and 3rd Dukes to January 1900 was £1052 000.

The Royal Society (founded 1662)
The longest term as an FRS (Fellow of the Royal Society) has been 61 years in the case of Bertrand Russell, 3rd Earl (1872–1970), who had been elected in 1908.

The longest-lived FRS has been Sir Rickard Christophers CIE, OBE (1873–1978) aged 104 years 84 days. John Lubbock (1834–1913), later 1st Baron Avebury, was elected at the age of 23 in 1857.

Erasmus Darwin was elected on 9 Apr 1761 and was followed by his son Robert (1788 to 1848), *his* son Charles (1879 to 1881), his sons Sir George (1879 to 1912), Francis (1882 to 1925) and Horace (1903 to 1928) and Sir George's son Sir Charles (1922 to 1962) so spanning over 200 years with 5 generations.

Who's Who
The longest entry in *Who's Who* (founded 1848) was that of the Rt Hon. Sir Winston Leonard Spencer Churchill KG, OM, CH, TD (1874–1965), who appeared in 67 editions from 1899 (18 lines) and had 211 lines by the 1965 edition.

Currently the longest entry in its wider format is that of Barbara Cartland, the romantic novelist, with 143 lines.

Apart from those who qualify for inclusion by hereditary title, the youngest entry has been Sir Yehudi Menuhin OM, KBE (b. New York City, USA, 22 Apr 1916), the concert violinist, who first appeared in the 1932 edition aged 15.

The longest entry of the 66 000 entries in *Who's Who in America* is that of Dr Glenn T. Seaborg (b. 19 Apr 1912) with an all-time record of 100 lines.

Oxford and Cambridge Unions
Four brothers were presidents of the Union in the case of the sons of the Rt Hon. Isaac Foot: Sir Dingle Foot (Balliol, 1927–8); John (Lord Foot) (Balliol, 1930–1) and the Rt Hon. Michael (Wadham, 1933–4) at Oxford and Hugh (Lord Caradon) (St John's, 1929) at Cambridge. The last named's son, the Hon. Paul, was president at Oxford (University College, 1960–1).

Sacred object ● The sacred object with the highest intrinsic value is this 15th-century gold Buddah in Wat Trimitr Temple in Bangkok, Thailand. It is 3·04 m *10 ft* tall and weighs an estimated 5½ tonnes. At $500 per fine ounce its intrinsic worth has been put at £28½ million. (Photo: Spectrum)

THE HUMAN WORLD
CHAPTER · ELEVEN

Political and Social

Largest political division

The British Commonwealth of Nations, a free association of 48 sovereign independent states together with 17 non-sovereign states and dependencies administered by them, covers an area of 27 171 608 km² *10 491 016 miles²* with a population estimated in 1988 to be 1 213 601 000. Fiji declared itself a Republic on 1 Oct 1987 and also severed links. The British Empire began to expand when Henry VII patented trade monopolies to John Cabot in March 1496 and when the East India Co. was incorporated on 31 Dec 1600.

COUNTRIES

The world comprises 170 sovereign countries and 63 separately administered non-sovereign or other territories, making a total of 233.

The United Nations still lists the *de jure* territories of East Timor (now incorporated into Indonesia), Western Sahara (now in Morocco), the former mandated territory of Palestine and the uninhabited Canton and Enderbury Islands (now disputed between the USA and Kiribati) but does not list the 3 Baltic states of Estonia, Latvia and Lithuania though their forcible incorporation into the USSR in 1940 has never been internationally recognised. Neither does it list the *de facto* territories of Taiwan, Mayotte or Spanish North Africa, the 4 Antarctic Territories or the Australian Territory of Coral Sea Islands and Heard and McDonald Islands. The USA's renunciation of the Pacific Islands' trusteeship on 3 Nov 1986 is resulting in the creation of Micronesia, Marshall Islands, Northern Mariana Islands and Palau as separate entities.

Largest

The country with the greatest area is the Union of Soviet Socialist Republics (the Soviet Union), comprising 15 Union (constituent) Republics with a total area of 22 402 200 km² *8 649 500 miles²*, or 15·0 per cent of the world's total land area, and a total coastline (including islands) of 106 360 km *66 090 miles*. The country measures 8980 km *5580 miles* from east to west and 4490 km *2790 miles* from north to south and is 91·8 times the size of the United Kingdom. Its population on 1 July 1987 was an estimated 284 000 000.

The United Kingdom covers 244 110 km² *94 251 miles²* (including 3100 km² *1197 miles²* of inland water), or 0·16 per cent of the total land area of the world. Great Britain is the world's 8th largest island, with an area of 218 040 km² *84 186 miles²* and a coastline 7930 km *4928 miles* long, of which Scotland accounts for 4141 km *2573 miles*, Wales 685 km *426 miles* and England 3104 km *1929 miles*.

Smallest

The smallest independent country in the world is the State of the Vatican City or Holy See (Stato della Città del Vaticano), which was made an enclave within the city of Rome, Italy on 11 Feb 1929. The enclave has an area of 44 ha *108·7 acres*. The maritime sovereign country with the shortest coastline is Monaco with 5·61 km *3·49 miles* excluding piers and breakwaters. The world's smallest republic is Nauru, less than 1 degree south of the equator in the western Pacific, which became independent on 31 Jan 1968. It has an area of 2129 ha *5263 acres* and a population of 8100 (latest estimate 1987).

The smallest colony in the world is Gibraltar (since 1969, the City of Gibraltar) with an area of 5·8 km² *2½ miles²*. However, Pitcairn Island, the only inhabited (59 people at 1 Jan 1987) island of a group of 4 (total area 48 km² *18½ miles²*), has an area of 388 ha *960 acres/1½ miles²*. It was named after Midshipman Robert Pitcairn of HMS *Swallow* in July 1767.

The official residence, since 1834, of the Grand Master of the Order of the Knights of Malta, totalling 1·2 ha *3 acres* and comprising the Villa del Priorato di Malta on the lowest of Rome's 7 hills, the 46 m *151 ft* Aventine, retains certain diplomatic privileges as does 68 via Condotti. The Order has accredited representatives to foreign governments and is hence sometimes cited as the world's smallest 'state'.

Flattest and most elevated

The country with the lowest highest point is the Republic of the Maldives which attains 2·4 m *8 ft*. The country with the highest lowest point is Lesotho. The egress of the Senqu (Orange) riverbed is 1381 m *4530 ft* above sea level.

Most impenetrable boundary

The 'Iron Curtain' (1380 km *858 miles*) dividing the Federal Republic of Germany (West) and the German Democratic Republic (East) utilises 2 230 000 land mines and 80 500 km *50 000 miles* of barbed wire, much of it of British manufacture, in addition to many watch-towers containing detection devices. The whole strip of 246 m *270 yd* wide occupies 344 km² *133 miles²* of East German territory and cost an estimated $7000 million to build and maintain. It reduced the westward flow from more than 200 000 in 1961 to a trickle of 30 (including 8 guards) in 1985. The death toll has been 184 since 1962. Construction of the second wall, 165·7 km *103 miles* in length, began in East Berlin in March 1984.

Longest and shortest frontier

The longest *continuous* frontier in the world is that between Canada and the United States, which (including the Great Lakes boundaries) extends for 6416 km *3987 miles* (excluding 2547 km *1538 miles* with Alaska). The frontier which is crossed most frequently is that between the United States and Mexico. It extends for 3110 km *1933 miles* and there are more than 120 000 000 crossings every year. The Sino-Soviet frontier, broken by the Sino-Mongolian border, extends for 7240 km *4500 miles*, with no reported figure of crossings. The 'frontier' of the Holy See in Rome measures 4·07 km *2·53 miles*. The land frontier between Gibraltar and Spain at La Linea, closed between June 1969 and February 1985, measures 1·53 km *1672 yd*. Zambia, Zimbabwe, Botswana and Namibia (South West Africa) almost merge.

Most frontiers

China has the most land frontiers with 13—Mongolia, USSR, North Korea, Hong Kong, Macau, Vietnam, Laos, Burma, India, Bhutan, Nepal, Pakistan and Afghanistan. These extend for 24 000 km *14 900 miles*. France, if all her *départements d'outre-mer* are included, may, on extended territorial waters, have 20. The United Kingdom's frontier with the Republic of Ireland measures 358 km *223 miles*.

WORLD POPULATION

Date	Millions	Date	Millions
8000 BC	c. 6	1970	3678
AD 1	c. 255	1975	4033
1000	c. 254	1980	4415
1250	416	1981	4530
1500	460	1982	4607
1600	579	1983	4685
1700	679	1984	4763
1750	770	1985	4837
1800	954	1986	4917
1900	1633	1987 (mid)	*5000
1920	1862	1988	5081
1930	2070	1990	5246
1940	2295	2000†	6122
1950	2513	2025	8206
1960	3049	2095	10 500

* *Population Institute of Washington, DC declared this landmark was reached on 7 July 1986 whereas the UN nominated 11 July 1987 'Baby Five Billion Day'.*

† *The UN publication State of World Population, 1984 forecast that the world population will not stabilise until 2095 at c. 10 500 million. In May 1988 a revised estimate put the likely world population in 2050 as high as 14 000 million. Note The all-time peak annual increase of 2·0 % c. 1958–1962 had declined to 1·73 % by 1975–1980. By 1990 this should decline to 1·5 %. This, however, now produces an annual increment of 87 million peaking to 90 million in the 1990s.*
On the estimates of the French demographer Biraben, A. R. Thatcher has calculated that 63 800 million people died between 40 000 BC and AD 1980. This indicates that there have thus been some 63 700 million specimens of Homo sapiens sapiens who ever lived i.e. the present population is about one thirteenth of those who have ever lived.

POPULATIONS

World

The daily increase in the world's population is 223 285, or 155 per minute. For past, present and future estimates see table.

Matej Gaspar, born 11 July 1987 in Yugoslavia, was symbolically named the world's 5 billionth inhabitant by the United Nations Secretary-General.

Most populous country

The most populated country is China, which in *pinyin* is written Zhongguo (meaning central land). The census of July 1982 was 1 008 175 288 while the mid-1987 estimate was 1 085 000 000. The rate of natural increase in the People's Republic of China is now estimated to be 35 068 a day or 12·8 million per year. The census of July 1982 required 5 100 000 enumerators to work for 10 days. India is set to overtake China in size of population by AD 2050 with 1590 million against 1554 million.

Least populous

The independent state with the smallest population is the Vatican City or the Holy See (see Smallest country, above), with 750 inhabitants in 1987 and a nil return for births.

Most densely populated

The most densely populated territory in the world is the Portuguese province of Macau (or Macao), on the southern coast of China. It has an estimated population of 392 000 (mid-1986) in an area of 16·05 km² *6·2 miles²*, giving a density of 24 423 per km² *63 225 per mile²*.

Of territories with an area of more than 1000 km², Hong Kong (1037 km² *400·5 miles²*) contains 5 533 000 (1986), giving the territory a density of 5169/km² *13 390/mile²*. Hong Kong is now the most populous of all colonies. The transcription of the name is from a local pronunciation of the Peking dialect version of Xiang gang (a port for incense). The 1976 by-census showed that the west area of the urban district of Mong Kok on the Kowloon Peninsula had a density of 252 090/km² *652 910/mile²*. In 1959, at the peak of the housing crisis, it was reported that in one house designed for 12 people the number of occupants was 459, including 104 in one room and 4 living on the roof.

Of countries over 2589 km² *1000 miles²* the most densely populated is Bangladesh with a population of 103 200 000 (1986) living in 142 775 km² *55 126 miles²* at a density of 727/km² *1882/mile²*. The Indonesian island of Java (with an area of 126 295 km² *48 763 miles²*) had a population of 100 300 000 (1987), which gives it a density of some 793/km² *2056/mile²*.

The United Kingdom (244 110 km² *94 251 miles²*) had an estimated population of 56 930 200 at mid-1987, giving a density of 233 persons/km² *604/mile²*. The mid-1986 population density for the Royal Borough of Kensington and Chelsea, London was 11 262/km² *29 168/mile²*.

Most sparsely populated

Antarctica became permanently occupied by relays of scientists from October 1956. The population varies seasonally and reaches 2000 at times.

The least populated territory, apart from Antarctica, is Kalaallit Nunaat (formerly Greenland), with a population of 53 406 (1986) in an area of 2 175 000 km² *840 000 miles²*, giving a density of one person to every 40·72 km² *15·72 miles²*. Some 84·3 per cent of the island comprises an ice-cap.

The lowest population densities in the United Kingdom are in the Highlands and Islands of Scotland with 13·1/km² *33·9/mile²*. The most sparsely populated county in England is Northumberland with 60·40/km² *156·45/ mile²*.

Emigration

More people emigrate from Mexico than from any other country. An estimated 800 000 emigrated illegally into

Distant and mystical China is the home of many records. This page shows just some of its record-breaking features.

Great Wall of China ● Built as a defensive system against the Huns, the Great Wall of China—above—is the largest building project in history. (Details are on page 122).

Largest legislative assembly ● The largest legislative assembly in the world is the National People's Congress of the People's Republic of China. (See left). The sixth congress, when convened in June 1983, had 2 978 members. Its standing committee has 197 members. The Congress meets in the auditorium of the Great Hall of the People in Beijing.

Photos are by Colorific, Gamma, Spectrum and Horizon.

China's army ● China's People's Liberation Army's strength in 1987 was estimated to be 3 200 000, some of whom are seen below. There are 4·4 million reserves and it is reckoned that her para-military forces of armed and unarmed militias number 'some 12 million'.

Most populous country ● The photo above shows crowds leaving a cinema in Kumning, China. More people go to the cinema in China than in any other country—in September 1987 it was reported that there had been 21 000 million cinema attendances during 1986.

WORLD'S MOST POPULOUS URBAN SETTLEMENTS

Population	Name	Country	Date
>100	Dolní Věstonice	Czechoslovakia	c. 27000 BC
c. 150	Chemi Shanidar	Iraq	8900 BC
27 000	Jericho (Aríhā)	Occupied Jordan	7800 BC
c. 5000	Çatal Huyuk, Anatolia	Turkey	c. 6800 BC
>5000	Hierakonopolis (Nekhen)	Egypt	c. 3200 BC
50 000	Uruk (Erech) (now Warka) from 3800 BC	Iraq	3000 BC
250 000	Greater Ur (now Tell Muqayyar)	Iraq	2200 BC
350 000	Babylon (now al-Hillah)	Iraq	600 BC
500 000	Pataliputra (Patna) Bihār	India	400–185 BC
600 000	Seleukia (near Baghdad)	Iraq	300 BC–165 AD
1 100 000	Rome (founded c. 510 BC)	Italy	133 BC
1 500 000	Angkor	Cambodia	900 AD
1·0–1·5 million	Hangchow (now Hangzhou)	China	1279
707 000	Peking (Cambaluc) (now Beijing)	China	1578
1 117 290	London	United Kingdom	1801
8 615 050	London (peak)	United Kingdom	1939
11 828 000	Tokyo	Japan	1985

Note: The UN projection for AD 2000 for Greater Mexico City is 31 616 000.

the USA in 1980 alone. The Soviet invasion of Afghanistan in December 1979 caused an influx of 2 900 000 refugees into Pakistan and a further 2 200 000 into Iran. A total of 108 000 emigrated from the UK in 1985. Her largest number of emigrants in any one year was 360 000 in 1852, mainly from Ireland.

Immigration

The country which regularly receives the most legal immigrants is the United States. It has been estimated that in the period 1820–1985, the USA has received 52 520 358 *official* immigrants. One in 24 of the US population is, however, an *illegal* immigrant. In 1986, 629 000 aliens were arrested by US patrol on the Mexican border.

The peak year for immigration into the United Kingdom was the 12 months from 1 July 1961 to 30 June 1962, when about 430 000 Commonwealth citizens arrived. The number of immigrants in the year 1987 was 45 500. The estimated total of 'non-whites' for Great Britain was 2 430 000 or 4·5 per cent of the population, averaged over surveys in 1984–86.

Most patient 'Refusenik'

The USSR citizen who waited longest for an exit visa was Benjamin Bogomolny (b. 7 Apr 1946) who first applied in 1966. He arrived in Vienna on 14 Oct 1986. Vladimir Slepak (b. 29 Oct 1927) became the new champion, having waited since June 1970.

Tourism

The record influx of tourists into the United Kingdom was

15 600 000 in 1987 and their record spending was £6300 million plus £1500 on British carriers in 1987.

Birth rate

The rate for the whole world was 28·0 per 1000 in 1987. The highest estimated by the UN is 55·1 per 1000 for Kenya for 1980–85. A worldwide survey published in 1985 showed no country with a rising birth rate—the last being Nepal.

Excluding Vatican City, where the rate is negligible, the lowest recorded rate is 9·3 per 1000 (1985) for San Marino.

The crude birth rate—the number of births per thousand population—for the United Kingdom was 13·6 in 1987 (13·6 for England and Wales, 12·9 for Scotland and 17·7 for Northern Ireland), whilst for the Republic of Ireland it was 16·6 registered live births per thousand population. (All figures for 1987 are provisional). The annual number of births in England and Wales was highest this century in 1920 at 957 782 (since the first full year of 463 787) and lowest in 1977 at 569 259. After falling each year since 1964 when there were 875 972 births, the number started to rise again in 1978. In 1987 there were 682 000 births (on average 1867 per day or 78 per hour).

Death rate

The death rate for the whole world was 10·0 per 1000 in

> **Highest capital** ● Before the domination of Tibet by China, Lhasa, at 3684 m *12 087 ft* above sea level, was the highest capital in the world. (Photo: Spectrum)

1987. The estimated death rate in Kampuchea of 40·0 per 1000 from 1975–80 subsided to 19·7 from 1980–85. The estimated figure for Sierra Leone from 1980–85 was 29·7.

The lowest of the latest available recorded rates is 3·5 deaths/1000 in Tonga in 1985.

The crude death rate—the number of deaths per thousand population of all ages—for the United Kingdom was 11·3 in 1987 (11·3 for England and Wales, 12·1 for Scotland and 9·7 for Northern Ireland). The local authority district with the highest SMR (Standard Mortality Ratio, where the national average is 100) was Castle Morpeth, Northumberland where the SMR was 135 in 1986. Wealden, East Sussex had the lowest SMR in 1986 at 75. The provisional 1987 rate for the Republic of Ireland was 8·8 registered deaths per 1000.

Natural increase

The rate of natural increase for the whole world is estimated to be 28·0 − 10·0 = 18·0 per 1000 in 1987 compared with a peak 22 per 1000 in 1965. The highest of the latest available recorded rates is 41·1 (55·1 − 14·0) from Kenya in 1980–85.

The 1986 rate for the United Kingdom was 1·5 (1·5 in England and Wales, 0·5 in Scotland and 7·4 in Northern Ireland). The rate for the first time in the first quarter of 1975 became temporarily one of natural decrease. The figure for the Republic of Ireland was 7·9/1000 in 1986.

The lowest rate of natural increase in any major independent country is in the Federal Republic of Germany with a negative figure of −1·3 per 1000 (10·2 births and 11·5 deaths) for 1986. On the Isle of Man the figure is –3·8 (11·0 births and 14·8 deaths).

Marriage ages

The lowest average age for marriage is India, with 20·0 years (males) and 14·5 years (females). At the other extreme is Ireland, with 26·8 (males) and 24·7 (females). In the mid 16th century the average age for first marriages by women in England was 26·7 years. In the People's Republic of China the *recommended* age for marriage for men has been 28 and for women 25. In England and Wales the average (modal) age at marriage in 1986 was 24 years (bridegrooms) and 22 years (brides). The average ages in 1986 were 30·5 (bridegrooms) and 27·8 (brides).

Divorces

The country with most divorces is the United States with a total of 1 157 000 in 1987—a rate of 4·8 per cent per thousand marriages. In 1986 some 2 per cent of all *existing* marriages in the USA broke up. In England and Wales, since 1980 more than one in nine marriages have ended in divorce before a fifth anniversary. By 1985 13 per cent of families had one parent.

Sex ratio

There were estimated in 1981 to be 1006·7 males in the world for every 1000 females. The country with the largest recorded shortage of males is the USSR, with 1132·1 females to every 1000 males (1985 census). The country with the largest recorded woman shortage is Pakistan, with 906 to every 1000 males in 1981. The figures are, however, probably under-enumerated due to *purdah*. The ratio in the United Kingdom was 1053 females to every 1000 males at mid 1986, and is expected to be 1034/1000 by AD 2000.

Infant mortality

The world rate in 1987 was 80 per 1000 live births. Based on deaths before one year of age, the lowest of the latest recorded rates is 4·9 in Japan in 1987.

In Ethiopia the infant mortality rate was unofficially estimated to be nearly 550/1000 live births in 1969. The highest rate recently estimated is 180/1000 in Sierra Leone (1980-85).

The rate of infant mortality—the number of deaths at ages under one year per thousand live births—for the

United Kingdom was 9·1 in 1987 (9·2 for England and Wales, 8·5 for Scotland and 8·6 for Northern Ireland). The corresponding rate in 1986 for the Republic of Ireland was 8·7.

Expectation of life at birth

World expectation of life is rising from 47·4 years (1950–55) towards 64·5 years (1995–2000). There is evidence that life expectation in Britain in the 5th century AD was 33 years for males and 27 years for females. In the decade 1890–1900 the expectation of life among the population of India was 23·7 years. Based on the latest available data, the highest recorded expectation of life at age 12 months is 74·8 years for males and 80·0 years for females (1987). The lowest recorded expectation of life at birth is 36·6 years for males and 37·3 years for females in Afghanistan.

The latest available figures for England and Wales (1983–85) are 71·8 years for males and 77·7 years for females, 70·1 and 76·3 in Scotland (1985) and 70·1 and 76·3 in Northern Ireland, (1984–86). For the Republic of Ireland, the figure (1980) was 69·5 years for males and 75 for females. The British figure for 1901–10 was 48·5 years (males) and 52·4 years (females).

Housing

For comparison, dwelling units are defined as a structurally separated room or rooms occupied by private households of one or more people and having separate access or a common passageway to the street.

The first country to surpass 100 000 000 housing units was India in 1972. In 1981 the figure was 142 954 921.

Great Britain had a stock of 22 272 000 dwellings as at 1 Dec 1987, of which 64·0 per cent were owner-occupied. The record number of permanent houses built in a year has been 413 715 in 1968.

Physicians

The country with the most physicians is the USSR, with 831 300, or one to every 307 persons. China had an estimated 1·4 million para-medical personnel, known as 'barefoot doctors', by 1981. There were 128 983 doctors on the General Medical Council's Principal List, and therefore entitled to practise in the United Kingdom as at 1 Jan 1988.

Dentists

The country with the most dentists is the United States, where 145 800 were registered members of the American Dental Association in 1987. The number of dentists registered in the United Kingdom as at 1 Jan 1988 was 25 286.

Psychiatrists

The country with the most psychiatrists is the United States. The registered membership of the American Psychiatric Association (inst. 1894) was 32 000 in 1987. The membership of the American Psychological Association (inst. 1892) was 60 000 in 1987. The No. 1 city in the 1987 couch rankings is Boston, Massachusetts with 1 shrink for 328 heads.

Largest hospital *World*

The largest mental hospital in the world is the Pilgrim State Hospital, West Brentwood, Long Island, NY, USA, with 3618 beds. It formerly contained 14 200 beds. The largest psychiatric institute is at the University of California, Los Angeles, USA.

The busiest maternity hospital in the world has been the Mama Yemo Hospital, Kinshasa, Zaïre with 41 930 deliveries in 1976. The record 'birthquake' occurred on a day in May 1976 with 175 babies born. The hospital had 599 beds.

Great Britain

The largest hospital of any kind in Great Britain is Hartwood Hospital near Shotts, Lanarkshire with 1600 staffed beds for mentally ill patients.

The largest acute hospital in Great Britain is the St

James's University Hospital (which is also a teaching hospital), Leeds, West Yorkshire, with 1432 staffed beds.

The largest maternity hospital in Great Britain is the Simpson Memorial Maternity Pavilion, Edinburgh with 218 staffed beds.

The largest children's hospital in Great Britain is Queen Mary's Hospital for Children, at Carshalton, Sutton, Surrey, with 340 staffed beds.

Longest stay in hospital

Miss Martha Nelson was admitted to the Columbus State Institute for the Feeble-Minded in Ohio, USA in 1875. She died in January 1975 aged 103 years 6 months in the Orient State Institution, Ohio after spending more than 99 years in institutions.

TOWNS AND CITIES
Oldest

The oldest known walled town in the world is Arīhā (Jericho). The Radio-carbon dating on specimens from the lowest levels reached by archaeologists indicate habitation there by perhaps 3000 people as early as 7800 BC. The settlement of Dolní Věstonice, Czechoslovakia, has been dated to the Gravettian culture c. 27 000 BC. The oldest capital city in the world is Dimashq (Damascus), Syria. It has been continuously inhabited since c. 2500 BC.

The oldest town in Great Britain is often cited as Colchester, the old British Camulodunum, headquarters of Belgic chiefs in the 1st century BC. However, the name of the tin trading post Salakee, St Mary's, Isles of Scilly is derived from pre-Celtic roots and hence *ante* 550 BC. The oldest borough in Britain is reputed to be Barnstaple, Devon whose charter was granted by King Athelstan (927–939) in AD 930.

The only one of the United Kingdom's 58 cities with a Saxon charter is Ripon, North Yorkshire which was a bishopric in 672 and had a charter dated 886.

Most populous

The most populous 'urban agglomeration' in the world is the 'Keihin Metropolitan Area' (Tokyo-Yokohama Metropolitan Area) of 2800 km^2 *1081 miles^2* containing an estimated 29 272 000 people in 1985. The municipal population of Greater Tokyo in 1985 was 11 828 000. The population of the metropolitan area of Greater Mexico City in 1985 was published as 17 321 800 with the city proper at 10 499 000 in 1984.

The most populous conurbation in Britain is London, with a population of 6 775 500 (mid 1986). The residential population of the City of London (274 ha *677·3 acres* plus 24·9 ha *61·7 acres* foreshore) is 5750 (1987 estimate) compared with 128 000 in 1801. The daytime figure is 330 000. The peak figure for London was 8 615 050 in 1939.

Largest in area

The world's largest town, in area, is Mount Isa, Queensland, Australia. The area administered by the City Council is 40 978 km^2 *15 822 miles^2*. The largest conurbation in the United Kingdom is Greater London with an area of 1579·5 km^2 *609·8 miles^2*.

Towns, villages and hamlets *Great Britain*

The smallest place with a town council is Llanwrtyd Wells, Powys (pop. 528 at 1981 census). The smallest town with a Royal Charter (granted in 1290) is Caerwys, Clwyd, Wales with a civil parish population of 1040. The strongest claimant to be Britain's oldest village is Thatcham, Berkshire. The earliest Mesolithic settlement there has been dated to 7720 BC. Kidlington, in Oxfordshire (population 17 200) claimed to be 'England's largest village' until 1987 when it ceased to be run by a parish council.

Highest

The highest capital in the world, before the domination of Tibet by China, was Lhasa, at an elevation of 3684 m

12 087 ft above sea level. La Paz, administrative and *de facto* capital of Bolivia, stands at an altitude of 3631 m *11 916 ft* above sea level. El Alto airport is at 4080 m *13 385 ft*. The city was founded in 1548 by Capt. Alonso de Mendoza on the site of an Indian village named Chuquiaṗu. It was originally called Ciudad de Nuestra Señora de La Paz (City of Our Lady of Peace), but in 1825 was renamed La Paz de Ayacucho, its present official name. Sucre, the legal capital of Bolivia, stands at 2834 m *9301 ft* above sea level. The new town of Wenchuan, founded in 1955 on the Chinghai–Tibet road, north of the Tangla range, is the highest in the world at 5100 m *16 732 ft* above sea level.

The highest village in Britain is Flash, north Staffordshire, at 462 m *1518 ft* above sea level. The highest in Scotland is Wanlockhead, in Dumfries and Galloway, at 420 m *1380 ft* above sea level.

Lowest

The settlement of Ein Bokek, which has a synagogue, on the shores of the Dead Sea is the lowest in the world at 393·5 m *1291 ft* below sea level.

Northernmost and southernmost

The world's most northerly town with a population of more than 10 000 is the Arctic port of Dikson, USSR in 73° 32′ N, so named in 1875 after a Swedish brewer. The northernmost village is Ny Ålesund (78° 55′ N), a coalmining settlement on King's Bay, Vest Spitsbergen, in the Norwegian territory of Svalbard, inhabited only during the winter season. The northernmost capital is Reykjavik, Iceland in 64° 08′ N. Its population was estimated to be 91 394 in 1986.

The world's southernmost village is Puerto Williams (population about 350) on the north coast of Isla Navarino, in Tierra del Fuego, Chile, 1090 km *680 miles* north of Antarctica. Wellington, North Island, New Zealand, with a 1987 population of 325 700 is the southernmost capital city on 41° 17′ S. The world's southernmost administrative centre is Port Stanley, with a population of 1200, (51° 43′ S) in the Falkland Islands.

Most remote from the sea

The largest town most remote from the sea is Wu–lu–mu-chi (formerly Ürümqi) in Xinjiang (formerly Tihwa, Sinkiang), capital of the Uighur autonomous region of China, at a distance of about 2250 km *1400 miles* from the nearest coastline. Its population was estimated to be 947 000 in 1987.

Royalty and Heads of State

Oldest ruling house and longest span

The Emperor of Japan, Hirohito (born 29 Apr 1901), is the 124th in line from the first Emperor, Jimmu Tenno or Zinmu, whose reign was traditionally from 660 to 581 BC, but more probably from c. 40 BC to c. 10 BC. The present Emperor, who succeeded on 25 Dec 1926, is currently the world's longest-reigning monarch.

Her Majesty Queen Elizabeth II (b. 21 Apr 1926) represents dynasties historically traceable back at least to the 4th century AD in the case of Tegid, great grandfather of Cunedda, founder of the House of Gwynedd in Wales; she is 54th in the line. If the historicity of some early Scoto-Irish and Pictish kings were acceptable, the lineage could be extended to about 70 generations.

Reigns *Longest all-time*

The longest recorded reign of any monarch is that of Phiops II or Neferkare, a Sixth Dynasty Pharaoh of ancient Egypt. His reign began c. 2281 BC, when he was aged 6, and is believed to have lasted c. 94 years. Minhti, King of Arakan (Burma), is reputed to have reigned for 95 years between 1279 and 1374. Musoma Kanijo, chief of the Nzega district of western Tanganyika (now part of

Tanzania), reputedly reigned for more than 98 years from 1864, when aged 8, until his death on 2 Feb 1963. The longest reign of any European monarch was that of Afonso I Henrigues of Portugal who ascended the throne on 30 Apr 1112 and died on 6 Dec 1185 after a reign of 73 years 220 days, first as a Count and then as King.

Roman occupation
During the 369-year-long Roman occupation of England, Wales and parts of southern Scotland there were 40 sole and 27 co-emperors of Rome. Of these the longest reigning was Constantinus I (The Great) from 31 Mar 307 to 22 May 337—30 years 2 months.

Shortest
The Crown Prince Luis Filipe of Portugal was mortally wounded at the same time that his father was killed by a bullet which severed his carotid artery, in the streets of Lisbon on 1 Feb 1908. He was thus technically King of Portugal (Dom Luis III) for about 20 minutes.

Highest post-nominal numbers
The highest post-nominal number ever used to designate a member of a royal house was 75, briefly enjoyed by Count Heinrich LXXV Reuss (1800 to 1801). All male members of this branch of the German family are called Heinrich and are successively numbered from I upwards *each* century.

British regnal numbers date from the Norman Conquest. The highest is 8, used by Henry VIII (1509–1547) and by Edward VIII (1936) who died as HRH the Duke of Windsor on 28 May 1972. Jacobites liked to style Henry Benedict, Cardinal York (b. 1725), the grandson of James II, as Henry IX in respect of his 'reign' from 1788 to 1807

Ronald Reagan and Lee Kuan Yew ● The oldest US President of all time was Ronald Reagan, who was 77 at the end of his term of office. He is seen here with Lee Kuan Yew, Hon. GCMG, Hon. CH (b. 16 Sept 1923) of Singapore, currently the longest serving Prime Minister, who has been 6 times re-elected and remains in office after 29 years. (Photo: Gamma)

BRITISH MONARCHY RECORDS

LONGEST REIGN OR TENURE
Kings
59 years 96 days[1] George III 1760–1820
Queens Regnant
63 years 216 days Victoria 1837–1901
Queens Consort
57 years 70 days Charlotte 1761–1818 (Consort of George III)

SHORTEST REIGN OR TENURE
Kings
77 days[2] Edward V 1483
Queens Regnant
13 days[3] Jane, 6–19 July 1553
Queens Consort
154 days Yoleta (1285–6) (Second Consort of Alexander III)

LONGEST LIVED
Kings
81 years 239 days[4] George III (b. 1738–d. 1820)
Queens Regnant
81 years 243 days Victoria (b. 1819–d. 1901)
Queens Consort
87 years Lady Elizabeth Bowes Lyon, Queen Elizabeth, the Queen Mother: (b. 4 Aug 1900)

MOST CHILDREN (LEGITIMATE)[5]
Kings
18 Edward I 1272–1307
Queens Regnant
9[6] Victoria (b. 1819–d. 1901)
Queens Consort
15 Eleanor (c. 1244–90) and Charlotte (b. 1744–d. 1818)

OLDEST TO START REIGN OR CONSORTSHIP
Kings
64 years 10 months William IV 1830–7
Queens Regnant
37 years 5 months Mary I 1553–8
Queens Consort
56 years 53 days Alexandra (b. 1844–d. 1925) (Consort of Edward VII)

YOUNGEST TO START REIGN OR CONSORTSHIP
Kings
269 days Henry VI in 1422
Queens Regnant
6 or 7 days Mary, Queen of Scots in 1542
Queens Consort
6 years 11 months Isabella (Second Consort of Richard II in 1396)

MOST MARRIED
Kings
6 times Henry VIII 1509–47
Queens Regnant
3 times Mary, Queen of Scots 1542–67 (Executed 1587)
Queens Consort
4 times Catherine Parr (b. c. 1512–d. 1548) (Sixth Consort of Henry VIII)

MOST ALIVE SIMULTANEOUSLY
Between 30 Oct 1683 (birth of George Augustus of Hanover, later George II) and 6 Feb 1685 (death of Charles II) there were 8 heads of state living simultaneously (Charles II, James II, William and Mary, Anne, George I and II) and also Richard Cromwell (d. 1712), the 2nd Lord Protector and *de facto* head of state in 1658–59.

Notes (Dates are of reigns or tenures unless otherwise indicated)
[1] James Francis Edward, the Old Pretender, known to his supporters as James III, styled his reign from 16 Sept 1701 until his death 1 Jan 1766 (i.e. 64 years 109 days).
[2] There is the probability that in pre-Conquest times Sweyn 'Forkbeard', the Danish King of England, reigned for only 40 days in 1013–14.
[3] She accepted the allegiance of the Lords of the Council (9 July) and was proclaimed on 10 July so is often referred to as the '9 (or 10) day Queen'.
[4] Richard Cromwell (b. 4 Oct 1626), the 2nd Lord Protector from 3 Sept 1658 until his abdication on 24 May 1659, lived under the alias John Clarke until 12 July 1712 aged 85 years 9 months and was thus the longest lived head of state.
[5] Henry I (b. 1068–d. 1135) in addition to one (possibly two) legitimate sons and a daughter had at least 20 bastard children (9 sons, 11 daughters), and possibly 22, by six mistresses.
[6] Queen Anne (b. 1665–d. 1714) had 17 pregnancies, which produced only 5 live births.

---

when he died as last survivor in the male line of the House of Stuart.

Longest-lived 'royals'
The longest life among the blood royal of Europe has been that of the Princess Pauline Marie Madeleine von Croy, who uniquely celebrated her 100th birthday in her birthplace of Le Roeulx, Belgium on 11 Jan 1887. The greatest age among European royal consorts is the 101 years 268 days of HSH Princess Leonilla Bariatinsky (b. Moscow, 9 July 1816), who married HSH Prince Louis of Sayn-Wittgenstein-Sayn and died in Ouchy, Switzerland on 1 Feb 1918. The longest-lived queen on record has been the Queen Grandmother of Siam, Queen Sawang (b. 10 Sept 1862), 27th daughter of King Mongkut (Rama IV); she died on 17 Dec 1955 aged 93 years 3 months.

HRH Princess Alice Mary VA, GCVO, GBE, Countess of Athlone (b. 25 Feb 1883) became the longest ever lived British 'royal' on 15 July 1977 and died aged 97 years 313 days on 3 Jan 1981. She fulfilled 20 000 engagements, including the funerals of 5 British monarchs.

Youngest king and queen
Forty-six of the world's 170 sovereign states are not republics. They are led by 1 emperor, 14 kings, 3 queens, 4 princely rulers, 1 sultan, 3 amirs, the Pope, a shaik, a ruler and one elected monarch. Queen Elizabeth II is head of state of 16 other Commonwealth countries. That with the youngest king is Swaziland where King Mswati III was crowned on 25 Apr 1986 aged 18 yr 6 day. He was born Makhosetive, the 67th son of King Subhusa II. That with the youngest queen is Denmark with Queen Margrethe II (b. 16 Apr 1940).

Heaviest monarch
The world's heaviest monarch is the 1·90 m *6 ft 3 in* tall King Taufa'ahau of Tonga who in September 1976 was weighed on the only adequate scales in the country at the airport, recording 209·5 kg *(33 st/462 lb)*. By 1985 he was reported to have slimmed down to 139·7 kg *(22 st/308 lb)*. His embassy car in London has the number plate '1 TON'.

Most prolific
The most prolific monogamous 'royals' have been Prince Hartmann of Liechtenstein (1613–86) who had 24 children, of whom 21 were live born, by Countess Elisabeth zu Salm-Reifferscheidt (1623–88). HRH Duke Roberto I of Parma (1848–1907) also had 24 children but by 2 wives. One of his daughters, HIM Empress Zita of Austria (b. 9 May 1892), was exiled on 23 Mar 1919 but visited Vienna, her titles intact, on 17 Nov 1982 reminding republicans that her father succeeded to the throne of Parma in 1854.

Head of state *Oldest and youngest*
The oldest head of state in the world is the Emperor of Japan (b. 29 Apr 1901). The youngest is King Mswati III of Swaziland (b. 19 Apr 1968).

Legislatures

PARLIAMENTS—WORLD

Earliest and oldest
The earliest known legislative assembly or *ukkim* was a bicameral one in Erech, Iraq c. 2800 BC. The oldest legislative body is the *Althing* of Iceland founded in AD 930. This body, which originally comprised 39 local chieftains at Thingvellir, was abolished in 1800, but restored by Denmark to a consultative status in 1843 and a legislative status in 1874. The legislative assembly with the oldest continuous history is the Court of Tynwald in the Isle of Man, which celebrated its millennium in 1979.

Smallest quorum
The House of Lords has the smallest quorum, expressed as a percentage of eligible voters, of any legislative body in the world, namely less than one-third of 1 per cent. The number of peers in 1988 was 1 244. To transact

business there must be 3 peers present, including the
Lord Chancellor or his deputy. The House of Commons'
quorum of 40 MPs, including the Speaker or his deputy,
is 20 times as exacting.

Highest-paid legislators

The most highly paid of all the world's legislators are
members of the US Congress whose basic annual salary
is $89 500 with limited honoraria of $20 940. In addition,
up to $1 021 167 per annum is allowed for office help, with
a salary limit of $50 000 for any one staff member (limited
to 16 in number). Senators are allowed up to $143 000 per
annum for an official office expense account from which
official travel, telegram, long-distance telephone, air
mail, postage, stationery, newspapers and office
expenses in home state are paid. They also command
very low rates for filming, speech and radio transcrip-
tions and, in the case of women senators, beauty
treatment. When abroad they have access to 'counter-
part funds'. The President has a salary of $200 000 taxable
plus $170 000 non-taxable for travel or entertainment,
and a lifetime pension of $69 630 per annum.

Longest membership

The longest span as a legislator was 83 years by József
Madarász (1814–1915). He first attended the Hungarian
Parliament in 1832–6 as *oblegatus absentium* (i.e. on
behalf of an absent deputy). He was a full member in
1848–50 and from 1861 until his death on 31 Jan 1915.

Longest UN speech

The longest speech made in the United Nations has
been one of 4 hr 29 min on 26 Sept 1960 by President Dr
Fidel Castro Ruz (b. 13 Aug 1927) of Cuba.

Filibusters

The longest continuous speech in the history of the
United States Senate was that of Senator Wayne Morse
(1900–74) of Oregon on 24–25 Apr 1953, when he spoke
on the Tidelands Oil Bill for 22 hr 26 min without
resuming his seat. Interrupted only briefly by the
swearing-in of a new senator, Senator Strom Thurmond
(b. 1902) (South Carolina, Democrat) spoke against the
Civil Rights Bill for 24 hr 19 min on 28–29 Aug 1957. The
US national duration record is 43 hr by Texas State
Senator Bill Meier against non-disclosure of industrial
accidents in May 1977.

Oldest treaty

The Anglo-Portuguese Treaty of Alliance was signed in
London over 615 years ago on 16 June 1373. The text was
confirmed 'with my usual flourish' by John de Banketre,
Clerk.

Constitutions

The world's oldest constitution is that of the United States
of America ratified by the necessary Ninth State (New
Hampshire) on 21 June 1788 and declared to be in effect
on 4 Mar 1789. The only countries without one-document
constitutions are Israel, Libya, New Zealand, Oman and
the United Kingdom.

Women's suffrage

The earliest legislature with female voters was the
Territory of Wyoming, USA in 1869, followed by the Isle
of Man in 1881. The earliest country to have universal
suffrage was New Zealand in 1893. The vote of Mrs Lily
Maxwell in Manchester on 26 Nov 1867 was declared
illegal on 9 Nov 1868.

PARLIAMENTS—UNITED KINGDOM
Earliest

The earliest known use of the term 'parliament' is in an
official royal document, in the meaning of a summons to
the King's (Henry III's) Council, dating from 19 Dec 1241.

The Houses of Parliament of the UK in the Palace of
Westminster, London had 1841 members (House of
Lords 1191, House of Commons 650) in July 1988.

Longest

The longest English Parliament was the 'Pensioners'
Parliament of Charles II, which lasted from 8 May 1661 to
24 Jan 1679, a period of 17 years 8 months and 16 days.
The longest United Kingdom Parliament was that of
George V, Edward VIII and George VI, lasting from 26
Nov 1935 to 15 June 1945, a span of 9 years 6 months and
20 days.

Shortest

The parliament of Edward I, summoned to Westminster
for 30 May 1306, lasted only 1 day. That of Charles II at
Oxford lasted 7 days from 21–28 Mar 1681. The shortest
United Kingdom Parliament was that of George III,
lasting from 15 Dec 1806 to 29 Apr 1807, a period of only 4
months and 14 days.

Longest sittings

The longest sitting in the House of Commons was one of 41½ hr from 4 p.m. on 31 Jan 1881 to 9.30 a.m. on 2 Feb 1881, on the question of better Protection of Person and Property in Ireland. The longest sitting of the Lords has been 19 hr 16 min from 2.30 p.m. on 29 Feb to 9.46 a.m. on 1 Mar 1968 on the Commonwealth Immigrants Bill (committee stage). The longest sitting of a standing committee occurred from 10.30 a.m. on 11 May to 12.08 p.m. on 13 May 1948 when Standing Committee D considered the Gas Bill through two nights for 49 hr 38 min.

Longest speeches

The longest recorded continuous speech in the Chamber of the House of Commons was that of Henry Peter Brougham (1778–1868) on 7 Feb 1828, when he spoke for 6 hr on Law Reform. He ended at 10.40 p.m. and the report of this speech occupied 12 columns of the next day's *Times*. Brougham, created the 1st Lord Brougham and Vaux on 22 Nov 1830, then set the House of Lords record, also with 6 hours, on 7 Oct 1831, when speaking on the second reading of the Reform Bill, 'fortified by 3 tumblers of spiced wine'.

The longest back-bench speech under present, much stricter standing orders has been one of 4 hr 23 min by Ivan John Lawrence QC, MP (b. 24 Dec 1936), Conservative Member for Burton, opposing the Water (Fluoridation) Bill on 6 Mar 1985. John Golding MP (b. 9 Mar 1931) (then Labour, Newcastle-under-Lyme) spoke for 11 hr 15 min in committee on small amendments to the British Telecommunications Bill on 8–9 Feb 1983.

The longest speech in Stormont, Northern Ireland was one of 9 hr 26 min by Thomas Gibson Henderson MP (1887–1970) on the Appropriations Bill from 6.32 p.m. on 26 to 3.58 a.m. on 27 May 1936.

Greatest parliamentary petition

The greatest petition has been supposed to be the Great Chartist Petition of 1848 but of the 5 706 000 'signatures' only 1 975 496 were valid. The largest of all time was for the abolition of Entertainment Duty with 3 107 080 signatures, presented on 5 June 1951.

Most and least time-consuming legislation

The most profligate use of parliamentary time was on the Government of Ireland Bill of 1893–4, which required 82 days in the House of Commons of which 46 days were in committee. The record for a standing committee is 59 sessions for the Police and Criminal Evidence Bill from 17 Nov 1983 to 29 Mar 1984.

The Abdication Bill (of King Edward VIII) passed all its stages in the Commons (2 hr) and the Lords (8 min) on 11–12 Dec 1936 and received the Royal Assent at 1.52 a.m. on the latter date.

Private Members' Bills

Balloting by private members for parliamentary time was in being at least as early as 1844. The highest recorded number of public Bills introduced by private members was 226 in 1908 but the highest number to receive Royal Assent was 27 in the Commons and 7 in the Lords in 1963–64. The worst session was 1973–74 with nil from 42 presented in the Commons and nil from 10 in the Lords.

Divisions

The record number of divisions in the House of Commons is 64 on 23–24 Mar 1971 including 57 in succession between midnight and noon. The largest division was one of 350–310 on the vote of no confidence on 11 Aug 1892.

ELECTIONS—WORLD

Largest

The largest elections in the world were those beginning on 24 Dec 1984 for the Indian *Lok Sabha* (Lower House)

UNITED KINGDOM ELECTORAL RECORDS

VOTES

MOST: 75 205, Sir Cooper Rawson (Con), Brighton, Sussex, 1931.
LEAST: Nil, F. R. Lees (Temperance Chartist), Ripon, Yorkshire, Dec 1860.
LEAST SINCE UNIVERSAL FRANCHISE: 5, Lt Cdr W. Boaks, RN, DSC (Public Safety Democratic Monarchist White Resident), Glasgow, Hillhead, 25 Mar 1982.

MAJORITY

HIGHEST: *Man*: 62 253, Sir Cooper Rawson (Con), Brighton, Sussex, 1931. *Woman*: 38 823, Countess of Iveagh (Con), Southend, Essex, 1931.
NARROWEST: 1 vote, Matthew Fowler (Lib), Durham, 1895 and 1 vote H. E. Duke (Unionist), Exeter, Devon, Dec 1910. *Since Universal Franchise*: 2 votes, A. J. Flint (National Labour), Ilkeston, Derbyshire, 1931.

YOUNGEST MP

EVER: Aged 15/16, Edmund Waller (1606–87), Amersham, Bucks, 1621.
SINCE 1832: James Dickson (Lib) (1859–1941), returned for Dungannon Tyrone on 25 June 1880, aged 21 years 67 days.

MOST RECOUNTS

7: Brighton, Kemptown 1964 and Peterborough 1966.

GENERAL ELECTION POLL

HIGHEST: 93·42%, Fermanagh & S Tyrone, 1951.
LOWEST: 29·7%, Kennington, London, 1918.

FASTEST EVER RESULT

57 min, Billericay, Essex, 1959 (9.57 p.m.).

LAST UNOPPOSED RETURNS

25 Oct 1951, Antrim N and S: R. W. H. O'Neill and D. L. Savory; Armagh: Major J. R. E. Horden and Londonderry: W. Wellwood (all Ulster Unionists).

LARGEST CONSTITUENCY BY AREA

Ross, Cromarty & Skye, 954 680 ha *2 472 260 acres*.

LARGEST ELECTORATE

217 900, Hendon (Barnet), 1941.

MOST ROTTEN BOROUGH

(8 Electors for 2 unopposed members) 1821 Old Sarum, Wiltshire—No elections contested 1295–1831.

MOST BY-ELECTION CANDIDATES

17: Chesterfield, 1 Mar 1984. Rt Hon. A. N. Wedgwood-Benn contested for a current record 14th time (12 times returned).

LONGEST GAP BETWEEN BY-ELECTIONS

No writ was moved for any by-election between that for Truro on 12 Mar 1987 and that for Kensington and Chelsea on 14 July 1988—1 year 125 days later.

---

which has 542 elective seats. The government of Rajiv Gandhi was returned in polls in which 379 000 000 electors were eligible to vote for 5301 candidates at 480 000 polling stations manned by 2½ million staff. In Maduranthkam (electorate 120 021) there were 90 candidates.

Closest

The ultimate in close general elections occurred in Zanzibar (now part of Tanzania) on 18 Jan 1961, when the Afro-Shirazi Party won by a single seat, after the seat of Chake-Chake on Pemba Island had been gained by a single vote.

The narrowest recorded percentage win in an election would seem to be for the office of Southern District Highway Commissioner in Mississippi, USA on 7 Aug 1979. Robert E. Joiner was declared the winner over W. H. Pyron with 133 587 votes to 133 582. The loser got more than 49·9999 per cent of the votes.

Most decisive

North Korea recorded a 100 per cent turn-out of electors and a 100 per cent vote for the Workers' Party of Korea in the general election of 8 Oct 1962. The next closest

---

approach was in Albania on 14 Nov 1982 when a single voter spoiled national unanimity for the official (and only) Communist candidates, who thus obtained only 99·99993 per cent of the poll in a 100 per cent turn-out of 1 627 968.

Most bent

In the Liberian presidential election of 1927 President Charles D. B. King (1875–1961) was returned with a majority over his opponent, Mr Thomas J. R. Faulkner of the People's Party, officially announced as 234 000. President King thus claimed a 'majority' more than 15½ times greater than the entire electorate.

Highest personal majority

The highest ever personal majority by any politician has been 424 545 by Ram Bilas Paswan, 30, the Janata candidate for Hajipur in Bihar, India in March 1977. The electorate was 625 179. In 1956 W. R. D. Bandaranaike achieved 91·82 per cent of the poll with 45 016 votes in Attanagalla constituency of Sri Lanka (then Ceylon).

Communist parties

The largest national Communist party outside the USSR (18 500 000 members in 1987) and communist states has been the Partito Comunista Italiano, with a membership of 2 300 000 in 1946. The total was 1 600 000 in 1986. The membership in mainland China was estimated to be 44 000 000 in 1987. The Communist Party of Great Britain, formed on 31 July 1920 in Cannon Street Station Hotel, London, attained its peak membership of 56 000 in December 1942, compared with 20 599 in 1979 and 8378 in 1988. The decline has been caused by doctrinal disputes and divisions over relations with the USSR leading to expulsions and the formation of new parties or groups within the Labour movement.

Largest ballot paper

On 5 Mar 1985 in the State Assembly (Vidha Sabha) elections in Karnataka, India there were 301 candidates for Belguum City.

Most mature electorate

The eligibility for voting in Andorra is 25 years.

Most coups

Statisticians contend that Bolivia, since it became a sovereign country in 1825, had its 191st coup on 30 June 1984 when President Hernan Siles Zuazo, 70, was kidnapped from his official residence by more than 60 armed men.

PRIME MINISTERS AND STATESMEN

Oldest

The longest-lived prime minister of any country was Dr. Willem Drees (Social Democrat), Prime Minister of the Netherlands in 1948–58. He was born on 5 July 1886 and died on 13 May 1988, aged 101 years 313 days. The Hon. Richard Gavin Reid (b. Glasgow, 17 Jan 1879), Premier of Alberta, Canada in 1934–35, died on 17 Oct 1980 aged 101 years 274 days.

El Hadji Muhammad el Mokri, Grand Vizier of Morocco, died on 16 Sept 1957 at a reputed age of 116 Muslim (*Hijri*) years, equivalent to 112·5 Gregorian years. The oldest age of first appointment has been 81 by Morarji Ranchhodji Desai of India (b. 29 Feb 1896) in March 1977.

Longest term of office

Enver Hoxha (b. 16 Oct 1908), First Secretary of the Central Committee of the Albania Party of Labour, ruled from October 1944 to his death on 11 Apr 1985.

Marshal Kim Il Sung (*né* Kim Sung Chu) (b. 15 Apr 1912) has been Head of Government or Head of State of the Democratic People's Republic of Korea since 25 Aug 1948.

Andrey Andreyevich Gromyko (b. 6 July 1909) had been Minister of Foreign Affairs of the USSR since 15 Feb 1957, having been Deputy Foreign Minister since 1946, when he was elected President of the USSR on 2 July 1985.

Lady legislators ● This record-breaking photograph is of the largest assemblage of British women MP's ever taken in one shot.

Forty-one of the record 327 women who stood in 1987 were returned at the last General Election. Of these 31 were able to join the Prime Minister on the terrace at the Palace of Westminster.

Seated: left to right—Jo Richardson (Lab), Dame Peggy Fenner (Con), Miss Janet Fookes (Con), Dame Jill Knight (Con), Rt. Hon. Margaret Thatcher (Con), Ms. Joan Lestor (Lab), Dame Elaine Kellett-Bowman (Con), Miss Betty Boothroyd (Lab) and Rt. Hon. Lynda Chalker (Con).

Middle Row: left to right—Miss Ann Widdecombe (Con), Mrs Ann Clwyd (Lab), Hon Gwyneth Dunwoody (Lab), Mrs Ann Taylor (Lab), Mrs Angela Rumbold (Con), Mrs Elizabeth Peacock (Con), Mrs Marion Roe (Con), Mrs Margaret Ewing (SNP), Marjorie Mowlam (Lab), Mrs Mildred Gordon (Lab), Mrs Llin Golding (Lab), Mrs Gillian Shephard (Con) and Clare Short (Lab).

Back Row: left to right—Mrs Margaret Beckett (Lab), Mrs Edwina Currie (Con), Mrs Teresa Gorman (Con), Mrs Joan Ruddock (Lab), Joan Walley (Lab), Mrs Ann Winterton (Con), Mrs Virginia Bottomley (Con), Emma Nicholson (Con), Ms Diane Abbott (Lab) and Mrs Rosie Barnes (SDP).

Absent due to parliamentary commitments were: Hilary Armstrong (Lab), Ms Maria Fyfe (Lab), Ms Harriet Harman (Lab), Mrs Maureen Hicks (Con), Mrs Alice Mahon (Lab), Mrs Ray Michie (Lib), Ms Dawn Primarolo (Lab), Ms Joyce Quin (Lab) and Mrs Audrey Wise (Lab). (Photo: Guinness Publishing/R. Chapman and C. Dobson)

PRIME MINISTERIAL RECORDS

Though given legal warrant in the instrument of the Congress of Berlin in 1878 and an established place in the Orders of Precedence in England and Scotland in 1904, the office of Prime Minister was not statutorily recognised until 1917. All previous acknowledged First Ministers had tenure as First Lords of the Treasury with the exception of No 12, William Pitt, Earl of Chatham, who controlled his ministers as Secretary of State of the Southern Department or as Lord Privy Seal. The first to preside over his fellow King's ministers was Walpole from 1721, and undisputedly from 15 May 1730.

Record	Value	No	Name	Dates
LONGEST SERVING	20 years 326 days	1st	Sir Robert Walpole KG (1676–1745)	3 Apr 1721–12 Feb 1742
LONGEST SERVING (20th century)	>9 years	52nd	Margaret Thatcher (née Roberts) (b. 13 Oct 1925)	from 3 May 1979
MOST MINISTRIES	5 times	41st	Earl Baldwin KG (1867–1947)	22 May 1923–28 May 1937
SHORTEST SERVICE IN OFFICE	120 days	22nd	George Canning (1770–1827)	10 Apr–8 Aug 1827
YOUNGEST TO ASSUME OFFICE	24 years 205 days	17th	Hon. William Pitt (1759–1806) (declined when 23 yr 275 days)	19 Dec 1783
OLDEST FIRST TO ASSUME OFFICE	70 years 109 days	31st	Viscount Palmerston KG, GCB (1784–1865)	6 Feb 1855
GREATEST AGE IN OFFICE	84 years 64 days	33rd	William Gladstone (1809–1898)	3 Mar 1894 (elected at 82 yr 171 days)
LONGEST LIVED	92 years 322 days	47th	Earl of Stockton OM (1894–1986)	from 6 Apr 1984 (so surpassing No 44)
LONGEST SURVIVAL AFTER OFFICE	41 years 45 days	13th	Duke of Grafton KG (1735–1811)	from 28 Jan 1770
SHORTEST LIVED	44 years	7th	Duke of Devonshire KG (1720–1764)	d. 2 Oct 1764 (exact birth date unknown)
SHORTEST MINISTRY	22 days	24th	Duke of Wellington KG, GCB, GCH (1769–1852)	17 Nov–9 Dec 1834
SHORTEST POSSESSION OF SEALS	c. 48 hours	4th	Earl of Bath (1684–1764)	10–12 Feb 1746
SHORTEST PRIOR SERVICE AS MP	2 years 11 months	17th	Hon. William Pitt (1759–1806)	19 Dec 1783
LONGEST PRIOR SERVICE AS MP	47 years	31st	Viscount Palmerston KG, GCB (1784–1865)	1807–6 Feb 1855
LONGEST SUBSEQUENT SERVICE AS MP	22 years 156 days	39th	Earl Lloyd George OM (1863–1945)	22 Oct 1922–26 Mar 1945
LONGEST SPAN AS MP	63 years 360 days	44th	Sir Winston Churchill KG, OM, CH (1874–1965)	1 Oct 1900–25 Sep 1964
RICHEST	£7¼ million (now say £200 million)	29th	Earl of Derby KG, GCMG (1799–1869)	Annual rent roll in 1869 £170 000
POOREST	£40 000 in debt (now>£1 million)	17th	Hon. William Pitt (1759–1806)	Level of personal debt by 1800
TALLEST	1·83 m 6 ft 1½ in	51st	Lord Callaghan KG (b. 27 Mar 1912)	
SHORTEST	1·64 m 5 ft 4¾ in	28th	Lord John Russell KG, GCMG (1792–1878)	7 month baby: max. wt. 50·7 kg 8 stone
MOST CHILDREN (fathered)	15 or 16	13th	Duke of Grafton (1735–1811)	Twice married
MOST CHILDREN (uniquely mothered)	2	52nd	Margaret Thatcher (b. 13 Oct 1925)	Twins born 21 Aug 1953
MOST LIVING SIMULTANEOUSLY	19	8th, 11th–26th, 29th–30th	from birth of Peel (26th) to death of Chatham (11th)	5 Feb–11 May 1788
	19	12th, 14th–31st	from birth of Disraeli (31st) to death of Shelburne (14th)	21 Dec 1804–7 May 1805
MOST LIVING EX PRIME MINISTERS	5	9th, 13–16th	Bute, Grafton, North, Shelburne, Portland (Pitt) till Bute died	19 Dec 1783–10 Mar 1792
	5	46–50th	Eden, Macmillan, Home, Wilson, Heath (Callaghan) till Eden d.	5 Apr 1976–14 Jan 1977
	5	47–51st	Macmillan, Home, Wilson, Heath, Callaghan (Thatcher) till Macmillan died	4 May 1979–29 Dec 1986
MOST PRINCIPAL OFFICES	4	51st	Lord Callaghan KG uniquely served also as Foreign and Home Secretary and as Chancellor of the Exchequer	16 Oct 1964–4 May 1979

Pyotr Lomako (b. 1904) has served in the government of the USSR as Minister for Non-Ferrous Metallurgy from 1940. He was relieved of his post after 46 years on 1 Nov 1986, aged 82, having served on the Central Committee of the CPSU since 1952.

EUROPEAN ASSEMBLY ELECTION RECORDS

In the European Assembly elections of 14 June 1984 the highest majority in the 81 UK constituencies was 95 557 (L. Smith, Lab) in Wales South-East. Lowest was 2625 (Sir Peter Vanneck, Con) in Cleveland and Yorkshire North. Largest and smallest electorates were 574 022 in Essex North-East and 307 265 in Highlands and Islands. Highest turn-out was 42·4 per cent in Wales North. Lowest was 25·2 per cent in London North-East. Northern Ireland voted by proportional representation.

MAJORITIES—UNITED KINGDOM
Party

The largest single party majority was that of the Liberals in 1832, of 307 seats, with a record of 66·7 per cent of the vote. In 1931 the Coalition of Conservatives, Liberals and National Labour candidates had a majority of 491 seats and 60·5 per cent of the vote. The narrowest party majority was that of the Whigs in 1847, with a single seat. The highest popular vote for a single party was 13 948 883 for Labour in 1951.

The largest majority on a division was one of 463 (464 votes to 1), on a vote of confidence in the conduct of World War II, on 29 Jan 1942. Since the war the largest has been one of 461 (487 votes to 26) on 10 May 1967, during the debate on the government's application for Britain to join the European Economic Community (the 'Common Market').

HOUSE OF LORDS
Oldest member
The oldest member ever was the Rt Hon. Lord Shinwell

PC, CH (1884–1986) who first sat in the Lower House in November 1922 and lived to be 101 years 202 days. The oldest peer to make a maiden speech was Lord Maenan 1854–1951) aged 94 years 123 days (see Peerage p. 186).

Youngest member
The youngest present member of the House of Lords is HRH the Prince Charles Philip Arthur George KG, PC, KT, GCB, the Prince of Wales (b. 14 Nov 1948) because Dukes of Cornwall, Prince Charles being the 24th, are technically eligible to sit, regardless of age—in his case from his succession on 6 Feb 1952, aged 3. The 20th and 21st holders, later King George IV (b. 1762) and King Edward VII (b. 1841), were technically entitled to sit from birth.

POLITICAL OFFICE HOLDERS
Chancellorship *Longest and shortest tenures*
The Rt Hon. Sir Robert Walpole KG, later the 1st Earl of Orford (1676–1745), served 22 years 5 months as Chancellor of the Exchequer, holding office continuously from 12 Oct 1715 to 12 Feb 1742, except for the period from 16 Apr 1717 to 2 Apr 1721. The briefest tenure of this office was 26 days in the case of the Baron (later the 1st Earl of) Mansfield (1705–93), from 11 Sept to 6 Oct 1767. The only man with 4 terms was the Rt Hon. William Ewart Gladstone (1809–98).

The longest budget speech was that of the Rt Hon. David (later Earl) Lloyd George PC, OM (1863–1945) on 29 Apr 1909 which lasted 4 hr 51 min but was interrupted by a 30-min laryngeal tea break. He announced *inter alia* the introduction of car tax and petroleum duty. Mr Gladstone spoke for 4¾ hours on 18 Apr 1853.

Foreign Secretaryship *Longest tenures*
The longest continuous term of office of any Foreign Secretary has been the 10 years 359 days of Sir Edward Grey KG, MP (later Viscount Grey of Fallodon) from 11 Dec 1905 to 5 Dec 1916. The Rt Hon. Sir Henry John Temple, 3rd Viscount Palmerston KG, PC, GCB, in three

spells in 1830–34, 1835–41 and 1846–51, aggregated 15 years 296 days.

Speakership *Longest*
Arthur Onslow (1691–1768) was elected Mr Speaker on 23 Jan 1728, aged 36. He held the position for 33 years 43 days, until 18 Mar 1761, allowing for the 'lost' 11 days (3–13 Sept 1752).

MPs *Youngest*
The youngest ever woman MP has been Josephine Bernadette Devlin now Mrs Michael McAliskey (b. 23 Apr 1947), elected for Mid Ulster (Ind. Unity) aged 21 years 359 days on 17 Apr 1969. Henry Long (1420–90) was returned for an Old Sarum seat at the age of 15. His precise date of birth is unknown. Minors were debarred in law in 1695 and in fact in 1832.

Oldest
Sir Francis Knollys (c. 1550–1648), 'the ancientest Parliament man in England', was elected for Reading in 1640 when apparently aged 90 and was probably 97 or 98 at the time of his death.

The oldest of 20th-century members has been Samuel Young (b. 14 Feb 1822), Nationalist MP for East Cavan (1892 to 1918), who died on 18 Apr 1918, aged 96 years 63 days. The oldest 'Father of the House' in parliamentary history was the Rt Hon. Charles Pelham Villiers (b. 3 Jan 1802), member for Wolverhampton South when he died on 16 Jan 1898, aged 96 years 13 days. He was a member for 63 years 6 days, having been returned at 17 elections. The oldest current member is Robert Edwards MP (Lab) for Wolverhampton South-East (b. 16 Jan 1905).

Longest span
Sir Francis Knollys (c. 1550–1648) was elected for Oxford in 1575 and died a sitting member for Reading 73 years later in 1648.

The longest span of service of any 20th-century MP is 63 years 11 months (1 Oct 1900 to 25 Sept 1964) by the Rt Hon. Sir Winston Leonard Spencer Churchill KG, OM,

CH, TD (1874–1965), with breaks only in 1908 and 1922–24. The longest continuous span was that of C. P. Villiers (see p.196). The longest span in the Palace of Westminster (both Houses of Parliament) has been 72 years by the 10th Earl of Wemyss and March GCVO, who, as Sir Francis Wemyss-Charteris-Douglas, served as MP for East Gloucestershire (July 1841 to 1846) and Haddingtonshire (1847 to 1883) and then took his seat in the House of Lords, dying on 30 June 1914 aged 95 years 330 days. The longest living of all parliamentarians was Theodore Cooke Taylor (1850–1952), Liberal MP for Batley 1910 to 1918.

Briefest span

There are two 18th-century examples of posthumous elections. Capt. the Hon. Edward Legge, RN (1710–47) was returned unopposed for Portsmouth on 15 Dec 1747. News came later that he had died in the West Indies 87 days before polling. In 1780 John Kirkman, standing for the City of London, expired before polling had ended but was nonetheless duly returned. A. J. Dobbs (Lab, Smethwick), elected on 5 July 1945, was killed on the way to take his seat.

Women

The first woman to be elected to the House of Commons was Mme Constance Georgine Markievicz (*née* Gore Booth). She was elected as member (Sinn Fein) for St Patrick's Dublin, on 28 December 1918. The first woman to take her seat was the Viscountess Astor CH (1879–1964) (*née* Nancy Witcher Langhorne at Danville, Virginia, USA; formerly Mrs Robert Gould Shaw), who was elected Unionist member for the Sutton division of Plymouth, Devon on 28 Nov 1919, and took her seat 3 days later. The first woman to take her seat from the island of Ireland was Lady Fisher (*née* Patricia Smiles) as unopposed Ulster Unionist for North Down on 15 Apr 1953, as Mrs Patricia Ford.

The first woman cabinet minister was the Rt Hon. Margaret Grace Bondfield PC, CH (1873–1953), appointed Minister of Labour in 1929.

Heaviest and tallest

The heaviest MP of all time is believed to be Sir Cyril Smith MBE, Liberal member for Rochdale since October 1972, when in January 1976 his peak reported weight was 189·60 kg *29 st 12 lb.*

Sir Louis Gluckstein GBE, TD, QC (1897–1979), Conservative member for East Nottingham (1931–45), was an unrivalled 2·02 m *6 ft 7½ in.* Currently the tallest is the Hon. Archie Hamilton, Conservative member for Epsom and Ewell, at 1·98 m *6 ft 6 in.*

Mayoralties

The longest recorded mayoralty was that of Edmond Mathis (1852–1953), *maire* of Ehuns, Haute-Saône, France for 75 years (1878 to 1953). The mayoralty of the City of London dates from 1192 with the 20-year term of Henry Fitz Ailwyn until 1212. The most elections, since these became annual in 1215, has been 8 by Gregory de Rokesley (1274/5 to 1280/1). The earliest recorded mayor of the City of York, Nigel, dates from 1142. Alderman G. T. Paine served as Mayor of Lydd, Kent for 29 consecutive years from 1931 to 1961. Cllr Denis Martineau took office as Lord Mayor of Birmingham on 20 May 1986 following in office his father, grandfather, great grandfather and great great grandfather.

Local government service duration records

The oldest local office was that of reeve to supervise villeins. First mentioned in AD 787, it evolved to that of shire reeve, hence sheriff.

Major Sir Philip Barber Bt, DSO, TD, DL (1876–1961) served as county councillor for Nottinghamshire for 63 years 41 days from 8 Mar 1898 to 18 Apr 1961. Matthew Anderson was a member of the Borough Council of Abingdon, Oxfordshire for 69 years 4 months from April 1709 until August 1778. Henry Winn (1816–1914) served

as parish clerk for Fulletby near Horncastle, Lincolnshire for 76 years.

Clifford Tasker (1906–1980) of Pontefract, West Yorkshire was appointed as presiding officer for elections in 1921 when aged 15, and served for 59 years until March 1980.

Weight of legislation

The greatest amount of legislation in a year has been 11 453 pages (83 Public General Acts and 2251 Statutory Instruments) in 1975. This compares with 46 Acts and 1130 Instruments of 1998 pages in 1928. The most Acts were 123 in 1939 and the fewest 39 in 1929 and 1942. The peak for Statutory Instruments was 2916 in 1947.

Military & Defence

Last battle on British soil

The last pitched land battle in Britain was at Culloden Field, Drummossie Moor, near Inverness on 16 Apr 1746. The last clan battle in Scotland was between Clan Mackintosh and Clan MacDonald at Mulroy, Invernessshire in 1689. The last battle on English soil was the Battle of Sedgemoor, Somerset on 6 July 1685, when the forces of James II defeated the supporters of Charles II's illegitimate son, James Scott (formerly called Fitzroy or Crofts), the Duke of Monmouth (1649–85). During the Jacobite rising of 1745–6, there was a skirmish at Clifton Moor, Cumbria on 18 Dec 1745, when the English forces under Prince William, the Duke of Cumberland (1721–65), brushed with the rebels of Prince Charles Edward Stuart (1720–88) with about 12 killed on the King's side and 5 highlanders. This was a tactical victory for the Scots under Lord George Murray.

Bloodiest Battle *British*

The bloodiest battle fought on British soil was the battle of Towton, near Tadcaster, North Yorkshire on 29 Mar 1461, when 36 000 Yorkists defeated 40 000 Lancastrians. The total loss has been estimated at between 28 000 and 38 000 killed. A figure of 80 000 British dead was attributed by Tacitus to the battle of AD 61 between Queen Boudicca (Boadicea) of the Iceni and the Roman Governor of Britain Suetonius Paulinus, for the reputed loss of only 400 Romans in an army of 10 000. The site of the battle is unknown but may have been near Borough Hill, Daventry, Northamptonshire, or more probably near Hampstead Heath, London. Prior to this battle the Romans had lost up to 70 000 in Colchester and London.

Invasion *Last on the soil of Great Britain*

The last invasion of Great Britain occurred on 12 Feb 1797, when the Irish-American adventurer General Tate landed at Carreg Gwastad with 1400 French troops. They surrendered near Fishguard, Dyfed to Lord Caw-

dor's force of the Castlemartin Yeomanry and some local inhabitants armed with pitchforks. The UK Crown Dependency of the Falkland Islands was invaded by Argentine troops on 2 Apr 1982. British troops re-landed at San Carlos on 21 May and accepted the surrender of Brig. Gen. Mario Menéndez 24 days later on 14 June 1982.

DEFENCE SPENDING

In May 1988 it was estimated that the world's spending on armaments was running at the annual rate of some $660 000 million. This represents £72 per person per annum, or 10 per cent of the world's total production of goods and services. In 1987 there were 28 123 000 full-time armed force regulars or conscripts plus 40 289 400 reservists to total 68 412 400. The budgeted expenditure on defence by the US Government for the fiscal year 1988 was $283 159 million.

The defence burden on the USSR has been estimated by official sources in the USA and the UK as a percentage of GNP (Gross National Product) to be between 13 and 17 per cent, and thus may be nearly treble the rate of that of the USA (5·9 per cent of GNP in 1988). The UK defence estimate for 1988–89 was £19 200 million.

ARMED FORCES
Largest

Numerically the largest regular armed force in the world is that of the USSR with 5 225 000 (1987). The USA's military manpower is 2 158 000 (1987) and that of the United Kingdom 318 700 (1987/88).

Navies *Largest*

The largest navy in the world in terms of manpower is the United States Navy, with a manpower of 583 800 and 199 600 Marines in mid-1987. The active strength in 1987 included 5 nuclear-powered aircraft carriers, with 10 others, 3 battleships, 92 nuclear attack submarines and 4 diesel attack submarines, 36 cruisers, 68 destroyers, 115 frigates and 60 amphibious warfare ships. The USSR's navy has a larger submarine fleet of 375 vessels (including 127 nuclear attack). The Red Fleet has 6 aircraft carriers, 37 cruisers and 63 destroyers.

The strength of the Royal Navy in mid-1987 included 3 *Invincible* class carriers, 4 nuclear submarines with strategic atomic missiles, 15 other nuclear and 12 diesel attack submarines, 14 guided weapon destroyers and 35 frigates. The uniformed strength was 66 500 including Royal Naval Air Service and Royal Marines (7700) in 1987–88. In 1914 the Royal Navy had 542 warships including 72 capital ships with 16 building, thus being the largest navy in the world.

Longest-serving admiral

Admiral of the Fleet Sir Provo Wallis GCB (1791–1892) first served on HMS *Cleopatra* in October 1804. Because of his service on HMS *Cleopatra* in 1805 against the French he was kept on the active list in 1870 for life. He thus was 87 years 4 months on paid active service though he was earlier on the books as a volunteer from

The Somme ● French infantry in the first Battle of the Somme. (Photo: Robert Harding Associates)

Earliest conflict ● The oldest known offensive weapon is a broken wooden spear found in April 1911 at **Clacton-on-Sea, Essex** by S. Hazzledine Warren. Beyond the limit of carbon-dating it is estimated to have been fashioned before 200 000 BC.

Longest ● The longest war was the 'Hundred Years War' between **England and France,** which lasted from 1338 to 1453 (115 years), although it may be said that the 9 Crusades from the First (1096–1104) to the Ninth (1270–91), extending over 195 years, comprised a single holy war.

Greatest evacuation ● The greatest evacuation in military history was that carried out by 1200 Allied naval and civil craft from the beach-head at **Dunkerque (Dunkirk), France** between 27 May and 4 June 1940. A total of 338 226 British and French troops were taken off.

Most costly ● The material cost of World War II far transcended that of the rest of history's wars put together and has been estimated at $1·5 million million. The total cost to the Soviet Union was estimated in May 1959 at 2 500 000 000 000 roubles while a figure of $530 000 million has been estimated for the USA. For the United Kingdom the cost of £34 423 million was over 5 times that of World War I (£6700 million) and 158·6 times that of the Boer War of 1899–1902 (£217 million).

Bloodiest battle *Modern* ● The battle with the greatest recorded number of *military* casualties was the first Battle of the Somme, France from 1 July to 19 Nov 1916, with 1 043 896— 623 907 Allied (of which 419 654 were British) and 419 989 German. The published German figure of *c.* 670 000 is not now accepted. Gunfire was heard on Hampstead Heath, London. An estimated *c.* 2 100 000 died in the Battle of Stalingrad ending with the German surrender on 31 Jan 1943 by Field Marshal Friedrich von Paulus (1890–1957). Additionally, only 1515 civilians from a pre-war population of more than 500 000 were found alive after the battle. The final investment of Berlin by the Red Army from 16 Apr–2 May 1945

involved 3 500 000 men; 52 000 guns and mortars; 7750 tanks and 11 000 aircraft on both sides.

Ancient ● Modern historians give no credence, on logistic grounds, to the casualty

figures attached to ancient battles, such as the 250 000 reputedly killed at Plataea (Greeks v Persians) in 479 BC or the 200 000 allegedly killed in a single day at Châlons, France (Huns v Romans) in AD 451.

Greatest airborne invasion ● The largest airborne invasion was the Anglo-American assault of 3 divisions (34 000 men), with 2800 aircraft and 1600 gliders, near **Arnhem, Netherlands,** on 17 Sept 1944.

Greatest seaborne invasion ● The greatest invasion in military history was the Allied land, air and sea operation against the **Normandy** coasts of France on D-day, 6 June 1944. Thirty-eight convoys of 745 ships moved in on the first 3 days, supported by 4066 landing craft, carrying 185 000 men, 20 000 vehicles and 347 minesweepers. The air assault comprised 18 000 paratroopers from 1087 aircraft. The 42 available divisions possessed an air support from 13 175 aircraft. Within a month 1 100 000 troops, 200 000 vehicles and 750 000 tons of stores were landed. The Allied invasion of Sicily from 10–12 July 1943 involved the landing of 181 000 men in 3 days.

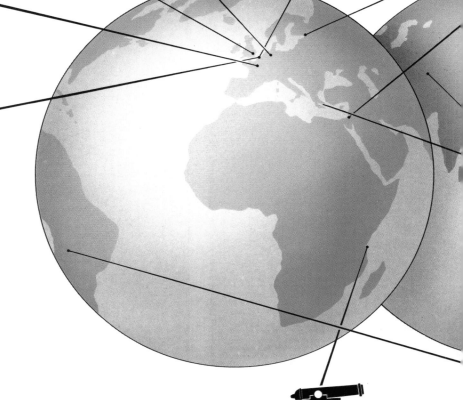

Shortest ● The shortest war on record was that between the United Kingdom and **Zanzibar** (now part of Tanzania) from 9.02 to 9.40 a.m. on 27 Aug 1896. The UK battle fleet under Rear-Admiral (later Admiral Sir) Harry Rawson (1843–1910) delivered an ultimatum to the self-appointed Sultan Sa'id Khalid to evacuate his palace and surrender. This was not forthcoming until after 38 minutes of bombardment. Admiral Rawson received the Brilliant Star of Zanzibar (first class) from Hamud ibn Muhammad, the new Sultan.

It was proposed at one time that elements of the local populace should be compelled to defray the cost of the broadsides fired.

Worst sieges ● The worst siege in history was the 880-day siege of **Leningrad, USSR** by the German Army from 30 Aug 1941 until 27 Jan 1944. The best estimate is that between 1·3 and 1·5 million defenders and citizens died.

The longest recorded siege was that of **Azotus** (now Ashdod), **Israel** which according to Herodotus was invested by Psamtik I of Egypt for 29 years in the period 664–610 BC.

Bloodiest civil ● The bloodiest civil war in history was the T'ai-p'ing ('Great Peace') rebellion, in which peasant sympathisers of the southern Ming dynasty fought the Manchu government troops in China from 1851 to 1864. The rebellion was led by the deranged Hung Hsiu-ch'üan (executed) who imagined himself to be a younger brother of Jesus Christ. His force was named *T'ai-p'ing T'ien Kuo* (Heavenly Kingdom of Great Peace). According to the best estimates, the loss of life was between 20 000 000 and 30 000 000 including more than 100 000 killed by government forces in the sack of Nanking on 19–21 July 1864.

Longest march ● The longest march in military history was the famous Long March by the Chinese Communists in 1934–5. In 368 days, of which 268 days were days of movement, from October to October, their force of 90 000 covered 9650 km *6000 miles* from Kiangsi to Yenan in Shensi via Yünnan, **China.** They crossed 18 mountain ranges and 6 major rivers and lost all but 22 000 of their force in continual rear-guard actions against nationalist Kuo-min-tang (KMT) forces.

Greatest naval battle ● The greatest number of ships and aircraft ever involved in a sea–air action was 231 ships and 1996 aircraft in the Battle of Leyte Gulf, in the **Philippines.** It raged from 22 to 27 Oct 1944, with 166 Allied and 65 Japanese warships engaged, of which 26 Japanese and 6 US ships were sunk. In addition, 1280 US and 716 Japanese aircraft were engaged. The greatest purely naval battle of modern times was the Battle of Jutland on 31 May 1916, in which 151 Royal Navy warships were involved against 101 German warships. The Royal Navy lost 14 ships and 6097 men and the German fleet 11 ships and 2545 men. The greatest of ancient naval battles was the Battle of **Salamis, Greece** on 23 Sept 480 BC. There were an estimated 800 vessels in the defeated Persian fleet and 310 in the victorious Greek fleet with a possible involvement of 190 000 men. The death toll at the Battle of Lepanto on 7 Oct 1571 has been estimated at 33 000.

Bloodiest ● By far the most costly war in terms of human life was World War II (1939–45), in which the total number of fatalities, including battle deaths and civilians of all countries, is estimated to have been 54 800 000 assuming 25 million USSR fatalities and 7 800 000 Chinese civilians killed. The country which suffered most was Poland with 6 028 000 or 22·2 per cent of her population of 27 007 000 killed. Total combatant death toll from World War I was 9 700 000 compared with the 15 600 000 of World War II.

In the case of the United Kingdom, however, the heavier armed forces fatalities occurred in World War I (1914–18), with 765 399 killed out of 5 500 000 engaged (13·9 per cent),

compared with 265 000 out of 5 896 000 engaged (4·49 per cent) in World War II.

In the **Paraguayan war** of 1864–70 against Brazil, Argentina and Uruguay, their population was reduced from 1 400 000 down to 220 000 survivors of whom only 30 000 were adult males.

Surgeon Major William Brydon CB (1811–1873) was the sole survivor of the 7-day retreat of 16 000 soldiers and camp followers from **Kabul, Afghanistan.** His horse died 2 days after his arrival at Jellalabad, India on 13 Jan 1842.

Artwork by Rhoda and Robert Burns

1795–1804 for a further 9 years—a system by which even infants could gain seniority on joining.

Armies *Oldest*
The oldest army in the world is the 83-strong Pontifical Swiss Guard in the Vatican City, with a regular foundation dating back to 21 Jan 1506. Its origins, however, extend back before 1400.

Largest
Numerically, the world's largest army is that of the People's Republic of China, with a total strength of some 2 300 000 in mid-1987. The total size of the USSR's army in mid-1987 was estimated by the International Institute of Strategic Studies at 2 000 000 men (including 28 500 Spetsnaz), believed to be organised into 209 divisions. The strength of the British Army was 158 700 in 1987–88. The basic strength maintained in Northern Ireland in 1988 is 11 400. Between 1969 and mid-1988, 1829 civilians and 827 armed forces and police personnel had been killed in the province.

Oldest soldiers
The oldest old soldier of all time was probably John B. Salling of the army of the Confederate States of America and the last accepted survivor of the US Civil War (1861–5). He died in Kingsport, Tennessee, USA on 16 Mar 1959, aged 113 years 1 day. The oldest Chelsea pensioner, based *only* on the evidence of his tombstone, was 111-year-old William Hiseland (b. 6 Aug 1620, d. 7 Feb 1732). The longest-serving British soldier has been Field Marshal Sir William Gomm GCB (1784–1875), who was an ensign in 1794 and Constable of the Tower of London at his death aged 91.

Youngest soldiers
Marshal Duke of Caxias (b. 25 Aug 1803, d. 7 May 1880), Brazilian military hero and statesman, entered his infantry regiment at the age of 5 in 1808.

Dr Kenneth Vernon Bailey MC (b. 14 Dec 1897) served as a 2nd lieutenant in the 2/8th Btn Manchester Regt for some 6 weeks before his 17th birthday. Probably the youngest enlistment in the 20th century was of William Frederick Price (b. 1 June 1891), who was enlisted into the army at Aldershot on 23 May 1903, aged 11 years 356 days.

Youngest conscripts
President Francisco Macias Nguema of Equatorial Guinea (deposed in August 1979) decreed in March 1976 compulsory military service for all boys aged between 7 and 14. The edict stated that any parent refusing to hand over his or her son 'will be imprisoned or shot'.

Tallest soldiers
The tallest soldier of all time was Väinö Myllyrinne (1909–63) who was inducted into the Finnish Army when he was 2·21 m *7 ft 3 in* and later grew to 2·51 m *8 ft 3 in*. The British Army's tallest soldier was Benjamin Crow who was signed on at Lichfield in November 1947 when he was 2·15 m *7 ft 1 in* tall. Edward Evans (1924–58), who later grew to 2·35 m *7 ft 8½ in*, was in the army when he was 2·08 m *6 ft 10 in*.

British regimental records
The oldest regular regiment in the British Army is the Royal Scots, raised in French service in 1633, though the Buffs (Royal East Kent Regiment) can trace back their origin to independent companies in Dutch pay as early as 1572. The Coldstream Guards, raised in 1650, were, however, placed on the establishment of the British Army before the Royal Scots and the Buffs. The oldest armed body in the United Kingdom is the Queen's Bodyguard of the Yeomen of the Guard formed in 1485. The Honourable Artillery Company, senior regiment of the Territorial Army, formed from the Fraternity of St George, Southwark, received its charter from Henry VIII in 1537 but this lapsed until re-formed in 1610. The infantry regiment with most battle honours is the Queen's Lancashire Regiment with 188.

The most senior regiment of the Reserve Army is the Royal Monmouthshire Royal Engineers (Militia) formed on 21 Mar 1577 and never disbanded, with battle honours at Dunkirk, 1940 and Normandy, 1944.

Greatest mutiny

In the 1914–18 War 56 French divisions comprising some 650 000 men and their officers refused orders on the Western Front sector of General Robert Nivelle in April 1917 after the failure of his offensive.

Longest march

On the night of 12–13 Sept 1944 a team of 9 from B Company 4th Infantry Battalion of the Irish Army made a night march of 67·59 km *42 miles* in full battle order carrying 18·1 kg *40 lb* in 11 hr 49 min.

A team of the 29 Commando Regiment, each man carrying a 18·14 kg *40 lb* pack, including a rifle, covered the Plymouth Marathon in 4 hr 35 min 47·28 sec on 1 Nov 1987.

Army drill

On 8–9 July 1987 a 90-man squad of the Queen's Colour Squadron, RAF, performed a total of 2 722 662 drill movements (2 001 384 rifle and 721 278 foot) at RAF Uxbridge from memory and without a word of command in 23 hr 55 min.

Air forces *Oldest*

The earliest autonomous air force is the Royal Air Force which owes its origins to the Corps of Royal Engineers Balloon Section (founded 1878), to the Air Battalion of the Royal Engineers (1 Apr 1911) and to the Royal Flying Corps (13 May 1912). The RAF took its place alongside the Navy and the Army as a separate service with its own ministry on 1 Apr 1918. The Prussian Army used a balloon near Strasbourg, France as early as 24 Sept 1870.

Largest

The greatest air force of all time was the United States Army Air Corps (now the US Air Force), which had 79 908 aircraft in July 1944 and 2 411 294 personnel in March 1944. The US Air Force including strategic air forces had 605 805 personnel and 4887 combat aircraft in mid-1986. The USSR Air Force had 453 000 men in mid-1986. It had 5150 combat aircraft. In addition, the USSR's Offensive Strategic Rocket Forces had about 298 000 operational personnel in mid-1986. The strength of the Royal Air Force was 93 300 with 50 operational squadrons in 1988.

BOMBS
Heaviest

The heaviest conventional bomb ever used operationally was the Royal Air Force's 'Grand Slam', weighing 9975 kg *22 000 lb* and measuring 7·74 m *25 ft 5 in* long, dropped on Bielefeld railway viaduct, Germany on 14 Mar 1945. In 1949 the United States Air Force tested a bomb weighing 19 050 kg *42 000 lb* at Muroc Dry Lake, California. The heaviest known nuclear bomb has been the 4 tonne 9 megatonne carried by US B-52 bombers. These bombs 3·67 m *12 ft 0½ in* in length were phased out by January 1984.

Atomic

The first atom bomb dropped on Hiroshima, Japan by the United States at 8.16 a.m. on 6 Aug 1945 had an explosive power equivalent to that of 12·5 kilotons *12 500 short tons* of trinitrotoluene ($C_7H_5O_6N_3$), called TNT. Code-named 'Little Boy' it was 3·04 m *10 ft* long and weighed 4080 kg *9000 lb* and burst 580 ± 15 m *c. 1900 ft* above the city centre. The most powerful thermonuclear device so far tested is one with a power equivalent of 57 000 000 short tons of TNT, or 57 megatons, detonated by the USSR in the Novaya Zemlya area at 8.33 a.m. GMT on 30 Oct 1961. The shock wave circled the world 3 times, taking 36 hr 27 min for the first circuit. Some estimates put the power of this device at between 62 and 90 megatons. The largest US H-Bomb tested was the 18–22 megaton 'Bravo' at Bikini Atoll, Marshall Islands on 1 Mar 1954. On 9 Aug

1961, Nikita Khrushchyov, then the Chairman of the Council of Ministers of the USSR, declared that the Soviet Union was capable of constructing a 100-megaton bomb, and announced the possession of one in East Berlin, Germany on 16 Jan 1963. Such a device could make a crater in rock 107 m *355 ft* deep and 2·9 km *1·8 miles* wide and a fireball 13·9 km *46 000 ft* or *8·7 miles* in diameter.

Atom bomb theory began with Einstein's publication of the $E = mc^2$ formula published in *Annalen der Physik* in Leipzig on 14 May 1907. This postulated that the latent energy of 1 gram of matter was 89 875 517 873·781 dynes. It became a practicality with the mesothorium experiments of Otto Hahn (1879–1968), Fritz Strassman (1902–1980) and Lise Meitner (1878–1968) on 17 Dec 1938. Work started in the USSR on atomic bombs in June 1942 although their first chain reaction was not achieved until December 1945 by Dr Igor Vasilyevich Kurchatov (1903–1960). The concept of a thermonuclear fusion bomb belonged to Edward Teller (b. 1908) in 1942. Development was ordered by President Truman on 30 Jan 1950 and code-named 'Super'. The bomb became practical only as a result of a calculation by the Polish-born American Stanislaw Ulam (1909–1984).

Largest nuclear weapons

The most powerful ICBM (inter-continental ballistic missiles) are the USSR's SS–18s (Model 5), believed to be armed with 10 750-kiloton MIRVs (multiple independently targetable re-entry vehicles). Earlier models had a single 20-megaton warhead. The US Titan II carrying a W-53 warhead was rated at 5 to 9 megatons but is now withdrawn leaving the 1–2 megaton W-56 as the most powerful US weapon.

'Star wars'

The first reported successful 'high frontier' interception test in outer space by the United States Strategic Defense Initiative occurred over the Pacific on 10 June 1984.

Largest 'conventional' explosion

The largest use of conventional explosive was for the demolition of the fortifications and U-boat pens at Helgoland on 18 Apr 1947. A net charge of 4061 tonnes (7122 tonnes gross) was detonated by Commissioned Gunner E. C. Jellis of the naval team headed by Lt F. T. Woosnam RN aboard HMS *Lasso* lying 14·5 km *9 miles* out to sea.

TANKS
Earliest

The first tank was 'No. 1 Lincoln' modified to become 'Little Willie' built by William Foster & Co Ltd of Lincoln. It first ran on 6 Sept 1915. Tanks were first taken into action by the Heavy Section, Machine Gun Corps, which later became the Royal Tank Corps, at the battle of Flers-Courcelette in France on 15 Sept 1916. The Mark I Male tank, armed with a pair of 6-pounder guns and 4 machine guns, weighed 28·4 tonnes and was driven by a motor developing 105 hp which gave it a maximum road speed of 4·8–6·4 km/h *3–4 mph*.

Heaviest and fastest

The heaviest tank ever constructed was the German Panzer Kampfwagen Maus II, which weighed 192 tonnes. By 1945 it had reached only the experimental stage and was not proceeded with. The heaviest operational tank used by any army was the 75·2 tonne 13-man French Char de Rupture 2C bis of 1922. It carried a 155-mm howitzer and had two 250 hp engines giving a maximum speed of 12 km/h *8 mph*. The world's most heavily armed tank since 1972 has been the Soviet T-72 with a 125 mm *4·92 in* high velocity gun. The British AVRE 'Centurion' has a 165 mm *6·5 in* low-velocity demolition gun. The world's fastest tank is the British Scorpion AFV which can touch 80·5 km/h *50 mph* with 75 per cent payload.

The heaviest British armoured vehicle ever built was the

79 tonne prototype 'Tortoise'. With a crew of seven and a designed speed of 19 km/h *12 mph*, this tank had a width 5 cm *2 in* less than that of the one-time operational 66 tonne 'Conqueror'.

GUNS
Earliest

Although it cannot be accepted as proven, the best opinion is that the earliest guns were constructed in both China and in north Africa in *c.* 1250. The earliest representation of an English gun is contained in an illustrated manuscript dated 1326 at Oxford.

The earliest anti-aircraft gun was an artillery piece on a high-angle mounting used in the Franco-Prussian War of 1870 by the Prussians against French balloons.

Largest

The 2 most massive guns ever constructed were used by the Germans in the siege of Sevastopol on the Eastern Front in July 1942. They were of a calibre of 800 mm *31·5 in* with barrels 28·87 m *94 ft 8½ in* long and named *Dore* and *Gustav*. Their remains were discovered, one near Metzenhof, Bavaria in August 1945 and the other in the Soviet zone. They were built by Krupp as railway guns carried on 24 cars, 2 of which had 40 wheels each. The whole assembly of the gun was 42·9 m *141 ft* long and weighed 1344 tonnes with a crew of 1500. The range for an 8·1 tonne projectile was 46·67 km *29 miles*.

During the 1914–18 War the British Army used a gun of 457 mm *18 in* calibre. The barrel alone weighed 127 tonnes. In World War II the 'Bochebuster', a train-mounted howitzer with a calibre of 457 mm *18 in* firing a 1133 kg *2500 lb* shell to a maximum range of 20 850 m *22 800 yd*, was used from 1940 onwards as part of the Kent coast defences.

Greatest range

The greatest range ever attained by a gun was achieved by the HARP (High Altitude Research Project) gun consisting of two 419 mm *16·5 in* calibre barrels in tandem 36·4 m *119·4 ft* long weighing 150 tonnes at Yuma, Arizona, USA. On 19 Nov 1966 an 84 kg *185 lb* projectile was fired to an altitude of 180 km *111·8 miles* or *590 550 ft*. The static V3 underground firing tubes built in 50-degree shafts near Mimoyècques, near Calais, France to bombard London were never operative.

The famous long-range gun which shelled Paris in World War I was the 'Kaiser Wilhelm geschütz' with a calibre of 220 mm *8·66 in*, a designed range of 127·9 km *79·5 miles* and an achieved range of 122 km *76 miles* from the Forest of Crépy in March 1918. The 'Big Berthas' were mortars of 420 mm *16·53 in* calibre and with a range of less than 14 500 m *9 miles*.

Mortars

The largest mortars ever constructed were Mallets mortar (Woolwich Arsenal, London, 1857), and the 'Little David' of World War II, made in the USA. Each had a calibre of 920 mm *36¼ in*, but neither was ever used in action. The heaviest mortar used was the tracked German 600 mm *23·6 in* siege piece known as 'Karl' before Stalingrad, USSR.

Largest cannon

The highest-calibre cannon ever constructed is the 'Tsar Puchka' (King of Cannons), now housed in the Kremlin, Moscow, USSR. It was built in the 16th century with a bore of 920 mm *36·2 in* and a barrel 3·18 m *10 ft 5 in* long. It weighs 40 tonnes or 2400 pouds (*sic*). The Turks fired up to 7 shots per day from a bombard 7·92 m *26 ft* long, with an internal calibre of 1066 mm *42 in* against the walls of Constantinople (now Istanbul) from 12 Apr to 29 May 1453. It was dragged by 60 oxen and 200 men and fired a 543 kg *1200 lb* stone cannon ball.

Military engines

The largest military catapults, or onagers, could throw a missile weighing 27 kg *60 lb* a distance of 457 m *500 yd*

Conscientious objector *Most obdurate*

The only conscientious objector to be 6 times court-martialled in World War II was Gilbert Lane of Wallington, Surrey. He served 31 months' detention and 183 days' imprisonment.

Nuclear delivery vehicles

As of mid-1987 the USSR deployed 2511 strategic nuclear delivery vehicles while the USA on the same date deployed 1957 vehicles or 340 below the 2250 SALT II limit. The comparative number of warheads has been estimated by the International Institute for Strategic Studies at USSR 11 044 and USA 13 873.

Judicial

LEGISLATION AND LITIGATION

Statutes *Oldest*

The earliest surviving judicial code was that of King Ur-Hammu during the third dynasty of Ur, Iraq, c. 2110 BC. The oldest English statute in the Statute Book is a section of the Statute of Marlborough of 1267, retitled in 1948 'The Distress Act, 1267' and last cited in the High Court in 1986. Some statutes enacted by Henry II (d. 1189) and earlier kings are even more durable as they have been assimilated into the Common Law. An extreme example is Ine's Law concerning the administration of shires. Ine reigned AD 689–726.

Longest in the United Kingdom

The weightiest piece of legislation ever written is the Income and Corporation Taxes bill of more than 1000 pages and weighing 2·5 kg *5½ lbs.* Lord Houghton of Sowerby appealed to fellow peers in November 1987 'not to walk about with it' for fear of ruptures. Lord Houghton was 89. Of old statutes, 31 George III XIV, the Land Tax Act of 1791, written on parchment, consists of 780 skins forming a roll 360 m *1170 ft* long.

Shortest

The shortest statute is the Parliament (Qualification of Women) Act 1918, which runs to 27 operative words: 'A woman shall not be disqualified by sex or marriage from being elected to or sitting or voting as a Member of the Commons House of Parliament.' Section 2 contains a further 14 words giving the short title.

Most inexplicable

Certain passages in several Acts have always defied interpretation and the most inexplicable must be a matter of opinion. A judge of the Court of Session of Scotland once sent the Editor his candidate which reads: *'In the Nuts (unground), (other than ground nuts) Order, the expression nuts shall have reference to such nuts, other than ground nuts, as would but for this amending Order not qualify as nuts (unground) (other than ground nuts) by reason of their being nuts (unground).'*

Earliest English patent

The earliest of all known English patents was that granted by Henry VI in 1449 to Flemish-born John of Utyman for making the coloured glass required for the windows of Eton College. The peak number of applications for patents filed in the United Kingdom in any one year was 63 614 in 1969. The shortest, concerning a harrow attachment, of 48 words was filed on 14 May 1956 while the longest, comprising 2318 pages of text and 495 pages of drawings, was filed on 31 Mar 1965 by IBM to cover a computer.

Most protracted litigation

The longest contested law suit ever recorded ended in Poona, India on 28 Apr 1966, when Balasaheb Patloji Thorat received a favourable judgement on a suit filed by his ancestor Maloji Thorat 761 years earlier in 1205. The points at issue were rights of presiding over public functions and precedences at religious festivals.

The dispute over the claim of the Prior and Convent (now the Dean and Chapter) of Durham Cathedral to adminis-ter the spiritualities of the diocese during a vacancy in the See grew fierce in 1283. It flared up again in 1672 and 1890; an attempt in November 1975 to settle the issue, then 692 years old, was unsuccessful. Neither side admits the legitimacy of writs of appointment issued by the other even though identical persons are named.

Fastest trial

The law's shortest delay occurred in *Duport Steel and Others* v. *Sirs and Others* heard in the High Court on 25 Jan 1980; the appeal was heard on 26 Jan and the appeal heard in the House of Lords on 1 Feb (a.m.) with the decision given p.m.

Longest trial

The longest jury trial in legal history is *Kemner* v. *Monsanto Co.* which started on 6 Feb 1984. The trial, at St. Clair County Court House, Belleville, Illinois, USA before Circuit Judge Richard P. Goldenhersh, ended on 26 Aug 1987 after 657 days and jury deliberation of two months. The verdict was returned on 22 Oct when the plaintiffs secured sums of $1 nominal compensatory damage and $16 250 000 punitive damage in a case concerning an alleged toxic spill in Sturgeon, Illinois in 1979.

Longest British trials

The longest trial in the annals of British justice was the Tichborne personation case. The civil trial began on 11 May 1871, lasted 103 days and collapsed on 6 Mar 1872. The criminal trial went on for 188 days, resulting in a sentence on 28 Feb 1874 for 2 counts of perjury (two 7-year consecutive terms of imprisonment with hard labour) on London-born Arthur Orton, *alias* Thomas Castro (1834–98), who claimed to be Roger Charles Tichborne (1829–54), the elder brother of Sir Alfred Joseph Doughty-Tichborne, 11th Bt (1839–66). The whole case thus spanned 1025 days. The jury were out for only 30 minutes.

The impeachment of Warren Hastings (1732–1818), which began in 1788, dragged on for 7 years until 23 Apr 1795, but the trial lasted only 149 days. He was appointed a member of the Privy Council in 1814.

The fraud case *R* v. *Bouzaglo and Others* ended before Judge Brian Gibbens (1912–1985) on 1 May 1981 having lasted 274 days. They appealed on 10 Dec 1981. Trial costs were estimated at £2·5 million. The fluoridation case *McColl* v. *Strathclyde Regional Council* lasted 204 days ending on 27 July 1982 before Lord Jauncey, whose judgement in the £1 million case ran to 400 pages.

The longest case in the House of Lords was *Armstrong Patents* v. *British Leyland*—7 weeks ending on 27 Feb 1986.

Murder

The longest murder trial in Britain was that at the Old Bailey, London of Reginald Dudley, 51, and Robert Maynard, 38, in the Torso Murder of Billy Moseley and Micky Cornwall which ran before Mr Justice Swanwick from 11 Nov 1976 to 17 June 1977 with 136 trial days. Both men were sentenced to life imprisonment (minimum 15 years). Costs were estimated to exceed £500 000 and the evidence amounted to 3 500 000 words.

Longest tribunal *Divorce*

The longest trial of a divorce case in Britain was *Gibbons* v. *Gibbons and Roman and Halperin.* On 19 Mar 1962, after 28 days, Mr Alfred George Boyd Gibbons was granted a decree *nisi* against his wife Dorothy for adultery with Mr John Halperin of New York City, NY, USA.

Shortest trials

The shortest recorded British murder hearings were *R.* v. *Murray* on 28 Feb 1957 and *R.* v. *Cawley* at Winchester assizes on 14 Dec 1959. Proceedings occupied only 30 seconds on each occasion.

Litigants in person

Since the Union of the Parliaments in 1707 the only Scot to win an appeal in person before the House of Lords has been Mr Jack Malloch, an Aberdeen schoolmaster. In 1971 he was restored to his employment with costs under the dormant but operative Teachers Act 1882 securing also a professional status in law for all qualified Scottish teachers.

Dr Mark Feldman, a podiatric surgeon, of Lauderhill, Florida, USA became the first litigant in person to secure 7 figures ($1 million) before a jury in compensatory and punitive damages in September 1980. The case concerned conspiracy and fraud alleged against 6 other doctors.

Longest address

The longest address in a British court was in *Globe and Phoenix Gold Mining Co Ltd* v. *Amalgamated Properties of Rhodesia.* Mr William Henry Upjohn KC (1853–1941) concluded his speech on 22 Sept 1916, having addressed the court for 45 days.

Highest bail

The world record for bail was set at $5000 million by Judge J. Dominique Olcomendy of San Francisco Municipal Court on Dorothy M. Toines, 25, for soliciting prostitution on 8 Feb 1988. She was unable to pay the 10 per cent or $500 million necessary for her release after repeated failures to appear in court. The bail figure was reduced on 25 Feb by a Superior Court judge to a more affordable $500 but she was re-arrested on 21 Mar 1988 for a fifth time. The Assistant District Attorney's comment was 'See what happens when you reduce a $5 billion bail'.

The highest bail figure in a British court is £1·2 million in the case of *Inland Revenue* v. *Piggott* at Newmarket, Cambridgeshire on 19 Dec 1986 which was reduced to £500 000 on 23 Dec 1986. This amount was subsequently equalled in the Guinness PLC affair at Bow Street Court, London in the cases of Ernest Walter Saunders, former chief executive (7 May 1987); Sir Isidore (Jack) Lyons (9 Oct 1987); Gerald Ronson (14 Oct 1987); Roger Seelig (16 Oct 1987); Lord (3rd Baron) Spens (11 Mar 1988); Anthony Parnes (24 Mar 1988) and David Mayhew (8 Apr 1988); Shabtai Kalmanowitch, who was charged with dishonestly procuring $2 030 000, was also allowed £500 000 bail at Bow Street Magistrates Court, London on 3 July 1987.

Longest arbitration

The longest arbitration (under the 1950 Act) on record has been the Royce Arbitr'tion. It lasted 239 days and concerned Mitchell Construction Co and the East Anglian Regional Hospital Board over the building of Peterborough Hospital.

Longest inquiry

The longest and most expensive public inquiry has been that over the projected £1200-million Sizewell B nuclear power station, Suffolk under Sir Frank Layfield QC. It began on 11 Jan 1983 and finished after 340 days of hearings on 7 Mar 1985 in the Snape Maltings, Aldeburgh. The cost to public funds was £20 million and the 3000-page 8-volume report weighed 13·6 kg *30 lb* and cost £30.

Best attended trial

The greatest attendance at any trial was that of Major Jesús Sosa Blanco, aged 51, for an alleged 108 murders. At one point in the 12½-hr trial (5.30 p.m. to 6 a.m., 22–23 Jan 1959), 17 000 people were present in the Havana Sports Palace, Cuba. He was executed on 18 Feb 1959.

Greatest damages *Personal injury*

The greatest personal injury damages ever awarded were $78 million to the model Maria Hanson, 26, on 29 Sept 1987 whose face was slashed with razors in Manhattan, New York City in June 1987. The 3 men convicted and now serving 5–15 years have no assets and Miss Hanson is entitled to 10 per cent of their post-prison earnings.

On 18 July 1986 a Bronx Supreme Court jury awarded

$65 086 000 to Mrs Agnes Mae Whitaker against the New York City Health and Hospitals Corporation for medical malpractice.

On 24 Nov 1983 a jury in Corpus Christi, Texas, USA awarded punitive damages of $106 million against the Ford Motor Co for alleged design faults in the Ford Mustang II in which Bevary Durrill, 20, died in 1974. The case was appealed.

Samer Aboul-Hosn, 23, was awarded £1 032 000 by Mr Justice Hirst in the High Court, London on 10 July 1987 against the Italian Hospital, Norman Grant, Peter Crawford and Zuhair Nouri for post-operative medical negligence.

Civil damages
The largest damages awarded in legal history were $11 120 million to Pennzoil Co against Texaco Inc. concerning the latter's allegedly unethical tactics in January 1984 to break up a merger between Pennzoil and Getty Oil Co, by Judge Solomon Casseb Jr in Houston, Texas on 10 Dec 1985. The 2 leading counsels were Joe Jamail (Pennzoil) and Richard Miller (Texaco). An out-of-court settlement of $5 500 million was reached after a 48 hour negotiation on 19 Dec 1987.

Breach of promise
The largest sum involved in a breach of promise suit in the United Kingdom was £50 000, accepted in 1913 by Miss Daisy Markham, *alias* Mrs Annie Moss (d. 20 Aug 1962, aged 76), in settlement against the 6th Marquess of Northampton DSO (1885–1978).

Defamation
A sum of $16 800 000 was awarded to Dr John J. Wild, 58, at the Hennepin District Court, Minnesota, USA on 30 Nov 1972 against The Minnesota Foundation and others for defamation, bad-faith termination of a contract, interference with a professional business relationship, along with $10·8 million in punitive damages. The Supreme Court of Minnesota granted an option of a new trial or a $1·5 million *remittitur* to Dr Wild on 10 Jan 1975. There was a no-disclosure clause in the settlement. The $39·6 million awarded in Columbus, Ohio, USA on 1 Mar 1980 to Robert Guccione, publisher of *Penthouse*, for defamation against Lowry Flynt, publisher of *Hustler*, was reduced by Judge Craig Wright to $4 million on 17 Apr 1980. The hearing ended in May 1982 with *Penthouse* being cleared of libel.

The greatest damages for defamation ever awarded in the United Kingdom have been £327 000 in the courts in Edinburgh in favour of Capital Life Assurance Co against the *Scottish Daily Record* and the *Sunday Mail* for articles published in the latter in 1975.

The most expensive defamation trial in Great Britain has been the 87-day-long case of *Gee* v. *British Broadcasting Corporation* which ran before Lord Justice Croom-Johnson from 22 Oct 1984 to 2 May 1985. The costs have been estimated at £1·5 million excluding the BBC's internal costs over the 681 days from the offending transmission of *That's Life* on 26 June 1983. Dr Gee, who was in the witness stand for 27 days, received a record settlement of £100 007.

A $640-million libel suit was brought by the California resort La Costa against *Penthouse* in March 1975. In May 1982 a jury found for the magazine, but in July their verdict was set aside by a Californian judge, who was then removed from the case. Costs exceeded $10 million.

Greatest compensation for wrongful imprisonment
Isadore Zimmerman (1917–1983) of New York City, USA accepted an award of $1 000 000 in 1982 for wrongful imprisonment for 24 years following a false conviction for slaying a policeman. After deduction of legal fees and expenses he took home some $600 000 or some $25 000 for each year in jail. He died some 14 months later.

The greatest Crown compensation in Britain for wrongful imprisonment has been £17 500 paid to Laszlo Virag, 35, who had been sentenced to 10 years' imprisonment at Gloucester assizes in 1969 for theft and shooting and wounding a police officer. His acceptance of this sum was announced on 23 Dec 1974 after he was released in April 1974 on grounds of mistaken identity.

Greatest alimony suit
Belgian-born Sheika Dena Al-Fassi, 23, filed the highest ever alimony claim of $3000 million against her former husband Sheik Mohammed Al-Fassi, 28, of the Saudi Arabian royal family, in Los Angeles, California, USA in February 1982. Mr Marvin Mitchelson, explaining the size of the settlement claim, alluded to the Sheik's wealth which included 14 homes in Florida alone and numerous private aircraft. On 14 June 1983 she was awarded $81 million and declared she would be 'very very happy' if she was able to collect.

Greatest divorce settlement
The reported settlement achieved by the lawyers of Soraya Khashóggi was £500 million plus property from her husband Adnan. Mrs Anne Bass, former wife of Sid Bass of Texas, USA was reported to have rejected $535 million as inadequate to live in the style to which she had been made accustomed.

The highest High Court divorce award received was £700 000 on 13 Nov 1980 for 'Mrs P' after 23 years of marriage, against her former husband from Jersey from whom she had been receiving £6000 per annum. In *Edgar* v. *Edgar* in 1980, £750 000 was awarded but this was set aside on appeal when Mrs Edgar accepted a much lesser figure.

Patent case
On 13 Mar 1986 Hughes Tool Co of Houston, Texas was awarded $205 381 259·40 in a suit involving Smith International Inc. over an infringement of their patent for the 'O' ring seal used in drilling. The inventor was Edward M. Galle.

Largest suit
The highest amount of damages ever sought to date is $675 000 000 000 000 (then equivalent to 10 times the US national wealth) in a suit by Mr I. Walton Bader brought in the US District Court, New York City, USA on 14 Apr 1971 against General Motors and others for polluting all 50 states.

Largest law firm
The world's largest law firm is Baker & McKenzie with 920 lawyers in 37 offices in 25 countries. It was founded in Chicago in 1949.

Highest costs
The 119-day trial of 7 servicemen from Cyprus under the Official Secrets Act 1911 ending at the Old Bailey, London on 29 Oct 1985 cost an estimated £3½ –£5 million. All the defendants were acquitted.

The most expensive man-hunt in police history was one costing £4 million terminating on 13 June 1981 with the arrest of Peter William Sutcliffe (the 'Yorkshire Ripper'), in Sheffield, South Yorkshire. His trial at the Old Bailey, London cost £250 000 and resulted in his being sentenced to a minimum of 30 years for 13 murders and 7 attempted murders which orphaned 25 children.

Longest lease
The longest lease on record is one concerning a plot for a sewage tank adjoining Columb Barracks, Mullingar, County Westmeath, Ireland signed on 3 Dec 1868 for 10 000 000 years. It is to be assumed that a future civil servant will bring up the matter for review early in AD 10 001 868.

Greatest lien
The greatest lien by a court is 40 000 million lire on 9 Apr 1974 upon Vittorio and Ida Riva in Milan for back taxes allegedly due on a chain of cotton mills around Turin, Italy.

Wills *Shortest and longest*
The shortest valid will in the world is 'Vše zene', the Czech for 'All to wife', written and dated 19 Jan 1967 by Herr Karl Tausch of Langen, Hessen, West Germany. The shortest will contested but subsequently admitted to probate in English law was the case of *Thorne* v. *Dickens* in 1906. It consisted of the 3 words 'All for mother' in which 'mother' was not his mother but his wife. The smallest will preserved by the Record Keeper is an identity disc 3·8 cm *1½ in* in diameter belonging to A.B. William Skinner, killed aboard HMS *Indefatigable* at Jutland in 1916. It had 40 words engraved on it including the signatures of 2 witnesses and was proved on 24 June 1922.

The longest will on record was that of Mrs Frederica Evelyn Stilwell Cook, proved at Somerset House, London on 2 Nov 1925. It consisted of 4 bound volumes containing 95 940 words.

Most durable judges
The oldest recorded active judge was Judge Albert R. Alexander (1859–1966) of Plattsburg, Missouri, USA. He was the magistrate and probate judge of Clinton County until his retirement aged 105 years 8 months on 9 July 1965.

The greatest recorded age at which any British judge has sat on a bench was 93 years 9 months in the case of Sir William Francis Kyffin Taylor GBE, KC (later Lord Maenan), who was born on 9 July 1854 and retired as presiding judge of the Liverpool Court of Passage in April 1948, having held that position since 1903. Sir Salathiel Lovell (1619–1713) was, however, still sitting when he died on 3 May 1713 in his 94th or 95th year. The greatest age at which a House of Lords judgement has been given is 92 in the case of the 1st Earl of Halsbury (b. 3 Sept 1823) in 1916. Lord Chief Baron of Exchequer in Ireland, the Rt Hon. Christopher Palles (1831–1920) served for 42 years from 17 Feb 1874 until 1916.

Master of the Rolls
The longest tenure of the Mastership of the Rolls since the office was inaugurated in 1286 has been 24 years 7 months by David de Wollore from 2 July 1346 to 27 March 1371. The longest tenure since the Supreme Court Judicature Act of 1881 has been that of 20 years by the Rt Hon. Lord Denning PC (b. 23 Jan 1899) from 1962 to Sept 1982. He had been first appointed a high court judge in 1944. William Morland held the office for 77 days, while in 1629 Sir Humphrey May died 'soon after' his appointment on 10 April.

Youngest judge
No collated records on the ages of judicial appointments exist. However, David Elmer Ward had to await the legal age of 21 before taking office after nomination in 1932 as Judge of the County Court at Fort Myers, Florida, USA.

The youngest certain age at which any English judge has been appointed is 28, in the case of Sir Ernest Wild KC (b. 1 Jan 1869) who was appointed Judge of the Norwich Guildhall Court of Record in 1897 at that age. The lowest age of appointment this century has been the 42 years 2 months of Lord Hodson in 1937.

Most judges
Lord Balmerino was found guilty of treason by 137 of his peers on 28 July 1746. In *R* v. *Canning* at the Old Bailey in 1754 Elizabeth Canning was deported to Connecticut, USA for wilful perjury by 19 judges voting 10 to 9. In *Young, James and Webster* v. *United Kingdom*, the British Rail 'closed shop' case, before the European Court of Human Rights in Strasbourg on 3–4 Mar 1981, Mr David Calcutt QC won a judgement for the railwaymen by 18 to 3.

Most offices
The most high judicial offices held by one man has been by Alexander Wedderbarn (1733–1805), later Lord Loughborough and Earl of Rosslyn, who was Solicitor General in 1771, Attorney General in 1778, Chief-Justice

of common pleas 1780–93 and Lord Chancellor from 27 Jan 1793 until he resigned in 1801.

Youngest English QC

The earliest age at which a barrister has taken silk this century is 33 years 8 months in the case of Mr (later the Rt Hon. Sir) Francis Raymond Evershed (1899–1966) in April 1933. He was later Lord Evershed, Master of the Rolls. Buller was nepotistically given silk aged 31, being a nephew of the then Lord Chancellor, Lord Bathurst.

Most successful

Sir Lionel Luckhoo KCMG, CBE, senior partner of Luckhoo and Luckhoo of Georgetown, Guyana, succeeded in getting his 245th successive murder charge acquittal by 1 Jan 1985.

Most durable solicitors

William George (1865–1967), brother of Prime Minister David Lloyd George, passed his preliminary law examination in May 1880 and was practising until December 1966 aged 101 years 9 months. The most durable firm is Thomson, Snell & Passmore of Tonbridge, Kent, begun by the Reverend Nicholas Hooper, a part-time scrivener, in 1570.

CRIME

Mass killings *China*

The greatest massacre ever imputed by the government of one sovereign nation against the government of another is that of 26 300 000 Chinese during the regime of Mao Tse-tung between 1949 and May 1965. This accusation was made by an agency of the USSR government in a radio broadcast on 7 Apr 1969. The broadcast broke down the figure into 4 periods: 2·8 million (1949–52); 3·5 million (1953–7); 6·7 million (1958–60); and 13·3 million (1961–May 1965). The highest reported death figures in single monthly announcements on Peking radio were 1 176 000 in the provinces of Anhwei, Chekiang, Kiangsu and Shantung, and 1 150 000 in the central south provinces. Po I-po, Minister of Finance, is alleged to have stated in the organ *For a lasting peace, for a people's democracy*: 'in the past three years [1950–2] we have liquidated more than 2 million bandits'. Général Jacques Guillermaz, a French diplomat, estimated the total executions between February 1951 and May 1952 at between 1 million and 3 million. In April 1971 the executive cabinet or *Yuan* of the implacably hostile government of the Republic of China in Taipei, Taiwan announced its official estimate of the mainland death toll in the period 1949–69 as 'at least 39 940 000'. This figure, however, excluded 'tens of thousands' killed in the Great Proletarian Cultural Revolution, which began in late 1966. The Walker Report published by the US Senate Committee of the Judiciary in July 1971 placed the parameters of the total death toll within China since 1949 between 32·25 and 61·7 million. An estimate of 63·7 million was published by Jean-Pierre Dujardin in *Figaro* magazine of 19–25 Nov 1978.

USSR

The total death toll in the Great Purge, or *Yezhovshchina*, in the USSR from 1936–38 has never been published. Evidence of its magnitude may be found in population statistics which show a deficiency of males from *before* the outbreak of the 1941–45 war. The reign of terror was administered by the *Narodny Kommissariat Vnutrennykh Del* (NKVD), or People's Commissariat of Internal Affairs, the Soviet security service headed by Nikolay Ivanovich Yezhov (1895–1939), described by Nikita Khrushchyov in 1956 as a 'degenerate'. S. V. Utechin regarded estimates of 8 000 000 or 10 000 000 victims as 'probably not exaggerations'. On 17 Aug 1942 Stalin indicated to Churchill in Moscow that 10 million *kulaks* had been liquidated for resisting the collectivisation of their farms. Prof. Igor Bestuzhev-Lada published an estimate of Stalin's victims in 1929–53 in the *Nedelya* supplement to *Izvestia* of 16 Apr 1988 of 50 million dead. Nobel prizewinner Alexander Solzhenitsyn estimated the loss of life from state repression and terrorism from

October 1917 to December 1959 under Lenin, Stalin and Khrushchyov at 66 700 000.

Nazi Germany

The best estimate of the number of Jewish victims of the Holocaust or the genocidal 'Final Solution' or *Endlösung* ordered by Adolf Hitler (1889–1945) in April 1941 and continuing into May 1945 is 5·8 million. Obersturmbannführer (Lt-Col.) Karl Adolf Eichmann (b. Solingen, Germany, 19 Mar 1906) of the SS was hanged in a small room inside Ramleh Prison, near Tel Aviv, Israel at just before midnight (local time) on 31 May 1962, for his complicity in the deaths of an indeterminably massive number of Jews.

At the SS (*Schutzstaffel*) extermination camp (*Vernichtungslager*) known as Auschwitz-Birkenau (Oświecim-Brzezinka), near Oświecim (Auschwitz) in southern Poland, where a minimum of 920 000 people (Soviet estimate is 4 000 000) were exterminated from 14 June 1940 to 18 Jan 1945, the greatest number killed in a day was 6000. The man who operated the release of the 'Zyklon B' cyanide pellets into the gas chambers there during this time was Sgt Major Moll (variously Mold). The Nazi (*Nationalsozialistische Deutsche Arbeiterpartei*) Commandant during the period 1940–3 was Rudolph Franz Ferdinand Höss who was tried in Warsaw from 11 Mar to 2 Apr 1947 and hanged, aged 47, at Oświecim on 15 Apr 1947.

Forced labour

No official figures have been published of the death toll in Corrective Labour Camps in the USSR, first established in 1918. In 1956 many were converted to less severe Corrective Labour Colonies. An estimate published in the Netherlands puts the death toll

> **Highest kidnapping ransom** ● Historically the greatest ransom paid was that for Atahualpa by the Incas to Francisco Pizarro in 1532–3 at Cajamarca, Peru – as depicted here. This constituted a hall full of gold and silver, worth in modern money some $170 million .

between 1921 and 1960 at 19 000 000. The camps were administered by the *Cheka* until 1922, the OGPU (1922–34), the NKVD (1934–46), the MVD (1946–53) and the KGB (*Komitet Gosudarstvennoi Bezopasnosti*) since 1953. A study published in 1985 estimated that there are 289 labour camp zones with a population of 4½ million. The largest is believed to be the Dubrovlag Complex of 15 camps centred on Pot'ma, Moldavian SSR.

In China there are no published official statistics on the numbers undergoing *Lao Jiao* (Education through Labour) nor *Lao Dong Gai Zao* (Reform through Manual Labour). An estimate published by Bao Ruo-wang, who was released in 1964 due to his father having been a Corsican, was 16 000 000, which then approached 3 per cent of the population.

Genocide

As a percentage of a nation's total population the worst genocide appears to have been that in Kampuchea, formerly Cambodia. According to the Khmer Rouge Foreign Minister, Ieng Sary, more than a third of the 8 million Khmers were killed between 17 Apr 1975 and January 1979. The highest 'class' ideals induced indifference to individual suffering to the point of serving as a warrant for massacre. Under the rule of Saloth Sar *alias* Pol Pot, a founder member of the CPK (Communist Party of Kampuchea, formed in September 1960) towns, money and property were abolished and economical execution by bayonet and club introduced for such offences as falling asleep during the day, asking too many questions, playing non-communist music, being old and feeble, being the offspring of an 'undesirable' or being too well educated. Deaths at the Tuol Sleng interrogation centre reached 582 a day.

In Chinese history of the 13th–17th centuries there were 3 periods of wholesale massacre. The numbers of victims attributed to these events are assertions rather than reliable estimates. The figure put on the Mongolian invasions of northern China from 1210–19 and from 1311–40 are both of the order of 35 million, while the number of victims of the bandit leader Chang Hsien-

chung (c. 1605–47), known as the 'Yellow Tiger', from 1643–47 in the Zechuan province has been put at 40 million.

Saving of life

The greatest number of people saved from extinction by one man is an estimated 90 000 Jews in Budapest, Hungary from July 1944 to January 1945 by the Swedish diplomat Raoul Wallenberg (b. 4 Aug 1912). After escaping an assassination attempt by the Nazis, he was imprisoned without trial in the Soviet Union. On 6 Feb 1957 Mr Gromyko said prisoner 'Wallenberg' had died in a cell in Lubyanka Jail, Moscow on 16 July 1947. Sighting reports within the Gulag system have persisted for 41 years after his disappearance. He was made an Honorary Citizen of the USA on 5 Oct 1981 and on 7 May 1987 a statue was unveiled to him in Budapest to replace an earlier one which had been removed.

Largest criminal organisation

The largest syndicate of organised crime is the Mafia or La Cosa Nostra, which has infiltrated the executive, judiciary and legislature of the United States. It consists of some 3000 to 5000 individuals in 25 'families' federated under 'The Commission', with an annual turnover in vice, gambling, protection rackets, tobacco, bootlegging, hijacking, narcotics, loan-sharking and prostitution which was estimated by *US News & World Report* in December 1982 at $200 billion and a profit estimated in March 1986 by the Attorney Rudolph Giuliani at $75 billion. Its origin in the USA dates from 1869 in New Orleans. The biggest Mafia (derived from an arabic expression connoting beauty and excellence allied with bravery) killing was from 11–13 Sept 1931 when 40

DRUGS BUST

Britain's giant cocaine haul ● Britain's biggest cocaine seizure – 208 kg *458·56 lbs* – worth £51 million, was realised in September 1987, and started off an international operation, code-named Harbinger II, involving British customs investigators, together with their counterparts in the Netherlands, France and West Germany.

On 22 Aug, the container ship the MV *Tagama* left Santa Marta **1** in Colombia, including in its cargo a container of ceramic tiles bound for the Netherlands. When it berthed at Southampton **2** on 22 Sept, customs officers had to off-load the Rotterdam-bound container as it had been positioned wrongly, on top of the ones which were to be delivered to Britain. On inspecting the rusty container, the officers noticed that the padlocks had been tampered with so that the doors could be opened without the seals being broken. Using the cover of darkness, they removed the container to a secure shed so that it could be thoroughly examined. There it was found that the interior had been freshly painted, and in the roof was a 10·16 cm *4 in* deep compartment containing the 263 packages of cocaine. These were removed, and bags of grain put in their place. The compartment was re-welded and re-painted, and the boxes of tiles put back. The container was then loaded back on to the *Tagama*, and customs at the next ports of call alerted. When the ship visited these ports – Le Havre in France **3** and Bremen in West Germany **4** – constant surveillance was maintained.

Meanwhile, British investigators had flown to Rotterdam to work alongside their Dutch colleagues. It was on 2 Oct that the *Tagama* docked in Rotterdam **5** and the container with its tiles and grain off-loaded. For over a month a close watch was kept up, and then on 10 Nov it was collected and driven to a caravan site at nearby Spijkenisse **6** where the Dutch authorities arrested eight men as they were cutting open the ceiling. (Artwork: Peter Harper)

mafiosi were liquidated following the murder in New York of Salvatore Maranzano, *Il Capo di Tutti Capi*, on 10 Sept. The greatest breaches of *omerta* (the vow of silence) were by Joseph Valachi who 'sang like a canary' in 1963, and by the much bereaved Tommaso Buschetta, 56, in 1984. The latter's information led to 329 convictions and 2655 years' imprisonment, and $9·6 million in fines plus 19 life sentences in the Sicilian Mafia or Cupola trial in Palermo from 10 Feb 1986 to 16 Dec 1987. Michele 'the Pope' and his brother Salvatore 'the Senator' Greco had been accused of slaying the Carabinieri General Dalla Chiesa in Palermo on 3 Sept 1982.

Murder rate *Highest and lowest*

The country with the highest recorded murder rate is Brazil, with 104 homicides for each 100 000 of the population in 1983, or 370 per day. A total of 592 deaths was attributed to one Colombian bandit leader, Teófilo ('Sparks') Rojas, aged 27, between 1948 and his death in an ambush near Armenia on 22 Jan 1963. Some sources attribute 3500 slayings to him during *La Violencia* of 1945–62. The highest homicide rates recorded in New York City have been 58 in a week in July 1972 and 13 in a day in August 1972. In 1973 the total for Detroit, Michigan (pop. then 1·5 million) was 751. The Chicago Crime Commission published in March 1983 a list of 1081 unsolved gang slayings since 1919. The country with the lowest officially recorded rate in the world is the Maldives with a nil rate among its naturals since its independence in July 1965. In the Indian state of Sikkim, in the Himalayas, murder is practically unknown, while in the Hunza area of Kashmir, in the Karakoram, only one definite case by a Hunzarwal has been recorded since 1900.

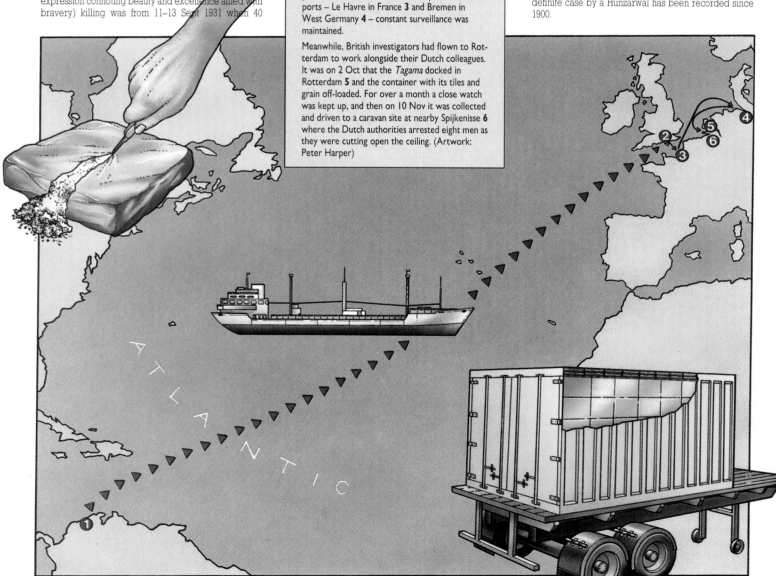

In Great Britain the total number of homicides and deaths from injuries purposely inflicted by other persons in the year 1986 was 826. This figure compares with a murder total of 124 in 1937 and 125 in 1958.

Most prolific murderers

It was established at the trial of Behram, the Indian Thug, that he had strangled at least 931 victims with his yellow and white cloth strip or *ruhmal* in the Oudh district between 1790 and 1840. It has been estimated that at least 2 000 000 Indians were strangled by Thugs (*burtotes*) during the reign of the Thugee (pronounced tugee) cult from 1550 until its final suppression by the British raj in 1853. The greatest number of victims ascribed to a murderess has been 650 in the case of Countess Erzsebet Bathory (1560–1614) of Hungary. At her trial, which began on 2 Jan 1611, a witness testified to seeing a list of her victims in her own handwriting totalling this number. All were alleged to be young girls from near her castle at Csejthe where she died on 21 Aug 1614. She had been walled up in her room for 3½ years after being found guilty.

20th century

Pedro Alonso López (b. Colombia, 1949) known as the 'Colombian Monster', was reported captured by the villagers of Ambato, Ecuador in early March 1980. He admitted to more than 300 murders of pre-teenage girls in Colombia, Peru and Ecuador since 1973. The remains of 53 victims of the 110 admitted to in Ecuador were rapidly detected after his confession.

In a drunken rampage lasting 8 hours on 26–27 Apr 1982 policeman Wou Bom-Kon, 27, killed 57 people and wounded 35 with 176 rounds of rifle ammunition and hand grenades in the Kyong Sang-Namdo province of South Korea. He blew himself up with a grenade.

Six men were each charged with 21 murders at Lancaster Crown Court on 9 June 1975 concerning the bombing of the 2 Birmingham public houses Mulberry Bush and Tavern in the Town on 21 Nov 1974. They were John Walker, Patrick Hill, Robert Hunter, Noel McIlkenny, William Power and Hugh Callaghan. These convictions were sent on 20 Jan 1987 by the Home Secretary to the Court of Appeal which unanimously confirmed the verdicts on 28 Jan 1988. The self-confessed arsonist Bruce Lee was sent to a mental hospital by Leeds Crown Court in January 1981 but on 14 Mar 1982 he retracted his confessions to starting fires in which 26 perished. On 2 Dec 1983 the Court of Appeal quashed charges of causing 11 of the deaths.

Judith Minna Ward, 25, of Stockport, Cheshire was convicted on 11 separate murder charges on 4 Nov 1974 making 12 in all arising from the explosion in an army coach on the M62 near Drighlington, West Yorkshire on 4 Feb 1974. Mary Ann Cotton (*née* Robson) (b. 1832, East Rainton, County Durham), hanged in Durham Jail on 24 Mar 1873, is believed to have poisoned 14, possibly 20, people.

Dennis Andrew Nilsen (b. 1948), then of 23 Cranley Gardens, Muswell Hill, north London, admitted to 15 one-at-a-time murders between December 1978 and February 1983. He was sentenced to life imprisonment with a 25-year minimum on 4 Nov 1983 at the Old Bailey by the Rt Hon. Lord Justice Croom-Johnson PC, DSC for 6 murders and 2 attempted murders.

Dominic McGlinchey (b. 1955) in November 1983 admitted in a press interview to at least 30 killings in Northern Ireland. He was jailed for 10 years at Dublin's Special Criminal Court on 11 Mar 1986 for shooting with intent to resist arrest in County Clare on 17 Mar 1984. On 7 May 1981 John Thompson of Hackney, London was found guilty at the Old Bailey of the 'specimen' murder by arson of Archibald Campbell and jailed for life. There were 36 other victims at the Spanish Club, Denmark St, London.

The worst armed rampage in Britain was at Hungerford, Berkshire on 19 Aug 1987 during which Michael Ryan, 27, shot dead 15 people and wounded 15 others before shooting himself.

Suicide

The estimated daily rate of suicides throughout the world surpassed 1000 in 1965. The country with the highest suicide rate is Denmark with 28·6 per 100 000 in 1986. The number in Japan rose to 69·9 per day in 1986. The country with the lowest recorded rate is Jordan with a single case in 1970 and hence a rate of 0·04 per 100 000. In England and Wales there were 4315 suicides in 1984—11·7 per day. In the northern hemisphere, they tend to peak in April and May.

Mass suicide

The total number of victims of the mass cyanide poisoning of the People's Temple cult near Port Kaituma, Guyana on 18 Nov 1978 was 913. The leader was the paranoid 'Rev' Jim Jones of San Francisco, who had deposited 'millions of dollars' overseas.

The volcanic crater of Mt Mihara on an island in Sagami Bay, south of Yokohama was the scene of more than 1000 suicides from 1933–36.

Mass poisoning

On 1 May 1981 the first of some 600 victims of the Spanish cooking oil scandal died. On 12 June it was discovered that this 8 year old boy's cause of death was the use of 'denatured' industrial colza from rape seed. The trial of 38 defendants including the manufacturers Ramon and Elias Ferrero lasted from 30 Mar 1987 to 28 June 1988 on 586 counts on which the prosecution demanded jail sentences totalling 60 000 years.

Robbery

The greatest robbery on record was that of the Reichsbank following Germany's collapse in April/May 1945. The Pentagon in Washington described the event, first published in the *Guinness Book of Records* in 1957, as 'an unverified allegation'. *Nazi Gold* by Ian Sayer and Douglas Botting, published in 1984, however, finally revealed full details and estimated the total haul at current values as £2500 million.

The robbery in the Knightsbridge Safety Deposit Centre, London on 12 July 1987 was estimated at £30 million for 80 of the 126 boxes robbed. The managing director Parvez Latiff, 30, was among those charged on 17 Aug 1987.

At 6.40 a.m. on 26 Nov 1983 six masked men raided the Brinks Mat Unit 7 warehouses at the Heathrow Trading Estate, removing 6 800 bars of gold and platinum together with diamonds and travellers' cheques worth £26 369 778. Michael McAvoy, 32, of East Dulwich and Brian Robinson, 41, of Lewisham were each sentenced to 25 years at the Old Bailey on 3 Dec 1984. Others were found guilty of related offences while further cases were pending in 1988.

Art

It is arguable that the *Mona Lisa*, though never valued, is the most valuable object ever stolen. It disappeared from the Louvre, Paris on 21 Aug 1911. It was recovered in Italy in 1913 when Vincenzo Perruggia was charged with its theft.

On 27 Oct 1985 nine paintings by Corot, Monet and Utrillo, valued at 100 million francs, were removed from the Mermotte Museum, Paris. They turned up less than a month later in a gallery in Ginza, Tokyo. On 25 Dec 1985 140 'priceless' gold, jade and obsidian artifacts were stolen from the National Anthropology and History Institute, Mexico City, Mexico.

Bank

During the extreme civil disorder prior to 22 Jan 1976 in Beirut, Lebanon a guerilla force blasted the vaults of the British Bank of the Middle East in Bab Idriss and cleared out safe deposit boxes with contents valued by former Finance Minister, Lucien Dahadah, at $50 million and by another source at an 'absolute minimum' of $20 million.

Train

The greatest recorded train robbery occurred between about 3.03 a.m. and 3.27 a.m. on 8 Aug 1963, when a General Post Office mail train from Glasgow, Scotland was ambushed at Sears Crossing and robbed at Bridego Bridge near Mentmore, Buckinghamshire. The gang escaped with about 120 mailbags containing £2 631 784 worth of bank notes being taken to London for destruction. Only £343 448 was recovered.

Jewels

The greatest recorded theft of jewels was from the bedroom of the 'well-guarded' villa of Prince Abdel Aziz bin Ahmed Al-Thani near Cannes, France on 24 July 1980 valued at $16 000 000 . The haul from Bond Jewellers, Conduit St, London on 20 June 1983 was estimated to be worth £6 million.

Greatest kidnapping ransom

The greatest ransom ever reported in modern times is 1500 million pesos for the release of the brothers Jorge Born, 40, and Juan Born, 39, of Bunge and Born, paid to the left-wing urban guerila group Montoneros in Buenos Aires, Argentina on 20 June 1975. The youngest person kidnapped has been Carolyn Wharton, born at 12.46 p.m. on 19 Mar 1955 in the Baptist Hospital, Texas, USA and kidnapped, by a woman disguised as a nurse, at 1.15 p.m. aged 29 minutes.

Greatest hijack ransom

The highest amount ever paid to aircraft hijackers has been $6 million by the Japanese government in the case of a JAL DC-8 at Dacca Airport on 2 Oct 1977 with 38 hostages. Six convicted criminals were also exchanged. The Bangladesh government had refused to sanction any retaliatory action.

Largest narcotics haul

In October 1983 it was estimated that the narcotics crime in the USA was running at $80 000 million per annum with cocaine dealers turning a profit of $35 000 million and illegal domestic 'green collar' marijuana growers netting $13 900 million.

The greatest drug haul ever achieved was 1320·8 kg *1·3 tons* of top-grade heroin inside bales of natural rubber at the docks in Bangkok, Thailand, on 13 Feb 1988, registered for shipment to New York City, USA on 25 Feb. The value was put at $2000 million by the Thai authorities.

The bulkiest haul was 2 903 000 kg *2850 long tons* of Colombian marijuana in the 14-month-long 'Operation Tiburon' concluded by the DEA with the arrest of 495 people and the seizure of 95 vessels announced on 5 Feb 1982.

In Britain, the Home Office disclosed on 23 Dec 1977 that 13 million LSD tablets with a street value approaching £100 million had been destroyed on the conclusion of 'Operation Julie'. A press report on 22 Nov 1986 named the operation to track down a drug trafficking syndicate, said to be masterminded from Iver, in Buckinghamshire, as Operation Fulmer and the worth of the drugs also at £100 million.

Greatest banknote forgery

The greatest forgery was the German Third Reich government's forging operation, code name 'Bernhard', engineered by SS Sturmbannführer Alfred Naujocks of the Technical Dept of the German Secret Service Amt VI F in Berlin in 1940–1. It involved £150 000 000 worth of £5 notes.

Biggest bank fraud

The largest amount of money named in a defalcation case has been a gross SwFr 222 million at the Lugano branch of Lloyd's Bank International in Switzerland on 2 Sept 1974. Mark Colombo and Egidio Mombelli were tried and found guilty in Lugano on 30 Oct 1975 on charges of mismanagement and falsification of accounting documents.

Computer fraud

Between 1964 and 1973, 64 000 fake insurance policies were created on the computer of the Equity Funding Corporation in the USA, involving $2000 million.

Stanley Mark Rifkin (b. 1946) was arrested in Carlsbad, California, USA by the FBI on 6 Nov 1978 charged with defrauding a Los Angeles bank of $10·2 million by manipulation of a computer system. He was sentenced to 8 years' imprisonment in June 1980.

Theft

It was estimated in November 1983 that the greatest theft in the world is running at $160 000 million per annum. This is the value of 'bosses' time' paid for but not worked in the United States in 1983/84.

The government of the Philippines announced on 23 Apr 1986 that they had succeeded in identifying $860·8 million 'salted' by the former President Ferdinand Edralin Marcos (b. 11 Sept 1917) and his wife Imelda. It was asserted that the total since November 1965 was believed to be between $5 and $10 billion.

Largest object stolen by a single man

On a moonless night at dead calm high water on 5 June 1966, armed with only a sharp axe, N. William Kennedy slashed free the mooring lines at Wolfe's Cove, St Lawrence Seaway, Canada of the 10 639-dwt SS *Orient Trader* owned by Steel Factors Ltd of Ontario. The vessel drifted to a waiting blacked-out tug thus escaping a ban on any shipping movements during a violent wild-cat waterfront strike. She sailed for Spain.

Maritime fraud

A cargo of 180 000 tonnes of Kuwaiti crude oil on the supertanker *Salem* at Durban was sold without title to the South African government in December 1979. The ship mysteriously sank off Senegal on 17 Jan 1980 leaving the government to pay £148 million to Shell International, who owned the shipment.

CAPITAL PUNISHMENT

Capital punishment is known to date at least from the Iron Age, as evidenced by the finding of Tollund man in Denmark. The countries in which capital punishment is still prevalent include China (hundreds of shootings per annum); South Africa (about 100 hangings for rape, robbery and murder); Turkey; Iran; USA (reintroduced in 38 states since January 1983 for the most heinous murders); USSR (23 capital offences including profiteering, speculation and currency offences for which some 400 persons have been reportedly shot annually).

Capital punishment was first abolished *de facto* in 1798 in Liechtenstein. The death penalty for murder was formally abolished in Britain on 18 Dec 1969.

Capital punishment in the British Isles dates from AD 450, but was abolished by William I and reimposed by Henry I, reaching a peak in the reign of Edward VI (1547–53), when an average of 560 persons were executed annually at Tyburn alone. Even into the 19th century there were 223 capital crimes, but these resulted in only 25 hangings. Between 1830 and 1964 the most murderers hanged in a year was 27 (24 men, 3 women) in 1903. In 1956 there were no executions.

Largest hanging

The most people hanged from one gallows were 38 Sioux Indians by William J. Duly outside Mankato, Minnesota, USA for the murder of unarmed citizens on 26 Dec 1862. The Nazi Feldkommandant simultaneously hanged 50 Greek resistance men as a reprisal in Athens on 22 July 1944.

Last hangings

The last public execution in England took place outside Newgate Prison, London at 8 a.m. on 26 May 1868, when Michael Barrett was hanged for his part in the Fenian bomb outrage on 13 Dec 1867, when 12 were killed outside the Clerkenwell House of Detention, London. The earliest non-public execution was of the murderer Thomas Wells on 13 Aug 1868. The last public hanging in Scotland was that of the murderer Robert Smith outside Dumfries Gaol on 12 May 1868 by the hangman Mr Askern. The last in the United States occurred in Owensboro, Kentucky in 1936. The last hangings in the United Kingdom were those of Peter Anthony Allen (b. 4 Apr 1943), hanged at Walton Prison, Liverpool by Mr Leslie Stewart, and John Robson Walby (b. 1 Apr 1940), *alias* Gwynne Owen Evans, at Strangeways Gaol, Manchester, both on 13 Aug 1964. They had been found guilty of the capital murder of John Alan West, on 7 Apr 1964. The 15th, youngest and last woman executed this century was Mrs Ruth Ellis (*née* Neilson), 28, for the murder of David Blakely, 25, shot outside the Magdala, Hampstead on 10 Apr 1955. She was executed on 13 July at Holloway Prison, London. The last hanging in the Republic of Ireland took place in 1954.

Last from yard-arm

The last naval execution at the yard-arm was the hanging of Private John Dalliger, Royal Marines, aboard HMS *Leven* in Victoria Bay near Lu-ta, China, on 13 July 1860. Dalliger had been found guilty of 2 attempted murders.

Youngest

On 26 June 1885 James Arcene was executed for a crime he committed when aged 10. In Britain the hanging of persons under 18 was expressly excluded in the Children's and Young Persons' Act 1933 (Sec. 33). No person under that age was, in fact, executed more recently than 1887. The lowest satisfactorily recorded age was of a boy aged 8 'who had malice, cunning and revenge' in firing 2 barns and who was hanged at Abingdon, Oxfordshire in the 17th century. The youngest persons hanged since 1900 have been six 18-year-olds, the most recent of whom was Francis Robert George ('Flossie') Forsyth on 10 Nov 1960.

Oldest

The oldest person hanged in the United Kingdom since 1900 was a man of 71 named Charles Frembd (*sic*) at Chelmsford Gaol on 4 Nov 1914, for the murder of his wife at Leytonstone, London. In 1822 John Smith, said to be 80, of Greenwich, south-east London, was hanged for the murder of a woman.

Last guillotinings

The last person to be publicly guillotined in France was the murderer Eugene Weidmann before a large crowd at Versailles, near Paris at 4.50 a.m. on 17 June 1939. The executioner was Henri Desfourneaux, who was succeeded by his nephew André Obrecht (1897–1983) in 1951, who was in turn succeeded by his niece's husband Marcel Chevalier in January 1978. Dr Joseph Ignace Guillotin (1738–1812) died a natural death. He had advocated the use of the machine designed by Dr Antoine Louis in 1789 in the French constituent assembly. The last use before abolition on 9 Sept 1981 was on 10 Sept 1977 at Baumettes Prison, Marseille for torturer and murderer Hamida Djandoubi, 28.

Death Row

The longest sojourn on Death Row was the 39 years of Sadamichi Hirasawa (1893–1987) in Sendai Jail, Japan. He was convicted in 1948 of poisoning 12 bank employees with potassium cyanide to effect a theft of £100, and died aged 94. Willie Jasper Darden, 54, survived a record six death warrants in 14 years on Death Row for the murder of a shopkeeper in 1973. His final TV interview was interrupted by a power failure caused by a test of the Florida electric chair in which he died on 15 Mar 1988. On 31 Oct 1987 Liong Wie Tong, 52, and Tan Tian Tjoen, 62, were executed for robbery and murder by firing squad in Jakarta, Indonesia after 25 years on Death Row.

Executioners

The longest period of office of a public executioner was that of William Calcraft (1800–79), who was in action from 1828 to 25 May 1874 and officiated at nearly every hanging outside and later inside Newgate Prison, London. On 2 Apr 1868 he hanged the murderess Mrs Frances Kidder, 25, outside Maidstone Jail, Kent—the last public execution of a woman. For 56 years from 1900 to the retirement of Albert in February 1956, the Pierrepoint family largely monopolised the task of executing murderers and war criminals. Henry Albert (1876–1922) officiated from 1900–1911 with a record 20 executions in Britain in 1909 and the last double female execution (the baby farmers Mrs Amelia Sachs and Mrs Annie Walters) on 3 Feb 1903. The longest-serving executioner has been his eldest brother Thomas Pierrepoint from 1903 to 1948. Albert Pierrepoint, son of Henry Albert, officiated at the hanging of 530 men and 20 women in his career in 9 countries including a record 27 war criminals in one day in Germany. Britain's 9th and last chief prison hangman was Henry B. Allen who was on call until the abolition of hanging for murder in 1969.

Lynching

The worst year in the 20th century for lynchings in the United States has been 1901, with 130 lynchings (105 Negroes, 25 Whites), while the first year with no reported cases was 1952. The last lynching case recorded in Britain was that of *R* v. *Caskie and Stevenson* on 29 Dec 1922. The accused were discharged after a verdict of not proven for murder by assault of Robert Alexander Stewart, 32, at Dalmarnock Bridge, Glasgow on 11 Sept 1922. Stewart was falsely thought by a tram conductor to be kidnapping Alistair John Sinclair, 5, who gave evidence not under oath standing on a seat.

Corporal punishment

The last use of corporal punishment in one of HM Prisons was on 26 June 1962 and it was abolished in the United Kingdom by the Criminal Justice Act 1967. The treadmill which 14 prisons operated in 1878 was finally suspended on 1 Apr 1902. Men on the 36-man wheel at Northallerton, Yorkshire raised themselves 2937 m *9639 ft* in an 8-hour day, equivalent to reaching within 33·8 m *111 ft* of the summit of Everest in 3 days.

PRISON SENTENCES
Longest sentences

A 10 000-year sentence was imposed on Deuel Wilhelm Davies, 40, on 4 Dec 1981 in Tuscaloosa, Alabama, USA for a triple murder (including his mother-in-law) in 1976. A sentence of 384 912 years was *demanded* at the prosecution of Gabriel March Grandos, 22, at Palma de Mallorca, Spain on 11 Mar 1972 for failing to deliver 42 768 letters, or 9 years per letter.

Juan Corona, a Mexican-American, was sentenced to 25 consecutive life terms, for murdering 25 farm workers in 1970–1 around Feather River, Yuba City, California, USA at Fairfield on 5 Feb 1973. His 20th-century record was surpassed by Dean Corll (27) in 1974 and John Wayne Gacy (33 victims) in 1980.

Kevin Mulgrew from the Ardoyne district of Belfast was sentenced on 5 Aug 1983 to life imprisonment for the murder of Sergeant Julian Connolley of the UDR. In addition he was given a further 963 years to be served concurrently on 84 other serious charges including 13 conspiracies to murder and 8 attempted murders.

The longest single period served by a reprieved murderer in Great Britain this century was 40 years 11 months by John Watson Laurie, the Goat Fell or Arran murderer, who was reprieved on the grounds of insanity in November 1889. He died in Perth Penitentiary on 4 Oct 1930.

The longest specific minimum period recommended by a judge under the Murder (Abolition of Death Penalty) Act 1965 has been 45 years in the case of Jordanian terrorist Nezar Hindawi for his abortive bomb plot against an El Al airliner on 24 Oct 1986.

The longest single sentence passed on a woman under English law was 20 years for Mrs Lona Teresa Cohen *née*

Petra (b. 1913) at the Old Bailey on 2 Mar 1961 for conspiring to commit a breach of the Official Secrets Act 1911. The sentence of this KGB agent was remitted by the Foreign Secretary on no known lawful authority on 24 July 1969. Ward (see Most prolific murderers) was sentenced to 20 years for a single offence and an aggregate 30 years on 4 Nov 1974.

Longest time served
Paul Geidel (b. 21 Apr 1894) was convicted of second degree murder on 5 Sept 1911 as a 17-year-old porter in a New York, USA hotel. He was released from the Fishkill Correctional Facility, Beacon, New York aged 85 on 7 May 1980 having served 68 years 8 months and 2 days—the longest recorded term in US history. He first refused parole in 1974. Rudolph Hess, formerly Hitler's deputy, was captured at Eaglesham on 10 May 1941 and died in Spandau Prison on 17 Aug 1987 aged 93, having entered his 47th year in prison.

The longest-serving prisoner in Britain is John Straffen (b. 1930), now in his 33rd year behind bars for 3 child murders.

Longest in Broadmoor Special Hospital
The longest period for which any person has been detained in the Broadmoor Hospital for the Criminally Insane, near Crowthorne, Berkshire, is 76 years in the case of William Giles. He was admitted as an insane arsonist at the age of 11 and died there on 10 Mar 1962, at the age of 87.

The longest escape from Broadmoor was one of 39 years by the Liverpool wife murderer James Kelly, who got away on 28 Jan 1888, using a pass key made from a corset spring. After an adventurous life in Paris, in New York and at sea he returned in April 1927, to ask for readmission. After some difficulties this was arranged. He died in 1930.

Most appearances
A record for arrests was set by Tommy Johns (1922–88) in Brisbane, Queensland, Australia on 9 Sept 1982 when he faced his 2000th conviction for drunkenness since 1957. His total at the time of his last drink on 30 Apr 1988 was 'nearly 3000'.

Greatest mass arrests
The greatest mass arrest reported in a democratic country was of more than 13 000 people in an anti-war demonstration designed to block rush-hour traffic in Washington DC, USA from 3–5 May 1971. The largest in the United Kingdom occurred on 17 Sept 1961, when 1314 demonstrators supporting unilateral nuclear disarmament were arrested for obstructing highways leading to Parliament Square, London by sitting down. As a consequence of the 1926 General Strike there were 3149 prosecutions: incitement (1760) and violence (1389).

FINES
Heaviest
The US Securities and Exchange Commission on 14 Nov 1986 fined Ivan Boesky, 49, the New York arbitrageur, $100 million for breaching their regulations on 'insider dealing'.

The heaviest fine ever imposed by a United Kingdom court is £525 000 on 10 Dec 1983 on the National Graphical Association (NGA) for illegal picketing of the *Messenger* newspaper plant, Warrington, Cheshire owned by Mr Eddie Shah.

On 6 Feb 1985 Lloyd's of London fined Peter Dixon, chairman of the PCW (Peter Cameron-Webb) Syndicate, £1 000 000 in connection with alleged misappropriation of £38·17 million. A High Court judgement of £8·2 million against Mr Dixon was also made in chambers.

The highest fine ever imposed on a UK company is 10 million ECUs (equivalent to £5·7 million) on ICI by the EEC for irregular trading concerning polypropylene from 1977–83, on 24 Apr 1986.

Rarest prosecution
There is a number of crimes in English law for which there have never been prosecutions. Among unique prosecutions are *Rex* v. *Crook* in 1662 for the praemunire of disputing the King's title and *Rex* v. *Gregory* for selling honours under the Honours (Prevention of Abuses) Act 1924, on 18 Feb 1933. John Maundy Gregory (d. 3 Oct 1941 in France as 'Sir' 'Arthur' Gregory) was an honours broker during 6 administrations from 1919 to 1932 and was sentenced to 2 months in Wormwood Scrubs, London.

PRISONS
Largest
The most capacious prison in Great Britain is Wandsworth, south London, with a certified normal accommodation of 1266. Peak occupation of 1519 was reached on 30 April 1988. The highest prison walls in Great Britain are those of Lancaster Prison, measuring 11–15·85 m *36–52 ft*. The Maze Prison, near Lisburn, Northern Ireland, opened in 1974, covers 53·8 ha *133 acres* with eight 100-cell blocks surrounded by a 9·1 m *30 ft* wall. The largest prison in Scotland is Barlinnie, Glasgow, with 750 single cells. Ireland's largest prison is Mountjoy Prison, Dublin, with 808 cells.

Devil's Island
The largest French penal settlement was that of St Laurent du Maroni, which comprised the notorious Iles du Diable, Royale and St Joseph (for incorrigibles) off the coast of French Guiana in South America. It remained in operation for 99 years from 1854 until the last group of repatriated prisoners, including Théodore Rouselle, who had served 50 years, was returned to Bordeaux on 22 Aug 1953. It has been estimated that barely 2000 *bagnards* (ex-convicts) of the 70 000 deportees ever returned. These, however, included the executioner Ladurelle (imprisoned 1921–37), who was murdered in Paris in 1938.

Highest population
The peak average prison population, including police cell occupation, for England and Wales was the figure for the week beginning 17 July 1987 with 51 239. In Scotland the prison population record was 5400 in 1972 and in Northern Ireland 2934 on 16 Nov 1975.

Most expensive prison
Spandau Prison, Berlin, originally built in 1887 for 600 prisoners, was used solely for the Nazi war criminal Rudolf Hess (b. 26 Apr 1894, d. 17 Aug 1987) for the last twenty years of his life. On 19 Aug 1987 it was announced that he had strangled himself with a piece of electrical flex and that he had left a note in old German script. He remained in lone confinement at Spandau for a total of forty years. The cost of maintenance of the staff of 105 was estimated at $415 000 per annum in 1987.

Longest escape
The longest recorded escape by a recaptured prisoner

was that of Leonard T. Fristoe, 77, who escaped from Nevada State Prison, USA on 15 Dec 1923 and was turned in by his son on 15 Nov 1969 at Compton, California. He had had 46 years of freedom under the name of Claude R. Willis. He had killed 2 sheriff's deputies in 1920. The longest period of freedom achieved by a British gaol breaker is more than 32 years by Irish-born John Patrick Hannan, who escaped from Verne Open Prison at Portland, Dorset on 22 Dec 1955. He had served only 1 month of a 21 month term for car stealing and assaulting 2 policemen.

Greatest gaol break
In February 1979 a retired US Army colonel, Arthur 'Bull' Simons, led a band of 14 to break into Gasre prison, Tehran, Iran to rescue 2 fellow Americans. Some 11 000 other prisoners took advantage of this and the Islamic revolution in what became history's largest ever gaol break.

In July 1971, Raoul Sendic and 105 other Tupamaro guerillas escaped from a Uruguayan prison through a tunnel 91 m *298 ft* long.

The greatest gaol break in the United Kingdom was that from the Maze Prison on 25 Sept 1983, when 38 IRA prisoners escaped from Block H-7. By June 1988 10 were still at large. The Provisional IRA had been first set up in Ballinamore, County Leitrim, Ireland in 1967.

Economics

MONETARY AND FINANCIAL
Largest budget
The greatest governmental expenditure ever made by any country has been $1004·6 billion by the United States Government for the fiscal year 1987. The highest ever revenue figure was $854·1 billion in this same US fiscal year.

The world's greatest fiscal surplus was $8 419 469 844 in the United States in 1947–8. The worst deficit was the $237·9 billion in the US fiscal year 1987.

The greatest general UK government expenditure is £183·0 billion planned for the fiscal year 1988–89. The highest general government receipts are expected to be £184·9 billion for the same fiscal year. The Public Sector Borrowing Requirement, running at a peak £11 628 million in 1983, was reduced to –£0·6 billion in May 1988.

Foreign aid

The total net foreign aid given by the United States Government between 1 July 1945 and 1 Jan 1986 was $256 516 million. The country receiving most US aid in 1987 was Israel with $3808 million. US foreign aid began with $50 000 to Venezuela for earthquake relief in 1812.

Least taxed

The lowest income-taxed sovereign countries in the world are Bahrain, Brunei, Kuwait and Qatar where the rate, regardless of income, is nil. No tax is levied on the Sarkese (inhabitants of Sark) in the Channel Islands or on the inhabitants of Tristan da Cunha.

Highest taxation rates

The country with the most confiscatory taxation is Norway where in January 1974 the Labour Party and Socialist Alliance abolished the 80 per cent limit. Some 2000 citizens were then listed in the *Lignings Boka* as paying more than 100 per cent of their taxable income. The shipping magnate Hilmar Reksten (1897–1980) was assessed at 491 per cent.

In the United Kingdom until 1979 the former top earned and unearned rates were 83 per cent and 98 per cent. The standard rate of tax was reduced to 25 per cent and the higher rate to 40 per cent in the 1988 budget. The all-time record was set in 1967–68, when a 'special charge' of up to 9s. (45p) in the £ additional to surtax brought the top rate to 27s. 3d. (or 136 per cent) in the £ on investment income.

Balance of payments

The record deficit for any country for a fiscal year is $140 569 million in 1986 by the USA. The record surplus was $96 460 million in 1987 by Japan.

The most favourable current balance of payments figure for the United Kingdom has been a surplus of £7272 million in 1981 (best quarter Jan–Mar £2698 million). The worst figure was a deficit of £3591 million in 1974. Monthly figures are regarded as too erratic to be of great significance.

Highest tax demands

The highest recorded personal tax demand is one for $336 million on 70 per cent of the estate of Howard Hughes. The highest disclosed UK personal income tax demand raised is one for £5 371 220 against international merchant banker Nicholas van Hoogstraten, then 34, for 1981.

Highest and lowest rates in Great Britain

Income tax was first introduced in Great Britain in 1799 for incomes above £60 per annum. It was discontinued in 1815, only to be reintroduced in 1842 at the rate of 7d. (2·91p) in the £. It was at its lowest at 2d. (0·83p) in the £ in 1875, gradually climbing to 1s. 3d. (6·24p) by 1913. From April 1941 until 1946 the record peak of 10s. (50p) in the £ was maintained to assist in the financing of the war effort.

National debt

The largest national debt of any country in the world is that of the United States, where the gross federal public debt of the federal government surpassed the 'trillion' (10^{12}) dollar mark on 30 Sept 1981. By the end of 1987 it had reached $2355·3 billion with net interest payments on the debt of $138·6 billion. The national debt in Great Britain was less than £1 million during the reign of James II in 1687. It was £197 295 million or £3464 per person at 31 Mar 1988.

Most foreign debt

The country most heavily in overseas debt at 1 Jan 1988 was Brazil with $113 billion. The suspension of interest payments was announced on 20 Feb 1987.

Gross national product

The country with the largest gross national product is the United States which, having reached $3 trillion ($3 × 10^{12}$) in 1981, was running at $4598 billion at the end of the fiscal year 1987. The GNP of the United Kingdom at factor cost in 1987 was £352 205 million.

National wealth

The richest territory in the 1988 World Bank rankings is Bermuda with $20 420 measured by average per caput. The USA, which had taken the lead in 1910, was 3rd behind Switzerland. The United Kingdom stood 23rd with $8920. It has been estimated that the value of all physical assets in the USA on 1 Jan 1983 was $12·5 trillion ($12·5 × 10^{12}$) or $53 800 per caput. The latest estimated figure for private wealth in the UK is £1 172 000 million or £53 000 per household.

Poorest country

The lowest published annual income per caput of any country in the world is that of Chad at $59 in 1983, but the World Bank has no publishable data for 17 marxist countries.

Gold and foreign currency reserves

The country with the greatest monetary gold reserve is the United States, whose Treasury had 263·90 million fine oz of the world's 949·86 million fine oz on hand in March 1987. Valued at $400 per fine oz, these amounts would translate to $105 560 million and $379 944 million respectively. The United States Bullion Depository at Fort Knox, 48 km *30 miles* south-west of Louisville, Kentucky, USA, has been the principal federal depository of US gold since December 1936. Gold is stored in 446 000 standard mint bars of 12·4414 kg *400 troy ounces* measuring 17·7 × 9·2 × 4·1 cm, *7 × 3⅝ × 1⅝ in*. Gold's peak price was $850 on 21 Jan 1980.

The lowest published figure for the sterling area's gold and convertible currency reserves was $298 000 000 on 31 Dec 1940. The valuation in July 1987 was a peak $34 915 million and the peak figure for gold was $7334 million on 31 Dec 1981.

Minimum Lending Rate

The highest ever figure for the British bank rate (since 13 Oct 1972, the Minimum Lending Rate) has been 17 per cent from 15 Nov 1979 to 3 July 1980. The longest period without a change was the 12 years 13 days from 26 Oct 1939 to 7 Nov 1951, during which time the rate stayed at 2 per cent. This lowest ever rate had been first attained on 22 Apr 1852.

Worst inflation

The world's worst inflation occurred in Hungary in June 1946, when the 1931 gold pengő was valued at 130 trillion ($1·3 × 10^{20}$) paper pengős. Notes were issued for 'Egymillard billion' (one milliard billion or 10^{21}) pengős on 3 June and withdrawn on 11 July 1946. Vouchers for 1000 billion billion (10^{27}) pengős were issued for taxation payment only. On 6 Nov 1923 the circulation of Reichsbank marks reached 400 338 326 350 700 000 000 and inflation was 755 700 million fold on 1913 levels. The country with the highest recent rate of inflation was Bolivia, with 8000 plus per cent for 1985. It peaked in October with >24 000 per cent, and there was a yearly rate of 23 503 per cent for Sept 1984–Sept 1985.

The United Kingdom's worst rate in a year has been for August 1974 to August 1975 when inflation ran at a rate of 26·9 per cent compared with the recent low point of 2·8 per cent for the 12 months to May 1986. The Tax and Price Index (allowing for tax reliefs) was 2·1 per cent for the 12 months to May 1988. The peak TPI extrapolated figure was 31·9 per cent in August 1975.

Least inflation

For 1987 Japan's inflation rate averaged 0·1 per cent.

WEALTH AND POVERTY

The comparison and estimations of extreme personal wealth are beset with intractable difficulties. Quite apart from reticence and the element of approximation in the valuation of assets, as Jean Paul Getty (1892–1976) once said: 'If you can count your millions you are not a billionaire.' The term millionaire was invented *c.* 1740 and billionaire (in the original American sense of one thousand million) in 1861. The earliest dollar centi-millionaire was Cornelius Vanderbilt (1794–1877) who left $100 million in 1877. The earliest billionaires were John Davison Rockefeller (1839–1937); Henry Ford (1863–1947) and Andrew William Mellon (1855–1937). In 1937, the last year in which all 3 were alive, a billion US dollars were worth £205 million, but that amount of sterling would today have a purchasing power exceeding £5000 million.

Richest men

Many of the riches of most of the world's 29 remaining monarchs are national rather than personal assets. The least fettered and most monarchical is HM Sir Muda Hassanal Bolkiah Mu'izzaddin Waddaulah Hon GCMG (b. 15 July 1946) of Brunei. He appointed himself Prime Minister, Finance and Home Affairs Minister on 1 Jan 1984. *Fortune Magazine* reported in September 1987 that his fortune was $25 000 million.

Forbes Magazine estimated on 13 July 1987 that Yoshiaki Tsutsumi, chairman of the Seiba Group, is the world's richest man from 70 real-estate and transport companies with assets of $21 000 million.

The richest man in the United States is Sam Moore Walton, founder in 1962 of Wal-Mart discount stores of Bentonville, Arkansas, whose personal worth was estimated in early 1988 to be $8·8 billion. He is said still to drive his old pick-up truck 25 miles for a $2 haircut.

The richest man in Great Britain is reputed to be Sir John Moores CBE, the co-founder (in 1923) and president of the Littlewoods Organisation. In 1973 he was estimated to be worth about £400 million. His first job after leaving school at 14 was as a telephone operator. He was born in Eccles, Lancashire on 25 Jan 1896. Other British-born men to whom fortunes in excess of £1½ billion have been attributed are the 6th Duke of Westminster and Sir James Goldsmith.

Highest incomes

The greatest incomes derive from the collection of royalties per barrel by rulers of oil-rich sheikhdoms who have not abrogated personal entitlement. Shaikh Zayid ibn Sultan an-Nuhayan (b. 1918), head of state of the United Arab Emirates, arguably has title to some $9000 million of the country's annual gross national product.

The highest gross income ever achieved in a single year by a private citizen is an estimated $105 000 000 in 1927 by the Neapolitan-born Chicago gangster Alphonse ('Scarface Al') Capone (1889–1947). This was derived from illegal liquor trading and alky-cookers (illicit stills), gambling establishments, dog tracks, dance halls, 'protection' rackets and vice from 1925–27. There were no convictions from 915 murders by his 'Italian Mob' in south Chicago. On his business card the former 'bouncer' and brothel-keeper described himself as a 'second-hand furniture dealer'. The highest gross earned income in a year by a UK subject is reputedly in excess of £25 million earned by Paul McCartney MBE in the years since 1979.

Proved wills and death duties

Sir John Reeves Ellerman, 2nd Bt (1909–73) left £53 238 370 on which all-time record death duties were payable. This is the highest-valued will ever proved in the United Kingdom. On 29 Apr 1985 the estate of Sir Charles Clore (1904–79) was agreed at £123 million. The Inland Revenue claimed £84 million but settled for £67 million. The greatest will proved in Ireland was that of the 1st Earl of Iveagh (1847–1927), who left £13 486 146.

Richest women

The title of the world's wealthiest woman has been

wrongly conferred upon the recluse Hioleko (b. 1930), widow since October 1986 of Kenji Osano. The US press first estimated her wealth at $25 000 million. In fact much of her husband's wealth was diverted from her. HM the Queen is asserted by some to be the wealthiest woman but few of her assets under the perpetual succession of the Crown are either personal or disposable. The largest amount proved in the will of a woman in the United Kingdom has been the £7 607 168 of the Rt Hon. Countess of Sefton in 1981. Mrs Anna Dodge (later Mrs Hugh Dillman), who was born in Dundee, Scotland, died on 3 June 1970 in the United States, aged 103, and left an estate of £40 million.

The cosmetician Madame C. J. Walker *née* Sarah Breedlove (b. Delta, Louisiana, USA 23 Dec 1867, d. 1919) is reputed to have become the first self-made millionairess. She was an uneducated Negro orphan scrub-woman whose fortune was founded on a hair straightener.

The youngest person ever to accumulate a million dollars was the child film actor Jackie Coogan (b. Los Angeles, USA 26 Oct 1914), co-star with Sir Charles Chaplin (1889–1977) in *The Kid*, made in 1920. Shirley Temple (b. Santa Monica, California, USA 23 Apr 1928), formerly Mrs John Agar Jr, now Mrs Charles Black, accumulated wealth exceeding $1 000 000 before she was 10. Her child acting career spanned the years 1934–9.

Richest families

It has been tentatively estimated that the combined value of the assets nominally controlled by the du Pont family of some 1600 members may be of the order of $150 000 million. The family arrived in the USA from France on 1 Jan 1800. Capital from Pierre du Pont (1730–1817) enabled his son Eleuthère Irénée du Pont to start his explosives company in the United States.

Largest dowry

The largest recorded dowry was that of Elena Patiño, daughter of Don Simón Iturbi Patiño (1861–1947), the Bolivian tin millionaire, who in 1929 bestowed £8 000 000 from a fortune at one time estimated to be worth £125 000 000.

Greatest miser

If meanness is measurable as a ratio between expendable assets and expenditure then Henrietta (Hetty) Howland Green (*née* Robinson) (1835–1916), who kept a balance of over $31 400 000 in one bank alone, was the all-time world champion. Her son had to have his leg amputated because of her delays in finding a *free* medical clinic. She herself ate cold porridge because she was too thrifty to heat it. Her estate proved to be of $95 million.

Return of cash

The largest amount of *cash* ever found and returned to its owners was $500 000 (US) found by Lowell Elliott, 61, on his farm at Peru, Indiana, USA. It had been dropped in June 1972 by a parachuting hijacker. Jim Priceman, 44, assistant cashier at Doft & Co Inc., returned an envelope containing $37·1 million in *negotiable* bearer certificates found outside 110 Wall Street to A. G. Becker Inc. of New York, USA on 6 April 1982. In announcing a reward of $250 Beckers were acclaimed as 'being all heart'.

Greatest bequests

The greatest bequests in a lifetime of a millionaire were those of Ryoichi Sasakawa, chairman of the Japanese Shipbuilding Industry Foundation, who made total donations of 405 732 907 012 yen during the years 1962–84, and the late John Davison Rockefeller (1839–1937), who gave away sums totalling $750 million. The greatest benefactions of a British millionaire were those of William Richard Morris, later the Viscount Nuffield GBE, CH (1877–1963), which totalled more than £30 000 000 between 1926 and his death on 22 Aug 1963. The Scottish-born US citizen Andrew Carnegie (1835–1919)

is estimated to have made benefactions totalling £70 million during the last 18 years of his life. These included 7689 church organs and 2811 libraries. He had started life in a bobbin factory at $1·20 per week.

The largest bequest in the history of philanthropy was the $500 000 000 gift, announced on 12 Dec 1955, to 4157 educational and other institutions by the Ford Foundation (established 1936) of New York, USA.

Highest salary

The highest reported remuneration of any US businessman was $51 544 000 in salary, bonus and stock options received by Mr Frederick W. Smith, board chairman of Federal Express, in 1982. The highest amount in salary in 1987 was $26 300 000 paid in salary, bonuses and stock options to Jim P. Manzi, chairman of the Lotus Development Corp. who are in computer software manufacture.

Britain's top earner was revealed on 6 Oct 1987 to be Christopher Heath, 41, who built up Baring Securities, the Far Eastern dealing branch of Baring Brothers, with 1986–87 earnings of £2 512 596.

Largest cheque ● The largest cheque drawn in Britain was one for £667 571 952·08p drawn on 31 December 1987 signed by Iain Vallance of British Telecom, payable to the Inland Revenue as part of its corporation tax payments. The picture shows Iain Vallance, BT Chairman, and Norris McWhirter, Founder Editor of the *Guinness Book of Records*, with an enlarged replica of the cheque. (Photo: TeleFocus)

Highest fees

The highest-paid investment consultant in the world is Harry D. Schultz, who operates from Monte Carlo. His standard consultation fee for 60 minutes is $2400 on weekdays and $3400 at weekends. His quarterly retainer permitting calls on a daily basis is $28 125. His 'International Harry Schultz Letter', instituted in 1964, now sells at $50 per copy. A life subscription costs $2400.

Golden handshake

In October 1986 it was confirmed that 'being fired well' in US industry can be more lucrative than working, with an alleged severance payment of $32 million to Michael C. Bergerac, former chairman of Revlon. In the United Kingdom, Sir George Jefferson CBE (b. 1921), retiring chairman of British Telecom, became the beneficiary of a £866 088 annuity in June 1988. John Barkshire, former chairman of Mercantile House Holdings was reported in August 1987 to have received between £750 000 and £1 000 000.

PAPER MONEY
Earliest

Paper money is an invention of the Chinese, first tried in

AD 812 and prevalent by AD 970. The world's earliest bank-notes (*banco-sedler*) were issued in Stockholm, Sweden in July 1661, the oldest survivor being one of 5 dalers dated 6 Dec 1662. The oldest surviving printed Bank of England note is one for £555 to bearer, dated 19 Dec 1699, 11·4 × 19·6 cm *(4½ × 7½ in)*.

Largest and smallest

The largest paper money ever issued was the 1-kwan note of the Chinese Ming dynasty issue of 1368–99, which measured 22·8 × 33·0 cm *9 × 13 in.* In October 1983 one sold for £340. The smallest national note ever issued was the 10-bani note of the Ministry of Finance of Romania, in 1917. It measured (printed area) 27·5 × 38 mm *1·09 × 1·49 in.* Of German *Notgeld* the smallest are the 1–3 pfg of Passau (1920–21) measuring 18 × 18·5 mm *0·70 × 0·72 in.*

Highest denominations

The highest denomination notes in circulation are US Federal Reserve bank-notes for $10 000. They bear the head of Salmon Portland Chase (1808–73). None has been printed since July 1944 and the US Treasury announced in 1969 that no further notes higher than $100 would be issued. Only 348 $10 000 bills remain in circulation or unretired.

Two Bank of England notes for £1 000 000 still exist, dated before 1812, but these were used only for internal accounting. In November 1977 the existence of a Treasury £1-million note dated 30 Aug 1948 came to light and it was sold by private treaty for $A18 500 in Australia. On 19 Feb 1987 a 50-tickal overprinted on a 1-tickal dark grey on grey Siamese note of 25 June 1918 was sold at an auction at Spinks in Singapore for $51 000 to Jan Olav Aamlid of Oslo Mynthandel A/S, Norway. The highest issued denominations have been £1000 notes, first printed in 1725, discontinued on 22 Apr 1943 and withdrawn on 30 Apr 1945. At least 16 of these notes were still unretired up to November 1979 (last data to be published). Of these perhaps 10 are in the hands of collectors or dealers.

Lowest denomination

The lowest denomination legal tender bank-note is the 1-sen (or 1/100th of a rupiah) Indonesian note. Its exchange value in mid-1984 was 140 to the new penny.

The lowest denomination Bank of England notes ever printed were the black on pale blue half-crown (now 12½ p) notes in 1941, signed by the late Sir Kenneth Peppiatt. Very few examples have survived and they are now valued at from £750.

Highest circulation

The highest ever Bank of England note circulation in the United Kingdom was £14 400 million worth on 24 Dec 1986—equivalent to a pile 230·34 km *143·13 miles* high in £5 notes.

CHEQUES AND COINS
Largest

The greatest amount paid by a single cheque in the history of banking has been one for Rs. 16 640 000 000, equivalent to £852 791 660, handed over by the Hon. Daniel P. Moynihan, US Ambassador to India in New Delhi, on 18 Feb 1974. An internal US Treasury cheque for $4 176 969 623·57 was drawn on 30 June 1954.

Greatest collection

The highest price paid for a coin collection has been $18 000 000 for 100 484 gold coins of Norwegian, Swedish, Danish and Finnish origin from the period 1873–1926. They were purchased by Jan Olav Aamlid (see above) through Spink & Son in London in June 1988.

Largest hoards

The largest hoard was one of about 80 000 aurei in Brescello near Modena, Italy in 1814, believed to have been deposited c. 37 BC. The numerically largest hoard ever found was the Brussels hoard of 1908 containing *c.* 150 000 coins. A hoard of 56 000 Roman coins was found at Cunetio near Marlborough, Wiltshire on 15 Oct 1978.

On 10 Dec 1986 the Irish High Court ruled that Michael Webb, farmer of Clonmel, Tipperary, have a hoard discovered by him in 1980 returned by the National Museum or be paid £5 225 000 in lieu. He had been offered £9500 for the Christian Derrynaflan chalice and 3 other pieces.

On 20 July 1985 two sons of Mel Fisher found the main cargo of the Spanish *Nuestra Senhora de Atocha* sunk off Key West, Florida, USA in 1622. The value of the cargo already recovered has been $80 million but is now expected to be close to $400 million, mainly in silver bars.

The greatest discovery of treasure is the estimated $2000 million of gold coins and platinum ingots from the sunken Tsarist battleship *Admiral Nakhimov* (8524 tonnes) 60 m *200 ft* down off the Japanese island of Tsushima. She sank on 27 May 1905. A figure of $2000 million has also been ascribed to the *San Jose* which sank in 210–365 m *700–1200 ft* of water off Colombia in 1708. Diving began in August 1984.

Largest mint

The largest mint in the world is the US Treasury's mint built from 1965–9 on Independence Mall, Philadelphia, covering 4·65 ha *11½ acres* with an annual production capacity on a 3-shift 7-day week of 8000 million coins. A single stamping machine can produce coins at a rate of 10 000 per hour.

Charity fund raising

The globally televised 'Live Aid' concerts, organised by Bob Geldof and Bill Graham, with 60 rock acts in Philadelphia and London on 13 July 1985, raised £35 million within 2 weeks. The estimated viewership, via a record 12 satellites, was 1·6 billion or one-third of the world's population. The 'Sport Aid' event, conceived by Chris Long and organised by Bob Geldof (Hon. KBE), took place in 277 cities in 78 countries on 25 May 1986 and raised a world-wide figure of over £67 million. The greatest recorded amount raised by a charity walk or run is (Can)$24·7 million by Terry Fox (1958–81) of Canada who ran with an artificial leg from St John's, Newfoundland to Thunder Bay, Ontario in 143 days from 12 Apr–2 Sept 1980. He covered 5373 km *3339 miles.*

Longest and most valuable line of coins

The most valuable column of coins amassed for charity was worth £13 628 and was knocked over by Frankie Vaughan at Mecca's Club, Bolton, Lancashire on 18 Aug 1984. The highest-valued line of coins was 16·12 km *10 miles, 5 feet, 7 inches* made up of 662 353 US quarters to a value of $165 788 on 16 Mar 1985 at Central City Park, Atlanta, Georgia, USA, and sponsored by the National Kidney Foundation of Georgia Inc. A line of 1 978 414 one-cent coins 34·425 km *21·391 miles* in length and totalling $19 784·14 was laid by residents and visitors to Boulder City, Nevada, USA on 21 Sept 1985. The longest line of coins laid in Britain was 23·55 km *14·63 miles* long, achieved by friends and pupils of Brumby Comprehensive School, Scunthorpe, South Humberside with 1·3 million 1p coins on 29 Mar 1987. The Copper Mountain, devised by Terry Pitts Fenby for the NSPCC at Selfridges, Oxford Street, London amassed over 3 million coins in 350 days (24 May 1984–7 May 1985), valued at £57 051·34.

LABOUR

Trade union *Oldest*

The oldest of the 84 trade unions affiliated to the Trades Union Congress (founded 1868) is the Educational

---

Oldest coin ● The oldest known coin in the world is the Electra coin of Lydia, Turkey, which dates from around 600 BC (shown here). The oldest known British one is the Westerham type gold stater – this dates from around 95 BC. (Photo: Ancient Art & Architecture Collection)

Institute of Scotland (EIS), founded in Edinburgh on 18 Sept 1847, with 44 596 members.

Largest

The world's largest union has been Solidarność (Solidarity), founded in Poland in November 1980, which by October 1981 was reported to have 8 000 000 members at the time it was outlawed.

The largest union in the United Kingdom is the Transport and General Workers' Union, with 1 348 712 members at 1 Jan 1988. Its peak membership was 2 086 281 in 1979.

Smallest

The ultimate in small unions was the Jewelcase and Jewellery Display Makers Union (JJDMU) founded in 1894. It was dissolved on 31 Dec 1986 by its general secretary, Charles Evans. The motion was seconded by Fergus McCormack, its only surviving member.

Longest name

The union with the longest name is the International Association of Marble, Slate and Stone Polishers, Rubbers and Sawyers, Tile and Marble Setters' Helpers and Marble Mosaic and Terrazzo Workers' Helpers, or the IAMSSPRSTMSHMMTWH of Washington DC, USA.

Labour dispute *Earliest*

A labour dispute concerning monotony of diet and working conditions was recorded in 1153 BC in Thebes, Egypt. The earliest recorded strike was one by an orchestra leader named Aristos from Greece, in Rome *c.* 309 BC. The cause was meal breaks.

Largest

The most serious single labour dispute in the United Kingdom was the General Strike of 4–12 May 1926, called by the Trades Union Congress in support of the Miners' Federation. During the 9 days of the strike 1 580 000 people were involved and 14 500 000 working days were lost.

During the year 1926 a total of 2 750 000 people were involved in 323 different labour disputes and the working days lost during the year amounted to 162 300 000, the highest figure ever recorded. Provisional figures for 1987 were 2 260 000 working days lost involving 785 stoppages with 597 000 workers involved.

Longest

The world's longest recorded strike ended on 4 Jan 1961, after 33 years. It concerned the employment of barbers' assistants in Copenhagen, Denmark. The longest recorded major strike was that at the plumbing fixtures factory of the Kohler Co in Sheboygan, Wisconsin, USA, between April 1954 and October 1962. The strike is alleged to have cost the United Automobile Workers' Union about $12 000 000 to sustain.

Britain's most protracted national strike was called by the National Union of Mineworkers from 8 Mar 1984 to 5 Mar 1985. HM Treasury estimated the cost to be £2625 million or £118·93 per household.

Unemployment *Highest*

The highest recorded percentage unemployment in Great Britain was on 23 Jan 1933, when the total of unemployed persons on the Employment Exchange registers was 2 903 065, representing 22·8 per cent of the insured working population. The peak figure for the post-war period has been 12·3 per cent (3 407 729) on 9 Jan 1986, falling to 9 per cent by the summer of 1988.

Lowest

In Switzerland in December 1973 (pop. 6·6 million), the total number of unemployed was reported to be 81. The lowest recorded peace-time level of unemployment in Britain was 0·9 per cent on 11 July 1955, when 184 929 persons were registered. The peak figure for the employed labour force in the United Kingdom has been 25 520 000 in December 1979.

ASSOCIATION

Oldest club

Britain's oldest gentleman's club is White's, St James's, London, opened *c.* 1697 by Francis White (d. 1711) as a Chocolate House, and moved to its present site in 37 St James's in 1755. This has been described as an 'oasis in a desert of democracy'.

Britain's oldest known dining club is the Charterhouse School Founder's Day Dinner held each twelfth of December. The 1984 dinner to commemorate Old Etonian coal-owner Thomas Sutton (1532–1611) was the 358th.

London clubland's most senior member is Sir Walter

Howard MBE who joined the United Oxford and Cambridge University Club in 1912 and who was born in 1888.

ENERGY CONSUMPTION

To express the various forms of available energy (coal, liquid fuels and water power, etc., but omitting vegetable fuels and peat), it is the practice to convert them all into terms of coal.

The highest consumption in the world is in the United States, with an average of 13 011 kg *255·6 cwt* per person per annum. With only 5·3 per cent of the world's population, the USA consumes 44 per cent of the world's gasoline and 32·9 per cent of the world's electric power. The UK average was 5956 kg *117·2 cwt* per person in 1987. The lowest recorded average was in 1974 at 13 kg *28·6 lb* per person in Rwanda.

MASS COMMUNICATIONS

Airline

The country with the busiest airlines system is the United States of America where 404 307 784 000 revenue passenger miles were flown on larger US certificated air carriers in domestic operations in 1987. This was equivalent to an annual trip of 2685 km *1668 miles* for every one of the inhabitants of the USA. United Kingdom airlines flew 705 424 000 km *438 330 086 miles* and carried 87 517 397 passengers on all services excluding air taxi operations in 1987. The longest air ticket was one of 12 m *39 ft 4½ in* issued for $4500 to M. Bruno Leunen of Brussels, Belgium in December 1984 for an 85 623 km *53 203 mile* trip on 80 airlines with 109 stopovers.

Merchant shipping

The world total of merchant shipping, excluding vessels of less than 100 gross tonnage, sailing vessels and barges, was 75 240 vessels of 403 498 122 gross tonnage on 1 July 1987. The largest merchant fleet in the world as at mid-1987 was that under the flag of Liberia with 1574 ships of 51 412 029 gross tonnage. The UK figure for mid-1987 was 2165 ships of 8 504 605 gross tonnage.

Largest and busiest ports

Physically, the largest port in the world is the Port of New York and New Jersey, USA. The port has a navigable waterfront of 1215 km *755 miles* (474 km *295 miles* in New Jersey) stretching over 238 km² *92 miles²*. A total of 261 general cargo berths and 130 other piers gives a total berthing capacity of 391 ships at one time. The total warehousing floor space is 170·9 ha *422·4 acres*. The world's busiest port and largest artificial harbour is Rotterdam-Europoort in the Netherlands which covers 100 km² *38 miles²* with 122·3 km *76 miles* of quays. It handled 22 600 sea-going vessels carrying a total of 255 million tonnes of sea-going cargo, and about 182 000 barges in 1986. It is able to handle 310 sea-going vessels simultaneously of up to 318 000 tonnes and 21·96 m *72 ft* draught.

Railways

The country with the greatest length of railway is the United States, with 296 489 km *184 235 miles* of track. The farthest anyone can get from a railway on the mainland island of Great Britain is 155·6 km *97·3 miles* by road in the case of Southend, Mull of Kintyre. The number of journeys made on British Rail in the 12 months to 31 Mar 1988 was 727 000 000 (average 45·5 km *28·3 miles*) compared with the peak year of 1957, when 1101 million journeys (average 33 km *20·51 miles*) were made.

Road *Mileages*

The country with the greatest length of road is the United States (all 50 states), with 6 263 210 km *3 891 781 miles* of graded roads at 31 Dec 1986. Regular driving licences are issuable at 15 without a driver education course only in Hawaii and Mississippi. Thirteen US states issue restricted juvenile licences at 14. Great Britain has 352 292 km *218 904 miles* of road including 2980 km *1851 miles* of motorway at June 1988, and 22 151 831 vehicles as at December 1987.

The first sod on Britain's first motorway, the M6 Preston bypass, was cut by bulldozer driver Fred Hackett on 12 June 1956 on the section between junctions 29 and 32 opened in December 1958. Britain's longest uninterrupted dual carriageway is from Plymouth to Exeter (A38) and thence by the M5 and M6 for 829 km *515 miles* terminating at Dunblane Fourways Restaurant, Stirling, Scotland. The oldest of the 46 motorway service stations is Watford Gap on the M1, opened on 2 Nov 1959.

Oldest

The oldest known trackway is the Sweet Way in the Somerset levels, England dated to *c*. 4000 BC.

Widest

The widest street in the world is the Monumental Axis running for 2·4 km *1½ miles* from the Municipal Plaza to the Plaza of the Three Powers in Brasilia, the capital of Brazil. The 6-lane boulevard was opened in April 1960 and is 250 m *273·4 yd* wide. The San Francisco–Oakland Bay Bridge Toll Plaza has 23 lanes (17 west-bound) serving the Bridge in Oakland, California, USA.

The only instance of 17 carriageway lanes side by side in Britain occurs on the M61 at Linnyshaw Moss, Worsley, Greater Manchester.

Longest

The longest motorable road in the world is the Pan-American Highway, from north-west Alaska to Santiago, Chile, thence eastward to Buenos Aires, Argentina and terminating in Brasilia, Brazil. There remains a gap known as the Tapon del Darién, in Panama and the Atrato Swamp, Colombia. This was first traversed by the Land Rover *La Cucaracha Carinosa* (The Affectionate Cockroach) of the Trans-Darién Expedition 1959–60 crewed by former SAS man Richard E. Bevir (UK) and engineer Terence John Whitfield (Australia). They left Chepo, Panama on 3 Feb 1960 and reached Quibdó, Colombia on 17 June, averaging 201 m *220 yd* per hour of indescribable difficulty. Garry Sowerby (Canada), with Tim Cahill (USA) as co-driver and navigator, drove a 1988 GMC Sierra K3500 4-wheel-drive pick-up truck powered by a 6·2 litre V8 Detroit diesel engine from Ushuaia, Tierra del Fuego, Argentina to Prudhoe Bay, Alaska, USA, a distance of 23 720 km *14 739 miles*, in a total elapsed time of 23 days 22 hr 43 min from 29 Sept to 22 Oct 1987. The vehicle and team were surface freighted from Cartagena, Colombia to Balboa, Panama so as to by-pass the Darién Gap.

Highest

The highest trail in the world is a 13 km *8 mile* stretch of the Kang-ti-suu between Khaleb and Hsin-chi-fu, Tibet which in two places exceeds 6080 m *20 000 ft*. The highest carriageable road in the world is one 1180 km *733·2 miles* long between Tibet and south-western Sinkiang, completed in October 1957, which takes in passes of an altitude up to 5632 m *18 480 ft* above sea level. Europe's highest pass (excluding the Caucasian passes) is the Col de Restefond (2802 m *9193 ft*), completed in 1962 with 21 hairpins between Jausiers and Saint Etienne-de-Tinée, France. It is usually closed between early October and early June. The highest motor road in Europe is the Pico de Veleta in the Sierra Nevada, southern Spain. The shadeless climb of 36 km *22·4 miles* brings the motorist to 3469 m *11 384 ft* above sea level and became, on completion of a road on its southern side in 1974, arguably Europe's highest 'pass'.

The highest road in the United Kingdom is the A6293 unclassified tarmac private extension at Great Dun Fell, Cumbria (847 m *2780 ft*) leading to a Ministry of Defence and Air Traffic Control installation. A permit is required to use it. The highest public classified road in England is the A689 at Killhope Cross (626 m *2056 ft*) on the Cumbria–Durham border near Nenthead. The highest classified road in Scotland is the A93 road over the Grampians through Cairnwell, a pass between Blairgowrie, Perthshire and Braemar, Aberdeenshire, which reaches a height of 670 m *2199 ft*. The highest classified road in Wales is the Rhondda-Afan inter-valley road

(A4107), which reaches 533 m *1750 ft* 4 km *2½ miles* east of Abergwynfi, Mid Glamorgan. An estate track exists to the summit of Ben a'Bhuird (1176 m *3860 ft*) in Grampian, Scotland. The highest motorway in Great Britain is the trans-Pennine M62, which, at the Windy Hill interchange, reaches an altitude of 371 m *1220 ft*. Its Dean Head cutting is the deepest roadway cutting in Europe at 55·7 m *183 ft*.

Lowest

The lowest road in the world is that along the Israeli shores of the Dead Sea, 393 m *1290 ft* below sea level. The world's lowest 'pass' is Rock Reef Pass, Everglades National Park, Florida, USA which is 91 cm *3 ft* above sea level.

The lowest surface roads in Great Britain are just below sea level in the Holme Fen area of Cambridgeshire.

Street *Longest*

The longest designated street in the world is Yonge Street running north and west from Toronto, Canada. The first stretch, completed on 16 Feb 1796, ran 55·783 km *34 miles 53 chains*. Its official length now extended to Rainy River at the Ontario–Minnesota border is 1896·2 km *1178·3 miles*.

The longest designated road in Great Britain is the A1 from London to Edinburgh, of 650 km *404 miles*. The longest Roman road was Watling Street, from Dubrae (Dover), 346 km *215 miles* through Londinium (London) to Viroconium (Wroxeter), and Fosse Way, which ran 350 km *218 miles* from Lindum (Lincoln) through Aquae Sulis (Bath) to Isca Dumnoniorum (Exeter). However, a 16 km *10 mile* section of Fosse Way between Ilchester and Seaton remains indistinct.

Commonest name

The commonest street name in Greater London is High Street (122) followed by Station Road (100).

Narrowest

The world's narrowest street is in the village of Ripatransone in the Marche region of Italy. It is called Vicolo della Virilita (Virility Alley) and is 43 cm *16·9 in* wide.

Shortest

The title of 'The Shortest Street in the World' is claimed by Bacup in Lancashire where 'Elgin Street', situated by the old market ground, measures just 5·18 m *17 ft 0 in*. It is not a carriageway, but a railed close.

Steepest

The steepest street in the world is Baldwin Street, Dunedin, New Zealand which has been surveyed to have a maximum gradient of 1 in 1·266. Britain's steepest motorable road is the unclassified Chimney Bank at Rosedale Abbey, North Yorkshire which is signposted '1 in 3'. The county surveyor states that it is 'not quite' a 33 per cent gradient. Of the 5 unclassified roads with 1 in 3 gradients the most severe is Hard Knott Pass between Boot and Ambleside, Cumbria.

Traffic volume *Highest*

The highest traffic volume of any point in the world is at the East Los Angeles interchange (Santa Ana, Pomona, Golden State, Santa Monica, Hollywood and San Bernardino Freeways), California, USA with a 24-hr average on weekdays of 522 020 vehicles—363 per minute. The most heavily travelled stretch of road is Route 101 Junction Route 405 Sherman Oaks and Haverhurst Ave, Encino, Los Angeles, California, with a weekday traffic volume of 288 000 vehicles.

The territory with the highest traffic density in the world is Hong Kong. By 1 Jan 1984 there were 302 118 motor vehicles on 1253 km *778·9 miles* of serviceable roads giving a density of 4·14 m *4·53 yd* per vehicle. The comparative figure for the United Kingdom in 1984 was 19·60 m *21·44 yd*. The world's busiest bridge is the Howrah Bridge across the river Hooghly in Calcutta. In addition to 57 000 vehicles a day it carries an incalculable number of pedestrians across its 457 m *1500 ft* long 21·9 m *72 ft* wide span.

The greatest traffic density at any one point in Great Britain is at Hyde Park Corner, London. The flow (including the underpass) for 24 hours in 1983 was 214 000 vehicles. The busiest Thames bridge is Twickenham Bridge, with a 24-hr average of 62 000 vehicles compared with 73 000 for the Dartford Tunnels. Britain's busiest and most heavily travelled motorway is the M25 between junctions 10 and 13 (towards Staines), which carries 160 000 vehicles a day or 58 400 000 per year.

Largest traffic jams

The longest traffic jam ever reported was that of 16 Feb 1980 which stretched northwards from Lyon 176 km *109·3 miles* towards Paris.

The longest in Britain were 2 of 64·3 km *40 miles* on the M1 from Junction 13 (Milton Keynes) to Junction 18 (Rugby) on 5 Apr 1985, and on the M6 between Charnock Richard and Carnforth, Lancashire on 17 Apr 1987 involving 200 000 people and a tailback of 50 000 cars and coaches.

Most complex interchange

The most complex interchange on the British road system is that at Gravelly Hill, north of Birmingham on the Midland Link Motorway section of the M6, opened on 24 May 1972. There are 18 routes on 6 levels together with a diverted canal and river, which consumed 26 000 tonnes of steel, 250 000 tonnes of concrete and 300 000 tonnes of earth, and cost £8 200 000.

Largest telephone ● The world's largest operational telephone was exhibited at the Glasgow Garden Festival, Strathclyde in May 1988. It was 3·96 m *13 ft* high and 4·57 m *15 ft* long, and weighed 3 tonnes. The handset, being 3·05 m *10 ft* long, is hydraulically operated to raise itself into a vertical position.

Longest bypass

The longest bypass in the world is the M25 6-lane London Orbital Motorway at 195·5 km *121½ miles* begun in 1972 and completed on 29 Oct 1986 at an estimated cost of £909 million or £8 million per mile. The first circumnavigation was by Terence Whelan, editor of *Ideal Home*, and Peter Cracknell (navigator).

Longest hill

The longest steep hill on any road in the United Kingdom is on the road westwards from Lochcarron towards Applecross in Ross and Cromarty. In 9·6 km *6 miles* this road rises from sea level to a height of 626 m *2054 ft* with an average gradient of 1 in 15·4, the steepest part of the hill being 1 in 4.

Longest viaduct

The longest elevated road viaduct on the British road system is the 4779 m *2·97 mile* Gravelly Hill to Castle Bromwich section of the M6 in the West Midlands. It was completed in May 1972.

Largest square

The Tian an men (Gate of Heavenly Peace) square in Beijing (Peking), described as the navel of China, extends over 39·6 ha *98 acres*. The Maiden e Shah in Isfahan, Iran extends over 8·1 ha *20·1 acres*.

Oldest square

The oldest London square is Lincoln's Inn Fields, dating to the mid-17th century. The largest is the 2·82 ha *6·99 acre* Ladbroke Square (open to residents only) constructed in 1842–45, while Lincoln's Inn Fields measures 2·76 ha *6·84 acres*.

Traffic lights

Semaphore-type traffic *signals* had been set up in Parliament Square, London in 1868 with red and green gas lamps for night use. It was not an offence to disobey traffic signals until assent was given to the 1930 Road Traffic Bill. Traffic *lights* were introduced in Great Britain with a one-day trial in Wolverhampton on 11 Feb 1928. They were first permanently operated in Leeds, West Yorkshire on 16 Mar and in Edinburgh, Scotland on 19 Mar 1928. The first vehicle-actuated lights were installed by Plessey at the Cornhill–Gracechurch junction, City of London in April 1932.

Parking meters

The earliest ever installed, put in the business district of Oklahoma City, Oklahoma, USA on 19 July 1935, were the invention of Carl C. Magee (US) and reached London in 1958.

Worst driver

It was reported that a 75-year-old male driver received 10 traffic tickets, drove on the wrong side of the road 4 times, committed 4 hit-and-run offences and caused 6 accidents, all within 20 minutes, in McKinney, Texas, USA on 15 Oct 1966.

The most heavily banned driver in Britain was John Hogg, 28, who, in the High Court, Edinburgh on 27 Nov 1975, received 5¾ years in gaol and his 3rd, 4th and 5th life bans for drunken driving in a stolen car while disqualified. For his previous 40 offences he had received bans of 71½ years plus 2 life bans.

Milestone

Britain's oldest milestone *in situ* is a Roman stone dating from AD 150 on the Stanegate, at Chesterholme, near Bardon Mill, Northumberland.

Longest ford

The longest ford in any classified road in England is in Violet's Lane north of Furneux Pelham, Hertfordshire, which measures 903 m *987½ yd* in length.

Inland waterways

The country with the greatest length of inland waterways is Finland. The total length of navigable lakes and rivers is about 50 000 km *31 000 miles*. In the United Kingdom the total length of navigable rivers and canals is 6340 km *3940 miles*.

Longest navigable river

Vessels can ascend on the river Amazon as far as Iquitos, in Peru, for 3598 km *2236 miles* from the Atlantic seaboard. On a National Geographic Society expedition ending on 10 Mar 1969, Helen and Frank Schreider navigated downstream from San Francisco, Peru, a distance of 6187 km *3845 miles* to Bélem.

TELECOMMUNICATIONS
Telephones

The country with the greatest number of telephone lines is the United States, with 114 349 000 lines, equivalent to 483 for every 1000 people. This compares with the British Telecom figure of 23 182 241 (March 1988) (6th largest in the world to the USA, Japan, USSR, West Germany and France), or 406 per 1000 people. The territory with fewest reported telephones is Pitcairn Island with 24.

The city with most access lines is New York City, NY, USA, with 4 337 890 at mid 1987. In 1983 Washington DC reached the level of 1730 telephones per 1000 people.

Longest telephone cable

The world's longest submarine telephone cable is the Commonwealth Pacific Cable (COMPAC), which runs for 15 032 km *9340 miles* from Sydney, Australia via Norfolk Island, Fiji and the Hawaiian Islands to Port Alberni, Canada. It cost about £35 000 000 and was inaugurated on 2 Dec 1963. The final splice was made on 24 Mar 1984.

Longest terrestrial call

A telephone call around the world, over an estimated 158 845 km *98 700 miles* was made on 28 Dec 1985 from, and back to, the Royal Institution, London, during one of the Christmas lectures given by David Pye, Professor of Zoology, Queen Mary College, London. (Cont. p.215)

POSTAGE STAMPS

EARLIEST

Put on sale at GPO 1 May 1840. 1d Penny Black of Great Britain, Queen Victoria, 68 158 080 printed. Available for prepayment of postage on 6 May 1840.

HIGHEST PRICE (TENDER) (WORLD)

$1·1 million. Lady McGill 2 cent local red-brown City Post stamp issued by AJ Dallas Co. in Pittsburgh, Pennsylvania, USA in 1852, sold by Marc Rousso's Coach Investments to a Japanese bank on 9 Oct 1987.

HIGHEST PRICE (AUCTION) (WORLD)

£615 000 (incl. buyer's premium). Baden 9-kr black on blue-green, colour error 1851 from the John R. Boker collection sold by Heinrich Köhler in Wiesbaden, West Germany on 16 Mar 1985.

HIGHEST PRICE (AUCTION) (UK)

£105 000. Norwegian 4-skilling Blue, 1855 block of 39 used—found in Trondheim railway station *c.* 1923 sold by Phillips, London on 5 Mar 1981.

LARGEST PHILATELIC PURCHASE

$11 000 000. Marc Haas collection of 3000 US postal and pre-postal covers to 1869 by Stanley Gibbons International Ltd of London in August 1979.

LARGEST (SPECIAL PURPOSE)

247·5 × 69·8 mm 9¾ × 2¾ in. Express Delivery of China, 1913.

LARGEST (STANDARD POSTAGE)

160 × 110 mm 6·3 × 4·33 in. Marshall Islands 75-cent issued 30 Oct 1979.

SMALLEST

8 × 9·5 mm 0·31 × 0·37 in. 10-cent and 1-peso Colombian State of Bolivar, 1863–6.

HIGHEST DENOMINATION (WORLD)

£100. Red and black, George V of Kenya, 1925–7.

HIGHEST DENOMINATION (UK)

£5. Orange, Victoria, issued 21 Mar 1882. Pink and blue Elizabeth II definitive 2 Feb 1977.

LOWEST DENOMINATION

3000 pengö of Hungary. Issued 1946 when 150 million million pengö = 1p.

RAREST (WORLD)

Unique examples include: British Guiana (now Guyana) 1-cent black on magenta of 1856; Swedish 3-skilling banco yellow colour error of 1855. Gold Coast provisional of 1885 and the US post-master stamp from Boscowen, New Hampshire and Lockport, NY.

RAREST (UK) (Issued for postal use)

11 or 12. 6d dull purple Inland Revenue Edward VII, issued on 14 Mar and withdrawn on 14 May 1904. Only unused specimen in private hands from W. H. Harrison-Cripps sold by Stanley Gibbons for £10 000 on 27 Oct 1972.

WORLD'S WORST DISASTERS

DISASTER	NUMBER KILLED	LOCATION	DATE
Pandemic	75 000 000	Eurasia: The Black Death (bubonic, pneumonic and septicaemic plague)	1347–51
Genocide	c. 35 000 000	Mongol extermination of Chinese peasantry	1311–40
Famine	c. 30 000 000[1]	Northern China	1959–61
Influenza	21 640 000	Worldwide	Apr–Nov 1918
Earthquake	1 100 000	Near East and E. Mediterranean (see p. 60)	c. July 1201
Circular Storm[2]	1 000 000	Ganges Delta Islands, Bangladesh	12–13 Nov 1970
Flood	900 000	Hwang-ho River, China	Oct 1887
Landslides (Triggered off by single earthquake)	180 000	Kansu Province, China	16 Dec 1920
Atomic Bomb	155 200	Hiroshima, Japan (including radiation deaths within a year)	6 Aug 1945
Conventional Bombing[3]	c. 140 000	Tokyo, Japan	10 Mar 1945
Volcanic Eruption	92 000	Tambora Sumbawa, Indonesia	5–7 Apr 1815
Avalanches	c. 18 000[4]	Yungay, Huascarán, Peru	31 May 1970
Marine (Single Ship)	c. 7700	*Wilhelm Gustloff* (25 484 tons) German liner torpedoed off Danzig by USSR submarine S-13 (only 903 survivors)	30 Jan 1945
Dam Burst	c. 5000[5]	Manchhu River Dam, Morvi, Gujaret, India	11 Aug 1979
Panic	c. 4000[6]	Chungking (Zhong qing) China, air raid shelter	c. 8 June 1941
Smog	2850	London fog, England (excess deaths)	5–13 Dec 1952
Tunnelling (Silicosis)	c. 2500	Hawk's Nest hydroelectric tunnel, W. Virginia, USA	1931–35
Industrial (Chemical)	2352[7]	Union Carbide methylisocyanate plant, Bhopal, India	2–3 Dec 1984
Explosion	1963[8]	Halifax, Nova Scotia, Canada	6 Dec 1917
Fire[9] (Single Building)	1670	The Theatre, Canton, China	May 1845
Mining[10]	1572	Hinkeiko Colliery, China (coal dust explosion)	26 Apr 1942
Riot	c. 1200	New York anti-conscription riots	13–16 July 1863
Road[11]	c. 1100	Petrol tanker explosion inside Salang Tunnel, Afghanistan	2 or 3 Nov 1982
Mass Suicide[12]	913	People's Temple cult by cyanide, Jonestown, Guyana	18 Nov 1978
Crocodiles	c. 900	Japanese soldiers, Ramree I., Burma (disputed)	19–20 Feb 1945
Railway	>800	Bagmati River, Bihar, India	6 June 1981
Fireworks	>800	Dauphin's wedding, Seine, Paris	16 May 1770
Tornado	689	South Central States, USA (3 hours)	18 Mar 1925
Aircraft (Civil)[13]	583	KLM-Pan Am Boeing 747 ground crash, Tenerife	27 Mar 1977
Man-eating Animal	436	Champawat district, India, tigress shot by Col. Jim Corbet (d. 1955)	1907
Terrorism	329	Bomb aboard Air-India Boeing 747, crashed into Atlantic south-west of Ireland. Sikh extremists suspected	23 June 1985
Bacteriological & Chemical Warfare	c. 300	Novosibirsk B & CW plant, USSR	Apr–May 1979
Hail	246	Moredabad, Uttar Pradesh, India	20 Apr 1888
Offshore Oil Platform	166[14]	Piper Alpha oil production platform, North Sea	6 July 1988
Submarine	130	*Le Surcouf* rammed by US merchantman *Thomas Lykes* in Caribbean	18 Feb 1942
Helicopter	54	Israel, military 'Sea Stallion', West Bank	10 May 1977
Ski Lift (Cable Car)	42	Cavalese resort, northern Italy	9 Mar 1976
Mountaineering	40[15]	USSR expedition on Mount Everest	Dec 1952
Nuclear Reactor	31[16]	Chernobyl No. 4, Ukraine, USSR	26 Apr 1986
Elevator (Lift)	23	Vaal Reefs gold mine lift fell 1·93 km *1·2 miles*	27 Mar 1980
Lightning	21	Hut in Chinamasa Krael nr Mutari, Zimbabwe (single bolt)	23 Dec 1975
Yacht Racing	19	28th Fastnet Race—23 boats sank or abandoned in Force 11 gale	13–15 Aug 1979
Space Exploration	7	US Challenger 51L Shuttle, Cape Canaveral, Florida, USA	28 Jan 1986
Nuclear Waste Accident	high but undisclosed[17]	Venting of plutonium extraction wastes, Kyshtym, USSR	c. Dec 1957

[1] It has been estimated that more than 5 million died in the post-World War I famine of 1920–1 in the USSR. The USSR government in July 1923 informed Mr (later President) Herbert Hoover that the ARA (American Relief Administration) had since August 1921 saved 20 million lives from famine and famine-related diseases.

[2] This figure published in 1972 for the Bangladeshi disaster was from Dr Afzal, Principal Scientific Officer of the Atomic Energy Authority Centre, Dacca. One report asserted that less than half of the population of the 4 islands of Bhola, Charjabbar, Hatia and Ramagati (1961 Census 1·4 million) survived. The most damaging hurricane recorded was Hurricane Gloria from 26-28 Sept 1985 with estimated insurance losses of £3500 million.

[3] The number of civilians killed by the bombing of Germany has been put variously at 593 000 and 'over 635 000' including some 35 000 deaths in the raids on Dresden, Germany from 13–15 Feb 1945. Total Japanese fatalities were 600 000 (conventional) and 220 000 (nuclear).

[4] A total of 18 000 Austrian and Italian troops was reported to have been lost in the Dolomite valleys of northern Italy on 13 Dec 1916 in more than 100 snow avalanches. Some of the avalanches were triggered by gun-fire.

[5] The dynamiting of a Yangtze Kiang dam at Huayuan Kou by the KMT during the Sino-Japanese war in 1938 is reputed to have resulted in 900 000 deaths.

[6] It was estimated that some 5000 people were trampled to death in the stampede for free beer at the coronation celebration of Czar Nicholas II in Moscow in May 1896.

[7] Certified total true figure obscured by litigation.

[8] Some sources maintain that the final death toll was over 3000 on 6–7 Dec. Published estimates of the 11 000 killed at the BASF chemical plant explosion at Oppau, West Germany on 21 Sept 1921 were exaggerated. The best estimate is 561 killed.

[9] >200 000 killed in the sack of Moscow, freed by the Tartars in May 1571. Worst ever hotel fire 162 killed, Hotel Daeyungak, Seoul, South Korea 25 Dec 1971. Worst circus fire 168 killed Hartford, Conn., USA 6 July 1944.

[10] The worst gold mining disaster in South Africa was when 182 were killed in Kinross gold mine on 16 Sept 1986.

[11] Some estimates ran as high as 2700 victims from carbon monoxide asphyxiation after Soviet military sealed both ends of the 2·7 km 1·7 mile long tunnel. The worst ever years for road deaths in the USA and the UK have been respectively 1969 (56 400) and 1941 (9169). The global aggregate death toll was put at 25 million by September 1975. The world's highest death rate is 29 per 100 000 in 1978 in Luxembourg and Portugal. The greatest pile-up on British roads was on the M6 near Lymm Interchange, near Thelwall, involving 200 vehicles on 13 Sept 1971 with 11 dead and 60 injured.

[12] 22 000 Japanese civilians jumped off a cliff to their deaths in June 1943 during the US Marines assault of the island of Tarawa (now in Kiribati). An unknown proportion may have been under duress of the defending troops.

[13] The crash of JAL's Boeing 747, flight 123, near Tokyo on 12 Aug 1985, in which 520 passengers and crew perished, was the worst single plane crash in aviation history.

[14] Reported figure at time of printing.

[15] According to Polish sources, not confirmed by the USSR. Also 23 died on Mount Fuji, Japan in blizzard and avalanche on 20 Mar 1972.

[16] Explosion at 0123 hrs Soviet European time 26 Apr 1986. The estimates for the eventual death toll vary between 200 and 600 by AD 2026 (per Nikolay Romanenko, Ukrainian Health Minister, on 4 Apr 1987) and 75 000 (per Dr Robert Gale, US bone transplant specialist). Izvestia published an estimate of consequential loss at 8000 million roubles to date on 4 Mar 1988.

[17] More than 30 small communities in a 1200 km² 460 mile² area eliminated from USSR maps since 1958. Possibly an ammonium nitrate-hexone explosion.

Accidents and Disasters

WORST IN THE BRITISH ISLES

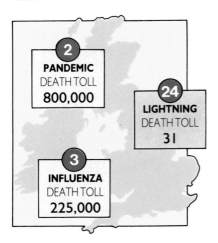

2
PANDEMIC
DEATH TOLL
800,000

3
INFLUENZA
DEATH TOLL
225,000

24
LIGHTNING
DEATH TOLL
31

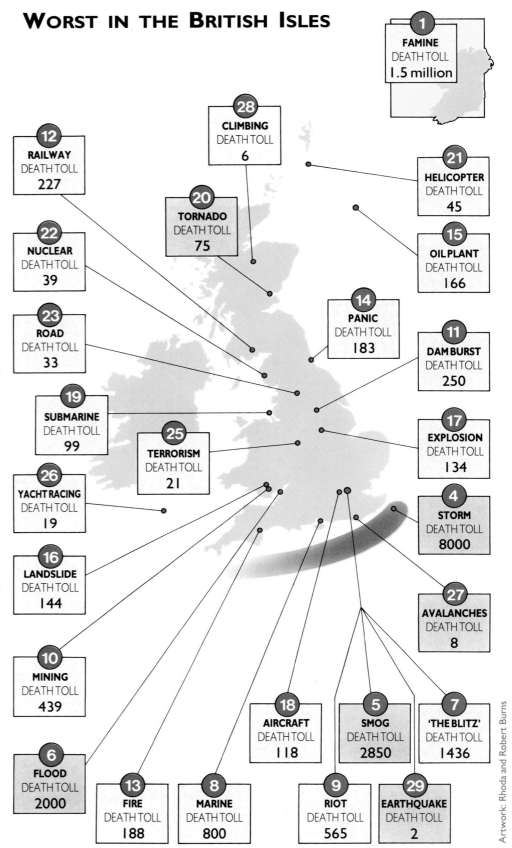

1
FAMINE
DEATH TOLL
1.5 million

28
CLIMBING
DEATH TOLL
6

12
RAILWAY
DEATH TOLL
227

20
TORNADO
DEATH TOLL
75

21
HELICOPTER
DEATH TOLL
45

22
NUCLEAR
DEATH TOLL
39

15
OIL PLANT
DEATH TOLL
166

23
ROAD
DEATH TOLL
33

14
PANIC
DEATH TOLL
183

11
DAM BURST
DEATH TOLL
250

19
SUBMARINE
DEATH TOLL
99

25
TERRORISM
DEATH TOLL
21

17
EXPLOSION
DEATH TOLL
134

26
YACHT RACING
DEATH TOLL
19

4
STORM
DEATH TOLL
8000

16
LANDSLIDE
DEATH TOLL
144

27
AVALANCHES
DEATH TOLL
8

10
MINING
DEATH TOLL
439

6
FLOOD
DEATH TOLL
2000

13
FIRE
DEATH TOLL
188

8
MARINE
DEATH TOLL
800

18
AIRCRAFT
DEATH TOLL
118

5
SMOG
DEATH TOLL
2850

9
RIOT
DEATH TOLL
565

7
'THE BLITZ'
DEATH TOLL
1436

29
EARTHQUAKE
DEATH TOLL
2

DISASTER No. KILLED LOCATION DATE

1 **Famine** 1 500 000[1], Ireland (famine and typhus), 1846–51
2 **Pandemic** (The Black Death) 800 000, 1347–50
3 **Influenza** 225 000, Sept–Nov 1918
4 **Circular Storm** c. 8000, 'The Channel Storm', 26 Nov 1703
5 **Smog** 2850, London fog, 5–13 Dec 1952
6 **Flood** c. 2000[2], Severn Estuary, 20 Jan 1606
7 **Bombing** 1436, London, 10–11 May 1941
8 **Marine** (Single Ship) c. 800[3], HMS *Royal George*, off Spithead, 29 Aug 1782
9 **Riot** 565 (min), London anti-Catholic Gordon riots, 2–13 June 1780
10 **Mining** 439, Universal Colliery, Senghenydd, Mid Glamorgan, 14 Oct 1913
11 **Dam Burst** 250, Bradfield Reservoir, Dale Dyke, near Sheffield, South Yorks (embankment burst), 12 Mar 1864
12 **Railway** 227[4], Triple collision, Quintins Hill, Dumfries & Galloway, 22 May 1915
13 **Fire** (single building) 188[5], Theatre Royal, Exeter, 5 Sept 1887
14 **Panic** (After outbreak of fire) 183, Victoria Hall, Sunderland, Tyne and Wear, 16 June 1883
15 **Offshore Oil Platform** 166[6], Piper Alpha oil production platform, North Sea, 6 July 1988
16 **Landslide** 144, Pantglas coal tip No. 7, Aberfan, Mid Glamorgan, 21 Oct 1966
17 **Explosion** 134[7], Chilwell, Notts (explosives factory), 1 July 1918
18 **Aircraft** (Civil) 118[8], BEA Trident 1C, Staines, Surrey, 18 June 1972
19 **Submarine** 99, HMS *Thetis*, during trials, Liverpool Bay, 1 June 1939
20 **Tornado** 75, Tay Bridge collapsed under impact of 2 tornadic vortices, 28 Dec 1879
21 **Helicopter** 45, Chinook, off Sumburgh, Shetland Islands, 6 Nov 1986
22 **Nuclear Reactor** 39, cancer deaths to 1977 Windscale (now Sellafield), Cumbria, 10 Oct 1957
23 **Road** 33, Coach crash, River Dibb, nr Grassington, North Yorks, 27 May 1975
24 **Lightning** 31, (Annual total) Worst year on record (annual av. 12), 1914
25 **Terrorism** 21, Birmingham pub bombs (IRA), 21 Nov 1974
26 **Yacht Racing** 19, 28th Fastnet Race—23 boats sank or abandoned in Force 11 gale. Of 316 starters only 128 finished, 13–15 Aug 1979
27 **Avalanches** 8, Lewes, East Sussex, 27 Dec 1836
28 **Mountaineering** 6, On Cairngorm, near Braemar (4084 ft), 21 Nov 1971
29 **Earthquake** 2, London earthquake, Christ's Hospital (Newgate), 6 Apr 1580

---

[1] Based on the net rate of natural increase between 1841 and 1851, a supportable case for a loss of population of 3 million can be made out if rates of under-enumeration of 25 per cent (1841) and 10 per cent (1851) are accepted. Potato rot (Phytophthora infestans) was first reported on 13 Sept 1845.

[2] Death tolls of 100 000 were reputed in England and Holland in the floods of 1099, 1421 and 1446.

[3] c. 4000 were lost on HM Troopship Lancastria, 16 243 tons, off St Nazaire on 17 June 1940. The Princess Alice collision in the Thames with the Bywell Castle off Woolwich on 3 Sept 1878 killed 786.

[4] The 194·7 m 213 yd long troop train was telescoped to 61·2 m 67 yd. Signalmen Meakin and Tinsley were sentenced for manslaughter. Britain's worst underground train disaster was the Moorgate Tube disaster of 28 Feb 1975 when 43 persons were killed.

[5] In July 1212, 3000 were killed in the crush, burned or drowned when London Bridge caught fire at both ends. The death toll in the Great Fire of London of 1666 was only 8. History's first 'fire storm' occurred in the Quebec Yard, Surrey Docks, Southwark, London during the 300-pump fire in the Blitz on 7–8 Sept 1940. Dockland casualties were 306 killed. Britain's most destructive fire was that leading to a £165-million loss at the Army Ordnance depot, Donnington, Shropshire in June 1982.

[6] Reported figure at time of printing.

[7] HM armed cruiser Natal blew up off Invergordon killing 428 on 30 Dec 1915.

[8] The worst crash by a UK operated aircraft was that of a Dan-Air Boeing 727 from Manchester which crashed into a mountain on the Canary Islands on 25 Apr 1980 killing 146 people. There were no survivors.

Artwork: Rhoda and Robert Burns

The international telecommunications 'rule', that only one communication satellite be used at a time, was suspended for the demonstration so that both geo-stationary Intelsats, one over the Indian Ocean and one over the Pacific, could be employed. The two 'telephonists', Anieka Russell and Alison Risk, experienced a delay in their conversation of 530 milliseconds.

Telephone directories
The world's most difficult directory to tear in half would be that for Houston, Texas which runs to 2889 pages for 939 640 listings. It is now issued in 2 sections. The easiest would be that for Knippa, Texas—221 listings on 2 pages. The directory for Anguilla in 1972 was of 26 numbers in typescript.

Largest switchboard
The world's biggest switchboard is that in the Pentagon, Washington DC, USA with 25 000 lines handling over 200 000 calls per day through 160 934 km *100 000 miles* of telephone cable. The 1988 phone bill was expected to be $11·2 million.

Optical fibre
The longest distance at which signals have been transmitted without repeaters is 251·6 km *156·3 miles* at the British Telecom research laboratory at Martlesham Heath, Suffolk in February 1985. The laser wavelength was 1525 nm and the rate was 35 megabits/sec.

Postal services
The country with the largest mail in the world is the United States, whose population posted 140·1 billion letters and packages in 1985 when the US Postal Service employed 744 490 people, with the world's largest civilian vehicle fleet of 200 811 cars and trucks. The United Kingdom total was 12 500 million letters and 192·2 million parcels in the year ending 31 Mar 1987. The record day was 15 Dec 1986 with 120 million items when Christmas cards coincided with the British Gas flotation.

The United States also takes first place in the average number of letters which each person posts during one year. The figure was 589 in 1985. The United Kingdom figure was 209 per head in 1986.

Postal address *Highest numbering*
The practice of numbering houses began on the Pont Notre Dame, Paris, France in 1463. The highest-numbered house in Britain is No. 2679 Stratford Road, Hockley Heath, West Midlands, owned since 1964 by Mr and Mrs Howard Hughes. The highest-numbered house in Scotland is No. 2629 London Road, Mount Vernon, Glasgow, which is part of the local police station.

Oldest pillar boxes
A cast iron posting box dating from *c.* 1690 was found at the White Hart coaching inn, Spilsby, Lincolnshire in January 1988. The oldest pillar box still in service in the British Isles is one dating from 8 Feb 1853 in Union Street, St Peter Port, Guernsey. It was cast by John Vaudin in Jersey and was restored to its original maroon livery in October 1981. The oldest box in mainland Britain is at Barnes Cross, Holwell (postally in Bishop's Caundle), Dorset, dating from probably later in 1853. The hexagonal-roofed pillar box in Kent Railway Station, Glanmere, Cork dates from 1857.

Post offices
The Post Office's northernmost post office is at Haroldswick, Unst, Shetland Islands. The most southerly in the British Isles is at Samarès, Jersey. The oldest is at Sanquhar, Dumfries and Galloway, which was first referred to in 1763. In England the post office at Shipton-under-Wychwood, Oxon dates back to April 1845. The highest post office in England is at Flash, Staffordshire at 462·6 m *1518 ft.*

The longest counter in Britain was one of 56·38 m *185 ft* with 33 positions when opened in 1962 at Trafalgar Square, London. Currently the longest is at George Square, Glasgow, being 47·8 m *157 ft* long with 27 positions.

Education

Compulsory education was first introduced in 1819 in Prussia. It became compulsory in the United Kingdom in 1870.

University *Oldest*
The Sumerians had scribal schools or *É-Dub-ba* soon after 3500 BC. The oldest existing educational institution in the world is the University of Karueein, founded in AD 859 in Fez, Morocco. The University of Bologna was founded in 1088.

The oldest university in the United Kingdom is the University of Oxford, which came into being *c.* 1167. The oldest of the existing colleges is probably University College (1249), though its foundation is less well documented than that of Merton in 1264. The earliest college at Cambridge University is Peterhouse, founded in 1284. The largest college at either university is Trinity College, Cambridge, founded in 1546. The oldest university in Scotland is the University of St Andrews, Fife. Established as a university in 1411, theology and medicine may have been taught there since *c.* AD 900.

Greatest enrolment
The university with the greatest enrolment in the world is the University of Rome (founded 1930) which reported 180 000 students in June 1987. Britain's largest university is the University of London with 51 296 internal students and 24 856 external students (1987) so totalling 76 152. The Open University, first called the University of the Air (Royal Charter 30 May 1969), at Walton Hall near Milton Keynes has 5083 part-time tutors and 149 672 students.

Largest
Tenders for the $3·4 billion University of Riyadh, Saudi Arabia closed in June 1978. The university will house 15 000 families and have its own mass transport system.

The largest existing university building in the world is the M. V. Lomonosov State University on the Lenin Hills, south of Moscow, USSR. It stands 240 m *787·4 ft* tall, has 32 storeys and 40 000 rooms. It was constructed from 1949–53.

Most northerly
The world's most northerly university is Inupiat University of the Arctic Barrow, Alaska, USA in Lat. 71° 16′ N. Eskimo subjects feature in the curricula.

Largest court or quadrangle
The largest college quadrangle at any Oxford or Cambridge college is the Great Court, Trinity College, Cambridge, completed in 1605. It averages 99·06 m × 83·2 m *325 ft × 273 ft.*

Professor *Youngest*
William Sidis (b. 1 Apr 1898, d. 1944), the mathematical and linguistic prodigy, entered Harvard University, Boston, USA aged 11 years 6 months, and at 17 was appointed Professor of Mathematics at Rice University, Houston, Texas, USA. The youngest at which anybody has been elected to a chair in a British university is 19 years in the case of Colin MacLaurin (1698–1746), who was elected to Marischal College, Aberdeen as Professor of Mathematics on 30 Sept 1717. In 1725 he was made Professor of Mathematics at Edinburgh University on the recommendation of Sir Isaac Newton, who was a professor at Cambridge aged 26. Henry Phillpotts (1778–1869) became a don at Magdalen College, Oxford on 25 July 1795 aged 17 years 80 days.

Most durable
Dr Joel Hildebrand (1881–1983), Professor Emeritus of Physical Chemistry at the University of California, Berkeley, USA, first became an assistant professor in 1913 and published his 275th research paper 68 years later in 1981. The longest period for which any professorship has been held in Britain is 63 years in the case of Thomas Martyn (1735–1825), Professor of Botany at Cambridge University from 1762 until his death. The last professor-for-life was the pathologist Professor Henry Roy Dean (1879–1961) for his last 39 years at Cambridge.

Senior Wranglers
Since 1910, the Wranglers (first-class honours students in the Cambridge University mathematical Tripos, part 2) have been placed in alphabetical order only. In 1890 Miss Philippa Garrett Fawcett (d. 1948) in Newnham was placed 'above the Senior Wrangler'.

Most graduates in family
Mr and Mrs Albert Kunz of Bloomington, Indiana, USA saw all their 8 daughters and 5 sons graduate from Indiana University between 1932 and 1956.

Youngest undergraduate and graduate
The most extreme recorded case of undergraduate juvenility was that of William Thomson (1824–1907), later Lord Kelvin OM, GCVO, who entered Glasgow University aged 10 years 4 months in October 1834 and matriculated on 14 Nov the same year. Dr Merrill Kenneth Wolf (b. 28 Aug 1931) of Cleveland, Ohio, USA took his BA in music from Yale University in September 1945 in the month of his 14th birthday. Ruth Lawrence (b. 1971) of Huddersfield, West Yorkshire passed Pure Mathematics O level at the age of 9 and Pure Mathematics A level and Grade 1 S level in June 1981, aged 10. She was accepted for entrance to Oxford at the age of 12 and graduated from St Hugh's with a first-class degree, top of 191 entrants, on 4 July 1985.

John Adams, (b. Dec 1977) of Asfordby, Leicestershire was the youngest person to have passed an A level when he achieved a grade C in A level Mathematics aged 10½ years on 1 June 1987 (announced on 13 Aug 1987).

Youngest doctorate
On 13 Apr 1814 the mathematician Carl Witte of Lochau was made a Doctor of Philosophy of the University of Giessen, Germany when aged 12.

School *Oldest in Britain*
The title of the oldest existing school in Britain is contested. It is claimed that King's School in Canterbury, Kent was a foundation of Saint Augustine, some time between his arrival in Kent in AD 597 and his death *c.* 604. Cor Tewdws (College of Theodosius) at Llantwit Major, South Glamorgan, reputedly burnt down in AD 446, was refounded, after an elapse of 62 years, by St Illtyd in 508, and it flourished into the 13th century. Winchester College was founded in 1382. Lanark Grammar School claims to have been referred to in a papal bull drawn up in 1183 by Lucius III.

Largest
In 1983/84 South Point High School, Calcutta, India (founded 1954) had an enrolment of 12 350 regular students.

The school with the most pupils in Great Britain was Exmouth Comprehensive, Devon with 2599 (1983/84). The highest enrolment in Scotland has been at Our Lady's Roman Catholic High School, Motherwell, Lanarkshire with a peak of 2325 in August 1977. The total in Holy Child School, Belfast, Northern Ireland reached 2752 in 1973 before being split up. The highest enrolment in 1986/87 is 2212 at the Methodist College, Belfast.

Most expensive
The annual cost of keeping a pupil at the Oxford Academy (founded 1906), Westbrook, Connecticut, USA for 1987/88 was $23 500. In the academic year 1987/88 St Andrew's Private Tutorial Centre, Cambridge, England (co-founders W. A. Duncombe and C. T. Easterbrook) charged £13 359 for full-time science students (tuition and accommodation). The most expensive school in Great Britain is Millfield (founded 1935) in Street, Somerset (headmaster C. R. M. Atkinson). The annual fee for boarding entries in 1987/88 is £7365. The most expensive girls' school in 1985 was Cobham Hall, near Gravesend, Kent (founded 1960) (headmistress Miss Susan Cameron), with annual fees of £5820.

Earliest comprehensive school
Lakes School, Cumbria, formed from an intake from

Religions

Windermere Grammar School and other Westmorland schools, adopted the non-selective comprehensive principle as early as 1945. Calder High School was established after formal rejection of the 11-plus examinations from 2 West Riding schools in 1950. The earliest purpose built school was Kidbrooke Comprehensive for Girls, in south-east London, opened in 1954.

Oldest old school tie

The practice of wearing distinctive neckties bearing the colours of registered designs of schools, universities, sports clubs, regiments, etc. appears to date from c. 1880. It originated in Oxford University, where boater bands were converted into use as 'ribbon ties'. The earliest definitive evidence stems from an order from Exeter College for college ties, dated 25 June 1880.

Oldest PTA

The parent-teacher association with the earliest known foundation date in Britain is that for Lawrence Sheriff School, Rugby, Warwickshire, formed in 1908.

Most schools

The greatest documented number of schools attended by a pupil is 265 by Wilma Williams, now Mrs R. J. Horton, from 1933–43 when her parents were in show business in the USA.

Most O and A levels

Dr Francis L. Thomason of Hammersmith, London had by August 1986 accumulated 70 O and O/A, 16 A and 1 S levels making a total of 87, of which 36 were in the top grade. A. F. Prime, a prisoner in HM Open Prison Sudbury, accumulated a total of 1 S, 14 As and 34 Os between 1968 and 1982. Environmental difficulties tend to make study harder in prison than elsewhere.

Stephen Murrell of Crown Woods School, Eltham passed 8 A levels at one sitting in June 1978 achieving 7 at grade A. Robert Pidgeon (b. 7 Feb 1959) of St Peter's School, Bournemouth secured 13 O level passes at grade A at one sitting in the summer of 1975. He then passed 3 A levels at grade A and 2 S levels with firsts. Andrew Maclaren (b. 1963) of Chelmsford, Essex passed 14 O levels, 5 A levels, all at grade A and 3 S levels at grade 1—making 22 top grades. At Queens' College, Cambridge he obtained first-class honours in 1983.

Youngest headmaster

The youngest headmaster of a major public school was Henry Montagu Butler (b. 2 July 1833), appointed Headmaster of Harrow School on 16 Nov 1859, when aged 26 years 137 days. His first term in office began in January 1860.

Most durable don

Dr Martin Joseph Routh (b. Sept 1755) was President of Magdalen College, Oxford from April 1791 for 63 years 8 months, until his death in his 100th year on 22 Dec 1854. He had previously been a fellow for 16 years and was thus a don for a span of 79 years.

Most durable teachers

David Rhys Davies (1835–1928) taught as a pupil teacher and latterly as teacher and headmaster of Dame Anna Child's School, Whitton, Powys for a total of 76 years 2 months. Col. Ernest Achey Loftus CBE, TD, DL (1884–1987) served as a teacher over a span of 73 years from May 1901 in York, England until 18 Feb 1975 in Zambia, retiring as the world's oldest civil servant aged 91 years 38 days. His father William was born in Hull in the reign of William IV in 1832.

Elsie Marguerite Touzel (1889–1984) of Jersey began her teaching career aged 16 in 1905 and was teaching at Les Alpes School, Faldonet until her retirement 75 years later on 30 Sept 1980.

Highest endowment

The greatest single gift in the history of higher education has been $125 million to Louisiana State University by C. B. Pennington in 1983.

Religions

Oldest

Human burial, which has religious connotations, is known from c. 60 000 BC among Homo sapiens neanderthalensis in the Shanidar cave, northern Iraq. The earliest named prophet was Zoroaster (Zarathustra) dated to c. 600 BC. He has 250 000 followers today.

Largest

Religious statistics are necessarily only approximate. The test of adherence to a religion varies widely in rigour, while many individuals, particularly in the East, belong to 2 or more religions.

Christianity is the world's prevailing religion, with some 1 619 272 560 adherents in 1987, or 32·9 per cent of the world's population. In 1987 there were 900 545 840 Roman Catholics, or 18·3 per cent of the world's population in the same year.

The largest non-Christian religion is Islam (Muslim) with some 860 000 000 followers in 1987.

In the United Kingdom the Anglicans comprise members of the Established Church of England, the Disestablished Church in Wales, the Episcopal Church in Scotland and the Church of Ireland. The Church of England has 2 provinces (Canterbury and York), 44 dioceses, 10 649 full-time diocesan clergymen and 13 369 parishes (mid-1987).

In Scotland the most numerous group is the Church of Scotland (12 synods, 47 presbyteries), which had 854 311 members as at 1 Jan 1987.

Largest clergies

The world's largest religious organisation is the Roman Catholic Church, with 138 cardinals, 729 archbishops, 3092 bishops, 403 480 priests and 917 432 nuns in 1987.

Jews

The total of world Jewry is estimated to be 16 million. The highest concentration is in the USA with 5 834 650 of whom 1 742 500 are in the New York area. The total in Israel is 3 537 000. The total of British Jewry is 330 000 of whom 201 000 are in London and 11 000 in Glasgow, the largest concentration in Scotland. The total in Tokyo, Japan is only 750.

PLACES OF WORSHIP
Earliest

A sculpted stone face, half primate/half feline, discovered by Dr Leslie Freeman of the University of Chicago in the El Juyo cave shrine, northern Spain, is claimed to be the oldest known religious shrine and is dated to c. 12 000 BC. The oldest surviving Christian church in the world is a converted house in Douro-Europos (now Qal'at es Salihiye) in eastern Syria, dating from AD 232.

Oldest Great Britain

The oldest ecclesiastical building in the United Kingdom is a 6th-century cell built by St Brendan in AD 542 on Eileachan Naoimh (pronounced Noo), Garvelloch Islands, Argyllshire. The church in Great Britain with the oldest origins is St Martin's Church in Canterbury, Kent. It was built in AD 560 on the foundations of a 1st-century Roman church. The chapel of St Peter on the Wall, Bradwell-on-Sea, Essex was built from AD 654–660. The oldest church in Ireland is the Gallerus Oratory, built c. 750 at Ballyferriter, near Kilmalkedar, County Kerry. Britain's oldest nunnery is St Peter and Paul Minster, on the Isle of Thanet, Kent. It was founded c. 748 by the Abbess Eadburga of Bugga. The oldest catholic church is St Etheldreda, Ely Place, Holborn, London, founded in 1251. The oldest non-conformist chapel is the thatched chapel at Horningsham, Wiltshire, dated 1566.

Largest temple

The largest religious structure ever built is Angkor Wat (City Temple), enclosing 162·6 ha 402 acres in Kampuchea, south-east Asia. It was built to the Hindu god Vishnu by the Khmer King Suryavarman II in the period 1113–50. Its curtain wall measures 1280 × 1280 m 1400 × 1400 yd and its population, before it was abandoned in 1432, was 80 000. The whole complex of 72 major monuments, begun c. AD 900, extends over 24 × 8 km 15 × 5 miles. The largest Buddhist temple in the world is Borobudur, near Jogjakarta, Indonesia, built in the 8th century. It is 31·5 m 103 ft tall and 123 m 403 ft square.

The largest Mormon temple is the Salt Lake Temple, Utah, USA dedicated on 6 Apr 1983 and with a floor area of 23 505 m² 253 015 ft² or 5·80 acres.

Largest cathedral

The world's largest cathedral is the cathedral church of the Diocese of New York, St John the Divine, with a floor area of 11 240 m² 121 000 ft² and a volume of 476 350 m³ 16 822 000 ft³. The cornerstone was laid on 27 Dec 1892, and work on the Gothic building was stopped in 1941. Work restarted in earnest in July 1979. In New York it is referred to as 'Saint John the Unfinished'. The nave is the longest in the world at 183·18 m 601 ft in length, with a vaulting 37·79 m 124 ft in height.

The cathedral covering the largest area is that of Santa Mariá de la Sede in Sevilla (Seville), Spain. It was built in Spanish Gothic style between 1402 and 1519 and is 126·18 m 414 ft long, 82·60 m 271 ft wide and 30·48 m 100 ft high to the vault of the nave.

The largest cathedral in the British Isles is the Cathedral Church of Christ in Liverpool. Built in modernised Gothic style, work was begun on 18 July 1904, and it was finally consecrated on 25 Oct 1978 after 74 years (cf. Exeter 95 years) using ½ million stone blocks and 12 million bricks at an actual cost of some £6 million. The building encloses 9687 m² 104 275 ft² and has an overall length of 193·85 m 636 ft. The Vestey Tower is 100·88 m 331 ft high. It contains the highest vaulting in the world—53·34 m 175 ft maximum at undertower, and the highest Gothic arches ever built, being 32·61 m 107 ft at apices.

Smallest

The smallest church in the world designated as a cathedral is that of the Christ Catholic Church, Highlandville, Missouri, USA. Consecrated in July 1983 it measures 4·26 × 5·18 m 14 × 17 ft and has seating for 18 people.

The smallest cathedral in use in the United Kingdom (of old foundation) is the Cathedral of the Isles on the Isle of Cumbrae, Strathclyde which was built 1849–51. The nave measures only 12·19 × 6·09 m 40 × 20 ft and the total floor area is 197·3 m² 2124 ft². Oxford Cathedral in Christ Church (College) is 47·24 m 155 ft long.

Largest church

The largest church in the world is the basilica of St Peter, built between 1492 and 1612 in the Vatican City, Rome. Its length, measured from the apse, is 186·33 m 611 ft 4 in. The area is 15 142 m² 162 990 ft². The inner diameter of the famous dome is 41·98 m 137 ft 9 in and its centre is 119 m 390 ft 5 in high. The external height is 139·52 m 457 ft 9 in.

The elliptical Basilique of St Pie X at Lourdes, France, completed in 1957 at a cost of £2 000 000, has a capacity of 20 000 under its giant span arches and a length of 200 m 656 ft.

The crypt of the underground Civil War Memorial Church in the Guadarrama Mountains, 45 km 28 miles from Madrid, Spain, is 260 m 853 ft in length. It took 21 years (1937–58) to build, at a reported cost of £140 000 000, and is surmounted by a cross 150 m 492 ft tall. The picture on page 218 shows the exterior of this most impressive building.

The largest Church in the United Kingdom is the Collegiate Church of St Peter at Westminster built AD 1050–1745. Its maximum dimensions are overall: length 161·5 m 530 ft; breadth across transept 61·87 m

203 ft and internal height 30·98 m *101 ft 8 in.* The largest parish church is the Parish Church of the Most Holy and Undivided Trinity at Kingston-upon-Hull, covering 2530 m² *27 235 ft²* and with an external length and width of 87·7×37·7 m *288 ft×124 ft.* It is also believed to be the country's oldest brick building serving its original purpose, dating from *c.* 1285. Both the former Cathedral of St Mungo, Glasgow and Beverley Minster, Humberside are now used as parish churches. The largest school chapel is that of the 45·7 m *150 ft* high Lancing College, West Sussex with a capacity of 600.

Smallest church
The world's smallest church is the Union Church at Wiscasset, Maine, USA, with a floor area of 2·92 m² *31½ ft²* (2·13×1·37 m *7×4½ ft*). St Gobban's Church, Portbradden, County Antrim, Northern Ireland measures 3·7×2·0 m *12 ft 1½ in×6 ft 6 in.*

The smallest church in use in England is Bremilham Church, Cowage Farm, Foxley near Malmesbury, Wiltshire which measures 3·65×3·65 m *12×12 ft* and is used for service once a year. The smallest completed mediaeval English church in regular use is that at Culbone, Somerset, which measures 10·66×3·65 m *35×12 ft.* The smallest Welsh chapel is St Trillo's Chapel, Rhôs-on-Sea (Llandrillo-yn-Rhos), Clwyd, measuring only 3·65×1·83 m *12×6 ft.* The smallest chapel in Scotland is St Margaret's, Edinburgh, measuring 5·02×3·20 m *16½×10½ ft,* giving a floor area of 16·09 m² *173¼ ft².*

Largest synagogue
The largest synagogue in the world is the Temple Emanu-El on Fifth Avenue at 65th Street, New York City, NY, USA. The temple, completed in September 1929, has a frontage of 45·72 m *150 ft* on Fifth Avenue and 77·11 m *253 ft* on 65th Street. The sanctuary proper can accommodate 2500 people, and the adjoining Beth-El Chapel seats 350. When all the facilities are in use, more than 6000 people can be accommodated.

The largest synagogue in Great Britain is the Edgware Synagogue, Barnet, London, completed in 1959, with a capacity of 1630 seats. That with the highest registered membership is Ilford Synagogue with 2492 at 1 Jan 1983.

Largest mosque
The largest mosque ever built was the now ruinous al-Malawiya mosque of al-Mutawakil in Samarra, Iraq built from AD 842–52 and measuring 3·72 ha *9·21 acres* with dimensions of 238·9×156·0 m *784×512 ft.* The world's largest mosque in use is the Umayyad Mosque in Damascus, Syria built on a 2000-year-old religious site measuring 157×97 m *515×318 ft* thus covering an area of 1·52 ha *3·76 acres.* The largest mosque is the Merdeka Mosque in Djakarta, Indonesia, which was begun in 1962. The cupola is 45 m *147·6 ft* in diameter and the capacity is in excess of 50 000 people.

Tallest minaret
The tallest minaret in the world is that for the £134 million Great Hassan II Mosque, Casablanca, Morocco measuring 175·6 m *576 ft.* The Qutb Minar, south of New Delhi, India, built in 1194, is 72·54 m *238 ft* tall.

Oldest pagoda
The oldest pagoda in China is Sung-Yo Ssu in Honan built with 15 12-sided storeys in AD 523, though the 99·3 m *326 ft* tall Shwedagon Pagoda, Rangoon, Burma is built on the site of an 8·2 m *27 ft* tall pagoda of 585 BC.

Longest nave
The longest nave in the United Kingdom is that of St Albans Cathedral, which is 86·86 m *285 ft* long. The central tower of Liverpool's Anglican Cathedral (internal overall length 193·85 m *636 ft*) interrupts the nave with an undertower space.

Tallest spire
The tallest cathedral spire in the world is that of the Protestant Cathedral of Ulm in West Germany. The building is early Gothic and was begun in 1377. The

tower, in the centre of the west façade, was not finally completed until 1890 and is 160·90 m *528 ft* high. The world's tallest church spire is that of the Chicago Temple of the First Methodist Church on Clark Street, Chicago, Illinois, USA. The building consists of a 22-storey skyscraper (erected in 1924) surmounted by a parsonage at 100·5 m *330 ft,* a 'Sky Chapel' at 121·92 m *400 ft* and a steeple cross at 173·12 m *568 ft* above street level.

The highest spire in Great Britain is that of the church of St Mary, called Salisbury Cathedral. The Lady Chapel was built in the years 1220–5 and the main fabric of the cathedral was finished and consecrated in 1258. The spire was added later, *ante* 1305, and reaches a height of 123·13 m *404 ft.* The central spire of Lincoln Cathedral, completed *c.* 1307 and which fell in 1548, was 160·02 m *525 ft* tall.

Stained glass *Oldest*
Pieces of stained glass dated before AD 850, some possibly even to the 7th century, excavated by Professor Rosemary Cramp, were placed into a window of that date in the nearby St Paul's Church, Jarrow, County Durham. The oldest complete stained glass in the world represents the Prophets in a window of the Cathedral of Augsburg, Bavaria, West Germany, dating from the second half of the 11th century. The oldest datable stained glass in the United Kingdom has been represented by a figure of St Michael in All Saints Church, Dalbury, Derbyshire of the late 11th century.

Largest
The largest stained-glass window is the complete mural of the Resurrection Mausoleum in Justice, Illinois, measuring 2079 m² *22 381 ft²* in 2448 panels, completed in 1971. The back-lit glass mural installed in 1979 in the atrium of the Ramada Hotel, Dubai is 41·14 m *135 ft* high. The largest single stained-glass window in Great Britain is the East Window in Gloucester Cathedral measuring 21·94×11·58 m *72×38 ft,* set up to commemorate the Battle of Crécy (1346), while the largest area of stained glass comprises the 128 lights, totalling 2322 m² *25 000 ft²,* in York Minster.

Brasses
The world's oldest monumental brass is that commemorating Bishop Yso von Wölpe in Andreaskirche, Verden, near Hanover, West Germany, dating from 1231. An engraved coffin plate of St Ulrich (d. 973), laid in 1187, was found buried in the Church of SS Ulrich and Afra, Augsburg, West Germany in 1979. The oldest brass in Great Britain is of Sir John D'Abernon (d. 1277) at Stoke D'Abernon, Surrey, dating from *c.* 1320.

A dedication brass dated 24 Apr 1241 in Ashbourne Church, Derbyshire has been cited as the earliest arabic writing extant in Britain.

CHURCH PERSONNEL
Saints
There are 1848 'registered' saints (including 60 St Johns) of whom 628 are Italians, 576 French and 271 from the United Kingdom and Ireland. Of these, 8 came from Cambridge and 7 from Oxford between 1535 and 1645, but none from the House of Commons. Britain's first Christian martyr was St Alban, executed *c.* AD 209. The first US-born saint was Mother Elizabeth Ann Bayley Seton (1774–1821), canonised 14 Sept 1975. The total includes 79 popes.

Most rapidly canonised
The shortest interval that has elapsed between the death of a saint and his canonisation was in the case of St Anthony of Padua, Italy, who died on 13 June 1231 and was canonised 352 days later on 30 May 1232. For the other extreme of 857 years see papal table.

Bishopric *Longest tenure*
The longest tenure of any Church of England bishopric is 57 years in the case of the Rt Reverend Thomas Wilson, who was consecrated Bishop of Sodar and Man on 16 Jan 1698 and died in office on 7 Mar 1755. Of English bishoprics the longest tenures, if one excludes the unsubstantiated case of Aethelwulf, reputedly Bishop of Hereford from 937 to 1012, are those of 47 years by Jocelin de Bohun (Salisbury) 1142–89 and Nathaniel Crew or Crewe (Durham) 1674–1721.

Religions

Bishop *Oldest*

The oldest serving bishop (excluding suffragans and assistants) in the Church of England as at June 1987 was the Right Reverend Richard David Say, Bishop of Rochester, who was born on 4 Oct 1914.

The oldest Roman Catholic bishop in recent years has been Bishop Angelo Teutonico, formerly Bishop of Aversa (b. 28 Aug 1874), who died aged 103 years 276 days on 31 May 1978. He had celebrated mass about 24 800 times. Bishop Herbert Welch of the United Methodist Church, who was elected a Bishop for Japan and Korea in 1916, died on 4 Apr 1969 aged 106.

Youngest

The youngest bishop of all time was HRH the Duke of York and Albany KG, GCB, GCH, the second son of George III, who was elected Bishop of Osnabrück, through his father's influence as Elector of Hanover, at the age of 196 days on 27 Feb 1764. He resigned after 39 years' enjoyment. The youngest serving bishop (excluding suffragans and assistants) in the Church of England is the Reverend Dr David Hope (b. 14 Apr 1940) whose appointment to the See of Wakefield was announced on 2 July 1985. When suffragans and assistants are counted, the youngest is Canon Michael Scott-Joynt, Bishop of Stafford, who was appointed on 21 Apr 1987 aged 44.

Oldest parish priest

Father Alvaro Fernandez (b. 8 Dec 1880, d. 6 Jan 1988) served as a parish priest at Santiago de Abres, Spain from 1919 continuing into his 108th year. The oldest Anglican clergyman, the Reverend Clement Williams (b. 30 Oct 1879), died aged 106 years 3 months on 3 Feb 1986. He lined the route at Queen Victoria's funeral and was ordained in 1904.

Longest service

Rev K. M. Jacob (b. 10 July 1880) was made a deacon in the Marthoma Syrian Church of Malabar in Kerala, southern India in 1897. He served his church until his death on 28 Mar 1984, 87 years later.

The longest Church of England incumbency on record is one of 75 years 357 days by the Reverend Bartholomew Edwards, Rector of St Nicholas, Ashill, Norfolk from 1813 to 1889. There appears to be some doubt as to whether the Reverend Richard Sherinton was installed at Folkestone from 1524 or 1529 to 1601. If the former is correct it would surpass the Norfolk record. The parish of Farrington, Hampshire had only 2 incumbents in a 122-year period *viz* Reverend J. Benn (28 Mar 1797 to 1857) and Reverend T. H. Massey (1857 to 5 Apr 1919). From 1675 to 1948 the incumbents of Rose Ash, Devon were from 8 generations of the family of Southcomb.

Longest-serving chorister

John Love Vokins (b. 19 June 1890) has been a chorister for 91 years. He joined the choir of Christ Church, Heeley, Sheffield in 1895 and that of St Michael's, Hathersage 35 years later.

Oldest warden

Having become a chorister in 1876 at the age of 9, Thomas Rogers was appointed vicar's warden in 1966 at Montacute, Somerset, aged 99.

Sunday school

Sunday schools were established by Congregationalists in Neath and Tirdwyncyn, Wales in 1697. Roland E. Daab (b. 25 Mar 1914) now of St Paul United Church of Christ, Columbia, Illinois, USA has attended for 3600 consecutive Sundays without a miss for 69 years to 22 Nov 1987.

Largest and smallest parishes

The smallest parish in the United Kingdom is The Scares, which consists of rocky islets in Luce Bay with an area of 0·44 ha *1·10 acres* and is included in Wigtown, Dumfries and Galloway.

In 1982 the parish of Dallinghoo Wield, Suffolk boasted a population of nil and an area of 14·6 ha *38 acres.*

The largest parish is Kilmonivaig in Inverness-shire with an area of 108 145·46 ha *267 233·03 acres.*

Oldest parish register

The oldest part of any parish register surviving in England contains entries from the summer of 1538. There is a sheet from that of Alfriston, East Sussex recording a marriage on 10 July 1504 but this is amid entries from 1547. Scotland's oldest surviving register is that for Anstruther-Wester, Fife, with burial entries from 1549.

Largest crowds

The greatest recorded number of human beings assembled with a common purpose was an estimated 12 700 000 at the Hindu festival of Kumbh-Mela, which

> **Longest crypt** ● The crypt of the underground Civil War Memorial Church in the Guadarrama Mountains, 45 km *28 miles* from Madrid, Spain, is 260 m *853 ft* in length. It is surmounted by a cross 150 m *492 ft* tall. (Photo: Robert Harding)

was held at the confluence of the Yamuna (formerly called the Jumna), the Ganges and the invisible 'Sarasvati' at Allahabad, Uttar Pradesh, India on 19 Jan 1977. The holiest time during this holiest day since 1833 was during the planetary alignment between 9.28 and 9.40 a.m. during which only 200 000 achieved immersion to wash away the sins of a lifetime.

Largest funerals

The funeral of the charismatic C. N. Annadurai (d. 3 Feb 1969), Madras Chief Minister, was, according to a police estimate, attended by 15 million.

The longest funeral in Britain was probably that of Vice Admiral Viscount Nelson on 9 Jan 1806. Ticket-holders were seated in St Paul's Cathedral by 8.30 a.m. Many were unable to leave until after 9 p.m. The queue at the grave of the chansonnier and guitarist Vladimir Visotsky (d. 28 July 1980), stretched 10 km *6·2 miles.*

Biggest demonstrations

A figure of 2·7 million was published from China for the demonstration against the USSR in Shanghai on 3–4 Apr 1969 following the border clashes, and one of 10 million for the May Day celebrations of 1963 in Peking.

Gymnastics/Aerobics display ● The annual Czechoslovak Spartakiad features gymnastics displays by about 180 000 participants. Held at the Strahov Stadium, Prague, there are 200 000 spectators for each of the four days. On the six hectare infield there are markers for 13 824 gymnasts at a time.

General Records

The origins of sport stem from the time when self-preservation ceased to be the all-consuming human preoccupation. Archery, although a hunting skill in Mesolithic times (by c. 8000 BC), did not become an organised sport until later, possibly as early as c. 1150 BC, as an archery competition is described in Homer's *Iliad*, and certainly by c. AD 300, among the Genoese. The earliest dated evidence is c. 2750–2600 BC for wrestling. Ball games by girls depicted on Middle Kingdom murals at Beni Hasan, Egypt have been dated to c. 2050 BC.

Fastest

The highest speed reached in a non-mechanical sport is in sky-diving, in which a speed of 298 km/h *185 mph* is attained in a head-down free-falling position, even in the lower atmosphere. In delayed drops speeds of 1005 km/h *625 mph* have been recorded at high, rarefied altitudes. The highest projectile speed in any moving ball game is c. 302 km/h *188 mph* in pelota. This compares with 273 km/h *170 mph* (electronically timed) for a golf ball driven off a tee.

Slowest

In wrestling, before the rules were modified towards 'brighter wrestling', contestants could be locked in holds for so long that a single bout once lasted for 11 hr 40 min. In the extreme case of the 2 hr 41 min pull in the regimental tug o' war in Jubbulpore, India, on 12 Aug 1889, the winning team moved a net distance of 3·6 m *12 ft* at an average speed of 0·00135 km/h *0·00084 mph.*

Longest

The most protracted sporting contest was an 'Earth-Moon' automobile duration test of 358 273 km *222 621 miles* (equivalent to 8·93 times around the equator) by Appaurchaux and others in a Ford Taunus 12M at

Largest sports contract ● In March 1982, the National Football League concluded a deal worth $2000 million for five years' coverage of American Football by the three major TV networks, ABC, CBS and NBC. This represented $14·2 million for each League team. (Photo: All-Sport/Duomo)

the Miranas circuit, France over 142 days in July–Nov 1963. The car averaged 106 km/h *65·33 mph.*

The most protracted human-powered sporting event is the *Tour de France* cycling race. In 1926 this was over 5743 km *3569 miles*, lasting 29 days, but the duration is now reduced to 21 days.

Largest pitch

The largest pitch of any ball game is that of polo, with 12·4 acres *5·0 ha*, or a maximum length of 300 yd *274 m* and a width, without side boards, of 200 yd *182 m*. With boards the width is 160 yd *146 m*. Twice a year in the Parish of St Columb Major, Cornwall, a game called hurling (not to be confused with the Irish game) is played on a 'pitch' which consists of the entire parish, approximately 25 square miles *64·7 km².*

Youngest and oldest world record breakers

The youngest at which anybody has broken a non-mechanical world record is 12 yr 298 days for Gertrude Caroline Ederle (USA) (b. 23 Oct 1906) with 13 min 19·0 sec for women's 880 yd freestyle swimming at Indianapolis, USA, on 17 Aug 1919. Gerhard Weidner (West Germany) (b. 15 Mar 1933) set a 20 mile walk record on 25 May 1974, aged 41 yr 71 days. Albert Rayner (GB) (b. 19 Apr 1923) was 59 yr 213 days when he broke the skipping record for most turns of the rope in 10 sec, on 19 Nov 1982.

Youngest and oldest champions

The youngest successful competitor in a world title event was a French boy, whose name is not recorded, who coxed the Netherlands' Olympic pair at Paris on 26 Aug 1900. He was not more than ten and may have been as young as seven. The youngest individual Olympic winner was Marjorie Gestring (USA) (b. 18 Nov 1922), who took the springboard diving title at the age of 13 yr 268 days at the Olympic Games in Berlin on 12 Aug 1936. Oscar Gomer Swahn (Sweden) (1847–1927) was aged 64 yr 258 days when he won a gold medal in the 1912 Olympic Running Deer team shooting competition.

Youngest internationals

The youngest age at which any person has won international honours is eight years in the case of Joy Foster, the Jamaican singles and mixed doubles table tennis champion in 1958. The youngest British international has been diver Beverley Williams (b. 5 Jan 1957), who was 10 yr 268 days old when she competed against the USA at Crystal Palace, London on 30 Sept 1967.

Oldest competitor at major games

William Edward Pattimore (b. 1 Mar 1892) competed for Wales at bowls at the 1970 Commonwealth Games in Edinburgh at the age of 78, the oldest competitor at such an international event open to competitors of all ages. Britain's oldest Olympian was Hilda Lorna Johnstone (b. 4 Sept 1902) who was 70 yr 5 days when she was placed twelfth in the Dressage competition at the 1972 Olympic Games.

Most versatile

Charlotte 'Lottie' Dod (1871–1960) won the Wimbledon singles tennis title five times between 1887 and 1893, the British Ladies' Golf Championship in 1904, an Olympic silver medal for archery in 1908, and represented England at hockey in 1899. She also excelled at skating and tobogganing. Mildred 'Babe' Zaharias (née Didrikson) (1914–56) (USA) won two gold medals (80 m hurdles and javelin) and a silver (high jump) at the 1932 Olympic Games. She set world records at those three events in 1930–32. She was an All-American basketball player for three years and set the world record for throwing the baseball 90·22 m *296 ft*. Switching to golf she won the US Women's Amateur title in 1946 and the US Women's Open in 1948, 1950 and 1954. She also excelled at several other sports. Charles Burgess Fry (GB) (1872–1956) was probably the most versatile male sportsman at the highest level. On 4 Mar 1893 he equalled the world long jump record of 7·17 m *23 ft 6½ in.* He represented England *v.* Ireland at soccer (1901) and played first-class rugby for the Barbarians. His greatest achievements, however, were at cricket, where he headed the English batting averages in six seasons and captained England in 1912. He was also an excellent angler and tennis player.

Most prolific record breaker

Between 24 Jan 1970 and 1 Nov 1977 Vasiliy Alekseyev (USSR) (b. 7 Jan 1942) broke 80 official world records in weightlifting.

Longest reign

The longest reign as a world champion is 33 years (1829–62) by Jacques Edmond Barre (France) (1802–73) at real tennis. The longest reign as a British champion is 41 years by the archer Alice Blanche Legh (1855–1948) who won 23 national titles between 1881 and 1922, the last when she was aged 67.

Shortest reign

Olga Rukavishnikova (USSR) (b. 13 Mar 1955) held the pentathlon world record for 0·4 sec at Moscow on 24 July 1980. That is the difference between her second-place time of 2 min 04·8 sec in the final 800 m event of the Olympic five-event competition, and that of third-placed Nadyezhda Tkachenko (USSR), whose overall points were better, 5083 to 4937.

Heaviest sportsman

The heaviest sportsman of all time was the professional wrestler William J. Cobb of Macon, Georgia, USA, who in 1962 was billed as the 363 kg *(802 lb 57 st 4 lb)* 'Happy Humphrey'. The heaviest player of a ball-game was Bob Pointer, the 221 kg *487 lb* US Football tackle formerly on the 1967 Santa Barbara High School Team, California, USA.

Greatest earnings

The highest-paid woman athlete in the world is tennis player Martina Navratilova (b. 18 Oct 1956) (USA, formerly Czechoslovakia) whose official career earnings passed $13 million in 1988. (Men's; see P.230)

Largest crowd

The greatest number of live spectators for any sporting spectacle is the estimated 2 500 000 who have lined the route of the New York Marathon. However, spread over 21 days, it is estimated that more than 10 000 000 see the annual *Tour de France* cycling race along the route.

The total attendance at the 1984 summer Olympic Games was given as 5 797 923 for all sports, including 1 421 627 for soccer and 1 129 465 for track and field athletics.

The largest crowd travelling to any single sporting venue is 'more than 400 000' for the annual *Grand Prix d'Endurance* motor race on the Sarthe circuit near Le Mans, France. The record stadium crowd was one of 199 854 for the Brazil *v.* Uruguay soccer match in the Maracaña Municipal Stadium, Rio de Janeiro, Brazil on 16 July 1950.

Most participants

An estimated 104 000 runners contested the 77th annual Examiner Bay to Breakers 7·6 mile race in San Francisco in 1986. The 1983 Women's International Bowling Congress Championship tournament attracted 75 480 bowlers for the 83-day event held 7 Apr–1 July at Showboat Lanes, Las Vegas, Nevada, USA.

Worst disasters

The worst sports disaster in recent history was when an estimated 604 were killed after stands at the Hong Kong Jockey Club racecourse collapsed and caught fire on 26 Feb 1918. During the reign of Antoninus Pius (AD 138–161) the upper wooden tiers in the Circus Maximus, Rome collapsed during a gladiatorial combat killing some 1112 spectators. Britain's worst sports disaster was when 66 were killed and 145 injured at the Rangers *v.* Celtic football match at Exit 13 of Ibrox Park Stadium, Glasgow on 2 Jan 1971.

GUINNESS HAVE PUBLISHED **THE ENCYCLOPAEDIA OF SPORTS RECORDS & RESULTS** PETER MATTHEWS AND IAN MORRISON **£9.95**

Aerobatics

The first aerobatic 'manoeuvre' is generally considered to be the sustained inverted flight in a Bleriot of Célestin-Adolphe Pégoud (1889–1915), at Buc, France on 21 Sept 1913, but Lt. Peter Nikolayevich Nesterov (1887–1914), of the Imperial Russian Air Service, performed a loop in a Nieuport Type IV monoplane at Kiev, USSR on 27 Aug 1913.

World Championships

Held biennially since 1960 (excepting 1974), scoring is based on the system devised by Col. José Aresti of Spain. The competition consists of two compulsory and two free programmes. The men's team competition has been won a record six times by the USSR. Petr Jirmus (Czechoslovakia) is the only man to become world champion twice, in 1984 and 1986. Betty Stewart (USA) won the women's competition in 1980 and 1982. Lidia Leonova (USSR) won a record three medals: first in 1976, second in 1978 and third in 1972. The only medal achieved by Britain has been a bronze in the team event at Kiev, USSR in 1976. The highest individual placing by a Briton is fourth by Neil Williams (1935–1977) in 1976.

Inverted flight

The duration record for inverted flight is 4 hr 9 min 5 sec by John 'Hal' McClain in a Swick Taylorcraft on 23 Aug 1980 over Houston International Raceways, Texas, USA.

Loops

On 21 June 1980, R. Steven Powell performed 2315⅚ inside loops in a Bellanca Decathalon over Almont, Michagan, USA. John McClain achieved 180 outside loops in Bellanca Super Decathalon on 2 Sept 1978 over Houston, Texas, USA.

Ken Ballinger completed 155 consecutive inside loops in a Bellanca Citabria on 6 Aug 1983 over Staverton Airport, Cheltenham, Gloucestershire.

American Football

American football, a direct descendant of the British games of soccer and rugby, evolved at American universities in the 19th century. The first match under the Harvard Rules was played by Harvard against McGill University of Montreal at Cambridge, Mass., USA in 1874. The Intercollegiate Football Association was founded in 1876.

The professional game dates from August 1895 when Latrobe played Jeanette at Latrobe, Pennsylvania. The American Professional Football Association was formed in 1919. This became the National Football League (NFL) in 1922. The American Football League (AFL) was formed in 1960; the NFL and AFL merged in 1970.

Super Bowl

First held in 1967 between the winners of the NFL and the AFL. Since 1970 it has been contested by the winners of the National and American Conferences of the NFL. Pittsburgh Steelers have most wins, four, 1975–6 and 1979–80. The highest aggregate score was in 1979 when Pittsburgh beat Dallas Cowboys 35–31. The highest team score and record victory margin was when the Chicago Bears beat the New England Patriots 46–10 at New Orleans, Louisiana on 26 Jan 1986. In their 42–10 victory over the Denver Broncos on 31 Jan 1988, the Washington Redskins scored a record 35 points in the second quarter. The Green Bay Packers won a record 11 NFL titles between 1929 and 1967.

College football *Highest team score*

Georgia Tech, Atlanta, Georgia scored 222 points, including a record 32 touchdowns, against Cumberland

---

PROFESSIONAL RECORDS
(NFL 1920–87, AFL 1960–9)

MOST POINTS

Career 2002, George Blanda (Chicago Bears, Baltimore Colts, Houston Oilers, Oakland Raiders), 1949–75. **Season** 176, Paul Hornung (Green Bay Packers), 1960. **Game** 40, Ernie Nevers (Chicago Cardinals), 28 Nov 1929.

MOST TOUCHDOWNS

Career 126, Jim Brown (Cleveland Browns), 1957–65. **Season** 24, John Riggins (Washington Redskins), 1983. **Game** 6: Ernie Nevers (Chicago Cardinals), 28 Nov 1929; William 'Dub' Jones (Cleveland Browns) 25 Nov 1951; Gale Sayers (Chicago Bears), 12 Dec 1965.

MOST YARDS GAINED RUSHING

Career 16 726, Walter Payton (Chicago Bears), 1975–88. **Season** 2105, Eric Dickerson (Los Angeles Rams), 1984. **Game** 275, Walter Payton (Chicago Bears), 20 Nov 1977.

MOST YARDS GAINED PASSING

Career 47 003, Fran Tarkenton (Minnesota Vikings, New York Giants), 1961–78. **Season** 5084, Dan Marino (Miami Dolphins), 1984. **Game** 554, Norm Van Brocklin (Los Angeles Rams), 28 Sept 1951.

MOST PASSES COMPLETED

Career 3686, Fran Tarkenton (Minnesota Vikings, New York Giants), 1961–78. **Season** 378, Dan Marino (Miami Dolphins), 1986. **Game** 42, Richard Todd (New York Jets), 21 Sept 1980.

PASS RECEPTIONS

Career 759, Steve Largent (Seattle Seahawks), 1975–88. **Season** 106, Art Monk (Washington Redskins), 1984. **Game** 18, Tom Fears (Los Angeles Rams), 3 Dec 1950.

FIELD GOALS

Career 373, Jan Stenerud (Kansas City Chiefs, Green Bay Packers, Minnesota Vikings), 1967–85. **Season** 35, Ali Haji-Sheikh (New York Giants), 1983. **Game** 7, Jim Bakken (St Louis Cardinals), 24 Sept 1967.

SUPER BOWL INDIVIDUAL RECORDS

POINTS 18	Roger Craig (San Francisco 49ers) 1985	
TOUCHDOWNS 3	Roger Craig (San Francisco 49ers) 1985	
YARDS GAINED RUSHING 204	Timmy Smith (Washington Redskins) 1988	
YARDS GAINED PASSING 340	Doug Williams (Washington Redskins) 1988	
PASSES COMPLETED 29	Dan Marino (Miami Dolphins) 1985	
PASS RECEPTIONS 11	Dan Ross (Cincinnati Bengals) 1982	
FIELD GOALS 4	Don Chandler (Green Bay Packers) 1968	
	Ray Wersching (San Francisco 49ers) 1982	

University, Lebanon, Tennessee (nil) in one game on 7 Oct 1916.

In Britain

The premier competition in Britain is the Budweiser Bowl which was inaugurated in 1986. It has been won twice by the London Ravens, 1986 and 1987.

The highest score, in a game in Britain, is by the East Kent Cougars, based in Folkestone, who beat the Maidstone M20's, 148-6 at Mote Park, Maidstone, Kent on 15 May 1988.

Angling

Oldest existing club

The Ellem fishing club was formed by a number of Edinburgh and Berwickshire gentlemen in 1829. Its first annual general meeting was held on 29 Apr 1830.

Largest single catch

The largest officially ratified fish ever caught on a rod was a man-eating Great white shark (*Carcharodon carcharias*) weighing 1208 kg *2664 lb* and measuring 5·13 m *16 ft 10 in* long, caught on a 58 kg *130 lb* test line

by Alf Dean at Denial Bay, near Ceduna, South Australia on 21 Apr 1959. A Great white shark weighing 1537 kg *3388 lb* was caught by Clive Green off Albany, Western Australia on 26 Apr 1976 but will remain unratified as whale meat was used as bait. The biggest ever rod-caught fish by a British angler is a 571·5 kg *1260 lb* Black marlin, by Edward A. Crutch off Cairns, Queensland, Australia on 19 Oct 1973.

In June 1978 a Great white shark measuring 6·2 m *20 ft 4 in* in length and weighing over 2268 kg *5 000 lb* was harpooned and landed by fishermen in the harbour of San Miguel, Azores.

The largest marine animal killed by *hand* harpoon was a Blue whale 29·56 m *97 ft* in

WORLD RECORDS; FRESHWATER AND SALTWATER
A selection of all-tackle records ratified by the International Game Fish Association as at June 1986

Species	Weight lb	oz	kg	Name of Angler	Location	Date	
BARRACUDA, GREAT	83	0	37·64	K. J. W. Hackett	Lagos, Nigeria	13 Jan	1952
BASS, EUROPEAN	20	11	9·40	Jean Baptiste Bayle	Stes Maries de la Mer, France	6 May	1986
BASS, LARGEMOUTH	22	4	10·09	George W. Perry	Montgomery Lake, Georgia, USA	2 June	1932
BASS, SMALLMOUTH	11	15	5·41	David L. Hayes	Dale Hollow Lake, Kentucky, USA	9 July	1955
BASS, STRIPED	78	8	35·60	Albert R. McReynolds	Atlantic City, New Jersey, USA	21 Sept	1982
BLUEFISH	31	12	14·40	James M. Hussey	Hatteras, North Carolina, USA	30 Jan	1972
BONEFISH	19	0	8·61	Brian W. Batchelor	Zululand, South Africa	26 May	1962
CATFISH, FLATHEAD	98	0	44·45	William O. Stephens	Lewisville, Texas, USA	2 June	1986
COD, ATLANTIC	98	12	44·79	Alphonse J. Bielevich	Isle of Shoals, New Hampshire, USA	8 June	1969
DOLPHIN	87	0	39·46	Manuel Salazar	Papagallo Gulf, Costa Rica	25 Sept	1976
HALIBUT (Pacific)	350	0	158·76	Vern S. Foster	Homer, Alaska, USA	30 June	1982
JACK, CREVALLE	54	7	24·69	Thomas F. Gibson Jr	Port Michel, Gabon	15 Jan	1982
JEWFISH	680	0	308·44	Lynn Joyner	Fernandina Beach, Florida, USA	20 May	1961
MACKEREL, KING	90	0	40·82	Norton I. Thomton	Key West, Florida, USA	16 Feb	1976
MARLIN, BLACK	1560	0	707·61	Alfred C. Glassell Jr	Cabo Blanco, Peru	4 Aug	1953
MARLIN, BLUE (Atlantic)	1282	0	581·51	Larry Martin	St Thomas, Virgin Islands	6 Aug	1977
MARLIN, BLUE (Pacific)	1376	0	624·14	Jay Wm de Beaubien	Kaaiwi Point, Kona Coast, Hawaii, USA	31 May	1982
MARLIN, STRIPED	494	0	224·10	Bill Boniface	Tutukaka, New Zealand	16 Jan	1986
MARLIN, WHITE	181	14	82·50	Evandro Luiz Coser	Vitoria, Brazil	8 Dec	1979
MUSKELLUNGE	69	15	31·72	Arthur Lawton	St Lawrence River, New York, USA	22 Sept	1957
PIKE, NORTHERN	55	1	25·00	Lothar Louis	Lake of Grefeern, West Germany	16 Oct	1986
SAILFISH (Atlantic)	128	1	58·10	Harm Steyn	Luanda, Angola	27 Mar	1974
SAILFISH (Pacific)	221	0	100·24	C. W. Stewart	Santa Cruz Island, Ecuador	12 Feb	1947
SALMON, ATLANTIC	79	2	35·89	Henrik Henriksen	Tana River, Norway		1928
SALMON, CHINOOK	97	4	44·11	Les Anderson	Kenia River, Alaska, USA	17 May	1985
SALMON, COHO	31	0	14·06	Mrs Lee Halberg	Cowichan Bay, BC, Canada	11 Oct	1947
SHARK, HAMMERHEAD	991	0	449·50	Allen Ogle	Sarasota, Florida, USA	30 May	1982
SHARK, MAKO	1080	0	489·88	James L. Melanson	Montauk, New York, USA	26 Aug	1979
SHARK, PORBEAGLE	465	0	210·92	Jorge Potier	Padstow, Cornwall, England	23 July	1976
SHARK, THRESHER	802	0	363·80	Dianne North	Tutukaka, New Zealand	8 Feb	1981
SHARK, TIGER	1780	0	807·40	Walter Maxwell	Cherry Grove, S. Carolina, USA	14 June	1964
SHARK, WHITE	2664	0	1208·38	Alfred Dean	Ceduna, South Australia	21 Apr	1959
SNAPPER, CUBERA	121	8	55·11	Mike Hebert	Cameron, Louisiana, USA	5 July	1982
SNOOK	53	10	24·32	Gilbert Ponzi	Parasmina Ranch, Costa Rica	18 Oct	1978
STURGEON	468	0	212·28	Joey Pallotta III	Benicia, California, USA	9 July	1983
SWORDFISH	1182	0	536·15	L. Marron	Iquique, Chile	17 May	1953
TARPON	283	0	128·36	M. Salazar	Lake Maracaibo, Venezuela	19 Mar	1956
TROUT, BROOK	14	8	6·57	Dr W. J. Cook	Nipigon River, Ontario, Canada	July	1916
TROUT, BROWN	35	15	16·30	Eugenio Cavaglia	Nahuel Huapi, Argentina	16 Dec	1952
TROUT, LAKE	65	0	29·48	Larry Daunis	Great Bear Lake, NWT, Canada	8 Aug	1970
TROUT, RAINBOW	42	2	19·10	David Robert White	Bell Island, Alaska, USA	22 June	1970
TUNA, BIGEYE (Pacific)	435	0	197·31	Dr Russel V. A. Lee	Cabo Blanco, Peru	17 Apr	1957
TUNA, BLUEFIN	1496	0	679·00	Ken Fraser	Aulds Cove, Nova Scotia, Canada	26 Oct	1979
TUNA, YELLOWFIN	388	12	176·35	Curt Wiesenhutter	San Benedicto I., Mexico	1 Apr	1977
WAHOO	149	0	67·58	John Pirovano	Cat Cay, Bahamas	15 June	1962
WALLEYE	25	0	11·34	Mabry Harper	Old Hickory Lake, Tennessee, USA	1 Apr	1960

BRITISH RECORDS—NATIONAL COARSE FISH
As recognised by the National Association of Specialist Anglers

Species	Weight lb	oz	dr	kg	Name of Angler	Location	Date
BARBEL	14	6	—	6·52	A. D. Tryon	Royalty Fishery, Hampshire Avon	1934
BLEAK		4	4	0·12	B. Derrington	River Monnow, Wye Mouth	1982
BREAM, COMMON	16	6	—	7·43	Anthony Bromley	Private water, Staffordshire	1986
CARP	51	8	—	23·36	C. Yates	Redmire Pool, Hertfordshire	1980
CARP, CRUCIAN	5	10	8	2·56	G. Halls	Lake near Kings Lynn, Norfolk	1976
CARP, GRASS	16	—	—	7·26	K. Crow	Lake near Canterbury, Kent	1986
CATFISH (WELS)	43	8	—	19·73	R. J. Bray	Wilstone Reservoir, Tring, Hertfordshire	1970
CHUB	8	4	—	3·74	G. F. Smith	Royalty Fishery, Hampshire Avon	1913
DACE	1	4	4	0·57	J. L. Gasson	Little Ouse, Thetford, Norfolk	1960
EEL	11	2	—	5·04	S. Terry	Kingfisher Lake, Ringwood, Hampshire	1978
GUDGEON		4	4	0·12	M. J. Brown	Fish Pond, Ebbw Vale, Gwent	1977
ORFE, GOLDEN	5	6	—	2·44	M. Foot	Kingsley, Hampshire	1978
PERCH	5	9	—	2·52	J. Shayler	Private water, Kent	1985
PIKE	44	14	—	20·35	Michael Linton	Ardleigh Reservoir	1987
ROACH	4	1	—	1·84	R. G. Jones	Gravel pit, Nottinghamshire	1975
RUDD *	4	8	—	2·04	Rev. E. C. Alston	Thetford, Norfolk	1933
RUFFE		5	4	0·148	R. J. Jenkins	West View Farm, Cumbria	1980
TENCH	14	3	—	6·43	Philip Gooriah	Wraysbury No.1 Reservoir, Berkshire	1987
WALLEYE	11	12	—	5·33	F. A. Adams	The Delph, Welney, Norfolk	1934
ZANDER	17	12	—	8·05	D. Litton	Great Ouse, Relief Channel, Norfolk	1977

Superior weight recognised by National Anglers' Council:
4 lb 10 oz, Dennis Webb at Pitsford Reservoir, Northamptonshire, 1986.

length, by Archer Davidson in Twofold Bay, New South Wales, Australia in 1910. Its tail flukes measured 6·09 m *20 ft* across and its jaw bone 7·11 m *23 ft 4 in.*

The largest fish ever taken underwater was an 804 lb *364 kg* Giant black grouper or jewfish by Don Pinder of the Miami Triton Club, Florida, USA in 1955. The British spear-fishing record is 89 lb *40·36 kg* for an Angler fish by James Brown (Weymouth Association Divers) in 1969.

World Freshwater Championship
The *Confédération Internationale de la Pêche Sportive* (CIPS) championships were inaugurated as European championships in 1953 and recognised as World Championships in 1957. France won 12 times between 1956 and 1981 and Robert Tesse (France) took the individual title uniquely three times, in 1959–60, 1965. The record weight (team) is 34·71 kg *76·52 lb* in 3 hr by West

Germany on the Neckar at Mannheim, West Germany on 21 Sept 1980. The individual record is 16·99 kg *37·45 lb* by Wolf-Rüdiger Kremkus (West Germany) at Mannheim on 20 Sept 1980. The most fish caught is 652 by Jacques Isenbaert (Belgium) at Dunajvaros, Yugoslavia on 27 Aug 1967.

Fly fishing

World fly fishing championships were inaugurated by the CIPS in 1981. The first British winner was Henry Anthony 'Tony' Pawson (b. 22 Aug 1921) at Salamanca, Spain in 1984. He also played amateur soccer for England and captained Oxford University at cricket.

British Championship

The National Angling Championship (instituted 1906) has been won seven times by Leeds (1909–10, 1914, 1928, 1948–9, 1952). James H. R. Bazley (Leeds) won the individual title twice (1909, 1927). Since 1972 the event has been split into divisions. Eddie Townsin (Cambridge) won the national title in 1967 and Div. 4 in 1982; Charlie Hibbs (Leigh) won Div. 2 in 1974 and 1984. The record catch is 34·72 kg *76 lb 9 oz* by David Burr (Rugby) in the Huntspill, Somerset in 1965. The largest single fish caught in the Championships is a carp of 6·41 kg *14 lb 2 oz* by John C. Essex on 13 Sept 1975 on the River Nene, Peterborough. The heaviest total produced by Division 1 team champions is 63·99 kg *141·07 lb* by the 12-angler team from Nottingham Federation.

Casting

The longest freshwater cast ratified under ICF (International Casting Federation) rules is 175·01 m *574 ft 2 in* by Walter Kummerow (West Germany), for the Bait Distance Double-Handed 30 g event held at Lenzerheide, Switzerland in the 1968 Championships. The British national record is 148·78 m *488 ft 1 in* by Andy Dickison on the same occasion. At the currently contested weight of 17·7 g, the longest Bait Distance Double-Handed cast is 139·31 m *457 ft ½ in* by Kevin Carriero (USA) at Toronto, Canada on 24 July 1984. The British National record is 138·79 m *455 ft 3 in* by Hugh Newton at Peterborough, Cambridgeshire on 21 Sept 1985. The longest Fly Distance Double-Handed cast, at the 17·7 g weight, is 97·28 m *319 ft 1 in* by Wolfgang Feige (West Germany) at Toronto, Canada on 23 July 1984. Hywel Morgan set a British national record of 91·22 m *299 ft 2 in* at Torrington, Devon on 27 Apr 1985.

The UK Surfcasting Federation record (150 g *5¼ oz* weight) is 257·32 m *844 ft 3 in* by Neil Mackellow at Peterborough, Cambridgeshire on 1 Sept 1985.

IGFA WORLD RECORDS

The International Game Fish Association (IGFA) recognises world records for game fish—both freshwater and saltwater—for a large number of species of fish. Their thousands of categories include all-tackle, various line classes and tippet classes for fly fishing. New records recognised by the IGFA reached an annual peak of 1074 in 1984.

The heaviest freshwater category recognised by the IGFA is for the sturgeon—212·28 kg *468 lb* by Joey Pallotta on 9 July 1983 off Benicia, California, USA.

Longest fight

The longest recorded individual fight with a fish is 32 hr 5 min by Donal Heatley (b. 1938) (New Zealand) with a Black marlin (estimated length 6 m *20 ft* and weight 680 kg *1500 lb*) off Mayor Island off Tauranga, North Island, New Zealand on 21–22 Jan 1968. It towed the 12 tonne launch 80 km *50 miles* before breaking the line.

Archery

Though the earliest pictorial evidence of the existence of bows is seen in the Mesolithic cave paintings in Spain, archery as an organised sport appears to have

World Records			Single FITA rounds	
Event	**Points**	**Name and Country**	**Possible**	**Year**
		MEN		
FITA	1341	Darrell Pace (USA)	1440	1979
90 m	322	Vladimir Yesheyev (USSR)	360	1980
70 m	343	Tomi Poikolainen (Finland)	360	1988
50 m	345	Richard McKinney (USA)	360	1982
30 m	357	Takayoshi Matsushita (Jap)	360	1986
Team	3948	USA (Richard McKinney, Darrell Pace, Jay Barrs)	4320	1987
		WOMEN		
FITA	1338	Kim Su Nyong (S. Korea)	1440	1988
70 m	330	Yelena Marfel (USSR)	360	1987
	330	Kim Su Nyung (S. Korea)	360	1988
60 m	342	Lessia Schan (USSR)	360	1988
50 m	335	Yanzhima Tsyrenzhapova (USSR)	360	1985
30 m	356	Kim Su Nyong (S. Korea)	360	1987
Team	3981	S.Korea (Kim Su Nyong, Lee Hae Young, Kyung Wook Kim)	4320	1988

Indoor Double FITA rounds at 25 m				
MEN	589	Darrell Pace (USA)	600	1984
WOMEN	588	Yelena Marfel (USSR)	600	1985

Indoor FITA round at 18 m				
MEN	590	Thierry Venant (France)	600	1987
WOMEN	583	Natalya Butuzova (USSR)	600	1983

developed in the 3rd century AD. Competitive archery may however date back to the 12th century BC. The oldest archery body in the British Isles is the Society of Archers in Yorkshire, formed on 14 May 1673, though the Society of Kilwinning Archers, in Scotland, has contested the Pa-pingo Shoot since 1488. The world governing body is the *Fédération Internationale de Tir à l'Arc* (FITA), founded in 1931.

Highest championship scores

The highest scores achieved in either a World or Olympic championship for Double FITA rounds are: men, 2617 points (possible 2880) by Darrell Pace (b. 23 Oct 1956) (USA) and Richard McKinney (b. 20 Oct 1963) (USA) at Long Beach, California, USA on 21–22 Oct 1983; and women, 2632 points by Wang Hee-kyung (S. Korea) at Adelaide, Australia in 1987. Park Jung-Ah (S. Korea) set a women's record of 2634 points at the 1986 Asian Games at Seoul, S. Korea.

British records

York round—possible 1296 pts: Single round, 1160 Steven Hallard at Meriden on 26 June 1983; Double round, 2240 Steven Hallard at Stoneleigh on 14 Aug 1983.

Hereford (Women)—possible 1296 pts: Single round, 1182 Elaine Tomkinson at Bingley on 10 Aug 1980; Double round, 2331 Sue Willcox at Oxford on 27–28 June 1979.

FITA round (Men): Single round, 1312 Richard Priestman (b. 16 July 1955) at Hesperange, Luxembourg on 26 June 1988; Double round, 2566 Steven Hallard at Castle Ashby, Nottinghamshire on 20 May 1983.

FITA round (Women): Single round, 1273 Pauline Edwards at Worcester on 23 July 1983; Double round, 2520 Rachel Fenwick at Brussels, Belgium on 12–13 Aug 1978.

Most titles *World*

The greatest number of world titles (instituted 1931) ever won by a man is four by Hans Deutgen (b. 28 Feb 1917) (Sweden) in 1947–50. The greatest number won by a woman is 7 by Janina Spychajowa-Kurkowska (b. 8 Feb 1901) (Poland) in 1931–4, 1936, 1939 and 1947. Oscar Kessels (Belgium) (1904–68) participated in 21 world championships.

Olympic
Hubert van Innis (1866–1961) (Belgium) won six gold and three silver medals at the 1900 and 1920 Olympic Games.

British
The greatest number of British Championships is 12 by Horace Alfred Ford (1822–80) in 1849–59 and 1867, and 23 by Alice Blanche Legh (1855–1948) in 1881, 1886–92, 1895, 1898–1900, 1902–9, 1913 and 1921–2. Miss Legh was inhibited from winning from 1882 to 1885—because her mother was champion—and for 4 further years 1915–18 because there were no Championships during World War I.

FLIGHT SHOOTING

UNLIMITED FOOTBOW: *Men*; 1854·40 m *1 mile 268 yd*, Harry Drake (b. 7 May 1915) (USA), Ivanpah Dry Lake, California, USA, 24 Oct 1971. *Female*; 1018·48 m *1113 yd 2 ft 6 in*, Arlyne Rhode (USA) (b. 4 May 1936), Wendover, Utah, USA, 10 Sept 1978.
HANDBOW: *Men*; 1222·01 m *1336 yd 1 ft 3 in*, Don Brown (USA), 'Smith Creek' Flight Range, near Austin, Nevada, USA, 2 Aug 1987. *Women*; 950·39 m *1039 yd 1 ft 1 in*, April Moon (USA), Wendover, 13 Sept 1981.
CROSSBOW: 1834·82 m *2006 yd 1 ft 9 in*, Harry Drake, 'Smith Creek' Flight Range, 1 Oct 1987.
CONVENTIONAL FOOTBOW: 1410·87 m *1542 yd 2 ft 10 in*, Harry Drake, Ivanpah Dry Lake, 6 Oct 1979.
COMPOUND BOW: *Men*; 1060·55 m *1159 yd 2 ft 6 in*, Bert McCune Jnr (USA), 'Smith Creek' Flight Range, 2 Aug 1987. *Women*; 738·30 m *807 yd 1 ft 3 in*, April Moon (USA), 'Smith Creek' Flight Range, 1 Aug 1987.
BROADHEAD FLIGHT BOWS: *Men*; 490·21 m *536 yd*, Arlan Reynolds (USA), Salt Lake City, Utah, USA, 27 June 1987. *Women*; 368·43 m *402 yd 2 ft 9 in*, April Moon (USA), Salt Lake City, 28 June 1987.

Greatest draw

Gary Sentman, of Roseberg, Oregon, USA drew a longbow weighing a record 79·83 kg *176 lb* to the maximum draw on the arrow of 72 cm *28¼ in* at Forksville, Penn., USA on 20 Sept 1975.

24 Hours—target archery

The highest recorded score over 24 hours by a pair of archers is 58 413 during 55 Portsmouth Rounds (60 arrows per round at 20 yd at 60 cm FITA targets) by Anton Hooymans and Wim van Eggelen at the Sportpark 'De Hoef', Rosemalen, The Netherlands on 19–20 Mar 1988.

Phyllis Griffiths, aged 64, achieved a score of 31 000 in 76 Portsmouth rounds in 24 hours at Holsworthy, Devon on 30–31 Mar 1986.

Badminton

A similar game was played in China in the 2nd millennium BC.

The modern game may have evolved *c.* 1870 at Badminton Hall in Avon, the seat of the Dukes of Beaufort, or from a game played in India. The first modern rules were codified in Pune in 1876.

Shortest game

In the 1969 Uber Cup in Tokyo, Japan, Noriko Takagi (later Mrs Nakayama) (Japan) beat Poppy Tumengkol (Indonesia) in 9 min.

Longest rallies

In the men's singles final of the 1987 All-England Championships between Morten Frost (Denmark) and Icuk Sugiarto (Indonesia) there were two successive rallies of over 90 strokes.

Most shuttles

In the final of the Indian National Badminton Championships 1986, when Syed Modi beat Vimal Kumar 15–12, 15–12, 182 shuttles were used in the 66-minute period.

World team championships

The most wins at the men's International Championship for the Thomas Cup (instituted 1948) is eight by Indonesia (1958, 1961, 1964, 1970, 1973, 1976, 1979 and 1984). The most wins at the ladies' International Championship for the Uber Cup (instituted 1956) is five by Japan (1966, 1969, 1972, 1978 and 1981).

Most titles

The All-England Championships were instituted in 1899. The men's singles have been won eight times by Rudy Hartono Kurniawan (Indonesia) (b. 18 Aug 1948) in 1968–74 and 1976. The greatest number of titles won (including doubles) is 21 by George Alan Thomas (1881–1972) between 1903 and 1928. The women's singles were won ten times by Judy Hashman (née Devlin) (USA) (b. 22 Oct 1935) in 1954, 1957–8, 1960–4, 1966–7. She also equalled the greatest number of titles won of 17 by Meriel Lucas (later Mrs King Adams) from 1899 to 1910.

Baseball

The Reverend Thomas Wilson, of Maidstone, Kent, England, wrote disapprovingly, in 1700, of baseball being played on Sundays.

The earliest baseball game under the Cartwright (Alexander Joy Cartwright Jr 1820–92) rules was at Hoboken, New Jersey, USA on 19 June 1846, with the New York Nine beating the Knickerbockers 23–1 in four innings.

There are two major leagues in the USA: the National League (NL), formed on 2 Feb 1876 at the Grand Central Hotel, New York, and the American League (AL), on 28 Jan 1901.

Most home runs

Henry Louis 'Hank' Aaron (Milwaukee and Atlanta Braves) (b. 5 Feb 1934) holds the major league career home run record of 755, from 1954 to 1976. George Herman 'Babe' Ruth (1895–1948) has the highest home run percentage, 8·5 per cent for 714 home runs from 8399 times at bat, 1914–38. Joshua Gibson (1911–47) of Homestead Grays and Pittsburgh Crawfords, Negro League clubs, achieved a career total of nearly 800 homers including an unofficial total of 75 in 1931.

The US major league record for home runs in a season is 61 by Roger Eugene Maris (1934–85) for New York Yankees in 162 games in 1961. 'Babe' Ruth hit 60 in 154 games in 1927 for the New York Yankees. The most official home runs in minor leagues is 72 by Joe Bauman of Rosewell, New Mexico in 1954.

Longest home run

The longest home run ever measured was one of 188·4 m *618 ft* by Roy Edward 'Dizzy' Carlyle (1900–56) in a minor league game at Emeryville Ball Park, California, USA on 4 July 1929. In 1919 'Babe' Ruth hit a 178·9 m *587 ft* homer in a Boston Red Sox *v.* New York Giants exhibition match at Tampa, Florida.

Longest throw

The longest throw (ball weighs 141–148 g *5–5¼ oz*) is 135·88 m *445 ft 10 in* by Glen Edward Gorbous (b. Canada 8 July 1930) on 1 Aug 1957. The longest throw by a woman is 90·2 m *296 ft* by Mildred Ella 'Babe' Didrikson (later Mrs Zaharias) (USA) (1914–56) at Jersey City, New Jersey, USA on 25 July 1931.

Fastest base runner

The fastest time for circling bases is 13·3 sec by Ernest Evar Swanson (1902–73) at Columbus, Ohio, USA in 1932, at an average speed of 29·70 km/h *18·45 mph*.

Fastest pitcher

The fastest recorded pitcher was Lynn Nolan Ryan (then of the California Angels) (b. 31 Jan 1947) who, on 20 Aug 1974 at Anaheim Stadium, California, USA, was measured to pitch at 162·3 km/h *100·9 mph*.

Youngest player

The youngest major league player of all time was the Cincinnati pitcher Joseph Henry Nuxhall (b. 30 July 1928), who played one game in June 1944, aged 15 yr 314 days. He did not play again in the NL until 1952.

Record attendances and receipts

The World Series record attendance is 420 784 (six games) when the Los Angeles Dodgers beat the Chicago White Sox 4–2 between 1–8 Oct 1959. The single game record is 92 706 for the fifth game at the Memorial Coliseum, Los Angeles, California, on 6 Oct 1959. The all-time season record for attendances for both leagues was 52 029 644 in 1987.

An estimated 114 000 spectators watched a game between Australia and an American Services team in a demonstration event during the Olympic Games at Melbourne on 1 Dec 1956.

Baseball ● Record-breaker Henry Louis 'Hank' Aaron (USA) (see below). (Photo: All-Sport)

US MAJOR LEAGUE RECORDS

AL American League
NL National League

BATTING

AVERAGE, Career, ·367 Tyrus Raymond Cobb (Detroit AL, Philadelphia AL) 1905–28. **Season**, ·438 Hugh Duffy (Boston NL) 1894.

RUNS, Career, 2245 Tyrus Raymond Cobb 1905–28.

HOME RUNS, Career[*1], 755 Henry 'Hank' Aaron (Milwaukee NL, Atlanta NL, Milwaukee AL) 1954–76. **Season**, 61 Roger Eugene Maris (New York NL) 1961.

RUNS BATTED IN, Career, 2297 Henry 'Hank' Aaron 1954–76. **Season**, 190 Lewis Rober 'Hack' Wilson (Chicago NL) 1930. **Game**, 12 James LeRoy Bottomley (St Louis NL) 16 Sept 1924. **Innings**, 7 Edward Cartwright (St Louis AL) 23 Sept 1890.

BASE HITS, Career, 4256 Peter Edward Rose (Cincinnati NL, Philadelphia NL) 1963–86. **Season**, 257 George Harold Sisler (St Louis AL) 1920.

TOTAL BASES, Career, 6856 Henry 'Hank' Aaron 1954–76. **Season**, 457 George Herman 'Babe' Ruth (New York AL) 1921.

HITS, Consecutive, 12 Michael Franklin 'Pinky' Higgins (Boston AL) 19–21 June 1938; Walter 'Moose' Dropo (Detroit AL) 14–15 July 1952.

CONSECUTIVE GAMES BATTED SAFELY, 56 Joseph Paul DiMaggio (New York AL) 15 May–16 July 1941.

STOLEN BASES, Career[*2], 938 Louis Clark Brock (Chicago NL, St Louis NL) 1961–79. **Season**, 130 Rickey Henley Henderson (Oakland AL) 1982.

CONSECUTIVE GAMES PLAYED[*3], 2130 Henry Louis 'Lou' Gehrig (New York AL) 1 June 1925–30 April 1939.

PITCHING

GAMES WON, Career, 511 Denton True 'Cy' Young (Cleveland NL, St Louis NL, Boston AL, Cleveland AL) 1890–1911. **Season**, 60 Charles Gardner Radbourn (Providence NL) 1884.

CONSECUTIVE GAMES WON, 24 Carl Owen Hubbell (New York NL) 1936–37.

SHUTOUTS, Career, 110 Walter Perry Johnson (Washington NL) 1907–27. **Season**, 16 George Washington Bradley (St Louis NL) 1876; Grover Cleveland Alexander (Philadelphia NL) 1916.

STRIKEOUTS, Career[*4], 4373 Lynn Nolan Ryan (New York NL, California AL, Houston NL) 1968–87. **Season**, 383 Lynn Nolan Ryan (California AL) 1973. **Game (9 innings)**, 20 Roger Clemens (Boston AL) *v.* Seattle 29 Apr 1986.

NO-HIT GAMES, Career, 5 Lynn Nolan Ryan 1966–81.

EARNED RUN AVERAGE, Season, 0·90 Ferdinand Schupp (140 inns) (New York NL) 1916; 1·01 Hubert 'Dutch' Leonard (222 inns) (Boston AL) 1914; 1·12 Robert Gibson (305 inns) (St Louis NL) 1968.

COMPLETE GAMES, Career, 751 Denton True 'Cy' Young 1890–1911.

Japanese League records that are superior to those in the US major leagues;
[1] *868 Sadaharu Oh (Yomiuri) 1959–80.*
[2] *1059 Yutaka Fukumoto (Hankyu) 1969–87.*
[3] *2215 Sachio Kinugasa (Hiroshima) 1970–87.*
[4] *4490 Masaichi Kaneda (Kokutesu, Yomiuri) 1950–69.*

WORLD SERIES RECORDS

AL American League, NL National League

Most wins	22 New York Yankees (AL)	1923–78
Most series played	14 Lawrence Peter 'Yogi' Berra (New York, AL)	1947–63
Most home runs in a game	3 George Herman 'Babe' Ruth (New York, AL)	6 Oct 1926
	3 Reginald Martinez Jackson (New York, AL)	18 Oct 1977
Only perfect pitch (in 9 innings)	Donald James Larson (New York, AL) v Brooklyn	8 Oct 1956

Basketball

Basketball

The game of 'Pok-ta-Pok' was played in the 10th century BC, by the Olmecs in Mexico, and closely resembled basketball in its concept. 'Ollamalitzli' was a variation of this game played by the Aztecs in Mexico as late as the 16th century. If the solid rubber ball was put through a fixed stone ring the player was entitled to the clothing of all the spectators. Modern basketball (which may have been based on the German game *Korbball*) was devised by the Canadian-born Dr James A. Naismith (1861–1939) at the Training School of the International YMCA College at Springfield, Massachusetts, USA in mid-December 1891. The first game played under modified rules was on 20 Jan 1892. The International Amateur Basketball Federation (FIBA) was founded in 1932; it has now dropped the word Amateur from its title.

Most titles *Olympic*
The USA have won nine men's Olympic titles. From the time the sport was introduced to the Games in 1936 until 1972 they won 63 consecutive matches in the Olympic Games until they lost 50–51 to the USSR in the disputed Final match in Munich. They won eighth and ninth titles in 1976 and 1984. The women's title was won by the USSR in 1976 and 1980 and by the USA in 1984.

World
The USSR has won most titles at both the men's World Championships (inst. 1950) with three (1967, 1974 and 1982) and women's (inst. 1953) with six (1959, 1964, 1967, 1971, 1975 and 1983).

European
The most European Champions Cup (instituted 1957) wins is seven by Real Madrid, Spain 1964–5, 1967–8, 1974, 1978 and 1980. The women's title has been won 18 times by Daugawa, Riga, Latvia, USSR between 1960 and 1982. The most wins in the European Nations Championships for men is 14 by the USSR, and in the women's event 19, also by the USSR, winning all but the 1958 championship since 1950, in this biennial contest.

American professional
The most National Basketball Association (NBA) titles (instituted 1947), played for between the leading professional teams in the United States, have been won by the Boston Celtics with 16 victories between 1957 and 1986.

English
The most English National Championship titles (instituted 1936) have been won by London Central YMCA, with eight wins in 1957–8, 1960, 1962–4, 1967 and 1969. The English National League title has been won seven times by Crystal Palace 1974, 1976–8, 1980 and 1982–3. Most English Women's Cup titles (instituted 1965) have been won by the Tigers with eight wins, 1972–3, 1976–80 and 1982.

Highest score *International*
The highest score recorded in a senior international match is 251 by Iraq against Yemen (33) at New Delhi in November 1982 at the Asian Games. The highest in a British Championship is 125 by England v. Wales (54) on 1 Sept 1978. England beat Gibraltar 130–45 on 31 Aug 1978.

Match
The highest aggregate score in an NBA match is 370 when the Detroit Pistons (186) beat the Denver Nuggets (184) in Denver on 13 Dec 1983. Overtime was played after a 145–145 tie in regulation time. The record in regulation time is 310, when Boston Celtics beat Minneapolis Lakers 173–139 on 27 Feb 1959. The highest score in a US college match is 210 when Essex County (Community) College beat Englewood Cliffs College (67) on 20 Jan 1979.

United Kingdom
The highest score recorded in a match is 250 by the Nottingham YMCA Falcons v. Mansfield Pirates at Nottingham on 18 June 1974. It was a handicap competition and Mansfield received 120 points towards their total of 145. The highest score in a senior National League match is 167 by West Bromwich Kestrels v. Milton Keynes (69) on 13 Feb 1983. The highest in the National Cup is 146 by Doncaster v. Cleveland (109) on 11 Feb 1976.

Individual
Mats Wermelin, 13 (Sweden), scored all 272 points in a 272–0 win in a regional boys' tournament in Stockholm, Sweden on 5 Feb 1974. The highest single game score in an NBA game is 100 points by Wilton Norman Chamberlin (b. 21 Aug 1936) for Philadelphia v. New York on 2 Mar 1962. The record score by a woman is 156 points by Marie Boyd (now Eichler) of Central HS, Lonaconing, Maryland, USA in a 163–3 defeat of Ursaline Academy, Cumberland on 25 Feb 1924.

The highest score by a British player is 124 points by Paul Ogden for St Albans School, Oldham (226) v. South Chadderton (82) on 9 Mar 1982. The highest individual score in a league match in Britain is 108 by Lewis Young for Forth Steel in his team's 154–74 win over Stirling in the Scottish League Division One at Stirling on 2 Mar 1985. The record in an English National League (Div. One) or Cup match is 73 points by Terry Crosby (USA) for Home Spare Bolton in his team's 120–106 defeat by Cottrills Manchester Giants at Altrincham, Cheshire on 26 Jan 1985 and by Billy Hungrecker in a semi-final play-off for Worthing v. Plymouth at Worthing, West Sussex on 20 Mar 1988.

Most points
Kareem Abdul-Jabbar (formerly Lewis Ferdinand Alcindor) (b. 16 Apr 1947) has scored a career record 37 570 points, including a record 15 496 field goals, in a record 1482 games and 186 play-offs from 1969 to 16 Apr 1988 for the Milwaukee Bucks and Los Angeles Lakers. The previous record holder, Wilt Chamberlain, had a record average of 30·1 points per game for his total of 31 419. He set a season's record 4029 for Philadelphia in 1962. The records for the most points scored in a college career are (women): 4061, Pearl Moore of Francis Marion College, Florence, S. Carolina, 1975–9; (men): 4045 by Travis Grant for Kentucky State in 1969–72. In the English National League, Ian Day (b. 16 May 1953) scored 3456 points in 203 games, 1973–84.

Tallest players
The tallest player of all time is reputed to be Suleiman Ali Nashnush (b. 1943) who played for the Libyan team in 1962 when measuring 2·45 m *8 ft*. Aleksandr Sizonenko of Kuibyshev Stroitel and USSR is 2·39 m *7 ft 10 in* tall. The tallest woman player was Iuliana Semenova (USSR) (b. 9 Mar 1952) at a reported 2·18 m *7 ft 2 in* and weighing 127 kg *281 lb*. The tallest British player has been the 2·29 m *7 ft 6¼ in* tall Christopher Greener of London Latvians whose international debut for England was v. France on 17 Dec 1969.

Shooting speed
The greatest goal-shooting demonstration has been by Ted St Martin of Jacksonville, Florida, USA who, on 25 June 1977, scored 2036 consecutive free throws.

In 24 hours Robert Browning scored 16 093 free throws from a total of 23 194 taken (69·38%) at St Mark's School, Dallas, Texas, USA on 21–22 Nov 1987.

Steve Bontrager (USA) (b. 1 Mar 1959) of Polycell Kingston scored 21 points in a minute from 7 positions in a demonstration for BBC TV's *Record Breakers* on 29 Oct 1986.

Longest goal
The longest recorded field goal in a match is a measured 28·17 m *92 ft 5¼ in* by Bruce Morris for Marshall University v. Appalachian State University at Huntington, West Virgina, USA on 8 Feb 1985. A British record of 23·10 m *75 ft 9½ in* is claimed by David Tarbatt (b. 23 Jan 1949) of Altofts Aces v. Harrogate Demons at Featherstone, West Yorkshire on 27 Jan 1980.

Billiards

The earliest recorded mention of billiards was in France in 1429, while Louis XI, King of France 1461–83, is reported to have had a billiard table. The first recorded public billiards room in England was the Piazza, Covent Garden, London, in the early part of the 19th century. Rubber cushions were introduced in 1835 and slate beds in 1836.

Most titles *Professional*
The greatest number of World Championships (instituted 1870) won by one player is eight by John Roberts Jr (1847–1919) (England) in 1870 (twice), 1871, 1875 (twice), 1877 and 1885 (twice). The greatest number of United Kingdom titles (instituted 1934) won is seven (1934–39 and 1947) by Joe Davis (1901–78) (England), who also won four world titles (1928–30 and 1932).

Amateur
The record for world amateur titles is four by Robert James Percival Marshall (Australia) (b. 10 Apr 1910) in 1936, 1938, 1951 and 1962. The greatest number of English Amateur Championships (instituted 1888) won is 15 by Norman Dagley (b. 27 June 1930) in 1965–66, 1970–75, 1978–84. The record number of women's titles is eight by Vera Selby (b. 13 Mar 1930), 1970–8.

Highest breaks
Tom Reece (1873–1953) made an unfinished break of 499 135, including 249 152 cradle cannons (two points each) in 85 hr 49 min against Joe Chapman at Burroughes' Hall, Soho Square, London between 3 June and 6 July 1907. This was not recognised because press and public were not continuously present. The highest certified break made by the anchor cannon is 42 746 by William Cook (England) from 29 May to 7 June 1907. The official world record under the then baulk-line rule is 1784 by Joe Davis in the United Kingdom Championship on 29 May 1936. Walter Albert Lindrum (Australia) (1898–1960) made an official break of 4137 in 2 hr 55 min against Joe Davis at Thurston's on 19–20 Jan 1932, before the baulk-line rule was in force. Davis had an unofficial personal best of 2502 (mostly pendulum cannons) in a match against Tom Newman (1894–1943) (England) in Manchester in 1930. The highest break recorded in amateur competition is 1149 by Michael Ferreira (India) at Calcutta, India on 15 Dec 1978. Under the more stringent 'two pot' rule, restored on 1 Jan 1983, the highest break is Ferreira's 962 unfinished in a tournament at Bombay, India on 29 Apr 1986.

Fastest century
Walter Lindrum made an unofficial 100 break in 27·5 sec in Australia on 10 Oct 1952. His official record is 100 in 46·0 sec set in Sydney in 1941.

3 CUSHION
This pocketless variation dates back to 1878. The world governing body, the *Union Mondiale de Billiard* (UMB), was formed in 1928. The most successful exponent spanning the pre- and post- international era from 1906 to 1952 was William F. Hoppe (USA) (1887–1959) who won 51 billiards championships in all forms. Most UMB titles have been won by Raymond Ceulemans (Belgium) (b. 12 July 1935) with 19 (1963–6, 1968–73, 1975–81, 1983, 1985).

BAR BILLIARDS *Scoring rates*
The record scoring rate in a league game has been 28 530 in 19 min 5 sec by Keith Sheard at the Crown and Thistle, Headington, Oxford on 9 July 1984. Sheard scored 1500 points in a minute on BBC TV's *Record Breakers* on 23 Sept 1986.

The highest bar billiards score in 24 hours by a team of five is 1 506 570 by John Burrows, Kent Murray, Ray Hussey, Roy Buckle and Brian Ray of The Hour Glass, Sands, High Wycombe, Buckinghamshire on 26–27 Nov 1983.

Board Games

BACKGAMMON

Forerunners of the game have been traced back to a dice and a board game found in excavations at Ur, dated to 3000 BC. Later the Romans played a game remarkably similar to the modern one. The name 'backgammon' is variously ascribed to Welsh 'little battle', or Saxon 'back game'.

Alan Malcolm Beckerson (b. 21 Feb 1938) devised the shortest game of 16 throws in 1982.

CHESS

The game originated in ancient India under the name Chaturanga (literally 'four-corps'—an army game). The name chess is derived from the Persian word *shah* (a king or ruler). The earliest reference is from the Middle Persian Karnamak (*c*. AD 590–628), though in December 1972, two ivory chessmen were found in the Uzbek Soviet Republic datable to AD 200. It reached Britain in *c*. 1255. The *Fédération Internationale des Echecs* (FIDE) was established in 1924.

Most world titles

World champions have been generally recognised since 1886. The longest undisputed tenure was 26 yr 337 days by Dr Emanuel Lasker (1868–1941) of Germany, from 1894 to 1921. The women's world championship title was held by Vera Francevna Menchik-Stevenson (1906–44) (USSR, later GB) from 1927 until her death, and was successfully defended a record seven times. Nona Terentievna Gaprindashvili (USSR) (b. 3 May 1941) held the title from 1962 to 1978 and defended successfully four times. Robert James 'Bobby' Fischer (USA) (b. 9 Mar 1943) is reckoned on the officially adopted Elo System to be the greatest Grand Master of all time with a 2785 rating. Gary Kimovich Kasparov (USSR) (b. 13 Apr 1963) at 2760 is currently the highest-ranked player. The highest-rated woman player is Maya Grigoryevna Chiburdanidze (USSR) (b. 17 Jan 1961), at 2555.

The USSR has won the men's team title (Olympiad) a record 16 times and the women's title 11 times (every time entered) to 1986.

The most active world champion has been Anatoliy Yevgenyevich Karpov (USSR) (b. 23 May 1951) who in his tenure as champion, 1975–85, averaged 45·2 competitive games per year, played in 32 tournaments and finished first in 26.

Youngest and oldest world champions

The youngest world champion has been Gary Kasparov, who won the title on 9 Nov 1985 at 22 yr 210 days. The oldest was Wilhelm Steinitz (Austria) (1836–1900) who was 58 yr 10 days when he lost his title to Lasker on 26 May 1894. Maya Chiburdanidze won the women's title in 1978 when only 17.

Most British titles

The most British titles have been won by Dr Jonathan Penrose (b. 7 Oct 1933) with ten titles in 1958–63, 1966–9. Rowena Mary Bruce (*née* Dew) (b. 15 May 1919) won 11 women's titles between 1937 and 1969. The first British player to attain official International Grand Master status was Anthony John Miles (b. 23 Apr 1955), on 24 Feb 1976. The top British player on the Elo list is Nigel David Short (b. 1 June 1965) on 2665. The top British woman is Susan Kathryn Arkell [*née* Walker] (b. 28 Oct 1965) on 2355.

Least games lost by a world champion

José Raúl Capablanca (Cuba) (1888–1942) lost only 34 games in his adult career, 1909–39. He was unbeaten from 10 Feb 1916 to 21 Mar 1924 and was world champion 1921–7.

Most opponents

The record for most consecutive games played is 663 by Vlastimil Hort (b. 12 Jan 1944) (Czechoslovakia) over 32½ hours at Porz, West Germany on 5–6 Oct 1984. He played 60–100 opponents at a time, scoring over 80 per cent wins and averaging 30 moves per game. He also holds the record for most games simultaneously, 201 during 550 consecutive games of which he only lost ten, in Seltjarnes, Iceland on 23–24 Apr 1977. Eric G. J. Knoppert (Netherlands) (b. 20 Sept 1959) played 500 games of 10-minute chess against opponents averaging 2002 on the Elo scale on 13–16 Sept 1985. He scored 413 points (1 for win, ½ for draw), a success rate of 82·6 per cent.

Slowest and longest games

The slowest reported moving (before modern rules) in an official event is reputed to have been by Louis Paulsen (Germany) (1833–91) against Paul Charles Morphy (USA) (1837–84) on 29 Oct 1857. The game ended in a draw on move 56 after 15 hours of play of which Paulsen used most of the allotted time. Grand Master Friedrich Sämisch (1896–1975) (Germany) ran out of the allotted time (2 hr 30 min for 45 moves) after only 12 moves, in Prague, Czechoslovakia, in 1938.

The slowest move played, since time clocks were introduced, was at Vigo, Spain in 1980 when Francisco Trois (b. 3 Sept 1946) took 2 hr 20 min for his seventh move *v.* Luis M. C. P. Santos (b. 30 June 1955).

The Master game with most moves on record was one of 194 moves, when Eugene Martinovsky (USA) (b. 3 Oct 1931) drew with Vlastimil Jansa (Czechoslovakia) (b. 27 Nov 1942) at the Gausdal International, Norway in August 1987.

DRAUGHTS

Draughts, known as checkers in North America, has origins earlier than chess. It was played in Egypt in the

---

Solitaire ● The shortest time taken to complete the game is 15·5 sec by Caroline Harrison of Sittingbourne, Kent at BBC Television Centre, London for BBC Television *Record Breakers* on 12 Oct 1987.

---

second millennium BC. The earliest book on the game was by Antonio Torquemada of Valencia, Spain in 1547.

Walter Hellman (USA) (1916–75) won a record 8 world titles during his tenure as world champion 1948–75. Dr Marion Tinsley (USA) (b. 3 Feb 1927), the current world champion, has been internationally undefeated in matchplay from 1947 to 1988.

The British Championship (biennial) was inaugurated in 1886. A record 6 titles were won by Samuel Cohen (London) (1905–72), 1924, 1927, 1929, 1933, 1937 and 1939. John McGill (Kilbride) (b. 1936) won six Scottish titles between 1959 and 1974. William Edwards (b. 28 Jan 1915) of Abercynon, Wales won the English open title on a record four successive occasions —1979, 1981, 1983 and 1985. In 1986, Andrew Knapp, (b. 19 Oct 1966) on his first attempt, became at 19 yr 322 days the youngest ever winner of the English Amateur Championship (instituted 1910).

Youngest and oldest national champion

Asa A. Long (b. 20 Aug 1904) became the youngest US national champion, aged 18 yr 64 days, when he won in Boston, Massachusetts on 23 Oct 1922. He became the oldest, aged 79 yr 334 days, when he won his sixth title in Tupelo, Mississippi on 21 July 1984.

Most opponents

Gary Davis played a record 177 games simultaneously, winning 175 and drawing two, at Marketown, Mt District, NSW, Australia on 4 July 1987. Newell W. Banks (1887–1977) played 140 games simultaneously, winning 133 and drawing seven, in Chicago, Illinois in 1933. His playing time was 145 min, so averaging about one move per sec. In 1947 he played blindfold for 4 hr per day for 45 consecutive days, winning 1331 games, drawing 54 and losing only two, while playing six games at a time.

Longest and shortest games

In competition the prescribed rate of play is not less than 30 moves per hour with the average game lasting about

90 min. In 1958 a game between Dr Marion Tinsley (USA) and Derek Oldbury (GB) lasted 7 hr 30 min (played under the 5-minutes-a-move rule). The shortest possible game is one of 20 moves composed by Alan Malcolm Beckerson (GB) in 1977.

SCRABBLE ® Crossword Game
The crossword game was invented by Alfred M. Butts in 1931 and was developed, refined and trademarked as Scrabble ® Crossword Game by James Brunot in 1948.

Highest scores
The highest competitive league game score is 849 by

Most titles *Olympic* ● The Olympic 4-man bob title (instituted 1924) has been won five times by Switzerland (1924, 1936, 1956, 1972 and 1988). This 1988 team was Ekkehard Fasser, Kurt Meier, Marcel Fassler and Werner Stocker. (Photo: All-Sport)

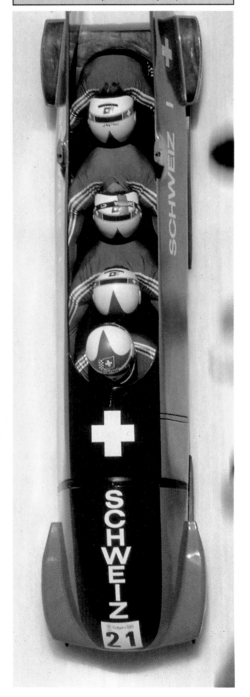

Maurice Rocker (GB) at Sheffield on 6 July 1985. The highest competitive single turn score recorded is 392 by Dr Saladin Karl Khoshnaw (of Kurdish origin) in Manchester in April 1982. He laid down 'CAZIQUES', which means 'native chiefs of West Indian aborigines'.

The greatest margin of victory in a league game was achieved by Ron Hendra when he beat Amber Sturdy 730–180 in a London League match in 1983.

Most titles
British National Championships were instituted in 1971. Olive Behan, 1972 and 1975, and Philip Nelkon, 1978 and 1981, have both won twice. The highest score in the Championship has been 1843 (three-game total) by Viraf Mehta in 1986.

BIGGEST BOARD GAME
The world's biggest board game, called Heartopoly, involved 4317 participants and stretched around the 403 m *440 yd* Flagler Dog Track in Miami, Florida, USA on 14–15 Sept 1985.

Bobsleigh and Tobogganing

BOBSLEDDING
The oldest known sledge is dated *c.* 6500 BC and came from Heinola, Finland. The first known bobsleigh race took place at Davos, Switzerland in 1889. The International Federation of Bobsleigh and Tobogganing was formed in 1923, followed by the International Bobsleigh Federation in 1957.

Most titles *Olympic*
The USA (1932, 1936), Switzerland (1948, 1980), Italy (1956, 1968), West Germany (1952, 1972) and GDR (1976, 1984) have won the Olympic 2-man bob (instituted 1932) event twice. The most gold medals won by an individual is three by Meinhard Nehmer (GDR) (b. 13 June 1941) and Bernhard Germeshausen (GDR) (b. 21 Aug 1951) in the 1976 2-man, 1976 and 1980 4-man events. The most medals won is six (two gold, two silver, two bronze) by Eugenio Monti (Italy) (b. 23 Jan 1928), 1956 to 1968. The only British victory was at 2-man bob in 1964 by the Hon. Robin Thomas Valerian Dixon (b. 21 Apr 1935) and Anthony James Dillon Nash (b. 18 Mar 1936).

Most titles *World and Olympic*
The world 4-man bob title (instituted 1924) has been won 17 times by Switzerland (1924, 1936, 1939, 1947, 1954–7, 1971–3, 1975, 1982–3, 1986–8). Italy won the two-man title 14 times (1954, 1956–63, 1966, 1968–9, 1971 and 1975). Eugenio Monti was a member of eleven world championship crews, eight 2-man and three 4-man in 1957–68.

TOBOGGANING
The word toboggan comes from the Micmac American Indian word *tobaakan*. The St Moritz Tobogganing Club, Switzerland, founded in 1887, is the oldest toboggan club in the world. It is notable for being the home of the Cresta Run, which dates from 1884, and for the introduction of the 1-man skeleton racing toboggan. The course is 1212·25 m *3977 ft* long with a drop of 157 m *514 ft* and the record is 50·91 sec (av. 85·72 km/h *53·27 mph*) by Franco Gansser of Switzerland on 22 Feb 1987. On 21 Feb 1986 Nico Baracchi (Switzerland) set a record from Junction (890·2 m *2920 ft*) of 41·58 sec. The greatest number of wins in the Grand National (instituted 1885) is eight by the 1948 Olympic champion Nino Bibbia (Italy) (b. 9 Sept 1924) in 1960–4, 1966, 1968 and 1973. The greatest number of wins in the Curzon Cup (instituted 1910) is eight by Bibbia in 1950, 1957–8, 1960, 1962–4, and 1969, who hence won the double in 1960 and 1962–4.

LUGEING
In lugeing the rider adopts a sitting, as opposed to a

prone, position. Official international competition began at Klosters, Switzerland in 1881. The first European championships were at Reichenberg, Germany, in 1914 and the first World Championships at Oslo, Norway in 1953. The International Luge Federation was formed in 1957. Lugeing became an Olympic sport in 1964.

Fastest speed
The highest recorded, photo-timed speed is 137·4 km/h *85·38 mph* by Asle Strand (Norway) at Tandådalens Linbane, Sälen, Sweden on 1 May 1982.

Most titles *World and Olympic*
The most successful riders in the World Championships

Most titles *Olympic* ● Steffi Walter (*née* Martin) (GDR) (b. 17 Sept 1962) became the first rider to win two Olympic single-seater luge titles, with victories at the women's event in 1984 and 1988. (Photo: All-Sport)

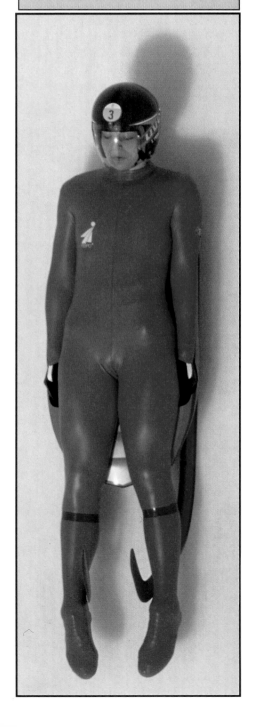

are Thomas Köhler (GDR) (b. 25 June 1940), who won the single-seater title in 1962, 1964 (Olympic), 1966 and 1967 and shared the 2-seater title in 1967 and 1968 (Olympic), and Hans Rinn (GDR) (b. 19 Mar 1953), Olympic champion 2-seater 1976 and 1980 and world champion at single-seater 1973 and 1977, 2-seater 1977 and 1980. Margit Schumann (GDR) (b. 14 Sept 1952) has won 5 women's titles, 1973–5, 1976 (Olympic) and 1977.

Bowling (Tenpin)

The ancient German game of nine-pins (*Heidenwerfen*—knock down pagans) was exported to the United States in the early 17th century. In 1841 the Connecticut State Legislature prohibited the game and other states followed. Eventually a tenth pin was added to evade the ban; but there is some evidence of ten pins being used in Suffolk, UK about 300 years ago. The first body to standardise rules was the American Bowling Congress (ABC), established in New York on 9 Sept 1895.

The world's largest bowling centre is the Fukuyama Bowl, Osaka, Japan which has 144 lanes. The Tokyo World Lanes Centre, Japan, now closed, had 252 lanes.

World Championships

The World (*Fédération Internationale des Quilleurs*) Championships were instituted for men in 1954 and for women in 1963. The highest pinfall in the individual men's event is 5963 (in 28 games) by Ed Luther (USA) at Milwaukee, Wisconsin, USA on 28 Aug 1971. For the current schedule of 24 games the men's record is 5261 by Rick Steelsmith and women's record is 4894 by Sandra Jo Shiery (USA), both at Helsinki, Finland in June 1987.

Highest scores *World*

The highest individual score for 3 sanctioned games (possible 900) is 886 by Albert 'Allie' Brandt of Lockport, New York, USA, on 25 Oct 1939. The record by a woman is 864 by Jeanne Maiden (b. 10 Nov 1957) at Solon, Ohio, USA on 23 Nov 1986. The record for consecutive strikes in sanctioned match play is 33, first achieved by John Pezzin (b. 1930) at Toledo, Ohio, USA on 4 Mar 1976. The highest number of sanctioned 300 games is 30 (to Apr 1988) by John Wilcox (b. 19 Jan 1947) of Lewisburg, Pennsylvania, USA; the women's record is 11 by Jeanne Maiden. The maximum 900 for a three-game series was achieved by Glenn Allison (b. 1930) at the La Habra Bowl in Los Angeles, California, USA on 1 July 1982, but this was not recognised by the ABC due to the oiling patterns on the boards. It has been recorded five times in unsanctioned games—by Leon Bentley at Lorain, Ohio, USA on 26 Mar 1931; by Joe Sargent at Rochester, New York State, USA in 1934; by Jim Murgie in Philadelphia, Pennsylvania, USA on 4 Feb 1937; by Bob Brown at Roseville Bowl, California, USA on 12 Apr 1980 and by John Strausbaugh at York, Pennsylvania, USA on 11 July 1987. Such series must have consisted of 36 consecutive strikes (i.e. all pins down with one ball).

The highest average for a season attained in sanctioned competition is 242 by John Ragard (b. 5 Feb 1954) of Susquehanna, Pennsylvania, USA for 66 games in 1981–82. The women's record is 232 by Patty Ann of Bloomington, Illinois, USA in 1983–84.

Great Britain

The British record for a 3-game series is 806 by Philip Anthony Scammell (b. 8 May 1962) at Worthing, West Sussex on 26 Sept 1986. Army Sergeant Michael Langley scored 835 at S.H.A.P.E., Belgium on 15 Apr 1985. The maximum score for a single game of 300 has been achieved on several occasions. The first man to do so was Albert Kirkham (b. 1931) of Burslem, Staffordshire, on 5 Dec 1965. The first woman was Georgina Wardle (b. 24 July 1948) at the Sheffield Bowl, South Yorkshire on 20 Jan 1985. The first person to achieve the feat twice is Patrick Duggan (b. 26 May 1944), in 1972 and 1986, both at Bexleyheath Bowl, Kent. The 3-game series record for a woman player is 740 by Elizabeth Cullen at the Astra

Highest number of pins in a world championship ● For the current schedule of 24 games, the men's record is 5261 by Rick Steelsmith (USA) (including a perfect 300 for one game) at Helsinki, Finland in June 1987. (Photo: Rory Gillespie)

Bowl, RAF Brize Norton, Oxfordshire, England, on 15 Mar 1983.

Highest earnings

Mark Roth (b. 1950) won a record $1 278 681 in Professional Bowlers Association (PBA) competition, 36 PBA titles to 1987. The season's record is $201 200 by Mike Aulby in 1985.

Highest score—24 hours

The Dragons team of six scored 75 223 in 24 hours at Nowra Tenpin Bowl and Leisure Centre, Nowra, NSW, Australia on 2–3 Apr 1988.

Bowls

OUTDOOR

Whilst bowling games date back some 7000 years, the game of bowls in recognisable form can be traced back to the 13th century in England. The Southampton Town Bowling was formed in 1299. A green dating back to 1294 is claimed by the Chesterfield Bowling Club. After falling into disrepute, the game was rescued by the bowlers of Scotland who, headed by William W. Mitchell (1803–84), framed the modern rules in 1848–9.

Most titles *World*

The only man to win two or more singles titles is David John Bryant (b. 27 Oct 1931) (England), who won in 1966, 1980 and 1988. With the triples 1980, and the Leonard

trophy 1984 and 1988, he has won six World Championship gold medals. At Johannesburg, South Africa, in February 1976, the South African team achieved an unprecedented clean sweep of all four titles plus the team competition (Leonard Trophy). The Leonard Trophy has been won on a record three occasions by England: 1972, 1984 and 1988.

Elsie Wilke (New Zealand) won 2 women's singles titles, 1969 and 1974. Merle Richardson (Australia) has won 3 women's gold medals: fours 1977, singles and pairs 1985.

English & British

The record number of English Bowls Association (founded 8 June 1903) championships is 16 won or shared by David Bryant, including six singles (1960, 1966, 1971–3, 1975), three pairs (1965, 1969, 1974), three triples (1966, 1977, 1985) and four fours championships (1957, 1968, 1969 and 1971). He has also won seven British Isles titles (four singles, one pairs, one triple, one fours) in the period 1957–86. The youngest ever EBA singles champion was David A. Holt (b. 9 Sept 1966) at 20 yr 346 days in 1987.

Highest score

The highest score achieved in an international bowls match is the 63–1 victory by Swaziland *v.* Japan during the World Championships at Melbourne, Australia on 16 Jan 1980.

Most eights

Freda Ehlers and Linda Bertram uniquely scored three consecutive eights in the Southern Transvaal pairs event at Johannesburg, South Africa on 30 Jan 1978.

International appearances

The greatest number of international appearances outdoors by any bowler is 78 by Syd Thompson (b. 29 Aug 1912) for Ireland, 1947–73 and David Bryant for England, 1958–87. He also had 50 indoor caps. The youngest bowler to represent England was Gerard Anthony Smyth (b. 29 Dec 1960) at 20 yr 196 days on 13 July 1981.

INDOOR

The English Indoor Bowling Association became an autonomous body in 1971. Prior to that it was part of the English Bowling Association.

Championships

The four-corner international championship was first held in 1936. England has won a record 23 titles. The National Singles title (instituted 1960) has been won most often by David Bryant with nine wins between 1964 and 1983. David Bryant has won the World Indoor singles (instituted 1979) three times, 1979–81 and with Tony Allcock (b. 11 June 1955) has won the doubles (instituted 1986) twice 1986–7.

The youngest EIBA singles champion, John Dunn (b. 6 Oct 1963), was 17 yr 117 days when he won in 1981.

Highest score

C. Hammond and B. Funnell of The Angel, Tonbridge beat A. Wise and C. Lock 55–0 over 21 ends in the second round of the EIBA National Pairs Championships on 17 Oct 1983 at The Angel, Tonbridge, Kent.

Boxing

Boxing with gloves was depicted on a fresco from the Isle of Thera, Greece which has been dated to 1520 BC.

The earliest prize-ring code of rules was formulated in England on 16 Aug 1743 by the champion pugilist Jack Broughton (1704–89), who reigned from 1734 to 1750.

Boxing, which had in 1867 come under the Queensberry Rules formulated for John Sholto Douglas, 8th Marquess of Queensberry (1844–1900), was not established as a legal sport in Britain until after the ruling, *R. v. Roberts and Others*, of Mr Justice Grantham, following the death of Billy Smith (Murray Livingstone) due to a fight on 24 Apr 1901.

Longest fights

The longest recorded fight with gloves was between Andy Bowen of New Orleans (1867–94) and Jack Burke in New Orleans, Louisiana, USA, on 6–7 Apr 1893. It lasted 110 rounds, 7 hr 19 min (9.15 p.m.–4.34 a.m.), and was declared a no contest (later changed to a draw). Bowen won an 85–round bout on 31 May 1893. The longest bare–knuckle fight was 6 hr 15 min between James Kelly and Jack Smith at Fiery Creek, Dalesford, Victoria, Australia on 3 Dec 1855. The greatest number of rounds was 276 in 4 hr 30 min when Jack Jones beat Patsy Tunney in Cheshire in 1825.

Shortest fights

There is a distinction between the quickest knock-out and the shortest fight. A knock-out in 10½ sec (including a 10 sec count) occurred on 23 Sept 1946, when Al Couture struck Ralph Walton while the latter was adjusting a gum shield in his corner at Lewiston, Maine, USA. If the time was accurately taken it is clear that Couture must have been more than half-way across the ring from his own corner at the opening bell. The shortest fight on record appears to be one in a Golden Gloves tournament at Minneapolis, Minnesota, USA on 4 Nov 1947, when Mike Collins floored Pat Brownson with the first punch and the contest was stopped, without a count, 4 sec after the bell.

The fastest officially timed knock-out in British boxing is 11 sec (including a doubtless fast 10 sec count) when Jack Cain beat Harry Deamer, both of Notting Hill, London, at the National Sporting Club on 20 Feb 1922. More recently, Hugh Kelly knocked out Steve Cook with the first punch of their contest at the Normandy Hotel, Glasgow on 14 May 1984, again in 11 sec, including the 10 sec count.

The shortest world title fight was 45 sec, when Lloyd Honeyghan (b. 22 Apr 1960) beat Gene Hatcher in an IBF welterweight bout at Marbella, Spain on 30 Aug 1987. The shortest ever heavyweight world title fight was the James J. Jeffries (1875–1953)-Jack Finnegan bout at Detroit, USA on 6 Apr 1900, won by Jeffries in 55 sec. The shortest ever British title fight was one of 40 sec (including the count), when Dave Charnley knocked out David 'Darkie' Hughes in a lightweight championship defence in Nottingham on 20 Nov 1961.

Most British titles

The most defences of a British heavyweight title is 14 by 'Bombardier' Billy Wells (1889–1967) from 1911 to 1919. The only British boxer

to win 3 Lonsdale Belts outright was Henry William Cooper (b. 3 May 1934), heavyweight champion. He retired after losing to Joe Bugner (b. Hungary, 13 Mar 1950), having held the British heavyweight title from 12 Jan 1959 to 28 May 1969 and from 24 Mar 1970 to 16 Mar 1971.

The fastest time to win a Lonsdale Belt, for 3 successive championship wins, is 203 days by Robert Dickie (b. 23 June 1964) at featherweight, 9 Apr–29 Oct 1986. The longest time for winning a Lonsdale belt outright is 8 yr 236 days by Kirkland Laing, 4 Apr 1979–26 Nov 1987.

Tallest

The tallest boxer to fight professionally was Gogea Mitu (b. 1914) of Romania in 1935. He was 233 cm *7 ft 4 in* and weighed 148 kg *327 lb*.

John Rankin, who won a fight in New Orleans, Louisiana, USA in November 1967, was reputedly also 233 cm *7 ft 4 in*.

Jim Culley, 'The Tipperary Giant', who fought as a boxer and wrestled in the 1940's is also reputed to have been 233 cm *7 ft 4 in*.

Most fights without loss

Edward Henry (Harry) Greb (USA) (1894–1926) was unbeaten in a sequence of 178 bouts, but these included 117 'no decision', of which 5 were unofficial losses, in 1916–23. Of boxers with complete records, Packey McFarland (USA) (1888–1936) had 97 fights (5 draws) in 1905–15 without a defeat.

Pedro Carrasco (Spain) (b. 7 Nov 1943) won 83 consecutive fights from 22 April 1964 to 3 Sept 1970, drew once and had a further nine wins before his loss to Armando Ramos in a WBC lightweight contest on 18 Feb 1972.

Most knock-outs

The greatest number of finishes classed as 'knock-outs' in a career (1936–63) is 145 (129 in professional bouts) by Archie Moore (USA) (b. Archibald Lee Wright, 13 Dec 1913 or 1916). The record for consecutive KO's is 44 by

> **Greatest earnings** ● The greatest fortune amassed by an individual in sport is an estimated $69 million by the boxer Muhammad Ali (USA) (b. 17 Jan 1942) from October 1960 to December 1981. This was from 61 fights (including exhibitions) comprising a total of 551 rounds.(Photo: All-Sport)

Lamar Clark (b. 1 Dec 1934) (USA) from 1958 to 11 Jan 1960. He knocked out 6 in one night (five in the first round) at Bingham, Utah, USA on 1 Dec 1958.

Largest purse

The total purse for the world heavyweight fight between Mike Tyson (USA) (b. 30 June 1966) and Michael Spinks (USA) (b. 22 July 1956) at Convention Hall, Atlantic City, New Jersey, USA on 27 June 1988, was estimated as at least $35·8 million, $22 m for Tyson and $13·8 m for Spinks, who was knocked out after 1 min 31 sec of the first round.

Attendances *Highest*

The greatest paid attendance at any boxing fight has been 120 757 (with a ringside price of $27·50) for the Tunney v. Dempsey world heavyweight title fight at the Sesquicentennial Stadium, Philadelphia, Pennsylvania, USA on 23 Sept 1926. The indoor record is 63 350 at the Ali v. Leon Spinks (b. 13 July 1956) fight in the Superdrome, New Orleans, Louisiana, USA on 15 Sept 1978. The British attendance record is 82 000 at the Len Harvey v. Jock McAvoy fight at White City, London on 10 July 1939.

The highest non-paying attendance is 135 132 at the Tony Zale v. Billy Pryor fight at Juneau Park, Milwaukee, Wisconsin, USA on 16 Aug 1941.

Lowest

The smallest attendance at a world heavyweight title fight was 2434 at the Clay v. Liston fight at Lewiston, Maine, USA on 25 May 1965.

WORLD HEAVYWEIGHT CHAMPIONS

Earliest title fight

The first world heavyweight title fight, with gloves and 3–min rounds, was that between John Lawrence Sullivan (1858–1918) and 'Gentleman' James John Corbett (1866–1933) in New Orleans, Louisiana, USA on 7 Sept 1892. Corbett won in 21 rounds.

Longest and shortest reigns

The longest reign of any world heavyweight champion is 11 years 252 days by Joe Louis (USA) (b. Joseph Louis Barrow, 1914–81), from 22 June 1937, when he knocked out James Joseph Braddock in the eighth round at Chicago, Illinois, USA, until announcing his retirement on 1 Mar 1949. During his reign Louis made a record 25 defences of his title.

The shortest reigns were 83 days for WBA champion James 'Bonecrusher' Smith (USA) (b. 3 Apr 1955), 13 Dec 1986 to 7 Mar 1987, Ken Norton (USA) (b. 9 Aug 1945), recognised by the WBC as champion for 83 days from 18 Mar–9 June 1978 and 64 days for Tony Tucker (USA) (b. 28 Dec 1958), IBF champion, 30 May–2 Aug 1987.

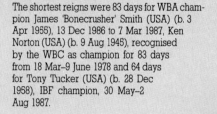

The longest lived world heavyweight champion was Jack Dempsey who died on 31 May 1983 aged 87 yr 341 days.

Most recaptures

Muhammad Ali (b. Cassius Marcellus Clay Jr, 17 Jan 1942) is the only man to regain the heavyweight championship twice. Ali first won the title on 25 Feb 1964 defeating Sonny Liston. He defeated George Foreman on 30 Oct 1974 having been stripped of the title by the world boxing authorities on 28 Apr 1967. He won the WBA title from Leon Spinks on 15 Sept 1978 having previously lost to him on 15 Feb 1978.

Undefeated

Rocky Marciano (b. Rocco Francis Marchegiano) (1923–69) is the only world heavyweight champion to have been undefeated during his entire professional career (1947–56). He won all his 49 fights, 43 by knock-outs or stoppages. Currently, Mike Tyson is undefeated, having won all 35 fights to June 1988.

Oldest and youngest

The oldest man to win the heavyweight crown was Jersey Joe Walcott (USA) (b. Arnold Raymond Cream, 31 Jan 1914), who knocked out Ezzard Mack Charles (1921–75) on 18 July 1951 in Pittsburgh, Pennsylvania, USA when aged 37 yr 168 days. Walcott was the oldest holder at 38 yr 236 days, losing his title to Rocky Marciano (1923–69) on 23 Sept 1952. The youngest age at which the world title has been won is 20 yr 144 days by Mike Tyson (USA) (b. 30 June 1966) when he beat Trevor Berbick (USA) to win the WBC version at Las Vegas, Nevada, USA on 22 Nov 1986. He added the WBA title when he beat James 'Bonecrusher' Smith on 7 Mar 1987 at 20 yr 249 days. He became universal champion on 2 Aug 1987 when he beat Tony Tucker (USA).

Heaviest and lightest

The heaviest world champion was Primo Carnera (Italy) (1906–67), the 'Ambling Alp', who won the title from Jack Sharkey in New York City, NY, USA on 29 June 1933. He scaled 118 kg *260½ lb* for this fight but his peak weight was 122 kg *270 lb*. He had an expanded chest measurement of 137 cm *54 in* and the longest reach at 217 cm *85½ in* (finger tip to finger tip). The lightest champion was Robert James 'Bob' Fitzsimmons (1863–1917), from Helston, Cornwall, England who at 75 kg *167 lb*, won the title by knocking out James J. Corbett at Carson City, Nevada, USA on 17 Mar 1897.

Tallest and shortest

The tallest world champion according to measurements by the physical education director of the Hemingway Gymnasium, Harvard University, was Carnera at 196·6 cm *6 ft 5·4 in*, although he was widely reported and believed to be up to 204 cm *6 ft 8½ in*. Jess Willard (1881–1968), who won the title in 1915, often stated to be 199 cm *6 ft 6¼ in* was in fact 196 cm *6 ft 5¼ in*. The shortest was Tommy Burns, world champion from 23 Feb 1906 to 26 Dec 1908, who stood 170 cm *5 ft 7 in* and weighed between 76–81 kg *168–180 lb*.

WORLD CHAMPIONS *Any weight*

Longest reign

Joe Louis's heavyweight duration record of 11 yr 252 days stands for all divisions.

Youngest and oldest

The youngest age at which any world championship has been won is 17 yr 176 days by Wilfred Benitez (b. New York, 12 Sept 1958) of Puerto Rico, who won the WBA light welterweight title in San Juan, PR on 6 Mar 1976. The oldest world champion was Archie Moore, who was recognised as a light heavyweight champion up to 10 Feb 1962 when his title was removed. He was then believed to be between 45 and 48. Bob Fitzsimmons had the longest career of any official world titleholder with over 31 years from 1883 to 1914. He had his last world title bout on 20 Dec 1905 at the age of 42 yr 208 days.

Regain a world title ● Lloyd Honeyghan (b. 22 Apr 1960) celebrates regaining his world welterweight title after knocking out Jorge Vaca (Mexico) in the third round on 29 Mar 1988. He was the second British boxer to have regained a world title, the first being Ted 'Kid' Lewis on 25 June 1917. Uniquely, Honeyghan was the first boxer, under the current ruling, to have lost a world title after a fight was stopped. This was also against Vaca, on 28 Oct 1987 when Vaca received a severe cut above the right eye following an accidental clash of heads. (Photo: All-Sport/John Gichigi)

Longest fight

The longest world title fight (under Queensberry Rules) was that between the lightweights Joe Gans (1874–1910), of the USA, and Oscar Matthew 'Battling' Nelson (1882–1954), the 'Durable Dane', at Goldfield, Nevada, USA on 3 Sept 1906. It was terminated in the 42nd round when Gans was declared the winner on a foul.

Most different weights

Thomas Hearns (USA) (b. 18 Oct 1958) beat Juan Roldan (Argentina) at Las Vegas, Nevada, USA on 29 Oct 1987 to win the WBC middleweight title. This made him the first man to win world titles at four weight categories, as he had previously won the WBA welterweight in 1980, WBC super welterweight in 1982 and WBC light heavyweight in 1987. The only boxer to win a world title five times at one weight is 'Sugar' Ray Robinson (USA) (b. Walker Smith Jr, 3 May 1921), who beat Carmen Basilio (USA) in the Chicago Stadium on 25 Mar 1958, to regain the world middleweight title for the fourth time. The record number of title bouts in a career is 37, of which 18 ended in 'no decision', by three-time world welterweight champion Jack Britton (USA) (1885–1962) in 1915–22.

The only man to hold world titles at three weights *simultaneously* was Henry 'Homicide Hank' Armstrong (b. 12 Dec 1912), now the Reverend Henry Jackson, of the USA, at featherweight, lightweight and welterweight from August to December 1938.

Greatest weight difference

When Primo Carnera (Italy) 122 kg *270 lb* fought Tommy Loughran (USA) 83 kg *184 lb* for the world heavyweight title at Miami, Florida, USA on 1 Mar 1934, there was a

Most Slalom World titles ● Richard Fox (GB) has won a record three K1 Slalom individual world titles in 1981, 1983 and 1985. He was also a member of the Great Britain team which won the K1 team world title on the same occasions and 1987.(Photo: Bob Martin/All-Sport)

weight difference of 39 kg *86 lb* between the two fighters. Carnera won the fight on points.

Greatest 'tonnage'

The greatest 'tonnage' recorded in any fight is 317 kg *700 lb* when Claude 'Humphrey' McBride (Oklahoma), 154 kg *340 lb*, knocked out Jimmy Black (Houston), who weighed 163 kg *360 lb* in the third round at Oklahoma City on 1 June 1971. The greatest 'tonnage' in a world title fight was 221½ kg *488¾ lb*, when Carnera, then 117½ kg *259½ lb* fought Paolino Uzcudun (Spain) 104 kg *229¼ lb* in Rome on 22 Oct 1933.

Most knock-downs in title fights

Vic Toweel (South Africa) (b. 12 Jan 1929) knocked down Danny O'Sullivan of London 14 times in ten rounds in their world bantamweight fight at Johannesburg on 2 Dec 1950, before the latter retired.

Twins

When Khaokor Galaxy (Thailand) won the WBA bantam-weight title on 8 May 1988, he and his twin brother, Khaosai, were the first twins ever to be world boxing champions. Khaosai Galaxy had been WBA super flyweight champion since 21 Nov 1984.

AMATEUR

Most Olympic titles

Only two boxers have won three Olympic gold medals: southpaw László Papp (b. 25 Mar 1926) (Hungary), middleweight 1948, light-middleweight 1952 and 1956; and Teofilo Stevenson (b. 23 Mar 1952) (Cuba), heavyweight 1972, 1976 and 1980. The only man to win 2 titles in one celebration was Oliver L. Kirk (USA), who won both bantam and featherweight titles in St Louis, Missouri, USA in 1904, but he needed only one bout in each class.

Oldest gold medallist

Richard Kenneth Gunn (1871–1961) (GB) won the Olympic featherweight gold medal on 27 Oct 1908 in London aged 37 yr 254 days.

World Championships

Two boxers have won three world championships (inst. 1974): Teofilo Stevenson (Cuba), heavyweight 1974, 1978 and super-heavyweight 1986, and Adolfo Horta (b. 3 Oct 1957) (Cuba) bantam 1978, feather 1982 and lightweight 1986.

Most titles *Great Britain*

The greatest number of ABA titles won by any boxer is seven by John Lyon (b. 9 Mar 1962) at light-flyweight 1981–4 and at flyweight 1986–8. Alex 'Bud' Watson (b. 27 May 1914) of Leith, Scotland won the Scottish heavyweight title in 1938, 1942–3, and the light-heavyweight championship 1937–9, 1943–5 and 1947, making ten in all. He also won the ABA light-heavyweight title in 1945 and 1947.

Longest span

The greatest span of ABA title-winning performances is that of the heavyweight Hugh 'Pat' Floyd (b. 23 Aug 1910), who won in 1929 and gained his fourth title 17 years later in 1946.

Canoeing

The acknowledged pioneer of canoeing as a modern sport was John Macgregor (1825–92), a British barrister, in 1865. The Canoe Club was formed on 26 July 1866.

Most titles *Olympic*

Gert Fredriksson (b. 21 Nov 1919) of Sweden won a record six Olympic gold medals, 1948–60. He added a silver and a bronze for a record eight medals. The most by a woman is three by Lyudmila Pinayeva (*née* Khvedosyuk) (b. 14 Jan 1936) (USSR), 1964–72. The most gold medals at one Games is three by Vladimir Parfeno-

River Rhine ● The fastest time for canoeing the River Rhine, solo and unsupported, is 10 days 12 hr 9 min by Frank Palmer, 15–25 May 1988. The 'Rhine Challenge', as organised by the International Long River Canoeists Club, begins from an official marker post in Chur, Switzerland and ends at Willemstad, Holland, a distance of 1149 km *714 miles.*

vich (b. 2 Dec 1958) (USSR) in 1980 and by Ian Ferguson (b. 20 July 1952) (New Zealand) in 1984.

World

Including the Olympic Games a men's record thirteen titles have been won by Gert Fredriksson, 1948–60, Rüdiger Helm (GDR) (b. 6 Oct 1956), 1976–83, and Ivan Patzaichin (Romania) (b. 26 Nov 1949), 1968–84. The women's record is 20 by Birgit Schmidt (*née* Fischer) (b. 25 Feb 1962), 1978–87. The most individual titles by a British canoeist is three by Alan Emus, canoe sailing 1961, 1965 and 1969, and by Richard Fox at K1 slalom in 1981, 1983 and 1985. Fox also won four gold medals at K1 team, in these years and 1987.

Highest speed

The Hungarian four-man kayak world champions in 1987 at Duisberg, West Germany covered 1000 m in 3 min 01·21 sec. This represents an average speed of 19·86 km/h *12·34 mph*. The USSR K4 that won the 1984 Olympic title achieved 21·15 km/h *13·14 mph* for the first 250 m.

Longest journey

The longest journey ever made by canoe is 19 603 km *12 181 miles* by father and son Dana and Donald Starkell from Winnipeg, Manitoba, Canada by ocean and river to Belem, Brazil from 1 June 1980 to 1 May 1982. All portages were human powered.

The longest journey without portages or aid of any kind is one of 9820 km *6102 miles* by Richard H. Grant and Ernest 'Moose' Lassy circumnavigating the eastern USA via Chicago, New Orleans, Miami, New York and the Great Lakes from 22 Sept 1930 to 15 Aug 1931.

Longest open sea voyage

Beatrice and John Dowd, Ken Beard and Steve Benson (Richard Gillett replaced him mid-journey) paddled 3491 km *2170 miles* (of a total 3527 km *2192 miles*) from Venezuela to Miami, Florida, USA, via the West Indies, 11 Aug 1977–29 Apr 1978 in two Klepper Aerius 20 kayaks.

Cross-Channel

The singles record across the English Channel is 3 hr

33 min 47 sec by Andrew William Dougall Samuel (b. 12 July 1937) of Glasgow, from Shakespeare Bay, Dover to Wissant, France on 5 Sept 1976. The doubles record is 2 hr 28 min 18 sec by Shaun Rice (Ireland) and Colin Simpkins (South Africa) in a K2 on 19 July 1986 from Shakespeare Bay, Dover to Cap Gris Nez, France.

North Sea

On 22–23 June 1986, a team of 5 in the 'Canadian Club Challenge' paddled K1s from Zeebrugge, Belgium to Felixstowe, England, over 177 km *110 miles* across open sea, in 28 hr 56 min 12 sec.

Devies-Westminister

The Senior Class record for the annual Challenge Cup race (instituted officially 1949) over 201 km *125 miles* with 76 locks on the River Thames is 15 hr 34 min 12 sec by Brian R. Greenham and Timothy J. Cornish (Reading/Leighton Park/Richmond) to win the 1979 race.

Loch Ness

The fastest time for a K1 from Fort Augustus to Lochend (36·5 km *22·7 miles*) is 2 hr 58 min 48 sec by Colin Simpkins (South Africa) in a Jaguar K1 on 26 July 1987.

Highest altitude

In September 1976 Dr Michael Leslie Jones (1951–78) and Michael Hopkinson of the British Everest Canoe Expedition canoed down the River Dudh Kosi, Nepal from an altitude of 5334 m *17 500 ft.*

Longest race

The longest race ever staged was 5283 km *3283 miles* from Rocky Mountain House, Alberta to the Expo 67 site at Montreal, Quebec as the Canadian Government Centennial Voyageur Canoe Pageant and Race. Ten canoes represented Canadian provinces and territories. The winner of the race, which took from 24 May to 4 Sept 1967, was the Province of Manitoba canoe *Radisson.*

24 hours

The solo 24-hour canoe record is 252·9 km *157·14 miles* by Zdzislaw Szubski (Poland) in a Jaguar K1 canoe on Vistula River, Włocławek to Gdansk, Poland on 11–12 Sept 1987. The women's record was set at 156·4 km *97·2 miles* by Lydia Formentin on the Swan River, Western Australia in 1979.

The record in flat water, without benefit of current, is 199·53 km *123·98 miles* by Thomas J. Mazuzan on the Barge Canal, New York State, USA on 24–5 Sept 1986.

The record in open sea is 194·1 km *120·6 miles* by Randy Fine (USA) along the Florida coast on 26–7 June 1986.

Card Games

Greatest lifetime distance
Fritz Lindner of Berlin, West Germany, totalled 103 444 km *64 278 miles* from 1928 to September 1987.

Eskimo rolls
Ray Hudspith (b. 18 Apr 1960) achieved 1000 eskimo rolls in 34 min 43 sec at the Elswick Pool, Newcastle-upon-Tyne, England on 20 Mar 1987. Julian Dean achieved 1555 continuous rolls at Casterton Swimming Pool, Cumbria, England taking 1 hr 49 min 45 sec on 6 Dec 1983. Colin Brian Hill (b. 16 Aug 1970) set a 'hand-rolling' record of 1000 rolls in 31 min 55·62 sec at Consett, Co. Durham, England on 12 Mar 1987. He achieved 100 rolls in 2 min 39·2 sec at Crystal Palace, London on 22 Feb 1987. Sarah Ashmead achieved 3500 continuous rolls at the College of St Mark and St John, Derriford, Plymouth, Devon on 30 Apr 1988.

Canoe raft
A raft of 302 kayaks and canoes, held together by hands only, while free floating for 30 seconds, was established on the Regatta Lake at Holme Pierrepont, Nottinghamshire on 15 Sept 1986.

Card Games

CONTRACT BRIDGE
Bridge (a corruption of Biritch, a now obsolete Russian word whose meanings include 'declarer') is thought either to be of Levantine origin, similar games having been played there in the early 1870s, or to have come from India.

Auction bridge (highest bidder names trump) was invented *c*. 1902. The contract principle, present in several games (notably the French game *Plafond, c.* 1917), was introduced to Bridge by Harold Sterling Vanderbilt (USA) on 1 Nov 1925 during a Caribbean voyage aboard the SS *Finland*. It became a world-wide craze after the USA *v.* Great Britain challenge match between Romanian-born Ely Culbertson (1891–1955) and Lt-Col Walter Thomas More Buller (1887–1938) at Almack's Club, London, in September 1930. The USA won the 200-hand match by 4845 points.

Biggest tournament
The Epson World Bridge Championship, held on 3 June 1988, was contested by 84 352 players playing the same hands at more than 1731 centres. It was won by Jan Horwitz and Barbara Norante of Butler, Pennsylvania, USA, with 76·33 %.

Most world titles
The World Championship (Bermuda Bowl) has been a won record 13 times by Italy's Blue Team (*Squadra Azzura*), 1957–9, 1961–3, 1965–7, 1969, 1973–5 and by the USA, 1950–1, 1953–4, 1970–1, 1976–7, 1979, 1981, 1983, 1985, 1987. Italy also won the Olympiad in 1964, 1968 and 1972. Giorgio Belladonna (b. 7 June 1923) was in all the Italian winning teams. The USA have a record four wins in the women's world championship for the Venice Trophy: 1974, 1976, 1978 and 1987 and three wins at the World Team Olympiad: 1976, 1980 and 1984.

Most world championship hands
In the 1987 Bermuda Bowl in Ocho Rios, Jamaica, Tony Forrester from Bradford, played a record 720 out of a possible 784 boards.

Most master points
In the latest ranking list based on Master Points awarded by the World Bridge Federation during the last ten years, the leading players in the world are (men) Robert Hamman (b. 1938) of Dallas, Texas, USA with 522½ and (women) Sally Horton (*née* Sowter) (GB) with 260¼. The all-time leading Master Point winner was Giorgio Belladonna (Italy) with 1821¼ points. The world's leading woman player is Jacqui Mitchell (USA) with 347 points.

Barry Crane of Los Angeles led the American Contract Bridge League rankings from 1968 to his murder in 1985. He amassed a record total of 35 137·6 Master Points. The current leader is Paul Soloway with 29 153 to June 1988. The most master points scored in a year is 3270 by Grant Baze (USA) in 1984.

The first man to win 10 000 Master Points was Oswald Jacoby (USA) (1902–84) in October 1967. He had been a member of the winning World Championship team in 1935 and on 4 Dec 1983 became the oldest member of a winning team of a major open team championship, in the Curtis Reisinger Trophy.

Youngest Life Master
Dougie Hsieh (b. 23 Nov 1969) of New York City became the world's youngest ever Life Master in 1981 at 11 yr 306 days. The youngest ever female Master is Patricia Thomas (b. 10 Oct 1968) at 14 yr 28 days in 1982.

Perfect deals
The mathematical odds against dealing 13 cards of one suit are 158 753 389 899 to 1, while the odds against a named player receiving a 'perfect hand' consisting of all 13 spades are 635 013 559 599 to 1. The odds against each of the four players receiving a complete suit (a 'perfect deal') are 2 235 197 406 895 366 368301 559 999 to 1.

Possible auctions
The number of possible auctions with North as dealer is 128 745 650 347 030 683 120 231 926 111 609 371 363 122 697 557.

CRIBBAGE
The invention of the game (once called Cribbidge) is credited to the English dramatist Sir John Suckling (1609–42).

Rare hands
Four maximum 29 point hands have been achieved by William E. Johnson of Waltham, Massachusetts, USA, 1974–81 and by Mrs Mary Matheson of Springhill, Nova Scotia, Canada, 1974–85. Paul Nault of Athol, Massachusetts, USA had two such hands within eight games in a tournament on 19 Mar 1977.

Most points in 24 hours
The most points scored by a team of four, playing singles in two pairs, is 111 201 by Christine and Elizabeth Gill, Jeanette MacGrath and Donald Ward at Grannie's Healin' Hame, Embo, Highland Region on 2–3 May 1987.

Caving

See also page 58

The world depth record was set by the Groupe Vulcain in the Gouffre Jean Bernard, France at 1535 m *5035 ft* in October 1983. However, this cave, explored via multiple entrances, has never been entirely descended, so the 'sporting' record for the greatest descent into a cave is recognised as 1408 m *4619 ft* in the Sima de la Puerta de Illamina in Spain by a team of Bulgarian cavers from the Speleo Club Studenz Pleven in 1987.

Cricket

The earliest evidence of a game similar to cricket is from a drawing depicting two men playing with a bat and ball dated *c.* 1250. The game was played in Guildford, Surrey, at least as early as 1550. The earliest major match of which the full score survives was one in which a team representing England (40 and 70) was beaten by Kent (53 and 58 for 9) by one wicket at the Artillery Ground in Finsbury, London on 18 June 1744. Cricket was played in Australia as early as 1803. The first international match was played between Canada and the USA in 1844. Fifteen years later those countries were host to the first

English touring team. The first touring team to visit England was an Australian Aborigine XI in 1868.

BATTING RECORDS
Teams
Highest innings
The highest recorded innings by a team was 1107 runs in 10 hr 30 min by Victoria *v.* New South Wales in an Australian Sheffield Shield match at Melbourne on 27–28 Dec 1926.

The highest innings in Test cricket and the highest made in England is 903 runs for seven wickets declared in 15 hr 17 min, by England *v.* Australia at Kennington Oval, London on 20, 22 and 23 Aug 1938. The highest innings in a County Championship match is 887 in 10 hr 50 min by Yorkshire *v.* Warwickshire at Edgbaston, Birmingham on 7–8 May 1896.

Lowest innings
The lowest recorded innings is 12 by Oxford University *v.* the Marylebone Cricket Club (MCC) at Cowley Marsh, Oxford on 24 May 1877, and by Northamptonshire *v.* Gloucestershire at Gloucester on 11 June 1907. On the occasion of the Oxford match, however, the University batted a man short. The lowest score in a Test innings is 26 by New Zealand *v.* England at Auckland on 28 Mar 1955.

The lowest aggregate for two innings is 34 (16 and 18) by Border *v.* Natal in the South African Currie Cup at East London on 19 and 21 Dec 1959.

Greatest victory
The greatest recorded margin of victory is an innings and 851 runs, when Pakistan Railways (910 for 6 wickets declared) beat Dera Ismail Khan (32 and 27) at Lahore on 2–4 Dec 1964. The largest margin in England is an innings and 579 runs by England over Australia at The Oval on 20–24 Aug 1938 when Australia scored 201 and 123 with two men short in both innings. The most one-sided county match was when Surrey (698) defeated Sussex (114 and 99) by an innings and 485 runs at The Oval on 9–11 Aug 1888.

Most runs in a day
The greatest number of runs scored in a day is 721 all out (ten wickets) in 5 hr 48 min by the Australians *v.* Essex at Southchurch Park, Southend-on-Sea on 15 May 1948. The Test record for runs in a day is 588 at Old Trafford, Manchester on 27 July 1936 when England added 398 and India were 190 for 0 in their second innings by the close.

BATTING RECORDS
Individuals
Highest innings
The highest individual innings is 499 in 10 hr 35 min by Hanif Mohammad (b. 21 Dec 1934) for Karachi *v.* Bahawalpur at Karachi, Pakistan on 8, 9 and 11 Jan 1959. The highest in England is 424 in 7 hr 50 min by Archibald Campbell MacLaren (1871–1944) for Lancashire *v.* Somerset at Taunton on 15–16 July 1895. The record for a Test match is 365 not out in 10 hr 14 min by Sir Garfield St Aubrun Sobers (b. 28 July 1936) for West Indies *v.* Pakistan at Sabina Park, Kingston, Jamaica on 27 Feb–1 Mar 1958. The England Test record is 364 by Sir Leonard Hutton (b. 23 June 1916) *v.* Australia at The Oval on 20, 22 and 23 Aug 1938.

Longest innings
The longest innings is one of 16 hr 10 min for 337 runs by Hanif Mohammad (Pakistan) *v.* West Indies at Bridgetown, Barbados on 20–23 Jan 1958. The English record is 13 hr 17 min by Len Hutton in his record Test score of 364.

Most runs *Off an over*
The first batsman to score 36 runs off a six ball over was Sir Garfield Sobers (Nottinghamshire) off Malcolm Andrew Nash (b. 9 May 1945) (Glamorgan) at

Swansea on 31 Aug 1968. His feat was emulated by Ravishankar Jayadritha Shastri (b. 27 May 1962) for Bombay v. Baroda at Bombay, India on 10 Jan 1985 off the bowling of Tilak Raj.

Most runs ● Graeme Ashley Hick (b. Zimbabwe 23 May 1966) scored a record 410 runs by the end of April in an English season and became the eighth player to score 1000 runs by the end of May, with a total of 1019 runs (av 101·9) from seven matches. The first player to score 1000 runs by the end of May was Dr William Gilbert Grace (1848–1915) with 1016 (av 112·88) in 1895, and the record number of runs is 1074 (av 97·63) by Thomas Walter Hayward (1871–1939) in 1900. Hick's 405 not out for Worcestershire v. Somerset at Taunton on 5–6 May 1988, was the highest score in England this century. (Photo: All-Sport/Gray Mortimore)

Off a ball

The most runs scored off a single hit is ten by Albert Neilson Hornby (1847–1925) off James Street (1839–1906) for Lancashire v. Surrey at The Oval on 14 July 1873, and by Samuel Hill Wood (later Sir Samuel Hill Hill-Wood) (1872–1949) off Cuthbert James Burnup (1875–1960) for Derbyshire v. MCC at Lord's, London on 26 May 1900.

Most sixes *In an innings*

The most sixes hit in an innings is 15 by John Richard Reid (b. 3 June 1928), in an innings of 296, lasting 3 hr 40 min, for Wellington v. Northern Districts in a Plunket Shield match at Wellington, New Zealand on 14–15 Jan 1963. The Test record is ten by Walter Hammond in an innings of 336 not out for England v. New Zealand at Auckland on 31 Mar and 1 Apr 1933.

Double hundreds

The only batsman to score double hundreds in both innings is Arthur Edward Fagg (1915–77), who made 244 and 202 not out for Kent v. Essex at Colchester from 13–15 July 1938. Sir Donald Bradman scored a career record 37 double hundreds, 1927–49.

Fastest scoring

The fastest 50 was completed off 13 balls in 8 min (1.22 to 1.30 p.m.) in 11 scoring strokes by Clive Clay Inman (b. 29 Jan 1936) in an innings of 57 not out for Leicestershire v. Nottinghamshire at Trent Bridge, Nottingham on 20 Aug 1965. Full tosses were bowled to expedite a declaration.

The fastest hundred was completed in 35 min off between 40 and 46 balls by Percy George Herbert Fender (1892-1987), when scoring 113 not out for Surrey v. Northamptonshire at Northampton on 26 Aug 1920. Steven Joseph O'Shaughnessy (b. 9 Sept 1961) also scored a hundred in 35 min for Lancashire v. Leices-

INDIVIDUAL RECORDS

FIRST-CLASS AND TEST CAREER

		Name	Team	Year
		BATTING		
MOST RUNS	First-Class ... 61 237	Sir John Berry 'Jack' Hobbs (1882–1963) (av. 50·65)	Surrey/England	1905–34
	Test ... 10,122	Sunil Manohar Gavaskar (b. 10 July 1949) (av. 51·12)	India (125 Tests)	1971–87
MOST CENTURIES	First-Class ... 197	Sir Jack Hobbs (in 1315 innings)	Surrey/England	1905–34
	Test ... 34	Sunil Gavaskar (in 214 innings)	India	1971–87
HIGHEST AVERAGE	First-Class ... 95·14	Sir Donald George Bradman (b. 28 Aug 1908) (28 067 runs in 338 innings, including 43 not out)	NSW/South Australia/Australia	1927–49
	Test ... 99·94	Sir Donald Bradman (6996 runs in 80 innings)	Australia (52 Tests)	1928–48
		BOWLING		
MOST WICKETS	First-Class ... 4187	Wilfred Rhodes (1877–1973) (av. 16·71)	Yorkshire/England	1898–1930
	Test ... 373	Ian Terrence Botham (b. 24 Nov 1955) (av. 27·86)	England (94 Tests)	1977–87
	... 373	Richard John Hadlee (b. 3 Jul 1951) (av. 22·46)	New Zealand (72 Tests)	1973–87
LOWEST AVERAGE (min 15 wkts)	Test ... 10·75	George Alfred Lohmann (1865–1901) (112 wkts)	England (18 Tests)	1886–96
		WICKET-KEEPING		
MOST DISMISSALS	First-Class ... 1648	Robert William Taylor (b. 17 July 1941)	Derbyshire/England	1960–86
	Test ... 355	Rodney William Marsh (b. 11 Nov 1947)	Australia (96 Tests)	1970–84
MOST CATCHES	First-Class ... 1473	Robert Taylor	Derbyshire/England	1960–86
	Test ... 343	Rodney Marsh	Australia	1970–84
MOST STUMPINGS	First-Class ... 415	Leslie Ethelbert George Ames (b. 3 Dec 1905)	Kent/England	1926–51
	Test ... 52	William Albert Stanley Oldfield (1894–1976)	Australia (54 Tests)	1920–37
		FIELDING		
MOST CATCHES	First-Class ... 1018	Frank Edward Woolley (1887–1978)	Kent/England	1906–38
	Test ... 122	Gregory Stephen Chappell (b. 7 Aug 1948)	Australia (87 Tests)	1970–84

IN A FIRST-CLASS SEASON IN ENGLAND

	Name	Team	Year
	BATTING		
MOST RUNS ... 3816	Denis Charles Scott Compton (b. 23 May 1918) (av. 90·85)	Middlesex/England	1947
MOST CENTURIES ... 18	Denis Compton (in 50 innings with 8 not outs)	Middlesex/England	1947
HIGHEST AVERAGE ... 115·66	Sir Donald Bradman (2429 runs in 26 innings, with 5 not outs)	Australians	1938
	BOWLING		
MOST WICKETS ... 304	Alfred Percy 'Tich' Freeman (1888–1965) (1976·1 overs) (av. 18·05)	Kent	1928
LOWEST AVERAGE (min 100 wkts) ... 8·54	Alfred Shaw (1842–1907) (186 wkts)	Nottinghamshire	1880
	WICKET-KEEPING		
MOST DISMISSALS ... 127	Leslie Ames (79 caught, 48 stumped)	Kent	1929
MOST CATCHES ... 96	James Graham Binks (b. 5 Oct 1935)	Yorkshire	1960
MOST STUMPINGS ... 64	Leslie Ames	Kent	1932
	FIELDING		
MOST CATCHES ... 78	Walter Reginald Hammond (1903–65)	Gloucestershire	1928

IN A TEST SERIES

	Name	Team	Year
	BATTING		
MOST RUNS ... 974	Sir Donald Bradman (av. 139·14)	Australia v. England (5 T)	1930
MOST CENTURIES ... 5	Clyde Leopold Walcott (b. 17 Jan 1926)	West Indies v. Australia (5 T)	1954–55
HIGHEST AVERAGE ... 563·00	Walter Reginald Hammond (563 runs, 2 inns, 1 n.o.)	England v. New Zealand (2 T)	1932–33
	BOWLING		
MOST WICKETS ... 49	Sydney Francis Barnes (1873–1967) (av. 10·93)	England v. South Africa (4 T)	1913–14
LOWEST AVERAGE (min 20 wkts) ... 5·80	George Alfred Lohmann (35 wkts)	England v. South Africa (3 T)	1895–96
	WICKET-KEEPING		
MOST DISMISSALS ... 28	Rodney Marsh (all caught)	Australia v. England (5 T)	1982–83
MOST STUMPINGS ... 9	Percy William Sherwell (1880–1948)	South Africa v. Australia (5 T)	1910–11
	FIELDING		
MOST CATCHES ... 15	Jack Morrison Gregory (1895–1973)	Australia v. England (5 T)	1920–21
	ALL-ROUND		
400 RUNS/ 30 WICKETS ... 475/34	George Giffen (1859–1927)	Australia v. England (5 T)	1894–95

tershire at Old Trafford, Manchester off 54 balls on 13 Sept 1983. In all he scored 105 and with Graeme Fowler (b. 20 Apr 1957) put on 201 runs for the first wicket in 45 mins. The match was 'dead' and irregular bowlers were used. The hundred in fewest recorded deliveries was by David William Hookes (b. 3 May 1955) in 34 balls, in 43 min, for South Australia v. Victoria at Adelaide on 25 Oct 1982. In all he scored 107 from 40 balls in this the second innings, following 137 in the first innings. The most prolific scorer of hundreds in an hour or less was Gilbert Laird Jessop (1874–1955), with 11 between 1897 and 1913. The fastest Test hundred was one off 56 balls by Isaac Vivian Alexander Richards (b. 7 Mar 1952) for the West Indies v. England at St John's, Antigua on 15 Apr 1986. His final score was 110 in 81 minutes. Edwin Boaler Alletson (1884–1963) scored 189 runs in 90 min for Nottinghamshire v. Sussex at Hove on 20 May 1911.

A double hundred in 113 min was scored by Ravi Shastri off 123 balls for Bombay v. Baroda at Bombay on 10 Jan 1985 (see most runs off an over). Clive Hubert Lloyd (b. 31 Aug 1944), for West Indians v. Glamorgan at Swansea on 9 Aug 1976, and Gilbert Jessop (286), for Gloucestershire v. Sussex at Hove on 1 June 1903, both scored 200 in 120 min. Lloyd received 121 balls, but the figure for Jessop is not known.

The fastest treble hundred was completed in 181 min by Denis Compton, who scored 300 for the MCC v. North-Eastern Transvaal at Benoni on 3–4 Dec 1948.

Slowest scoring
The longest time a batsman has ever taken to score his first run is 1 hr 37 min by Thomas Godfrey Evans (b. 18 Aug 1920), who scored 10 not out for England v. Australia at Adelaide on 5–6 Feb 1947. The longest innings without scoring is 87 min by Vincent Richard Hogg (b. 3 July 1952) for Zimbabwe–Rhodesia 'B' v. Natal 'B' at Pietermaritzburg in the South African Castle Bowl competition on 20 Jan 1980.

The slowest hundred on record is by Mudassar Nazar (b. 6 Apr 1956) for Pakistan v. England at Lahore on 14–15 Dec 1977. He required 9 hr 51 min for 114, reaching the 100 in 9 hr 17 min. The slowest double hundred is one of 10 hr 52 min (426 balls) by Anshuman Dattajirao Gaekwad (b. 23 Sept 1952) during an innings of 201 for India v. Pakistan at Jullundur on 25–29 Sept 1983.

Highest partnership
The record partnership for any wicket is the fourth-wicket stand of 577 by Gul Mahomed (b. 15 Oct 1921), 319, and Vijay Samuel Hazare (b. 11 Mar 1915), 288, for Baroda v. Holkar at Baroda, India on 8–10 Mar 1947. The highest in England is the first-wicket partnership of 555 by Percy Holmes (1886–1971) (224 not out) and Herbert Sutcliffe (1894–1978) (313) for Yorkshire v. Essex at Leyton on 15–16 June 1932.

The highest Test partnership is 451 for the second wicket by William Harold Ponsford (b. 19 Oct 1900) (266) and Sir Donald Bradman (244) for Australia v. England at the Oval on 18 Aug 1934, and for the third wicket by Mudassar Nazar (231) and Javed Miandad Khan (b. 12 Jun 1957) (280 not out) for Pakistan v. India at Hyderabad, Pakistan on 14–15 Jan 1983.

BOWLING
Most wickets *In an innings*
Only one bowler has taken all ten wickets in an innings on three occasions—Alfred 'Tich' Freeman of Kent, 1929–31. The fewest runs scored off a bowler taking all ten wickets is ten, off Hedley Verity (1905–43) for Yorkshire v. Nottinghamshire at Leeds on 12 July 1932. The only bowler to bowl out all ten was John Wisden (1826–84) for North v. South at Lord's in 1850.

In a match
James Charles Laker (1922–86) took 19 wickets for 90 runs (9–37 and 10–53) for England v. Australia at Old Trafford from 27–31 July 1956. No other bowler has taken more than 17 wickets in a first-class match.

Most consecutive wickets
No bowler in first-class cricket has yet achieved five wickets with five consecutive balls. The nearest approach was that of Charles Warrington Leonard Parker (1882–1959) (Gloucestershire) in his own benefit match against Yorkshire at Bristol on 10 Aug 1922, when he struck the stumps with five successive balls but the second was called as a no-ball. The only man to have taken four wickets with consecutive balls more than once is Robert James Crisp (b. 28 May 1911) for Western Province v. Griqualand West at Johannesburg on 24 Dec 1931 and against Natal at Durban, South Africa on 3 Mar 1934.

Patrick Ian Pocock (b. 24 Sep 1946) took five wickets in six balls, six in nine balls and seven in eleven balls for Surrey v. Sussex at Eastbourne on 15 Aug 1972. In his own benefit match at Lord's on 22 May 1907, Albert Edwin Trott (1873–1914) of Middlesex took four Somerset wickets with four consecutive balls and then later in the same innings achieved a 'hat trick'.

Most wickets ● Michael Anthony Holding (b. 16 Feb 1954) produced the best bowling analysis ever in a one-day game, when he took 8–21 for Derbyshire v. Sussex in a Nat West Trophy match at Hove, East Sussex on 22 June 1988. (Photo: All-Sport)

Most consecutive maidens
Hugh Joseph Tayfield (b. 30 Jan 1929) bowled 16 consecutive eight-ball maiden overs (137 balls without conceding a run) for South Africa v. England at Durban on 25–26 Jan 1957. The greatest number of consecutive six-ball maiden overs bowled is 21 (131 balls) by Rameshchandra Gangaram 'Bapu' Nadkarni (b. 4 Apr 1932) for India v. England at Madras on 12 Jan 1964. Alfred Shaw (1842–1907) of Nottinghamshire bowled 23 consecutive 4-ball maiden overs (92 balls) for North v. South at Trent Bridge on 17 July 1876.

Most balls
The most balls bowled in a match is 917 by Cottari Subbanna Nayudu (b. 18 Apr 1914), 6–153 and 5–275, for Holkar v. Bombay at Bombay on 4–9 Mar 1945. The most balls bowled in a Test match is 774 by Sonny Ramadhin (b. 1 May 1929) for the West Indies v. England, 7–49 and 2–179, at Edgbaston on 29 May–4 June 1957. In the second innings he bowled a world record 588 balls (98 overs).

Most expensive bowling
The greatest number of runs hit off one bowler in an innings is 362, off Arthur Alfred Mailey (1886–1967) of New South Wales by Victoria at Melbourne on 24–28 Dec 1926. The most runs conceded by a bowler in a match is 428 by Cottari Subbanna Nayudu in the Holkar v. Bombay match above. The most runs conceded in a Test innings is 298 by Leslie O'Brien 'Chuck' Fleetwood-Smith (1910–71) for Australia v. England at The Oval on 20–23 Aug 1938.

Fastest
The highest electronically measured speed for a ball bowled by any bowler is 160·45 km/h *99·7 mph* by Jeffrey Robert Thomson (b. 16 Aug 1950) (Australia) against the West Indies in December 1975.

ALL-ROUNDERS
The double
The 'double' of 1000 runs and 100 wickets in the same season was performed a record number of 16 times by Wilfred Rhodes between 1903 and 1926. The greatest number of consecutive seasons in which a player has performed the 'double' is 11 (1903–13) by George Herbert Hirst (1871–1954), of Yorkshire and England. Hirst is also the only player to score 2000 runs (2385) and take 200 wickets (208) in the same season (1906).

Test cricket
The best all-round Test career record is that of Ian Terrence Botham (b. 24 Nov 1955) with 5057 runs (av 34·87), 373 wickets (av 27·86) and 109 catches in 94 matches, 1977–87. Botham is the only player to score a hundred and take eight wickets in an innings in the same Test, with 108 and eight for 34 for England v. Pakistan at Lord's on 15–19 June 1978. He scored a hundred (114) and took more than ten wickets (6–58 and 7–48) in a Test, for England v. India in the Golden Jubilee Test at Bombay on 15–19 Feb 1980. This feat was emulated by Imran Khan Niazi (b. 25 Nov 1952) with 117, 6–98 and 5–82 for Pakistan v. India at Faisalabad on 3–8 Jan 1983.

Botham completed the double of 1000 runs and 100 wickets in the fewest Test matches (21) on 30 Aug 1979. Kapil Dev Nikhanj (India) (b. 6 Jan 1959) achieved his double in the shortest time span, 1 year 107 days, and at the youngest age, 21 yr 27 days, in his 25th Test. The double of 2000 runs and 200 wickets was achieved in fewest matches (42) by Botham and at the youngest age by Kapil Dev at 24 yr 68 days. Botham completed 3000 runs and 300 wickets in 71 Tests at 28 yr 259 days.

WICKET-KEEPING
Most dismissals *Innings*
The most dismissals by a wicket-keeper in an innings is eight (all caught) by Arthur Theodore Wallace 'Wally' Grout (1927–68) for Queensland v. Western Australia at Brisbane on 15 Feb 1960 and by David Edward East (b. 27 July 1959) for Essex v. Somerset at Taunton on 27 July 1985. The most stumpings in an innings is six by Henry 'Hugo' Yarnold (1917–74) for Worcestershire v. Scotland at Broughty Ferry, Tayside on 2 July 1951. The Test record is seven (all caught) by Wasim Bari (b. 23 Mar 1948) for Pakistan v. New Zealand at Auckland on 23 Feb 1979, and by Bob Taylor for England v. India at Bombay on 15 Feb 1980.

128·6 m *140 yd 2 ft* by Robert Percival, a left-hander, on Durham Sands racecourse on Easter Monday, 18 Apr 1881.

OTHER TEST RECORDS

Test appearances
Sunil Gavaskar played in a record 125 Tests, 1975–87, including a record 106 consecutive Tests. The English record for most Tests is 114 by Michael Colin Cowdrey (b. 24 Dec 1932) and for consecutive Tests is 65 by Alan Philip Eric Knott (b. 9 Apr 1946), 1971–77 and Ian Botham, 1978–84.

Longest match
The lengthiest recorded cricket match was the 'timeless' Test between England and South Africa at Durban on 3–14 Mar 1939. It was abandoned after ten days (eighth day rained off) because the boat taking the England team home was due to leave. The total playing time was 43 hr 16 min and a record Test match aggregate of 1981 runs was scored.

Largest crowds
The greatest attendance at a cricket match is about 394 000 for the Test between India and England at Eden Gardens, Calcutta on 1–6 Jan 1982. The record for a Test series is 933 513 for Australia v. and England (5 matches) in 1936–37. The greatest recorded attendance at a cricket match on one day was 90 800 on the second day of the Test between Australia and the West Indies at Melbourne on 11 Feb 1961. The English record is 159 000 for the Test between England and Australia at Headingley, Leeds on 22–27 July 1948, and the record for one day probably a capacity of 46 000 for Lancashire v. Yorkshire at Old Trafford on 2 Aug 1926. The English record for a Test series is 549 650 for the series against Australia in 1953. The highest attendance for a limited-overs game is 84 153 at the Benson and Hedges World Series Cup match between Australia and England at Melbourne on 23 Jan 1985.

Most successful Test captain
Clive Hubert Lloyd (b. 31 Aug 1944) led the West Indies in a record 74 Test matches from 22 November 1974 to 2 January 1985. Of these, 36 were won, 12 lost and 26 were drawn. His team set records for most successive Test wins, 11 in 1984, and most Tests without defeat, 27, between losses to Australia in December 1981 and January 1985 (through injury Lloyd missed one of those matches, when the West Indies were captained by Vivian Richards).

Most extras
The most extras conceded in a Test innings is 71 by the West Indies in Pakistan's 1st innings at Georgetown, Guyana on 3–4 Apr 1988. The figure consisted of 21 byes, 8 leg byes, 4 wides and 38 no-balls.

ONE-DAY INTERNATIONALS
The first 'limited overs' international was played at Melbourne Cricket Ground on 5 Jan 1971 between Australia and England. The Prudential Trophy series of one-day internationals began in England in 1972, matches being of 55 overs per side. The Benson and Hedges World Cup Series has been held annually in Australia since 1979–80.

World Cup
The World Cup was held in England in 1975, 1979 and 1983, and in India and Pakistan in 1987. The West Indies are the only double winners, in 1975 and 1979. Matches were played at 60 overs per side (except at 50 overs in 1987).

One-day international records *Team*
The highest innings score by a team is 360–4 (50 overs) by the West Indies v. Sri Lanka at Karachi, Pakistan on 13 Oct 1987. The lowest completed innings total is 45 by Canada v. England at Old Trafford, Lancashire on 14 June 1979. The largest victory margin is 232 by Australia

Match
The most dismissals by a wicket-keeper in a match is 12 by: Edward Pooley (1838–1907), eight caught, four stumped, for Surrey v. Sussex at The Oval on 6–7 July 1868; nine caught, three stumped by both Donald Tallon (1916–84) for Queensland v. New South Wales at Sydney, Australia on 2–4 Jan 1939, and by Hedley Brian Taber (b. 29 Apr 1940) for New South Wales v. South Australia at Adelaide on 13–17 Dec 1968.

The record for catches is 11 by: Arnold Long (b. 18 Dec 1940), for Surrey v. Sussex at Hove on 18 and 21 July 1964, by Rodney Marsh for Western Australia v. Victoria at Perth on 15–17 Nov 1975; and by David Leslie Bairstow (b. 1 Sept 1951) for Yorkshire v. Derbyshire at Scarborough on 8–10 Sept 1982.

The most stumpings in a match is nine by Frederick Henry Huish (1869–1957) for Kent v. Surrey at The Oval on 21–23 Aug 1911.

The Test record for dismissals is ten, all caught, by Robert Taylor for England v. India at Bombay, 15–19 Feb 1980.

FIELDING

Most catches *Innings and Match*
The greatest number of catches in an innings is seven, by Michael James Stewart (b. 16 Sept 1932) for Surrey v.

> **Most runs** ● The most runs scored in one-day internationals is 5852 (av. 51·78) by Isaac Vivian Alexander Richards (West Indies) (b. 7 Mar 1952) in 148 matches between 1975–88. He also holds the one-day international records for the highest individual score: 189 not out v. England at Old Trafford, Lancashire on 31 May 1984; most centuries: 11 and most catches by a fielder: 71. Here he is in action against Pakistan during the 1987 World Cup. (Photo: All-Sport/Chris Cole)

Northamptonshire at Northampton on 7 June 1957; and by Anthony Stephen Brown (b. 24 June 1936) for Gloucestershire v. Nottinghamshire at Trent Bridge on 26 July 1966.

The most catches in a Test match is seven by Greg Chappell for Australia v. England at Perth on 13–17 Dec 1974; and by Yajurvindra Singh (b. 1 Aug 1952) for India v. England at Bangalore on 28 Jan–2 Feb 1977.

Walter Hammond held a match record total of ten catches (four in the first innings, six in the second) for Gloucestershire v. Surrey at Cheltenham on 16–17 Aug 1928.

Longest throw
A cricket ball (155 g *5½ oz*) was reputedly thrown

v. Sri Lanka (323–2 to 91), at Adelaide, Australia on 28 Jan 1985.

Individual

The best bowling analysis is 7–51 by Winston Walter Davis (b. 18 Sept 1958) for the West Indies v. Australia at Headingley, Yorkshire on 12 June 1983. The best partnership is 224 by Dean Mervyn Jones (b. 24 Mar 1961) and Allan Robert Border (b. 27 July 1955) for Australia v. Sri Lanka at Adelaide, Australia on 28 Jan 1985

Career

The most matches played is 170 by Allan Border (Australia), 1979–88. The most wickets taken is 146 by Joel Garner (West Indies) (b. 16 Dec 1952) in 98 matches, 1977–87. The most dismissals is 150 (136 ct, 14 st) by Peter Jeffrey Leroy Dujon (West Indies) (b. 28 Mar 1956) in 119 matches, 1981–8.

ENGLISH COUNTY CHAMPIONSHIP

The greatest number of victories since 1890, when the Championship was officially constituted, has been by Yorkshire with 29 outright wins (the last in 1968), and one shared (1949). The record number of consecutive title wins is seven by Surrey from 1952 to 1958. The greatest number of appearances in County Championship matches is 763 by Wilfred Rhodes for Yorkshire between 1898 and 1930, and the greatest number of consecutive appearances is 423 by Kenneth George Suttle (b. 25 Aug 1928) of Sussex between 1954 and 1969. James Graham 'Jimmy' Binks (b. 5 Oct 1935) played in every County Championship match for Yorkshire between his debut in 1955 and his retirement in 1969—412 matches.

The seven sons of the Reverend Henry Foster, of Malvern, uniquely all played county cricket for Worcestershire between 1899 and 1934.

OLDEST AND YOUNGEST

The oldest man to play in a Test match was Wilfred Rhodes, aged 52 yr 165 days, for England v. West Indies at Kingston, Jamaica on 12 April 1930. Rhodes made his Test debut in the last Test of William Gilbert Grace (1848–1915), who at 50 yr 320 days at Nottingham on 3 June 1899 was the oldest ever Test captain. The youngest Test captain was the Nawab of Pataudi (later Mansur Ali Khan) at 21 yr 77 days on 23 Mar 1962 for India v. West Indies at Bridgetown, Barbados. The youngest Test player was Mushtaq Mohammad (b. 22 Nov 1943), aged 15 yr 124 days, for Pakistan v. West Indies at Lahore on 26 March 1959. England's youngest player was Dennis Brian Close (b. 24 Feb 1931) aged 18 yr 149 days v. New Zealand at Old Trafford on 23 July 1949.

The oldest player in first-class cricket was the Governor of Bombay, Raja Maharaj Singh (1878–19..) (India), aged 72 yr 192 days, when he batted, scoring 4, on the opening day of the match played on 25–27 Nov 1950 at Bombay for his XI v. Commonwealth XI at Brisbane, Australia. The youngest is reputed to be Qasim Feroze (Pakistan) (b. 21 Jan 1958) for Bahawalpur v. Karachi Whites on 19 Jan 1971, aged 12 yr 363 days. The oldest Englishman was George Robert Canning, the 4th Lord Harris (1851–1932) for Kent v. All India at Catford on 4 July 1911, aged 60 yr 151 days. The youngest English first-class player was Charles Robertson Young for Hampshire v. Kent at Gravesend on 13 June 1867, aged 15 yr 131 days.

WOMEN'S CRICKET

Earliest

The first recorded women's match took place at Gosden Common, Surrey, England on 26 June 1745. *Circa* 1807 Christina Willes is said to have introduced the roundarm bowling style. The first Test match was Australia v. England at Brisbane on 28–31 Dec 1934. The International Women's Cricket Council was formed in 1958.

Batting *Individual*

The highest individual innings recorded is 224 not out by

Mabel Bryant for Visitors v. Residents at Eastbourne, East Sussex in August 1901.

The highest innings in a Test match is 193 by Denise Annetts (b. 30 Jan 1964), in 381 minutes, for Australia v. England at Collingham, Nottinghamshire on 23–4 August 1987 in a 4-day Test. With Lindsay Reeler (110 not out) (b. 18 Mar 1961) she added 309 for the third wicket, the highest Test partnership.

The highest in a 3-day Test is 189 (in 222 minutes) by Elizabeth Alexandra 'Betty' Snowball (b. 1907) for

ENGLISH ONE–DAY RECORDS

GC/NWT : Gillette Cup (1963–1980); Nat West Trophy (1981–) (60-over matches).

SL (Sunday League) : John Player (1969–1986); Refuge Assurance (1987–) (40-over matches).

B & H : Benson & Hedges Cup (1972–) (55-over matches).

MOST WINS

GC/NWT 4, Lancashire 1970–2, 1975; Sussex 1963–4, 1978, 1986. **SL** 3, Kent 1972–3, 1976; Essex 1981, 1984–5; Hampshire 1975, 1978, 1986. **B & H** 3, Kent 1973, 1976, 1978; Leicestershire 1972, 1975, 1985.

HIGHEST INNINGS TOTAL

GC/NWT 404–3 Worcestershire v. Devon, Worcester, 1987. **SL** 310–5 Essex v. Glamorgan, Southend, 1983. **B & H** 350–3 Essex v. Oxford & Cambridge Universities, Chelmsford, 1979.

LOWEST INNINGS TOTAL

GC/NWT 39 Ireland v. Sussex, Hove, 1985. **SL** 23 Middlesex v. Yorkshire, Headingley, 1974. **B & H** 56 Leicestershire v. Minor Counties, Wellington, 1982.

HIGHEST INDIVIDUAL INNINGS

GC/NWT 206 Alvin Isaac Kallicharran (b. 21 Mar 1949), Warwickshire v. Oxfordshire, Edgbaston, 1984. **SL** 176 Graham Alan Gooch (b. 23 July 1953), Essex v. Glamorgan, Southend, 1983. **B & H** 198* Graham Gooch, Essex v. Sussex, Hove, 1982.

BEST INDIVIDUAL BOWLING

GC/NWT 8–21 Michael Anthony Holding (b. 16 Feb 1954), Derbyshire v. Sussex, Hove, 1988. **SL** 8–26 Keith David Boyce (b. 11 Oct 1943), Essex v. Lancashire, Old Trafford, 1971; Alan Ward (b. 10 Aug 1947) took 4 wickets in 4 balls, Derbyshire v. Sussex, Derby, 1970. **B & H** 7–12 Wayne Wendell Daniel (b. 16 Jan 1956), Middlesex v. Minor Counties (East), Ipswich, 1978.

MOST DISMISSALS IN INNINGS

GC/NWT 6, Robert William Taylor (b. 17 July 1941), Derbyshire v. Essex, Derby, 1981; Terry Davies (b. 25 Oct 1960), Glamorgan v. Staffordshire, Stone, 1986. **SL** 7, Bob Taylor, Derbyshire v. Lancashire, Old Trafford, 1975. **B & H** 8, Derek John Somerset Taylor (b. 12 Nov 1942), Somerset v. Combined Universities, Taunton, 1982.

RUNS IN CAREER

GC/NWT 1950, Dennis Leslie Amiss (b. 7 Apr 1943), Warwickshire 1969–87. **SL** 7040, Dennis Amiss, Warwickshire 1969–87. **B & H** 3007, Graham Gooch, Essex 1973–87.

WICKETS IN CAREER

GC/NWT 81, Geoffrey Graham Arnold (b. 3 Sept 1944), Surrey, Sussex 1963–80. **SL** 357, John Kenneth Lever (b. 24 Feb 1949), Essex 1969–87. **B & H** 137, John Lever, Essex 1972–87.

DISMISSALS IN CAREER

GC/NWT 66, Bob Taylor, Derbyshire 1963–84. **SL** 236, Bob Taylor, Derbyshire 1969–86. **B & H** 114, David Bairstow, Yorkshire 1972–87.

* Not out

England v. New Zealand at Christchurch, NZ on 16 Feb 1935.

Rachael Flint (*née* Heyhoe) (b. 11 June 1939) has scored the most runs in Test cricket with 1814 (av. 49·02) in 25 matches from December 1960 to July 1979.

Team

The highest innings score by any team is 567 by Tarana v. Rockley, at Rockley, NSW, Australia in 1896. The highest Test innings is 503 for five wickets declared by England v. New Zealand at Christchurch, NZ on 16 and 18 Feb 1935. The most in a Test in England is 379 by Australia v. England at The Oval, London on 26–27 July 1976. The highest innings total in England is 410 for two wickets declared by the South v. East at Oakham, Leicestershire on 29 May 1982.

The lowest innings in a Test is 35 by England v. Australia at St Kilda, Melbourne, Australia on 22 Feb 1958. The lowest in a Test in England is 63 by New Zealand at Worcester on 5 July 1954.

Bowling

Mary Beatrice Duggan (England) (1925–73) took a record 77 wickets (av. 13·49) in 17 Tests from 1949 to 1963. She recorded the best Test analysis with seven wickets for six runs for England v. Australia at St Kilda, Melbourne on 22 Feb 1958.

Rubina Winifred Humphries (b. 19 Aug 1915), for Dalton Ladies v. Woodfield SC, at Huddersfield, West Yorkshire on 26 June 1931, took all ten wickets for no runs. (She also scored all her team's runs.) This bowling feat was equalled by Rosemary White (b. 22 Jan 1938) for Wallington LCC v. Beaconsfield LCC in July 1962.

World Cup

Three women's World Cups have been staged. Australia won in 1978 and 1982 and England in 1973. The highest individual score in this series is 138 not out by Janette Ann Brittin (b. 4 July 1959) for England v. International XI at Hamilton, New Zealand on 14 Jan 1982.

MINOR CRICKET RECORDS

(where excelling those in first–class cricket)

Highest individual innings

In a Junior House match between Clarke's House (now Poole's) and North Town, at Clifton College, Bristol, 22–23, 26–28 June 1899, Arthur Edward Jeune Collins (1885–1914) scored an unprecedented 628 not out in 6 hr 50 min, over five afternoons' batting, carrying his bat through the innings of 836. The scorer, E. W. Pegler, gave the score as '628—plus or minus 20, shall we say'.

Fastest individual scoring

Stanley Keppel 'Shunter' Coen (South Africa) (1902–67) scored 50 runs (11 fours and one six) in 7 min for Gezira v. the RAF in 1942. The fastest hundred by a prominent player in a minor match was by Vivian Frank Shergold Crawford (1879–1922) in 19 min at Cane Hill, Surrey on 16 Sept 1899. David Michael Roberts Whatmore (b. 6 Apr 1949) scored 210 (including 25 sixes and 12 fours) off 61 balls for Alderney v. Sun Alliance at Alderney on 19 June 1983. His first 100 came off 33 balls and his second off 25 balls.

Successive sixes

Cedric Ivan James Smith (1906–79) hit nine successive sixes for a Middlesex XI v. Harrow and District at Rayner's Lane, Harrow in 1935. This feat was repeated by Arthur Dudley Nourse (1910–81) in a South African XI v. Military Police match at Cairo, Egypt in 1942–3. Nourse's feat included six sixes in one over.

Fastest and Slowest scoring rates

In the match Royal Naval College, Dartmouth v. Seale Hayne Agricultural College in 1923, Kenneth Anderson Sellar (b. 11 Aug 1906) and Leslie Kenneth Allen Block (1906–80) were set to score 174 runs in 105 min but achieved this total in 33 min, so averaging 5·27 runs per min.

Most runs off a ball

A scoring stroke of 11 (all run, with no overthrows) was achieved by Lt (later Lt-Col.) Philip Mitford (1879–1946), QO Cameron Highlanders, in a Malta Governor's Cup match on 28 May 1903.

Most runs off an over

H. Morely scored 62, nine sixes and two fours, off an eight-ball over from R. Grubb which had four no-balls, in a Queensland country match in 1968–9.

Bowling

Nine wickets with nine consecutive balls were taken by: Stephen Fleming, for Marlborough College 'A' XI v. Bohally Intermediate at Blenheim, New Zealand in December 1967; and by Paul Hugo for Smithfield School v. Aliwal North, South Africa in February 1931. In the Inter-Divisional Ships Shield at Purfleet, Essex on 17 May 1924, Joseph William Brockley (b. 9 Apr 1907) took all ten wickets, clean bowled, for two runs in 11 balls—including a triple hat trick. Jennings Tune took all ten wickets, all bowled, for 0 runs in five overs for Cliffe v. Eastrington in the Howden and District League at Cliffe, Yorkshire on 6 May 1922.

In 1881 Frederick Robert Spofforth (1835–1926) at Bendigo, Victoria, Australia clean bowled all ten wickets in both innings. J. Bryant for Erskine v. Deaf Mutes in Melbourne on 15 and 22 Oct 1887, and Albert Rimmer for Linwood School v. Cathedral GS at Canterbury, New Zealand in December 1925, repeated the feat. In the 1910 season, H. Hopkinson, of Mildmay CC London, took 99 wickets for 147 runs.

Maurice Hanes bowled 107 consecutive balls (17 overs and 5 balls) for Bedworth II v. A P Leamington II at Bedworth, Warwickshire on 16 June 1979, without conceding a run.

Wicket-keeping

Welihinda Badalge Bennett (b. 25 Jan 1933) caught four and stumped 6 batsmen in one innings, on 1 March 1953 for Mahinda College v. Galle CC, at the Galle Esplanade, Sri Lanka.

Fielding

In a Wellington, New Zealand secondary schools 11-a-side match on 16 Mar 1974, Stephen Lane, 13, held 14 catches in the field (7 in each innings) for St Patrick's College, Silverstream v. St Bernard's College, Lower Hutt.

GUINNESS HAVE PUBLISHED **CRICKET FACTS & FEATS** **(2nd EDITION)** BILL FRINDALL £11.95
CRICKET FIRSTS PETER MATTHEWS & ROBERT BROOKE £8.95

Croquet

Its exact origins are obscure, but croquet was probably derived from the French game *Jeu de Mail* first mentioned in the 12th century. A game resembling croquet, possibly of foreign origin, was played in Ireland in the 1830s, and was introduced to Hampshire 20 years later. The first club was formed in the Steyne Gardens, Worthing, West Sussex in 1865.

Most championships

The greatest number of victories in the Open Croquet Championships (instituted at Evesham, Worcestershire, 1867) is ten by John William Solomon (b. 1931) (1953, 1956, 1959, 1961, 1963–8). He also won ten Men's Championships (1951, 1953, 1958–60, 1962, 1964–5, 1971–2), ten Open Doubles (with Edmond Patrick Charles Cotter) (1954–5, 1958–9, 1961–5 and 1969) and one Mixed Doubles (with Freda Oddie) in 1954, making a total of 31 titles. Solomon has also won the President's Cup (inst. 1934, an invitation event for the best 8 players) on 9 occasions (1955, 1957–9, 1962–4, 1968 and 1971), and was Champion of Champions on all four occasions that this competition has been run (1967–70).

Dorothy Dyne Steel (1884–1965), fifteen times winner of the Women's Championship (1919–39), won the Open Croquet Championship four times (1925, 1933, 1935–36). She had also five Doubles and seven Mixed Doubles for a total of 31 titles.

> **Lowest score** ● At the World Cross Country Championships in Auckland, New Zealand on 26 March 1988, Kenya dominated the team events. Their senior team finished eight men in the first nine, with a record low score of 23 (six to score) and (seen here in the red strip) they also dominated the junior race to set a record low score, 11 (four to score) with six in the first seven. (Photo: All-Sport/Simon Bruty)

The MacRobertson International Shield (instituted 1925) has been won a record seven times by Great Britain, 1925, 1937, 1956, 1963, 1969, 1974 and 1982). A record six appearances have been made by John G. Prince (New Zealand), 1963, 1969, 1975, 1979, 1982 and 1986; on his debut he was the youngest ever international at 17 yr 190 days.

Cross-country Running

WORLD CHAMPIONSHIPS

The earliest recorded international cross-country race took place over 14·5 km *9 miles 18 yd* from Ville d'Avray, outside Paris on 20 Mar 1898 between England and France (England won by 21 points to 69). The inaugural International Cross-Country Championships took place at the Hamilton Park Racecourse, Scotland on 28 Mar 1903. The greatest margin of victory is 56 sec or 356 m *390 yd* by John 'Jack' Thomas Holden (England) (b. 13 Mar 1907) at Ayr Racecourse, Scotland on 24 Mar 1934. Since 1973 the events have been official world championships under the auspices of the International Amateur Athletic Federation.

Most wins

The greatest number of team victories has been by England with 45 for men, 11 for junior men and seven for women. The USA have a record eight women's team victories.

The greatest number of men's individual victories is four by: Jack Holden (England) in 1933–5 and 1939; by Alain Mimoun-o-Kacha (France) (b. 1 Jan 1921) in 1949, 1952, 1954 and 1956 and by Gaston Roelants (Belgium) (b. 5 Feb 1937) in 1962, 1967, 1969 and 1972. The women's race has been won five times by: Doris Brown-Heritage (USA) (b. 17 Sept 1942) 1967–71; and by Grete Waitz (*née* Andersen) (Norway) (b. 1 Oct 1953), 1978–81 and 1983.

Most appearances

Marcel van de Wattyne (Belgium) (b. 7 July 1924) ran in a record 20 races, 1946–65. The women's record is 16 by Jean Lochhead (Wales) (b. 24 Dec 1946), 1967–79, 1981, 1983–4.

English Championship

The English Cross-Country Championship was inaugurated at Roehampton, Wandsworth, London in 1877. The most individual titles won is four by Percy H. Stenning (1854–92) (Thames Hare and Hounds) in 1877–80 and Alfred E. Shrubb (1878–1964) (South London Harriers) in 1901–4. The most successful club in the team race has been Birchfield Harriers from Birmingham with 28 wins and one tie between 1880 and 1988. The largest field was the 2006 finishers in the senior race in 1987 at Luton, Bedfordshire.

Largest field

The largest recorded field in any cross-country race was 11 763 starters (10 810 finished) in the 30 km *18·6 miles* Lidingöloppet, near Stockholm, Sweden on 3 Oct 1982.

Curling

Although a 15th—century bronze figure in the Florence Museum appears to be holding a curling stone, the earliest illustration of the sport was in one of the Flemish painter Pieter Bruegel's winter scenes *c.* 1560. The game was probably introduced into Scotland by Flemings in the 15th century. The earliest documented club is Muthill, Tayside, Scotland, formed in 1739. Organised administration began in 1838 with the formation in Edinburgh of the Grand (later Royal) Caledonian Curling Club, the international legislative body until the foundation of the International Curling Federation in

1966. The first indoor ice rink to introduce curling was in Montreal, Canada in 1807, and the first in Britain was at Southport, Merseyside in 1878.

The USA won the first Gordon International Medal series of matches, between Canada and the USA, at Montreal in 1884. Curling has been a demonstration sport at the Olympic Games of 1924, 1932, 1964 and 1988.

Most titles

Canada has won the Men's World Championships (inst. 1959) 18 times, 1959–64, 1966, 1968–72, 1980, 1982–3, 1985–7. The most Strathcona Cup (inst. 1903) wins is seven by Canada (1903, 1909, 1912, 1923, 1938, 1957, 1965) against Scotland. The most Women's World Championships (inst. 1979) is six titles by Canada (1980, 1984–8).

'Perfect' games

Stu Beagle, of Calgary, Alberta, Canada, played a perfect game (48 points) against Nova Scotia in the Canadian Championships (Brier) at Fort William (now Thunder Bay), Ontario on 8 Mar 1960. Bernice Fekete, of Edmonton, Alberta, Canada, skipped her rink to two consecutive eight-enders on the same ice at the Derrick Club, Edmonton on 10 Jan and 6 Feb 1973. Two eight-enders in one bonspiel were scored at the Parry Sound Curling Club, Ontario, Canada from 6–8 Jan 1983.

Fastest game

Eight curlers from the Burlington Golf and Country Club curled an eight–end game in 47 min 24 sec, with time penalties of 5 min 30 sec, at Burlington, Ontario, Canada on 4 Apr 1986, following rules agreed with the Ontario Curling Association. The time is taken from when the first rock crosses the near hogline until the game's last rock comes to a complete stop.

Longest throw

The longest throw of a curling stone was a distance of 163·59 m *536 ft 8¾ in* by Tom Milne (Canada) at Park Lake, Neepawa, Manitoba, Canada on 7 Feb 1988. The attempt took place on a specially prepared sheet of curling ice on frozen Park Lake, a record 365·76 m *1200 ft* long.

Largest bonspiel

The largest bonspiel in the world is the Manitoba Curling Association Bonspiel held annually in Winnipeg, Canada. In 1988 there were 1424 teams of four men, a total of 5696 curlers, using 187 sheets of curling ice.

Largest rink

The world's largest curling rink is the Big Four Curling Rink, Calgary, Alberta, Canada, opened in 1959. Ninety-six teams and 384 players are accommodated on two floors each with 24 sheets of ice.

Cycling

The earliest recorded bicycle race was a velocipede race over 2 km *1·24 miles* at the Parc de St Cloud, Paris, on 31 May 1868, won by Dr James Moore (GB) (1847–1935) (later Chevalier de la Légion d'Honneur).

Highest speed

The highest speed ever achieved on a bicycle is 245·077 km/h *152·284 mph* by John Howard (USA) behind a wind-shield at Bonneville Salt Flats, Utah, USA on 20 July 1985. It should be noted that considerable help is provided by the slipstreaming effect of the lead vehicle. The British speed record is 158·05 km/h *98·21 mph* over 200 metres by David Le Grys (b. 10 Aug 1955) on a closed section of the M42 at Alvechurch, Warwickshire on 28 Aug 1985. Fred Markham, 29, recorded an official unpaced 6·832 sec for 200 m (105·386 km/h *65·484 mph*) on a streamlined bicycle on Highway 120, California, USA on 11 May 1986. The greatest distance ever covered in one hour is 122·771 km *76 miles 504 yd* by Leon Vanderstuyft (Belgium) (1890–1964) on the Montlhéry

---

WORLD RECORDS

Records are recognised by the Union Cycliste Internationale (UCI) *for both professionals and amateurs on open air and indoor tracks for a variety of distances at unpaced flying and standing starts and for motor-paced. In this list only the best are shown, with a † to signify those records set by a professional rather than an amateur.*

OPEN–AIR TRACKS

MEN

Distance	hr:min:sec	Name and country	Venue	Date	
Unpaced standing start					
1 km	1:02·091	Maic Malchow (GDR)	Colorado Springs, USA	28 Aug	1986
4 km	4:31·160	Gintautas Umaras (USSR)	Seoul, South Korea	18 Sept	1987
5 km	5:44·700	Gregor Braun (W. Germany)†	La Paz, Bolivia	12 Jan	1986
10 km	11:39·720	Francesco Moser (Italy)†	Mexico City	19 Jan	1984
20 km	23:21·592	Francesco Moser (Italy)†	Mexico City	23 Jan	1984
100 km	2:11:21·428	Beat Meister (Switzerland)	Zürich, Switzerland	14 Jul	1986
1 hour	51·151 km	Francesco Moser (Italy)†	Mexico City	23 Jan	1984
Unpaced flying start					
200 metres	10·118	Michael Hübner (GDR)	Colorado Springs, USA	27 Aug	1986
500 metres	26·993	Rory O'Reilly (USA)	La Paz, Bolivia	23 Nov	1985
1 km	58·269	Dominguez Rueda Efrain (Colombia)†	La Paz, Bolivia	13 Dec	1986
Motor-paced					
50 km	35:21·108	Aleksandr Romanov (USSR)	Tbilisi, USSR	6 May	1987
100 km	1:10:50·940	Alexsandr Romanov (USSR)	Tbilisi, USSR	6 May	1987
1 hour	84·710 km	Alexsandr Romanov (USSR)	Tbilisi, USSR	6 May	1987

WOMEN

Distance	hr:min:sec	Name and country	Venue	Date	
Unpaced standing start					
1 km	1:14·249	Erika Salumyae (USSR)	Tashkent, USSR	17 May	1984
3 km	3:49·780	Rebecca Twigg (USA)	Barcelona, Spain	29 Aug	1984
5 km	6:41·75	Amanda Jones (GB)	Leicester, England	31 Jul	1982
10 km	13:19·019	Jeannie Longo (France)	Colorado Springs, USA	20 Sept	1987
20 km	26:41·013	Jeannie Longo (France)	Colorado Springs, USA	23 Sept	1987
100 km	2:28:26·259	Francesco Galli (Italy)	Milan, Italy	26 Oct	1987
1 hour	44·933km	Jeannie Longo (France)	Colorado Springs, USA	23 Sept	1987
Unpaced flying start					
200 metres	11·383	Isabelle Gautheron (France)	Colorado Springs, USA	16 Aug	1986
500 metres	30·59	Isabelle Gautheron (France)	Cali, Colombia	14 Sept	1986
1 km	1:10·463	Erika Salumyae (USSR)	Tashkent, USSR	15 May	1984

Many of the above venues, such as La Paz, Colorado Springs, Cali and Mexico City, are at high altitude. The UCI recognises separate world records for the classic one-hour event at venues below 600 metres. These are: MEN 49·80193 km Francesco Moser on 3 Oct 1986, WOMEN 43·58789 km Jeannie Longo on 29 Sept 1986, both at Milan.

INDOOR TRACKS

MEN

Distance	hr:min:sec	Name and country	Venue	Date	
Unpaced standing start					
1 km	1:02·955	Lothar Thoms (GDR)	Moscow, USSR	22 Jul	1980
4 km	4:28·900	Vyacheslav Yekimov (USSR)	Moscow, USSR	20 Sept	1986
5 km	5:43·514	Vyachselav Yekimov (USSR)	Moscow, USSR	21 Aug	1987
10 km	11:50·360	Francesco Moser (Italy)†	Stuttgart, W. Germany	13 May	1988
20 km	23:52·098	Vyacheslav Yekimov (USSR)	Moscow, USSR	27 Oct	1986
100 km	2:11:47·255	Beat Meister (Switzerland)	Stuttgart, W. Germany	30 Oct	1987
4 km team	4:11·301	USSR	Moscow, USSR	15 Aug	1987
1 hour	50·644 km	Francesco Moser (Italy)†	Stuttgart, W. Germany	21 May	1988
Unpaced flying start					
200 metres	10·117	Nikolay Kovch (USSR)	Moscow, USSR	5 Feb	1988
500 metres	26·715	Nikolay Kovch (USSR)	Moscow, USSR	17 Aug	1987
1 km	58·364	Aleksandr Krichenko (USSR)	Moscow, USSR	29 May	1988
Motor-paced					
50 km	32:56·746	Aleksandr Romanov (USSR)	Moscow, USSR	21 Feb	1987
100 km	1:05:58·031	Aleksandr Romanov (USSR)	Moscow, USSR	21 Feb	1987
1 hour	91·131 km	Aleksandr Romanov (USSR)	Moscow, USSR	21 Feb	1987

WOMEN

Distance	hr:min:sec	Name and country	Venue	Date	
Unpaced standing start					
1 km	1:13·377	Erika Salumyae (USSR)	Moscow, USSR	21 Sept	1983
3 km	3:43·490	Jeannie Longo (France)	Paris (Bercy), France	14 Nov	1986
5 km	6:22·713	Jeannie Longo (France)	Grenoble, France	2 Nov	1986
10 km	13:29·395	Jeannie Longo (France)	Grenoble, France	7 Nov	1986
20 km	26:58·152	Jeannie Longo (France)	Grenoble, France	7 Nov	1986
100 km	2:31:30·043	Mieke Havik (Netherlands)	Rotterdam, Netherlands	19 Sept	1983
1 hour	44·718 km	Jeannie Longo (France)	Grenoble, France	7 Nov	1986
Unpaced flying start					
200 metres	11·232	Erika Salumyae (USSR)	Moscow, USSR	2 Aug	1987
500 metres	29·655	Erika Salumyae (USSR)	Moscow, USSR	6 Aug	1987
1 km	1:05·232	Erika Salumyae (USSR)	Moscow, USSR	30 May	1987
LONG DISTANCE BESTS (unpaced)					
24 hr	830·79 km	Michael L. Secrest (USA)	Montreal, Canada	13–14 Mar	1985
1000 km	32 hr 4 min	Herman de Munck (Belgium)	Keerbergen, Belgium	23–24 Sept	1983
1000 miles	51:12:32	Herman de Munck (Belgium)	Keerbergen, Belgium	23–25 Sept	1983

Motor Circuit, France, on 30 Sept 1928, achieved from a standing start paced by a motorcycle. The 24 hr record behind pace is 1384·367 km *860 miles 367 yd* by Hubert Ferdinand Opperman (later the Hon. Sir) (b. 29 May 1904) in Melbourne, Australia on 23 May 1932.

Most titles *Olympic*

The most gold medals won is three by Paul Masson (France) (1874–1945) in 1896, Francisco Verri (Italy) (1885–1945) in 1906; and Robert Charpentier (France) (1916–66) in 1936. Daniel Morelon (France) won two in 1968, and a third in 1972; he also won a silver in 1976 and a bronze medal in 1964. In the 'unofficial' 1904 cycling programme, Marcus Hurley (USA) (1884–1950) won four events.

World

World Championships are contested annually. They were first staged for amateurs in 1893 and for professionals in 1895. The most wins at a particular event is ten by Koichi Nakano (Japan) (b. 14 Nov 1955), professional sprint 1977–86. The most wins at a men's amateur event is seven by; Daniel Morelon (France) (b. 28 July 1944), sprint 1966–7, 1969–71, 1973, 1975; and Leon Meredith (UK) (1882–1930), 100 km motor paced 1904–5, 1907–9, 1911, 1913. The most women's titles is seven by; Beryl Burton (UK) (b. 12 May 1937), pursuit 1959–60, 1962–3, 1966 and road 1960, 1967; and by Yvonne Reynders (Belgium), pursuit 1961, 1964–5 and road 1959, 1961, 1963, 1966.

British

Beryl Burton (b. 12 May 1937), 25 times British all-round time trial champion (1959–83), has won 72 individual road TT titles, 14 track pursuit titles and 12 road race titles to 1986. Ian Hallam (b. 24 Nov 1948) won a record 25 men's titles, 1969–82.

Tour de France

The greatest number of wins in the *Tour de France* (inaugurated 1903) is five by Jacques Anquetil (France) (1934–1987), 1957, 1961–4; Eddy Merckx (Belgium) (b. 17 June 1945), 1969–72 and 1974; and Bernard Hinault (France) (b. 14 Nov 1954); 1978–9, 1981–2 and 1985. The closest race ever was in 1968 when after 4665 km *2898·7 miles* over 25 days (27 June–21 July) Jan Janssen (Netherlands) (b. 19 May 1940) beat Herman van Springel (Belgium) in Paris by 38 sec. The fastest average speed was 37·84 km/h *23·51 mph* by Bernard Hinault in 1981. The longest race was 5745 km *3569 miles* in 1926, and the most participants were 170 starters in

1982 and 1984. The longest ever stage was the 486 km from Les Sables d'Olonne to Bayonne in 1919.

Tour of Britain (Milk Race)

Four riders have won the Tour of Britain twice each—Bill Bradley (GB) (1959–60), Les West (GB) (1965, 1967), Fedor den Hertog (Netherlands) (1969, 1971) and Yuriy Kashurin (USSR) (1979, 1982). The closest race ever was in 1976 when after 1665·67 km *1035 miles* over 14 days

Most wins ● Sean Kelly (Ireland) (b. 24 May 1956) has won a record seven consecutive Paris-Nice Classics, 1982–8. (Photo: All-Sport/Vandystadt)

(30 May–12 June) Bill Nickson (GB) (b. 30 Jan 1953) beat Joe Waugh (GB) by 5 sec.

The fastest average speed is 42·185 km/h *26·213 mph* by Joey McLoughlin (GB) (b. 3 Dec 1964) in the 1986 race (1714 km *1065 miles*). Malcolm Elliott (b. 1 July 1961) won a record six stages in 1983 and had taken his total to 15 by 1987, after winning a record four in succession.

The longest Milk Race was in 1969 (2438·16 km *1515 miles*) although the longest ever Tour of Britain was in 1953 (2624·84 km *1631 miles* starting and finishing in London).

Six-day races

The most wins in 6-day races is 88 out of 233 events by Patrick Sercu (b. 27 June 1944), of Belgium, 1964–83.

Longest one-day race

The longest single-day 'massed start' road race is the 551–620 km *342–385 miles* Bordeaux–Paris, France, event. Paced over all or part of the route, the highest average speed was in 1981 with 47·186 km/h *29·32 mph* by Herman van Springel (Belgium) (b. 14 Aug 1943) for 584·5 km *363·1 miles* in 13 hr 35 min 18 sec.

Land's End to John O' Groats

The 'end to end' record for the 1363 km *847 miles* is 1 day 21 hr 3 min 16 sec (average speed 30·25 km/h *18·80 mph*) by John Woodburn (b. 22 Dec 1936) on 14–15 Aug 1982.

The women's record is 2 days 11 hr 7 min by Eileen Sheridan (b. 18 Oct 1923) on 9–11 July 1954. She completed 1609 km *1000 miles* in 3 days 1 hr.

Cross-America

The trans-America solo records recognised by the Ultra-Marathon Cycling Association are: men, Pete Penseyres 8 days 9 hr 47 min; women, Elaine Mariolle 10 days 2 hr 4 min, both in the McDonald's Race Across America, Huntingon Beach, California to Atlantic City, New Jersey, 5000 km *3107 miles*, starting on 6 July 1986.

The trans-Canada record is 14 days 22 hr 47 min by Wayne Phillips of Richmond, BC, 6115 km *3800 miles* from Vancouver, BC to Halifax, Nova Scotia on 13–28 June 1982.

One-legged cycling

Hugh G. E. Culverhouse (GB), who has an immobile left leg completed the trans-America race in 13 days 11 hr 1 min from 20 Sept–4 Oct 1986. He took 69 hr 5 min 4 sec for the journey from Land's End, England to John O'Groats, Scotland a total distance of 1363 km *847 miles*, from 31 Aug–3 Sept 1987.

Endurance

Thomas Edward Godwin (1912–75) (GB) in the 365 days of 1939 covered 120 805 km *75 065 miles* or an average of 330·96 km *205·65 miles* per day. He then completed 160 934 km *100 000 miles* in 500 days to 14 May 1940. Jay Aldous and Matt DeWaal cycled 22 997 km *14·290 miles* on a round-the-world trip from Place Monument, Salt Lake City, Utah, USA in 106 days, 2 Apr–16 July 1984. Nicholas Mark Sanders (b. 26 Nov 1957) of Glossop, Derbyshire, circumnavigated the world (20 977·8 km *13 035 road miles*) in 78 days 3 hr 30 min between 5 July and 21 Sept 1985. He cycled 7728 km *4802 miles* around Britain in 22 days, 10 June–1 July 1984.

Cycle touring

The greatest mileage amassed in a cycle tour was more than 643 700 km *402 000 miles* by the itinerant lecturer Walter Stolle (b. Sudetenland, 1926) from 24 Jan 1959 to 12 Dec 1976. He visited 159 countries starting from Romford, Essex, England. From 1922 to 25 Dec 1973 Tommy Chambers (1903–84) of Glasgow, rode a verified total of 1 286 517 km *799 405 miles*. Visiting every continent, John W. Hathaway (b. England, 13 Jan 1925) of Vancouver, Canada covered 81 300 km *50 600 miles* from 10 Nov 1974 to 6 Oct 1976. Veronica and Colin Scargill, of Bedford, travelled 29 000 km *18 020 miles* around the world on a tandem, 25 Feb 1974–27 Aug 1975. The most particpants in a bicycle tour was 27 300 in the 90 km *56 mile* London to Brighton Bike Ride on 15 June 1986.

Non-stop

Carlos Vieira cycled for 191 hr 'non-stop' at Leira, Portugal from 8–16 June 1983. The distance covered was 2407·64 km *1496·04 miles* and ·he was moving 98·7 per cent of the time.

Highest

Adrian Crane (UK) cycled from the lower summit of Mount Chimborazo, an altitude of 6267 m *20 561 ft*, to the town of Riobamba, Ecuador at *c.* 2750 m *9022 ft* on 11 May 1986. His brother Richard and cousin Nicholas Crane held the previous record, from Mount Kilimanjaro, Tanzania at 5894 m *19 340 ft.*

CYCLO-CROSS

The greatest number of World Championships (inst. 1950) has been won by Eric de Vlaeminck (Belgium) (b. 23 Aug 1945) with the Amateur and Open in 1966 and 6 Professional titles in 1968–73. British titles (inst. 1955) have been won most often by John Atkins (b. 7 Apr 1942) with 5 Amateur (1961–2, 1966–8), seven Professional (1969–75) and one Open title in 1977.

Pennine Way

John North (b. 18 Aug 1943) of Rawtenstall, Lancashire, cycled or carried his machine along the 271 miles *436 km* Pennine Way from Edale, Derbyshire to Kirk Yetholm, Borders in 2 days 8 hr 45 min on 9–11 June 1978.

Three Peaks

Stuart and Neil Shipley, Adrian Scholes and Richard Day, all of Derbyshire, cycled from sea level at Caernarvon, Gwynedd, via the peaks of Snowdon, Scafell Pike and Ben Nevis, to sea level Fort William, Inverness-shire in 74 hr 47 min, from 30 Apr–3 May 1988.

CYCLE SPEEDWAY

First mention of the sport is at Coventry in 1920 and it was first organised in 1945. The sport's governing body, the Cycle Speedway Council, was formed in 1973. Most British Senior Team Championships (inst. 1950) is 6 by; Wednesfield, Wolverhampton (1974, 1976–8, 1981 and 1983); and by Offerton, Cheshire (1962, 1964–5, 1969, 1972–3). The most individual titles is 4 by Derek Garnett (b. 16 July 1937) (1963, 1965, 1968 and 1972); he also won

the inaugural British Veterans' Championship, for the over 40s, in 1987.

ROLLER CYCLING

James Baker (USA) achieved a record speed of 207·8 km/h *129·1 mph* at the University of Arizona, Tucson, Arizona, USA on 6 Dec 1987.

STATIONARY CYCLING

Rudi Jan Jozef De Greef (b. 28 Dec 1955) stayed stationary without support for 10 hr at Meensel-Kiezegem, Belgium on 19 Nov 1982.

Darts

The origins of darts date from the use by archers of heavily weighted ten-inch throwing arrows for self-defence in close quarters fighting. The 'dartes' were used in Ireland in the 16th century and darts was played on the *Mayflower* by the Plymouth pilgrims in 1620. The modern game dates from at least 1896 when Brian Gamlin of Bury, Lancashire, is credited with inventing the present numbering system on the board. The first recorded score of 180 was by John Reader at the Highbury Tavern in Sussex in 1902.

Most titles

Eric Bristow (b. 25 Apr 1957) has most wins in the World Masters Championship (inst. 1974) with five, 1977, 1979,

World Professional champion ● Bob Anderson (b. 7 Nov 1947), the world's joint number one with John Lowe, won the World Professional tile in January 1988. He was also at the time World Masters champion and World Match Play champion, having won these titles in 1987. (Photo: All-Sport/Pascal Rondeau)

1981 and 1983–4, the World Professional Championship (inst. 1978) with five, 1980–1 and 1984–6, and the World Cup Singles (inst. 1977), two, 1983 and 1985. Seven men have won the annual *News of the World* Individual Championship twice; most recently by Mike Gregory (b. 16 Dec 1956) in 1987 and 1988. John Lowe (b. 21 July 1945) is the only other man to have won each of the four major titles: World Masters, 1976 and 1980; World Professional, 1979 and 1987; World Cup Singles, 1981; and *News of the World*, 1981.

World Cup

The first World Cup was held at the Wembley Conference Centre, London in 1977. England has a record 5 wins at this biennial tournament. A World Cup for women was instituted in 1983 and has been won twice by England.

Record prize

John Lowe won £102 000 for achieving the first 501 scored with the minimum nine darts in a major event on 13 Oct 1984 at Slough in the quarter-finals of the World Match-play Championships. His darts were six successive treble 20s, treble 17, treble 18 and double 18.

Speed records

The fastest time taken to complete 3 games of 301, finishing on doubles, is 1 min 47 sec by Keith Deller on BBC TV's *Record Breakers* on 22 Oct 1985.

The record time for going round the board clockwise in 'doubles' at arm's length is 9·2 sec by Dennis Gower at the Millers Arms, Hastings, East Sussex on 12 Oct 1975 and 14·5 sec in numerical order by Jim Pike (1903–60) at the Craven Club, Newmarket in March 1944. The record for this feat at the 9 ft 2·7 m throwing distance, retrieving own darts, is 2 min 13 sec by Bill Duddy (b. 29 Sept 1932) at The Plough, Haringey, London on 29 Oct 1972.

Least darts

Scores of 201 in 4 darts, 301 in 6 darts, 401 in 7 darts and 501 in 9 darts, have been achieved on various occasions.

Roy Edwin Blowes (Canada) (b. 8 Oct 1930) was the first person to acheive a 501 in nine darts, 'double-on, double-off', at the Widgeons pub, Calgary, Canada at 9 Mar 1987. His scores were; Bull, treble 20, treble 17, five treble 20s and a double 20 to finish. The lowest number of darts thrown for a score of 1001 is 19 by Cliff Inglis (b. 27 May 1935) (160, 180, 140, 180, 121, 180, 40) at the Bromfield Men's Club, Devon on 11 Nov 1975. A score of 2001 in 52 darts was achieved by Alan Evans (b. 14 June 1949) at Ferndale, Glamorgan on 3 Sept 1976. 3001 in 73 darts was thrown by Tony Benson at the Plough Inn, Gorton, Manchester on 12 July 1986. Linda Batten (b. 26 Nov 1954) set a women's 3001 record of 117 darts at the Old Wheatsheaf, Enfield, Middlesex on 2 Apr 1986. 100 001 was achieved in 3732 darts by Alan Downie of Stornoway on 21 Nov 1986.

Equestrian Sports

Evidence of horse-riding dates from a Persian engraving dated *c.* 3000 BC. Pignatelli's academy of horsemanship at Naples dates from the 16th century. The earliest jumping competition was at the Agricultural Hall, Islington, London, in 1869. Equestrian events have been included in the Olympic Games since 1912.

SHOW JUMPING
Olympic Games

The greatest number of Olympic gold medals is five by Hans-Günter Winkler (b. 24 July 1926) (West Germany), 4 team in 1956, 1960, 1964 and 1972 and the individual Grand Prix in 1956. The most team wins in the Prix des

> **Badminton 3-day event** ● Ian Stark (GB), seen here riding *Glenburnie*, became in May 1988 the first ever rider to ride first (*Sir Wattie*) and second (*Glenburnie*) in the same year at Badminton. (Photo: All-Sport/Bob Martin)

Nations is five by; Germany in 1936, 1956, 1960, 1964 and 1972. The lowest score obtained by a winner is no faults by; Frantisek Ventura (1895–1969) (Czechoslovakia) on *Eliot*, 1928 and Alwin Schockemöhle (b. 29 May 1937) (West Germany) on *Warwick Rex*, 1976. Pierre Jonquères d'Oriola (b. 1 Feb 1920) (France) uniquely won the individual gold medal twice, 1952 and 1964. Richard John Hannay Meade (b. 4 Dec 1938) (Great Britain) is the only British rider to win three gold medals—as an individual in 1972 and team titles in 1968 and 1972, all in the 3-day event.

World Championships

The men's World Championships (inst. 1953) have been won twice by Hans-Günter Winkler (West Germany) (1954–5) and Raimondo d'Inzeo (Italy) (1956 and 1960). The women's title (1965–74) was won twice by Jane 'Janou' Tissot (*née* Lefebvre) (France) (b. Saigon, 14 May 1945) on *Rocket* (1970 and 1974).

President's Cup

The World Team championship (inst. 1965) has been won a record twelve times by Great Britain, 1965, 1967, 1970, 1972–4, 1977–9, 1983, 1985–6.

World Cup

Instituted in 1979, the only double winner is Conrad Homfeld (USA) (b. 25 Dec 1951), 1980 and 1985.

King George V Gold Cup and Queen Elizabeth II Cup

David Broome (b. 1 Mar 1940) has won the King George V Gold Cup (first held 1911) a record five times, 1960 on *Sunsalve*, 1966 on *Mister Softee*, 1972 on *Sportsman*, 1977 on *Philco* and 1981 on *Mr Ross*. The Queen Elizabeth II Cup (first held 1949), for women, has been won five times by his sister Elizabeth Edgar (b. 28 Apr 1943), 1977 on *Everest Wallaby*, 1979 on *Forever*, 1981 and 1982 on *Everest Forever*, 1986 on *Everest Rapier*. The only horse to win both these trophies is *Sunsalve* in 1957 (with Elisabeth Anderson) and 1960.

Jumping records

The official *Fédération Equestre Internationale* records are: high jump 2·47 m *8 ft 4¼ in* by *Huasó*, ridden by Capt Alberto Larraguibel Morales (Chile) at Viña del Mar, Santiago, Chile on 5 Feb 1949; long jump over water 8·40 m *27 ft 6¾ in* by *Something*, ridden by André Ferreira (South Africa) at Johannesburg on 25 Apr 1975.

The British high jump record is 2·32 m *7 ft 7⁵/₁₆ in* by the 16·2 hands *167 cm* grey gelding *Lastic* ridden by Nick Skelton (b. 30 Dec 1957) at Olympia, London on 16 Dec 1978. On 25 June 1937, at Olympia, the Lady Wright (*née* Margery Avis Bullows) set the best recorded height for a British equestrienne on her liver chestnut *Jimmy Brown* at 2·23 m *7 ft 4 in*.

The greatest recorded height reached on bareback is 2·13 m *7 ft* by Michael Whitaker (b. 17 Mar 1960) on *Red Flight* at Dublin, Eire on 14 Nov 1982.

THREE-DAY EVENT

Olympic Games and World Championships

Charles Ferdinand Pahud de Mortanges (Netherlands) (1896–1971) won a record four Olympic gold medals, team 1924 and 1928, individual (riding *Marcroix*) 1928 and 1932, when he also won a team silver medal. Bruce Davidson (USA) (b. 13 Dec 1949) is the only rider to have won two world titles (inst. 1966), on *Irish Cap* in 1974 and *Might Tango* in 1978. Richard John Hannay Meade (b. 4 Dec 1938) is the only British rider to win three gold medals, individual 1972 and team 1968 and 1972.

Badminton

The Badminton Three-Day Event (inst. 1949) has been

won six times by Lucinda Green (*née* Prior-Palmer) (b. 7 Nov 1953) in 1973 (on *Be Fair*), 1976 (*Wide Awake*), 1977 (*George*), 1979 (*Killaire*), 1983 (*Regal Realm*) and 1984 (*Beagle Bay*).

DRESSAGE

Henri St. Cyr (Sweden) (1904–79) won a record four Olympic gold medals, both team and individual in 1952 and 1956. Germany (West Germany post-war) have won a record six team gold medals, 1928, 1936, 1964, 1968, 1976 and 1984, and have most team wins, five, at the World Championships (inst. 1966). Dr. Reiner Klimke (W. Germany) (b. 14 Jan 1936) is the only rider to win two world titles, on *Mehmed* in 1974 and *Ahlerich* in 1982.

CARRIAGE DRIVING

World Championships were first held in 1972. Three team titles have been won by Great Britain, 1972, 1974 and 1980, and Hungary 1976, 1978 and 1986. Two individual titles have been won by György Bárdos (Hungary), 1978 and 1980 and by Tjeerd Velstra (Netherlands), 1982 and 1986.

LONGEST RIDE

Henry G. Perry, a stockman from Mollongghip, Victoria, Australia rode 22 565 km *14 021 miles* around Australia in 157 days, 1 May to 4 Oct 1985, with six horses.

Fencing

'Fencing' (fighting with single sticks) was practised as a sport, or as a part of a religious ceremony, in Egypt as early as *c.* 1360 BC. The first governing body for fencing in Britain was the Corporation of Masters of Defence founded by Henry VIII before 1540, and fencing has been practised as sport, notably in prize fights, since that time. The modern foil was introduced in France as a practice weapon for the short court sword in the mid-17th century. In the late 19th century the épée was developed in France and the light fencing sabre in Italy.

Most titles *World*

The greatest number of individual world titles won is 5 by Aleksandr Romankov (USSR) (b. 7 Nov 1953), at foil 1974, 1977, 1979, 1982 and 1983, but Christian d'Oriola (France) won four world foil titles, 1947, 1949, 1953–4 as well as two individual Olympic titles. Four women foilists have won three world titles: Hélène Mayer (Germany) (1910–53) 1929, 1931, 1937; Ilona Schacherer-Elek (Hungary) (b. 17 May 1907) 1934–5, 1951; Ellen Müller–Preis (Austria) (b. 6 May 1912) 1947, 1949–50; and Cornelia Hanisch (West Germany) (b. 12 June 1952) 1979, 1981, 1985. Of these only Ilona Schacherer-Elek also won two individual Olympic titles (1936 and 1948).

Olympic

The most individual Olympic gold medals won is three by Ramón Fonst (Cuba) (1883–1959) in 1900 and 1904 (two) and by Nedo Nadi (Italy) (1894–1952) in 1912 and 1920 (two). Nadi also won three team gold medals in 1920 making a then unprecedented total of five gold medals at one celebration. Edoardo Mangiarotti (Italy) (b. 7 Apr 1919) with six gold, five silver and two bronze, holds the record of 13 Olympic medals. He won them for foil and épée from 1936 to 1960. The most gold medals by a woman is four (one individual, three team) by Elena Novikova (*née* Byelova) (USSR) (b. 28 July 1947) from 1968 to 1976, and the record for all medals is seven (two gold, three silver, two bronze) by Ildikó Sági (formerly Ujlaki, *née* Retjö) (Hungary) (b. 11 May 1937) from 1960 to 1976.

British Olympic records

The only British fencer to win a gold medal is Gillian Mary Sheen (b. 21 Aug 1928) in the 1956 foil. A record three Olympic medals were won by Edgar Seligman (1867–1958) with silver medals in the épée team event in 1906, 1908 and 1912.

Henry William Furse Hoskyns (b. 19 Mar 1931) has

competed most often for Great Britain with six Olympic appearances, 1956–76.

Amateur Fencing Association titles

The most won at one weapon is ten at women's foil by Gillian Sheen (now Donaldson), 1949, 1951–8, 1960.

Field Sports

FOXHUNTING

Hunting the fox in Britain became popular from the second half of the 18th century, though it is mentioned very much earlier. Prior to that time hunting was confined principally to the deer and the hare.

Pack *Earliest*

The Old Charlton Hunt (later the Goodwood) in West Sussex (now extinct), the Duke of Monmouth and Lord Grey of Werke at Charlton, Sussex, and the Duke of Buckingham in North Yorkshire owned packs which were entered to fox only during the reign (1660–85) of Charles II.

Largest

The pack with the greatest number of hounds has been the Duke of Beaufort's hounds maintained at Badminton, Avon since 1786. At times hunting six days a week, this pack once had 120 couples at hounds. It now meets four days a week.

Longest span

The 10th Duke of Beaufort (1900–84) was Master of Foxhounds from 1924 until his death in 1984 and hunted his hounds on 3895 days from 1920–67.

Longest hunt

The longest recorded hunt was one held by Squire Sandys which ran from Holmbank, northern Lancashire to Ulpha, Cumbria, a total of nearly 80 miles *128 km* in reputedly only 6 hr, in January or February 1743. The longest duration hunt was one of 10 hr 5 min by Charlton Hunt of West Sussex, which ran from East Dean Wood at 7.45 a.m. to a kill over 57 ¼ miles *92 km* away at 5.50 p.m. on 26 Jan 1738.

Most widespread hunting

Between 1969 and 1988, J. N. P. Watson, hunting correspondent to *Country Life*, hunted with 257 different packs of foxhounds, staghounds and harehounds in Britain, Ireland, USA and Europe.

GAME SHOOTING
Record heads

The world's finest head is the 23-pointer stag in the Maritzburg collection, East Germany. The outside span is 191 cm *75½ in*, the length 120 cm *47½ in* and the weight 18·824 kg *41½ lb*. The greatest number of points is probably 33 (plus 29) on the stag shot in 1696 by Frederick III (1657–1713), the Elector of Brandenburg, later King Frederick I of Prussia.

Largest tally to a single sportsman

556 813 head of game fell to the guns of the 2nd Marquess of Ripon between 1867 and when he dropped dead on a grouse moor after shooting his 52nd bird on the morning of 22 Sept 1923. This figure included 241 234 pheasants, 124 193 partridge and 31 900 hares. (His game books are held by the gunmakers James Purdey and Sons.)

Thomas, 6th Baron Walsingham bagged 1070 grouse, a one-day record for a single gun, in Yorkshire on 30 Aug 1888.

Fives

ETON FIVES

A handball game against the buttress of Eton College Chapel was first recorded in 1825. New courts were built

at Eton in 1840, the rules were codified in 1877, rewritten laws were introduced three times and last amended in 1981.

Most titles

One pair has won the amateur championship (Kinnaird Cup) eight times—Anthony Hughes and Arthur James Gordon Campbell (1958, 1965–8, 1971, 1973 and 1975). Hughes was also in the winning pair in 1963 and has played in 16 finals. Brian C. Matthews and John P. Reynolds won a record six successive titles, 1981–6.

RUGBY FIVES

As now known, this game dates from *c.* 1850 with the first inter-public school matches recorded in the early 1870s. The Oxford *v.* Cambridge contest was inaugurated in 1925 and the Rugby Fives Association was founded in the home of Dr Edgar Cyriax (1874–1954), in Welbeck Street, London on 29 Oct 1927. The dimensions of the standard rugby fives court were approved by the Association in 1931.

Most titles

The greatest number of Amateur Singles Championships (instituted 1932) ever won is 14 by Wayne Enstone in 1973–8 and 1980–7. The record for the Amateur Doubles Championship (instituted 1925) is eight by David Hebden and Ian Fuller in 1980–5 and 1987–88.

The invitation World Championships were first held in 1983. On the first three occasions Wayne Enstone won the singles and Enstone and Steve Ashton the doubles.

Football
(Association)

A game with some similarities termed *Tsu-chu* was played in China in the 4th and 3rd centuries BC. One of the earliest references to the game in England is a Royal Proclamation by Edward II in 1314 banning the game in the City of London. The earliest clear representation of football is an Edinburgh print dated 1672–3. The game was standardised with the formation of the Football Association in England on 26 Oct 1863. The oldest club is Sheffield FC, formed on 24 Oct 1857. The oldest in the Football League is Notts County, founded in 1862. Eleven per side became standard in 1870.

PROFESSIONAL
Longest match

The duration record for first–class fixtures is 3 hr 30 min (with interruptions), in the Copa Libertadores in Santos, Brazil, on 2–3 Aug 1962, when Santos drew 3–3 with Penarol FC of Montevideo, Uruguay.

The longest British match on record was one of 3 hr 23 min between Stockport County and Doncaster Rovers in the second leg of the Third Division (North) Cup at Edgeley Park, Stockport, Greater Manchester on 30 Mar 1946.

Longest unbeaten run

Nottingham Forest were undefeated in 42 consecutive First Division matches from 20 Nov 1977 to 9 Dec 1978. In Scottish Football Glasgow Celtic were undefeated in 62 matches (49 won, 13 drawn), 13 Nov 1915–21 April 1917.

Most postponements

The Scottish Cup tie between Inverness Thistle and Falkirk during the winter of 1978–9 was postponed a record 29 times due to weather conditions. Finally Falkirk won the game 4–0.

GOAL SCORING
Teams

The highest score recorded in a first-class match is 36. This occurred in the Scottish Cup match between

Arbroath and Bon Accord on 5 Sept 1885, when Arbroath won 36–0 on their home ground. But for the lack of nets and the consequent waste of retrieval time the score must have been even higher. Seven further goals were disallowed for offside.

The highest margin recorded in an international match is 17, when England beat Australia 17–0 at Sydney on 30 June 1951. This match is not listed by England as a *full* international. The highest in the British Isles was when England beat Ireland 13–0 at Belfast on 18 Feb 1882.

The highest score between English clubs in any major competition is 26, when Preston North End beat Hyde 26–0 in an FA Cup tie at Deepdale, Lancashire on 15 Oct 1887. The biggest victory in an FA Cup Final is six when Bury beat Derby County 6–0 at Crystal Palace on 18 Apr 1903, in which year Bury did not concede a single goal in the five Cup matches.

The highest score by one side in a Football League (First Division) match is 12 goals when West Bromwich Albion beat Darwen 12–0 at West Bromwich, West Midlands on 4 Apr 1892; when Nottingham Forest beat Leicester Fosse by the same score at Nottingham on 21 Apr 1909; and when Aston Villa beat Accrington 12–2 at Perry Barr, West Midlands on 12 Mar 1892.

The highest aggregate in League Football was 17 goals when Tranmere Rovers beat Oldham Athletic 13–4 in a Third Division (North) match at Prenton Park, Merseyside, on Boxing Day, 1935. The record margin in a League match has been 13 in the Newcastle United 13, Newport County 0 (Second Division) match on 5 Oct 1946 and in the Stockport County 13, Halifax 0 (Third Division (North)) match on 6 Jan 1934.

The highest number of goals by any British team in a professional league in a season is 142 in 34 matches by Raith Rovers (Scottish Second Division in the 1937–8 season. The English League record is 134 in 46 matches by Peterborough United (Fourth Division) in 1960–1.

Individual

The most scored by one player in a first-class match is 16 by Stephan Stanis (*né* Stanikowski, b. Poland, 15 July 1913) for Racing Club de Lens v. Aubry-Asturies, in Lens, France, in a wartime French Cup game on 13 Dec 1942.

> **Fastest League Hat-trick** ● Jimmy Scarth (b. 26 Aug 1920) scored a hat-trick in 2½ minutes for Gillingham v. Leyton Orient in a Division III (Southern) match on 1 Nov 1952. Here he is seen holding a present from the local paper detailing the achievement, for his wedding, which occured four weeks later. (Photo: David Roberts)

BRITISH GOAL-SCORING RECORDS

SCOTTISH CUP
13 John Petrie for Arbroath v. Bon Accord on 5 Sept 1885

FOOTBALL LEAGUE
10 Joe Payne (1914–77) for Luton Town v. Bristol Rovers (Div 3S) at Luton on 13 Apr 1936

FOOTBALL LEAGUE DIVISION ONE
7 Ted Drake (b. 16 Aug 1912) for Arsenal v. Aston Villa at Birmingham on 14 Dec 1935; James David Ross for Preston NE v. Stoke at Preston on 6 Oct 1888

FA CUP (PRELIMINARY ROUND)
10 Chris Marron for South Shields v. Radcliffe at South Shields on 20 Sept 1947

FA CUP
9 Edward 'Ted' MacDougall (b. 8 Jan 1947) for Bournemouth v. Margate at Bournemouth on 20 Nov 1971

SCOTTISH LEAGUE
8 James Edward McGrory (1904–82) for Celtic v. Dunfermline (Div 1) at Celtic Park, Glasgow on 14 Jan 1928

HOME INTERNATIONAL
6 Joe Bambrick (b. 3 Nov 1905) for Ireland v. Wales at Belfast on 1 Feb 1930

AMATEUR INTERNATIONAL
6 William Charles Jordan (1885–1949) for England v. France at Park Royal, London on 23 Mar 1908; Vivian John Woodward (1879–1954) for England v. Holland at Stamford Bridge, London on 11 Dec 1909; Harold A. Walden for Great Britain v. Hungary at Stockholm, Sweden on 1 July 1912

The record number of goals scored by one player in an international match is ten by Sofus Nielsen (1888–1963) for Denmark v. France (17–1) in the 1908 Olympics and by Gottfried Fuchs (1889–1972) for Germany who beat Russia 16–0 in the 1912 Olympic tournament (consolation event) in Sweden.

Most in a season
The most goals in a League season is 60 in 39 games by William Ralph 'Dixie' Dean (1907–80) for Everton (First Division) in 1927–8 and 66 in 38 games by James Smith (1902–76) for Ayr United (Scottish Second

Division in the same season. With three more in Cup ties and 19 in representative matches Dean's total was 82.

Career
Artur Friedenreich (1892–1969) (Brazil) scored an undocumented 1329 goals in a 43 year first–class football career. The most goals scored in a specified period is 1216 by Edson Arantes do Nascimento (Brazil) (b. 23 Oct 1940), known as Pelé, from 7 Sept 1956 to 2 Oct 1974 in 1254 games. His best year was 1959 with 126, and the *Milesimo* (1000th) came from a penalty for his club Santos in the Maracaña Stadium, Rio de Janeiro on 19 Nov 1969 when playing his 909th first–class match. He later played for New York Cosmos and on his retirement on 1 Oct 1977 his total had reached 1281, in 1363 games. He later added two more goals in special appearances. Franz 'Bimbo' Binder (b. 1 Dec 1911) scored 1006 goals in 756 games in Austria and Germany between 1930 and 1950.

The international career record for England is 49 goals by Robert 'Bobby' Charlton (b. 11 Oct 1937). His first was v. Scotland on 19 Apr 1958 and his last on 20 May 1970 v. Colombia.

The greatest number of goals scored in British first-class football is 550 (410 in Scottish League matches) by James McGrory of Glasgow Celtic (1922–38). The most scored in League matches is 434, for West Bromwich Albion, Fulham, Leicester City and Shrewsbury Town, by George Arthur Rowley (b. 21 Apr 1926) between 1946 and April 1965. Rowley also scored 32 goals in the F.A. Cup and one for England 'B'.

Fastest goals
The fastest Football League goals on record were scored in 6 sec by Albert E. Mundy (b. 12 May 1926) (Aldershot) in a Fourth Division match v. Hartlepool United at Victoria Ground, Hartlepool, Cleveland on 25 Oct 1958, by Barrie Jones (b. 31 Oct 1938) (Notts Co) in a Third Division match v. Torquay United on 31 Mar 1962, by Keith Smith (b. 15 Sept 1940) (Crystal Palace) in a Second Division match v. Derby County at the Baseball Ground, Derby on 12 Dec 1964 and by Tommy W. Langley (b. 8 Feb 1958) (Queen's Park Rangers) in a Second Division match v. Bolton Wanderers on 11 Oct 1980.

The fastest confirmed hat-trick is in 2½ minutes by Ephraim 'Jock' Dodds (b. 7 Sept 1915) for Blackpool v. Tranmere Rovers on 28 Feb 1942, and Jimmy Scarth (b. 26 Aug 1920) for Gillingham v. Leyton Orient in Third Division (Southern) on 1 Nov 1952. A hat-trick in 1 min 50 sec is claimed for Maglioni of Independiente v. Gimnasia y Escrima de la Plata in Argentina on 18 Mar 1973. John McIntyre (Blackburn Rovers) scored four goals in 5 min v. Everton at Ewood Park, Blackburn, Lancashire on 16 Sept 1922. William 'Ginger' Richardson (West Bromwich Albion) scored four goals in 5 min from the kick-off against West Ham United at Upton Park on 7 Nov 1931. Frank Keetley scored six goals in 21 min in the second half of the Lincoln City v. Halifax Town league match on 16 Jan 1932. The international record is three goals in 3½ min by Willie Hall (Tottenham Hotspur) for England against Ireland on 16 Nov 1938 at Old Trafford, Greater Manchester.

Fastest own goal
Torquay United's Pat Kruse (b. 30 Nov 1953) equalled the fastest goal on record when he headed the ball into his own net only 6 sec after kick-off v. Cambridge United on 3 Jan 1977.

GOALKEEPING
The longest that any goalkeeper has succeeded in preventing any goals being scored past him in international matches is 1142 min for Dino Zoff (Italy), from September 1972 to June 1974.

The British club record in all competitive matches is 1196 min by Chris Woods (b. 14 Nov 1959) for Glasgow Rangers from 26 Nov 1986 to 31 Jan 1987.

FA CHALLENGE CUP AND SCOTTISH FA CUP

Most wins

The greatest number of FA Cup wins is seven by: Aston Villa, 1887, 1895, 1897, 1905, 1913, 1920 and 1957 (nine Final appearances); and Tottenham Hotspur, 1901, 1921, 1961, 1962, 1967, 1981 and 1982 (eight appearances). Newcastle United and Arsenal have been in the final 11 times. The highest aggregate scores have been 6–1 in 1890 and 4–3 in 1953.

The greatest number of Scottish FA Cup wins is 28 by Celtic in 1892, 1899, 1900, 1904, 1907–8, 1911–12, 1914, 1923, 1925, 1927, 1931, 1933, 1937, 1951, 1954, 1965, 1967, 1969, 1971, 1972, 1974, 1975, 1977, 1980, 1985 and 1988.

Youngest player

The youngest player in an FA Cup Final was Paul Allen (b. 28 Aug 1962) for West Ham United *v.* Arsenal on 10 May 1980, aged 17 yr 256 days. Derek Johnstone (Rangers) (b. 4 Nov 1953) was 16 yr 11 months old when he played in the Scottish League Cup Final against Celtic on 24 Oct 1970. The youngest goal scorer in the FA Cup Final was Norman Whiteside (b. 7 May 1965) for Manchester United *v.* Brighton at 18 yr 19 days on 26 May 1983.

Most medals

Three players have won five FA Cupwinners' medals: James Forrest (Blackburn Rovers) (1884–6, 1890–1); the Hon. Sir Arthur Fitzgerald Kinnaird KT (Wanderers) (1873, 1877–8) and Old Etonians (1879, 1882); and Charles H. R. Wollaston (Wanderers) (1872–3, 1876–8).

The most Scottish Cupwinners' medals won is eight by Charles Campbell (Queen's Park) in 1874–6, 1880–2, 1884 and 1886.

Longest tie

The most protracted FA Cup tie in the competition proper was that between Stoke City and Bury in the third round, with Stoke winning 3–2 in the fifth meeting after 9 hr 22 min of play in January 1955. The matches were at Bury (1–1) on 8 Jan; Stoke-on-Trent on 12 Jan (abandoned after 22 min of extra time with the score 1–1); Goodison Park (3–3) on 17 Jan; Anfield (2–2) on 19 Jan; and finally at Old Trafford on 24 Jan. In the 1972 final qualifying round Alvechurch beat Oxford City after five previous drawn games (total playing time 11 hours).

FOOTBALL LEAGUE/MILK CUP/ LITTLEWOODS CUP

Instituted in 1960–1, the most wins is four by Liverpool, 1981–4.

SCOTTISH LEAGUE SKOL CUP

Instituted in 1946–7, the most wins is 15 by Rangers between 1947 and 1987.

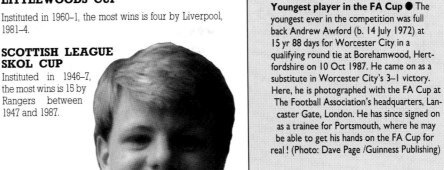

LEAGUE CHAMPIONSHIPS

The record number of successive national league championships is nine by: Celtic (Scotland) 1966–74; CSKA, Sofia (Bulgaria) 1954–62; and MTK Budapest (Hungary) 1917–25. The Sofia club holds a European post–war record of 23 league titles.

English

The greatest number of League Championships (First Division) is 17 by Liverpool in 1901, 1906, 1922–1923, 1947, 1964, 1966, 1973, 1976–7, 1979–80, 1982–84, 1986 and 1988. The record number of wins in a season is 33 from 42 matches by Doncaster Rovers in Third Division (North) in 1946–7. The First Division record is 31 wins from 42 matches by Tottenham Hotspur in 1960–1. In 1893–4 Liverpool won 22 and drew 6 in 28 Second Division games. They also won the promotion match.

The most points in a season under the current scoring system is 102 from 46 matches by Swindon in the Fourth Division in 1985–6. Under the new system the First Division record would have been Liverpool's 98 in 1978–9, when they won 30 and drew 8 of their 42 matches.

'Double'

The only FA Cup and League Championship 'doubles' are those of Preston North End in 1889, Aston Villa in 1897, Tottenham Hotspur in 1961, Arsenal in 1971 and Liverpool in 1986. Preston won the League without losing a match and the Cup without having a goal scored against them throughout the whole competition.

Scottish

Glasgow Rangers have won the Scottish League Championship 36 times between 1899 and 1987 and were joint champions in 1891. Their 76 points in the Scottish First Division in 1920–1 represent a record in any division.

Closest win

In 1923–4 Huddersfield won the First Division Championship over Cardiff by 0·02 of a goal with a goal average of 1·81.

THE FIFA WORLD CUP

Fédération Internationale de Football Association (FIFA), which was founded on 21 May 1904, instituted the first World Cup on 13 July 1930, in Montevideo, Uruguay. It is now held quadrennially. Three wins have been achieved by Brazil 1958, 1962 and 1970, and Italy 1934, 1938 and 1982. Brazil, uniquely, have taken part in all 13 finals tournaments.

Goal scoring and appearances

Antonio Carbajal (b. 1923) (Mexico) is the only player to have appeared in five World Cup finals tournaments, keeping goal for Mexico in 1950, 1954, 1958, 1962 and 1966, playing 11 games in all. The most appearances in finals tournaments is 21 by: Uwe Seeler (b. 5 Nov 1936) (West Germany), 1958–70; and by Wladyslaw Zmuda (Poland) (b. 6 June 1954), 1974–86. Pelé is the only player to have been with three World Cup–winning teams, in 1958, 1962 and 1970. The youngest ever to play in the World Cup is Norman Whiteside, who played for Northern Ireland v. Yugoslavia aged 17 yr 42 days on 17 June 1982.

Just Fontaine (b. Marrakesh, Morocco, 18 Aug 1933) of France scored 13 goals in six matches in the final stages of the 1958 competition in Sweden. Gerd Müller (b. 3 Nov 1945) (West Germany) scored 10 goals in 1970 and four in 1974 for the highest aggregate of 14 goals. Fontaine, Jairzinho (Brazil) and Alcide Ghiggia (Uruguay) are the only three players to have scored in every match in a final series. Jairzinho scored seven in six games in 1970 and Ghiggia, four in four games in 1950 .

The most goals scored in a final is three by Geoff Hurst (b. 8 Dec 1941) for England v. West Germany on 30 July 1966. Three players have scored in two finals: Vava (real name Edwaldo Izito Neto) (Brazil) in 1958 and 1962, Pelé in 1958 and 1970; and Paul Breitner (West Germany) in 1974 and 1982. The fastest goal in World Cup competition was one in 27 sec by Bryan Robson (b. 11 Jan 1957) for England v. France in Bilbao on 16 June 1982.

The highest score in a World Cup match occurred in a qualifying match in Auckland on 15 Aug 1981 when New

European Champion Clubs Cup

The European Cup for the league champions of the respective nations was approved by FIFA on 8 May 1955 and was run by the European governing body UEFA (Union of European Football Associations) which came into being in the previous year. Real Madrid won the first final, and have won a record six times 1956–60, 1966. The highest score in a Final was Real Madrid's 7–3 win over Eintracht Frankfurt at Hampden Park, Glasgow on 18 May 1960.

Glasgow Celtic became the first British club to win the Cup, beating Inter-Milan 2–1 in Lisbon, Portugal on 25 May 1967. They also became the first British club to win the European Cup and the two senior domestic tournaments (League and Cup) in the same season. Liverpool, winners in 1977, 1978, 1981 and 1984, have been the most successful British club and in the 1983–4 season emulated Celtic by also winning two domestic competitions—League and Milk Cup.

European Cup Winners Cup

A tournament for national cup winners started in 1960–1. Clubs to win twice have been: AC Milan 1968 and 1973; Anderlecht 1976 and 1978, Barcelona 1979 and 1982; and Dynamo Kiev 1975 and 1986. Tottenham Hotspur were the first British club to win the trophy, when they set a record score for the Final beating Atlético Madrid 5–1 in Rotterdam on 15 May 1963.

UEFA Cup

Originally known as the International Inter-City Industrial Fairs Cup, this club tournament began in 1955. The first competition lasted three years, the second two years. In 1960–1 it became an annual tournament and since 1971–2 has been replaced by the UEFA Cup. The most wins is three by Barcelona in 1958, 1960 and 1966. The first British club to win the trophy was Leeds United in 1968.

PLAYERS
Most durable

Norman John Trollope (b. 14 June 1943) made 770 League appearances for one club, Swindon Town, between 1960 and 1980. The most senior UK appearances is 1119 by Ray Clemence (b. 5 Aug 1948) for Scunthorpe United (50), Liverpool (665), Tottenham Hotspur (337) and 67 in representitives including internationals.

Transfer fees

The greatest transfer fee quoted for a player is 15 895

Zealand beat Fiji 13–0. The highest score during the final stages is 10, scored by Hungary in a 10–1 win over El Salvador at Elche, Spain on 15 June 1982. The highest match aggregate in the finals tournament is 12, when Austria beat Switzerland in 1954.

The highest scoring team in a finals tournament has been West Germany who scored 25 in six matches in 1954, for the highest average of 4·17 goals per game.

The best defensive record belongs to England, who in six matches in 1966 conceded only three goals. Curiously, no team has ever failed to score in a World Cup Final.

TOURNAMENT RECORDS
World Club Championship

This club tournament was started in 1960 between the winners of the European Cup and the Copa Libertadores, the South American equivalent. The most wins is three by Penarol, Uruguay in 1961, 1966 and 1982. Independiente, Argentina won in 1973 and 1984 and reached the Final in 1975, but couldn't agree dates for the matches with Bayern Munich.

European Championship (Nations Cup)

Held every four years from 1958. West Germany are the only country to have won twice, in 1972 and 1980. They also lost in the 1976 final, to Czechoslovakia.

million lire by Napoli in 1984 for Diego Maradona (Argentina) (b. 30 Oct 1960) from Barcelona. This exceeded the *c.* £5 million that Barcelona paid for Maradona in 1982.

The record fee between two British clubs is £2 million (including VAT and other levies) paid by Tottenham Hotspur to Newcastle United for Paul Gascoigne (b. 27 May 1967) on 7 July 1988 and by Everton to West Ham United for Tony Cottee (b. 11 July 1965) on 25 July 1988. The highest transfer fee for a British player is the estimated £3·2 million paid by Juventus of Italy to Liverpool for Ian Rush (b. 20 Oct 1961) in June 1986.

Heaviest goalkeeper

The biggest goalkeeper in representative football was the England international Willie J. 'Fatty' Foulke (1874–1916), who stood 1·90 m *6 ft 3 in* and weighed 141 kg *22 st 3 lb*. His last games were for Bradford City, by which time he was 165 kg *26 st.* He once stopped a game by snapping the cross bar.

INTERNATIONAL CAPS
Oldest and youngest

The oldest international has been William Henry 'Billy' Meredith (1874–1958) (Manchester City and United) who played outside right for Wales v. England at Highbury, London on 15 Mar 1920 when aged 45 yr 229 days. He played internationally for a record span of 26 years (1895–1920). The youngest British international was Norman Whiteside, who played for Northern Ireland v. Yugoslavia at 17 yr 42 days on 17 June 1982.

England's youngest international was Duncan Edwards (1936–58) (Manchester United) v. Scotland at Wembley on 2 Apr 1955, at 18 yr 183 days. The youngest Welsh cap was John Charles (b. 27 Dec 1931) (Leeds United) v. Ireland at Wrexham on 8 Mar 1950, aged 18 yr

71 days. Scotland's youngest international has been Johnny Lambie (Queen's Park), at 17 yr 2 days v. Ireland on 20 Mar 1886. The youngest for the Republic of Ireland was James Holmes (b. 11 Nov 1953) (Coventry City), at 17 yr 200 days v. Austria in Dublin on 30 May 1971.

Most international appearances

The greatest number of appearances for a national team is 150 by Hector Chumpitaz (b. 12 Apr 1943) (Peru) from 1963 to 1982. This includes all matches played by the national team. The record for full internationals against other national teams is 119 by Pat Jennings of Northern Ireland (as above).

The most international appearances by a woman is 56 (49 as captain) by Carol Thomas (b. 5 June 1955) for England, 1974–86.

ATTENDANCES
Greatest crowds

The greatest recorded crowd at any football match was 205 000 (199 589 paid) for the Brazil v. Uruguay World Cup match in the Maracaña Municipal Stadium, Rio de Janeiro, Brazil on 16 July 1950.

The record attendance for a European Cup match is 136 505 at the semi-final between Glasgow Celtic and Leeds United at Hampden Park, Glasgow on 15 Apr 1970.

The British record paid attendance is 149 547 at the Scotland v. England international at Hampden Park, Glasgow, on 17 Apr 1937. It is, however, probable that this total was exceeded (estimated 160 000) at the FA Cup Final between Bolton Wanderers and West Ham United at Wembley Stadium on 28 Apr 1923, when the crowd broke in on the pitch and the start was delayed

> **Most durable player** ● The most durable in League history has been Peter Leslie Shilton (b. 18 Sept 1949) who has made 826 League appearances up to 1988 playing; 286 for Leicester City (1966–74), 110 for Stoke City (1974–7), 202 for Nottingham Forest (1977–82), 188 for Southampton (1982–7) and 40 for Derby County (1987–8). (Photo: All-Sport)

40 min until the pitch was cleared. The counted admissions were 126 047.

The Scottish Cup record attendance is 146 433 when Celtic played Aberdeen at Hampden Park on 24 Apr 1937.

The record attendance for a League match in Britain is 118 567 for Rangers v. Celtic at Ibrox Park, Glasgow on 2 Jan 1939.

The highest attendance at an amateur match has been 120 000 in Senayan Stadium, Jakarta, Indonesia on 26 Feb 1976 for the Pre-Olympic Group II Final, North Korea v. Indonesia.

Smallest crowd

The smallest crowd at a full home international was 2315 for Wales v. Northern Ireland on 27 May 1982 at the Racecourse Ground, Wrexham, Clwyd.

The smallest paying attendance at a Football League fixture was for the Stockport County v. Leicester City match at Old Trafford, Greater Manchester on 7 May 1921. Stockport's own ground was under suspension and the 'crowd' numbered 13 but an estimated 2000 gained free admission.

When West Ham United beat Castilla of Spain (5–1) in the European Cup Winners Cup at Upton Park, Greater London on 1 Oct 1980 and when Aston Villa beat Besiktas of Turkey (3–1) in the European Cup at Villa Park on 15 Sept 1982, there were no paying spectators due to disciplinary action by the European Football Union.

PENALTIES

The greatest number of penalty kicks taken to decide a cup game under the jurisdiction of the Football League occurred in a Freight Rover Trophy, Southern Section quarter-final between Aldershot and Fulham on 10 Feb 1987, at the Recreation Ground, Aldershot, Hampshire. After 90 minutes play the score was 1–1. A further 30 minutes of extra time produced no further scoring. It needed 28 penalty kicks, of which only seven were missed, before Aldershot won 11–10.

In the Cyprus First-Division match in which Omonia beat Olympiakos 6–4 in Nicosia on 15 February 1987, FIFA referee Stafanos Hadjistefanou awarded six penalties, three to each side, all of which were converted by George Savvides (Omonia) and Sylvester Vernon (Olympiakos).

OLYMPIC GAMES

The only country to have won the Olympic football title three times is Hungary in 1952, 1964 and 1968. The United Kingdom won the unofficial tournament in 1900 and the official tournaments of 1908 and 1912. The highest Olympic score is by Denmark (17) v. France 'A' (1) in 1908.

OTHER MATCHES

Highest scores *Teams*

In a Felixstowe Sunday League match on 11 Mar 1984 Ipswich Exiles beat Seaton Rovers 45–0.

In an Under-14 League match between Midas FC and Courage Colts, in Kent, on 11 Apr 1976, the full-time score after 70 minutes play was 59–1. Top scorer for Midas was Kevin Graham with 17 goals. Courage had scored the first goal.

Needing to improve their goal 'difference' to gain promotion in 1979, Ilinden FC of Yugoslavia, with the collusion of the opposition, Mladost, and the referee, won their final game of the season by 134–1. Their rivals in the promotion race won their match, under similar circumstances, by 88–0.

Individual

Dean Goodliff scored 26 goals for Deleford Colts v. Iver Minors in the Slough Boys Soccer Combination Under-14 League at Iver, Buckinghamshire in his team's 33–0 win on 22 Dec 1985. The women's record is 22 goals by Linda Curl of Norwich Ladies in a 40–0 league victory over Milton Keynes Reserves at Norwich on 25 Sept 1983.

Season

The greatest number of goals in a season reported for an individual player in junior professional league football is 96 by Tom Duffy (b. 7 Jan 1937), for Ardeer Thistle FC, Strathclyde in 1960–1. Paul Anthony Moulden (b. 6 Sept 1967) scored 289 goals in 40 games for Bolton Lads Club in Bolton Boys Federation intermediate league and cup matches in 1981–2. An additional 51 goals scored in other tournaments brought his total to 340, the highest season figure reported in any class of competitive football for an individual. He made his Football League debut for Manchester City on 1 Jan 1986 and has played for the England Youth team.

Fastest goals

Wind-aided goals in 3 sec after kick-off have been scored by a number of players. Damian Corcoran (b. 25 Nov 1976) scored three goals within a minute for 7th Fulwood Cubs v 4th Fulwood Cubs on 1 Feb 1987.

Fastest own goal

The fastest own goals on record have been in 5 sec 'scored' by Peter Johnson of Chesham United v. Wycombe Wanderers on 21 Feb 1976 and by John Smythe of Vernon Carus v. Duke Williams Reserves in March 1986.

Longest ties

In the Hertfordshire Intermediate Cup, London Colney beat Leavesden Hospital after 12 hr 41 min play and seven ties from 6 Nov to 17 Dec 1971.

Largest tournament

The Metropolitan Police 5-a-side Youth Competition in 1981 attracted an entry of 7008 teams, a record for an FA sanctioned competition.

Most and least successful teams

Winlaton West End FC, Tyne and Wear, completed a run of 95 league games without defeat between 1976 and 1980. Penlake Junior Football Club remained unbeaten for 153 games (winning 152 including 85 in succession) in the Warrington Hilden Friendly League from 1981 until defeated in 1986. Stockport United FC, of the Stockport Football League, lost 39 consecutive League and Cup matches, September 1976 to 18 Feb 1978.

Most indisciplined

In the local cup match between Tongham Youth Club, Surrey and Hawley, Hampshire, on 3 Nov 1969, the referee booked all 22 players including one who went to hospital, and one of the linesmen. The match, won by Tongham 2–0, was described by a player as 'a good, hard game'.

In a Gancia Cup match at Waltham Abbey, Essex on 23 Dec 1973, the referee, Michael J. Woodhams, sent off the entire Juventus-Cross team and some club officials. Glencraig United, Faifley, nr Clydebank, had all 11 team members and two substitutes for their 2–2 draw against Goldenhill Boys' Club on 2 Feb 1975 booked in the dressing room before a ball was kicked. The referee, Mr Tarbet of Bearsden, took exception to the chant which greeted his arrival. It was not his first meeting with Glencraig.

Ball control

Allan Abuto Nyanjong (Kenya) juggled a regulation soccer ball for 16 hr 27 min 52 sec non-stop with feet, legs and head without the ball ever touching the ground at the Hyatt Regency Crystal City, Arlington, Virginia, USA on 16 Jan 1988. He also headed a regulation football non-stop for 5 hr at Coronado High School Gym, El Paso, Texas, USA on 25 Apr 1987. Janusz Chomontek of Gdanieck, Poland kept a football up while he travelled a distance of 30 km *18·641 miles* in 8 hr 25 min 20 sec on 19 Sept 1987.

GUINNESS HAVE PUBLISHED **SOCCER: RECORDS, FACTS AND CHAMPIONS (2nd EDITION)** JACK ROLLIN £8.95

Gaelic Football

The game developed from inter-parish 'free for all' with no time-limit, specific playing area or rules. The earliest reported match was Meath v. Louth, at Slane in 1712. Standardisation came with the formation of the Gaelic Athletic Association in Thurles, Ireland on 1 Nov 1884.

All-Ireland Championships

The greatest number of All-Ireland Championships won by one team is 30 by Ciarraidhe (Kerry) between 1903 and 1986. The greatest number of successive wins is four by Wexford (1915–18) and Kerry twice (1929–32, 1978–81).

The most finals contested is eleven, including eight wins by the Kerry players Pat Spillane, Michael Sheehy, Paudie O'Shea, Ger Power and Denis Moran, 1975–86.

The highest team score in a final was when Dublin, 27 (5 goals, 12 points) beat Armagh, 15 (3 goals, 6 points) on 25 Sept 1977. The highest combined score was 45 points when Cork (26) beat Galway (19) in 1973. A goal equals three points. The highest individual score in an All-Ireland final has been 2 goals, 6 points by Jimmy Keaveney (Dublin) v. Armagh in 1977, and by Michael Sheehy (Kerry) v. Dublin in 1979.

Largest crowd

The record crowd is 90 556 for the Down v. Offaly final at Croke Park, Dublin in 1961.

Gambling

World's biggest win

The world's biggest individual gambling win is $40 million by Mike Wittkowski in the Illinois State Lottery, announced on 3 Sept 1984. From $35 worth of 'Lotto' tickets bought by his family, the winning six numbers bring him $2 million for the next 20 years.

Largest casino

The largest casino in the world is the Burswood Island Casino, Perth, Western Australia opened on 30 Dec 1985. In an area of 7500 ^{2}m *80 729 ^{2}ft* has 200 video games and 142 gaming tables.

BINGO

Bingo is a lottery game which, as Keno, was developed in the 1880s from Lotto, whose origin is thought to be the 17th-century Italian game *tumbule*. It has long been known in the British Army (called Housey-Housey) and the Royal Navy (called Tombola). The winner was the first to complete a random selection of numbers from 1 to 90. The USA version called Bingo differs in that the selection is from 1 to 75. There are an estimated six million players in the United Kingdom.

Largest house

The largest 'house' in Bingo sessions was 15 756 at the Canadian National Exhibition, Toronto on 19 Aug 1983. Staged by the Variety Club of Ontario Tent Number 28, there was total prize money of $C250 000 with a record one-game payout of $C100 000.

Earliest and latest Full House

A 'Full House' call occurred on the 15th number by Norman A. Wilson at Guide Post Working Men's Club, Bedlington, Northumberland on 22 June 1978, by Anne Wintle of Brynrethin, Mid-Glamorgan, on a coach trip to Bath on 17 Aug 1982 and by Shirley Lord at Kahibah Bowling Club, New South Wales, Australia on 24 Oct 1983. 'House' was not called until the 86th number at the Hillsborough Working Men's Club, Sheffield, South Yorkshire on 11 Jan 1982. There were 32 winners.

ELECTIONS

The highest ever individual bet was £90 000 to win £20 000 for the Conservative party to return the most MPs in the 1983 General Election, by an unnamed man. A bet of £5000 at 200–1 was placed by Frank Egerton in April 1975 that his Centre Party would win the next General Election. It didn't.

FOOTBALL POOLS

Two unnamed punters won *c.* £1·5 million each in November 1972 on the state-run Italian pools. The winning dividend paid out by Littlewoods Pools in their first week in February 1923 was £2 12s 0d . In 1985–6 the three British Pools companies which comprise the Pool Promoters Association (Littlewoods, Vernons and Zetters) had a total record turnover of £550 434 000 of which Littlewoods contributed over 70 per cent.

Biggest win

The record payout from the British Pools—which is also the biggest ever prize paid in any British competition—is £1 339 358.30 paid by Littlewoods Pools to Jim Anderson, 51, of Anderton, Northants for matches on 11 July 1987.

The record double payout is £1 988 510 by Littlewoods on 13 Feb 1988 to John Clark of Bristol, Avon (£991 656) and an anonymous Strathclyde woman (£996 854). Littlewoods' record total payout for a single week is £3 149 116 on 5 Mar 1988.

HORSE RACING

Highest ever odds

The highest secured odds were 1 670 759 to 1 by George Rhodes of Aldershot, Hampshire. For a 5p bet, with a 10 per cent bonus for the ITV Seven, less tax, he was paid £86 024.42 by the William Hill Organisation on 30 Sept 1984. Edward Hodson of Wolverhampton landed a 3 956 748 to 1 bet for a 55p stake on 11 Feb 1984, but his bookmaker had a £3000 payout limit. The world record odds on a 'double' are 31 793 to 1 paid by the New Zealand Totalisator Agency Board on a five shilling tote ticket on *Red Emperor* and *Maida Dillon* at Addington, Christchurch in 1951.

Greatest payout

Anthony A. Speelman and Nicholas John Cowan (both Great Britain) won $1 627 084·40, after federal income tax of $406 768·00 was withheld, on a $64 nine-horse accumulator at Santa Anita racecourse, California, USA on 19 Apr 1987. Their first seven selections won and the payout was for a jackpot, accumulated over 24 days. The largest payout by a British bookmaker is £227 812·50 by William Hill, paid to a Mr. 'X' for three winners, all coupled in three £2000 doubles and a £9000 treble on 1 Aug 1985.

Biggest tote win

The best recorded tote win was one of £341 2s 6d to 2s

Biggest win ● The biggest beating handed to a 'one-armed bandit' was $6 814 823.48 by Cammie Brewer, 61, at the Club Cal-Neva, Reno, Nevada, USA on 14 Feb 1988. (Photo: Gamma)

representing odds of 3410¼ to 1, by Catharine Unsworth of Blundellsands, Liverpool at Haydock Park on a race won by *Coole* on 30 Nov 1929. The highest odds in Irish tote history were £289.64 for a 10p unit on *Gene's Rogue* at Limerick on 28 Dec 1981.

Largest bookmaker

The world's largest bookmaker is Ladbrokes with a turnover from gambling in 1987 of £1300 million. The largest chain of betting shops is that of Ladbrokes with 1766 shops in the United Kingdom and the Republic of Ireland at the end of 1987, as well as 1084 in Belgium and The Netherlands.

Topmost tipster

The only recorded instance of a racing correspondent forecasting ten out of ten winners on a race card was at Delaware Park, Wilmington, Delaware, USA on 28 July 1974 by Charles Lamb of the *Baltimore News American*.

The best performance by a British correspondent is seven out of seven winners for a meeting at York on 12 May 1988 by Fred Shawcross of the *Today* newspaper.

Gliding

Isadore William Deiches has researched evidence of the use of gliders in Ancient Egypt *c.* 2500–1500 BC. Emanuel Swedenborg (1688–1772) of Sweden made sketches of gliders *c.* 1714. The earliest man-carrying glider was designed by Sir George Cayley (1773–1857) and carried his coachman (possibly John Appleby) about 457 m *500 yd* across a valley in Brompton Dale, North Yorkshire in the summer of 1853.

Most titles *World*

The most World Individual Championships (inst. 1948) won is four by Ingo Renner (Australia) in 1976 (Standard class), 1983, 1985 and 1987 (Open).

British

The British National Championship (inst. 1939) has been won eight times by Ralph Jones (b. 29 Mar 1936). The first woman to win this title was Anne Burns (b. 23 Nov. 1915) of Farnham, Surrey on 30 May 1966.

Altitude records *Women*

The women's single-seater world record for absolute altitude is 12 637 m *41 449 ft* by Sabrina Jackintell (USA) in an Astir GS on 14 Feb 1979. The British single-seater record is 10 550 m *34 612 ft* by Anne Burns in a Skylark 3B over South Africa on 13 Jan 1961, when she set a world record for height gain of 9119 m *29 918 ft*.

HANG GLIDING

In the eleventh century the monk, Eilmer, is reported to have flown from the 18·3 m *60 ft* tower of Malmesbury Abbey, Wiltshire, England. The earliest modern pioneer was Otto Lilienthal (1848–96) (Germany) with about 2500 flights in gliders of his own construction between 1891 and 1896. In the 1950s Professor Francis Rogallo of the National Space Agency, USA, developed a flexible 'wing' from his space capsule re-entry researches.

World Championships

The World Team Championships have been won most often by Great Britain (1981 and 1985).

WORLD RECORDS

As officially recognised by the *Fédération Aéronautique Internationale*.

MEN

Greatest distance in straight line: (Flexwing) 321·47 km *199.76 miles* Randy Haney (Canada), Golden, Canada to Trego, USA, 2 June 1986; (Multiplace Flexwing) 161·904 km *100·607 miles* Larry Tudor (USA), Owens Valley, California, USA, 12 July 1985; (Rigid Wing) 167·83 km *104·28 miles* George Worthington (USA), Owens Valley, 23 July 1980;

Height gain: (Flexwing) 4343·4 m *14 250 ft* Larry Tudor (USA) at Owens Valley, 4 Aug 1985; (Multiplace Flexwing) 3169·92 m *10 399 ft* Larry Tudor (USA), Owens Valley, 12 July 1982; (Rigid Wing) 3820 m *12 532 ft* Rainer Scholl (West Germany) at Owens Valley, 5 Aug 1985.

Declared goal distance: 272·19 km *169·13 miles* Geoffrey R. Lyons (GB) (b. 23 Feb 1951) at Owens Valley, 11 June 1986.

Out and return distance: 172·6 km *107·25 miles* Klaus Kohmstedt (West Germany), 15 July 1985.

Triangular course distance: (Flexwing) 80·83 km *50.22 miles* Denis Cummings (Australia), Parks, NSW, 29 Dec 1985.

GLIDING WORLD RECORDS
(Single-seaters)

	DISTANCE	NAME	TYPE OF GLIDER	LOCATION	DATE
STRAIGHT DISTANCE	1460·8 km *907·7 miles*	Hans-Werner Grosse (West Germany)	ASW-12	Lübeck, W. Germany to Biarritz, France	25 Apr 1972
DECLARED GOAL DISTANCE	1254·26 km *779·4 miles*	Bruce Drake (New Zealand)	Nimbus 2	Te Anau to Te Araroa, New Zealand	14 Jan 1978
		David Speight (New Zealand)	Nimbus 2	Te Anau to Te Araroa, New Zealand	14 Jan 1978
		S. H. 'Dick' Georgeson (New Zealand)	Nimbus 2	Te Anau to Te Araroa, New Zealand	14 Jan 1978
GOAL AND RETURN	1646·68 km *1023·2 miles*	Tom Knauff (USA)	Nimbus 3	Williamsport, Pa to Knoxville, Tn USA	25 Apr 1983
ABSOLUTE ALTITUDE	14 938 m *49 009 ft*	Robert R. Harris (USA)	Grob G102	California, USA	17 Feb 1986
HEIGHT GAIN	12 849 m *42 303 ft*	Paul Bikle (USA)	Schweitzer SGS1–23E	Mojave, California, USA	25 Feb 1961

SPEED OVER TRIANGULAR COURSE

DISTANCE	SPEED KM/H	MPH	NAME	TYPE OF GLIDER	PLACE	DATE	
100 km	195·3	*121·35*	Ingo Renner (Australia)	Nimbus 3	Australia	14 Dec	1982
300 km	169·49	*105·32*	Jean-Paul Castel (France)	Nimbus 3	South Africa	15 Nov	1986
500 km	164·11	*101·97*	Jean-Paul Castel (France)	Nimbus 3	South Africa	10 Dec	1986
750 km	158·40	*98·43*	Hans-Werner Grosse (West Germany)	ASW-22	Australia	8 Jan	1985
1000 km	145·32	*90·29*	Hans-Werner Grosse (West Germany)	ASW-17	Australia	3 Jan	1979
1250 km	133·24	*82·79*	Hans-Werner Grosse (West Germany)	ASW-17	Australia	9 Jan	1980

BRITISH RECORDS

	DISTANCE	NAME	TYPE OF GLIDER	LOCATION	DATE
STRAIGHT DISTANCE	949·7 km *589·9 miles*	Karla Karel	LS-3	Australia	20 Jan 1980
DECLARED GOAL DISTANCE	859·2 km *534 miles*	M. T. Alan Sands	Nimbus 3	Ridge soaring to Chilhowee, Va, USA	23 Apr 1986
GOAL AND RETURN	1127·68 km *700·72 miles*	M. T. Alan Sands	Nimbus 3	Lock Haven, Pa to Bluefield, Va, USA	7 May 1985
ABSOLUTE ALTITUDE	11 500 m *37 729 ft*	H. C. N. Goodhart	Schweitzer 1–23	California, USA	12 May 1955
HEIGHT GAIN	10 065 m *33 022 ft*	D. Benton	Nimbus 2	Portmoak, Scotland	18 Apr 1980

SPEED OVER TRIANGULAR COURSE

DISTANCE	SPEED KM/H	MPH	NAME	TYPE OF GLIDER	PLACE	DATE	
100 km	143·3	*88·99*	E. Paul Hodge	Standard Cirrus	Rhodesia	30 Oct	1976
300 km	146·8	*91·2*	Edward Pearson	Nimbus 2	S. W. Africa	30 Nov	1976
500 km	141·3	*87·8*	Bradley James Grant Pearson	ASW-20	South Africa	28 Dec	1982
750 km	109·8	*68·2*	Michael R. Carlton	Kestrel 19	South Africa	5 Jan	1975
1250 km	109·01	*67·73*	Robert L. Robertson	Ventus A	USA	2 May	1986

WOMEN

Greatest distance: (Flexwing) 233·9 km *145·34 miles* Judy Leden (GB), Owens Valley, 13 July 1983.

Height gain: (Flexwing) 3291·84 m *10 800 ft* Page Pfieffer (USA), Owens Valley, 12 July 1979.

Out and return distance: 118·09 km *73·38 miles* Valerie Wallington (Australia), Australia, 4 Jan 1985.

Declared goal distance: 124·52 km *77·37 miles* Judy Lori (USA), Owens Valley, 15 July 1983.

Triangular course distance: 68·75 km *42·72 miles*, Jenny Canderton (GB), St Andre-les-Alpes, France, 23 June 1987.

BRITISH RECORDS

The British record for distance is held by John Pendry, 300·62 km *186·80 miles*, flying an Airwave Magic 3 from Horseshoe Meadows, Owens Valley, California to Summit Mountain, Nevada, USA on 13 July 1983. The best in Britain is 217·07 km *134·88 miles* by Patrick Laverty, Cemmaes Mountain, Wales on 31 Aug 1986. The out and return distance record is Judy Leden, 82·04 km *50·97 miles* at Owens Valley, California, USA on 15 June 1983. In 1987 Pendry became the first hang glider pilot to receive the Royal Aero Club's gold medal.

The British height gain record is 4145·33 m *13 600 ft* by Colin Rider at Wether Fell, North Yorkshire on 4 July 1987.

Greatest descent

John Bird piloted a hang glider from a height of 39 000 ft *11 887·2 m* when he was released from a hot-air balloon, to the ground, landing in Edmonton, Alberta, Canada on 29 Aug 1982. He touched down 80·4 km *50 miles* from his point of departure.

Golf

Although a stained glass window in Gloucester Cathedral, dating from 1350, portrays a golfer-like figure, the earliest mention of golf occurs in a prohibiting law passed by the Scottish Parliament in March 1457 under which 'goff be utterly cryit doune and not usit'. The Romans had a cognate game called *paganica* which may have been carried to Britain before AD 400. The Chinese Nationalist Golf Association claims the game is of Chinese origin (*Ch'ui Wan*—the ball hitting game) in the 3rd or 2nd century BC. There were official ordinances prohibiting a ball game with clubs in Belgium and Holland from 1360. Gutta percha balls succeeded feather balls in 1848 and by 1902 were in turn succeeded by rubber-cored balls, invented in 1899 by Coburn Haskell (USA). Steel shafts were authorised in the USA in 1925 and in Britain in 1929.

Oldest club

The oldest club of which there is written evidence is the Gentlemen Golfers (now the Honourable Company of Edinburgh Golfers) formed in March 1744—ten years prior to the institution of the Royal and Ancient Club of St Andrews, Fife. However, the Royal Burgess Golfing Society of Edinburgh claims to have been founded in 1735.

Highest course

The highest golf course in the world is the Tuctu Golf Club in Morococha, Peru, which is 4369 m *14 335 ft* above sea level at its lowest point. Golf has, however, been played in Tibet at an altitude of over 4875 m *16 000 ft*.

Highest earnings ● Ian Woosnam (Wales) (b. 2 Mar 1958) won a European record £253 717.10 in European Order of Merit tournaments in 1987, when in all events world-wide he won £1 042 662.76. This included the greatest first place prize money ever won by an individual, $1 000 000 on 6 Dec 1987, at Sun City, Bophuthatswana, South Africa. (Photo: All-Sport/ David Cannon)

The highest golf course in Great Britain is one of nine holes at Leadhills, Strathclyde, 457 m *1500 ft* above sea level.

The highest recorded golf shot played on Earth was at 6194 m *20 320 ft* from the summit of Mt McKinley, Alaska, USA by Timothy J. Ayers (USA) on 23 May 1984.

Longest hole

The longest hole in the world is the 7th hole (par-7) of the Sano Course, Satsuki GC, Japan, which measures 831 m *909 yd*. The longest hole on a championship course in Great Britain is the sixth at Troon, Strathclyde, which stretches 528 m *577 yd*.

Largest green

Probably the largest green in the world is that of the par-6 635 m *695 yd* fifth hole at International GC, Bolton, Massachusetts, USA, with an area greater than 2600 m² *28 000 ft².*

Longest course

The world's longest course is the par-77 7612 m *8325 yd* International GC (see also above) from the 'Tiger' tees, remodelled in 1969 by Robert Trent Jones.

Floyd Satterlee Rood used the United States as a course, when he played from the Pacific surf to the Atlantic surf from 14 Sept 1963 to 3 Oct 1964 in 114 737 strokes. He lost 3511 balls on the 5468 km *3397·7 mile* trail.

Longest drives

In officially regulated long driving contests over level ground the greatest distance recorded is 358 m *392 yd* by William Thomas 'Tommie' Campbell (b. 24 July 1927) (Foxrock Golf Club) at Dun Laoghaire, Co. Dublin, Ireland in July 1964.

On an airport runway Liam Higgins (Ireland) drove a Spalding Top Flite ball 579·8 m *634·1 yd* at Baldonnel military airport, Dublin, Ireland on 25 Sept 1984. The women's record is held by Helen Dobson (GB) who drove a Titleist Pinnacle 469·1 m *531 yd* at RAF Honnington, Suffolk on 31 Oct 1987. The greatest recorded drive on an ordinary course is one of 471 m *515 yd* by Michael Hoke Austin (b. 17 Feb 1910) of Los Angeles, California, USA, in the US National Seniors Open Championship at Las Vegas, Nevada on 25 Sept 1974. Austin, 1·88 m *6 ft 2 in* tall and weighing 92 kg *210 lb* drove the

ball to within a yard of the green on the par-4 412 m *450 yd* fifth hole of the Winterwood Course and it rolled 59 m *65 yd* past the flagstick. He was aided by an estimated 56 km/h *35 mph* tailwind.

A drive of 2414 m *2640 yd (1½ miles)* across ice was achieved by an Australian meteorologist named Nils Lied at Mawson Base, Antarctica in 1962. Arthur Lynskey claimed a drive of 182 m *200 yd* horizontal and 3200 m *2 miles* vertical off Pikes Peak, Colorado (4300 m *14 110 ft*) on 28 June 1968. On the Moon the energy expended on a mundane 274 m *300 yd* drive would achieve, craters permitting, a distance of 1·6 km *1 mile*.

Longest putt

The longest recorded holed putt in a major tournament was one of 26 m *86 ft* on the vast 13th green at the Augusta National, Georgia by Cary Middlecoff (b. 6 Jan 1921) (USA) in the 1955 Masters' Tournament. Robert Tyre 'Bobby' Jones Jr, (1902–71) was reputed to have holed a putt in excess of 30 m *100 ft* at the fifth green in the first round of the 1927 Open at St Andrews. Bob Cook (USA) sank a putt measured at 42·74 m *140 ft 2¾ in* on the 18th at St Andrews in the International Fourball Pro Am Tournament on 1 Oct 1976.

SCORES
Lowest 9 holes

Nine holes in 25 (4, 3, 3, 2, 3, 3, 1, 4, 2) was recorded by A. J. 'Bill' Burke in a round in 57 (32 + 25) on the 5842 m *6389 yd* par-71 Normandie course at St Louis, Missouri, USA on 20 May 1970. The tournament record is 27 by Mike Souchak (USA) (b. 10 May 1927) for the second nine (par-35), first round of the 1955 Texas Open (see 72 holes); Andy North (USA) (b. 9 Mar 1950) second nine (par-34), first round, 1975 BC Open at En-Joie GC, Endicott, NY; José Maria Canizares (Spain) (b. 18 Feb 1947), first nine, third round, in the 1978 Swiss Open on the 6228 m *6811 yd* Crans-Sur course; and Robert Lee (GB) (b. 12 Oct 1961) first nine, first round, in the Monte Carlo Open on the 5714 m *6249 yd* Mont Agel course on 28 June 1985.

Lowest 18 holes *Men*

At least four players have played a long course (over 6000 m *6561 yd*) in a score of 58, most recently Monte Carlo Money (USA) (b. 3 Dec 1954), the par-72, 6041 m *6607 yd* Las Vegas Municipal GC, Nevada, USA on 11 Mar 1981. Alfred Edward Smith (1903–85) achieved an 18-hole score of 55 (15 under bogey 70) on his home course on 1 Jan 1936. The course measured 3884 m *4248 yd.* The detail was 4, 2, 3, 4, 2, 4, 3, 4, 3 = 29 out, and 2, 3, 3, 3, 3, 2, 5, 4, 1 = 26 in.

The United States PGA Tournament record for 18 holes is 59 (30 + 29) by Al Geiberger (b. 1 Sept 1937) in the

second round of the Danny Thomas Classic, on the 72-par 6628 m *7249 yd* Colonial GC course, Memphis, Tennessee on 10 June 1977. Other golfers to have recorded 59 over 18 holes in major non-PGA tournaments include: Samuel Jackson Snead (b. 27 May 1912) in the third round of the Sam Snead Festival at White Sulphur Springs, West Virginia, USA on 16 May 1959; Gary Player (South Africa) (b. 1 Nov 1935) in the second round of the Brazilian Open in Rio de Janeiro on 29 Nov 1974; David Jagger (GB) (b. 9 June 1949) in a Pro-Am tournament prior to the 1973 Nigerian Open at Ikoyi Golf Club, Lagos; and Miguel Martin (Spain) in the Argentine Southern Championship at Mar de Plata on 27 Feb 1987.

Women

The lowest recorded score on an 18-hole course (over 5486 m *6000 yd*) for a woman is 62 (30 + 32) by Mary 'Mickey' Kathryn Wright (b. 14 Feb 1935) (USA) on the Hogan Park Course (par-71, 5747 m *6286 yd*) at Midland, Texas, USA, in November 1964. Wanda Morgan (b. 22 Mar 1910) recorded a score of 60 (31 + 29) on the Westgate and Birchington Golf Club course, Kent, over 18 holes (4573 m *5002 yd*) on 11 July 1929.

Great Britain

The lowest score recorded in a first-class professional tournament on a course of more than 5486 m *6000 yd* in Great Britain is 61 (29 + 32), by Thomas Bruce Haliburton (1915–75) of Wentworth GC in the Spalding Tournament at Worthing, West Sussex in June 1952, and 61 (32 + 29) by Peter J. Butler (b. 25 Mar 1932) in the Bowmaker Tournament at Sunningdale, Berkshire on 4 July 1967.

Lowest 36 holes

The record for 36 holes is 122 (59 + 63) by Sam Snead in the 1959 Sam Snead Festival on 16–17 May 1959. Horton Smith (1908–63), twice US Masters Champion, scored 121 (63 + 58) on a short course on 21 Dec 1928 (see 72 holes). The lowest score by a British golfer has been 124 (61 + 63) by Alexander Walter Barr 'Sandy' Lyle (b. 9 Feb 1958) in the Nigerian Open at the 5508 m *6024 yd* (par-71) Ikoyi Golf Club, Lagos in 1978.

Lowest 72 holes

The lowest recorded score on a first-class course is 255 (29 under par) by Leonard Peter Tupling (b. 6 Apr 1950) (GB) in the Nigerian Open at Ikoyi Golf Club, Lagos in February 1981, made up of 63, 66, 62 and 64 (average 63.75 per round).

The lowest 72 holes in a US professional event is 257 (60, 68, 64, 65) by Mike Souchak in the 1955 Texas Open at San Antonio.

The 72 holes record on the European tour is 258 (64, 69, 60, 65) by David Llewellyn (b. 18 Nov 1951) in the Biarritz Open on 1–3 Apr 1988. The lowest 72 holes in an open championship in Europe is 262 (67, 66, 66, 63) by Percy Alliss (GB) (1897–1975) in the 1932 Italian Open at San Remo, and by Lu Liang Huan (Taiwan) (b. 10 Dec 1935) in the 1971 French Open at Biarritz. Kelvin D. G. Nagle (b. 21 Dec 1920) of Australia shot 261 in the Hong Kong Open in 1961. The lowest for four rounds in a British first-class tournament is 262 (66, 63, 66 and 67) by Bernard Hunt in the Piccadilly Tournament on the par-68 5655 m *6184 yd* Wentworth East course, Virginia Water, Surrey on 4–5 Oct 1966.

Trish Johnson scored 242 (64, 60, 60, 56) (21 under par) in the Bloor Homes Eastleigh Classic at the Fleming Park Course (4025 m *4402 yd*) at Eastleigh, Hants on 22–25 1987. Horton Smith scored 245 (63, 58, 61 and 63) for 72 holes on the 4297 m *4700 yd* course (par-64) at Catalina Country Club, California, USA, to win the Catalina Open on 21–23 Dec 1928.

World one-club record

Thad Daber (USA), with a 6-iron, played the 5520 m *6037 yd* Lochmore GC, Cary, N. Carolina, USA in 73 on 10 Nov 1985 to win the world one-club championship.

Highest score

It is recorded that Chevalier von Cittern went round 18

Highest earnings ● The record for a year on the US PGA circuit was set by Curtis Northup Strange (b. 20 June 1955) (USA) in 1987 with $925 941, which was without winning a major title. However, he succeeded in winning his first major on 20 June 1988, when he won the US Open. (Photo: All-Sport/David Cannon)

holes in 316, averaging 17·55 per hole, at Biarritz, France in 1888. Steven Ward took 222 strokes for the 5680 m *6212 yd* Pecos course, Reeves County, Texas, USA on 18 June 1976—but he was aged only 3 years 286 days.

Most shots for one hole

A woman player in the qualifying round of the Shawnee Invitational for Ladies at Shawnee-on-Delaware, Pennsylvania, USA, *c.* 1912, took 166 strokes for the short 118 m *130 yd* 16th hole. Her tee shot went into the Binniekill River and the ball floated. She put out in a boat with her exemplary but statistically-minded husband at the oars. She eventually beached the ball 2·4 km *1½ miles* downstream but was not yet out of the wood. She had to play through one on the home run. In a competition at Peacehaven, Sussex, England in 1890, A. J. Lewis had 156 putts on one green without holing out.

The highest score for a single hole in the British Open is 21 by a player in the inaugural meeting at Prestwick in 1860. Double figures have been recorded on the card of the winner only once, when Willie Fernie (1851–1924) scored a ten at Musselburgh, Lothian in 1883. Ray Ainsley of Ojai, California, took 19 strokes for the par-4 16th hole during the second round of the US Open at Cherry Hills Country Club, Denver, Colorado on 10 June 1938. Most of the strokes were used in trying to extricate the ball from a brook. Hans Merell of Mogadore, Ohio took 19 strokes on the par-3 16th (203 m *222 yd*) during the third round of the Bing Crosby National Tournament at Cypress Point Club, Del Monte, California, USA on 17 Jan 1959.

Fastest rounds *Individual*

With such variations in lengths of courses, speed records, even for rounds under par, are of little comparative value. The fastest round played when the golf ball comes to rest before each new stroke is 27 min 9 sec by James Carvill (b. 13 Oct 1965) at Warrenpoint Golf Course, Co. Down, Northern Ireland (18 holes, 5628 m *6154 yd*) on 18 June 1987.

Team

Forty-eight players completed the 18-hole 6500 m *7108 yd* Kyalami course, near Johannesburg, South Africa in 9 min 51 sec on 23 Feb 1988 using only one ball. They scored 73!

Slowest rounds

The slowest stroke-play tournament round was one of 6 hr 45 min taken by South Africa in the first round of the 1972 World Cup at the Royal Melbourne GC, Australia. This was a four-ball medal round; everything holed out.

Most holes in 24 hours/1 week

The greatest number of rounds played on foot in 24 hr is 22 rounds and five holes (401 holes) by Ian Colston, 35, at Bendigo GC, Victoria, Australia (par-73, 5542 m *6061 yd*) on 27–8 Nov 1971.

The British record is 360 holes by Antony J. Clark at Childwall GC, Liverpool on 18 July 1983.

Using golf carts for transport Charles Stock played 783 holes in 24 hr at Acacia Country Club, Lyndhurst, Ohio, USA (9 holes, 2844 m *3110 yd*) on 20 July 1987.

Terry Zachary played 391 holes in 12 hours on the 6132 m *6706 yd* course at Connaught Golf Club, Alberta, Canada on 16 June 1986.

The most holes played on foot in a week (168 hr) is 1128 by Steve Hylton at the Mason Rudolph Golf Club (5541m *6060 yd*), Clarkesville, Tennessee, USA from 25–31 Aug 1980.

> **US and British Opens** ● Laura Davies (b. 5 Oct 1963), in 1987, became the first British woman golfer to win the US Womens' Open. Thus she simultaneously held both US and British titles. The trophy for the latter, won in October 1986, is on the left. (Photo: All-Sport/David Cannon)

Throwing the golf ball

The lowest recorded score for throwing a golf ball round 18 holes (over 5500 m *6000 yd*) is 82 by Joe Flynn (USA), 21, at the 5694 m *6228 yd* Port Royal course, Bermuda on 27 Mar 1975.

Most balls hit in one hour

The most balls driven in one hour, over 100 yds and into a target area, is 1064 (from 1290 attempts) by David Morris at Abergele Golf Club, Clwyd on 21 May 1988.

CHAMPIONSHIP RECORDS

The Open

The Open Championship was inaugurated in 1860 at Prestwick, Strathclyde, Scotland. The lowest score for 9 holes is 28 by Denis Durnian (b. 30 June 1950), at Royal Birkdale, Southport, Lancashire in the second round on 15 July 1983.

The lowest round in The Open is 63 by: Mark Stephen Hayes (b. 12 July 1949) (USA) at Turnberry, Strathclyde on 7 July 1977; Isao Aoki (b. 31 Aug 1942) (Japan) at Muirfield, East Lothian on 19 July 1980; and Gregory John Norman (b. 10 Feb 1955) (Australia) at Turnberry on 18 July 1986. Thomas Henry Cotton (1907–1987) at Royal St George's, Sandwich, Kent completed the first 36 holes in 132 (67 + 65) on 27 June 1934. The lowest 72-hole aggregate is 268 (68, 70, 65, 65) by Thomas Sturges Watson (b. 4 Sept 1949) (USA) at Turnberry in July 1977.

US Open

The United States Open Championship was inaugurated in 1895. The lowest 72-hole aggregate is 272 (63, 71, 70, 68) by Jack Nicklaus (b. 21 Jan 1940) on the lower course (6414 m *7015 yd*) at Baltusrol Country Club, Springfield, New Jersey from 12–15 June 1980. The lowest score for 18 holes is 63 by: Johnny Miller (b. 29 Apr 1947) on the 6328 m *6921 yd* par-71 Oakmont Country Club course, Pennsylvania on 17 June 1973; by Jack Nicklaus and Tom Weiskopf (USA) (b. 9 Nov 1942), both on 12 June 1980.

US Masters

The lowest score in the US Masters (instituted on the par-72 6382 m *6980 yd* Augusta National Golf Course, Georgia, in 1934) is 271 by Jack Nicklaus in 1965 and Raymond Loran Floyd (b. 4 Sept 1942) in 1976. The lowest round is 63 by Nicholas Raymond Leige Price (b. 28 Jan 1957) (Zimbabwe) in 1986.

World Cup (formerly Canada Cup)

The World Cup (instituted as the Canada Cup in 1953) has been won most often by the USA with 16 victories between 1955 and 1983. The only men to have been on six winning teams have been Arnold Palmer (b. 10 Sept 1929) (1960, 1962–4, 1966–7) and Jack Nicklaus (1963–4, 1966–7, 1971 and 1973). Only Nicklaus has taken the individual title three times (1963–4, 1971). The lowest aggregate score for 144 holes is 544 by Australia, Bruce Devlin (b. 10 Oct 1937) and Anthony David Graham (b. 23 May 1946), at San Isidro, Buenos Aires, Argentina from 12–15 Nov 1970.

The lowest individual score has been 269 by Roberto de Vicenzo (Argentina) (b. 14 Apr 1923), also in 1970.

Ryder Cup

The biennial Ryder Cup professional match between the USA and Europe (British Isles or Great Britain prior to 1979) was instituted in 1927. The USA have won 21 ½ to 5 ½ to date. William Earl 'Billy' Casper (b. San Diego, California, USA, 24 June 1931) has the record of winning most matches in the Trophy with 20 in 1961–75. Christy O'Connor, Sr (b. 21 Dec 1924) (Ireland) played in ten matches, 1955–73.

Walker Cup

The series was instituted in 1921 (for the Walker Cup since 1922 and now held biennially). Joseph Boynton Carr (GB&I) (b. 18 Feb 1922) played in ten contests, 1947–67. The USA have won 28, Great Britain & Ireland 2 (in 1938 and 1971) and the 1965 match was tied.

Curtis Cup

The biennial ladies' Curtis Cup match between the USA and Great Britain and Ireland was first held in 1932. The USA have won 19, GB&I four (1952, 1956, 1986 and 1988) and two matches have been tied. Mary McKenna (GB&I) (b. 29 Apr 1949) played in a record ninth match in 1986, when for the first time she was on the winning team.

Highest earnings US PGA and LPGA circuits

The all-time professional money-winner is Jack Nicklaus, with $4 976 980 to the end of 1987. The record for a year on the US PGA circuit was set by Curtis Northup Strange (b. 20 June 1955) (USA) in 1987 with $925 941.

The record career earnings for a woman is by Pat Bradley (b. 24 Mar 1951) with $2 430 000 to 1988, including a season's record $492 021 in 1986.

Most tournament wins

John Byron Nelson (b. 4 Feb 1912) (USA) won a record 18 tournaments (plus one unofficial) in one year, including a record 11 consecutively from 8 Mar to 4 Aug 1945. Sam Snead won 84 official US PGA tour events 1936–65, and has been credited with a total 134 tournament victories since 1934. The ladies' PGA record is 88 by Kathy Whitworth (b. 27 Sept 1939) from 1962 to 1985.

Biggest winning margin

The greatest margin of victory in a major tournament is 21 strokes by Jerry Pate (b. 16 Sept 1953) (USA), who won the Colombian Open with 262 from 10–13 Dec 1981. Cecilia Leitch won the Canadian Ladies' Open Championship in 1921 by the biggest margin for a major title, 17 up and 15 to play.

Youngest and oldest champions

The youngest winner of The Open was Tom Morris Jr (1851–75) at Prestwick, Strathclyde in 1868 aged 17 yr 249 days.

The oldest Open champion was 'Old Tom' Morris (1821–1908), aged 46 yr 99 days when he won at Prestwick in 1867. In recent times the 1967 champion, Roberto de Vicenzo, was aged 44 yr 93 days. The oldest US Open champion was Raymond Floyd (b. 4 Sept 1942) at 43 yr 284 days on 15 June 1986. Isabella 'Belle' Robertson (b. 11 Apr 1936) won the 1986 Scottish Women's Championship aged 50 yr 43 days.

Most club championships

Marjorie Edey (1913–81) was ladies champion at Charleswood Golf Club, Winnipeg, Manitoba, Canada, 36 times between 1937 and 1980. The men's record is 34 by Bernard Charles Cusack (b. 24 Jan 1920), including 33 consecutively, at the Narembeen GC, Western Australia, between 1943 and 1982. The British record is 32 by Helen Gray at Todmorden GC, Lancashire between 1952 and 1986.

Largest tournament

The Volkswagen Grand Prix Open Amateur Championship in the United Kingdom attracted a record 321 779 (206 820 men and 114 958 women) competitors in 1984.

HOLES IN ONE
Longest

The longest straight hole ever holed in one shot was, appropriately, at the tenth (408 m 447 yd) at Miracle Hills Golf Club, Omaha, Nebraska, USA by Robert Mitera (b. 1944) on 7 Oct 1965. Mitera stood 1·68 m 5 ft 6 in tall and weighed 75 kg 165 lb (11 st 11 lb). He was a two handicap player who normally drove 224 m 245 yd. A 80 km/h 50 mph gust carried his shot over a 265 m 290 yd drop-off. The longest 'dog-leg' hole achieved in one is the 439 m 480 yd fifth at Hope Country Club, Arkansas, USA by L. Bruce on 15 Nov 1962. The women's record is 359 m 393 yd by Marie Robie on the first hole of the Furnace Brook Golf Club, Wollaston, Mass., USA on 4 Sept 1949. The longest hole in one performed in the British Isles was the seventh (par-4, 359 m 393 yd) at West Lancashire GC by Peter Richard Parkinson (b. 26 Aug 1947) on 6 June 1972.

Consecutive

There are at least 16 cases of 'aces' being achieved in two consecutive holes, of which the greatest was Norman L. Manley's unique 'double albatross' on the par-4 301 m 330 yd seventh and par-4 265 m 290 yd eighth holes on the Del Valle Country Club course, Saugus, California, USA on 2 Sept 1964. The first woman to record consecutive 'aces' was Sue Prell, on the 13th and 14th holes at Chatswood Golf Club, Sydney, Australia on 29 May 1977.

The closest to achieving three consecutive holes in one were the late Dr Joseph Boydstone on the 3rd, 4th and 9th at Bakersfield GC, California, USA on 10 Oct 1962 and the Rev Harold Snider (b. 4 July 1900) who aced the 8th, 13th and 14th holes of the par-3 Ironwood course, Arizona, USA on 9 June 1976.

Youngest and oldest

The youngest golfer recorded to have shot a hole-in-one was Coby Orr (5 years) of Littleton, Colorado on the 94 m 103 yd fifth at the Riverside Golf Course, San Antonio, Texas, USA in 1975. The British record was set by Benjamin Robinson, aged 8 yr 337 days on the 132 m 144 yd second at the Cleveland Golf Club, Redcar, Cleveland on 21 Aug 1987. The oldest golfers to have performed this feat are: (men) 99 yr 244 days Otto Bucher (Switzerland) (b. 12 May 1885) on the 100 m 130 yd 12th at La Manga GC, Spain on 13 Jan 1985; (women) 95 yr 257 days Erna Ross (b. 9 Sept 1890) on the 102 m 112 yd 17th at The Everglades Club, Palm Beach, Florida, USA on 25 May 1986. The British record was set by Samuel Richard Walker (b. 6 Jan 1892) at the 143 m 156 yd 8th at West Hove GC, East Sussex at the age of 92 yr 169 days on 23 June 1984.

The oldest player to score his age is C. Arthur Thompson (1869–1975) of Victoria, British Columbia, Canada, who scored 103 on the Uplands course of 5682 m 6215 yd aged 103 in 1973.

GUINNESS HAVE PUBLISHED **GOLF: RECORDS, FACTS AND CHAMPIONS** DONALD STEEL £12.95

Greyhound Racing

The first greyhound meeting was staged at Hendon, north London with a railed hare operated by a windlass, in Sept 1876. Modern greyhound racing originated with the perfecting of the mechanical hare by Owen Patrick Smith at Emeryville, California, USA in 1919. St Petersburg Kennel Club, located in St Petersburg, Florida, USA, which opened on 3 Jan 1925, is the oldest greyhound track in the world still in operation on its original site. The earliest greyhound race behind a mechanical hare in the British Isles was at Belle Vue, Manchester, opened on 24 July 1926.

Derby

The only two greyhounds to have won the English Greyhound Derby twice (instituted 1927, now over 500 m 546 yd) are Mick the Miller (1926–39) on 25 July 1929, when owned by Albert H. Williams, and on 28 June 1930 when owned by Mrs Arundel H. Kempton, and Patricia's Hope on 24 June 1972 when owned by Gordon and Basil Marks and Brian Stanley and 23 June 1973 when owned by G. & B. Marks and J. O'Connor. The highest prize was £35 000 to Indian Joe for the Derby on 28 June 1980. The only greyhounds to win the English, Scottish and Welsh Derby 'triple' are Trev's Perfection, owned by Fred Trevillion, in 1947, Mile Bush Pride, owned by Noel W. Purvis, in 1959, and Patricia's Hope in 1972. The only two greyhounds to have won the American Derby, at Taunton, Mass., twice are Real Huntsman in 1950–51 and Dutch Bahama in 1984–5.

Grand National

The only greyhound to have won the Grand National (inst. 1927 over 480 m 525 yd, now 500 m 546 yd and five flights) three times is Sherry's Prince (1967–78) owned by Mrs Joyce Mathews of Sanderstead, Surrey in 1970–2.

Fastest greyhound

The highest speed at which any greyhound has been timed is 67·14 km/h 41·72 mph (374 m 410 yd in 20·1 sec) by The Shoe on the then straightaway track at Richmond, NSW, Australia on 25 Apr 1968. It is estimated that he covered the last 91·44 m 100 yd in 4·5 sec or at 73·14 km/h 45·45 mph. The highest speed recorded for a greyhound in Great Britain is 62·97 km/h 39·13 mph by Beef Cutlet, when covering a straight course of 457 m 500 yd in 26·13 sec at Blackpool, Lancashire on 13 May 1933.

Fastest speeds for four-bend tracks

The fastest automatically timed speed recorded for a full 4-bend race is 62·59 km/h 38·89 mph at Brighton, East Sussex by Glen Miner on 4 May 1982 with a time of 29·62 sec for 515 m 563 yd. The fastest overhurdles is 60·58 km/h 37·64 mph at Brighton by Wotchit Buster on 22 Aug 1978.

Most wins

The most career wins is 143 by the American greyhound, JR's Ripper in 1982–6. The world record for consecutive victories is 32 by Ballyregan Bob, owned by Cliff Kevern and trained by George Curtis from 1985 to 8 Dec 1986, including 16 track record times. His race wins were by an average of more than nine lengths.

Highest earnings

The career earnings record is held by Homspun Rowy with $297 000 in the USA, 1984–7. The richest first prize for a greyhound race is $200 000 won by Dacia in the Great Greyhound Race at Seabrook, New Hampshire, USA in 1987.

Longest odds

Apollo Prince won at odds of 250-1 at andown GRC, Springvale, Victoria, Australia on 14 Nov 1968.

Gymnastics

A primitive form of gymnastics was practised in ancient Greece and Rome during the period of the ancient Olympic Games (776 BC to AD 393) but Johann Friedrich Simon was the first teacher of modern gymnastics at Basedow's School, Dessau, Germany in 177.

Most titles World

The greatest number of individual titles won by a man in

Most Olympic gold medals ● Gymnast Vera Caslavska-Odlozil (b. 3 May 1942) (Czechoslovakia) has won most individual gold medals with seven, three in 1964 and four (one shared) in 1968. (Photo: All-Sport)

the World Championships (including Olympic Games) is ten by Boris Shakhlin (b. 27 Jan 1932) (USSR) between 1954 and 1964. He also had three team wins. The female record is 12 individual wins and five team titles by Larissa Semyonovna Latynina (b. 27 Dec 1934) of the USSR, between 1956 and 1964. Japan has won the men's team title a record ten times between 1960 and 1978, and the USSR the women's team title on 17 occasions (out of 20 titles since 1952).

The most overall individual titles in Modern Rhythmic Gymnastics is three by Maria Gigova (Bulgaria) in 1969, 1971 and 1973 (shared). Bulgaria has a record six team titles 1969, 1971, 1973, 1983, 1985 and 1987. Lilia Ignatova (Bulgaria) has won both the individual World Cup titles that have been held, 1983 and 1986. Bianka Panova (Bulgaria) uniquely won all four apparatus gold medals all with maximum scores, and won a team gold in 1987.

Olympic
Japan (1960, 1964, 1968, 1972 and 1976) has won the men's team title most often. The USSR has won the women's title eight times (1952–80). The most men's individual gold medals is six by: Boris Shakhlin (USSR), one in 1956, four (two shared) in 1960 and one in 1964; and Nikolay Andrianov (USSR) (b. 14 Oct 1952), one in 1972, four in 1976 and one in 1980.

Larissa Latynina won six individual gold medals and was in three winning teams from 1956–64, making nine gold medals. She also won five silver and four bronze making 18 in all—an Olympic record. The most medals for a male gymnast is 15 by Nikolay Andrianov (USSR), 7 gold, 5 silver and 3 bronze from 1972–80. Aleksandr Ditiatin (USSR) (b. 7 Aug 1957) is the only man to win a medal in all eight categories in the same Games, with 3 gold, 4 silver and 1 bronze at Moscow in 1980.

Highest score *Olympics*
Nadia Comaneci (Romania) (b. 12 Nov 1961) was the first to achieve a perfect score (10·00) and achieved seven in all at the Montreal Olympics in July 1976.

Youngest international and world champion
Pasakevi 'Voula' Kouna (b. 6 Dec 1971) was aged 9 yr 299 days at the start of the Balkan Games at Serres, Greece on 1 Oct 1981, when she represented Greece. Olga Bicherova (USSR) (b. 26 Oct 1966) won the women's world title at 15 yr 33 days on 28 Nov 1981. The youngest male world champion was Dmitriy Belozerchev (USSR) (b. 17 Dec 1966) at 16 yr 315 days at Budapest, Hungary on 28 Oct 1983.

Most titles *British*
The British Gymnastic Championship was won ten times by Arthur John Whitford (b. 2 July 1908) in 1928–36 and 1939. He was also in four winning teams. Wray 'Nik' Stuart (b. 20 July 1927) equalled the record of nine successive wins, 1956–64. The women's record is eight by Mary Patricia Hirst (b. 18 Nov 1918) (1947, 1949–50 and 1952–6). The most overall titles in Modern Rhythmic Gymnastics is by Sharon Taylor with five successive, 1977–81.

World Cup
Gymnasts who have won two World Cup (inst. 1975) overall titles are three men: Nikolay Andrianov (USSR), Aleksandr Ditiatin (USSR) and Li Ning (China) (b. 8 Sept 1963), and one woman: Maria Filatova (USSR) (b. 19 July 1961).

Somersaults
Ashrita Furman performed 8341 forward rolls in 10 hr 30 min over 19·67 km *12 miles 390 yards* from Lexington to Charleston, Massachusetts, USA on 30 Apr 1986. Shigeru Iwasaki (b. 1960) backwards somersaulted over 50 m *54·68 yd* in 10·8 sec at Tokyo, Japan on 30 Mar 1980.

Static wall 'sit' (or Samson's Chair)
Kevin DeWitt stayed in an unsupported sitting position against a wall for 76 min 12 sec in Kennewick, Washington, USA on 31 July 1986.

Handball

Handball was first played *c.* 1895 in Germany. It was introduced into the Olympic Games at Berlin in 1936 as an 11-a-side outdoor game, with Germany winning, but when re-introduced in 1972 it was an indoor game with seven-a-side, the standard size of team since 1952.

The International Handball Federation was founded in 1946. The first international match was held at Halle/Saale on 3 Sept 1925 when Austria beat Germany 6–3.

Most championships
Three Olympic titles have been won by the USSR—men 1976, women 1976 and 1980, and by Yugoslavia men 1972 and 1984, women 1984. The most victories won in world

Like father, like son ● Anthony Gildert (right) has continued the family tradition of holding gymnastic records, being the current holder of the squat thrust record. His father, Tommy, was a previous record holder for both press-ups and parallel bar dips in the early 1980's. (Photo: J. D. Photography)

EXERCISES
SPEED AND STAMINA

Records are accepted for the most repetitions of the following activities within the given time span.

CHINS (FROM DEAD-HANG POSITION)—**CONSECUTIVE** 170 Lee Chin-yong at Backyon Gymnasium, Seoul, South Korea on 10 May 1983.

CHINS ONE ARM (FROM A RING)—**CONSECUTIVE** 22 Robert Chisnall (b. 9 Dec 1952) at Queen's University, Kingston, Ontario, Canada on 3 Dec 1982. (Also 18 two-finger chins, 12 one-finger chins).

PARALLEL BAR DIPS—I HOUR 2569 Simon Kent (GB) at Pinella's Health Club, Lincoln, Lincolnshire on 12 Apr 1988.

PRESS-UPS (PUSH-UPS)—24 HOURS 33 600 Jeffrey Warwick (USA) at Buffalo YMCA, New York, USA on 10–11 June 1988.

PRESS-UPS (ONE ARM)—5 HOURS 4156 Colin Hewick (GB) at Costello Stadium, Hull, North Humberside on 8 July 1988.

PRESS-UPS (FINGER TIP)—5 HOURS 5010 John Decker (GB) at Kendal's Department Store, Manchester on 19 June 1987.

PRESS-UPS (ONE FINGER)—CONSECUTIVE 100 Harry Lee Welch Jr at Durham, N. Carolina, USA on 31 Mar 1985.

HAND-STAND PUSH-UPS—I HOUR 1985 by Chung Kwun Ying (Hong Kong) at Government City Hall, Hong Kong on 18 May 1986. Against a wall the record is 3300 by Chung Man Wah, aged 4, at the Chung Sze Kung Fu (HK) Association, Hong Kong on 4 Jan 1987.

SIT-UPS—24 HOURS 60 405 Louis Scripa Jr (USA) at Jack La Lanne's American Health & Fitness Spa, Sacramento, California, USA on 5–6 Aug 1985.

LEG RAISES—12 HOURS 25 000 Geoffrey Meyers at The Sports Connection Health Centre, Johannesburg, South Africa on 6 May 1988.

SQUATS—I HOUR 1810 Rodney Driver (GB) at the Guinness World of Records, Trocadero, London on 10 March 1988.

SQUAT THRUSTS—I HOUR 1803 Anthony Gildert (GB) at the Corporation Hotel, Burnley, Lancashire on 4 Feb 1988.

PUMMEL HORSE DOUBLE CIRCLES—CONSECUTIVE 75 by Lee Thomas (GB) on BBC television on 12 Dec 1985.

PRESS-UPS IN A YEAR Adam Parsons, a retired Lieutenant Colonel in the US Air Force, achieved a documented 1 293 850 press-ups in Akron, Ohio, USA in the calendar year of 1985.

championship (inst. 1938) competition are by Romania with four men's and three women's titles from 1956 to 1974. The GDR also have three women's titles, 1971, 1975 and 1978.

The most European Champions' Cup titles is thirteen in the women's event by Spartak Kiev, USSR between 1970 and 1988. VfL Gummersbach have won a record five men's titles. They are also the only club team to win all three European trophies; European Champions' Cup, European Cup Winners' Cup and IHF Cup.

Highest score
The highest score in an international match was recorded when the USSR beat Afghanistan 86–2 in the 'Friendly Army Tournament' at Miskolc, Hungary in August 1981.

British *Titles*
The most men's national championship titles is seven by Brentwood '72 (British Championship, 1974; English National League, 1979–83; British League, 1985). The most women's titles is seven by Wakefield Metros (English National League, 1982–87; British League, 1988).

Highest score
The highest score in a men's league match is by Glasgow University, who beat Claremont, 69–5 at

Glasgow, Strathclyde in March 1984. The record in a women's match is 45–0 by Dunfermline College when beating Satellites Strikers at Dunfermline, Fife in December 1985.

The highest score by an individual is 22 by Rolv Erichsen (b. 23 Aug 1963) for Glasgow University (63) against Claremont (3) at Claremont, East Kilbride, Strathclyde in November 1983. The women's record is 14 by Jacqueline Swan (b. 16 Jan 1963) for Wakefield Metros (40) against Kirkby Ladies (8) at Featherstone, West Yorkshire in October 1985.

Harness Racing

Trotting races were held in Valkenburg, Netherlands in 1554. In England the trotting gait (the simultaneous use of the diagonally opposite legs) was known in the 16th century. The sulky first appeared in 1829. Pacers thrust out their fore and hind legs simultaneously on one side.

Most successful driver

The most successful sulky driver in North American harness racing history has been Herve Filion (b. 1 Feb 1940) of Quebec, Canada, who has achieved 10 395 wins by the end of 1987. His career earnings (1953–87) at that time exceeded $56 million. The most wins in a year is 770 by Mike Lachance in 1986. The greatest earnings in a year is $10 207 372 by William O'Donnell (b. 4 May 1948) when he won 419 races in 1985.

Fastest trotter ● *Mack Lobell*, driven by John D. Campbell (USA) (b. 8 Apr 1955), set a record for the fastest trotting mile, 1 min 52·2 sec, at Springfield, Illinois, USA on 21 Aug 1987. John Campbell has record career earnings of $61 518 511 from 3112 wins, to May 1988.

HARNESS RACING MILE RECORDS

TROTTING

World mile record	1:52·2	*Mack Lobell* (driver, John Campbell)	Springfield, USA	21 Aug 1987
British record	2:06·2	*Silver Glorie* (driver, M. A. Strutter)	York	5 Aug 1986

PACING

World	1:49·2	*Niatross* (driver, Clint Galbraith)	Lexington, USA	1 Oct 1980
World race record	1:49·6	*Nihilator* (driver, William O'Donnell)	East Rutherford, USA	3 Aug 1985
British record	2:02·1	*Lydia M* (driver, James Pickard)	York	10 July 1982

Highest price

The highest price ever paid for a pacer is $19·2 million for *Nihilator* who was syndicated by Wall Street Stable and Almahurst Stud Farm in 1984. The highest price paid for a trotter is $5·25 million for *Mystic Park* by Lana Lobell Farms from Gerald and Irving Wechter of New York and Robert Lester of Florida, announced on 13 July 1982.

Greatest winnings

The greatest winnings for any harness horse is $3 225 653 by the pacer *Nihilator*, who won 35 of 38 races in 1984–5. The greatest amount won by a trotting horse is $2 753 666 by *Idéal du Gazeau* (France) to July 1983. The single season record is $1 864 286 by *Nihilator* in 1985.

The largest ever purse was $2 161 000 for the Woodrow Wilson two-year-old race over 1 mile at the Meadowlands, New Jersey on 16 Aug 1984. Of this sum a record $1 080 500 went to the winner *Nihilator*, driven by William O'Donnell.

Hockey

A representation of two players with curved snagging sticks apparently in an orthodox 'bully' position was found in Tomb No. 17 at Beni Hasan, Egypt and has been dated to c. 2050 BC. There is a British reference to the game in Lincolnshire in 1277. The modern game evolved in south London in the 1870s. An English Hockey Association was founded in 1875, but the current English men's governing body, the Hockey Association, was formed on 18 Jan 1886. The All-England Women's Hockey Association was founded in 1895. The *Fédération Internationale de Hockey* was formed on 7 Jan 1924.

The first organised club was the Blackheath Rugby and Hockey Club founded in 1861. The oldest club with a continuous history is Teddington HC formed in the autumn of 1871. They played Richmond on 24 Oct 1874 and used the first recorded circle *versus* Surbiton at Bushey Park on 9 Dec 1876.

The first international match was the Wales *v.* Ireland match at Rhyl on 26 Jan 1895. Ireland won 3–0.

Most Olympic medals

The Indians were Olympic champions from the re-introduction of Olympic hockey in 1928 until 1960, when Pakistan beat them 1–0 at Rome. They had their eighth win in 1980.

Of the seven Indians who have won three Olympic team gold medals two have also won a silver medal—Leslie Walter Claudius (b. 25 Mar 1927) in 1948, 1952, 1956 and 1960 (silver) and Udham Singh (b. 4 Aug 1928) in 1952, 1956, 1964 and 1960 (silver). A women's tournament was added in 1980 when Zimbabwe were the winners. The Netherlands won in 1984.

World Cup

The World Cup for men was first held in 1971, and for women in 1974.

The most wins are, (men) three by Pakistan, 1971, 1978 and 1982; (women) four by the Netherlands, 1974, 1978, 1983 and 1986.

Champions' Trophy

First held in 1978 and contested annually since 1980 by the top six men's teams in the world; the most wins is three by Australia 1983–5 and West Germany 1986–8. The first women's Champions' Trophy was won by the Netherlands in 1987.

MEN

Highest international score

The highest score in international hockey was when India defeated the USA 24–1 at Los Angeles, California, USA in the 1932 Olympic Games. The greatest number of goals in a home international match was when England defeated France 16–0 at Beckenham on 25 Mar 1922.

Most international appearances

Michael Peter (b. 7 May 1949) represented West Germany over 250 times between 1969 and 1984, indoors and out. The most by a player from the British Isles is 161 by Richard Leman (b. 13 July 1959), 118 for England and 43 for Great Britain, 1980–88. H. David Judge (b. 19 Jan 1936) played a record 124 times for Ireland, 1957–78. The first player to achieve 100 international appearances for England was Norman Hughes (b. 30 Sept 1952) on 21 Sept 1986.

Greatest scoring feats

The greatest number of goals scored in international hockey is 267 by Paul Litjens (Netherlands) (b. 9 Nov 1947) in 177 games. M. C. Marckx (Bowden 2nd XI) scored 19 goals against Brooklands 2nd XI (score 23–0) on 31 Dec 1910. He was selected for England in March 1912 but declined due to business priorities. Between 1923 and 1958, Fred H. Wagner scored 1832 goals for Beeston HC, Nottingham Casuals and the Nottinghamshire county side. David Ashman has scored 1592 goals for one club, Hamble Old Boys, Southampton, from 1958 to 1988. Ron Waterman has made 727 1st XI appearances for the same club, 1958–88. The fastest goal in an international was 7 sec after the bully-off by John French for England *v.* West Germany at Nottingham on 25 Apr 1971.

Greatest goalkeeping

Richard James Allen (b. 4 June 1902) (India) did not concede a goal during the 1928 Olympic tournament and only three in the Olympics of 1932 and 1936. In these three Games India scored a total of 102 goals.

Longest game

The longest international game on record was one of 145 min (into the sixth period of extra time), when the Netherlands beat Spain 1–0 in the Olympic tournament at Mexico City on 25 Oct 1968. Club matches of 205 min have twice been recorded: the Hong Kong Football Club beat Prison Sports Dept as the first to score in a 'sudden death' play-off after 2–2 at full time on 11 Mar 1979, and Gore Court beat Hampstead in the first round of the English Club Championships in 1983.

WOMEN

The earliest women's club was East Molesey in Surrey, England formed c. 1887. Two ladies' hockey clubs, Wimbledon and Ealing, each founded one year later, are still in existence. The first national association was the Irish Ladies' Hockey Union founded in 1894. The All England Women's Hockey Association held its first formal meeting in Westminster Town Hall, London on 23 Nov 1895. The first international match was an England *v.* Ireland game in Dublin in 1896. Ireland won 2–0.

Most international appearances

Valerie Robinson made a record 144 appearances for England, 1963–84.

Highest scores

The highest score in a women's international match was when England beat France 23–0 at Merton, Greater London on 3 Feb 1923. In club hockey, Ross Ladies beat Wyeside, at Ross-on-Wye, Herefordshire 40–0 on 24 Jan 1929, when Edna Mary Blakelock (b. 22 Oct 1904) scored a record 21 goals.

Highest attendance

The highest attendance at a women's hockey match was 65 165 for the match between England and the USA at Wembley, London on 11 Mar 1978.

Horse Racing

Horsemanship was an important part of the Hittite culture of Anatolia, Turkey dating from 1400 BC. The 33rd ancient Olympic Games of 648 BC in Greece featured horse racing.

The earliest races recorded in England were those held in about AD 200 at Netherby, Cumbria between Arab horses imported by the Romans.

Largest prizes

The highest prize money for a day's racing is $10 million for the Breeders' Cup series of seven races staged annually since 1984. Included each year is a record $3 million for the Breeders' Cup Classic.

Most runners

The most horses in a race has been 66 in the Grand National on 22 Mar 1929. The record for the flat is 58 in the Lincolnshire Handicap at Lincoln on 13 Mar 1948.

Most successful horses

The horse with the best win-loss record was *Kincsem*, a Hungarian mare foaled in 1874, who was unbeaten in 54 races (1876–9) throughout Europe, including the Goodwood Cup of 1878.

The longest winning sequence is 56 races by *Camarero*, foaled in 1951, in Puerto Rico from 19 Apr 1953 to his first defeat on 17 Aug 1955. (In his career to 1956 he won 73 of 77 races.)

The most wins in a career is 137 from 159 starts by *Galgo Jr* (foaled 1928) in Puerto Rico between 1930 and 1936; in 1931 he won a record 30 races in one year.

The only horse to win the same race in seven successive years was *Doctor Syntax* (foaled 1811) in the Preston Gold Cup, 1815–21.

> **Largest winning margin in the Derby** ● *Shergar*, ridden by Walter Swinburn, won by a record 10 lengths in 1981. (Photo: All-Sport)

Triple Crown winners

The English Triple Crown (2000 Guineas, Derby, St Leger) has been won 15 times, most recently by *Nijinsky* in 1970. The fillies' equivalent (1000 Guineas, Oaks, St Leger) has been won nine times, most recently by *Oh So Sharp* in 1985. Two of these fillies also won the 2000 Guineas: *Formosa* (in a dead-heat) in 1868 and *Sceptre* in 1902.

The American Triple Crown (Kentucky Derby, Preakness Stakes, Belmont Stakes) has been achieved 11 times, most recently by *Affirmed* in 1978.

Horses *Highest price*

Enormous valuations placed on potential stallions may be determined from sales of a minority holding, but such valuations would, perhaps, not be reached on the open market. The most paid for a yearling is $13·1 m on 23 July 1985 at Keeneland, Kentucky, USA by Robert Sangster and partners for *Seattle Dancer*.

Greatest winnings

The career earnings record is $6 597 947 by the gelding *John Henry* (foaled 1975) with 39 wins from 83 races, 1977–84. The leading money-winning mare is *Lady's Secret* (foaled 1982) with $3 021 425 in the USA, 1984–87.

The greatest amount earned in a year is $3 552 704 by *Spend A Buck* (USA) in 1985. This included a one race record of $2·6 million in the Jersey Derby, Garden State Park, New Jersey, USA on 27 May 1985, of which $2-million was a bonus for having previously won the Kentucky Derby and two preparatory races at Garden State Park.

Biggest weight

The biggest weight ever carried is 190 kg *30 stone* by both Mr Maynard's mare and Mr Baker's horse in a match won by the former over a mile at York on 21 May 1788.

Oldest winners

The oldest horses to win on the flat have been the 18-year-olds *Revenge* at Shrewsbury in September 1790, *Marksman* at Ashford, Kent in September 1826 and *Jorrocks* at Bathurst, Australia in February 1851. At the same age *Wild Aster* won three hurdle races in six days in March 1919 and *Sonny Somers* won two steeplechases in February 1980.

World speed records

The highest race speed recorded is 69·62 km/h *43·26 mph* by *Big Racket*, 20·8 sec for ¼ mile *409·26 m*, at Mexico City, Mexico on 5 Feb 1945. The 4-year-old carried 51·7 kg *114 lb*. The record for 1½ miles *2414 m* is 60·76 km/h *37·76 mph* by *Fiddle Isle* (carrying 56·2 kg *124 lb*) on 21 Mar 1970 and by *John Henry* (carrying 57·1 kg *126 lb*) on 16 Mar 1980, both at Santa Anita Park, Arcadia, California, USA in a time of 2 min 23 sec.

Over half a furlong (330 ft *100·6 m*), *Klute*, ridden by Lesley Bruce (58·9 kg *130 lb*), achieved a speed of 72·27 km/h *44·91 mph* at Haydock Park Racecourse on 17 June 1988.

Jockeys *Most successful*

Laffit Pincay (b. 29 Dec 1946, Panama City) has earned a career record $127 809 838 from 1966 to the start of 1988. He won $13 415 049 in 1985, a record for a jockey in one season.

The most races won by a jockey in a year is 546 from 2199 rides by Chris McCarron (USA) (b. 1955) in 1974.

Wins *One day*

The most winners ridden in one day is nine by Chris Antley (USA) on 31 Oct 1987. It consisted of four in the afternoon at Aqueduct, New York, USA and five in the evening at The Meadowlands, New Jersey, USA.

One card

The most winners ridden on one card is eight by Hubert S. Jones, 17, from 13 rides at Caliente, Cal., USA on 11 June 1944; Oscar Barattuci, at Rosario City, Argentina on 15

Dec 1957; Dave Gall, from ten rides at Cahokia Downs, East St Louis, Illinois, USA on 18 Oct 1978; Chris Loseth, from ten rides at Exhibition Park, Vancouver, BC, Canada on 9 Apr 1984; and Robert Williams from ten rides at Lincoln, Nebraska, USA on 29 Sept 1984.

Consecutive

The longest winning streak is 12 by: Sir Gordon Richards (1904–86) (one race at Nottingham on 3 Oct, six out of six at Chepstow on 4 Oct and the first five races next day at Chepstow) in 1933; and by Pieter Stroebal at Bulawayo, Southern Rhodesia (now Zimbabwe), 7 June–7 July 1958.

Trainers

Jack Van Berg (USA) has the greatest number of wins in a year, 496 in 1976, and in a career, 5116 from 1955 to start of 1988. The greatest amount won in a year is $17 502 206 by D. Wayne Lukas (USA) in 1987, when his horses won 343 races from 1737 starts.

The only trainer to saddle the first five finishers in a championship race is Michael Dickinson in the 1983 Cheltenham Gold Cup; on 27 Dec 1982 he won a record 12 races in one day.

Owners

The most lifetime wins by an owner is 4775 by Marion Van Berg in North America in the 35 years up to his death in 1971. The most wins in a year is 494 by Dan R. Lasater (USA) in 1974. The greatest amount won in a year is $5 451 201 by Eugene Klein (USA) in 1985.

BRITISH TURF RECORDS
Most successful horses

Eclipse (foaled 1764) still has the best win-loss record,

Most successful jockey ● The diminutive, but durable, William Lee 'Bill' Shoemaker (below)(USA), (born weighing 1·1 kg *2½ lb*, 19 Aug 1931), now weighing 43 kg *95 lb* and standing 1·50 m *4 ft 11 in*, has ridden a record 8759 winners from over 39 600 mounts from his first ride on 19 Mar 1949 and first winner on 20 Apr 1949 to 30 May 1988. Above, Shoemaker (wearing the pink cap) rides *Ferdinand* to victory by a nose in the Breeders' Cup Classic, the world's richest race, at Hollywood Park, Inglewood, California on 21 Nov 1987. It was his 8706th winner and his first in the Breeders' Cup series (see Largest prizes). (Photos: All-Sport)

being unbeaten in a career of 18 races between May 1769 and October 1770. The longest winning sequence is 21 races by *Meteor* (foaled 1783) between 1786 and 1788. The most races won in a season is 23 by three-year-old *Fisherman* in 1856. *Catherina* (foaled 1830) won a career record 79 out of 176 races, 1832–41. The most successful sire was *Stockwell* (foaled 1849) whose progeny won 1153 races (1858–76) and who in 1866 set a record of 132 races won. The greatest amount ever won by an English-trained horse is $1 182 140 by the filly *Pebbles* (foaled 1981) in 1983–5. In 1985 she won a record $1 012 611 in one season, including the Breeders' Cup Turf in New York. The biggest winning margin in a Classic is 20 lengths by *Mayonaise* in the 1000 Guineas in 1859.

Most successful jockeys

Sir Gordon Richards won 4870 races from 21 815 mounts from his first mount at Lingfield Park on 16 Oct 1920 to his last at Sandown Park on 10 July 1954. His first win was on 31 Mar 1921. In 1953, at his 28th and final attempt, he won the Derby, six days after his knighthood. He was champion jockey 26 times between 1925 and 1953 and won a record 269 races in 1947. Lester Piggott (b. 5 Nov 1935) won 4349 races in Great Britain, 1948–85, but his global total exceeded 5200.

The most Classic races won by a jockey is 29 by Lester Piggott from his first on *Never Say Die* in the 1954 Derby to the 1985 2000 Guineas on *Shadeed*. (Derby—9, St Leger—8, Oaks—6, 2000 Guineas—4, 1000 Guineas—2.)

Most successful Trainers

The record first-prize money earned in a season is

MAJOR RACE RECORDS

RACE (instituted)	RECORD TIME	MOST WINS			LARGEST FIELD
		Jockey	Trainer	Owner	

FLAT

RACE (instituted)	RECORD TIME	Jockey	Trainer	Owner	LARGEST FIELD
Derby (1780) 1½ miles *2414 m* Epsom	2 min 33·8 sec *Mahmoud* 1936 2 min 33·84 sec *Kahyasi* 1988 (Electronically timed)	9–Lester Piggott 1954, 57, 60, 68, 70, 72, 76, 77, 83	7–Robert Robson 1793, 1802, 09, 10, 15, 17, 23 7–John Porter 1868, 82, 83, 86, 90, 91, 99 7–Fred Darling 1922, 25, 26, 31, 38, 40, 41	5–3rd Earl of Egremont 1782, 1804, 05, 07, 26 5–HH Aga Khan III 1930, 35, 36, 48, 52	34 (1862)
2000 Guineas (1809) 1 mile *1609 m* Newmarket	1 min 35·8 sec *My Babu* 1948	9–Jem Robinson 1825, 28, 31, 33, 34, 35, 36, 47, 48	7–John Scott 1842, 43, 49, 53, 56, 60, 62	5–4th Duke of Grafton 1820, 21, 22, 26, 27 5–5th Earl of Jersey 1831, 34, 35, 36, 37	28 (1930)
1000 Guineas (1814) 1 mile *1609 m* Newmarket	1 min 36·85 sec *Oh So Sharp* 1985	7–George Fordham 1859, 61, 65, 68, 69, 81, 83	9–Robert Robson 1818, 19, 20, 21, 22, 23, 25, 26, 27	8–4th Duke of Grafton 1819, 20, 21, 22, 23, 25, 26, 27	29 (1926)
Oaks (1779) 1½ miles *2414 m* Epsom	2 min 34·21 sec *Time Charter* 1982	9–Frank Buckle 1797, 98, 99, 1802, 03, 05, 17, 18, 23	12–Robert Robson 1802, 04, 05, 07, 08, 09, 13, 15, 18, 22, 23, 25	6–4th Duke of Grafton 1813, 15, 22, 23, 28, 31	26 (1848)
St Leger (1776) 1 m 6 f 127 yd *2932 m* Doncaster	3 min 01·6 sec *Coronach* 1926 *Windsor Lad* 1934	9–Bill Scott 1821, 25, 28, 29, 38, 39, 40, 41, 46	16–John Scott 1827, 28, 29, 32, 34, 38, 39, 40, 41, 45, 51, 53, 56, 57, 59, 62	7–9th Duke of Hamilton 1786, 87, 88, 92, 1808, 09, 14	30 (1825)
King George VI and Queen Elizabeth Diamond Stakes (1951) 1½ miles *2414 m* Ascot	2 min 26·98 sec *Grundy* 1975	7–Lester Piggott 1965, 66, 69, 70, 74, 77, 84	4–Dick Hern 1972, 79, 80, 85	2–Nelson Bunker Hunt 1973, 74	19 (1951)
Prix de l'Arc de Triomphe (1920) 2400 metres *1 mile 864 yd* Longchamp, France	2 min 26·3 sec *Trempolino* 1987	4–Jacques Doyasbère 1942, 44, 50, 51 4–Frédéric 'Freddy' Head 1966, 72, 76, 79 4–Yves Saint-Martin 1970, 74, 82, 84 4–Pat Eddery 1980, 85, 86, 87	4–Charles Semblat 1942, 44, 46, 49 4–Alec Head 1952, 59, 76, 81 4–François Mathet 1950, 51, 70, 82	6–Marcel Boussac 1936, 37, 42, 44, 46, 49	30 (1967)
VRC Melbourne Cup (1861) 3200 metres *1 mile 1739 yd* Flemington, Victoria, Australia	3 min 19·1 sec *Rain Lover* 1968	4–Bobby Lewis 1902, 15, 19, 27 4–Harry White 1974, 75, 78, 79	7–Bart Cummings 1965, 66, 67, 74, 75, 77, 79	4–Etienne de Mestre 1861, 62, 67, 78	39 (1890)
Kentucky Derby (1875) 1¼ miles *2012 m* Churchill Downs, USA	1 min 59·4 sec *Secretariat* 1973	5–Eddie Arcaro 1938, 41, 45, 48, 52 5–Bill Hartack 1957, 60, 62, 64, 69	6–Ben Jones 1938, 41, 44, 48, 49, 52	8–Calumet Farm 1941, 44, 48, 49, 52, 57, 58, 68	23 (1974)
Irish Derby (1866) 1½ miles *2414 m* The Curragh	2 min 28·8 sec *Tambourine* 1962	6–Morny Wing 1921, 23, 30, 38, 42, 46	6–Vincent O'Brien 1953, 57, 70, 77, 84, 85	5–HH Aga Khan III 1925, 32, 40, 48, 49	24 (1962)

JUMPING

RACE (instituted)	RECORD TIME	Jockey	Trainer	Owner	LARGEST FIELD
Grand National (1839) 4½ miles *7242 m* Aintree, Liverpool	9 min 01·9 sec *Red Rum* 1973	5–George Stevens 1856, 63, 64, 69, 70	4–Fred Rimell 1956, 61, 70, 76	3–James Machell 1873, 74, 76 3–Sir Charles Assheton-Smith 1893, 1912, 13 3–Noel Le Mare 1973, 74, 77	66 (1929)
Cheltenham Gold Cup (1924) 3¼ miles *5230 m* Cheltenham	6 min 23·4 sec *Silver Fame* 1951	4–Pat Taaffe 1964, 65, 66, 68	5–Tom Dreaper 1946, 64, 65, 66, 68	7–Dorothy Paget 1932, 33, 34, 35, 36, 40, 52	22 (1982)
Champion Hurdle (1927) 2 miles *3218 m* Cheltenham	3 min 51·7 sec *See You Then* 1985	4–Tim Molony 1951, 52, 53, 54	5–Peter Easterby 1967, 76, 77, 80, 81	4–Dorothy Paget 1932, 33, 40, 46	24 (1964)

£1 896 689 by Henry Richard Amherst Cecil (b. 11 Jan 1943) from a record 180 winners (446 runners) in 1987. Michael Ronald Stoute (b. 22 Oct 1945) set a record for worldwide earnings of £2 778 405 in 1986.

The most Classics won by a trainer is 40 by John Scott (1794–1871) of Malton, Yorkshire between 1827 and 1863. James Croft of Middleham, Yorkshire trained the first four horses in the 1822 St Leger. Alec Taylor of Manton, Wiltshire headed the trainers' list for a record 12 seasons between 1907 and 1925.

Most successful owners

H H Aga Khan III (1877–1957) was leading owner a record 13 times between 1924 and 1952. The record first-prize money won in a season is £1 232 240 by Sheikh Mohammed bin Rashid al Maktoum as his horses won a record 126 races in 1987. The most Classics won is 20 by the 4th Duke of Grafton (1760–1844) between 1813 and 1831 and by the 17th Earl of Derby (1865–1948) between 1910 and 1945.

THE DERBY

The greatest of England's five Classics is the Derby Stakes, inaugurated on 4 May 1780, and named after the 12th Earl of Derby (1752–1834). The distance was increased in 1784 from a mile to 1½ miles *2·414 km*. The race has been run at Epsom Downs, Surrey, except for the two war periods, when it was run at Newmarket, and is for three-year-olds only. Since 1884 the weights have been: colts 57 kg *9 st*, fillies 55 kg *8 st 9 lb*. Geldings were eligible until 1904.

Smallest winning margins

There have been two dead-heats: in 1828 when *Cadland* beat *The Colonel* in the run-off, and in 1884 between *St Gatien* and *Harvester* (stakes divided).

Longest and shortest odds

Three winners have been returned at odds of 100–1: *Jeddah* (1898), *Signorinetta* (1908) and *Aboyeur* (1913). The shortest-priced winner was *Ladas* (1894) at 2–9 and the hottest losing favourite was *Surefoot*, fourth at 40–95 in 1890.

Largest prize

The richest prize on the British Turf was £296 500 in the 209th Derby on 1 June 1988, won by H H Aga Khan IV's *Kahyasi*.

JUMPING

Most successful horses

Triple champion hurdler *Sir Ken* (foaled 1947) won a record 16 hurdle races in succession, April 1951 to March 1953.

The greatest amount earned by a British or Irish-trained jumper is £278 837 in 1982–6 by the mare *Dawn Run* (k. 1986), the first horse ever to win both Champion Hurdle (1984) and Cheltenham Gold Cup (1986).

Most successful jockeys

John Francome (b. 13 Dec 1952) won a career record 1138 races over jumps (5072 mounts) from 1970 to 1985.

The record number of wins in a season is 149 by Jonjo O'Neill (b. 13 Apr 1952) in 1977–8. The most wins in a day is six by amateur Charlie Cunningham at Rugby on 29 Mar 1881. The record number of successive wins is ten by: John Alnam 'Johnny' Gilbert (b. 26 July 1920), 8–30 Sept 1959; and by Phil Tuck (b. 10 July 1956), 23 Aug–3 Sept 1986. The record number of championships is seven by: Gerald 'Gerry' Wilson (1903–68) 1933–8 and 1941; and by John Francome (one shared) in 1976, 1979, 1981–5.

Most successful trainers

The most first-prize money earned in a season is £358 837 from 120 wins (in just 259 races) by Michael Dickinson in 1982–3. The most wins in a season is 129 from 511 races by Martin Pipe in 1987-88. Fredrick Thomas Winter (b. 20 Sept 1926) won a record eight trainers' championships, 1971–5, 1977–8 and 1985.

GRAND NATIONAL

The first Grand National Steeple Chase may be regarded as the Grand Liverpool Steeple Chase of 26 Feb 1839 though the race was not given its present name until 1847. It became a handicap in 1843. Except for 1916–18, and 1941–5 the race has been run at Aintree, near Liverpool, over 30 fences.

Most wins

The only horse to win three times is *Red Rum* (foaled 1965) in 1973, 1974 and 1977, from five runs. He came second in 1975 and 1976. *Manifesto* ran a record eight times (1895–1904). He won in 1897 and 1899, came third three times and fourth once.

Highest prize

The highest prize and the richest ever over jumps in Great Britain was £68 740.50 won by *Rhyme 'N' Reason* on 9 Apr 1988.

Highest weight

The highest weight ever carried to victory is 79·4 kg *12 st 7 lb* by *Cloister* (1893), *Manifesto* (1899), *Jerry M.* (1912) and *Poethlyn* (1919).

Hurling

A game of very ancient origin, hurling was included in the Tailteann Games (inst. 1829 BC). It only became standardised with the formation of the Gaelic Athletic Association in Thurles, Ireland, on 1 Nov 1884. The Irish Hurling Union was formed on 24 Jan 1879.

Most titles *All-Ireland*

The greatest number of All-Ireland Championships won by one team is 26 by Cork between 1890 and 1986. The greatest number of successive wins is four by Cork (1941–4).

Inter-provincials

Munster holds the greatest number of inter-provincial (Railway Cup) championships with 34 (1928–77).

Most appearances

The most appearances in All-Ireland finals is ten shared by Christy Ring (Cork and Munster) and John Doyle (Tipperary). They also share the record of All-Ireland medals won with eight each. Ring's appearances on the winning side were in 1941–4, 1946 and 1952–4, while Doyle's were in 1949–51, 1958, 1961–2 and 1964–5. Ring also played in a record 22 inter-provincial finals (1942–63) and was on the winning side 18 times.

Highest and lowest scores

The highest score in an All-Ireland final (60 min) was in 1896 when Tipperary (8 goals, 14 points) beat Dublin (no goals, 4 points). The record aggregate score was when Cork (6 goals, 21 points) defeated Wexford (5 goals, 10 points) in the 80-minute final of 1970. A goal equals three points. The highest recorded individual score was by Nick Rackard (Wexford), who scored 7 goals and 7 points against Antrim in the 1954 All-Ireland semi-final. The lowest score in an All-Ireland final was when

Tipperary (1 goal, 1 point) beat Galway (nil) in the first championship at Birr in 1887.

Longest stroke

The greatest distance for a 'lift and stroke' is one of 117 m *129 yd* credited to Tom Murphy of Three Castles, Kilkenny, in a 'long puck' contest in 1906.

Largest crowd

The largest crowd was 84 865 for the All-Ireland final between Cork and Wexford at Croke Park, Dublin in 1954.

Ice Hockey

There is pictorial evidence that a hockey-like game (*kalv*) was played on ice in the early 16th century in The Netherlands. The game was probably first played in North America on 25 Dec 1855 at Kingston, Ontario, Canada, but Halifax also lays claim to priority. The International Ice Hockey Federation was founded in

Most points and goals *Individual* ● The most goals scored in a season in the NHL is 92 in the 1981–2 season by Wayne Gretzky (b. 26 Jan 1961) (Edmonton Oilers). He scored a record 215 points, including a record 163 assists in 1985–6. In 1981–2 in all games, adding Stanley Cup play-offs and for Canada in the World Championship, he scored 238 points (103 goals, 135 assists). In 815 NHL and Stanley Cup play-off games to June 1988, he has a record 1257 assists and in NHL games alone Gretzky has reached 1844 points, just six points short of the record held by Gordie Howe (see text for details). (Photo: All-Sport/Mike Powell)

Ice Hockey

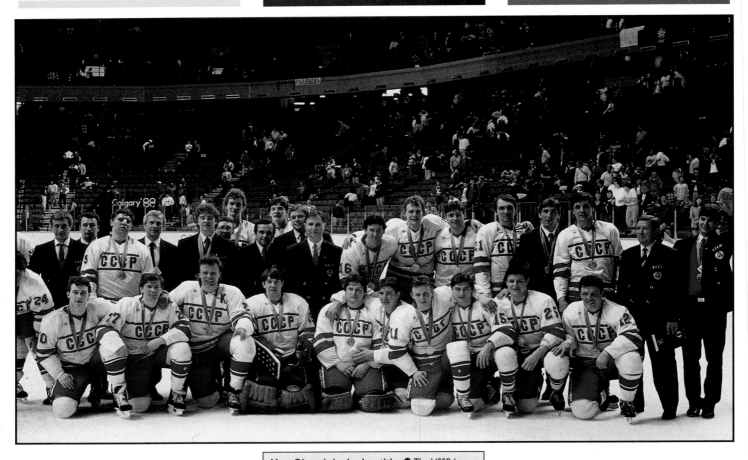

World Championships and Olympic Games

World Championships were first held for amateurs in 1920 in conjunction with the Olympic Games, which were also considered as world championships up to 1968. From 1977 World Championships have been open to professionals. The USSR won 20 world titles between 1954 and 1986, including the Olympic titles of 1956, 1964 and 1968. The longest Olympic career is that of Richard Torriani (b. 1 Oct 1911) (Switzerland) from 1928 to 1948. The most gold medals won by any player is three, achieved by USSR players Vitaliy Davidov, Anatoliy Firssov, Viktor Kuzkin and Aleksandr Ragulin in 1964, 1968 and 1972, and by Vladislav Tretyak in 1972, 1976 and 1984.

Stanley Cup

The Stanley Cup, presented by the Governor-General, Lord Stanley (original cost $48.67), became emblematic of National Hockey League supremacy 33 years after the first contest at Montreal in 1893. It has been won most often by the Montreal Canadiens with 23 wins in 1916, 1924, 1930–1, 1944, 1946, 1953, 1956–60, 1965–6, 1968–9, 1971, 1973, 1976–9, 1986.

British competitions

The English National (later British) League Championship (inst. 1935) has been won by the Wembley Lions four times, in 1936–7, 1952 and 1957 and by Streatham (now Redskins) in 1950, 1953, 1960 and 1982. Murrayfield Racers have won the Northern League (inst. 1966) seven times, 1970–2, 1976, 1979–80 and 1985. The Icy Smith Cup (first held 1966), the premier British club competition until 1981, was won by Murrayfield Racers nine times, 1966, 1969–72, 1975 and 1979–81. The British Club Championship (inst. 1982) was won by Dundee Rockets in 1982, 1983 and 1984.

Most goals *Team*

The greatest number of goals recorded in a world

Most Olympic ice hockey titles ● The USSR have won a record seven Olympic titles in 1956, 1964, 1968, 1972, 1976, 1984 and here they celebrate their success in Calgary in 1988. (Photo: All-Sport/David Cannon)

---

championship match was when Australia beat New Zealand 58–0 at Perth on 15 Mar 1987. The NHL record is 21 goals when Montreal Canadiens beat Toronto St Patrick's, at Montreal, 14–7 on 10 Jan 1920.

Most goals and points *Individual*

The North American career record for goals is 1071 (a record 801 in the NHL) by Gordie Howe (b. 31 Mar 1928) (Detroit Red Wings, Houston Aeros, New England Whalers and Hartford Whalers) from 16 Oct 1946 in 32 seasons ending in 1979–80. He took 2204 games to achieve the 1000th goal, but Robert Marvin 'Bobby' Hull (b. 3 Jan 1939) (Chicago Black Hawks and Winnipeg Jets) scored his 1000th in 1600 games on 12 Mar 1978. Wayne Gretzky is establishing a much faster rate: 664 goals in 815 NHL and Stanley Cup play-off games to June 1988. The NHL points record is 1850 by Gordie Howe, 1946–71.

British

The highest score and aggregate in a British League match was set when Medway Bears beat Richmond Raiders 48–1 at Gillingham in a Second Division fixture on 1 Dec 1985, when Kevin McNaught scored a record 25 points from seven goals and 18 assists.

The most individual goals scored in a senior game is 14 by Ron Halpin (Canada) (b. 18 Oct 1955) for Dundee Rockets in a 24–1 win over Durham Wasps at Dundee on 4 Apr 1982. Steve Moria (Canada) (b. 1960) achieved the highest number of assists, 13, for Fife Flyers at Cleveland on 28 Mar 1987.

Rick Fera (Canada) (b. 1964) set British season's records of 165 goals and 318 points for Murrayfield Racers in 48 games in 1986–7.

Tim Salmon (Canada) (b. 27 Nov 1964) achieved a season's record 183 assists in 47 games for Ayr Bruins in 1985–6.

Most points one game

The North American major league record for most points scored in one game is ten (3 goals, 7 assists) by Jim Harrison (b. 9 July 1947) (for Alberta, later Edmonton Oilers) in a World Hockey Association match at Edmonton on 30 Jan 1973, and by Darryl Sittler (b. 18 Sept 1950) (6 goals, 4 assists) for Toronto Maple Leafs in an NHL match at Toronto on 7 Feb 1976.

Fastest scoring *World*

In the NHL the fastest goal was after 4 seconds in the second period by Joseph Antoine Claude Provost (b. 17 Sept 1933) (Montreal Canadiens) *v.* Boston Bruins at Montreal on 9 Nov 1957. Doug Smail of the Winnipeg Jets scored 5 seconds from the opening whistle against St Louis on 20 Dec 1981. Canadian Bill Mosienko (b. 2 Nov 1921) (Chicago Black Hawks) scored three goals in 21 sec *v.* New York Rangers on 23 Mar 1952. Toronto scored eight goals in 4 min 52 sec *v.* New York Americans on 19 Mar 1938.

In minor leagues, Kim D. Miles scored in 3 seconds for University of Guelph *v.* University of W. Ontario on 11 Feb 1975. Three goals in 12 seconds was achieved by Steve D'Innocenzo for Holliston *v.* Westwood in a high school match in Massachusetts, USA on 9 Jan 1982. The Skara Ishockeyclubb, Sweden, scored three goals in 11 seconds against Örebro IK at Skara on 18 Oct 1981. The Vernon Cougars scored five goals in 56 seconds against Salmon Arm Aces at Vernon, BC, Canada on 6 Aug 1982. The Kamloops Knights of Columbus scored seven goals in 2 min 22 sec *v.* Prince George Vikings on 25 Jan 1980.

Great Britain

The fastest goal in the Heineken League was scored by Steve Johnson for Durham Wasps after four seconds *v.* Ayr Bruins at Ayr, Scotland on 6 Nov 1983. Kenny Westman (Nottingham Panthers) scored a hat-trick in 30 seconds *v.* Brighton Tigers on 3 Mar 1955.

In an English Junior League (under-16) game Jonathan Lumbis scored a hat-trick in 13 seconds for Nottingham Cougars *v.* Peterborough Jets on 4 Nov 1984.

Most successful goaltending

The most matches played by a goaltender in an NHL career without conceding a goal is 103 by Terrance 'Terry' Gordon Sawchuck (1929–70) of Detroit, Boston, Toronto, Los Angeles and New York Rangers, between 1950 and 1967. Gerry Cheevers (b. 2 Dec 1940) (Boston Bruins) went a record 33 successive games without a defeat in 1971–2.

Longest match

The longest match was 2 hr 56 min 30 sec (playing time) when Detroit Red Wings beat Montreal Maroons 1–0 in the sixth period of overtime at the Forum, Montreal, at 2.25 a.m. on 25 Mar 1936. Norm Smith, the Red Wings goaltender, turned aside 92 shots for the NHL's longest single shutout.

Ice Skating

The earliest reference to ice skating is in early Scandinavian literature referring to the 2nd century though its origins are believed, on archaeological evidence, to be ten centuries earlier still. The earliest English account of 1180 refers to skates made of bone. The earliest club was the Edinburgh Skating Club formed in about 1742.

The first recorded race was from Wisbech to Whittlesey, Cambridge in 1763. The earliest artificial rink in the world was opened at the Baker Street Bazaar, Portman Square, London on 7 Dec 1842, although the surface was not of ice. The first artificial ice rink was opened in the King's Road, Chelsea, London on 7 Jan 1876.

The National Skating Association of Great Britain was founded in 1879. The International Skating Union was founded at Scheveningen, Netherlands in 1892.

FIGURE SKATING

Most titles *Olympic*

The most Olympic gold medals won by a figure skater is three by: Gillis Grafström (1893–1938) of Sweden in 1920, 1924 and 1928 (also silver medal in 1932); by Sonja Henie (1912–69) of Norway in 1928, 1932 and 1936; and by Irina Rodnina (b. 12 Sept 1949) (USSR) with two different partners in the Pairs in 1972, 1976, and 1980.

World

The greatest number of individual world figure skating titles (inst. 1896) is ten by Ulrich Salchow (1877–1949) of Sweden, in 1901–5 and 1907–11. The women's record (inst. 1906) is also ten individual titles by Sonja Henie between 1927 and 1936. Irina Rodnina has won ten pairs titles (inst. 1908), four with Aleksey Ulanov (b. 4 Nov 1947), 1969–72, and six with her husband Aleksandr Zaitsev (b. 16 June 1952), 1973–8. The most ice dance titles (inst. 1952) won is six by Lyudmila Pakhomova (1946–86) and her husband Aleksandr Gorshkov (b. 8 Oct 1946) (USSR), 1970–4 and 1976. They also won the first ever Olympic ice dance title in 1976.

British

The most individual British titles are: (men) 11 by Jack Ferguson Page (1900–47) (Manchester SC) in 1922–31 and 1933; and (women) six by Cecilia Colledge (b. 28 Nov 1920) (Park Lane FSC, London) in 1935–6, 1937 (two), 1938 and 1946. Page and Ethel M. Muckelt (1885–1953) won nine pairs titles, 1923–31. The most by an ice dance couple is six by Jayne Torvill (b. 7 Oct 1957) and Christopher Dean (b. 27 July 1958), 1978–83.

Triple Crown

The only British skaters to win the 'Grand Slam' of World, Olympic and European titles in the same year are John Anthony Curry (b. 9 Sept 1949) in 1976 and the ice dancers Jayne Torvill and Christopher Dean in 1984. Karl Schäfer (Austria) (1909–76) and Sonja Henie achieved double 'Grand Slams', both in the years 1932 and 1936.

Highest marks

The highest tally of maximum six marks awarded in an

international championship was 29 to Jayne Torvill and Christopher Dean (GB) in the World Ice Dance Championships at Ottawa, Canada on 22–24 Mar 1984. This comprised seven in the compulsory dances, a perfect set of nine for presentation in the set pattern dance and 13 in the free dance, including another perfect set from all nine judges for artistic presentation. They previously gained a perfect set of nine sixes for artistic presentation in the free dance at the 1983 World Championships in Helsinki, Finland and at the 1984 Winter Olympic Games in Sarajevo, Yugoslavia. In their career Torvill and Dean received a record total of 136 sixes.

The most by a soloist was seven to Donald Jackson (b. 2 Apr 1940) (Canada) in the World Men's Championship at Prague, Czechoslovakia in 1962.

Quadruple turn

Kurt Browning (Canada) (b. 18 June 1966) was the first to achieve a quadruple jump in competition–a toe loop in the World Championships at Budapest, Hungary on 25 Mar 1988.

Distance

Robin Cousins (GB) (b. 17 Mar 1957) achieved 5·81 m *19 ft 1 in* in an axel jump and 5·48 m *18 ft* with a back flip at Richmond Ice Rink, Surrey on 16 Nov 1983.

Largest rink

The world's largest indoor ice rink is in the Moscow Olympic arena which has an ice area of 8064 m² *86 800 ft²*. The five rinks at Fujikyu Highland Skating Centre, Japan total 26 500 m² *285 243 ft²*.

SPEED SKATING

Most titles *Olympic*

The most Olympic gold medals won in speed skating is six by Lidiya Skoblikova (b. 8 Mar 1939) of Chelyabinsk,

---

SPEED SKATING WORLD RECORDS

MEN

Metres	min sec	Name (Country)	Place	Date	
500	36·45	Uwe-Jens Mey (GDR)	Calgary, Canada	14 Feb	1988
1000	1:12·05	Nick Thometz (USA)	Medeo, USSR	27 Mar	1987
1500	1:52·06	André Hoffmann (GDR)	Calgary, Canada	20 Feb	1988
3000	3:59·27	Leo Visser (Netherlands)	Heerenveen, Netherlands	19 Mar	1987
5000	6:43·59	Geir Karlstad (Norway)	Calgary, Canada	6 Dec	1987
10 000	13:48·2	Tomas Gustafson (Sweden)	Calgary, Canada	21 Feb	1988

WOMEN

Metres	min sec	Name (Country)	Place	Date	
500	39·10	Bonnie Blair (USA)	Calgary, Canada	22 Feb	1988
1000	1:17·65	Christa Rothenberg (GDR)	Calgary, Canada	26 Feb	1988
1500	1:59·30	Karin Kania (GDR)	Medeo, USSR	22 Mar	1986
3000	4:11·94	Yvonne van Gennip (Netherlands)	Calgary, Canada	23 Feb	1988
5000	7:14·13	Yvonne van Gennip (Netherlands)	Calgary, Canada	28 Feb	1988
10 000	15:25·25	Yvonne van Gennip (Netherlands)	Heerenveen, Netherlands	19 Mar	1988

Note that Medeo, Alma Ata, USSR is situated at an altitude of 1691 m above sea level.

WORLD SHORT TRACK SPEED SKATING RECORDS

MEN

Metres	min sec	Name (Country)	Place	Date	
500	44·46	Orazio Fagone (Italy)	Budapest, Hungary	15 Jan	1988
1000	1:32·83	Peter van der Velde (Netherlands)	Budapest, Hungary	16 Jan	1988
1500	2:25·25	Michel Daignault (Canada)	Calgary, Canada	22 Feb	1988
3000	5:04·24	Tatsuyoshi Ishihara (Japan)	Amsterdam, Netherlands	17 Mar	1985

WOMEN

Metres	min sec	Name (Country)	Place	Date	
500	47·77	Christina Sciolla (Italy)	Budapest, Hungary	16 Jan	1988
1000	1:39·00	Yan Li (China)	Calgary, Canada	25 Feb	1988
1500	2:34·85	Yan Li (China)	Calgary, Canada	23 Feb	1988
3000	5:18·33	Maria-Rosa Candido (Italy)	Budapest, Hungary	17 Jan	1988

BRITISH SHORT TRACK SPEED SKATING RECORDS

MEN

Metres	min sec	Name	Place	Date	
500	44·80	Wilfred O'Reilly	Calgary, Canada	23 Feb	1988
1000	1:33·44	Wilfred O'Reilly	Calgary, Canada	24 Feb	1988
1500	2:31·51	Wilfred O'Reilly	Calgary, Canada	17 Oct	1988
3000	5:17·47	Wilfred O'Reilly	Chamonix, France	6 Apr	1986

WOMEN

Distance	min sec	Name	Place	Date	
500	51·78	Kim Ferran	Brugge, Belgium	18 Mar	1984
1000	1:46·63	Nicky Bell	Chamonix, France	5 Apr	1986
1500	2:46·88	Amanda Worth	Tokyo, Japan	8 Apr	1983
3000	5:59·08	Amanda Worth	Richmond, England	1 Mar	1985

Ice and Sand Yachting

USSR, in 1960 (two) and 1964 (four). The male record is by Clas Thunberg (1893–1973) (Finland) with five gold (including one tied), and also one silver and one tied bronze, in 1924 and 1928. Eric Heiden (USA) (b. 14 June 1958) also won five gold medals, uniquely at one Games at Lake Placid, NY, USA in 1980.

World

The greatest number of world overall titles (inst. 1893) won by any skater is five; by Oscar Mathisen (Norway) (1888–1954) in 1908–9 and 1912–14; and Clas Thunberg in 1923, 1925, 1928–9 and 1931. The most titles won in the women's events (inst. 1936) is five by Karin Kania (*née* Enke) (b. 20 June 1961) (GDR) 1982, 1984, 1986–8. Kania has also won a record six overall titles at the World Sprint Championships 1980–1, 1983–4, 1986–7.

The record score achieved in the world overall title is 159·356 points by Nikolay Gulyayev (USSR) at Heeren-veen, Netherlands on 14–15 Feb 1987. The title record women's score is 171·760 points by Andrea Schöne (GDR) (b. 1 Dec 1960) at Medeo, USSR, 23–24 Mar 1984.

Longest race

The 'Elfstedentocht' ('Tour of the Eleven Towns') was held in the Netherlands from the 1800s to 1963 and again in 1985, covering 200 km *124 miles 483 yd.* It was transferred first to Lake Vesijärvi, near Lahti, Finland and in 1984 to Canada as the International Race of 11 Cities on the Ottawa River. The record time for 200 km is 6 hr 5 min 12 sec by Jan-Roelof Kruithof (Netherlands) (b. 1936) on 25 Feb 1979 at Oulu, Finland. Kruithof won the race eight times, 1974, 1976–7, 1979–83. An estimated 16 000 skaters took part in 1986.

24 hours

Martinus Kuiper (Netherlands) skated 546·650 km *339·681 miles* in 24 hr in Alkmaar, Netherlands on 12–13 Dec 1988.

Ice and Sand Yachting

The sport originated in the Low Countries from the year 1600 (earliest patent granted) and along the Baltic coast. The earliest authentic record is Dutch, dating from 1768. Land or sand yachts of Dutch construction were first reported on beaches (now in Belgium) in 1595. The earliest international championship was staged in 1914.

Largest yacht

The largest ice yacht was *Icicle*, built for Commodore John E. Roosevelt for racing on the Hudson River, New York in 1869. It was 21 m *68 ft 11 in* long and carried 99 m² *1070 ft²* of canvas.

Highest speeds *Ice*

The highest speed officially recorded is 230 km/h *143 mph* by John D. Buckstaff in a Class A stern-steerer on Lake Winnebago, Wisconsin, USA in 1938. Such a speed is possible in a wind of 115 km/h *72 mph.*

Sand

The official world record for a sand yacht is 107 km/h *66·48 mph* set by Christian-Yves Nau (b. 1944) (France) in *Mobil* at Le Touquet, France on 22 Mar 1981, when the wind speed reached 120 km/h *75 mph.* A speed of 142·26 km/h *88·4 mph* was attained by Nord Embroden (USA) in *Midnight at the Oasis* at Superior Dry Lake, California, USA on 15 Apr 1976.

Judo

Judo is a modern combat sport which developed out of an amalgam of several old Japanese fighting arts, the most popular of which was ju-jitsu (jiu-jitsu), which is thought to be of Chinese origin. Judo has greatly developed since 1882, when it was first devised by Dr Jigoro Kano (1860–1938). The International Judo Federation was founded in 1951.

Most titles *World and Olympic*

World Championships were inaugurated in Tokyo in 1956. Women's championships were first held in 1980 in New York. Yashiro Yamashita won nine consecutive Japanese titles 1977–85, four world titles; Over 95 kg 1979, 1981 and 1983, Open 1981, and the Olympic Open category in 1984. He retired undefeated after 203 successive wins, 1977–85.

Two other men have won four world titles, Wilhelm Ruska (b. 29 Aug 1940) (Netherlands), Over 93 kg 1967, 1971 and 1972 Olympic and Open titles, and Shozo Fujii (Japan) (b. 12 May 1950), Under 80 kg 1971, 1973 and 1975, Under 75 kg 1979.

Ingrid Berghmans (Belgium) has won a record five

women's world titles (first held 1980): Open 1980, 1982, 1984 and 1986 and Under 72 kg in 1984. She has also won three silver medals and a bronze.

Karen Briggs (b. 11 Apr 1963) is the most successful British player, with three world titles, Under 48 kg in 1982, 1984 and 1986.

British
The greatest number of titles (inst. 1966) won is nine by David Colin Starbrook (b. 9 Aug 1945) (6th dan): Middle-weight 1969–70, Light-heavyweight 1971–5 and the Open division 1970–1. A record six titles in the women's events (inst. 1971) were won by Christine Gallie (*née* Child) (b. 1946) (6th dan): Heavyweight in 1971–5 and the Open division in 1973. Neil Adams (b. 27 Sept 1958) has the most successful international record of any British player. He has won two junior (1974 and 1977) and five senior (1979–80, 1983–5) European titles; four World Championships medals (one gold, one silver, two bronze) and two Olympic silver medals. He has won eight British senior titles.

Highest grades
The efficiency grades in judo are divided into pupil (*kyu*) and master (*dan*) grades. The highest awarded is the extremely rare red belt *Judan* (10th dan), given to only 13 men so far. The Judo protocol provides for an 11th dan (*Juichidan*) who also would wear a red belt, a 12th dan (*Junidan*) who would wear a white belt twice as wide as an ordinary belt, and the highest of all, *Shihan* (ductor), but these have never been bestowed, save for the 12th dan to the founder of the sport Dr Jigoro Kano. The highest British native Judo grade is 8th dan by Charles Stuart Palmer (b. 1930). Christine Gallie was awarded her 6th Dan in 1983.

10 hours
The brothers Carl and Peter Udry completed 18 779 judo throwing techniques in a ten-hour period at Hendra Sports Field, Truro, Cornwall, England on 29 Aug 1987.

Jiu-Jitsu
The World Council of Jiu-Jitsu Organisations have staged two World Championships, in 1984 and 1986. The Canadian team were the team winners on each occasion.

Karate

Based on techniques devised from the 6th century Chinese art of Shaolin boxing (Kempo), Karate was developed by an unarmed populace in Okinawa as a weapon against armed Japanese oppressors *c.* 1500. Transmitted to Japan in the 1920s by Funakoshi Gichin, this method of combat was refined into karate and organised into a sport with competitive rules. The five major styles of karate in Japan are: *Shotokan*, *Wado-ryu*, *Goju-ryu*, *Shito-ryu* and *Kyokushinkai*, each of which places different emphasis on speed and power, etc. Other styles include *Sankukai*, *Shotokai* and *Shukokai*. *Wu shu* is a comprehensive term embracing all Chinese martial arts. *Kung fu* is one aspect of these arts popularised by the cinema.

The governing body for the sport in Britain is the Martial Arts Commission, upon which all the martial arts are represented.

World Championships
Great Britain have won a record four world titles (inst. 1970) at the Kumite team event, 1975, 1982, 1984 and 1986. Pat McKay (GB) is the only man to win two individual kumite titles, at Under 80 kg, 1982 and 1984. Three women's titles have been won by Guus van Mourik (Netherlands) at Over 60 kg, and by Mie Nakayama (Japan) at individual Kata, both 1982, 1984 and 1986.

Top exponents
The leading exponents among karateka are a number of

10th dans in Japan. The leading exponents in the United Kingdom are Tatsuo Suzuki (8th dan, *Wado-ryu*) (b. 27 Apr 1928), Keinosuke Enoeda (8th dan, *Shotokan*), Steve Arneil (8th dan, *Kyokushinkai*), Shiro Asano (7th dan, *Shokotan*), Thomas Morris (7th dan, *Shito-ryu*), David Donovan (7th dan, *Ishin-ryu*) and James Rosseau (6th dan, *Goju-ryu*).

Lacrosse

MEN'S LACROSSE

The game is of American Indian origin, derived from the inter-tribal game *baggataway*, and was played before 1492 by Iroquois Indians in lower Ontario, Canada and upper New York State, USA. The French named it after their game of *chouler à la crosse*, known in 1381. It was introduced into Great Britain in 1867. The English Lacrosse Union was formed in 1892. Lacrosse was included in the Olympic Games of 1904 and 1908 and featured as an exhibition sport in the 1928, 1932 and 1948 Games.

Most titles *World*
The United States have won four of the five World Championships, in 1967, 1974, 1982 and 1986, and also won the pre-Olympic tournament in 1984. Canada won the other world title in 1978 beating the USA 17–16 after extra time—this was the first drawn international match.

English
The English Club Championship (Iroquois Cup inst. 1890), has been won most often by Stockport with 16 wins between 1897 and 1987. The record score in a final is 33 by Stockport v. London University (4) on 9 May 1987.

Most international appearances
The record number of international representations is 33 for England by James Michael 'Mike' Roberts (Urmston) (b. 22 Feb 1946), to 1982. He is the only Englishman to play in four World Championships.

Highest scores
The highest score in an international match was the United States' 32–8 win over England at Toronto, Canada in 1986. England's highest score was their 19–11 win over Canada at Melbourne in August 1974.

Fastest scoring
Rod Burns scored only 4 seconds into the game for South Manchester and Wythenshawe v. Sheffield University on 6 Dec 1975.

WOMEN'S LACROSSE

The first reported playing of lacrosse by women was in 1886. The All-England Women's Lacrosse Association was formed in 1912. The game has evolved from the men's game so that the rules now differ considerably.

World Championships/World Cup
The first World Cup was held in 1982, when the winners were the USA, and Australia won in 1986.

Most international appearances
Caro Macintosh (b. 18 Feb 1932) played in 56 internationals (52 for Scotland and four for Great Britain) and Barbara Dootson (b. 24 Aug 1955) in 54 (41 England, 13 Great Britain), 1974–86.

Highest score
The highest score by an international team was by Great Britain and Ireland with their 40–0 defeat of Long Island during their 1967 tour of the USA.

Marbles

Origins
The game of marbles became a competitive sport under the British Marbles Board of Control at the Greyhound

Marbles ● The name derives from the practice in the 18th century of making the ball from marble chips. However, marbles dates from ancient times and may have been a children's game in ancient Egypt, where pebbles or nuts were used. It was introduced into Britain by the Romans (the Emperor Augustus Ceasar is believed to have played as a child with nuts) in the 1st century AD. The popularity amongst children continues to this day and it has become a highly competitive sport. (Photo: All-Sport)

Hotel, at Tinsley Green, Crawley, West Sussex, England in 1926.

Most championships
The British Championship (established 1926) has been won most often by the Toucan Terribles with 20 consecutive titles (1956–75). Three founder members, Len Smith, Jack and Charlie Dempsey, played in every title win. They were finally beaten in 1976 by the Pernod Rams, captained by Len Smith's son, Paul. Len Smith (b. 13 Oct 1917) won the individual title 15 times (1957–64, 1966, 1968–73) but lost in 1974 to his son Alan.

Speed record
The record for clearing the ring (between 5¾ and 6¼ ft *1·75–1·90 m* in diameter) of 49 marbles is 2 min 56 sec by the Black Dog Boozers of Crawley, West Sussex at BBC Television Centre, London for BBC Television's *Record Breakers* on 14 Sept 1987.

Microlighting

The *Fédération Aéronautique Internationale* have established two classes of aircraft for which records are accepted, C1 a/o and R 1-2-3, and the following are the overall best of the two classes, in fact all of which are the C1 a/o class.

WORLD RECORDS

Distance in a straight line: 777 miles *1249·52 km* Norman E. Howell (USA), 9 Apr 1987.
Distance in a closed circuit: 1032 miles *1661·13 km* Wilhelm Lischak (Austria), 24 May 1987.
Altitude: 7906·5 m *25 939·64 ft* Richard J. Rowley (USA), 17 Sept 1983.
Speed over a 100 km closed circuit: 297·72 km/h *185 mph* C. T. Andrews (USA), 3 Aug 1982.
Speed over a 500 km closed circuit: 293·04 km/h *182 mph* C. T. Andrews (USA), 3 Aug 1982.

Bob Calvert set a British altitude record of 5791·27 m *19 000 ft* on 19 Feb 1983 at Middleton Sands, Lancashire.

Endurance

Eve Jackson flew from Biggin Hill, Kent to Sydney, Australia from 26 Apr–1 Aug 1986 in a Shadow Series B (nicknamed *Gertie*), powered by a 40 hp Rotax 447 two stroke engine. The flight took 279 hr 55 min, required 3360 litres *887 gallons* of petrol and covered 26 553 km *16 500 miles*.

Modern Pentathlon & Biathlon

Points scores in riding, fencing, cross country and hence overall scores have no comparative value between one competition and another. In shooting and swimming (300 m) the scores are of record significance and the best achievements are shown.

The Modern Pentathlon (Riding, Fencing, Swimming, Shooting and Running) was inaugurated into the Olympic Games at Stockholm in 1912. The Modern Pentathlon Association of Great Britain was formed in 1922. *L'Union Internationale de Pentathlon Moderne et Biathlon* (UIPMB) was founded in 1948. Originally the UIPM, the administration of Biathlon (cross-country skiing and shooting) was added in 1957, and the name modified accordingly.

MODERN PENTATHLON

Most titles *World*

András Balczó (Hungary) (b. 16 Aug 1938) won the record number of world titles (inst.1949), six individual and seven team. He won the world individual title in 1963, 1965–7 and 1969 and the Olympic title in 1972. His seven team titles (1960–70) comprised five world and two Olympic. The USSR has won a record 12 world and three Olympic team titles.

Women's World Championships were first held in 1981. Great Britain won three team titles 1981–83, with Sarah Parker (b. 16 July 1956) a member of each of those teams. Wendy Johana Norman (b. 20 Feb 1965) won the individual title in 1982 and team golds in 1981–2. She also won the individual World Cup title in 1980 and Great Britain won three World Cup team titles, 1978–80.

Olympic

The greatest number of Olympic gold medals won is three by András Balczó, a member of the winning team in 1960 and 1968 and the 1972 individual champion. Lars Hall (b. 30 Apr 1927) (Sweden) has uniquely won two individual championships (1952 and 1956). Pavel Lednyev (USSR) (b. 25 Mar 1943) won a record seven medals (two gold, two silver, three bronze), 1968–80. The best British performance is the team gold medal in 1976 by Jim Fox, Adrian Philip Parker and Daniel Nightingale. The best individual placing is fourth by Jeremy Robert 'Jim' Fox (b. 19 Sept 1941) in 1972.

MODERN PENTATHLON HIGHEST SCORES
In major competition

WORLD

SHOOTING
200/200: Charles Leonard (USA) (b. 23 Feb 1913)[1], Berlin, Germany, 3 Aug 1936. Daniele Masala (Italy) (b. 12 Feb 1955), 1132 points, Jönkoping, Sweden, 21 Aug 1978. George Horvath (Sweden) (b. 14 Mar 1960), 1132 points, Moscow, USSR, 22 July 1980.

SWIMMING
3 min 08·22 sec: John Scott (USA) (b. 14 Apr 1962), 1368 points, London, England, 27 Aug 1982.

BRITISH

SHOOTING
198/200: Timothy Kenealy (b. 3 Mar 1950), 1088 points, Helsinki, Finland, 4 June 1979.

SWIMMING
3 min 09·02 sec: Graham Brookhouse, 1360 points, Milton Keynes, England, 4 July 1987.

[1] *points not given in 1936 Olympic Games.*

Probably the greatest margin of victory was by William Oscar Guernsey Grut (b. 17 Sept 1914) (Sweden) in the 1948 Games, when he won three events and was placed fifth and eighth in the other two.

British

The pentathlete with most British titles is Jim Fox, with ten (1963, 1965–8, 1970–4). Wendy Norman won a record four women's titles, 1978–80 and 1982.

BIATHLON

The biathlon, which combines cross-country skiing and rifle shooting, was first included in the Olympic Games in 1960, and World Championships were first held in 1958.

Most titles *Olympic Games*

Two Olympic individual titles have been won by: Magnar Solberg (Norway) (b. 4 Feb 1937), in 1968 and 1972; and by Franz-Peter Rötsch (GDR) at both 10 km

---

and 20 km in 1988. The USSR has won all six 4 × 7·5 km relay titles, 1968–88. Aleksandr Tikhonov (b. 2 Jan 1947) who was a member of the first four teams also won a silver in the 1968 20 km.

World Championship

Frank Ullrich (GDR) (b. 24 Jan 1958) has won a record six individual world titles, four at 10 km, 1978–81, including the 1980 Olympics, and two at 20 km, 1982–3. Aleksandr Tikhonov was in ten winning USSR relay teams, 1968–80 and won four individual titles.

The Biathlon World Cup (inst.1979) was won three times by Frank Ullrich, 1980–2. He was second in 1979 and third in 1983.

Motorcycle Racing

Earliest race

The first motorcycle race was held over a mile *1·6 km* on an oval track at Sheen House, Richmond, Surrey on 29 Nov 1897, won by Charles Jarrott (1877–1944) on a Fournier.

The oldest motorcycle races in the world are the Auto-Cycle Union Tourist Trophy (TT) series, first held on the 25·44 km *15·81 mile* 'Peel' (St John's) course in the Isle of Man on 28 May 1907, and still run in the island on the 'Mountain' circuit.

Fastest circuits

The highest average lap speed attained on any closed circuit is 257·958 km/h *160·288 mph* by Yvon du Hamel (Canada) (b. 1941) on a modified 903 cc 4-cylinder Kawasaki Z1 at the 31-degree banked 4·02 km *2·5 mile* Daytona International Speedway, Florida, USA on March 1973. His lap time was 56·149 sec.

The fastest road circuit was the Francorchamps circuit near Spa, Belgium, then 14·12 km *8·74 miles* in length. It was lapped in 3 min 50·3 sec (average speed 220·721 km/h *137·150 mph*) by Barry Stephen Frank Sheene (GB) (b. 11 Sept 1950) on a 495 cc 4-cylinder Suzuki during the Belgian Grand Prix on 3 July 1977. The world's fastest now is the Portstewart-Coleraine-Portrush circuit in Londonderry, Northern Ireland. The lap record (10·1 mile *16·26 km* lap) is 4 min 53·2 sec (average speed 199·655 km/h *124·060 mph*) by John Glyn Williams (1946–78) on a 747 cc four-cylinder Yamaha on lap five of the 750 cc event of the North-West 200, on 21 May 1977. Minor circuit changes prior to 1986 have resulted in slower times.

The lap record for the outer circuit (4·453 km *2·767 miles*) at the Brooklands Motor Course, near Weybridge, Surrey (open between 1907 and 1939) was 80·0 sec (average speed 200·37 km/h *124·51 mph*) by Noel Baddow 'Bill' Pope (later Major) (1909–71) of the United Kingdom on a Brough Superior powered by a supercharged 996 cc V-twin '8-80' JAP engine developing 110 bhp, on 4 July 1939.

Fastest race *World*

The fastest road race is the 500 cc Belgian Grand Prix held on the Francorchamps circuit (see above). The record time for this ten-lap (141·20 km *87·74 mile*) race is 38 min 58·5 sec (average speed 217·370 km/h *135·068 mph*) by Barry Sheene, on a 495 cc 4-cylinder Suzuki, on 3 July 1977.

United Kingdom

The fastest race in the United Kingdom is the 750 cc event of the North-West 200 held on the Londonderry circuit (see above). The record lap speed is 205·395 km/h *127·63 mph* by Tom Herron (1949–79) on a 747 cc Yamaha in 1978.

Longest race

The longest race was the Liège 24 hr, run on the old Francorchamps circuit. The greatest distance ever covered is 4444·8 km *2761·9 miles* (average speed

185·20 km/h *115·08 mph*) by Jean-Claude Chemarin and Christian Leon, both of France, on a 941 cc 4-cylinder Honda on the Francorchamps circuit on 14–15 Aug 1976.

Longest circuit

The 60·72 km *37·73 mile* 'Mountain' circuit on the Isle of Man, over which the principal TT races have been run since 1911 (with minor amendments in 1920), has 264 curves and corners and is the longest used for any motorcycle race.

Most successful riders *Tourist Trophy*

The record number of victories in the Isle of Man TT races is 14 by Stanley Michael Bailey Hailwood (1940–81) between 1961 and 1979. The first man to win three consecutive TT titles in two events was James A. Redman (Rhodesia) (b. 8 Nov 1931). He won the 250 cc and 350 cc events in 1963–5. Mike Hailwood won three events in one year, in 1961 and 1967.

World championships

The most World Championship titles (instituted by the *Fédération Internationale Motocycliste* in 1949) won is 15 by Giacomo Agostini (Italy) (b. 16 June 1942), seven at 350 cc, 1968–74, and eight at 500 cc in 1966–72, 1975. He is the only man to win two World Championships in five consecutive years (350 cc and 500 cc titles 1968–72).

Agostini won 122 races (68 at 500 cc, 54 at 350 cc) in the World Championship series between 24 Apr 1965 and 25 Sept 1977, including a record 19 in 1970, also achieved by Mike Hailwood in 1966.

Angel Roldan Nieto (Spain) (b. 25 Jan 1947) won a record seven 125 cc titles, 1971–2, 1979, 1981–4 and Klaus Enders (West Germany) (b. 1937) won six world side-car titles, 1967, 1969–70, 1972–4.

In 1985 Freddie Burdette Spencer (USA) (b. 20 Dec 1961), riding for Honda, became the first man ever to win the 250 cc and 500 cc titles in the same year.

Trials

A record three World Trials Championships have been won by Yrjö Vesterinen (Finland), 1976–8 and by Eddie Lejeune (Belgium), 1982–4.

Moto-cross

Joël Robert (Belgium) (b. 11 Nov 1943) won six 250 cc Moto-cross World Championships (1964, 1968–72). Between 25 Apr 1964 and 18 June 1972 he won a record fifty 250 cc Grand Prix. The youngest moto-cross world champion was Dave Strijbos (Netherlands) (b. 9 Nov 1968), who won the 125–cc title aged 18 yr 296 days on 31 Aug 1986.

Most successful machines

Italian MV-Agusta machines won 37 World Championships between 1952 and 1973, and 276 World Championship races between 1952 and 1976.

Youngest and oldest world champions

Alberto 'Johnny' Cecotto (Venezuela) (b. 25 Jan 1956) is the youngest to win a World Championship. He was 19 yr 211 days when he won the 350 cc title on 24 Aug 1975. The oldest was Hermann-Peter Müller (1909–76) of West Germany, who won the 250 cc title in 1955 aged 46.

Highest speeds

Official world speed records must be set with two runs over a measured distance made in opposite directions within a time limit—1 hr for FIM records and 2 hr for AMA records.

Donald A. Vesco (USA) (b. 8 Apr 1939), riding his 21 ft *6·4 m* long *Lightning Bolt* streamliner, powered by two 1016 cc Kawasaki engines on Bonneville Salt Flats, Utah, USA on 28 Aug 1978 set AMA and FIM absolute records averaging 512·733 km/h *318·598 mph* and had a fastest run at an average of 513·165 km/h *318·66 mph.*

The highest speed achieved over two runs in the UK is 308·82 km/h *191·897 mph* by Roy Francis Daniel (b. 7 Dec

1938) on his 998 cc supercharged twin-engined RDS Triumph at Elvington, North Yorkshire, England on 29 July 1978. His average time for the flying 402 m *440 yd* was 4·69 sec.

The world record for 1 km *1·093·6 yd* from a standing start is 16·68 sec by Henk Vink (b. 24 July 1939) (Netherlands) on his supercharged 984 cc four-cylinder Kawasaki, at Elvington Airfield, North Yorkshire, England on 24 July 1977. The faster run was made in 16·09 sec.

The world record for 402 m *440 yd* from a standing start is 8·805 sec by Henk Vink on his supercharged 1132 cc four-cylinder Kawasaki at Elvington Airfield, North Yorkshire on 23 July 1977. The faster run was made in 8·55 sec.

The fastest time for a single run over 402 m *440 yd* from a standing start is 7·08 sec by Bo O'Brechta (USA) riding a supercharged 1200 cc Kawasaki-based machine at Ontario, California, USA in 1980. The highest terminal velocity recorded at the end of a 402 m *440 yd* run from a standing start is 321·14 km/h *199·55 mph* by Russ Collins (USA) at Ontario on 7 Oct 1978.

Motor Racing

Earliest races

There are various conflicting claims, but the first automobile race was the 323 km *201 mile* Green Bay to Madison, Wisconsin, USA run in 1878 won by an Oshkosh steamer. In 1887 Count Jules Félix Philippe Albert de Dion de Malfiance (1856–1946) won the *La Vélocipéde* 31 km *19·3 miles* race in Paris in a De Dion steam quadricycle in which he is reputed to have exceeded 59 km/h *37 mph.* The first 'real' race was from Paris to Bordeaux and back (1178 km *732 miles*) on 11–13 June 1895. The first to finish was Emile Levassor (1844–97) of France, in a Panhard-Levassor two-seater, with a 1·2-litre Daimler engine developing 3½ hp. His time was 48 hr 47 min (average speed 24·15 km/h *15·01 mph*). The first closed circuit race was held over five laps of a mile *1·6 km* dirt track at Narragansett Park, Cranston, Rhode Island, USA on 7 Sept 1896, won by A. H. Whiting, driving a Riker electric.

The oldest race in the world still regularly run, is the RAC Tourist Trophy, first staged on 14 Sept 1905, in the Isle of Man. The oldest continental race is the French Grand Prix, first held on 26–27 June 1906. The Coppa Florio, in Sicily, has been irregularly held since 1906.

Fastest circuits

The highest average lap speed attained on any closed circuit is 403·878 km/h *250·958 mph* in a trial by Dr Hans Liebold (b. 12 Oct 1926) (Germany) who lapped the 12·64 km *7·85 mile* high-speed track at Nardo, Italy in 1 min 52·67 sec in a Mercedes-Benz C111-IV experimental coupé on 5 May 1979. It was powered by a V8 engine with two KKK turbochargers with an output of 500 hp at 6200 rpm.

The fastest road circuit was the Francorchamps circuit near Spa, Belgium, then 14·10 km *8·76 miles* in length which was lapped in 3 min 13·4 sec (average speed 163·086 mph *262·461 km/h*) on 6 May 1973, by Henri Pescarolo (France) (b. 25 Sept 1942) driving a 2993-cc V12 Matra-Simca MS670 Group 5 sports car. The race lap average speed record at Berlin's AVUS track was 276·38 km/h *171·75 mph* by Bernd Rosemeyer (Germany) (1909–38) in a 6-litre V16 Auto Union in 1937.

Fastest pit stop

Robert William 'Bobby' Unser (USA) (b. 20 Feb 1934) took 4 seconds to take on fuel on lap 10 of the Indianapolis 500 on 30 May 1976.

Fastest race

The fastest race is the Busch Clash at Daytona, Florida over 80·5 km *50 miles* on a 4 km *2½ mile* 31-degree banked track. In 1987 Bill Elliott (b. 8 Oct 1955) averaged 318·322 km/h *197·802 mph* in a Ford Thunderbird. Bill Elliott set the world record for a 805 km *500 mile* race in 1985 when he won at Talladega, Alabama at an average

> **Most successful driver** ● The eyes of a determined man. Alain Prost, 'le Professeur' waits while adjustments are made to his McLaren minutes before the 1988 British Grand Prix. He has had more Formula One victories than any other driver. (See p.270) (Photo: Rob Burns).

speed of 299·793 km/h *186·288 mph*. The NASCAR (National Association for Stock Car Automobile Racing) qualifying record is 342·482 km/h *212·809 mph* by Bill Elliott in a Ford Thunderbird at Alabama International Motor Speedway, Talladega, Alabama, USA, a 4·28 km *2·66 mile* oval speedway with 33-degree banked turns, on 30 Apr 1987.

NASCAR records

Richard Lee Petty (USA) (b. 2 July 1937) won 200 NASCAR Winston Cup races in 1024 starts from 1958 to 1 May 1988. His best season was 1967 with 27 wins. Petty, on 1 Aug 1971, was the first driver to pass $1 million career earnings. The NASCAR career money record is $8 136 963 to 25 May 1988 by Darrell Waltrip (b. 5 Feb 1949). Bill Elliott won a year's record $2 383 187 in NASCAR events in 1985. Geoff Bodine (b. 18 Apr 1949) won 55 races in NASCAR Modified racing in 1978.

WORLD CHAMPIONSHIP GRAND PRIX MOTOR RACING

Most successful Drivers

The World Drivers' Championship, inaugurated in 1950, has been won a record five times by Juan-Manuel Fangio

---

Le Mans ▼ The record for the greatest distance ever covered for the current circuit is 5332 km *3313·241 miles* (av speed 221·63 km/h *137·718 mph*) by Jan Lammers (Holland), Johnny Dumfries and Andy Wallace (both GB) in a Jaguar XJR9 on 11–12 June 1988. Jan Lammers (No. 2) is escorted across the finishing line by the two remaining Jaguars, the three cars having formed up for the last couple of laps, to the obvious delight of the British contingent. (Photo: All-Sport/Vandystadt)

▶ It was Jaguar's first success for 31 years, the last being when Ron Flockhart (GB) (seen here driving) and Ivor Beub (GB) (sat over the back wheel) drove to victory in a D-type in 1957.

(Argentina) (b. 24 June 1911) in 1951 and 1954–7. He retired in 1958, after having won 24 Grand Prix races (two shared) from 51 starts.

Alain Prost (France) (b. 24 Feb 1955) holds the records for both the most Grand Prix points in a career, 465·5 and the most Grand Prix victories, 32 from 130 Grand Prix races, 1980–88. The most Grand Prix victories in a year is seven by James 'Jim' Clark (GB) (1936–68) in 1963 and by Alain Prost in 1984.

The most Grand Prix starts is 176 (out of a possible 184) between 18 May 1958 and 26 Jan 1975 by Norman Graham Hill (GB) (1929–75) and by Jacques Laffite (France) (b. 21 Nov 1943), 1974–86. Between 20 Nov 1960

and 5 Oct 1969 Hill took part in 90 consecutive Grands Prix.

Oldest and youngest

The youngest world champion was Emerson Fittipaldi (Brazil) (b. 12 Dec 1946) who won his first World Championship on 10 Sept 1972 aged 25 yr 273 days. The oldest world champion was Juan-Manuel Fangio who won his last World Championship on 18 Aug 1957 aged 46 yr 55 days.

The youngest Grand Prix winner was Bruce Leslie McLaren (1937–70) of New Zealand, who won the United States Grand Prix at Sebring, Florida on 12 Dec 1959,

aged 22 yr 104 days. Troy Ruttmann (USA) was 22 yr 80 days when he won the Indianapolis 500 on 30 May 1952, which was part of the World Championships at the time.

The oldest Grand Prix winner (in pre-World Championship days) was Tazio Giorgio Nuvolari (Italy) (1892–1953), who won the Albi Grand Prix at Albi, France on 14 July 1946, aged 53 yr 240 days.

The oldest Grand Prix driver was Louis Alexandre Chiron (Monaco) (1899–1979), who finished 6th in the Monaco Grand Prix on 22 May 1955, aged 55 yr 292 days.

The youngest driver to qualify for a Grand Prix was Michael Christopher Thackwell (New Zealand) (b. 30 Mar 1961) at the Canadian GP on 28 Sept 1980, aged 19 yr 182 days.

Manufacturers

Ferrari have won a record eight manufacturers' World Championships, 1961, 1964, 1975–7, 1979, 1982–3. Ferrari have 93 race wins in 432 Grands Prix, 1950–88.

Fastest race

The fastest overall average speed for a Grand Prix race on a circuit in current use is 235·421 km/h *146·284 mph* by Nigel Mansell (GB) in a Williams at Zeltweg in the Austrian Grand Prix on 16 Aug 1987.

The qualifying lap record was set by Keke Rosberg (Finland) at 1 min 05·59 sec, an average speed of 258·803 km/h *160·817 mph*, in a Williams-Honda at Silverstone in the British Grand Prix on 20 July 1985.

Closest finish

The closest finish to a World Championship race was when Ayrton Senna (Brazil) in a Lotus beat Nigel Mansell (GB) in a Williams by 0·014 sec in the Spanish Grand Prix at Jerez de la Frontera on 13 Apr 1986. In the Italian Grand Prix at Monza on 5 Sept 1971, 0·61 sec separated winner Peter Gethin (GB) from the fifth placed driver.

BRITISH GRAND PRIX

First held in 1926 as the RAC Grand Prix, and held annually with the above name since 1949. The venues having been Aintree, Merseyside; Brands Hatch, Kent; Brooklands, Surrey; Donington, Leicestershire and Silverstone, Northamptonshire.

Fastest speed

The fastest race time is 1 hr 18 min 10·436 sec, when Alain Prost won in a McLaren at Silverstone on 21 July 1985.

Longest Annual Rally ● The Safari Rally was first run in 1953 as the Coronation Rally, through Kenya, Tanzania and Uganda, but is now restricted to Kenya. The race has covered up to 6234 km *3874 miles*, as in the 17th Safari held from 8–12 Apr 1971. It has been won a record five times by Shekhar Mehta (b. Uganda 1945) in 1973, 1979–82. The local wildlife provide, on occasions, unusual spectators! (Photo: All-Sport/ Vandystadt)

Most wins

The most wins by a driver is five by Jim Clark, 1962–5 and 1967, all in Lotus cars. Ferrari have most wins with ten, 1951–4, 1956, 1958, 1961, 1976 and 1978.

LE MANS

The greatest distance ever covered in the 24-hour *Grand Prix d'Endurance* (first held on 26–27 May 1923) on the old Sarthe circuit at Le Mans, France is 5333·724 km *3314·222 miles* by Dr Helmut Marko (Austria) (b. 27 Apr 1943) and Gijs van Lennep (Netherlands) (b. 16 Mar 1942) in a 4907-cc flat-12 Porsche 917K Group 5 sports car, on 12–13 June 1971.

The race lap record (now 13·535 km *8·410 mile* lap) is 3 min 22·5 sec (average speed 240·622 km/h *149·519 mph* by Hans Stück (West Germany) in a Porsche 962C on 11 June 1988. He also set the practice lap record of 3 min 14·8 sec (av. speed 252·05 km/h *156·62 mph*) on 14 June 1985.

Most wins

The race has been won by Porsche cars twelve times, in 1970–1, 1976–7, 1979, 1981–7. The most wins by one man is six by Jacques Bernard 'Jacky' Ickx (Belgium) (b. 1 Jan 1945), 1969, 1975–7 and 1981–2.

INDIANAPOLIS 500

The Indianapolis 804 km *500 mile* race (200 laps) was inaugurated in the USA on 30 May 1911. Two drivers have four wins: Anthony Joseph 'A.J.' Foyt, Jr (USA) (b. 16 Jan 1935) in 1961, 1964, 1967 and 1977; and Al Unser, Snr (USA) (b. 29 May 1939) in 1970–1, 1978 and 1987. The record time is 2 hr 55 min 42·48 sec (average speed 274·743 km/h *170·722 mph*) by Bobby Rahal (USA) driving a Penske March-Cosworth on 31 May 1986. The record average speed for four laps pre-qualifying is 352·755 km/h *219·198 mph* by Rick Mears (USA) (b. 3 Dec 1951) in a Penske-Chevrolet V8 on 22 May 1988. The one-lap record is 356·565 km/h *221·565 mph* by Mario

Gabriele Andretti (USA) (b. 28 Feb 1940) in a Lola-Chevrolet on 11 May 1988. The record prize fund is $5 016 799 and the individual prize record is $804 853 by Rick Mears, both in 1988.

RALLYING

The earliest long rally was promoted by the Parisian daily *Le Matin* in 1907 from Peking, China to Paris over about ·12 000 km *7500 miles* on 10 June. The winner, Prince Scipione Borghese (1872–1927) of Italy, arrived in Paris on 10 Aug 1907 in his 40-hp Itala accompanied by his chauffeur, Ettore, and Luigi Barzini.

Longest

The longest ever rally was the *Singapore Airlines* London–Sydney Rally over 31 107 km *19 329 miles* from Covent Garden, London on 14 Aug 1977 to Sydney Opera House, won on 28 Sept 1977 by Andrew Cowan, Colin Malkin and Michael Broad in a Mercedes 280E.

Monte Carlo

The Monte Carlo Rally (first run 1911) has been won a record four times by: Sandro Munari (b. 1940) (Italy) in 1972, 1975, 1976 and 1977; and Walter Röhrl (b. 7 Mar 1947) (with co-driver Christian Geistdorfer) in 1980, 1982–4, each time in a different car.

The smallest car to win was an 851-cc Saab driven by Erik Carlsson (Sweden) (b. 5 Mar 1929) and Gunnar Häggbom (Sweden) on 25 Jan 1962, and by Carlsson and Gunnar Palm on 24 Jan 1963.

Britain

The RAC Rally (first held 1932) has been recognised by the FIA since 1957. Hannu Mikkola (Finland) (b. 24 May 1942) (with co-driver Arne Hertz) has a record four wins, in a Ford Escort, 1978–9 and an Audi Quatro, 1981–2.

World Championship

World Championships (instituted 1979) have been won by two drivers, Walter Röhrl in 1980 and 1982 and by Juha Kaukkunen (Finland) (b. 2 Apr 1959) in 1986-7. The most wins in World Championship races is 19 by Hannu Mikkola to February 1988.

DRAG RACING

Piston engined

The world record for two runs in opposite directions over 440 yd *402 m* from a standing start is 6·70 sec by Dennis Victor Priddle (b. 1945) of Yeovil, Somerset, England driving his 6424-cc supercharged Chrysler dragster developing 1700 bhp using nitromethane and

methanol, at Elvington Airfield, North Yorkshire on 7 Oct 1972. The faster run was made in 6·65 sec.

Rocket or jet engined

The highest terminal velocity recorded by any dragster is 631·732 km/h *392·54 mph* by Kitty O'Neil (USA) at El Mirage Dry Lake, California, USA on 7 July 1977. The lowest elapsed time is 3·58 sec by Sammy Miller in a Pontiac 'Funny Car' in 1986.

Highest speeds *See also p.164*

The most successful land speed record breaker was Sir Malcolm Campbell (1885–1948) (GB). He broke the official record nine times between 25 Sept 1924, with 235·216 km/h *146·157 mph* in a Sunbeam, and 3 Sept 1935, when he achieved 480·620 km/h *301·129 mph* in the Rolls–Royce-engined *Bluebird*.

Duration record

The greatest distance ever covered in one year is 400 000 km *248 548·5 miles* by François Lecot (1879–1949), an innkeeper from Rochetaillée, near Lyon, France, in a 1900-cc 66-bhp Citroën 11 sedan, mainly between Paris and Monte Carlo, from 22 July 1935 to 26 July 1936. He drove on 363 of the 370 days allowed.

GUINNESS HAVE PUBLISHED **MOTOR RACING: THE RECORDS** IAN MORRISON £8.95

Mountaineering

Although bronze-age artifacts have been found on the summit of the Riffelhorn, Switzerland (2927 m *9605 ft*), mountaineering as a sport has a continuous history dating back only to 1854. Isolated instances of climbing for its own sake exist back to the 13th century. The Atacamenans built sacrificial platforms near the summit of Llullaillaco (6723 m *22 058 ft*) in late pre-Columbian times c. 1490. The earliest recorded rock climb in the British Isles was of Stac na Biorrach, St Kilda (71·9 m *236 ft*) by Sir Robert Moray in 1698.

Mount Everest

Mount Everest (8848 m *29 028 ft*) was first climbed at 11.30 a.m. on 29 May 1953, when the summit was reached by Edmund Percival Hillary (b. 20 July 1919), created KBE, of New Zealand, and the Sherpa, Tenzing Norgay (1914–86, formerly called Tenzing Khumjung Bhutia), who was awarded the GM. The successful expedition

---

Fastest Top Fuel dragster ● The lowest elapsed time recorded by a piston-engined dragster is 4·99 sec from a standing start for 440 yd *402 m* by Eddie Hill (USA) at Ennis, Texas, USA on 9 Apr 1988. The highest terminal velocity recorded at the end of a 440 yd run is 464·65 km/h *288·73 mph* by Eddie Hill (USA) at Gainesville, Florida, USA on 18 Mar 1988. (Photo: Les Welch)

was led by Col. (later Hon. Brigadier) Henry Cecil John Hunt CBE, DSO (b. 22 June 1910), who was created a Knight Bachelor in 1953, a life Baron on 11 June 1966 and KG on 23 Apr 1979.

The Sherpa, Sundare (or Sungdare) (b. 1955) has climbed Everest a record five times in 1979, 1981, 1982, 1985 and 1988. Ang Rita Sherpa (b. 1939), with ascents in 1983, 1984, 1985 and 1987, is the first person to scale Everest four times without the use of bottled oxygen. Reinhold Messner (b. 17 Sept 1944) (Italy) was the first to make the entire climb solo on 20 Aug 1980. Messner and Peter Habeler (b. 22 July 1942) (Austria) made the first entirely oxygen-less ascent on 8 May 1978.

The first Britons to reach the summit were Douglas Scott (b. 29 May 1941) and Dougal Haston (1940–77) on 24 Sept 1975. The first woman to reach the summit was Junko Tabei (b. 22 Sept 1939) (Japan) on 16 May 1975. The oldest person was Richard Daniel Bass (b. 21 Dec 1929) aged 55 yr 130 days on 30 Apr 1985.

Reinhold Messner with his ascent of Kanchenjunga in 1982, became the first person to climb the world's three highest mountains, having earlier reached the summits of Everest and K2. He has successfully scaled all 14 of the world's mountains of over 8000 m *26 250 ft*, all without oxygen.

All continents

The first person to climb the highest mountain in each of the seven continents (Africa; Kilimanjaro 5895 m *19 340 ft*. Antarctica; Vinson Massif 5140 m *16 863 ft*. Asia; Mount Everest 8848 m *29 029 ft*. Europe; El'brus 5642 m *18 510 ft*. North and Central America; McKinley 6194 m *20 320 ft*. South America; Aconcagua 6960 m *22 834 ft* and Australia; Kosciusko 2230 m *7316 ft*) was Richard Bass (USA) (b. 21 Dec 1929). He completed the last of the peaks with his conquest of Everest on 30 Apr 1985.

However, the above definition excludes New Zealand, Tasmania, New Guinea and the Pacific Islands from continental classification. These land masses, along with

---

Australia, are sometimes known as Australasia (Oceania). In this case, the highest peak is Carstensz Pyramid 5030 m *16 502 ft*, Irian Jaya, New Guinea and the first person to climb the six other peaks and Carstensz was Patrick Morrow (Canada) (b. 18 Oct 1952). He completed the last of the seven mountains, with his successful conquest of Carstensz Pyramid on 7 May 1986.

Greatest walls

The highest final stage in any wall climb is that on the south face of Annapurna I (8091 m *26 545 ft*). It was climbed by the British expedition led by Christian John Storey Bonington (b. 6 Aug 1934) when from 2 Apr to 27 May 1970, using 5500 m *18 000 ft* of rope, Donald Whillans (1933–85) and Dougal Haston scaled to the summit. The longest wall climb is on the Rupal-Flank from the base camp at 3560 m *11 680 ft* to the South Point 8042 m *26 384 ft* of Nanga Parbat—a vertical ascent of 4482 m *14 704 ft*. This was scaled by the Austro-German-Italian expedition led by Dr Karl Maria Herrligkoffer (b. 13 June 1916) in April 1970.

Europe's greatest wall is the 2000 m *6600 ft* north face of the Eigerwand (Ogre wall) first climbed by Heinrich Harrer and Fritz Kasparek of Austria and Anderl Heckmair and Wiggerl Vörg of Germany from 21–24 July 1938. The north-east face of the Eiger had been climbed on 20 Aug 1932 by Hans Lauper, Alfred Zurcher, Alexander Graven and Josef Knubel. The greatest alpine solo climb was that of Walter Bonatti (b. 22 June 1930) (Italy) of the South-West Pillar of the Dru, Montenvers, now called the Bonatti Pillar, with five bivouacs in 126 hr 7 min from 17–22 Aug 1955.

The most demanding free climbs in the world are those rated at 5·13, the premier location for these being in the Yosemite Valley, California, USA. The top routes in Britain are graded E7·7b, which relates closely to 5·13.

Highest bivouac

Douglas Scott and Dougal Haston bivouacked in a snow hole at 8747 m *28 700 ft* on the south summit of Everest on the night of 24 Sept 1975. Two Japanese, Hironobu Kamuro (1951–83) and Hiroshi Yoshino (1950–83), bivouacked at 8800 m *28 870 ft* on Everest on the night of 8/9 Oct 1983, but neither survived beyond the following day.

Oldest

Teiichi Igarashi (b. 21 Sept 1886) (Japan) climbed Mount Fuji (3776 m *12 388 ft*) at the age of 99 years 302 days on 20 July 1986.

MOUNTAIN RACING

Mount Cameroun

Reginald Esuke (Cameroun) descended from the summit 4095 m *13 435 ft* to Buea at 915 m *3002 ft* in 1 hr 2 min 15 sec on 24 Jan 1988, achieving a vertical rate of 51 m *167·5 ft* per min.

Timothy Leku Lekunze (Cameroun) set the record for the race to the summit and back of 3 hr 46 min 34 sec on 25 Jan 1987, when the temperature varied from 35°C at the start to 0°C at the summit. The record time for the ascent is 2 hr 25 min 20 sec by Jack Maitland (GB) in 1988.

Ben Nevis

The record time for the race from Fort William Town Park to the cairn on the summit of Ben Nevis 1346·6 m *4418 ft* and return is 1 hr 25 min 34 sec by Kenneth Stuart (b. 25 Feb 1957), and the feminine record is 1 hr 43 min 25 sec by Pauline Haworth (b. 1 Aug 1956), both on 1 Sept 1984. The full course by the bridle path is about 22 km *14 miles* but distance is saved by crossing the open hillside. The mountain was first climbed c. 1720 and the earliest run, by William Swan in 2 hr 41 min, was in 1895.

Snowdon

The Snowdon Race (Ras Yr Wyddfa) has been run annually since 1976 from Llanberis to the summit of Snowdon and back. The fastest time is 1 hr 2 min 29 sec

Mount Everest ● The most successful expedition to Mount Everest is the Norwegian Everest Expedition in 1985. It succeded in putting the greatest number of people on the summit for an expedition, 17, six on 21 April, eight on 29 April, which itself is a record for one day, and three on 30 April 1985. It was during this expedition that Richard Bass became the oldest man to climb Everest and the Sherpa Sundare completed the fourth of his record five ascents (see text for details). The photo shows three of the men who reached the summit on 21 April, from left, Odd Eliassen, Bjørn Myrer Lund (both Norway) and Sherpa Pertemba, and the photo was taken by Chris Bonnington (GB).
(Photo: Norwegian Everest Expedition)

by Kenny Stuart (Keswick) in 1985. Carol Haigh set a women's record of 1 hr 14 min 36 sec in 1986.

FELL RUNNING

In the 1972 Skiddaw Fell Race (930 to 107 m *3053 ft to 250 ft*) a vertical descent rate of 39 m *128 ft* per min was achieved by George Jeffrey Norman (b. 6 Feb 1945) (Altrincham AC).

Joss Naylor (b. 10 Feb 1936) won the Ennerdale mountain race (37 km *23 miles*) nine times, 1968–77. The fastest time is 3 hr 20 min 57 sec by Kenny Stuart (b. 25 Feb 1957) of Keswick AC in 1985.

The Yorkshire three-peak record for the current 24-mile course is 2 hr 49 min 13 sec by Hugh Symonds of Kendal AC in 1985. The record for the former 23-mile course was 2 hr 37 min 30 sec by John Wild on 25 Apr 1982.

The Lakeland 24-hr record is 76 peaks (approximately 40 000 ft *12 192 m* of ascents and descents) achieved by Mark McDermott on 19–20 June 1988.

The Scottish 24-hr record is 26 Munro (mountains over 914 m *3000 ft*) summits achieved by Martin Stone, on 25–26 June 1987. He covered 70 miles *112 km*, with 31 000 ft *9 449 m* of ascents and descents in 23 hr 24 min.

The record for the Bob Graham Round of 42 lakeland peaks covering a total distance of 116 km *72 miles* and 8230 m *27 000 ft* of ascent and descent, is 13 hr 54 min by Billy Bland, 34, on 19 June 1982. Ernest Roger Baumeister (b.17 Dec 1941) (Dark Peak Fell Runners Club) ran the double Bob Graham Round in 46 hr 34½ min on 30 June–1 July 1979.

The record for traversing the 136·79 km *85 mile* cross-country route of the nine 1219·2 m *4000 ft* Scottish peaks is 21 hr 39 min by Martin Stone (Dark Peak Fell Runners) on 4 Jul 1987

The 'Three Thousander' record over the 15 Welsh peaks of over 914 m *3000 ft* is 4 hr 19 min 56 sec, by Colin Donnelly on 11 June 1988.

The Ten Peaks run is from Burnthwaite Farm, Wasdale Head, Cumbria to the top of Skiddaw via England's nine other highest mountains and tops. The record time is 6 hr 56 min by Joss Naylor, wholly on foot, in May 1975.

Three Peaks record

The Three Peaks route from sea level at Fort William, Inverness-shire, to sea level at Caernarvon, via the summits of Ben Nevis, Scafell Pike and Snowdon, was walked by Arthur Eddleston (1939–84) (Cambridge H) in 5 days 23 hr 37 min from 11–17 May 1980. Peter and David Ford, David Robinson, Kevin Duggan and John O'Callaghan, of Luton and Dunstable, ran the distance in relay in 54 hr 39 min 14 sec from 7–9 Aug 1981. The fastest individual total time for climbing the three mountains is 4 hr 16 min by Joss Naylor from 8–9 July 1971.

On 23 June 1984 a team of 3 from the Greater Manchester Police Tactical Aid Group covered the distance in 8 hr 22 min, being transported between the peaks by helicopter. Their running time was 5 hr 4 min.

A total climbing time of 7 hr 47 min was achieved by Brian Stadden from 13–15 Aug 1982 for Five Peaks, adding the highest points in Northern Ireland—Slieve Donard (852 m *2796 ft*) and in the Republic of Ireland—Carrauntaul (1041 m *3414 ft*) to the Three Peaks.

A team of four from West Midlands Police climbed the Three peaks and the highest peaks in the Isle of Skye and the Isle of Man; Sgurr Alasdair 992 m *3257 ft* and Snaefell 620 m *2036 ft*, travelling by bicycle, ferry and helicopter in a time of 77 hr 43 min (climbing time; 17 hr 57 min and cycling time; 58 hr 6 min) from 7–12 May 1988. They took short rests between climbing and cycling and slept overnight.

Pennine Way

The record for traversing the 436 km *271 mile* long

Pennine Way is 2 days 21 hr 55 min by Michael Cudahy, 43, from 1–3 June 1984. The club relay record for a team of 24 is 29 hr 7 min 58 sec by Holmfirth Harriers from 28–29 June 1986.

Multiple peaks

Three members of the 'Climathon' team, Mick Cottam, Matthew Beresford and Andrew Curson, completed a climb of all 349 peaks in England over 609·6 m *2000 ft* (walking a distance of 647·76 km *402·5 miles*) from 21 July–11 Aug 1985.

Craig Caldwell took 377 days to cycle, walk and climb to the top of the 277 Munros (mountains over 914 m *3000 ft*) and the 222 Corbetts (762-914 m *2500-3000 ft*) in Scotland. In all he cycled 6682 km *4152 miles*, walked 4876 km *3030 miles* and climbed 252 542 m *828 491 ft.*

Top to bottom

Clive Johnson and Les Heaton of 'Mountain Adventure' climbed the highest peaks and descended the deepest caves in each of England, Scotland and Wales in 44 hr 50 min from 16–18 Sept 1986.

Netball

The game was invented in the USA in 1891 and introduced into England in 1895 by Dr Toles. The All England Women's Netball Association was formed in 1926. The oldest club in continuous existence is the Polytechnic Netball Club of London founded in 1907.

Most titles *World*

Australia has won the World Championships (inst. 1963) a record five times, 1963, 1971, 1975, 1979 and 1983.

English

The National Club's Championships (inst. 1966) have been won eight times by Sudbury Netball Club (1968–70, 1971 (shared), 1973, 1983–5). Surrey has won the County Championships (inst. 1932) a record 19 times (1949–64, 1966, 1981; 1969 and 1986 (both shared)).

Most international appearances

The record number of internationals is 90 by June Wightman (b. 28 June 1946) for Northern Ireland, 1964–85. The record for England is 83 by Jillean Hipsey, 1978–86.

Highest scores

The World Tournament record score was in Auckland, New Zealand in 1975 when England beat Papua New Guinea 114 goals to 16. The record number of goals in the World Tournament is 402 by Judith Heath (England) (b. 1942) in 1971.

Orienteering

The first indications of orienteering as a competitive sport have been found in the Swedish army (1888) and the Norwegian army (1895).

The first civilian competition seems to have been organised on 31 Oct 1897 (with 8 participants) by the sport club Tjalve, outside Oslo, Norway.

In spite of a number of other small events up to 1910, the sport died out in Norway but in Sweden survived World War I.

On 25 Mar 1919, the first large competition with more than 200 participants was organised in the forest of Nacka, outside Stockholm. From there the sport spread rapidly throughout Sweden and later (about 1925) to Finland, Norway and (especially post–1945) to other countries in Europe and elsewhere. The initiator was Major Ernst Killander, who is known as 'The Father of Orienteering'.

World Championships were instituted in 1966. Annual

British Championships were instituted in 1967 following the formation of the British Orienteering Federation.

Most titles *World*

Sweden has won the men's relay six times between 1966 and 1979 and the women's relay seven times, 1966, 1970, 1974, 1976, 1981, 1983 and 1985. Three women's individual titles have been won by Annichen Kringstad-Svensson (Sweden) (b. 15 July 1960), 1981, 1983 and 1985. The men's title has been won twice by: Åge Hadler (Norway) (b. 14 Aug 1944), in 1966 and 1972; Egil Johansen (Norway) (b. 18 Aug 1954), 1976 and 1978; and Öyvin Thon (Norway) (b. 25 Mar 1958), in 1979 and 1981.

British

Geoffrey Peck (b. 27 Sept 1949) won the men's individual title a record five times, 1971, 1973, 1976–7 and 1979 as well as the over-35s title in 1985–6. Carol McNeill (b. 20 Feb 1944) won the women's title six times, 1967, 1969, 1972–6. She also won the over-35s title in 1984 and 1985.

Lorna Collett (b. 2 Sept 1922) of South Ribble OC and Terry Dooris (b. 22 Sept 1926) of Southern Navigators have both competed in all 21 British individual championships 1967–87.

Most competitors

The most competitors at an event in one day is 22 510 on the first day of the Swedish O-Ringen at Småland on 18 July 1983.

Parachuting

See also p.181

Parachuting became a regulated sport with the institution of World Championships in 1951. A team title was introduced in 1954 and women's events were included in 1956.

Most titles *World*

The USSR won the men's team title in 1954, 1958, 1960, 1966, 1972, 1976 and 1980, and the women's team title in 1956, 1958, 1966, 1968, 1972 and 1976. Nikolay Ushamyev (USSR) has won the individual title twice, 1974 and 1980.

British

Sgt Ronald Alan 'Scotty' Milne (b. 5 Mar 1952) of the Parachute Regiment won the British title five times in 1976–7, 1979–81.

Rob Colpus and Geoff Sanders have each shared ten British titles for Relative Work parachuting, the 4-Way and 8-Way titles won by their team 'Symbiosis' in 1976–7, 1979, 1981–2.

Greatest accuracy

Jacqueline Smith (GB) (b. 29 Mar 1951) scored ten consecutive dead centre strikes (10 cm *4 in* disc) in the World Championships at Zagreb, Yugoslavia, 1 Sept 1978. At Yuma, Arizona, USA, in March 1978, Dwight Reynolds scored a record 105 daytime dead centres, and Bill Wenger and Phil Munden tied with 43 night time DCs, competing as members of the US Army team, the Golden Knights.

With electronic measuring the official FAI record is 50 DCs by Aleksandr Aasmiae (USSR) at Ferghana, USSR in October 1979.

The Men's Night Accuracy Landing record on an electronic score pad is 27 consecutive dead centres by Cliff Jones (USA) in 1981.

Parascending

Andrew Wakelin (UK) at Artesia Airport, New Mexico, USA on a Sorcerer 33 canopy on a 488 m *1600 ft* line on 1 Aug 1985 set records for distance: 7300 m *23 950 ft*, and height gain: 400 m *1312 ft.* The duration record is 21 min 8 sec by Pat Sugrue on a Paramount 9 in South Wales on 12 Apr 1986. Nigel Horder scored four successive dead centres at the Dutch Open, Flevhof, Netherlands on 22 May 1983.

Highest speed ● The highest speed in a non-mechanical sport is that in sky-diving, where a speed of 298 km/h *185 mph* is possible in the head-down free-falling position in the lower atmosphere, but speeds of 1005 km/h *625 mph* have been recorded in higher, rarefied altitudes. (Photo: All-Sport/Simon Ward)

Pelota Vasca
(Jaï Alaï)

The game, which originated in Italy as *longue paume* and was introduced into France in the 13th century, is said to be the fastest of all ball games. The glove or *gant* was introduced *c.* 1840 and the *chistera* was invented by Jean 'Gantchiki' Dithurbide of Ste Pée, France. The *grand chistera* was invented by Melchior Curuchague of Buenos Aires, Argentina in 1888. The world's largest *frontón* (enclosed stadium) is the World Jaï Alaï at Miami, Florida, USA, which had a record attendance of 15 052 on 27 Dec 1975.

World Championships

The *Federacion Internacional de Pelota Vasca* stage World Championships every four years (first in 1952). The most successful pair have been Roberto Elias and Juan Labat (Argentina), who won the *Trinquete Share* four times, 1952, 1958, 1962 and 1966. Labat won a record seven world titles in all. The most wins in the long court game *Cesta Punta* is three by Hamuy of Mexico, with two different partners, 1958, 1962 and 1966.

Highest speed

An electronically-measured ball velocity of 302 km/h *188 mph* was recorded by José Ramon Areitio at the Newport Jai Alai, Rhode Island, USA on 3 Aug 1979.

Longest domination

The longest domination as the world's No. 1 player was enjoyed by Chiquito de Cambo (*né* Joseph Apesteguy)

Highest speed ● The highest projectile speed for a moving ball game is for pelota vasca, somtimes known as jai alai (pronounced *hi-ali*), in which a speed of 302 km/h *188 mph* has been recorded. The curved wicker basket from where the high ball-speed is generated is known as a *grand chistera* or *cesta*. (Photo: All-Sport/Bill Frakes)

(France) (1881–1955) from the beginning of the century until succeeded in 1938 by Jean Urruty (France) (b. 19 Oct 1913).

Pétanque

The origins of pétanque or boules can be traced back over 2000 years, but it was not until 1945 that the *Fédération Française de Pétanque et Jeu Provençal* was formed, and subsequently the *Fédération Internationale* (FIPJP). The first recognised British club was formed on 30 Mar 1966 as the Chingford Club de Pétanque and the British Pétanque Association was founded in 1974.

World Championships

Winner of the most World Championships (inst. 1959) has been France with eight titles to 1985.

Highest score in 24 hours

David Gyton, Paul Gyton and Michael Morris scored a record 1767 points in 24 hours (159 games) at the Gin Trap, Ringstead, Norfolk on 27–8 June 1986.

Pigeon Racing

Pigeon racing developed from the use of homing pigeons for carrying messages. The sport originated in Belgium from commercial services and the earliest long-distance race was from London to Antwerp in 1819, involving 36 pigeons.

Longest flights

The longest confirmed distances, flown in opposite directions, by a single pigeon were north from Rome, Italy, 1474·38 km *916·16 miles*, and south from The Faroes, 1178·82 km *732·5 miles*, by a dark cock, GB83X 03693, to the loft of Marley Westrop of Hitchin, Hertfordshire.

The greatest recorded homing flight by a pigeon was made by one owned by the 1st Duke of Wellington (1769–1852). Released from a sailing ship off the Ichabo Islands, West Africa on 8 April, it dropped dead a mile from its loft at Nine Elms, Wandsworth, London on 1 June 1845, 55 days later, having flown an airline route of 8700 km *5400 miles*, but an actual distance of possibly 11 250 km *7000 miles* to avoid the Sahara Desert.

The official British duration record (into Great Britain) is 1887 km *1173 miles* in 15 days by *C.S.O.*, owned by Rosie and Bruce of Wick, in the 1976 Palamos Race. In the 1975 Palamos Race, *The Conqueror*, owned by Alan Raeside, homed to Irvine, Strathclyde, 1625 km *1010 miles*, in 43 hr 56 min.

The greatest number of flights over 1000 miles flown by one pigeon is that of *Dunning Independence*, owned by D. Smith, which annually flew from Palamos to Dunning, Perthshire, Scotland 1662 km *1039 miles* between 1978 and 1981.

Highest speeds

In level flight in windless conditions it is very doubtful if any pigeon can exceed 96 km/h *60 mph*. The highest race speed recorded is one of 2952 m *3229 yd* per min (177·14 km/h *110·07 mph*) in the East Anglian Federation race from East Croydon on 8 May 1965 when the 1428 birds were backed by a powerful south-south-west wind. The winner was owned by A. Vigeon & Son, Wickford, Essex.

The highest race speed recorded over a distance of more than 1000 km is 2224·5 m *2432·7 yd* per min (133·46 km/h *82·93 mph*) by a hen in the Central Cumberland Combine race over 1099·316 km *683 miles 147 yd* from Murray Bridge, South Australia to North Ryde, Sydney on 2 Oct 1971.

24-hr records

The world's longest reputed distance in 24 hr is 1292 km *803 miles* (velocity 1394 m *1525 yd* per min) by E. S. Petersen's winner of the 1941 San Antonio R.C. event in Texas, USA.

The best 24-hr performance into the United Kingdom is 1165·3 km *724 miles 219 yd* by E. Cardno's *Mormond Lad*, on 2 July 1977, from Nantes, France to Fraserburgh, Grampian. Average speed was 1507 m *1648 yd* per min (90.41 km/h *56·18 mph*).

Career records

Owned by R. Green, of Walsall Wood, West Midlands, *Champion Breakaway* won 59 first prizes from 1972 to May 1979. The greatest competitive distance flown is 32 318 km *20 082 miles* by *Nunnies*, a chequer cock owned by Terry Haley of Abbot's Langley, Hertfordshire, England.

Highest– priced bird

Champion racing pigeons commonly change hands for £30 000 or more. Currency fluctuations mean that a record price in sterling may not reflect the true price paid. Recent high-priced pigeons include *Keiser* sold by Arthur Leflere to Masahiko Ohta of Japan in 1985; *Sproetekop*, also sold by Arthur Leflere to Japan in 1986, and *Peter Pau* sold by Silvere Toye of Belgium to Louis Massarella of Loughborough, England in 1986.

Polo

Polo is usually regarded as being of Persian origin, having been played as *Pulu c.* 525 BC. Other claims have come from Tibet and the Tang Dynasty of China AD 250. Modern polo originated in Manipur, India and the first club was the Cachar Club (founded in 1859) in Assam, India. The oldest club still in existence is the Calcutta Polo Club (1862). The game was introduced into England from India in 1869 by the 10th Hussars at Aldershot, Hampshire and the earliest match was one between the 9th Lancers and the 10th Hussars on Hounslow Heath, Greater London in July 1871. The earliest international match between England and the USA was in 1886. The game's governing body is the Hurlingham Polo Association, which drew up the first English rules in 1875.

Most titles

The British Open Championship for the Cowdray Park Gold Cup (inst. 1956) has been won five times by Stowell Park, 1973–4, 1976, 1978 and 1980.

Highest handicap

The highest handicap based on eight 7½ min 'chukkas' is ten goals introduced in the USA in 1891 and in the United Kingdom and in Argentina in 1910. A total of 55 players have received ten-goal handicaps. The only two currently playing in Britain are the Mexicans Guillermo and Carlos Gracida. The latter, with Ernesto Trotz (Argentina) in 1985 is the most recent recipient of this handicap. The last (of six) ten-goal handicap players from Great Britain was Gerald Balding in 1939. A match of two 40-goal teams was staged, for the only time, at Palermo, Buenos Aires, Argentina in 1975. The highest handicaps of current United Kingdom players are eight by: Julian Hipwood (b. 23 June 1946); and by Howard Hipwood (b. 24 Mar 1950). Claire J. Tomlinson of Gloucestershire attained a handicap of five, the highest ever by a woman, in 1986.

Highest score

The highest aggregate number of goals scored in an international match is 30, when Argentina beat the USA 21–9 at Meadow Brook, Long Island, New York, USA in September 1936.

Pool

Pool or championship pocket billiards with numbered balls began to become standardised c. 1890. The greatest exponents were Ralph Greenleaf (USA) (1899–1950), who won the 'world' professional title 19 times (1919–37), and William Mosconi (USA) (b. 27 June 1913), who dominated the game from 1941 to 1957.

The longest consecutive run in an American straight pool match is 625 balls by Micheal Eufemia at Logan's Billiard Academy, Brooklyn, New York, USA on 2 Feb 1960. The greatest number of balls pocketed in 24 hr is 15 780 by Vic Elliott at the Royal George, Lincoln, England on 2–3 Apr 1985.

The record times for potting all 15 balls in a speed competition are: (men) 37·9 sec by Rob McKenna at Blackpool, Lancashire on 7 Nov 1987; (women) 53·29 sec by Susan Thompson, at Oldham, Greater Manchester on 5 June 1988.

A record break of 132 for 14–1 pool was set by Ross McInnes at Pontin's, Heysham, Lancashire, England on 3 Oct 1984.

Powerboat Racing

A petrol engine was first installed in a boat by Jean Joseph Etienne Lenoir (1822–1900) on the River Seine, Paris in 1865. Actual powerboat racing started in about 1900, the first prominent race being from Calais to Dover in 1903.

International racing was largely established by the presentation of a Challenge Trophy by Sir Alfred Harmsworth in 1903. Thereafter, racing developed mainly as a 'circuit' or short, sheltered course type competition. Offshore or sea-passage races also developed, initially for displacement (non-planing) cruisers.

Offshore events for fast (planing) cruisers began in 1958 with a 273 km *170 mile* passage race from Miami, USA to Nassau, Bahamas. Outboard motor, i.e. the combined motor/transmission detachable propulsion unit type racing began in the USA in about 1920. Both inboard and outboard motor boat engines are mainly petrol fuelled, but since 1950 diesel (compression ignition) engines have appeared and are widely used in offshore sport.

Highest speeds

The highest speed recorded by a propeller-driven boat is 368·52 km/h *229 mph* by *The Texan*, a Kurtis Top Fuel Hydro Drag boat, driven by Eddie Hill (USA). He also set a 440 yd *402 m* elapsed time record of 5·16 sec in the same boat at Firebird Lake, Arizona, USA on 13 Nov 1983.

The official American Drag Boat Association record is 360·29 km/h *223·88 mph* by *Final Effort*, a Blown Fuel Hydro boat driven by Robert T. Burns at Creve Coeur Lake, St Louis, Missouri, USA on 15 July 1985 over a 402 m ¼ mile course.

The fastest speed recognised by the *Union Internationale Motonautique* for an outboard- powered boat is in Class (e): 285·83 km/h *177·61 mph* by P. R. Knight in a Chevrolet-engined Lautobach hull on Lake Ruataniwha, New Zealand in 1986. Robert F. Hering (USA) set the world Formula One record at 266·085 km/h *165·338 mph* at Parker, Arizona on 21 Apr 1986.

The fastest speed recognised for an offshore boat is 248·537 km/h *154·438 mph* for one way and 238·559 km/h *148·238 mph* for two runs by Tom Gentry (USA), in his 15 m *49 ft* catamaran, powered by four Gentry Turbo Eagle V8 Chevrolets.

The fastest speed recorded for a diesel (compression ignition) boat is 218·26 km/h *135·62 mph* by the hydroplane *Iveco World Leader*, powered by an Aifo-Fiat engine, driven by Carlo Bonomi at Venice, Italy in 1985.

Highest race speeds

The highest speed recorded in an offshore race is 166·22 km/h *103·29 mph* by Tony Garcia (USA) in a Class I powerboat at Key West, Florida, USA in November 1983.

Longest races

The longest offshore race has been the Port Richborough London to Monte Carlo Marathon Offshore international event. The race extended over 4742 km *2947 miles* in 14 stages from 10–25 June 1972. It was won by *H.T.S.* (GB) driven by Mike Bellamy, Eddie Chater and Jim Brooker in 71 hr 35 min 56 sec for an average of 66·24 km/h *41·15 mph*. The longest circuit race is the 24-hour race held annually since 1962 on the River Seine at Rouen, France. The 1983 winners François Greens, Jan van Brockels and Roger Robin of Belgium drove a Johnson outboard-engined Piranha boat at an average speed of 75·02 km/h *46·63 mph*.

Longest jetboat jumps

The longest ramp jump achieved by a jetboat has been 36·57 m *120 ft* by Peter Horak (USA) in a Glastron Carlson CVX 20 Jet Deluxe with a 460 Ford V8 engine (take-off speed 88 km/h *55 mph*) for a documentary TV film, at Salton Sea, California, USA on 26 Apr 1980. The longest leap on to land is 38·7 m *172 ft* by Norm Bagrie (NZ) from the Shotover River on 1 July 1982 in the 1½ ton jetboat *Valvolene*.

Rackets

There is record of the sale of a racket court at Southernhay, Exeter, Devon dated 12 Jan 1798. The game, which is of 17th-century origin, was played by debtors in the Fleet Prison, London in the middle of the 18th century, and an inmate, Robert Mackay, claimed the first 'world' title in 1820. The first closed court champion was Francis Erwood at Woolwich, London in 1860.

World Championships

Of the 22 world champions since 1820 the longest reign is by Geoffrey Willoughby Thomas Atkins (b. 20 Jan 1927)

> **Ambidexterous world rackets champion** ● James Simpson Male (GB) (b. 25 Mar 1964) became the youngest world rackets champion this century, at 23 yr 246 days when he defeated William Boone (USA), 4–1 (15–2, 15–4, 7–15, 14–4, 15–6), at The Racquet Club of Chicago, USA on 27 Feb 1988 and 2–0 (17–15, 15–10), to win 6–1 overall, at Queen's Club, West Kensington, London on 5 Mar 1988. His method is unique as he plays double-handed and serves ambidextrously.(Photo: Dave Page for Guinness Publishing)

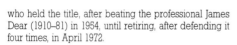

who held the title, after beating the professional James Dear (1910–81) in 1954, until retiring, after defending it four times, in April 1972.

Most Amateur titles

Since the Amateur Singles Championship was instituted in 1888 the most titles won by an individual is nine by Edgar Maximilian Baerlein (1879–1971) between 1903 and 1923.

Since the institution of the Amateur Doubles Championship in 1890 the most shares in titles has been eleven by: David Sumner Milford (1905–84), between 1938 and 1959; and John Ross Thompson (b. 10 May 1918), between 1948 and 1966; they won ten titles together. Milford also won seven Amateur Singles titles (1930–51), an Open title (1936) and held the World title from 1937 to 1946.

Thompson has additionally won an Open Singles title and five Amateur Singles titles.

Racketball

Racquetball using a 40 ft by 20 ft court was invented in 1950 by Joe Sobek at the Greenwich YMCA, Connecticut, USA, originally as Paddle Rackets.

The International Racquetball Association was founded in 1968 by Bob Kendler (USA). John Treharne won three British titles, 1981–3.

Racketball using a 32 ft by 21 ft court (as for squash) was introduced to Britain by Ian Wright in 1976. The British Racketball Association was formed and staged inaugural British National Championships in 1984. Three titles have been won at the women's event by Bett Dryhurst, 1985–7.

Rodeo

Rodeo, which developed from 18th-century *fiestas*, came into being in the early days of the North American cattle industry.

The sport originated in Mexico and spread from there into the cattle regions of the USA. Steer wrestling came in with Bill Pickett (1870–1932) of Texas in 1900.

The largest rodeo in the world is the Calgary Exhibition and Stampede at Calgary, Alberta, Canada. In 1981 the total paid attendance for the rodeo events over ten days was 122 268.

The National Finals Rodeo was first held in 1959 in Dallas, Texas. This annual event is organised by the Professional Rodeo Cowboys Association (PRCA).

In 1987 a record of over $2 million in prize money was offered for the event, staged in Las Vegas, Nevada, USA.

Most world titles

The record number of all-around titles in the PRCA World Championships is six by Larry Mahan (USA) (b. 21 Nov 1943) in 1966–70 and 1973 and, consecutively, 1974–9 by Tom Ferguson (b. 20 Dec 1950). Tom Ferguson had record career earnings of $1 089 428, 1972–87.

Jim Shoulders (b. 1928) of Henryetta, Oklahoma, USA has won a record 16 World Championships at all events between 1949 and 1959.

The record figure for prize money in a single season is $166 042 by Lewis Feild (b. 28 Oct 1956) in 1986. Feild won a record $75 219 for one rodeo ($47 449 for saddle bronc riding and $27 770 for bareback riding) at the 1987 National Finals Rodeo, Las Vegas, Nevada, USA.

Youngest champions

The youngest winner of a world title is Metha Brorsen of Oklahoma, USA, who won the International Rodeo Association cowgirls barrel-racing event in 1975 at 11 years old. The youngest champion in Professional Rodeo Cowboys Association/Women's Professional Rodeo Association competition is Jackie Jo Perrin of Antlers, Oklahoma, USA, who won the barrel-racing title in 1977 at age 13.

Time records

Records for PRCA timed events, such as calf-roping and steer-wrestling, are not always comparable, because of the widely varying conditions due to the sizes of arenas and amount of start given the stock.

The fastest time recorded for roping a calf is 5·7 sec by Lee Phillips at Assiniboia, Saskatchewan, Canada in 1978, and the fastest time for overcoming a steer is 2·4 sec by: James Bynum, at Marietta, Oklahoma, USA in 1955; Carl Deaton at Tulsa, Oklahoma, USA in 1976; and Gene Melton at Pecatonica, Illinois, USA in 1976.

The highest score in bull riding was 98 points out of a possible 100 by Denny Flynn on *Red Lightning* at Palestine, Illinois, USA in 1979.

Champion bull

The top bucking bull *Red Rock*, who had dislodged 312 riders during an eight year career since 1980, was finally ridden to the eight-second bell by Lane Frost on 20 May 1988. Frost had already had two unsuccessful attempts. *Red Rock* retired at the end of the 1987 season having been voted Bull of the Year, but he still makes guest appearances.

Champion bronc

Traditionally, a bronc called *Midnight* owned by Jim McNab of Alberta, Canada was never ridden in 12 appearances at the Calgary Stampede.

Amateur Rink Hockey Association was formed in 1908, and in 1913 became the National Rink Hockey (now Roller Hockey) Association. England won the first World Championships, 1936–9, since when Portugal has won most titles with 12 between 1947 and 1982. Portugal also won a record 16 European (inst. 1926) titles between 1947 and 1987.

Rowing

The Sphinx stela of Amenhotep II (1450–1425 BC) records that he *stroked* a boat for some three miles.

The earliest established sculling race is the Doggett's Coat and Badge, which was first rowed on 1 Aug 1716 from London Bridge to Chelsea as a race for apprentices, and is still contested annually. Although rowing regattas were held in Venice in 1300 the first English regatta probably took place on the Thames by the Ranelagh Gardens, near Putney in 1775.

Most Olympic medals

Six oarsmen have won three gold medals: John B. Kelly (USA) (1889–1960), father of the late HSH Princess Grace of Monaco, Single Sculls (1920) and Double Sculls (1920 and 1924); his cousin Paul Vincent Costello (USA) (b. 27 Dec 1899), Double Sculls (1920, 1924 and 1928); Jack Beresford, Jr (GB) (1899–1977), Single sculls (1924), Coxless fours (1932) and Double Sculls (1936), Vyacheslav Ivanov (USSR) (b. 30 July 1938), Single Sculls (1956, 1960 and 1964); Siegfried Brietzke (GDR) (b. 12 June 1952), Coxless Pairs (1972) and Coxless Fours (1976, 1980); and Pertti Karppinen (Finland) (b. 17 Feb 1953), Single Sculls 1976, 1980 and 1984.

World Championships

World rowing championships distinct from the Olympic Games were first held in 1962, at first four yearly, but from 1974 annually, except in Olympic years.

Roller Skating

The first roller skate was devised by Jean Joseph Merlin (1735–1803) of Huy, Belgium in 1760 and demonstrated by him in London but with disastrous results. James L. Plimpton of New York produced the present four-wheeled type and patented it in January 1863. The first indoor rink was opened in the Haymarket, London in about 1824.

Most titles

Speed

The most world speed titles won is 18 by two women: Alberta Vianello (Italy), eight track and ten road 1953–65; and Annie Lambrechts (Belgium), one track and 17 road 1964–81, at distances from 500 m to 10 000 m. The most British national individual men's titles have been won by Michael Colin McGeogh (b. 30 Mar 1946) with 19 in 1966–85. Chloe Ronaldson (b. 30 Nov 1939) won 40 individual and 14 team women's senior titles from 1958 to 1985.

Figure

The records for figure titles are: five by Karl Heinz Losch in 1958–9, 1961–2 and 1966; and four by Astrid Bader in 1965–8, both of West Germany. The most world pair titles is four by Dieter Fingerle (West Germany) in 1959, 1965–7 with two different partners.

Speed skating

The fastest speed put up in an official world record is 43·05 km/h *26·75 mph* when Patrizio Sarto (b. 19 Jan 1964) recorded 25·088 sec for 300 m on a road at Bogotá, Colombia in 1984. The world records on a rink for 10 000 m are: (men) 15 min 49·7 sec, Roberto Marotta (b. 6 Mar 1948) (Italy) at Inzell, West Germany 1968; (women) 16 min 30·484 sec, Annie Lambrechts (Belgium) at Louvain, Belgium on 1 July 1985. Lambrechts went on to skate 37·097 km *23·051 miles* in 1 hr and 50 km in 1 hr 21 min 25 sec. The men's 1-hour record on a track is 37·230 km *23·133 miles* by Alberto Civolani (Italy) (b. 16 Mar 1933) at Inzell, West Germany on 28 Sept 1968. He went on to skate 80·46 km *50 miles* in 2 hr 20 min 33·1 sec.

Largest rink

The greatest indoor rink ever to operate was located in the Grand Hall, Olympia, London. Opened in 1890 and closed in 1912, it had an actual skating area of 6 300 m² *68 000 ft²*. The current largest is the main arena of 3250 m² *34 981 ft²* at Guptill Roll-Arena, Boght Corner, New York, USA. The total rink area is 3844 m² *41 380 ft²*.

Endurance

Theodore James Coombs (b. 1954) of Hermosa Beach, California, USA skated 8357 km *5193 miles* from Los Angeles to New York and back to Yates Center, Kansas from 30 May to 14 Sept 1979.

Land's End to John o'Groats

Steve Fagan, 20, roller skated the distance, 1488 km *925 miles*, in 9 days 10 hr 25 min from 1–10 May 1984, averaging 157 km *98 miles* a day. The fastest time by a woman was 12 days 4 hr 15 min by Cheryl Fisher, 17, from 19 Sept–1 Oct 1987.

ROLLER HOCKEY

Roller hockey (previously known as rink hockey in Europe) was introduced to Britain as rink polo, at the old Lava rink, Denmark Hill, London in the late 1870s. The

---

Rowing

The most gold medals won at World Championships and Olympic Games is six by the GDR oarsmen: the twins Bernd and Jörg Landvoigt (b. 23 Mar 1951); Joachim Dreifke (b. 26 Dec 1952); Karl-Heinz Bussert (b. 8 Jan 1955); Ulrich Diessner (b. 27 Dec 1954); Siegfried Brietzke (b. 12 June 1952); and Wolfgang Mager (b. 24 Aug 1952); and at lightweight events by Ruggero Verroca (Italy) (b. 3 Jan 1961).

The most wins at Single Sculls is five, by Peter-Michael Kolbe (West Germany) (b. 2 Aug 1953), 1975, 1978, 1981, 1983 and 1986, and by Pertti Karppinen, 1979 and 1985 with his three Olympic wins (above), and in the women's events by Christine Hahn (*née* Scheiblich) (GDR) (b. 31 Dec 1954), 1974–5, 1977–8 (and the 1976 Olympic title).

Boat Race

The earliest University Boat Race, which Oxford won, was from Hambledon Lock to Henley Bridge on 10 June 1829. Outrigged eights were first used in 1846. In the 134 races to 1988, Cambridge won 69 times, Oxford 64 times and there was a dead heat on 24 Mar 1877.

The race record time for the course of 6·779 km *4 miles 374 yd* (Putney to Mortlake) is 16 min 45 sec by Oxford on 18 Mar 1984. This represents an average speed of 24·28 km/h *15·09 mph*. The smallest winning margin has been by a canvas by Oxford in 1952 and 1980. The greatest margin (apart from sinking) was Cambridge's win by 20 lengths in 1900.

Boris Rankov (Oxford, 1978–83) rowed in a record six winning boats. Susan Brown (b. 29 June 1958), the first woman to take part, coxed the winning Oxford boats in 1981 and 1982. Daniel Topolski coached Oxford to ten successive victories, 1976–85.

The largest man ever to row in a University boat has been Gavin Stewart (Wadham, Oxford), the tallest at 2·04 m *6 ft 8½ in* in 1987–8 and the heaviest at 105 kg *231 lb* in 1987. The 1988 Oxford crew averaged a record 94·12 kg *207·5 lb*. The lightest oarsman was the 1882 Oxford Stroke, Alfred Herbert Higgins, at 60 kg *9 st 6½ lb*. The lightest coxes, Francis Henry Archer (Cambridge) (1843–89) in 1862 and Hart Parker Vincent Massey (Oxford) (b. Canada, 30 Mar 1918) in 1939, were both 32·6 kg *5 st 2 lb*.

The youngest 'blue' ever was Matthew John Brittin (Cambridge) (b. 1 Sept 1968) at 18 yr 208 days, in 1986.

Head of the River

A processional race for eights instituted in 1926, the Head has an entry limit of 420 crews (3780 competitors). The record for the course Mortlake–Putney (the reverse of the Boat Race) is 16 min 37 sec by the ARA National Squad in 1987.

Henley Royal Regatta

The annual regatta at Henley-on-Thames, Oxfordshire, was inaugurated on 26 Mar 1839. Since then the course, except in 1923, has been about 2112 m *1 mile 550 yd* varying slightly according to the length of boat. In 1967 the shorter craft were 'drawn up' so all bows start level.

The most wins in the Diamond Challenge Sculls (inst. 1844) is six consecutively by Stuart A. Mackenzie (b. 5 Apr 1937) (Australia and GB) 1957–62. The record time is 7 min 40 sec by Sean Drea (Neptune RC, Ireland) on 5 July 1975. The record time for the Grand Challenge Cup (inst. 1839) event is 6 min 13 sec by Harvard University, USA, and a combined Leander/Thames Tradesmen crew, both on 5 July 1975.

Sculling

The record number of wins in the Wingfield Sculls (Putney to Mortlake) (inst. 1830) is seven by Jack Beresford, Jr from 1920 to 1926. The fastest time for the course has been 21 min 1 sec by Steven Redgrave (b. 23 Mar 1962) in winning his fourth Wingfield Sculls in 1988.

Highest speed

The highest recorded speed on non-tidal water for

River Thames ● Malcom Knight, Simon Leifer and Kevin Thomas rowed the navigable length of the Thames, 299·14 km *185·88 miles*, from Lechlade Bridge, Gloucestershire to Southend Pier, Essex in 39 hr 27 min 12 sec in a skiff from 10–11 May 1988. Here they are approaching Clifton Hampden Bridge, Oxfordshire.

2000 m *2187 yd* is by an American eight in 5 min 27·14 sec (22·01 km/h *13·68 mph*) at Lucerne, Switzerland on 17 June 1984. A crew from Penn AC, USA, was timed in 5 min 18·8 sec (22·58 km/h *14·03 mph*) in the FISA Championships on the River Meuse, Liège, Belgium on 17 Aug 1930.

24 hours

The greatest distance rowed in 24 hours (upstream and downstream) by an eight is 209 km *130 miles* by members of the Renmark Rowing Club, South Australia on 20–1 Apr 1984.

Cross Channel

Ivor Lloyd sculled across the English Channel in a record 3 hr 35 min 1 sec on 4 May 1983.

River Thames

The fastest time from Folly Bridge, Oxford to Westminster Bridge, London (180 km *112 miles*) is 14 hr 25 min 15 sec by an eight from Kingston Rowing Club on 1 Feb 1986.

Longest race

The longest annual rowing race is the annual Tour du Lac Leman, Geneva, Switzerland for coxed fours (the five-man crew taking turns as cox) over 160 km *99 miles*. The record winning time is 12 hr 52 min by LAGA Delft, Netherlands on 3 Oct 1982.

International Dragon Boat Races

Instituted in 1975 and held annually in Hong Kong, the fastest time achieved for the 640 metres *700 yd* course is 2 min 27.45 sec by the Chinese Shun De team on 30 June 1985. The best time for a British team was 2 min 51.8 sec by an Amateur Rowing Association team in 1984. Teams have 28 members—26 rowers, one steersman and one drummer.

Rugby League

There have been four different scoring systems in Rugby League football. For the purpose of these records all points totals remain as they were under the system in operation at the time they were made.

The Northern Rugby Football Union was formed on 29 Aug 1895 at the George Hotel, Huddersfield, West Yorkshire. Twenty-one clubs from Yorkshire and Lancashire were present and all but one agreed to resign from the Rugby Union. Payment for loss of wages was the major cause of the breakaway and full professionalism was allowed in 1898. A reduction in the number of players from 15 to 13 took place in 1906. The title 'Rugby Football League' was adopted in 1922.

Most titles

There have been seven World Cup Competitions. Australia have most wins, with four, 1957, 1968, 1970 and 1977 as well as a win in the International Championship of 1975.

The Northern Rugby League was formed in 1901. The word 'Northern' was dropped in 1980. Wigan have won the League Championship a record ten times (1909, 1922, 1926, 1934, 1946, 1947, 1950, 1952, 1960 and 1987).

In the Rugby League Challenge Cup (inaugurated 1896–7 season) Leeds have most wins with ten, 1910, 1923, 1932, 1936, 1941–2 (wartime), 1957, 1968, 1977–8. Oldham is the only club to appear in four consecutive Cup Finals (1924–7).

Since 1974 there have been five major competitions for RL clubs: Challenge Cup, League Championship, Premiership, John Player Special Trophy and County Cups. Wigan has a record 42 wins in these competitions, and won four, the League Championship, John Player Special Trophy, Lancashire Cup and Premiership in 1986–7.

Three clubs have won all possible major Rugby League trophies in one season: Hunslet, 1907–8 season, Huddersfield, 1914–15 and Swinton, 1927–8, all won the Challenge Cup, League Championship, County Cup and County League (now defunct).

HIGHEST SCORES
Senior match

The highest aggregate score in a game where a senior club has been concerned was 121 points, when Huddersfield beat Swinton Park Rangers by 119 (19 goals, 27 tries) to 2 (one goal) in the first round of the Northern Union Cup on 28 Feb 1914. The highest score in League football is 112 points by Leeds v. Coventry (nil) on 12 Apr 1913. St Helens beat Carlisle 112–0 in the Lancashire Cup on 14 Sept 1986.

Challenge Cup Final

The highest score in a Challenge Cup Final is 38 points (8 tries, 7 goals) by Wakefield Trinity v. Hull (5) at Wembley on 14 May 1960. The record aggregate is 52 points when Wigan beat Hull 28–24 at Wembley on 4 May 1985. The greatest winning margin was 34 points when Huddersfield beat St Helens 37–3 at Oldham on 1 May 1915.

International match

The highest score in an international match is Australia's 70–8 defeat of Papua New Guinea in World Cup match at Wagga Wagga, Australia on 20 July 1988. Great Britain's highest score in an international is the 53–19 win over New Zealand at Hameau, Paris on 4 Nov 1972.

Touring teams

The record score for a British team touring Australasia is 101 points by England v. South Australia (nil) at Adelaide in May 1914. The record for a touring team in Britain is 92 (10 goals, 24 tries) by Australia against Bramley 7(2 goals and 1 try) at the Barley Mow Ground, Bramley, near Leeds on 9 Nov 1921.

Most points *Season*

Leigh scored a record 1436 points (258 tries, 199 goals, 6 drop goals) in the 1985–6 season, playing in 43 Cup and League games.

HIGHEST INDIVIDUAL SCORES
Most points, goals and tries in a game

George Henry 'Tich' West (1882–1927) scored 53 points

(10 goals and a record 11 tries) for Hull Kingston Rovers (73) in a Challenge Cup tie v. Brookland Rovers (5) on 4 Mar 1905.

The record for a League match is 39 (5 tries, 12 goals) by Jimmy Lomas (1880–1960) in Salford's 78–0 win over Liverpool City on 2 Feb 1907.

The most goals in a Cup match is 22 kicked by James 'Jim' Sullivan (1903–77) for Wigan v. Flimby and Fothergill on 14 Feb 1925. The most goals in a League match is 15 by Michael Stacey (b. 9 Feb 1953) for Leigh v. Doncaster on 28 Mar 1976. The most tries in a League match is 10 by Lionel Cooper (b. Australia, 1922–87) for Huddersfield v. Keighley on 17 Nov 1951.

Most points *Season & career*
The record number of points in a season was 496 by Benjamin Lewis Jones (Leeds) (b. 11 Apr 1931), 194 goals, 36 tries, in 1956–7.

Neil Fox (b. 4 May 1939) scored 6220 points (2575 goals, 358 tries, 4 drop goals) in a senior Rugby League career from 10 Apr 1956 to 19 Aug 1979.

Most tries *Season & career*
Albert Aaron Rosenfeld (1885–1970) (Huddersfield), an Australian-born wing-threequarter, scored 80 tries in 42 matches in the 1913–14 season.

Brian Bevan (b. Australia, 24 Apr 1924), a wing-threequarter, scored 796 tries in 18 seasons (16 with Warrington, two with Blackpool Borough) from 1945 to 1964. He scored 740 for Warrington, 17 for Blackpool and 39 in representative matches.

Most goals *Season & career*
The record number of goals in a season is 221, in 47 matches, by David Watkins (b. 5 Mar 1942) (Salford) in the 1972–3 season.

Jim Sullivan (Wigan) kicked 2859 goals in his club and representative career, 1921–46.

Most consecutive scores
David Watkins (Salford) played and scored in every club game during seasons 1972–3 and 1973–4, contributing 41 tries and 403 goals—a total of 929 points, in 92 games.

Individual international records
Jim Sullivan (Wigan) played in most internationals (60 for Wales and Great Britain, 1921–39), kicked most goals (160) and scored most points (329).

Michael Sullivan (no kin) (b. 12 Jan 1934) of Huddersfield, Wigan, St Helens and York played in 51 international games for England and Great Britain and scored a record 45 tries, 1954–63.

Michael O'Connor (b. 30 Nov 1960) scored a record 30 points for Australia v. Papua New Guinea at Wagga Wagga, Australia on 20 July 1988.

Most Challenge Cup Finals
Eric Batten (b. 13 June 1914) (Leeds, Bradford Northern and Featherstone Rovers) played in a record eight Challenge Cup Finals including war-time guest appearances between 1941 and 1952 and was on four winning sides.

Seven players have been in four Challenge Cup winning sides—Alan Edwards, Eric Batten, Alex Murphy, Brian Lockwood, Mick Adams, Keith Elwell and Eric Hughes. Alan Edwards (b. 15 May 1916) was the only one to do so with four different clubs, Salford 1938, Leeds 1942, Dewsbury 1943, Bradford Northern 1949.

Youngest and oldest players
Harold Wagstaff (1891–1939) played his first League game for Huddersfield at 15 yr 175 days, for Yorkshire at 17 yr 141 days, and for England at 17 yr 228 days.

The youngest player in a Cup Final was Shaun Edwards (b. 17 Oct 1966) at 17 yr 201 days for Wigan when they

lost 6–19 to Widnes at Wembley on 5 May 1984. He became the youngest Great Britain international when he played against France at Headingley, Leeds on 1 Mar 1985 at 18 yr 135 days. The oldest player for Great Britain was Jeffrey Grayshon (b. 4 Mar 1949) at 36 yr 250 days v. New Zealand at Elland Road, Leeds on 9 Nov 1985.

Most durable player
The most appearances for one club is 774 by Jim Sullivan for Wigan, 1921–46. He played a record 928 first-class games in all. The longest continuous playing career is that of Augustus John 'Gus' Risman (b. 21 Mar 1911), who played his first game for Salford on 31 Aug 1929 and his last for Batley on 27 Dec 1954.

Keith Elwell (b. 12 Feb 1950) played in 239 consecutive games for Widnes from 5 May 1977 to 5 September 1982.

In his career, 1972–85, he received a record 28 winners' or runners-up medals in major competitions.

Most and least successful teams
Wigan won 31 consecutive league games from February 1970 to February 1971. Huddersfield were undefeated for 40 league and cup games in 1913–14. Hull is the only club to win all League games in a season, 26 in Division II 1978–9. Doncaster holds the record of losing 40 consecutive League games from 16 Nov 1975 to 21 Apr 1977.

Greatest crowds
The greatest attendance at any Rugby League match is 102 569 for the Warrington v. Halifax Challenge Cup Final replay at Odsal Stadium, Bradford on 5 May 1954. The record attendance for any international match is 70 204 for the First Test between Australia and England on the Sydney Cricket Ground on 6 June 1932. The highest international attendance in Britain is 50 583 for the First Test between Great Britain and Australia at Old Trafford, Manchester on 25 Oct 1986.

AMATEUR RUGBY LEAGUE
The British Amateur Rugby League Association

(BARLA) was formed in 1973 'to foster, develop, extend and control amateur rugby league football in Great Britain'. Prior to that year the ultimate control of amateurs as well as professionals rested with the Rugby Football League. A National League was formed in 1986–7.

National Cup

Pilkington Recreation (St Helens, Merseyside) have won the National Cup four times (1975, 1979, 1980, 1982). John McCabe (b. 26 Jan 1952) has played in a record five National Cup finals, winning on each occasion. He played for Pilkington Recreation in each of their four successes and captained Thatto Heath (St Helens, Merseyside) to victory in 1987.

Highest score *Major competition*

Humberside beat Carlisle by 138 points to nil in the second round of the National Inter-league Competition on 20 Oct 1984.

Rugby Union

Records are determined in terms of present-day scoring values, i.e. a try at 4 points; a dropped goal, penalty or goal from a mark at 3 points; and a conversion at 2 points. The *actual* score, in accordance with whichever of the eight earlier systems was in force at the time, is also given, in brackets.

Although there are records of a game with many similarities to rugby dating back to the Roman occupation, the game is traditionally said to have originated from a breach of the rules of the football played in November 1823 at Rugby School by William Webb Ellis (later the Rev) (c. 1807–72). This handling code of football evolved gradually and was known to have been played at Cambridge University by 1839. The Rugby Football Union was founded on 26 Jan 1871. The International Rugby Football Board (IRFB) was founded in 1886.

WORLD CUP

The inaugural World Cup was contested in Australia and New Zealand by 16 national teams in 1987. The final in

---

Most wins ● The Middlesex Seven-a-sides were inaugurated in 1926 and have been won a record eleven times by Harlequins, 1926–9, 1933, 1935, 1967, 1978, 1986–8. Here Harlequins' Everton Davies swerves past Bristol's Kelvin Wyles during Harlequins' 20–18 victory in the 1988 final on 7 May 1988. A week earlier, in the final of the John Player Cup (15-a-side), Harlequins had defeated Bristol 28–22, for a unique double. (Photo: All-Sport/Pascal Rondeau)

MOST INTERNATIONAL APPEARANCES

IRELAND	69	Cameron Michael Henderson Gibson (b. 3 Dec 1942)	1964–79
NEW ZEALAND	55	Colin Earl Meads (b. 3 June 1936)	1957–71
WALES	55*	John Peter Rhys 'JPR' Williams (b. 2 Mar 1949)	1969–81
FRANCE	52	Roland Bertranne (b. 6 Dec 1949) (in all matches—69)	1971–81
SCOTLAND	51	Andrew Robertson Irvine (b. 16 Sept 1951)	1973–82
	51	James Menzies 'Jim' Renwick (b. 12 Feb 1952)	1972–83
AUSTRALIA	49	Simon Paul Poidevin (b. 31 Oct 1958)	1980–88
ENGLAND	43	Anthony Neary (b. 25 Nov 1948)	1971–80
SOUTH AFRICA	38	Frederick Christoffel Hendrick Du Preez (b. 28 Nov 1935)	1960–71
	38	Jan Hendrik Ellis (b. 5 Jan 1943)	1965–76

* Gareth Owen Edwards (b. 12 July 1947) made a record 53 consecutive international appearances, never missing a match throughout his career for Wales, 1967–78.

Auckland on 20 June 1987 was won by New Zealand, who beat France 29–9. The highest team score was New Zealand's 74–13 victory over Fiji at Christchurch on 27 May 1987. They scored ten goals, two tries and two penalty goals. The individual match record was 30 (3 tries, 9 conversions) by Didier Camberabero (France) (b. 9 Jan 1961) v. Zimbabwe at Auckland on 2 June 1987. The leading scorer in the tournament was the New Zealand goal-kicker Grant James Fox (b. 6 June 1962), with 126 points.

INTERNATIONAL CHAMPIONSHIP

The International Championship was first contested by England, Ireland, Scotland and Wales in 1884. France first played in 1910.

Wales has won a record 21 times outright and tied for first a further eleven times to 1988. Since 1910 Wales has 15 wins and 10 ties and England 15 wins and 7 ties. The most Grand Slams, winning all four matches, is eight by England. Wales also have eight but these include two in 1908–9, before the entry of France.

Highest team score

The highest score in an International Championship match was set at Swansea on 1 Jan 1910 when Wales beat France 49–14 or 59–16 on present-day scoring values (8 goals, 1 penalty goal, 2 tries, to 1 goal, 2 penalty goals, 1 try).

Season's scoring

Jean-Patrick Lescarboura (France) (b. 12 Mar 1961) scored a record 54 points (10 penalty goals, 6 conversions, 4 dropped goals) in 1984.

Individual match records

William John 'Billy' Bancroft (1871–1959) kicked a record 9 goals (8 conversions and 1 penalty goal) for Wales v. France at Swansea in 1910.

HIGHEST TEAM SCORES
Internationals

The highest score in any full international was when New Zealand beat Japan by 106–4 at Tokyo, Japan on 1 Nov 1987, although New Zealand did not award caps. France beat Paraguay 106–12 at Asuncion, Paraguay on 28 June 1988.

The highest aggregate score for any international match between the Four Home Unions is 69 when England beat Wales by 69 points (7 goals, 1 drop goal and 6 tries) to nil at Blackheath, London on 19 Feb 1881. (Note: there was no point scoring in 1881.) The highest score under the modern points system between IRFB members is 63, when New Zealand beat Wales 54–9 at Auckland, New Zealand on 11 June 1988.

The highest score by any overseas side in an international in the British Isles is 53 points (7 goals, 1 drop goal and 2 tries) to nil when South Africa beat Scotland at Murrayfield, Edinburgh on 24 Nov 1951 (44–0).

Tour match

The record score for any international tour match is 125–0 (17 goals, 5 tries and 1 penalty goal) (103–0) when New Zealand beat Northern New South Wales at Quirindi, Australia on 30 May 1962. The highest under scoring in use for the game is 117–6 for New Zealand's defeat of South Australia on 1 May 1974.

Match

In Denmark, Comet beat Lindo by 194–0 on 17 Nov 1973. The highest British score is 174–0 by 7th Signal Regiment v. 4th Armoured Workshop, REME, on 5 Nov 1980 at Herford, West Germany. Scores of over 200 points have been recorded in school matches, for example Radford School beat Hills Court 214 points (31 goals and 7 tries) to nil (200–0) on 20 Nov 1886. The highest score in the Courage Club Championship is 146–0 by Billingham against Hartlepool Athletic in a Durham/Northumberland Division 3 match at Billingham, Durham on 3 Oct 1987.

Season

The highest number of points accumulated in a season by a club is 1607 points by Pontypool, Gwent in 1983–4. The record number of tries is 269 by Bridgend, Mid Glamorgan, 1983–4.

HIGHEST INDIVIDUAL SCORES
Internationals

Phil Bennett (Wales) (b. 24 Oct 1948) scored 34 points (2 tries, 10 conversions, 2 penalty goals) for Wales v. Japan at Tokyo on 24 Sept 1975, when Wales won 82–6. The highest individual points score in any match between members of the International Board is 26 by Allan Roy Hewson (b. 6 June 1954) (1 try, 2 conversions, 5 penalty goals and a drop goal) for New Zealand against Australia at Auckland on 11 Sept 1982.

Patrick Lagisquet scored seven tries for France v. Paraguay on 28 June 1988. The most tries in an international match between IRFB members is five by George Campbell Lindsay (1863–1905) for Scotland *v.* Wales on 26 Feb 1887, and by Douglas 'Daniel' Lambert (1883–1915) for England *v.* France on 5 Jan 1907. Ian Scott Smith (Scotland) (1903–72) scored a record six consecutive international tries in 1925, comprising the last three *v.* France and two weeks later, the first three *v.* Wales. The most tries in an international career is 26 by David Campese (b. 21 Oct 1962) for Australia, 28 Aug 1982–11 June 1988.

In all internationals Hugo Porta (b. 1951) scored a record 479 points in 48 matches for Argentina, 1973–88, including 376 in 39 against IRB teams. Andrew Robertson Irvine (Heriots) (b. 16 Sept 1951) scored 301 points in his career, 273 for Scotland (including 12 *v.* Romania) and 28 for the British Lions, from 1973 to 1982.

Season

The first-class season scoring record is 581 points by Samuel Arthur Doble (1944–77) of Moseley, in 52 matches in 1971–2. He also scored 47 points for England in South Africa out of season.

Andy Higgin (b. 4 Mar 1963) scored a record 28 drop goals in a season in first-class rugby, for the Vale of Lune in 1986–7.

Career

William Henry 'Dusty' Hare (b. 29 Nov 1952) scored 6693 points in first-class games from 1971–88, comprising 1800 for Nottingham, 3922 for Leicester, 240 for England, 88 for the British Lions and 643 in other representative matches.

Match

Jannie van der Westhuizen scored 80 points (14 tries, 9 conversions, 1 dropped goal, 1 penalty goal) for Carnarvon (88) *v.* Williston (12) at North West Cape, South Africa on 11 March 1972.

In a junior house match in February 1967 at William Ellis School, Edgware, Greater London, between Cumberland and Nunn, Thanos Morphitis, 12, contributed 90 points (13 tries and 19 conversions) (77) to Cumberland's winning score.

All-rounder

Canadian international Barrie Burnham scored all possible ways—try, conversion, penalty goal, drop goal, goal from mark—for Meralomas *v.* Georgians (20–11) at Vancouver, BC on 26 Feb 1966.

Most international appearances

Cameron Michael Henderson Gibson (b. 3 Dec 1942) played in 69 internationals for Ireland, 1964–79, a record for matches between the seven member countries of the 'International Rugby Football Board' and France. Including 12 appearances for the British Lions, he played in a total of 81 international matches. Willie John McBride (b. 6 June 1940) made a record 17 appearances for the British Lions, as well as 63 for Ireland.

Youngest international

Edinburgh Academy pupils Ninian Jamieson Finlay (1858–1936) and Charles Reid (1864–1909) were both 17 yr 36 days old when they played for Scotland *v.* England in 1875 and 1881 respectively. However, as Finlay had one less leap year in his lifetime up to his first cap, the outright record must be credited to him. Daniel Brendan Carroll (b. 17 Feb 1892) was aged only 16 yr 149 days when he played for Australia in the 1908 Olympic Games rugby tournament—not considered to be a 'full' international.

County Championships

The County Championships (inst. 1889) have been won most often by Gloucestershire with 15 titles (1910, 1913, 1920–2, 1930–2, 1937, 1972, 1974–6 and 1983–4).

The most individual appearances is 104 by Richard Trickey (Sale) (b. 6 Mar 1945) for Lancashire between 1964 and 1978.

Club Championships

The most outright wins in the RFU Club Competition (John Player Cup, inst. 1971–2) is four by Bath, 1984–7. The Courage Clubs Championship was founded in the 1987–8 season, when the inaugural winners of the National League were Leicester.

The most wins in the Welsh Rugby Union Challenge Cup (Schweppes Welsh Cup, inst. 1971–2) is six, by Llanelli, 1973–6, 1985 and 1988. The most wins in the Scottish League Division One (inst. 1973–4) is ten by Hawick between 1973 and 1987.

Seven-a-sides *Origins*

Seven-a-side rugby dates from 28 Apr 1883 when Melrose RFC Borders, in order to alleviate the poverty of a club in such a small town, staged a seven-a-side tournament. The idea was that of Ned Haig, the town's butcher.

Hong Kong Sevens

This, the world's most prestigious international tournament for seven-a-side teams, was first held in 1976. The record of five wins is held by Australia, 1979, 1982–3, 1985 and 1988.

Greatest crowd

The record paying attendance is 104 000 for Scotland's 12–10 win over Wales at Murrayfield, Edinburgh on 1 Mar 1975.

Highest posts

The world's highest rugby union goal posts are 33·54 m *110 ft ½ in* high at the Roan Antelope Rugby Union Club, Luanshya, Zambia. The posts at Brixham RFC, Devonshire, England are 17·37 m *57 ft* high with an additional 0·30 m *1 ft* spike.

Longest kicks

The longest recorded successful drop goal is 82 m *90 yd* by Gerald Hamilton 'Gerry' Brand (b. 8 Oct 1906) for South Africa *v.* England at Twickenham, Greater London, on 2 Jan 1932. This was taken 6 m *7 yd* inside the England 'half', 50 m *55 yd* from the posts, and dropped over the dead ball line.

The place kick record is reputed to be 91 m *100 yd* at Richmond Athletic Ground, London, by Douglas Francis Theodore Morkel (1886–1950) in an unsuccessful penalty for South Africa *v.* Surrey on 19 Dec 1906. This was not measured until 1932. In the match Bridlington School 1st XV *v.* an Army XV at Bridlington, Humberside on 29 Jan 1944, Ernie Cooper (b. 21 May 1926), captaining the school, landed a penalty from a measured 74 m *81 yd* from the post with a kick which carried over the dead ball line. The record in an international was set at 21·55 m *70 yd 8½ in* by Paul Huw Thorburn (b. 24 Nov 1962) for Wales *v.* Scotland on 1 Feb 1986.

Fastest try

The fastest try in an international game was when Herbert Leo 'Bart' Price (1899–1943) scored for England *v.* Wales at Twickenham on 20 Jan 1923 less than 10 sec after kick-off.

Most tries

Alan John Morley (b. 25 June 1950) has scored 473 tries in senior rugby in 1968–86 including 378 for Bristol, a record for one club. John Huins scored 85 tries in 1953–4, 73 for St Luke's College, Exeter and 12 more for Neath and in trial games.

Longest try

The longest 'try' ever executed was by a team of 15, from Power-House RUFC, Victoria, Australia, who ran a try of 2366·7 km *1470·6 miles* from 4–13 Mar 1983 around Albert Park Lake, Victoria. There were no forward passes or knock-ons, and the ball was touched down between the posts in the prescribed manner (Law 12).

Most successful team

The Feilding junior team of New Zealand played 93

successive games without defeat from 1984–8. The Chiltern under-ten mini rugby side have, since their formation as an under-eight side, played 140 games without defeat to the end of the 1988 season. They have conceded points in only twelve of these matches and averaged 25·86 points a match.

GUINNESS HAVE PUBLISHED **RUGBY: THE RECORDS** CHRIS RHYS £8.95

Shinty

Shinty (from the Gaelic *sinteag*, a bound) has roots reaching back more than 2000 years to the ancient game of *camanachd*, the sport of the curved stick, the diversion of the heroes of Celtic history and legend. It was effective battle training, exercising speed and co-ordination of eye and arm along with aggression and cool self-control. In spite of the break-up of the clan system in the Highlands of Scotland, the 'ball plays', involving whole parishes, without limit in number or time except the fall of night, continued in areas such as Lochaber, Badenoch and Strathglass. Whisky and the inspiration of the bagpipes were important ingredients of these occasions. The ruling body of this apparently ungovernable game was established in 1893 when the Camanachd Association was set up at Kingussie, Highland.

Most titles

Newtonmore, Highland has won the Camanachd Association Challenge Cup (instituted 1896) a record 28 times, 1907–86. Johnnie Campbell, David Ritchie and Hugh Chisholm, all of Newtonmore, have won a record 11 winners' medals. In 1923 the Furnace Club, Argyll won the cup without conceding a goal throughout the competition.

In 1984 Kingussie Camanachd Club won all five senior competitions, including the Camanachd Cup Final. This feat was equalled by Newtonmore in 1985.

Highest scores

The highest Scottish Cup Final score was in 1909 when Newtonmore beat Furnace 11–3 at Glasgow, Dr Johnnie Cattanach scoring eight hails or goals. In 1938 John Macmillan Mactaggart scored ten hails for Mid-Argyll in a Camanachd Cup match.

Shooting

The Lucerne Shooting Guild (Switzerland) was formed *c.*1466 and the first recorded shooting match was at Zurich in 1472.

Most Olympic medals

The record number of medals won is 11 by Carl Townsend Osburn (USA) (1884–1966) in 1912, 1920 and 1924, consisting of five gold, four silver and two bronze. Six other marksmen have won five gold medals. The only marksman to win three individual gold medals has been Gudbrand Gudbrandsönn Skattebo (Norway) (1875–1965) in 1906. Separate events for women were first held in 1984.

Bisley

The National Rifle Association was instituted in 1859. The Queen's (King's) Prize has been shot since 1860 and has only once been won by a woman—Marjorie Elaine Foster (1894–1974) (score 280) on 19 July 1930. Arthur George Fulton (1887–1972) won three times (1912, 1926, 1931). Both his father and his son also won the Prize.

The highest score (possible 300) for the final of the Queen's Prize is 295 by Lindsay Peden (Scotland) on 24 July 1982. The record for the Silver Medals is 150 (possible 150) by Martin John Brister (City Rifle Club) (b. 1951) and (Lord) John Swansea (b. 1 Jan 1925) on 24 July

SHOOTING–INDIVIDUAL WORLD RECORDS

World records are accepted only when set at major international events

MEN

FREE RIFLE
Three positions 3×40 shots at 300 m

	1174/1200 Malcolm Cooper (GB)	Skövde, Sweden	30 Aug 1986
	1174/1200 Glenn Dubis (USA) (twice)	Skövde, Sweden	29 & 30 Aug 1986
Prone 60 shots at 300 m	599/600 Malcolm Cooper (GB)	Skövde, Sweden	28 Aug 1986

STANDARD RIFLE
Three positions 3×20 shots at 300 m

	586/600 Malcolm Cooper (GB)	Skövde, Sweden	1 Sept 1986

SMALL-BORE RIFLE
Three positions 3×40 shots at 50 m
Prone 60 shots at 50 m

	1183/1200 Petr Kurka (Czechoslovakia)	Seoul, South Korea	1 Oct 1987
	600/600 Thirteen men		
	First Alistair Allan (GB)	Titograd, Yugoslavia	21 Sept 1981

FREE PISTOL 60 shots at 50 m

	581/600 Aleksandr Melentiev (USSR)	Moscow, USSR	20 July 1980

RAPID-FIRE PISTOL 60 shots at 25 m

	599/600 Igor Puzyrev (USSR)	Titograd, Yugoslavia	21 Sept 1981

CENTRE-FIRE PISTOL
60 shots at 25 m

	597/600 Thomas D. Smith III(USA)	Sao Paulo, Brazil	20 Apr 1963

STANDARD PISTOL 60 shots at 25 m

	584/600 Eric Buljung (USA)	Caracas, Venezuela	20 Aug 1983

RUNNING GAME TARGET
60 shots at 50 m with small-bore rifle

	596/600 Nikolay Lapin (USSR)	Lahti, Finland	25 July 1987

OLYMPIC TRAP 200 birds

	200/200 Daniel Carlisle (USA)	Caracas, Venezuela	21 Aug 1983

OLYMPIC SKEET 200 birds

	200/200 Matthew Dryke (USA)	Sao Paulo, Brazil	11 Nov 1981
	200/200 Jan Hula (Czechoslovakia)	Zaragoza, Spain	16 June 1984

AIR RIFLE 60 shots at 10 m

	596/600 Jean-Pierre Amat (France)	Zürich, Switzerland	4 June 1987

AIR PISTOL 60 shots at 10 m

	590/600 Vladas Turla (USSR)	Caracas, Venezuela	4 Nov 1982
	590/600 Igor Basinskiy (USSR)	Bratislava, Czechoslovakia	1 Mar 1987
	590/600 Igor Basinskiy (USSR)	Stavanger, Norway	27 Feb 1988

WOMEN

STANDARD RIFLE
Three positions 3×20 shots at 50 m
Prone 60 shots at 50 m

	592/600 Marlies Helbig (GDR)	Titograd, Yugoslavia	17 Sept 1981
	598/600 Eulalia Rolinska (Poland)	Suhl, GDR	28 Aug 1971
	598/600 Margaret Murdock (USA)	Thun, Switzerland	21 Sept 1974
	598/600 Nonka Matova (Bulgaria)	Osijek, Yugoslavia	8 Sept 1985
	598/600 Eva Forian (Hungary)	Suhl, GDR	9 Sept 1986

SMALL-BORE SPORT PISTOL
60 shots at 25 m

	595/600 Nino Salukvadze (USSR)	Seoul, South Korea	28 Sept 1987

OLYMPIC TRAP 200 birds

	195/200 Susan Nattrass (Canada)	Seoul, South Korea	4 Oct 1978

OLYMPIC SKEET 200 birds

	197/200 Svetlana Yakimova (USSR)	Zaragoza, Spain	16 June 1984

AIR RIFLE 40 shots at 10 m

	399/400 Vessela Letcheva (Bulgaria)	Suhl, GDR	30 May 1987
	399/400 Eva Joo (Hungary)	Stavanger, Norway	26 Feb 1988

AIR PISTOL 40 shots at 10 m

	388/400 Svetlana Smirnova (USSR)	Suhl, GDR	29 May 1987

1971. This was equalled by John Henry Carmichael (WRA Bromsgrave RC) on 28 July 1979 and Robert Stafford on 26 July 1980, with the size of the bullseyes reduced.

Small-bore

The National Small-Bore Rifle Association, of Britain, was formed in 1901. The British team record (1966 target) is 1988 × 2000 by Lancashire in 1968–9 and London in 1980–1. The British individual small-bore rifle record for 60 shots prone is 600×600, first achieved by John Palin (b. 16 July 1934) in Switzerland in 1972. Richard Hansen shot 5000 bullseyes in 24 hr at Fresno, California, USA on 13 June 1929.

Clay pigeon

Most world titles have been won by Susan Nattrass (Canada) (b. 5 Nov 1950) with six, 1974–5, 1977–9, 1981.

The record number of clay birds shot in an hour is 2312 by Colin Hewish at the Street and District Gun Club, Ivythorn, Street, Somerset on 8 May 1988.

Graham Douglas Geater (b. 21 July 1947) shot 2264 targets in an hour on a trapshooting range at the NILO Gun Club, Papamoa, New Zealand on 17 Jan 1981.

The maximum 200/200 was achieved by Ricardo Ruiz Rumoroso at the Spanish Clay Pigeon Championships at Zaragossa on 12 June 1983.

Noel D. Townend achieved the maximum 200 consecutive down-the-line targets at Nottingham on 21 Aug 1983.

Bench rest shooting

The smallest group on record at 914 m *1000 yd* is 11·11 cm *4·375 in* by Earl Chronister with a ·30–378 Weatherby Magat Williamsport, Pennsylvania, USA on 12 July 1987

Highest score in 24 hr

The Easingwold Rifle and Pistol Club team of John Smith, Edward Kendall, Phillip Kendall and Paul Duffield scored 120 242 points (averaging 95·66 per card) on 6–7 Aug 1983.

Skiing

The most ancient ski in existence was found well preserved in a peat bog at Hoting, Sweden, dating from *c.* 2500 BC. The earliest recorded military use of skiing was at the Battle of Isen, near Oslo, Norway in 1200. The Trysil Shooting and Skiing Club, founded in Norway in 1861, claims it is the world's oldest. The oldest ski competitions are the Holmenkøllen Nordic events which were first held in 1866. The first downhill races were staged in Australia in the 1850s. The International Ski Federation (FIS) was founded on 2 Feb 1924, succeeding the International Skiing Commission, founded at Christiania (Oslo), Norway on 18 Feb 1910. The Ski Club of Great Britain was founded on 6 May 1903. The National Ski Federation of Great Britain was formed in 1964 and changed its name to the British Ski Federation in 1981.

Most titles

World/Olympic Championships—Alpine
The World Alpine Championships were inaugurated at Mürren, Switzerland, in 1931. The greatest number of titles won has been by Christel Cranz (b. 1 July 1914) of Germany, with seven individual—four slalom (1934, 1937–9) and three downhill (1935, 1937, 1939), and five combined (1934–5, 1937–9). She also won the gold medal for the Combined in the 1936 Olympics. The most won by a man is seven by Anton 'Toni' Sailer (b. 17 Nov 1935) (Austria), who won all four in 1956 (giant slalom, slalom, downhill and the non-Olympic Alpine combination) and the downhill, giant slalom and combined in 1958.

World/Olympic Championships—Nordic
The first World Nordic Championships were those of the 1924 Winter Olympics in Chamonix, France. The greatest number of titles won is nine by Galina Kulakova (b. 29 Apr 1942) (USSR) in 1970–8. The most medals is 21 by Raisa Smetania (USSR) (b. 29 Feb 1952) including six gold, 1974–88. She also won four silver and four bronze medals for a record 17 in total. The most won by a man is eight, including relays, by Sixten Jernberg (b. 6 Feb 1929) (Sweden) in 1956–64. Johan Grøttumsbraaten (1899–1942) of Norway won six individual titles (two 18 km cross-country, four Nordic combined) in 1926–32. The record for a jumper is five by Birger Ruud (b. 23 Aug 1911) of Norway, in 1931–2 and 1935–7. Ruud is the only person to win Olympic events in each of the dissimilar Alpine and Nordic disciplines. In 1936 he won the Ski-jumping and the Alpine downhill (which was not then a separate event, but only a segment of the Combined event).

WORLD CUP

The World Cup was introduced for Alpine events in 1967 and for Nordic events in 1981.

The most individual event wins is 85 by Ingemar Stenmark (Sweden) (b. 18 Mar 1956) in 1974–87, including a record 10 in one season in 1978–9, part of a record 14 successive giant slalom wins from 18 Mar 1978, his 23rd birthday, to 21 Jan 1980. Franz Klammer (Austria) (b. 3 Dec 1953) won a record 25 downhill races, 1974–84.

Annemarie Moser (*née* Pröll) (Austria) (b. 27 Mar 1953) won a women's record 62 individual event wins, 1970–9. She had a record 11 consecutive downhill wins from Dec 1972 to Jan 1974.

Ski-jumping

The longest ski-jump ever recorded is one of 194 m *636 ft* by Piotr Fijas (Poland) at Planica, Yugoslavia on 14 Mar 1987. The women's record is 110 m *361 ft* by Tiina Lehtola (b. 3 Aug 1962) (Finland) at Ruka, Finland on 29 Mar 1981.

Fastest skier ● A determined looking Michael Prufer of Monaco (b. France), who holds the record for being the fastest person on skis, achieved a speed of 223·741 km/h *139·030 mph* at Les Arcs, France on 16 Apr 1988.

The picture clearly shows the adapted helmet, skin-tight suit and leg-fins, so important for aerodynamics. (Photo: All-Sport/Vandystadt)

MOST WORLD CUP TITLES

ALPINE

MEN

OVERALL	4	Gustavo Thoeni (Italy)	1971–3, 1975
DOWNHILL	5	Franz Klammer (Austria)	1975–8, 1983
SLALOM	8	Ingemar Stenmark (Sweden)	1975–81, 1983
GIANT SLALOM	7	Ingemar Stenmark	1975–6, 1978–81, 1984

Two men have won four titles in one year: Jean-Claude Killy (France) (b. 30 Aug 1943) won all four possible disciplines (downhill, slalom, giant slalom and overall) in 1967; and Pirmin Zurbriggen (Switzerland) (b. 4 Feb 1963) won four of the five possible disciplines (downhill, giant slalom, Super G [added 1982–3] and overall) in 1987.

WOMEN

OVERALL	6	Annemarie Moser (Austria)	1971–5, 1979
DOWNHILL	7	Annemarie Moser	1971–5, 1978–9
SLALOM	4	Erika Hess (Switzerland)	1981–3, 1985
GIANT SLALOM	3	Annemarie Moser	1971–2, 1975

NORDIC

MEN

JUMPING	4	Matti Nykänen (Finland)	1983, 1985–6, 1988
CROSS-COUNTRY	4	Gunde Svan (Sweden)	1984–6, 1988

WOMEN

CROSS-COUNTRY	3	Marjo Matikainen (Finland)	1986–8

The longest dry ski-jump is 92 m *302 ft* by Hubert Schwarz (West Germany) at Berchtesgarten, West Germany on 30 June 1981.

Highest speed

The official world record, as recognised by the International Ski Federation for a skier, is 223·741 km/h *139·030 mph* by Michael Prufer (Monaco) and the fastest by a woman is 214·413 km/h *133·234 mph* by Tarja Mulari (Finland), both at Les Arcs, France on 16 Apr 1988. On the same occasion, Graham Wilkie (GB) (b. 21 Sept 1959) set a Britsh men's record of 219·914 km/h *136·651 mph* and Patrick Knaff (France) set a one-legged record of 185·567 km/h *115·309 mph*. On 18 Apr 1987, a British women's record was set by Divina Galica (b. 13 Aug 1944) at 191·99 km/h *119·30 mph*, also at Les Arcs, France. The highest average speed in the Olympic downhill race was 104·53 km/h *64·95 mph* by William D. Johnson (USA) (b. 30 Mar 1960) at Sarajevo, Yugoslavia on 16 Feb 1984. The fastest in a World Cup downhill is 107·82 km/h *67·00 mph* by Harti Weirather (Austria) (b. 25 Jan 1958) at Kitzbühl, Austria on 15 Jan 1982.

Highest speed—cross-country

Bill Koch (USA) (b. 13 Apr 1943) on 26 Mar 1981 skied ten times round a 5 km *3·11 mile* loop on Marlborough Pond, near Putney, Vermont, USA. He completed the 50 km in 1 hr 59 min 47 sec, an average speed of 25·045 km/h *15·57 mph*. A race includes uphill and downhill sections; the record time for a 50 km race in World Championships or Olympic Games is 2 hr 4 min 30·9 sec by Gunde Svan (Sweden) (b. 12 Jan 1962) in 1988, an average speed of 24·09 km/h *14·97 mph*.

Closest verdict

The narrowest winning margin in a championship ski race was one hundredth of a second by Thomas Wassberg (Sweden) over Juha Mieto (Finland) (b. 20 Nov 1949) in the Olympic 15-km cross-country race at Lake Placid, USA on 17 Feb 1980. His winning time was 41 min 57·63 sec.

Highest altitude

Jean Afanassieff and Nicolas Jaeger skied from 8200 m *26 900 ft* to 6200 m *20 340 ft* on the 1978 French expedition on Mt Everest.

Steepest descent

The steepest descents in alpine skiing history have been by Sylvâin Saudan. At the start of his descent from Mont Blanc on the north-east side down the Couloir Gervasutti from 4248 m *13 937 ft* on 17 Oct 1967 he skied to gradients of *c.* 60°.

Longest run

The longest all-downhill ski run in the world is the Weissfluhjoch-Küblis Parsenn course, near Davos, Switzerland, which measures 12·23 km *7·6 miles*. The run from the Aiguille du Midi top of the Chamonix lift (vertical lift 2759 m *9052 ft*) across the Vallée Blanche is 20·9 km *13 miles*.

Most competitors – *Alpine*

1700 downhill skiers competed at Åre, Jämtland, Sweden on 30 Apr 1984.

The most competitors in a skiing competition in Britain are the 450 who took part in the Army Ski Association (Scotland) Championships at Aviemore, Grampian from 29 Feb–5 Mar 1988.

Longest races–*Nordic*

The world's greatest Nordic ski race is the Vasaloppet, which commemorates an event of 1521 when Gustav Vasa (1496–1560), later King Gustavus Eriksson, fled 85·8 km *53·3 miles* from Mora to Sälen, Sweden. He was overtaken by loyal, speedy scouts on skis, who persuaded him to return eastwards to Mora to lead a rebellion and become the king of Sweden. The re-enactment of this return journey is now an annual event at 89 km *55·3 miles*. There were a record 10 934 starters on 6 Mar 1977 and a record 10 633 finishers on 4 Mar 1979. The fastest time is 3 hr 48 min 55 sec by Bengt Hassis (Sweden) on 2 Mar 1986.

The Finlandia Ski Race, 75 km *46·6 miles* from Hämeenlinna to Lahti, on 26 Feb 1984 had a record 13 226 starters and 12 909 finishers.

The longest downhill race is the *Inferno* in Switzerland, 15·8 km *9·8 miles* from the top of the Schilthorn to Lauterbrunnen. The record entry was 1401 in 1981 and the record time 15 min 26·44 sec by Ueli Grossniklaus (Switzerland) in 1987.

Long-distance Nordic

In 24 hours Teuvo Rantanen covered 401·28 km *249·35 miles* at Jyväskylä, Finland on 1–2 Feb 1986. The women's record is 330 km *205·05 miles* by Sisko Kainulaisen at Jyväskylä, Finland on 23–24 Mar 1985.

In 48 hours Bjørn Løkken (Norway) (b. 27 Nov 1937) covered 513·568 km *319 miles 205 yd* on 11–13 Mar 1982.

Longest lift

The longest gondola ski lift is 6239 m *3·88 miles* long at Grindelwald-Männlichen, Switzerland (in two sections, but one gondola). The longest chair lift in the world was the Alpine Way to Kosciusko Chalet lift above Thredbo, near the Snowy Mountains, New South Wales, Australia. It took from 45 to 75 min to ascend the 5·6 km *3·5 miles*, according to the weather. It has now collapsed. The highest is at Chacaltaya, Bolivia, rising to 5029 m *16 500 ft*.

Ski-bob *Origins*

The ski-bob was invented by J. C. Stevenson of Hartford, Connecticut, USA in 1891, and patented (No. 47334) on 19 Apr 1892 as a 'bicycle with ski-runners'.

The *Fédération Internationale de Skibob* was founded on 14 Jan 1961 in Innsbruck, Austria and the first World Championships were held at Bad Hofgastein, Austria in 1967.

The Ski-Bob Association of Great Britain was registered on 23 Aug 1967. The highest speed attained is 166 km/h *103·4 mph* by Erich Brenter (b. 1940) (Austria) at Cervinia, Italy in 1964.

World Championships

The only ski-bobbers to retain a world championship are: men—Alois Fischbauer (Austria) (b. 6 Oct 1951), 1973 and 1975, Robert Mühlberger (West Germany), 1979 and 1981; women—Gerhilde Schiffkorn (Austria)

MOST OLYMPIC TITLES

MEN

ALPINE	3	Anton 'Toni' Sailer (Austria) (b. 17 Nov 1935)	Downhill, slalom, giant slalom, 1956
	3	Jean-Claude Killy (France) (b. 30 Aug 1943)	Downhill, slalom, giant slalom, 1968
NORDIC	4[1]	Sixten Jernberg (Sweden) (b. 6 Feb 1929)	50 km, 1956; 30 km, 1960; 50 km and 4×10 km, 1964

WOMEN

ALPINE	2	Andrea Mead-Lawrence (USA) (b. 19 Apr 1932)	Slalom, giant slalom, 1952
	2	Marielle Goitschel (France) (b. 28 Sept 1945)	Giant slalom, 1964; slalom, 1968
	2	Marie-Thérèse Nadig (Switz) (b. 8 Mar 1954)	Downhill, giant slalom, 1972
	2[2]	Rosi Mittermaier (now Neureuther) (West Germany) (b. 5 Aug 1950)	Downhill, slalom, 1976
	2[3]	Hanni Wenzel (Liechtenstein) (b. 14 Dec 1956)	Giant slalom, slalom 1980
NORDIC	4[4]	Galina Kulakova (USSR) (b. 29 Apr 1942)	5 km, 10 km and 3×5 km relay, 1972; 4×5 km relay, 1976
(individual)	3	Marja-Liisa Hämäläinen (Finland) (b. 10 Aug 1955)	5 km, 10 km and 20 km 1984

[1] ***Most medals*** *9, Sixten Jernberg, four golds, three silver and two bronze and Raisa Smetanina, three gold, five silver and one bronze at women's Nordic skiing 1976–88.*

[2] *Also won silver medal in giant slalom in 1976.*

[3] *Wenzel won a silver in the 1980 downhill and a bronze in the 1976 slalom.*

[4] *Kulakova also won two silver and two bronze medals in 1968, 1976 and 1980.*

(b. 22 Mar 1950), 1967 and 1969, Gertrude Geberth (Austria) (b. 18 Oct 1951), 1971 and 1973.

Snowmobile

A record speed of 239·1 km/h *148·6 mph* was set by Tom Earhart (USA) in a Budweiser-Polaris snowmobile designed and owned by Bob Gaudreau at Lake Mille Lacs, Minnesota, USA on 25 Feb 1982. (*See p.132*).

GRASS SKIING

Grass skis were first manufactured by Josef Kaiser (West Germany) in 1963. World Championships (awarded for Super G, giant slalom, slalom and combined) were first held in 1979. The most titles won is nine by Ingrid Hirschhofer (Austria) to 1987. The most by a man is seven by Erwin Gansner (Switzerland) to 1987.

The speed record is 86·88 km/h *53·99 mph* by Erwin Gansner on 5 Sept 1982; the British record is 79·49 km/h *43·39 mph* by Laurence Beck on 8 Sept 1985, both at Owen, West Germany.

Skipping

MARATHON

The longest recorded skipping marathon (5 min per hour breaks) was one of 22 hr 5 min 2 sec by Randall R. Schneider at State Fair Park, West Allis, Wisconsin, USA on 7 May 1988.

Other records made without a break:

MOST TURNS IN 10 SEC 128 by Albert Rayner (b. 19 Apr 1923), Stanford Sports, Birmingham, England, 19 Nov 1982.

MOST TURNS IN 1 MIN 418 by Tyrone Krohn at Middletown High School, New York, USA, 10 July 1984.

MOST DOUBLES (WITH CROSS) 2411 by Ken Solis (USA) at the North Shore-Elite Fitness and Racquets Club, Glendale, Wisconsin, USA, 29 Mar 1988.

DOUBLE TURNS 10 133 by Katsumi Suzuki, Saitama, Japan, 27 Sept 1979.

TREBLE TURNS 423 by Shozo Hamada, Saitama, Japan, 1 June 1987.

QUADRUPLE TURNS 51 by Katsumi Suzuki, Saitama, Japan, 29 May 1975.

QUINTUPLE TURNS 6 by Hideyuki Tateda (b. 1968), Aomori, Japan, 19 June 1982.

DURATION 2034 km *1264 miles* by Tom Morris, Brisbane-Cairns, Queensland, 1963.

MOST ON SINGLE ROPE (minimum 12 turns obligatory) 181 by a team at the International Rope Skipping Competition, Greeley, Colorado, USA, 28 June 1988.

MOST TURNS ON SINGLE ROPE, TEAM OF 90 160 by students from the Nishigoshi Higashi Elementary School, Kumamoto, Japan, 27 Feb 1987.

ON A TIGHTROPE 58 (consecutive) by Bryan Andro (*né* Dewhurst), TROS TV, the Netherlands, 6 Aug 1981.

MOST TURNS IN 1 HOUR 13 160 Robert Commers (USA) at Connellsville, Pennsylvania, USA, 19 March 1988

Skittles

24 hours

The highest score at West Country skittles by a team of eight is 99 051 by the 'Alkies' Skittles team at Courtlands Holiday Inn, Torquay, Devon on 4–5 Apr 1987; they reset the skittles after every ball. The highest hood skittle score in 24 hr is 118 951 pins by 12 players from the White Hart, Grafton Regis, Northamptonshire on 9–10 April 1986. The highest long alley score is 61 781 by a team of eight from the RAF Digby, Lincolnshire on 16–17 Mar 1988. The highest table skittle score in 24 hr is 90 446 skittles by 12 players at the Finney Gardens Hotel, Hanley, Staffordshire on 27–28 Dec 1980.

Maximum break ● Willie Thorne (b. 4 Mar 1954) achieved one of the more recent 147 breaks in tournament play in the Tennent's UK Open at Preston, Lancashire on 17 Nov 1987. (Photo: All-Sport/Pascal Rondeau)

Snooker

Origins

Research shows that snooker was originated by Colonel Sir Neville Francis Fitzgerald Chamberlain (1856–1944) as a hybrid of 'black pool', 'pyramids' and billiards, in Jubbulpore, India in 1875. It did not reach England until 1885, where the modern scoring system was adopted in 1891. Championships were not instituted until 1916. The World Professional Championship was instituted in 1927.

Skipping marathon ● The longest skipping marathon is 22 hr 5 min 2 sec by Randall R. Schneider (USA) at State Fair Park, West Allis, Wisconsin on 7 May 1988

Most titles *World*

The world professional title (inst 1927) was won a record 15 times by Joe Davis, 1927–40 and 1946. The most wins in the Amateur Championships (inst. 1963) have been two by: Gary Owen (England) in 1963 and 1966; Ray Edmonds (England) 1972 and 1974; and Paul Mifsud (Malta) 1985–6.

Women

Maureen Baynton (*née* Barrett) won a record eight Women's Amateur Championships between 1954 and 1968, as well as seven at billiards.

World Championships *Youngest*

The youngest man to win a world title is Jimmy White (GB) (b. 2 May 1962), who was 18 yr 191 days when he won the World Amateur Snooker Championship in Launceston, Tasmania, Australia on 9 Nov 1980. Stacey Hillyard (GB) won the Women's World Amateur Championship in October 1984 at the age of 15.

The youngest winner of a major title was Stephen Hendry (b. 13 Jan 1969) at 18 yr 285 days, when he won the Rothmans Grand Prix on 25 Oct 1987.

Highest breaks

Over 200 players have achieved the 'maximum' break of 147. The first to do so was E. J. 'Murt' O'Donoghue (b. New Zealand 1901) at Griffiths, NSW, Australia on 26 Sept 1934. The first officially ratified 147 was by Joe Davis against Willie Smith at Leicester Square Hall, London on 22 Jan 1955.

The first maximum achieved in a major tournament was by John Spencer (b. 18 Sept 1935) at Slough, Berkshire on 13 Jan 1979, but the table had oversized pockets. Steve Davis (b. 22 Aug 1957) had a ratified break of 147 against John Spencer in the Lada Classic at Oldham on 11 Jan 1982. The first 147 scored in the World Championships was by Cliff Thorburn (Canada) (b. 16 Jan 1948) against Terry Griffiths at the Crucible Theatre, Sheffield on 23 April 1983, thereby winning a £10 000 jackpot prize. The other 147s in tournament play were by Kirk Stevens (Canada) (b. 17 Aug 1958) in the Benson & Hedges Masters at Wembley, London on 28 Jan 1984, Willie Thorne (b. 4 Mar 1954) in the Tennent's UK Open at Preston, Lancashire on 17 Nov 1987 and Tony Meo (b. 4 Oct 1959) in the Rothmans Matchroom League at Chesterfield, Derbyshire on 20 Feb 1988.

Steve Duggan (b. 10 Apr 1958) made a break of 148 in a witnessed practice frame in Doncaster, South Yorkshire on 27 Apr 1988. The break involved a free ball, which therefore created an 'extra' red, when all fifteen reds were still on the table. In these very exceptional circumstances, the maximum break is 155.

The world amateur record break is 147 by Geet Sethi (India) in the Indian Amateur Championships on 21 Feb 1988. David Taylor (b. 29 July 1943) made three consecutive frame clearances of 130, 140, and 139 at Minehead, Somerset on 1 June 1978. Jim Meadowcroft (b. 15 Dec 1946) made four consecutive frame clearances of 105, 115, 117 and 125 at Connaught Leisure Centre, Worthing on 27 Jan 1982.

The first century break by a woman in competitive play was 114 by Stacey Hillyard in a league match at Bournemouth on 15 Jan 1985.

Softball

Softball, the indoor derivative of baseball, was invented by George Hancock at the Farragut Boat Club of Chicago, Illinois in 1887. Rules were first codified in Minneapolis, Minnesota, USA in 1895 as Kitten Ball. The name Softball was introduced by Walter Hakanson at a meeting of the National Recreation Congress in 1926. The name was adopted throughout the USA in 1930. Rules were formalised in 1933 by the International Joint Rules Committee for Softball and adopted by the Ama-

Speedway

teur Softball Association of America. The International Softball Federation was formed in 1950 as governing body for both fast pitch and slow pitch. It was reorganised in 1965.

Most titles

The USA has won the men's world championship (inst. 1966) four times, 1966, 1968, 1976 (shared), and 1980. The USA won the women's title (inst. 1965) in 1974, 1978 and 1986. The world's first slow-pitch championships for men's teams was held in Oklahoma City, USA in 1987, when the winners were the USA.

Speedway

Motorcycle racing on large dirt track surfaces has been traced back to 1902 in the United States. The first organised 'short track' races were at the West Maitland (New South Wales, Australia) Agricultural Show on 22 Dec 1923, promoted by Johnnie Hoskins (NZ) (1892–1987), who brought the sport to Britain, where it evolved with small diameter track racing at Droylsden, Manchester on 25 June 1927 and a cinder track event at High Beech, Essex on 19 Feb 1928.

British championships

League racing was introduced to British speedway in 1929 and consisted of a Southern League and Northern Dirt Track League, the National League was formulated in 1932 and continued to 1964. The Wembley Lions who won in 1932, 1946–7, 1949–53, had a record eight victories. In 1965 it was replaced by the British League which Belle Vue have won four times, including three times in succession (1970–2). Wimbledon is the only club to have competed every year since 1929 in Southern, National and British Leagues.

In league racing the highest score recorded was when Crayford beat Milton Keynes 76–20 in the then 16-heat formula for the National League on 26 Oct 1982. A maximum possible score was achieved by Bristol when they defeated Glasgow (White City) 70–14 on 7 Oct 1949 in the National League Division Two. The highest number of League points scored by an individual in a season was 516 by Stephen Faulder Lawson (b. 11 Dec 1957) for Glasgow in the National League in 1982. The League career record is 6471 points by Nigel Boocock (b. 17 Sept 1937), 1955–80.

Oxford set a record of 28 successive wins in the British League in 1986.

Belle Vue (Manchester) had a record nine victories (1933–7, 1946–7, 1949 and 1958) in the National Trophy Knock-out Competition (held 1931–64). This was replaced in 1965 by the Knock-Out Cup, which has been won five times by Cradley Heath. The highest recorded score in this competition is 81–25, when Hull beat Sheffield in 1979.

The British League riders Championship was instituted in 1965 and is an annual event contested by the top scorers from each team. Ivan Gerald Mauger (New Zealand) (b. 4 Oct 1939) holds the records for appearances, 15 and points scored, 146, 1965–79. The National League Riders Championship was instituted in 1968. Stephen Lawson has made a record 9 appearances and John Jackson (b. 26 June 1952) has scored a record 67 points.

World championships

The World Speedway Championship was inaugurated at Wembley, London on 10 Sept 1936. The most wins have been six by Ivan Mauger in 1968–70, 1972, 1977 and 1979. Barry Briggs (New Zealand) (b. 30 Dec 1934) made a record 17 consecutive appearances in the finals (1954–70) and won the world title in 1957–8, 1964 and 1966. He also scored a record 201 points in world championship competition from 87 races.

England has most wins in the World Team Cup (inst.

1960) with eight, and the World Pairs Championship (inst. 1968) with seven. Poland uniquely competed in 21 successive World Team Cup finals, 1960–80 and in a 22nd in 1984. The maximum 30 points were scored in the World Pairs Championship by: Jerzy Szczakiel (b. 28 Jan 1949) and Andrzej Wyglenda (Poland) at Rybnik, Poland in 1971; and Arthur Dennis Sigalos (b. 16 Aug 1959) and Robert Benjamin 'Bobby' Schwartz (b. 10 Aug 1956) (USA) at Liverpool, New South Wales, Australia on 11 Dec 1982.

Ivan Mauger also won four World Team Cup, two World Pairs (including one unofficial) and two world long track titles. Ove Fundin (Sweden) (b. 23 May 1933) won twelve world titles: five individual, one Pairs, and six World Team Cup medals in 1956–70. Erik Gundersen (Denmark) (b. 8 Oct 1959) became in 1985 the first man to hold simultaneously world titles at individual, pairs, team and long-track events.

Tests—*maximum points*

The only rider to have scored maximum points in every match of a Test series was Arthur 'Bluey' Wilkinson (b. 27 Aug 1911) in five matches for Australia v. England in Sydney in 1937–8.

Squash Rackets

Although rackets (US spelling racquets) with a soft ball was played in 1817 at Harrow School, Harrow, London, there was no recognised champion of any country until John A. Miskey of Philadelphia won the American Amateur Singles Championship in 1907.

World Championships

Jahangir Khan (b. 10 Dec 1963) (Pakistan) won 6 World Open (inst. 1976) titles, 1981–5 and 1988, and the ISRF world individual title (formerly World Amateur, inst. 1967) in 1979, 1983 and 1985. Geoffrey B. Hunt (b. 11 Mar 1947) (Australia) won four World Open titles, 1976–7 and 1979–80 and three World Amateur, 1967, 1969 and 1971.

Pakistan have won five men's team titles, 1977, 1981, 1983, 1985 and 1987, and Australia have won three women's, 1976, 1981 and 1983.

Most titles *Open Championship*

The most wins in the Open Championship held annually in Britain, is eight by Geoffrey Hunt in 1969, 1974, 1976–81. Jahangir Khan has won seven consecutive titles, 1982–88. Hashim Khan (Pakistan) (b. 1915) won seven times, 1950–5 and 1957, and also won the Vintage title six times in 1978–83.

The most British Open women's titles is 16 by Heather Pamela McKay (*née* Blundell) (Australia) (b. 31 July 1941) from 1961 to 1977. She also won the World Open title in 1976 and 1979.

Amateur Championship

The most wins in the Amateur Championship is six by Abdelfattah Amr Bey (Egypt) (b. 14 Feb 1910), who won in 1931–3 and 1935–7. Norman Francis Borrett (b. 1 Oct 1917) of England won in 1946–50.

Unbeaten sequences

Heather McKay was unbeaten from 1962 to 1980. Jahangir Khan was unbeaten from his loss to Geoff Hunt at the British Open on 10 Apr 1981 until Ross Norman (New Zealand) ended his sequence in the World Open final on 11 Nov 1986.

Longest and shortest championship matches

The longest recorded competitive match was one of 2 hr 45 min when Jahangir Khan beat Gamal Awad (Egypt) (b. 8 Sept 1955) 9–10, 9–5, 9–7, 9–2, the first game lasting a record 1 hr 11 min, in the final of the Patrick International Festival at Chichester, West Sussex, England on 30 Mar 1983. Lucy Soutter beat Hugolein van Hoorn (Netherlands) in just 7½ min (9–0, 9–0, 9–0) in the British

Under-21 Open Championship at Lamb's Squash Club, London on 17 Jan 1988.

Most international appearances

The men's record is 121 by David Gotto (b. 25 Dec 1948) for Ireland. The women's record is 71 by Geraldine Barniville (b. 7 Nov 1942) for Ireland, 1973–83.

Highest speed

In tests at Wimbledon Squash and Badminton Club in January 1988, Ray Buckland (b. 25 March 1953) hit a squash ball by an overhead service at a measured speed of 232·7 km/h *144·6 mph* over the distance to the front wall. This is equivalent to an initial speed at the racket of 242·6 km/h *150·8 mph*.

Largest crowd and tournament

The finals of the ICI 'Perspex' World Team Championships at Royal Albert Hall, London had a record attendance for squash of 3526 on 18 Apr 1988.

The InterCity National Squash Challenge was contested by 9588 players in 1988, a knock-out tournament record.

Surfing

The traditional Polynesian sport of surfing in a canoe (*ehorooe*) was first recorded by Captain James Cook, RN, FRS (1728–79) on his first voyage at Tahiti in December 1771. Surfing on a board (*Amo Amo iluna ka lau oka nalu*) was first described 'most perilous and extraordinary . . . altogether astonishing and is scarcely to be credited' by Lt (later Capt.) James King, RN, FRS in March 1779 at Kealakekua Bay, Hawaii Island. A surfer was first depicted by this voyage's official artist John Webber. The sport was revived at Waikiki by 1900. Hollow boards were introduced in 1929 and the light plastic foam type in 1956.

Most titles

World Amateur Championships were inaugurated in May 1964 at Sydney, Australia. The most titles is three by Michael Novakov (Australia) who won the Kneeboard event in 1982, 1984 and 1986. A World Professional series was started in 1975 and Mark Richards (Australia) has won the men's title five times, 1975 and 1979–82.

Highest waves ridden

Makaha Beach, Hawaii provides the reputedly highest consistently high waves often reaching the ridable limit of 9–10 m *30–35 ft*. The highest wave ever ridden was the *tsunami* of 'perhaps 15·24 m *50 ft*', which struck Minole, Hawaii on 3 Apr 1868, and was ridden to save his life by a Hawaiian named Holua.

Longest ride *Sea wave*

About four to six times each year rideable surfing waves break in Matanchen Bay near San Blas, Nayarit, Mexico which makes rides of *c.* 1700 m *5700 ft* possible.

Longest ride *River bore*

The longest recorded rides on a river bore have been set on the Severn bore, England. The official British Surfing Association record for riding a surfboard in a standing position is 1·3 km *0·8 mile* by Nick Hart (b. 11 Dec 1958) from Lower Rea to Hempsted on 26 Oct 1984. The longest ride on a surfboard standing or lying down is 4·73 km *2·94 miles* by Colin Kerr Wilson (b. 23 June 1954) on 23 May 1982.

Swimming

In Japan, swimming in schools was ordered by Imperial edict of Emperor Go-Yozei (1586–1611) in 1603 but competition was known from 36 BC. Sea-water bathing was fashionable at Scarborough, North Yorkshire as early as 1660. The earliest pool was Pearless Pool, north London, opened in 1743. In Great Britain competitive

World records: women's freestyle ● Janet Evans (USA) (b. 28 Aug 1971) holds the long-course records for 400 m (4:05·45), 800 m (8:17·12) and 1500 m (15:52·10), all set at Orlando, Florida, USA. (Photo: All-Sport/Mike Powell)

swimming originated from at least 1791. Swimming races were particularly popular in the 1820s in Liverpool, where the first pool opened at St George's Pier Head in 1828.

Largest pools

The largest swimming pool in the world is the sea-water Orthlieb Pool in Casablanca, Morocco. It is 480 m *1574 ft* long and 75 m *246 ft* wide, and has an area of 3·6 ha *8·9 acres*. The largest land-locked swimming pool with heated water was the Fleishhacker Pool on Sloat Boulevard, near Great Highway, San Francisco, California, USA. It measured 304·8 × 45·7 m *1000 × 150 ft* and up to 4·26 m *14 ft* deep and contained 28 390 hectolitres *7 500 000 US gal* of heated water. It was opened on 2 May 1925 but has now been abandoned. The greatest spectator accommodation is 13 614 at Osaka, Japan. The largest in use in the United Kingdom is the Royal Commonwealth Pool, Edinburgh, completed in 1970 with 2000 permanent seats, but the covered over and unused pool at Earls Court, London (opened 1937) could seat some 12 000 spectators.

Fastest swimmer

The fastest speed measured in a 50 m pool is by Peter Williams (South Africa) who achieved a speed of 8·12 km/h *5·04 mph* at Indianapolis, USA on 10 April 1988. The women's record is by Yang Wenyi (China), 7·21 km/h *4·48 mph* (see World Record table).

Most world records

Men: 32, Arne Borg (Sweden) (1901–87), 1921–9. Women: 42, Ragnhild Hveger (Denmark) (b. 10 Dec 1920), 1936–42. Under modern conditions (only metric distances in 50 m pools) the most is 26 by Mark Andrew Spitz (USA) (b. 10 Feb 1950), 1967–72, and 23 by Kornelia Ender (GDR) (b. 25 Oct 1958), 1973–6.

Most world titles

In the World Championships (inst 1973) the most medals won is ten by Kornelia Ender with eight gold and two silver in 1973 and 1975. The most by a man is eight by Ambrose 'Rowdy' Gaines (USA) (b. 17 Feb 1959), five gold and three silver, in 1978 and 1982. The most gold medals is six by James Montgomery (USA) (b. 24 Jan 1955) in 1973 and 1975. The most medals at a single championship is seven by Matthew Biondi (USA) (b. 8 Oct 1965), three gold, one silver, three bronze, in 1986.

OLYMPIC RECORDS
Most medals *Men*

The greatest number of Olympic gold medals won is

nine by Mark Spitz (USA): 100 m and 200 m freestyle 1972; 100 m and 200 m butterfly 1972; 4 × 100 m freestyle 1968 and 1972; 4 × 200 m freestyle 1968 and 1972; 4 × 100 m medley 1972. *All but one of these performances (the 4 × 200 m freestyle of 1968) were also new world records.* He also won a silver (100 m butterfly) and a bronze (100 m freestyle) in 1968 for a record eleven medals.

Women

The record number of gold medals won by a woman is four shared by: Patricia McCormick (*née* Keller) (USA) (b. 12 May 1930), the high and springboard diving double in 1952 and 1956 (also the female record for individual golds); Dawn Fraser (Australia) (b. 4 Sept 1937), the 100 m freestyle (1956, 1960 and 1964) and the 4 × 100 m freestyle (1956); and Kornelia Ender (GDR) the 100 and 200 m freestyle, 100 m butterfly and 4 × 100 m medley in 1976. Dawn Fraser is the only swimmer to win the same event on three successive occasions.

The most medals won by a woman is eight by: Dawn Fraser, who in addition to her four golds won four silvers (400 m freestyle 1956, 4 × 100 m freestyle 1960 and 1964, 4 × 100 m medley 1960), Kornelia Ender who in addition to her four golds won four silvers (200 m individual medley 1972, 4 × 100 m medley 1972, 4 × 100 m freestyle 1972 and 1976) and Shirley Babashoff (USA) (b. 3 Jan 1957), who won two golds (4 × 100 m freestyle 1972 and 1976) and six silvers (100 m freestyle 1972, 200 m freestyle 1972 and 1976, 400 m and 800 m freestyle 1976, 4 × 100 m medley 1976).

Most individual gold medals

The record number of individual gold medals won is four by: Charles M. Daniels (USA) (1884–1973) (100 m freestyle 1906 and 1908, 220 yd freestyle 1904, 440 yd freestyle 1904); Roland Matthes (GDR) (b. 17 Nov 1950) with 100 m

Diving: Highest score ● Greg Louganis (USA) (b. 29 Jan 1960) achieved record scores at the 1984 Olympic Games in Los Angeles, with 754·41 points for the 11-dive springboard event and 710·91 for the highboard. At the world championships in Guayaquil, Ecuador in 1984 he was awarded a perfect score of 10·0 by all seven judges for his highboard inward 1 ½ somersault in the pike position. (Photo: All-Sport)

SWIMMING—WORLD RECORDS (set in 50 m pools)
MEN

Event	Time	Name, country and date of birth	Place	Date	
FREESTYLE					
50 metres	22·18	Peter Williams (South Africa) (b. 20 June 1968)	Indianapolis, USA	10 Apr	1988
100 metres	48·74	Matthew Biondi (USA) (b. 8 Oct 1965)	Orlando, Florida, USA	24 June	1986
200 metres	1:47·44	Michael Gross (W. Germany) (b. 17 June 1964)	Los Angeles, California, USA	29 July	1984
400 metres	3:47·38	Artur Wojdat (Poland) (b. 20 May 1968)	Orlando, Florida, USA	25 Mar	1988
800 metres	7:50·64	Vladimir Salnikov (USSR) (b. 21 May 1960)	Moscow, USSR	4 July	1986
1500 metres	14:54·76	Vladimir Salnikov (USSR)	Moscow, USSR	22 Feb	1983
4 × 100 metres relay	3:17·08	United States (Scott McAdam, Michael Heath, Paul Wallace, Matthew Biondi)	Tokyo, Japan	17 Aug	1985
4 × 200 metres relay	7:13·10	W. Germany (Peter Sitt, Rainer Henkel, Thomas Fahrner, Michael Gross)	Strasbourg, France	19 Aug	1987
BREASTSTROKE					
100 metres	1:01·65	Steven Lundquist (USA) (b. 20 Feb 1961)	Los Angeles, California, USA	29 July	1984
200 metres	2:13·34	Victor Davis (Canada) (b. 19 Feb 1964)	Los Angeles, California, USA	2 Aug	1984
BUTTERFLY					
100 metres	52·84	Pedro Pablo Morales (USA) (b. 5 Dec 1964)	Orlando, Florida, USA	23 June	1986
200 metres	1:56·24	Michael Gross (W. Germany)	Hannover, W. Germany	28 June	1986
BACKSTROKE					
100 metres	55·00	Igor Polyanskiy (USSR) (b. 20 Mar 1967)	Moscow, USSR	16 July	1988
200 metres	1:58·14	Igor Polyanskiy (USSR)	Erfurt, GDR	3 Mar	1985
MEDLEY					
200 metres	2:00·56	Tamas Darnyi (Hungary)	Strasbourg, France	23 Aug	1987
400 metres	4:15·42	Tamas Darnyi (Hungary)	Starsbourg, France	19 Aug	1987
4 × 100 metres relay	3:38·28	United States (Richard Carey, John Moffet, Pedro Pablo Morales, Matthew Biondi)	Tokyo, Japan	18 Aug	1985

WOMEN

Event	Time	Name, country and date of birth	Place	Date	
FREESTYLE					
50 metres	24·98	Yang Wenyi (China) (b. 1972)	Guangzhou, China	10 Apr	1988
100 metres	54·73	Kristin Otto (GDR) (b. 7 Feb 1965)	Madrid, Spain (relay first leg)	19 Aug	1986
200 metres	1:57·55	Heike Friedrich (GDR) (b. 18 Apr 1970)	East Berlin, GDR	18 June	1986
400 metres	4:05·45	Janet Evans (USA) (b. 28 Aug 1971)	Orlando, Florida, USA	20 Dec	1987
800 metres	8:17·12	Janet Evans (USA)	Orlando, Florida, USA	22 Mar	1988
1500 metres	15:52·10	Janet Evans (USA)	Orlando, Florida, USA	26 Mar	1988
4 × 100 metres relay	3:40·57	GDR (Kristin Otto, Manuela Stellmach, Sabine Schulze, Heike Friedrich)	Madrid, Spain	19 Aug	1986
4 × 200 metres relay	7:55·47	GDR (Manuela Stellmach, Astrid Strauss, Anke Möhring, Heike Friedrich)	Strasbourg, France	18 Aug	1987
BREASTSTROKE					
100 metres	1:07·91	Silke Hörner (GDR) (b. 12 Sept 1965)	Strasbourg, France	21 Aug	1987
200 metres	2:27·27	Allison Higson (Canada) (b. 13 Mar 1973)	Montreal, Canada	29 May	1988
BUTTERFLY					
100 metres	57·93	Mary T. Meagher (USA) (b. 27 Oct 1964)	Milwaukee, Wisconsin, USA	16 Aug	1981
200 metres	2:05·96	Mary T. Meagher (USA)	Milwaukee, Wisconsin, USA	13 Aug	1981
BACKSTROKE					
100 metres	1:00·59	Ina Kleber (GDR) (b. 29 Sept 1964)	Moscow, USSR	24 Aug	1984
200 metres	2:08·60	Betsy Mitchell (USA) (b. 15 Jan 1966)	Orlando, Florida, USA	27 June	1986
MEDLEY					
200 metres	2:11·73	Ute Geweniger (GDR) (b. 24 Feb 1964)	East Berlin, GDR	4 July	1981
400 metres	4:36·10	Petra Schneider (GDR) (b. 11 Jan 1963)	Guayaquil, Ecuador	1 Aug	1982
4 × 100 metres relay	4:03·69	GDR (Ina Kleber, Sylvia Gerasch, Ines Geissler, Birgit Meineke)	Moscow, USSR	24 Aug	1984

and 200 m backstroke 1968 and 1972; Mark Spitz, and Pat McCormick. The most individual golds by a British swimmer is three by Henry Taylor.

Most medals *British*
The record number of gold medals won by a British swimmer (excluding water polo, *q.v.*) is four by Henry Taylor (1885–1951) in the mile freestyle (1906), 400 m freestyle (1908), 1500 m freestyle (1908) and 4 × 200 m freestyle (1908). Henry Taylor won a record eight medals in all with a silver (400 m freestyle 1906) and three bronzes (4 × 200 m freestyle 1906, 1912, 1920). The most medals by a British woman is four by M. Joyce Cooper (now Badcock) (b. 18 Apr 1909) with one silver (4 × 100 m freestyle 1928) and three bronze (100 m freestyle 1928, 100 m backstroke 1928, 4 × 100 m freestyle 1932).

Closest verdict
The closest verdict in the Olympic Games was in Los Angeles on 29 July 1984, when Nancy Hogshead (b. 17 Apr 1962) and Carrie Steinseifer (b. 12 Feb 1968) (both USA) dead-heated for the women's 100 m freestyle gold medal in 55·92 sec. In the 1972 men's 400 m individual medley Gunnar Larsson (Sweden) (b. 12 May 1951) beat Tim McKee (USA) (b. 14 Mar 1953) by just 2/1000th second, just 3 mm. Now timings are determined only to hundredths.

DIVING
Most Olympic medals *World*
The most medals won by a diver is five (three gold, two silver) by Klaus Dibiasi (b. Austria, 6 Oct 1947) (Italy) in the four Games from 1964 to 1976. He is also the only diver to win the same event (highboard) at three successive Games (1968, 1972 and 1976). Pat McCormick (*see above*) won four gold medals.

British
The highest placing by a Briton has been the silver medal by Beatrice Eileen Armstrong (later Purdy) (1894–1981) in the 1920 highboard event. The best placings by male divers are the bronze medals by Harold Clarke (b. 1888) (plain high diving, 1924) and Brian Phelps (b. 21 Apr 1944) (highboard, 1960).

Most world titles
Greg Louganis (USA) (b. 29 Jan 1960), won a record five world titles, highboard in 1978, and both highboard and springboard in 1982 and 1986, as well as two Olympic gold medals in 1984. Three gold medals at one event have also been won by Phil Boggs (USA) (b. 29 Dec 1949), springboard 1973, 1975 and 1978.

Highest scores
The first diver to be awarded a score of 10·0 by all seven judges was Michael Finneran (b. 21 Sept 1948) in the 1972 US Olympic Trials, in Chicago, Illinois, for a backward 1½ somersault, 2½ twist, from the 10 m board.

CHANNEL SWIMMING
The first to swim the English Channel from shore to shore

BRITISH NATIONAL RECORDS
MEN

Event	Time	Name and date of birth	Place	Date	
FREESTYLE					
50 metres	23·13	Mark Foster (b. 12 May 1970)	Crystal Palace, England	1 Aug	1987
100 metres	50·57	Andrew Jameson (b. 19 Feb 1965)	Orlando, Florida, USA	25 Mar	1988
200 metres	1:51·52	Andrew Astbury (b. 29 Nov 1960)	Brisbane, Australia	2 Oct	1982
400 metres	3:51·93	Kevin Boyd (b. 23 June 1966)	Madrid, Spain	21 Aug	1986
800 metres	8:01·87	Kevin Boyd	Orlando, Florida, USA	26 Mar	1988
1500 metres	15:20·87	Kevin Boyd	Monte Carlo, Monaco	3 June	1988
4×100 metres relay	3:22·76	GB (Andrew Jameson, Mark Foster, Michael Fibbens, Roland Lee)	Strasbourg, France	21 Aug	1987
4×200 metres relay	7:24·78	GB (Neil Cochran, Paul Easter, Paul Howe, Andrew Astbury)	Los Angeles, USA	30 July	1984
BREASTSTROKE					
100 metres	1:01·78	Adrian Moorhouse (b. 24 May 1964)	Orlando, Florida, USA	26 Mar	1988
200 metres	2:15·11	David Andrew Wilkie (b. 8 Mar 1954)	Montreal, Canada	24 July	1976
BUTTERFLY					
100 metres	53·49	Andrew Jameson	Strasbourg, France	19 Aug	1987
200 metres	2:00·21	Philip Hubble (b. 19 July 1960)	Split, Yugoslavia	11 Sept	1981
BACKSTROKE					
100 metres	57·72	Gary Abraham (b. 8 Jan 1959)	Moscow, USSR	24 July	1980
200 metres	2:04·16	John Davey (b. 29 Dec 1964)	Crystal Palace, England	30 July	1987
MEDLEY					
200 metres	2:03·20	Neil Cochran (b. 12 Apr 1965)	Orlando, Florida, USA	25 Mar	1988
400 metres	4:24·20	John Davey (b. 29 Dec 1964)	Crystal Palace, England	31 July	1987
4×100 metres relay	3:42·01	GB (Neil Cochran, Adrian Moorhouse, Andrew Jameson, Roland Lee)	Strasbourg, France	23 Aug	1987

WOMEN

Event	Time	Name and date of birth	Place	Date	
FREESTYLE					
50 metres	26·39	Caroline Cooper (b. 26 May 1966)	Austin, Texas	12 June	1985
100 metres	56·60	June Croft (b. 17 June 1963)	Amersfoort, Netherlands	31 Jan	1982
200 metres	1:59·74	June Croft	Brisbane, Australia	4 Oct	1982
400 metres	4:07·68	Sarah Hardcastle (b. 9 April 1969)	Edinburgh, Scotland	27 July	1986
800 metres	8:24·77	Sarah Hardcastle	Edinburgh, Scotland	29 July	1986
1500 metres	16:43·95	Sarah Hardcastle	Montreal, Canada	18 Apr	1985
4×100 metres relay	3:49·65	England (Caroline Cooper, Nicola Fibbens, Zara Long, Annabelle Cripps)	Edinburgh, Scotland	27 July	1986
4×200 metres relay	8:13·70	England (Annabelle Cripps, Sarah Hardcastle, Karen Mellor, Zara Long)	Edinburgh, Scotland	25 July	1986
BREASTSTROKE					
100 metres	1:10·39	Susannah 'Suki' Brownsdon (b. 16 Oct 1965)	Strasbourg, France	21 Aug	1987
200 metres	2:31·57	Jean Hill (b. 15 July 1964)	Strasbourg, France	19 Aug	1987
BUTTERFLY					
100 metres	1:01·48	Nicola Fibbens (b. 29 Apr 1964)	Los Angeles, USA	2 Aug	1984
200 metres	2:11·97	Samantha Purvis (b. 24 June 1967)	Los Angeles, USA	4 Aug	1984
BACKSTROKE					
100 metres	1:03·61	Beverley Rose (b. 21 Jan 1964)	Los Angeles, USA	31 July	1984
200 metres	2:14·87	Katharine Read (b. 30 June 1969)	Coventry, England	30 May	1986
MEDLEY					
200 metres	2:17·21	Jean Hill	Edinburgh, Scotland	21 July	1986
400 metres	4:46·83	Sharron Davies (b. 1 Nov 1962)	Moscow, USSR	26 July	1980
4×100 metres relay	4:12·24	GB (Helen Jameson, Margaret Kelly, Ann Osgerby, June Croft)	Moscow, USSR	20 July	1980

(without a life jacket) was the Merchant Navy captain Matthew Webb (1848–83) who swam from Dover, England to Calais Sands, France, in 21 hr 45 min from 12.56 p.m. to 10.41 a.m., 24–25 Aug 1875. He swam an estimated 61 km *38 miles* to make the 33 km *21 mile* crossing. Paul Boyton (USA) had swum from Cap Gris-Nez to the South Foreland in his patent life-saving suit in 23 hr 30 min on 28–29 May 1875. There is good evidence that Jean-Marie Saletti, a French soldier, escaped from a British prison hulk off Dover by swimming to Boulogne in July or August 1815. The first crossing from France to England was made by Enrico Tiraboschi, a wealthy Italian living in Argentina, in 16 hr 33 min on 12 Aug 1923, to win the *Daily Sketch* prize of £1000.

The first woman to succeed was Gertrude Caroline Ederle (USA) (b. 23 Oct 1906) who swam from Cap Gris-Nez, France to Deal, England on 6 Aug 1926, in the then overall record time of 14 hr 39 min. The first woman to swim from England to France was Florence Chadwick (USA) (b. 1918) in 16 hr 19 min on 11 Sept 1951. The first

British record: men's 100 m butterfly ● Andrew Jameson (b. 19 Feb 1965) set a long-course record of 53·49 sec. (Photo: All-Sport/Bob Martin)

Englishwoman to succeed was Mercedes Gleitze (later Carey) (1900–81) who swam from France to England in 15 hr 15 min on 7 Oct 1927.

Fastest

The official Channel Swimming Association (founded 1927) record is 7 hr 40 min by Penny Dean (b. 21 Mar 1955) of California, USA, from Shakespeare Beach, Dover to Cap Gris-Nez, France on 29 July 1978.

The fastest crossing by a relay team is 7 hr 17 min, by six Dover lifeguards, from England to France on 9 Aug 1981.

Earliest and latest

The earliest date in the year on which the Channel has been swum is 6 June by Dorothy Perkins (England) (b. 1942) in 1961, and the latest is 28 Oct by Michael Peter Read (GB) (b. 9 June 1941) in 1979.

Youngest and oldest

The youngest conqueror is Marcus Hooper (GB) (b. 14

June 1967) who swam from Dover to Sangatte, France in 14 hr 37 min on 5–6 Aug 1979, when he was aged 12 yr 53 days. The youngest girl is Samantha Claire Druce (GB) (b. 21 Apr 1971) who was 12 yr 119 days on 18 Aug 1983 when she swam from Dover to Cap Gris-Nez in 15 hr 27 min.

The oldest has been Bertram Clifford Batt (b. 22 Dec 1919), of Australia at 68 yrs 241 days when he swam from Cap Gris–Nez to Dover in 18 hr 37 min from 19–20 Aug 1987. The oldest woman was Stella Ada Rosina Taylor (b. 20 Dec 1929) aged 45 yr 350 days when she did the swim in 18 hr 15 min on 26 Aug 1975.

Double crossing

The first double crossing was by Antonio Abertondo (Argentina) (b. 1919), in 43 hr 10 min on 20–22 Sept 1961. Kevin Murphy (b. 1949) completed the first double crossing by a Briton in 35 hr 10 min on 6 Aug 1970. The first swimmer to achieve a crossing both ways was Edward Harry Temme (1904–78) on 5 Aug 1927 and 19 Aug 1934.

The fastest double crossing was in 16 hr 10 min by Philip Rush (New Zealand) (b. 6 Nov 1963) on 17 Aug 1987. In setting this record, Philip Rush completed the fastest ever crossing by a man, 7 hr 55 min and the fastest ever crossing France to England, 8 hr 15 min. He went on to complete the fastest ever triple crossing 28 hr 21 min on 17–18 Aug 1987.

The women's record is 18 hr 15 min by Irene van der Laan (Netherlands) (b. 27 Dec 1960) on 18 Aug 1983. The first British woman to achieve the double crossing was Alison Streeter (b. 29 Aug 1964) in 21 hr 16 min on 4 Aug 1983. The fastest by a relay team is 15 hr 36 ½ min by the six-man West One International Team (GB) on 24 Sept 1985.

Triple crossing

The first triple crossing was by Jon Erikson (USA) (b. 6 Sept 1954) in 38 hr 27 min on 11–12 Aug 1981.

Most conquests

The greatest number of Channel conquests is 31 by Michael Read (GB) from 24 Aug 1969 to 19 Aug 1984, including a record six in one year. The most by a woman

---

is 19 (including five two-way) by Cynthia 'Cindy' M. Nicholas (Canada) (b. 20 Aug 1957) from 29 July 1975 to 14 Sept 1982.

LONG–DISTANCE SWIMMING
Longest swims

The greatest recorded distance ever swum is 2938 km *1826 miles* down the Mississippi, USA between Ford Dam near Minneapolis and Carrollton Ave, New Orleans, Louisiana, by Fred P. Newton, (b. 1903) of Clinton, Oklahoma from 6 July to 29 Dec 1930. He was 742 hr in the water.

The greatest distance covered in a continuous swim is 481·5 km *299 miles* by Ricardo Hoffmann (b. 5 Oct 1941), from Corrientes to Santa Elena, Argentina in the River Parana in 84 hr 37 min on 3–6 Mar 1981.

The longest ocean swim is one of 207·3 km *128·8 miles* by Walter Poenisch Snr (USA) (b. 1914) who started from Havana, Cuba, and arrived at Little Duck Key, Florida, USA (in a shark cage and wearing flippers) 34 hr 15 min later on 11–13 July 1978.

In 1966 Mihir Sen of Calcutta, India uniquely swam the Palk Strait from Sri Lanka to India (in 25 hr 36 min on 5–6 Apr); the Straits of Gibraltar (in 8 hr 1 min on 24 Aug); the length of the Dardanelles (in 13 hr 55 min on 12 Sept); the Bosphorus (in 4 hr on 21 Sept), and the length of the Panama Canal (in 34 hr 15 min on 29–31 Oct).

Irish Channel

The swimming of the 37 km *23 mile* wide North Channel from Donaghadee, Northern Ireland to Portpatrick, Scotland was first accomplished by Tom Blower of Nottingham in 15 hr 26 min in 1947. A record time of 11 hr 21 min was set by Kevin Murphy on 11 Sept 1970. The first Irish-born swimmer to achieve the crossing was Ted Keenan on 11 Aug 1973 in 11–13°C *52–56°F* water in 18 hr 27 min.

Bristol Channel

The first person to achieve a crossing of the Bristol Channel was Kathleen Thomas (now Mrs Day) (b. Apr 1906) who swam from Penarth, South Glamorgan to Weston-super-Mare, Avon in 7 hr 20 min on 5 Sept 1927. The record for the longer swim from Glenthorne Cove, Devon to Porthcawl, Mid-Glamorgan is 10 hr 46 min by Jane Luscombe (b. 13 Jan 1961) of Jersey, CI on 19 Aug 1976.

Lake swims

The fastest time for swimming the 36·5 km *22·7 mile* long

Loch Ness is 9 hr 57 min by David Trevor Morgan (b. 25 Sept 1963) on 31 July 1983. The first successful swim was by Brenda Sherratt (b. 1948) of West Bollington, Cheshire on 26–27 July 1966. David Morgan achieved a unique double crossing of Loch Ness in 23 hr 4 min on 1 Aug 1983. The fastest time for swimming Lake Windermere, 16·9 km *10·5 miles* is 3 hr 49 min 56 sec by Karen Toole, 17, of Darlington on 5 Sept 1981. The fastest time for the Lake Windermere International Championship, 26·5 km *16·5 miles*, is 6 hr 10 min 33 sec by Mary Beth Colpo (USA) (b. 1961) on 5 Aug 1978.

Longest duration

The longest duration swim ever achieved was one of 168 continuous hours, ending on 24 Feb 1941, by the legless Charles Zibbelman, *alias* Zimmy (b. 1894) in a pool in Honolulu, Hawaii, USA. The longest duration swim by a woman was 129 hr 45 min by Vicki Keith (Canada) at the Artillery Pool, Kingston, Ontario, Canada from 5–10 June 1986

24 hours

Evan Barry (Australia) swam 96·7 km *60·08 miles*, in a 50 m pool, at the Valley Pool, Brisbane, Australia on 19–20 Dec 1987. The women's record is 80·82 km *50·22 miles* by Irene van der Laan (Netherlands) at Brussels, Belgium in January 1982.

Greatest lifetime distance

Gustave Brickner (b. 10 Feb 1912) of Charleroi, Pennsylvania, USA in 59 years to November 1986 had recorded 61 977 km *38 512 miles*.

Long–distance relays

The New Zealand national relay team of 20 swimmers swam a record 182·807 km *113·59 miles* in Lower Hutt, New Zealand in 24 hours, passing 160 km *100 miles* in 20 hr 47 min 13 sec on 9–10 Dec 1983. The 24 hours club record by a team of five is 154·93 km *96·27 miles* by the City of Newcastle ASC on 16–17 Dec 1986. A women's team from the club swam 143·11 km *88·93 miles* on the same occasion.

The most participants in a one-day swim relay is 2135, each swimming a length, organised by Syracuse YMCA in Syracuse, New York, USA on 11 Apr 1986. The longest duration swim relay was 216 hr 50 min 16 sec for 601·180km by a team of 20 at Katowice, Poland from 17-26 Feb 1987.

Underwater Swimming

Paul Cryne (UK) and Samir Sawan al Awami of Qatar swam 78·92 km *49·04 miles* in a 24 hr period from Doha, Qatar to Umm Said and back on 21–22 Feb 1985 using sub–aqua equipment. They were swimming underwater for 95·5 per cent of the time.

A relay team of six swam 151·987 km *94·44 miles* in a swimming pool at Olomouc, Czechoslovakia on 17–18 Oct 1987. Tony Boyle, Eddie McGettigan, Laurence Thermes and Gearoid Murphy swam a relay of 535·71 km *332·88 miles* underwater in 168 hr using sub-aqua equipment at the Mosney Holiday Centre, Co. Meath, Ireland, 22–29 June 1985.

The first underwater cross-Channel swim was achieved by Fred Baldasare (b. 1924) (USA), who completed a 67·5 km *42 mile* distance from France to England with scuba equipment in 18 hr 1 min on 10–11 July 1962.

Sponsored swimming

The greatest amount of money collected in a charity swim was £91 552.05 in 'Splash '86' organised by the Royal Bank of Scotland Swimming Club for the 1986 Commonwealth Games Appeal. Held at the Royal Commonwealth Pool, Edinburgh, Scotand on 11–12 Jan 1986, 3559 swimmers took part. The record for an event staged at several pools was £548 006.14 by 'Penguin Swimathon '88' for the Wishing Well Appeal for Great Ormond Street Children's Hospital. It took place at 43 pools throughout London on 26–28 Feb 1988, 5482 swimmers participated.

Mass relay ● The most participants in a swimming relay race is 2000 at the Ibirapuera pool, São Paulo, Brazil on 27 Mar 1988. The photo shows a section of the 40 lanes in which the teams of 50 competed.

Youngest international ● The youngest ever to play for England was Carl Prean (b. 20 Aug 1967), aged 14 yr 191 days, against Portugal at Lisbon on 27 Feb 1982. Here he is in his attic with his collection of trophies and memorabilia. (Photo:All-Sport/Trevor Jones)

Counter hitting

The record number of hits in 60 sec is 170 by English Internationals Alan Cooke (b. 23 Mar 1966) and Desmond Douglas at Scotswood Sports Centre, Newcastle–upon–Tyne on 28 Feb 1986.

The women's record is 168 by the sisters Lisa (b. 9 Mar 1967) and Jackie (b. 9 Sept 1964) Bellinger at Crest Hotel, Luton, Bedfordshire on 14 July 1987. With a bat in each hand, Gary D. Fisher of Olympia, Washington, USA completed 5000 consecutive volleys over the net in 44 min 28 sec on 25 June 1979.

Highest speed

No conclusive measurements have been published but in a lecture M. Sklorz (West Germany) stated that a smashed ball had been measured at speeds up to 170 km/h *105·6 mph.*

Taekwon-Do

The founder and father of this martial art is General Choi Hong Hi 9th Dan, the highest dan awarded. Taekwon-Do was officially recognised as part of Korean tradition and culture on 11 Apr 1955.

The International Taekwon-Do Federation was formed in 1966, and has staged world championships from 1974.

Taekwon-Do is being staged as a demonstration sport at the 1988 Olympic Games.

The highest dan in Britain is Master Rhee Ki Ha 8th Dan, the Chief Instructor of the United Kingdom Taekwon-Do Association.

Table Tennis

The earliest evidence relating to a game resembling table tennis has been found in the catalogues of London sports goods manufacturers in the 1880s. The old Ping Pong Association was formed in 1902 but the game proved only a temporary craze until resuscitated in 1921.

The International Table Tennis Federation was founded in 1926 and the English Table Tennis Association was formed on 24 Apr 1927.

Table Tennis is to be included at the Olympic Games for the first time in 1988.

Most English titles

The highest total of English men's titles (instituted 1921) is 20 by G. Viktor Barna (1911–72) (b. Hungary, Gyözö Braun). The women's record is 17 by Diane Rowe (b. 14 Apr 1933), now Mrs Eberhard Scholer. Her twin Rosalind (now Mrs Cornett) has won nine (two in singles).

The most titles won in the English Closed Championships is 23 by Desmond Douglas (b. 20 July 1955), a record ten men's singles, 1976 and 1979–87, nine men's doubles and four mixed doubles. A record seven women's singles were won by Jill Patricia Hammersley (now Parker, *née* Shirley) (b. 6 Dec 1951) in 1973–6, 1978–9, 1981.

Internationals

The youngest ever international was Joy Foster, aged 8 when she represented Jamaica in the West Indies Championships at Port of Spain, Trinidad in Aug 1958.

Jill Parker played for England on a record 413 occasions, 1967–83.

TABLE TENNIS TITLES

MOST WINS IN WORLD CHAMPIONSHIPS

Event	Name and Nationality	Times	Years
MEN			
Singles (St Bride's Vase)	G. Viktor Barna (Hungary) (1911–72)	5	1930, 1932–5
Doubles	G. Viktor Barna (Hungary)	8	1929–35,1939
Mixed Doubles	Ferenc Sido (Hungary) (b. 1923)	4	1949–50, 1952–3
WOMEN			
Singles (G. Geist Prize)	Angelica Rozeanu (Romania) (b. 15 Oct 1921)	6	1950–5
Doubles	Maria Mednyanszky (Hungary) (1901–79)	7	1928, 1930–5
Mixed Doubles	Maria Mednyanszky (Hungary)	6	1927–8, 1930–1, 1933–4

G. Viktor Barna gained a personal total of 15 world titles, while 18 have been won by Maria Mednyanszky. Note: With the staging of championships biennially the breaking of the above records would now be virtually impossible.

MOST TEAM TITLES

Event	Team	Times	Years
MEN (Swaythling Cup)	Hungary	12	1927–31, 1933–5, 1938, 1949, 1952, 1979
WOMEN (Marcel Corbillon Cup)	Japan	8	1952, 1954, 1957, 1959, 1961, 1963, 1967, 1971
	China	8	1965, 1975, 1977, 1979, 1981, 1983, 1985, 1987

MOST WINS IN ENGLISH OPEN CHAMPIONSHIPS

Event	Name and Nationality	Times	Years
MEN			
Singles	Richard Bergmann (Austria, then GB) (1920–70)	6	1939–40, 1948, 1950, 1952, 1954
Doubles	G. Viktor Barna (Hungary, then GB)	7	1931, 1933–5, 1938–9, 1949
Mixed Doubles	G. Viktor Barna (Hungary, then GB)	8	1933–6, 1938, 1940, 1951, 1953
WOMEN			
Singles	Maria Alexandru (Romania) (b. 1941)	6	1963–4, 1970–2, 1974
Doubles	Diane Rowe (GB) (now Scholer) (b. 14 Apr 1933)	12	1950–6, 1960, 1962–5
Mixed Doubles	Diane Rowe (GB)	4	1952, 1954, 1956, 1960

Tennis (Lawn)

The modern game is generally agreed to have evolved as an outdoor form of the indoor game of tennis (see Tennis [Real]). 'Field tennis' is mentioned in an English magazine—*Sporting Magazine*—of 29 Sept 1793.

The earliest club for such a game, variously called Pelota or Lawn Rackets, was the Leamington Club founded in 1872 by Major Harry Gem.

The earliest attempt to commercialise the game was by Major Walter Clopton Wingfield (1833–1912) who patented a form called 'sphairistike' on 23 Feb 1874. It soon became called lawn tennis. Amateur players were permitted to play with and against professionals in 'open' tournaments in 1968.

Grand Slam

The grand slam is to hold at the same time all four of the world's major championship singles: Wimbledon, the United States, Australian and French championships.

The first man to have won all four was Frederick John Perry (GB) (b. 18 May 1909) when he won the French title in 1935.

The first man to hold all four championships simultaneously was John Donald Budge (USA) (b. 13 June 1915) in 1938, and with Wimbledon and US in 1937, he won six successive grand slam tournaments. The first man to achieve the grand slam twice was Rodney George Laver (Australia) (b. 9 Aug 1938) as an amateur in 1962 and again in 1969 when the titles were open to professionals.

Three women have achieved the grand slam and all won six successive grand slam tournaments: Maureen Catherine Connolly (USA) (1934–69), in 1953; Margaret Jean Court (*née* Smith) (Australia) (b. 16 July 1942) in 1970; and Martina Navratilova (USA) (b. 18 Oct 1956) in 1983–4. Pamela Howard Shriver (USA) (b. 4 July 1962) with Navratilova won eight successive grand slam tournament women's doubles titles and 109 successive matches in all events from April 1983 to July 1985.

The most singles championships won in grand slam tournaments is 24 by Margaret Court (eleven Australian, five French, five USA, three Wimbledon), 1960–73. The men's record is 12 by Roy Emerson (Australia) (b. 3 Nov 1936) (six Australian, two each French, USA, Wimbledon), 1961–7.

The most succesful doubles partnership has been Althea Louise Brough (USA) (b. 11 Mar 1923) and Margaret Evelyn Du Pont (*née* Osborne) (USA) (b. 4 Mar 1918) who won 20 grand slam tournaments, (12 USA, 5 Wimbledon, 3 French), 1942–57.

Fastest service

The fastest service timed with modern equipment is 222 km/h *138 mph* by Steve Denton (USA) (b. 5 Sept 1956) at Beaver Creek, Colorado, USA on 29 July 1984. The fastest *ever* measured was one of 263 km/h *163·6 mph* by William Tatem Tilden (USA) (1893–1953) in 1931.

Longest game

The longest known singles game was one of 37 deuces (80 points) between Anthony Fawcett (Rhodesia) and Keith Glass (GB) in the first round of the Surrey Championships at Surbiton, Surrey on 26 May 1975. It lasted 31 min. Noëlle van Lottum and Sandra Begijn played a game lasting 52 min in the semi-finals of the Dutch Indoor Championships at Ede, Gelderland on 12 Feb 1984.

The longest rally in tournament play was one of 643 times over the net between Vicky Nelson and Jean Hepner at Richmond, Virginia, USA in October 1984. The 6 hr 22 min match was won by Nelson 6–4, 7–6. It concluded with a 1 hr 47 min tiebreak, 13–11, for which one point took 29 minutes.

The longest tiebreak was 26–24 for the fourth and decisive set of a first round men's doubles at the Wimbledon Championships on 1 July 1985. Jan Gunnarsson (Sweden) and Michael Mortensen (Denmark) defeated John Frawley (Australia) and Victor Pecci (Paraguay) 6–3, 6–4, 3–6, 7–6.

Greatest crowd

A record 30 472 people were at the Astrodome, Houston, Texas, USA on 20 Sept 1973, when Billie-Jean King (*née* Moffitt) (USA) (b. 22 Nov 1943) beat Robert Larimore Riggs (USA) (b. 25 Feb 1918). The record for an orthodox tennis match is 25 578 at Sydney, NSW, Australia on 27 Dec 1954 in the Davis Cup Challenge Round (first day) Australia *v.* USA.

Highest earnings

Ivan Lendl (Czechoslovakia) (b. 7 Mar 1960) won a men's season's record $2 028 850 in 1982 and has career earnings of $12·5 million. The season's record for a

Grand slam ● Steffi Graf (West Germany) (b. 14 June 1969) completed the third part of the grand slam when she defeated Martina Navratilova (USA) at Wimbledon on 2 July 1988. She had already succeeded in winning the Australian and French championships earlier in the year. The fourth and final part of the grand slam, the United States championship, had not been completed at the time of going to press. (Photo: Sporting Pictures)

woman is $2 173 556 in 1984 (including a $1 million Grand Slam bonus) by Martina Navratilova. Earnings from special restricted events and team tennis are not included. Navratilova's lifetime earnings by July 1988 reached $13·3 million.

The one-match record is $583 200 by Ivan Lendl (Czechoslovakia) when he beat Pat Cash (Australia) in the final of the four-man Stakes Match tennis exhibition at West Palm Beach, USA on 30 Nov 1987. The highest total prize money was $3 979 294 for the 1987 US Open Championships.

Longest span as national champion
Keith Gledhill (b. 17 Feb 1911) won the US National Boy's Doubles Championship with Sidney Wood in August 1926. Sixty-one years later he won the US National 75 and over Men's Doubles Championship with Elbert Lewis at Goleta, California, USA in August 1987.

Dorothy May Bundy-Cheney (USA) (b. Sept 1916) won 180 US titles at various age groups from 1941 to March 1988.

International contest *Longest span*
Jean Borotra (France) (b. 13 Aug 1898) played in every one of the twice yearly contests between the International Club of France and the I.C. of Great Britain from the first in 1929 to his 100th match at Wimbledon on 1–3 Nov 1985. On that occasion he played a mixed doubles against Kitty Godfree (GB) (b. 7 May 1896). Both were former Wimbledon singles champions, and aged 87 and 89 respectively.

INTERNATIONAL TEAM COMPETITIONS
Davis Cup (inst. 1900)
The most wins in the Davis Cup, the men's international team championship, has been 28 by the USA. The most appearances for Cup winners is eight by Roy Emerson (Australia), 1959–62, 1964–7. The British Isles/Great Britain have won nine times, in 1903–6, 1912, 1933–6.

Nicola Pietrangeli (Italy) (b. 11 Sept 1933) played a record 163 rubbers (66 ties), 1954 to 1972, winning 120. He played 109 singles (winning 78) and 54 doubles (winning 42). The record number of rubbers by a British player is 65 (winning 43) by Michael J. Sangster (b. 9 Sept 1940), 1960–8; the most wins is 45 from 52 rubbers by Fred Perry, including 34 of 38 singles, 1931–6.

Wightman Cup (inst. 1923)
The Wightman Cup has been won 49 times by the United States and 10 times by Great Britain. Virginia Wade (GB) (b. 10 July 1945) played in a record 21 ties and 56 rubbers, 1965–85. Christine Marie Evert (USA) (b. 21 Dec 1954) won all 26 of her singles matches, 1971 to 1985.

Federation Cup (inst. 1963)
The most wins in the Federation Cup, the women's international team championship, is 12 by the USA. Virginia Wade (GB) played each year from 1967 to 1983, in a record 57 ties, playing 100 rubbers, including 56 singles (winning 36) and 44 doubles (winning 30). Chris Evert won her first 29 singles matches, 1977–86. Her overall record, 1977–87 is 35 wins in 37 singles and 16 wins in 18 doubles matches.

WIMBLEDON CHAMPIONSHIPS
Most wins *Women (see above)*
Billie-Jean King (USA) (*née* Moffit) (b. 22 Nov 1943) won a record 20 titles between 1961 and 1979, six singles, ten women's doubles and four mixed doubles. Elizabeth Montague Ryan (USA) (1892–1979) won a record 19 doubles (12 women's, 7 mixed) titles from 1914 to 1934.

Men
The greatest number of titles by a man has been 13 by Hugh Laurence Doherty (GB) (1875–1919) with five singles titles (1902–6) and a record eight men's doubles (1897–1901, 1903–5) partnered by his brother Reginald Frank (1872–1910).

Singles
Helen Newington Moody (*née* Wills) (USA) (b. 6 Oct 1905) won 8 in 1927–30, 1932–3, 1935 and 1938, a record shared with Martina Navratilova, 1978–9, 1982–7. The most men's singles wins since the Challenge Round was abolished in 1922 is five consecutively, by Bjørn Borg (Sweden) in 1976–80. William Charles Renshaw (GB) (1861–1904) won seven singles in 1881–6 and 1889.

Mixed doubles
The male record is four titles shared by: Elias Victor Seixas (USA) (b. 30 Aug 1923) in 1953–6; Kenneth Norman Fletcher (Australia) (b. 15 June 1940) in 1963, 1965–6, 1968; and Owen Keir Davidson (Australia) (b. 4 Oct 1943) in 1967, 1971, 1973–4. The female record is seven by Elizabeth Ryan (USA) from 1919 to 1932.

Most appearances
Arthur William Charles 'Wentworth' Gore (1868–1928) (GB) made a record 36 appearances at Wimbledon between 1888 and 1927. In 1964, Jean Borotra (b. 13 Aug 1898) of France made his 35th appearance since 1922. In 1977 he appeared in the Veterans' Doubles aged 78.

Youngest champions
The youngest champion was Charlotte 'Lottie' Dod (1871–1960), who was 15 yr 285 days when she won in 1887. The youngest male champion was Boris Becker (W. Germany) (b. 22 Nov 1967) who won the men's singles title in 1985 at 17 yr 227 days. The youngest ever player at Wimbledon was reputedly Mita Klima (Austria) who was 13 yr in the 1907 singles competition. The youngest player to win a match at Wimbledon was Kathy Rinaldi (USA) (b. 24 Mar 1967), at 14 yr 91 days on 23 June 1981.

Oldest champions
The oldest champion was Margaret Evelyn du Pont (*née* Osborne) (USA) (b. 4 Mar 1918) at 44 yr 125 days when she won the mixed doubles in 1962 with Neale Fraser (Australia). The oldest singles champion was Arthur Gore (GB) in 1909 at 41 yr 182 days.

Greatest crowd
The record crowd for one day was 39 813 on 26 June 1986. The record for the whole championship was 400 032 in 1986.

UNITED STATES CHAMPIONSHIPS
Most wins
Margaret Evelyn du Pont (*née* Osborne) won a record 25 titles between 1941 and 1960. She won a record 13 women's doubles (12 with Althea Louise Brough), nine mixed doubles and three singles. The men's record is 16 by William Tatem Tilden, including seven men's singles, 1920–5, 1929—a record for singles shared with: Richard Dudley Sears (1861–1943), 1881–7; William A. Larned (1872–1926), 1901–2, 1907–11, and at women's singles by: Molla Mallory (*née* Bjurstedt) (1892–1959), 1915–16, 1918, 1920–2, 1926; and Helen Moody (*née* Wills), 1923–5, 1927–9, 1931.

Youngest and oldest
The youngest champion was Vincent Richards (1903–59), who was 15 yr 139 days when he won the men's doubles with Bill Tilden in 1918. The youngest singles champion was Tracy Ann Austin (b. 12 Dec 1962) who was 16 yr 271 days when she won the women's singles in 1979. The oldest champion was Margaret du Pont who won the mixed doubles at 42 yr 166 days in 1960. The oldest singles champion was William Larned at 38 yr 242 days in 1911.

FRENCH CHAMPIONSHIPS
Most wins (from international status 1925)
Margaret Court won a record 13 titles, five singles, four women's doubles and four mixed doubles, 1962–73. The men's record is nine by Henri Cochet (France) (1901–87), four singles, three men's doubles and two

mixed doubles, 1926–30. The singles record is seven by Chris Evert, 1974–5, 1979–80, 1983, 1985–6. Bjørn Borg won a record six men's singles, 1974–5, 1978–81.

Youngest and oldest
The youngest champions were the 1981 mixed doubles winners, Andrea Jaeger (b. 4 June 1965) at 15 yr 339 days and Jimmy Arias (b. 16 Aug 1964) at 16 yr 296 days. The youngest singles winner was Mats Wilander (Sweden) (b. 22 Aug 1964) at 17 yr 288 days in 1982. The oldest champion was Elizabeth Ryan who won the 1934 women's doubles with Simone Mathieu (France) at 42 yr 88 days. The oldest singles champion was Andres Gimeno in 1972 at 34 yr 301 days.

GRAND PRIX MASTERS
The first Grand Prix Masters Championships were staged in Tokyo, Japan in 1970. They have been held in New York annually from 1977. Qualification to this annual event is by relative success in the preceding year's Grand Prix tournaments. A record five titles have been won by Ivan Lendl, 1982–3, two in 1986 (January and December) and 1987. James Scott Connors (USA) (b. 2 Sept 1952) uniquely qualified for 14 consecutive years, 1972–85. He chose not to play in 1975, 1976 and 1985, and won in 1977. He played again in 1987.

A record seven doubles titles were won by John Patrick McEnroe (b. 16 Feb 1959) and Peter Fleming (b. 21 Jan 1955) (both USA), 1979–85

OLYMPIC GAMES
Tennis is being re-introduced to the Olympic Games in 1988, having originally been included at the Games from 1896 to 1924. It was also a demonstration sport in 1968 and 1984.

A record four gold medals as well as a silver and a bronze, were won by Max Decugis (France) (1882–1978), 1900–20. A women's record five medals (one gold, two silver, two bronze) were achieved by Kitty McKane (later Mrs Godfree) (GB) (b. 7 May 1897) in 1920 and 1924.

Tennis (Real/Royal)

The game originated as *jeu de paume* in French monasteries c. 1050. A tennis court is mentioned in the sale of the Hôtel de Nesle, Paris bought by King Philippe IV of France in 1308. The oldest of the surviving active courts in Great Britain is that at Falkland Palace, Fife, Scotland, built by King James V of Scotland in 1539.

Most titles *World*
The first recorded world tennis champion was Clerge (France) c. 1740. Jacques Edmond Barre (France) (1802–73) held the title for a record 33 yr from 1829 to 1862. Pierre Etchebaster (1893–1980), a Basque, holds the record for the greatest number of successful defences of the title with eight between 1928 and 1952.

The first two Women's World Championships in 1985 and 1987 were won by Judith Anne Clarke (Australia) (b. 28 Dec 1954).

British
The Amateur Championship of the British Isles (inst. 1888) has been won 16 times by Howard Rea Angus (b. 25 June 1944) 1966–80 and 1982. He also won eight Amateur Doubles Championships with David Warburg (1923–1987), 1967–70, 1972–4 and 1976, and was world champion 1976–81.

Tiddlywinks

National Championships
Alan Dean (Edwinstowe, Notts) (b. 22 July 1949) has won the singles title six times, 1971–3, 1976, 1978 and 1986, and the pairs title five times. Jonathan Mapley (b. 1947)

has won the pairs title six times, 1972, 1975, 1977, 1980 and 1983–4.

Potting records

The record for potting 24 winks from 18 in *45 cm* is 21·8 sec by Stephen Williams (Altrincham Grammar School) in May 1966. Allen R. Astles (University of Wales) potted 10 000 winks in 3 hr 51 min 46 sec at Aberystwyth, Cardiganshire, Wales in February 1966.

A record 35 winks were potted in relay in three minutes (24 in two minutes) by Duncan Budd, Tim Hedger, Alex Satchell and Nick Inglis of the Cambridge University Tiddlywinkers Club at Queen's College, Cambridge on 20 July 1987.

Track and Field Athletics

The earliest evidence of organised running was at Memphis, Eygpt *c.* 3800 BC. The earliest accurately dated Olympic Games was in July 776 BC, at which celebration Coroibos won the foot race. The oldest surviving measurements are a long jump of 7·05 m *23 ft 1 ½ in* by Chionis of Sparta in *c.* 656 BC and a discus throw of 100 cubits (about 46·30 m *152 ft*) by Protesilaus.

Fastest speed

The fastest speed recorded in an individual world record is 36·62 km/h *22·76 mph* by Ben Johnson, but this does not allow for the effects of the delay in reaching peak speed from a standing start. An analysis of each 10 m split in the 1987 World Championship final in Rome showed that both Ben Johnson (first in 9·83) and Carl Lewis (second in 9·93) reached a peak speed (50 m–70 m and 80 m–90 m respectively) of 0·85 sec for 10 m, i.e. 42·35 km/h *26·32 mph.*

Highest jump above own head

The greatest height cleared above an athlete's own head is 59 cm *23 ¼ in* by Franklin Jacobs (USA) (b. 31 Dec 1957), who cleared 2·32 m *7 ft 7 ¼ in* at New York, USA, on 27 Jan 1978. He is 1·73 m *5 ft 8 in* tall. The greatest height cleared by a woman above her own head is

WORLD RECORDS *MEN*

World records for the men's events scheduled by the International Amateur Athletic Federation. Fully automatic electric timing is mandatory for events up to 400 metres.

RUNNING

	min sec	Name and country	Place	Date
100 metres	9·83	Ben Johnson (Canada) (b. 30 Dec 1961)	Rome, Italy	30 Aug 1987
200 metres	19·72A	Pietro Mennea (Italy) (b. 28 June 1952)	Mexico City, Mexico	12 Sept 1979
400 metres	43·86A	Lee Edward Evans (USA) (b. 25 Feb 1947)	Mexico City, Mexico	18 Oct 1968
800 metres	1:41·73	Sebastian Newbold Coe (GB) (b. 29 Sept 1956)	Florence, Italy	10 June 1981
1000 metres	2:12·18	Sebastian Newbold Coe (GB)	Oslo, Norway	11 July 1981
1500 metres	3:29·46	Saïd Aouita (Morocco) (b. 2 Nov 1960)	West Berlin, West Germany	23 Aug 1985
1 mile	3:46·32	Steven Cram (GB) (b. 14 Oct 1960)	Oslo, Norway	27 July 1985
2000 metres	4:50·81	Saïd Aouita (Morocco)	Paris, France	16 July 1987
3000 metres	7:32·1	Henry Rono (Kenya) (b. 12 Feb 1952)	Oslo, Norway	27 June 1978
5000 metres	12:58·39	Saïd Aouita (Morocco)	Rome, Italy	22 July 1987
10 000 metres	27:13·81	Fernando Mamede (Portugal) (b. 1 Nov 1951)	Stockholm, Sweden	2 July 1984
20 000 metres	57:24·2	Josephus Hermens (Netherlands) (b. 8 Jan 1950)	Papendal, Netherlands	1 May 1976
25 000 metres	1 hr 13:55·8	Toshihiko Seko (Japan) (b. 15 July 1956)	Christchurch, New Zealand	22 Mar 1981
30 000 metres	1 hr 29:18·8	Toshihiko Seko (Japan)	Christchurch, New Zealand	22 Mar 1981
1 hour	20 944 m *13 miles 24 yd 2 ft*	Josephus Hermens (Netherlands)	Papendal, Netherlands	1 May 1976

A *These records were set at high altitude—Mexico City 2240 m 7349 ft. Best marks at low altitude have been: 200 m: 19·75 sec, Frederick Carlton 'Carl' Lewis (USA) (b. 1 July 1961), Indianapolis, Indiana, USA, 19 June 1983. 400 m: 43·93 sec, Harry Lee 'Butch' Reynolds (USA) (b. 8 Aug 1964), Indianapolis, USA, 20 July 1988.*

HURDLING

		Name and country	Place	Date
110 metres (3' 6" *106 cm*)	12·93	Renaldo Nehemiah (USA) (b. 24 Mar 1959)	Zürich, Switzerland	19 Aug 1981
400 metres (3' 0" *91,4 cm*)	47·02	Edwin Corley Moses (USA) (b. 31 Aug 1955)	Koblenz, West Germany	31 Aug 1983
3000 metres steeplechase	8:05·4	Henry Rono (Kenya)	Seattle, Washington, USA	13 May 1978

RELAYS

		Name and country	Place	Date
4 × 100 metres	37·83	United States National Team: Sam Graddy, Ronald James Brown, Calvin Smith, Frederick Carlton Lewis	Los Angeles, USA	11 Aug 1984
4 × 200 metres	1:20·26†	University of Southern California, USA: Joel Andrews, James Sanford, William Mullins, Clancy Edwards	Tempe, Arizona, USA	27 May 1978
4 × 400 metres	2:56·16A	United States National Team: Vincent Edward Matthews, Ronald J. Freeman, George Lawrence James, Lee Edward Evans	Mexico City, Mexico	20 Oct 1968
4 × 800 metres	7:03·89	Great Britain: Peter Elliott, Garry Peter Cook, Steven Cram, Sebastian Newbold Coe	Crystal Palace, London	30 Aug 1982
4 × 1500 metres	14:38·8	West Germany: Thomas Wessinghage, Harald Hudak, Michael Lederer, Karl Fleschen	Cologne, West Germany	17 Aug 1977

† *Texas Christian University ran 1:20·20 at Philadelphia, Pa, USA on 26 Apr 1986. This time could not be ratified as their team was composed of different nationalities: Roscoe Tatum (USA), Andrew Smith (Jamaica), Leroy Reid (Jamaica), Greg Sholars (USA).*
A *Best result at low altitude: 2:57·29 USA (Danny Everett, Roderick Haley, Antonio McKay, Harry Lee 'Butch' Reynolds) Rome, Italy, 6 Sept 1987.*

FIELD EVENTS

	m	ft in	Name and country	Place	Date
High Jump	2·42	7 11¼	Jan Niklas Patrik Sjöberg (Sweden) (b. 5 Jan 1965)	Stockholm, Sweden	30 June 1987
Pole Vault	6·06	19 10½	Sergey Bubka (USSR) (b. 4 Dec 1963)	Nice, France	10 July 1988
Long Jump	8·90A	29 2	Robert Beamon (USA) (b. 29 Aug 1946)	Mexico City, Mexico	18 Oct 1968
Triple Jump	17·97	58 11	William Augustus 'Willie' Banks (USA) (b. 11 Mar 1956)	Indianapolis, USA	16 June 1985
Shot 7·26 kg *16 lb*	23·06	75 8	Ulf Timmermann (GDR) (b. 1 Nov 1962)	Khania, Greece	22 May 1988
Discus 2 kg *4 lb 6·55 oz*	74·08	243 0	Jürgen Schult (GDR) (b. 11 May 1960)	Neubrandenburg, GDR	6 June 1986
Hammer 7·26 kg *16 lb*	86·74	284 7	Yuriy Georgiyevich Sedykh (USSR) (b. 11 Jun 1955)	Stuttgart, West Germany	30 Aug 1986
Javelin 800 g *28·22 oz*	87·66†	287 7	Jan Zelezný (Czechoslovakia) (b. 16 June 1966)	Nitra, Czechoslovakia	31 May 1987

† *With the new javelin, which has the centre of gravity moved back, introduced in 1986. The best performance with the old javelin was 104·80 m 343 ft 10 in by Uwe Hohn (GDR) (b. 16 July 1962) at East Berlin, GDR on 20 July 1984.*
A *Set at high altitude; the low altitude best: 8·79 m 28 ft 10¼ in, Carl Lewis at Indianapolis, Indiana, USA on 19 June 1983.*

DECATHLON

		Name and country	Place	Date
8847 points		Francis Morgan 'Daley' Thompson (GB) (b. 30 July 1958)	Los Angeles, USA	8–9 Aug 1984

(1st day: 100 m 10·44 sec, Long Jump 8·01 m *26' 3½"*, Shot Put 15·72 m *51' 7"*, High Jump 2·03 m *6' 8"*, 400 m 46·97 sec)   (2nd day: 110 m Hurdles 14·33 sec, Discus 46·56 m *152' 9"*, Pole Vault 5·00 m *16' 4¾"*, Javelin 65·24 m *214' 0"*, 1500 m 4:35·00 sec)

30·5 cm *12 in* by Cindy John Holmes (USA) (b. 29 Aug 1960), 1·525 m *5 ft* tall, who jumped 1·83 m *6 ft* at Provo, Utah, USA on 1 June 1982.

Most Olympic titles *Men*

The most Olympic gold medals won is ten (an absolute Olympic record) by Ray C. Ewry (USA) (1874–1937) in the standing high, long and triple jumps in 1900, 1904, 1906 and 1908.

Women

The most gold medals won by a woman is four shared by: Francina 'Fanny' E. Blankers-Koen (Netherlands) (b. 26 Apr 1918) with 100 m, 200 m, 80 m hurdles and 4 × 100 m relay, 1948; Betty Cuthbert (Australia) (b. 20 Apr 1938) with 100 m, 200 m, 4 × 100 m relay, 1956 and 400 m, 1964; and Bärbel Wöckel (*née* Eckert) (GDR) (b. 21 Mar 1955) with 200 m and 4 × 100 m relay in 1976 and 1980.

Most wins at one Games

The most gold medals at one celebration is five by Paavo Johannes Nurmi (Finland) (1897–1973) in 1924; 1500 m, 5000 m, 10 000 m cross-country, 3000 m team and cross-country team. The most at individual events is four by Alvin C. Kraenzlein (USA) (1876–1928) in 1900: 60 m, 110 m hurdles, 200 m hurdles and long jump.

Most Olympic medals *Men*

The most medals won is 12 (nine gold and three silver)

World record ● Pole vaulter Sergey Bubka (USSR) (b. 4 Dec 1964) cleared an aptly named bar to set a new world record at 6·05 m *19 ft 10¼ in* at Bratislava, Czechoslovakia on 9 June 1988. He improved further to 6·06 m *19 ft 10½ in* at Nice, France on 10 July 1988. He is the only vaulter to have cleared six metres.

by Paavo Nurmi (Finland) in the Games of 1920, 1924 and 1928.

Women

The most medals won by a woman athlete is seven by Shirley de la Hunty (*née* Strickland) (Australia) (b. 18 July 1925) with three gold, one silver and three bronze in the 1948, 1952 and 1956 Games. A recently discovered photo-finish indicates that she finished third, not fourth, in the 1948 200 metres event, thus unofficially increasing her medal haul to eight. Irena Szewinska (*née* Kirszenstein) (Poland) (b. 24 May 1946) won three gold, two silver and two bronze in 1964, 1968, 1972 and 1976, and is the only woman athlete to win a medal in four successive games.

Most Olympic titles *British*

The most gold medals won by a British athlete (excluding tug of war and walking, *q.v.*) is two by: Charles Bennett (1871–1949) (1500 m and 5000 m team, 1900); Alfred Edward Tysoe (1874–1901) (800 m and 5000 m team, 1900); John Rimmer (1879–1962) (4000 m steeplechase and 5000 m team, 1900); Albert George Hill (1889–1969) (800 m and 1500 m, 1920); Douglas Gordon Arthur Lowe (1902–81) (800 m 1924 and 1928); Sebastian Newbold Coe (b. 29 Sept 1956) (1500 m 1980 and 1984) and Francis Morgan 'Daley' Thompson (b. 30 July 1958) (decathlon 1980 and 1984). Daley Thompson was also world champion at the decathlon in 1983.

WORLD RECORDS *WOMEN*

World records for the women's events scheduled by the International Amateur Athletic Federation. The same stipulation about automatically timed events applies in the six events up to 400 metres as in the men's list.

RUNNING

	min sec	Name and country	Place	Date
100 metres	10·49	Florence Griffith-Joyner (USA) (b. 21 Dec 1959)	Indianapolis, USA	16 July 1988
200 metres	21·71	Marita Koch (GDR) (b. 18 Feb 1957)	Karl-Marx-Stadt, GDR	10 June 1979
		Marita Koch (GDR)	Potsdam, GDR	21 July 1984
		Heike Drechsler [*née* Daute] (GDR) (b. 16 Dec 1964)	Jena, GDR	29 June 1986
400 metres	47·60	Marita Koch (GDR)	Canberra, Australia	6 Oct 1985
800 metres	1:53·28	Jarmila Kratochvilova (Czechoslovakia)	Munich, West Germany	26 July 1983
1000 metres	2:30·6	Tatyana Providokhina (USSR) (b. 26 Mar 1953)	Podolsk, USSR	20 Aug 1978
1500 metres	3:52·47	Tatyana Kazankina (USSR) (b. 17 Dec 1951)	Zürich, Switzerland	13 Aug 1980
1 mile	4:16·71	Mary Slaney [*née* Decker] (USA) (b. 4 Aug 1958)	Zürich, Switzerland	21 Aug 1985
2000 metres	5:28·69	Maricica Puica (Rumania) (b. 29 July 1950)	Crystal Palace, London	11 July 1986
3000 metres	8:22·62	Tatyana Kazankina (USSR)	Leningrad, USSR	26 Aug 1984
5000 metres	14:37·33	Ingrid Kristiansen [*née* Christensen] (Norway) (b. 21 Mar 1956)	Stockholm, Sweden	5 Aug 1986
10 000 metres	30:13·74	Ingrid Kristiansen (Norway)	Oslo, Norway	5 July 1986

HURDLING

	min sec	Name and country	Place	Date
100 metres (2′ 9″ *84 cm*)	12·25	Ginka Zagorcheva (Bulgaria) (b. 12 Apr 1958)	Drama, Greece	8 Aug 1987
400 metres (2′ 6″ *76 cm*)	52·94	Marina Styepanova [*née* Makeyeva] (USSR) (b. 1 May 1950)	Tashkent, USSR	17 Sept 1986

RELAYS

	min sec	Name and country	Place	Date
4 × 100 metres	41·37	GDR: Silke Gladisch, Sabine Rieger [now Günther], Ingrid Auerswald [*née* Brestrich], Marlies Göhr [*née* Oelsner]	Canberra, Australia	6 Oct 1985
4 × 200 metres	1:28·15	GDR: Marlies Göhr [*née* Oelsner], Romy Müller [*née* Schneider], Bärbel Wöckel [*née* Eckert], Marita Koch	Jena, GDR	9 Aug 1980
4 × 400 metres	3:15·92	GDR: Gesine Walther, Sabine Busch, Dagmar Rübsam [now Neubauer], Marita Koch	Erfurt, GDR	3 June 1984
4 × 800 metres	7:50·17	USSR: Nadezha Olizarenko [*née* Mushta], Lyubov Gurina, Lyudmila Borisova, Irina Podyalovskaya	Moscow, USSR	4 Aug 1984

FIELD EVENTS

	m	ft in	Name and country	Place	Date
High Jump	2·09	6 10¼	Stefka Kostadinova (Bulgaria) (b. 25 Mar 1965)	Rome, Italy	30 Aug 1987
Long Jump	7·52	24 8¼	Galina Chistyakova (USSR) (b. 26 July 1962)	Leningrad, USSR	11 June 1988
Shot 4 kg *8 lb 13 oz*	22·63	74 3	Natalya Lisovskaya (USSR) (b. 16 July 1962)	Moscow, USSR	7 June 1987
Discus 1 kg *2 lb 3·27 oz*	76·80	252 0	Gabriele Reinsch (GDR) (b. 23 Sept 1963)	Neubrandenburg, GDR	9 July 1988
Javelin 600 g *24·74 oz*	78·90	258 10	Petra Felke (GDR) (b. 30 July 1959)	Leipzig, GDR	29 July 1987

HEPTATHLON

		Name and country	Place	Date
7215 points		Jackie Joyner-Kersee (USA) (b. 3 Mar 1962)	Indianapolis, USA	16–17 July 1988

(100 m hurdles 12·71 sec; High Jump 1·93 m *6 ft 4 in*; Shot 15·65 m *51 ft 4¼ in*; 200 m 22·30 sec; Long Jump 7·00 m *22 ft 11½ in*; Javelin 50·08 m *164 ft 4 in*; 800 m 2 min 20·70 sec)

HIGH JUMP MEN
selected milestones

2.42 metres	Sjöberg (Sweden), 1987	*current world record*
2.39 metres	Zhu Jianhua (China), 1984	
2.34 metres	Yashchenko (USSR), 1978	
	last straddler to set WR	
2.30 metres	Stones (USA), 1973	
	first 'flop' world record	
2.25 metres	Brumel (USSR), 1961	
	straddle	
2.22 metres	Thomas (USA), 1960	
	4 outdoor and 11 indoor bests	
2.15 metres	Dumas (USA), 1956	
	straddle, first 7 ft jump	
	lasted a record 12 years	
2.11 metres	Steers (USA), 1941	
2.09 metres	Walker (USA), 1937	
2.07 metres	Marty (USA), 1934	
2.03 metres	Larsen (USA), 1917	
	unofficial	
2.00 metres	Horine (USA), 1912	
	first to use Western Roll	
1.97 metres	Sweeney (USA), 1895	
	Eastern cut-off technique	
1.93 metres	Byrd Page (USA), 1887	
	Scissors style	
1.90 metres	Davin (Ireland), 1880	
1.83 metres	Brooks (UK), 1876	
	Scissors style, first 6 ft jump	

Most Olympic medals *British*

The most medals won by a British athlete is four by Guy M. Butler (1899–1981) gold for the 4×400 m relay and silver for 400 m in 1920 and bronze for each of these events in 1924, and by Sebastian Coe, who also won silver medals at 800 m in 1980 and 1984. Three British women athletes have won three medals: Dorothy Hyman (b. 9 May 1941) with a silver (100 m, 1960) and two bronze (200 m, 1960 and 4×100 m relay, 1964), Mary Denise Rand (now Toomey, *née* Bignal), (b. 10 Feb 1940) with a gold (long jump), a silver (pentathlon) and a bronze (4×100 m relay), all in 1964 and Kathryn Jane Cook (*née* Smallwood) (b. 3 May 1960), all bronze—at 4×100 m relay 1980 and 1984, and at 400 m in 1984.

Olympic champions *Oldest and youngest*

The oldest athlete to win an Olympic title was Irish-born Patrick J. 'Babe' McDonald (USA) (1878–1954) who was aged 42 yr 26 days when he won the 25.4 kg *56 lb* weight throw at Antwerp, Belgium on 21 Aug 1920. The oldest female champion was Lia Manoliu (Romania) (b. 25 Apr 1932) aged 36 yr 176 days when she won the discus at Mexico City on 18 Oct 1968. The youngest gold medallist was Barbara Pearl Jones (USA) (b. 26 Mar 1937) who at 15 yr 123 days was a member of the winning 4×100 m relay team, at Helsinki, Finland on 27 July 1952. The youngest male champion was Robert Bruce Mathias (USA) (b. 17 Nov 1930) aged 17 yr 263 days when he won the decathlon at the London Games on 5–6 Aug 1948.

The oldest Olympic medallist was Tebbs Lloyd Johnson (1900–84), aged 48 yr 115 days when he was third in the 1948 50 000 m walk. The oldest woman medallist was Dana Zátopkova (b 19 Sept 1922) aged 37 yr 348 days when she was second in the javelin in 1960.

World record breakers *Oldest and youngest*

For the greatest age at which anyone has broken a world record under IAAF jurisdiction *see p.220.* The female record is 36 yr 139 days for Marina Styepanova (*née* Makeyeva) (USSR) (b. 1 May 1950) with 52.94 sec for the 400 m hurdles at Tashkent, USSR on 17 Sept 1986. The youngest individual record breaker is Wang Yang (China) (b. 9 Apr 1971) who set a women's 3000 m walk record at age 14 yr 334 days with 21 min 33.8 sec at Jian, China on 9 Mar 1986. The youngest male is 17 yr 198 days Thomas Ray (1862–1904) when he pole-vaulted 3.42 m *11 ft 2¾ in* on 19 Sept 1879 (prior to IAAF ratification).

Most records in a day

Jesse Owens (1913–80) (USA) set six world records in 45 min at Ann Arbor, Michigan on 25 May 1935 with a 9.4 sec 100 yd at 3.15 p.m., a 8.13 m *26 ft 8¼ in* long jump at 3.25 p.m., a 20.3 sec 220 yd (and 200 m) at 3.45 p.m. and a 22.6 sec 220 yd low hurdles (and 200 m) at 4.00 p.m.

Most national titles *Great Britain*

The greatest number of senior AAA titles (excluding those in tug of war events) won by one athlete is 14 individual and one relay title by Emmanuel McDonald Bailey (Trinidad) (b. 8 Dec 1920), between 1946 and 1953. The most won outdoors in a single event is 13 by Denis Horgan (Ireland) (1871–1922) in the shot put between 1893 and 1912. 13 senior titles were also won by: Michael Anthony Bull (b. 11 Sept 1946) at pole vault, eight indoor and five out, and by Geoffrey Lewis Capes (b. 23 Aug 1949) at shot, six indoor and seven out.

The greatest number of WAAA outdoor titles won by one athlete is 14 by Suzanne Allday (*née* Farmer) (b. 26 Nov 1934) with seven each at shot and discus between 1952 and 1962. She also won two WAAA indoor shot titles. Judith Miriam Oakes (b. 14 Feb 1958) at the shot won seven WAAA outdoor, ten WAAA indoor and six UK titles, 1977–88.

Most international appearances

The greatest number of international matches contested for any nation is 89 by shot-putter Bjørn Bang Andersen (b. 14 Nov 1937) for Norway, 1960–81.

The greatest number of full Great Britain international appearances (outdoors and indoors) is 73 by Verona Marolin Elder (*née* Bernard) (b. 5 Apr 1953), mostly at 400 m, from 1971 to 1983. The men's record is 67 by shot-putter Geoff Capes, 1969–80. At pole vault and decathalon Mike Bull had 66 full internationals or 69 including the European Indoor Games, before these were official internationals. The most outdoors is 61 by hammer thrower Andrew Howard Payne (b. South Africa, 17 Apr 1931) from 1960 to 1974.

Oldest and youngest internationals

The oldest full Great Britain international was Hector Harold Whitlock (1903–85) at 50 km walk at the 1952 Olympic Games, aged 48 yr 218 days. The oldest woman was Christine Rosemary Payne (*née* Charters) (b. 19 May 1933) at discus in the Great Britain *v.* Finland match on 26 Sept 1974, aged 41 yr 130 days. The youngest man was high jumper Ross Hepburn (b. 14 Oct 1961) *v.* the USSR on 26 Aug 1977, aged 15 yr 316 days, and the youngest woman was Janis Walsh (b. 28 Mar 1960) *v.* Belgium (indoor) at 60 m and 4 × 200 m relay on 15 Feb 1975, aged 14 yr 324 days.

Longest career

Duncan McLean (1884–1980) of Scotland set a world age (92) record of 100 m in 21·7 sec in August 1977, over 73 years after his best ever sprint of 100 yd in 9·9 sec in South Africa in February 1904.

Longest winning sequence

Iolanda Balas (Romania) (b. 12 Dec 1936) won a record 140 consecutive competitions at high jump from 1956 to 1967. The record at a track event was 122 at 400 m

hurdles by Edwin Corley Moses (USA) (b. 31 July 1955) between his loss to Harold Schmid (West Germany) (b. 29 Sept 1957) at Berlin on 26 Aug 1977 and that to Danny Harris (USA) (b. 7 Sept 1965) at Madrid on 4 June 1987.

London to Brighton race

Ian Thompson (b. 16 Oct 1949) (Luton United H) won the 87·4 km *54·3 miles* race (inst. 1951) in 5 hr 15 min 15 sec on 28 Sept 1980, averaging 16·62 km/h *10·33 mph.* The most wins is four by Bernard Gomersall (b. 28 Aug 1932) in 1963–6. The women's record is 6 hr 37 min 8 sec by Ann Franklin (b. 26 Apr 1951) on 25 Sept 1983.

'End to end'

The fastest confirmed run from John o'Groats to Land's End is 12 days 1 hr 59 min by Kenneth John Craig (S. Africa) (b. 27 Nov 1935) from 29 Aug–10 Sept 1984. A faster 10 days 3 hr 30 min was claimed by Fred Hicks (GB) for 1410 km *876 miles* on 20–30 May 1977. The fastest by a women is 13 days 17 hr 42 min by walker Ann Sayer (see Walking). A relay team of 10 from Aberdeen A. A. C. covered the distance in 77 hr 26 min 18 sec from 3–6 Apr 1982.

Longest non-stop run

Bertil Järläker (Sweden) (b. 1936) ran 568 km *352·9 miles* in 121 hr 54 min at Norrköping, Sweden, 26–31 May 1980. He was moving for 95·04 per cent of the time.

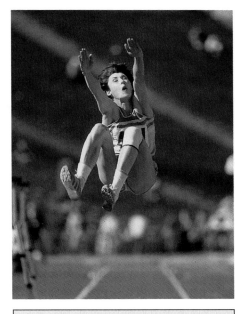

World record: women's long jump ● Galina Chistyakova (USSR) (b. 26 July 1962) set a record for the long jump of 7·52 m *24 ft 8 ¼ in* at Leningrad, USSR on 11 June 1988. (Photo: All-Sport/Gray Mortimore)

HIGH JUMP WOMEN
selected milestones

current world record	Kostadinova (Bul), 1987 / 1987	**2.09 metres**
	Andonova (Bulgaria), 1984	**2.07 metres**
10 years after her first WR	Meyfarth, 1982	**2.02 metres**
	Ackermann (GDR), 1977	**2.00 metres**
first over 2m, her 7th WR		
first 'flop' world record	Meyfarth (W. Germany), 1972	**1.92 metres**
	Balas, 1961	**1.91 metres**
lasted a record 10 years		
	Balas (Romania), 1958	**1.83 metres**
	Cheng Feng-jung (China), 1957	**1.77 metres**
Western Roll		
	Blankers-Koen (Hol), 1943	**1.71 metres**
scissors style		

Artwork: Rhoda and Robert Burns

Longest running race

The longest races ever staged were the 1928 (5507 km *3422 miles*) and 1929 (5898 km *3665 miles*) transcontinental races from New York City, NY to Los Angeles, California, USA. The Finnish-born Johnny Salo (1893–1931) was the winner in 1929 in 79 days, from 31 Mar to 18 June. His elapsed time of 525 hr 57 min 20 sec (averaging 11·21 km/h *6·97 mph*) left him only 2 min 47 sec ahead of Englishman Pietro 'Peter' Gavuzzi (1905–81).

The longest race staged annually is Australia's Westfield Run from Paramatta, New South Wales to Doncaster, Victoria (Sydney to Melbourne). The distance run has varied slightly, but the record is by Yiannis Kouros (Greece) (b. 13 Feb 1956) in 5 days 14 hr 47 min in 1987, when the distance was 1060 km *658 miles* .

Longest runs

The longest ever solo run is 17 072 km *10 608 miles* by Robert J. Sweetgall (USA) (b. 8 Dec 1947) around the perimeter of the USA starting and finishing in Washington, DC, 9 Oct 1982–15 July 1983. Ron Grant (Australia) (b. 15 Feb 1943) ran around Australia, 13 383 km *8316 miles* in 217 days 3 hr 45 min, running every day from 28 Mar to 31 Oct 1983. Max Telford (NZ) (b. Hawick, Scotland, 2 Feb 1935) ran 8224 km *5110 miles* from Anchorage, Alaska to Halifax, Nova Scotia, in 106 days 18 hr 45 min from 25 July to 9 Nov 1977.

The fastest time for the cross-America run is 46 days 8 hr 36 min by Frank Giannino Jr (USA) (b. 1952) for the 4989 km *3100 miles* from San Francisco to New York from 1 Sept–17 Oct 1980. The women's trans-America record is 69 days 2 hours 40 min by Mavis Hutchison (South Africa) (b. 25 Nov 1924) from 12 Mar–21 May 1978.

Greatest mileage

Douglas Alistair Gordon Pirie (GB) (b. 10 Feb 1931), who set five world records in the 1950s, estimated that he had run a total distance of 347 600 km *216 000 miles* in 40 years to 1981.

Dr. Ron Hill (b. 21 Sept 1938), the 1969 European and 1970 Commonwealth marathon champion, has not missed a day's training since 20 Dec 1964. Since then he has run twice a day, except once on Sundays and 23 Dec 1964. His meticulously compiled training log shows a total of 186 931 km *116 157 miles* from 3 Sept 1956 to 14 July 1988. He has finished 111 marathons, all sub 2:52 and has raced in 49 nations.

The greatest competitive distance run in a year is 8855 km *5502 miles* by Malcolm Campbell (GB) (b. 17 Nov 1934) in 1985.

Mass relay records

The record for 100 miles *160·9 km* by 100 runners from one club is 7 hr 53 min 52·1 sec by Baltimore Road Runners Club, Towson, Maryland, USA on 17 May 1981. The women's record is 10 hr 47 min 9·3 sec on 3 Apr 1977 by the San Francisco Dolphins Southend Running Club, USA.

The longest relay ever run was 16 936 km *10 524 miles* by 2660 runners at Trondheim, Norway from 26 Aug–20 Oct 1985. Twenty members of the Melbourne Fire Brigade ran 15 059 km *9357 miles* around Australia on Highway No. 1 in 43 days 23 hr 58 min, 10 July–23 Aug 1983. The most participants is 4800, 192 teams of 25, in the Batavierenrace, 167·2 km *103·89 miles* from Nijmegan to Enschede, Netherlands on 23 Apr 1983. The greatest distance covered in 24 hr by a team of ten is 425·595 km *264·459 miles* by Gerrit Maritz High School at Johannesburg, South Africa on 28–9 Aug 1987.

Highland Games

The weight and height of cabers (Gaelic *cabar*) vary considerably. Extreme values are 7·62 m *25 ft* and 127 kg *280 lb*. The Braemar caber (5·86 m *19 ft 3 in* and 54·4 kg *120 lb*) in Grampian, Scotland was untossed from 1891 until 1951 when it was tossed by George Clark (1907–86). The best authentic mark recorded for throwing the 56 lb

World records ▲ Florence Griffith-Joyner (USA) (b. 21 Dec 1959) ran the fastest women's 100 m, 10·49 sec, during the US Olympic trials at Indianapolis on 16 July 1988. ▼ On the same occasion, her sister-in-law, Jackie Joyner-Kersee (USA) (b. 3 Mar 1962), set a new heptathlon record of 7215 points, 16–17 July 1988. Here she prepares to put the shot, the third of the seven disciplines. (Photos: All-Sport/Tony Duffy)

World record: women's marathon ● Ingrid Kristiansen (*née* Christensen) (Norway) (b.21 Mar 1955) is seen here on the course of the 1985 London Marathon on 21 April 1985. It was on this occasion that she set a world record for the marathon completing the course in 2 hr 21 min 6 sec. (Photo: All-Sport/Mike King)

weight for height, using one hand only is 5·23 m *17 ft 2 in* by Geoffrey Lewis Capes (GB) (b. 23 Aug 1949) at Lagos, Nigeria on 5 Dec 1982. The best throw recorded for the Scots hammer is 46·08 m *151 ft 2 in* by William Anderson (b. 6 Oct 1938) at Lochearnhead on 26 July 1969.

Backwards running

Anthony 'Scott' Weiland, 27, ran the Detroit marathon backwards in 4 hr 7 min 54 sec on 13 Oct 1982. Donald Davis (USA) (b. 10 Feb 1960) ran 1 mile backwards in 6 min 7·1 sec at the University of Hawaii on 21 Feb 1983. Ferdie Adoboe (USA) ran 100 yd backwards in 12·8 sec (100 m in 14·0 sec) at Amherst, Mass, USA on 28 July 1983.

Arvind Pandya of India ran backwards across America, Los Angeles to New York, in 107 days, 18 Aug–3 Dec 1984. He also ran backwards from John O'Groats to Land's End, 1416·2 km *880 miles* in 29 days 5 hr 39 min, 2–31 Oct 1985.

MARATHON

The marathon is run over a distance of 42·195 km *26 miles 385 yd*. This distance was that used for the race at the 1908 Olympic Games, run from Windsor to the White City stadium, and which became standard from 1924. The marathon (of 40 km) was introduced to the 1896 Olympic Games to commemorate the legendary run of Pheidippides (or Philippides) from the battlefield of Marathon to Athens in 490 BC. The 1896 Olympic marathon was preceded by trial races that year. The first Boston marathon, the world's longest-lasting major marathon, was held on 19 Apr 1897 at 39 km *24 miles 1232 yd* and the first national marathon championship was that of Norway in 1897.

It is only in the past decade that marathon running by women has become widespread, following the pioneering efforts, particularly in the USA, of some determined women who had quite a struggle to overcome prejudices against their participation. The first championship marathon for women was organised by the Road Runners Club of America on 27 Sept 1970.

WORLD INDOOR RECORDS

From 1 Jan 1987, the International Amateur Athletics Federation recognised world indoor records. The best performances made before that date have been noted as world bests, and world records must better these to be officially accepted. Track performances around a turn must be made on a track no longer than 200 metres.

MEN

RUNNING	min:sec	Name and country	Place	Date	
50 metres	5·55	Ben Johnson (Canada) (b. 30 Dec 1961)	Ottawa, Canada	31 Jan	1987
60 metres	6·41	Ben Johnson (Canada)	Indianapolis, USA	7 Mar	1987
200 metres	20·36	Bruno Marie-Rose (France) (b.20 May 1965)	Lievin, France	22 Feb	1987
400 metres	45·41	Thomas Schönlebe (GDR) (b. 6 Aug 1965)	Vienna, Austria	9 Feb	1986
800 metres	1:44·91	Sebastian Coe (GB) (b. 29 Sept 1956)	Cosford, Shropshire	12 Mar	1983
1000 metres	2:16·62	Robert Druppers (Holland) (b. 1964)	The Hague, Holland	20 Feb	1988
1500 metres	3:35·82	José Luis Gonzalez (Spain) (b. 8 Dec 1957)	Oviedo, Spain	3 Jan	1986
	3:35·4 u	Marcus O'Sullivan (Ireland) (b. 22 Dec 1961)	East Rutherford, New Jersey, USA	13 Feb	1988
1 mile	3:49·78	Eamonn Coghlan (Ireland) (b. 21 Nov 1952)	East Rutherford, USA	27 Feb	1983
2000 metres	4:54·07	Eamonn Coghlan (Ireland)	Inglewood, California, USA	21 Feb	1987
3000 metres	7:39·2	Emiel Puttemans (Belgium) (b. 8 Oct 1947)	West Berlin	18 Feb	1973
5000 metres	13:20·4	Suleiman Nyambui (Tanzania) (b. 13 Feb 1953)	New York, USA	6 Feb	1986
50 metres hurdles	6·25	Mark McKoy (Canada) (b. 10 Dec 1961)	Kobe, Japan	5 Mar	1986
60 metres hurdles	7·46	Greg Foster (USA) (b. 4 Aug 1958)	Indianapolis, USA	6 Mar	1987

RELAYS

	min:sec		Place	Date	
4 × 200 metres	1:22·32	Italy	Turin, Italy	11 Feb	1984
		(Pierfrancesco Pavoni, Stefano Tilli, Giovanni Bongiorni, Carlo Simionato)			
4 × 400 metres	3:05·9 *	USSR	Vienna, Austria	14 Mar	1970
		(Yevgeniy Borisenko, Yuriy Zorin, Boris Savchuk, Aleksandr Bratchikov)			
	3:06·01	USA	Cosford, Shropshire	15 Mar	1987
		(Walter McCoy, Chip Jenkins, Ken Lowery, Clarence Daniel)			
4 × 800 metres	7:17·8	USSR	Sofia, Bulgaria	14 Mar	1971
		(Valentin Tartynov, Stanislav Mesherskikh, Aleksey Taranov, Viktor Semyashkin)			

WALKING

	min:sec		Place	Date	
5000 metres	18:11·41	Roland Weigel (GDR) (b. 8 Aug 1959)	Vienna, Austria	13 Feb	1988

FIELD EVENTS

	m	ft in		Place	Date	
High Jump	2·42	7 11¼	Carlo Thränhardt (West Germany)	West Berlin	26 Feb	1988
Pole Vault	5·97	19 7	Sergey Bubka (USSR) (b. 4 Dec 1963)	Turin, Italy	17 Mar	1987
Long Jump	8·79	28 10	Carl Lewis (USA) (b. 1 July 1961)	New York, USA	27 Feb	1984
Triple Jump	17·76	58 3¼	Mike Conley (USA) (b. 5 Oct 1962)	New York, USA	27 Feb	1987
Shot	22·26	73 0½	Werner Günthör (Switzerland) (b. 1 June 1961)	Magglingen, Switzerland	8 Feb	1987

WOMEN

RUNNING	min:sec	Name and Country	Place	Date	
50 metres	6·06	Angella Issajenko (Canada) (b. 28 Sept 1958)	Ottawa, Canada	31 Jan	1987
60 metres	7·00	Nelli Cooman-Fiere (Holland) (b. 6 June 1964)	Madrid, Spain	23 Feb	1986
200 metres	22·27	Heike Dreschler (GDR) (b. 16 Dec 1964)	Indianapolis, USA	7 Mar	1987
400 metres	49·59	Jarmila Kratochvilova (Czechoslovakia) (b. 26 Jan 1955)	Milan, Italy	7 Mar	1982
800 metres	1:56·40	Christine Wachtel (GDR) (b. 6 Jan 1965)	Vienna, Austria	13 Feb	1988
1000 metres	2:34·8	Brigitte Kraus (GDR) (b. 12 Aug 1956)	Dortmund, West Germany	19 Feb	1978
1500 metres	4:00·8	Mary Decker-Slaney (USA) (b. 4 Aug 1958)	New York, USA	8 Feb	1980
1 mile	4:18·86	Doina Melinte (Romania) (b. 27 Dec 1956)	East Rutherford, USA	13 Feb	1988
3000 metres	8:39·79	Zola Budd (GB) (b. 26 May 1966)	Cosford, Shropshire	8 Feb	1986
5000 metres	15:25·02	Brenda Webb (USA) (b. 30 May 1954)	Gainesville, Florida, USA	30 Jan	1988
50 metres hurdles	6·58	Cornelia Oschekenat (GDR) (b. 29 Oct 1961)	Berlin, GDR	21 Feb	1988
60 metres hurdles	7·74	Yordanka Donkova (Bulgaria) (b. 28 Sept 1961)	Sofia, Bulgaria	14 Feb	1987

RELAYS

	min:sec		Place	Date	
4 × 200 metres	1:32·55	S. C. Eintracht Hamm (West Germany)	Dortmund, West Germany	19 Feb	1988
		(Helga Arendt, Silke Knoll, Mechthild Kluth, Gisela Kinzel)			
4 × 400 metres	3:34·38	West Germany	Dortmund, West Germany	30 Jan	1981
		(Heide-Elke Gaugel, Christina Sussiek, Christiane Brinkmann, Gaby Bussmann)			
4 × 800 metres	8:24·72	Villanova University (USA)	Oklahoma City, USA	14 Mar	1987
		(Gina Procaccio, Debbie Grant, Michelle DiMuro, Celeste Halliday)			

WALKING

	min:sec		Place	Date	
3000 metres	12:05·49	Olga Krishtop (USSR) (b. 8 Oct 1957)	Indianapolis, USA	6 Mar	1987

u *not officially recognised.* * *hand timed.*

FIELD EVENTS

	m	ft in		Place	Date	
High jump	2·06	6 9¼	Stefka Kostadinova (Bulgaria) (b. 25 Nov 1965)	Piraeus, Greece	20 Feb	1988
Long jump	7·37	24 2¼	Heike Dreschler (GDR) (b. 16 Dec 1964)	Vienna, Austria	13 Feb	1988
Shot	22·50	73 9¾	Helena Fibingerova (Czechoslovakia) (b. 13 July 1959)	Jablonec, Czechoslovakia	19 Feb	1988

Fastest

There are as yet no official records for the marathon, and it should be noted that courses may vary in severity. The following are the best times recorded, all on courses whose distance has been verified.

The world records are: (men) 2 hr 6 min 50 sec by Belayneh Dinsamo (Ethiopia) (b. 1965) at Rotterdam, Netherlands on 17 Apr 1988 and (women) 2 hr 21 min 6 sec by Ingrid Kristiansen (*née* Christensen) (Norway) (b. 21 Mar 1956) at London on 21 Apr 1985. The British records are: (men) 2 hr 7 min 13 sec by Stephen Henry Jones (b. 4 Aug 1955) at Chicago, Illinois, USA on 20 Oct 1985 and (women) 2 hr 26 min 51 sec by Priscilla Welch (b. 22 Nov 1944) at London on 10 May 1987.

Most competitors

The record number of confirmed finishers in a marathon is 21 141 (from 22 523 starters) in the New York marathon on 1 Nov 1987. A record 93 men ran under 2 hr 20 min and 29 under 2 hr 15 min at London in 1983, and a record 6 men ran under 2 hr 10 min at Fukuoka, Japan on 4 Dec 1983. A record 9 women ran under 2 hr 30 min in the first Olympic marathon for women at Los Angeles, USA on 5 Aug 1984.

Three in three days

The fastest combined time for three marathons in three days is 8 hr 22 min 31 sec by Raymond Hubbard, (Belfast 2 hr 45 min 55 sec, London 2 hr 48 min 45 sec and Boston 2 hr 47 min 51 sec) on 16–18 Apr 1988.

Highest altitude

The highest start to a marathon was one run in the

United Kingdom (National) Records *Men*

RUNNING	min sec	Name	Place	Date	
100 metres	10·03	Linford Christie (b. 10 Apr 1960)	Budapest, Hungary	4 July	1987
200 metres	20·18	John Paul Lyndon Regis (b. 13 Oct 1966)	Rome, Italy	3 Sept	1987
400 metres	44·50	Derek Antony Redmond (b. 3 Sept 1965)	Rome, Italy	1 Sept	1987
800 metres	1:41·73	Sebastian Newbold Coe (b. 29 Sept 1956)	Florence, Italy	10 June	1981
1000 metres	2:12·18	Sebastian Newbold Coe	Oslo, Norway	11 July	1981
1500 metres	3:29·67	Steven Cram (b. 14 Oct 1960)	Nice, France	16 July	1985
1 mile	3:46·32	Steven Cram	Oslo, Norway	27 July	1985
2000 metres	4:51·39	Steven Cram	Budapest, Hungary	4 Aug	1985
3000 metres	7:32·79	David Robert Moorcroft (b. 10 Apr 1953)	London (Crystal Palace)	17 July	1982
5000 metres	13:00·41	David Robert Moorcroft	Oslo, Norway	7 July	1982
10 000 metres	27:23·06	Eamonn Thomas Martin (b. 9 Oct 1958)	Oslo, Norway	2 July	1988
20 000 metres	58:39·0	Ronald Hill (b. 25 Sept 1938)	Leicester	9 Nov	1968
25 000 metres	1 hr 15:22·6	Ronald Hill	Bolton, Lancashire	21 July	1965
30 000 metres	1 hr 31:30·4	James Noel Carroll Alder (b. 10 June 1940)	London (Crystal Palace)	5 Sept	1970
1 hour	12 miles 1268 yd *20 472m.*	Ronald Hill	Leicester	9 Nov	1968

HURDLING

	min sec	Name	Place	Date	
110 metres	13·23	Colin Ray Jackson (b. 18 Feb 1967)	Belfast	27 June	1988
400 metres	48·12	David Peter Hemery (b. 18 July 1944)	Mexico City, Mexico	15 Oct	1968
3000 metres Steeplechase	8:12·11	Colin Robert Reitz (b. 5 April 1960)	Brussels, Belgium	5 Sept	1987

RELAYS

	min sec	Name	Place	Date	
4×100 metres	38·62	United Kingdom: Michael Anthony McFarlane, Allan Wipper Wells, Robert Cameron Sharp, Andrew Emlyn McMaster	Moscow, USSR	1 Aug	1980
4×200 metres	1:22·42	UK 'B': Adeoye Mafe, Philip Goedluck, Donovan Reid, John Regis	Gateshead	16 July	1988
4×400 metres	2:58·86	United Kingdom: Kriss Akabusi, Derek Redmond, Todd Bennett, Phil Brown	Rome, Italy	6 Sept	1987
4×800 metres	7:03·89	United Kingdom: Peter Elliott, Gary Peter Cook, Steven Cram, Sebastian Newbold Coe	London (Crystal Palace)	30 Aug	1982
4×1500 metres	14:56·8	United Kingdom: Alan David Mottershead. Geoffrey Michael Cooper, Stephen John Emson, Roy Wood	Bourges, France	24 June	1979

FIELD EVENTS	m	ft	in	Name	Place	Date	
High Jump	2·29*	7	6	Dalton Grant (b. 8 Apr 1966)	Portsmouth, Hampshire	19 June	1988
Pole Vault	5·65	18	6½	Keith Frank Stock (b. 18 Mar 1957)	Oslo, Norway	7 July	1981
Long Jump	8·23	27	0	Lynn Davies (b. 20 May 1942)	Bern, Switzerland	30 June	1968
Triple Jump	17·57	57	7¾	Keith Leroy Connor (b. 16 Sept 1957)	Provo, Utah, USA	5 June	1982
Shot 7·26 kg *16 lb*	21·68	71	1½	Geoffrey Lewis Capes (b. 23 Aug 1949)	Cwmbran, Gwent	18 May	1980
Discus 2 kg *4 lb 6·55 oz.*	64·32†	211	0	William Raymond Tancred (b. 6 Aug 1942)	Woodford, Essex	10 Aug	1974
Hammer 7·26 kg *16 lb*	77·54	254	5	Martin Girvan (b. 17 Apr 1960)	Wolverhampton, West Midlands	12 May	1984
Javelin 800 g *28·22 oz*	85·24‡	279	8	Michael Christopher Hill (b. 22 Oct 1964)	Stockholm, Sweden	30 June	1987

* Also 2·30 m 7 ft 6½ in indoors by Geoff Parsons at Cosford, Shropshire on 25 Jan 1986.

† William Raymond Tancred threw 64·94 m 213 ft 1 in at Loughborough on 21 July 1974 and Richard Charles Slaney (b. 16 May 1956) threw 65·16 m 213 ft 9 in at Eugene, Oregon, USA on 1 July 1985 but these were not ratified.

‡ New javelin; best with old javelin 91·40 m 299 ft 10 in by Arne-Roald Bradstock (b. 24 Apr 1962) at Arlington, Texas, USA on 4 May 1985.

DECATHLON

8847 points		Francis Morgan 'Daley' Thompson (GB) (b. 30 July 1958)	Los Angeles, USA	8–9 Aug 1984

(1st day: 100 m 10·44 sec, Long Jump 8·01 m *26 ft 3½ in*, Shot Put 15·72 m *51 ft 7 in*, High Jump 2·03 m *6 ft 8 in*, 400 m 46·97 sec)

(2nd day: 110 m Hurdles 14·33 sec, Discus 46·56 m *152 ft 9 in*, Pole Vault 5·00 m *16 ft 4¾ in*, Javelin 65·24 m *214 ft 0 in*, 1500 m 4:35·00 sec)

United Kingdom (National) Records *Women*

RUNNING	Min sec	Name and country	Place	Date	
100 metres	11·10	Kathryn Jane Smallwood [now Cook] (b. 3 May 1960)	Rome, Italy	5 Sept	1981
200 metres	22·10	Kathryn Jane Cook [*née* Smallwood]	Los Angeles, USA	9 Aug	1984
400 metres	49·43	Kathryn Jane Cook [*née* Smallwood]	Los Angeles, USA	6 Aug	1984
800 metres	1:57·42	Kirsty Margaret McDermott [now Wade] (b. 6 Aug 1962)	Belfast, N. Ireland	24 June	1985
1000 metres	2:33·70	Kirsty Margaret McDermott [now Wade]	Gateshead, Tyne and Wear	9 Aug	1985
1500 metres	3:59·96	Zola Budd (b. 26 May 1966)	Brussels, Belgium	30 Aug	1985
1 mile	4:17·57	Zola Budd	Zürich, Switzerland	21 Aug	1985
2000 metres	5:29·58	Yvonne Carol Grace Murray (b. 4 Oct 1964)	Crystal Palace, London	11 July	1986
3000 metres	8:28·83	Zola Budd	Rome, Italy	7 Sept	1985
5000 metres	14:48·07	Zola Budd	Crystal Palace, London	26 Aug	1985
10000 metres	31:06·99	Elizabeth McColgan [*née* Lynch (b. 24 May 1964)	Oslo, Norway	2 July	1988

RELAYS

	Min sec	Name and country	Place	Date	
4×10 metres	42·43	United Kingdom: Heather Regina Hunte [now Oakes], Kathryn Jane Smallwood [now Cook], Beverley Lanita Goddard [now Callender], Sonia May Lannaman	Moscow, USSR	1 Aug	1980
4×200 metres	1:31·57	United Kingdom: Donna-Marie Louise Hartley [*née* Murray], Verona Marolin Elder [*née* Bernard], Sharon Colyear [now Danville], Sonia May Lannaman	Crystal Palace, London	20 Aug	1977
4×400 metres	3:25·51	United Kingdom: Michelle Scutt [*née* Probert], Helen Catherine Barnett [now Burkart], Gladys Taylor, Joslyn Yvonne Hoyte-Smith	Los Angeles, USA	11 Aug	1984
4×800 metres	8:23·8	Great Britain: Joan Florence Allison [*née* Page], Sheila Janet Carey [*née* Taylor], Patricia Barbara Lowe [now Cropper], Rosemary Olivia Stirling [now Wright]	Paris, France	2 Oct	1971

Cont.
HURDLING

100 metres	12·87	Shirley Elaine Strong (b. 18 Nov 1958)	Zürich, Switzerland	24 Aug	1983
400 metres	56·04	Susan Anita Jayne Morley [now Chick] (b. 6 Jan 1960)	Helsinki, Finland	10 Aug	1983

FIELD EVENTS

	m	ft	in				
High Jump	1·95	6	4¾	Diana Clare Elliot (now Davies) (b. 7 May 1961)	Oslo, Norway	26 June	1982
Long Jump	6·90	22	7¾	Beverly Kinch (b. 14 Jan 1964)	Helsinki, Finland	14 Aug	1983
Shot 4 kg 8 lb 13 oz	19·26	63	2¼	Judith Miriam Oakes (b. 14 Feb 1958)	Edinburgh, Scotland	16 July	1988
Discus 1 kg 2 lb 3·27 oz	67·48	221	5	Margaret Elizabeth Ritchie (b. 6 July 1952)	Walnut, California, USA	26 Apr	1981
Javelin 600 g 21·16 oz	77·44	254	1	Fatima Whitbread (b. 3 Mar 1961)	Stuttgart, W. Germany	28 Aug	1987

HEPTATHLON

6623 points	Judy Earline Veronica Simpson [née Livermore] (b. 14 Nov 1960)	Stuttgart, W. Germany	29–30 Aug	1986

(100 m hurdles 13·05 sec; High Jump 1·92 m 6 ft 3½ in ; Shot
14·75 m 48 ft 4ft; 200 m 25·09 sec; Long Jump 6·56 m 21 ft 6¼ in;
Javelin 40·92 m 134 ft 3 in; 800 m 2 min 11·70 sec)

Himalayas on 27 Nov 1987. It began at Gorak Shep, 5212 m *17 100 ft* and ended at Namche Bazar, 3444 m *11 300 ft.* The winner from the field of 45 was Stewart Dutfield (GB), aged 32, in a time of 4 hr 53 min 10 sec.

Oldest finishers

The oldest man to complete a marathon was Dimitrion Yordanidis (Greece), aged 98, in Athens, Greece on 10 Oct 1976. He finished in 7 hr 33 min. Thelma Pitt-Turner (New Zealand) set the women's record in August 1985, completing the Hastings, New Zealand marathon in 7 hr 58 min at the age of 82.

WALKING

Most Olympic medals

Walking races have been included in the Olympic events since 1906. The only walker to win three gold medals has been Ugo Frigerio (Italy) (1901–68) with the 3000 m in 1920, and 10 000 m in 1920 and 1924. He also holds the record of most medals with four (he won the bronze medal at 50 000 m in 1932), a total shared with Vladimir Golubnichiy (USSR) (b. 2 June 1936), who won gold medals for the 20 000 m in 1960 and 1968, the silver in 1972 and the bronze in 1964.

The best British performance has been two gold medals by George Edward Larner (1875–1949) for the 3500 m and the 10 miles in 1908, but Ernest J. Webb (1872–1937) won three medals, being twice 'walker up' to Larner and finishing second in the 10 000 m in 1912.

Most titles

Four-time Olympian, Ronald Owen Laird (b. 31 May 1938) of the New York AC, USA, won a total of 65 US national titles from 1958 to 1976, plus four Canadian Championships. The greatest number of UK national titles won by a British walker is 27 by Vincent Paul Nihill (b. 5 Sept 1939) from 1963 to 1975.

Longest race

The Paris–Colmar, until 1980 Strasbourg–Paris, event (inst. 1926 in the reverse direction), now about 519 km *322 miles* is the world's longest annual race walk.

The fastest performance is by Robert Pietquin (Belgium) (b. 1938) who walked 507 km *315 miles* in the 1980 race in 60 hr 1 min 10 sec (after deducting 4 hr compulsory stops). This represents an average speed of 8·45 km/h *5·25 mph.* Two men have won a record six times: Gilbert Roger (France) (b. 1914), 1949, 1953–4, 1956–8 and Roger Quémener (France), 1979, 1983, 1985–8. The first woman to complete the race was Annie van der Meer (Netherlands) (b. 24 Feb 1947), who was 10th in 1983 in 82 hr 10 min.

Dumitru Dan (1890–1978) of Romania was the only man of 200 entrants to succeed in a contest in walking 100 000 km *62 137 miles* organised by the *Touring Club de France* on 1 Apr 1910. He covered 96 000 km *59 651 miles* up to 24 Mar 1916, so averaging 43·85 km *27·24 miles* a day.

TRACK WALKING—*WORLD RECORDS*

The International Amateur Athletic Federation recognises men's records at 20 km, 30 km, 50 km and 2 hours, and women's at 5 km and 10 km. This table also includes world bests for other standard distances.

Event	Time hr:min:sec	Name, country and date of birth	Place	Date	
MEN					
3 km	10:54·6 *	Carlo Mattioli (Italy) (b. 23 Oct 1954)	Milan, Italy	6 Feb	1980
10 km	38:02·6	Jozef Pribilinec (Czechoslovakia) (b. 6 July 1960)	Banska Bystrica, Czechoslovakia	30 Aug	1985
20 km	1:18:40·0	Ernesto Canto (Mexico) (b. 18 Oct 1959)	Fana, Norway	5 May	1984
30 km	2:06:07·3 †	Maurizio Damilano (Italy) (b. 6 Apr 1957)	San Danato Milanese, Italy	5 May	1985
50 km	3:41:38·4	Raul Gonzalez (Mexico) (b. 29 Feb 1952)	Fana, Norway	25 May	1979
1 hour	15 547 m	Josef Pribilinec (Czechoslovakia)	Hildesheim, W. Germany	6 Sept	1986
2 hours	28 565 m†	Maurizio Damilano (Italy)	San Danato Milanese, Italy	5 May	1985
WOMEN					
3 km	12:05·49*	Olga Krishtop (USSR) (b. 23 June 1957)	Indianapolis, USA	6 Mar	1987
5 km	20:45·32	Kerry Ann Saxby (Australia) (b.2 June 1961)	Perth, Australia	26 Mar	1988
10 km	42:14·2	Kerry Saxby (Australia)	Canberra, Australia	26 Jan	1988

*indoors. †unratified.

ULTRA LONG DISTANCE WORLD RECORDS

TRACK (Men)

Event	hr:min:sec	Name	Place		Date
50 km	2:48:06	Jeff Norman (UK)	Timperley, Manchester	7 June	1980
50 miles	4:51:49	Don Ritchie (UK)	Hendon, London	12 Mar	1983
100 km	6:10:20	Don Ritchie (UK)	Crystal Palace, London	28 Oct	1978
100 miles	11:30:51	Don Ritchie (UK)	Crystal Palace, London	15 Oct	1977
200 km	15:11:10	Yiannis Kouros (Greece)	Montauban, France	15–16 Mar	1985
200 miles	27:48:35	Yiannis Kouros (Greece)	Montauban, France	15–16 Mar	1985
500 km	60:23:00	Yiannis Kouros (Greece)	Colac, Australia	26–29 Nov	1984
500 miles	105:42:09	Yiannis Kouros (Greece)	Colac, Australia	26–30 Nov	1984
1000 km	136:17:00	Yiannis Kouros (Greece)	Colac, Australia	26 Nov–1 Dec	1984

	kilometres				
24 hours	283·600	Yiannis Kouros (Greece)	Montauban, France	15–16 Mar	1985
48 hours	452·270	Yiannis Kouros (Greece)	Montauban, France	15–17 Mar	1985
6 days	1023·200	Yiannis Kouros (Greece)	Colac, Australia	26 Nov–1 Dec	1984

ROAD (Men)

Where superior to track bests and run on properly measured road courses.

	hr:min:sec				
50 km	2:43:38	Thompson Magawana (SAf)	Claremont–Kirstenbosch	2 Apr	1988
50 miles	4:50:21	Bruce Fordyce (SAf)	London–Brighton	25 Sept	1983
1000 miles	10d 10hr 30min 35sec	Yiannis Kouros (Greece)	New York, USA	21–30 May	1988

	kilometres				
24 hours	286·463	Yiannis Kouros (Greece)	New York, USA	28–29 Sept	1985
6 days	1028·300	Yiannis Kouros (Greece)	New York, USA	21–26 May	1988

TRACK (Women)

	hr:min:sec				
15 km	49:44·0	Silvana Cruciata (Italy)	Rome, Italy	4 May	1981
20 km	1:06:55·5	Rosa Mota (Portugal)	Lisbon, Portugal	14 May	1983
25 km	1:31:04·3	Chantal Langlacé (France)	Amiens, France	3 Sep	1983
30 km	1:49:55·7	Chantal Langlacé (France)	Amiens, France	3 Sep	1983
50 km	3:36:58	Ann Franklin (UK)	Barry, Wales	9 Mar	1986
50 miles	6:17:30†	Monika Kuno (W. Germany)	Vogt, W. Germany	8–9 July	1983
100 km	8:01:01	Monika Kuno (W. Germany)	Vogt, W. Germany	8–9 July	1983
100 miles	15:25:46	Eleanor Adams (UK)	Honefoss, Norway	12–13 July	1986

cont.	hr:min:sec				
200 km	20:09:28†	Eleanor Adams (UK)	Honefoss, Norway	12–13 July	1986
200 miles	43:38:41	Arlette Touchard (Fr)	Montauban, France	14–16 Mar	1986
500 km	86:26:02	Eleanor Adams (UK)	Colac, Australia	24–28 Feb	1986
500 miles	143:49:00	Eleanor Adams (UK)	Colac, Australia	24 Feb–2 Mar	1984

kilometres					
1 hour	18·084	Silvana Cruciata (Italy)	Rome, Italy	4 May	1981
24 hours	229·459	Marion Savage (GB)	Birmingham	2–3 July	1988
48 hours	347·420	Arlette Touchard (France)	Montauban, France	14–16 Mar	1986
6 days	838·800	Eleanor Adams (UK)	Colac, Australia	16–22 Nov	1987

†Timed on one running watch only.

ROAD (Women)
Where superior to track bests and run on properly measured road courses.

	hr:min:sec				
30 km	1:47:06	Karolina Szabo (Hungary)	Budapest, Hungary	23 Apr	1988
50 km	3:15:51	Janis Klecker (USA)	Tallahassee, USA	17 Dec	1983
40 miles	4:43:22	Marcy Schwam (USA)	Chicago, USA	3 Oct	1982
50 miles	5:59:26	Marcy Schwam (USA)	Chicago, USA	3 Oct	1982
100 km	7:47:28*	Marcy Schwam (USA)	Santander, Spain	19 Sept	1981
100 miles	15:07:45	Christine Barrett (UK)	Forthampton, Gloucestershire	14 Apr	1984
200 km	20:08:44	Hilary Walker (UK)	Feltham, Middlesex	23–24 May	1987
500 km (actually 518 km)	82:10	Annie van der Meer (Hol)	Paris–Colmar	8–11 June	1983
24 hours	230·618 km	Hilary Walker (UK)	Feltham, Middlesex	14–15 May	1987
1000 miles	14d 20hr 45min 16sec	Sandra Barwick (N. Zealand)	New York, USA	21 May–3 June	1988

It should be noted that road times must be assessed with care as course conditions can vary considerably.

* On a road course of unverified measurement: 7:26:01 by Chantal Langlacé (France) at Migennes, France on 17 June 1984.

ROAD WALKING WORLD BEST PERFORMANCES

It should be noted that severity of road race courses and the accuracy of their measurement may vary, sometimes making comparisons of times unreliable.

MEN
20 km: 1 hr 19 min 8 sec, Mikhail Shchennikov (USSR) (b. 24 Dec 1967) at Kiev, USSR on 30 July 1988.
30 km: 2 hr 03 min 06 sec, Daniel Bautista (Mexico) (b. 4 Aug 1952) at Cherkassy, USSR on 27 Apr 1980.
50 km: 3 hr 38 min 17 sec, Ronald Weigel (GDR) (b. 8 Aug 1950) at Potsdam, GDR on 25 May 1986.

WOMEN
10 km: 42 min 52 sec, Kerry Ann Saxby (Australia) (b. 2 June 1961) at Hobart, Australia on 19 July 1987.
20 km: 1 hr 29 min 40 sec, Kerry Saxby at Värnamo, Sweden on 13 May 1988.
50 km: 5 hr 01 min 52 sec, Lillian Millen (GB) (b. 5 Mar 1945) at York, Yorkshire on 16 Apr 1983.

BRITISH BEST PERFORMANCES

MEN
20 km: 1 hr 22 min 37 sec, Ian Peter McCombie (b. 11 Jan 1961) at Thamesmead, London on 11 May 1985.
30 km: 2 hr 7 min 56 sec, Ian Peter McCombie at Edinburgh on 27 Apr 1986.
50 km: 3 hr 58 min 25 sec, Leslie Morton (b. 1 July 1958) at Puerto Pollensa, Majorca, Spain on 20 Mar 1988.

WOMEN
10 km: 45 min 42 sec, Lisa Martine Langford (b. 15 Mar 1967) at New York, USA on 3 May 1987.
20 km: 1 hr 40 min 45 sec, Irene Lillian Bateman (b. 13 Nov 1947) at Basildon, Essex on 9 Apr 1983.

'End to end'
The fastest Land's End to John o'Groats walk is 12 days 3 hr 45 min for 1426·4 km 886·3 miles by WO2 Malcolm Barnish of the 19th Regiment, Royal Artillery from 9–21 June 1986. The women's record is 13 days 17 hr 42 min by Ann Sayer (b. 16 Oct 1936) from 20 Sept–3 Oct 1980. The Irish 'end to end' record over the 644 km 400·2 miles from Malin Head, Donegal to Mizen Head, Cork is 5 days

22 hr 30 min, set by John 'Paddy' Dowling (b. 15 June 1929) on 18–24 Mar 1982.

London to Brighton
The record time for the 85 km 53 mile walk is 7 hr 35 min 12 sec by Donald James Thompson (b. 20 Jan 1933) on 14 Sept 1957. Richard Esmond Green (b. 22 Apr 1924) completed the course a record 44 times from 1950 to 1980.

Longest non-stop walk
Georges Holtyzer (Belgium) walked 673·48 km 418·49 miles in 6 days 10 hr 58 min, 452 laps of a 1·49–km circuit, at Ninove, Belgium from 19–25 July 1986. He was not permitted any stops for rest and was moving 98·78 per cent of the time.

24 hours
The greatest distance walked in 24 hr is 226·432 km 140 miles 1229 yd by Paul Forthomme (Belgium) on a road course at Woluwé, Belgium on 13–14 Oct 1984. The best by a woman is 202·3 km 125·7 miles by Annie van der Meer at Rouen, France on 30 Apr–1 May 1984 over a 1·185–km lap road course.

Backwards walking
The greatest ever exponent of reverse pedestrianism has been Plennie L. Wingo (b. 24 Jan 1895) then of Abilene, Texas, who completed his 12 875 km 8000 mile trans-continental walk from Santa Monica, California, USA to Istanbul, Turkey, from 15 Apr 1931 to 24 Oct 1932. The longest distance recorded for walking backwards in 24 hr is 135·18 km 84·0 miles by Anthony Thornton (USA) in Minneapolis, Minnesota, USA on 31 Dec 1985–1 Jan 1986.

Trampolining

Trampolines were used in show business at least as early as 'The Walloons' of the period 1910–12. The sport of trampolining (from the Spanish word trampolin, a springboard) dates from 1936, when the prototype 'T' model trampoline was developed by George Nissen (USA).

Most titles
World Championships were instituted in 1964. A record five titles were won by Judy Wills (USA) (b. 1948) in the women's event, 1964–8. Five men have won two titles.

A record seven United Kingdom titles have been won by Wendy Wright (1969–70, 1972–5, 1977). The most by a man has been five by Stewart Matthews (b. 19 Feb 1962) (1976–80).

Youngest international Great Britain
Andrea Holmes (b. 2 Jan 1970) competed for Britain at 12 yr 131 days in the World Championships at Montana, USA on 13 May 1982.

Somersaults
Richard Cobbing of Gateshead Metro Tampolining Club performed 1988 consecutive somersaults at BBC Television Centre, London for The Guinness Book of Records Hall of Fame on 22 Dec 1987.

The most somersaults completed in one minute is 78 by Zoe Finn of Chatham, Kent at BBC Television Centre, London for Blue Peter on 25 Jan 1988.

Triathlon

The Triathlon combines long–distance swimming, cycling and running. Distances for each of the phases can vary, but for the best established event, the Hawaii Ironman (inst. 1978), competitors first swim 3·8 km 2·4 miles, then cycle 180 km 112 miles, and finally run a full marathon of 42·195 km 26 miles 385 yards.

Record times for the Hawaii Ironman are: (men) 8 hr 28 min 37 sec Dave Scott (USA) (b. 1953) on 19 Oct 1986; (women) 9 hr 35 min 25 sec Erin Baker (New Zealand) on 10 Oct 1987.

Dave Scott has won a record six races, 1980, 1982–4 and 1986–7.

For the same distances as in the Ironman, Scott Tinley (USA) (b. 1956), 8 hr 27 min 46 sec and Erin Baker (New Zealand) (b. 23 May 1961), 9 hr 27 min 36 sec, set records for men and women respectively in the 1986 European Championships at Sofia, Bulgaria.

World Championships
The Triathlon Federation International was founded in Amsterdam in Nov 1987. It staged the first official World Championships in 1988.

A 'World Championship' race has been held annually in Nice, France from 1982; the distances 3200 m, 120 km and 32 km respectively. Mark Allen (USA) won five times 1982–6, setting a record time of 5 hr 46 min 10 sec in 1986. The women's record is 6 hr 37 min 21 sec by Erin Baker in 1985.

Largest field
The largest field in a triathlon race has been 3888 finishers at Chicago in 1987. This series encompasses races over 1500 m, 40 km and 10 km for the three phases.

Tug of War

Though ancient China and Egypt have been suggested as the originators of the sport, it is known that Neolithic flint miners in Norfolk, England practised 'rope-pulling'. The first rules were those framed by the New York AC in 1879. Tug of War was an Olympic sport from 1900 until 1920. In 1958 the Tug-of-War Association was formed to administer Britain's 600 clubs. World Championships have been held annually from 1975, with a women's event introduced in 1986.

Most titles
The most successful team at the World Championships have been the Sheen Farmers, competing for England, who won at 640 kg in 1975–6 and at 720 kg in 1977–8 and 1980.

The Wood Treatment team (formerly the Bosley Farmers) of Cheshire won 20 consecutive AAA

Catchweight Championships 1959–78, two world titles (1975–6) and ten European titles at 720 kg. Hilary Brown (b. 13 Apr 1934) was in every team. Trevor Brian Thomas (b. 1943) of British Aircraft Corporation Club is the only holder of three winners' medals in the European Open club competitions.

Longest pulls *Duration*

The longest recorded pull (prior to the introduction of AAA rules) is one of 2 hr 41 min when 'H' Company beat 'E' Company of the 2nd Battalion of the Sherwood Foresters (Derbyshire Regiment) at Jubbulpore, India on 12 Aug 1889. The longest recorded pull under AAA rules (in which lying on the ground or entrenching the feet is not permitted) is one of 13 min 4 sec for the first pull between the Republic of Ireland and England during the world championships (560 kg class) at Slagharen, The Netherlands on 13 Sept 1986. The record time for 'The Pull' (inst. 1898), across the Black River, between freshman and sophomore teams at Hope College, Holland, Michigan, USA, is 3 hr 51 min on 23 Sept 1977, but the method of bracing the feet precludes this replacing the preceding records.

Distance

The longest tug of war is the 2·6 km *1·616 miles* Supertug across the Little Traverse Bay, Lake Michigan, USA. It has been contested annually since 1980 between two teams of 20 from Bay View Inn and Harbor Inn. Bay View leads 4–3.

Volleyball

The game was invented as *mintonette* in 1895 by William G. Morgan at the YMCA gymnasium at Holyoke, Massachusetts, USA. The International Volleyball Association was formed in Paris in April 1947. The Amateur (now English) Volleyball Association of Great Britain was formed in May 1955.

Most world titles

World Championships were instituted in 1949 for men and 1952 for women. The USSR has won six men's titles (1949, 1952, 1960, 1962, 1978 and 1982) and four women's (1952, 1956, 1960 and 1970). Japan (1962, 1967, 1974 and 1987) have also won four women's titles.

Most Olympic titles

The sport was introduced to the Olympic Games for both men and women in 1964. The USSR has won a record three men's (1964, 1968 and 1980) and three women's (1968, 1972 and 1980) titles. The only player to win four medals is Inna Ryskal (USSR) (b. 15 June 1944), who won women's silver medals in 1964 and 1976 and golds in 1968 and 1972. The record for men is held by Yuriy Poyarkov (USSR) (b. 10 Feb 1937) who won gold medals in 1964 and 1968 and a bronze in 1972, and by Katsutoshi Nekoda (Japan) (b. 1 Feb 1944) who won gold in 1972, silver in 1968 and bronze in 1964.

Most internationals *Great Britain*

Ucal Ashman (b. 10 Nov 1957) made a record 153 men's international appearances for England, 1976–86. The women's record is 171 by Ann Jarvis (b. 3 June 1955) for England, 1974–87.

Water Polo

Water polo was developed in England as 'water soccer' in 1869 and first included in the Olympic Games in Paris in 1900.

Most Olympic titles

Hungary has won the Olympic tournament most often with six wins in 1932, 1936, 1952, 1956, 1964 and 1976. Great Britain won in 1900, 1908, 1912 and 1920.

Five players share the record of three gold medals; Britons George Wilkinson (1879–1946) in 1900, 1908,

Fastest skier ● The fastest speed recorded by a British woman is 122·187 km/h *75·92 mph* by Elizabeth Hobbs at Lake Windermere, Cumbria on 14 Oct 1982. She has also won the World Ski Racing championships a record two times, 1981 and 1983. (Photo: All-Sport)

1912; Paulo 'Paul' Radmilovic (1886–1968), and Charles Sidney Smith (1879–1951) in 1908, 1912, 1920; and Hungarians Deszö Gyarmati (b. 23 Oct 1927) and György Kárpáti (b. 23 June 1935) in 1952, 1956, 1964. Paul Radmilovic also won a gold medal for the 4×200 m freestyle swimming in 1908.

World Championships

First held at the World Swimming Championships in

1973. The USSR is the only double winner, 1975 and 1982. A women's competition was introduced in 1986, when it was won by Australia.

Most goals

The greatest number of goals scored by an individual in an international is 13 by Debbie Handley for Australia (16) *v.* Canada (10) at the World Championship in Guayaquil, Ecuador in 1982.

Most international appearances

The greatest number of international appearances is 412 by Aleksey Barkalov (USSR) (b. 18 Feb 1946), 1965–80. The British record is 126 by Martyn Thomas, of Cheltenham, Gloucestershire, 1964–78.

Water Skiing

The origins of water skiing derive from walking on planks and aquaplaning. A 19th-century treatise on sorcerers refers to Eliseo of Tarentum who, in the 14th century, 'walks and dances' on the water. The first report of aquaplaning was on America's Pacific coast in the early 1900s. At Scarborough, Yorkshire on 15 July 1914, a single plank-gliding contest was won by H. Storry.

The present day sport of water skiing was pioneered by Ralph W. Samuelson (1904–77) on Lake Pepin, Minnesota, USA, on two curved pine boards in the summer of 1922, although claims have been made for the birth of the sport on Lake Annecy (Haute Savoie), France at about the same time. The first world organisation, the *Union Internationale de Ski Nautique*, was formed in Geneva on 27 July 1946.

Most titles

World Overall Championships (inst. 1949) have been won four times by Sammy Duvall (USA) in 1981, 1983, 1985 and 1987 and three times by two women, Willa McGuire (*née* Worthington) of the USA in 1949–50 and 1955 and Elizabeth 'Liz' Allan-Shetter (USA) in 1965, 1969 and 1975. Liz Allan-Shetter has won a record eight individual championship events and is the only person to win all four titles—slalom, jumping, tricks and overall in one year, at Copenhagen, Denmark in 1969. The USA have won the team championship on 16 successive occasions, 1957–87. The most British Overall titles (instituted 1953) won by a man is seven by Michael Hazelwood (b. 14 Apr 1958) in 1974, 1976–9, 1981, 1983; the most by a woman is nine by Karen Jane Morse (b. 14 Aug 1956) in 1971–6, 1978, 1981, 1984.

Highest speed

The fastest water skiing speed recorded is 230·26 km/h *143·08 mph* by Christopher Michael Massey (Australia) on the Hawkesbury River, Windsor, New South Wales, Australia on 6 Mar 1983. His drag boat driver was Stanley Charles Sainty (b. 1953). Donna Patterson Brice (b. 1953) set a feminine record of 178·8 km/h *111·11 mph* at Long Beach, California, USA on 21 Aug 1977. The fastest recorded speed by a British skier over a measured kilometre is 141·594 km/h *87·984 mph* (average) on Lake Windermere, Cumbria on 14 Oct 1987 by Steven Moore (b. 3 Mar 1963).

Longest run

The greatest distance travelled is 2099·7 km *1304·6 miles* by Will Coughey on 18–19 Feb 1984 on Lake Tikitapu, New Zealand.

Most skiers towed by one boat

A record 100 water skiers were towed on double skis over a nautical mile by the cruiser *Reef Cat* at Cairns, Queensland, Australia on 18 Oct 1986. This feat, organised by the Cairns and District Powerboat and Ski Club, was then replicated by 100 skiers on single skis.

Barefoot

The first person to water ski barefoot is reported to be Dick Pope Jr at Lake Eloise, Florida, USA on 6 Mar 1947.

The barefoot duration record is 2 hr 42 min 39 sec by Billy Nichols (USA) (b. 1964) on Lake Weir, Florida on 19 Nov 1978. The backward barefoot record is 39 min by Paul McManus (Australia). The British duration record is 67 min 5 sec by John Doherty on 1 Oct 1974. The official barefoot speed record is 192·08 km/h *119·36 mph* by Scott Michael Pellaton (b. 8 Oct 1956) over a quarter-mile course at Chowchilla, California, USA on 4 Sept 1983. The fastest by a woman is 118·56 km/h *73·67 mph* by Karen Toms (Australia) on the Hawkesbury River, Windsor, New South Wales on 31 Mar 1984. The British records are: (men) 114·86 km/h *71·37 mph* by Richard Mainwaring (b. 4 June 1953) at Holme Pierrepont, Notts. on 2 Dec 1978; (women) 80·25 km/h *49·86 mph* by Michele Doherty (b. 28 May 1964) (also 71·54 km/h *44·45 mph* backwards), both at Witney, Oxfordshire on 18 Oct 1986. The fastest official speed backwards barefoot is 100 km/h *62 mph* by Robert Wing (Australia) (b. 13 Aug 1957) on 3 Apr 1982.

The barefoot jump record is: men 20·50 m *67 ft 3 in* by Quentin Posthumus (South Africa) at Kimberley, South Africa on 5 Apr 1986 and women 12·40 m *40 ft 8¼ in* by Jaqueline Pfeiffer (Switzerland) at Lago di Orta, Italy on 28 June 1986. The British record is: men 19·10 m *62 ft 8 in* by Chris Harris in Germany in 1986 and women 9·9 m *32 ft 5¾ in* by Michele Doherty at Thorpe Park, Surrey in 1986.

Weightlifting

Competitions for lifting weights of stone were held in the ancient Olympic Games. The first championships entitled 'world' were staged at the Café Monico, Piccadilly, London on 28 Mar 1891 and then in Vienna, Austria on 19–20 July 1898, subsequently recognised by the IWF. Prior to that time, weightlifting consisted of professional exhibitions in which some of the advertised poundages were open to doubt.

The *Fédération Internationalé Haltérophile et Culturiste*, now the International Weightlifting Federation (IWF), was established in 1905, and its first official cham-

WORLD WEIGHTLIFTING RECORDS

Bodyweight class	Lift	kg	lb	Name and country	Place	Date	
52 kg 114½ lb FLYWEIGHT	Snatch	119·5	263¼	He Zhuqiang (China)	Xilong, China	16 June	1988
	Jerk	153	337¼	He Zhuqiang (China)	Ostrava, Czechoslovakia	6 Sept	1987
	Total	267·5	589¾	He Zhuqiang (China)	Xilong, China	16 June	1988
56 kg 123¼ lb BANTAMWEIGHT	Snatch	134	295¼	He Yingqiang (China)	Xilong, China	16 June	1988
	Jerk	171	377	Neno Terziiski (Bulgaria)	Ostrava, Czechoslovakia	6 Sept	1987
	Total	300	661¼	Neum Shalamanov (Bulgaria)	Varna, Bulgaria	11 May	1984
60 kg 132¼ lb FEATHERWEIGHT	Snatch	150	330¾	Naim Suleimanoglou (Turkey)*	Cardiff, South Glamorgan	27 Apr	1988
	Jerk	188	414¼	Neum Shalamanov (Bulgaria)	Sofia, Bulgaria	9 Nov	1986
	Total	335	738½	Neum Shalamanov (Bulgaria)	Sofia, Bulgaria	9 Nov	1986
67·5 kg 148¾ lb LIGHTWEIGHT	Snatch	158·5	349¼	Israil Militosyan	Athens, Greece	24 May	1988
	Jerk	200·5	442	Mikhail Petrov (Bulgaria)	Ostrava, Czechoslovakia	8 Sept	1987
	Total	355	782½	Mikhail Petrov (Bulgaria)	Seoul, South Korea	5 Dec	1987
75 kg 165¼ lb MIDDLEWEIGHT	Snatch	170	374¾	Angel Guenchev (Bulgaria)	Miskolc, Hungary	11 Dec	1987
	Jerk	215½	475	Aleksandr Varbanov (Bulgaria)	Seoul, South Korea	5 Dec	1987
	Total	382·5	843¼	Aleksandr Varbanov (Bulgaria)	Plovdiv, Bulgaria	20 Feb	1988
82·5 kg 181¾ lb LIGHT-HEAVYWEIGHT	Snatch	183	403¼	Asen Zlatev (Bulgaria)	Melbourne, Australia	7 Dec	1986
	Jerk	225	496	Asen Zlatev (Bulgaria)	Sofia, Bulgaria	12 Nov	1986
	Total	405	892½	Yurik Vardanyan (USSR)	Varna, Bulgaria	14 Sept	1984
90 kg 198¼ lb MIDDLE-HEAVYWEIGHT	Snatch	195·5	431	Blagoi Blagoyev (Bulgaria)	Varna, Bulgaria	1 May	1983
	Jerk	235	518	Anatoliy Khrapatiy (USSR)	Cardiff, South Glamorgan	29 Apr	1988
	Total	422·5	931¼	Viktor Solodov (USSR)	Varna, Bulgaria	15 Sept	1984
100 kg 220½ lb	Snatch	200·5	442	Nicu Vlad (Romania)	Sofia, Bulgaria	14 Nov	1986
	Jerk	242·5	532¼	Aleksandr Popov (USSR)	Tallinn, USSR	5 Mar	1988
	Total	440	970	Yuriy Zakharevich (USSR)	Odessa, USSR	4 Mar	1983
110 kg 242½ lb HEAVYWEIGHT	Snatch	203·5	448½	Yuriy Zakharevich (USSR)	Cardiff, South Glamorgan	30 Apr	1988
	Jerk	250·5	552¼	Yuriy Zaharevich (USSR)	Cardiff, South Glamorgan	30 Apr	1988
	Total	452·5	997½	Yuriy Zakharevich (USSR)	Cardiff, South Glamorgan	30 Apr	1988
Over 110 kg 242½ lb SUPER-HEAVYWEIGHT	Snatch	216	476	Antonio Krastev (Bulgaria)	Ostrava, Czechoslovakia	13 Sept	1987
	Jerk	265·5	585¼	Leonid Taranenko (USSR)	Ostrava, Czechoslovakia	13 Sept	1987
	Total	472·5	1041½	Aleksandr Kurlovich (USSR)	Ostrava, Czechoslovakia	13 Sept	1987

* Formerly Naim Suleimanov or Neum Shalamanov of Bulgaria

Weightlifting ● Judith Miriam Oakes (b. 14 Feb 1958) holds several British records for both weightlifting and powerlifting. She is also the current holder of the British shot put record. (Photo: All-Sport)

pionships were held in Tallinn, Estonia on 29–30 Apr 1922. The first Women's World Championships were held in Daytona Beach, USA in October 1987.

There are two standard lifts: the 'snatch' and the 'clean and jerk' (or 'jerk'). Totals of the two lifts determine competition results. The 'press', which was a standard lift, was abolished in 1972.

Most Olympic medals

Norbert Schemansky (USA) (b. 30 May 1924) won a record four Olympic medals: gold, middle-heavyweight 1952; silver, heavyweight 1948; bronze, heavyweight 1960 and 1964.

Most titles *World*

The most world title wins, including Olympic Games, is eight by: John Davis (USA) (1921–84) in 1938, 1946–52; Tommy Kono (USA) (b. 27 June 1930) in 1952–9; and by Vasiliy Alekseyev (USSR) (b. 7 Jan 1942), 1970–7.

Youngest world record holder

Naim Suleimanov (later Neum Shalamanov) (Bulgaria) (b. 23 Nov 1967) (now Naim Suleimanoglou of Turkey) set 56-kg world records for clean and jerk (160 kg) and total (285 kg) at 15 yr 123 days at Allentown, New Jersey, USA on 26 Mar 1983.

Most successful British lifter

The only British lifter to win an Olympic title has been Launceston Elliot (1874–1930), the open one-handed lift

BRITISH WEIGHTLIFTING RECORDS (in kg)

MEN

Class	Snatch		Date	Jerk		Date	Total		Date
52 kg	92·5	Precious McKenzie	25 Jan 1974	122·5	Precious McKenzie	25 Jan 1974	215	Precious McKenzie	25 Jan 1974
56 kg	105	Dean Willey	15 June 1981	132·5	Geoff Laws	1982	235	Geoff Laws	1982
60 kg	122·5	Dean Willey	26 Feb 1983	152·5	Dean Willey	26 Mar 1983	272·5	Dean Willey	26 Feb 1983
67·5 kg	145	Dean Willey	26 July 1986	170	Dean Willey	1 Aug 1984	315	Dean Willey	1985
75 kg	155	David Morgan	11 Nov 1986	190	David Morgan	11 Nov 1986	345	David Morgan	11 Nov 1986
82·5 kg	165·5	David Morgan	9 July 1988	205	David Morgan	13 June 1987	365	David Morgan	13 June 1987
90 kg	162	David Mercer		202·5	David Mercer		360	David Mercer	
100 kg	165	Andrew Davies		212·5	Peter Pinsent	17 Sept 1983	362·5	Peter Pinsent	17 Sept 1983
110 kg	185·5	Andrew Davies	30 Apr 1988	220	Andrew Davies	30 Apr 1988	405	Andrew Davies	30 Apr 1988
Super	190	Andrew Davies	9 July 1988	220	Andrew Davies	9 July 1988	410	Andrew Davies	9 July 1988

WORLD POWERLIFTING RECORDS (All weights in kilograms)

Class	Squat	Bench Press	Deadlift	Total
MEN				
52 kg	243 Hideaki Inaba (Jap) 1986	146·5 Joe Cunha (USA) 1982	237·5 Hideaki Inaba 1987	587·5 Hideaki Inaba 1987
56 kg	240 Hideaki Inaba 1987	155 Hiroyaki Isagawa (Jap) 1986	289·5 Lamar Gant (USA) 1982	625 Lamar Gant 1982
60 kg	295 Joe Bradley (USA) 1980	180 Joe Bradley 1980	302·5 Lamar Gant 1987	707·5 Joe Bradley 1982
67·5 kg	300 Jessie Jackson (USA) 1987	200 Kristoffer Hulecki (Swe) 1985	313 Daniel Austin (USA) 1987	735 Daniel Austin 1987
75 kg	327·5 Mike Bridges (USA) 1980	217·5 James Rouse (USA) 1980	332·5 John Inzer (USA) 1987	850 Rick Gaugler (USA) 1982
82·5 kg	379·5 Mike Bridges 1982	240 Mike Bridges 1981	357·5 Veli Kumpuniemi (Fin) 1980	952·5 Mike Bridges 1982
90 kg	375 Fred Hatfield (USA) 1980	255 Mike MacDonald (USA) 1980	372·5 Walter Thomas (USA) 1982	937·5 Mike Bridges 1980
100 kg	400 Fred Hatfield 1982	261·5 Mike MacDonald 1977	377·5 James Cash (USA) 1982	952·5 James Cash 1982
110 kg	393·5 Dan Wohleber (USA) 1981	270 Jeffrey Magruder (USA) 1982	395 John Kuc (USA) 1980	1000 John Kuc 1980
125 kg	412·5 David Waddington (USA) 1982	278·5 Tom Hardman (USA) 1982	387·5 Lars Noren (Swe) 1987	1005 Ernie Hackett (USA) 1982
125+ kg	445 Dwayne Fely (USA) 1982	300 Bill Kazmaier (USA) 1981	405 Lars Noren 1987	1100 Bill Kazmaier 1981
WOMEN				
44 kg	142·5 Delcy Palk (USA) 1988	75 Teri Hoyt (USA) 1982	165 Nancy Belliveau (USA) 1985	352·5 Marie Vassart (Bel) 1985
48 kg	147·5 Keiko Nishio (Japan) 1987	82·5 Michelle Evris (USA) 1981	182·5 Majik Jones (USA) 1984	390 Majik Jones 1984
52 kg	173 Sisi Dolman (Neth) 1986	95 Mary Ryan (USA) 1984	197 Diana Rowell (USA) 1984	427·5 Diana Rowell 1984
56 kg	190 Vicki Steenrod (USA) 1984	115 Mary Jeffrey (née Ryan) 1988	200 Diana Rowell 1984	482·5 Vicki Steenrod 1984
60 kg	200·5 Ruthi Shafer (USA) 1983	105 Vicki Steenrod 1985	213 Ruthi Shafer 1983	502·5 Vicki Steenrod 1985
67·5 kg	230 Ruthi Shafer 1984	115 Heidi Wittesch (Aus) 1987	244 Ruthi Shafer 1984	565 Ruthi Shafer 1984
75 kg	215·5 Heidi Wittesch 1988	140 Beverley Francis (Aus) 1981	215 Marie Geldhof (Bel) 1988	550 Beverley Francis 1981
82·5 kg	230 Juanita Trujillo (USA) 1986	150 Beverley Francis 1981	227·5 Vicky Gagne (USA) 1981	577·5 Beverley Francis 1983
90 kg	252·5 Lorraine Constanzo (USA) 1988	130 Lorraine Constanzo 1988	227·5 Lorraine Constanzo 1988	607·5 Lorraine Constanzo 1988
90+ kg	262·5 Lorraine Constanzo 1987	135 Myrtle Augee (GB) 1988	237·5 Lorraine Constanzo 1987	622·5 Lorraine Constanzo 1987

champion in 1896 at Athens. Louis George Martin (b. Jamaica, 11 Nov 1936) won four world and European mid-heavyweight titles in 1959, 1962–3, 1965. He won an Olympic silver medal in 1964 and a bronze in 1960 and three Commonwealth gold medals in 1962, 1966, 1970. His total of British titles was 12.

Heaviest lift to body weight

The first man to clean and jerk more than three times his body weight was Stefan Topurov (Bulgaria), who lifted 180 kg *396¾ lb* at Moscow, USSR on 24 Oct 1983. The first man to snatch two-and-half times his own body weight was Naim Suleimanoglou (Turkey), who lifted 150 kg *330½ lb* at Cardiff, South Glamorgan on 27 Apr 1988.

Heaviest weight

The greatest weight ever raised by a human being is 6270 lb *2844 kg* (2·80 tons *2·84 tonnes*) in a back lift (weight raised off trestles) by the 26 st *165 kg* Paul Anderson (USA) (b. 17 Oct 1932), the 1956 Olympic heavyweight champion, at Toccoa, Georgia, USA on 12 June 1957. The greatest lift by a woman is 3564 lb *1616 kg* with a hip and harness lift by Josephine Blatt (*née* Schauer) (1869–1923) at the Bijou Theater, Hoboken, New Jersey, USA on 15 Apr 1895.

POWERLIFTING

The sport of powerlifting was first contested at national level in Great Britain in 1958. The first US Championships were held in 1964. The International Powerlifting Federation was founded in 1972, a year after the first, unofficial world championships were held. Offical championships have been held annually for men from 1973 and for women from 1980. The three standard lifts are squat,

bench press and dead lift, the totals from the three lifts determining results.

Most world titles

The winner of the most world titles is Hideaki Inaba (Japan) with 13, at 52 kg 1974–83, 1985–7. The most by a British lifter is seven by Ron Collins: 75 kg 1972–4, 82 kg 1975–7 and 1979. The most by a women is six by Beverley Francis (Australia) (b. 15 Feb 1955) at 75 kg 1980, 1982; 82·5kg 1981, 1983–5.

Powerlifting feats

Paul Anderson, as a professional, reportedly achieved 1200 lb *544 kg* in a squat so aggregating, with a 627 lb *284 kg* press and an 820 lb *371 kg* dead lift, a career total of 2647 lb *1200 kg*. Lamar Grant (USA) was the first man to deadlift five times his own body weight, lifting 299·5 kg *661 lb* when 59·5 kg *132 lb* in 1985.

The greatest power lift by a woman is a squat of 262·5 kg *578·7 lb* by Lorraine Constanzo (USA) at Perth, Australia on 2 June 1987. Cammie Lynn Lusko (USA) (b. 5 Apr 1958) became the first woman to lift more than her body weight with one arm, with 59·5 kg *131 lb* at a body weight of 58·3 kg *128·5 lb*, at Milwaukee, Wisconsin, USA on 21 May 1983.

24-hr and 1-hr lifts

A deadlifting record of 2 392 150 kg *5 273 699 lb* in 24 hr was set by a team of ten from HM Prison Frankland at Finchale Weightlifting Club, Co. Durham on 8–9 May 1987. The 24 hr deadlift record by an individual is 329 611 kg *726 655 lb* by Roy A. Marshall at 'The Gym', Woodstock, USA on 17–18 May 1986.

A bench press record of 3 869 011 kg *8 529 565 lb* was set

by a nine-man team from the Hogarth Barbell Club, Chiswick, London on 18–19 July 1987. A squat record of 2 168 625 kg *4 780 919 lb* was set by a ten-man team from St Albans Weightlifting Club and Ware Boys Club, Hertfordshire on 20–21 July 1986. A record 63 600 arm-curling repetitions using three 22 kg *48¼ lb* weightlifting bars and dumb-bells were achieved by a team of nine from Heathfield Strength and Fitness Club at Wandsworth, London on 22–23 Jan 1988.

Jack Atherton achieved 1052 repetitions of his bodyweight (60·5 kg *133·4 lb*) in one hour by bench presses on 1 Apr 1988 at HM Prison, Featherstone, Wolverhampton, West Midlands.

Strandpulling

The International Steel Strandpullers' Association was founded by Gavin Pearson (Scotland) in 1940. The greatest ratified poundage to date is a super-heavyweight right-arm push of 815 lb *369·5 kg* by Malcolm Bartlett (b. 9 June 1955) of Oldham, Lancashire. The record for the back press anyhow is 645 lb *292·5 kg* by Barry Anderson, of Leeds, in 1975. A record 21 British Open titles have been won by Ian Storton (b. 2 Feb 1951) of Morecambe, Lancashire, 1974–87.

Wrestling

The earliest depictions of wrestling holds and falls on wall plaques and a statue indicate that organised wrestling dates from *c.* 2750–2600 BC. It was the most popular sport in the ancient Olympic Games and victors were recorded from 708 BC. The Greco-Roman style is of French origin and arose about 1860. The International

Amateur Wrestling Federation (FILA) was founded in 1912.

Most titles *Olympic*

Three Olympic titles have been won by: Carl Westergren (1895–1958) (Sweden) in 1920, 1924 and 1932; Ivar Johansson (1903–79) (Sweden) in 1932 (two) and 1936; and Aleksandr Medved (USSR) (b. 16 Sept 1937) in 1964, 1968 and 1972.

Four Olympic medals were won by: Eino Leino (b. 7 Apr 1891) at freestyle 1920–32; and by Imre Polyák (Hungary) (b. 16 Apr 1932) at Greco-Roman in 1952–64.

World

The freestyler Aleksandr Medved (USSR) won a record ten World Championships, 1962–4, 1966–72 at three weight categories. The only wrestler to win the same title in seven successive years has been Valeriy Rezantsev (USSR) (b. 2 Feb 1947) in the Greco-Roman 90 kg class in 1970–6, including the Olympic Games of 1972 and 1976.

Most titles and longest span *British*

The most British titles won in one weight class is ten by heavyweight Kenneth Alan Richmond (b. 10 July 1926) between 1949 and 1960.

The longest span for BAWA titles is 24 years by George Mackenzie (1890–1957) between 1909 and 1933. He represented Great Britain in five successive Olympiads, 1908 to 1928.

Most wins

In international competition, Osamu Watanabe (b. 21 Oct 1940), of Japan, the 1964 Olympic freestyle 63 kg champion, was unbeaten and unscored-upon in 189 consecutive matches. Outside of FILA sanctioned competition, Wade Schalles (USA) won 821 bouts from 1964 to 1984, with 530 of these victories by pin.

Longest bout

The longest recorded bout was one of 11 hr 40 min when Martin Klein (1885–1947) (Estonia representing Russia) beat Alfred Asikáinen (1888–1942) (Finland) for the Greco-Roman 75 kg 'A' event silver medal in the 1912 Olympic Games in Stockholm, Sweden.

Heaviest heavyweight

The heaviest wrestler in Olympic history is Chris Taylor (1950–79), bronze medallist in the super-heavyweight class in 1972, who stood 1·96 m *6 ft 5 in* tall and weighed over 190 kg *420 lb*. FILA introduced an upper weight limit of 130 kg *286 lb* for international competition in 1985.

SUMO WRESTLING

The sport's origins in Japan date from *c.* 23 BC. The heaviest ever *rikishi* is Samoan-American Salevaa Fuali Atisnoe of Hawaii, *alias* Konishiki, who in 1988 had a peak weight of 252 kg *556 lb*. He is also the first foreign *rikishi* to attain the second highest rank of *ozeki* or champion. Weight is amassed by over-alimentation with a high-protein stew called *chankonabe*.

The most successful wrestlers have been *yokozuna* Sadaji Akiyoshi (b. 1912) *alias* Futabayama, winner of 69 consecutive bouts in the 1930s, *yokozuna* Koki Naya (b. 1940) *alias* Taiho ('Great Bird'), who won the Emperor's Cup 32 times up to his retirement in 1971 and the *ozeki* Tameemon Torokichi *alias* Raiden (1767–1825), who in 21 years (1789–1810) won 254 bouts and lost only ten for the highest ever winning percentage of 96·2. Taiho and Futabayama share the record of eight perfect tournaments without a single loss. The youngest of the 62 men to attain the rank of *yokozuna* (grand champion) was Toshimitsu Ogata (b. 16 May 1953) *alias* Kitanoumi, in July 1974 aged 21 years and two months. He set a record in 1978 winning 82 of the 90 bouts that top *rikishi* fight annually and had a record 804 wins in the top *Makunouchi* division.

Yokozuna Mitsugu Akimoto (b. 1 June 1955), *alias* Chiyonofuji, set a record for domination of one of the six annual tournaments by winning the Kyushu Basho for seven

successive years, 1981–7. Hawaiian-born Jesse Kuhaulua (b. 16 June 1944), now a Japanese citizen named Daigoro Watanabe, *alias* Takamiyama, was the first non-Japanese to win an official top-division tournament, in July 1972 and in 1981 he set a record of 1231 consecutive top-division bouts. He weighed in at 204 kg *450 lb* before his retirement in 1984.

Yukio Shoji (b. 14 Nov 1948), *alias* Aobajo, did not miss a single bout in his 22-year career, 1964–86, and contested a record 1631 consecutive bouts. Kenji Hatano (b. 4 Jan 1948) *alias* Oshio, contested a record 1891 bouts in his 26-year career, 1962–88, the longest in modern sumo history. He holds the record for the most career wins with 964.

Yachting

Yachting in England dates from the £100 stake race between Charles II and his brother James, Duke of York, on the Thames on 1 Sept 1661 over 23 miles from Greenwich to Gravesend. The oldest club in the world is the Royal Cork Yacht Club which claims descent from the Cork Harbour Water Club, established in Ireland by 1720. The oldest active club in Britain is the Starcross Yacht Club at Powderham Point, Devon. Its first regatta was held in 1772. The oldest exsiting club to have been truly formed as a yacht club is the Royal Yacht Squadron, Cowes, Isle of Wight, instituted as 'The Yacht Club' at a meeting at the Thatched House Tavern, St James's Street, London on 1 June 1815.

Olympic titles *World*

The first sportsman ever to win individual gold medals in four successive Olympic Games was Paul B. Elvström (Denmark) (b. 24 Feb 1928) in the Firefly class in 1948 and the Finn class in 1952, 1956 and 1960. He also won eight other world titles in a total of six classes. The lowest number of penalty points by the winner of any class in an Olympic regatta is three points (five wins, one disqualified and one second in seven starts) by *Superdocious* of the Flying Dutchman class (Lt. Rodney Stuart Pattisson, RN (b. 5 Aug 1943) and Iain Somerled Macdonald-Smith (b. 3 July 1945)) at Acapulco Bay, Mexico in October 1968.

British

The only British yachtsman to win in two Olympic regattas is Rodney Pattisson in 1968 (see above and again with *Superdoso* crewed by Christopher Davies (b. 29 June 1946) at Kiel, West Germany in 1972. He gained a silver medal in 1976 with Julian Brooke Houghton (b. 16 Dec 1946).

Admiral's Cup and ocean racing

The ocean racing series with the most participating nations (three boats allowed to each nation) is the Admiral's Cup held by the Royal Ocean Racing Club. A record 19 nations competed in 1975, 1977 and 1979. Britain has a record eight wins.

Modern ocean racing (in moderate or small sailing yachts, rather than professionally manned sailing ships) began with a race from Brooklyn, New York, USA to Bermuda, 630 nautical miles *1166 km* organised by Thomas Fleming Day, editor of the magazine *The Rudder* in June 1906. The race is still held today in every even numbered year, though the course is now Newport, Rhode Island, USA to Bermuda.

The race still regularly run with the earliest foundation for any type of craft and either kind of water (fresh or salt) is the Chicago to Mackinac race on Lakes Michigan and Huron, first sailed in 1898. It was held again in 1904, then annually until the present day, except for 1917–20. The record for the course (333 nautical miles *616 km*) is 1 day 1 hr 50 min (average speed 12·89 knots *23·84 km/h*) by the sloop *Pied Piper*, owned by Dick Jennings (USA) in 1987.

The current record holder of the elapsed time records

for both the premier American and British ocean races, the Newport, Rhode Island, to Bermuda race and the Fastnet race: the sloop *Nirvana*, owned by Marvin Green (USA). The record for the Bermuda race, 635 nautical miles *1176 km*, is 2 days 14 hr 29 min and for the Fastnet race, 605 nautical miles *1120 km*, is 2 days 12 hr 41 min, an average speed of 10·16 knots *18·81 km/h* and 9·97 knots *18·45 km* respectively.

Longest race

The longest regular sailing race is the quadrennial Whitbread Round the World race (inst. Aug 1973) organised by the Royal Naval Sailing Association. The distance is 26 180 nautical miles *48 465 km* from Portsmouth and return, with stops and re-starts at Cape Town, Auckland and Mar del Plata. The record (sailing) time, obtained by adding the elapsed time of the three legs of the course, is 117 days 14 hr 31 min by *UBS Switzerland*, skipper Pierre Fehlmann (Switzerland), finishing on 9 May 1986 (*see also p. 166*).

Greatest distance

The greatest distance claimed for a day's run under sail was set by the trimaran *Fleury–Michon VIII* (skipper Philippe Poupon) at 520 nautical miles *963 km* on 16–17 June 1987 during a transatlantic crossing (7 days 12 hr 50 min), thus averaging 21·67 knots *40·10 km/h*.

America's Cup

The America's Cup was originally won as an outright prize by the schooner *America* on 22 Aug 1851 at Cowes and was later offered by the New York Yacht Club as a challenge trophy. On 8 Aug 1870 J. Ashbury's *Cambria* (GB) failed to capture the trophy from the *Magic*, owned by F. Osgood (USA). The Cup has been challenged 26 times, the United States were undefeated winning 77 races and only losing eight until 1983 when *Australia II*, skippered by John Bertrand and owned by a Perth syndicate headed by Alan Bond beat *Liberty* 4–3, the narrowest series victory, at Newport, RI, USA.

The most times a single helmsman has steered a cup defender is in three separate series. This was achieved by Charlie Barr (USA) who defended in 1899, 1901 and 1903 and again by Harold S. Vanderbilt (USA) in 1930, 1934 and 1937. Dennis Conner has been helmsman of American boats three times in succession: in 1980, when he successfully defended; in 1983, when he steered the defender, but lost, and in 1987 when he steered the American challenger *Stars and Stripes* to a 4–0 win over *Kookaburra III* (Australia) to regain the trophy.

The largest yacht to have competed in the America's Cup was the 1903 defender, the gaff rigged cutter *Reliance* with an overall length of 43·89 m *144 ft*, a sail area of 1501 m² *16 160 ft²* and a rig of 53·3 m *175 ft* high.

Regattas

The most consistently sailed regatta is that at Cowes, where the first race for a gold cup took place on 10 Aug 1826. Since then there has been a regatta with one or more races in early August every year except for 1915–18 and 1940–5. At present, Cowes 'Week' runs for 9 days and there are about 20 races for different classes of yacht each day.

Yacht and dinghy classes

The oldest racing class still sailing is the Water Wag class of Dublin, formed in 1887. The design of the boat was changed in 1900 to that which is still used today. The oldest classes in Britain, both established in 1898 and both still racing in the same design of boat are the Seabird Half Rater, centreboard sailing dinghy of Abersoch and other north-west ports, and the Yorkshire One-design keel boat which race from the Royal Yorkshire Yacht Club at Bridlington, Humberside.

The first international class for racing dinghies was the 14 foot International, whose principal trophy in Britain is the Prince of Wales Cup which has been contested annually since 1927 (except 1940–5). The most win is 12 by Stewart Morris between 1932 and 1965.

Highest speeds

The highest speed reached under sail on water by any craft over a 500-metre timed run is by a boardsailer Pascal Maka (France) at 38·86 knots *71·96 km/h* in a 50-knot wind at Fuerteventura, Canary Islands on a Gaastra 4-m² limited edition speed trial sailboard on 21 July 1986. The women's record was set at Saintes-Maries-de-la-Mer on 25 Mar 1988 when Elisabeth Coquelle (France) achieved 34·72 knots *64·37 km/h*.

The previous sailing speed record was 36·04 knots (41·50 mph *66·78 km/h*) by the 22·40 m *73½ ft* proa *Crossbow II* over a 500 m *547 yd* course in Portland Harbour, Dorset, on 17 Nov 1980. The vessel (sail area 130·06 m² *1400 ft²*) was designed by Rod McAlpine-Downie and owned and steered by Timothy Colman. In an unsuccessful attempt on the record in October 1978, *Crossbow II* is reported to have momentarily attained a speed of 45 knots (51 mph *83 km/h*).

Most competitors

The most boats ever to start in a single race was 2072 in the Round Zeeland (Denmark) race on 21 June 1984, over a course of 235 nautical miles *435 km*. The greatest number to start in a race in Britain was 1536 keeled yachts and multihulls on 25 June 1988 from Cowes in the Annual Round-the-Island Race. The fastest time achieved in this annual event is 3 hr 55 min 28 sec by the trimaran *Paragon*, owned and sailed by Michael Whipp on 31 May 1986.

The largest trans-oceanic race was the ARC (Atlantic Rally for Cruisers), when 204 boats of the 209 starters from 24 nations completed the race from Las Palmas de Gran Canaria to Barbados

Highest

The greatest altitude at which sailing has taken place is 4910 m *16 109 ft* on Laguna Huallatani, Bolivia, in Mirror Dinghy 55448, variously by Peter Williams, Gordon Siddeley, Keith Robinson and Brian Barrett, on 19 Nov 1977. The highest for boardsailing is 4970 m *16 300 ft* by Juan Felipe Marti, Juan Ojeda, Fermin Tarres and Philippe Levrel on Tilicho's Lake, Nepal on 20 Oct 1983.

BOARDSAILING

The High Court ruled on 7 Apr 1982 that Peter Chilvers (when aged 12) had devised a prototype of a boardsailer in 1958 in England. In 1968 Henry Hoyle Schweitzer and Jim Drake pioneered the sport, often termed windsurfing, in California, USA. World Championships were first held in 1973 and the sport was added to the Olympic Games in 1984 when the winner was Stephan van den Berg (Netherlands), who also won five world titles 1979–83.

English Channel

The record time for boardsailing across the English Channel is 1 hr 4 min 33 sec by Baron Arnaud de Rosnay (France) on 4 July 1982 from Cap Gris Nez to Dover at an average speed of 16·9 knots (19·5 mph *31·3 km/h*). After 45 min rest he returned to Wissant, France in 1 hr 4 min 37 sec.

Highest speed

See above for highest sailing speeds. Peter Bridgeman set a British record of 31·89 knots *59·10 km/h* at Port-Saint-Louis, Marseille, France on 17 Apr 1985.

Endurance

Neil Marlow (GB) set an endurance record of 107 hr in Braye Bay, Alderney and Pembroke Bay, Guernsey, Channel Islands from 4–8 Aug 1987.

Longest sailboard

The longest 'snake' of boardsails was set by 60 windsurfers in tandem at the 'International Windsurfing Week' event in Balk, Netherlands on 2 July 1985.

The world's longest sail board, 50·2 m *165 ft*, was constructed at Fredrikstad, Norway, and first sailed on 28 June 1986.

Sport Endurance Marathons

Board Games, Card Games and Other Pastimes

BACKGAMMON
Dick Newcombe and Greg Peterson at Rockford, Illinois, USA, 30 June–6 July 1978.
151 hr 11 min

BRIDGE (*CONTRACT*)
Johnathan Noad, Jeremy Cohen, Robert Pinder and Andrew Bale at Ariel Hotel, Hayes, Middlesex, 20–8 Sept 1986.
186 hr 38 min

CHESS
Roger Long and Graham Croft at Dingles, Bristol, Avon, 11–19 May 1984.
200 hr

CRIBBAGE
Four students from St Anselm's College, Wirral, Merseyside, 14–19 July 1986.
124 hr 15 min

DRAUGHTS
Greg Davis and Mark Schumacher at Denny's Restaurant, Nunawading, Victoria, Australia, 26 Aug–1 Sept 1985.
138 hr 28 min

DUNGEONS & DRAGONS (*TSR*)
5–9 Players; A team from Ogden, Utah, USA in 1983.
209 hr

SCRABBLE ®
Peter Finan and Neil Smith at St. Anselm's College, Wirral, Merseyside, 18–25 Aug 1984.
153 hr
(Ken Cardozo played for 155 hr 48 min against various opponents at 'Perfect Pizza', London, 5–11 Dec 1984.)

SNAKES & LADDERS
4 Players: A team from Essex Young Farmers Club, West Mersea, Essex, 29 Jan–9 Feb 1982.
260 hr

SUBBUTEO ® TABLE FOOTBALL
Shaun Unterslak and Jay Boccia in South Africa, 5–9 Apr 1987.
91 hr 20 min

TIDDLYWINKS
6 Players: Southampton University Tiddlywinks Club, Hampshire, 20 Feb–5 Mar 1981.
300 hr

TRIVIAL PURSUIT ™
2–6 Players: Six students at St Anselm's College, Wirral, Merseyside, 9–15 Aug 1987.
141 hr 56 min

Pub Games

BAR BILLIARDS
David Lillie and Mark Whitehart at The Waggon And Horses, Sudbury, Suffolk, 1–4 Apr 1988
84 hr 46 min

DARTS
David Dingley and Michael Poole at The Three Horseshoes, Malvern, Worcestershire, November 1986.
168 hr 4 min

DOMINOES
Neil Thomas and Tim Beesley at St Anselm's College, Wirral, Merseyside, 5–11 Aug 1985.
150 hr 5 min

POOL
Gary Drummond and John Small at Clackmannan College of Further Education, Alloa, Central, 17 June–1 July 1988.
345 hr 52 min

SKITTLES
6 Players: Gloucester & District Irish Society at Gloucester, 15–22 Aug 1981.
168 hr

SNOOKER
Nick Burgess and Paul Reid at Snookerlodge, Exeter, Devon, 8–23 July 1988.
366 hr 13 min

TABLE FOOTBALL
Binesh Lad and Spencer Hughes at Marcher Sound, Wrexham, Clywd, 1–4 Apr 1988
72 hr 20 min

Racket sports

BADMINTON
Singles: Henry Marais and Jaco Visser at Quartermaster, Pretoria, South Africa, 1–4 Jan 1988.
83 hr 25 min
Doubles: Cameron McMullen, Michael Patterson, Stephen Breuer and Michael Bain at Rhyl, Clywd 18–21 July 1987.
86 hr 22 min

RACQUETBALL
Robert Sauve and Vic Sabramsky in Whitby, Ontario, Canada, 20–2 Aug 1987.
50 hr 2 min

SQUASH
P. Etherton and L. Davies at Tannum Sands, Queensland, Australia, 7–12 July 1987.
126 hr 1 min

TABLE TENNIS
Singles: Shaun Unterslak and Jay at Dewaal Hotel, Cape Town, South Africa, 12–18 Nov 1983.
147 hr 47 min
Doubles: Lance, Phil and Mark Warren and Bill Weir at Sacramento, California, USA, 9–13 Apr 1979.
101 hr 1 min

TENNIS (*LAWN*)
Singles: Mark Humes and Bill Victor at The City of Reno Plumas Tennis Centre, Reno, Nev., USA, 20–5 May 1987.
120 hr 9 min
Doubles: Ann Wilkinson, Peter Allsopp, John Thorpe and David Dicks at Mansfield Lawn Tennis Club, Notts. 17–21 Aug 1983.
96 hr 25 min

Individual Records

BOWLING (*TEN PIN*)
Jim Webb at Gosford City Bowl, New South Wales, Australia, 1984.
195 hr 1 min

HORSEMANSHIP
Ken Northdruft at Kingsthorpe, Queensland, Australia 31 Aug–4 Sept 1985
112 hr 30 min

ICE SKATING
Austin McKinley at Christchurch, New Zealand 21–5 June 1977.
109 hr 5 min

ROLLER CYCLING
Gilbert Bil at De Weesper, Amsterdam, Netherlands, 10–14 Oct 1986.
85 hr 24 min

ROLLER SKATING
Isamu Furugen at Naha Roller Skate Land, Okinawa, Japan, 11–27 Dec 1983.
344 hr 18 min

SKIING (*ALPINE*)
Luc Labrie at Daie Comeau, Quebec, Canada 20–5 Feb 1984.
138 hr
With no waiting for lifts—John Mordini at Kissing Bridge, New York, USA, 11–14 Jan 1988.
87 hr 28 min

TRAMPOLINING
Jeff Schwartz at Glenview, Illinois, USA, 14–25 Aug 1981.
266 hr 9 min

Team Records

BASKETBALL
Sigma Nu Fraternity at Indiana University, Pennsylvania, USA, 13–17 Apr 1983.
102 hr

BOWLS
Outdoor: Two teams from Kirkcaldy Police Station at Kirkcaldy, Fife, 19–23 Aug 1987.
103 hr 47 min
Indoor: Two teams from R.O.T.A. Bowling Club, Ramelton, Letterkenny, Republic of Ireland, 9–14 May 1988.
113 hr 16 min

CRICKET
Two teams from Belper, Derbyshire, 14–27 Aug 1983.
316 hr
Indoor: Two teams from Isandis CC, Edenvale, South Africa, 14–19 July 1987.
129 hr 40 min

Netball ● Fourteen players from the Farnham Sports Centre, Surrey successfully played netball for a record 45 hr 25 min from 22–4 July 1988. Here, just about to drop in, is one of the 2087 goals scored during this marathon.

CROQUET
Jane Langan, Miles Harbot, Jo Gill and Daryl Shorthose at Birmingham University, 14–19 June 1986.
120 hr 25 min

CURLING
4 Players: Capital Winter Club, Fredericton, New Brunswick, Canada, 9–12 Apr 1982.
67 hr 55 min
Brian Rankin and David Senior at Bradford, West Yorkshire, 5–7 July 1988.
43 hr 2 min

FIVES (*RUGBY*)
Robert Ridgwell, Justin Khraushar, Tegid Matthews and David Spencer at Highgate School, London 12–14 Sept 1986.
35 hr

FOOTBALL
Two teams from Stewart's, Lake Park, Florida, USA 31 Aug– 3 Sept 1984.
64 hr 44 min
Outdoor 5–a–side: Two teams at Liswerry Leisure Centre, Newport, Gwent, 23–6 June 1983.
74 hr 30 min
Indoor 5–a–side: Two teams from Rockhampton, Queensland, Australia, 17–22 Nov 1985.
106 hr 10 min

GAELIC FOOTBALL
Two teams from Kilcornan GAA. Club, Kilcornan, Co. Limerick, Ireland, 23–5 May 1986.
60 hr 5 min

HANDBALL
Castlebridge Handball Club, Castlebridge, Co. Wexford, Ireland 26–8 Sept 1986.
45 hr 50 min

HOCKEY
Outdoor: Two teams from Hood College, Fredrick, Maryland, USA, 3–5 Oct 1987
44 hr 30 min
Indoor: Two teams from Queen's University, Belfast, Stramillis Gardens, Belfast, 28–30 Dec 1987
55 hr 10 min

JUDO
Five of six people at Smithfield RSL Youth Club, New South Wales, Australia, 3–13 Jan 1984.
245 hr 30 min

RUGBY UNION
Tongario High School and Taupo-Nua-A-Tia Grade College School at Turangi Park, New Zealand, 27–8 Mar 1987.
24 hr

SOFTBALL
Fast Pitch: Two teams from Campbelltown District Association at Ingleburn, New South Wales, Australia 6–8 Dec 1986.
60 hr
Slow Pitch: Brigade Service Support Group-1 and Marine Aircraft Group-24 at Kareohe Marine Corps Air Station, Hawaii, USA, 3–8 Sept 1986.
111 hr 2 min

VOLLEYBALL
Students from Krugersdorp High School, Krugerdorp, South Africa, 30 Mar–4 Apr 1988.
118 hr 30 min

WATER POLO
Two teams from Shrewsbury School at Shrewsbury Baths, Shropshire, 29–30 Nov 1986.
25 hr 34 min

IMPORTANT
Rest breaks of five minutes for each completed hour played (not calculated according to a running total) are permitted in these endurance marathons. Such breaks are aggregable but at no time can the earned rest period be exceeded. The number of participants in team events is shown in the table, all must be in action throughout the attempt, except that a drop out rate of up to 20% of the people is permitted. No substitutes are allowed. Claims for new records must be accompanied by full authentication.

Stop Press

Chapter 1

Super heavyweights ● (p. 9) Welshman Melvyn Jones (b. 1934), who died in Liverpool on 25 July 1988 and was buried in Bangor, Gwynedd recorded a posthumous weight of 329 kg *52 st*. He was 1.70 m *5 ft 7 in* tall.

Walter Hudson reportedly lost 286 kg *45 st* during the 9 month period to June 1988 on a spartan diet of powdered vitamins and minerals. His target is a weight of 86 kg *13.5 st* by 1991.

Oldest living person ● (p. 11) Authentication was received in July 1988 to show that Jeanne Calment of Arles, France, was born on 21 Feb 1875.

Youngest living great-great-great-grandmother ● (p. 14) Harriett Holmes of Newfoundland, Canada (b. 17 Jan 1899) was 88 years 50 days old when she became a 3 greats grandmother on 8 Mar 1987.

Memory ● (p. 16) Allan Griffith memorised a random sequence of seven shuffled packs of cards with only 2 errors at the Carmondean Library, Livingston, West Lothian on 1 Aug 1988.

Fastest Talker ● (p. 17) John Moschitta recited 545 words in 55·8 sec or 586 words per minute on 24 May 1988, in Los Angeles, California, USA.

Talking backwards ● (p. 17) Steve Briers recited the entire lyrics of Queen's 1975 album *A Night at the Opera* on the Radio 1 Roadshow at Tenby, Dyfed on 26 July 1988. He achieved the 2343 words in 15 min 7 sec.

Highest mortality rate ● (p. 18) The World Health Organisation reported 108 176 cases up to July 1988. The UK total of fatalities to 1 July 1988 was 897 with 8 794 infected.

Chapter 2

Oldest mammal ● (p. 24) Rajah died on 16 July 1988 allegedly aged 81 years.

Smallest pinniped ● (p. 24-25) The Common seal has been measured up to 1·98 m *6 ft 6 in* in length and up to 149·6 kg *330 lb* in weight.

Largest rodent ● (p. 26) On 18 July 1988 the corpse of an old male Coypu was found at Barton Bendish, Norfolk. Until then there had been no sightings for 15 months.

Top trainer ● (p. 30) Barbara Woodhouse died at Great Missenden, Buckinghamshire on 9 July 1988 aged 78 years.

Most talkative bird ● (p. 33) Lyn Logue, owner of 'Prudle', died in January 1988.

Longest segmented worm ● (p. 40) In May 1988 an unconfirmed length of c. 1·98 m *6 ft 6in* was reported for a *live* earthworm found at Brambles Wildlife Park near Canterbury, Kent.

Largest flying creature ● (p. 43) Weight recalculations indicate this pterosaur weighed in the region of 113 kg *250 lb*.

Tallest dahlia ● (p. 46) R. D. Blythe of Nannup, Western Australia grew a dahlia which was 6·3 m *20 ft 8 in* tall on 9 June 1988.

Tallest lupin ● (p. 46) K. S. Barnes of Guildford, Surrey grew a lupin measured in June 1988 at 1·90 m *6 ft 3 in*.

Heaviest pears ● (p. 46) It was reported in the 4 Nov 1831 edition of *The Standard* that Mrs G. Chambers of Faversham, Kent had grown seven 'extraordinary large pears', the heaviest weighing 2 lb 14½ oz *1·318 kg*.

Chapter 3

Shortest river ● (p. 57) The world's shortest river with a name is the Roe River, near Great Falls, Montana, USA which flows into the Missouri River and has an official length of 61 m *200·13 ft*.

Chapter 4

Stellar planets ● (p. 70) It was announced on 3 Aug 1988 that the star HB 114762, 90 light-years distant in Coma Berenice, had a planet 20 times larger than Jupiter orbiting it every 84 days. The discovery by Dr. David Latham from Oak Ridge Observatory, Massachusetts, USA was challenged by other astronomers as being a binary small brown dwarf star.

Jeanne Calment with Pierre Gorin of *Le Livre Guinness des Records*.

Remotest object ● (p. 72) Galaxy 4C41.17 was announced from Kitt Peak, Arizona, USA on 9 Aug 1988 to have a red shift of $z=3·8$ which is held to correspond to 15 000 000 000 light-years.

Chapter 5

Bottle collections ● (p. 77) At 9 July 1988 Ted Schuler of Germantown, Tennessee, USA, had a collection of 1850 different bottled beers with specimens from 83 countries.

Largest Topaz ● (p. 79) *The American Golden Topaz* weighs 22 892·5 carats. It has been on display at the Smithsonian Institution, Washington DC, USA since 4 May 1988.

Chapter 6

Most spellings ● (p. 86) Mr B. Cook of Edinburgh has recorded that in the period 1955-88 he has seen 259 different spellings of the word isosceles.

Top-selling ● (p. 89) *Year of Royal Days* by Barbara Cartland brought her total global sales past the 500 000 000 mark over 478 titles by July 1988.

Largest pan pipes ● (p. 93) The world's largest pan pipes created by Simon Desorgher and Lawrence Casserley consisted of 5 contra-bass pipes, each 100 mm in diameter with lengths of 4790 mm, 4160 mm, 3606 mm, 3104 mm and 2666 mm respectively and 5 bass pipes of 50 mm diameter with lengths of 2395 mm, 2080 mm, 1803 mm, 1522 mm and 1333 mm. Their first public appearance was at Jubilee Gardens, London on 9 July 1988.

Broadway ● (p. 97) The Broadway record for advance sales was set in 1987 by *Phantom of the Opera* at \$19 000 000.

Largest output ● (p. 100) Indian production of feature length films was a record 807 in 1987.

Most violent film ● (p. 100) The National Coalition on Television Violence has listed 123 deaths and 245 separate acts of violence in 109 minutes of *Rambo III*. Sylvester Stallone, as a one man fighting machine, fends off the Soviet Army single-handedly.

Most expensive personal movie prop ● (p. 103) The ruby slippers, worn by Judy Garland in the 1939 film *The Wizard of Oz*, were sold on 2 June 1988 to a mystery buyer at Christie's, New York USA for \$165 000.

Largest single screen auditorium ● (p. 103) The Grays State Theatre, Grays, Essex has 2200 seats and was opened in 1938.

Most durable show ● (p. 104) By 15 April 1988 TV personality Hugh Downs had appeared on camera for 10 037 ½hours.

Chapter 7

Oldest inhabited house in Britain ● (p. 110) There is evidence that the Manor Farm, Nyetimber, Pagham, West Sussex, includes the remains of a hall or *aula*, built in early Saxon times c. 800 AD.

Largest non-palatial residence ● (p. 110) St. Emmeram Castle, Regensburg, West Germany valued at more than \$177 million contains 517 rooms with a floor space of 21 460 m² *231 000 ft²*. Only 95 rooms are personally used by its owner Prince Johannes von Thurm und Taxis and his family.

Largest scarecrow ● (p. 122) A scarecrow of 27·5 m *90 ft 1 in* high with an arm span of 19·8 m *65 ft* was erected by a team of 20 men from Ward Building Systems Ltd on 30 May 1988 in the grounds of Castle Howard, North Yorkshire.

Oil fields ● (p. 122) In 1987 the world's largest oil producer was the USSR with 12·5 million barrels per day, followed by the USA with 9·9 million with the UK sixth with 2.6 million barrels.

Oil platforms ● (p. 123) The \$500 000 000 off-shore oil rig *Bullwinkle*, towed out from Corpus Christi, Texas, USA to a site 241 km *150 miles* south of New Orleans on 27 May 1988, measured 492·2 m *1615 ft* tall.

Chapter 8

Largest tanker ● (p. 126) The world's largest tanker and ship of any kind is the 555 051 tonne deadweight *Hella Foss*, a steam turbine tanker built in 1979. Of 274 826 gross registered tonnage and 225 011 net registered tonnage, she is Greek-owned by the Bilinder Marine Corporation of Athens and has been laid up at Piræeus since July 1987.

Motor cars ● (p. 128) The number of automobiles constructed worldwide in 1987 was 14 300 000 of which 3 860 000 were made in Japan and 3 430 000 in the USA.

Number plates ● (p. 128) The number plate NEW 1 was bought at auction at Phillips, London on 20 July 1988 for £17 600.

Fuel economy ● (p. 130) An experimental Japanese vehicle achieved the equivalent of 2269 km/litre, *6409 mpg* in the Shell Mileage Marathon at Silverstone, Northamptonshire on 30 June 1988.

Longest fuel range ● (p. 130) The greatest distance driven without refuelling on a single fuel fill 185·1 litre *40·7 gal* carried in factory optional twin fuel tanks is 2094·9 km *1300·9 miles* in a Toyota LandCruiser diesel pickup driven by Ewan Kennedy and Ray Barker with John Windass (observer) from Sydney, Australia, to a point on the Eyre Highway west of Wirrulla in South Australia in 31 hr 8 min in May 1988.

Stop Press

Longest taxi ride ● (p. 130) Ned Kelly left London on 19 Aug 1988 on a 20 100 km *12 500 mile* ride to Australia to raise £250 000 for Irish children's charities.
Most durable cabbie ● (p. 130) Charles Kerslake (b. 27 June 1895) held a London Metropolitan cab licence from February 1922 until his retirement in May 1988.
Battery-powered vehicle ● (p. 131) Joe Schwarzkopf-Bowers drove a complete circuit of the M25 (195·5 km *121·5 miles*) at an average speed of 64·36 km/h *40 mph* on a single charge of his specially designed car on 5 July 1988.
Oldest motorcyclist ● (p. 134) Leonard Hart of Tonbridge, Kent, (b. 10 Aug 1889) is still riding his Puch moped.
Bicycle parade ● (p. 135) The greatest percentage participation in a bicycle parade is one of 2·75 per cent of the total population of San Juan, Puerto Rico (1 816 300) on 17 April 1988. It was organised by TV personality 'Pacheco' aka Joaquin Monserrat.
Trains — fastest ● (p. 135) Design of the 237 km/h *140 mph* £1 129 000 Class 91 Electra locomotive, tested in July 1988, calls for an eventual schedule for the 632 km *393 miles* London-Edinburgh route of 210 minutes, to average 180·6 km/h *112·28 mph.*
Underwater cycling ● (p. 135) A team of 32 divers achieved a distance of 187·7 km *116·66 miles* in 75 hr 20 min at Divers Den, Santa Barbara, California, USA on 16-19 June 1988 to raise money for The Muscular Dystrophy Association.
Rail travel ● (p. 137) Matthew Youell of Leeds, West Yorkshire travelled 11 374 km *7069 miles* using a British Rail 7-day Rover ticket from 11-17 July 1988.

John Byrne and Lisa Shelley covered the entire passenger networks of Iarnrod Eireann and Northern Ireland Railways in 4 days 2 hr 47 min from 4-8 July 1988.
Flights in a day ● (p. 139) Brother Michael Bartlett, O.G.S. travelled on 18 scheduled flights in 23 hr 52 min (14 of these being achieved in 11 hr 6 min) in the Channel Isles and south coast of England on 15-16 June 1988.
Hot-air balloon ● (p. 142) Per Lindstrand (GB) achieved a new altitude record of 19811 m *64 996 ft* over Laredo, Texas, USA on 6 June 1988.

Chapter 9

Menwsear store ● (p. 150) The world's largest store selling only men's suits and accessories is Slater Menswear of Howard Street, Glasgow, Strathclyde with a weekly turnover in excess of 2000 suits per week. The premises cover 2600 m^2 *28 000* ft^2 and carry a stock of over 14 000 suits at any one time.
English furniture *UK* ● (p. 152) A record price of £407 000 was paid for a George II bombe commode on 7 July 1988 at Christie's, London.
Bottle caps ● (p. 153) Helge Friholm's collection contained 50 008 different bottle caps from 158 countries as at 12 July 1988.
Sheep shearing ● (p. 160) At Lesmahagow, Strathclyde on 25 June 1988, a British record for 9 hr was set at 706 by David Galloway (373) and Andrew Muirhead (333) (sheep caught *for* shearers).

Chapter 10

Auctioneering ● (p. 170) The longest one-man auction on record is one of 57 hr by John Martin at Romany City, Manchester from 21-23 Aug 1987.
Balloon release ● (p. 170) The British record is 115 000 helium balloons released simultaneously on 30 May 1988 from Castle Howard, near Malton, North Yorkshire.
Bed race ● (p. 170) The record time for the annual Knaresborough Bed Race (established 1966) in North Yorkshire is now 12 min 25 sec fo the 3.27 km *2 mile 63 yd* course crossing the River Nidd, achieved by the Bebra Beevers' team on 11 June 1988.
Best man ● (p. 170) The world champion 'best man' is Ting Ming Siong, from Sibu, Sarawak, in Malaysia, who officiated for the 408th time since 1976 on 7 May 1988.

The World Bus starting a run of 246.8 metres *810 feet* at North Weald Airfield, Essex, on 21 May 1988.

Bicycle (most mounting simultaneously) ● (p. 170) On 30 June 1988 at Semarang, Central Java, Indonesia 19 members of the Jago Sport Club mounted and rode a single bicycle a distance of 200 m *656 ft 2 in.*
Bubble ● (p. 171) David Stein of New York, USA created a 15·24 m *50 ft* long bubble on 6 June 1988. He made the bubble using a bubble wand, washing-up liquid and water.
Clapping ● (p. 171) The duration record for continuous clapping (sustaining an average of 160 claps per min audible at 109·7 m *120 yd*) is now 58 hr 9 min, by V. Jeyaraman of Tamil Nadu, India from 12-15 Feb 1988.
Juggling ● (p. 171) Sam Scurfield juggled 3 oranges without a drop for 6 hours 24 minutes 50 seconds on 21 Mar 1988 at Bradford, West Yorkshire.
Crawling ● (p. 172) The longest continuous voluntary crawl (progression with one or other knee in unbroken contact with the ground) on record is 45·87 km *28.5 miles* by Reg Morris of Brownhills, West Midlands on 29 July 1988. The crawl took place on a measured course 2·41 km *1½ miles* long. It took 9½ hours and 19 laps of the track to gain the record.
Dancing — High kicking ● (p. 174) The world record for high kicks (heel to ear level) is 10 508 in 5 hr 30 min by Keith Nesbitt at Rochester, New York, USA on 16 Apr 1988. Tony Higo set heel to ear level high kick records of 94 in 10 seconds, 190 in 25 seconds and 213 in 1 minute on Yorkshire TV's Telethon 1988, in Leeds, West Yorkshire on 30 May 1988.
Cheese ● (p. 175) The largest cheese ever created was a cheddar of 18 171 kg *40 060 lb*, made on 13-14 Mar 1988 at Simon's Specialty Cheese, Little Chute, Wisconsin, USA. It was subsequently taken on tour in a specially designed, refrigerated 'Cheesemobile'.
Ice cream sundae ● (p. 175) The largest ice cream sundae was one weighing 24 908.8 kg *54 914.8 lb* made by Palm Dairies Ltd under the supervision of Mike Rogiani in Edmonton, Alberta, Canada on 24 July 1988. It consisted of 20 270.7 kg *44 689·5 lb* of ice-cream, 4394·4 kg *9688·1 lb* of syrup and 243.7 kg *537·2 lb* of topping.
Kebab ● (p. 175) The longest kebab ever made was one 139.3 m *457 ft* long, by staff of Ruwi Novotel at the Oman Exhibition Centre, Muscat, Sultanate of Oman on 20 May 1988.
Milk shake ● (p. 175) The largest milk shake was one of 2029.8 litres *446·5 gal* containing 1136·5 litres *250 gal* of strawberry ice cream, 838·75 litres *184·5 gal* of milk and 54·55 litres *12 gal* of strawberry syrup, made at a charity party held in Bamford, Derbyshire on 17 July 1988.
Strawberry bowl ● (p. 175) The largest strawberry bowl ever picked was by children from various schools at Hewitts Farm, Chelsfield, Kent on 7 July 1988, having a net weight of 1218·0 kg *2685·2 lb.*
Sausage ● (p. 176) The longest continuous sausage ever made was one of 21·12 km *13·125 miles* made at the premises of Keith Boxley at Wombourne, near Wolverhampton in 15 hr 33 min on 18-19 June 1988.
Joke cracking ● (p. 178) Felipe Carbonell of Lima, Peru told jokes for 72 hr at the Alfa Hotel, Lisbon, Portugal from 18-21 Mar 1988.
Kiss of life ● (p. 178) Christopher Currie and Kevin Pilkington completed an 80 hr CPR (cardiopulmonary resuscitation — 15 compressions alternating with 2 breaths) marathon between 7-10 July 1988 in Penrith, Cumbria.
Kissing ● (p. 178) James Whale kissed 4525 women in 8 hr at the *Yorkshire TV* Telethon garden party in Leeds, West Yorkshire on 30 May 1988, a rate of 1 each 6·36 sec.
Leapfrogging ● (p. 178) The greatest distance covered was 1429·2 km *888·1 miles* by fourteen members of The Class of 1988 of Hanover High School, in Hanover, New Hampshire, USA, who started leapfrogging on 10 June 1988 and stopped 189 hr 49 min later, on 18 June.
Milk bottle balancing ● (p. 179) The greatest distance walked by a person continuously balancing a full pint milk bottle on the head is 38·6 km *31½ miles* by Reg Morris of Brownhills, West Midlands on 23 July 1988.
Musical chairs ● (p. 179) The largest game on record was one starting with 6500 participants, ending with Christine Hick on the last chair, which was held on the beach at Weymouth, Dorset on 30 May 1988.
Riding in armour ● (p. 180) The longest ride in armour is one of 288·47 km *179·25 miles* by Gary Bourne and David Ward, from 10-14 July 1988, around Kent. Their riding time was 41 hr 5 min.
Parachuting ● (p. 181) Longest delayed drop over UK, man, civilian — 10 180 m *33 400 ft* from 10 851 m *35 600 ft* by Mark Child and Rory McCarthy in King's Lynn, Norfolk on 18 Sept 1986.
Parachuting ● (p. 181) 24-hour total (under the rules of the United States Parachute Association) — 301 by Dale Nelson, Pennsylvania, USA, 26-27 May 1988.
Shaving ● (p. 181) Denny Rowe shaved 1994 men in 60 min at Herne Bay, Kent on 19 June 1988, taking on average 1.8 sec per volunteer, and drawing blood 4 times.
Shoe-shining ● (p. 181) In this category (limited to a team of 4 teenagers; duration of 8 hr; shoes 'on the hoof') the record is 9403 pairs by 4 members of the COGS Youth Group of Crofton Park Baptist Church at Lewisham, London on 6 Aug 1988.
Teeth-pulling ● (p. 183) John Massis died on 11 July 1988

Chapter 11

Infant mortality ● (p. 190) In June 1988 UNICEF reported that infant mortality in Mozambique had reached 350 per thousand for the age group 0-5 years.
Expectation of life at birth ● (p. 191) By January 1988 the average expectation of life in Japan reached 81·39 years for women and 75·61 years for men.
United Kingdom Electoral Records ● (p. 194) Votes — least since universal franchise. At the Kensington by-election on 14 July 1988, Dr Kailish Trivedi (Independent Janata) equalled the all-time low with 5 votes.
Greatest mass arrest ● (p. 207) South Korean police rounded up 15 617 potential troublemakers on 11 July 1988 to ensure security in advance of the 1988 Olympic Games in Seoul.
Billionaires ● (p. 208) It was reported in July 1988 that among the world's private billionaires, 68 were in the USA, 34 in Japan and 5 in Britain. The latest official estimate of the number of millionaires in the UK in 1975 (published in July 1988) was 'about 10 000'.
Richest men ● (p. 208) *Forbes Magazine* estimated on 8 July 1988 that Yoshiaki Tsutsumi, chairman of the Seiba Group, is the world's richest man with assets of $18 900 million. The richest man in the United States is Sam Moore Walton, founder in 1962 of Wal-Mart discount stores of Bentonville, Arkansas, whose personal worth was estimated by *Forbes Magazine* on 8 July 1988 to be $6.5 billion.
Longest and most valuable lines of coins ● (p. 210) A carpet of 1 945 223 Belgian One Franc coins (21 mm *0·83 in* in diameter) and thus with a total length of 40·849 km *25·384 miles* was laid in Geel, Belgium by members of Mepp-Stegeta on 25 June 1988.
Youngest graduates and undergraduates ● (p. 215) Adragon Eastwood De Mello (b. 5 Oct 1976) of Santa Cruz, California, USA obtained his BA in Mathematics from the University of California in Santa Cruz on 11 June 1988 at the age of 11 years 8 months.

Chapter 12

Cycling ● (p. 242) Tour de France, most participants, 198 in 1988.
Golf ● (p. 256) Most holes in a week, 1260 by Colin Young, using a golf cart for transport, at Patshull Park Golf Club (5863 m *6412 yd*), Pattingham, Shropshire from 2-9 July 1988.
Gymnastics ● (p. 258) Parallel bar dips, 2682 by Michael Williams at Don Styler's Gymnasium, Gosport, Hampshire on 29 July 1988.
Motor Racing ● (p. 270) Alain Prost's point total is 471.5 from 131 Grand Prix races to 7 Aug 1988.
Swimming ● (p. 290) World records: Men: 100 m freestyle, 48·42 Matthew Biondi (USA) on 10 Aug 1988; 100 m backstroke, 54·91. David Berkoff (USA) on 13 Aug 1988 both at Austin, Texas, USA.
Track and field ● (p. 296) World record: Men: 400 m, 43·29 Harry Lee 'Butch' Reynolds (USA) at Zürich, Switzerland on 17 Aug 1988.
(p. 302) British records: Men: 110 m hurdles, 13·11 Colin Jackson at Sestriere, Italy on 11 Aug 1988. (Set at high altitude)
(p. 303) Women: 100 m hurdles, 12·29 Sally Jane Janet Gunnell (b. 29 July 1966) at Zürich, Switzerland on 17 Aug 1988; 400 m hurdles, 55·40 Sally Jane Janet Gunnell at Birmingham on 6 Aug 1988: Shot, 19·36 m *63 ft 6¼in*, Judith Oakes at Gateshead on 14 Aug 1988.
Endurance marathons ● (p. 309-10) Hockey *Outdoor;* 48 hr by two teams from K.M.H.C. Waalwijk at Waalwijk, The Netherlands from 24-26 June 1988.

Index

DEATH DUTIES, highest 208
DEATH RATE, highest, lowest, infant mortality 190
DEATH ROW, longest stay 206
DEBATE, most protracted 172
DEBT, largest national, most foreign 208
DECAPLETS, 13
DECATHLON, world record 296, UK 302
DECORATIONS, see **Medals** 184-6
DEEP-SEA DIVING, record depth 165
DEER, largest wild 22, fastest, largest herd 24, largest, largest antler span, smallest, rarest, oldest 27, record heads 245
DEFAMATION, highest damages 202
DEFENCE, world expenditure 197
DEGREES, most honorary 186
DELTA, largest 58
DEMOLITION WORK, by hand 172
DEMONSTRATION, largest 218
DENTISTS, most dedicated 15, most 191
DEPARTMENT STORE, largest world, UK, most profitable, most 149
DEPRESSIONS, deepest world, GB, largest 56
DESCENDANTS, most 14
DESPATCHES, most mentions 185
DESTROYER, fastest 125
DIAMOND, largest, rarest coloured, price, highest auction price, smallest, largest cut 79
DIARY, longest 88
DICTIONARY, largest 87
DINING OUT, 169
DINOSAUR, largest, smallest, longest trackway, fastest, largest footprints, earliest, most brainless, largest eggs, largest claws, largest skull, largest flying creatures 41-3
DIRECTOR, most prolific film 102
DIRECTORSHIPS, most 148
DISASTERS AND ACCIDENTS, worst world, UK 213-14, sports 221
DISCO, dancing marathon 174
DISEASE, commonest 17, rarest 17-18, most infectious, Parkinson's 18
DISH, largest 175
DISTILLERY, largest 149
DIVE, deepest animal 22, highest 177-8
DIVING, Deep-sea, record depth 165, deepest salvage, flexible dress 167, (sport) 290
DIVORCE, highest rate 190, longest case 201, highest settlements 202, oldest 169
DOCK, largest dry, largest gate 117
DOCTORATE, youngest 215
DOCTORS, highest percentage, 191, most in family 169
DOG, canine population, heaviest, tallest, smallest, oldest 28, strength and endurance 28-9, rarest, guide, largest litter, most prolific, most valuable, highest and longest jump, ratting record, tracking feat record, top show dog, top trainer*, drug sniffing 29-30
DOG SHOW, largest 30
DOLLS, most expensive 152
DOME, largest world, UK 117
DOMESTICATED ANIMALS, 28-31
DOMINOES, 172, 309
DON, most durable 216
DONKEY, lowest price 161
DOOR, largest, oldest 117
DOUBLE BASS, largest, most players 93
DOUGHNUTS, eating record 177
DOW JONES AVERAGE, peak 151
DOWRY, biggest 209
DRAGLINE, largest 144
DRAGON, longest dancing 172
DRAGONFLY, largest, smallest 39
DRAUGHTS, 227-8, 309
DRAWING, highest price 83
DREAM, longest 18
DREDGER, largest 127
DRESS, most expensive 156
DRILLING, deepest world, deepest ocean, progressive records 122-3
DRINK, most alcoholic, oldest vintage wine, strongest, weakest beer, most expensive wine, greatest wine auction, biggest tasting, most expensive wine, greatest wine auction, biggest tasting, most expensive, spirits 76, top-selling brand (spirits) 149, (soft) 150, biggest round 172
DRINKER, hardest 17
DRINKING, records 176-7
DRIVER, (car) oldest 131-2, youngest, most durable 132, worst 212
DRIVING, fastest round the world, Cape to Cape, round Britain economy, fastest mountain driving, farthest in reverse, battery-powered, longest, fastest on two wheels 131, longest tow 133, motor racing 269-72
DRIVING TEST, most failures 132
DROUGHT, longest 64
DRUG, most powerful, most prescribed 77, haul 204, 205
DRUG SNIFFING, top dog 30
DRUM, largest kit, largest drum 94
DRUMMING, duration record 172
DRY DOCK, largest 117
DUCK, most eggs 162
DUCKS AND DRAKES, 172
DUMPER TRUCK, largest 134
DUNGEONS AND DRAGONS, 309
DWARF, shortest, lightest 8-9, oldest, most variable stature 9

EAR, longest rabbit 31
EARNINGS, see **Income**
EARTH, largest diameter, greatest circumference, area, axial rotation, weight, density, volume, most abundant element 54, deepest penetration 167 (see also **Structure and Dimensions** 54-61)
EARTH MOVER, largest 134
EARTHQUAKE, greatest 60-61, highest seismic (tidal) wave 55, worst world, UK 213-14
EARTHWORK, most massive, most extensive single site GB 117
EARTHWORM, longest in world, GB 40
EASTER EGG, heaviest and tallest 175
EATING, most prodigious animal 22, records 176-7
EATING OUT, world champion 169
ECHO, longest 80
ECLIPSES, earliest, longest, most and least frequent 69
ECONOMICS, 207-12
EDITORSHIP, longest 91
EDUCATION, 215-16
EELS, most electric 38, eating record 177, largest caught 223
EGG, largest 22, 33, smallest bird 33, most, least (fish) 37, largest dinosaur 43, laying records 162, biggest drop, hunt, shelling, longest distance thrown 172, eating records 177
EGG AND SPOON RACE, marathon 172
ELECTION, largest, closest, most decisive, most bent, highest personal majority, UK records* 194, betting 251
ELECTORATES, European Parliament 196, most mature 194
ELECTRIC CURRENT, most powerful, highest voltage 80
ELECTRIC GENERATOR, largest 143
ELECTRIC LIGHT BULB, oldest 80
ELECTRIC RAILWAY, first, fastest train 135, longest line underground 137
ELECTRONIC BRAIN, see **Computer**
ELECTRON MICROSCOPE, most powerful 80
ELEMENTS, 75
ELEPHANT, largest 22, longest lived*, longest gestation period 24, longest, heaviest tusks 27
ELEVATOR, worst disaster 213-14, **Grain,** largest, largest collection 108, **Lock,** highest 115
EMBASSY, largest 108
EMBROIDERY, longest 159
EMERALD, largest, highest price 79
EMIGRATION, most UK, most 188, 190
EMPEROR, longest dynasty 191
EMPLOYER, largest 148
EMPLOYMENT, highest 210
EMPLOYMENT AGENCY, biggest 149
ENCORE, longest operatic 95
ENCYCLOPAEDIA, earliest 87-8, largest, most comprehensive 88
ENDOWMENT, biggest educational 216
ENDURANCE MARATHONS*, (sport) 309-10
ENERGY, world average, highest, lowest consumption 211
ENGAGEMENT, longest 169
ENGINE, (car) largest, fastest change 129
ENGINE, (jet) see **Jet Engine**
ENGINE, (military) largest 200
ENGINE, (railway) first, fastest electric, steam 135, most powerful 135-6
ENGINE, (ship) earliest steam 125
ENGINE, (steam) oldest 143
ENGINEERING 144-6
ENGLISH CHANNEL, (first crossing) aircraft 137, canoeing 233, rowing 280, swimming 290-92
EPONYMOUS RECORD, largest object named after human 184
EQUESTRIAN SPORTS, 244-5, horsemanship marathon 310
EQUITY, largest, smallest 152
ERUPTION, greatest volcanic 61
ESCALATOR, first, longest 144, longest ride 172
ESCAPE, deepest underwater 165, longest prison, greatest gaol break 207
ESCAPOLOGY, greatest artist 172
ESKIMO ROLLS, 234
E.S.P., best performance 20
ESTUARY, longest 57
ETON FIVES, 245
EUROPEAN ASSEMBLY, election records 196
EVACUATION, greatest military 198
EXAMINATIONS, youngest 'A' level achiever 215, most 'O' and 'A' levels passed 216
EXCAVATOR, largest 144
EXECUTION, most, largest hanging, last public hanging, last public guillotining, youngest, oldest, longest stay on Death Row 206
EXECUTIONER, longest in office 206
EXECUTIVE, highest-paid 209
EXHIBITION, largest centre 108
EXPECTATION OF LIFE, highest and lowest at birth* 191
EXPLOSION, greatest volcanic 61, largest 'conventional' 200, worst world, UK 213-14
EXTINCT ANIMALS, largest, smallest dinosaur, longest trackway, fastest, largest footprints, earliest, most brainless, largest dinosaur eggs, largest claws, largest skull, flying creature* 43, marine reptile 43-4, crocodile, chelonians, tortoise, longest snake, largest amphibian, insect, largest bird, largest mammal, mammoth, largest primate 44, longest, heaviest tusks 44-5, antlers, greatest span 44
EXTRA-SENSORY PERCEPTION, see **E.S.P.**
EYE, smallest visible object 15-16, colour sensitivity, colour blindness 16

FABRIC, earliest, most expensive, finest cloth 156-7
FACTORY, largest whale ship 126, earliest motor-cycle 134, largest chocolate 149
FAIR, earliest, largest, record attendance, big wheel, fastest, longest switchback, longest slide 111
FALL, greatest altitude without parachute 181
FAMILY, richest 209
FAMILY TREE, largest 172-3
FAMINE, worst world, UK 213-14
FANGS, largest (snake) 35
FARM, earliest site, largest 160
FASHION SHOW, most prolific producer 98, longest 173
FAST, longest 19
FATTEST, man 9-10, woman 10
FAUX PAS, greatest 173
FEATHERS, longest, most 33
FEES, highest 209
FEET, largest 15
FELINE, largest, smallest 24
FELL RUNNING, 274
FENCE, longest, highest 117-18
FENCING, 245
FERN, largest, smallest 48
FERRY, largest car 126, fastest cross-Channel 127-8
FIDDLER, most durable 93-4
FIELD, oil 122, largest wheat, hop 161
FIELD GUN, competition 173
FIELD SPORTS, 245
FIGURE SKATING, see **Ice Skating**
FILIBUSTER, longest 193
FILLING STATION, largest 132
FILM*, earliest, most, least expensive, most expensive rights, longest, longest running, highest box-office gross, largest loss, most violent*, longest series 100, longest make-up jobs, largest studios 102, most Oscar awards, most seen 103
FINE, heaviest 207
FINGER NAILS, longest 15
FINGERS, greatest number, most sensitivity of 15
FIRE, human endurance 18, worst disaster 213-14
FIREBALL, brightest 67
FIRE BREATHER, most voracious 18
FIRE EXTINGUISHER, most voracious 18
FIRE ENGINE, most powerful 134
FIRE PUMP, greatest gallonage, pulling 173
FIREWORK, largest 157, worst disaster 213-14
FIRST NIGHTS, most 98
FISH, most ferocious 35, largest, smallest 35-6, fastest 36, longest lived 36-7, oldest goldfish, shortest lived, most abundant, deepest, most, least eggs 37, most valuable 37-8, most venomous, most electric 38, largest prehistoric 43
FISH AND CHIPS, largest shop 151
FISHERIES, highest recorded catch 149
FISHING, see **Angling**
FIVES, 245, 310
FJORD, longest 54
FLAG, oldest, largest 157
FLAGSTAFF, tallest 118
FLAME, hottest 80
FLAMENCO, fastest dancer 174
FLARE, greatest 123
FLATS, tallest block, largest, most expensive, mobile 111
FLEA, largest, longest and highest jumps 39
FLIGHT, fastest, longest, highest (bird) 32, fastest insect 39, space 72-3, hovercraft 128, aircraft, earliest, cross-Channel, jet-engined, supersonic 137, trans-Atlantic, first non-stop, solo, most flights, first trans-Pacific, circumnavigational, fastest, longest, shortest scheduled 139, speed records 139-40, duration record 140, greatest distance human-powered 143, kite 178, gliding 252-3
FLOAT, largest 157
FLOATING BRIDGE, longest 113
FLOOD, worst world, UK, alluvian 213-14
FLOTATION, greatest 152
FLOWER, rarest, northernmost, southernmost, highest 45, earliest, largest, most valuable, largest arrangement, slowest flowering plant 47, largest, tallest, smallest, highest priced orchid, largest rhododendron, largest rose 48, tallest dahlia*, gladiolus, hollyhock, lupin*, petunia, sunflower 46
FLUTE, marathon 173
FLYING-BOAT, first North Atlantic air crossing 138, largest aircraft wing span 138, fastest, highest 142
FLYING CREATURE, largest extinct 43
FLYING DISC, records 173
FLYING TRAPEZE, 171
FOG, longest 64
FOOD, survival without 19, most expensive 175, heaviest, longest, tallest* 175-6
FOOD CONSUMPTION, gluttony records 176-7
FOOT-AND-MOUTH DISEASE, worst outbreak 160
FOOTBAG, records 174
FOOTBALL, American 221-2, association 245-51, five-a-side 310, Gaelic 251, 310, rugby league 280-82, rugby union 282-3, seven-a-side 283, World Cup 248-9
FOOTBALL POOLS, 251
FOOTBALL STADIUM, largest 111
FORD, longest in England 212
FOREIGN AID, total given by US 208
FOREIGN DEBT, most 208
FOREIGN SECRETARYSHIP, longest tenures 196
FOREST, largest world, GB 50
FORGERY, greatest 205
FORGING, largest 144
FORK-LIFT TRUCK, largest 144
FORT, largest 109
FOSSIL, oldest human 10, biggest animal 41
FOUNTAIN, tallest 118, tallest champagne 171
FOXHUNTING, 245
FRANKFURTERS, eating record 177
FRAUD, biggest bank 205, largest computer, biggest maritime 206
FREEDOMS, most conferred 186
FREEZE, longest 62
FREIGHT TRAIN, longest, heaviest 136
FREQUENCY, highest 80
FRICTION, lowest 80
FROG, largest, smallest, rarest, most posionous, longest jump 35
FROGMAN, longest submergence 183, farthest underwater 165
FRONTIERS, most impenetrable, longest continuous, shortest, country with most 188
FROST FAIR, first recorded 62-3
FRUIT, most and least nutritive, biggest, peach, pineapple 48, record dimensions and weight UK* 46, most expensive 175
FUEL ECONOMY, world car record 130
FUEL RANGE, longest car 130
FUNERAL, largest attendance 218
FUNGUS, largest, most poisonous 52
FURNACE, (blast) largest 144, solar 143
FURNITURE, most expensive* 152, largest item 157-8

GAELIC FOOTBALL, 251
GALAXIES, most distant, number of, Milky Way, progressive records, farthest visible 72
GALLANTRY, civilian 185, see also **Medals**
GALLERY, largest art 82
GALLEY, largest 125
GAMBLING, 251-2
GAME RESERVE, largest 52
GAME SHOOTING, 245
GAOL, see **Prison**
GARAGE, largest, largest bus 133, see also **Filling Station**
GARBAGE DUMP, biggest 118
GARDEN, largest community 161
GAS, most powerful nerve, lightest, heaviest, lowest melting point, commonest 75
GAS DEPOSIT, largest 123
GAS FLARE, greatest 122
GAS HOLDER, largest 118-19
GAS PIPELINE, longest 146
GASTROPODS, largest, fastest 41
GASWORKS, largest 144
GAUGE, widest and narrowest railway track, highest standard, highest GB 136
GEMS, largest opal, amber, largest, rarest, smallest, largest cut, most expensive diamond, largest jade, topaz, largest gold nugget, largest emerald, ruby, pearl, largest, largest cut, most expensive sapphire 79
GENERATING PLANT, see **Power Station**
GENERATOR, largest 143
GENOCIDE, greatest 203-4
GERBIL, largest litter, oldest 30
GESTATION PERIOD, mammalian longest and shortest 24
GEYSER, tallest 61
G FORCE, highest sustained, momentary 19, highest animal 22, highest bird 32
GHERKINS, eating record 177
GHOSTS, most durable 20
GIANT, tallest 6-7

Indexing by Anna Pavord

Acknowledgements

CONTRIBUTORS: Andrew Adams; C V Appleton; John W Arblaster AIM; Glenn A Baker; Moira Banks; Howard Bass; Pat Besford; Henry G Button; A C Carder; Bryan Castle; Sq Ldr D H Clark DFC, AFC; Colin Dyson; Keith Escott; Clive Everton,; Frank L Forster; Bill Frindall; Tim Furniss; Ian Goold; Steven Goldberg; Stan Greenberg; J C Greetham; Elizabeth Hawley; Albert Herbert; Ron Hildebrandt; Sir Peter Johnson; Alan Jones (Gallup); Peter Lunn; John Marshall; Andy Milroy; Alan Mitchell BA, BAgr (For); David Mondey; John Moody; Ian Morrison; Susann Palmer; Tessa Pocock; John Randall; Chris Rhys; Patrick Robertson; Jack Rollin; Irvin Saxton; Robert Shopland; Colin C Smith; Graham Snowdon; William Stephens; Lance Tingay; Juhani Virola; Dr A C Waltham; David Wells; Rick Wilson; Gerald L Wood FZS; Tony Wood.

Grateful acknowledgement is made to the governing bodies and organisations who have helped in our researches.

OVERSEAS EDITORS: *Denmark*-Per Theil Hansen; *Finland*-Juhani Stenqvist; *France*-Philippe Scali; *Germany*-Hans Heinrich Kummel; *Greece*-Athanasios Rigas; *Hindi*-Ashok Gupta; *Hungary*-Robert Stein; *Iceland*-Orlygur Halfdanarson; *India*-Desu Subrahmanyam; *Israel*-Daphna Hausman; *Italy*-Maurizio Orlandi; *Middle East*-Antoine Naufal; *Netherlands*-Klaas de Boer; *Norway*-Anne Fjeldberg; *Spain*-Margarita Jordán; *Sweden*-Lisbet Ekberg; *Thailand*-Aphai Prakobpol; *USA*-David A Boehm and to D Richard Bowen (Europe); Bob Burton (Australia); Ben Matsumoto (Far East).

COVER DESIGN: 20/20 Graphics, Iver, Buckinghamshire: Cover illustrations, All-Sport; Bruce Coleman; Matthew Hillier.

ARTWORK, MAPS AND DIAGRAMS: Rhoda and Robert Burns; Matthew Hillier; Peter Harper; Eddie Botchway; Ashley Hamilton-Lloyd; Suzanne Alexander.

The Editor of The Guinness Book of Records wishes to thank

Deputy Editors
Nicholas Heath-Brown
Stewart Newport
Alex E Reid
Sheelagh Thomas

Sports Editor
Peter J Matthews

Art Editor
David L Roberts

Picture Editor
P Alex Goldberg

Production Manager
Chris Lingard

Editorial Assistants
Sheila Goldsmith
Muriel Ling

Secretarial Support
Bernadette Bidwell
Tracey Brown
Ann Collins
Lisa Webster

Press Officer
Anna Nicholas

Computer Consultant
Simon Johnson